KEY TO EXERCISE ICONS

The exercises in this text are drawn from a variety of contexts—mostly business-related. One of these icons appears next to each end-of-chapter exercise to indicate its subject area:

   Accounting/Finance

   General Management

   Operations Management

   Marketing

   Economics/Policy

   Other Business

   Non-Business

STATISTICS FOR BUSINESS PROBLEM SOLVING

HARVEY BRIGHTMAN
REGENTS' PROFESSOR OF
DECISION SCIENCES
GEORGIA STATE UNIVERSITY

HOWARD SCHNEIDER
ASSOCIATE PROFESSOR OF
DECISION SCIENCES
GEORGIA STATE UNIVERSITY

SECOND EDITION

COLLEGE DIVISION South-Western Publishing Co.

Cincinnati Ohio

Developmental Editor: Dennis Hanseman
Production Editor: Mark Sears
Production Service: Bookman Productions
Internal Designer: Lesiak/Crampton Design
Cover Designer: Diane Sullivan/Siebart Design
Cover Artist: © John Pearson
         Fresnell Proposition #32
         1985 Oberlin, Ohio

ME60BA
Copyright ©1994

by South-Western Publishing Co.
Cinncinati, Ohio

IP

International Thomson Publishing
South-Western Publishing Co. is an ITP Company.
The ITP trademark is used under license.

ISBN: 0-538-83130-8
1 2 3 4 5 6 7 K 9 8 7 6 5 4 3
Printed in the United States of America

Library of Congress Cataloging-in-Publication Data

Brightman, Harvey J.
    Statistics for business problem solving / Harvey Brightman, Howard Schneider.—2nd ed.
      p.   cm.
    Includes bibliographical references and index.
    ISBN 0-538-83130-8
    1. Problem Solving—Statistical methods. 2. Decision-making—Statistical methods. I. Schneider, Howard C., 1941–.
II. Title.
HD30.29.B744   1993
658.4'033—dc20   93-36429
                                               CIP

PREFACE

Statistics for Business Problem Solving, Second Edition, introduces the student to statistical methods and reasoning that aid in problem detection, problem diagnosis, and decision making and that improve managerial performance. The first edition incorporated novel elements such as

- The use of statistical methods to improve business problem solving
- An early introduction to, and analysis of, time series data
- An emphasis on graphics and descriptive statistics
- A chapter on data collection methods and questionnaire design
- The use of integrating frameworks to help students see the "big picture" and interconnect the material
- A stress on communicating statistical results to management
- An extensive set of interesting, real-world problems taken from all the functional fields of business
- A readable and discovery-based presentation style

The second edition represents our effort to improve upon the first edition. The changes and additions we made were based on suggestions from teachers, colleagues, and students.

Added Topics

We have added three new chapters to the text—hypothesis testing, advanced topics in regression analysis, and chi-square methods. Our colleagues convinced us that one section on hypothesis testing was not sufficient for business students, and so we added an entire chapter (Chapter 9). We also added a second chapter on regression analysis in which we cover model building, indicator variables, and multicollinearity. We removed the chi-square test of independence from the regression chapter and included it and the goodness-of-fit test in a new chapter on chi-square methods (Chapter 14.)

From the first edition, however, we have retained the parallel presentation of parametric and nonparametric methods. After presenting the parametric method, we then present a nonparametric alternative when the assumptions underlying the former have not been met. For example, in Chapter 7 we present confidence intervals on the mean followed by confidence intervals on the median. In Chapter 8 we present F-based confidence intervals on two variances followed by the Mood test for dispersion. In Chapter 10, we present the one-way ANOVA and Tukey HSD confidence intervals followed by the Kruskal–Wallis test and Dunn's multiple comparison method.

Computer Output

In the second edition most chapters have appendices that present examples using either MINITAB or SAS. The appendices present a problem, followed by the necessary input statements (with explanation) and the statistical software output (with explanation). We believe that this will aid those teachers who use MINITAB or SAS in statistics courses. This will also acquaint students with real-world statistical software packages.

More Exercises

We have increased by 50% the number of end-of-section exercises and problems. The exercises range from demonstration of simple mechanics and skills to real-world business applications taken from all the functional fields of business, including the statistical quality-assurance area.

User-Friendly Statistical Tables

We have simplified the student t-table (Appendix 5) to help students easily select the correct t-values for one-sided and two-sided confidence intervals. We have also added .025 and .050 percentile values for the F-distribution in Appendix 7. These two percentiles are necessary for constructing 90% and 95% confidence intervals on the variance ratio in Chapter 8.

New Ancillaries

For the instructor the second edition offers a revised and extended instructor's manual. In addition, we have developed over 350 new professional transparency masters using Microsoft's *Powerpoint* software. If you want color slides, we will send you the *Powerpoint* slide files, which can then be printed using one of the software's 170 templates. We have used the transparencies in classes of up to 120 students with great success.

We have revised the test bank and added over 1,500 new questions. The second edition test bank now contains over 2,000 questions cross-classified by section of text and the Bloom levels of learning (knowledge, exercise solving, and comprehension). The inclusion of the Bloom taxonomy will help faculty construct tests across multiple learning levels. The questions have been "debugged" through testing in our classes.

An instructor can order the text with COMSTAT, a user-friendly software package for IBM-compatible microcomputers, which can be used to solve most problems in the book. For the second edition, we have added the chi-square goodness-of-fit test, Cramer's measure of association, and some additional statistical quality-assurance measures. In addition, we have improved COMSTAT's data- and file-handling capability and its ability to output graphics.

Many of the changes and improvements incorporated into the second edition of *Statistics for Business Problem Solving* resulted from the constructive comments we received from many individuals:

Ronald Bremer
Texas Tech University

Sangit Chatterjee
Northeastern University

Joe Coleman
Wright State University

Eugene Enneking
Portland State University

Samuel Graves
Boston College

Jack Hayya
Pennsylvania State University

Der-Ann Hsu
University of Wisconsin, Milwaukee

Marie Klugman
Drake University

Susan Lenker
Central Michigan University

Robert Mogull
California State University, Sacramento

Herbert Moskowitz
Purdue University

Sharon Neidert
University of Tennessee

Jack Wilson
North Carolina State University

David Ronen
University of Missouri, St. Louis

Jimmie Woods
The Hartford Graduate Center

Brian Schott
Georgia State University

Douglas Zahn
Florida State University

Penny Verhoeven
Kennesaw State College

We thank them for helping improve the text.

There are several others we wish to thank. Penny Verhoeven did an outstanding job in reviewing and correcting our exercises and problems. John Pickett at Georgia Southern University developed what we believe is a first-rate test bank. Finally, we wish to thank Dennis Hanseman, Managing Editor, for his professional and editorial assistance.

The first edition was successful because it addressed the needs of both faculty and students. In writing the first edition we drew upon many of the ideas expressed at the annual conferences on improving the teaching of statistics. Moreover, students found the text readable (and dare we say, even enjoyable). We believe that the second edition retains these strengths. But we have listened to our customers—teachers and students—and have attempted to improve the product. We think we have; we hope you will agree.

Harvey J. Brightman
Howard C. Schneider
Atlanta, Georgia

About the Authors

Harvey Brightman is Regents' Professor of Decision Sciences at Georgia State University. He is Past President and a Fellow of the Decision Sciences Institute. His work has appeared in *Decision Sciences, The American Statistician, Interfaces, Journal of the Academy of Management*, and many other journals. A renowned educator, Professor Brightman has won numerous teaching excellence awards at Miami University and at Georgia State. He has consulted with major corporations such as IBM, Armco Steel, Arco Oil and Gas, and Georgia Power. His *Problem Solving: A Logical and Creative Approach* was a selection of the Executive Book of the Month Club and has been translated into Japanese.

Howard Schneider is Associate Professor of Decision Sciences at Georgia State University. Professor Schneider received his Ph.D. from the University of Virginia and is a specialist in multivariate statistics, forecasting, and survey design. He has served as consultant to the U.S. Office of Personnel Management, Wachovia Bank, The Southern Company, Deloitte & Touche, General Electric, the U.S. Department of Transportation, and the Georgia Department of Offender Rehabilitation. He has developed and taught more than 100 seminars and short courses in statistical methods.

CONTENTS

1 Improving Business Problem Solving
Through Statistics   1

    1.1   Introduction, 2
    1.2   Problem Sensing in Business, 2
    1.3   The Role of Statistics in Problem Sensing, 3
    1.4   Problem Diagnosis and Alternative Generation in Business, 5
    1.5   The Role of Statistics in Diagnosis and Alternative Generation, 7
    1.6   Decision Making in Business, 11
    1.7   The Role of Statistics in Decision Making, 12
    1.8   Integrating Problem Solving and Statistics, 12
    Appendix: Brief Description of the COMCEL Organization, 16

2 Descriptive Statistics I: Problem Sensing   18

    2.1   Introduction, 20
    2.2   Displaying Cross-Sectional Data Using Tables and Graphs, 22
    2.3   Recognizing the Shape of a Histogram, 31
    2.4   Displaying Time-Ordered Data: The Line Graph, 38
    2.5   Summarizing Cross-Sectional Data: The Mean and Standard
           Deviation, 44
    2.6   Interpreting the Mean and Standard Deviation: The Empirical
           and Chebyshev Rules, 53
    2.7   Summarizing Cross-Sectional Data: The Median, Trimmed
           Mean, and Interquartile Range, 58
    2.8   Interpreting the Median and Interquartile Range, 66
    2.9   Summarizing Time-Ordered Data, 71
    2.10 Key Ideas and Overview, 82
    Appendix: Statistical Software, 95

3 Descriptive Statistics II: Problem Diagnosis   98

    3.1   Introduction, 100
    3.2   Types of Variables, 103
    3.3   Analyzing Mixed Cross-Sectional Data, 105
    3.4   Analyzing Categorical Cross-Sectional Data, 110
    3.5   Analyzing Quantitative Cross-Sectional Data, 121
    3.6   Analyzing Quantitative Time-Ordered Data, 134
    3.7   Correlation and Cross-Correlation, 146
    3.8   Key Ideas and Overview, 155
    Appendix: Statistical Software, 170

4 Basic Probability Concepts   174

4.1 Introduction, 176
4.2 Probability Concepts, 176
4.3 Picturing Probabilities: Introduction to the Probability Tree, 185
4.4 Joint and Union Probabilities, 193
4.5 Conditional Probabilities and Statistical Independence, 198
4.6 Computing Conditional Probabilities, 202
4.7 Using Probability Trees to Minimize Managerial Judgment Errors, 210
4.8 Nonstatistical Judgment Errors, 218
4.9 Key Ideas and Overview, 220

5 Probability Distributions   232

5.1 Probability Distributions and Problem Solving, 234
5.2 Random Variables and Discrete Probability Distributions, 235
5.3 The Binomial Distribution, 244
5.4 Problem Solving and the Binomial Distribution, 253
5.5 The Poisson Distribution, 261
5.6 The Normal Distribution, 268
5.7 Integrating Framework and Key Ideas, 284

6 Data Collection Methods   294

6.1 Data and Managerial Performance, 296
6.2 Sampling Principles and Statistical Inferences, 296
6.3 Basic Sampling Terminology, 300
6.4 Planning and Conducting a Survey: An Overview, 301
6.5 Simple Random Sampling Design, 304
6.6 Stratified Random Sampling Design, 307
6.7 Selecting a Survey Method, 312
6.8 General Principles for Writing Questions, 315
6.9 Basic Principles of Experimental Design, 321
6.10 Avoiding Problems in Experimental Design, 326
6.11 Key Ideas of Data Collection, 330

7 Making Inferences About One Population   336

7.1 Problem Solving and Statistical Inferences,   338
7.2 The Distribution of the Sample Mean, 342
7.3 Confidence Intervals on an Unknown Population Mean, 355
7.4 One-Sided Confidence Intervals on an Unknown Population Mean, 368
7.5 Stratified Random Sampling, 373
7.6 Confidence Intervals on an Unknown Population Proportion, 376
7.7 Determining the Sample Size, 380
7.8 Sign Test-Based Nonparametric Confidence Interval for an Unknown Population Median, 384

7.9 Confidence Intervals on an Unknown Population Variance and Standard Deviation, 390

7.10 Key Ideas and Overview, 394

Appendix: Statistical Software, 403

8 Making Inferences About Two Populations   406

8.1 Improving Departmental Performance, 408

8.2 Comparing Two Populations of Data, 408

8.3 Inferences on the Difference Between Two Population Means, 417

8.4 Inferences on the Difference Between Two Population Proportions, 428

8.5 The Mann-Whitney Nonparametric Confidence Interval for the Difference Between Two Population Medians, 432

8.6 Inferences on Two Population Variances for Normal Populations, 438

8.7 A Nonparametric Method for Comparing Two Population Variabilities, 445

8.8 Key Ideas and Overview, 451

Appendix: Statistical Software, 463

9 Hypothesis Testing   466

9.1 Introduction to Hypothesis Testing, 468

9.2 Hypothesis Testing on One Population Mean, 468

9.3 Hypothesis Testing on One Population Proportion, 488

9.4 Hypothesis Testing on the Difference Between Two Population Means, 494

9.5 Hypothesis Testing on the Difference Between Two Population Proportions, 505

9.6 Key Ideas and Overview, 511

Appendix A: Relationships Between Type I and Type II Errors, 521

Appendix B: Statistical Software, 523

10 Analysis of Variance   526

10.1 The Role of Experimentation in Problem Solving, 528

10.2 Exploratory Data Analysis, 531

10.3 Analysis of Variance for a One-Factor, k-Level Study, 538

10.4 Testing for Significant Differences Between Pairs of Population Means, 550

10.5 The Kruskal–Wallis Nonparametric Analysis of Variance, 556

10.6 The Two-Factor, Completely Random Factorial Study, 563

10.7 Key Ideas and Overview, 575

Appendix: Statistical Software, 587

11 Regression Analysis   590

11.1 Looking for Relationships Among Variables, 592
11.2 Collecting Data for a Regression Study, 600
11.3 Plotting Scatter Diagrams and Measuring the Strength of Relationships, 602
11.4 Curve Fitting: Estimating Conditional Means, 611
11.5 Evaluating the Regression Model, 620
11.6 Evaluating the Regression Model Assumptions: Residual Analysis, 635
11.7 Using Regression Models for Prediction, 648
11.8 Integrating Framework, 652
Appendix A: COMCEL Job Satisfaction and Salary Data, 662
Appendix B: Statistical Software, 664

12 Advanced Topics in Regression Analysis   670

12.1 Introduction, 672
12.2 Indicator Variables, 672
12.3 Nonlinear Regression, 687
12.4 The Extra Sum of Squares Principle and the General Linear Test, 695
12.5 Multicollinearity, 705
Appendix A: COMCEL Personnel Data, 731
Appendix B: HICOMM Job Satisfaction Data, 733

13 Forecasting   734

13.1 Data Patterns and Forecasting, 736
13.2 Alternative Forecasting Approaches, 738
13.3 Forecasting Using Regression Analysis, 741
13.4 Forecasting Using the Classical Decomposition Method, 753
13.5 Qualitative Forecasting Methods, 774
13.6 Key Ideas and Overview, 777
Appendix: Statistical Software, 787

14 Chi-Square Methods   790

14.1 Introduction, 792
14.2 The Need for Nonparametric Methods, 792
14.3 The Chi-Square Goodness-of-Fit Test, 798
14.4 The Chi-Square Test of Independence, 811
14.5 Key Ideas and Overview, 819
Appendix: Statistical Software, 826

15 Quality Improvement   828

15.1 The Strategic Importance of Quality, 830
15.2 Types of Quality, 830
15.3 Control Charting for Variables, 834
15.4 Control Charts for Attributes, 852
15.5 Tools for Controlling and Improving Quality, 858
15.6 Vendor Certification and Acceptance Sampling, 867
15.7 General Principles, 872
Appendix: Statistical Software, 883

Appendices   A-1

Appendix 1 The Binomial Table, A-1
Appendix 2 Cumulative Poisson Distribution, A-16
Appendix 3 The Normal Table, A-22
Appendix 4 Table of Random Numbers, A-23
Appendix 5 Student t-Table, A-25
Appendix 6 Percentiles of the χ^2 Distribution, A-26
Appendix 7 The F Distribution, A-27
Appendix 8 Table of Studentized Range Values, A-34
Appendix 9 Data Sets for Application Problems, A-36

Answers to Odd-Numbered Exercises and Problems   B-1

Index   C-1

CHAPTER

1

IMPROVING BUSINESS PROBLEM SOLVING THROUGH STATISTICS

1.1   Introduction
1.2   Problem sensing in business
     Pounds's strategies
1.3   The role of statistics in problem sensing
     Data collection
     Data organizing and summarizing
     Data interpretation
1.4   Problem diagnosis and alternative generation
     in business
1.5   The role of statistics in diagnosis and
     alternative generation
     Data collection
     Data organizing and summarizing
     Data interpretation

1.6   Decision making in business
1.7   The role of statistics in decision making
     Data collection
     Data organizing and summarizing
     Data interpretation
1.8   Integrating problem solving and statistics
     Philosophy of data analysis
Appendix: Brief description of the COMCEL
     organization

CHAPTER OUTLINE

1.1 ≡ Introduction

Statistics. We know what you're thinking—plugging numbers into unreadable formulas; sadistics; irrelevant. You are mistaken. Statistics can improve the problem-solving performance of salaried and professional workers, supervisors, and managers in every business field.

Solving problems quickly is essential to business and personal success. Business professionals face two major types of problems. A disturbance, or crisis, problem is a gap between a previous or budgeted level of performance and the present performance. For example, when a retail department's sales show a sudden and dramatic decline from the previous quarter, we must diagnose the problem's causes and take corrective action to solve the problem permanently. A managerial problem, on the other hand, is a gap between the present level of performance and a desired higher level of performance. For example, a support staff takes three hours to type and mail a letter, a task that the supervisor believes should take only one hour. This is a managerial problem, and we must seek ways to improve performance. In summary, solving a disturbance problem means asking, "How can we restore performance to previous levels?" Solving a managerial problem means asking, "How can we improve performance to the desired level?"

American managers and business professionals are often not effective problem solvers. One reason is that the mass of data that daily crosses their desks overwhelms them. But it need not! We can learn how to organize and analyze the data to develop mental models of the state of the department or firm. A mental model describes how an area is doing, where the opportunities lie, and what the emerging problems are. Mental models need not be complex or mathematical. Rather, they should be simple, verbal, or visual. In short, mental models describe how an area is operating, how it used to operate, and how it should operate. **Statistics** can play an essential role in building mental models.

Whether solving disturbance problems or managerial problems, we must follow a plan of attack. Consider the approach outlined in Figure 1.1. The three phases incorporated in this problem solving model are explained in this chapter.

Statistics is a way of thinking that helps collect or create, organize, analyze, summarize, and interpret data to improve problem solving.

1.2 ≡ Problem Sensing in Business

Problem solving begins with problem finding. Problem sensing is crucial, because we cannot solve a problem until we know it exists. Effective business professionals

FIGURE 1.1   A Problem-Solving Model

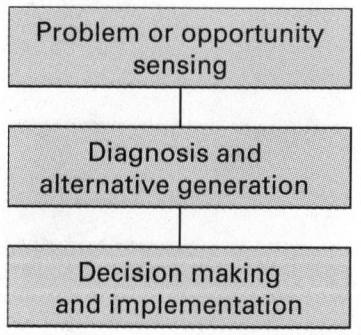

detect emerging problems before they become crises. How do they do it? Management theorist William Pounds (1969) studied problem sensing and found that four strategies are used.

Pounds's Strategies

Historic Strategy   Under the assumption that the best prediction of the future is the recent past, we expect continuity of performance: Whatever happened in the recent past should continue into the near future. If it does not, then a performance gap exists. For example, why is our safety record better this quarter than last quarter? Why is there a drop in the profits to earnings ratio? Why has the age of our accounts receivables increased? Much of the data necessary for problem solving can be found in a firm's management information system.

Budget Variance Strategy   Plans and budgets provide detailed projections of performance for upcoming years. When actual performance falls short of budgeted levels, a potential gap may result. Unfortunately, budgeted performance levels are often set so low that departments easily exceed them. Thus, we detect few, if any, performance gaps. When planning is based on realistic goals, however, variances between actual and budgeted performance can help highlight hidden problems.

Other People's Strategy   Often, a problem comes to light from outside sources. A customer who purchases a product and is disappointed with it will notify the firm of his disappointment with the poor quality. Now the firm knows it has a problem! That is what happened to General Motors in the late 1970s and early 1980s. Potential customers told GM to make reliable, fuel-efficient, front-wheel-drive cars, or they would purchase them from firms that did. Another source of problem sensing is when a senior manager's brainstorm becomes an improvement project for her subordinates to investigate. The organization channels the problems identified by some (usually senior people) to others who are qualified to solve them (junior people).

Extra-Organizational Strategy   Trade journals, competitors, other divisions within the organization, or professional conferences can sometimes identify performance gaps. Why is there a difference between our performance and our competitor's? Should we adopt a competitor's practices? Should we adopt a new procedure seen at a trade show? How do we compare with published performance levels for the industry? The extra-organizational strategy focuses on the external environment. Here the data in the management information system are less useful. Instead, a business person's informal network of contacts within the industry or country will provide much of the data needed for sensing problems or opportunities.

Effective business professionals evaluate current performance using Pounds's four strategies. Next they identify important differences, select one for examination, and begin the problem solving process. Statistics can play an essential role in problem sensing, as we shall see next.

1.3≣ The Role of Statistics in Problem Sensing

The following example illustrates how statistics helps in problem sensing. Note that problem sensing includes data collection, data organizing and summarizing, and data interpretation.

Data Collection

COMCEL's Norcross, Georgia, manufacturing plant employs 300 workers (see the Appendix at end of Chapter 1 for the organizational chart). Each month Sarah Teman, the manufacturing manager, receives two attendance reports from the management information system. The January 1994 monthly report just crossed her desk and showed that workers had only a 90% attendance rate. The second report, Table 1.1, shows the attendance percentages for the last 12 months. What, if anything, are the data trying to say?

Table 1.1

1993 Monthly Attendance Data:
Routine Management Information System Report

Period	Attendance
January	97.7%
February	99.0%
March	95.0%
April	98.3%
May	98.3%
June	97.0%
July	97.7%
August	95.0%
September	99.0%
October	96.3%
November	97.0%
December	95.1%

Data Organizing and Summarizing

Statistics helps to organize and summarize the data. One simple and effective way to view a data set is to graph it. Using the data in Table 1.1, assign monthly attendance percentages to the vertical axis, and months to the horizontal axis. Examining Figure 1.2, Teman develops the following mental model of how her plant has been operating:

> Using last year's data, I expect monthly attendance to be between 95% and 99%. The mean is slightly over 97%, and there is no upward, downward, or systematic pattern in the data. As long as monthly attendance is within the above limits, there is no disturbance problem. There is no need for problem solving.

Data Interpretation

January's attendance dropped to 90%. Is this an important, or major, deviation from the historic data? Does it signify a disturbance problem? That is, if Teman could afford to wait until next month without taking any action, would monthly attendance recover to historic levels?

FIGURE 1.2

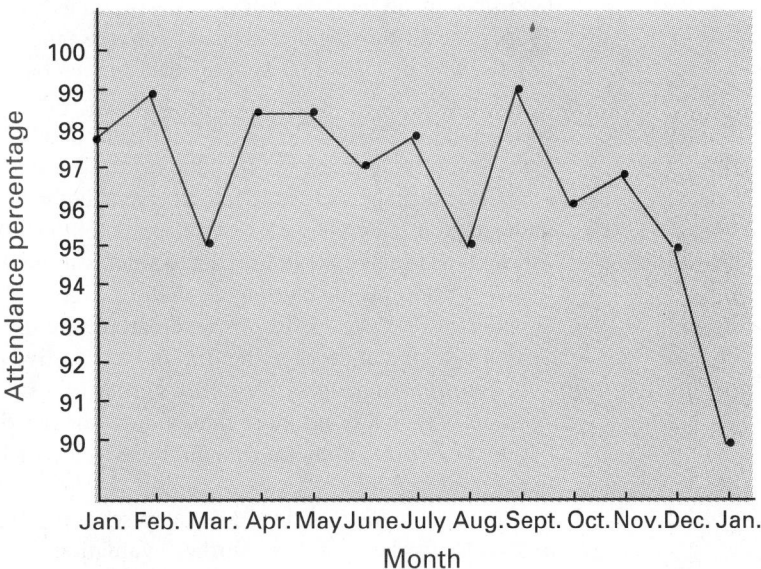

There are two possible reasons why the January attendance fell to 90%. It may be due to **random variation** or to **assignable**, or **special cause variation**. Distinguishing between random and assignable cause variation is difficult, requires statistical training and insight, and is absolutely essential to problem sensing and effective performance. It may be the greatest contribution that statistics makes to business problem solving.

1.4 ▇ Problem Diagnosis and Alternative Generation in Business

According to Peter Drucker (1971), a leading management theorist, American managers are ineffective diagnosticians, being "solution-minded" instead of "problem-minded." Often they attempt (and fail) to solve a problem before considering its root causes. Even when they do manage to diagnose problems, they promptly jump to conclusions. Dewitt Dearborn and Herbert Simon (1958) asked a group of 23 senior executives to analyze the problems facing the Castengo Steel Company. Five of the six sales executives thought that the major problem was related to sales, but only five of the remaining 17 executives considered sales to be a major cause. When four of the five operations executives concluded that the major problem was related to production, only four of the 18 other executives agreed. Just three executives thought that the major problem involved human relations. Interestingly, their departments were public relations, industrial relations, and health.

As this example illustrates, our training dictates our view of a problem. However, just because we are accountants does not mean all problems are accounting problems! Decision scientists call this narrow view selective perception. Selective perception is hard to overcome because what is observed partly depends on who we are. We see with the mind as well as the eyes.

Another human failing that may hamper the search for causes of a disturbance problem is the tendency to blame others. If a worker's performance has dropped significantly, what may be the special (assignable) causes? The worker may initially

Random variation is a minor departure from the average historic level of performance. Random variation results from the thousands of factors that make it impossible to predict exactly the level of a variable. Random variation does not require immediate problem solving action.

Special cause variation is a major departure from the average historic level of performance. The major departure is due to an assignable or special cause and must be corrected.

blame such external factors as recent task changes: "I was doing fine until they changed my job. Now I don't know what they expect me to do." Supervisors whose bonuses depend on their workers' performances often blame their workers (Brown, 1984). The all-too-familiar scenario is to pass the buck: "I'm not to blame. The cause lies elsewhere, with other people, or in factors beyond our control."

Jumping to conclusions, like blaming others or dodging responsibility, is a common phenomenon. In fact, we may not be able to stop from jumping to conclusions—and sometimes true insights result. But it is not a formal method of analysis.

Once managers are able to perceive accurately the causes of a problem and thus understand it, they must seek or design potential solutions. In seeking a solution, we ask what has been done in the past to solve similar problems. In designing a solution, we ask what kinds of solutions could be designed if there were no constraints of time or money. Then we modify these creative options to reflect the actual constraints. Search is a logical process and design is a creative process.

Too often managers seek only one or two solutions to a problem. The second solution is typically no more than a clone of the first one: a variation on the same theme. Moreover, both are frequently recycled old solutions and often fail to solve the current problem.

Instead, managers should develop several different skeletal ideas, screen them, and select the best ones for further evaluation. A skeletal idea can be written on a single page. It includes a brief description of the idea, its rationale, and very rough estimates of the costs and benefits.

Alternative generation is related to problem diagnosis because the alternatives that are generated also depend on the perception of the root causes.

The Case of the Missing Information   Many product managers within a firm were complaining that they did not have the necessary information to make good decisions when introducing new products. They had never complained before. Sensing that an important problem existed, the president contacted the information systems group. They, of course, chose to define the root causes as technological and proposed three alternative computerized systems. Each was very expensive and required extensive user training.

Despite some misgivings, the president installed one of the recommended systems. Although the product managers showed little enthusiasm during the six-month installation, the president assumed that once the information system was in place it would be used. He was wrong. One year later, few product managers were using the computer system. Not even half had attended the training sessions. Moreover, the system had no impact on product decision making.

Perhaps the problem was not technological. The president had not considered that he might be facing a human problem. He sent a psychologist from corporate planning to interview the product managers. The psychologist concluded that the problem was not what they complained of—lack of information. Rather, the product managers were uneasy making risky decisions involving huge sums of money. Over the past several years the cost of introducing a new product had skyrocketed. The product managers realized that now any mistake could be costly to them and the firm. Viewing the problem as a human problem, the psychologist suggested two alternatives: either modify the reward system to emphasize overall departmental performance, or require managers to approve product introduction decisions jointly, in groups, rather than as individuals.

The president tried the shared risk approach, with astonishing results. Product managers grew enthusiastic and sought creative ways to promote their products. The supposed lack of information was never mentioned again.

The moral of the story: Almost any solution to the right problem beats the best solution to the wrong problem. A correct diagnosis is essential.

1.5 ≡ The Role of Statistics in Diagnosis and Alternative Generation

On reflection, Sarah Teman concludes that January 1994 90% attendance figure signifies a real problem. That is, it is due to a special or assignable cause. She must now determine this cause or causes.

Data Collection

Teman's hunch is that monthly attendance and workers' attitudes are related. When workers feel good about their jobs, they come to work; when dissatisfied with the job or management, they take paid sick leave. How can she test this belief? She needs a measure of workers' attitudes. Fortunately, COMCEL conducts a monthly worker attitude, or climate, sampling survey. Each month a sample of ten workers anonymously completes the survey shown in Table 1.2. The responses are stored in the management information system, which generates a routine monthly report on overall job attitudes. The Data Processing Department will also provide special reports on the responses to the eight questions, if requested. Teman obtains a summary of the overall attitudes averaged month by month over the past year, according to the 10-point rating system used in the survey. Table 1.3 displays the summary data.

Table 1.2

Climate Study Questionnaire

Instructions: For each of the following statements, please circle the number that best describes your situation.

1 = Strongly disagree	4 = Agree
2 = Disagree	5 = Strongly agree
3 = Neutral	

Workers in this plant:

1.	Help one another.	1	2	3	4	5
2.	Share information to help one another.	1	2	3	4	5
3.	Encourage creativity.	1	2	3	4	5
4.	Always try to improve.	1	2	3	4	5
5.	Join in social activities.	1	2	3	4	5
6.	Get to know one another.	1	2	3	4	5
7.	Comply with all rules.	1	2	3	4	5
8.	Live for their job.	1	2	3	4	5

Overall Job Attitude:

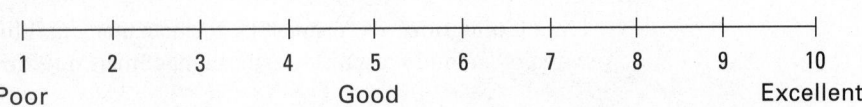

Table 1.3

Mean Overall Job Attitude for Last 12 Months

Period	Mean Job Attitude
January	7
February	3
March	6
April	6
May	5
June	5
July	3
August	6
September	5
October	5
November	6
December	1

Data Organizing and Summarizing

Again we begin by graphing the data, assigning mean overall job attitude to the vertical axis and months to the horizontal axis. We have placed monthly attendance in the upper panel and overall job attitudes in the lower panel of Figure 1.3 on page 9.

The mean overall job attitude ranged from 1 to 7, with no obvious pattern. Overall, the workers had a good attitude, although in February, July, and December it deteriorated. The lower graph by itself is not very useful, but remember: Teman wants to determine if monthly attendance and overall job attitude are related. She will compare the two graphs in Figure 1.3.

Data Interpretation

Now a pattern emerges. In January the workers' mean job attitude was very good (a rating of 7). In February monthly attendance was also very high—99%. In February workers' attitudes dropped to a mean rating of 3, and one month later monthly attendance dropped to 95%. The pattern continued throughout the year. It appears that the mean attitude rating in one month predicts the monthly attendance in the following month. Thus the mean attitude rating leads monthly attendance by one month, or monthly attendance lags the mean attitude rating by one month. Given the lead-lag relationship, we should not be surprised that monthly attendance dropped to 90% in January 1994. After all, in December the plant had the worst attitude rating all year, predicting a major drop in the following month's attendance.

Now, what can Sarah Teman conclude about all this? The drop in monthly attendance was only a symptom of a more serious problem. Aided by statistical analysis and graphing, Teman has separated the symptom from its underlying cause. She must now refine her new diagnosis. If Teman is correct, she has to address the problem not of absenteeism but of improving workers' attitudes on the job. What causes their attitudes to vary monthly? Why were attitudes so positive in November and negative in December? The diagnosis is not yet complete. She must repeat the cycle of data collection, organization, and interpretation.

Data Collection   Fortunately, the management information system preserved the workers' monthly responses to the eight climate questions shown in Table 1.2. Teman

FIGURE 1.3

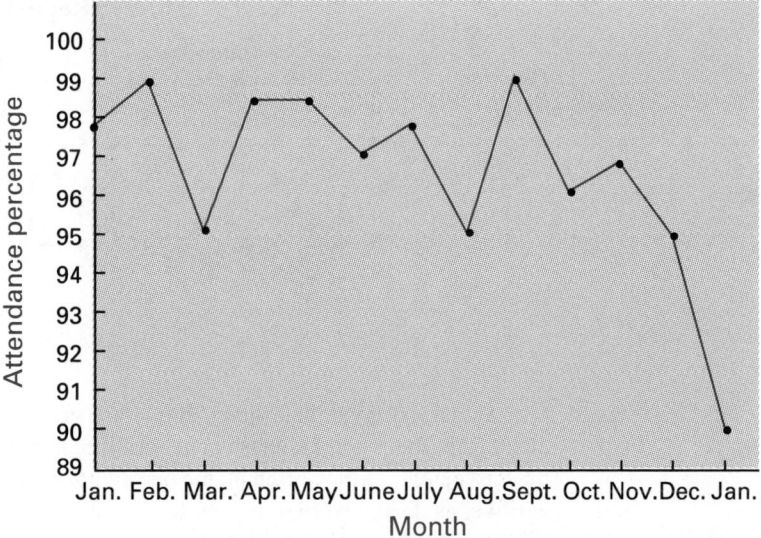

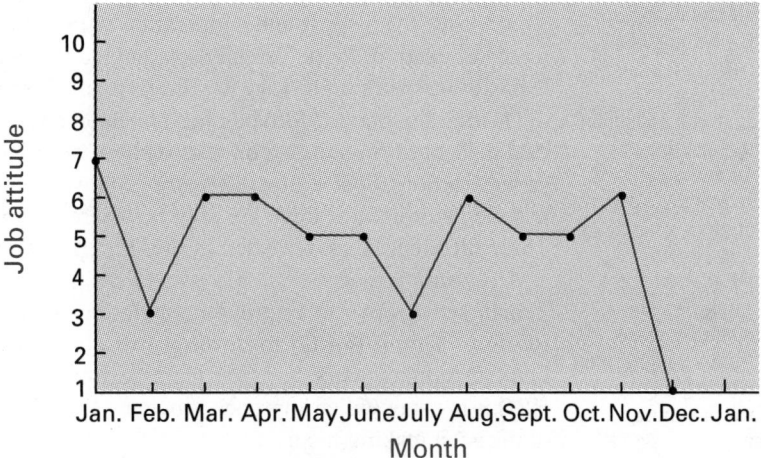

now requests a special report comparing the November and December data for all eight questions. The results are shown in Table 1.4.

Data Organizing and Summarizing   The raw data in Table 1.4 are difficult to interpret. We need to organize and summarize them. One useful way is simply to compute means for the ten responses to each question. The means are given in Table 1.5.

Data Interpretation   The biggest change from November to December is the response to the first two attitude questions. Both concern task support, the degree to which workers cooperate with one another. Teman therefore suspects that a change in the level of worker cooperation caused the poor overall job attitudes. She reasons that some months the workers are cooperative and friendly to one another. Other months, it's like a war zone. After the bad times, the workers find reasons to stay home the following month.

Table 1.4

Raw Data on Responses to Eight Climate Questions: Special Report

Question	November Data (Sample size = 10)	December Data (Sample size = 10)
1	5, 5, 5, 4, 5, 4, 5, 4, 5, 5	2, 3, 2, 1, 2, 3, 3, 2, 1, 2
2	4, 4, 5, 4, 5, 4, 4, 5, 5, 5	1, 2, 2, 1, 2, 3, 2, 1, 1, 2
3	3, 3, 3, 4, 3, 2, 3, 4, 3, 3	3, 4, 3, 2, 3, 4, 3, 3, 4, 3
4	4, 4, 3, 4, 3, 3, 4, 3, 4, 4	4, 4, 4, 3, 3, 4, 3, 3, 4, 4
5	5, 4, 4, 5, 4, 5, 4, 4, 5, 4	4, 5, 5, 5, 5, 4, 4, 4, 5, 4
6	4, 4, 4, 5, 4, 4, 5, 4, 4, 5	4, 5, 4, 5, 4, 4, 4, 5, 4, 4
7	3, 3, 2, 3, 4, 3, 2, 3, 4, 3	3, 3, 4, 3, 2, 3, 3, 2, 3, 4
8	2, 3, 2, 3, 4, 3, 3, 3, 2, 3	3, 3, 2, 4, 3, 3, 2, 3, 3, 3

Teman believes that when things are going well in the plant the workers get along fine. But when glitches occur—falling behind schedule or producing too many defective items—they often blame one another. She sees the work groups as too competitive, as if they were opposing teams rather than squads on the same side. Teman decides that the goal should be to develop a team spirit throughout the entire plant.

Having completed the diagnosis, Teman asks the following question: How can we improve team spirit and cooperation within the plant? Let us pause here for two words of caution. First, Teman has assumed that worker competitiveness caused the levels of task support to vary within the plant. Perhaps she is right . . . or is she guilty of shifting the blame? Maybe poor management practices are to blame. Second, the data in Table 1.5 are based on a **sample** of only 20 workers. Yet Teman is making a generalization about a **population** of 300 workers in the plant. The generalization may be incorrect, for there are always differences between samples and populations. These differences are reflected in the **margin of error**.

Assuming that the sample results are indeed representative of the population, Teman seeks ways to improve cooperation within the plant. She asks the Human Resource Group (HRG) to develop two alternative solutions. Both its approaches involve training workshops on team building or on interpersonal communication. HRG is not sure which approach is better. How can it decide? We consider the process of decision making next.

A sample is a representative collection of some, but not all, elements of a population.

A population is a collection of elements—people or objects—about which we wish to make generalizations.

The margin of error is the possible difference we allow between the result obtained from a sample and what we would get if we could check the entire population.

Table 1.5

Mean Responses to Climate Questions for November and December

Question	November	December
1	4.7	2.1
2	4.5	1.7
3	3.1	3.2
4	3.6	3.6
5	4.4	4.5
6	4.3	4.3
7	3.0	3.0
8	2.8	2.9

1.6 ▤ Decision Making in Business

Decision makers should select those options that best accomplish their goals. Now that may seem obvious. Yet decisions are not always made that way.

Decision making is not usually a formal competition among competing ideas to accomplish a set of goals. Quite often managers do not set explicit goals in advance. Instead they create them once they have chosen a course of action. The goals then serve to justify the decision. For example, a chief executive officer (CEO) desires a sports franchise. To create a seeming need for action, he guides his Board of Directors to the discovery of a previously unknown crucial problem. Then he shows how the franchise would solve the problem. To the Board, the sports franchise will seem like a match made in heaven (Brightman, 1985).

That is not all. Sometimes the point in time when a decision is made cannot even be identified. It just happens. Marion Folsom (1962, p. 210), a top executive in business, has observed: It is often hard to pinpoint the exact stage at which a decision is reached. More often than not the decision comes about naturally during the discussions, when the consensus seems to be reached among those whose judgment and opinion the executive seeks.

By now, one wonders if decision making really can be treated as an orderly process. Yes, it can, despite all the problems in real-world practice, and statistics again plays an important role in sorting out the information. Statistics can provide objective and unbiased data that can influence the final decision. Properly used, statistics minimizes some of the problems in real-world decision making.

Even if a decision seems optimal—in accord with our goals as well as with our statistical data—we have another point to consider in decision making: implementation. Too frequently managers assume that they can easily install whatever option they select. But anyone who neglects implementation is living in a dream world. When the installation proves complex or the solution controversial, managers may face many problems, from coordination and scheduling conflicts to the political maneuverings of those opposed to the decision.

The decision maker should develop an implementation plan by:

1.   listing every task required to install the option;
2.   estimating the total installation time;
3.   estimating the time to complete each task; and
4.   comparing the time required to complete the tasks to the total time available.

Suppose there is insufficient time. Then various options exist. We may eliminate tasks, do several tasks simultaneously, obtain additional resources to reduce task time, or simply request more time to install the option.

The only sure thing in a complex installation is that something unexpected will occur. Be ready for it! Develop an implementation plan describing the steps to installing a solution. It should cover who, when, what, where, and how. Who will install the solution? What will motivate them to do their best? Who will oppose it? Why will they object? What are the crucial components in the installation? Why are they crucial? Where will the greatest coordination problems arise? Why will these coordination problems be so acute? When must each step of the installation be completed? Why can't the steps be rescheduled and thereby reduce potential problems? A decision that cannot be put into place solves no problems and meets no goals—except the unintended goal of exposing a poor decision maker.

1.7≣ The Role of Statistics in Decision Making

COMCEL's Human Resources Group has proposed two alternative workshops to improve worker cooperation. HRG is not sure which approach is better, so Teman authorizes a pilot (small-scale) study. Based on the results, she will make the final choice and then require all workers to attend the selected workshop.

Data Collection

HRG selects two work teams of five workers each. It assigns one team to the team-building workshop and the other to the communication workshop. The workshop assignments are made by flipping a coin, to ensure that each work group has an equal chance of being in each workshop. HRG will evaluate both programs by comparing the mean job attitudes before and after the workshops.

Data Organizing and Summarizing

Table 1.6 contains the results of the pilot study.

Table 1.6

Changes in Mean Job Attitudes of Teams by Workshop

	Before Means	Workshop	After Means
Team 1	4.50	Team Building	7.90
Team 2	4.57	Communication	4.65

Data Interpretation

Table 1.6 indicates that members of team 1 appear to have improved their job attitudes, whereas members of team 2 show little overall improvement. Of course, these are inferences from a small sample and generalized to the entire plant. They may be wrong. Nevertheless, the data suggest that Teman should choose the team-building workshop. She did, and the attendance problem was corrected.

1.8≣ Integrating Problem Solving and Statistics

Figure 1.4 integrates the problem solving model presented in this chapter with statistics. We begin with problem sensing. By organizing and summarizing routine reports, we can develop mental models that describe how a department operates under normal conditions. Chapters 2 and 13 are especially helpful for developing mental models. Any major disturbance signals a problem. Failing to sense a major disturbance (assignable cause variation) is as serious as sensing a bogus problem (mere random variation). Chapters 2, 3, 13, and 15 will show how to distinguish between random and assignable cause variation, a critical skill in effective problem sensing.

Having detected a major disturbance, we must diagnose it. We ask: "What factor or factors caused the deviation from budgeted or historical levels of performance?" Seeking root causes is like finding a needle in a haystack—hard but not impossible, if we are methodical, persistent, and perceptive. Chapters 3, 11, 12, and 15 focus on problem diagnosis.

FIGURE 1.4   Integrating Statistics Within a Problem-Solving Framework

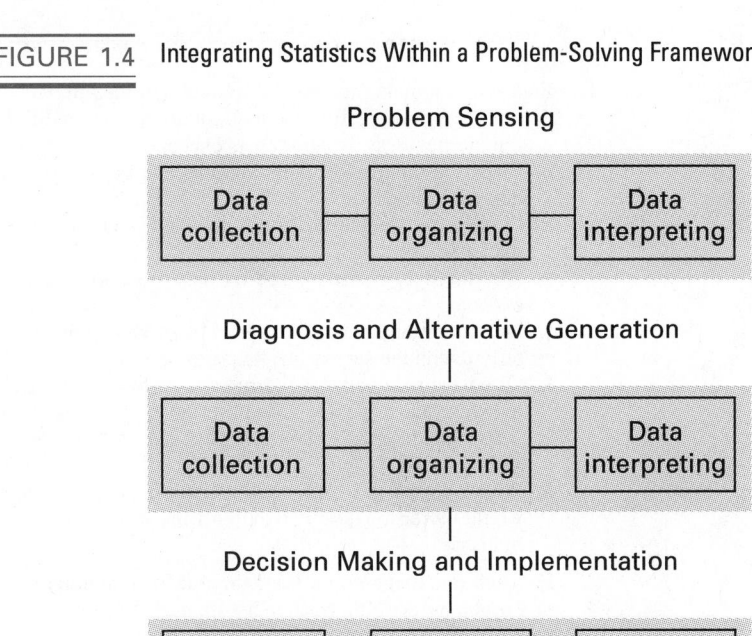

After generating several possible solutions we must choose one and implement it. Chapters 4 and 5 provide basic probability concepts and the background to understand statistical analysis, a tool in making decisions. Chapter 6 shows how to collect data by conducting sampling surveys or pilot studies. Chapters 7–10 and 14 examine how we analyze and interpret the study results.

Philosophy of Data Analysis

The underlying theme of this book is that we must learn how to explore and analyze data to solve business problems. We suggest the following pattern of data analysis:

1. Plot or graph the data; then study it. What are the data trying to tell us? Do we have a problem, or is the variation merely random?
2. If there is a problem, select an appropriate method of analysis.
3. Check the assumptions underlying the statistical method. If the assumptions are not valid, choose another method.
4. Collect or create the data, analyze them, interpret the findings, and take corrective action.

Data exploration and analysis can help in many ways: to separate opinions from facts; to develop mental models of departmental performance; to sense emerging problems long before they become crises; to prevent overreaction to random variation; to diagnose problems better by tracing causality, thus countering the tendency to jump from symptoms to false conclusions; and to make better decisions. In summary, statistics is a way of thinking about and improving business problem solving. It is too useful to be left only to statisticians.

CHAPTER 1 EXERCISES

1. For each statement indicate the source(s) of the implied standard. Use H, historical precedent; B, budgeted performance; O, other people; and E, extra-organizational.
    a. "In our business, if labor costs exceed 10% of total cost, we can't make a profit."
    b. "Japanese-managed plants making television sets in this country average only a 3% defective rate."
    c. "I want the company I run to have a reputation for the highest quality product in the industry."
    d. "Productivity has increased by only 1.5% this year, not by the 2% increase that was expected."
    e. "A major manufacturer monitors its service division by commissioning impartial quarterly telephone surveys of its customers."
    f. "We have received letters from our customers complaining that our warranty period is too short and coverage is too limited."
    g. "Our outside people should have some form of instant recognition just like the white shirts of IBM."
    h. "Our labor costs are expanding faster than those of anyone else in the industry. Profits would increase faster if we didn't insist on making the highest quality product in the industry."

2. For each statement indicate whether the information received suggests an opportunity (O) or a problem resulting from a disturbance (D).
    a. "Weekly figures show we are 15% over standard cost."
    b. "Weekly figures show we are 15% under standard cost."
    c. "Customers have been telling our retail outlets that our two best-selling programs should be combined into one."
    d. "If the mail-order catalog sent out last week was well-received, our switchboard would be very busy by now."
    e. "By this time of year, we should have $2 million in sales instead of $1.5 million."

3. The accompanying table indicates your department's quarterly performance over the past three years. It shows the rate of return of items sold as a percentage of dollar value.

    | | Year | | |
Quarter	1	2	3
1	3.0%	3.5%	4.0%
2	4.5%	4.0%	4.5%
3	2.5%	2.5%	2.5%
4	6.5%	6.2%	7.0%

    Write down the mental models you would use as standards for detecting problems or opportunities in these data.

4. The goal of statistics is to aid the manager in deciding which deviations from mental models are problems or opportunities and which are the result of random variation. A manufacturer produces an object that is supposed to be 100 cm wide. After hundreds of measurements, she has found that 68% of the items measured between 99.9 cm and 100.1 cm; 95% measured between 99.8 cm and 100.2 cm; and all of the measurements fell within the interval from 99.7 cm to 100.3 cm. Using this historical experience, should she conclude there is a problem if a selected item measures 100.7 cm? 99.5 cm? 100.25 cm? 100.05 cm?

CHAPTER 1 QUESTIONS

1. What is a mental model?
2. Describe how Pounds's four strategies help salaried staff, professionals, and managers sense problems and opportunities.
3. Distinguish between problem sensing and diagnosis.

4. Why is problem diagnosis essential to problem solving success?

5. How are disturbance and managerial problems similar? Different?

6. Name three sources of data that can be used to detect and solve problems.

7. We use historical data to form mental models of how things ought to be. For example, our mental model says that the defective rate should average 0.4%. But the actual rate will vary from day to day or week to week. If the primary use of mental models is to detect problems or opportunities, how can statistics be helpful?

8. Provide an example from your own experience that illustrates random variation and assignable cause variation.

9. How does statistics—data collection, data organizing and summarizing, and data interpretation—help identify and solve problems?

10. Looking for relationships between data sets is an essential diagnostic skill. For example, Sarah Teman had to determine what factor(s) affected monthly attendance. How can you generate these factors?

REFERENCES

Brightman, Harvey. "The Structure of the Unstructured Acquisition Decision." Presented at the Annual Meeting of the Decision Sciences Institute, Las Vegas, 1985.

Brown, Karen. "Explaining Group Poor Performance: An Attributional Analysis." *Academy of Management Review* 9, no. 1 (1984): 54–63.

Dearborn, Dewitt, and Herbert A. Simon. "Selective Perception: A Note on the Departmental Identifications of Executives." *Sociometry* 21 (1958): 140–144.

Drucker, Peter. "What We Can Learn from Japanese Management." *Harvard Business Review* (March–April 1971): 110–122.

Folsom, Marion B. *Executive Decision Making*. New York: McGraw-Hill, 1962.

Pounds, William. "The Process of Problem Finding." *Industrial Management Review* (Fall 1969): 1–19.

APPENDIX   Brief Description of the COMCEL Organization

COMCEL manufactures, sells, and services high-quality car phones and runs one of the major mobile phone communications networks in the United States. COMCEL's corporate headquarters are in Atlanta, Georgia, and it has about 1,000 employees. It has manufacturing plants in Norcross, Georgia, and Dallas, Texas. Both plants employ about 300 workers.

Ann Tabor is CEO of the firm, and her senior team includes herself and five direct supports. Howard Bright, the plant manager in Norcross, and Arlene Taylor, the plant manager in Dallas, directly report to Nat Gordon, Vice President of Manufacturing. Pam Ascher, National Sales Manager, and Cherian Jain, Manager of Marketing Research, directly report to Bill O'Hara, Vice President of Marketing. Ms. Ascher manages four sales regions that include 30 markets. The southern region, which is the largest, includes 12 cities. The other three regions include six cities each. There are at least five to ten competitors in each sales region. However, COMCEL has been very successful. Sales have grown by 15–20% each year and recently exceeded $200 million.

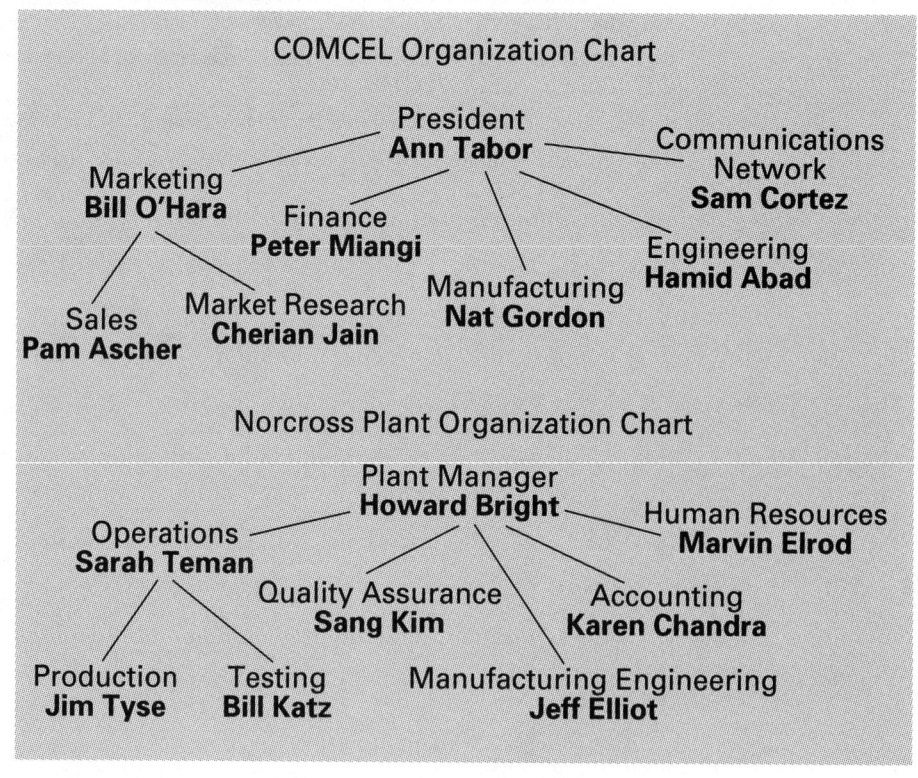

2

DESCRIPTIVE STATISTICS I: PROBLEM SENSING

2.1   Introduction
      Cross-sectional data
      Time-ordered data
2.2   Displaying cross-sectional data using tables
      and graphs
      The stem-and-leaf display
      The relative frequency distribution and
      histogram
      The cumulative frequency distribution and
      ogive
2.3   Recognizing the shape of a histogram
      Symmetric histograms
      Bell-shaped histograms
      Impact of rescaling data
      Skewed or nonsymmetric histograms
      The outlier
2.4   Displaying time-ordered data: the line graph
      Stationary time-ordered data
      Nonstationary time-ordered data
2.5   Summarizing cross-sectional data: the mean
      and standard deviation
      Distinguishing the sample from the
      population
      The mean
      Approximating the mean of histogram data
      The range
      The variance and standard deviation
2.6   Interpreting the mean and standard deviation:
      the Empirical and Chebyshev rules
      Bell-shaped histograms: the Empirical rule

      The outlier
      Skewed histograms: Chebyshev's rule
      Weakness of the mean and standard
      deviation
2.7   Summarizing cross-sectional data: the median,
      trimmed mean, and interquartile range
      The median
      Approximating the median of a frequency
      histogram
      Differences between the mean and median
      The trimmed mean
      The interquartile range
      Which set of summarizing measures?
2.8   Interpreting the median and interquartile range
      Identifying outliers using the median and
      interquartile range
      Drawing box plots
      Recognizing symmetry or skewness
2.9   Summarizing time-ordered data
      Are the mean and median informative for
      nonstationary data?
      Single moving averages
      Smoothing by moving averages
      Repeated smoothing by moving averages
      of three
      Residuals
      Impact of outliers on moving averages
2.10 Key ideas and overview
Appendix: Statistical Software

COMCEL INTEROFFICE COMMUNICATION

Date: April 1, 1994
To: Howard Bright, Manager, Norcross Plant
From: Ann Tabor, CEO
Re: Analysis of Work Group Productivity

In looking over the most recent industrial engineering report for the work groups at the Norcross plant, I was disappointed to see that so many are performing below industry standards. I note on the positive side that one work group is performing at 123% of standard. If one group can perform this well, why can't they all?

Please look into this and report back as soon as possible.

2.1 ≡ Introduction

Aspiring managers must learn to identify opportunities as well as potential problems. Problem sensing is a crucial managerial activity, since we cannot solve a problem until we know it exists. Effective managers detect emerging problems long before they become crises; they also uncover opportunities before their competitors do.

How can managers become more effective in problem sensing? As noted in Chapter 1, they must learn to organize, summarize, and interpret large quantities of data. Simple descriptive statistics that organize and summarize data can help build mental models.

Where do managers get data to build their mental models? If they do not already have the data set, they create it or buy it. The firm's management information system provides much of the in-house data in the form of routine structured reports. Typically, these reports contain financial, accounting, marketing, and operations data. The data describe the state of the firm and are historical, aggregated, and internal to the firm. (An example is the monthly attendance report from Chapter 1.)

Managers can also purchase external data bases, undertake surveys, or conduct planned change studies. A survey is a sampling of facts or opinions that is used to estimate how an entire group would respond. Typical business examples are attitude surveys and marketing research studies. Surveys are especially important in uncovering emerging business opportunities. To seek ways of improving departmental performance, managers may run small-scale planned change experiments or pilot projects and study the results. If the planned change is an improvement, they may implement it permanently.

Once managers uncover problems, they must diagnose them quickly and accurately. Diagnosis is the ability to understand the problem and discover its root causes. Many managers are poor diagnosticians who jump to conclusions about problem causality, blame others, or totally ignore problem diagnosis in their rush to solve a problem.

Over the next two chapters, we will discuss the role of statistics—that is, of summarizing, organizing, and interpreting data—in problem sensing and diagnosis. The management information system, external data bases, surveys, and planned change studies are the sources of data. They provide two types of data-cross-sectional and time-ordered data. We shall examine each kind in turn.

Cross-Sectional Data

Cross-sectional data are measurements taken *at one time period* on different persons, places, or things, such as four plants, 50 workers, or several departments. Here are two examples.

Example 1: Absenteeism data from four plants during January

Example 2: Job attitude and productivity data for 50 workers during the second week of July

The cross-sectional data for the two examples differ. In Example 1 data are collected on only *one* variable—absenteeism. A *variable* is a characteristic that has different values, all measured in the same units, such as dollars, number of sales, productivity, sick hours lost, or consulting hours. In Example 2 data are collected on multiple variables—job attitude and productivity. Both examples contain cross-sectional data, however, since all the data describe a person, place, or thing at one point in time.

Time-Ordered Data

Time-ordered, or time series, data are data collected over time, in chronological sequence. Here are three examples.

Example 1:   Absenteeism data for plant 1 from March to December

Example 2:   Absenteeism data and productivity data for plant 1 from March to December

Example 3:   Absenteeism data and productivity data for plants 3 and 4 from March to December

The first example illustrates time-ordered data for one place (plant 1) on one variable (absenteeism). The second example shows time-ordered data for one plant on two variables (absenteeism and productivity). Example 3 involves *panel data*, which combine features of cross-sectional data and time-ordered data. The data are cross-sectional because measurements are taken in two plants in any one month. The data are time-ordered because the measurements are taken over time.

Cross-sectional and time-ordered data are both important to managers, but most routine data that management information systems deliver are time-ordered. Figure 2.1 visualizes the differences between time-ordered and cross-sectional data and how panel data are related to both.

It is the aim of these next two chapters to show how to decipher the information embodied by cross-sectional and time-ordered data. In plain English, what are the data trying to say, and what can be learned from them? The remainder of this chapter will demonstrate how to organize, summarize, and interpret cross-sectional and

---

FIGURE 2.1   Differences Between Cross-Sectional and Time-Ordered Data

Period	Plant 1	Plant 2	Plant 3	Plant 4
Jan.	Cross-sectional data			
Feb.				
Mar.	Time-ordered data on one place		Time-ordered data on two places (panel data)	
Apr.				
May				
June				
July				
Aug.				
Sept.				
Oct.				
Nov.				
Dec.				

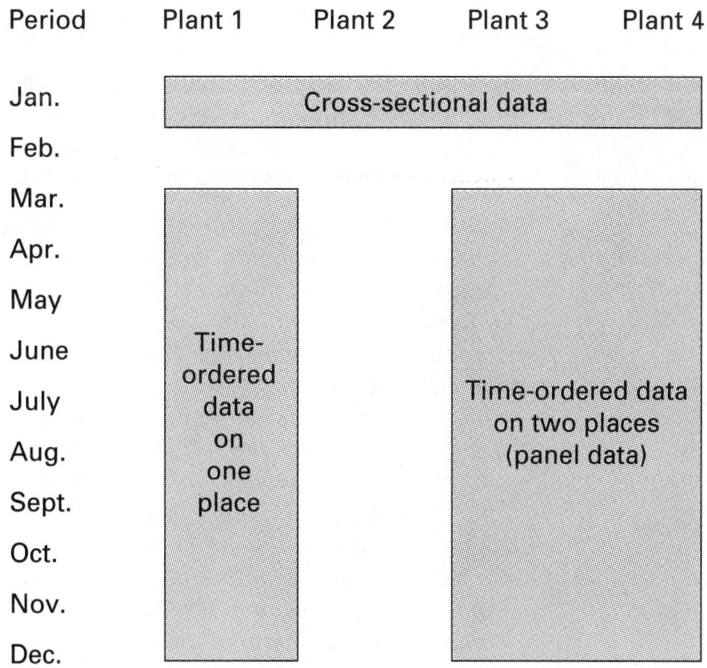

time-ordered data in order to sense problems. In Chapter 3 the emphasis will be on how to use the data to diagnose problems.

SECTION 2.1 EXERCISES

1. For each of the data sets listed indicate whether they are cross-sectional data (C) or time-ordered data (T).
    a. Daily Dow-Jones industrial averages
    b. The results of a Gallup poll on presidential preferences
    c. Mean salaries by department of a college for the academic year 1993–1994
    d. The Consumer Price Index by year since 1967

2. Explain the difference between problem sensing and problem diagnosis.

3. Explain why problem sensing can be done with one variable, while problem diagnosis usually requires the study of two or more variables. (See Chapter 1.)

2.2 ≡ Displaying Cross-Sectional Data Using Tables and Graphs

Displaying cross-sectional data helps managers see the structure underlying the data. They can then begin developing simple mental models of how their departments are operating—the first step of effective problem sensing. By the end of this section you should be able to:

1. draw a stem-and-leaf display for a small data set;
2. draw a frequency histogram for a large data set;
3. convert a frequency histogram into a relative frequency histogram and interpret it; and
4. construct and interpret a cumulative frequency distribution, a cumulative percent distribution, and an ogive.

The Stem-and-Leaf Display

No matter how small the data set, always draw a diagram. A picture conveys more than words or numbers can. It can help you to see the structure or underlying pattern within the data, which is, after all, the purpose of organizing and displaying the data. For a small data set, consider the **stem-and-leaf display**.

A stem-and-leaf display shows the number of observations that share a common stem and the value of each observation.

Example: Claims Adjustment Data   As manager of an insurance claims department, you must set performance standards. You ask 30 experienced claims adjusters to record the number of claims they process in the coming week. The totals are listed in Table 2.1.

To create a stem-and-leaf display draw a vertical line, and separate each number into its first digit, the stem, and its second digit, the leaf. Put a stem on the left side of the vertical line and all of its attached leaves on the right. Do the same with the other stems and their leaves. The stem-and-leaf display should look like Figure 2.2.

In Figure 2.2, the stem-and-leaf display has only three stems, so much detail is lost. It is redrawn in Figure 2.3 with two improvements. First, the stem is repeated for the two large classes and the leaf digits are arranged in order from the smallest to the largest on each stem. Second, digits from 0 to 4 go in the first row of a repeating stem and digits 5 to 9 go in the second row. These changes make the display more understandable and will be useful later in calculating measures of the center and variability.

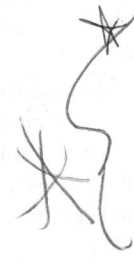

FIGURE 2.5   Frequency Histogram for Number of Claims Processed by 30 Adjusters

? I think this should
be # of adjusters
not days.

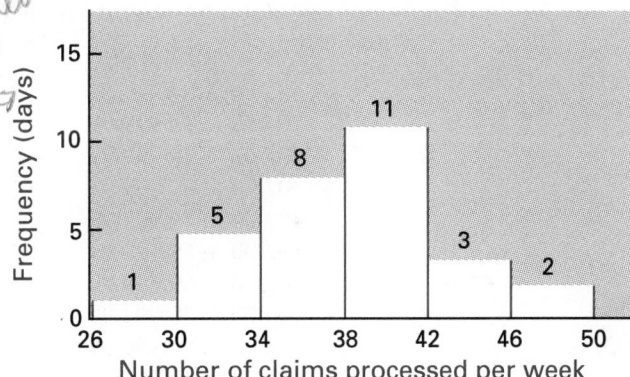

misleading. Since the purpose of the display is to compare frequency counts between classes, the basis of comparison will not be the same when classes have unequal widths.

Steps in Constructing a Frequency Distribution

1. Decide on the number of classes.
2. Find the range of the data—the largest data value minus the smallest data value.
3. Divide the range by the desired number of classes to find the class width. Round if necessary to a number that is easily interpretable.
4. Choose a lower limit for the first class so that the smallest data value falls slightly above the lower limit.
5. Record the number of data points that fall in each class.

In constructing Table 2.2, we decided on six classes. The range for the claims data is $48 - 28 = 20$, so the class width must be about $20/6 = 3.3$. An easily interpreted class width was 4. As mentioned, we chose 26 as a convenient starting point.

Figure 2.5 is a frequency histogram for the claims data set as grouped in the frequency table. The number of claims processed is on the horizontal axis. Place the lower limits of each class on the horizontal axis. The vertical axis shows the frequency count of each class (the number of adjusters). In Figure 2.5, the height of the vertical lines represents the number of observations in each class.

Open-Ended Classes   Sometimes it is impractical to use class intervals of equal width over the entire range of the frequency distribution. For example, how would we classify a sample of 1,000 household incomes ranging from $0 to $4,000,000 into ten classes? If we divide the range by 10, each class would have a width of $400,000. More than 99% of the data values would fall in the first class, and less than 1% would be distributed over the other nine classes—a very uninformative depiction of the data. How then should we set up the classes for a useful frequency distribution of household incomes? Table 2.3 shows one possibility. The last class is *open-ended*. This does not distort the frequency distribution, since the classes in the middle of the distribution all have the same width of $10,000, and 980 of the 1,000 data values fall into classes with equal widths. An open-ended class is a good solution for displaying some data sets.

Table 2.3

Histogram for Income (in Dollars) with an Open-Ended Class

Income Class ($)	Number of Families
$0 to 9,999.99	80
10,000 to 19,999.99	130
20,000 to 29,999.99	145
30,000 to 39,999.99	185
40,000 to 49,999.99	130
50,000 to 59,999.99	105
60,000 to 69,999.99	80
70,000 to 79,999.99	70
80,000 to 89,999.99	55
90,000 and above	20
Total:	1,000

The Relative Frequency Distribution and Histogram

A frequency table shows how many data points from a sample fall into each class. But the actual frequency counts would change as the sample size changed, thus obscuring the development of a simple mental model of the department's performance. One way around the problem of changing sample sizes is to construct a *relative* frequency table or *relative* frequency distribution.

Start with a frequency table as shown in Table 2.2. Divide each frequency count by the total number of data points and then multiply by 100. The resulting percentages are relative frequencies: the proportional occurence of each class of observations.

Table 2.4 shows the relative frequency or percentage distribution for the experienced claims adjusters. From it, the manager might formulate several mental models.

Model 1. Over one-third of the time (36.7%), an experienced claims adjuster can process from 38 to 41 claims per week.

Model 2. Over one-fourth of the time (26.7%), an experienced claims adjuster can process from 34 to 37 claims per week.

Model 3. An experienced claims adjuster rarely (3.3% of the time) completes fewer than 30 claims per week.

Model 4. An experienced claims adjuster seldom (6.6% of the time) completes 46 or more claims per week.

Table 2.4

Frequency and Relative Frequency Distribution

Claims Processed Classes	Number of Adjusters	Percentage
26 to 29	1	1/30 = 3.3
30 to 33	5	5/30 = 16.7
34 to 37	8	8/30 = 26.7
38 to 41	11	11/30 = 36.7
42 to 45	3	3/30 = 10.0
46 to 49	2	2/30 = 6.6
Totals:	30	100.0

FIGURE 2.6   Relative Frequency Histogram for Number of
Claims Processed by 30 Adjusters

This graph is exactly the same as 2.5 only the heading is different. Why?

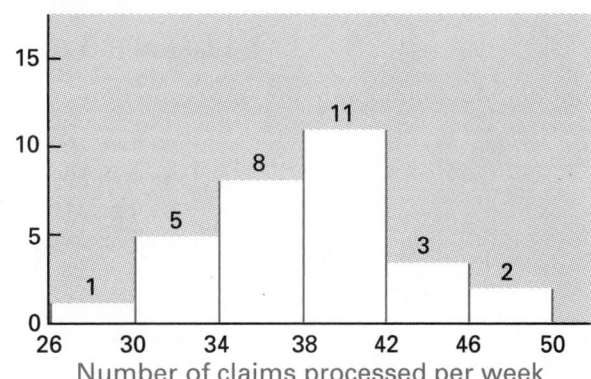

A relative frequency histogram is similar to a frequency histogram, as Figure 2.6 shows. The horizontal axis again represents the number of claims. The vertical axis shows the percentages (rather than the actual frequencies) of the data set falling into each class.

The Cumulative Frequency Distribution and Ogive

Problem sensing involves examining the numbers at the extremes, or tails, of a frequency distribution. By slightly modifying the relative frequency table we can focus attention on the data at either tail of the distribution. The aim is to show how the data accumulate, their cumulative distribution.

In Table 2.5 two new columns have been added to Table 2.4. The first new column is labeled the cumulative frequency. Each row entry is the sum of the entries in the frequency column up to and including that row. For example, the entry in the third row of the cumulative frequency column is the sum of the entries in the first three rows of the frequency column, 1 + 5 + 8 = 14. That is, 14 adjusters processed fewer than 38 claims. Similarly, the cumulative percentage column is the cumulative sum of the percentage column. Row 5 tells the manager that 93.3% of the adjusters processed fewer than 46 claims a week.

Table 2.5

Constructing a Cumulative Frequency and
Cumulative Percentage Distribution

Claims Processed Classes	Number of Adjusters	Percentage	Cumulative Frequency	Cumulative Percentage
26 to 29	1	3.3	1	3.3
30 to 33	5	16.7	6 (1+5)	20.0
34 to 37	8	26.7	14 (1+5+8)	46.7
38 to 41	11	36.7	25	83.3
42 to 45	3	10.0	28	93.3
46 to 49	2	6.6	30	100.0

An ogive is a graph of the cumulative frequency or cumulative percentage distribution.

An **ogive** is a graph of a cumulative frequency or cumulative percentage distribution. To plot an ogive for the cumulative percentage distribution of processed claims, we must modify the first and fifth columns of Table 2.5 as shown.

Claims Processed Class	Cumulative Percentage
Less than 26	0.0
Less than 30	3.3
Less than 34	20.0
Less than 38	46.7
Less than 42	83.3
Less than 46	93.3
Less than 50	100.0

The revised entries are then plotted in Figure 2.7 below. To have the ogive start at 0, the first point is an additional one placed at the intersection of the horizontal axis value of 26 claims and the vertical axis value of 0%. The second point is at the intersection of the horizontal axis value of 30 claims and the vertical axis value of 3.3%. Recall that 30 is the smallest number of claims in the second class, so *less than* 30 matches up with the cumulative percentage in the first class, or 3.3%. The rest of the ogive is constructed in a similar fashion.

Managers could use Figure 2.7 to sense problems and to make routine staffing decisions. Suppose that an experienced claims adjuster completes only 20 claims in a week. Figure 2.7 shows that the sample of 30 experienced claims adjusters never processed fewer than 26 claims. The low value of 20 claims may signal a disturbance problem. Alternatively, if an adjuster completes 55 claims in a week, this may signal

FIGURE 2.7   Ogive for Number of Claims Processed by 30 Adjusters

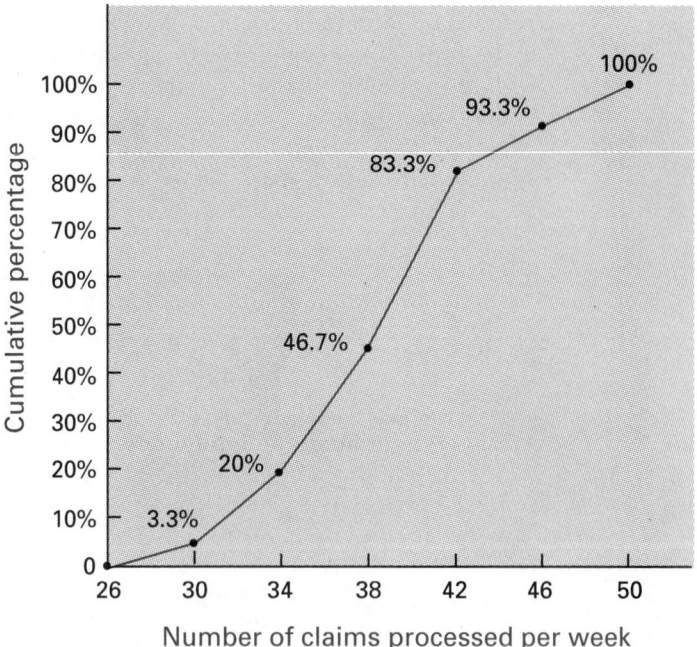

an opportunity. Perhaps this worker is doing something differently that could improve the entire staff's productivity. Knowing that adjusters process under 38 claims per week about half the time (46.7%) will also help the manager determine staffing needs.

In summary, use stem-and-leaf displays, frequency histograms, or ogives to develop mental models. The mental models will then help to sense emerging disturbance problems, to recognize opportunities, or to make routine decisions.

SECTION 2.2 EXERCISES

1. Shown below are interest percentage rates charged on 30-year fixed-rate mortgage loans at 15 San Antonio banks. Construct a stem-and-leaf display to show the data.

10.75	10.25	9.75	11.1	13.0
10.5	9.85	12.25	10.25	10.5
10.1	10.75	12.0	12.75	10.75

2. A comparison shopper found the following prices per pound on the same cut of meat at 30 different grocery stores and specialty food shops.

5.23	5.65	6.30	6.72	7.00
5.26	5.95	6.50	6.72	7.00
5.30	5.95	6.65	6.74	7.15
5.45	6.13	6.69	6.90	7.15
5.49	6.20	6.70	7.00	7.20
5.55	6.30	6.70	7.00	7.20

    a. Make a stem-and-leaf display.
    b. Construct a frequency table with five classes.

3. Construct a stem-and-leaf display using 3 stems for the following data.

32.5	33.2	33.5	41.5	40.3	25.1	42.9	32.7	23.2	36.6
34.5	33.8	42.6	26.5	36.8	28.3	45.8	34.0	36.1	34.7

4. Construct a stem-and-leaf display using 4 stems for the following GPA data for seniors majoring in Business at Louisiana State University.

2.41	3.44	3.47	3.71	3.95	2.82	2.71	2.68	3.19	2.91
2.21	2.67	2.89	3.21	3.31	2.78	2.89	3.04	3.40	2.89

5. The two tables below indicate the number of arrests for DUI in 32 states (matched on the number of DUIs before the test program) for a test month. The test program involves mandatory loss of driving license for a first DUI offense.

No Test Program					Test Program			
820	1021	900	889		760	707	814	678
706	967	934	904		550	606	890	603
945	812	834	967		790	678	900	657
806	906	781	978		678	704	678	734

    a. Draw two stem-and-leaf displays using hundreds digits as stems.
    b. Do the displays suggest that the mandatory loss of driving license affects the number of DUIs?

6. In constructing a frequency distribution you must decide how to group the numbers into classes. Each data point must belong to one and only one class. The classes should be of equal width unless there are open classes at the tails of the distribution. Suppose you are classifying sales receipts at a grocery store. What, if anything, is wrong with the class groupings shown.

a.	b.	c.
$0 to $9	$0 to $19.99	$0 to under $20.00
$10 to $29	$20 to $59.99	$20 to under $40.00
$20 to $39	$60 to $79.99	$40 to under $60.00
$30 to $39	$80 to $99.99	$60 to under $80.00
$40 and over	$100 and over	$80.00 and over

7. The data shown below are price earnings ratios for 30 common stocks. Classify the data using the classes shown and determine the frequency and relative frequency distributions.

						Class	Frequency	Percentage
14.2	2.9	15.5	11.3	15.2	20.4	0 to 4.99	____	____
16.5	4.5	23.2	11.6	21.7	16.8	5 to 9.99	____	____
12.1	6.7	22.5	12.0	22.5	18.9	10 to 14.99	____	____
11.4	8.7	19.3	7.4	23.1	9.6	15 to 19.99	____	____
9.5	9.8	19.5	14.1	24.4	8.2	20 to 24.99	____	____

8. COMCEL'S management wishes to construct a frequency histogram to investigate the length of service of its employees. The smallest number of years of service is 1.5, and the largest number of years of service is 25.7. Begin the first class with zero years and use integer class widths.
a. If six classes are desired, what should the classes be?
b. If four classes are desired, what should the classes be?
c. If five classes are desired, what should the classes be?

9. A plant manager recorded the number of accidents occurring in 24 work groups. The resulting frequency table is shown.

Accidents	Frequency	Accidents	Cumulative Frequency	Cumulative Percentage
1 to 2	6	Less than 1	____	____
3 to 4	10	Less than 3	____	____
5 to 6	5	Less than 5	____	____
7 to 8	2	Less than 7	____	____
9 to 10	1	Less than 9	____	____
	24	Less than 11	____	____

a. Complete the table and plot a graph of the cumulative percentages—the ogive.
b. What mental model could a manager develop based on these data?
c. Suppose a work group experienced 11 accidents. What might that suggest?

10. A company with two branch offices wished to compare sales commissions paid to employees during the 1990 calendar year. The data are shown.

Sales Commission	Office 1	Office 2
Up to $5,000	15	2
$5,000 to $9,999.99	100	23
$10,000 to $14,999.99	65	13
$15,000 or over	20	12
	200	50

a. Convert these frequency tables to percentage tables.

b. Convert these frequency tables to cumulative frequency tables.

c. Convert the percentage tables from part a to cumulative percentage tables.

d. Which of the tables provides the easiest means of comparison of sales commissions between the two offices? Explain.

11. The accompanying table shows gas prices at 20 stations for unleaded gasoline in Atlanta on Memorial Day 1993.

1.13	1.05	1.21	1.06	1.31
1.23	1.25	1.17	1.19	1.24
1.19	1.27	1.24	1.23	1.14
1.18	1.29	1.28	1.09	1.34

a. Construct a relative frequency histogram for the data. Use four classes and a class width of 10 cents. Begin the first interval at $1.00.

b. What percentage of the stations sampled charged $1.30 or more?

c. Would you expect the percentage of all stations charging $1.30 or more in Atlanta to be the same percentage that you computed in part **b**? Discuss.

12. Shown are two cumulative percentage distributions for the number of incorrect accounting postings before and after a quality improvement training program.

a. Draw two ogives to represent the data on the same graph.

b. Interpret the two ogives, and determine if the quality training program had been effective.

Incorrect Postings	Before Cum %	After Cum %
0	5	60
1	20	80
2	50	90
3	80	95
4	95	98
5	100	100

13. Consider the following data set of 5-year average percent return on equity for the following 30 high-performing firms with sales under $100 million dollars.

13.5	24.5	34.5	10.8	45.6	24.9
35.8	23.9	14.9	40.7	50.7	37.8
38.7	26.6	17.9	42.8	37.9	24.8
58.7	39.5	36.7	21.5	42.6	58.7
11.4	32.6	37.9	42.4	35.8	47.1

a. Construct a frequency histogram with 5 classes. Begin the first class at 10.0%.

b. Construct a frequency ogive.

c. Construct a percentage ogive.

d. What percentage of the 30 firms in the sample had 5-year average returns on equity of 50% or more.

e. Would you expect the percentage of all small firms with a 5-year average return on equity of 50% or more to be the same as your answer in part **d**? Explain.

14. Refer to Figure 2.6 in the text. If a recently hired claims adjuster processes 28 claims per week, what reaction as manager would you have in terms of his performance? if he processed 54 claims per week?

2.3 ≡ Recognizing the Shape of a Histogram

The shape of a histogram is important in summarizing and understanding data. By the end of this section you should be able to:

1. recognize symmetric, bell-shaped, and skewed histograms;
2. explain how rescaling can affect the shape of a histogram; and
3. explain what outliers are and what they could mean.

Symmetric Histograms

In a symmetric histogram the classes left of center are mirror images of those right of center.

What characterizes a **symmetric histogram**? Consider the two frequency histograms shown in Figure 2.8. First find the centers, or balance points. Think of the number of observations in each class as weights and the horizontal axis of the histogram as a wooden board. In each class there is a stack of weights, one for each observation. Below the wooden board is a steel rod. Move the rod back and forth. The point where the board balances is the center of the frequency histogram and the mean of the data points, as depicted in Figure 2.9. It is evident that both histograms of Figure 2.8 balance at the value of 40. The classes to the right of the centers of both histograms are mirror images of the classes to the left. It is the mirror image characteristic of these histograms that makes them symmetric.

You should not expect real data sets to be perfectly symmetric. That happens only in statistics books. Yet many real-world histograms are close to symmetric.

FIGURE 2.8   Two Frequency Histograms

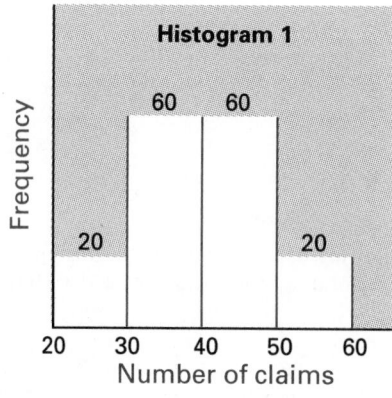
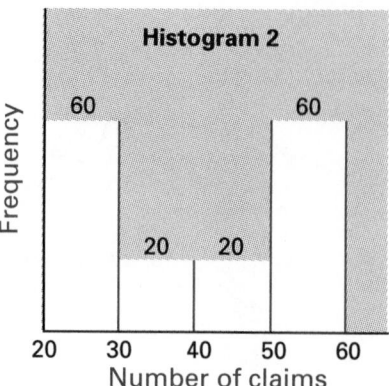

FIGURE 2.9   Balance Point for Histogram

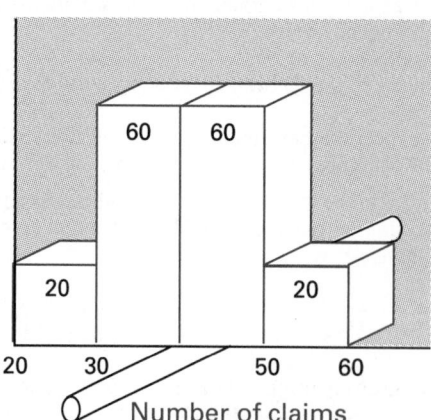
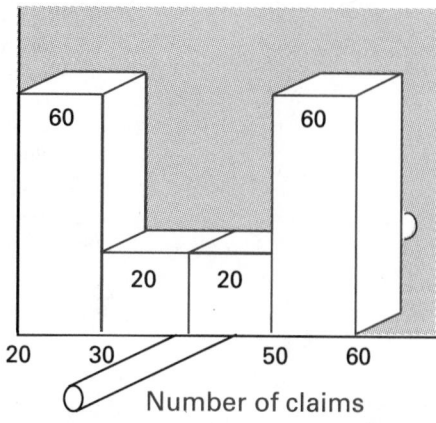

Bell-Shaped Histograms

Bell-shaped histograms are symmetric, have one peak, and are mound-shaped.

The **bell-shaped histogram** is one special type of symmetric histogram. One is presented in Figure 2.10 below for data on the values of loans at a bank. The center of the histogram is halfway between $500 and $550; that is, $525 is the mean loan. While the histogram is symmetric, it is also bell-shaped. Notice the following features:

1. Many of the dollar values of loans are at or near the center.
2. There are successively fewer values away from the center.
3. Moving in either direction from the center, the numbers of loans first drop off slowly, then more rapidly, and then more slowly again.

The bell-shaped histogram is very important in data analysis because it allows us to make precise statements regarding how far particular data values are from the histogram's center. This is a powerful way to summarize data, as will be shown in Section 2.6.

Impact of Rescaling Data

There are two reasons why a histogram may not look bell-shaped. One is that the class intervals chosen may hide the bell shape. The other, of course, is that data are not bell-shaped and no degree of rescaling them will make the histogram bell-shaped.

An example of the first situation can be demonstrated using the data in Table 2.6. The data represent the number of days needed to complete a project. By varying the class intervals, we can observe its effect on the appearance of the data.

Begin by constructing an initial frequency distribution and a histogram. Use the balance point idea to estimate the mean of the data set. For example, histogram A of Figure 2.11 is a graph of distribution A of Table 2.7. The histogram is not bell-shaped. The estimated mean of the dataset from histogram A is slightly more than 10. When the classes are changed so that 10 is the middle value, or midpoint, of the middle class of distribution B, histogram B becomes bell-shaped.

The impact of changing class limits or the class width on the shape of the histogram is clearly significant. If rescaling does not result in a bell-shaped histogram, then the second situation—the underlying data are not bell-shaped—holds.

FIGURE 2.10   A Normal-Shaped Frequency Histogram

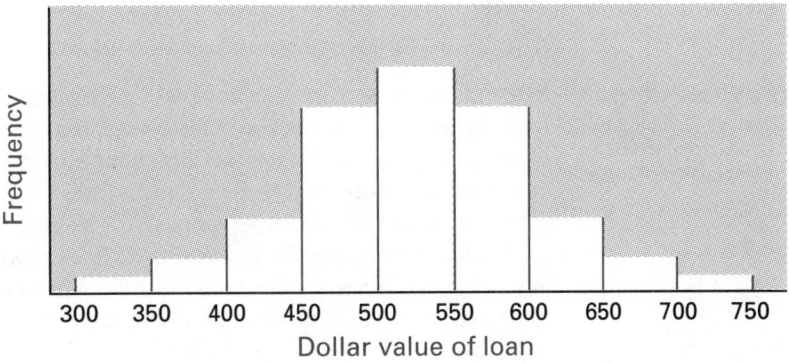

Table 2.6

Days Needed to Complete a Project

2.6	5.7	10.2	11.0	15.2
3.5	5.9	10.4	11.1	15.3
3.9	6.7	10.6	12.2	16.3
4.3	8.0	10.8	13.7	17.8
5.4	8.4	10.9	14.6	19.5

Table 2.7

Two Frequency Distributions for Project Completion Data

A		B	
Class	Days	Class	Days
0 to 4.9	4	0 to 3.9	3
5 to 9.9	6	4 to 7.9	5
10 to 14.9	10	8 to 11.9	9
15 to 19.9	5	12 to 15.9	5
	25	16 to 19.9	3
			25

FIGURE 2.11   Impact of Scaling on Shape of Frequency Histogram

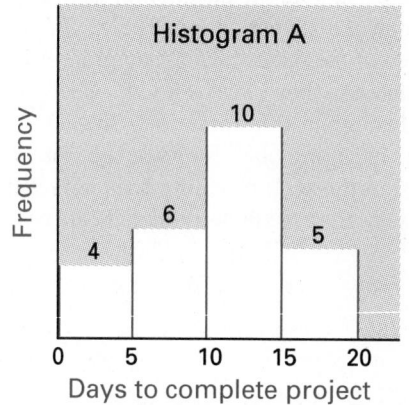
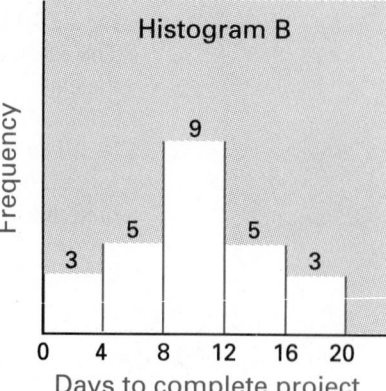

Skewed or Nonsymmetric Histograms

Skewed distributions fall off more slowly on one side of the class with the highest frequency than on the other side.

Skewed histograms are not symmetric. This can be seen readily by using the class with the highest frequency as a reference point. If more classes lie to the left of this class than to the right, then the distribution is skewed to the left. That is, the data values fall off more slowly toward the left than toward the right. If a histogram falls off more slowly toward larger values, it is skewed to the right.

Table 2.8 on page 35 shows COMCEL's productivity data for 36 work groups at its Norcross plant for the month of July. A frequency histogram for the cross-sectional data using a class width of 5 is shown in Figure 2.12. What does the histogram say about the various work groups?

Table 2.8

Work Group Productivity as a Percentage of Industrial Engineering Standards

Group	Productivity	Group	Productivity
1	106	19	110
2	95	20	123
3	103	21	104
4	95	22	100
5	95	23	101
6	97	24	95
7	95	25	97
8	105	26	94
9	102	27	102
10	89	28	102
11	105	29	106
12	99	30	110
13	95	31	97
14	100	32	101
15	106	33	95
16	101	34	98
17	97	35	97
18	104	36	94

FIGURE 2.12   Frequency Histogram for Productivity Data for 36 Work Groups

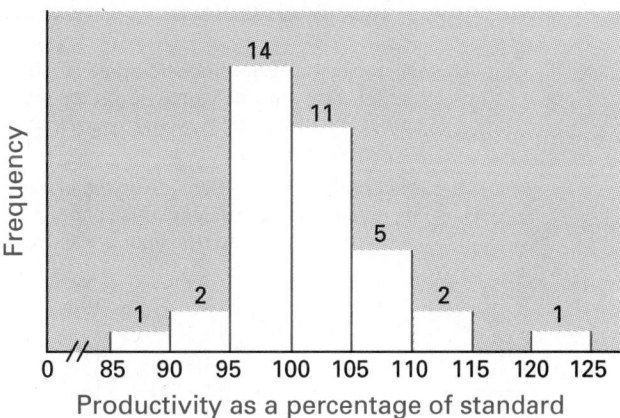

The histogram is skewed toward higher values, or skewed to the right. The frequencies for the higher productivity classes fall off more slowly than those for the lower classes. Most work groups produced from 95% to under 110%. The productivity of 123% for work group 20 stands out from the rest; perhaps it is an outlier.

The Outlier

A rudimentary definition of an outlier is any value that is much larger or smaller than most of the other values. Outliers can signify major deviations from standard or historic performance, and thus are essential to effective problem sensing. We say "can" for there are three possible explanations for an outlier.

1. The outlier is due to a coding error.
2. The outlier is due to chance, or random variation.
3. The outlier signifies the onset of a problem or an opportunity—assignable cause variation.

Outliers can be the result of coding errors in the form of inaccurate record keeping. A supervisor records work group 20's productivity as 123% when it is really 103%. If coding errors are eliminated as a cause, then the outlier may signify a chance happening. If a monkey sitting at a typewriter types the alphabet in the correct order, it is due to chance. We don't expect it to happen, but it could. Chance involves probabilities, which are presented in Chapters 4 and 5.

Assuming that chance can also be ruled out, then the outlier indicates either a disturbance problem or an opportunity. We must determine the cause(s) of the outlier. Suppose that the workers in group 20 had learned each other's jobs and thus could frequently switch jobs. Job switching might then account for their exceptional productivity. Alternatively, perhaps there is something distinctive about the group members—seniority, level of cooperation, or amount of schooling—that accounts for their high productivity. Later in this chapter we will demonstrate how to identify outliers using descriptive statistics.

In summary, knowing a histogram's shape is informative. For example, telling a colleague that COMCEL's work group productivities are skewed toward higher values provides him or her with a clear picture of the data. After identifying a distribution's shape, look for outliers, as they may signal an emerging problem or opportunity.

SECTION 2.3 EXERCISES

1. On a recent test in a statistics class of 20 students, 19 of the students scored between 70 and 95. One student scored 45 on the test, and the teacher said that this student was an outlier. What questions would you ask to determine why the student did so poorly—that is, was an outlier?

2. A worker selects 30 items from the assembly line every hour and measures the width of the item to the nearest tenth of a centimeter. The width should be 15 ± 1 centimeters. The measurements for the first hour are shown below.

13.8	14.6	14.8	15.1	15.3	15.5
14.2	14.7	14.9	15.1	15.3	15.6
14.3	14.7	14.9	15.2	15.4	15.7
14.4	14.8	15.0	15.2	15.4	15.8
14.5	14.8	15.1	15.3	15.4	16.1

    a. Construct a frequency table with four classes.
    b. Sketch the histogram for the frequency table and estimate the mean or balance point of the distribution.
    c. Construct a frequency table with six classes with the estimated mean as the lower limit of the fourth class.
    d. Sketch the histogram for the revised frequency table.
    e. Do the data appear to be bell-shaped?

3. Must bell-shaped histograms be symmetric? Must symmetric histograms be bell-shaped?

4. Refer to Exercise 2. Suppose several hours later, you obtain the following frequency distribution on widths.

Class	Frequency
13 to 13.99	8
14 to 14.99	20
15 to 15.99	60
16 to 16.99	12

    a. Given the acceptable width of 15 ± 1 centimeters, what can you conclude?

    b. What action should you take now?

5. You are recording family incomes in a typical large city. Family incomes range from $7,200 to $750,000. Would you expect that the frequency histogram for family incomes would be skewed toward lower incomes, be symmetric, or be skewed toward higher incomes?

6. Below is a histogram on the number of claims processed per week.

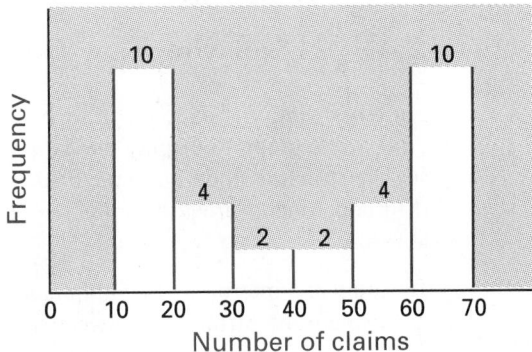

    a. Is the above frequency histogram symmetric?

    b. Using the balance point idea, approximate the mean number of claims.

    c. Interpret the histogram. That is, what information can you derive from it?

    d. What factors might account for a "U-shaped" histogram.

7. Below is a frequency histogram of the number of incorrect postings per day by an operator over the last 30 workdays.

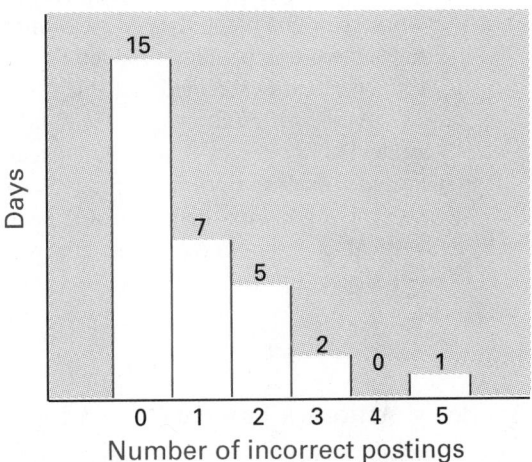

    a. Are the data skewed right or skewed left?

    b. Using the balance point idea, approximate the mean number of incorrect postings.

8. Refer to Exercise 2.7. The five errors made in one of the days appears to be an outlier. What are two other possible explanations for this observation?

9. The accompanying frequency table represents the number of women directors in the Fortune 1,000 firms.

Number of Firms	481	386	113	15	3	2
Number of Women Directors	0	1	2	3	4	5

Source: Catalyst.

a. Draw the histogram. Is the histogram skewed right or left?
b. Using the balance point idea, approximate the mean number of women directors in the Fortune 1,000 firms.
c. Construct a cumulative percentage distribution.
d. What percent of the 1,000 firms have more than 3 women directors?

2.4 ≡ Displaying Time-Ordered Data: The Line Graph

For cross-sectional data, we draw histograms or ogives. For time-ordered data, we draw a line graph to display the data. Displaying time-ordered data helps managers see the structure underlying the data. Then they can develop simple models of how their departments are performing *over time*. By the end of this section you should be able to:

1. draw and interpret a line graph; and
2. explain the difference between stationary and nonstationary time-ordered data.

Stationary Time-Ordered Data

The following example illustrates how managers can use time-ordered data to develop simple mental models.

Example: Job Attitude Data   As part of its continual job climate assessment, COMCEL collects monthly data on the mean responses of ten workers to statement 4 from the climate study questionnaire shown in Table 1.2. The statement, "The workers in this plant always try to improve," is designed to assess the workers' attitudes toward improving productivity. COMCEL's monthly attitude data for the past three years are presented in Table 2.9.

A *line graph* to display the data's structure is shown in Figure 2.13. The horizontal axis measures time in months, and the vertical axis is the level of the variable, attitude toward improving productivity. Attitude level varies from 1 (poor attitude) to 5 (very good attitude). Equal distances between grid marks on the horizontal and vertical axes should represent equal differences in amounts. Using unequal distances will distort the line graph.

Table 2.9

Mean of Ten Workers' Attitudes Toward Improving Productivity over the Past 36 Months

Year	Jan.	Feb.	Mar.	Apr.	May	June	July	Aug.	Sept.	Oct.	Nov.	Dec.
1990	4.81	2.60	3.12	3.66	2.80	3.60	2.94	1.87	2.30	1.80	4.60	2.56
1991	4.60	2.41	3.46	3.50	2.21	3.82	2.08	2.06	2.20	2.20	4.30	2.91
1992	4.60	2.73	3.38	3.46	2.43	3.60	2.39	1.99	2.17	2.01	4.40	2.36

FIGURE 2.13   COMCEL's Monthly Attitude Data, 1990–1992

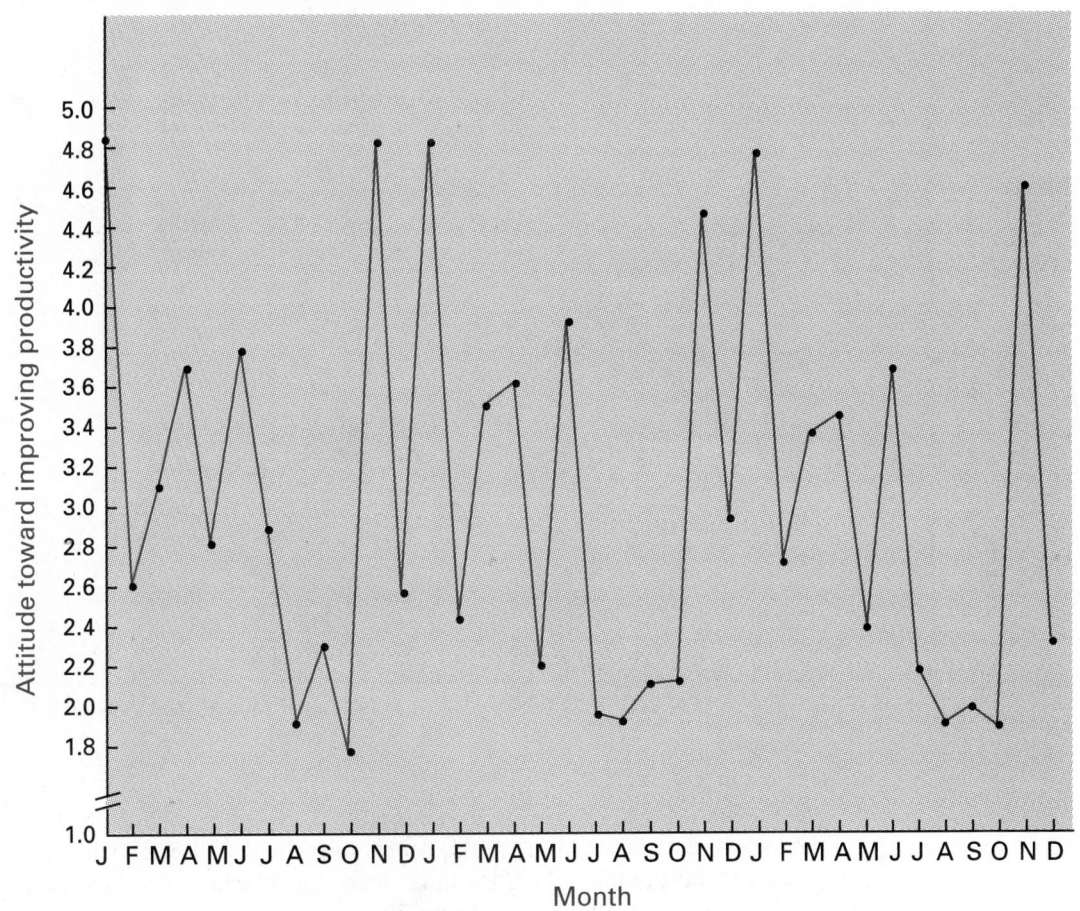

What does the line graph reveal? Look for patterns! First, the data are **stationary**, because there is no upward or downward trend over time. While attitudes vary from month to month, the graph shows no systematic tendency for attitudes to improve or deteriorate over the 36 months. Specifically, the mean attitude score over the 3-year period is 3.00. The mean attitude scores for each of the 3 years, 1990, 1991, and 1992, are 3.06, 2.98, and 2.96, respectively. Thus the mean score over the 3-year period is virtually the same as that of any given year. The mean value of the series has remained constant over time.

> A time-ordered series is stationary when the general level of the series remains nearly constant over the entire time period. The values of a stationary series fluctuate around a constant mean value.

The second thing to note is that attitudes are highest for the same two months—namely, January and November—each year. Monthly attitudes are lowest from August to October each year. Effective managers should now ask why attitudes toward improving productivity are highest in January and November and lowest in August through October each year. Asking why is the beginning of problem diagnosis.

Nonstationary Time-Ordered Data

Next, consider the line graphs in Figure 2.14 and compare them with the line graph in Figure 2.13. Immediately, one notices that the line graphs in Figure 2.14 display

FIGURE 2.14   Examples of Nonstationary Time-Ordered Data

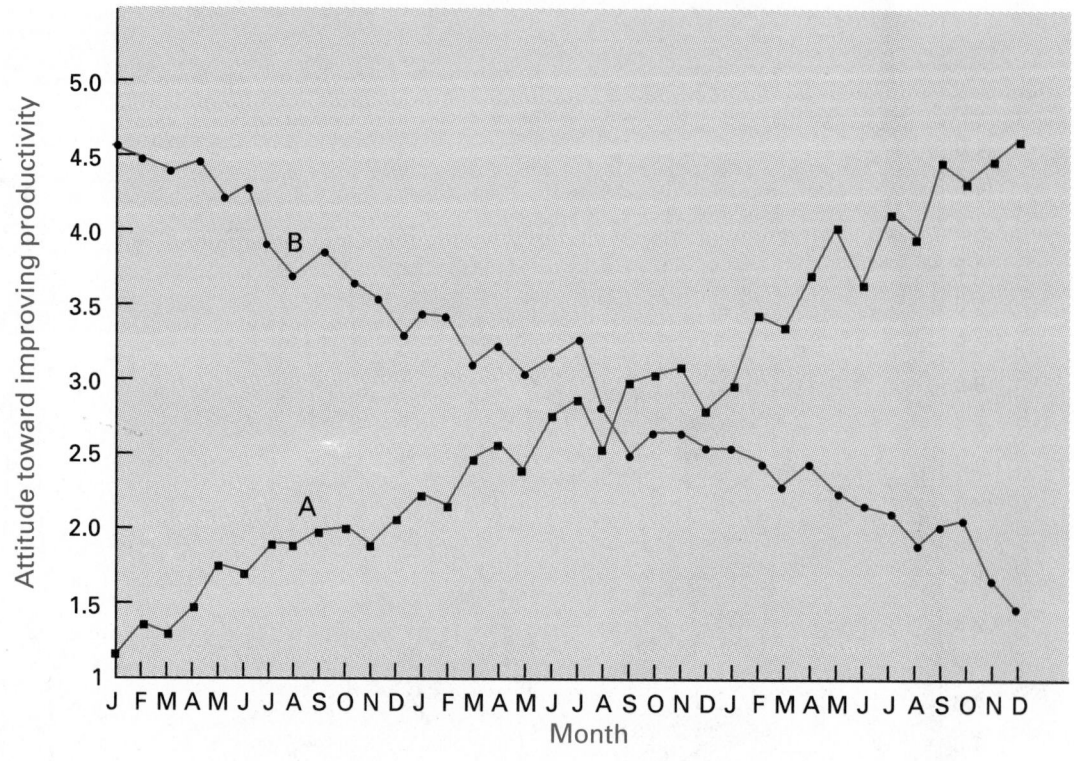

clear tendencies, in contrast to that in Figure 2.13. Line graph A shows an overall increase or upward trend in attitude scores over the three years. Although there are peaks and valleys throughout the three years, the attitudes tend to improve. In this case, the overall mean attitude for the 36-month period is *not* a good description of the level of the series from beginning to end. The mean attitude scores for each of the three years are increasing. The series is **nonstationary**.

> A time-ordered series is nonstationary when the general level of the series either systematically increases or decreases over time. ▪

Likewise, line graph B is also nonstationary, as it shows an overall decrease in attitude scores, or downward trend. The mean attitude scores for each of the three years are decreasing, rather than remaining stationary.

In summary, managers use stem-and-leaf displays or frequency histograms to display cross-sectional data and line graphs to display time-ordered data. Managers describe cross-sectional data as symmetric or skewed and time-ordered data as stationary or nonstationary. Both sets of descriptors are essential for obtaining a clear understanding of the data.

SECTION 2.4 EXERCISES

1. Explain what we mean by a stationary series.

2. Plot the following time-ordered data. Decide whether the series is stationary or nonstationary.

Quarter	1	2	3	4	1	2	3	4
Sales	30	60	70	40	30	60	70	40

3. Plot the following time-ordered data. Decide whether the series is stationary or non-stationary.

Quarter	1	2	3	4	1	2	3	4
Sales	12	24	25	30	28	48	45	50

4. Your summer job is to make sure a cola vending machine is working properly. For 50 cents, the machine should dispense 7 ounces of soda. Your job is to test the machine twice an hour and write down amounts of soda actually dispensed. The 16 measurements made over your 8-hour shift are shown here.

Time Period	1	2	3	4	5	6	7	8
Soda (ounces)	6.9	7.0	7.1	7.4	7.2	6.7	7.1	6.0

Time Period	9	10	11	12	13	14	15	16
Soda (ounces)	6.9	7.1	7.4	6.7	6.9	7.3	6.7	6.9

a. Before plotting the data, would you expect this time series to be stationary or non-stationary? Explain.
b. How is the concept of stationarity related to your job as quality control inspector?
c. Plot the data to check your expectations.

5. A sales manager was quoted as saying that sales of computer products have increased by 2% per month over the last 24 months. Would the sales data by month be stationary or nonstationary?

6. Two graphs are shown that record the percentage of pages with errors typed daily by the staff. Both graphs indicate that for the past week typists' errors are increasing. At week two, the firm took corrective action that solved the problem. Which graph reflects the successful problem solving?

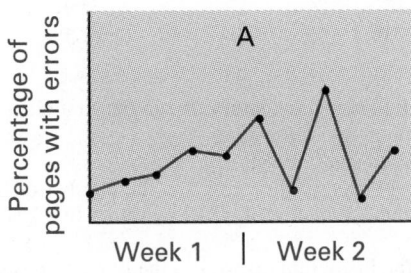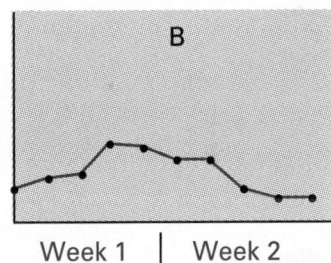

7. Shown are data of total production of electrical energy in trillion kilowatt-hours by utility companies for various years.

Year	1912	1920	1930	1940	1950	1960	1970	1980	1986
Energy	12	39	91	142	329	755	1,532	2,286	2,489

Sources: Historical Statistics of the United States, Colonial Times to 1970, p. 821; and Statistical Abstract of the United States 1988, p. 547.

a. Plot the data in a line graph. Are the data stationary?
b. Describe the relationship.
c. Estimate the time it has taken to double our energy production. For example, how long did it take to go from 100 trillion kwh to 200 trillion? From 200 trillion to 400 trillion? From 400 trillion to 800 trillion? From 800 trillion to 1,600 trillion?
d. Estimate the year when energy production should have reached 3,200 trillion kwh. What are some reasons that it did not?

8. Shown are the percentages of people living in urban areas in the United States since colonial times.

Year	1800	1830	1860	1890	1920	1950	1980
Percentage	6	9	20	35	51	64	73.7

Source: Statistical Abstract of the United States 1985, p. 22.

   a. Plot the data. Are the data stationary?
   b. Describe the relationship.

9. The accompanying table represents the percentage of satisfied customers at Hechts department store in Washington D.C. The data are based on surveys taken over a 20-month period.

Month	J	F	M	A	M	J	JL	A	S	O
Percent	85	84	86	87	86	88	89	90	90	92

Month	N	D	J	F	M	A	M	J	JL	A
Percent	91	92	94	94	93	95	97	96	99	98

   a. Draw a frequency histogram. Begin the first class at 80% and use a class width of 5%.
   b. Plot a line graph of the data.
   c. You are trying to explain the growth or decline in the percentage of satisfied customers to your manager. Which tool—histogram or line graph—would you use?
   d. Why is the histogram **misleading** in displaying nonstationary time-ordered data?

10. The accompanying table represents the number of Decision Science majors at a state university in Illinois from 1985 to 1994.

Year	85	86	87	88	89	90	91	92	93	94
Majors	75	85	70	72	65	78	65	70	73	75

   a. Draw a frequency histogram. Begin the first class at 65 and use a class width of 7.
   b. Plot a line graph of the data.
   c. Are the data stationary?
   d. What proportion of the years was the number of Decision Science majors from 65 to 71 students? Which tool—histogram or line graph—would you use to answer this question?
   e. Why is the histogram (as well as the line graph) useful for displaying stationary time-ordered data?

11. Shown are approximate Dow Jones Industrial averages from December 1991 to May 1992.

December 1	2910
December 15	3050
January 2	3200
January 15	3250
February 1	3260
February 15	3240
March 1	3270
March 15	3250
April 1	3240
April 15	3340
May 1	3340
May 15	3390

a. Plot the time-ordered Dow Jones data.
b. Are the data stationary?
c. Describe the movement of the data over the six-month period.
d. Construct a frequency histogram. The first class should start at 2,900 and use a class width of 200.
e. Can you tell from the histogram that the Dow Jones Index increased over the six-month period? Should a frequency histogram be constructed for nonstationary data?

12. In making temples (the part that fits behind the ear) for eyeglasses, the hardness of the metal should be between 85 and 95. Below are the average hardness measures of five randomly selected temples within a shift over the past 20 shifts.

Shift	Hardness	Shift	Hardness
1	94	11	91
2	95	12	90
3	93	13	88
4	93	14	89
5	91	15	87
6	92	16	88
7	90	17	89
8	91	18	87
9	90	19	86
10	91	20	85

a. Plot the time-ordered temple hardness data.
b. Are the data stationary?
c. Describe the movement of the data over the last 20 shifts.
d. Construct a frequency histogram. The first class should start at 85, and the class width should equal 2.
e. Can you tell from the histogram that the temple hardness has decreased over the 20 shifts? Should a frequency histogram be constructed for nonstationary data?

13. The acceptable maximum G-force measurement on a Federal Express parcel during sorting is 12. Each hour of a shift the firm sends a "dummy" parcel containing a G-force measuring device through the sorting conveyor belt. Shown are the G-force data for the past 8 hours.

Hour	G-Force
1	9.6
2	7.5
3	8.9
4	14.4
5	10.6
6	11.4
7	11.8
8	15.8

a. Plot the time-ordered G-force hourly data.
b. Are the data stationary?
c. Describe the movement of the data over the last 8 hours.
d. Construct a frequency histogram. The first class should start at 6, and the class interval should equal 3.
e. Can you tell from the histogram that the G-force was unacceptably high at hour 4 (lunch break) and hour 8 (shift change)? Should a frequency histogram be constructed for nonstationary data?

14. Consider the following quality/customer feedback data on the percentage of bank customers satisfied with First South banking services. The data are monthly customer survey
data over two years. At the end of year 1, the bank initiated a Total Quality Management
(TQM) effort.

Month	Percentage Satisfied	Month	Percentage Satisfied
JAN	75%	JAN	78
FEB	74	FEB	81
MAR	76	MAR	84
AP	75	AP	85
MY	78	MY	85
JN	72	JN	90
JL	76	JL	91
AU	71	AU	95
SE	76	SE	94
OCT	75	OCT	96
NOV	76	NOV	95
DEC	74	DEC	95

a. Are the data stationary?

b. Describe the line graph. Has the TQM effort been useful?

15. Consider the following lockbox processing errors as a percentage of transactions at the
First South Bank. The data are monthly accounting data over two years. At the end of year
1, the bank initiated a Total Quality Management (TQM) effort.

Month	Percentage Error Rates	Month	Percentage Error Rates
JAN	2.6%	JAN	2.3
FEB	2.4	FEB	2.1
MAR	2.6	MAR	2.0
AP	2.5	AP	1.5
MY	2.7	MY	1.4
JN	2.4	JN	1.2
JL	2.5	JL	0.9
AU	2.5	AU	0.7
SE	2.6	SE	0.8
OCT	2.4	OCT	0.6
NOV	2.7	NOV	0.7
DEC	2.5	DEC	0.8

a. Are the data stationary?

b. Describe the line graph. Has the TQM effort been useful?

2.5 Summarizing Cross-Sectional Data: The Mean and Standard Deviation

The main purpose of summarizing cross-sectional data is to help problem solvers
answer the following questions more precisely:

How are we doing on average? Most of the time? The majority of the time?

Is there much variation from one plant to the next, one work group to the
next? If so, how much?

How far away from the rest of the data must a data value be before we label it as an outlier? What constitutes an extraordinary, or unusual, event?

We have shown how to organize cross-sectional data by drawing histograms and ogives. Now we will explain how to summarize the data to help the problem solver answer the questions. By the end of this section, you should be able to:

1. compute the sample mean;
2. approximate the sample mean of data that have already been displayed in a frequency histogram;
3. explain the need for a measure of spread;
4. explain why the range is not an effective measure of spread;
5. compute the sample standard deviation;
6. compute the mean and standard deviation for yes/no data;
7. use the standard deviation to explain how far particular data values are from the mean; and
8. explain why the mean can be misleading as a measure of the center.

Distinguishing the Sample from the Population

Problem solvers generally deal with sample data. For example, COMCEL selects 10 workers and determines that their mean attitude toward improving productivity is 3.50 (on a 5-point scale). If COMCEL selected 10 other workers, the mean attitude might be 4.25. The two numbers are **sample means** and are affected by random events, which include many factors that can cause the sample means to vary.

The sample mean is the sum of all the data values in the sample divided by the sample size.

The *population mean* is the average attitude of *all* workers in the company. We rarely know the population mean because it is either too costly or too time-consuming to determine. We must use the sample mean to estimate the population mean. The distinction between samples and populations is very important in statistics, and will be discussed further in Chapters 6–15.

The Mean

Suppose we compute the sample mean for the weekly claims data for the 30 adjusters shown in Figure 2.4. To do so, we add up all the data values and divide by the number of observations. Use expression (2.1) to calculate the sample mean:

$$\text{Sample mean} = \bar{x} = \frac{\sum_{i=1}^{n} x_i}{n} \tag{2.1}$$

The sample mean is called *x-bar*. The expression says: Sum the data values in the sample and divide by the total number of data values, n. The Greek letter sigma means "sum." The sample mean for the number of claims processed by the 30 claims adjusters is

$$\bar{x} = \frac{28 + 30 + 30 + 31 + \cdots + 44 + 45 + 46 + 48}{30}$$

$$= \frac{1{,}124}{30} = 37.5 \text{ claims per week}$$

The average adjuster processes 37.5 claims per week.

Approximating the Mean of Histogram Data

Suppose we are given only Figure 2.5, a histogram for the claims adjustment data, without the original data. We could approximate the histogram's mean by using the balance point idea, as shown in Figure 2.15.

Figure 2.15 shows a steel rod underneath a three-dimensional view of the histogram in Figure 2.5. Move the rod from left to right. At what claims processing rate would the frequency histogram balance? It wouldn't balance at 34 claims per week, because there would be too much weight (data values) to the right, and the histogram would tilt down to the right. It wouldn't balance at 42 claims per week, because there would be too much weight to the left, and the histogram would tilt down to the left. The balance point, or the approximate mean, is somewhere between 37 and 39 claims per week.

The sample mean is a very important measure in summarizing a data set. However, it does not measure the spread of values in a data set.

The Range

A new manager is placed in charge of two production lines. His goals are to increase the mean production rates to above 50 units per hour and to achieve a relatively constant hourly output. Table 2.10 presents a sample of hourly data for the two departments.

Table 2.10

Hourly Production Data

	Department A	Department B
	60	80
	59	40
	61	0
	60	120
	60	60
Mean	60 units per hour	60 units per hour

While both data sets have the same mean, the hourly production rate in department A is stable whereas that of department B is not. For department B, the sample mean simply does not typify the data. How can we measure the spread or variability in the two data sets?

The **sample range** is the simplest measure of spread. It equals the difference between the largest and smallest data values. The ranges for the two data sets are $61 - 59 = 2$ for department A and $120 - 0 = 120$ for department B. Thus, there is a very narrow spread in the production rate of department A and a very wide spread in that of department B.

Although the range is a useful measure of spread, it has three weaknesses. First, it uses only two data values, ignoring the remaining data. At best, it is a quick estimate of spread. Second, you can be easily misled by the range. Consider the two data sets in Table 2.11. The range is 50 for both data sets, but the departments are quite different. Department C produced at a high level for four of the five sample hours. It may have experienced a temporary problem which produced a outlier, but it recovered. Department D appears to produce less per hour than C and has experienced wide

The sample range is the difference between the largest and smallest data values.

FIGURE 2.15   Frequency Histogram of Claims Adjustment Data

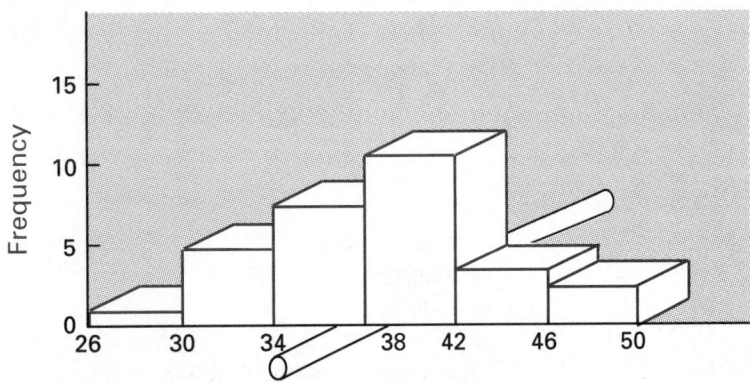

variation in hourly production. The third weakness is that the range ignores the mean in calculating the spread in a data set. A useful measure of spread should tell us how close the data values are to the mean. Why? In order to solve a problem, managers often need to know if groups differ in their mean performance or in their variability around that mean performance. We turn to such a measure next.

Table 2.11

Hourly Production Data

	Department C	Department D
	60	60
	60	10
	10	60
	60	10
	60	30
Range	50 units per hour	50 units per hour

The Variance and Standard Deviation

The sample variance overcomes the three weaknesses of the range. The sample variance is the sum of the squared differences between each observation and the sample mean divided by the sample size minus 1:

$$\text{Sample variance} = s^2 = \frac{\sum_{i=1}^{n}(x_i - \bar{x})^2}{n - 1} \tag{2.2}$$

The computations needed to calculate the sample variances for Departments C and D are shown below.

	Department C			Department D	
x	$(x - \bar{x})$	$(x - \bar{x})^2$	x	$(x - \bar{x})$	$(x - \bar{x})^2$
60	$(60 - 50) = 10$	100	60	$(60 - 34) = 26$	676
60	$(60 - 50) = 10$	100	10	$(10 - 34) = -24$	576
10	$(10 - 50) = -40$	1600	60	$(60 - 34) = 26$	676
60	$(60 - 50) = 10$	100	10	$(10 - 34) = -24$	576
60	$(60 - 50) = 10$	100	30	$(30 - 34) = -4$	16
250		2,000	170		2,520

$$\bar{x} = 250/5 = 50 \qquad\qquad \bar{x} = 170/5 = 34$$
$$s^2 = 2000/(5 - 1) = 500 \qquad s^2 = 2520/(5 - 1) = 630$$
$$s = \sqrt{500} = 22.36 \qquad\qquad s = \sqrt{630} = 25.1$$

The variance has the following properties:

1. Unlike the range, all the data are used.
2. Unlike the range, the variance does not measure only spread or dispersion, but measures spread or dispersion around the mean.
3. The variance can never be negative because the squared differences around the mean are summed. When the variance equals zero, all the numbers are equal to the mean and there is no dispersion.

The sample variance has no direct physical meaning because it is measured in squared units such as units^2 and dollars^2. A more informative measure of the spread is the **sample standard deviation**. The standard deviation, s, is the square root of the variance. The standard deviations for the two departments are 22.36 and 25.1, respectively.

The sample standard deviation is the square root of the sum of the squared differences between the data values and the sample mean divided by the sample size minus 1.

What does the standard deviation tell us? Like the variance, the standard deviation measures the variability in the number of units produced over the five-hour periods. But the standard deviation is measured in the same units as the original data. It has a direct physical interpretation. It indicates how far away the numbers in each sample are from the sample mean. If the number of units produced each hour was the same, the standard deviation would be zero. The larger the standard deviation, the greater the spread in hourly production rates around the mean. In general, very few data values will fall beyond two or three standard deviations from the sample mean.

A comparison of the means and standard deviations for the two departments confirms what we see in the data, and tells us what the range could not. Department C has a larger mean and smaller standard deviation than Department D. The values in Department C are closer to its mean of 50 than the values of Department D are to its mean of 34.

Claims Data Example: Returning again to the claims data in Figure 2.4, we know from above that the mean number of claims processed was 37.5. The sample variance is

$$s^2 = \frac{(28 - 37.5)^2 + \cdots + (48 - 37.5)^2}{30 - 1} = 24 \text{ claims}^2$$

The sample standard deviation is the square root of 24 or 4.9 claims. Refer back to Figure 2.4 and note that all but one of the data values fall within two standard deviations of the mean. That is, there are no values below 27.7 (37.5 − 2(4.9)), and only one value, 48, above 47.3 (37.5 + 2(4.9)) claims.

Yes/No Data

Managers are often asked to respond to questions such as: Did your department have any discipline cases last year? Is your department planning to purchase additional computers? Do any of your employees use the firm's aerobic facilities? Unlike the previous examples, a response to any of these questions is either yes or no. Much of the data crossing a manager's desk are yes/no data. We must learn how to organize and summarize them.

Example: COMCEL's Benefits Survey Results   COMCEL recently surveyed 500 employees to determine the number who are interested in a flexible benefits package. Presently, every employee has the same package. COMCEL is considering allowing employees to design their own benefits package. Thus, one worker could select the base life and health coverage insurance plans plus three weeks vacation, while another could select the extended insurance coverage and only one week vacation.

To quantify the yes/no data we assign a 1 to each person who said yes, favoring the proposed new benefits system, and a 0 to those who said no. The usual practice is to assign a 1 to the group of interest. Four hundred employees said yes, and 100 employees said no.

Figure 2.16 is a frequency histogram of the survey's results. Code the data as follows:

Let x_i = 1 if person responded yes;
      0 if person responded no;

and

X = the number of people who respond yes, assigned as the 1s

Y = the number of people who respond no, assigned as the 0s

$n = X + Y$ = the total number of observations

FIGURE 2.16   Histogram for Response to Proposed Flexible Benefits Package

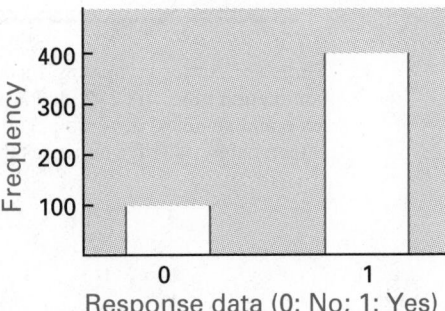

Use expression (2.3) to compute the sample mean, or the fraction of yes responses:

$$\bar{x} = \frac{\sum\limits_{i=1}^{n} x_i}{n} = \frac{X}{n} \tag{2.3}$$

The sum of x_i represents the number of people who responded yes to the survey. The sum of y_i represents the number of people who responded no. For the benefits survey, the data and the resulting sample mean are as follows:

$$X = 400 \text{ workers}$$

$$Y = 100 \text{ workers}$$

$$n = 500 \text{ workers}$$

$$\bar{x} = \frac{X}{n} = \frac{400}{500} = .80$$

In other words, 80% of the workers want a flexible benefits package. Use expression (2.4) to compute the sample variance:

$$s^2 = \frac{X \cdot Y}{n \cdot (n-1)} \tag{2.4}$$

For the benefits survey data we obtain the following:

$$s^2 = \frac{400 \cdot 100}{500 \cdot 499} = .16$$

$$s = \sqrt{.16} = .40$$

What does the .40 mean? The standard deviation measures the variability in the attitudes of the 500 workers. If all favored (or did not favor) the new benefits package, the sample standard deviation would be zero. (Please check this for yourself!) The smaller the sample standard deviation, the greater the workers' agreement about the new benefits package. But what does the .40 mean? We address that issue in the next section.

In brief, the three common measures used to summarize a data set are the sample mean, the sample range, and the sample standard deviation.

SECTION 2.5 EXERCISES

1. Three secretaries competing for a position are asked to type the same document. Their completion times are 1, 2, and 3 minutes, respectively. We wish to find the sample variance and standard deviation. The variance can be found by using the shortcut formula shown below. The formula uses the mean and the sum of the **squared** values.

x	x^2
1	1
2	4
3	9
6	14

$$\bar{x} = \frac{\Sigma x}{n} = \frac{6}{3} = 2$$

$$s^2 = \frac{[\Sigma x^2 - n\bar{x}^2]}{(n-1)}$$

$$= \frac{[14 - (3)(4)]}{(3 - 1)}$$

$$= \frac{[14 - 12]}{2}$$

$$= 1$$

$$s = \sqrt{s^2} = \sqrt{1} = 1$$

Use expression 2.2 in the text to calculate the sample variance and verify that the shortcut formula gives the same result.

2. Without doing any computation, what is the standard deviation of the following set of numbers: {1, 1, 1}?

3. The hourly wages of three employees are $4.00, $4.50, and $5.00. What would happen to the mean and standard deviation of these wages if the following occurred:
   a. each got a $.50 per hour raise?
   b. the hourly wage of each was doubled?

4. Consider the following sample of data values: {4, 8, 6, 6, 5, 7, 3, 9, 2, 10}.
   a. Find the sample mean.
   b. Find the range.
   c. Find the sample variance and standard deviation.

5. Shown are two frequency histograms for the size of consumer loans at two banks. Without doing any computation, which has the greater mean? The greater standard deviation?

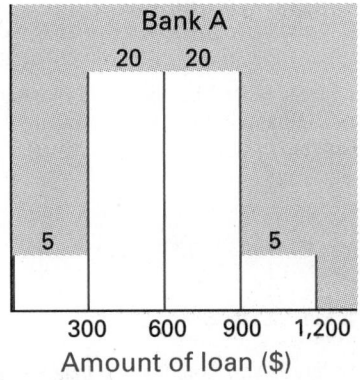

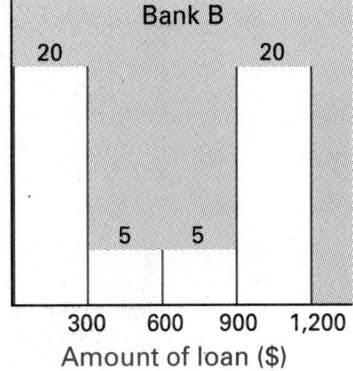

6. The following histogram shows the number of days to complete construction of houses in a development. One histogram block is missing. Given that the mean number of days to build a house is 75, estimate how many houses took 60 to under 70 days to build?

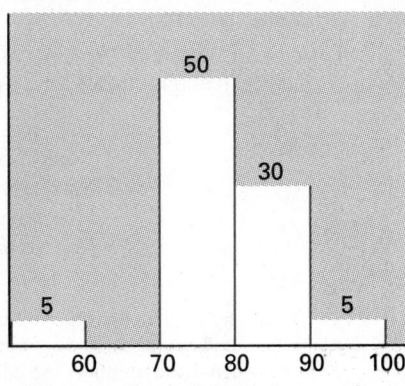

7. When many data values are repeated, it is sometimes easier to find the mean by constructing a frequency disribution of single values and using the formula for the **weighted mean**. To get the total, each value is weighted, or multiplied, by its frequency and the results are summed. For example, to find the mean of {2, 2, 2, 3, 3, 3, 3, 4}, we proceed as shown.

x	f	xf
2	3	6
3	4	12
4	1	4
	8	22

$$\bar{x} = \frac{\Sigma xf}{n} = \frac{22}{8} = 2.75$$

A telephone survey of 200 homes found that 25 homes had no television set, 100 had one television set, 50 had two television sets, and 25 had three television sets. Find the mean number of television sets per household for this sample.

8. The accompanying table represents the number of Decision Science majors at a state university in Illinois from 1985 to 1994.

Year	85	86	87	88	89	90	91	92	93	94
Majors	75	85	70	72	65	78	65	70	73	75

   a. Compute the mean, variance, standard deviation, and range for the number of Decision Science majors.
   b. From Section 2.4 you know that the above time-ordered data are stationary. Is the mean a relevant measure for stationary time-ordered data?

9. The accompanying table represents the approximate number of defects per 100 cars built at General Motors's Oklahoma City factory from 1985 to 1992. Defects range from rattling windows to engine failures.

Year	85	86	87	88	89	90	91	92
Defects (per 100)	143	132	125	120	110	90	81	71

   a. Compute the mean, variance, standard deviation, and range for the number of defects per 100 cars.
   b. Plot the time-ordered data. Note that the data are nonstationary. Is the mean a relevant measure for nonstationary time-ordered data?

10. Can a standard deviation ever be
   a. zero? Explain.
   b. larger than the variance for a set of data? Explain.
   c. negative? Explain.

11. A report to the Vice President for Human Resources contained the following statistics for medical reimbursements for a single department.

Number of employees	10
Max. reimbursement	$3000
Min. reimbursement	$0
Mean reimbursement	$250

The vice president sent the report back and asked that the figures be recalculated. Why? Note: Good managers **always** check the reasonableness of any numbers presented to them, even when these numbers are calculated by computers.

12. The manager of the downtown hotel received information on occupancy rates over the past week.

Day	S	M	T	W	T	F	S
Percent occupied	75	93	90	86	85	65	42

Calculate the mean occupancy rate and its standard deviation.

13. Workers in a nonunion company recently voted whether to join a national union. Of the 300 employees who voted, 90 voted in favor of union representation. Find the mean and standard deviation for the data set consisting of 210 values of 0 (those who did not favor union representation) and 90 values of 1 (those who favored union representation).

14. Mankato State University conducts a survey of its recent Business school graduates to determine what percent are in favor of a required course in business problem solving. They obtain the following data.

Yes	100
No	650
Total	750

a. Draw a histogram for the responses to the survey.
b. Compute the mean and standard deviation for the survey data. Interpret the results.
c. Is it meaningful to compute the range? Explain.

15. Would you like to work for a firm whose mean salary is $100,000? If your answer is "not sure," what additional descriptive data would you need to have before making your decision? Explain.

16. The Gallup Poll conducts a survey to determine attitudes toward a balanced budget amendment to the U.S. constitution. A random sample of 1,500 voters are interviewed, and the following results are obtained.

Yes	900
No	600

a. Draw a histogram for the responses to the survey.
b. Compute the mean and standard deviation for the survey data. Interpret the results.
c. Is it meaningful to compute the range? Explain.

2.6 Interpreting the Mean and Standard Deviation: The Empirical and Chebyshev Rules

The sample mean and sample standard deviation quickly and accurately describe a data set. But what exactly does the standard deviation mean? How should we interpret it? It depends on whether the histogram for the data set is bell-shaped or not. By the end of this section you should be able to:

1. use the Empirical rule and the standard deviation to describe the variation of bell-shaped data around the sample mean;
2. use the Empirical rule and the standard deviation to detect outliers;
3. use Chebyshev's rule and the standard deviation to describe the variation of data that are not bell-shaped; and
4. use Chebyshev's rule and the standard deviation to detect outliers.

(margin handwritten notes: "mean ± 3 std. dev.", "use when bell-shaped!")

Bell-Shaped Histograms: The Empirical Rule

When a data set's histogram is approximately bell-shaped, we can use the mean and standard deviation to describe the distribution of values using the Empirical rule. The Empirical rule says that:

About 68% of the data values will lie within a distance of one standard deviation on either side of the mean.

About 95% of the data values will lie within a distance of two standard deviations on either side of the mean.

Nearly all (99% or more) data values will lie within a distance of three standard deviations on either side of the mean. *(handwritten: Anything outside is outlier.)*

Let's apply the Empirical rule to the project completion data in Table 2.6. Figure 2.11 (Histogram B) shows that the data set is reasonably bell-shaped. The mean and standard deviation for the data in Table 2.6 are given by:

$$\bar{x} = \frac{2.6 + 3.5 + 3.9 + 4.3 \cdots + 15.3 + 16.3 + 17.8 + 19.5}{25}$$

$$= 10.2 \text{ days}$$

$$s = \sqrt{\frac{(2.6 - 10.2)^2 + \cdots + (19.5 - 10.2)^2}{25 - 1}}$$

$$= 4.7 \text{ days}$$

On the basis of the Empirical rule we can surmise that:

1. About 68% of the data will lie between 5.5 days and 14.9 days. This is a distance of one standard deviation on each side of the mean.
2. About 95% of the data will lie between .8 day and 19.6 days. This is a distance of two standard deviations on each side of the mean.

The Empirical rule is especially useful when we do not have the original data values. If we know only the mean and standard deviation of a bell-shaped data set, we could determine what percentage of the data lies within various distances from the mean.

The Outlier

If the histogram for a data set is approximately bell-shaped, a data value more than three standard deviations away from the mean should be considered an outlier.

Until now **outliers** have been defined as data values that lie far away from the mean. But how far is far? According to the Empirical rule, it would be rare for a data value to fall more than two standard deviations from the mean. We should expect this to happen only 5% of the time. Data values beyond three standard deviations from the mean are even rarer (occurring less than 1% of the time). This leads to the definition given in the margin.

But how do we handle data sets that are skewed? The next section will demonstrate the application of Chebyshev's rule for such data.

Skewed Histograms: Chebyshev's Rule

If a histogram is not bell-shaped, we can use Chebyshev's rule to determine what percentage of the data may lie at various distances from the mean. Chebyshev's rule states that:

At least $(100 - 100/h^2)\%$ of the observations of any data set must lie within a distance of h standard deviations from the mean. This expression is true for all values of h greater than 1.

Table 2.12 illustrates how Chebyshev's rule summarizes data that are not bell-shaped.

Table 2.12

Summarizing a Data Set with Chebyshev's Rule

Number of Standard Deviations	Computation	Interpretation
$h = 2$	$100 - \dfrac{100}{4} = 75\%$	At least 75% of the data values must lie within a distance of plus or minus two standard deviations from the mean.
$h = 3$	$100 - \dfrac{100}{9} = 88.9\%$	At least 88.9% of the data values must lie within a distance of plus or minus three standard deviations from the mean.
$h = 4$	$100 - \dfrac{100}{16} = 93.8\%$	At least 93.8% of the data values must lie within a distance of plus or minus four standard deviations from the mean.

Use Chebyshev's rule to summarize the work group productivity data in Table 2.8. The corresponding Figure 2.12 shows that the data are skewed toward higher values. Work group 20 was identified as a possible outlier. That is, based on the frequency histogram alone, work group 20's productivity was extraordinarily high. Now we can calculate the mean and standard deviation to check if it is an outlier:

$$\bar{x} = \frac{106 + 95 + \cdots + 97 + 94}{36}$$

$$= 100.42\% \text{ of industry standard}$$

$$s = \sqrt{\frac{(106 - 100.42)^2 + \cdots + (94 - 100.42)^2}{36 - 1}}$$

$$= 6.22\% \text{ of industry standard}$$

Now, using Table 2.12, we can determine if work group 20's productivity is an outlier.

For bell-shaped data, the rare data value or outlier is defined as happening 1% or less of the time. For non–bell-shaped data, rarely would a data value fall more than a distance of four standard deviations from the mean, or at most $100\% - 93.8\% = 6.2\%$ of the time. If such an event happened, consider it an outlier.

When a data set is not bell-shaped, consider a value more than four standard deviations away from the mean as an outlier.

Let's determine the productivities that are four standard deviations on each side of the mean:

> Four standard deviations below the mean: $100.42\% - 4(6.22\%) = 75.5\%$
>
> Four standard deviations above the mean: $100.42\% + 4(6.22\%) = 125.3\%$

Work group 20's productivity of 123% is very close to four standard deviations above the mean and thus very close to being an outlier. Based on the frequency histogram, mean, standard deviation, and Chebyshev's rule, we can develop the following expanded mental model:

> The mean productivity for the 36 work groups is 100.42% of industry standard, and the standard deviation is 6.22% of industry standard.
>
> At least 75% of the work groups should have productivities between the mean minus two standard deviations and the mean plus two standard deviations—that is, between 87.9% ($100.42\% - 2(6.22\%)$) and 112.9% ($100.42\% + 2(6.22\%)$).
>
> Work group 20's productivity of 123% may be an outlier, since it is so close to a productivity of 125.3%, the value at four standard deviations above the mean.

Even without these statistical tools ($\bar{x}$, s, and Chebyshev's rule), a mental model of performance for the 36 work groups had been developed. However, the tools have refined and added precision to the initial mental model without an excessive amount of work.

In summary, we can apply Chebyshev's rule to any data set. When the data are bell-shaped, use the Empirical rule for a more precise description of the distribution. And what have we accomplished by using these rules? We have summarized a data set in terms of two numbers—the mean and standard deviation—without losing much information. Managers build their mental models about how their departments are doing from such summarizing statistics. Moreover, these rules help to define more precisely which data values are outliers.

Weakness of the Mean and the Standard Deviation

Sometimes the mean can be misleading. Suppose a company has 10 employees whose mean salary is $100,000 per year. Would you like to work for such a company? Your inclination is probably to say: "Where do I sign up?" But think again. Although the mean salary is $100,000, there is no guarantee that you will be getting the mean salary! One scenario for such a mean is that nine employees earn $10,000 per year and the boss earns $910,000 per year. The moral is that, unless you are the boss, the mean can be misleading.

A more informative measure of the average or typical salary for this company would be the mode. The mode is the data value that occurs most frequently. Since nine of the 10 salaries are $10,000, the mode of the data set would be $10,000.

The mode does have some drawbacks. If all data set values are different, there is no mode. Also, the mode has no corresponding measure of spread like the mean does. Thus, the mode provides no assistance in detecting outliers. We must look for another measure to overcome the shortcomings of the mean.

SECTION 2.6 EXERCISES

1. Given the following sample of {0, 3, 2, 6, 1, 2, 3, 4, 3, 5}.
    a. Find the mean.
    b. Find the variance and standard deviation.
    c. How many values fall within one standard deviation of the mean?
    d. How many values fall within two standard deviations of the mean?

2. The mean and standard deviation of a bell-shaped data set are 16 and 4, respectively. If an outlier is defined as any data point falling beyond three standard deviations from the mean, are any of these data points outliers: 13, 22, 281?

3. Suppose you received a computer printout showing the mean and standard deviation for a variable as MEAN = 100 and S.D. = 10. Describe what the distribution for the variable looks like, first assuming that the histogram is skewed, and then assuming the histogram is bell-shaped.

4. The mean score on a college entrance examination is 500 and the standard deviation is 100. Assume that the test scores are bell-shaped.
    a. Approximately what percentage of the scores will fall below 400 or above 600?
    b. Approximately what percentage of the scores will fall beyond 700?

5. A set of measurements taken from an assembly line is bell-shaped with a mean of 65.0 inches and a standard deviation of .1 inch.
    a. Approximately what percentage of the measurements will fall above 65.1 inches?
    b. Between 64.6 and 65.2 inches?
    c. Below 64.8 inches?

6. The mean amount paid out in workers' compensation claims is $750 and the standard deviation is $1,800. Is the distribution of claims bell-shaped? Explain.

7. The accompanying table represents the number of Decision Science majors at a state university in Illinois from 1985 to 1994.

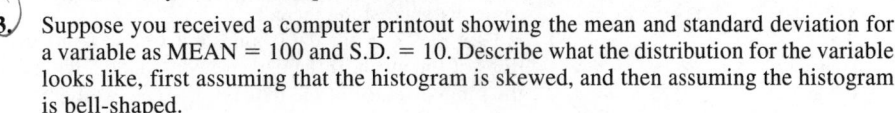

Year	85	86	87	88	89	90	91	92	93	94
Majors	75	85	70	72	65	78	65	70	73	75

    a. Compute the mean and standard deviation.
    b. Assume that the frequency histogram for the data are approximately bell-shaped. What percent of the data should fall within ± one standard deviation of the mean? What percent of the data should fall within ± two standard deviations of the mean? What percent of the data should fall within ± three standard deviations of the mean?
    c. Use the Empirical rule to determine if there are any outliers in the above data set? Discuss.

8. The accompanying table contains the productivity for 15 workers at the COMCEL Dallas plant.

102	104	95	114	100
103	98	104	107	102
97	101	103	104	109

    a. Construct a frequency histogram. The first class should begin at 95 and have a class width of five.
    b. Compute the mean and standard deviation for the data set.
    c. Between what two data values must at least 75% of the data lie?
    d. Between what two data values must at least 88.9% of the data lie?
    e. Between what two data values must at least 93.8% of the data lie?
    f. Using Chebyshev's rule, are there any outliers?

Tukey

① Compute median rank $\left(\dfrac{n+1}{2}\right)$ $n = $ # of observations

② Find median:
count up from smallest
value using median rank

③ Quartile Rank
$\left(\dfrac{med.\ rank + 1}{2}\right)$

④ Find Quartile values
Q_1: count up from smallest
Q_3: count down from largest

⑤ Find IQR
$Q_3 - Q_1$

⑥ Tukey's
$LF = Q_1 - 1.5(IQR)$
    step
$UF = Q_3 + 1.5(IQR)$
    step

9. The frequency histograms for two data sets are skewed. The mean productivity is 105 for both data sets.
   a. Determine the standard deviation for data set 1 so that at least 75% of the data lies between 95 and 115.
   b. Determine the standard deviation for data set 2 so that at least 88.9% of the data lies between 95 and 115.
   c. Use Chebyshev's rule to determine when a data point would be an outlier for data set 1.
   d. Use Chebyshev's rule to determine when a data point would be an outlier for data set 2.

10. The mean productivity for a data set is 105.
    a. The histogram for the data set is bell-shaped. Determine the standard deviation for the data set given that about 68% of the data lies between 95 and 115.
    b. The shape of the histogram is unknown. Determine, if possible, the standard deviation for the data set given that about 68% of the data lies between 95 and 115.

11. Chebyshev's rule states that
    a. at least 75% of the data values must lie within a distance of $\pm$ two standard deviations of the mean. If the data are bell-shaped, what percent of the data must lie within the same distance of the mean?
    b. at least 88.9% of the data values must lie within a distance of $\pm$ three standard deviations of the mean. If the data are bell-shaped, what percent of the data must lie within the same distance of the mean?

12. A process control inspector reported that a sample of 50 fuses had a mean life of 96.5 hours and a standard deviation of .75 hour. He was later asked the fraction of the fuses that lasted more than 95 hours. The inspector did not have the data with him and could not answer the question. Can you place a lower and an upper bound on the desired proportion?

13. Chebyshev's rule is useful in inventory control when little is known about the shape of a demand distribution. Suppose a retailer is selling an item for the first time and has only one week of sales data. A mean of 9 units per day was sold, with the standard deviation of 3 units. How many units should be on-hand at the beginning of each day of the coming week so that stockout will occur no more than 5% of the time.

2.7 ▤ Summarizing Cross-Sectional Data: The Median, Trimmed Mean, and Interquartile Range

In the previous example, why did the mean fail to give an accurate picture of the average salary in the firm? It failed because the boss's salary was an outlier. Outliers strongly affect the mean and the standard deviation. One therefore needs alternative measures of the center and spread that are less affected by outliers. By the end of this section you will be able to:

1. determine the median;
2. approximate the median for data that have already been displayed in a frequency histogram;
3. compute the trimmed mean;
4. discuss when to use the mean, median, and trimmed mean;
5. compute the interquartile range; and
6. explain when to use the mean and standard deviation or the median and interquartile range.

The Median

An alternative measure to the mean is the median, the *middle data value* in an ordered data set. Recall that we must rank order the data from the smallest to the largest value before drawing an ordered stem-and-leaf display.

The median is the middle value in a rank-ordered data set. That means that half the data values are larger than or equal to the median, and half the data values are smaller than or equal to the median.

Consider the data in Table 2.13. Is the median age of accounts receivable equal to 37 days? No, because there are four numbers below it—namely, 31, 33, 36, and 36—and five numbers above it—namely, 38, 39, 41, 44, and 47. The **median** is that number such that half the data values are larger and half are smaller than it. Thus the median must be between 37 days and 38 days. Arbitrarily we say that the median is halfway between the two values or 37.5 days.

How do we determine the middle value? Begin by distinguishing between the ranks of data values and the data values themselves. For example, in Table 2.13, data value 31 ranks first (the lowest) and data value 47 ranks 10th (the highest).

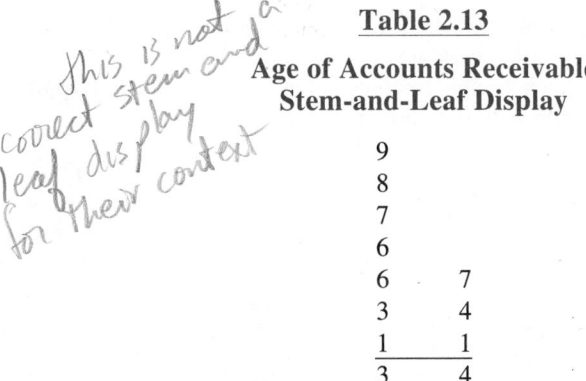

this is not a correct stem and leaf display for their context

Table 2.13

Age of Accounts Receivable Stem-and-Leaf Display

9	
8	
7	
6	
6	7
3	4
1	1
3	4

Formally, we can compute the rank using the following expression:

$$\text{Rank of median value} = (1 + \text{Number of data values})/2 \qquad (2.5)$$

For the data in Table 2.13, the *rank* of the median value is $(1 + 10)/2 = 5.5$. Thus, a *rank* of 5.5 means that the median lies halfway between the fifth and sixth rank-ordered data values, or 37.5 days. Five data values are below 37.5 days and five data values are above 37.5 days.

Approximating the Median of a Frequency Histogram

How can we approximate the median of a histogram such as the one shown for the work group productivity data in Figure 2.12? Use Figure 2.12 to develop the cumulative frequency table shown in Table 2.14. Note that the eight classes will contain all the data values because productivity data are integer values.

Table 2.14

Cumulative Frequency Table for Work Group Productivity Data as Percentage of Standard

Productivity Classes	Number of Groups	Cumulative Frequency
85 to 89	1	1
90 to 94	2	3
95 to 99	14	17
100 to 104	11	28
105 to 109	5	33
110 to 114	2	35
115 to 119	0	35
120 to 124	1	36
Total:	36	

Cumulative frequencies are useful in approximating the median of frequency data. With 36 data values, expression (2.5) gives the rank of the median as $(1 + 36)/2 = 18.5$. The cumulative frequency column shows that the 17 smallest data values lie in the first three classes. The 18th and 19th data values are at the beginning of the 100% to 104% productivity class. In fact, they are the first two data values in that class. Therefore, we approximate the median to be just over 100% of industry standard.

We can check the approximation in this instance since the actual data are available from Table 2.8. In Table 2.15 the productivities of the 36 work groups are rank-ordered. Notice that since the rank is 18.5, the actual median is 100, which is very close to the approximation using the cumulative frequency table.

In summary, when only frequency data are available, develop a cumulative frequency table to approximate the median. The approximation will be almost as accurate as having the raw data.

Table 2.15

Determining the Actual Median for the 36 Work Group Productivities

Group	Data Value	Rank Order from Bottom	Group	Data Value	Rank Order from Bottom
10	89	1	22	100	19
26	94	2	16	101	20
36	94	3	23	101	21
33	95	4	32	101	22
24	95	5	9	102	23
4	95	6	27	102	24
7	95	7	28	102	25
5	95	8	3	103	26
2	95	9	21	104	27
13	95	10	18	104	28
6	97	11	8	105	29
17	97	12	11	105	30
35	97	13	29	106	31
31	97	14	1	106	32
25	97	15	15	106	33
34	98	16	30	110	34
12	99	17	19	110	35
14	100	18	20	123	36

Differences Between the Mean and Median

The mean and median were relatively close—38.2 days vs. 37.5 days—for the age of accounts receivable data set in Table 2.13. Please verify this. In the salary example the mean was $100,000, but the median was only $10,000. Why does the median not always lie close to the mean even though both are measures of the center of a data set? Consider, what is the major difference between how we compute the mean and how we determine the median?

In determining the median, we are not concerned with the actual data values that lie above and below the median. We are concerned only that the number of observations that lie at or above the median be the same as the number that lie **at or** below it. In computing the mean, we sum the actual data values and divide by the sample size. If there are outliers or if the data are skewed, the median may differ widely from the mean.

The median is often used to summarize demographic data, such as the median family income level within a city. We use the median because a few very rich families can distort the average. If a few wealthy families move into a small community, the mean income level will be shifted upward but the median will be relatively unaffected. Thus the median provides a more accurate picture of the typical income level.

In the presence of outliers the mean and median will be different. As has been shown in the varied examples, the mean is sensitive to outliers while the median is robust, or unaffected, by outliers.

The Trimmed Mean

To compute a trimmed mean: Rank order a data set from the smallest to the largest data value. Delete an equal number of the smallest and largest data values. Calculate the mean for the remaining data.

Up to this point we have had two choices for determining the center of a data set. The mean is sensitive to outliers but sacrifices robustness. The median is robust against outliers but sacrifices sensitivity. A third choice, the **trimmed mean**, is a compromise. It is based on the actual data values, but ignores an equal number of the lowest and highest values. If there are no outliers, then the trimmed mean and the mean will be similar. If there are outliers, the two statistics will differ.

The idea behind the trimmed mean is illustrated with the following two data sets. One has an outlier and one does not. We will compute the mean, median, and the 10% trimmed mean. A 10% trimmed mean requires eliminating the lowest 10% and highest 10% of the data values. We ignore 20% of the data—the price of compromise.

Begin by putting the numbers in order from the smallest to the largest:

Data with Outlier

20, 40, 50, 80, 100, 130, 140, 190, 200, 300, 3,000

Data with No Outlier

20, 40, 50, 80, 100, 130, 140, 190, 200, 240, 300

There are 11 observations in each data set. To determine the 10% trimmed mean, trim, or eliminate, the one lowest and one highest data values. (Ten percent of 11 observations is 1.1, which is rounded to one observation.)

Statistics for the Data with Outlier

$$\bar{x} = \frac{20 + 40 + 50 + 80 + 100 + 130 + \cdots + 3{,}000}{11}$$

$$= 386.4$$

$$\text{Rank of median} = \frac{1 + 11}{2}$$

$$\text{Median} = 130$$

$$\text{Trimmed mean} = \frac{40 + 50 + 80 + \cdots + 300}{9}$$

$$= 136.7$$

Statistics for the Data with No Outlier

$$\bar{x} = \frac{20 + 40 + 50 + 80 + \cdots + 300}{11}$$

$$= 134.5$$

$$\text{Median} = 130$$

$$\text{Trimmed mean} = \frac{40 + 50 + 80 + 100 + \cdots + 240}{9}$$

$$= 130$$

These statistics show that the mean and 10% trimmed mean are quite different when there is an outlier, but are very similar when there is none. In both data sets the median and 10% trimmed mean are similar or identical. This may not always be the case. It depends on the number of extreme values and the spread of the remaining 80% of the data values—those that were not trimmed.

One major advantage of the 10% trimmed mean over the median is that we use 80% of the actual data values to calculate it. When we ignore the values of the observations, some information is lost. It is as if the data are trying to speak but no one is listening. The trimmed mean has much to recommend it. It is less affected by outliers than the mean, but is more affected than the median. It is a compromise between the two traditional measures of the center.

Nevertheless, the median is still a commonly used and often appropriate alternative measure to the mean. We also need a measure of the spread around the median that, like the median itself, is unaffected by outliers.

The Interquartile Range

The interquartile range is a measure that is easy to determine and interpret, and unaffected by outliers. We begin by defining the quartiles. The quartiles are three numbers that divide a data set that has been rank ordered from the smallest to the largest value into four equal parts. The second quartile, Q_2, is the same as the median value. The first and third quartiles, Q_1, and Q_3, are the data values that are about a quarter of the way in from each end of the ordered data set. Just as the median is halfway in from each end, the quartiles are halfway between the end values and the median value.

The interquartile range measures the width of the middle half of the data between Q_1 and Q_3. Figure 2.17 shows a general diagram of the interquartile range.

FIGURE 2.17   The Interquartile Range

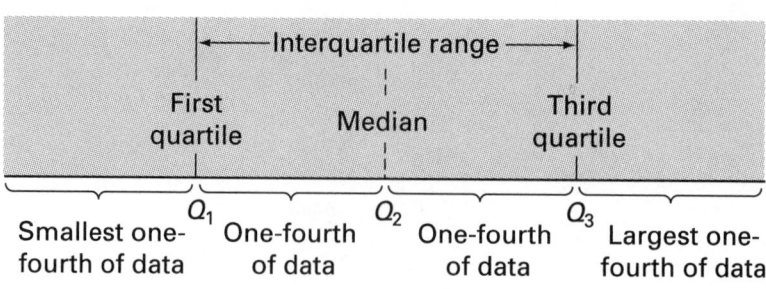

In Table 2.16 the accounts receivable data from Table 2.13 have been ranked. The rank of the median is 5.5. Drop any fraction from the rank of the median value (drop the .5 and keep the 5), and use expression (2.6) to compute the rank of the quartile value:

$$\text{Rank of quartile value} = \frac{1 + \text{Median value rank}}{2} \qquad (2.6)$$

Table 2.16

Ages of Accounts Receivable in Rank Order

Data Values	Rank of Data Values
31	1
33	2
36.	3
36	4
37	5
38	6
39	7
41	8
44	9
47	10

Thus, the rank of the quartile value is $(1 + 5)/2 = 3$. Count up three data values from the lowest data value. The first quartile data value is 36. If the rank falls between two data values, take the mean as is done in finding the median. Now count down three values from the largest data value. The third quartile data value is 41. The **interquartile range** is the difference, or distance, between the first and third quartiles: $Q_3 - Q_1$ or $41 - 36 = 5$.

The interquartile range measures the spread around the median in a data set and equals Q_3 minus Q_1.

The interquartile range is less affected by outliers than the standard deviation is. Table 2.17 demonstrates this. Note that one data set has no outliers while the other has two outliers. For both data sets, the rank of the median value is $(1 + 6)/2$ or 3.5 for a median value of 350. The rank of first and third quartiles is $(1 + 3)/2 = 2$. For both data sets, the first quartile value is the second smallest data value or 200 and the third quartile value is the second largest data value or 500. For both data sets, the interquartile range is $500 - 200 = 300$. It is unaffected by the two outliers in data set 1. Thus, the interquartile range, unlike the standard deviation, is not affected by outliers.

Table 2.17

Impact of Outliers on Interquartile Range

Data Set 1 Two Outliers	Data Set 2 No Outliers
−20,000	100
200	200
300	300
400	400
500	500
60,000	600

In summary, the interquartile range has the following properties:

1. It must be greater than or equal to zero. Since the data are ordered from the smallest to largest value, the third quartile must always be greater than or equal to the first quartile. The interquartile range, like the standard deviation, can never be negative.

2. It is not affected by outliers.

Which Set of Summarizing Measures?

Suppose we want to summarize a data set. Should the mean and standard deviation or the median and interquartile range be used? It depends, of course, on whether the data are highly skewed. The mean and standard deviation are very sensitive to highly skewed data because the actual data values are included in the calculations. So if one or more values are very far from the rest of the data, both measures will be affected.

The median and interquartile range are insensitive to highly skewed data because we use only the ranks of the data.

In summary, use the following guidelines to treat a given data set:

1. If the data are highly skewed, determine the median and interquartile range.
2. If the data are nearly symmetric, calculate the mean and standard deviation.

SECTION 2.7 EXERCISES

1. We determine the rank of the median value for a data set to be 13.5.
   a. Does this mean that the median value is 13.5?
   b. What does the rank of the median value indicate?
   c. How many data values are in the data set?

2. We determine the rank of the median value for a data set to be 6.
   a. Does this mean that the median value is 6?
   b. What does the rank of the median value indicate?
   c. How many data values are in the data set?

3. Shown is the number of traffic citations issued by 15 police officers in a single month.

21	34	43
23	34	45
26	37	45
31	37	52
33	38	68

   a. Find the median number of citations issued in a month.
   b. Find the interquartile range.

4. Shown below is the number of times ritalin, a controversial drug that affects the behavior of hyperactive children, was prescribed by 10 pediatricians in the past year.

0	0	1	4	3	20	0	2	6	30

   Determine the median number of prescriptions, the first and third quartiles, and the interquartile range.

5. The ages of 15 participants in a training seminar are shown. The data have already been rank ordered.

27	33	40
28	35	41
28	35	41
29	36	46
29	37	62

     a. Find the median age, the first and third quartiles, and the interquartile range.
     b. Find the mean age and the 10% trimmed mean age.
     c. How does the 10% trimmed mean compare to the mean and the median?

6. The first quartile of a set of data values is 15, the median is 33, and the third quartile is 49.
     a. Find the interquartile range and explain its meaning.
     b. What fraction of the values are greater than 49?

7. Complete the following table using the data: {0, 3, 2, 6, 1, 2, 3, 4, 3, 5, 7, 5}

Class	Frequency	Percentage	Cumulative Frequency	Cumulative Percentage
0 to 1	_____	_____	_____	_____
2 to 3	_____	_____	_____	_____
4 to 5	_____	_____	_____	_____
6 to 7	_____	_____	_____	_____

Use the table to approximate the median for the set of values. Now use the raw data to calculate the median.

8. For the following data set:

$$1,5,5,6,6,7,8,9,10,12,12,14,15,18,19,20,24,26,30,500$$

     a. Compute the mean.
     b. Compute the 10% trimmed mean.
     c. Compute the 20% trimmed mean.
     d. Compute the median.
     e. Why does the mean differ from the other three measures of the center?
     f. Which are the most and least useful measures of the center? Why?

9. For the following data set:

$$1,5,5,6,6,7,8,9,10,12,12,14,15,18,19,20,24,26,30,500$$

     a. Compute the standard deviation.
     b. Compute the interquartile range.
     c. Use Chebyshev's rule to determine if there are any outliers.
     d. Which, the standard deviation or the interquartile range, is the more useful measure of spread? Why?

10. The rank of the first quartile value is 3.
     a. Does this mean that the first quartile value is 3?
     b. From the rank of the quartile value, can you determine the number of observations in the data set? Explain.

11. The rank of the first quartile value is 3.5.
     a. Does this mean that the first quartile value is 3.5?
     b. From the rank of the quartile value, can you determine the number of observations in the data set? Explain.

12. The median and interquartile range for a data set are 100 and 10, respectively.
     a. Determine the approximate percentage of the data that lies above 105.
     b. Determine the approximate percentage of the data that lies below 95.
     c. Knowing the median and interquartile range, can you determine the number of observations in the data set? Explain.

13. The median, first quartile, and third quartile are 100, 95, and 105 respectively.
     a. Determine the approximate percentage of the data that lies above 105.
     b. Determine the approximate percentage of the data that lies below 95.
     c. Knowing the median, first quartile, and third quartile, can you determine the number of observations in the data set? Explain.

14. Incomes in the city of Los Angeles are highly skewed toward the right (or toward higher incomes). What measures of the center and spread should be used to describe accurately this data set?

15. Personnel managers usually want to know where a job applicant ranked in his or her graduating class. With a grade point average of 3.75, Mary Smith graduated in the 90th percentile of her graduating class. This means that 90% of the graduating class had GPAs of 3.75 or less. What percentile rank would a student be in if the student's GPA was:
    a. the median GPA?
    b. the first quartile?
    c. the third quartile?

16. Refer to exercise 15. The first quartile, median, and interquartile range of GPAs in Mary Smith's graduating class were 2.40, 3.00, and 1.25, respectively.
    a. Determine the 75th percentile.
    b. What percentage of the GPAs is above 2.40?
    c. What percentage of the GPAs is above 3.00?

17. The accompanying frequency distribution portrays the number of women directors in the Fortune 1,000 firms.

Number of Women Directors	Number of Firms
0	481
1	386
2	113
3	15
4	3
5	2
	1,000

Source: Catalyst

Develop a cumulative percent table and approximate the first quartile, median, and third quartile for the number of women directors in the Fortune 1,000 firms.

2.8 Interpreting the Median and Interquartile Range

An important step in interpreting a data set is the ability to identify outliers. When the mean and standard deviation are used to summarize a bell-shaped data set, the Empirical rule helps to determine outliers. Recall that outliers in a bell-shaped distribution are data values that are more than three standard deviations away from the mean. This section shows how to determine outliers in a non–bell-shaped distribution using the median and interquartile range. By the end of this section you should be able to:

1. identify outliers using Tukey's rule;
2. draw a box plot to visualize the important features of a data set; and
3. distinguish symmetric and skewed data sets from a box plot.

Identifying Outliers Using the Median and Interquartile Range

Table 2.15 on page 60 shows the productivities for 36 work groups at COMCEL's Norcross plant. Are any of the work group productivities outliers? Begin by computing the median and interquartile range. In Table 2.15, the rank of the median value is 18.5, which leads to a median value of 100%. The rank of the first and third quartiles is (1

+ 18)/2 = 9.5. Count up 9.5 values from the smallest value of 89% to the first quartile value of 95%. Count down 9.5 values from the largest value of 123% to the third quartile value of 104%. The interquartile range is $104 - 95 = 9\%$.

John Tukey, the creator of exploratory data analysis, has developed an approach to determine outliers. He uses the interquartile range and first and third quartiles to define outliers. In his definition of **outliers**, a *step* is the number that is 1.5 times the interquartile range.

Now return to the productivity data. A step for the productivity data is given by

$$1.5 \cdot 9\% = 13.5\%$$

Thus, outliers are work groups whose productivities are

Lower than (First quartile value $-$ One step) or $95 - 13.5 = 81.5\%$

Higher than (Third quartile value $+$ One step) or $104 + 13.5 = 117.5\%$

By this definition, work group 20's productivity of 123% is an outlier. Next we will show how to draw a box plot that displays the quartile values, the median, and outliers, if any.

> **Outliers** are data values that are more than one step lower than the first quartile value or more than one step higher than the third quartile value.

Drawing Box Plots

Refer to Figure 2.18 to see how the following directions for drawing a box plot are applied to the work group productivity data.

1. Draw a horizontal scale. Label its units and indicate the number of values in the data set.
2. Draw a rectangular box above the horizontal scale with sides at the first and third quartiles. The box height is unimportant.
3. Draw a vertical line through the box at the median value.
4. Draw horizontal lines from the box to the smallest and largest data values.
5. Draw a vertical line (called a fence) *one step* above the third quartile. Any data points to the right of this fence are outliers. Plot, circle, and label them.
6. Draw a vertical line (called a fence) *one step* below the first quartile. Any data points to the left of this fence are outliers. Plot, circle, and label them.

Box plots display important features of a data set. Figure 2.18 shows that:

1. The median work group productivity is 100% of standard, and the productivity varies between 89% and 123% of standard.
2. The lowest one-quarter, or nine work groups, produces at between 89% and 95% of standard.
3. The middle half, or 18 work groups, produces at between 95% and 104% of standard.
4. The highest one-quarter, or nine work groups, produces at between 104% and 123% of standard.
5. There are no outliers on the low side. None of the 36 work group productivities is below 81.5%.
6. Work group 20, which has the highest productivity at 123%, is an outlier. We should determine what factors account for this work group's high monthly productivity.

Given the above insights, the following mental models emerge:

- If a work group's productivity falls below 81.5%, we have a potential disturbance problem and we should take action. Unless someone has incorrectly coded a work group's monthly productivity, we should begin problem diagnosis. If we do not, we will fail to nip an emerging problem in the bud.

- If a work group's productivity exceeds 117.5%, we have a potential opportunity. If there is no coding error, begin problem diagnosis. If we do not, we may let an opportunity to improve the productivities of other groups slip through our fingers.

In summary, the box plot is a powerful visual way of summarizing data and of developing mental models. As we've said before, pictures are better than words.

FIGURE 2.18   Box Plot of Productivity Data for 36 Work Groups

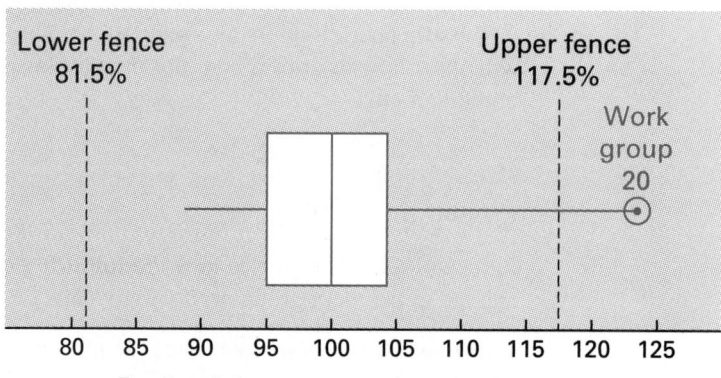

Productivity as a percentage of standard
(Based on 36 work groups)

FIGURE 2.19   Two Box Plots

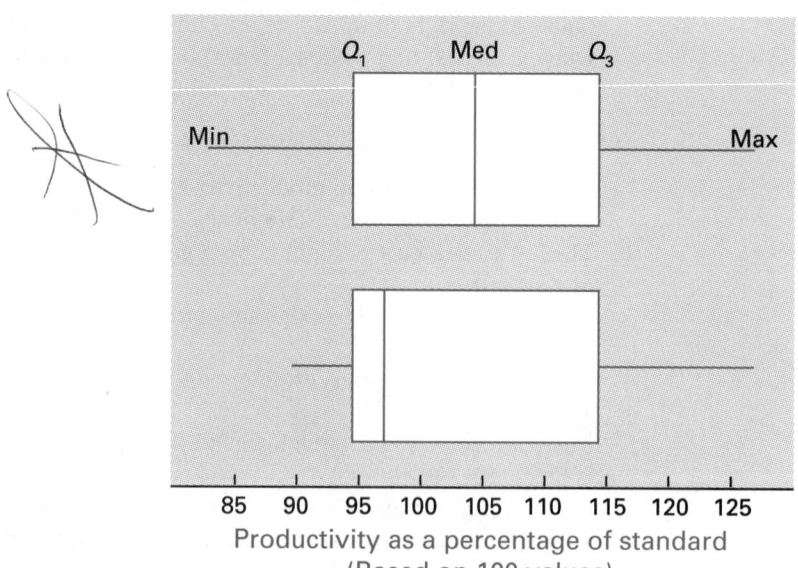

Productivity as a percentage of standard
(Based on 100 values)

Recognizing Symmetry or Skewness

Box plots show more than quartiles and outliers. They also indicate the distribution's shape—whether it is symmetric or skewed. Figure 2.19 shows two box plots with the fences omitted. One box plot displays a nearly symmetric distribution, and the other box plot displays a skewed distribution. Which is which? Think about it before reading on.

The top box plot shows symmetric data. Notice that the median is exactly in the middle of the box and the extreme values are at equal distances from the first and third quartiles. Using the median as the center, the left side of the plot is an exact mirror image of the right side of the plot. The data are symmetric.

The bottom box plot shows skewed data. Notice that the median is not in the middle of the box. Nor are the extreme values at equal distances from the first and third quartiles. The data are not symmetric. In fact, the data are skewed toward higher values, or to the right.

In summary, when using the median and quartiles to summarize data, always draw a box plot. We can determine if the data are symmetric or skewed and can easily spot outliers. Remember, outliers are data values that are above the upper fence or below the lower fence. A box plot provides much information about a data set in a single picture.

SECTION 2.8 EXERCISES

1. The first and third quartiles are 90 and 105, respectively, and the median is 104. Determine
   a. the interquartile range.
   b. the size of a step.
   c. the lower and upper fences.

2. The third quartile is 1,500 and the interquartile range is 400. Determine
   a. the first quartile value
   b. the median, if possible.
   c. the size of a step.
   d. the lower and upper fences.

3. A report contains the following information.

Minimum	5	Maximum	25
Mean	15	Median	19
First Quartile	10	Third Quartile	20

   a. Are the data symmetric or skewed?
   b. Are the minimum or maximum data values outliers?

4. A data set contains a first quartile value of 100 and a lower fence of 55. The minimum and maximum values are 50 and 180.
   a. Determine the third quartile value and upper fence.
   b. If the data are symmetric, determine the median.
   c. Are the maximum or minimum values outliers?

5. A manager received a report containing the following summary statistics on the number of complaints from customers from her 20 branch offices last month:

Minimum	0	First quartile	3
Maximum	22	Median	6
Mean	7.5	Third quartile	13

   a. Draw a box plot to display these data. Is the distribution symmetric or skewed? Why?
   b. Are either of the extreme values, 0 or 22, to be considered outliers?

6. A personnel manager is interested in the performance rankings assigned to middle-level managers. The performance scale ranges from 1 to 10, where a rating of 5 indicates average performance and 10 indicates exceptional performance. The summary statistics for 15 middle managers' ratings are shown.

Minimum	5	First quartile	8
Maximum	10	Median	9
Mean	8.7	Third quartile	10

a. Draw a box plot to display these data. Is the distribution symmetric or skewed? Why?
b. Should the minimum value be considered an outlier?
c. Note that the median is 9 (on a 10-point scale). What are two possible explanations for this very high median value?

7. A marketing manager wishes to develop a box plot on the performance of his seven sales-people. The data are the number of sales in excess of $1,000 for the past week.

The data are shown here.

| Salesperson | 1 | 2 | 3 | 4 | 5 | 6 | 7 |
| Number of Sales | 3 | 6 | 2 | 4 | 5 | 15 | 1 |

a. Why might the manager wish to develop a box plot?
b. Determine the median, first quartile, third quartile, and interquartile range.
c. Are there any outliers? If so, what action would you take?

8. You are recording times to build houses in a major development. You construct a box plot for the data and find one outlier, a point far below the first quartile. This means that one house took much less time to build than any of the other houses.
a. Should you investigate the causes of this outlier?
b. Do outliers always signify that something bad has happened?

9. Is it possible that the first quartile, median, and third quartile values are all the same? What does that tell you about the data?

10. Below are starting salaries of 1994 MBAs with a concentration in Quality Assurance from Rice University.

| $31,000 | 30,500 | 36,750 | 28,500 | 42,500 |
| $34,000 | 33,500 | 36,000 | 38,750 | 51,000 |

a. Determine the median, first and third quartiles.
b. Draw a box plot and label the upper and lower fences.
c. Are any of the starting salaries possible outliers?
d. If you were the placement director for Rice's Business School, why would you want to investigate the outlier(s)?

11. The accompanying table shows the average price of unleaded gas (excluding excise tax) in 20 states as of March 1989.

State	Price	State	Price
Alaska	92.5	Nevada	64.9
Arkansas	63.3	New Hampshire	74.7
Connecticut	76.8	New York	70.6
Delaware	68.5	North Dakota	72.4
Louisiana	67.6	Oklahoma	64.6
Maine	76.8	Oregon	70.8
Massachusetts	74.9	Pennsylvania	65.5
Michigan	63.9	Texas	64.6
Missouri	63.4	Wisconsin	65.7
Montana	69.0	Wyoming	69.7

Source: Petroleum Marketing Monthly, March 1989, in *Statistical Abstract of the United States, 1989.*

   a. Develop a box plot.
   b. Are the any of the gas prices for the 20 states possible outliers?
   c. From the box plot do the data appear to be symmetric or skewed?

12. Investors use earnings per share (EPS) to monitor the financial performance of firms. Below are hypothetical, but realistic, EPSs for 11 firms.

$$-.30, .56, .75, 1.40, 1.70, 2.45, 2.89, 3.05, 3.60, 4.05, 5.78$$

   a. Construct a box plot. Identify any outliers.
   b. Why would a financial analyst be interested in low EPS outliers and high EPS outliers?

13. On the first two exams in a Statistics course, Joe Johnson's scores are outliers (below the lower fence). Is his poor performance merely chance or does it signify a serious problem and that he or the instructor must take corrective action? Explain.

14. A data set contains a third quartile value of 500 and a median of 400. The minimum and maximum values are 200 and 600. Furthermore, the data are symmetric.
   a. Determine the first quartile.
   b. Determine the lower and upper fences.

2.9≡ Summarizing Time-Ordered Data

Summarizing time-ordered data enables problem solvers to answer the following questions more precisely:

How are we doing, on the average, over time?

Is our department's performance declining, staying the same, or improving over time?

Is there any pattern to our department's performance over time? When do we do well? When do we do poorly?

How can I identify an outlier? What constitutes an extraordinary, or unusual, event?

   The first step in analyzing time-ordered data—drawing line graphs—was explained in Section 2.4. By the end of this section you should be able to:

1. explain why the mean and standard deviation, or the median and interquartile range, should not be used to summarize nonstationary time-ordered data;
2. compute a single, double, or triple moving average;
3. interpret a moving, or smoothed, average and use it to build a mental model;
4. explain the problems of computing double or triple moving averages, and so on;
5. compute residuals from the smoothed data;
6. interpret residuals to help sharpen mental models; and
7. explain how data outliers can distort the residuals.

Are the Mean and Median Informative for Nonstationary Data?

Two years of nonstationary monthly sales data are presented in Table 2.18 and graphed in Figure 2.20. We have computed the mean and median for each year and for the two-year period. Please verify the calculations.

Table 2.18

Monthly Sales Data (in Thousands of Dollars) over Two Years

	Jan.	Feb.	Mar.	Apr.	May	June	July	Aug.	Sept.	Oct.	Nov.	Dec.
Year 1	100	90	80	80	60	70	50	60	50	45	50	45
Year 2	50	40	30	40	30	25	35	20	20	30	10	5

FIGURE 2.20   Nonstationary Data

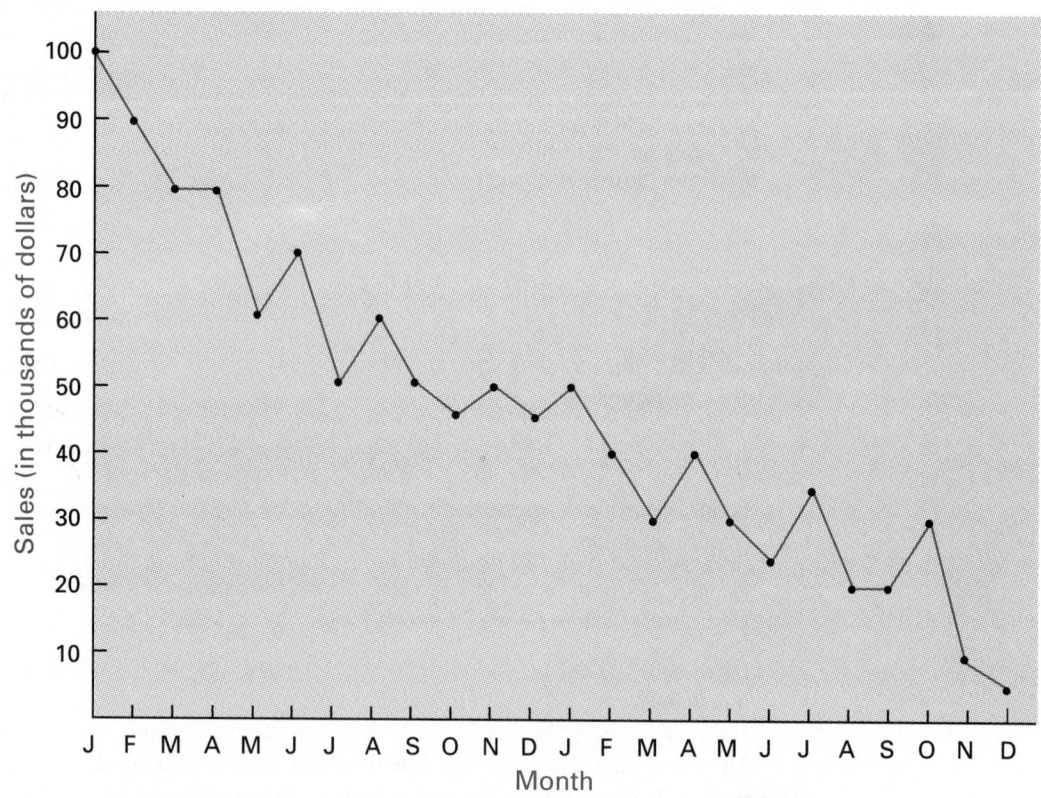

Comparison of Means and Medians for Sales Data over Two Years

	Mean	Median
Year 1	$65.0	$60
Year 2	$27.9	$30
Two years	$46.5	$45

Notice that the means and medians for each year differ dramatically from the mean and median for the entire two-year period. The two-year mean and median are not informative and useful for these data. Why? Please think about it before reading on.

An "average" should accurately summarize the data. It should provide a typical value that characterizes the series. The two-year mean and median are too low for the first year and too high for the second year. In short, do not use the mean and median to summarize time-ordered data that are nonstationary. Nonstationary data do not have a constant mean or median over time.

If the data are stationary, then the overall mean or median will accurately reflect the average performance each and every year. Thus, we can use the mean and standard deviation or the median and interquartile range for stationary time-ordered data.

In conclusion:

Summarize stationary time-ordered data by computing either the mean and standard deviation or the median and interquartile range. Use the latter pair of statistics when the data are highly skewed. Treat stationary time-ordered data the same as cross-sectional data.

Do not compute the mean and standard deviation or median and interquartile range for nonstationary time-ordered data.

How then can we describe nonstationary time-ordered data? The solution is to use a moving average series.

Single Moving Averages

A moving average replaces each data value with a mean of what is happening around it. A moving average of three or five time periods (days, weeks, months, years, or the like) is often used to describe nonstationary data.

Table 2.19 contains nonstationary data for the number of personal hours taken for the past 48 months. Table 2.20, which contains only one of the four years of data, illustrates how to construct a **single moving average** of three months, MA(3). For now, ignore the double moving average column.

A single moving average of length n, MA(n), contains a series of means based on n successive data points. The term single means that a moving average series is constructed from the original data.

For a moving average of three periods, a period's moving average value is the mean of the values for that period, the period before, and the period after. Thus, February's moving average value is the mean of January, February, and March's data values, and March's moving average value is the mean of March and its neighbors, February and April.

We cannot compute a moving average for the first data value (see Table 2.20, Undeterminable entry) and the last data value (not shown), since there are no values before the first data point or after the last data point. Two data values are lost when computing a single moving average of three.

In general, to compute a single moving average of 3, MA(3), series:

1. Set up a three-period moving average column.
2. Leave the first and last rows of the moving average column blank.
3. Note that any period's moving average is the sum of its data value, that of the period before it, and that of the period after it, divided by 3.
4. Place the mean of the three numbers opposite the middle of the three numbers averaged. This is called centering.

Table 2.19

Personal Hours Taken

Year	J	F	M	A	M	J	J	A	S	O	N	D
1989	50	120	60	150	80	180	50	120	250	130	190	390
1990	120	200	270	150	280	290	200	350	300	310	400	350
1991	300	375	250	350	200	150	250	140	100	190	170	150
1992	250	200	150	170	270	170	200	300	150	250	250	200

Table 2.20

Moving Averages of Three Periods

Month	Time-Ordered Data Personal Hours	Single Moving Average of Three	Double Moving Average of Three
Jan.	50	Undeterminable	Undeterminable
Feb.	120	76.7	Undeterminable
Mar.	60	110.0	94.4
Apr.	150	96.7	114.4
May	80	136.7	112.2
June	180	103.3	118.9
July	50	116.7	120.0
Aug.	120	140.0	141.1
Sept.	250	166.7	165.6
Oct.	130	190.0	197.8
Nov.	190	236.7	220.0
Dec.	390	233.3	235.6

Smoothing by Moving Averages

Moving averages expose underlying trends that tell whether the time-ordered data are increasing or decreasing over the long term. Sometimes the raw data contain many peaks and valleys, and it may be difficult to see the long-term upward or downward changes over time. Such is the case for the rough data from Table 2.19 graphed in Figure 2.21 on page 75. In contrast, Figure 2.22 shows the moving average of the original data.

What does the smoothed line graph in Figure 2.22 reveal? It shows that the mean number of personal hours increased from under 80 hours in February to about 350 hours in November of the second year, when it peaked. The mean personal hours then dropped quickly and reached a low of about 150 hours in September of the third year. Since then, mean personal hours have increased to about 240 hours.

It's not that we couldn't see the pattern in Figure 2.21, but with all the roughness, it was somewhat hidden and more difficult to detect. The underlying data pattern is more obvious in the smoothed line graph of the moving average.

Repeated Smoothing by Averages of Three

If smoothing the data once is useful, is smoothing more than once better? We can smooth the single moving average of three to reduce the remaining roughness. This is called a double moving average—a moving average of a moving average. For example, see the double moving average column in Table 2.20. The double moving average for March is simply (76.7 + 110.0 + 96.7)/3 = 94.4. The other double moving averages were computed in a similar fashion. The double moving average will be smoother than the MA(3). We can go a step further and also compute a triple moving average—a moving average of the double moving average.

Figure 2.23 on page 76 shows a double moving average for personal hours data. Compare this line graph with the single moving average of Figure 2.22. The double moving average is indeed smoother. The big picture is very easy to detect.

Does this mean that we should always compute double or higher moving averages when looking for a pattern in the data? Are double or higher moving averages better than single moving averages? Not necessarily!

FIGURE 2.21   Raw Data—Personal Hours Taken Each Month

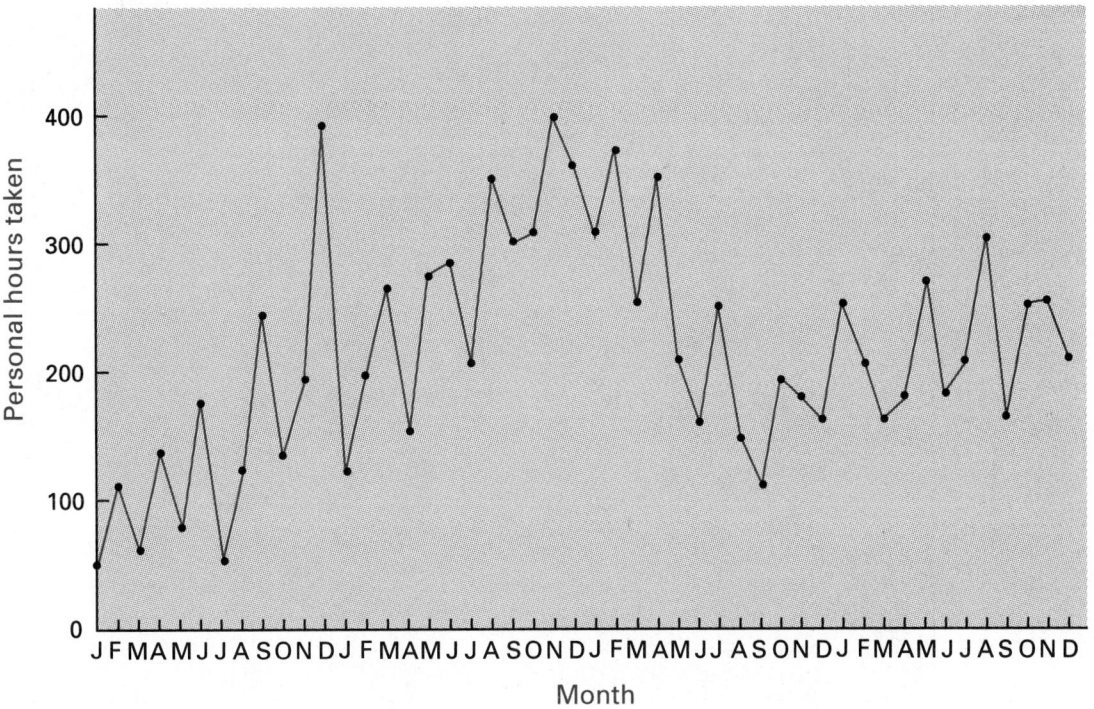

FIGURE 2.22   MA(3)—Personal Hours Taken Each Month

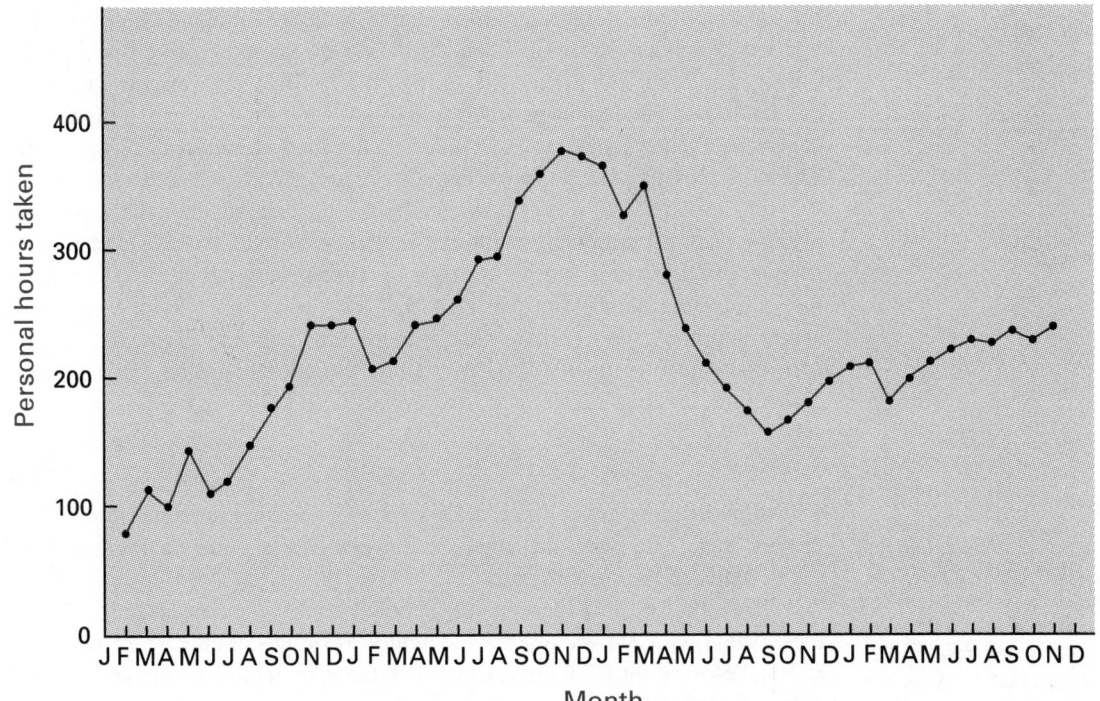

FIGURE 2.23   Double MA(3)—Personal Hours Taken Each Month

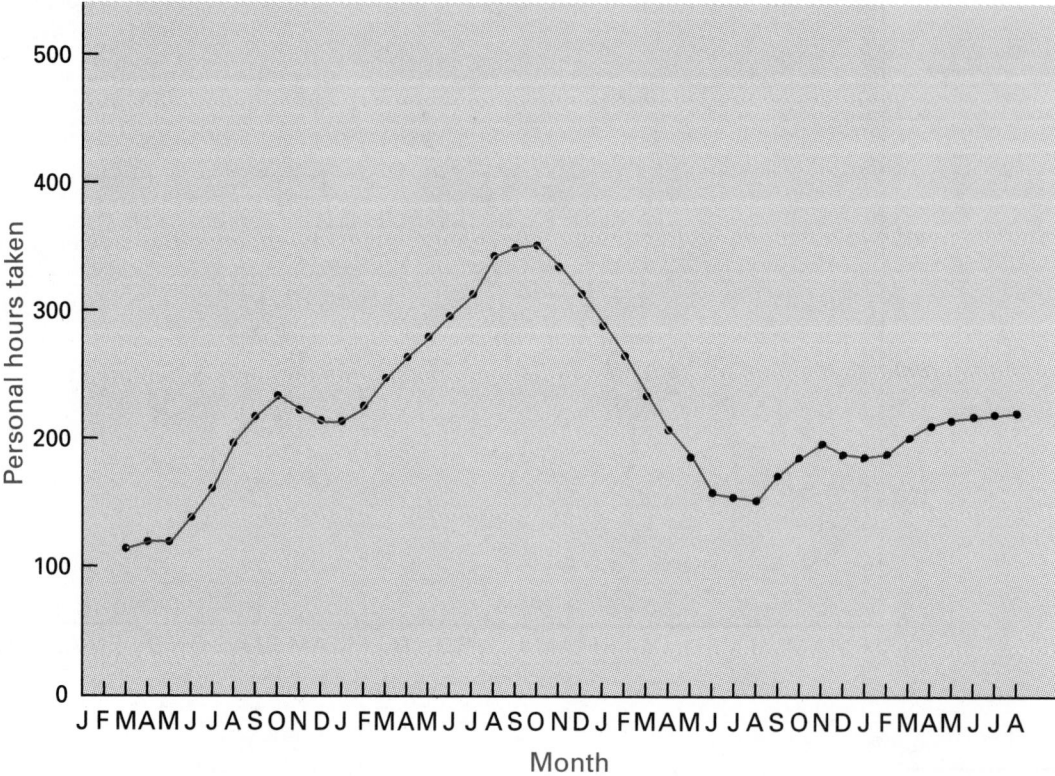

The unbroken line in Figure 2.24 shows a line graph of 48 numbers taken from the random numbers table in Appendix 4. Random numbers exhibit no pattern nor upward or downward trend. Then the data were smoothed five times using moving averages of three. The dashed line in Figure 2.24 illustrates this moving average. Note that the moving average smoothed five times suggests a pattern in the data. But there cannot be a pattern since the original data are random numbers. What is happening? The more moving averages we compute, the more likely we are to see bogus patterns.

The rougher—more peaks and valleys—the original data, the higher the moving average we must compute to smooth the data to see the data's pattern. However, be forewarned! In computing higher moving averages, we obtain smoother line graphs that expose the underlying pattern—the good news; but we lose more data points at the beginning and end of the time-ordered data and begin to see nonexistent patterns—the bad news. Statistics alone cannot determine the right amount of smoothing. It is a judgment call, that comes with knowing the issues.

Residuals

The smoothed line graph is a crucial step in developing a mental model, but it is not the last step. We must also analyze the **residuals**—the differences between the rough data and the smooth data.

A residual is the difference between an original data value and its corresponding smoothed value. A large negative or positive residual suggests that an extraordinary event has happened.

The data for the 48 months of personal hours taken are used to illustrate residuals. Table 2.21 shows several calculated residuals. Figure 2.25 on page 78 is a residual plot for the 48 months of data. Time is on the horizontal axis, and the residuals are on the vertical axis.

FIGURE 2.24   Plot of Random Numbers and Moving Average of 3 Smoothed Five Times

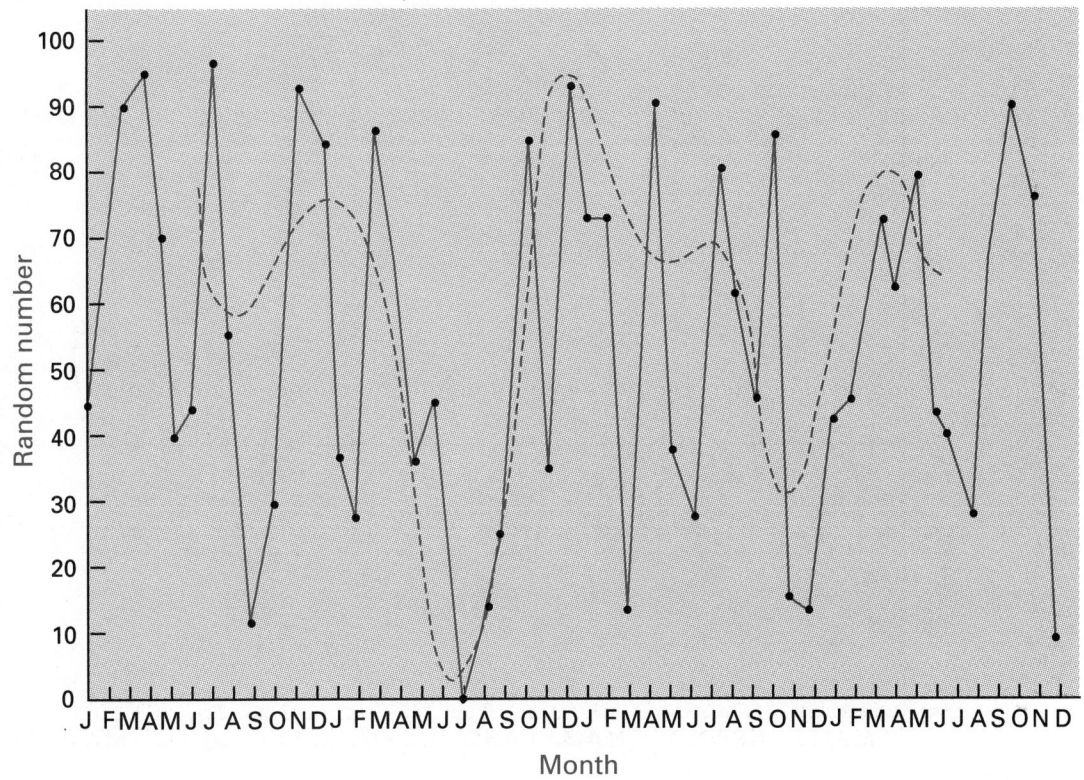

Table 2.21

Computing Residuals

Month	Original Data	Moving Average	Residual
Jan.	50	Undeterminable	
Feb.	120	76.7	+43.3
Mar.	60	110.0	−50.0
Apr.	150	96.7	+53.3
May	80	136.7	−56.7
June	180	103.3	+76.7

Look for sudden jumps or drops in the residuals. They suggest something out of the ordinary happened. In Figure 2.25, two large residuals stand out from the rest. In December of the first year, the actual number of personal hours taken was much higher than the moving average. In the following month, the actual number of personal hours taken was much lower than the moving average. What has caused these extraordinary residuals? The moving average and residual line graphs suggest the two mental models described below.

Insight from Smoothed Graph

Average personal hours increased steadily from under 80 hours in February to about 350 hours in November of the second year, when it peaked. Then

FIGURE 2.25   Residual Plot: Personal Hours Taken

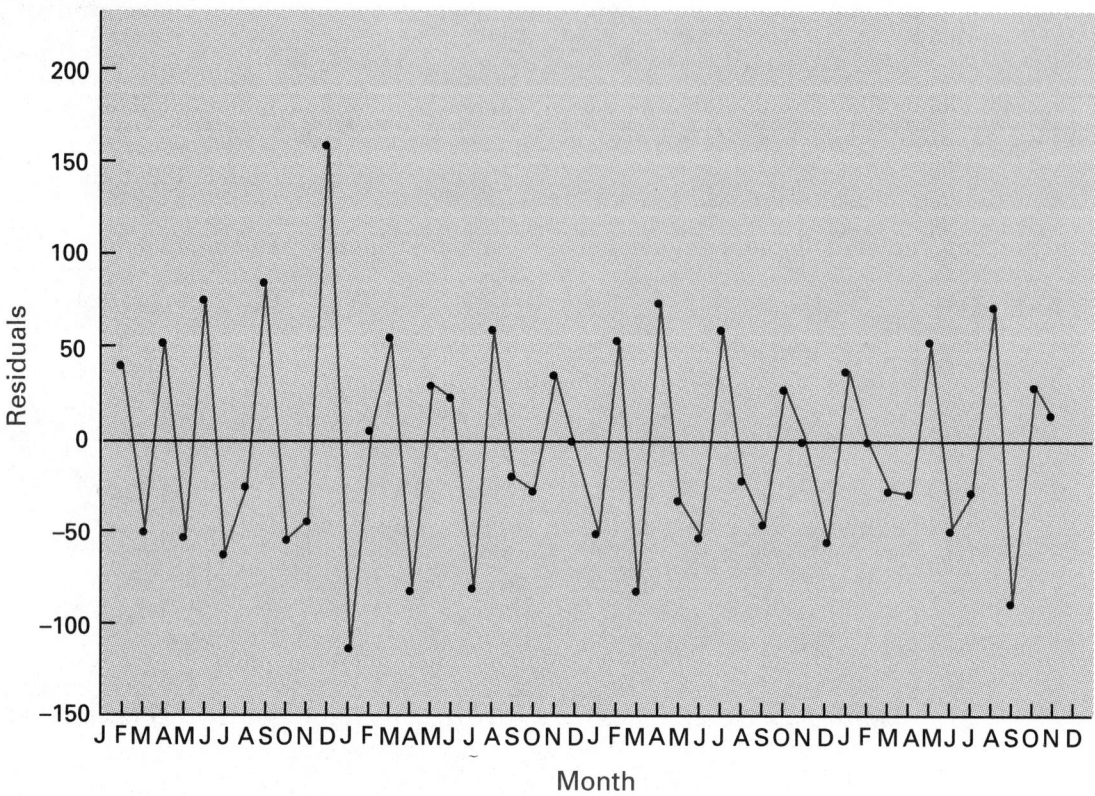

it dropped quickly and reached a low of about 150 hours in September of the third year. Average personal hours have again increased steadily to about 240 hours.

What accounts for these changes over time?

Insight from Residual Plot

Workers took an unusually large number of personal hours in December of the first year. The next month they took an unusually small number of personal hours.

What could account for the large positive and negative residuals? Did this occur during the time when the firm considered and then rejected a wage cut? Did the accounting department mistakenly credit some of January's hours to December? Was there a flu epidemic?

The residual plot has sharpened the mental model first developed from the moving average line graph. Both moving averages and residual plots are essential tools in building mental models. The former reveals the big picture or pattern over time, and the latter identifies unusual events in the form of large positive or negative residuals.

The residual plot for the 48 months of personal hours data suggests that both in December of the first year and in January of the second year something out of the ordinary happened. However, as we will now demonstrate, only one month may have been an outlier.

Impact of Outliers on Moving Averages

In Table 2.22, the original data contain an outlier (see the data point for 1984). What impact does it have on the single moving average series and residuals?

The residual column indicates large negative and positive residuals for the three years from 1983 to 1985. Large positive and negative residuals suggest that something unusual happened over those three years. But we can see from the original data that in only one year was there an unusual happening, namely, 1984. But due to the smoothing by averages of three, the outlier's impact was spread over three years. Remember, one data value affects three moving average calculations.

Table 2.22 demonstrates that if we find large positive and negative residuals, one or more of them may not signify outliers. Here, the two large residuals for 1983 and 1985 are simply due to averaging. The large residual for 1984 signifies an outlier, and thus a potential real problem or opportunity.

In summary, smooth the data to detect the underlying data pattern. Develop a residual plot and identify large positive and negative residuals. Some of these large residuals may not indicate outliers. But some do. Effective managers investigate all large residuals, determine which residuals suggest real problems, and then solve them.

Table 2.22

Impact of an Outlier in Time-Ordered Data on the Residuals

Year	Original Data	Moving Average of Three	Residual
1980	10	Undeterminable	
1981	12	11.7	.3
1982	13	12.3	.7
1983	12	25.0	−13.0
1984	50	25.7	24.3
1985	15	27.0	−12.0
1986	16	15.0	1.0
1987	14	15.7	−1.7
1988	17	16.3	.7
1989	18	18.0	.0
1990	19	19.0	.0
1991	20	Undeterminable	

SECTION 2.9 EXERCISES

 1. Below are time-ordered data on the number of customer complaints per month before and after the implementation of a total quality management program (TQM). The goal of TQM is reduce complaints, improve service, and ultimately increase net profits.

Before

J	F	M	A	MY	J	JL	AU	SE	O	N	D
45	46	45	45	43	46	47	42	45	43	48	43

After

J	F	M	A	MY	J	JL	AU	SE	O	N	D
41	39	40	37	36	35	36	32	31	31	28	29

a. Use a line graph to plot the time-ordered data.
b. Are the data stationary? Why?
c. Compute the mean number of complaints for the first year, the second year, and for both years combined.
d. Does the mean for both years accurately represent the average number of complaints for years 1 and 2?
e. What lesson have you just learned about using the mean for nonstationary data?

2. Below are time-ordered data on sales over a two-year period.

1993

J	F	M	A	MY	J	JL	AU	S	O	N	D
120	170	140	150	150	170	120	160	140	160	135	165

1994

J	F	M	A	MY	J	JL	AU	S	O	N	D
140	160	130	140	170	160	150	150	130	170	135	135

a. Use a line graph to plot the time-ordered data.
b. Are the data stationary? Why?
c. Compute the mean sales for the first year, the second year, and for both years combined.
d. Does the mean for both years accurately represent the average sales for years 1993 and 1994?
e. What lesson have you just learned about using the mean for stationary data?

3. Construct a three-period moving average series for the sales data shown.

Time Period	Sales
1	3
2	5
3	7
4	6
5	8
6	12
7	15
8	18
9	8
10	14
11	16
12	20

4. Using the same data given in Exercise 3, compute a three-period double moving average series.

5. Compute the residuals for the data in Exercise 3. Do any residuals appear to be outliers?

6. Construct a five-period moving average for the data in Exercise 3. How many data values are lost? Now construct a seven-period moving average for the data in Exercise 3. Now how many data values are lost? What serious problem occurs as you increase the length of the moving average?

7. Under what conditions will a moving average of three be a horizontal line?

8. Calculate a three-month moving average series and the residuals for the given data. Describe the pattern in the data. Do any residuals appear to be outliers?

Month	J	F	M	A	M	J	J	A	S	O	N	D
Claims	4	8	7	15	6	9	5	3	8	7	6	5

9. Calculate a three-quarter moving average series and calculate the residuals for the sales data shown. Describe the pattern in the data. Do any residuals appear to be outliers?

Year	Quarter	Sales	Year	Quarter	Sales
1989	1	240	1990	1	350
	2	260		2	330
	3	250		3	370
	4	290		4	390

10. Compute and plot three-period moving averages for the number of complaints received by a retail store over the past 16 weeks as shown below. Are the data stationary?

Week	1	2	3	4	5	6	7	8	9	10	11	12	13	14	15	16
Complaints	15	20	7	15	24	8	9	15	36	12	11	10	16	8	19	18

11. Compute and plot the residuals for the moving averages in Exercise 10. Do there appear to be any outliers?

12. Since the residual plot in Exercise 11 is stationary, use the Empirical rule and Tukey's rule to determine if any residuals are outliers. If the results of the two rules differ, why do they differ?

13. Consider the following time-ordered data set consisting of quarterly sales data (in thousands) for three years.

Q1	Q2	Q3	Q4	Q5	Q6	Q7	Q8	Q9	Q10	Q11	Q12
25	35	30	120	40	45	40	50	55	60	65	70

    a. Plot the quarterly data.
    b. Construct a three-quarter moving average.
    c. Determine the residuals from the moving averages.
       Note that the residuals for quarters 3, 4, and 5 are large. That would suggest that in all three quarters unusually low or high sales occurred. However, the original data indicate that only in quarter 4 were sales exceptionally high in comparison to other quarters.
    d. Why were the residuals for three quarters affected when only the sales for quarter 4 were exceptionally high?
    e. To overcome the problems of misleading residuals, construct a three-period **moving median**. Take the data for the first three periods. Instead of computing an average, determine the median. Now do the same for the data for periods 2, 3, and 4. Now do the same for the data for periods 3, 4, and 5. Repeat this procedure for all the data. You have just constructed a moving median.
    f. Determine the residuals from the moving median. Note that only in quarter 4 is the residual exceptionally large, indicating a potential outlier period.

14. The following data set represents the approximate percentage of electoral votes cast in presidential elections by California this century.

Year	1900	1910	1920	1930	1940	1950	1960	1970	1980	1990
Percent	2%	2%	3%	4%	4%	4%	6%	8%	9%	10%

Source: Congressional Quarterly's Guide to U.S. Elections

    a. Construct a three-period moving average.
    b. Using the answer from part **a**, describe the growth of California's clout in the Electoral College over the past 90 years.

2.10 ≡ Key Ideas and Overview

We conclude this chapter on problem sensing through descriptive statistics and graphics with the diagram in Figure 2.26. It will help integrate the material within Chapter 2, as it recapitulates the following general ideas:

FIGURE 2.26   Integrating Framework for Chapter 2

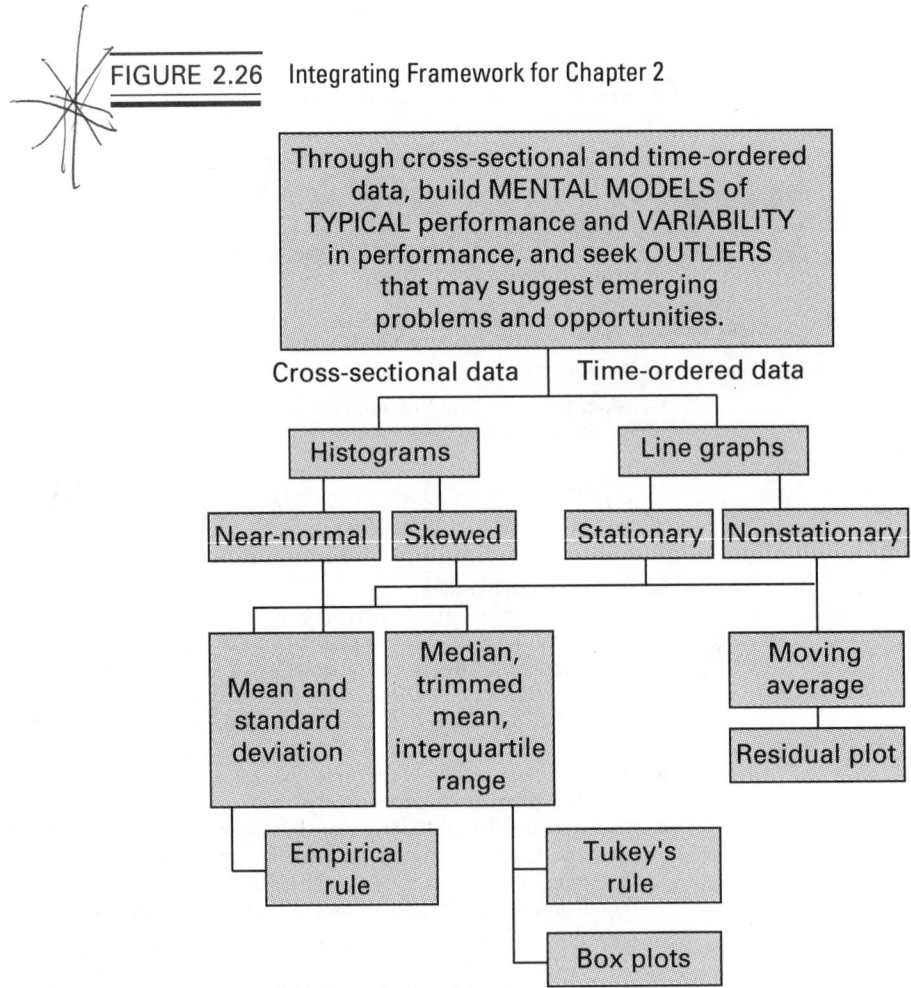

1. As problem solvers, start with the following questions: How do we (myself, group, department, division, or firm) compare to others? Or, how are we doing over time? Have any extraordinary events happened? Are there outliers?

2. Organize cross-sectional data by drawing stem-and-leaf displays, frequency and relative frequency histograms, and ogives.

3. Summarize and interpret cross-sectional data by computing the mean and standard deviation or the median, trimmed mean, and interquartile range. Which statistics we use depends on the skewness of the data.

4. Use either the Empirical rule or Tukey's rule to identify outliers in cross-sectional data.

5. Organize time-ordered data by drawing line graphs.

6. Treat stationary time-ordered data as cross-sectional data. Compute the mean and standard deviation or the median and interquartile range. Which set of descriptive statistics we use depends on the skewness of the data.

7. For nonstationary time-ordered data, use a single-or higher-order moving average series to smooth the data and to detect its underlying pattern.

8. Use residual plots to seek outliers. Determine the root causes of the outliers.

9. Keep mental models simple. Use pictures (histograms or line graphs) when discussing a model with others. Many managers and business professionals prefer pictures or words to numbers alone.

COMCEL

Date: April 15, 1994
To: Ann Tabor, CEO
From: Howard Bright, Manager, Norcross Plant
Re: Analysis of Work Group Productivity Data

SUMMARY
Your April 1 memo asked why one group can perform at 123% of standard when so many work groups are producing below standard. Work group 20's performance is an outlier. They are an exceptionally high-performing group.

I have found one difference between work group 20 and the other 35 groups. Group 20 members often switch jobs with one another. Apparently the group decided that job switching was something they wanted to do. Other groups have members that occasionally switch jobs, but not to the extent of work group 20. I am investigating this potential explanation. If job switching does explain their high performance, we should encourage and train other groups to do likewise.

SUPPORTING ANALYSIS

Since the productivity data pertain to a single month, I used a statistical software package, to construct a frequency table and histogram to understand the data. The distribution is skewed to the right and appeared to contain an outlier—the group that produced at 123% of industry standard.

Because of the potential outlier, I calculated the median and the interquartile range. The median is 100. The first quartile is 95 and the third quartile is 104. Thus the interquartile range is 9. Tukey's rule tells us that an outlier is any data point that is more than 1 step below the first quartile or more than 1 step above the third quartile. So an outlier is any number less than 81.5% (95 − 1.5 · 9) or above 117.5% (104 + 1.5 · 9). This analysis confirms that only work group 20's productivity is an outlier.

CHAPTER 2 QUESTIONS

1. Why would you use histograms to display cross-sectional data?

2. How can a relative frequency histogram help you quickly and easily identify unusual or rare occurrences?

3. Why is it important to managers to identify unusual happenings?

4. A outlier might not signal the onset of a problem or opportunity. What are two other possible explanations for an outlier?

5. Why do we use line graphs for time-ordered data and histograms for cross-sectional data? That is, why can't we use line graphs for displaying cross-sectional data and frequency histograms for displaying nonstationary time-ordered data?

6. Distinguish between yes/no data and numerical data.

7. Why is the standard deviation more useful than the range as a measure of spread or variability?

8. Without resorting to math, how could you quickly approximate the mean of a frequency histogram?

9. What would a frequency histogram with a near-zero variance look like?

10. As the variance increases, what happens to the shape of the frequency distribution?

11. Explain the logic of defining an outlier as an observation that is more than three standard deviations away from the mean.

12. Under what conditions can the mean and standard deviation be misleading summary statistics?

13. The mean is *sensitive* to outliers and the median is *robust* to outliers. What do these terms mean?

14. Explain why the interquartile range is not affected by outliers.

15. When should you use the mean and standard deviation and when the median and interquartile range to summarize cross-sectional data?

16. Explain why Tukey's definition of an outlier as a data point that is either one step above the third quartile or one step below the first quartile makes sense.

17. What problems will you have if you use the mean and standard deviation or the median and interquartile range to summarize nonstationary time-ordered data?

18. What are two problems in using triple- or higher-order moving averages to smooth time-ordered data to see the underlying pattern in time-ordered data?

19. How does a residual analysis aid in problem sensing?

20. What can go wrong if you use a moving average to smooth a time series that has outliers?

CHAPTER 2 APPLICATION PROBLEMS

1. Best Dairy Inc. has segmented its market into eight groups. Among these separate markets are the Machos and the Status Seekers. Machos are young, male, blue-collar workers with high school degrees who live in the city. Status Seekers are young, male, white-collar workers with college degrees who live in the suburbs. Best Dairy Inc. takes a sample of ten from both market segments and asks each person his annual income. The data below show the results. Are there any differences in incomes between the Machos and Status Seekers?

Machos	Status Seekers
$22,500	$29,000
22,000	28,500
21,000	28,000
22,000	27,500
23,000	28,500
23,750	29,000
20,000	27,500
22,500	28,000
23,500	28,000
21,500	28,000

a. Draw stem-and-leaf displays.
b. Compute the appropriate measures of the center and spread.
c. What are the differences between the two segments?

2. The following list presents the number of computer crimes each year for the period 1962–1978. [*Source: Computer Crimes—Criminal Justice Resource Manual*; Bureau of Justice Statistics, 1979.] What is the underlying trend and are there any years when the number of crimes was unusual or extraordinary?

1962	2	1971	59
1963	2	1972	73
1964	6	1973	75
1965	8	1974	84
1966	3	1975	59
1967	4	1976	87
1968	12	1977	42
1969	20	1978	20
1970	38		

a. Plot the raw data.
b. Smooth the data with an MA(3).
c. Develop a residual plot.
d. Develop a mental model on the increase in computer crimes in the United States during 1962–1978.
e. As director of the Computer Crimes Division, should you be seeking additional personnel for your department based on your answer in part **d**?

3. The administrator of the emergency room in Safehaven Hospital in Chicago has recorded the amount of time a patient waits before receiving treatment. The length of time that a patient must wait for treatment is important in determining the size of the emergency room staff. He records the wait times for 200 patients in a typical week. The data follow.

Class	Frequency
Less than 10 minutes	5
10 up to 15 minutes	25
15 up to 20 minutes	70
20 up to 25 minutes	70
25 up to 30 minutes	25
30 or more minutes	5

a. What percentage of patients receive treatment in less than 10 minutes?
b. What percentage of patients receive treatment after 30 or more minutes?
c. Experience indicates that if 30% of wait times are less than 10 minutes, the emergency room is overstaffed. If 20% of the wait times are 30 or more minutes, the emergency room is understaffed. What can you conclude about Safehaven's emergency staffing?
d. Construct a frequency data set that would suggest that the emergency room is both understaffed and overstaffed.

4. Historically, over 40% of the accounts receivable at Apex Inc. have been in excess of 35 days. Apex recently started a program of inducements to reduce the age of the accounts receivable. Two months later a sample of 15 accounts receivable is taken. Given the following data, has the age of the accounts receivable been reduced?

Number of Days

20	15	20	16	19
15	22	21	20	17
21	30	20	18	15

a. Plot a stem-and-leaf display.
b. Compute the appropriate measures of the center and spread.
c. Has the inducements program been successful? Explain.

5. Length-of-tenure discounts are the difference between the rents charged long-time tenants and newer tenants. Landlords give discounts because they want to keep good tenants and minimize turnover. The American Housing Group wants to know if the size of the discount is the same in Atlanta and Houston. It collects the following data, which are the percentage discounts at selected apartment complexes in the two cities. Do the discounts differ in the two cities?

Atlanta		Houston	
3.4	1.5	6.2	3.5
6.5	2.0	7.2	4.6
11.5	3.4	5.4	5.3
2.7	2.5	6.8	4.2
2.3	3.9	7.1	6.9
2.9	1.1	10.9	7.4
3.9	2.2	23.0	5.6
3.2		5.8	

a. Construct box plots for the two cities.
b. Compute the appropriate measures of the center and spread.
c. Do the discounts differ between Atlanta and Houston? How?
d. What economic and demographic variables might account for the difference between Atlanta and Houston?

 6. The financial manager at COMCEL wants to know how profit margins, net profit after taxes divided by sales, have done for the past 16 quarters. Data are given below. Are profit margins increasing or decreasing?

Quarter	Profit Margin
1	5.05
2	4.10
3	5.15
4	5.20
5	6.75
6	5.30
7	5.35
8	5.40
9	5.95
10	5.50
11	5.15
12	5.60
13	5.65
14	6.70
15	5.75
16	5.80

a. Develop a line graph.
b. Smooth the data using an MA(3).
c. Develop a residual plot.
d. Develop a mental model on profit margin performance.
e. Based on your answer to part **d**, what do you expect should happen to profit margin for the next four quarters? If your expectations are not met, what might that mean?

 7. American Breakfast sells 10-ounce boxes of its cereals. Each hour the Statistical Process Control Department takes a sample of four boxes from the production line and weighs the contents. It computes the hourly mean and the range of the four data values. This is to ensure that they do have 10 ounces in their boxes.

Hour	Weight of Four Boxes off the Line				Hourly Mean	Hourly Range
0800–0900	9.8	10	10.1	9.9	9.95	.30
0900–1000	9.9	10	10.2	10	10.03	.30
1000–1100	9.8	10	9.7	10.2	9.93	.50
1100–1200	10.1	10	9.9	9.8	9.95	.30
1200–1300	9.7	10	9.9	10	9.90	.30
1300–1400	10.4	10	9.8	9.8	10.00	.60
1400–1500	9.9	10.2	9.7	10.3	10.03	.60
1500–1600	9.8	10	10	10	9.95	.20
1600–1700	10	9.9	9.8	10.2	9.98	.40
1700–1800	9.9	10	10.1	10	10.00	.20

a. Plot the hourly mean and range in two separate line graphs.
b. Compute the mean and standard deviation of the hourly sample means and ranges.

Assuming that the means and ranges are bell-shaped, 95% of the hourly means (and hourly ranges) should lie within a distance of two standard deviations of their respective means.

c. Suppose that the hourly mean weight of the four boxes for hour 1900–2000 is 9.5 ounces. What might that signify? Why?

d. Suppose that the hourly mean range is 1.2 ounces for hour 2100–2200. What might that signify? Why?

e. Given your answers to parts **c** and **d**, what action would you take if you were the plant manager?

8. Industrywide figures show that for plants with 200 to 300 workers, the mean number of grievances filed per month is 75. Midwest Electric Company, which has 250 employees, has been tracking grievances. Data for the last 12 months are given. Do we have a possible disturbance problem?

Month	Grievances
1	75
2	70
3	73
4	78
5	65
6	73
7	97
8	94
9	99
10	93
11	100
12	93

a. Use descriptive statistics and graphics to defend and support your position.

b. How would you go about solving the disturbance problem?

9. Pan-Pacific Power Company wishes to know if its employees want the flexibility of designing their own benefits package. A flexible package allows employees to make choices among amount of vacation, type and amount of insurance, number of personal days, etc. Pan-Pacific conducts a survey of its managers and professionals, administrative support people, and hourly employees. The survey data are given here.

Group	Sample Size	Number in Favor
Managers and professionals	50	40
Administrative staff support	100	30
Hourly employees	1,000	250

a. Compute the mean and the standard deviation for the three groups of data.

b. Do the three groups appear to differ in the mean or the standard deviation?

c. Based on your answers to parts **a** and **b**, how should Pan-Pacific deal with the flexible benefits issue?

10. For bell-shaped data, the mean and standard deviation together with the Empirical rule permit you to estimate specific values of the original data. I.Q. scores are bell-shaped with a mean of 100 and a standard deviation of 15.

a. Describe the data using the Empirical rule.

b. If 16% of the population has a higher I.Q. than Mr. Jones, what is Jones's I.Q.?

11. The sales of motor homes for Mobile Homes Inc. for a 20-month period are shown. The sales manager wants to develop a model of sales for the past 20 months. She may wish to use the model to make predictions for the next several months.

Month	Sales in Units	Month	Sales in Units
1	628	11	1,117
2	652	12	1,214
3	495	13	762
4	344	14	846
5	405	15	1,228
6	586	16	937
7	403	17	1,396
8	700	18	1,174
9	837	19	628
10	1,224	20	1,753

a. Plot the raw data.
b. Compute the 10% trimmed mean, median, and interquartile range.
c. Do any of the measures summarize the data accurately? Why?
d. Compute an MA(3) series and plot it. Are the time-ordered data stationary? Describe the overall pattern of the moving average series.

 12. Centex Industries maintains data on the number of service calls its technicians make each day. Below is a frequency distribution of the data. The service manager wants to develop a simple mental model for the typical and the unusual number of calls per day (outliers).

Number of Calls	Frequency
0 to 4.99 calls	1
5 to 9.99 calls	3
10 to 14.99 calls	7
15 to 19.99 calls	17
20 to 24.99 calls	8
25 to 29.99 calls	2
30 to 34.99 calls	1

a. Plot the frequency histogram.
b. Develop a cumulative frequency distribution.
c. Plot the frequency ogive.
d. Develop a mental model on the typical and the rare or unusual number of calls per day.

 13. The Arbitration Association collects data on the number of grievances filed by plants with between 200 and 300 workers. Shown are the data for the January survey. They want to identify firms with exceptionally low and high numbers of filed grievances. They plan to study these firms.

Firms	Grievances
1	70
2	74
3	65
4	45
5	78
6	69
7	99
8	76
9	72
10	62

a. Compute the median and interquartile range.
b. Draw a box plot.

c. Identify outliers and label the box plot.

d. Having identified two plants that are outliers (problem sensing), what would you do next?

14. The given data set is the number of children per household in a survey of 10 families taken in the 1950s.

0   1   1   1   2   2   2   2   3   3

a. Compute the mean, 10% trimmed mean, and the median.

b. The mean and median are relatively close. What does that imply about the data set?

c. Compute the standard deviation and the interquartile range.

15. The data set below is the number of defective fuses in ten boxes of 100 fuses.

Box Number	Number of Defectives
1	0
2	1
3	1
4	1
5	2
6	2
7	2
8	2
9	5
10	25

a. Compute the mean, 10% trimmed mean, and the median.

b. The mean and median are relatively far apart. What does that imply about the data set?

c. Compute the standard deviation and the interquartile range.

16. COMCEL wants to compare the sales-to-salary ratio for salespeople in two of its southern sales regions—Charlotte and New Orleans. Sales-to-salary ratio is an employee's sales divided by his or her base salary. Historically, New Orleans has had the highest sales-to-salary ratios. Recently, the Charlotte region has taken measures to increase the ratio. Summary data for all employees in both regions are presented.

	New Orleans	Charlotte	Charlotte (one year ago)
Population size	5	5	5
Minimum	9	9	3
Maximum	25	24	15
First quartile	10	10	7
Median	12	11	7
Third quartile	15	15	11

a. Has Charlotte been successful? Defend your position.

b. How would you attempt to further improve both Charlotte's and New Orleans's sales-to-salary ratio?

17. Managers at Zentron Inc. maintain a database on the number of personal hours taken in the plant at the end of each month. They want to determine the trend over the past two years. They also want to determine a normal number of hours taken so they can identify a month when the number of hours is out of line. If so, they will investigate.

Month	Number of Hours Taken	Month	Number of Hours Taken
January	51	January	65
February	56	February	66
March	60	March	65
April	68	April	68
May	72	May	65
June	69	June	63
July	57	July	66
August	67	August	63
September	63	September	59
October	55	October	60
November	62	November	65
December	51	December	59

a. Plot the data in a line graph.
b. Are the time-ordered data stationary? Why?
c. Compute the mean and standard deviation.
d. Assume that no changes occur within the plant. Use the Empirical rule to determine how many personal hours taken you should expect in 95% of the months.
e. If, in the following January, workers took over 100 hours, what might that mean? Why?

 18. Each day the process control group takes 10 cans of the company's best-selling beverage and checks to see if the cans contain 300 ml. The mean results for a 10-day period on the filling volume are listed. This procedure is to ensure that proper filling volume is maintained.

Day	Filling Volume	Day	Filling Volume
1	301	6	295
2	300	7	290
3	297	8	291
4	299	9	287
5	295	10	285

a. Plot the daily means of the filling volumes in a line graph.
b. Compute an MA(3) and plot it.
c. Does it appear that the firm is having trouble with its filling volume operation? What action should the firm take? Explain your position.

 19. The finance manager of XYZ Inc. wishes to compare her firm's current ratio to those of other firms in the industry. Current ratio is current assets divided by current liabilities. A frequency distribution for a sample of 32 firms' current ratios is presented.

Current Ratio	Frequency
Less than 1.0	1
1.00 to 1.49	2
1.50 to 1.99	7
2.00 to 2.49	14
2.50 to 2.99	7
3.00 and above	1

a. Plot the frequency histogram.
b. Develop a cumulative percentage distribution.

   c. Plot the percentage ogive.
   d. XYZ's current ratio is .95. How does XYZ compare with the other 32 firms? Is it typ-
      ical or unusual? What action should XYZ take next if it concludes that its current ratio
      is out of line with the rest of the industry?

 20. Financial analysts agree that for an industrial bond to be a safe investment, the firm's total
   income should be more than three or four times its interest payment. Shown are the interest
   coverage data, total income divided by bond interest, for the past ten years. Are the firm's
   bonds a safe investment?

Year	Interest Coverage
1982	8.5*
1983	7.9
1984	8.2
1985	6.5
1986	6.6
1987	5.7
1988	5.8
1989	6.9
1990	7.5
1991	8.5

* In 1982 the firm's total income was
  8.5 times as large as its interest on bonds.

   a. Plot the interest coverage for the past ten years.
   b. Compute an MA(3) and plot it.
   c. Describe the overall pattern of the interest coverage ratio for the past ten years. Using
      only the above time-ordered data, have the firm's industrial bonds been a safe invest-
      ment for the past ten years?

 21. The product life cycle tells us that the sales for a product are slow right after introduction,
   increase at an increasing rate, increase at a constant rate, begin to level off, and may even
   decline. Do the following sales data behave as the life cycle predicts?

Year	Sales (in thousands)	Year	Sales (in thousands)
1975	5	1984	54
1976	7	1985	57
1977	10	1986	61
1978	19	1987	60
1979	31	1988	59
1980	47	1989	57
1981	49	1990	55
1982	52	1991	56
1983	50	1992	54

   a. Compute an MA(3) for the yearly sales and plot it.
   b. Use the moving average series to describe the growth of your product. Do sales follow
      the product life cycle model?
   c. Given the stage of the product, what actions should the firm consider?

 22. Shown are two frequency distributions of cholesterol levels of 100 people who eat similar foods with only one exception. Group B people take 7 grams of fiber (oat bran) daily.
   Cholesterol levels over 200 indicate a potential problem. Levels over 240 are considered
   serious enough to warrant medication.

Group A		Group B	
Class	Frequency	Class	Frequency
Under 160	5	Under 160	10
160 to 179	10	160 to 179	25
180 to 199	35	180 to 199	55
200 to 219	30	200 to 219	5
220 to 239	10	220 to 239	5
240 or over	10	240 or over	0

a. Construct a frequency histogram for each group.
b. Determine the approximate mean for both histograms.
c. Does it appear that fiber affects a person's cholesterol level? Defend your position.

23. The accompanying scatter diagram contains a plot of the number of students in an elective Managerial Communications course in a College of Business Administration at an urban university. It also contains a plot of a moving average of length three. The instructor must make predictions on enrollment for the next year. If the class size tops 40, he will have to find a second instructor.

Term	Enrollment	Term	Enrollment
F88	12	SP90	12
W89	10	SU90	24
SP89	14	F90	30
SU89	20	W91	31
F89	17	SP91	34
W90	30	SU91	35

a. Since the moving average series is much smoother than the original data, let's use it to make our predictions. What is the predicted enrollment for the fall term of '91? Begin with an estimate of the moving average for SU91 and determine an estimate of enrollment for fall '91.
b. Now predict the enrollment for the winter term of '92.

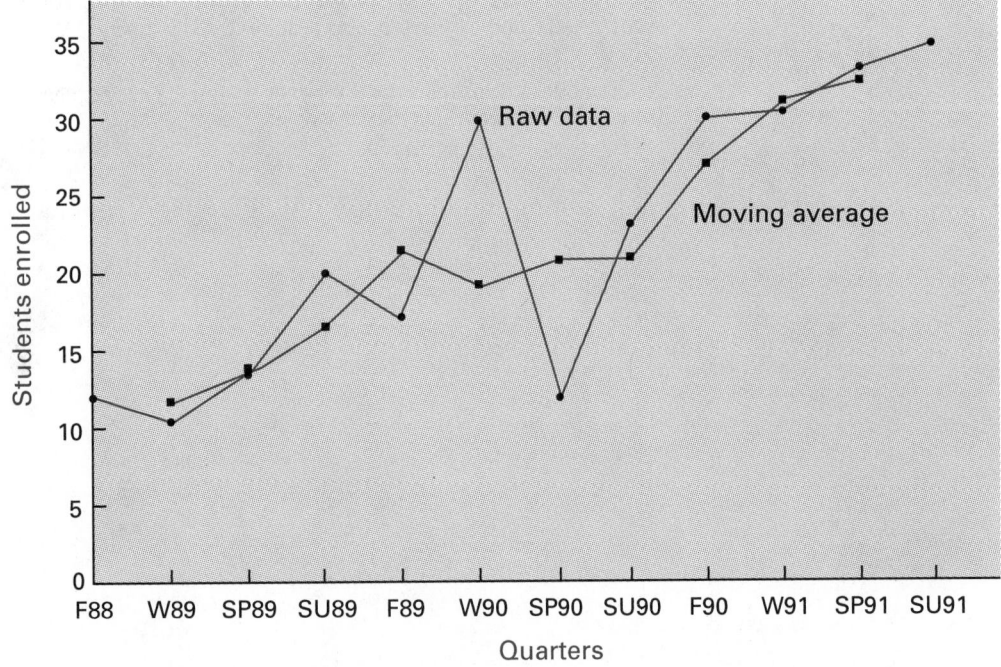

24.

Date: June 5, 1992
To: Nat Gordon, Vice President of Manufacturing
From: Ann Tabor, CEO
Re: Monthly Attendance at Two Operating Plants

It has recently come to my attention that monthly attendance at our two operating plants may differ. Both may be below our desired goal of 98%. You will recall the emphasis that we placed on monthly attendance at our Annual Goal-Setting Retreat. Please have one of your staff members look into the situation. I need the answers to the following questions:

1. Do both plants have similar monthly attendance figures?
2. Is monthly attendance of males and females, or hourly and management employees the same?

Are there any other differences between the two plants? I need the report by June 12.

Use Data Base I in Appendix 9 for your analysis. Your response to Ann Tabor should include a brief memo and your analysis.

25.

Date: January 7, 1992
To: Pam Ascher, National Sales Manager
From: Bill O'Hara, Vice President of Marketing
Re: Tracking Unit Sales in the Atlanta Sales Territory

Ann Tabor has asked me to provide her with an executive summary of our unit sales performance for Atlanta for the past 36 months. She wants to know how fast sales are increasing, which are our strong and weak quarters, and if there have been any months when sales were unusually high or low. I'm sorry to add this to your other duties, but Ann needs the report on her desk by January 15.

Use Data Base II in Appendix 9 for your analysis. Your response to Bill O'Hara should include a brief memo and your analysis.

APPENDIX   Statistical Software

Example: Here we use SAS, the **S**tatistical **A**nalysis **S**ystem, to generate descriptive statistics for the work group productivity data in Table 2.8.

Input

```
01   DATA TEST;
02   INPUT PRODUCT @@;
03   LABEL PRODUCT = 'PRODUCTIVITY';
04   CARDS;
05         106   95 103   95   95   97   95 105 102
06          89 105   99   95 100 106 101   97 104
07         110 123 104 100 101   95   97   94 102
08         102 106 110   97 101   95   98   97   94
09   PROC UNIVARIATE PLOT FREQ; VAR PRODUCT;
```

Explanation of Input

01   SAS uses two different types of statements: DATA statements and PROCess statements. DATA tells SAS to build a temporary data file and gives the file the name TEST. Note: except for data entry (lines 5–8), each line ends with a semicolon. Also semi-colons are used within the PROC statements (see line 9).

02–03   The INPUT statement defines the variable(s) that will be read into the temporary file TEST. A single variable called PRODUCT will be read into TEST. SAS limits the names of variables to eight characters, so PRODUCTIVITY was renamed PRODUCT. The @@ symbols allow the user to put data for many observations on the same line (see lines 5–8). A fuller description of the variable is obtained by providing a label for the variable, that is PRODUCTIVITY (see headings in the output section).

04   CARDS tells SAS that data will follow.

09   Instructs SAS to PROCess the data for the VARiable called PRODUCT. UNIVARIATE is the name of a statistical subroutine that provides descriptive statistics on one (uni) variable at a time.

Output

```
                                   SAS
                               UNIVARIATE
          VARIABLE=PRODUCT     PRODUCTIVITY

                                 MOMENTS

A              N                36     SUM WGTS          36
               MEAN        100.417     SUM             3615
               STD DEV     6.22151     VARIANCE     38.7071
               SKEWNESS    1.35283     KURTOSIS     3.70409
               USS          364361     CSS          1354.75
               CV          6.19569     STD MEAN     1.03692
               T:MEAN=0    96.8415     PROB>|T|      0.0001
               SGN HANK        333     PROB>|S|      0.0001
               NUM ^= 0         36
```

B   QUANTILES   EXTREMES

```
100%   MAX        123      99%      123      LOWEST    HIGHEST
 75%   Q3         104      95%   111.95         89        106
 50%   MED        100      90%   107.2          94        106
 25%   Q1          95      10%    94.7          94        110
  0%   MIN         89       5%    93.25         95        110
                            1%      89          95        123


RANGE            34
Q3-Q1             9
MODE             95
```

C
```
STEM LEAF                              #                                    BOXPLOT
  12  3                                1 ------------------->                  0
  11
  11  00                               2                          |
  10  55666                            5                          |
  10  00111222344                     11 ------------------->    *--+--*
   9  55555557777789                  14                         +-----+
   9  44                               2                          |
   8  9                                1                          |
      ----+----+----+----+
MULTIPLY STEM.LEAF BY 10**+01
```

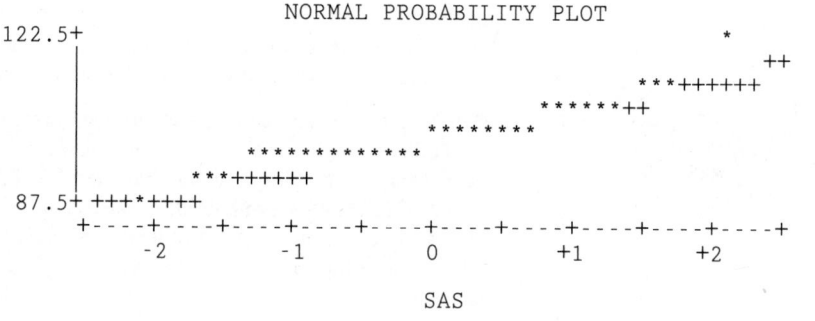

NORMAL PROBABILITY PLOT

SAS

D   UNIVARIATE

VARIABLE=PRODUCT   PRODUCTIVITY

FREQUENCY TABLE

VALUE	COUNT	PERCENTS CELL	PERCENTS CUM	VALUE	COUNT	PERCENTS CELL	PERCENTS CUM
89	1	2.8	2.8	102	3	8.3	69.4
94	2	5.6	8.3	103	1	2.8	72.2
95	7	19.4	27.8	104	2	5.6	77.8
97	5	13.9	41.7	105	2	5.6	83.3
98	1	2.8	44.4	106	3	8.3	91.7
99	1	2.8	47.2	110	2	5.6	97.2
100	2	5.6	52.8	123	1	2.8	100.0
101	3	8.3	61.1				

Interpretation of Output

A   The output (in bold) presents the descriptive statistics found in the text. The remaining statistics are beyond the text's scope.

B   The "quantiles" or percentiles include Q_1 = 25%, the median = 50%, and Q_3 = 75%. The values are the same as in the text, but this will not always be true.

Percentiles in some SAS output may vary slightly from the text. The reason is that there are several equally correct, but slightly different, formulas for computing the first and third quartiles.

C   UNIVARIATE produces a stem-and leaf display and a box plot. The box plot uses the stems from the stem-and-leaf display for its scaling. The SAS box plot does not look like Figure 2.18 because both the median of 100 and Q_3 of 104 are in the same stem. That is, the first 10 stem contains data values from 100 to 104. Thus, we cannot visually determine both the median and the 75th percentile. SAS uses the "0" symbol to indicate an **outlier**—a value that is one step below Q_1 or one step above Q_3. SAS uses the "*" symbol to indicate a **super outlier**—a value that is two steps below Q_1 or two steps above Q_3.

UNIVARIATE also produces a normal probability plot that is beyond the text's scope.

D   SAS constructs a frequency table with classes of "unit" width. The COUNT indicates how many values in the data set equal each single value. For example, there were seven 95% productivity values in the data set. The text's frequency tables have class widths greater than one, and are more informative. If all values in the data set are different, a SAS frequency table will simply print all the values and will not summarize the data.

DESCRIPTIVE STATISTICS II: PROBLEM DIAGNOSIS

3.1   Introduction
        Univariate and bivariate data
        Problem sensing
        Problem diagnosis
3.2   Types of variables
3.3   Analyzing mixed cross-sectional data
        One-way table display
        Multiple box plots
3.4   Analyzing categorical cross-sectional data
        Cross-tabs tables
        Joint percentage tables
        Column percentage tables
        Row percentage tables
        Inductive inference
        Intervening variables
3.5   Analyzing quantitative cross-sectional data
        Scatter diagrams

        Linear relationships
        The circle vs. ellipse test
        Nonlinear relationships
        Clusters
3.6   Analyzing quantitative time-ordered data
        Multiple line graphs
        Lagged relationships
3.7   Correlation and cross-correlation
        The correlation coefficient
        Determining lagged relationships using
          cross-correlations
        Interpreting cross-correlations
3.8   Key ideas and overview
Appendix: Statistical Software

 INTEROFFICE
COMMUNICATION

Date: July 21, 1995
To: Cherian Jain, Vice President of Marketing Research
From: Ann Tabor, CEO
Re: Market Share in the Southern Region

In checking the latest report on market share, I was pleased to see that we have captured 55% of the Dallas market and 50% of the Birmingham market. However, we have only 5% of the Washington market and 20% of the Atlanta market. What are we doing right in Birmingham and Dallas, and wrong in Washington, D.C., and Atlanta?

Please look into this for me and make some recommendations on how to improve our market share in the Southern Region.

3.1 ≡ Introduction

There are two major differences between Chapters 2 and 3. From a *statistical* viewpoint, we focus here on *bivariate* data, whereas we focused on *univariate* data in Chapter 2. From a problem-solving perspective, we focus now on both *problem sensing* and *diagnosis,* whereas we focused only on *problem sensing* in Chapter 2. By the end of this section you should be able to:

1. distinguish between bivariate and univariate data;
2. distinguish between problem sensing and diagnosis; and
3. distinguish between diagnosing disturbance problems and entrepreneurial opportunities.

Univariate and Bivariate Data

In Chapter 2 we presented productivity data for 36 work groups. Shown are data for four of these work groups.

Work Group	Productivity (% of standard)
1	106%
2	95%
3	103%
4	95%

These are univariate data. Each work group is described by *one variable,* group productivity. Thus, univariate data represent observations on *one* variable that are all measured in the same units, such as dollars, productivity, or personal hours taken.

Table 3.1 presents bivariate cross-sectional data for 12 sales regions of COMCEL. Each region is described by four variables—market share, advertising, mean years of experience of the sales force, and relative price of product as compared to the competition's price. Note that the units of the four variables need not be the same. Bivariate (or multivariate) data represent observations on *two (or more)* variables that can be expressed in different units. However, each set of data values is measured on the *same* person, region, month, or thing. For example, the data set for the Atlanta region includes the following four values with different units: 20%, $13,000, 3 years, and 1.50.

Problem Sensing

Problem sensing is a critical managerial capability. Effective managers and business professionals must detect emerging disturbance problems and be *pathfinders.* They need to be able to create new opportunities and goals for their departments. Consider the market share data in Table 3.1. What are the data trying to say to the Charlotte regional sales manager?

The mean market share is 29.4%, and the standard deviation is 15.2%. None of the data points is more than three standard deviations from the mean. Even Washington's and Dallas's market shares are not outliers. Charlotte's market share is very close to the mean for the 12 regions. Should the Charlotte manager be satisfied to be in the middle of the pack? Perhaps, but he might also be curious to learn why the market shares vary so much among the 12 regions. If he can determine what causes market share to vary, he may be able to improve the Charlotte region's share. Looking for ways to improve performance is pathfinding.

Thus, a situation perceived as a problem can also be viewed as an opportunity. The Charlotte manager should ask himself: How can I improve my market share? Opportunity sensing begins with asking the question. Problem diagnosis involves answering the question.

Table 3.1
Multivariate Data

Region	Market Share	Advertising	Mean Years Sales Experience	Relative Price
Atlanta	20%	$13,000	3	1.50
Birmingham	50%	$28,000	12	.60
Charlotte	30%	$17,000	15	1.00
Jacksonville	10%	$8,000	1	1.75
New Orleans	25%	$16,000	18	1.30
Orlando	30%	$18,000	7	.90
Miami	35%	$21,000	8	2.00
Washington	5%	$6,000	23	2.90
Baltimore	45%	$25,000	9	1.50
Dallas	55%	$32,000	11	1.10
Houston	20%	$11,000	20	2.50
Austin	28%	$16,000	17	2.25

$\bar{x} = 29.4\%$
$s = 15.2\%$

Problem Diagnosis

Diagnosis begins once we have discovered a disturbance problem (an outlier) or have decided to attempt to improve performance (an entrepreneurial opportunity). For disturbance problems, diagnosis means determining the root causes of an outlier. To do so, ask the following two questions.

1.   What is *unique* about the outlier group or the outlier time period?

Examples

What is unique or distinctive about work group 20 that might account for its very high productivity?

What is unique or distinctive about December 1990 that might account for the unusually high number of personal hours taken that month?

2.   What has *changed* that might account for the outliers?

Examples

Has work group 20 undergone any changes recently that might explain its very high productivity?

Were there any changes in the plant around December that might explain why so many personal hours were taken?

That is, when diagnosing disturbance problems, look for *differences* and *changes*.

Diagnosing entrepreneurial opportunities means determining what variables affect the goals we are trying to attain. Table 3.1 indicates that the Charlotte manager believes that market share is affected by level of advertising, mean years of sales force experience, and relative price. How do managers identify such potential variables? They draw upon their own judgment, creativity, and past experiences as well as advice from customers, vendors, and consultants. Diagnosis means identifying variables that might explain large variations from one region to the next in cross-sectional data or large variations from one time period to the next in time-ordered data. In short, diagnosis answers the question: "What affects what?"

In summary, you will learn how to diagnose disturbance problems and opportunities using bivariate cross-sectional and time-ordered data.

SECTION 3.1 EXERCISES

1. Why do we usually need to do a bivariate data analysis in order to perform problem diagnosis?

2. Suppose your univariate analysis has identified an outlier—a potential problem or an opportunity. What two questions will you ask in determining possible causes of the outlier?

3. A company has divided its market area into regions. For some time each region has contributed equally to the revenues of the firm. Last month one region's contribution to the company's revenue dropped. Assuming that this drop is more than a chance effect, how would you assist the company in diagnosing the causes of the problem?

4. List two variables that might explain the variation in the ratio of annual sales to total salary data.

Salesperson	Ratio of Annual Sales to Total Salary
1	8.0
2	7.5
3	8.4
4	6.7
5	7.5

5. Are the following quality and cost data univariate or bivariate data?

Year	Cost per Unit	Number of Quality Control Groups
1989	$1.45	100
1990	1.40	103
1991	1.30	110
1992	1.24	110
1993	1.28	107
1994	1.10	129
1995	1.05	145

6. Refer to Table 3.1.
   a. Explain how a manager can use the large standard deviation in market share (15.2%) to sense a potential opportunity.
   b. How could managers identify the three other variables (advertising dollars, mean years experience, and relative price) in Table 3.1. What other variables might affect market share?
   c. If the standard deviation in market share were small (1%), should managers attempt to determine what possible variables are associated with the variation among the twelve regions.

7.   Consider the following data.

Year	Sales (thousands)	Sales (hundreds)
1991	2.0	20
1992	2.5	25
1993	2.4	24
1994	2.9	29
1995	3.2	32

   a. Are the data cross-sectional or time-ordered?
   b. Are the data univariate or bivariate?
   c. If the data are not bivariate, add an additional variable that might be related to sales to make the data bivariate.

8.   Consider the following time-ordered production data. An acceptable strength for an eyeglass frame is between 4,700 pounds per square inch (ppsi) and 4,900 ppsi. The data shown below are the mean strength of five eyeglass frames (thousands) taken at random times and the average temperature within the plant in each shift.

Shift	1	2	3	4	5	6	7	8
Strength (thousands)	4.75	4.81	4.72	4.78	4.77	4.70	4.69	4.68
Temperature	72	74	73	74	73	79	80	80

   a. Is the data set univariate or bivariate?
   b. Is the data set time-ordered or cross-sectional?
   c. Use a line graph (Section 2.4) to plot the strength data. Is there a problem with eyeglass strength, and, if so, in what shift did it happen?
   d. Is the problem a disturbance problem or opportunity?
   e. Does it appear that the sudden increase in plant temperature might have caused the problem? Defend.

3.2 ▤ Types of Variables

Diagnosis means identifying variables that affect goals, such as improving market share or determining the reasons for one group's very high productivity. This section describes two types of variables—*quantitative* and *categorical.* By the end of this section you should be able to:

1.   distinguish between quantitative and categorical variables;
2.   explain why you might consider assigning numbers to categorical variables; and
3.   explain why numbers you assign to categorical variables may not be meaningful.

   A variable is a quantity that can take on more than one value. Consider the four variables—job productivity, job switching, number of grievances, and leadership style—to describe three work groups. Productivity is measured as a percentage of the management standard. Job switching assesses whether work group members do or do not switch jobs. Grievances record the number of complaints filed against management. Leadership style assesses the managers' styles of supervision along two dimensions—importance in achieving production (high productivity) and concern for workers (high people).

Work Group	Job Productivity	Job Switching	Number of Grievances	Leadership Style
1	106%	Yes	4	High productivity/High people
2	95%	No	8	High people/Low productivity
3	103%	Yes	4	High productivity/Low people

Productivity and number of grievances are both quantitative variables. Group 2 filed twice as many grievances as groups 1 and 3. Work group 1's productivity is 11% higher than group 2's. Measurements for the productivity and grievances variables are meaningful because they are quantitative. That is, one can add, subtract, multiply, and divide two numbers, and the result makes sense.

The job-switching and leadership variables are qualitative, or categorical, variables, because they cannot be meaningfully represented by numbers. Job switching within the group either has or has not happened. The group leadership style focuses on concern (or lack of it) for productivity and people. Differences in the leadership styles cannot be meaningfully expressed by numbers. Rather, we express the differences qualitatively, in words.

We can assign numbers to categorical variables, but the numbers are not quantitatively meaningful. For example, we can assign values from 1 to 4 to the leadership style categories:

Low on productivity and people	1
Low on productivity and high on people	2
Low on people and high on productivity	3
High on people and productivity	4

The four numbers are useful for *coding* the data in a management information system, as it takes less space to store the four numbers than it does to store the full leadership descriptions. However, the numbers are not meaningful as numerical measurements. We cannot say that a high on people and productivity leadership style has a value that is 3 more than a low on productivity and people style. The mathematical operations of addition, subtraction, multiplication, and division have no meaning for coded categorical variables.

SECTION 3.2 EXERCISES

1. Classify each of the following variables as either quantitative or categorical.
   a. age of employee
   b. monthly income
   c. gender
   d. leadership style
   e. race
   f. number of years of formal schooling
   g. month of the year
   h. occupation

2. Explain how educational level could be either a categorical variable or a quantitative variable.

3. The quantitative variable, annual income, could be transformed into a categorical variable with six levels as follows.

   less than 20,000
   20,000 to 39,999.99
   40,000 to 59,999.99
   60,000 to 79,999.99
   80,000 to 99,999.99
   100,000 and above

Note that the levels, with the exception of the last level, are of equal width ($20,000). Also note that the six levels capture all the possible annual incomes.

a. Transform annual income into a categorical variable with only three levels.

b. Transform annual income into a categorical variable with seven levels.

4. For purposes of computer storage, the states are assigned numbers from 1 to 50 rather than typing the names of the states. On a computer output, the mean value of the state variable was $\bar{x} = 25.5$. What meaning can you place on this output?

5. Transform the quantitative variable, number of years with firm, into a categorical variable with three levels.

6. Below is a list of variables one would find on a survey of attitudes toward a balanced-budget amendment to the U.S. Constitution. Classify the variables as quantitative or categorical.

party affiliation	Democrat, Republican, etc.
attitude	pro, con, no opinion
college attendance	yes, no
number of children	
age	

7. In the text the categorical variable, leadership style, is presently coded as 1 through 4. Would changing the coding to -1 to -4 affect future data analyses?

8. In the text the categorical variable, leadership style, was described along four levels, and the job-switching variable was described along two levels. Note in both cases that the levels cover all the leadership styles and job-switching possibilities. Describe the race variable along two levels, three levels, and four levels.

9. In the text the categorical variable, leadership style, was described along four levels, and the job-switching variable was described along two levels. Note in both cases that the levels cover all the leadership styles and job-switching possibilities. Describe the categorical variable, level of job satisfaction, along two levels, three levels, four levels, and five levels.

10. The following data describe important characteristics of a state. Which of the following is *not* a variable? Classify the remaining characteristics as quantitative or qualitative variables.

a. size in square miles   e. major products
b. population   f. number of counties
c. state motto   g. number of U.S. senators
d. state flag   h. population increase since last Census

3.3 ≡ Analyzing Mixed Cross-Sectional Data

Why is it important to distinguish between categorical and quantitative variables? There are different ways to display and interpret categorical, quantitative, and mixed variables. We will address these methods next. By the end of this section you should be able to:

1. explain what mixed data are;
2. explain what explanatory and dependent variables are; and
3. construct a one-way table and multiple box plot for mixed data.

In Chapter 2 a statistical analysis determined that work group 20's productivity of 123% of standard was an outlier. Assuming it was not due to a coding error or chance, what factor(s) might account for the very high productivity? Have there been any changes in the work group lately? Has it recently received specialized training? Have group members learned new techniques? Do group members switch jobs with one another to maintain their morale and skills? In short, what is *unique* or *different* about this group as compared with the other 35 groups?

Suppose further investigation of work group 20 revealed the following:

1. Its members continually switch jobs with one another. No other group does this as frequently. Job switching may be a cause of work group 20's very high productivity.
2. There are no other recent changes inside or outside the plant that might explain work group 20's high productivity.

We might surmise that job switching—a categorical variable—affects productivity—a quantitative variable. This pairing of different types of variables creates a *mixed data set*. One variable is categorical while the other is quantitative.

How can we determine if the two variables are related? The answer is to construct a *one-way table*.

One-Way Table Display

A one-way table displays the impact of one categorical explanatory variable on a quantitative dependent variable. A one-way table contains the sample sizes and measures of the center and spread. Use a one-way table to determine whether an explanatory variable affects the dependent variable.

An explanatory variable is a variable that affects the variation in another variable. It is also called the independent variable.

A dependent variable is a variable whose variation depends upon another variable.

Before developing **one-way tables**, we must designate the **explanatory** and **dependent variables**. In the work group study, we should ask the following two questions. Could job switching explain why some groups are high producers and other groups are low producers? Could high or low productivity explain the absence or presence of job switching? The former makes more sense. Thus, job switching is the explanatory variable and productivity is the dependent variable. That is, productivity depends on job switching.

Table 3.2 contains the bivariate data on productivity and job switching.

Table 3.2

Bivariate Data for Productivity and Job Switching

Group	Productivity (%)	Job Switch	Group	Productivity (%)	Job Switch
1	106	Yes	19	110	Yes
2	95	No	20	123	Yes
3	103	Yes	21	104	Yes
4	95	No	22	100	Yes
5	95	Yes	23	101	Yes
6	97	No	24	95	No
7	95	No	25	97	No
8	105	Yes	26	94	No
9	102	Yes	27	102	No
10	89	No	28	102	Yes
11	105	Yes	29	106	Yes
12	99	Yes	30	110	Yes
13	95	No	31	97	No
14	100	Yes	32	101	Yes
15	106	Yes	33	95	No
16	101	Yes	34	98	Yes
17	97	No	35	97	Yes
18	104	Yes	36	94	No

Table 3.3

One-Way Two-Level Table for Work Group Productivity Data

	Categorical Variable	
	No Job Switching	Job Switching
Number of Groups	14	22
$\bar{x}$	95.5%	103.5%
s	2.8%	5.8%
Median	95.0%	102.5%
Interquartile Range	2.0%	6.0%

Table 3.3 is a one-way table for the same data which includes the sample sizes, the means, the medians, and measures of variability. Please verify the calculations for yourself.

One-way tables may contain more than two levels of a categorical variable. For example, to look for differences in sick leave hours taken by workers within a firm, we could divide the categorical variable—type of workers—into the three levels of management and professionals, administrative support, and production workers.

Multiple Box Plots

If we compute the median and interquartile range for a set of data, we can also draw a multiple box plot, with or without the fences. Figure 3.1 shows a multiple box plot for the bivariate data. The base line measures the quantitative variable—productivity. One box plot is drawn for each level of the categorical variable—job switching.

Both the one-way table and the multiple box plot suggest that the two measures of the center (mean and median) and the two measures of spread (standard deviation and interquartile range) *appear* to be different between the groups that did and did not switch jobs. Shortly, we will discuss why we must use the term *appears*. If job switching is a cause of high productivity, then management should encourage and train other groups to rotate jobs among their members.

FIGURE 3.1   A Multiple Box Plot Without Fences

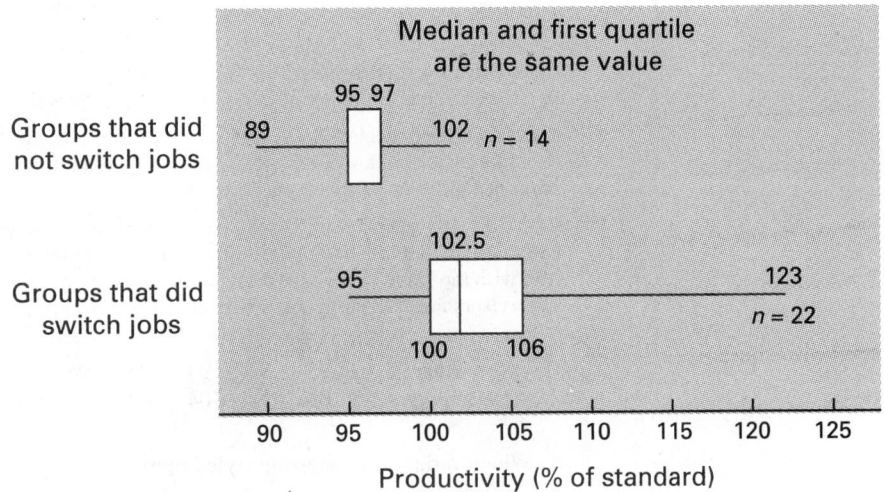

SECTION 3.3 EXERCISES

1. A work group is composed of 11 men and 9 women. You want to know whether the number of sick days is related to gender. Listed are the number of sick days each person took during the past year.

Men	6	5	9	2	3	0	1	3	2	1	3
Women	0	2	1	3	4	8	2	11	2		

   a. Construct a one-way table by finding the mean number of sick days and standard deviation for each gender.
   b. Find the median number of sick days and interquartile range for each gender. Construct a multiple box plot.

2. The numbers of insurance claims processed by two branch offices for the past two weeks are listed. The general manager wants to know if the offices differ in their claims processing.

Office 1	25	30	32	38	37	31	33	29	32	34
Office 2	28	34	32	44	40	34	37	32	35	38

   a. Construct a one-way table for the number of claims processed by each office using the mean and standard deviation for each group.
   b. Find the median number of claims processed and the interquartile range for each office. Construct a multiple box plot.
   c. Does it appear that one office processes more claims than the other?

3. An insurance association conference was held for agents specializing in life and property insurance. The ages of the attendees are shown.

Life		Property	
23	41	29	43
25	42	30	43
28	42	30	44
30	43	32	44
30	44	34	48
33	44	36	54
35	45	38	55
37	49	40	56
39	50	43	56
40	52	43	57

   a. Construct a multiple box plot for both groups.
   b. Does it appear that the distribution of ages differs between the two groups?

4. You find an unexpected large variation in salaries among 50 men, all working as loan officers in a major bank in Chicago. Suggest two potential explanatory variables that might account for the large variation.

5. COMCEL believes participative leadership is more effective (higher productivity) than autocratic leadership. Below are productivity data taken from one shift on two supervisors with the same years of experience and similar backgrounds. The workers under both supervisors are also similar in experience and background.

Autocratic	93	94	94	95	95	96	96	98
Participative	103	104	104	103	102	103	104	102

   a. Which variable—leadership style or productivity—is the explanatory variable?

    b. Which variable—leadership style or productivity—is the dependent variable?

    c. Develop a one-way table similar to Table 3.3.

    d. Draw a multiple box plot for the data.

    e. What conclusions can be drawn from your table and box plot?

6. Market research personnel believe that in selling VCRs informative advertising is more effective (higher monthly sales) than persuasive advertising. Below are VCR sales data for 16 stores of a national chain. Informative advertising was used in eight stores in Atlanta, and persuasive advertising was used in eight stores (with similar size and sales history) in Houston.

Informative	630	644	640	652	632	645	651	638
Persuasive	533	546	549	534	527	534	548	529

    a. Which variable—monthly sales or type of advertising—is the explanatory variable?

    b. Which variable—monthly sales or type of advertising—is the dependent variable?

    c. Develop a one-way table similar to Table 3.3.

    d. Draw a multiple box plot for the data.

    e. What conclusions can be drawn from your table and box plot?

7. Physiologists believe that exercising for at least 20 minutes three times a week reduces cholesterol. A research team selects 16 men with similar cholesterol levels. Eight men are placed on an exercise program. Both groups of eight continue their normal diet. The following data indicate the drop in cholesterol levels for the 16 men over a 2-month period.

Exercise	9.5	8.6	9.8	7.6	6.5	6.3	8.5	7.6
No Exercise	2.3	3.5	3.2	4.2	1.4	2.4	3.5	3.6

    a. Which variable—exercise or drop in cholesterol—is the explanatory variable?

    b. Which variable—exercise or drop in cholesterol—is the dependent variable?

    c. Develop a one-way table similar to Table 3.3.

    d. Draw a multiple box plot for the data.

    e. What conclusions can be drawn from your table and box plot?

8. Abbott Rental Properties believes that a toll-free 800 number will increase the number of units rented. They select two condos on the same beach. Each condo has the same number of 2- and 3-bedroom units. They establish and advertise a 800 number for the Mainsail; no 800 number is used for the Sunset. Below are the number of units rented over the past 9 weeks.

800 number	30	32	28	25	34	38	34	31	34
No 800 number	10	12	10	14	15	12	14	10	8

    a. Which variable—the presence or absence of an 800 number or number of units rented—is the explanatory variable?

    b. Which variable—the presence or absence of an 800 number or number of units rented—is the dependent variable?

    c. Develop a one-way table similar to Table 3.3.

    d. Draw a multiple box plot for the data.

    e. What conclusions can be drawn from your table and box plot?

9. Suppose you believe that previous performance rating—outstanding, good, mediocre, and poor—affects salary. You want to develop a one-way table. Which is the explanatory variable and which is the dependent variable? How many levels of the explanatory variable will there be?

10. Draw a multiple box plot that shows that outstanding performers have higher median salaries and lower variability in salaries than poor performers.

11. Draw a multiple box plot that shows that firms with quality circles (groups of workers who get together to solve problems) have a higher median returns on investments and lower variability in returns on investments than firms without quality circles.

12. Which of the following bivariate data sets contain mixed data?

Set 1	Level of productivity and job-switching status
Set 2	Level of productivity and type of leadership
Set 3	Level of productivity and number of hours of training
Set 4	Promotion status and gender
Set 5	Promotion status and number of hours of training
Set 6	Party affiliation and gender
Set 7	Party affiliation and annual income
Set 8	Annual income and number of years of schooling
Set 9	Return on investment and type of organizational structure
Set 10	Type of advertising and market share

3.4 ≡ Analyzing Categorical Cross-Sectional Data

Managers often collect categorical data on both the explanatory and dependent variables. Moreover, they sometimes convert quantitative variables into categorical variables. For example, we can convert the quantitative work group productivity variable into a categorical variable as follows:

Low-productivity teams	Teams whose productivity is *below* the median productivity of the 36 work groups
High-productivity teams	Teams whose productivity is *at* or *above* the median productivity of the 36 work groups

From Table 2.15 (page 60), the median productivity for the 36 work groups is 100%. Note that the above definitions ensure that all 36 work groups will fall into either the low- or high-productivity team subcategory.

When the explanatory and dependent variables are both categorical, managers use *cross-tabs* tables to determine whether two variables are related. By the end of this section you should be able to:

1. construct a cross-tabs table;
2. explain joint, row, and column percentages in a cross-tabs table;
3. determine whether two categorical variables appear to be related to one another by using the row or column percentages;
4. explain why you might need to qualify your conclusion about the relationship between two variables;
5. control for the impact of a potential intervening variable; and
6. assess the potential relationship between two variables after accounting for an intervening variable.

Cross-Tabs Tables

We want to determine whether productivity is in fact related to the absence or presence of job switching within work groups. The two categorical variables are job switching and level of productivity (converted to a categorical variable). The subcategories for both categorical variables should not overlap and should include all the observations. That is, the subcategories must be *mutually exclusive and exhaustive*. Job switching is assessed as yes or no, productivity as low or high.

Table 3.2 includes the data needed to count the number of work groups that fall into the following four subcategories. Remember, the median productivity for all 36 work groups is 100%. Please verify the counts.

Description of Work Groups Using Both Variables	Number of Groups
No job switching and low productivity	13
Job switching and low productivity	4
No job switching and high productivity	1
Job switching and high productivity	18

A cross-tabs-table shows the number of observations that have been cross-classified according to two categorical variables. Use a cross-tabs table to determine whether two categorical variables are related .

Table 3.4 is a two-by-two (2 × 2) **cross-tabs table.** Each categorical variable is broken down into two mutually exclusive and exhaustive subcategories.

What do the entries in the body of Table 3.4 represent? Entries within the four cells of the table represent the number of work groups with two attributes—level of productivity *and* presence or absence of job switching. Thus, we see that there are 13 groups that had low productivity *and* did not switch jobs, while there are 4 groups that had low productivity *and* did switch jobs.

What do the entries in the margins represent? They are row and column totals found by summing across rows and down columns. Thus, there are 14 groups that did not switch jobs and 22 that did, while there are 17 groups that had low productivity and 19 that had high productivity. Margin entries represent the number of work groups with one attribute—level of productivity *or* presence or absence of job switching.

The 2 × 2 table is the simplest cross-tabs table. However, we can divide categorical variables into more than two subcategories. Table 3.5 on page 112 is a four-by-three cross-tabs table. We developed it to explore the impact of class standing on the desirability of an honor code. The undergraduate students were divided into four class standings and three opinions about having an honor code. An undergraduate student is either a freshman, sophomore, junior, or senior. A student either favors the code, does not favor the code, or has no opinion. Note that for both categorical variables, the subcategories are mutually exclusive and exhaustive.

Having developed the cross-tabs table, we can now determine whether the two categorical variables appear to be related. Does job switching seem to affect productivity? Or, does class standing affect one's position on an honor code?

Table 3.4

Cross-Tabs Table for Productivity and Job-Switching Data

	No Job Switching	Job Switching	Total
Low Productivity	13	4	17
High Productivity	1	18	19
Total	14	22	36

marginal

Table 3.5

4 × 3 Cross-Tabs Table for Desirability of an Honor Code

	Favor	Do Not Favor	No Opinion	
Freshman	100	300	600	1,000
Sophomore	150	200	600	950
Junior	200	150	550	900
Senior	250	100	550	900
	700	750	2,300	3,750

To answer these questions, consider computing the following three important percentage tables:

1. Joint percentage table
2. Column percentage table
3. Row percentage table

Each table highlights a different aspect of the data. Use these three tables to answer the question: Does the absence or presence of job switching affect work group productivity?

Joint Percentage Tables

Table 3.6 shows joint percentages for the work group data. To create Table 3.6, Table 3.4, the initial cross-tabs table, was used. Each entry in Table 3.4 was divided by the total number of observations. For example, the top left entry in the joint percentage table is 13/36 = 36.1%. That is, 36.1% of the work groups had low productivity *and* did not switch jobs. The lower right entry indicates that 50% of the work groups had high productivity *and* did switch jobs. The marginal percentages found by summing across rows and down columns are also informative. They show that 47.2% of the work groups had low productivity and 38.9% of the work groups did not switch jobs.

While the joint percentages are informative, they do not tell whether productivity and job switching are related. We must explore further the cross-tabs data.

Table 3.6

Joint Percentages for Productivity and Job-Switching Data

	No Job Switching	Job Switching	
Low Productivity	36.1%	11.1%	47.2%
High Productivity	2.8%	50%	52.8%
	38.9%	61.1%	100%

Column Percentage Tables

Table 3.7 shows the column percentages for the cross-tabs data. To obtain column percentages, divide each entry in Table 3.4 by its *column* total. For example, the top left entry in Table 3.7 is 13/14 = 92.9%. *One final note:* Notice that the marginal percentages on the right are not obtained by summing across the rows.

Table 3.7

Column Percentages for Productivity and Job-Switching Data

	No Job Switching	Job Switching	
Low Productivity	92.9%	18.2%	47.2%
High Productivity	7.1%	81.8%	52.8%
	100%	100%	100%

This breakdown is very informative. We can analyze either row of the table. If we focus on the low-productivity teams in the upper row, we learn the following:

1. Overall, 47.2% of the work groups were low-productivity teams.
2. Of the groups that did not switch, 92.9% were low-productivity teams.
3. Of the groups that did switch, only 18.2% were low-productivity teams.

If job switching were not related to productivity, the above three column percentages would be similar.

Row Percentage Tables

Table 3.8 shows the row percentages for the cross-tabs data. To obtain row percentages, divide each entry in Table 3.4 by its *row* total. For example, the top left entry in Table 3.8 is 13/17 = 76.5%. Again, note that the marginal percentages at the bottom are not obtained by summing down the columns.

Table 3.8

Row Percentages for Productivity and Job-Switching Data

	No Job Switching	Job Switching	
Low Productivity	76.5%	23.5%	100%
High Productivity	5.3%	94.7%	100%
	38.9%	61.1%	100%

This breakdown is also informative. We can analyze either *column* of the table. If we choose to focus on the job-switching teams in the right column, we surmise the following:

1. Overall, 61.1% of the teams switched jobs.
2. Of the low-producing teams, only 23.5% switched jobs.
3. Of the high-producing teams, 94.7% switched jobs.

If productivity were not related to job switching, the above three row percentages would be about the same. Both row and column percentages suggest that job switching and productivity appear to be related.

Which percentages—row or column—are more informative? It is often a matter of individual taste. Which one is more helpful in understanding the potential relationship between the two categorical variables? A safe rule is to compute both.

Now consider how row and column percentage tables can be used to determine whether a firm has discriminated against women in its promotional practices.

Example: Gender Discrimination Case   A large company is being sued for discrimination in its promotion practices. The suit alleges that women have been systematically denied promotion. The lawyers for the women have obtained access to the company's personnel records for the past 5 years. However, the court has allowed only limited access since the information is highly personal. It will allow the plaintiff to select a sample of 200 employees hired 5 years ago and follow their careers within the firm. The evidence from the sample will be used to determine whether the company is discriminating. Both sides have agreed to the procedure.

In this case, we are dealing with bivariate categorical data. We have two pieces of data for each employee: gender and whether the employee has been promoted. Note that the subcategories are mutually exclusive and exhaustive for each categorical variable.

Table 3.9 is a cross-tabs table for the gender discrimination suit data. Table 3.10 is the row percentage table for the data. It shows that 52.5% of the total sample were promoted. Of the males, 72.7% were promoted; of the females, only 27.8% were promoted. If there were no relationship between gender and promotion, we would expect the two row percentages to be relatively close to one another and to the overall percentage of 52.5%. In other words, whether an employee is a male or female, the chance of being promoted would be the same—52.5%. Thus it *appears* that the company is discriminating against women. Why is it again necessary to qualify the diagnosis with the word *appears?* The next two sections will shed some light on the types of arguments that could be used to call into question this *apparent* relationship.

Inductive Inference

The firm could make two arguments in its defense. One argument involves *inductive inference,* and the other involves the impact of *intervening variables.* Consider first the inductive inference argument. Table 3.9 is based upon only a sample of all the employees. Assume that the firm had not discriminated in its promotional practices. In that case, if Table 3.9 included data on *all* the employees, we would find that the row percentages were the same. Now take a *sample* of employees from the firm, assuming no discrimination. Will the row percentages for the sample equal the row percentages for all the employees? Not necessarily, because there could be differences depending upon which particular employees were selected for the sample. We would expect the two row percentages to be close but not necessarily equal. When we take a small sample and attempt to draw conclusions about the population from

Table 3.9

Cross-Tabs Table for Gender Discrimination Suit Data

	Promoted	Not Promoted	
Male	80	30	110
Female	25	65	90
	105	95	200

Table 3.10

Row Percentages for Gender Discrimination Suit Data

	Promoted	Not Promoted	
Male	72.7%	27.3%	100%
Female	27.8%	72.2%	100%
	52.5%	47.5%	100%

which the sample was taken, we must allow room for a *margin of error*. The margin of error is the difference between the sample result and what would be obtained if everyone in the population were sampled. Inductive inference involves making educated guesses about a population based upon a small sample.

Returning to the gender discrimination data, we must ask the following question: Is 72.7% so much larger than 27.8% that the difference is beyond the margin of error?

In Chapter 14 we will present the chi-square test of independence. It incorporates the margin of error into the analysis of row percentages. We can use the test of independence to answer the previous question. In summary, the judge would not use sample data alone to make a ruling. Rather, he or she would draw an inference from the sample data to apply to the target population.

Intervening Variables

The second argument that the firm could make follows this line of reasoning. It is true that, historically, a higher sample percentage of men have been promoted than women, but the difference in promotion percentages is not based on gender. Suppose that most promotions occurred in the firm's overseas divisions. Furthermore, suppose the promoted men had taken more course work in International Business (IB). The firm might argue that, therefore, the men were better qualified and thus more deserving of promotion. By so arguing, the firm would be suggesting reasons other than gender discrimination that could account for the differences in the promotion percentages of each gender. A judge would rule then on the validity of these alternative explanations.

> Intervening variables are substitute explanatory variables. They are alternative variables that one can logically argue should have an impact on the dependent variable.

The firm is suggesting that International Business course work is an **intervening variable.** That is, IB course work, not gender, explains the difference in the row percentages of men and women promoted.

Can IB course work explain why a higher sample percentage of men were promoted? Before developing cross-tabs tables, construct a *tree diagram*. Figure 3.2 displays a tree diagram, which is a breakdown of the total sample according to the categorical variables of interest—IB course work, gender, and promotion status.

To construct a tree diagram, divide the entire sample of 200 into two groups by the intervening variable, IB course work. Then divide each of these groups into either male or female and then into promoted or not promoted or vice versa.

Use Figure 3.2 to construct Table 3.11, *two* cross-tabs row percentage tables. In this case, once we have accounted for the intervening variable—IB course work taken—the row percentages within each cross-tabs table are very close. For example, of those who had IB course work, 96.2% of the males were promoted as were 95% of females. Of those who did not have IB course work, 10% of the males were promoted and 8.6% of the females. With inclusion of the intervening variable, there no longer appears to be a relationship between gender and promotion.

In summary, Table 3.10 suggested that gender and promotion are related. Males appeared to have a greater likelihood of being promoted than females. However, Table 3.11 indicates that after accounting for IB courses, gender and promotion do not appear to be related.

How would the judge rule in the gender discrimination case? First, the judge would use the statistical test of independence to draw conclusions about company-wide discrimination. Second, if the test suggested discrimination, the judge would evaluate the reasonableness of the intervening variable(s). A variable such as IB course work could be reasonably related to overseas promotions. However, height of the employee or color of hair would not be reasonable intervening variables. An intervening variable must pass the reasonableness test. Third, the judge would look for additional evidence of discrimination within the firm. This includes:

1. There are other gender-based harassment suits pending in the courts.
2. The company has an outdated maternity leave policy.
3. The firm was previously found guilty of racial discrimination in promotion practices.

Given that the intervening variable is reasonable and assuming that the company has no history of discrimination, the judge might rule in favor of the firm.

There can be more than one intervening variable. For example, we could classify people by course work and overseas experience. Here we are using two intervening variables as potential explanations for the differences in percentages of males and females that have been promoted. As more intervening variables are included, the number of cross-tabs tables increases while the sample size for each table decreases. The sample size for *each cell* of the cross-tabs table may become so small that we cannot reach valid conclusions about potential gender discrimination.

FIGURE 3.2   Tree Diagram for One Intervening Variable

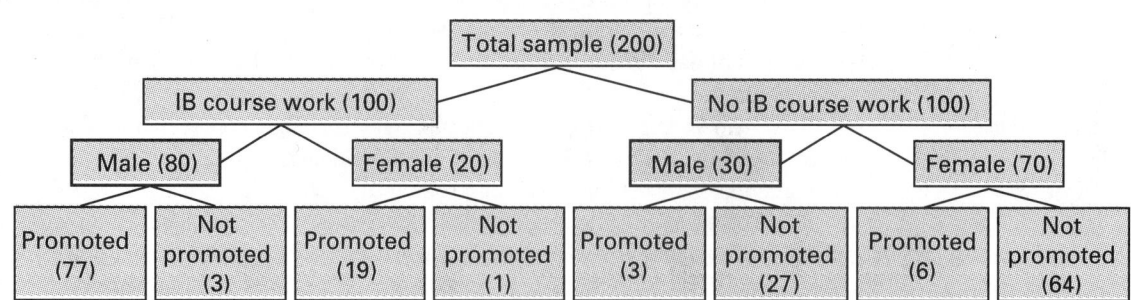

Table 3.11

Cross-Tabs Tables and Row Percentages for Gender Discrimination Data with an IB Course Work Intervening Variable

IB Course Work

	Promoted	Not Promoted	
Male	77 96.2%	3 3.8%	100%
Female	19 95%	1 5%	100%
	96 96%	4 4%	100%

No IB Course Work

	Promoted	Not Promoted	
Male	3 10%	27 90%	100%
Female	6 8.6%	64 91.4%	100%
	9 9%	91 91%	100%

One final point remains. How do we determine potential intervening variables? They do not walk up and say: "Here I am!" Rather we must consider possible *logical* alternative variables that might account for the differences. Bear in mind that intervening variables must pass the reasonableness test.

SECTION 3.4 EXERCISES

1. A consulting firm administered the same questionnaire to 30 managers and 50 nonmanagers. On one of the yes/no questions, 15 managers answered yes and 15 nonmanagers answered yes. Construct a cross-tabs table to display these data.

2. A financial analyst wishes to determine if there is a connection between relative level of product quality and return on investments, ROIs, (below 20%, 20% and above). She obtains the following data on 273 firms.

Description of Firms Using Both Variables	Number
Low product quality and below 20%	100
Low product quality and 20% and above	25
High product quality and below 20%	41
High product quality and 20% and above	107

   a. Construct a 2 × 2 cross-tabs table.
   b. What is the percentage of firms with (1) low product quality and ROIs below 20% and (2) low product quality and ROIs of 20% and above?

    c. What percentage of the total sample are high-product-quality firms?

    d. What percentage of the firms with ROIs of 20% and above are high-product-quality firms?

    e. What percentage of firms with ROIs of 20% and above are low-product-quality firms?

    f. Based on parts **c–e**, does it appear that relative level of product quality and ROI are related?

    g. Would you expect the percentage of high-product-quality firms in the United States to equal the percentage of high-product-quality firms in the sample? Why?

3. A management consultant wishes to determine if participative decision making leads to a more positive job climate. He obtains the following data on 400 firms.

Description of Firms Using Both Variables	Number
Autocratic and poor job climate	150
Participative and poor job climate	50
Autocratic and good job climate	10
Participative and good job climate	190

    a. Construct a 2 × 2 cross-tabs table.

    b. What is the percentage of firms with (1) autocratic decision making and a good job climate and (2) participative decision making and a poor job climate?

    c. What percentage of the total sample are good job climate firms?

    d. What percentage of the firms that use autocratic decision making are good job climate firms?

    e. What percentage of the firms that use participative decision making are good job climate firms?

    f. Based on parts **c–e,** does it appear that decision making style and job climate are related?

    g. Would you expect the percentage of good job climate firms in the United States to equal the percentage of good job climate firms in the sample? Why?

4. Below are data on 10 people taken from the Human Resource department data bank.

Person	Promotion	Overseas Assignment
1	yes	yes
2	yes	yes
3	no	no
4	no	no
5	yes	no
6	yes	yes
7	no	yes
8	no	no
9	yes	yes
10	no	no

    a. Construct a 2 × 2 cross-tabs table.

    b. What percentage of the total sample are promoted?

    c. What percentage of the people with an overseas assignment are promoted?

    d. What percentage of the people with no overseas assignment are promoted?

    e. Based on parts **b–d,** does it appear that an overseas assignment and job promotion are related?

5. Gallup conducts a survey of 1,500 voters: 500 Democrats, 300 Republicans, and 700 Independents. Each is asked his or her position on a constitutional amendment for a balanced budget. One hundred Democrats, 250 Republicans, and 250 Independents favor the amendment.

    a. Construct a cross-tabs table to display the data.

    b. What percentage of the voters favor the balanced budget amendment?

    c. What percentage of Democrats favor the amendment?
    d. What percentage of Republicans favor the amendment?
    e. What percentage of Independents favor the amendment?
    f. Based on parts **b–e,** does it appear that party affiliation and position on the amendment are related?

6. A credit agency must distinguish good from bad credit risks. The credit manager believes that home ownership should be a good predictor of credit worthiness. The following table was constructed from the records of 300 previous clients.

	Credit-Risk Group		
	Good	Bad	Total
Owns home	225	30	255
Rents	25	20	45
	250	50	300

    a. What percentage of the total sample are homeowners?
    b. What percentage of the good risks are homeowners?
    c. What percentage of the bad risks are homeowners?
    d. Based on parts **a–c,** does it appear that credit worthiness is related to home ownership?

7. A parole authority has constructed the next table showing success or failure in completing parole vs. the parolee's age at first conviction.

		Parole Outcome		
		Success	Failure	Total
Age at	Under 18	270	630	900
First	18–21	750	750	1,500
Conviction	Over 21	420	180	600
		1,440	1,560	3,000

    a. Of the parolees who were first convicted at age under 18, what percentage are successes?
    b. What percentage of the 18–21 age group are successes?
    c. What percentage of the over 21 age group are successes?
    d. What percentage of parolees are successes?
    e. Based on parts **a–d,** does it appear that age at first conviction is related to the success of parole outcomes?

8. The president of a university wants to know the extent to which undergraduates in the two largest colleges—Arts and Sciences, and Business—want a required course in interpersonal communications. A total of 100 students are surveyed.
    a. Complete the table by filling in the blanks.
    b. What is the overall percentage that favor the communications requirement?

Major		Position on Course Requirement	
		Yes	No
Sciences	Count	10	_____
	Row %	33.3	_____
	Column %	25.0	_____
	Cell %	10.0	_____
Business	Count	_____	_____
	Row %	_____	_____
	Column %	_____	_____
	Cell %	_____	_____
		40	60

   c. What percentage of business students favor the communications requirement?
   d. What percentage of science students favor the communications requirement?
   e. From parts **b–d,** what can you conclude?

9. A small sample of consumers was selected for a pilot study to see if household income is related to whether the households owe money on revolving charge accounts. The data are shown here.

Household income (in $1,000s)	10	15	18	20	20	25	27	29
Owes money	N	Y	Y	Y	Y	Y	N	Y
Household income (in $1,000s)	32	35	35	35	37	39	35	40
Owes money	N	Y	Y	N	Y	Y	N	Y
Household income (in $1,000s)	42	43	50	55	60	62	70	80
Owes money	N	Y	N	N	Y	Y	N	N

   a. Using the given data, complete the following table:

	Owes Money	**Does Not Owe Money**
Above Median		
Median and Below		

   b. Does it appear that owing money is related to income level?
   c. Why do we have to say *appear* in part **b?**

10. Three years ago 50 new people were hired at plant A and at plant B. A recent review showed that 15 of 50 are still working at plant A and 25 of 50 are still working at plant B.

Table 1

	Plant A	Plant B	Total
Still Employed	15	25	40
Left Employment	35	25	60
	50	50	100

Table 2

	Nonmanagers			Managers		
	Plant A	Plant B	Total	Plant A	Plant B	Total
Still Employed	7	9	16	8	16	24
Left Employment	33	21	54	2	4	6
	40	30	70	10	20	30

   a. Based on the information in Table 1, does it appear that labor retention is related to place of employment? Explain using either row or column percentages.
   b. Table 2 shows the same data broken down by whether the new employees were in managerial or nonmanagerial positions. Does it appear that employee retention is related to place of employment after controlling for type of position? Explain.

11. An aide to a state legislator is interested in determining attitude toward increasing starting salaries for teachers. One hundred people are interviewed on their position toward increasing starting salaries (for = 40, against = 40, no opinion = 20) and the party affiliation (Democrat = 30, Republican = 30, Independent = 40). Construct a 3 × 3 cross-tabs table that would indicate that the two variables are not related. Explain.

12. Using the same data as in Exercise 11, construct a 3 × 3 table that shows that Democrats prefer increasing starting salaries, but not Republicans and Independents. Defend.

13. Using the same data as in Exercise 11, construct a 3 × 3 table that shows that Republicans prefer increasing starting salaries, but not Democrats and Independents. Defend.

14. Suppose the percentage of African Americans suffering from excessive stress is twice that of White Americans. Suggest possible intervening variables, beyond race, that could explain the disparity.

15. Does the following cross-tabs table suggest a gender gap, a difference between the attitudes of men and women on the death penalty? Compute the relevant row or column percentages.

	Oppose Death Penalty	Favor Death Penalty	
Male	330	670	1,000
Female	490	510	1,000
	820	1,180	2,000

16. Refer to the cross-tabs table in Exercise 15. Without changing the row totals, determine the frequencies within the body of the table if 41% of the total sample oppose the death penalty and there is no relationship between gender and death penalty position.

17. Refer to the cross-tabs table in Exercise 15. Without changing the row totals, determine the frequencies within the body of the table if 70% of the total sample oppose the death penalty and there is no relationship between gender and death penalty position.

18. Which of the following data sets must be displayed by a cross-tabs table?

Set 1	Type of store (independent or chain) and competitive focus (price or service)
Set 2	Gender and attitude toward increased spending for social programs
Set 3	Monthly sales and years of training
Set 4	Valuation method (LIFO of FIFO) and economic outlook (recession or boom)
Set 5	Type of advertising (informative or persuasive) and industry classification (manufacturing, banking, other)

3.5 Analyzing Quantitative Cross-Sectional Data

One-way tables and cross-tabs tables are effective in showing relationships between two variables when one or more variables are categorical. However, when both variables are quantitative, we need an additional tool—the scatter diagram. By the end of this section you should be able to:

1. construct a scatter diagram;
2. interpret a scatter diagram;
3. apply the ellipse test to determine whether two quantitative variables appear to be related;
4. look for clusters in a scatter diagram; and
5. interpret clusters accurately.

We will use the data in Table 3.1 to introduce the scatter diagram. The table shows that last month the Charlotte sales region had a 30% market share and spent $17,000 on media advertising. Its sales force had, on the average, 15 years of experience. Charlotte's retail price for its product was $1,000 (not shown), and the mean competitors' retail price was also $1,000. Thus the relative price variable for Charlotte was 1.00. Atlanta, on the other hand, had a retail price of $1,000, but the mean price of its competitors was $667. So Atlanta's relative price was 1.5 (1,000/667).

Question: Do advertising expenditures, mean sales force experience, and relative price affect market share? *Answer:* Plot scatter diagrams.

Scatter Diagrams

A scatter diagram is a graph of two quantitative variables plotted against one another.

Since *all* the variables—advertising expenditures, years of experience, relative price, and market share—are quantitative, consider drawing **scatter diagrams** or *XY* plots.

Shown are the steps to construct a scatter diagram.

1. Place the dependent variable on the vertical axis and label it. The dependent variable is called Y and its values are denoted as y.

   We believe that advertising expenditures affect market share, or market share *depends* on advertising expenditures. Therefore market share is the dependent variable, y. Its 12 values are called $y_1, y_2, \ldots, y_{12}$.

2. Select one explanatory, or independent, variable. The explanatory variable is called X and its values are denoted as x. Place it on the horizontal axis and label it.

   Advertising expenditure is an explanatory variable, X. Its 12 values are called $x_1, x_2, \ldots, x_{12}$. Average years of sales force experience and relative price are two other explanatory variables that could also be plotted against market share, Y.

3. Plot each observation by its x and y values. Each observation will be one point in the scatter diagram. Label each point.

   Each observation is the advertising expenditure and market share for a city in the Southern Region. For example, the Charlotte observation is

$$x_1 = \text{Advertising} = \$17,000$$
$$y_1 = \text{Market share} = 30\%$$

Label the point ($17,000, 30%) as CHAR.

Figure 3.3 is a scatter plot of market share and advertising expenditures for the 12 sales regions. What does a scatter diagram show? It may indicate that the two variables are related to one another. However, as there are several types of relationships, look for:

1. a linear relationship between the two variables;
2. a nonlinear relationship between the two variables; and
3. clusters or groups of observations that are distinct from one another.

FIGURE 3.3   Market Share vs. Advertising Expenditures for 12 Southern Sales Regions

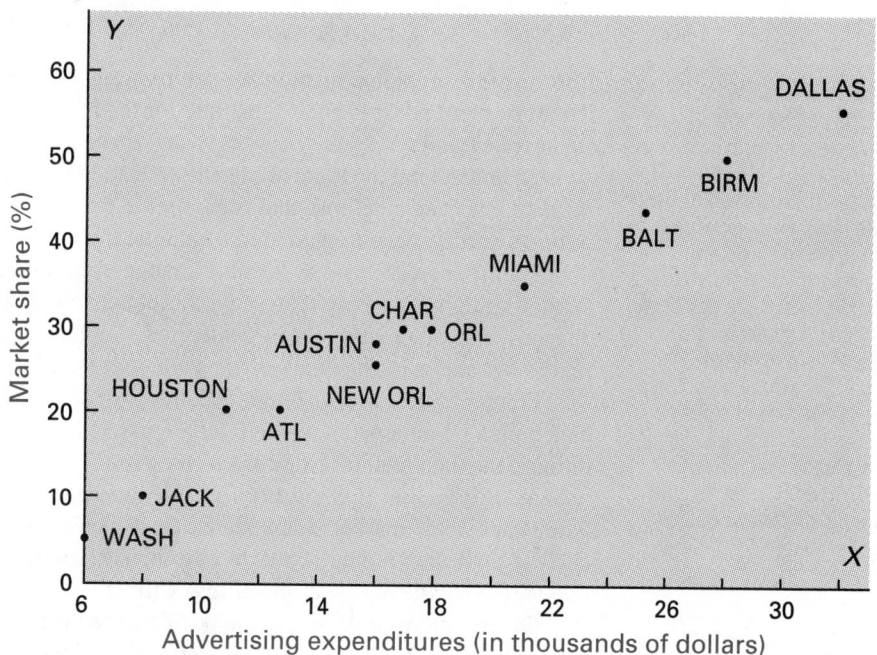

Linear Relationships

We can ascertain readily if there is a linear, or straight-line, relationship between two quantitative variables using a scatter diagram. In Figure 3.3, as advertising expenditures, *X,* increase, does market share, *Y,* increase by a *constant amount?* Yes. Moreover, there is a *positive* linear relationship. As advertising expenditures increase, so does market share. Advertising expenditures appear to be an important explanatory variable.

What might the Charlotte manager conclude from the scatter diagram? Increasing advertising *may* improve market share. In other COMCEL markets, higher advertising expenditures result in higher market shares. However, do not jump to conclusions, since one or more intervening variables could account for this apparent relationship. Still, the relationship between these two variables makes marketing sense. As an initial action, the manager could present the scatter diagram to senior management and convince them to authorize the increased advertising expenditures on a *trial basis.* Then the impact of increased advertising could be determined. If Charlotte's market share increases, more advertising dollars would be requested on a permanent basis.

Now consider the scatter diagram in Figure 3.4 on page 125, which plots market share against mean January temperature. It appears that there is no linear relationship between the two variables. As the mean January temperature increases, market share neither increases nor decreases. The diagram consists of a shapeless cloud of data points that slope neither up nor down in either direction. Mean January temperature does not explain market share variation. This is not a surprising finding.

One issue remains. Is there a way to determine whether there is a linear relationship? Yes, we can use the quick and simple *circle vs. ellipse test.*

The Circle vs. Ellipse Test

This test is a graphical method for determining whether two variables are probably **linearly related**. It is not a substitute for the regression analysis to be discussed in Chapters 11 and 12.

To understand the logic of the ellipse test, look at Figure 3.4. In order to enclose the data, we need an ellipse that is parallel to the horizontal axis. There is no upward or downward pattern to the cloud of points; they are widely scattered. As the mean temperature increases, no systematic change occurs in the market share. Thus a horizontal straight line best represents the pattern, which means that as one variable changes, the other variable is unaffected. Subject to statistical verification using regression analysis, the two variables are not related.

Figure 3.5 reproduces Figure 3.3, but with an ellipse drawn around the data. The data points lie on a path and are tightly clustered. An unbroken straight line running through the data would be upward sloping to the right. This indicates, subject to statistical verification, that the two variables are positively related. That is, as advertising increases, market share increases. When two variables are related, we can enclose their data points in a tight ellipse. The stronger the association between the two variables, the narrower the ellipse will be.

Given a set of data, always look first to see if the data exhibit a straight-line or **linear relationship**, since linear relationships are easiest to understand and explain. However, sometimes relationships are not linear, and we must learn how to identify and interpret those that are not.

> If one can enclose all the data points in the scatter diagram with a tight ellipse, then the two variables are probably linearly related. If the ellipse is upward sloping to the right, then the two variables are positively related. If the ellipse is downward sloping to the right, the two variables are negatively related. If it takes a circle or an ellipse parallel to the horizontal axis to enclose all the data points, the two variables are probably not linearly related. ∎

> A linear relationship means that as the explanatory variable increases, the dependent variable increases or decreases by a constant amount. ∎

Nonlinear Relationships

Figure 3.6 is a scatter diagram of another quantitative variable, mean years of sales experience, vs. market share. Are the two variables related? Please think about it before reading on.

Using the circle vs. ellipse test, we would conclude that there is no straight-line relationship between market share and mean number of years of experience. We would be right! But, there is a nonlinear relationship that can be represented by an inverted U. This means that as the number of years of experience increases, market share initially increases. Market share, however, peaks between 11 and 13 years of experience and then drops off.

How can we make sense of the nonlinear relationship? As the sales force gains more experience, it grabs more market share from the competition. However, after 13 years, salespeople experience burnout; they lose enthusiasm, and the market share decreases. The nonlinear relationship does make sense.

For the Charlotte sales manager, how is the scatter diagram in Figure 3.6 useful? What managerial action should he take? Please think about the possibilities before reading on.

The sales force has, on the average, 15 years of experience. The scatter diagram in Figure 3.6 shows that they are in the burnout stage. Here are several options.

1. Hire some new salespeople who are enthusiastic.

FIGURE 3.4   Market Share vs. Mean Temperature

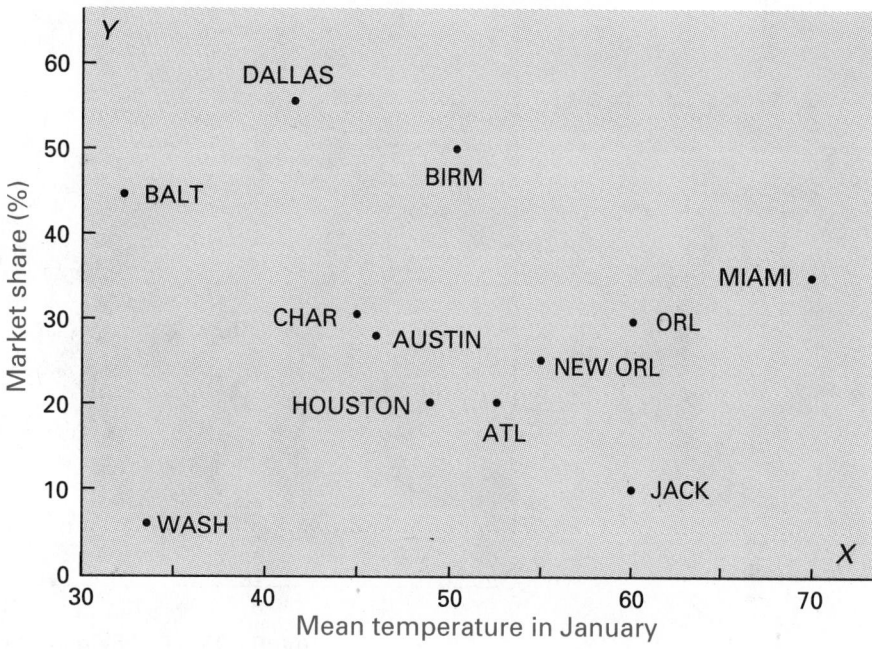

FIGURE 3.5   Market Share vs. Advertising Expenditures

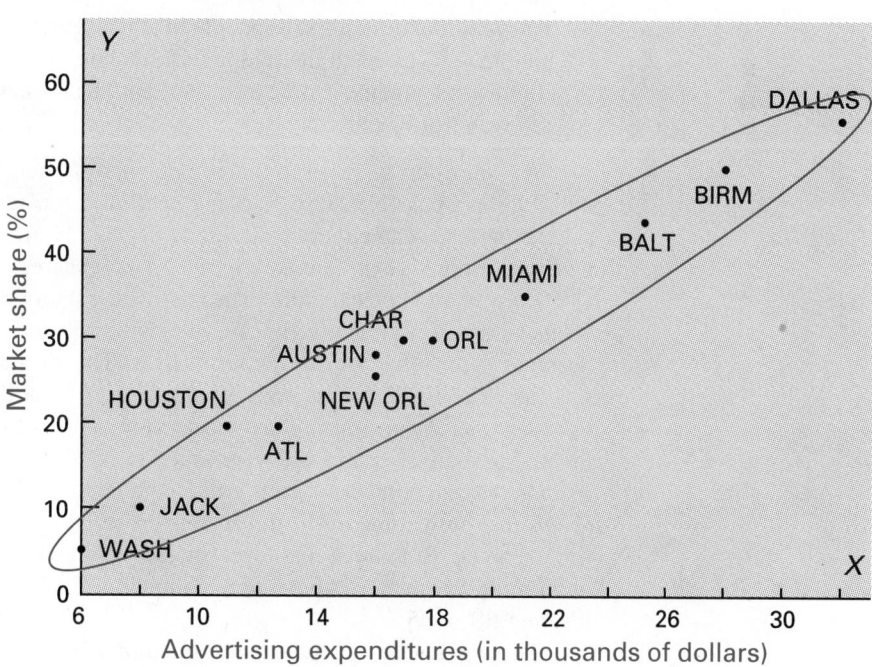

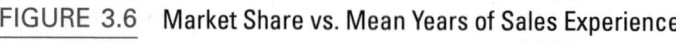

FIGURE 3.6   Market Share vs. Mean Years of Sales Experience

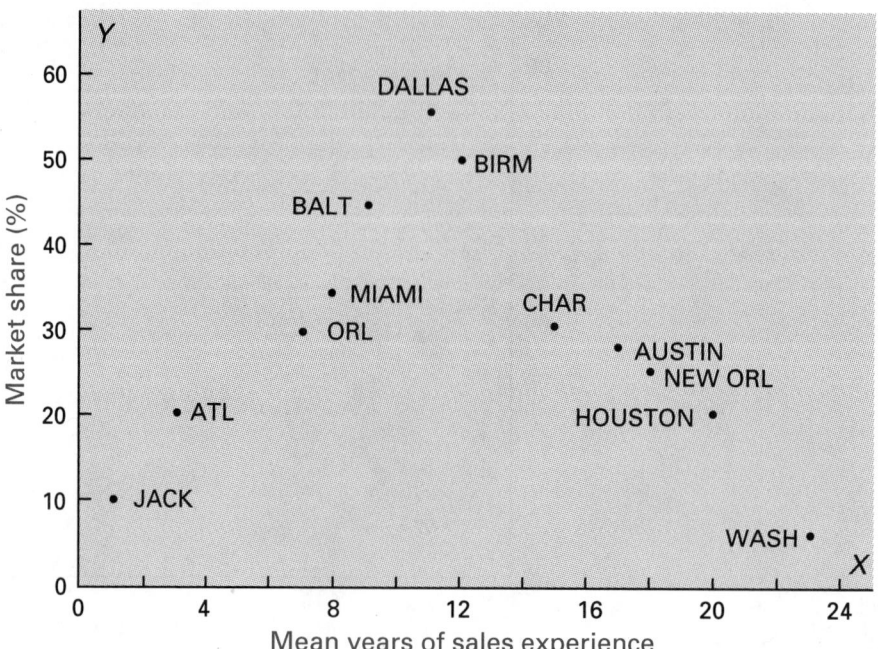

2. Talk to the senior salespeople and determine how they can regain enthusiasm. A different pay schedule, less travel within the region, earned days off, or vacation bonuses could be considered.
3. Pair junior and senior salespeople in teams. Perhaps the enthusiasm of the junior people will spread to the senior staff. Of course, the opposite could also happen.
4. Review management practices. Perhaps the manager himself is an ineffective motivator or leader.

    We are often inclined to blame poor performance on others, rarely looking at ourselves as a possible cause. Perhaps we should consider option 4 first! In summary, sales experience can either positively or negatively affect market share. Now we can generate alternative options to improve market share.

    Here is another example of a nonlinear relationship. A market research firm wants to know how many times a television viewer would have to see an advertisement before that viewer could recall it. The firm selects 10 groups of 100 TV viewers. The firm assigns each group of 100 to one of the following 10 conditions—view ad once during test week, view ad twice, . . . , view ad 10 times. One month later, all 1,000 people were asked to recall the ad. The market research firm records the percentages of each group who could correctly recall the ad. Figure 3.7 shows that only about 5% could remember an ad if it was viewed from one to three times a week. But above that level, the percentage increased as the commercial was aired more frequently. Above nine commercials per week, the graph appears to be leveling off at 35%.

    These examples show nonlinear relationships and what they mean.

FIGURE 3.7   Percentage Recall vs. Number of Times Commercial Viewed per Week

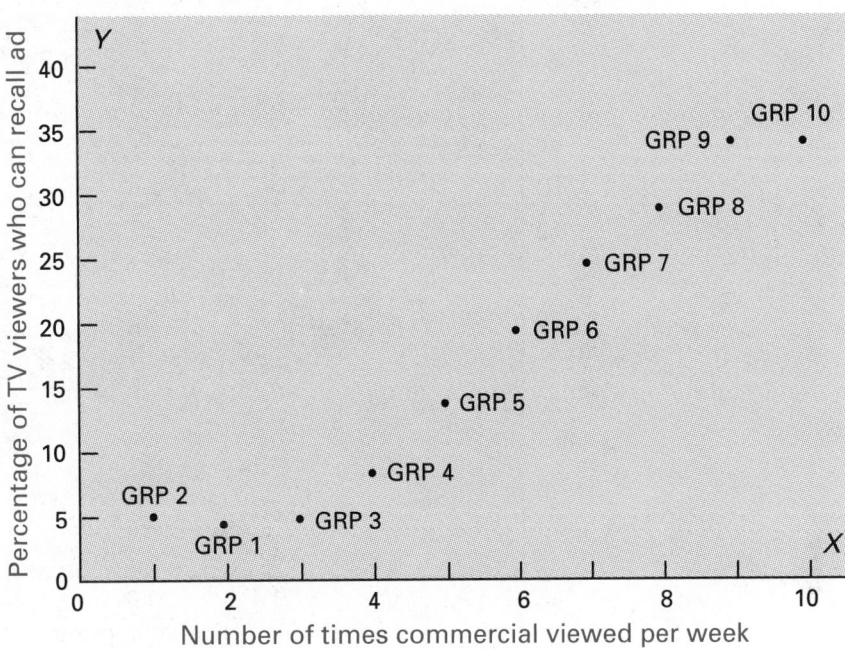

Clusters

Figure 3.8a is a scatter diagram of market share vs. relative price for the 12 sales regions. At first glance there appears to be no relationship between relative price and market share. We would need a circle to enclose all the data points. Moreover, there is not a nonlinear relationship. Can we conclude that the two variables are not related? Please think about it before reading on.

Look again carefully at Figure 3.8a. There are two distinct clusters, or groups, of data points, each consisting of six cities as shown in Figure 3.8b. The lower cluster includes the Atlanta, Birmingham, Charlotte, Jacksonville, New Orleans, and Orlando sales regions. The upper cluster includes the other six cities. What do the clusters mean?

Both clusters slope downward from left to right. Within each cluster, the higher COMCEL's price vs. the competitions' prices, the lower its market share. That makes economic sense. Now compare two cities—one in each cluster that have the same relative price. In the lower cluster, Atlanta has a 1.5 relative price, as does Baltimore in the upper cluster. In both regions, COMCEL's price is 50% higher than the mean of its competitors. Then why does Baltimore have a 45% market share and Atlanta only a 20% share? There must be other variables that explain the different market shares for the same relative price.

Begin the diagnosis. First, what is similar about the six cities within each cluster? What is different between the two clusters? For example, perhaps sales offices in the upper-cluster cities provide better after-sales service, have a more effective reward structure, have more efficient sales organizations, or sell to different clientele. Second, have there been any changes in the six cities in the upper cluster that might

FIGURE 3.8a   Market Share vs. Relative Price

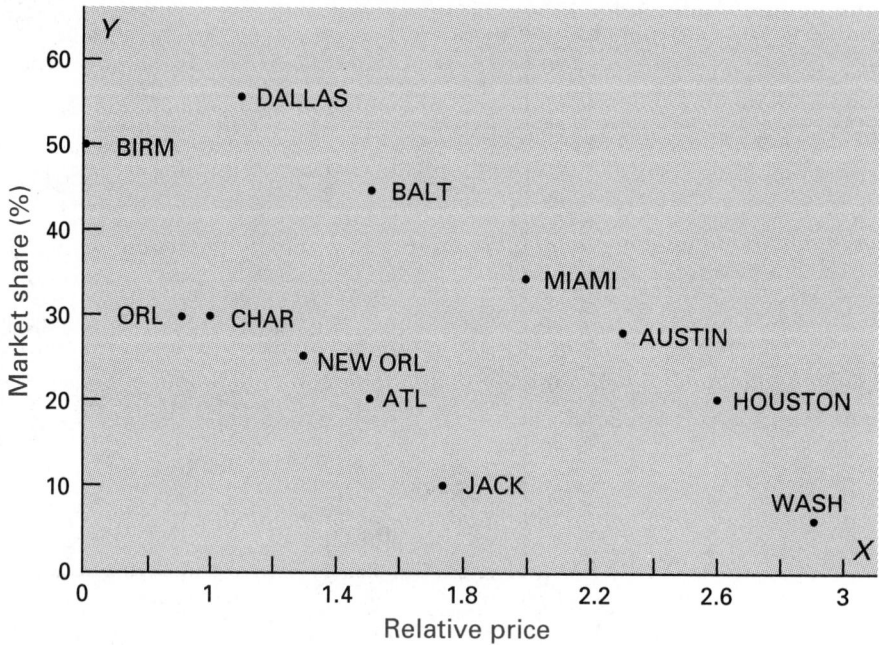

FIGURE 3.8b   Market Share vs. Relative Price

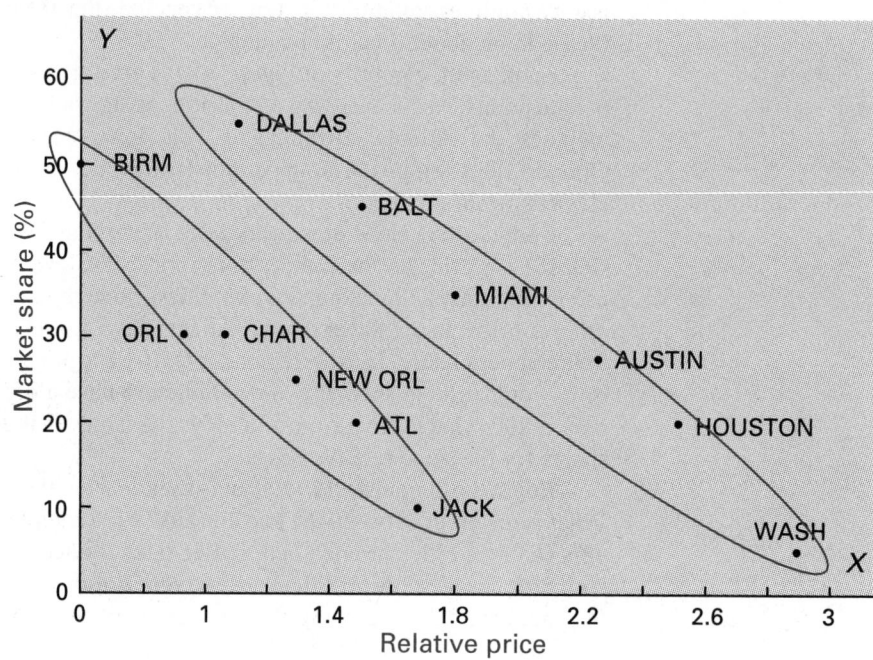

account for their superior performance? For example, have they recently run sales promotion campaigns? Have they recently restructured their sales forces?

Sales managers in the lower-cluster cities should evaluate these potential differences and changes. If they find that the clustering is caused by factors over which they have control, they might be able to raise market share to the level of the higher cluster. They would have found a pathway to better sales performance.

Consider another example. Figure 3.9 shows productivity versus the number of training hours during the year for 12 work groups. Try to interpret Figure 3.9 before reading on.

Again, there appears to be no linear or nonlinear relationship between the two quantitative variables. But there are two distinct clusters. In the lower cluster of six work groups, there is no relationship between productivity and amount of training. Groups that had the most training, G7 and G9, had the same productivity as those with fewer hours of training, such as G2 and G11. However, the upper cluster does show a positive relationship between productivity and training. Groups that had the most training, G6 and G10, had higher productivities than those with fewer hours of training, G3 and G8.

The question to ask, of course, is: What is unique or distinctive about the six groups for which productivity varied with amount of training versus those that did not? Were both given the same type of training? Have there been any changes that might account for the two clusters?

In summary, diagnosing why a quantitative variable, such as market share, varies involves (1) identifying potential explanatory variables, (2) looking for linear and nonlinear relationships and clusters, and (3) if clustering occurs, finding the reasons for it.

FIGURE 3.9   Productivity vs. Training Hours

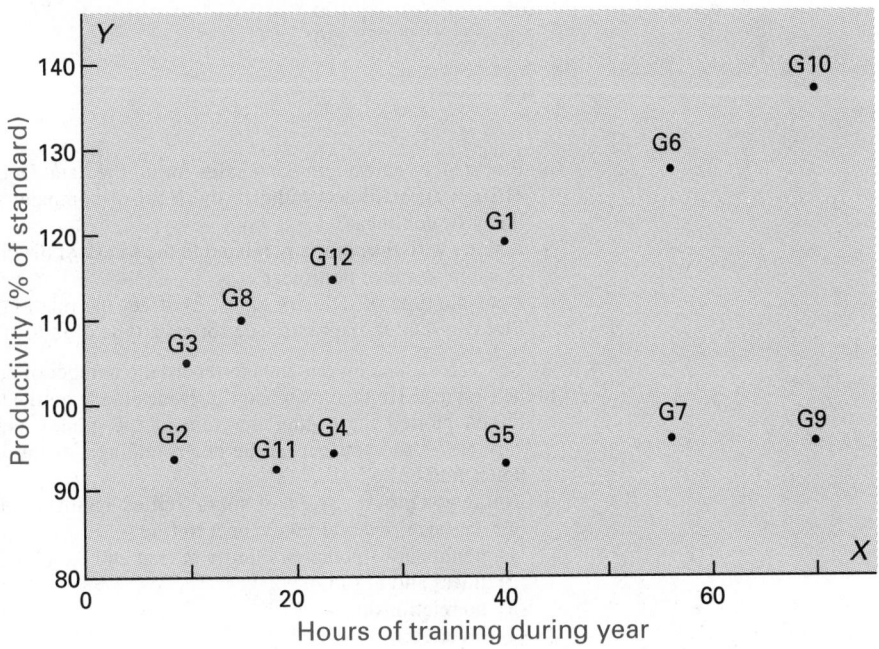

SECTION 3.5 EXERCISES

1. On which axis is the dependent variable placed? On which axis is the independent variable placed? How do you determine the dependent and independent variables in a data set or study?

2. In the following six data sets, identify the dependent and independent variables. Can a scatter diagram be used to display each data set?

Set 1	Market share and number of retail outlets
Set 2	Hours studied and score on exam
Set 3	Hours of training and number of defectives
Set 4	Annual salary and number of years of school
Set 5	Number of Xrays taken per month and mean daily patient load
Set 6	Position on the environment and gender

3. A survey was done to compare the base salaries (in hundreds of thousands of dollars) of chief executives in two industries. The results are shown.

Salary	Company Sales (millions of dollars)	Industry Type	Years with Company
4.6	60	1	8
14.3	400	2	3
5.4	90	1	12
5.6	150	1	12
4.1	180	2	18
4.8	75	1	6
5.6	130	1	10
21.5	500	2	9
3.3	130	2	12
8.1	300	2	15
5.7	105	1	16
5.6	100	1	14
5.6	230	2	8
5.7	115	1	15
9.7	330	2	20

a. Plot salary against company sales for all the data. Does it appear that chief executive officers are paid according to the level of company sales? If so, is the relationship linear or nonlinear?

b. Is years with the company related to the salary of the chief executive? If so, is the relationship linear or nonlinear?

c. Does the type of industry (1 vs. 2) affect the relationship between sales and salary? Plot two scatter diagrams, one for each type of industry.

4. An instructor asked his students to record the number of hours spent studying statistics up to the first test. He then matched the grades made on the test with hours studied.

a. If you plotted the scatter diagram of the grades against the hours studied, which variable would you put on the horizontal axis as the independent variable, grades or hours studied?

b. Before you plot the graph of hours studied against grade, which of the following types of relationship would you expect to find?

(1) nonlinear—increases rapidly at first and then levels off

(2) linear and negative

(3) no relationship

(4) inverted U

Explain.

5. An operations manager suspects a positive linear relationship between lot size and cost. Use the given data to plot a scatter diagram of lot size, X, and the cost to produce the lot, Y.

Lot Size (hundreds)	10	20	30	40	50	60	70	80
Cost (thousands)	34	47	53	68	75	88	98	110

Perform an ellipse test to determine if cost and lot size are linearly related. What do you conclude?

6. The ellipse test can only be used to determine if two variables *appear to be linearly* related. This is shown in the following example.

Job Experience (years)	1	3	5	7	9	11	13
Sales (thousands)	2	3	6	11	17	25	45

a. Which is the dependent variable? Put this variable on the vertical axis. What is the independent variable? Put this variable on the horizontal axis.
b. Plot the data.
c. Perform an ellipse test to determine if the two variables appear to be *linearly related*. What can you conclude?
d. Does it appear that the two variables are related at all?

7. A publishing company measures the effectiveness of advertising on the sales of its magazine in 16 cities. It records the annual total advertising expenditure in tens of thousands of dollars and the number of copies sold over the same period. The data are shown here.

City	A	B	C	D	E	F	G	H
Advertising ($10,000s)	4	5	10	15	16	12	20	6
Total Copies Sold (thousands)	10	9	40	12	11	35	10	8

City	I	J	K	L	M	N	O	P
Advertising ($10,000s)	11	9	5	30	8	40	45	11
Total Copies Sold (thousands)	38	38	8	7	41	6	74	7

a. Plot a scatter diagram and label the points.
b. Describe the relationship between advertising and number of copies sold. If the data appear to cluster, explain how you would proceed from here.

8. Shown is a graph of students' SAT scores and their GPAs after the first year of college. Does SAT score appear to affect GPA?

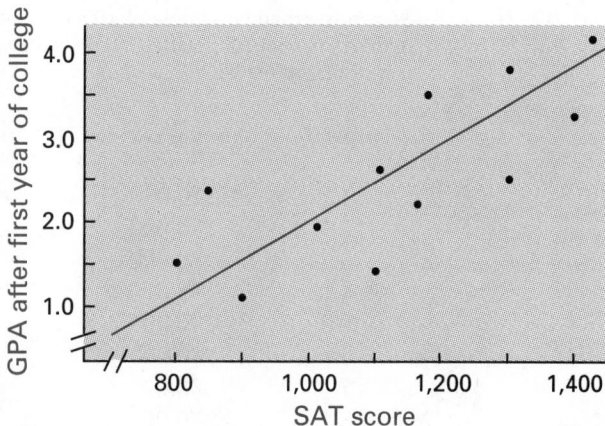

9. Refer to Exercise 8. If SAT score was the only variable that affected GPA, redraw the scatter plot.

10. Why would it be inappropriate to draw a scatter diagram for the following cross-sectional data? What is the most appropriate way to determine if the absence or presence of a Total Quality Management program affects sales.

Region	Sales	Total Quality Management Program
Northeast	250,000	yes
Mid Atlantic	275,000	yes
Southeast	175,000	no
Midwest	187,500	no
Far West	215,000	yes
Southwest	154,000	no
International	165,000	yes

11. Is cost per unit related to the size of the production run? And if so, what is the best size of a production run to minimize cost per unit? The data are taken over 10 shifts in which different size production runs were made.

Cost per Unit	Size of Production Run
$1.90	1,000
$1.85	900
$1.70	800
$1.65	700
$1.55	600
$1.75	500
$1.85	400
$1.95	300
$2.05	200
$2.15	100

12. Consider the following data on years of experience and productivity. Plot the data and describe the experience-productivity relationship.

Experience	1	3	5	7	9	11	13	15
Productivity	100	106	112	115	116	117	115	110

13. Shown is a random sample of 10 surgeons. We have recorded their annual incomes, the numbers of years in practice, and whether they are board-certified (passed a certification test similar to the CPA in accounting).

Surgeon	Annual Income	Years of Experience	Board-Certified
1	$170,000	4	no
2	190,000	6	no
3	180,000	8	no
4	195,000	10	no
5	210,000	12	no
6	240,000	3	yes
7	300,000	5	yes
8	370,000	7	yes
9	430,000	9	yes
10	510,000	11	yes

a. Develop a scatter diagram between annual income and years of experience. Does there appear to be a linear relationship between the two variables?

b. Label each point in the scatter diagram with the Board certification status of the surgeon as Y or N. Are there distinct clusters? What can you conclude about the impact of Board certification on the annual income-years of experience relationship of surgeons.

14. Shown are the data for a study of product innovation in the insurance industry.

Firm	Number of Innovations over a 3-year period	Asset Size (millions)	Decentralized
1	10	200	no
2	14	300	no
3	12	400	no
4	13	500	no
5	12	600	no
6	10	215	yes
7	13	290	yes
8	16	405	yes
9	19	510	yes
10	23	580	yes

a. Develop a scatter diagram between number of innovations and asset size. Does there appear to be a linear relationship between the two variables?

b. Label each point in the scatter diagram as (C)entralized or (D)ecentralized. Are there distinct clusters? What can you conclude about the impact of decentralization on the asset size-number of product innovations relationship of insurance firms?

15. Shown are data on the number of Xrays taken per month and mean daily patient load for teaching and nonteaching hospitals.

Hospital	Number of Xrays	Patient Load	Hospital Type
1	2,100	16	nonteaching
2	4,350	15	teaching
3	9,100	50	nonteaching
4	21,000	60	teaching
5	17,800	100	nonteaching
6	31,000	90	teaching
7	30,500	200	nonteaching
8	55,500	225	teaching
9	60,000	300	nonteaching
10	105,000	275	teaching

a. Develop a scatter diagram between number of Xrays taken per month and the mean daily patient load. Does there appear to be a linear relationship between the two variables?

b. Label each point in the scatter diagram with the hospital type as (N)onteaching or (T)eaching. Are there distinct clusters? What can you conclude about the impact of hospital type on the number of Xrays-mean daily patient load relationship?

16. Refer to Figure 3.9 on page 129 of the text. Note that there are two distinct clusters—G2, G11, G4, G5, G7, and G9 are in one cluster. Suggest some realistic differences between the pairs of six groups that could account for the two distinct clusters. Also suggest some possible changes that might explain the two distinct clusters.

17. In 1982 American Telephone and Telegraph Company was required to break into 21 "Baby Bell" companies. Listed at the top of page 134 are data on revenue in billions and number of phones in millions in late 1982 for 10 of the 21 firms. [*Source: New York Times,* Jan. 9, 1982, p. 35.]

Firm	Telephones (millions)	Revenues (billions of dollars)
Bell—PA	8.0	1.97
Chesapeake	3.6	.96
Diamond State	.5	.14
Indiana Bell	2.7	.75
Mountain States	7.9	2.69
New Jersey	6.6	1.91
Northwestern	5.7	1.82
Pacific Northwest	3.9	1.39
South Central	10.6	3.56
Southwestern Bell	16.7	5.84

a. Which variable should be the explanatory variable?
b. Plot the data and describe the data set.

18. A market research firm wants to determine how much it must offer in dollars to get respondents to complete a survey and return it. The firm selects 11 groups of 100 people. One group receives no money, another group receives $1, and so on. The last group receives $10. The firm then distributes the survey and records the percentage of surveys returned in each group. The data are shown in the graph. What does the graph tell you?

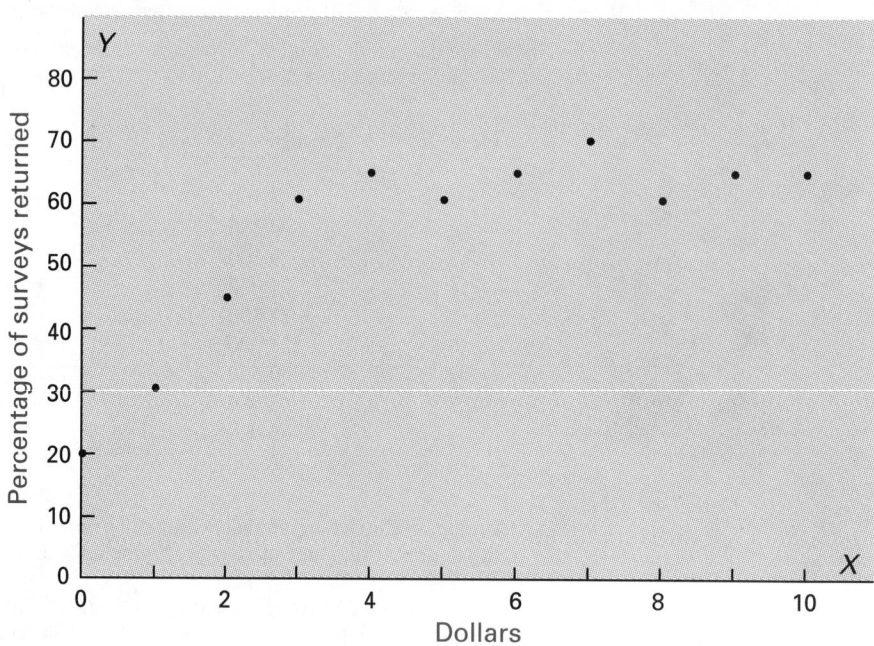

3.6 ≡ Analyzing Quantitative Time-Ordered Data

Cross-sectional data can be either categorical, as in the gender discrimination example, or quantitative, as in the market share example. Time-ordered data are generally quantitative. Thus, we can extend the cross-sectional quantitative techniques presented in the preceding section to time-ordered data also. These include drawing scatter diagrams and looking for linear or nonlinear relationships and clusters. But, because the data are time-ordered, we also recommend drawing *multiple line graphs*. By the end of this section you should be able to:

1. construct and interpret multiple line graphs for time-ordered data;
2. construct and interpret scatter diagrams for time-ordered data; and
3. explain a leading or lagging relationship between two variables.

An example involving time-ordered data analyzes COMCEL's Atlanta market share and advertising expenditures data for the past 16 months. The data are found in Table 3.12. The table shows that market share ranges from 15% to 25%. Suppose COMCEL believes that the dollars spent on advertising account for the large variation. How can COMCEL evaluate that potential relationship?

Table 3.12

Atlanta's Market Share for Past 16 Months

Period	Advertising Expenditures (thousands of dollars)	Market Share(%)
JA90	13	24
FE90	11	18
MA90	17	16
AP90	20	22
MY90	20	24
JU90	16	24
JL90	15	20
AU90	13	21
SE90	17	18
OC90	11	22
NO90	19	16
DE90	15	24
JA91	21	20
FE91	10	25
MA91	15	15
AP91	13	20
$\bar{x}$	15.38	20.56
s	3.44	3.24

Begin by plotting a scatter diagram. As in cross-sectional scatter diagrams, each data point represents an X value, advertising expenditure, and a Y value, market share. Remember to place advertising expenditures—the independent variable—on the horizontal axis, since COMCEL believes that it affects market share. After plotting the data, label each data point with its corresponding calendar date, as shown in Figure 3.10.

It is clear from the scatter diagram that there is no linear or nonlinear relationship, nor are there any clusters. The data are totally scattered. However, since the data are time-ordered, we should also draw a *multiple line graph* before reaching a final conclusion. A multiple line graph can help determine if the two variables have a leading or lagging relationship.

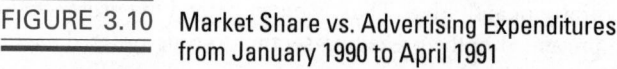

FIGURE 3.10   Market Share vs. Advertising Expenditures from January 1990 to April 1991

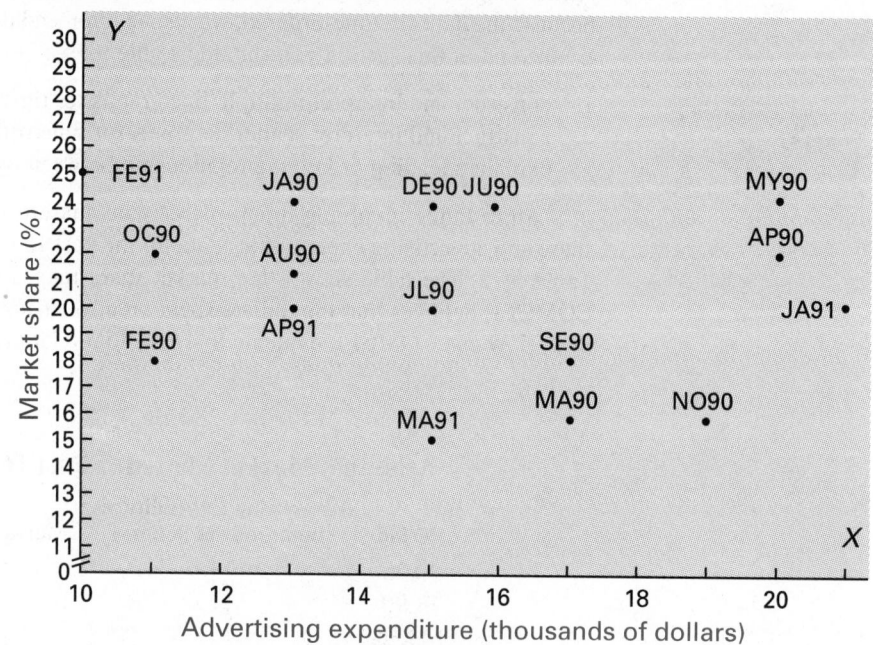

Multiple Line Graphs

We first presented line graphs in Chapter 2. In a line graph, the horizontal axis shows time measured in days, months, or years and the vertical axis shows the value of a quantitative variable. A line graph of the market share data would present months on the horizontal axis and the percentage market share on the vertical axis. Each data point would represent one month's experience. The line graph would show how market share changed *over time.*

Multiple line graphs contain more than one quantitative variable. Figure 3.11 is a multiple line graph of market share *and* advertising expenditures. Time is still shown on the horizontal axis. The first variable—market share—is shown in the upper graph. The first data point is at the intersection of JA90 and 24%. The second variable—advertising expenditures—is shown in the lower graph. The first data point is at the intersection of JA90 and $13,000.

Lagged Relationships

The upper line graph shows how market share varied monthly. The lower line graph shows how advertising expenditures varied monthly. What insights does the multiple line graph provide? Please think about this before reading on.

From February to March of 1990 COMCEL increased advertising from $11,000 to $17,000. Market share did not increase in March, but it did increase in April. From August to September of 1990 COMCEL increased advertising from $13,000 to $17,000, but market share dropped in September. However, market share then

FIGURE 3.11   Multiple Line Graph—Market Share and Advertising Expenditure vs. Time

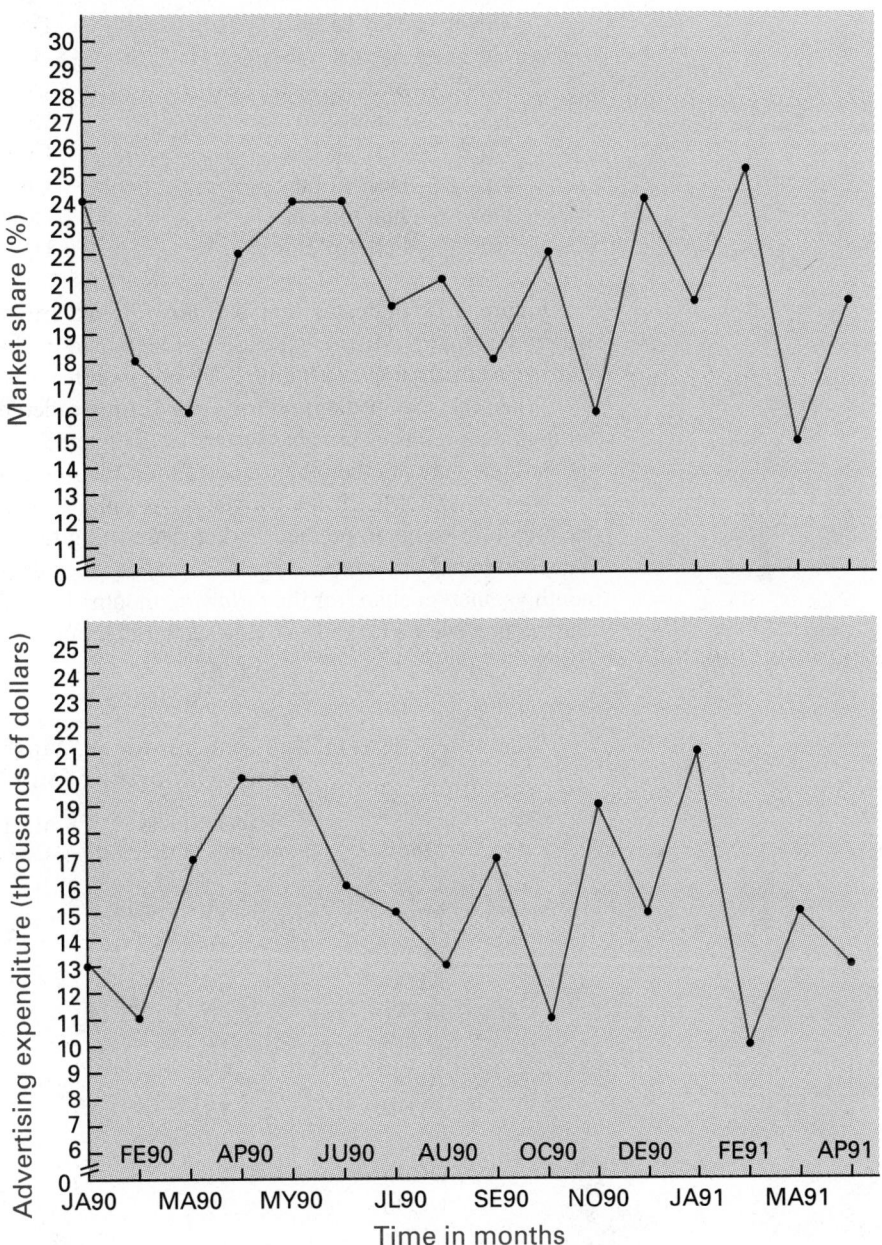

increased in October. From September to October COMCEL reduced advertising from $17,000 to $11,000, yet market share in October actually increased. However one month later, market share dropped.

Figure 3.11 shows that advertising expenditures are related to market share. How? Upturns or downturns in the advertising line graph always occur *one month* before the corresponding turns in the market share line graph.

Turns in Advertising Line Graph	Turns in Market Share Line Graph
Up —Feb. to March	Up —March to April
Down —May to June	Down —June to July
Up —August to Sept.	Up —Sept. to Oct.
Down —Sept. to Oct.	Down —Oct. to Nov.
Up —Oct. to Nov.	Up —Nov. to Dec.
Down —Nov. to Dec.	Down —Dec. to Jan.
Up —Dec. to Jan.	Up —Jan. to Feb.
Down —Jan. to Feb.	Down —Feb. to March
Up —Feb. to March	Up —March to April

Figure 3.11 indicates that *one month's* advertising affects the *next month's* market share. Advertising expenditures lead market share by one month, or market share *lags* advertising expenditures by one month.

When the scatter diagram for a set of time-ordered data shows neither a linear nor nonlinear relationship nor clusters as in Figure 3.10, consider the possibility that one variable may lag the other. Draw a multiple line graph to verify.

Now that COMCEL knows that advertising expenditures lead market share by one month, it wants to predict market share using level of advertising expenditures. We recommend drawing a *lagged-variable* scatter diagram of advertising for each month vs. market share for the *following* month. Table 3.13 contains the data set for constructing such a lagged-variable scatter diagram.

Table 3.13

Advertising in a Month vs. Market Share in the Following Month

Month	Expenditures (thousands of dollars)	Market Share (%) One Month Later
JA90	13	18
FE90	11	16
MA90	17	22
AP90	20	24
MY90	20	24
JU90	16	20
JL90	15	21
AU90	13	18
SE90	17	22
OC90	11	16
NO90	19	24
DE90	15	20
JA91	21	25
FE91	10	15
MA91	15	20
AP91	13	Unknown

Note that the first month's advertising is paired with the second month's market share, the second month's advertising with the third month's market share, etc. See Table 3.12 for the original data.

The scatter diagram in Figure 3.12 indicates that advertising expenditures for a month and market share one month later are linearly and positively related. We can envision the data encompassed by a tight ellipse that slopes upward to the right. We have drawn freehand a straight line through the data points in Figure 3.12. Note that it passes through many of them. The line seems to fit the data well, although some points are above or below the line.

COMCEL can now use Figure 3.12 to estimate its market share for different levels of advertising. For example, if it spends $16,000 for advertising this month, its market share next month should be between 20% and 21%. That is COMCEL's expectation based on the past 16 months of data. If it actually spends $16,000 and its market share is very much less or more than 20%–21%, there may be a disturbance problem (or it may be random variation). Recall that a disturbance problem is a deviation between expected and actual performance. Diagnosing a disturbance problem calls for determining why there was a deviation. For example, could competitors' price cuts explain the deviation between expected and actual market share?

Next, consider an example where two variables lag each other by two periods. We can detect this by drawing a multiple line graph. Table 3.14 on page 141 contains the data for the two variables—monthly sales and research and development (R&D) expenditures for a firm. Figure 3.13 on page 140 shows the multiple line graph for these data. The upper line graph in Figure 3.13 shows how sales varied monthly. The lower line graph shows how research and development expenditures varied monthly. Are the two time series lagged and by how many periods?

The two time series are related. More specifically, R&D expenditures lead sales by two months. Note that R&D expenditures increased from February to June 1991. Sales increased from April to August—two months later. R&D expenditures dropped

FIGURE 3.12   Advertising Expenditure vs. Market Share One Month Later

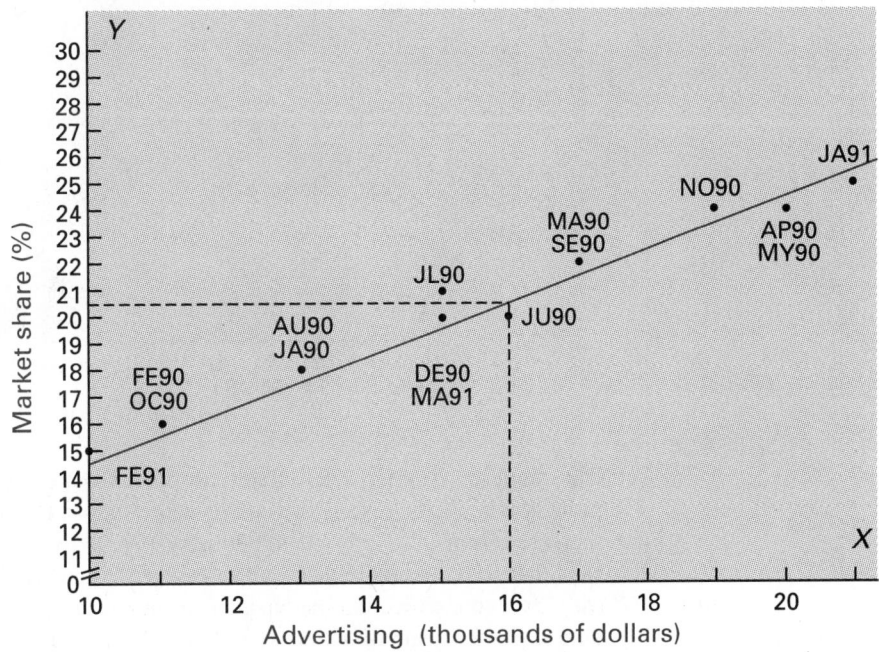

FIGURE 3.13   Multiple Line Graph—Monthly Sales and Expenditures for Research and Development vs. Time

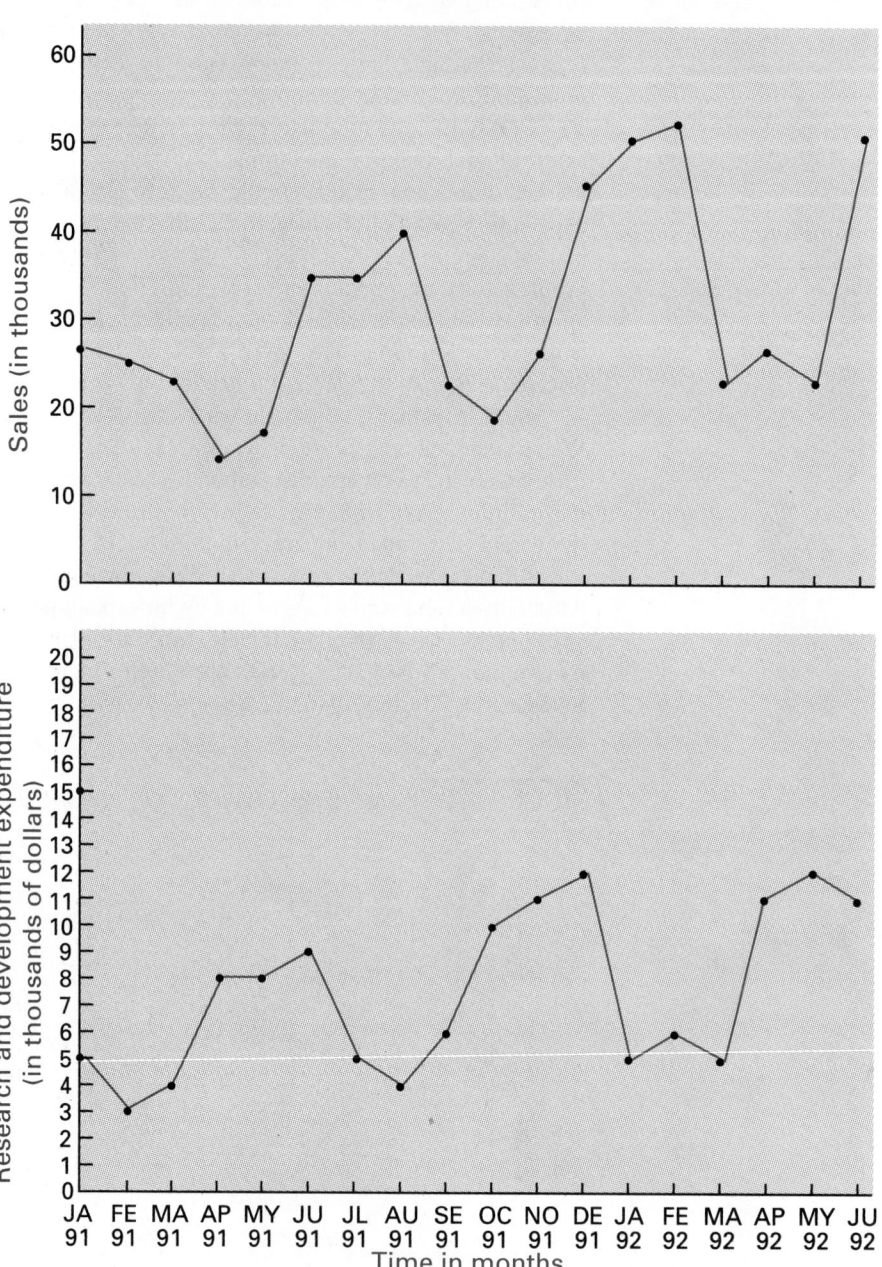

from June to August 1991. Sales dropped from August to October 1991—two months later. R&D again increased from August to December 1991. Sales again increased from October 1991 to February 1992—two months later. In summary, one says that R&D expenditures lead sales by two months, or sales lag R&D expenditures by two months. On the basis of this analysis, we could develop a lagged-variable scatter diagram of R&D expenditures for each month vs. sales two months later from which future sales estimates could be made.

In summary, with time-ordered data, begin by plotting a scatter diagram to check for linear or nonlinear relationships or clusters. If no relationships or clusters are found, then plot a multiple line graph to determine if the two time series are lagged and by how many periods. If a lagged relationship is found, then we can develop a lagged-variable scatter diagram. Draw a straight line through the data points in the lagged-variable scatter diagram. Use the line to estimate values of the dependent variable. *Warning:* Drawing a straight line through data by hand is easy to do, but different people will draw different straight lines. Different lines will yield different estimates. Chapter 11 presents a technique that produces the best fitting line for a set of data points.

Table 3.14

Monthly Sales and R&D Expenditures

Month	Sales (thousands of units)	Research and Development (thousands of dollars)
JA91	26	5
FE91	24	3
MA91	23	4
AP91	14	8
MY91	18	8
JU91	36	9
JL91	36	5
AU91	41	4
SE91	23	6
OC91	18	10
NO91	27	11
DE91	45	12
JA92	50	5
FE92	54	6
MA92	23	5
AP92	27	11
MY92	23	12
JU92	50	11

SECTION 3.6 EXERCISES

1. Consider the following time-ordered data on advertising expenditures and sales.

Month	Sales (thousands of units)	Advertising Expenditures (thousands of dollars)
January	6.5	10
February	4.0	9
March	3.8	15
April	5.1	12
May	4.4	20
June	6.0	25
July	7.1	30
August	8.1	27
September	7.6	20
October	6.1	30
November	7.8	35
December	9.1	7

a. Plot a scatter diagram of sales against advertising expenditures using sales as the dependent variable. Perform an ellipse test to determine if the two variables are related.

b. Plot a multiple line graph of sales and advertising with time on the horizontal axis. Do you notice any lead-lag relationship?

c. It appears that advertising expenditures in one month affect sales in the following month. Reorder the data points so that the advertising expenditure data values in one month align with the sales data values in the following month. For example:

Month	Sales (thousands of units) One Month Later	Advertising Expenditures (thousands of dollars) in One Month
January	4.0	10
February	3.8	9
⋮	⋮	⋮
November	9.1	35

Draw a scatter diagram for the above data.

d. Use an ellipse test to determine if the two variables are related.

e. Interpret the scatter diagram in part **d** so a nontechnical manager could understand the marketing implications.

2. Below are time-ordered data on the number of quality circle (a group of workers who work together to solve problems) ideas on reducing scrap that were accepted by top management and the percentage of scrap in a production process.

Month	Percentage of Scrap	Number of Ideas
1	4.5%	10
2	2.8%	6
3	3.4%	2
4	3.9%	15
5	2.6%	12
6	2.7%	3
7	3.7%	15

a. Plot a scatter diagram of percentage of scrap against number of ideas using percentage of scrap as the dependent variable. Perform an ellipse test to determine if the two variables are related.

b. Plot a multiple line graph of scrap percentage and number of ideas with time on the horizontal axis. Do you notice any lead-lag relationship?

c. It appears that number of ideas in one month affect percentage of scrap in the following month. Reorder the data points so that the number of ideas data values in one month align with the scrap percentage in the following month. For example:

Month	Scrap One Month Later	Number of Ideas Accepted in One Week
1	2.8	10
2	3.4	6
⋮	⋮	⋮
6	3.7	3

Draw a scatter diagram for the above data.

d. Use an ellipse test to determine if the two variables are related.

e. Interpret the scatter diagram in part **d** so a nontechnical manager could understand the production or cost implications.

3. Assume that advertising expenditures in one quarter affect sales one quarter later.
    a. Complete the following table (fill in the sales for quarters 2–8) if the relationship is that the sales in one period is 10 times larger than the advertising expenditures *one period earlier*.

Quarter	Sales (thousands)	Advertising Expenditures (thousands of dollars)
1	140	12
2		15
3		10
4		17
5		20
6		14
7		21
8		16

    b. Reorder the data points so that advertising expenditures in one quarter align with sales in the following month. Draw a scatter diagram of advertising expenditures vs. sales one quarter later. Does your scatter plot indicate the desired relationship; namely, that sales in one quarter are ten times larger than advertising one quarter earlier?

4. Assume that advertising expenditures in one quarter affects sales two quarters later.
    a. Complete the following table (fill in the sales for quarters 3–8) if the relationship is that the sales in one period are ten times larger than the advertising expenditures *two periods earlier*.

Quarter	Sales (thousands)	Advertising Expenditures (thousands of dollars)
1	140	12
2	120	15
3		10
4		17
5		20
6		14
7		21
8		16

    b. Reorder the data points so that advertising expenditures in one quarter align with sales two quarters later. Draw a scatter diagram of advertising expenditures vs. sales two quarters later. Does your scatter plot indicate the desired relationship; namely, that sales in one quarter are ten times larger than advertising two quarters earlier?

5. An economist is studying the relationship between consumption, C, and disposable personal income, Y, over the past year.

Month	J	F	M	A	M	J	J	A	S	O	N	D
Y	20	30	10	20	40	10	20	5	30	40	10	20
C	15	16	21	9	16	23	11	14	7.5	28	26	10

    a. Plot a scatter diagram of C against Y using C as the dependent variable. Perform an ellipse test to determine whether the variables are linearly related.
    b. Plot the C and Y series on a multiple line graph with time on the x-axis. Does one series appear to lead or lag the other? If so, by how many months?

    c. If you notice a lead-lag relationship, reorder the data and pair the value of C with the value of Y that affects it. Plot the reordered pairs in a lagged-variable scatter diagram.

    d. What conclusions can you draw about the relationship between Y and C?

6. Consider the following time series data.

Month	Sales	Training Hours
January	1.0	2
February	.4	5
March	2.5	10
April	10	6
May	3.6	8
June	6.4	12
July	14.4	4
August	1.6	9
September	8.1	7
October	4.9	15
November	22.5	11
December	12.1	13

    a. Plot sales vs. training hours as a scatter diagram with sales as the dependent variable. Can you draw any conclusions from the scatter diagram?

    b. Plot a multiple line graph of sales and training hours with time on the horizontal axis. Do you notice any lead-lag relationships?

    c. Reorder the data to match the value of sales with the value of training hours the month before. Plot a lagged-variable scatter diagram for the reordered data.

    d. On the basis of your graphical analysis, how would you describe the relationship between sales and training hours?

7. Why couldn't we develop multiple line graphs for quantitative cross-sectional data?

8. Suppose that research and development expenditures lead sales by nine months—a positive relationship. Explain what that means to a sales manager.

9. Shown is a multiple line graph of two variables, sales of a firm and Gross National Product. Does it appear that the two series are related? Discuss.

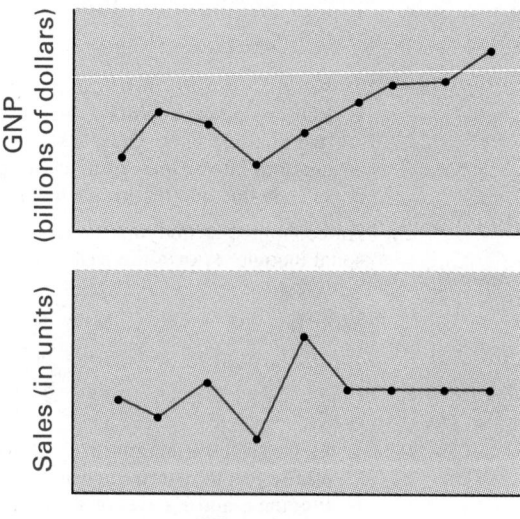

10. A political scientist believes that the percentage of total state legislative seats held by women and the percentage of mayoralties (mayors) held by women in cities of more than 30,000 population are related.

Year	State Legislators	Mayors
1971	4.8%	1.1%
1973	5.6%	1.6%
1975	8.1%	4.6%
1977	9.2%	6.2%
1979	10.3%	6.9%
1981	12.1%	9.1%
1983	13.3%	8.8%
1985	14.8%	9.6%
1987	15.6%	11.1%
1989	16.9%	12.7%
1991	18.2%	17.1%

Source: New York Times, 1992.

   a. Develop a scatter plot and interpret it.
   b. Perform an ellipse test to determine if the two percentages appear to be linearly related? What can you conclude?
   c. Draw two line graphs, one for the percentage of state legislators over time (1971 to 1991) and one for the percentage of mayoralties over time (1971 to 1991).
   d. Interpret the two line graphs. What do they indicate?
   e. What different information did the line graphs and the scatter plot provide?

11. Consider the following quality control data. The data in the mean and standard deviation columns are based on a sample of five units taken from the production line. The data are in hours to failure. Acceptable hours to failure (within product specification) for the mean are 1,450 to 1,650 hours and for the standard deviation are 30 to 50 hours.

Shift	Mean	Standard Deviation
1	1,625	45
2	1,575	47
3	1,580	47
4	1,520	54
5	1,500	57
6	1,510	57
7	1,425	63
8	1,420	63

   a. Plot and describe the multiple line graph of the mean and standard deviation in hours to failure with time on the horizontal axis. Do you notice any lead-lag relationship?
   b. Plot a scatter diagram of the mean time to failure against the standard deviation using the standard deviation as the dependent variable. Perform an ellipse test to determine if the two variables are related.
   c. Explain your answer from part **b** in words that a nontechnical operations manager could understand. That is, as the mean drops below the acceptable limit, what, if anything, happens to the standard deviation in hours to failure?

12. For which of the following data sets can a **multiple** line graph be drawn?

   Set 1   Monthly data on the value of Dow Jones Index and IBM stock
   Set 2   Quarterly data on percentage of voters who think the president is doing an outstanding job and the value of the gross national product
   Set 3   Hourly data on the temperature at DFW airport in Dallas-Fort Worth

Set 4   The six regions of the country and regional sales for April
Set 5   Shift data on the fraction defective products and the number of adjustments made to production equipment

13. Often forecasters believe that one quarter's sales affect the next quarter's sales. That is, sales in the first quarter affect sales in the second quarter, sales in the second quarter affect sales in the third quarter, and so on. Below are twelve quarters (3 years) of sales data.

Column 1 Year/Qtr	Column 2 Sales(thousands)	Column 3 Sales One Month Before	
93–1	3.40	—	
93–2	2.00	3.40	Sales from Quarter 1
93–3	1.90	2.00	Sales from Quarter 2
93–4	3.20	1.90	
94–1	4.80	3.20	
94–2	3.75	4.80	
94–3	4.13	3.75	
94–4	4.51	4.13	
95–1	5.61	4.51	
95–2	4.05	5.61	
95–3	4.63	4.05	
95–4	5.01	4.63	Sales from Quarter 3

a. Draw a line graph of sales over the 12 quarters (column 2 vs. time on the horizontal axis). Describe the growth of sales over the past 3 years. In which quarters are sales relatively high and relatively low each year?

b. To determine if there is a relationship between sales for a quarter and sales for a previous quarter, draw a scatter plot for the data in columns 2 and 3 for periods 93–2 to 95–4. Place the sales from the previous quarter (column 3) on the horizontal axis and the sales for the present quarter (column 2) on the vertical axis. We have developed a scatter diagram for an **autoregressive model,** which we present more fully in Chapter 13.

c. Use the ellipse test to determine if the two variables—sales for a quarter and sales for the previous quarter—are linearly related.

3.7 ▤ Correlation and Cross-Correlation

Graphs are useful in identifying lagged relationships between two time series. But an easier method can be used if a computer is available. We can calculate cross-correlation coefficients for the two series at different lags. Cross-correlation is an application of the general idea of correlation, a numerical index measuring the degree of linear association between two variables. By the end of this section you should be able to:

1. explain the relationship between the ellipse test and a correlation coefficient;
2. estimate the correlation coefficient for different data patterns;
3. define covariance and explain how it relates to the correlation coefficient;
4. explain when the cross-correlation coefficient should be used and how to interpret it; and
5. distinguish between correlation and cause and effect.

The Correlation Coefficient

The correlation coefficient, r, is a numerical measure of the strength of a linear relationship between two variables. Correlation coefficients can vary from -1 to $+1$. The graphs in Figure 3.14 show different degrees of *linear* associations and their r values.

In scatter diagram (a), $r = +1$. There is a *perfect positive* linear relationship between the two variables. It is perfect because r equals 1 and positive because of the plus sign. All the data points fall on a straight line. The relationship is perfect in the sense that if we knew the equation of the straight line and the value of the variable X, we could predict the Y value with perfect certainty. The relationship is positive because as variable X increases, variable Y also increases. Graph (e) shows a *perfect inverse* linear relationship, and r has a value of -1.

Scatter diagrams (b) and (d) show lines that fit the pattern of data points quite well, but not perfectly. A tight ellipse can enclose the data points. Correlation coefficients are close to $+1$ and -1. Scatter diagram (c) shows a pattern of points that can only be enclosed by a circle. The correlation coefficient is 0, indicating no linear relationship. That is, as variable X increases, variable Y neither increases nor decreases. A horizontal line is drawn to reflect the lack of a linear relationship between the two variables.

FIGURE 3.14   Examples of the Range of Correlation Coefficients

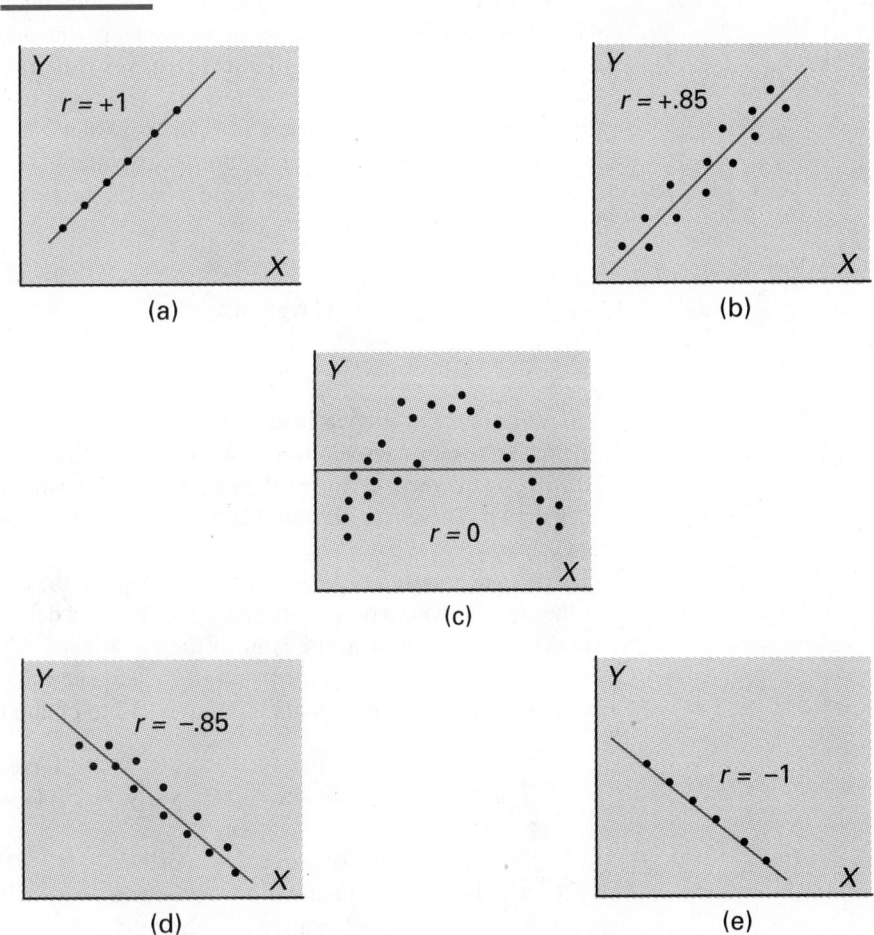

Cross-correlations
measure the linear
association between two
variables *at different lags*.

Correlations measure the linear association between two variables. **Cross-correlations** build upon the correlation concept.

We will use Atlanta's sales data for the past 16 months, found in Table 3.12, to compute cross-correlations between market share and advertising expenditures. Recall from Figures 3.10 and 3.11 that advertising expenditures do not affect market share in the month, but rather in the following month. This example will demonstrate that cross-correlations of lag 0 and 1 provide the same information.

Determining Lagged Relationships Using Cross-Correlations

We will use expression (3.1) to compute the cross-correlation between market share and advertising expenditures for a lag of 0. Here we are determining if advertising expenditures in one month affect market share in the same month. Since Figure 3.10 indicates that the two variables are not linearly related, the correlation coefficient should be close to 0.

$$r = \frac{\text{Covariance (X, Y)}}{s_X s_Y} \tag{3.1}$$

The terms s_X and s_Y are the sample standard deviations for the advertising expenditures and market share data. The numerator, the *covariance,* is an extension of the variance. Covariance measures the extent to which the advertising and market share data move together, or covary. When the advertising and market share data points in a scatter diagram move upward to the right (as in Figure 3.14a or 3.14b), the covariance and the correlation will be positive. When the data points move downward to the right (as in Figure 3.14d or 3.14e), the covariance and the correlation will be negative. When the data points show no *linear* pattern (as in Figure 3.14c), the covariance and the correlation will be close to 0. Expression (3.2) shows how to compute the covariance.

$$\text{Covariance} = \frac{\sum_i (x_i - \bar{x})(y_i - \bar{y})}{n - 1} \tag{3.2}$$

where n *always* equals the original number of data points.

Visualizing the covariance graphically is important. Figure 3.15 reproduces Figure 3.10 with two additions. A horizontal line at the mean for market share, 20.56%, and a vertical line at the mean for advertising expenditures, $15,380, have been drawn. These two lines divide the scatter diagram into four quadrants labeled A, B, C, and D.

From expression (3.1), we see that the sign of the covariance determines the sign of the correlation coefficient, because the standard deviations in the denominator are always positive. In turn, the sign of the covariance depends on the cross-products term in the numerator of expression (3.2). To determine the sign of the cross-products, one can use the quadrants in Figure 3.15 to obtain the following results:

Quadrant	$x - \bar{x}$	$y - \bar{y}$	Cross-Products $(x - \bar{x})(y - \bar{y})$
A	Negative	Positive	Negative
B	Positive	Positive	Positive
C	Negative	Negative	Positive
D	Positive	Negative	Negative

FIGURE 3.15   Four Quadrants of Market Share vs. Advertising Expenditures

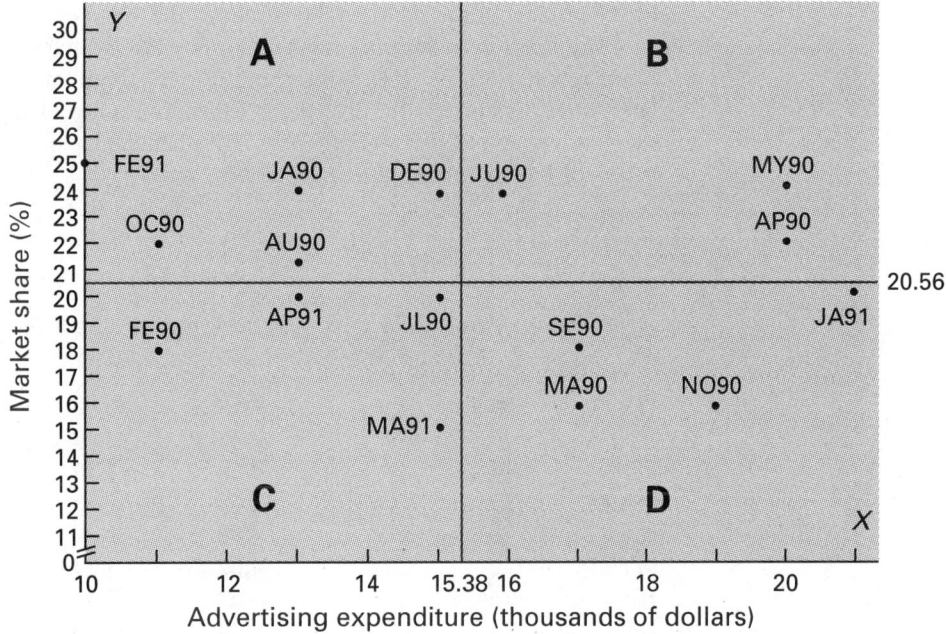

In quadrant B, both the advertising and market share values are larger than their respective means. From expression (3.2), the cross-products terms for these data points will be positive. In quadrant C, both the advertising and market share values are less than their respective means. The cross-products terms will also be positive. Cross-products terms for data points in quadrants A and D are negative.

When there is a positive linear relationship, most data points lie in quadrants B and C. The covariance term and thus the correlation will be positive. When there is a negative linear relationship, most data points lie in quadrants A and D. The covariance term and thus the correlation will be negative. When there is no linear relationship, it takes a circle or an ellipse parallel to the horizontal axis to encompass the data. That is, there are roughly equal numbers of data points in the four quadrants. The positive cross-products for data points in quadrants B and C will cancel out the negative cross-products from quadrants A and D. The covariance and thus the correlation coefficient will be approximately 0.

In Figure 3.15, we see that there are five data points in quadrant A, three data points in quadrant B, four data points in quadrant C, and four data points in quadrant D. Thus the correlation should be close to 0. Table 3.15 on page 150 shows the computations for the cross-correlation for the advertising and market share data for lag 0.

The cross-correlation at lag 0, $r(0)$, is only $-.19$, which suggests no linear relationship between market share and advertising expenditures, since r is close to 0. Advertising expenditures are not a *coincident indicator* of market share. A variable X is a *coincident indicator* when values of X in one period affect the values of Y in the *same* period.

Table 3.16 on page 151 contains the calculations for the cross-correlation for lag 1. Here we are determining if advertising in one month affects market share in the next month. As in Table 3.13, we match up January's advertising with February's market share, February's advertising with March's market share, etc. Note that we compute the cross-product terms about the means of the *original* two series even though one point has been eliminated due to lagging. We also divide the covariance by the product of the standard deviations of the *original* time series.

The cross-correlation at lag 1, $r(1)$, is $+.93$, which suggests a strong positive linear relationship between advertising in one month and market share one month later, since r is close to 1. Advertising expenditures are a leading indicator of market share. A variable X is a *leading indicator* when values of X in one period affect the values of Y in one or more *later* periods.

Table 3.15

Computing the Cross-Correlation at Lag 0 for the Variables X, Advertising Expenditures, and Y, Market Share

Period	x	y	$x - \bar{x}$	$y - \bar{y}$	Cross-Product Terms
JA90	13	24	-2.38	3.44	-8.19
FE90	11	18	-4.38	-2.56	11.21
MA90	17	16	1.62	-4.56	-7.39
AP90	20	22	4.62	1.44	6.65
MY90	20	24	4.62	3.44	15.89
JU90	16	24	.62	3.44	2.13
JL90	15	20	$-.38$	$-.56$	.21
AU90	13	21	-2.38	.44	-1.05
SE90	17	18	1.62	-2.56	-4.15
OC90	11	22	-4.38	1.44	-6.31
NO90	19	16	3.62	-4.56	-16.51
DE90	15	24	$-.38$	3.44	-1.31
JA91	21	20	5.62	$-.56$	-3.15
FE91	10	25	-5.38	4.44	-23.89
MA91	15	15	$-.38$	-5.56	2.11
AP91	13	20	-2.38	$-.56$	1.33
Sum					-32.42

$\bar{x} = 15.38$

$\bar{y} = 20.56$

Standard deviation in market share (see Table 3.12)	$=$	3.24
Standard deviation in advertising expenditures (see Table 3.12)	$=$	3.44
Covariance (see expression (3.2))	$=$	$\dfrac{-32.42}{16-1}$
	$=$	-2.16

$$r(0) = -\frac{-2.16}{(3.24)(3.44)} \qquad = \quad -.19$$

These cross-correlations confirm that:

1. Advertising expenditures do not affect market share in the same month; $r(0) = -.19$.

2. Advertising expenditures in a month affect market share in the following month; $r(1) = +.93$.

Interpreting Cross-Correlations

Shown are cross-correlations at lags 0, 1, 2,..., 6 for the advertising expenditures and market share data in Table 3.12.

Lag (months)	0	1	2	3	4	5	6
$r(k)$	−.19	+ .93	−.20	+ .11	−.48	+ .10	−.20

Table 3.16

Computing the Cross-Correlation at Lag 1 for the Variables X, Advertising Expenditures, and Y, Market Share, One Month Later

Period	x	y	$x - \bar{x}$	$y - \bar{y}$	Cross-Product Terms
JA90	13	18	−2.38	−2.56	6.09
FE90	11	16	−4.38	−4.56	19.97
MA90	17	22	1.62	1.44	2.33
AP90	20	24	4.62	3.44	15.89
MY90	20	24	4.62	3.44	15.89
JU90	16	20	.62	− .56	− .35
JL90	15	21	−.38	.44	− .17
AU90	13	18	−2.38	−2.56	6.09
SE90	17	22	1.62	1.44	2.33
OC90	11	16	−4.38	−4.56	19.97
NO90	19	24	3.62	3.44	12.45
DE90	15	20	− .38	− .56	.21
JA91	21	25	5.62	4.44	24.95
FE91	10	15	−5.38	−5.56	29.91
MA91	15	20	− .38	−.56	.21
AP91	13	Unknown			
Sum					155.77

$\bar{x} = 15.38$
$\bar{y} = 20.56$

$$\text{Covariance} = \frac{155.77}{16-1} = 10.38$$

$$r(1) = +\frac{10.38}{(3.24)(3.44)} = +.93$$

Use the following rule to determine if a cross-correlation is large enough to indicate an important linear relationship between the two variables.

Based on n data points, two variables are linearly related at lag k if, ignoring the sign of the cross-correlation,

$$r(k)\sqrt{(n - k)} > 2$$

The largest of the above six cross-correlations are

$$r(1) = +.93; \qquad .93\sqrt{16 - 1} = 3.6 > 2$$
$$r(4) = -.48; \qquad .48\sqrt{16 - 4} = 1.7 < 2$$

The rule demonstrates that advertising expenditures affect market share at lag 1 but not lag 4. Advertising expenditures affect market share one month later. Moreover, the positive coefficient, $+.93$, means that increases in advertising expenditures are associated with increases in market share.

The cross-correlation for lag 4 does not indicate a relationship. However, suppose that $r(4)\sqrt{12}$ was greater than 2. How would you interpret a negative cross-correlation? Please think about it before reading on.

An important negative $r(4)$ cross-correlation would mean that an increase in advertising expenditures this month is associated with a reduction (negative coefficient) in market share four months later.

Warning: Correlation is different from cause and effect. A high correlation does not mean that one variable causes another to vary. The high cross-correlation for lag 1 of $+.93$ indicates only that variation in advertising is associated with variation in market share one month later. However, the term cause has been used because we can make a *logical* connection between the two variables. Marketing theory predicts that advertising expenditures should affect market share. However, if we computed cross-correlations for different lags between the Dow Jones Index and length of women's dresses, we might find one or more negative correlations. The shorter dresses are, the higher the stock prices. Yet no one would seriously argue that short dresses cause the Dow Jones Index to increase. Remember, high correlations only establish a linear association between variables. Judgment or theory establishes cause and effect.

In summary, when looking for relationships between two variables for which we have time-ordered data, compute cross-correlations for lags of 0, 1, 2, 3, or more periods. Use our rule to determine which cross-correlation coefficients indicate important linear associations between the two variables. Try to make sense of the cross-correlations. That is, why should variable X affect variable Y k periods later? Knowledge of cross-correlations helps managers understand their firm and its market place. For example, knowing that advertising expenditures lead market share by one month is essential to timing of advertising expenditures. Managers who understand their environment are better performers and can bring about better performance from others.

SECTION 3.7 EXERCISES

1. Explain the difference between variance and covariance. Which is likely to be more important in problem diagnosis?

2. A recent article in the newspaper noted: "There is a definite correlation between alcohol consumption and lung cancer." Does that mean that alcohol consumption causes lung cancer? Discuss.

3. Consider the following pairs of numbers:

x	1	3	5	7
y	5	9	13	17

    a. Find the mean and standard deviation for each variable.
    b. Find the covariance of the two variables at lag (0).

   c. Find the correlation of x and y, $r(0)$.

   d. Interpret the correlation and plot the data.

4. Consider the following data relating sales and advertising for six quarters.

Quarter	Advertising (millions of dollars)	Sales (millions of dollars)
1	2	8
2	3	9
3	4	11
4	5	12
5	6	13
6	7	14

Write the pairs of numbers you would use to calculate the covariance of the cross-correlation coefficient to determine whether:

a. advertising leads sales by one quarter.

b. advertising leads sales by two quarters.

c. sales lead advertising by one quarter.

5. Calculate cross-correlations at lags 0, 1, and 2 for the sales and training hours data in Exercise 6 of Section 3.6.

6. If $r = 0$, does that mean that two variables are not related? Discuss.

7. Draw a scatter diagram where the covariance is

a. positive.

b. negative.

c. close to 0.

Defend your three diagrams.

8. Consider the following cross-sectional data set.

Mean Student Evaluation of Instructor Rating (on 5-point scale)	4.8	4.6	4.4	4.3	4.2	3.9	3.8
Class Size	10	20	30	40	50	60	70

a. Find the mean and standard deviation for each variable.

b. Plot a scatter diagram. Place class size on the horizontal axis. Count the number of data points in the four quadrants of the scatter plot (review Figure 3.15 for help). Do the counts suggest that the two variables are positively, negatively, or not related?

c. Find the covariance of the two variables.

d. Find the correlation of mean evaluation and class size.

e. Does increasing class size cause lower student evaluation ratings of instructors?

9. Consider the following time-ordered data set.

Day	1	2	3	4	5	6	7
Change in Dow Jones	+10.5	+3.5	−10.1	+2.5	+6.1	−12.5	+30.5
Change in IBM price	+1.5	+.75	−1.0	+.25	+.63	−1.25	+4.25

a. Find the mean and standard deviation for each variable.

b. Plot a scatter diagram. Place change in DJ on the horizontal axis. Count the number of data points in the four quadrants of the scatter plot (review Figure 3.15 for help). Do the counts suggest that the two variables are positively, negatively, or not related?

   c. Find the covariance of the two variables at lag (0).
   d. Find the correlation of the daily price change of the DJ and IBM, $r(0)$.
   e. Does price changes in the DJ cause price changes in IBM?

10. Consider the following cross-sectional data set.

Years in Teaching	1	3	5	7	9	11
Annual Salary (thousands)	68	63	58	65	67	75

   a. Find the mean and standard deviation for each variable.
   b. Find the covariance of the two variables.
   c. Find the correlation of years in teaching and annual salary.
   d. Plot the data and interpret the correlation coefficient.

11. Consider the following cross-sectional data set.

College GPA	2.3	2.7	2.9	3.1	3.4	3.8	4.0
Salary (thousands) 10 Years after Graduation	49	51	43	52	50	49	46

   a. Find the mean and standard deviation for each variable.
   b. Plot a scatter diagram. Place GPA on the horizontal axis. Count the number of data points in the four quadrants of the scatter plot (review Figure 3.15 for help). Do the counts suggest that the two variables are positively, negatively, or not related?
   c. Find the covariance of the two variables.
   d. Find the correlation of GPA and salary ten years after graduation.

12. Refer to the time-ordered data set in Exercise 1 of Section 3.6 in which sales and advertising expenditures are recorded for a one-year period. A scatter plot showed no relationship between the two variables for lag 0. A second scatter plot of advertising expenditures vs. sales one period later (for lag 1) showed a linear relationship. Calculate the cross-correlations at lag 0 and 1. Use the cross-correlation rule on page 151 to determine if the two variables are related at either lag 0 or lag 1.

13. Refer to the time-ordered data set in Exercise 10 of Section 3.6 in which the percentage of state legislative seats and mayoralties held by women over the past 20 years are recorded. Calculate the cross-correlation at lag 0. Use the cross-correlation rule on page 151 to determine if the two variables are related at lag 0.

14. Following are the closing levels of the Dow Jones Index and beer production (both rounded off) for the years 1971–1983.

Year	Dow Jones Closing Value	Beer Production (millions of barrels)
1971	884	133
1972	951	137
1973	924	149
1974	759	156
1975	802	161
1976	975	164
1977	835	171
1978	805	179
1979	839	184
1980	963	194
1981	899	194
1982	1047	196
1983	1259	195

Source: Standard & Poor's Current Statistics, 1986.

  a. Draw a scatter plot. Place beer production on the horizontal axis.
  b. Draw a scatter plot of beer production in one year and the Dow Jones Index for the fol-
     lowing year. Interpret the graph.
  c. Draw a scatter plot of beer production in one year and the Dow Jones Index two years
     later. Interpret the graph.
  d. Compute the cross-correlations for lags 0,1,and 2.
  e. Use the cross-correlation rule on page 151 to determine if the two variables are related
     at lag 0,1, or 2.
  f. Does it make sense to cross-correlate annual beer production and the closing Dow
     Jones Index values? That is, would you expect a relationship—concurrent or lagged—
     between these two variables?

15. Below are data on the mean number of hours to failure and the range in the number of
   hours to failure of a computer component (based on a sample of 5 components) over 15
   successive shifts.

Shift	Mean Failure Time (thousands of hours)	Range in Failure Times (thousands of hours)
June 7 A.M.	2.5	.5
June 7 P.M.	2.4	.6
June 8 A.M.	2.3	.7
June 8 P.M.	2.4	.7
June 9 A.M.	2.2	.9
June 9 P.M.	2.1	.8
June 10 A.M.	2.0	1.1
June 10 P.M.	1.9	1.2

  a. Plot a multiple line graph of mean time to failure and range in time to failure with time
     on the horizontal axis. Interpret the multiple line graph.
  b. Draw a scatter diagram of mean failure time vs. range in failure times. What happens,
     in general, to the range in failure times as the mean failure time decreases?
  c. Compute the correlation, $r(0)$, between the two variables. Based on part **b**, do you
     expect the correlation to be negative, close to zero, or positive? Why?
  d. Correlation rule on page 151 to determine if the two variables are related at lag 0.
  e. Interpret the correlation coefficient to a nontechnical operations manager. The man-
     ager wants the mean and range to be stable over time (no upward or downward move-
     ment). Given the correlation, as the mean time to failure decreases, is the range
     affected? Describe how the range is affected.

3.8 ≡ Key Ideas and Overview

Table 3.17 integrates problem sensing and diagnosis with the graphical techniques
and descriptive statistics presented in Chapters 2 and 3.
   Managers and business professionals must learn to sense and diagnose problems
quickly and accurately. Sensing begins with building mental models of the department's performance for a single time period (day, week, month) and over time.
Sensing also involves looking for outliers in departmental, product, or people performance. Diagnosis means finding potential explanatory variables that account for
performance differences or outliers. Look for distinctions between groups or changes
that might explain the performance differences or outliers. Collect data and use one-
way or cross-tabs tables or scatter diagrams to display the findings. For time-ordered
data plot multiple line graphs and compute cross-correlations.

We conclude this chapter with a set of key ideas:

1. To answer the question of why two or more departments differ, first seek an explanatory categorical variable. Then compute descriptive statistics such as the mean and standard deviation or the median and interquartile range for different levels of the explanatory variable. Display the results in a one-way table.

Table 3.17

Integrating Framework for Chapters 2 and 3

Problem-Solving Activity	Typical Managerial Questions	Statistical and Graphical Tools
Problem sensing	Sensing begins with understanding the performance of the department, product, people, etc. *Ask:* What is the:	
	• distribution of performances?	Stem-and-leaf, frequency tables and histograms, ogives, box plots
	• average performance?	Mean, median, or trimmed mean
	• variability of performances?	Range, standard deviation, and interquartile range
	• performance over time?	Line graphs
	Sensing continues with seeking outliers in departmental, product, or people performance. *Ask:* Are there:	
	• outliers?	Empirical and Tukey's rules
	• outliers over time?	Moving average and residuals
Problem diagnosis	Diagnosis seeks variables that will explain differences between two or more departments or groups that have different performance distributions, averages, or variabilities. Diagnosis also seeks explanations for outliers. *Ask:*	
	Does an explanatory variable explain differences in average performance or variability in performance?	One-way tables
	Are two categorical variables related?	Cross-tabs tables, row or column percentages
	Are two quantitative variables related?	Scatter diagrams, ellipse vs. circle test, clusters, correlations
	Are two quantitative variables related over time?	Multiple line graphs, cross-correlations

2. Multiple box plots are an effective way of presenting one-way table data. Many managers prefer pictures to tables.

3. Cross-tabs tables help answer the question of whether two categorical variables are related to one another. Compute the row or column percentages.

4. Scatter diagrams help answer the question of whether two quantitative variables are related to one another. Look for linear or nonlinear relationships or clusters. The circle vs. ellipse test is effective for detecting possible linear relationships.

5. For time-ordered data, always draw a multiple line graph and scatter diagrams. Compute cross-correlations for zero, one, two, or more lags between the two variables.

6. High correlations do not mean that one variable causes another variable to vary. Correlation only establishes an association among variables. Judgment or theory establishes cause and effect.

Date: August 10, 1995
To: Ann Tabor, CEO
From: Cherian Jain, VP Marketing Research
Re: Analysis of the factors affecting market share

SUMMARY
Our recommendations are to:

1. increase advertising expenditures in selected cities on a trial basis; and
2. reduce burnout of our senior sales force and improve performance of more junior salespeople.

We also found that the 12 cities form two distinct clusters when relative price and market share are plotted. We continue to seek an explanation. Finally, we discovered that advertising expenditures lead market share by one month. That is, a month's advertising affects market share in the following month.

SUPPORTING ANALYSIS
My staff brainstormed and generated three potential explanatory variables—advertising expenditures, mean years of sales force experience, and relative product price. We examined the relationship between market share and these variables from both a cross-sectional and time-ordered perspective.

CROSS-SECTIONAL ANALYSIS
Market share and advertising appear to be positively related, at least within the range of our data. Increasing advertising should produce market share increases.

Market share and mean years of sales experience have an inverted U relationship. Regions whose sales force have 11 years' experience obtain the largest market share. More or less experience reduces market share. Intervening variable(s) may be responsible for this apparent relationship. But we should consider ways to season our younger sales forces and rejuvenate our more senior sales forces.

We found two distinct clusters when we plotted relative price vs. market share. We are looking for differences in the markets themselves and in our policies which would explain the two clusters.

TIME-SERIES ANALYSIS

Our data base included 16 months of market share and advertising data for Atlanta. Our initial scatter diagram found no relationship. Since this didn't make sense, we plotted both market share and advertising expenditures against time on a multiple line graph. Advertising expenditures appeared to lead market share by one month. That is, advertising in one month affects our market share the next month. The cross-correlation for lag 1, $r(1)$, of +.93 confirmed our analysis.

The analysis continues. We are working on a time-ordered data analysis for relative price vs. market share for Washington for the past 16 months. Other reports to follow.

CHAPTER 3 QUESTIONS

1. What is the difference between univariate and bivariate data?

2. Why are bivariate data necessary in problem diagnosis?

3. In your own words, distinguish between quantitative and categorical data.

4. Explain how one-way tables or multiple box plots help in problem diagnosis.

5. Construct your own data to show how a column percentage table provides insight into the possible connections between two categorical variables such as homeowner and renter vs. for and against tax increase.

6. What are intervening variables?

7. What role do intervening variables play in a cross-tabs table analysis?

8. How can managers develop lists of variables that might help them explain variation among multiple groups?

9. Explain the logic of the ellipse test in determining if two variables are linearly related.

10. Does a finding of no linear relationship between two variables mean no relationship at all?

11. Explain how the presence of distinct clusters in a scatter diagram helps in problem diagnosis.

12. In simple terms, what are leading and lagging relationships?

13. How do multiple line graphs help in problem diagnosis?

14. Correct, if necessary, the following statement:

    Problem diagnosis determines if groups differ in their mean performance or how much variation there is among groups. Problem sensing determines why groups differ or explains the variation among groups.

15. Does a high correlation mean that one variable causes another variable to vary?

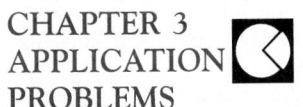

CHAPTER 3 APPLICATION PROBLEMS

1. Best Dairy Inc. knows that the Macho consumers have lower incomes than do the Status Seeker consumers. They wonder if Machos and Status Seekers also have different preferences for skim and whole milk. The marketing manager conducts a survey to determine if Machos and Status Seekers prefer skim and whole milk equally. He wants to verify that Best Dairy has meaningfully segmented its market. Best Dairy Inc. interviews 200 customers and cross-classifies them along the following two dimensions:

	Machos	Status Seekers	Total
Skim	30	80	110
Whole	70	20	90
	100	100	200

   a. Compute the row and the column percentages.
   b. Using either percentages, do Machos and Status Seekers prefer skim and whole milk equally?
   c. Why should you qualify your conclusion? That is, why could you be wrong?

2. Length-of-tenure discounts are the differences between the rents charged long-time tenants and newer tenants. Landlords give discounts because they want to keep good tenants and minimize turnover. The length-of-tenure discounts in Chicago vary from 1.5% to 11.5%. Why is there so much variability? The American Housing Association believes that it is due to the size of the apartment complex. Larger complexes (more than 10 units) are owned by corporations and can afford to have vacant apartments. Thus they give smaller discounts. Small complexes owned by families cannot afford to have unrented apartments, and so give higher discounts for tenants to stay.

Discount (%)	Size of Complex	Discount (%)	Size of Complex
1.5	Small	6.5	Large
2.0	Small	11.5	Large
5.4	Large	2.7	Small
2.5	Small	10.7	Large
3.9	Large	2.9	Small
1.7	Small	6.7	Large
5.5	Large	3.2	Small
3.4	Small		

   a. Develop a one-way table using size of complex as the explanatory variable. Compute only the mean and standard deviation.
   b. Does complex size seem to explain why discounts vary widely in Chicago?
   c. Why couldn't you use a scatter diagram to organize and summarize the data?

3. Apex wants to reduce its age of accounts receivable from a mean of about 35 days. They try a program of inducements (discounts for prompt payment) in Hartford and no inducements in New Haven. They then select six accounts from both cities. Does the discount program appear to be successful?

Age of Accounts Receivable in Days

With Inducement	Without Inducement
20	30
15	28
20	31
16	35
19	25
24	30

    a. Set up a one-way table with presence or absence of inducements as the explanatory variable. Compute the mean and standard deviation for both groups.

    b. Has the inducement reduced the age of the accounts receivable? Explain in terms that an accounting manager could understand.

    c. Why couldn't you use a cross-tabs table to organize the above data?

 4. The financial manager at COMCEL wants to know how profit margin, the net profit after taxes divided by sales, has done for the past 16 quarters in comparison to the industry average profit margin. Here are the data.

Quarter	COMCEL(%)	Industry(%)	Quarter	COMCEL(%)	Industry(%)
1	5.34	5.40	9	5.40	5.80
2	5.19	5.45	10	5.47	5.85
3	5.17	5.60	11	5.20	6.00
4	5.41	5.55	12	5.12	5.90
5	5.25	5.56	13	5.28	6.00
6	5.49	5.65	14	5.21	6.10
7	5.46	5.80	15	5.31	6.30
8	5.34	5.75	16	5.16	6.20

    a. Draw a multiple line graph that shows the profit margin at COMCEL and the industry average for the past 16 quarters.

    b. How do COMCEL's profit margins compare with the industry? Explain in terms that a financial manager could understand.

    c. Does the multiple line graph signal a problem for COMCEL?

 5. Length-of-tenure discounts are the differences between the rents charged long-time tenants and newer tenants. Is the discount size related to length of residence? Shown are data taken from 15 San Francisco apartment dwellers.

Size of Discount (%)	Years in Residence	Size of Discount (%)	Years in Residence
1.5	2	6.5	7
2.0	3	11.5	10
3.4	3	2.7	3
2.5	2	7.6	8
3.9	4	2.9	1
10.0	9	3.9	5
2.2	3	4.7	6
3.4	4		

    a. Draw a scatter plot for the cross-sectional data. Which is the more likely explanatory variable?

    b. Do the variables appear to be related? Explain the relationship in terms that a real estate broker could understand.

    c. Why shouldn't you use a one-way table to organize the data?

 6. An advertising manager wants to determine whether level of advertising is positively related to sales. If so, she may increase advertising. If the two variables are not related, she may reduce advertising. Shown are the most recent 20 months of sales and level of advertising data. Are the two variables related?

    a. Draw a scatter diagram for sales and level of advertising.

    b. Draw a scatter diagram for sales and the previous month's advertising.

    c. Which scatter diagram is more suggestive of a relationship between sales and level of advertising? Explain the relationship in terms that a marketing manager could understand.

Month	Sales (hundreds of units)	Advertising (thousands of dollars)
1	210	23.0
2	210	25.5
3	235	26.5
4	220	27.0
5	250	27.0
6	250	32.5
7	270	28.0
8	260	29.5
9	290	34.0
10	320	29.0
11	270	36.0
12	320	33.0
13	310	34.0
14	340	32.0
15	300	38.0
16	360	30.0
17	330	40.0
18	380	43.0
19	410	42.0
20	400	30.0

7. A stock analyst specializing in the retail industry wants to know if chain stores, such as JC Penney, stress the same focus—service or price—as do independents. She surveys 30 independents and 20 chains and determines if they are price- or service-oriented. Here are the data.

	Service	Price	Total
Independents	25	5	30
Chains	4	16	20
	29	21	50

a. Compute either row or column percentages.
b. Do chains have a different orientation than independents? Explain in terms that a marketing manager could understand.
c. Why shouldn't you use a one-way table to organize the data?

8. Most experts believe that the number of grievances filed increases with increasing numbers of employees. You wish to determine if this is true. You suspect that the statement may be true for plants in the Midwest but not in the South. You collect data on the following ten plants, five in each region.

Plant	Region	Workers	Grievances
1	S	200	50
2	S	400	55
3	S	250	55
4	S	150	60
5	MW	160	60
6	S	300	65
7	MW	210	70
8	MW	240	85
9	MW	310	90
10	MW	390	100

a. Draw a scatter plot with number of workers as the explanatory variable and the number of grievances as the dependent variable. Be sure to label the ten data points as either a Midwestern or Southern plant.

b. Does there appear to be any relationship between number of grievances and number of workers? Describe how the two variables are related in terms that a personnel manager could understand.

c. What is a logical follow-up question given your answer in part **b?**

9. The Arbitration Association collects data on the number of grievances filed by plants with between 200 and 300 workers. It wonders why the number of grievances varies from 45 to 99 among the ten firms. Could the large variability be related to a firm's use of participative management? It determines whether each firm uses participative management in the ten plants through a survey. Shown are the data.

Firms	Grievances	Participative Management
1	70	No
2	74	No
3	65	Yes
4	45	Yes
5	78	No
6	69	Yes
7	99	No
8	76	No
9	56	Yes
10	62	Yes

a. Using the absence or presence of participative management as an explanatory variable, construct a one-way table for the mean and standard deviation in the number of grievances filed.

b. Does it appear that participative management has an impact on the number of grievances? Explain in terms a manager could understand.

10. Is job attitude related to salary? Are people with higher salaries happier on the job than low-salaried people? Ten accounting managers are asked to indicate how satisfied they are on the job along a 5-point scale from 1 (very unsatisfied) to 5 (very satisfied). We also collect their salary data. Here are the cross-sectional data.

Manager	Salary	Job Attitude
1	38	1
2	38	4
3	40	3
4	36	2
5	46	2
6	43	5
7	50	2
8	52	2
9	54	4
10	56	2

a. Plot a scatter diagram with job attitude as an explanatory variable.

b. Does there appear to be a relationship between the two variables? Explain in simple terms.

c. Why do we need to use the word *appear* in part **b?**

d. Why can't you use a cross-tabs table to organize the data?

11. Do stress management programs minimize absenteeism? ABC Research conducts a study in which it selects 200 firms. One hundred firms have stress-reduction programs, and 100 do not have programs. It subdivides each group into firms with high and low absenteeism using industrywide average absenteeism figures.

	Absenteeism		
	Low	High	Total
Programs	40	60	100
No Programs	10	90	100
	50	150	200

a. Compute either the row or column percentages.

b. Do stress-reduction programs appear to affect absenteeism? Explain your conclusion to a human resources manager.

12. Each day the U.S. Park Service recorded the number of cars entering a beach area. After day 10, the number of cars began to drop. Could that drop be related to the mean daily temperature?

Day	Cars (thousands)	Mean Temperature
1	20	75
2	21	77
3	19	74
4	21	75
5	20	78
6	18	82
7	22	78
8	21	75
9	20	77
10	21	72
11	19	68
12	17	63
13	16	64
14	15	65
15	14	60

a. Draw a multiple line graph for both variables—number of cars and mean temperature. Remember, time in days is the independent variable.

b. What does the multiple line graph tell you? Explain your conclusion to the park administrator.

 13. Suppose a cross-tabs table suggests that market segment and milk preference appear to be related. Does including an intervening variable (weight of consumer) affect the relationship between the two market segments (Machos and Status Seekers) and their milk preferences (skim or whole milk)? Here are the data.

	Underweight Consumers		
	Machos	Status Seekers	Total
Skim	5	7	12
Whole	35	33	68
	40	40	80

Overweight Consumers

	Machos	Status Seekers	Total
Skim	50	48	98
Whole	10	12	22
	60	60	120

a. Compute row or column percentages for both cross-tabs tables.
b. With weight as an intervening variable, does it now appear that market segment and milk preference are related? Explain your conclusion to a marketing manager.

 14. The production manager of a COMCEL division is looking for a better way to plan production and to reduce excess inventory. Sales of the division are generated by "cold calling" by the sales staff and from calls initiated by potential customers. The manager hopes she can predict sales based on the quotes made by the sales staff. She collected data on the total dollar value of quotes given to prospective clients and also recorded the dollar volume of sales in that month over the past year. The data are shown.

Month	Quotes (thousands of dollars)	Sales (thousands of dollars)
1	20	13
2	15	12
3	10	9
4	17	7
5	25	11
6	15	15
7	18	10
8	20	12
9	20	12
10	14	11
11	18	9
12	12	11

a. Plot a scatter diagram for sales vs. quotes. Is quotes a coincident indicator of sales? Explain.
b. Is quotes a leading indicator of sales? Calculate the cross-correlation between sales and quotes for lag 1 and lag 2. Plot the scatter diagrams for lags 1 and 2.
c. How would you describe the relationship, if any, between sales and quotes?

 15. People with credit cards often mistakenly pay more than they owe and are given positive credit balances. Some people pay with bad checks, run up a credit balance, and then withdraw the credit balance in cash. An analyst with a small bank wonders whether there is a relationship between the number of credit balances over $1,000 in any week and the percentage of these accounts that are fraudulent. The only data at hand are the number of accounts showing credit balances above $1,000 and the number of fraud cases involving cash withdrawal for each week.
a. Plot scatter diagrams of the data at lags 0, 1, and 2. Treat fraud cases as the dependent variable and accounts as the independent variable.
b. Calculate cross-correlations for these lags.
c. Does there appear to be a relationship between the number of accounts with credit balances over $1,000 and the number of fraud cases involving withdrawal of credit balances in cash?

Week	Accounts with More than $1,000 in Credit	Fraud Cases Involving Cash Withdrawal
1	12	17
2	20	17
3	14	8
4	17	10
5	16	9
6	12	10
7	15	9
8	13	7
9	7	9
10	14	8
11	20	4
12	16	7

16. A marketing manager runs a study in which he tries two advertising strategies to sell tooth-paste. His goal is to increase market share. He selects ten test markets and tries each marketing approach in five test markets. He records the change in market share from last quarter's market share.

Strategy	Test Market	Increase in Market Share (%)
Comparison to Other Brands	1	3
	2	4
	3	5
	4	6
	5	12
Use of Star Performers	6	0
	7	1
	8	1
	9	2
	10	5

a. Draw a multiple box plot for both marketing strategies.
b. Which marketing strategy should the manager implement? Discuss.

17. A financial analyst believes that firms that produce high-quality products have higher returns on investment than those firms that produce less-reliable products. Product quality is rated from 50 for low-quality to 100 for high-quality. Shown are data collected on 10 firms in 2 different industries.

Firm	Industry	Average Product Quality	Return on Investment
1	Stereo	90	17.5
2	Stereo	50	8.7
3	Paper	50	8.8
4	Paper	70	7.8
5	Paper	90	8.0
6	Stereo	70	15.4
7	Stereo	100	22.5
8	Paper	100	7.8
9	Stereo	60	13.5
10	Paper	60	8.2

a. Plot the data.

b. Is product quality related to return on investment across both industries or in either industry?

18. Is the use of LIFO (Last In First Out) and FIFO (First In First Out) affected by the rate of inflation? That is, do firms tend to use LIFO in times of high inflation (above 6%) and FIFO in times of lower inflation ($\leq 6\%$)? Here are hypothetical results of a survey of firms.

	Low Inflation	High Inflation
LIFO	10	190
FIFO	100	100

a. Compute either row or column percentages.

b. Is use of LIFO or FIFO related to the level of inflation? Explain in terms that an accounting manager could understand.

19. Will small farms survive into the 21st century? The multiple line graph shown on page 167 illustrates the number of farms and the mean number of acres per farm since 1920. [*Source: Empty Breadbasket?*, The Cornucopia Project of the Rodale Press, 1981, p. 16.]

a. What does the multiple line graph show?

b. If both trends continue, describe the farming community in the 21st century.

20. The Myers-Briggs Type Indicator (MBTI) measures four dimensions of human behavior. One dimension is how people make judgments. They are either thinkers (T) or feelers (F). Thinkers use logic and analysis; feelers stress feelings and impacts on people. Do thinkers and feelers choose different careers? One hundred preschool teachers and 86 computer systems analysts are interviewed. Each completes the MBTI. The cross-tabs data are shown here. [*Source: Manual: A Guide to the Development of the Myers-Briggs Type Indicator,* Myers and McCaulley, 1985, pp. 248–250.]

	Thinker	Feeler	Total
Preschool Teacher	21	79	100
Computer Analyst	66	20	86

a. Is the thinker-feeler dimension related to job preference?

b. Does it appear that thinkers and feelers choose different careers?

21. The Consumer Price Index (CPI) is the most commonly used measure of inflation. The index measures the average change in prices relative to a base year for a common bundle of goods and services bought by a consumer on a regular basis. Two important groups within the index are energy costs and medical care costs. Are both groups rising at the about the same rate over the past 27 years? Shown are data of the CPI for energy costs and medical care for 1960–1987. [*Source: U.S. Bureau of Labor Statistics, Monthly Labor Review, and Handbook of Labor.*]

Year	1960	1965	1970	1975	1980	1981	1982	1983	1984	1985	1986	1987
Energy	22.4	22.9	25.5	42.1	86.0	97.7	99.2	99.9	100.9	101.6	88.2	88.6
Medical	22.3	25.2	34.0	47.5	74.9	82.9	92.5	100.6	106.8	113.5	122.0	130.1

a. Construct a scatter diagram. Plot the energy price index on the horizontal axis.

b. Interpret the graph. What can you conclude?

c. What other format could you use to show how the two components of the CPI have varied over the past 27 years?

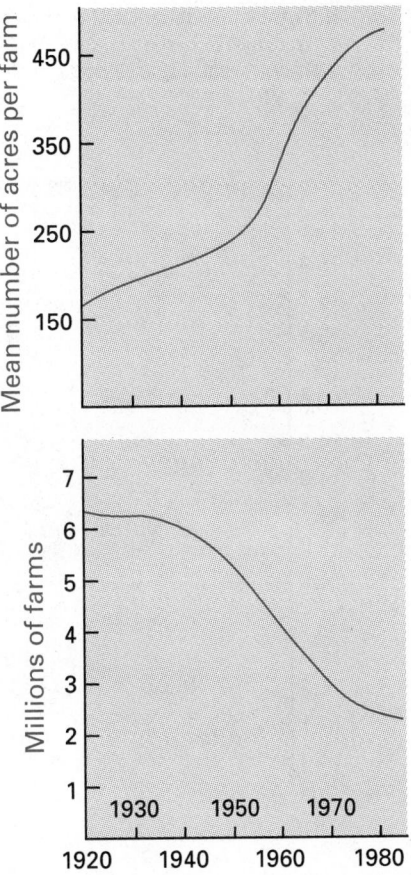

 22. The multiple line graphs on page 168 contain the mean and standard deviation of weights of boxes of cereal taken each day off a production line. On day 5 the process mean was too low, meaning that the boxes were being underfilled. The firm took corrective action. On day 10 the standard deviation increased, meaning the variability in weights was beyond what the firm desired. Again the firm took action. Did the actions correct the problem? Explain.

23. Franchised businesses represent about 40% of all U.S. retail sales. Is the franchise fee affected by the number of franchises? Shown are data on the 10 largest franchisers in America. [*Source: The Franchise Handbook, 1989.*]

Name of Company	Franchise Fee (dollars)	Number of Franchises
Century 21 Real Estate	18,000	7,005
Dairy Queen	30,000	5,122
Wendy's	25,000	2,597
TCBY Yogurt	20,000	1,240
Jiffy Lube	35,000	1,000
Computerland	25,000	800
West Coast Video	40,000	700
Thrift Rent-a-Car	7,500	655
Supercuts	17,500	508
Merry Maids	17,500	425

a. Is franchise fee related to the number of franchises? That is, do firms that have more
franchises charge greater franchise fees?

b. If not, what might the cost of the franchise be related to?

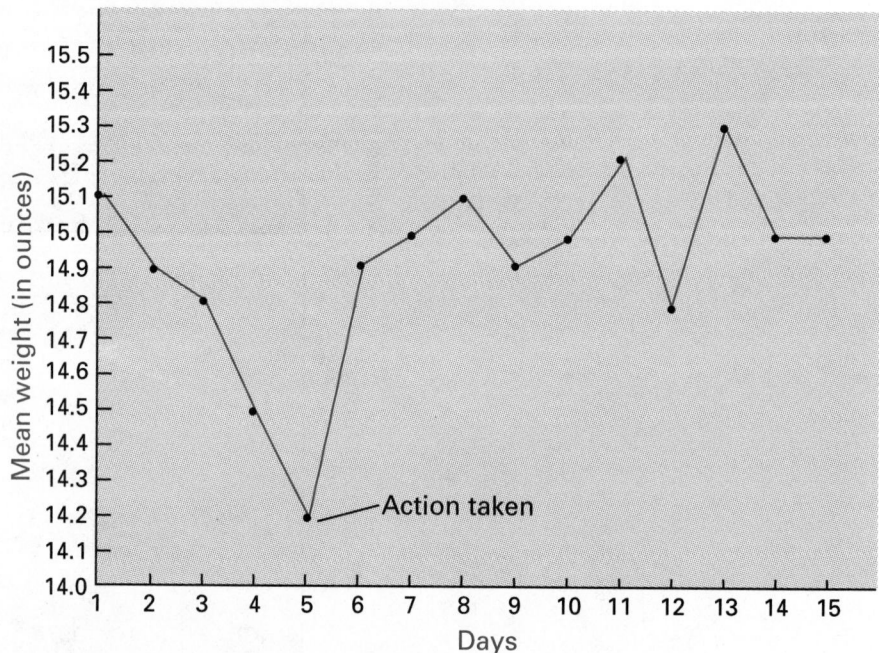

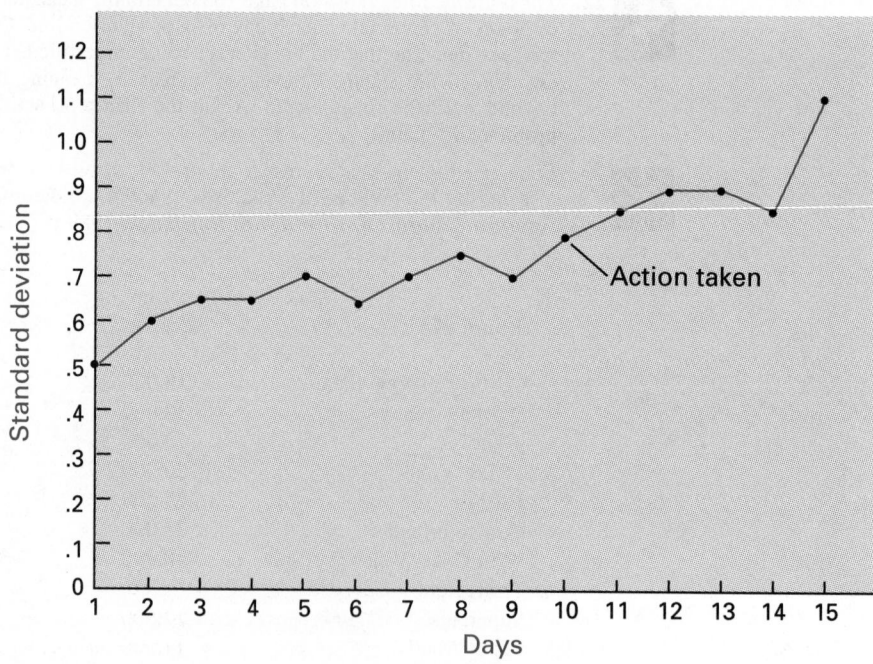

24.

Date: June 23, 1992
To: Nat Gordon, Vice President of Manufacturing
From: Ann Tabor, CEO
Re: Monthly Attendance at Two Operating Plants

I received your report that noted that the Dallas plant monthly attendance figures exceed those of the Norcross plant. I noticed that management employees in both plants have higher monthly attendance figures. That, of course, does not surprise me. However, I am disturbed that there is so much variation in monthly attendance within each plant and between the two plants. We must determine the underlying root causes.

Please assign your best analysts to investigate the situation to determine possible reasons for the differences within and between plants. Once we know some causes, we can consider possible corrective actions. As always, I need your analysis quickly—no later than July 10.

Use Data Base I in Appendix 9 for your analysis. Your response to Ann Tabor should include a brief memo and your analysis.

25.

Date: January 7, 1991
To: Pam Asher, Manager of South Marketing Region
From: Bill O'Hara, Vice President of Marketing
Re: Analysis of Atlanta Sales Growth

Both Ann and I appreciated your informative report. Also, congratulations on the excellent sales growth. We noted that sales have been steadily increasing and that the second and third quarters tend to be strong sales periods. What accounts for our increasing sales in Atlanta? What are you doing to obtain this growth? If we can determine what influences sales, we can help other regions experience the same growth as Atlanta.

I also noticed that you had unusually high and low sales in the fourth quarter of 1988 and the third quarter of 1990, respectively. Any ideas as to what caused these? Did anything unusual happen during those quarters? Did you or your competition make any changes? Don't spend too much time on this as our first concern is to understand what factors influence your sales growth.

We will need a preliminary analysis by February 10.

Use Data Base II in Appendix 9 for your analysis. Your response to Bill O'Hara should include a brief memo and your analysis.

APPENDIX Statistical Software

Example: Here we use SAS to study the relationship between work group productivity and job switching behavior. Table 3.2 contains the input data. SAS provides summary statistics for the job switching and no job switching groups. It also constructs a one-way, two-level table. (Table 3.3.) After converting the productivity variable into a categorical variable, SAS constructs the cross-tabs table shown in Table 3.4. Recall that the median productivity level for the 36 work groups was 100% of standard.

Input

```
01      DATA TEST;
02      INPUT PRODUCT SWITCH $ @@;
03      LABEL PRODUCT = 'PRODUCTIVITY'
04           SWITCH = 'JOB SWITCHING';
05      GROUP = "LOW";
06      IF PRODUCT >= 100 THEN GROUP = "HIGH";
07      LABEL GROUP = 'PRODUCTIVITY LEVEL';
08      CARDS;
09         106  YES   95  NO 103 YES   95  NO   95 YES   97  NO
10          95  NO  105 YES 102 YES   89  NO  105 YES   99 YES
11          95  NO  100 YES 106 YES 101 YES   97  NO  104 YES
12         110  YES 123 YES 104 YES 100 YES 101 YES   95  NO
13          97  NO   94  NO 102  NO 102 YES 106 YES 110 YES
14          97  NO  101 YES  95  NO  98 YES  97 YES   94  NO
15   PROC SORT; BY GROUP;
16   PROC UNIVARIATE; VAR PRODUCT; BY GROUP;
17   PROC FREQ; TABLES GROUP*SWITCH;
```

Explanation of Input

01   See Chapter 2 Appendix for explanation of line 1.

02   Two variables, PRODUCT and SWITCH, will be read into the TEST file. SAS expects the SWITCH variable to be non-numeric because it is followed by a $ sign. See Chapter 2 Appendix for more explanation of line 2.

03–04   See Chapter 2 Appendix for explanation of lines 3-4.

05   This line defines a new nonnumeric variable called GROUP and assigns it the value "LOW". GROUP refers to productivity level of a work group. Enclose referenced or assigned values of nonnumeric variables in double quotes.

06   If the value of the PRODUCT variable is greater than or equal to the median value of 100, then the value of the GROUP variable will be changed from "LOW" to "HIGH".

08   CARDS tells SAS that data will follow.

15   Instructs SAS to sort the TEST file into two subfiles, one containing cases where GROUP = "LOW" productivity and the other where GROUP = "HIGH" productivity.

16   Instructs SAS to provide UNIVARIATE statistics for the PRODUCTivity data for each subfile or GROUP.

17   Instructs SAS to produce a cross-tabs table using GROUP productivity as the row variable and SWITCH as the column variable.

Interpretation of Output

A&B   Shows univariate statistics for each group (SWITCH=YES and SWITCH=NO). The statistics are the very similar to Table 3.3 with one exception. The IQR for the no job switch group is 2.0% in the text and 2.25% in SAS. For an explanation of the difference, see interpretation of B section of SAS output for Chapter 2.

C   Refer to the cell at the intersection of the first row and first column. The 1 is the number of groups that did not switch jobs and were high producing (above 100%). The cell frequency of 1 is 2.78% (1/36) of all the cases in the table. The cell frequency of 1 is 5.26% of the GROUP="HIGH" cases (1/19), and is 7.14% of the cases (1/14) that did not switch jobs. Note: The row headers in Table 3.4 and the SAS output are reversed.

Output

A
```
                              JOB SWITCHING=NO

                               UNIVARIATE

VARIABLE=PRODUCT              PRODUCTIVITY


                               MOMENTS

        N               14    SUM WGTS             14
        MEAN          95.5    SUM                1337
        STD DEV    2.76656    VARIANCE        7.65385
        SKEWNESS 0.0254293    KURTOSIS        3.68139
        USS         127783    CSS                99.5
        CV         2.89692    STD MEAN       0.739394
        T:MEAN=0    129.16    PROB>|T|         0.0001
        SGN RANK      52.5    PROB>|S|    .000959969
        NUM ^= 0        14
```
```
          QUANTILES(DEF=4)                                        EXTREMES

100%  MAX      102      99%          102          LOWEST      HIGHEST
 75%  Q3        97      95%          102              89           97
 50%  MED       95      90%         99.5              94           97
 25%  Q1     94.75      10%         91.5              94           97
  0%  MIN       89       5%           89              95           97
                         1%           89              95          102

RANGE           13
Q3-Q1         2.25
MODE            95
```
```
                                 SAS
```

B
```
                             JOB SWITCHING=YES

                               UNIVARIATE

VARIABLE=PRODUCT              PRODUCTIVITY


                               MOMENTS

        N               22    SUM WGTS             22
        MEAN        103.545    SUM               2278
        STD DEV     5.7795    VARIANCE        33.4026
        SKEWNESS   1.80073    KURTOSIS        5.37443
        USS         236578    CSS             701.455
```

```
CV              5.5816   STD MEAN      1.23219
T:MEAN=0       84.0335   PROB>|T|       0.0001
SGN RANK        126.5    PROB>|S|       0.0001
NUM ^= 0          22
```

QUANTILES(DEF=4)   EXTREMES

					LOWEST	HIGHEST
100% MAX	123	99%	123		95	106
75% Q3	106	95%	121.05		97	106
50% MED	102.5	90%	110		98	110
25% Q1	100	10%	97.3		99	110
0% MIN	95	5%	95.3		100	123
		1%	95			

```
RANGE           28
Q3-Q1            6
MODE           101
```

SAS

C

TABLE OF GROUP BY SWITCH

GROUP(PRODUCTIVITY LEVEL)
     SWITCH(JOB SWITCHING)

FREQUENCY PERCENT ROW PCT COL PCT	NO	YES	TOTAL
HIGH	1 2.78 5.26 7.14	18 50.00 94.74 81.82	19 52.78
LOW	13 36.11 76.47 92.86	4 11.11 23.53 18.18	17 47.22
TOTAL	14 38.89	22 61.11	36 100.00

BASIC PROBABILITY CONCEPTS

4.1   Introduction
4.2   Probability concepts
      Event
      Frequency of an event
      Relative frequency of an event
      The law of large numbers
      Probability of an event
      Basic rules of probability
      What the law of large numbers does not say
      Personal probability
4.3   Picturing probabilities: Introduction to the
          probability tree
      Joint probability table
      Probability tree diagram
4.4   Joint and union probabilities
      Union probability: Combining two events
          using OR

4.5   Conditional probabilities and statistical
          independence
      Conditional probability
      Statistical independence and dependence
4.6   Computing conditional probabilities
      Distinguishing between conditional and joint
          probabilities
      Conditional probabilities and row or column
          percentage tables
4.7   Using probability trees to minimize
          managerial judgment errors
      The error of overlooking the base rate
      Noncoherency error
4.8   Nonstatistical judgment errors
      Availability error
      Concreteness error
4.9   Key ideas and overview

COMCEL INTEROFFICE COMMUNICATION

Date: September 4, 1992
To: Sarah Teman, Manager of Operations
From: Howard Bright, Plant Manager
Re: Improving Work Group Productivity

An article in Forbes indicated that companies have been successful in improving productivity by encouraging members of work groups to learn each others' jobs. Switching jobs reduces the monotony and boredom of performing a single task, eight hours a day, and leads to less reworking and improved productivity.

I know that some of our work groups have, on their own initiative, started switching jobs. Is there any evidence that these work groups have higher productivity levels than those groups that have not?

Please look into this for me, and give me your recommendation. The fact that job switching was successful in other companies does not mean it will work for us. However, if job switching is related to higher productivity, I will put it on the agenda for the next meeting of the Senior Team. We may want to make job switching a company policy.

176

4.1 ≡ Introduction

Chapter 2 showed how to use the mean, range, standard deviation, trimmed mean, median, and interquartile range to sense possible emerging problems. Chapter 3 described how to organize and interpret data through one-way tables, multiple box plots, cross-tabs tables, scatter diagrams, and multiple line graphs. These tools help you sense and diagnose problems. Chapter 4 will help you to use probability to make estimates, or judgments, under *uncertain* conditions.

Consider the following situation. The director of planning for a utility company must determine if additional power generating plants are needed for the year 2000. She believes that it depends on whether (1) consumers will increase their conservation efforts and (2) the federal government will change tax policy to permit taxpayers to deduct conservation costs, such as installing insulation, double-pane windows, and power-saving thermostats, from their tax bills.

The director is uncertain about future conservation efforts and federal tax policies. She personally believes there is a .50 chance of increased consumer conservation efforts and a .60 chance that the federal government will allow taxpayers to deduct conservation costs. If the federal tax policy does permit deductions for conservation costs, the chance of increased conservation will be higher than her .50 estimate, say .85.

The three probability estimates—.50, .60, and .85—cannot all be correct. They violate one of the rules of probability. You will know why by the end of the chapter.

Managers talk about chances everyday. What is the chance that consumers will increase conservation efforts? What is the chance that the federal tax policy will permit deducting conservation costs? The official name for chance is probability. Managers must understand probability. They may make poor decisions if they base future plans on questionable probabilities.

4.2 ≡ Probability Concepts

A random experiment is an action that, when repeated over many trials, produces a set of definite outcomes or values. We cannot predict with certainty which value will occur on any trial. However, there is a predictable long-run pattern in the values.

To understand probability, we introduce the concept of a **random experiment**. Consider the following random experiment: Walk into a store that has 35 salespeople on its staff and count the number of salespeople on the floor. Now repeat this experiment many times. You will find that the number of salespeople on the floor can be one of 36 possible values—0, 1, 2, . . . , 35. However, we cannot predict with certainty the number of salespeople we will find in any one visit. There is randomness or unpredictability. However, over many trials or visits, we would find a long-run pattern. Perhaps most of the time there are between 20 and 25 salespeople on the floor, and rarely are there fewer than 10 salespeople on the floor.

By the end of this section you should be able to:

1. explain in your own words the following terms: event, frequency of an event, relative frequency of an event, and probability of an event;
2. distinguish between relative frequency and probability;
3. explain what the law of large numbers is and is not;
4. explain the two basic rules of probability; and
5. distinguish between relative frequency-based probability and personal probability.

Here are five random experiments that we have repeated many times and a list of their possible values.

Random Experiment	Possible Values	Example of Values
Walk into a store with 35 salespeople once. Count the number of salespeople on the floor.	Any integer number between 0 and 35, inclusive	0, 1, 6, 20
Select a work group. Record whether the group members switched jobs or not.	Two possibilities— Switch or Not switch	Switch
Flip a coin five times. Count the number of heads.	Any integer number between 0 and 5, inclusive	0, 3, 5
Ask one family its annual income.	Any number between $0 and $100 million	$3,345, $152,000.06
Select one 12-ounce can of peaches and weigh the contents.	Any number between 11.90 ounces and 12.10 ounces	11.965 oz., 12.04 oz.

As was noted earlier, the number of salespeople on the floor can be any of 36 possible values—0, 1, 2, 3, 4, . . . , 35. The status of job switching can be either of two possible values—yes or no. The number of heads in five flips can be any of six possible values—0, 1, 2, 3, 4, or 5 heads. There are millions of possible values for the fourth random experiment. Remember, one must include Bill Cosby's annual family income of over $70 million. The fifth experiment has an uncountable number of possible values. For example, the weight could be 12.00456745 ounces. If we round off weight to the nearest hundredth of an ounce, then only 21 values are possible—11.90, 11.91, 11.92, . . . , 12.10.

Given the definition of a random experiment, we are now ready to define an **event**.

An event is a collection of one or more values from a random experiment.

Event

There are several types of events. A *simple event* can take on only one value out of all possible values of the repeated random experiment. Finding exactly zero salespeople is a simple event. So is getting five heads in five coin flips or recording an income of $13,345.00.

A *compound event* includes two or more values from a repeated random experiment. Entering a store and finding between four and seven salespeople is a compound event. Selecting a family and recording an annual income between $10,000 and $15,000 is also a compound event. The first compound event contains four values—four, five, six, and seven salespeople. If we round off annual income to the nearest dollar and include the $10,000 and $15,000 figures, the second compound event contains 5,001 values.

For any simple or compound event there is a *complementary event* that consists of all other possible values of a repeated random experiment. Following is a list of two events and their complements. $13,454 is a simple event. Its complement is a compound event that includes all possible values of the repeated random experiment except $13,454. The event, more than 30 salespeople on the floor, is a compound event. Its complement is also a compound event—namely, 30 or fewer salespeople on the floor. Note that an event, simple or compound, and its complement together account for all possible outcomes of a repeated random experiment.

Event	Complementary Event
Income of $13,454	All incomes other than $13,454
More than 30 salespeople on the floor	30 or fewer salespeople on the floor

Frequency of an Event

The frequency of an event, A, is the number of times the event occurs over a number of trials, or repetitions, of a random experiment. Suppose we walk into a store $n = 100$ times and record the number of times we find at least 20 salespeople on the floor. Or suppose we interview $n = 1,000$ families and count the number of families whose income is greater than $50,000. We use the following notation to record the data.

$$\text{Frequency}_{100} \text{ (at least 20 salespeople)} = 90$$

$$\text{Frequency}_{1,000} \text{ (income greater than \$50,000)} = 50$$

In 90 out of the 100 trials, we counted at least 20 salespeople on the floor. In 50 out of the 1,000 trials, we found families with incomes greater than $50,000.

Relative Frequency of an Event

When we conduct a random experiment n times (over n trials), the relative frequency of an event A is equal to the number of times A happens divided by the number of trials.

The **relative frequency** of an event is the fraction of times that an event occurs in a given number (n) of trials. The following notation is used to express relative frequency:

$$\text{Relative frequency } (A) = \frac{\text{Frequency } (A)}{n} \tag{4.1}$$

The relative frequency of finding at least 20 salespeople is simply the number of times we found 20 or more salespeople divided by the total number of trials, or store visits. The relative frequency of finding families with incomes greater than $50,000 is the number of times we found a family with an income greater than $50,000 divided by the total number of trials, or number of families interviewed. Thus,

$$\text{Relative frequency (at least 20 salespeople)} = \frac{90}{100} = .90$$

$$\text{Relative frequency (income greater than \$50,000)} = \frac{50}{1,000} = .05$$

Rare events, those that are not likely to occur, will have small relative frequencies. For example, in only 5% of the 1,000 trials or interviews did we find a family with an income greater than $50,000.

Common events, those that occur often, will have relative frequencies near 1. For example, the relative frequency of finding at least 20 salespeople on the floor is .90.

The Law of Large Numbers

According to the law of large numbers, every event has a fixed value called a probability, such that if a random experiment is repeated a very large number of times, then the relative frequency of the event will approach the fixed value. The more times the random experiment is repeated, the greater the stability of the relative frequency.

The relative frequency of an event is a useful indicator of the chance that an event will occur. But relative frequency has one drawback. It will change as the number of trials of the repeated random experiment increases. Fortunately, the relative frequency is more stable if the random experiment is repeated many times. Stability means the following. If two people interview two sets of 10 families and count the number with incomes greater than $50,000, they may get very different relative frequencies. If they interview two sets of 100,000 families and count the number with incomes greater than $50,000, then the two relative frequencies will be nearly identical. This demonstrates the **law of large numbers**.

Figure 4.1 illustrates the law of large numbers. Consider an event that has a probability of .8. The probability is represented by the horizontal line. The jagged line represents how the relative frequency tends to stabilize and in general becomes closer to the probability of the event. However, note that even after 150 trials, the relative frequency and probability of the event are not yet equal.

Probability of an Event

The probability, or chance, of an event represents the proportion of trials in which the event will happen in the long run. It is a fixed, or nonchanging, number between 0 and 1, inclusive, that represents the relative frequency of the event if the random experiment were repeated an infinite number of times.

Probabilities are precise descriptions of randomness. An event may be unpredictable and yet have a probability of .80. The event would occur in 80% of the trials if the random experiment were repeated forever and ever. A probability near 0 suggests a rare event, whereas a probability near 1 suggests a nearly certain event. A probability of .5 suggests an event that has the same chance of occurring as not occurring.

Basic Rules of Probability

In probability, there are two very basic and simple rules or principles to remember.

Rule 1:   Probabilities are numbers whose values lie between 0 and 1.0 inclusive.

If there is absolutely no chance of an event occurring, it happens in 0% of the trials. If the event always occurs, it happens in 100% of the trials. Since an event cannot occur in less than 0% of the trials, it cannot have a negative probability, and since an event cannot occur more often than in all the trials, it cannot have a probability greater than 1.

FIGURE 4.1

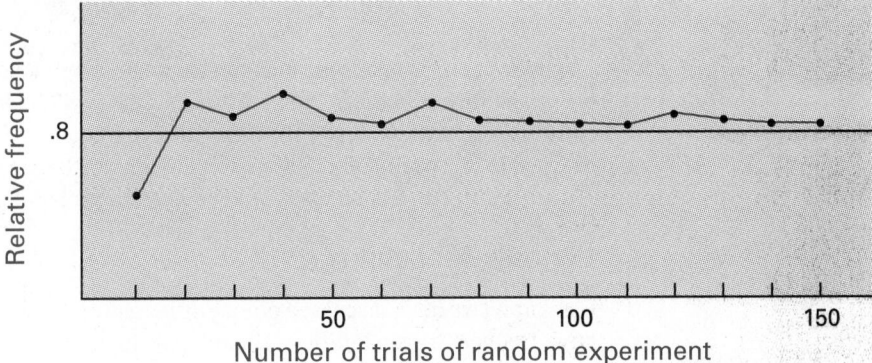

Rule 2: The sum of the probabilities of all the possible non-overlapping events that can occur must be 1.0.

Recall the random experiment where 1,000 families were surveyed. Suppose we define two events—incomes of $50,000 or less and incomes greater than $50,000. Now we interview 100,000 families. Isn't it clear that the sum of the two relative frequencies must be 1.0? Similarly, the sum of the probabilities of the two events must also equal 1.0.

From Rule 2, we also know that the sum of the probabilities of an event, A, and its complement, $\bar{A}$, (read as not A) must be 1.0. Remember, an event and its complement include all the possible non-overlapping events. Thus, by Rule 2,

$$P(A) + P(\bar{A}) = 1.0 \tag{4.2}$$

$$P(A) = 1.0 - P(\bar{A}) \tag{4.3}$$

The notation $P(A)$ means the probability of event A happening.

What the Law of Large Numbers Does Not Say

What is wrong with the following reasoning? You toss a fair coin 10 times and get 10 consecutive heads. A friend argues that the "law of averages" says you are very likely to get a tail on the 11th flip. Is he correct?

Contrary to what would-be gamblers, muddleheaded managers, or confused friends say, the answer is no. The coin has no memory. It does not remember what happened on the first 10 trials. Statistically speaking, we say that the trials, or coin flips, are independent. The probability of getting a head with a fair coin always remains ½. Now the chance of getting 10 heads in a row is very small. But if you did, the chance of getting a tail on the next trial does not increase.

Since the probability of getting a head for a fair coin is .5, shouldn't we expect some tails to balance out the 10 heads obtained? Yes, but that does not increase the probability of getting a tail in any individual trial. Suppose that we flip the coin an additional 9,990 times for a total of 10,000 flips. Imagine that half (4,995) of the next 9,990 flips are heads and the other half are tails. These events are tabulated here along with their relative frequencies of heads.

Number of Trials	Relative Frequency of Heads
10	10/10 = 1.0000
9,990	4,995/9,990 = .5000
10,000	(10 + 4,995)/10,000 = .5005

Now it is true that in the long run the relative frequency of getting a head must equal the probability of getting a head. which is .5. If you obtained an equal number of heads and tails over the next 9,990 flips, the relative frequency for the 10,000 trials would still be close to .5, specifically .5005, even though you began with 10 straight heads.

In short, there is no "law of averages" in probability.

Personal Probability

Until now, we have discussed probabilities estimated from relative frequencies or relative frequency probabilities. The relative frequency viewpoint is useful when valid historical data are available. The relative frequency viewpoint is not useful when assessing the chance of a never-before-happened event. For example, what is the probability that a new boss will change the dress policy? What is the probability that a new microcomputer will outsell its major competitors in the next quarter? For a first-time event we need personal, or subjective, probabilities. Personal probabilities are also numbers whose values lie between 0 and 1, inclusive, but they reflect one's personal beliefs and biases about the chance of an event happening.

Personal probabilities are still subject to the same two basic rules as are relative frequency probabilities. That is, personal probability is a number between 0 and 1, and the sum of the personal probabilities for all the possible non-overlapping events must be 1. We would assign a personal probability of 0 if we were *absolutely* sure that the event would not occur; we would assign a personal probability of 1 if we were *absolutely* sure that the event would occur. The more certain we are that the event will occur, the greater would be our personal probability of the event.

There's good news and bad news regarding personal probabilities. The good news is that they are very easy to assign. The bad news is that they are very easy to assign. Irrelevant factors (see Section 4.7) often influence a manager's personal probability estimates.

Let's illustrate how irrelevant factors may affect personal probability estimates. For example, is a person more likely to die from an accidental fall or from an accidental discharge of a firearm? What are your personal probability estimates for both events? Please think about it before reading on.

Many people believe that death due to an accidental discharge of a firearm is more likely. That is because such deaths make the evening news. According to psychologists Amos Tversky and Daniel Kahneman (1974, 1981), the probabilities of dramatic, sensational causes of death that get heavy media coverage are overestimated. Data from the U.S. Public Health Service show that the probability of accidental death from falling is many times greater than from a discharge of a firearm. People's probability beliefs may be biased by the amount of media exposure—an irrelevant factor.

Personal probabilities are subject to all the biases that humans have. A manager might overestimate future sales because he reads in the *Wall Street Journal* that a competing firm has recently had greater-than-expected sales, or a manager may underestimate sales because a friend's firm had a sudden drop in sales. The friend's firm is in an unrelated industry and so the manager has been influenced by what may be an irrelevant factor. Now it is true that there are no "correct" personal probabilities. Unlike relative frequency probabilities, we cannot determine them by running a random experiment over many trials. However, to be useful, personal probabilities must be free of irrelevant factors.

Managers often develop erroneous personal probability estimates. Previously a case was discussed where a director of planning generated three personal probability estimates—.50, .60, and .85. While these estimates reflect her thinking about the future, they are not valid for they violate the first rule of probability. This will be explained further in Section 4.7.

In summary, managers use relative frequencies to estimate probabilities of events. Managers also use personal probabilities when reliable historical data are unavailable. Both probabilities must obey the two rules of probability. However, personal probability has one singular drawback. Irrelevant factors may influence a manager's personal probability assessments. To avoid this problem to some degree, have several managers *independently* generate personal probabilities and then develop *consensus* probability estimates. This may minimize the impact of irrelevant factors on personal probabilities.

SECTION 4.2 EXERCISES

1. State which of the following could be classified as a random experiment and explain why.
   a. Buying five state lottery tickets and recording the amount won
   b. Observing and recording the temperature at any time of the day
   c. Driving to work
   d. Selecting an item from an assembly line and counting the number of defects
   e. Watching the World Series and recording whether the National League team wins or loses
   f. Entering a store and watching the people
   g. Reading the paper and enjoying it.
   h. Selecting five items from a production line and computing their mean weight.

2. Consider the following random experiment: record the parcel delivery time for an intracity courier service.
   a. Explain why recording delivery times is a random experiment.
   b. What type of event is a delivery time of 45.0 minutes?
   c. What type of event is delivery times between 45 and 50 minutes?
   d. What is the complementary event to part **b?**
   e. What is the complementary event to part **c?**
   f. Under what conditions, if any, can the relative frequency of the event in part **c** be less than zero, or greater than one?
   g. Suppose that in 100 deliveries, there were 15 deliveries between 45 and 50 minutes. Compute the relative frequency.
   h. If we recorded 10,000 delivery times, would we expect the relative frequency of a delivery time of between 45 and 50 minutes to be the same as in part **g?** Explain using the Law of Large Numbers.
   i. Based on the Law of Large Numbers, would you expect your answer in part **g** or part **h** to be closer to the true probability of a delivery time between 45 and 50 minutes?

3. Consider the following random experiment: A COMCEL operator records if the phone handset s(he) completed is an acceptable or defective (one or more scratches on the phone) unit.
   a. List all the possible values of this random experiment.
   b. Suppose that of 100 phones inspected, there are 3 defectives. Compute the relative frequency for defectives.
   c. Suppose that of 1,000 phones inspected, there are 22 defectives. Compute the relative frequency for defectives.
   d. Would you expect the relative frequencies in parts **b** and c to be the same? Why?
   e. Based on the Law of Large Numbers, would you expect your answer in part **b** or part **c** to be closer to the actual probability of finding a defective phone handset?

4. Consider the following random experiment: interview a head-of-household and record the household's annual income.
   a. What type of event is an income over $100,000?
   b. What type of event is an income of $17,456?
   c. What is the complementary event to part **a?**
   d. What is the complementary event to part **b?**
   e. Under what conditions, if any, can the relative frequency of the event in part **a** be less than zero, or greater than one?
   f. Suppose that in 100 families, there were 6 families with incomes over $100,000. Compute the relative frequency.
   g. If we interviewed 10,000 families, would we expect the relative frequency of a family with an income of over $100,000 to be the same as in part **f?** Explain using the Law of Large Numbers.
   h. Based on the Law of Large Numbers, would you expect your answer in part **f** or part **g** to be closer to the true probability of a family income of over $100,000?

5. Consider the following random experiment: select five electronic components from a production line and compute their mean time to failure.
   a. What type of event is a mean time to failure of 1,500 hours?
   b. What type of event is a mean time to failure below 2,500 hours?
   c. What is the complementary event to part **a?**
   d. What is the complementary event to part **b?**

e. Under what conditions, if any, can the relative frequency of the event in part **b** be less than zero, or greater than one?

f. If the relative frequency of the event in part **b** is .95, is this a rare or common event?

g. Suppose that in 100 samples of size 5, 90 had mean times to failure below 2,500 hours. Compute the relative frequency.

h. If we examined 100,000 samples of size five, would we expect the relative frequency of a mean time to failure of below 2,500 hours to be the same as in part **g**? Explain using the Law of Large Numbers.

i. Based on the Law of Large Numbers, would you expect your answer in part **h** or part **g** to be closer to the true probability of a mean time to failure below 2,500 hours?

6. Over the past year a firm has purchased 10,000 replacement parts from the Acme Company. Approximately 5% of these parts were defective and had to be replaced by Acme. A shipment of 20 parts has just arrived from Acme. Can you predict the exact number of defective parts in this shipment? Explain.

7. A group of five people contains three females and two males. Suppose we put the peoples' names in a hat and select three people. The following outcomes are possible.

$$
\begin{array}{ccc}
F_1 & F_2 & F_3 \\
F_1 & F_2 & M_1 \\
F_1 & F_2 & M_2 \\
F_1 & F_3 & M_1 \\
F_1 & F_3 & M_2 \\
F_2 & F_3 & M_1 \\
F_2 & F_3 & M_2 \\
F_1 & M_1 & M_2 \\
F_2 & M_1 & M_2 \\
F_3 & M_1 & M_2
\end{array}
$$

a. Is selecting three people a random experiment? Why?

b. Is selecting three people and counting the number of females a random experiment? Why?

c. Suppose you decide to draw three people and count the number of females. List the possible numerical outcomes of this random experiment and calculate the relative frequency of each.

d. Why are the relative frequencies in part **c** equal to the true probabilities of each numerical outcome?

8. Suppose you rolled a single fair die and recorded the number of times each side came up. A fair die is one in which the chances of getting a 1, 2, 3, 4, 5, and 6 are the same. After 60 rolls, the frequencies were as shown below:

Die Face	Frequency
1	5
2	8
3	12
4	6
5	10
6	19
Total	60

a. Find the relative frequency of each outcome.

b. Is the relative frequency of the occurrence of 6 equal to the probability of rolling a 6? Why?

c. Make a relative frequency histogram of the data for 60 rolls.

d. Sketch what you think the relative frequency histogram might look like if you rolled the die 600 times. If it were rolled 6,000 times.

9. Suppose that 12% of U.S. households include four or more children. You select a random sample of 400 families and record the number of children in each household. The results are shown below.

Number of Children	Frequency
0	60
1	88
2	132
3	80
4 or more	40
Total	400

   a. What is the relative frequency of four or more children in the sample of households?
   b. What is the probability of selecting a family with four or more children from the whole U.S. population?
   c. Explain why the answers to parts **a** and **b** differ.

10. A newly formed consulting firm is preparing its first presentation to a prospective client. One member of the team says, "We have better than a 50% chance of making this sale." Why does this statement represent a personal probability, rather than a relative frequency probability?

11. An automobile salesperson claims to have a 20% chance of selling no cars today, a 50% chance of selling one car, and a 40% chance of selling two or more cars. Comment on the salesperson's knowledge of probability.

12. For Exercise 11, identify a simple event and a compound event.

13. A random experiment involves selecting an item from an assembly line and counting the number of defects. Suppose that the number of defects can vary between 0 and 5, inclusive.
   a. Is the event of one defect a simple event or a compound event?
   b. Define the complementary event to finding one defect.

14. We say that a probability is a fixed and nonchanging number between 0 and 1, inclusive. Given that definition, why doesn't the relative frequency of an event generally equal the probability of the event?

15. A real estate manager estimates the following probabilities for a condominium under construction.

Number of Units Sold in First Year	Probability
under 20	.10
20–29	.20
30–39	.30
40–49	.40
50 or more	.20

   a. Are the five probabilities personal or relative frequency-based?
   b. What, if anything, is wrong with the five probabilities?

16. A marketing manager has been asked to estimate the following three personal probabilities: sales significantly below expectations, close to expected sales, and sales significantly above expectations. She has trouble assigning numbers to the three events, but does provide the following qualitative information about her thinking.
   a. The probability of significantly below and significantly above expected sales are equal to one another.
   b. The probability of obtaining close to expected sales is twice as large as the other two probabilities.

Given this information and the second rule of probability, determine the manager's probabilities for the three events. *Hint:* Use either trial and error (try different probabilities and see if either rule 2 or the above two conditions is violated) or simple algebra.

17. A personnel manager has been asked to estimate the following four personal probabilities: no wildcat strike, a strike within the next month, a strike one to six months from now, and a strike more than six months from now. He has trouble assigning numbers to the four events, but does provide the following qualitative information about his thinking.
    a. The chances of no strike is "an even bet"—that is, equivalent to a flip of a fair coin.
    b. The chances of a strike within the next month is three times as likely as a strike more than six months from now.
    c. The chances of a strike one to six months from now is twice as likely as a strike more than six months from now.

    Given this information and the second rule of probability, determine the manager's probabilities for the four events. *Hint:* Use either trial and error (try different probabilies and see if either rule 2 or the above three conditions are violated) or simple algebra.

4.3 ▤ Picturing Probabilities: Introduction to the Probability Tree

In Chapter 3 you learned how to develop cross-tabs tables to cross-classify groups using two attributes or variables. We now extend the cross-tabs table to the joint probability table and construct probability trees. Probability trees help to visualize probabilities. By the end of this section you should be able to:

1. explain how the cross-tabs table and the joint probability table are similar and how they are different;
2. draw a probability tree from a joint probability table and vice versa; and
3. interpret the probabilities of a joint probability table or probability tree.

In Chapter 3, a 2 × 2 cross-tabs table for two categorical variables—productivity and job switching—was presented for 36 work groups. It is reproduced here.

Joint Probability Table

We can transform the cross-tabs frequency data in Table 4.1 into joint probabilities by simply dividing each entry by the total sample size, 36. The resulting numbers are between 0 and 1 and are shown in Table 4.2.

A joint probability is the probability of the joint event, event *A* and event *B*. The joint probability of event *A* and *B* is expressed as $P(A \text{ AND } B)$.

The four probabilities within the body of Table 4.2 are called **joint probabilities**. Let event *A* be a low-productivity group. Let event B be a group that does not switch jobs. Define a particular joint event as a group with low productivity and no job switching. From Table 4.2, that joint probability is .361. The joint probability is .50 that a work group will have high productivity and will switch jobs.

Table 4.1

Cross-Tabs Table for Productivity and Job-Switching Data

	No Job Switching	Job Switching	
Low Productivity	13	4	17
High Productivity	1	18	19
	14	22	36

Table 4.2

Joint Probability Table for Productivity and Job-Switching Data

marginal

	No Job Switching	Job Switching	
Low Productivity	.361	.111	.472
High Productivity	.028	.500	.528
	.389	.611	1.000

Table 4.1 is based on 36 work groups. Since there are only 36 work groups in COMCEL's Norcross plant, the sample equals the entire population. When cross-tabs tables are based on the entire population, frequency counts convert directly to joint probabilities. When cross-tabs tables are based on a portion of the population, dividing the frequency counts by 36 produces joint relative frequencies, which are only *estimates* of joint probabilities.

Probability Tree Diagram

We can use the joint probability table, Table 4.2, to build a probability tree as shown in Figure 4.2. In this case, it does not make any difference which categorical variable is placed near the top of the tree—productivity or job switching. In Figure 4.2, the productivity variable has been placed closer to the top of the tree. The two boxes are labelled low productivity and high productivity. For each level of productivity we draw two more boxes that represent no job switching and job switching. Thus there are four *end boxes* at the bottom of the tree.

Insert the following joint probabilities from Table 4.2 into the four end boxes of the probability tree.

Not switching jobs AND having low productivity .361
Switching jobs AND having low productivity .111
Not switching jobs AND having high productivity .028
Switching jobs AND having high productivity .500

The four joint probabilities sum to 1.0, because these four joint events are non-overlapping and cover all possible outcomes. That is, two levels of productivity and two levels of job switching produce four possible events. Thus, by the second rule of probability, the four probabilities must sum to 1.0.

Now we can compute the probabilities for the remaining boxes as shown in Figure 4.3. The probability for the low-productivity box equals .361 + .111 = .472. The probability for the high-productivity box equals .028 + .500 = .528. The probability for the uppermost box equals .472 + .528 = 1.0, which is the sum of the probabilities of all boxes below it in the tree. Why? Please think about it before reading on.

There are two ways to be a low-productivity group:

1. Low productivity AND no job switch
2. Low productivity AND job switch

The sum of the two probabilities must be the probability of being a low productivity group:

Conditional probability

$$P(\text{low productivity}) = P(\text{low productivity AND no job switch})$$
$$+ P(\text{low productivity AND job switch})$$
$$= .361 + .111 = .472$$

Similarly, the probability of being a high-productivity group must be the sum of the joint probabilities, .028 + .500 = .528.

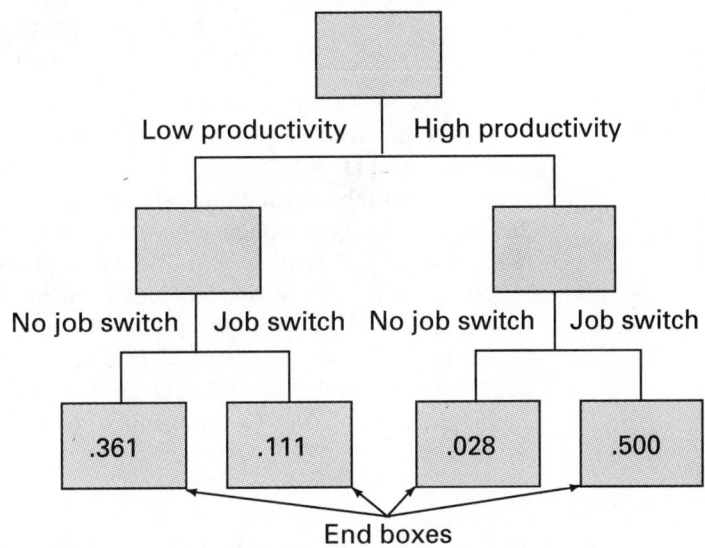

FIGURE 4.2   Partially Completed Probability Tree for Productivity and Job-Switching Data

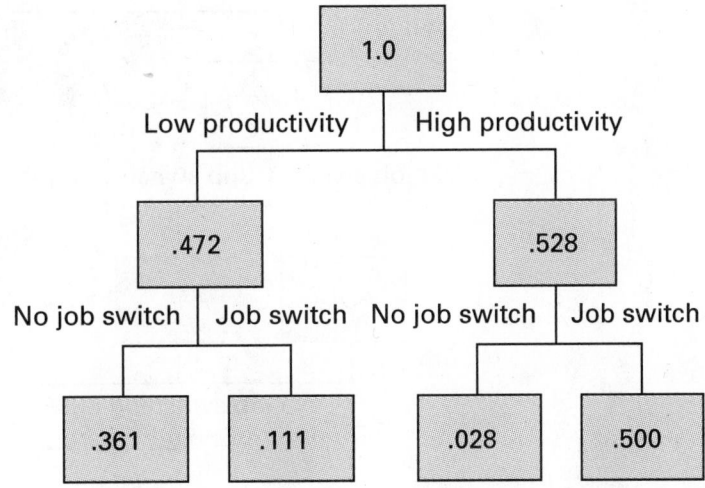

FIGURE 4.3   Probability Tree for Productivity and Job-Switching Data

Note that the probability of being a low-productivity or high-productivity group can also be found along the *row margins* of the joint probability table, Table 4.2.

But how can we determine the probability of job switch or the probability of no job switch from the probability tree?

There are two ways to be a no-job-switch group:

1. No job switch AND low productivity
2. No job switch AND high productivity

The sum of the two probabilities must be the probability of being a no-job-switch group:

$$P(\text{no job switch}) = P(\text{no job switch AND low productivity})$$
$$+ P(\text{no job switch AND high productivity})$$

$$= .361 + .028 = .389$$

Similarly, the probability of being a job-switch group must be the sum of the joint probabilities, .111 + .500 = .611. Figure 4.4 shows how the probabilities for the job-switch and no-job-switch groups are obtained from the probability tree. Please note that the probability of being a job-switch group or a no-job-switch group can also be found along the *column margins* of the joint probability table, Table 4.2.

In summary, this section has demonstrated how to convert cross-tabs tables into joint relative frequency or joint probability tables. Joint probabilities are probabilities of the joint event—event A AND event B. You can then construct a probability tree from a joint probability table. Of course, you could convert a probability tree into a joint probability table. The probability tree helps to visualize probabilities.

FIGURE 4.4   Probability Tree for Productivity and Job-Switching Data

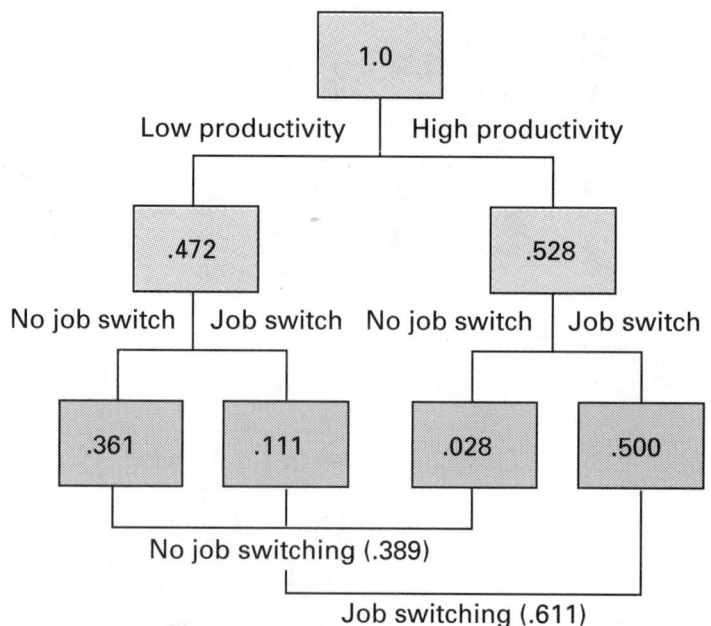

SECTION 4.3 EXERCISES

1. How many joint probabilities are there in a 4×5 joint probability table?

2. Consider the following categorical variables: personality type and job satisfaction.

   Personality Type   Extrovert or introvert
   Job Satisfaction   Satisfied or dissatisfied

   Which of the following are joint probabilities?
   a. $P(\text{extrovert})$
   b. the probability of being an introvert and satisfied on the job
   c. $P(\text{introvert AND dissatisfied on the job})$
   d. the probability of being a dissatisfied extrovert.
   e. the probability of being dissatisfied on the job.
   f. $P(\text{dissatisfied})$

3. Consider the following categorical variables: gender and job satisfaction.

   Gender   Male or female
   Job Satisfaction   Satisfied or dissatisfied

   Which of the following are joint probabilities?
   a. the probability of being a male and satisfied on the job
   b. $P(\text{male})$
   c. the probability of being a dissatisfied female.
   d. the probability of being dissatisfied on the job.
   e. $P(\text{female AND satisfied})$

4. Consider the following categorical variables: gender and promotion status. Consider the following joint frequencies for a sample of 200 employees at a large firm:

$$\text{Frequency(male AND promoted)} = 90$$

$$\text{Frequency(male AND not promoted)} = 30$$

$$\text{Frequency(female AND promoted)} = 20$$

$$\text{Frequency(female AND not promoted)} = 60$$

   a. Develop a 2×2 cross-tabs table.
   b. Develop a 2×2 joint probability table.
   c. Are the joint probabilities in part **b** true probabilities? Explain.
   d. Develop a probability tree and place the gender variable higher in the tree.
   e. Develop a probability tree and place the promotion status variable higher in the tree.
   f. Determine the estimated probability of selecting a promoted male (male AND promoted), a female, a promoted person, and an unpromoted female.

5. Refer to Figure 4.4 in the text.
   a. Why is the probability in the box at the top of the tree 1.0?
   b. What are the probabilities in the end boxes called?
   c. What is the probability of being a low-productivity group? Is this a joint probability?
   d. What is the probability of being a job-switching low-productivity group? Is this a joint probability?

6. Consider the following categorical variables: overseas assignment status and promotion status. Consider the following estimated joint probabilities based on a sample of 500 employees:

$$P(\text{no overseas assignment AND promoted}) = .16$$

$$P(\text{overseas assignment AND promoted}) = .24$$

$$P(\text{no overseas assignment AND not promoted}) = .22$$

$$P(\text{overseas assignment AND not promoted}) = .38$$

a. Develop a 2 × 2 joint probability table.
b. Are the joint probabilities in part **a** true probabilities? Explain.
c. Develop a probability tree and place the overseas assignment status variable higher in the tree.
d. Develop a probability tree and place the promotion status variable higher in the tree.
e. Use the probability table or tree to determine the estimated probability of selecting (1) a person who has been promoted and had an overseas assignment, (2) a promoted person, and (3) a person who has had an overseas assignment.
f. Develop a 2 × 2 cross-tabs table.

7. Shown is a joint probability tree for two categorical variables: type of supervision and level of job satisfaction.

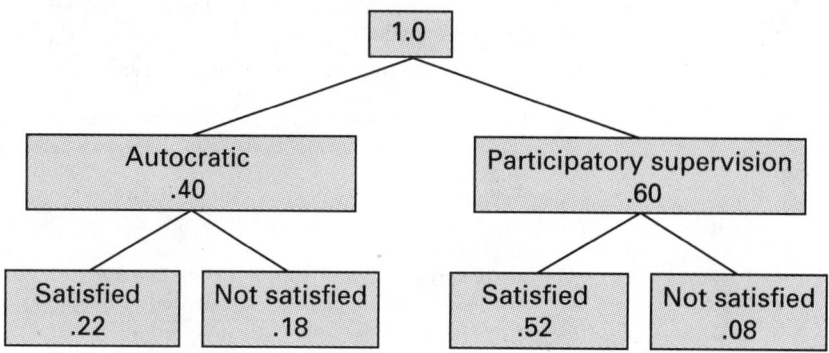

a. Redraw the probability tree and place the job satisfaction variable higher in the tree.
b. Convert the probability tree diagram into a joint probability table.
c. What are the probabilities in the end boxes for the above probability tree called?
d. Given a sample size of 5,000 employees, convert the probability tree into a cross-tabs table.

8. Shown is a partially completed joint probability tree for two categorical variables: personality type and management level.

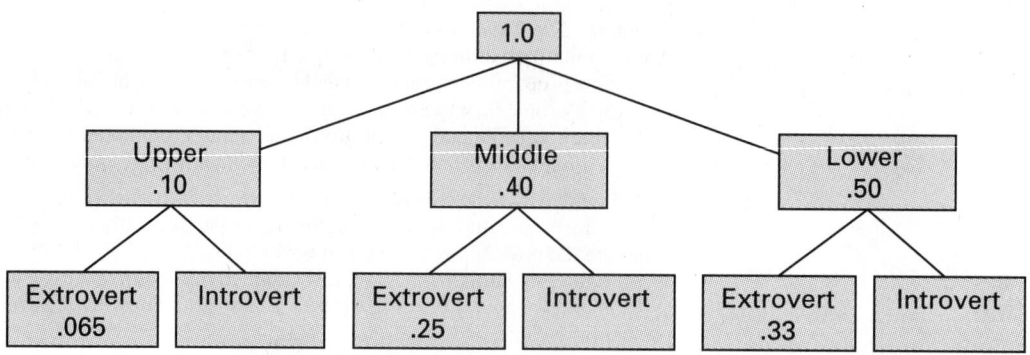

a. Determine the missing joint probabilities.
b. Redraw the probability tree and place the personality type variable higher in the tree.
c. Convert the probability tree diagram into a joint probability table.
d. Given a sample size of 2,000 employees, convert the probability tree into a cross-tabs table.

9. Shown is a partially completed joint probability tree for two categorical variables: personality type and management level.

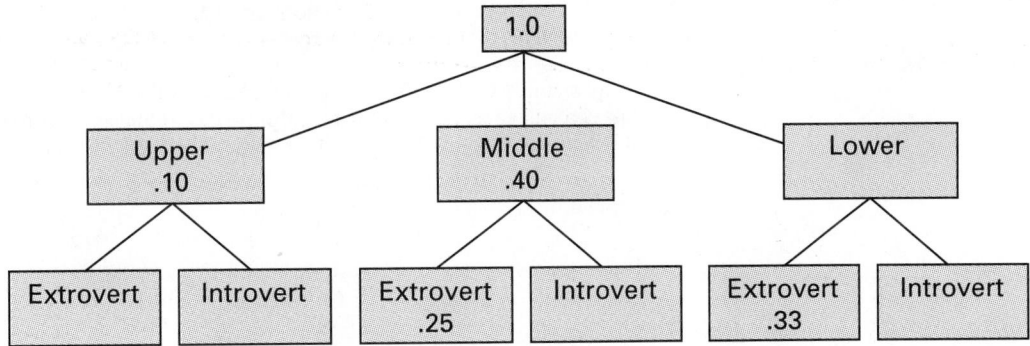

a. The joint probability of being an extroverted-upper management employee is .08. The joint probability of being an introverted-lower management employee is .40. Given this information, complete the probability tree.
b. Redraw the probability tree and place the personality type variable higher in the tree.
c. Convert the probability tree diagram into a joint probability table.
d. Given a sample size of 3,500 employees, convert the probability tree into a cross-tabs table.

10. Consider the following two categorical variables: gender and college major. Consider these four hypothetical joint probabilities:

$$P(\text{male AND major in physical sciences}) = .35$$

$$P(\text{male AND not major in physical sciences}) = .20$$

$$P(\text{female AND major in physical sciences}) = .15$$

$$P(\text{female AND not major in physical sciences}) = .30$$

a. Construct a probability tree for the events shown. Place the gender variable higher in the tree.
b. Find $P(\text{male})$ and $P(\text{female})$.
c. Redraw the probability tree and place the college major variable higher in the tree.
d. Find $P(\text{major in physical sciences})$ and $P(\text{not major in physical sciences})$.
e. Construct a joint probability table.
f. Given a sample size of 5,000 students, convert the joint probability table into a cross-tabs table.

11. A night student must decide whether to take a difficult course next term. If she gets promoted she will not be able to spend as much time studying and could get a grade of C or worse. She thinks that the probability of getting promoted and getting a grade of B or better is only .10. The probability of not getting promoted and getting a C or worse is only .05. She estimates that her overall probability of getting a B or better is .8.
a. Construct a joint probability table from the data.
b. What is the student's personal probability assessment that she will be promoted?

12. The day shift on a production line produced 400 units, of which 28 were defective. The night shift produced 350 items over the same time period, of which 35 were defective. The results are shown.

	Day	Night	Total
Acceptable	372	315	687
Defective	28	35	63
	400	350	750

a. Of the 750 items produced, what percentage were defective?
b. Of the 750 items produced, what percentage were defective and produced by the night shift?
c. What percentage of the 750 items were produced by the day shift and were acceptable? Is this percentage the same as the probability of selecting an item of output and finding that it was produced by the day shift and was acceptable? Explain.

13. A real estate company cross-classifies its 500 agents by experience and membership in the million dollar club. The results are shown.

Club Member	<2 Years	Experience 2 to 5 Years	Over 5 Years	Total
Yes	20	30	50	100
No	100	200	100	400
	120	230	150	500

a. Construct a joint probability table from the data.
b. If an agent is selected, what is the probability that the agent is a member of the million dollar club? the agent is not a member of the million dollar club and has over 5 years of experience? the agent is a member of the million dollar club and has less than 2 years of experience?
c. Construct a probability tree from the joint probability table.

14. We wish to study two categorical variables: type of leadership (participative or autocratic) and level of employee morale (high or low). We have cross-classified 180 employees by type of leadership and level of morale and developed the following probability tree.

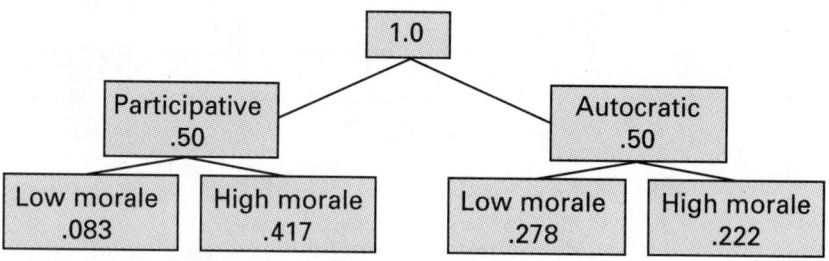

a. Develop a cross-tabs table from the probability tree.
b. Develop a joint probability table from the probability tree.

15. We are preparing to develop a probability tree that represents methods of financing a car purchase and the cost of the car. What, if anything, is wrong with the following cross-classification?

Type of Financing	Cost of Car
Installment loan of 36 months or less	Less than $10,000
Installment loan of more than 36 months	$10,000 to under $25,000
	More than $25,000

16. We are preparing to develop a joint probability table that represents number of years employed at a firm and the level of job satisfaction. What, if anything, is wrong with following cross-classification? If wrong, correct the cross-classification.

Number of Years	Job Satisfaction
Less than 5 years	Satisfied
5 to 9.99 years	Dissatisfied
More than 10 years	

4.4 ≡ Joint and Union Probabilities

In Section 4.3 we focused solely on joint probabilities. They use the logical connector AND. Recall that joint probabilities are found at the end boxes of the probability tree. In this section we introduce the union probability, P(event A OR event B). By the end of this section you should be able to:

1. explain in your own words what a union probability is;
2. distinguish between joint and union probabilities;
3. determine union probabilities from a probability tree; and
4. explain the addition rule that relates joint and union probabilities.

Union Probability: Combining Two Events Using OR

The probability of event A or event B is called a union probability. Both union and joint probabilities are probabilities of compound events. So how are they different?

Begin by computing the union probability,

$$P(\text{low productivity OR no job switch})$$

In Table 4.3 are listed the joint events taken from the four end boxes of Figure 4.4. We then determine how many of the joint events are part of the union event—low productivity OR no job switch. The union event—low productivity OR no job switch—is the sum of the probabilities for the first three joint events. The only joint event that is not part of the union event is where neither event happened—the fourth joint event.

From Figure 4.4, the union probability of low productivity OR no job switch is

$$P(\text{low productivity OR no job switch}) = P(\text{low productivity AND no job switch})$$
$$+ P(\text{low productivity AND job switch})$$
$$+ P(\text{high productivity AND no job switch})$$
$$= .361 + .111 + .028 = .500$$

Use Table 4.3 to compute P(high productivity OR job switch). This is the probability of selecting either a high-productivity group or a group whose members switch jobs. You should obtain $.111 + .028 + .500 = .639$.

In summary, a union event includes events where only event A happened, only event B happened, or both events happened.

Table 4.3

Joint and Union Events Table

Joint Events	Is Joint Event a Part of the Union Event —Low Productivity OR No Job Switch?
Low productivity AND no job switch	Yes, both events happened.
Low productivity AND job switch	Yes, first event happened.
High productivity AND no job switch	Yes, second event happened.
High productivity AND job switch	No, neither event happened.

Here's another way to compute the union probability. Expression (4.4) is called the addition rule.

$$P(A \text{ OR } B) = P(A) + P(B) - P(A \text{ AND } B) \qquad (4.4)$$

Verify it by recomputing P(low productivity OR no job switch). Use Figure 4.4 or Table 4.2 to obtain the three necessary probabilities.

$$
\begin{aligned}
P(\text{low productivity OR no job switch}) &= P(\text{low productivity}) + P(\text{no job switch}) \\
&\quad - P(\text{low productivity AND no job switch}) \\
&= .472 + .389 - .361 \\
&= .500
\end{aligned}
$$

Note that we obtain the same answer as when Table 4.3 was used.

Why does the addition rule work? From Figure 4.4, note that P(low productivity) equals $.361 + .111$. Also note that P(no job switch) equals $.361 + .028$. Thus when these two pairs of probabilities were added, the joint probability—P(low productivity AND no job switch) $= .361$—appeared twice. Therefore we must subtract it once to correct for the double counting.

SECTION 4.4 EXERCISES

1. Indicate if items **a–i** are joint probabilities, union probabilities, or neither. What is the probability that the person is a
   a. highly satisfied and highly paid worker.
   b. highly satisfied or poorly paid worker.
   c. highly satisfied worker.
   d. highly satisfied or highly paid worker.
   e. highly satisfied worker if he is highly paid.
   f. highly satisfied but highly paid worker.
   g. highly satisfied-highly paid worker.
   h. highly satisfied worker if she is poorly paid.
   i. poorly paid worker.

2. Construct a 2×2 joint probability table—gender and promotion status. Insert hypothetical data and determine if the following expressions are correct. Let M represent male, F represent female, P represent promoted, and NP represent not promoted.
   a. $P(M \text{ OR } P) = P(M \text{ AND } P)$
   b. $P(M \text{ OR } P) = P(M \text{ AND } P) + P(M \text{ AND } NP) + P(F \text{ AND } P)$
   c. $P(M \text{ OR } P) = P(M) + P(P) - P(M \text{ AND } P)$
   d. $P(M \text{ OR } P) = P(P) + P(M)$
   e. $P(M \text{ OR } P) = 1 - P(F \text{ AND } NP)$
   f. $P(M \text{ OR } P) = P(M) - P(P)$

3. Using the Figure 4.4 probability tree, determine if the following expressions are correct. Let L represent low productivity, H represent high productivity, JS represent job switching, and NJS represent no job switching.
   a. $P(L \text{ OR } JS) = P(L) + P(JS) - P(L \text{ AND } JS)$
   b. $P(L \text{ OR } JS) = P(L \text{ AND } JS)$
   c. $P(L \text{ OR } JS) = P(L) + P(JS)$
   d. $P(L \text{ OR } JS) = 1 - P(H \text{ AND } NJS)$
   e. $P(L \text{ OR } JS) = P(L)/P(JS)$
   f. $P(L \text{ OR } JS) = P(L \text{ AND } JS) + P(L \text{ AND } NJS) + P(H \text{ AND } JS)$

4. Consider the following probability tree that represents the two categorical variables—do formal strategic planning and return on equity.

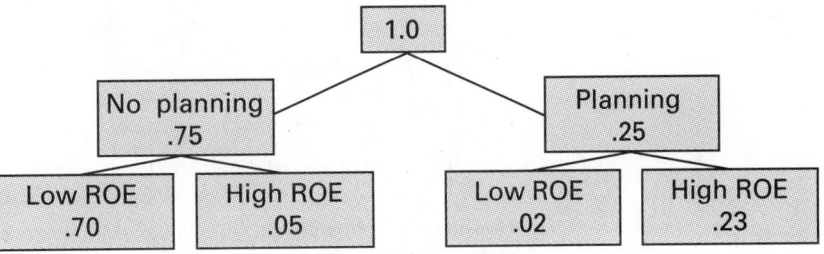

a. Find P(low *ROE* AND no planning).
b. Use the Addition Rule to find P(high *ROE* OR planning).
c. Which one of the four joint probabilities in the end boxes is not a part of the union event—high *ROE* OR planning?
d. Explain why the following expression is correct.
P(high *ROE* OR planning) $= 1 - P$(low *ROE* AND no planning)

5. Consider the following probability tree that represents the two categorical variables—personality type and management level.

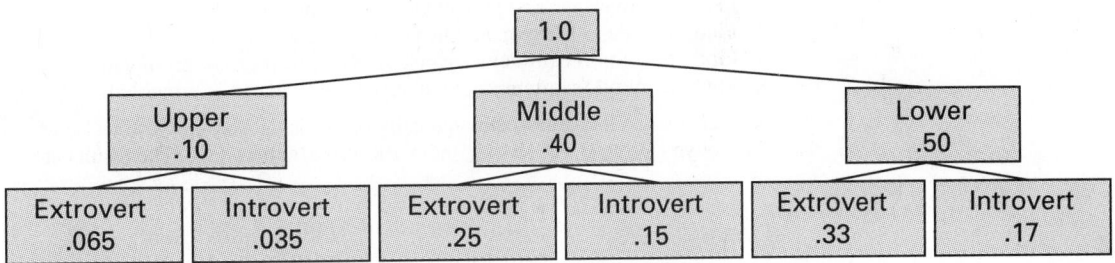

a. Find P(upper management AND extrovert).
b. Use the tree to find P(upper management OR extrovert).
c. Which of the six joint probabilities in the end boxes are not a part of the union event—upper management or extrovert?

6. Consider the following probability tree that represents the two categorical variables—leadership style and job satisfaction.

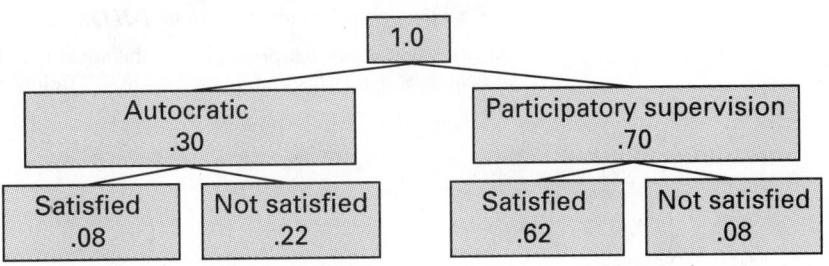

a. Find P(autocratic AND not satisfied).
b. Use the Addition Rule to find P(autocratic OR not satisfied).
c. Use the above tree to determine which of the following expressions are correct. The first letters for each categorical variable are used in the following expression. For example, A represents autocratic supervision.

(1) $P(A \text{ OR } S) = P(A \text{ AND } S) + P(A \text{ AND } NS) + P(P \text{ AND } NS)$

(2) $P(A \text{ OR } S) = P(A) + P(S) - P(A \text{ AND } S)$

(3) $P(A \text{ OR } S) = P(A) + P(S)$

(4) $P(A \text{ OR } S) = 1 - P(P \text{ AND } NS)$

7. Consider the following categorical variables: overseas assignment status and promotion status. Consider the following joint relative-frequency-based probabilities based on a sample of 500 employees:

$$P(\text{no overseas assignment AND promoted}) = .16$$

$$P(\text{overseas assignment AND promoted}) = .24$$

$$P(\text{no overseas assignment AND not promoted}) = .22$$

$$P(\text{overseas assignment AND not promoted}) = .38$$

a. Develop a 2×2 joint probability table.
b. Find $P(\text{no overseas assignment OR promoted})$.
c. Find $P(\text{no overseas assignment OR not promoted})$.
d. Find $P(\text{overseas assignment OR not promoted})$.
e. Find the union **frequency**—overseas assignment or not promoted.
f. Find the union **frequency**—no overseas assignment or promoted.

8. A stock analyst has cross-tabulated daily price changes of the (D)ow (J)ones (I)ndex and the Tokyo (N)ikkei 225-stock (I)ndex for thirty trading days. The results are shown.

| | | Nikkei Index Change | |
		Up	Not Up
Dow Jones	Up	15	5
Index Change	Not Up	2	8

a. Develop a 2×2 joint probability table.
b. Find $P(\text{up } DJI \text{ AND up } NI)$.
c. Find $P(\text{up } DJI \text{ OR up } NI)$.
d. Find $P(\text{up } DJI \text{ OR not up } NI)$.
e. Find the union *frequency*—up DJI OR up NI.
f. Find the union *frequency*—not up DJI OR not up NI.

9. Do firms that apply the principles of statistical quality control (SQC) have lower scrap percentages than firms that do not use SQC? Below are survey data on 1,000 American firms.

| | Apply SQC Principles | | |
	No	Yes	Total
Below Industry Median Scrap Percentage	350	150	500
At/Above Median Scrap Percentage	50	450	500
	400	600	1,000

a. Develop a 2×2 joint probability table.
b. Use the addition rule to find $P(\text{below OR no SQC})$.

    c. Sum up the appropriate joint probabilities to find P(at/above OR yes SQC).

    d. Find P(at/above AND yes SQC).

    e. Find the union *frequency*—below OR no SQC.

    f. Find the union *frequency*—at/above OR yes SQC.

10. Consider the following categorical variables: gender and job satisfaction.

Gender   Male or female

Job Satisfaction   Satisfied or dissatisfied

You are provided the following information.

1. The probability of selecting a male is .60.
2. The probability of selecting a satisfied male worker (male and satisfied) is .40.
3. The probability of selecting a dissatisfied worker is .55.

    a. Develop a 2 × 2 joint probability table.

    b. Use the addition rule to find P(male OR satisfied).

    c. Sum up the appropriate joint probabilities to find P(female OR dissatisfied).

11. Consider the following categorical variables: personality type and job satisfaction.

Personality Type   Extrovert or introvert

Job Satisfaction   Satisfied or dissatisfied

You are provided the following information.

1. The probability of selecting an extrovert is .70 .
2. The probability of selecting an extrovert and satisfied (satisified extrovert) worker is .35.
3. The probability of selecting a dissatisfied worker is .50.

    a. Develop a 2 × 2 joint probability table.

    b. Use the addition rule to find P(extrovert OR satisfied).

    c. Sum up the appropriate joint probabilities to find P(introvert OR dissatisfied).

12. Consider the following probability tree that represents the two categorical variables: level of inflation and method for valuing inventories.

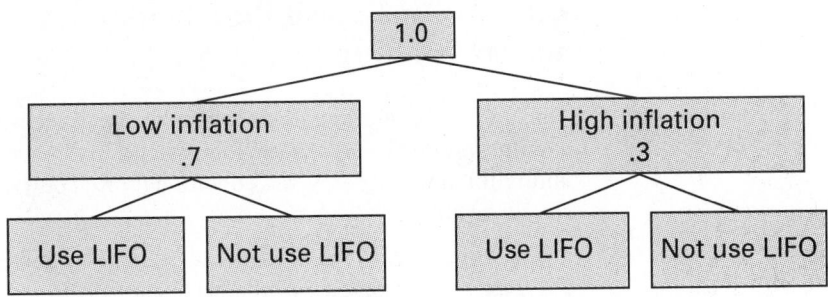

    a. Find P(low inflation OR not use LIFO).

    b. Find P(low inflation AND use LIFO).

13. A company has cross-tabulated its 350 employees by line/staff position and gender. The results are shown.

	Male	Female	Total
Line	40	10	50
Staff	230	70	300
	270	80	350

    a. Construct a probability tree from the data. Place the gender variable nearer the top of the tree.

    b. If one person is selected, what is the probability that the person is female and has a line position?

    c. How many of the four joint events are members of the union event—male or a staff-person?

    d. Use the probability tree to determine the union probability in part **c.**

    e. Use the addition rule to obtain the union probability in part **d.**

14. A restaurant has collected data on its customers' orders. They report that 30% had coffee only, 50% had dessert only, and 20% had both coffee and dessert.

    a. Construct a probability tree.

    b. What is the probability of a person ordering coffee?

    c. What is the probability of a person ordering neither coffee nor dessert?

    d. What is the probability of a person ordering coffee or dessert?

15. Suppose that a product manager estimates the following subjective probabilities for different levels of profit for a new product:

Event	Probability
Profit of $100,000 or more	.40
Profit of $50,000 or more but less than $100,000	.20
Profit of $0 or more but less than $50,000	.10
Loss of more than $0 but less than $50,000	.05
Loss of $50,000 or more but less than $100,000	.10
Loss of $100,000 or more	.15

    a. What is the probability of making a profit of $100,000 or more?

    b. What is the probability of losing $50,000 or more?

    c. Explain how the probability in part **b** is a union probability.

    d. What is the probability of making a profit of $100,000 or more and a loss of $100,000 or more on this product?

    e. Explain how the probability in part **d** is a joint probability.

4.5≣ Conditional Probabilities and Statistical Independence

Thus far, in discussing simple events we have focused solely on probabilities, such as P(low productivity) or P(no job switch). In this section we introduce another probability for simple events, the conditional probability. By the end of this section you should be able to:

1. distinguish between conditional probability and unconditional probability; and
2. explain, in your own words, what statistical independence is.

Conditional Probability

Here are three sets of statements describing probabilities regarding the job switching and productivity data example we have been using:

1. Select one team. Given no other additional information, what is the probability that it is a high-productivity group?
2. Select one team. Before assessing its probability of being a high-productivity group, we tell you that the members often switch jobs.
3. Select one team. Before assessing its probability of being a high-productivity group, we tell you that the group's mean shoe size is 7C.

The unconditional
probability of event *A*
is denoted by $P(A)$.

The conditional probability
of event *A* given that event
B is known is denoted by
$P(A \mid B)$.

If/given

All three statements describe probabilities of a simple, or single, event—a high-productivity group. What is different about the three statements? In the last two statements additional information about the group has been provided. The first statement provides no additional information. The first statement describes an **unconditional probability**. The last two statements describe **conditional probabilities**. A conditional probability is the probability of a simple event, event *A,* given that event *B* is known. Event *B* in statement 2 is that team members switch jobs. Event *B* in statement 3 is that the mean shoe size is 7C. Following are the three statements translated into probability notation:

1. Unconditional probability P(high productivity)
2. Conditional probability P(high productivity | members switch jobs)
3. Conditional probability P(high productivity | mean shoe size is 7C)

From Figure 4.4 we can readily determine that the unconditional probability of being a high-productivity group is P(high productivity) = .528.

Section 4.6 will show how to use Figure 4.4 to determine conditional probabilities. But for now, use logic to approximate them. *Warning*: Logic is not a substitute for determining conditional probabilities from actual data. However, logic will help to intuitively understand the concept of statistical independence, which we will present shortly.

As mentioned before, the probability of being a high-productivity group is .528. Given in statement 2 that team members switch jobs, doesn't it seem logical that the conditional probability of being a high-productivity group should be higher than .528? That is,

$$P(\text{high productivity} \mid \text{team members switch jobs}) > .528$$

Exactly how much higher is not yet clear. But logically we expect it to be higher because groups whose members switch jobs may be more motivated, more knowledgeable about the group's jobs, and thus have higher productivities.

In statement 3, we are told that the team members of the high-productivity group have a mean shoe size of 7C. What would you logically say is the conditional probability of being a high-productivity group with this fact in mind? Think about it before reading on.

Presumably, you wouldn't change the probability figure of .528 upon knowing that the group's mean shoe size is 7C. After all, a team's mean shoe size should not affect its productivity. Thus, one might logically conclude that

$$P(\text{high productivity} \mid \text{mean shoe size is 7C}) = .528$$

So what has been learned? We have logically concluded that productivity and mean shoe size of 7C are *statistically independent* events. Knowing that event *B* happened did not cause us to revise the original unconditional probability of .528. We have also concluded that productivity and job switching are statistically dependent events. That is, the conditional probability is not .528.

Probability revision means that we believe that the two events, *A* and *B,* are statistically dependent. When event *B* is pertinent information, we should increase or decrease the unconditional probability. When the information is irrelevant, we do not revise the unconditional probability. The two events are statistically independent.

Statistical Independence and Dependence

Events that are statistically independent are not related to one another and do not affect each other. Events that are statistically dependent are related to one another, and the occurrence of one event affects the probability of the occurrence of the other event.

Two events can be **statistically independent** or **dependent**. The following table distinguishes independent and dependent events.

Independent Events	Dependent Events
$P(A \mid B) = P(A)$	$P(A \mid B) \neq P(A)$
The probability of the occurrence of A does not change if event B is known.	The probability of the occurrence of A changes if event B is known.
$P(B \mid A) = P(B)$	$P(B \mid A) \neq P(B)$
The probability of the occurrence of B does not change if event A is known.	The probability of the occurrence of B changes if event A is known.

When the conditional probability, $P(A|B)$, and unconditional probability, $P(A)$, are equal, event B is independent of event A. Knowing event B does not affect the probability that A occurs.

On the other hand, when the conditional and unconditional probabilities are not the same, then knowing event A or event B will cause us to revise the probability that the other will occur.

In summary, conditional and unconditional probabilities deal with a simple event. Conditional probabilities are denoted as $P(A \mid B)$, the probability of event A given that we know event B. If $P(A \mid B)$ does not equal the unconditional probability, $P(A)$, then events A and B are statistically dependent. In this section we have surmised statistical independence using logic and intuition. But in real-world situations logic and intuition are usually not enough. We must calculate conditional probabilities to establish statistical independence.

SECTION 4.5 EXERCISES

1. What does it mean to say that two events are statistically independent?

2. Given the following list of events, indicate whether you think events A and B are likely to be independent or dependent.
   a. A = A two-spot face comes up on the first roll of a die.
      B = A two-spot face comes up on the second roll of a die.
   b. A = Accountant wears a red tie to work.
      B = Accountant passes CPA examination.
   c. A = Person enjoys work.
      B = Person does good work.
   d. A = Person owns place of residence.
      B = Person will pay credit card bills on time.
   e. A = Person has missed payments three times in the last six months.
      B = Person will pay credit card bill this month.

3. Which of the following are conditional, joint, union, or unconditional probabilities? Also write the probability expression for each subproblem.
      What is the probability that the person is
   a. a highly satisfied and highly paid worker?
   b. highly satisfied?
   c. a highly paid worker?
   d. a highly satisfied or highly paid worker?
   e. a highly satisfied worker given that he is highly paid?
   f. highly satisfied if she is highly paid?

    g. a highly satisfied, highly paid worker?

    h. a highly satisfied worker if she is poorly paid?

    i. a poorly paid worker?

    j. a dissatisfied worker given that she is poorly paid?

4. Translate the following probability expressions into everyday language a financial analyst could understand.

    a. P(high earnings per share (EPS) AND high performing stock)

    b. P(low performing stock | low EPS)

    c. P(low performing stock)

    d. P(high performing OR high EPS)

    e. P(high EPS | high performing stock)

    f. P(high EPS)

    g. P(low EPS | high performing stock)

    h. P(low EPS) + P(high performing stock)

    i. P(high performing stock | low EPS)

5. The following probabilities reflect earnings per share (EPS) and stock performance. Given the probabilities, which statement is correct for each subproblem?

    1. The events appear to be statistically independent.

    2. The events appear to be statistically dependent.

    3. We cannot tell—insufficient data.

    a. P(high stock performance) = .30
       P(high stock performance | high EPS) = .80

    b. P(low stock performance) = .40
       P(low stock performance AND low EPS) = .25

    c. P(high EPS | high stock performance) = .70
       P(high stock performance | high EPS) = .50

    d. P(high stock performance) = .30
       P(high stock performance | low EPS) = .05

    e. P(high stock performance) = .30
       P(high stock performance | low EPS) = .30

    f. P(high EPS | high stock performance) = .70
       P(high stock performance | high EPS) = .70

    g. P(high stock performance) = .30
       P(high EPS) = .30

6. Using logic only, would you expect that the second probability for each subproblem would be greater than, equal to, or less than the first probability? In one subproblem we cannot even make an educated guess. Which subproblem is it and why?

    a. P(high GPA) = .25
       P(high GPA | always attends class)

    b. P(high GPA) = .25
       P(high GPA | never attends class)

    c. P(on time arrival) = .50
       P(on time arrival | bad weather)

    d. P(on time arrival) = .50
       P(on time arrival | extrawide seating)

    e. P(on time arrival | extrawide seating) = .70
       P(extrawide seating | on time arrival)

    f. P(get desired job) = .30
       P(get desired job | internship during school)

    g. P(low scrap percentage) = .10
       P(low scrap percentage | quality improvement program)

    h. P(high GPA) = .25
       P(high GPA | over 6 feet tall)

7. A marketing organization varies its advertising among different zip codes to reflect differences in family income levels. Consider the following marketing research questions and state whether each suggests an unconditional, conditional, or joint probability.

a. How many BMW 733s can we sell to families if their annual incomes are in excess of $100,000?

b. How many potential car buyers are there who want a BMW 733 and have the $50,000 to pay for it?

c. How many BMW 733s can we sell to the 50,000 families in this area?

8. Assume that the level of pollutants in the air depends on whether power is generated from coal-burning plants. Let:

A_1 = Level of pollutants below Environmental Protection Agency standards

A_2 = Level of pollutants at or above standards

B_1 = Coal-burning plants used

B_2 = Coal-burning plants not used

a. Suppose $P(A_2) = .20$. Using only logic, would you estimate $P(A_2 \mid B_1)$ to be less than, equal to, or greater than .20? Explain.

b. Explain why we cannot rely merely on logic to estimate the desired conditional probability.

9. Assume that the franchise fee is independent of the number of franchises that are currently operating. Let:

A_1 = Franchise fee > $15,000

A_2 = Franchise fee ≤ $15,000

B_1 = Number of franchises > 2,000

B_2 = Number of franchises ≤ 2,000

Suppose $P(A_1 \mid B_1) = .45$. Using only logic, would you estimate that $P(A_1)$ is less than, equal to, or greater than .45?

4.6 ▤ Computing Conditional Probabilities

In the business world, we do not use logic or intuition to determine statistical dependence; we compute conditional probabilities. Why is it important to know whether two variables are statistically related? It is because managers are always looking for relationships between variables. For example, is job switching related to productivity? Does gender affect promotional status? Does advertising affect sales? Does serving internships during college help students obtain the jobs they want? By the end of this section you should be able to:

1. compute conditional probabilities using a probability tree and determine whether two events appear to be statistically dependent;
2. distinguish between conditional and joint probabilities; and
3. explain in your own words how conditional probabilities are similar to and different from row or column percentage tables.

We continue to use the job-switching and productivity data in this section. Recall from the previous section that logic was used to argue that the probability of high productivity, given that members switch jobs, should be greater than .528. Now use expression (4.5) to compute the desired conditional probability.

if / given

$$P(A \mid B) = \frac{P(A \text{ AND } B)}{P(B)} \tag{4.5}$$

Let event A = high productivity and event B = switch jobs. Then

$$P(\text{high productivity} \mid \text{switch jobs}) = \frac{P(\text{high productivity AND switch jobs})}{P(\text{switch jobs})}$$

The probability tree, Figure 4.4, provides the desired joint and unconditional probabilities. The unconditional probability of switching jobs is .611, which is the denominator for expression (4.5). The joint probability of high productivity and job switching is .500 (see the end box), which is the numerator of expression (4.5). Thus,

$$P(\text{high productivity} \mid \text{switch jobs}) = \frac{.500}{.611} = .818$$

There are two important observations. First, the calculated conditional probability is greater than .528. The data support our intuition. Second, the conditional probability of .818 is different from the unconditional probability of .528 of being a high-productivity group. Thus, high productivity and job switching are statistically dependent events.

Why does expression (4.5) work? What is the logic behind it? Although expression (4.5) deals with probabilities, we can understand its logic by studying the cross-tabs table, Table 4.1. The denominator of expression (4.5) focuses on event B—namely, groups whose members switch jobs. How many groups switch jobs? From Table 4.1, there are 22 such groups. Thus the denominator of expression (4.5) is $^{22}/_{36}$. The numerator focuses on groups that switch jobs and have high productivity. How many of the 22 groups also had high productivity? Look at the job-switching column of Table 4.1. Note that of the 22 groups, 18 also had high productivity. Thus the numerator of expression (4.5) is $^{18}/_{36}$. Therefore, the conditional probability of having high productivity given that a group switches jobs is $^{18}/_{36}$ divided by $^{22}/_{36}$, or .818.

One additional example is presented to demonstrate how to calculate conditional probabilities from data.

Example: Internships and the Hiring Decision Case   Does *serving internships* during college help graduates obtain their *desired jobs* upon graduation? That is, is the unconditional probability of obtaining a desired job the same as the conditional probability of obtaining a desired job given that the student had an internship? The placement officer has collected data on 500 students over the past 5 years. He recorded whether they had internships and whether they got their desired jobs upon graduation.

Table 4.4 is the joint probability table based on a sample size of 500 students. In the sample, 38% of the students had no internships *and* did not get their desired jobs; 28% had internships *and* did get their desired jobs.

Now we can build a probability tree. In this case, it makes no difference which categorical variable we place higher in the tree. In Figure 4.5, the internship variable is placed higher. We encourage you to build a different tree by placing the desired job event higher in the tree. Then it can be used to check the following calculations. The four joint probabilities have been inserted into the end boxes to complete the tree.

Table 4.4

Joint Probability Table

	No Internship	Internship	Total
No Desired Job	.38	.02	.40
Desired Job	.32	.28	.60
	.70	.30	1.00

FIGURE 4.5   Probability Tree for Internship and Desired Job Data

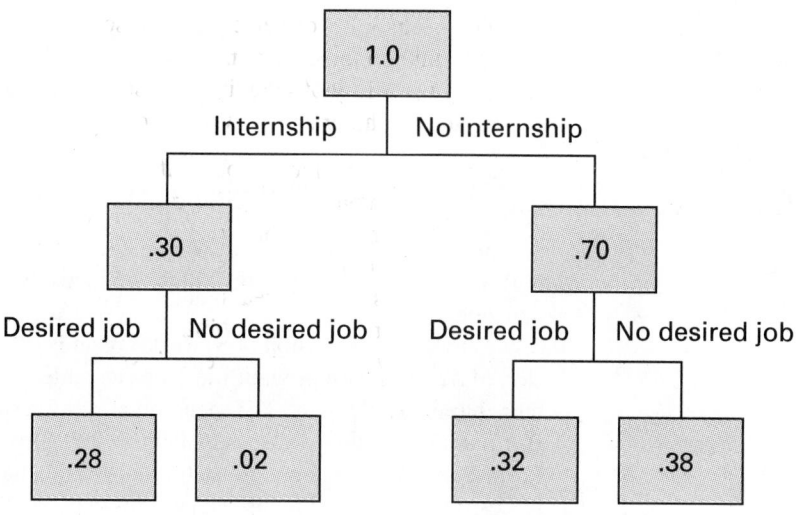

The unconditional probability of getting a desired job is

$$P(\text{Desired job}) = .28 + .32 = .60$$

Does an internship increase the probability of getting a desired job? If the conditional probability, $P(\text{Desired job} \mid \text{Internship})$ is still .60, then having an internship has no effect on getting a desired job. Now use expression (4.5) to compute the conditional probability:

$$P(A \mid B) = \frac{P(A \text{ AND } B)}{P(B)}$$

$$P(\text{Desired job} \mid \text{Internship}) = \frac{P(\text{Desired job AND Internship})}{P(\text{Internship})} = \frac{.28}{.30} = .933$$

The denominator for expression (4.5) is $P(\text{Internship})$, or .30. The numerator, the joint probability of getting the desired job and having an internship, is .28. The result yields a conditional probability of .933.

The conditional probability strongly suggests that internships do increase students' chances of getting desired jobs, because the conditional and unconditional probabilities of getting a desired job are very different. The chance of getting a desired job increases from .60 to .933 if students have had an internship. Thus, having an internship and getting a desired job appear to be statistically related events (see margin of error concept, Section 3.4).

Distinguishing Between Conditional and Joint Probabilities

It is easy to distinguish between an unconditional probability, $P(A)$, and a joint probability, $P(A \text{ AND } B)$. But differentiating between joint and conditional probabilities is more difficult. A joint probability is the probability of two or more events, A and B, happening. A conditional probability is the probability of a single event A, given that we know event B.

Two statements are given here. One statement is a joint probability and the other is a conditional probability. Which is which and why?

1. The probability of selecting a person over 35 years old who favors increased spending on the environment.
2. The probability of selecting a person who favors increased spending on the environment if he or she is over 35 years old.

Statement 1 is the joint probability. It is a joint probability because two events describe the person—over 35 years old *and* in favor of increased spending. Statement 2 is a conditional probability because we are interested only in a single event—a person who favors increased spending. However, we know event B about the person —the person is over 35 years old.

In summary, joint probabilities deal with two or more events. Conditional probabilities deal with only one event, A, where we are given a second piece of information by way of another event, B.

Conditional Probabilities and Row or Column Percentage Tables

Conditional probabilities have been introduced before, although not in the same terms. We first presented them in the discussion of row and column percentage tables in Chapter 3. Row and column percentages are similar to conditional probabilities in the following respect.

Return to the job productivity and job switching data. First use Figure 4.4 to compute the following four conditional probabilities where event B is the level of job switching:

$$P(\text{low productivity} \mid \text{no job switch}) = \frac{.361}{.389} = .929$$

$$P(\text{high productivity} \mid \text{no job switch}) = \frac{.028}{.389} = .071$$

$$P(\text{low productivity} \mid \text{job switch}) = \frac{.111}{.611} = .182$$

$$P(\text{high productivity} \mid \text{job switch}) = \frac{.500}{.611} = .818$$

Now note that these four conditional probabilities are similar to the column percentages in Table 3.7 (page 113). One difference is that percentages are numbers between 0 and 100, and probabilities are numbers between 0 and 1. A second difference is that column percentages, which are based on a sample of the population, are only estimates of the true conditional probabilities.

Please verify that the four conditional probabilities where event B is the level of productivity are similar to the row percentages in Table 3.8.

SECTION 4.6 EXERCISES

1. Decide whether each of the following is a conditional or a joint probability:
   a. The probability of selecting a promoted male
   b. The probability of selecting a male if the person has been promoted
   c. The probability of selecting an individual with high cholesterol if you already know that the person eats eggs six times a week
   d. The probability of selecting a six-times-a-week egg eater with high cholesterol

2. Decide whether each of the following is an unconditional, conditional, or joint probability.
   a. The probability that the Tokyo Nikkei Index is up if the Dow Jones Index is up
   b. The probability that both the Tokyo Nikkei and Dow Jones Indices are up
   c. If the Dow Jones Index is up, the probability that the Tokyo Nikkei is down
   d. The probability that the Dow Jones Index is up
   e. The probability that the Dow Jones Index is up if the Tokyo Nikkei Index is up
   f. The probability that neither Indices are up
   g. If the Dow Jones Index is up, the probability that the Tokyo Nikkei Index is up
   h. The probability that the Tokyo Nikkei Index is down if the Dow Jones Index is up

3. Consider the following probability data:

$$P(\text{high EPS}) = .60$$

$$P(\text{high EPS AND high performing stock}) = .40$$

$$P(\text{low performing stock}) = .50$$

$$P(\text{low EPS AND low performing stock}) = .30$$

   Construct a joint probability table and use Equation 4.5 to determine
   a. The $P(\text{high performing stock} \mid \text{high EPS})$.
   b. The probability of a high performing stock if the firm has a high EPS.
   c. The $P(\text{low EPS} \mid \text{low performing stock})$
   d. The probability of a low performing stock if the firm has a low EPS.

4. Consider the following probability data:

$$P(\text{Total Quality Management [TQM] emphasis}) = .10$$

$$P(\text{low turnover}) = .13$$

$$P(\text{TQM emphasis AND low turnover}) = .08$$

$$P(\text{no TQM emphasis AND high turnover}) = .85$$

   Construct a joint probability table and use equation (4.5) to determine
   a. The $P(\text{low turnover} \mid \text{TQM emphasis})$.
   b. The probability of TQM emphasis if the firm has low turnover.
   c. The $P(\text{high turnover} \mid \text{no TQM emphasis})$
   d. The probability of no TQM emphasis given the firm has high turnover.

e. Does it appear that a TQM emphasis and turnover are statistically related? Explain.

5. A stock analyst has cross-tabulated daily price changes of the Dow Jones Index and the Tokyo Nikkei 225-stock Index for 120 trading days. The results are shown.

		Nikkei Index Change	
		Up	Not Up
Dow Jones	Up	60	6
Index Change	Not Up	12	42

a. Develop a 2 × 2 joint probability table.
b. Calculate the probability that the Nikkei Index is up if the Dow Jones Index is up.
c. Calculate the probability that the Nikkei Index is up if the Dow Jones Index is down.
d. What is the probability that the Nikkei Index is up?
e. Given your answers to **b–d,** does it appear that the movement of the two stock indices are statistically related?

6. Consider the following probability tree that represents the two categorical variables—personality type and management level.

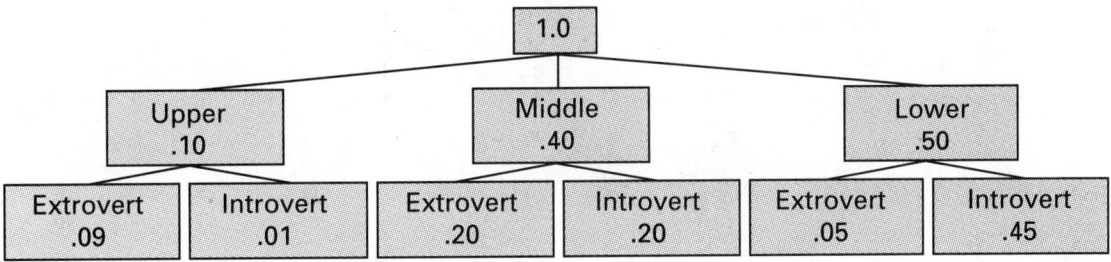

a. What is the probability of selecting an upper-level professional?
b. What is the probability of selecting an upper-level professional if the person is an extrovert?
c. Find the P(upper-level professional | introvert).
d. Given your answers to **a–c,** does it appear that personality type and management level are statistically related?

7. Do firms that apply the principles of statistical quality control (SQC) have lower scrap percentages than firms that do not use SQC? Below are survey data on 1,000 American firms.

	Apply SQC Principles		
	No	Yes	Total
Below-Industry-Median Scrap Percentage	350	150	500
At/Above Median Scrap Percentage	50	450	500
	400	600	1,000

a. Develop a 2 × 2 joint probability table.
b. Calculate the probability that a firm has a below-industry-median scrap percentage if it applies SQC principles.
c. Calculate the probability that a firm has a below-industry-median scrap percentage if it does not apply SQC principles.
d. What is the probability that a firm has a below-industry-median scrap percentage?
e. Given your answers to **b–d,** does it appear that the use of SQC principles is statistically related to the scrap percentage within a firm?

8. Are leadership style and job satisfaction statistically related? Consider the probability tree based on survey data.

a. What is the probability of selecting a satisfied worker?
b. What is the probability of selecting a satisfied worker if the person's boss is autocratic?
c. Find the P(satisfied worker | participatory supervision).
d. Given your answers to **a–c,** does it appear that leadership and job satisfaction are statistically related?

9. Is personality type and performance in an industrial sales job statistically related? Below is a joint probability table.

	Personality Type		
	Extrovert	Introvert	Total
Ineffective Performance	.32	.48	.80
Effective Performance	.08	.12	.20
	.40	.60	1.00

a. What is the probability of selecting an effective performance salesperson?
b. Compute the P(effective performance | extrovert).
c. Compute the P(effective performance | introvert).
d. Given your answers to **a–c,** does it appear that personality type and sales performance level are statistically related?
e. Now note that the following is true when any events—such as personality type and performance level—are statistically independent.

$$P(A \text{ AND } B) = P(A) \cdot P(B)$$

Verify this by computing the

$$P(\text{effective AND introvert}) = P(\text{effective}) \cdot P(\text{introvert})$$

using the general expression in **e.**
f. Note that the $P(A \text{ AND } B) = P(A) \cdot P(B)$ expression is only true if events are *statistically independent.* Verify this by referring to Exercise 8. The exercise indicated that supervision style and job satisfaction level appeared to be statistically related. Now determine if

$$P(\text{autocratic AND satisfied}) = P(\text{autocratic}) \cdot P(\text{satisfied})$$

You will find that the equality sign does not hold.

10. Is formal strategic planning related to financial performance, specifically return on equity (ROE)?

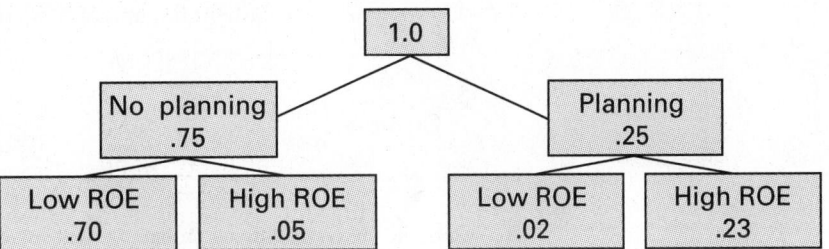

a. What is the probability of selecting a high ROE firm?
b. What is the probability of selecting a high ROE firm given the firm does formal strategic planning?
c. Find the *P*(high ROE | no formal planning).
d. Given your answers to **a–c,** does it appear that formal strategic planning and ROE are statistically related?

11. Consider the following probability tree: ≤

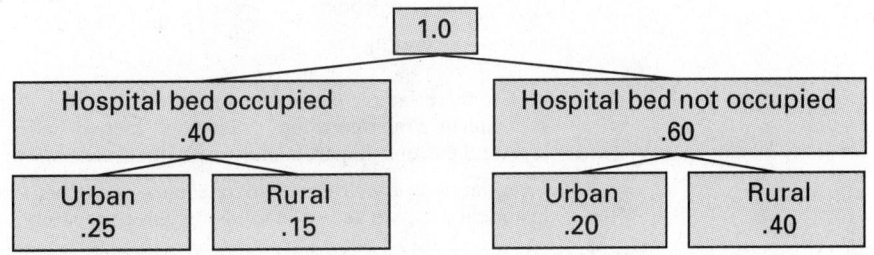

a. Calculate *P*(bed occupied | urban county).
b. Calculate *P*(bed not occupied | rural county).
c. Are the events—hospital bed occupied and location of county—statistically independent?

12. Consider the following probability tree:

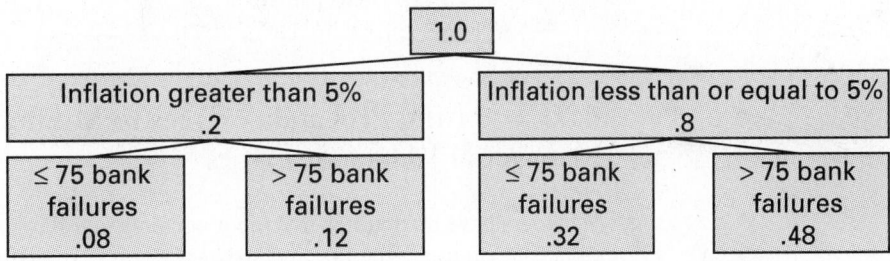

a. Calculate *P*(inflation greater than 5% | ≤75 bank failures).
b. Calculate *P*(>75 bank failures | inflation rate less than or equal to 5%).
c. Are the events—inflation rate >5% and number of bank failures > 75—statistically independent?
d. Convert the probability tree into a joint probability table.

13. A major bank wishes to distinguish between good and bad credit risks. One variable the bank thinks might be related to credit worthiness is whether the applicant has worked for the same company for 5 years or more. The following joint probability (relative frequency) table was estimated based on the bank's experience with existing clients.

Client Company Affiliation

		<5 years	≥5 years	
Credit	Good	.25	.60	.85
	Bad	.10	.05	.15
		.35	.65	1.00

a. Determine the unconditional probability that an account will be a bad risk account.
b. Calculate the conditional probability that an account will be a bad risk if the applicant has worked for a company less than five years.
c. Are the events "Account will be bad" and "Applicant worked for the same company less than five years" statistically independent? Explain.

14. The following table shows the results of a sample of 200 students cross-classified on two variables: internship—yes or no—and grade point average—under 3.0 or 3.0 and above.

	Internship	No Internship	Total
Under 3.0	20	30	50
3.0 and Above	60	90	150
	80	120	200

a. Use these sample data to estimate the probability of an internship.
b. Estimate P(an internship | grade point average under 3.0).
c. Are the events in part **b** statistically independent?

15. Consider two variables: studied for exam—yes or no—and partied—yes or no. Based on historical data, we know the following three probabilities:

$$P(\text{studied}) = .40$$

$$P(\text{partied}) = .42$$

$$P(\text{partied} \mid \text{studied}) = .75$$

a. Construct a probability tree. Place the studied variable nearer the top of the tree.
b. Compute P(studied | partied).
c. Compute P(not studied | not partied).

4.7 ≡ Using Probability Trees to Minimize Managerial Judgment Errors

Managers have difficulties making judgments involving probability data. Their judgments are often plagued by inconsistency and systematic error. One source of error is that managers use rules of thumb. Probability trees can be used by managers to minimize such errors. By the end of this unit you should be able to:

1. explain in your own words the errors of *ignoring the base rate* and *noncoherency;*
2. construct a probability tree from unconditional and conditional probabilities; and
3. explain the logic of the two general principles of constructing probability trees.

A rule of thumb helps us to arrive at a judgment about some event or to make a decision. It serves to simplify making judgments. We all use rules of thumb. For example, in the child's game of tic-tac-toe, we learned that whoever goes first should place an X in the center square. This rule of thumb makes it difficult to lose the game.

As another example, suppose you must develop a food expense budget for next year. You could develop 365 daily meal plans and then price them out. Or you could use the following rule of thumb: Take last year's food expenses and multiply by an inflation factor.

Rules of thumb are useful and they do simplify judgment making in some situations. However, they can also cause us to make mistakes in others. Fortunately, you can use the probability tree to help minimize some of the most common errors that managers make when using probability data.

The Error of Overlooking the Base Rate

Managers often use probability information poorly. They tend to develop rules of thumb based entirely on conditional probabilities and ignore unconditional probabilities or base rate information. The following example illustrates the error of overlooking the base rate data.

Example: Seismic Testing Case   Before a well is drilled, oil companies often conduct seismic tests to determine if there is oil. They drill a hole in the ground, insert a dynamite charge, and detonate it. The sonic waves indicate whether oil is present or not. An *open structure* means that either oil, water, or air is present. A *closed structure* tends to rule out oil.

ABC Oil has drilled over 100 wells in a west Texas site. It has determined that the probability of finding oil at a given site is 20%. Furthermore, of those wells where oil was found, 70% had an open structure seismic test. Of those wells where oil was not found, 75% had a closed structure.

Estimate within 10% the chance of finding oil given that a site has an open structure.

Many managers would estimate the probability at between 70% and 80% because they are influenced solely by the 70% and 75% figures in the example. They formulate a rule of thumb that uses only the conditional probabilities and **ignore the base rate data**—the unconditional probability of finding oil, the 20% figure.

The error of ignoring the base rate data occurs when managers use the following rule of thumb: When estimating probabilities, use only the conditional probabilities ▪

The rule of thumb given in the margin generates poor probability estimates. Instead we will use a probability tree to determine the probability of finding oil, given an open structure. The example deals with two categorical variables—presence of oil and seismic test results. Begin by dividing each variable into mutually exclusive and exhaustive levels:

Categorical Variables	Levels
Oil found	Yes or no
Seismic test results	Open or closed

We have the following information:

1. The probability of finding oil at a site is 20%. This is an unconditional, or base rate, probability. It applies to all wells that ABC has drilled.

$$P(\text{oil found}) = .20$$

2. Of those wells where oil was found, 70% had an open structure. This is a conditional probability. We focus on only that subset of wells where oil was found.

$$P(\text{open structure} \mid \text{oil found}) = .70$$

3. Of those wells where oil was not found, 75% had a closed structure. This is also a conditional probability.

$$P(\text{closed structure} \mid \text{no oil found}) = .75$$

Until now, it made no difference which categorical variable we placed closer to the top of the probability tree. Is this still true? Before reading on, try constructing a probability tree in which the seismic test results—open or closed—are the first entries in the tree. You will find that you do not have enough information to fill in the probability boxes.

Now, draw the tree in which the results—oil or no oil—are the first data entered. You do have the unconditional probability data for these first entries—namely, the .20 and .80 base rate figures, as shown in Figure 4.6.

Oil Entries   Next, consider the conditional probabilities. Of those wells where oil was found, 70% had an open structure. Simply multiply .20 × .70 to find the joint probability (.14) of having an open structure AND finding oil. Insert the .14 figure into the end box that represents an open structure and oil found. The joint probability of finding oil AND having a closed seismic structure must then be .06.

Why do we multiply the .20 and .70 probabilities to get the joint probability? Please think about it before reading on.

The conditional probability expression (4.5) is used to calculate the joint probability by rewriting it in the form of expression (4.6). In this form it is called the *multiplication rule:*

$$P(A \mid B) = \frac{P(A \text{ AND } B)}{P(B)} \qquad (4.5)$$

$$P(A \text{ AND } B) = P(A \mid B)P(B) \qquad (4.6)$$

We can use the multiplication rule to determine the joint probability of an open structure and finding oil:

$$P(\text{open structure} \mid \text{oil found}) \cdot P(\text{oil found}) = .70 \cdot .20 = .14$$

That's why we multiplied the two probabilities.

No Oil Entries   Of those wells where oil was not found, 75% had a closed structure. In other words, 75% of the 80% that had no oil also had a closed structure. Therefore, the joint probability of having a closed structure AND finding no oil is .75 × .80 = .60. Insert the .60 figure into the end box. The joint probability of finding no oil AND an open structure must equal .20. This completes the probability tree for the seismic study, as shown in Figure 4.7.

Now compute the probability of finding oil given an open structure.

$$P(\text{oil found} \mid \text{open structure}) = \frac{.14}{.14 + .20} = .412$$

If you estimated that this probability would be between .70 and .75, you fell prey to the error of ignoring the base rate.

FIGURE 4.6   Probability Tree for Seismic Study: Base Rate Data Only

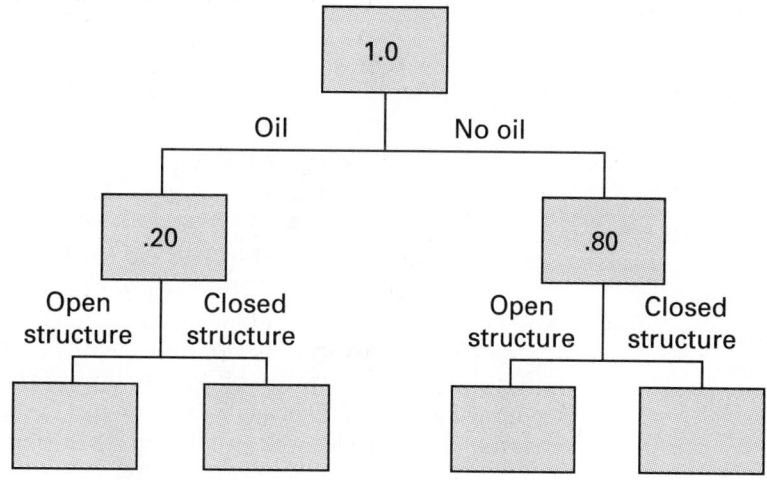

FIGURE 4.7   Completed Probability Tree for Seismic Study

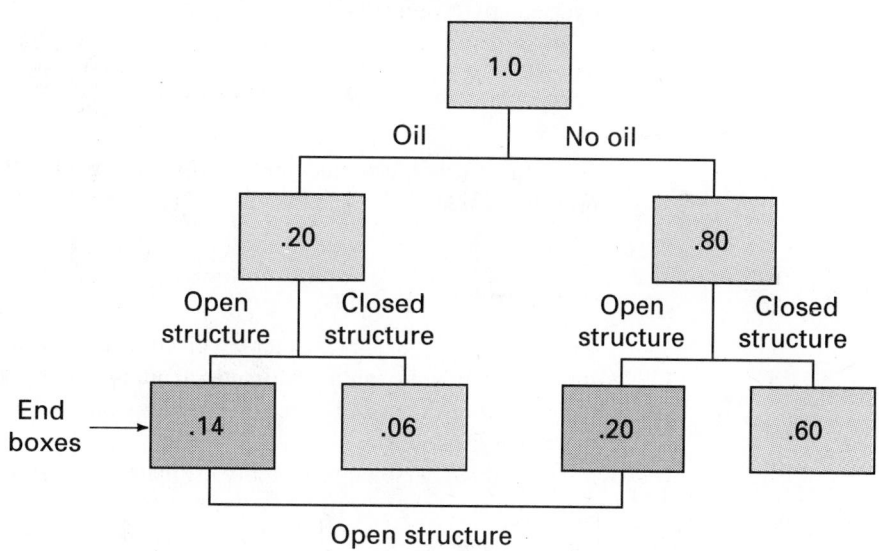

Consider a second case that illustrates the error of ignoring the base rate or unconditional probability data.

Example: Scanner Problem Case   A computer company uses a scanning device that places a mark on each defective chip it spots on the production line. The quality control department reports that 10% of all chips are defective. When a chip is good, the scanner correctly leaves it unmarked 90% of the time. When a chip is defective, the scanner marks it as defective 90% of the time.

Estimate within 10% the probability that a computer chip is really defective if the scanner marks it as defective.

The two categorical variables are chip quality and the result of the scanner test. Chip quality is good or defective—complementary events. The scanner results are marked defective or not marked—also complementary events.

Categorical Variables	Levels
Chip quality	Good or defective
Scanner result	Not marked or marked as defective

The categorical variable for which we have unconditional probability data, chip quality—good or defective chips—is placed closer to the top of the tree, which is shown in Figure 4.8. Ten percent of all chips are defective and 90% are good.

Good Chip Entries   Of the 90% good chips, 90% are not marked by the scanner. Thus, the joint probability of a good chip AND not being marked is $.90 \times .90 = .81$. Since the probability in any box must equal the sum of the probabilities below it, .09 is the joint probability of a good chip AND being marked defective.

Defective Chip Entries   Of the 10% defective chips, 90% are marked defective by the scanner. Thus the joint probability of having a defective chip AND being marked as defective is $.10 \times .90 = .09$. Then .01 is the joint probability of a defective chip AND not being marked. Therefore, the probability that a chip marked defective actually is defective is

$$P(\text{defective chip} \mid \text{marked defective}) = \frac{.09}{.09 + .09} = .50$$

Again, if you estimated about 90%, you ignored the base rate data. By using a probability tree, you avoid the error of ignoring the base rate data.

Noncoherency Error

At the beginning of this chapter we discussed a director of planning who had made three subjective probability estimates about the future. All her estimates fell between 0 and 1. Nevertheless, all three probabilities cannot be correct. We will use a probability tree to show why.

Her three personal probability estimates are restated here:

Unconditional probability:	$P(\text{increased conservation})$	$= .50$
Unconditional probability:	$P(\text{deducting expenses})$	$= .60$
Conditional probability:	$P(\text{increased conservation} \mid \text{deducting expenses})$	$= .85$

The three personal probabilities are numbers between 0 and 1. Taken together, do these three probabilities violate the two basic rules of probability? Might they imply that one or more joint probabilities are negative or greater than 1? If so, all three personal probabilities cannot be valid. Determining if joint probabilities are less than 0 or greater than 1 is very difficult by mere inspection. But we can use a probability tree.

As always, define the two categorical variables and divide them into mutually exclusive and exhaustive levels:

Categorical Variables	Levels
Increased conservation	Yes or no
Deducting expenses	Yes or no

Again, we place our base rate, or unconditional probability, data nearer the top of the tree. However, in this example there are two unconditional probabilities—P(increased conservation) and P(deducting expenses). Which categorical variable goes first? Please think about it before reading on.

We place the deducting expenses categorical variable nearer the top of the tree, as shown in Figure 4.9. Then we can use the conditional probability data (given

FIGURE 4.8   Completed Probability Tree for Scanner Problem

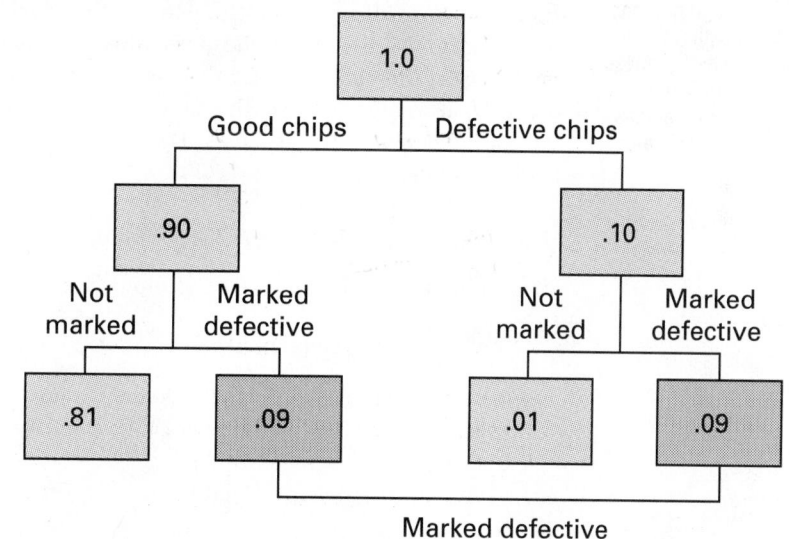

FIGURE 4.9   Probability Tree for Conservation Problem

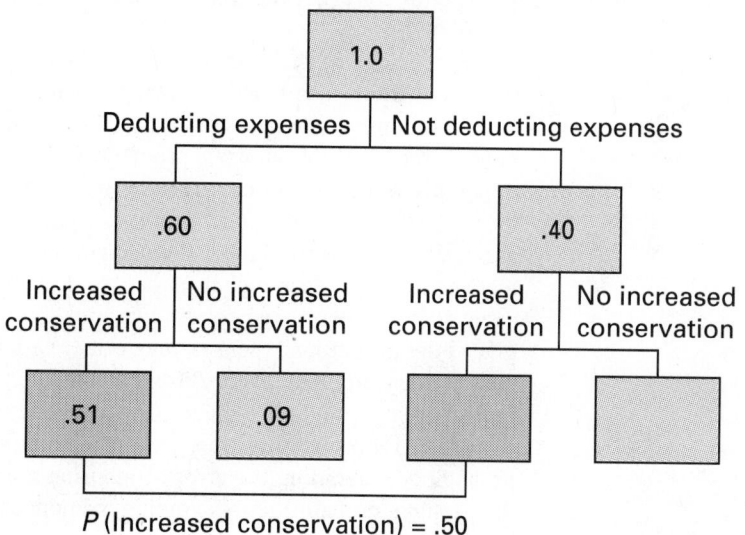

deducting expenses) to determine the joint probabilities for the end boxes. If we place the increased conservation variable nearer the top of the tree, we cannot compute joint probabilities in this example. Try it and you'll see.

Now, we use the multiplication rule, expression (4.6). The joint probability of deducting expenses AND increased conservation is $.6 \cdot .85 = .51$. The second joint probability of the deducting branch, the probability of deducting expenses AND no increased conservation, is then $.60 - .51 = .09$. Remember, the director of planning estimated the unconditional probability of increased conservation as .50. Thus, the two boxes shaded in gray must sum to .5. But that cannot be, because the third joint probability would need to equal $-.01$, which violates the first rule of probability. Therefore, the three personal probabilities are not valid. The director must change one or more personal probabilities.

Let's consider a second case that illustrates the **noncoherency error**.

Managers make the noncoherency error when they assign personal probabilities without determining whether these probabilities imply that one or more joint probabilities are less than 0 or greater than 1.

Example: COMCEL and the Knoxville Market Case   COMCEL's senior management is discussing the possibility of entering the Knoxville, Tennessee, market. Management believes that its chance of successfully entering the market depends on whether COMCEL can develop a new communications technology that will significantly reduce its costs. The group has made the following personal probability assessments:

Unconditional probability:	$P(\text{successful entry})$	$= .70$
Unconditional probability:	$P(\text{technological breakthrough})$	$= .20$
Conditional probability:	$P(\text{successful entry} \mid \text{technological breakthrough})$	$= .95$

Are these three probabilities valid? Do they imply that one or more of the joint probabilities are less than 0 or greater than 1? We begin by defining the categorical variables:

Categorical Variables	Levels
Successful entry into Knoxville	Yes or no
Technological breakthrough	Yes or no

Try to construct the tree before reading on. Then compare your tree to that in Figure 4.10.

Since none of the four-joint probabilities is negative or greater than 1, there is no noncoherency error. Thus COMCEL can use the three probability estimates.

In summary, managers often fall prey to the errors of ignoring the base rate and noncoherency. They can use a probability tree to overcome these errors. In building a tree, place the categorical variable with known unconditional probabilities nearer the top of the tree. If the unconditional probabilities for both categorical variables are known, let event B from the estimated conditional probability dictate which categorical variable you place higher in the tree. For example, in the conservation problem, event B for the estimated conditional probability was deducting expenses. Thus we placed the deducting expenses categorical variable nearer the top of the tree. In the market entry problem, event B for the estimated conditional probability was technological breakthrough. We placed this categorical variable higher in the tree. Having constructed a probability tree, we can determine either (1) the desired conditional probability—avoiding the error of ignoring the base rate—or (2) the validity of all the personal probabilities—avoiding the noncoherency error.

FIGURE 4.10   Completed Probability Tree for Knoxville Expansion

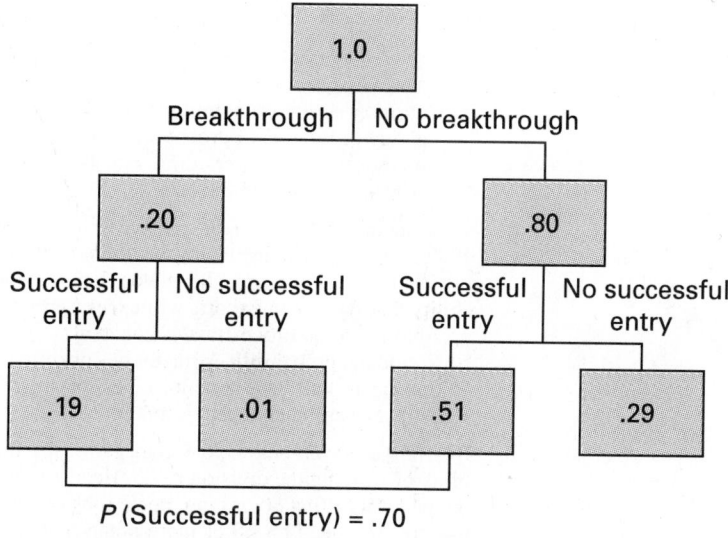

P (Successful entry) = .70

SECTION 4.7 EXERCISES

1. A nationwide client survey showed that 5% of the clients were dissatisfied with the service received. Of those clients who were dissatisfied, 80% said they intended to change vendors. Of those who said they were satisfied, 90% said they did not intend to change vendors.
    a. Given the information above, what is the probability that a client from the survey list will be dissatisfied and want to change vendors?
    b. What is the probability that the person selected will be satisfied and not want to change?
    c. Construct a probability tree.
    d. Use the probability tree to find the probability that a person is dissatisfied, given that she tells you she intends to change vendors.

2. We survey firms to determine whether they use quality circles, small groups of employees who try to improve productivity, and their level of profitability. We obtain the following relative frequency-based probabilities.

    $$P(\text{have quality circles}) = .10$$

    $$P(\text{above-average profit} \mid \text{have quality circles}) = .40$$

    $$P(\text{average or below-average profit} \mid \text{have no quality circles}) = .80$$

    a. Construct a probability tree.
    b. Construct a joint probability table.
    c. Calculate:

    $$P(\text{have quality circles} \mid \text{above-average profit})$$

    $$P(\text{have quality circles} \mid \text{average or below-average profit})$$

3. Three different managers were asked for their personal probabilities of events A, B, and the joint probability of A AND B. Their responses are shown. Event A is family branding and $\bar{A}$ is not family branding. Event B is 10% or less market share and $\bar{B}$ is more than 10% market share.

Manager	$P(A)$	$P(B)$	$P(A \text{ AND } B)$
1	.6	.4	.24
2	.8	.3	.70
3	.3	.5	0

    a. Construct a joint probability table for each manager's set of probabilities.
    b. Are any of the sets of probabilities noncoherent?
    c. Do any of the managers think events A (family branding) and B (amount of market share) are unrelated? Explain.

4. An economist estimates that the probability that American exports will exceed imports in 1992 is .10. She also estimates that the probability that Japan will have a major recession in 1991 is .20. However, if Japan does have a major recession, she estimates that the probability that American exports will exceed imports in 1992 will increase to .50.
    a. Are the probability estimates coherent?
    b. Would the probability estimates be coherent if the economist estimated the probability that Japan will have a major recession in 1991 as .40? Assume all other probability estimates are unchanged. Explain.

5. Before the season begins, the manager of the Boston Red Sox estimates that the probability of winning the division is .65. He also estimates the probability of two new players on the team hitting 60 or more home runs is .70. Finally, he estimates that if the two new players do indeed hit 60 or more home runs, the chance of winning the division would then increase to .90.
    a. Are the probability estimates coherent?
    b. If the probability estimates are coherent, then compute the following probability:

$$P(\text{not winning the division} \mid \text{two new players hit less than 60 home runs})$$

4.8 ≡ Nonstatistical Judgment Errors

The probability tree is an effective tool for minimizing some managerial judgment errors. Managers can overcome other errors simply by knowing that they exist. We describe two common errors that managers make.

Availability Error

Please answer the following question:

Is the letter k more likely to be the first or third letter in an English word?

If you think that k is more likely to occur at the beginning of a word, you are not alone. That's how most people respond. When asked why, they usually say that they can recall more words that start with k than they can those that have k as their third letter. These people have made the **availability error**. The letter k is twice as likely to be the third letter as it is to be the first.

Ready recollections of an event happening do not mean that it has a high probability of happening. Likewise, vague or few recollections of an event happening do not mean that it has a low probability of happening. Memories are faulty and subjective. Instead, look for supporting data before making probability estimates.

> The availability error occurs when managers' judgments of an event's probability are based on or biased by the number of instances of that event that they recall and the ease with which these events come to mind.

Concreteness Error

Several years ago, a college professor decided to purchase a used automobile. He studied the surveys that *Consumer Reports* conducts to determine which cars have the fewest repair problems. He then decided to purchase one of their recommended vehicles. Several days before purchasing the car, he was discussing his choice with a colleague. The colleague happened to own that particular model car, and told the professor that it was the worst lemon in the world. In one instant the professor changed his mind. He made the **concreteness error**.

Review the professor's decision-making process. The survey, based upon repair records from several thousand people, reported that the model needed very few repairs. On the other hand, a close friend told him that the car was a real lemon. The professor valued his colleague's information—a sample of one—much more heavily than the *Consumer Reports* data—a sample of several thousand. The professor did not know the survey people, but he knew his friend. His friend's personal and concrete experiences caused the professor to change his mind—the concreteness error in action. Unless survey data are questionable (see Chapter 6 for details), large size samples are more meaningful than a sample size of one.

The concreteness error occurs also in the business world. A pharmaceutical firm must reverse a precipitous drop in the market share of its major profit maker. Its patents had recently expired, and competitors who sold generic equivalents were eroding the firm's sales and profits. The company was considering maintaining its price in hopes of convincing doctors and pharmacists that it produced the high-quality product. It had recently conducted a scientific market research study showing that maintaining its current price would convince no one. During the deliberations, a senior manager strongly argued that he *personally* believed that the high-price strategy would work. Without much discussion, the group accepted his personal opinion and rejected the marketing research results. They had fallen prey to the concreteness error and as a result they suffered the consequences.

Do not value highly personal concrete data more than impersonal survey data. Rather, what is important is the validity of each, and the amount of evidence that supports each position. Generally, large-size samples are more informative than small-size samples. There is one exception to that rule. If the survey uses improper sampling designs or asks poorly worded questions, then of course do not trust the data.

> The concreteness error occurs when a person places greater weight on highly personal data than on abstract or survey data. Decision making is erroneously based on the source of the data, rather than the sample size.

SECTION 4.8 EXERCISES

1. You tell a friend that 95% of all paroled felons complete parole without rearrest, thus saving millions of dollars of prison expenditures. The friend responds: "That's not true. There was a case reported in the paper where a parolee committed a heinous crime." Assuming you are correct, what's wrong with your friend's reasoning?

2. In a national survey, 93% of all customers surveyed reported being "satisfied" or "very satisfied" with the repair service of a major appliance firm, the best record of any major appliance company. A friend of yours tells you that he had a service call and the work was awful. Would you buy an appliance from this company if it had to service the appliance? Discuss your reasoning.

3. According to the National Safety Council's *Accident Facts* (1988 edition), the probability of death due to firearms is about one-eleventh of the probability of death due to falls. Explain why most people estimate the probability of dying due to firearms as higher than that of dying due to falls.

4. Tom Taylor has high intelligence. However, he lacks true creativity. He has a need for order and clarity, and for neat and tidy systems in which every detail finds its appropriate place. His writing is rather dull and mechanical, occasionally enlivened by flashes of imagination of the science fiction type. He has a strong drive for competence. He seems to have little feeling and sympathy for other people, and does not enjoy interacting with

others. He has a deep moral sense of right and wrong. Tom is currently a graduate student. What is he majoring in?

Suppose we asked you to rank the listed majors from 1 = most likely to 8 = least likely. You shouldn't rank the majors because you do not yet have enough information. You know much about Tom and his interests and this is important information. However, you are missing a second important piece of information—base rate data. What are the missing base rate data?

Business administration	_____	Physical sciences	_____
Engineering	_____	Law	_____
Computer sciences	_____	Social work	_____
Humanities education	_____	Library sciences	_____

4.9 Key Ideas and Overview

Except in statistics books, managers are not given probabilities. So where do they come from? There are two methods for assigning probabilities:

1. the relative frequency approach, and
2. the personal, or subjective, probability approach.

Experience is the basis for the relative frequency approach. If we observe a random experiment, we can determine the relative frequency of an event. That, in turn, is an estimate of the probability. Relative frequency probabilities come from observation.

Intuition is the basis for personal probabilities. A manager "guesstimates" a probability based on knowledge and insight about an event. Managers' intuitive powers are often weak and so they make errors in assessing personal probabilities. Probability trees can improve their judgment making. Any probability—relative frequency or subjective—must satisfy the following two rules of probability:

RULE 1:   Probabilities are numbers between 0 and 1.0 inclusive.

RULE 2:   The sum of the probabilities of all non-overlapping possible events that can occur must be 1.0.

Table 4.5 captures some of the similarities between this chapter and the preceding descriptive statistics chapters.

SECTION 4.9 EXERCISES

1.   In each of the following scenarios, the word *probability* is mentioned. For each situation state whether the probability is a relative frequency or personal probability. Explain your answer.
  a.   After producing 10,000 items over a period of 5 years, a manufacturer found that 5% of these items were defective. Therefore, the probability that any part is defective is 5%.
  b.   A top executive states that there is an almost zero probability that her competitor will beat her firm to market with a competing product.
  c.   The probability is greater than .5 that the Seattle Seahawks will win the Super Bowl by 1994.

2.   The National Aeronautics and Space Administration (NASA) plans to purchase parts from several current vendors to construct its sixth space shuttle. Each vendor reports the probability that its part(s) will be defective. From these probabilities, NASA engineers calculate that the probability of a shuttle failure is .0001. Is this probability based on personal or relative frequency considerations?

Table 4.5

A Comparison of Descriptive Statistics and Basic Probability Concepts

	Descriptive Statistics	**Basic Probability**
Goals	To collect, organize, summarize, and intepret data To detect possible relationships between variables To describe a data set by a few numbers—mean, standard deviation, median, and interquartile range	To compute or assess probabilities To detect possible relationships between variables To describe the unpredictability of an event by its probability
Starting Point	A representative set of cross-sectional or time-ordered data. Compute measures of the central tendency and variability	A random experiment. Compute a relative frequency probability or estimate a personal probability
Relationship Detection	Use a cross-tabs table to display descriptive data. Determine relationship by computing row or column percentages.	Use a probability tree to display probability data. Determine relationship by computing conditional probabilities.
Problem Solving	Helps managers build mental models, sense outliers, and diagnose root causes of disturbance problems.	Helps managers make decisions in a logical and systematic fashion. Probability trees help managers minimize information-processing errors.

COMCEL

Date: September 10, 1992
To: Howard Bright, Plant Manager
From: Sarah Teman, Manager of Operations
Re: Effects of Job Switching on Productivity

Summary. Although the work group productivity varies both by group and by month, work groups that switch jobs appear, on average, to outperform work groups that don't switch jobs. The Operations Analysis Group is now reviewing my analysis. Subject to their confirmation, I recommend you ask Marvin Elrod to determine the potential training costs as his Human Resources group will do the job training.

Supporting analysis. I obtained productivity data for all 36 work groups from the production information system. I assigned work groups to the "high" productivity category if they produced at the median level of productivity or higher. I assigned work groups to the "low" productivity category if they produced below the median productivity. I then determined how many groups in each category switched or had not switched jobs during the quarter.

Job switching appears to be related to high performance: 52.8% of my sample were high producers, but among the groups that switched jobs, 81.8% are high producers. So, the chance that a group is producing at or above the median level increases among the groups that switch jobs.

A note of caution. I have made two assumptions in my analysis. First, the above percentages are stable from month to month. Second, work groups worked on a normal mix of products.

Although the percentage of job-switching groups that are high producers is dramatically higher than the percentage of high producers overall— 81.8% vs. 52.8%—a definite conclusion must wait until we have more data. Since the total number of work groups is only 36, a shift of two or three groups from the high- to low-productivity categories could dramatically affect the percentages. All work groups have off-months, job switching or not. I have sent the data over to our statistical wizards to see what conclusions they can draw from the data. I will report as soon as I have their results.

CHAPTER 4 QUESTIONS

1. How do inaccurate probability estimates affect your problem-solving ability?
2. Which of the following are random experiments and why?
   a. Determine the time it takes for products to reach the market place.
   b. Watch a ball game at a company picnic.
   c. Find out the promotional status of a worker.
   d. Assess the cholesterol levels of workers who exercise at least four times a week.
3. Illustrate a simple and a compound event for a random experiment where you interview random households and ask them how many cars they own.
4. Do relative frequencies of events always equal their respective probabilities? Explain.
5. How are relative frequency and personal probabilities similar and different?
6. The categorical variable, gender, has two levels: male or female. The two levels are mutually exclusive events. Are the events male and female also statistically independent?
7. Under what conditions can a joint probability be greater than 0?
8. Compare unconditional, joint, and conditional probabilities showing similarities and differences.
9. If $P(A \mid B)$ equals $P(A)$, what can you conclude about event B's impact on event A?
10. What is the multiplication rule? What is the multiplication rule when two events are statistically independent?

11. What is the addition rule? What is the addition rule when two events are statistically independent?

12. In your own words, what is the error of ignoring the base rate?

13. Explain the logic of placing the base rate, or unconditional probability, data as the first entry in a probability tree (nearer the top of the tree) when using it to overcome the error of ignoring the base rate.

14. In your own words, what is the noncoherency error?

15. You must estimate the probability of an airplane crash. You read that morning of a major air disaster and you increased your original probability estimate. What error have you just made?

CHAPTER 4 APPLICATION PROBLEMS

1. Best Diary Inc. has collected the following frequency data on market segment and milk preference. Do different segments have different milk preferences?

	Machos	Status Seekers	Total
Skim	30	80	110
Whole	70	20	90
	100	100	200

a. Develop a probability tree from the cross-tabs table.

b. What is P(preferring skim milk OR being a Status Seeker)?

c. What is the following unconditional probability: P(being a Macho)?

d. What is the following conditional probability: P(being a Macho | preferring whole milk)?

e. Are the probabilities in parts **b–d** true probabilities or only estimated probabilities—that is, relative frequencies?

f. Based on your answers to parts **c** and **d,** does milk preference appear to be independent of market segment? Explain.

g. Develop one marketing/advertising strategy the manager should consider given the answer in part **f.**

2. Based on 2,000 accounts, an accounting manager develops the following probability table on the size of accounts payable (rounded to the nearest dollar).

Less than $1,500	.05
$1,500 to $1,999	.15
$2,000 to $2,499	.30
$2,500 to $2,999	.30
$3,000 to $3,499	.15
$3,500 and above	.05

a. What is the probability of an account payable being between $1,500 and $2,999?

b. What is the probability of an account payable being less than $2,500?

c. What is the probability of an account payable being more than $2,999?

d. Why must the six probabilities in the table sum to 1? Explain.

e. How would you develop the table?

f. One year later, the manager finds that 40% of the accounts payable are $3,500 or more. Given the data in this problem, what might the accounting manager conclude?

3. A firm is considering using a nondiscriminatory test to predict which employees will be very successful on the job. Presently, 60% of the employees are very successful on the job. The firm asked each employee to take the test. The firm obtained the following conditional probability data:

$$P(\text{passing score} \mid \text{very successful}) = .80$$

$$P(\text{failing score} \mid \text{not very successful}) = .90$$

Is the test a good predictor? Can it be used to evaluate potential employees? That is, what is the probability of being very successful on the job given you get a passing score? What is the probability of not being very successful given you get a failing score?

a. Construct a probability tree. *Hint:* Place the categorical variable—job success—nearer the top of the tree.

b. Compute the following two conditional probabilities:

$$P(\text{very successful} \mid \text{passing score})$$

$$P(\text{not very successful} \mid \text{failing score})$$

c. Is the test a good predictor of (1) very successful and (2) not very successful job performance? Explain in simple terms.

4. A civil rights group has collected the following hypothetical probability data on hiring practices in an industry:

$$P(\text{hiring an applicant}) = .10$$

$$P(\text{hiring an applicant} \mid \text{applicant is white male}) = .10$$

$$P(\text{hiring an applicant} \mid \text{applicant is black male}) = .10$$

The Civil Rights Act says that a person cannot be discriminated against in hiring based on sex, race, creed, or place of national origin. Given the above data, are hiring and the applicant's race statistically independent in the industry? Explain.

5. Restaurants must determine the number of waiters to hire. If there are too few, customers will have to wait more than 20 minutes for service. They may leave and never return. Too many waiters can increase the restaurant's operating costs. Consider the following wait times:

less than 5 minutes
5 minutes to 20 minutes
more than 20 minutes

a. What must the sum of the probabilities for the three events be?

b. Assign personal probabilities that indicate that the restaurant has too few waiters. Discuss.

c. Assign personal probabilities that indicate that the restaurant has too many waiters. Discuss.

6. A real estate manager provides personal, or subjective, probability estimates about the chances of selling several tracts of land to a major developer.

Tracts	Personal Probability
0	.05
1	.60
2	.15
3	.50
4	.35
5 or more	.45

a. What, if anything, is incorrect about her six subjective probability estimates?

b. How could you change the probability estimates to eliminate the problem you described in part **a?**

7. A product manager develops the following three personal probability estimates about the sales potential for high resolution TVs:

$$P(\text{meeting sales goals}) = .60$$

$$P(\text{positive market research finding}) = .70$$

$$P(\text{meeting sales goals} \mid \text{positive market research finding}) = 1.00$$

    a. Do the three probabilities imply that any of the joint probabilities is greater than 1 or less than 0? Use a probability tree to support your position.

    b. Suppose the product manager believes that the first and third probability estimates reflect his best thinking. Change the second probability estimate so that no joint probability is negative.

    c. Based on the third conditional probability, what is the product manager saying about the effectiveness or impact of the marketing research findings? Explain.

 8. A stock analyst specializing in the retail industry wants to know if chain stores have the same focus—service or price—as do independents. In statistical terms, is focus statistically independent of type of store? The data are shown.

	Service	Price	Total
Independents	25	5	30
Chains	4	16	20
	29	21	50

    a. Develop a probability tree from the cross-tabs table.

    b. What is $P(\text{having a service focus OR being a chain})$?

    c. What is the following unconditional probability: $P(\text{having a price focus})$?

    d. What is the following conditional probability: $P(\text{having a price focus} \mid \text{being a chain})$?

    e. Based on your answers to parts **c** and **d,** is focus independent of type of store? Explain.

    f. Are the probabilities in parts **b–d** true probabilities or estimated probabilities—that is, relative frequencies? Explain.

 9. A firm is considering two methods for purchasing microcomputers. One method will permit divisions to centralize the purchases. That is, all division purchases will be made by one person. The second method will allow individual employees within a division to purchase any computer they wish. The MIS manager develops the following subjective joint probability estimates regarding the presence or absence of centralized purchasing and the purchasing of three different computer brands:

$$P(\text{decentralized purchasing AND buy IBM micros}) = .20$$

$$P(\text{centralized purchasing AND buy IBM micros}) = .30$$

$$P(\text{decentralized purchasing AND buy Macintosh micros}) = .20$$

$$P(\text{centralized purchasing AND buy Macintosh micros}) = .10$$

$$P(\text{decentralized purchasing AND buy other micros}) = .05$$

$$P(\text{centralized purchasing AND buy other micros}) = .05$$

    a. What, if anything, is improper about the six subjective joint probability estimates?

    b. The manager wants to maintain the relative sizes of the six probabilities. For example, she believes that the first probability is three times greater than the third probability and six times greater than the fourth and fifth probabilities. How can you do this without violating the basic rules of probability?

10. Does taking a workshop in problem solving improve on-the-job problem-solving skills? Overall only 30% of all managers are rated as having high on-the-job problem-solving skills. Of those who are highly rated, 90% took the problem-solving-course. Of those who are not highly rated, only 10% took the course. What is the conditional probability of being highly rated on the job if you have taken the problem-solving course?
   a. Construct a probability tree.
   b. Compute the following conditional probability:

   P(highly rated on the job | taken problem-solving course)

   c. Would you recommend that the firm require the course of all managers? Assume that costs are negligible.
   d. Explain how you would collect the data in this problem.
   e. Use the probability tree to determine what P(taken problem-solving course | not highly rated) must be if P(highly rated | taken course) = .90. Assume that all other probabilities remain the same.

 11. Using data obtained from a sample of students at a college, you have computed the following three probabilities:

   P(GPA above 3.5) = .15

   P(GPA above 3.5 | SAT score at or above 1,200) = .30

   P(GPA above 3.5 | SAT score below 1,200) = .03

   a. Does it appear that GPA and SAT scores are statistically dependent? Explain.
   b. How would you determine the above three probabilities for a sample of 1,500 students?
   c. Are the probabilities true probabilities or relative frequencies? Explain.

 12. A project manager estimates the following three subjective probabilities for building a new warehouse:

   P(completing project on time) = .90

   P(rainy weather) = .50

   P(completing project on time | rainy weather) = .80

   a. Do the three probabilities imply that any of the joint probabilities is greater than 1 or less than 0? Use a probability tree to support your position.
   b. Given your probability tree from part **a,** what is P(completing project on time | no rainy weather)?

 13. Do company-run stress-management programs minimize absenteeism? ABC Research collects the following cross-tabs data. Low absenteeism is defined as less than 1% of total man-hours lost.

	Absenteeism		
	Low	High	Total
Program	40	60	100
No Program	10	90	100
	50	150	200

   a. Develop a probability tree from the cross-tabs table.
   b. What is P(having no stress-management program OR having high absenteeism)?
   c. What is the unconditional probability: P(having low absenteeism)?
   d. What is the conditional probability: P(having low absenteeism | having stress-management program)?

e. Based on your answers to parts **c** and **d,** is level of absenteeism independent of running stress-management programs? Explain.

14. An airline's most popular flight is the shuttle from New York to Washington, D.C. Each plane can hold 150 passengers, and each flight is always sold out in advance. However, the airline has noted that often there are one or more vacant seats. Apparently, some passengers catch an earlier flight or "double book" flights. The airline records the number of empty seats over a 1-week period.

Empty Seats	Probability
0	.10
1	.10
2	.20
3	.20
4	.20
5	.20

a. Given the above data, is the airline losing revenues by selling only 150 seats per flight?
b. Should the airline consider selling more than 150 tickets per flight? Discuss.
c. Suppose it sells 155 tickets per flight. Given the above data, will it ever have any empty seats on a flight?
d. What problem would the airline now experience if it sold 155 tickets per flight?

15. An economist makes the following subjective probability estimates. (High inflation is defined as an inflation rate over 5%.)

$$P(\text{high inflation}) = .20$$

$$P(\text{increased federal spending}) = .40$$

$$P(\text{high inflation} \mid \text{increased federal spending}) = .30$$

a. Do the three probabilities imply that any of the joint probabilities must be greater than 1 or less than 0? Use a probability tree to support your position.
b. Given the above data, what is $P(\text{high inflation} \mid \text{no increased spending})$?

16. The probability of having disease X in the general population is only .05. The Sagman Test is a newly discovered method for early detection. Of those who have disease X, the test indicates the disease for 90% of them. Of those who do not have the disease, the test indicates no disease for 90% of them. Is the test a good predictor of whether you actually have the disease or not? Should its use be widespread?

a. Which of the following conditional probabilities is most appropriate to determine the test's effectiveness? Explain.

$$P(\text{have disease X} \mid \text{test says you have the disease})$$

$$P(\text{test says you have the disease} \mid \text{have the disease})$$

$$P(\text{test says you have the disease})$$

b. Set up a joint probability table and compare the unconditional probability of having the disease to the conditional probability of having the disease given the test says you have the disease.
c. Compare the unconditional probability of not having the disease to the conditional probability of not having the disease given the test says you do not have the disease.
d. Based on parts **b** and **c,** is the test a good predictor? Explain.
e. Suppose that to use the test, $P(\text{have disease} \mid \text{test says you have disease})$ must be 90% or greater. What must the following conditional probability be: $P(\text{test says you do not have the disease} \mid \text{no disease})$?

17. An MIS manager had determined the following relative frequency probabilities for the age of microcomputers in the firm:

Age of Microcomputer	Probability
Less than 1 year	.05
1 year but less than 2 years	.10
2 years but less than 3 years	.10
3 years but less than 4 years	.15
4 or more years	.60

a. Find the probability that a microcomputer is less than 2 years old.
b. Find the probability that a microcomputer is at least 1 year old.
c. Find the probability that a microcomputer is 3 years old or more.
d. Given that the mean useful life of a computer is 4 years due to technical obsolescence, what can you conclude about the need for capital investment in microcomputers from the probability data?

 18. An organizational behavior consulting firm has collected the following data on leadership style for 200 firms in the United States and Canada. Do American and Canadian firms prefer the same leadership styles?

	Leadership Style	
	Participative	Autocratic
United States	30	70
Canada	50	50

a. What is the following unconditional probability: P(having participative leadership)?
b. What is the following conditional probability: P(having participative leadership | firm in United States)?
c. Based on your answers to parts **a** and **b,** is leadership style independent of the country where the firm is located? Explain in terms that a manager could understand.

 19. You are told that men and women have the same chances of being promoted in a firm.
a. What must be true about the following three probabilities? Explain in simple terms.

$$P(\text{promoted})$$

$$P(\text{promoted} \mid \text{male})$$

$$P(\text{promoted} \mid \text{female})$$

b. Must the following two probabilities equal one another for gender and promotion to be statistically independent? Explain.

$$P(\text{promoted} \mid \text{female})$$

$$P(\text{female} \mid \text{promoted})$$

 20. Fifty percent of all undergraduate students major in Business Administration. Given that you are a Business major, there is a .70 probability of being an extrovert—a person who likes to interact with others. If you are not a Business Administration major, there is an .80 chance that you are an introvert—a person who likes to concentrate on ideas. Suppose you select an extrovert; what is the chance that he or she is a Business major?
a. Write the unconditional probability in the first sentence in probability notation.
b. Write the two conditional probabilities in the next two sentences in probability notation.
c. Write the conditional probability in the last sentence in probability notation.
d. Develop a probability tree and determine the conditional probability P(Business major | Extrovert).

21. Shown here is a cross-tabs table of the age and race of the male inmate population in Georgia in 1988. [*Source: Georgia Criminal Justice Data, 1988.*] Does it appear that race and age are statistically independent?

| | | | Age | | |
	0–21	22–39	40–54	55–99	Total
White Male	639	4,335	1,224	270	6,468
Nonwhite Male	1,200	8,631	1,385	228	11,444
	1,839	12,966	2,609	498	17,912

   a. What is the probability of a nonwhite male inmate?
   b. What is the probability of a white male inmate?
   c. What is the probability of an inmate being of age 0–21, given that he is a white male?
   d. What is the probability of an inmate being of age 0–21, given that he is a nonwhite male?
   e. Considering only your answers in parts **c** and **d,** does it appear that age and race are related? Discuss.

 22. Cablebest is preparing to apply to the Federal Communications Commission (FCC) for a license. The FCC has three options: (1) grant a restricted license, (2) grant an unrestricted license, (3) do not grant a license. Cablebest believes that the FCC ruling will depend on its ability to recruit a knowledgeable general manager. Cablebest is presently seeking such a person. The firm is not sure whether it will have such a person when it submits the application. Following are the firm's subjective probability estimates.

$$P(\text{will recruit}) = .70$$

$$P(\text{won't recruit}) = .30$$

$$P(\text{unrestricted license}) = .50$$

$$P(\text{restricted license}) = .40$$

$$P(\text{no license}) = .10$$

   a. Explain how a firm might estimate the probabilities.
   b. The firm also estimates that $P(\text{unrestricted license} \mid \text{will recruit}) = .90$. Are all the probability estimates coherent?

 23. BHJ Inc. is one of Apex's largest customers. Here are historical probability data on the number of sales made to BHJ Inc. of more than 1,000 units over the 52 weeks of 1991:

$$P(\text{zero sales}) = .02$$

$$P(\text{one sale}) = .10$$

$$P(\text{two sales}) = .10$$

$$P(\text{three sales}) = .30$$

$$P(\text{four sales}) = .48$$

   a. Suppose that in the first week of 1992, Apex has zero sales of more than 1,000 units to BHJ. Given the historical probability data, should Apex be concerned about lack of sales to BHJ Inc.? Discuss.
   b. Suppose that for the first two weeks of 1992, Apex. has zero sales of more than 1,000 units to BHJ. Should Apex now be concerned? Discuss. Assume that each week's sales are statistically independent events.

24. According to data from the National Center for Health Statistics, in 1986, the probability of an infant (one year old or less) dying in the United States was .0104. The probability of a white infant dying within the first year was .0089. The probability of a black infant dying within the first year was .0180.
   a. Which are unconditional probabilities and which are conditional probabilities?
   b. Given the above data, does it appear that infant mortality and race are related? Discuss.
   c. What might account for the fact that black babies are more than twice as likely to die within the first year as white babies?

25. A college tracks 200 students enrolled in a basic management course. Seventy percent of the students received a grade of B or better. Of those students who received a grade of B or better, 90% had prepared for exams by using study groups. Of those who received a grade of C or worse, only 30% had used study groups.
   a. What is the probability of receiving a grade of B or better if you use a study group?
   b. What is the probability of receiving a grade of C or worse if you do not use a study group?
   c. If you want to maximize your chance of receiving a grade of B or better, should you use a study group? Discuss.

REFERENCES

Tversky, Amos, and Daniel Kahneman. "Judgment under Uncertainty." *Science* (September 25, 1974): 1124–1131.

Tversky, Amos, and Daniel Kahneman. "The Framing of Decisions and the Psychology of Choice." *Science* (January 30, 1981): 453–458.

PROBABILITY DISTRIBUTIONS

5.1   Probability distributions and problem solving
5.2   Random variables and discrete probability
         distributions
      Random variables
      Relative frequency and personal probability
         distributions and histograms
      Mean and standard deviation
5.3   The binomial distribution
      Calculating probabilities
      The binomial expression
      The binomial table
      Mean and standard deviation of a binomial
         distribution
5.4   Problem solving and the binomial distribution
      Assessing consequences
      Problem sensing
      Assessing the Bernoulli processs assumption

5.5   The Poisson distribution
      The Poisson expression
      The Poisson table
      Problem sensing and the Poisson distribution
      Assessing the Poisson process assumptions
      Mean and standard deviation of a Poisson
         distribution
5.6   The normal distribution
      Why is the normal distribution so useful?
      Characteristics of the normal distribution
      z-scores and finding probabilities
      The normal distribution and decision making
      Validity of the normal distribution
         assumptions
5.7   Integrating framework and key ideas

COMCEL INTEROFFICE COMMUNICATION

Date: February 12, 1994
From: Howard Bright, Plant Manager
To: Sang Kim, Quality Assurance
Re: Quality of circuit breakers

I received a call from a good friend of mine who is also one of our best customers. She wanted to know if we are relaxing our quality control standards. In a box of 25 circuit breakers purchased from us last week, three turned out to be defective, a defective rate of 12%. She reminded me that our competitors guarantee a defect rate of no more than 5%.

Are our quality standards slipping? We should strive to ship no defective products, but we must certainly meet or exceed the quality levels of our competitors.

Please look into this and report back ASAP.

5.1 ▤ Probability Distributions and Problem Solving

Chapter 4 demonstrated two ways managers can obtain probabilities—namely, using intuition and judgment to generate personal probabilities, and survey data to provide relative frequency probabilities. Managers *generate* personal probabilities based on their knowledge and insight about an event. However, their intuitive powers are usually weak, and so they often make errors in determining personal probabilities. Survey data *provide* relative frequency probabilities. If we observe a random experiment many times, we can determine the relative frequency of an event, which is an approximation of the true probability.

In this chapter we will discuss a third probability source. Theoretical probability distributions are mathematical expressions that we use to *calculate* probabilities. These expressions are based on sets of underlying assumptions that must be satisfied if the calculated probabilities are to be valid. We will discuss three important theoretical probability distributions—the binomial, the Poisson, and the normal.

Thus, managers can use empirical (data-based), personal, or theoretical probabilities to become more effective problem solvers and decision makers. Figure 5.1 reproduces our problem-solving model.

Problem or Opportunity Sensing   From Chapter 1, we know that effective managers use Pounds's four strategies to sense problems. The following example illustrates the historic model, in which managers look for deviations from past performance.

EXAMPLE 1:   From historical data, Georgia Stationery Supplies knows that 40% of orders received from ABC Inc. will be for more than 1,000 boxes of paper. Of ABC's last six orders, none has been for more than 1,000 boxes. Could Georgia Stationery Supplies be facing a problem with declining business from ABC Inc.?

Diagnosis   Once a problem happens, managers suggest changes that might explain the deviation. After determining the root causes, they take corrective action and determine if the problem has been solved.

FIGURE 5.1   Problem-Solving Model

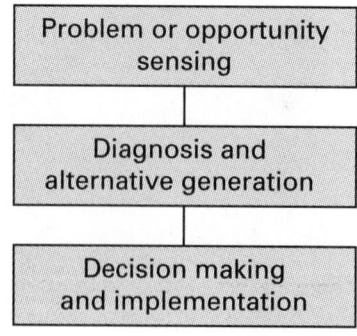

EXAMPLE 2:   Recently the number of accidents per month on a highway has increased from one to ten per month. After a major investigation, the Highway Patrol thought they identified the cause—rapid road deterioration. They repaired the road and over the next month, there was only one accident. Was their diagnosis accurate?

Decision Making—Evaluating Alternatives   Managers must evaluate alternative actions before selecting the best one to implement. Evaluating alternatives sometimes means making predictions about the consequences of an alternative action. Theoretical probability models can provide objective and unbiased information.

EXAMPLE 3:   COMCEL buys electronic components from ZT Audio for its cellular phones. COMCEL requires that each lot of 1,000 components contain 10% or fewer defectives. COMCEL inspects every shipment from ZT by selecting and testing a sample of 10 components. It is considering two acceptance rules: Accept the lot of 1,000 if (1) one or no components are defective or (2) two or fewer components are defective.

Evaluating alternatives sometimes means determining which action is more likely to accomplish the desired goals. Again we can use probability effectively.

EXAMPLE 4:   Two overnight express services are in head-to-head competition. Federal Service advertises a mean delivery time of 30 hours, while United Express claims that its mean delivery time is 34 hours. However United Express's arrival times are more consistent because its standard deviation is only 2 hours, whereas Federal's is 5 hours. Which service should you use if your documents must always arrive within 36 hours?

Sensing problems, verifying diagnoses, evaluating alternative actions, and making choices are problem-solving activities. Later, we will show how theoretical probability distributions can improve problem-solving and decision-making skills.

5.2 ≣ Random Variables and Discrete Probability Distributions

In Chapter 3 we introduced the random experiment. Now we build upon that idea and introduce two new terms—a random variable and its probability distribution. By the end of this section you should be able to:

1. explain what a random variable is;
2. explain the similarities and differences between discrete and continuous random variables;
3. describe the properties common to all discrete probability distributions;
4. draw a discrete probability histogram; and
5. compute the mean and standard deviation of a discrete probability distribution.

Random Variables

Table 5.1 lists four random experiments along with the variables for which we would like to compute probabilities.

How many values can the first variable take on? Since there are only 36 work groups in the plant, the variable can take on 37 different possible values: 0, 1, 2, 3, . . . , 36.

In the second example the random variable is the number of correct answers obtained on a 15-question exam. If there is no partial credit, this variable can take on 16 possible values: 0, 1, 2, 3, . . . , 15.

In the third example the random variable is the lifetime of a computer chip. Suppose that no chip has ever lasted less than 800 hours or more than 1,300 hours. What are all the possible lifetimes within this interval? Since fractions of hours are possible, the life of a computer chip can take on any value between 800 and 1,300 hours. There is an infinite, or uncountable, number of possible values.

Table 5.1

Variables Defined in Random Experiments

Random Experiment	Variable
From a total of 36 work groups, count the number of work groups that exceed 100% productivity	The number of high-producing work groups
Count the number of correct answers on a 15-question exam.	The number of correct answers on exam
Record the life of a computer chip.	The number of hours a computer chip lasts
Record the weight of a box of cereal that has a nominal weight of 16 oz.	The actual weight of the box

In the last example the random variable is the box weight. Suppose that no box has ever weighed less than 15.9 ounces or more than 16.1 ounces. How many values are possible within this interval? There is an infinite, or uncountable, number of values.

In summary, the four random experiments in Table 5.1 have one thing in common. There may be a finite or an infinite number of outcomes, but the outcomes are numbers.

A random variable is defined in a random experiment that has numerical outcomes. Describing a random variable means (1) stating the variable (for which we would like to determine or compute probabilities) and (2) listing all its possible values.

Now we are ready for a working definition of a **random variable.**

The number of high-producing work groups in a plant and the number of correct answers on an exam are examples of *discrete* random variables. Discrete random variables can take on a finite or countable number of values. Often the values are *counts*. For example, we can count the number of high-producing groups or the number of questions answered correctly on an exam. We write discrete random variables as follows:

The random variable	X = the number of high-producing work groups
Listing of values	Possible values: {0, 1, 2, 3, . . . , 36}

In the other two random experiments, the number of hours that a chip lasts and the weight of the cereal box are *continuous* random variables. They can take on an uncountable number of values. Other examples of continuous random variables are length, weight, and speed. Continuous random variables can be *measured*. In measuring weight, for example, the scale may permit a determination only to the nearest pound. Thus the resulting data will be discrete in units of 1 pound. Nevertheless we treat weight as continuous because it could take on an uncountable number of values. We write continuous random variables as follows:

The random variable X = the number of hours that a chip lasts

Listing of values   Possible values: {$800 < x < 1,300$}

The notation "<" indicates that there is an uncountable number of possible values between 800 and 1,300 hours.

Relative Frequency and Personal Probability Distributions and Histograms

Assume that no family in Omaha owns more than four cars. Consider the following discrete random variable:

X = the number of cars owned by families in Omaha

Possible values: {0, 1, 2, 3, 4}

We conduct a survey and obtain the relative frequency probabilities. Table 5.2 presents the **discrete probability distribution** results. Note that the sum of the five probabilities equals 1. This is because of the families interviewed, all had either 0, 1, 2, 3, or 4 cars. These are all the possible events in the survey. As the second rule of probability says, the sum of the probabilities of all possible nonoverlapping events that can occur must equal 1.

A discrete probability distribution consists of all the possible numerical values of a discrete random variable together with their associated probabilities.

Table 5.2

Relative Frequency Distribution

Number of Cars	Relative Frequency Probability
0	.10
1	.40
2	.40
3	.08
4	.02

We can describe a discrete probability distribution by listing the allowable values and their probabilities or by drawing a picture called a *probability histogram.* We first talked about histograms in Chapter 2 to show how managers could use them to organize and summarize a mass of data into meaningful information. Figure 5.2 depicts a histogram for the number of cars owned by families in Omaha, using the same data given in Table 5.2.

Like frequency histograms, probability histograms consist of bars or rectangles. The base of each rectangle is centered on one of the values of the random variable— for example, 0, 1, 2, 3, and 4 cars in Figure 5.2. Each rectangle is 1 unit wide; its height is equal to the probability of getting that value. The total area under the probability histogram is 1 by the second rule of probability.

In Chapter 2, we analyzed groups of numbers using the mean and standard deviation. Now we extend these statistical tools to probability distributions for discrete random variables.

FIGURE 5.2   Probability Histogram: Survey of Number of Cars per Family in Omaha

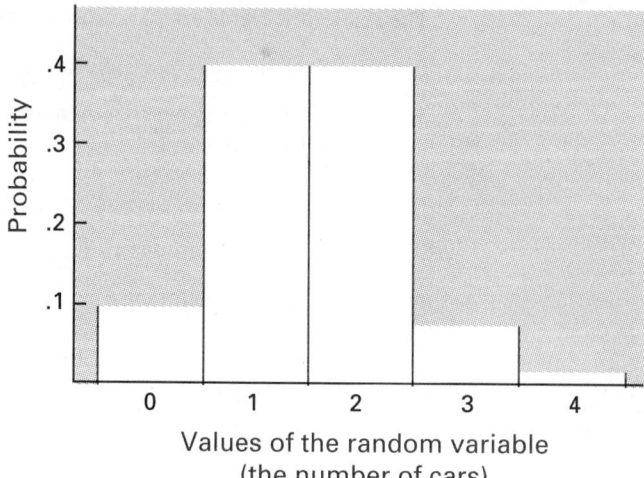

Values of the random variable
(the number of cars)

Mean and Standard Deviation

The mean is a measure of the central tendency of a probability distribution. As with frequency histograms, we can use the balance point idea from Chapter 2 to *approximate* the mean. Place a steel rod underneath the probability histogram in Figure 5.2 and move it from left to right. At what number of cars would the probability histogram balance? It would not balance at one car, for there would be too much weight (probability) to the right, and the histogram would tilt down to the right. It would not balance at three cars, for there would be too much weight to the left, and the histogram would tilt down to the left. The balance point is slightly more than 1.5 cars, and that is our approximation of the mean.

We can use expression (5.1) to compute the actual mean or expected value of the random variable X:

$$\text{Mean}^* = \mu = E(X) = \sum_i x_i \cdot P(x_i)$$
$$= x_1 \cdot P(x_1) + x_2 \cdot P(x_2) + \cdots + x_n \cdot P(x_n) \qquad (5.1)$$

The expected value of the random variable X, denoted $E(X)$, is a weighted mean of the values of X, where the weights are the probabilities of each value occurring. We see from expression (5.1), the term x_1 represents the first value that the discrete random variable X can take on. That is, we use capital letters to denote a random variable and lowercase letters to denote the individual values of the random variable. $P(x_1)$ represents the probability that the random variable takes on a value of x_1. We multiply each value, x_i, by its probability, $P(x_i)$, and then sum the products.

Now compute the mean, or expected value, for the discrete random variable—the number of cars owned by Omaha families. The results are shown in Table 5.3.

---

*We use the Greek letter μ (mu) to denote a population mean or the mean of a probability distribution.

Table 5.3

Computing the Mean

Value of x	Probability	Value · Probability
0	.10	.00
1	.40	.40
2	.40	.80
3	.08	.24
4	.02	.08
		Mean = 1.52 cars

Does the mean indicate that each family owns exactly 1.52 cars? No, the mean value of 1.52 cars is the *long-run* average; it is the *average* number of cars per family over many thousands of families.

The mean, however, does not completely describe a probability distribution. It provides no insight about the amount of variability in the number of cars among families. That is, do *most* families own *close* to 1.52 cars? Figure 5.2 suggests that outcomes far away from the mean of 1.52 are not likely to occur. For example, owning four cars is not likely since the probability is only .02. Owning one or two cars is very likely since the probability is .40 + .40 = .80. The standard deviation, which is a measure of the concentration of the values about the mean, should be small. If numerical values far from the mean had large probabilities, then the standard deviation would be large.

For all types of data—whether raw data, histogram data, or probability data—the standard deviation is still the square root of the weighted sum of the squared deviations of the data around the mean. That is,

$$\text{Standard deviation}^* = \sigma = \sqrt{\sum_i (x_i - \mu)^2 \cdot P(x_i)} \qquad (5.2)$$

where μ is the mean of the probability distribution. Table 5.4 shows that the standard deviation for the number of cars owned per family in Omaha is $\sigma = .85$.

Table 5.4

Computing the Standard Deviation

Value of x	Probability	Deviation $(x - \mu)$	Squared Deviation	Squared Deviation · Probability
0	.10	$(0 - 1.52)$	2.31	$(2.31)(.10) = .231$
1	.40	$(1 - 1.52)$	.27	$(.27)(.40) = .108$
2	.40	$(2 - 1.52)$	.23	$(.23)(.40) = .092$
3	.08	$(3 - 1.52)$	2.19	$(2.19)(.08) = .175$
4	.02	$(4 - 1.52)$	6.15	$(6.15)(.02) = \underline{.123}$
				Variance = σ^2 = .729

$$\sigma = \sqrt{.729} = .85 \text{ car per family}$$

---

*We use the Greek letter σ (sigma) to denote a population standard deviation or the standard deviation of a probability distribution. σ^2 is the population variance.

In summary, the mean gives the long-run average, and the standard deviation describes the variability about that average. The Empirical rule aids in interpreting the standard deviation. It says that if the probability distribution for cars owned is approximately normal (see Figure 5.2), 95% of the families will own between $-.18$ car $(1.52 - 2(.85))$ and 3.22 cars $(1.52 + 2(.85))$. Since a negative number of cars or parts of cars are not possible values for the random variable here, we would round off the values to between zero and three cars.

Our final example illustrates a personal discrete probability distribution. Consider two possible stocks—U.S. Conversion and AeroTech. The rates of return on both stocks are uncertain since they depend on the state of the economy. There are three possible future economic scenarios—boom, neutral, and recession. A stockbroker predicts the rates of return on both stocks as follows:

X = rate of return on U.S. Conversion stock
Possible values: $\{100\%, 15\%, -70\%\}$

Y = rate of return on AeroTech stock
Possible values: $\{20\%, 15\%, 10\%\}$

Table 5.5 shows the computations for the mean and standard deviation of rate of return for the U.S. Conversion stock. The personal probability distribution shown in the second column is based on the stockbroker's personal probabilities.

The mean rate of return for U.S. Conversion stock is 15% and its standard deviation is 65.8%. The mean rate of return for AeroTech stock is also 15% (calculations not shown) and its standard deviation is 3.9%. In the long run, both stocks have the same mean rate of return. But which stock is the riskier investment?

The U.S. Conversion stock is riskier because it has a much larger standard deviation. Its actual rate of return may be much higher or much lower than the mean rate of return of 15%. That is not true for the AeroTech stock. Its small standard deviation says that whether there is a boom, neutral, or recession economy, the actual return will be quite close to the mean return of 15%. Note that if both stocks had different mean rates of return, determining which is the riskier stock would be more difficult.

In summary, a discrete random variable can take on a finite number of numerical values. Its probability distribution includes the probability for each value of the random variable. Together with the mean and standard deviation, the probability distribution reveals nearly everything of interest about a random variable.

Table 5.5

Computation of Mean and Standard Deviation for Rates of Return on U.S. Conversion Stock

Value of x	$P(x)$	$xP(x)$	Deviation from Mean	Squared Deviation	Squared Deviation $\cdot$ $P(x)$
100%	.3	30%	$(100 - 15)$	7,225	$7,225(.3) = 2,167.5$
15%	.4	6%	$(15 - 15)$	0	$0(.4) = 0$
-70%	.3	-21%	$(-70 - 15)$	7,225	$7,225(.3) = 2,167.5$
		$\mu = 15\%$			Variance $= \sigma^2 = 4,335$

$\sigma = \sqrt{4,335} = 65.8\%$

SECTION 5.2 EXERCISES

1. Suppose a movie theater has 100 seats and movie tickets cost $6 each. Let X = number of tickets sold on a single Friday night. Let Y = total dollar sales resulting from selling the X tickets.
   a. Is X a random variable? If so, is it discrete or continuous? Describe the range of outcomes possible on any Friday night.
   b. Is Y a random variable? If so, is it discrete or continuous? Describe the range of outcomes on any Friday night.

2. Decide which of the following statements describe a random variable and whether the random variable is discrete or continuous.
   a. Number of accidents per month in a factory
   b. Time required to complete a typing test
   c. Selecting five items from an assembly line
   d. Dollar sales in a single week
   e. Return on investment for a company in a single year

3. Decide which of the following statements describe a random variable and whether the random variable is discrete or continuous. Explain.
   a. Number of engines in an American-made car.
   b. Percentage of defective items per shift.
   c. Type of defective items per shift.
   d. Time to failure of an electronic assembly.
   e. Number of repairs under warranty for a week.

4. What is the difference between a random variable and a probability distribution?

5. Are the following legitimate probability distributions?

   a.

Number of Cars	Probability
0	.5
1	.3
2	.3
3	.2

   b. X = the fraction defective during a shift

   c.

Number of Lockbox Processing Errors per Month	Probability
0	.25
1	.50
2	.25

   d.

Delivery Time	Probability
less than 30 minutes	.75
30 to 59.99 minutes	.25
60 or more minutes	.05

   e. Draw a probability histogram for each legitimate probability distribution in parts **a–d.**

6. Construct histograms and approximate the mean (expected value) for the following probability distributions.

a.

Number of Cars	Probability
0	.20
1	.30
2	.30
3	.20

b.

Number of Bent Fans/Shift	Probability
1	.70
2	.25
3	.05

c.

Return on Investment	Probability
−10%	.50
0%	.25
+10%	.25

7. Find the mean and standard deviation for the probability distributions in Exercise 6. Are the approximate means from Exercise 6 similar to the computed means in this exercise?

8. Sketch a histogram for the following probability distribution for X, the number of workshops offered during the quarter:

x	0	1	2	3
$P(x)$	.2	.3	.3	.2

a. Approximate the expected value of this probability distribution.
b. Find the expected value and standard deviation for the probability distribution.
c. Explain why the expected value is not what you would expect as an outcome of any single quarter.

9. You are offered two investment opportunities:

I		II	
Outcome	Probability	Outcome	Probability
−$1,000	.6	−$500	.4
$0	.3	$0	.1
+$7,000	.1	+$600	.5
	1.0		1.0

a. Find the mean and standard deviation of each investment opportunity.
b. Which of the two investments is less risky?

10. A national CD (compact disk) chain obtains the following data on the number of CDs purchased per week and their associated relative frequencies. They have segmented their market by musical taste.

Number of CDs per Week	Rock	Segments Classical	Blues
0	.30	.10	.25
1	.20	.10	.25
2	.15	.20	.25
3	.15	.25	.20
4	.10	.15	.05
5	.05	.10	—
6	.05	.10	—

a. Explain how the chain might obtain the above data.
b. Draw a probability histogram for the number of CDs purchased per week for each of the three market segments.
c. Examine your probability histograms and without using expression (5.1), which market segment has the highest expected number of CDs sold per week? Explain.
d. Verify your answer in part **c** by using expression (5.1).
e. Examine your probability histograms and without using expression (5.2), which market segment has the lowest standard deviation in the number of CDs purchased per week? Explain.
f. Explain what the lowest standard deviation in the number of CDs sold per week means in terms a manager could understand.
g. Verify your answer in part **e** by using expression (5.2).

11. Through careful record keeping over thousands of guests, a large hotel has determined the probability distribution for the random variable X, the length of stay (measured in days), as

x	$P(X = x)$	$P(X \leq x)$
1	.45	—
2	.25	—
3	.15	—
4	.10	—
5	.05	—
	1.00	

a. In Chapter 2, you learned how to construct a cumulative percentage distribution. Construct a cumulative probability distribution by filling in the blanks.
b. What is the probability that a person about to check into this hotel will stay three days or less?
c. Find the probability that a new guest will stay more than four days.

12. Calculate the mean and standard deviation for the probability distribution in Exercise 11. Show that Chebyshev's rule applies to this probability distribution by showing that the probability that a length of stay will be outside 3 standard deviations from the mean is less than .11.

13. The number of defective parts produced per hour in a plant has the following empirical probabilities:

Defects per Hour	Probability
0	.50
1	.25
2	.15
3	.08
4	.02

  a. Find the mean and standard deviation.
  b. Why shouldn't you use the Empirical rule from Chapter 2 to interpret the standard deviation? That is, why can't you say that 95% of the number of defects per hour should be between the mean plus or minus 2 standard deviations?

14. Refer to Exercise 13. What is the probability that in a single hour more than one defective part will be produced? At least one defective part will be produced?

15. The borrower's creditworthiness is a factor in determining if he will receive a loan. Creditworthiness is typically determined by regression models, a technique we will learn in Chapter 11. The higher one's creditworthiness score, the higher is the creditworthiness of the potential borrower. Below are creditworthiness scores (coded) and their associated relative frequency probabilities for 1,000 potential borrowers at the First South Bank and the Midwest National Bank.

Midwest National Bank		First South Bank	
Credit Score	Relative Frequency	Credit Score	Relative Frequency
0	.10	0	.14
1	.10	1	.15
2	.10	2	.14
3	.40	3	.15
4	.10	4	.14
5	.10	5	.14
6	.10	6	.14

  a. Draw a probability histogram for the Midwest National Bank and the First South Bank data.
  b. Examine your probability histograms and without using expression (5.1), which bank customers have the higher expected creditworthiness score? Explain.
  c. Verify your answer in part **b** by using expression (5.1).
  d. Examine your probability histograms and without using expression (5.2), which bank customers have the greater variance or standard deviation in creditworthiness scores? Explain.
  e. Explain what a higher standard deviation in creditworthiness scores means in terms a bank manager could understand.
  f. Verify your answer in part **d** by using expression (5.2).

5.3 ≡ The Binomial Distribution

Probability distributions based on relative frequencies (Table 5.2) or intuition (Table 5.5) are useful. But there are other distributions—theoretical probability distributions—that play a critical role in business problem solving. We turn next to an important discrete theoretical distribution—the binomial distribution. By the end of this section you should be able to:

1. define a success and a failure;
2. calculate and interpret binomial probabilities;
3. use the binomial probability table in Appendix 1; and
4. compute and interpret the mean and standard deviation for a binomially distributed random variable.

Calculating Probabilities

To use the binomial probability distribution, a Bernoulli process must describe the repeated trials of a random experiment. A Bernoulli process has two characteristics:

1. The possible outcomes of a single trial must be classified into two mutually exclusive and exhaustive categories. For example: flip a coin—heads, tails; select a group—high productivity, low productivity; or inspect a product—good, defective.

2. The probability of any particular outcome (getting a head or finding a defective product) must remain constant from trial to trial.

The second condition requires that the probability of the outcome will not be affected by what happened on preceding trials. For example, suppose the probability of getting a head, *p,* on one flip of a fair coin is .5. The chance of getting a head on the first flip is .5. What is the chance of getting a head on the second coin flip *given* a head on the first coin flip? What is the chance of getting a head on the third flip *given* two heads on the first two flips? Since the coin has no memory, the probability of getting a head does not change over the three trials no matter what happens. It always remains .5. *Conclusion:* Flipping a fair coin is a Bernoulli process. Using terminology from Chapter 4, we say that a Bernoulli process requires that the outcomes on successive trials must be *statistically independent.* In actual business problems, we will settle for situations that are near-Bernoulli processes. We will discuss this important idea in Section 5.4.

Now we will derive the algebraic expression for computing binomial probabilities using the coin flip example. Flip a fair coin ($p = .5$) three times and compute the probability of getting exactly one head (and two tails). Since we are interested in computing the probability of getting *one* head in *three* coin flips, define the problem in terms of the following discrete random variable:

The random variable	$X =$ the number of heads in three coin flips
Possible values	$\{0, 1, 2, 3\}$
Known quantities	$n = 3, \quad p = .5, \quad x = 1$
Unknown quantity	$P(X = 1)$

One way to get one head and two tails in three coin flips is H AND T AND T. We know from the multiplication rule (expression (4.6)) that

$$P(A \text{ AND } B) = P(A \mid B)P(B)$$

In a Bernoulli process, the conditional probability of event A given event B equals the unconditional probability of event A. Remember, event B has no impact on the probability of event A happening. Therefore, for statistically independent events, we can rewrite the multiplication rule as

$$P(A \text{ AND } B) = P(A)P(B) \tag{5.3}$$

Expression (5.3) says that the joint probability of two independent events is equal to the product of the unconditional probabilities for each event. Now extend the multiplication rule to more than two independent events:

$$P(\text{H AND T AND T}) = P(\text{H})P(\text{T})P(\text{T})$$

$$= .5(1 - .5)(1 - .5) = .125 \tag{5.4}$$

The H AND T AND T sequence is only one of several ways of getting one head and two tails in three coin flips. In fact, there are three possible ways of getting exactly one head in three tosses of the coin, namely, HTT, THT, and TTH. Each sequence has the same probability, .125. Thus, the probability of getting exactly one head in three coin flips, $P(X = 1)$ is $.125 + .125 + .125$, or $.375$. Alternatively, we can multiply expression (5.4) by 3:

$$P(X = 1) = 3(.125) = .375 \qquad (5.5)$$

If we repeatedly flip a fair coin, for which $p = .5$, three times and count the number of heads, 37.5% of the time we will get exactly one head. We do not have to run a study or use intuition. We have used expression (5.5), which is the binomial probability expression, to determine the probability.

The Binomial Expression

Each flip of a fair coin is a single trial. On a single trial, two outcomes are possible. We define the outcome we are interested in as a "success" and the other outcome as a "failure." The terms are in quotes because a success could be selecting a defective item and a failure could be selecting a good item. The "success" outcome does not necessarily mean a desirable outcome. It is the one for which we want to calculate a probability of a given number of successes.

Given that n is the number of trials, p is the probability of a success, and $(1 - p)$ is the probability of a failure, we can generalize expression (5.5) to get exactly x successes in n trials:

$$P(X = x) = {_nC_x}p^x(1 - p)^{n-x} \qquad (5.6)$$

When the number of trials is small (for example, three coin flips), we can simply list the different sequences and count them. For a large number of trials, use the *combinations* expression (5.7) to determine the number of different ways to get x successes in n trials:

$$_nC_x = \frac{n!}{x!(n - x)!} \qquad (5.7)$$

The term n is the number of trials and x is the number of successes. The symbol "!" stands for factorial, which means multiply the number before the factorial symbol by each positive integer lower than it. For example, 3! equals $3 \cdot 2 \cdot 1$ or 6. Zero factorial equals 1. In the coin flip example, we have

$$_3C_1 = \frac{3!}{1!(3 - 1)} = \frac{3 \cdot 2 \cdot 1}{1 \cdot 2 \cdot 1} = 3$$

This is the number of different ways to get one head in three coin tosses.

Expression (5.6) generates binomial probabilities. We will now use the binomial expression for two miniproblems.

Example: Credit Classification   A department store classifies its charge customers as either high-volume or low-volume purchasers. Ten percent are high-volume purchasers. If a sample of four charge customers is selected, what is the chance that none of them is a high-volume purchaser?

Define success as selecting a high-volume purchaser, and failure, the other outcome, as selecting a low-volume purchaser. For this example, the two assumptions underlying the binomial expression are the following:

ASSUMPTION 1:   There is a .10 chance of selecting a high-volume purchaser (success, $p = .10$) and a .90 chance of selecting a low-volume purchaser (failure, $1 - p = .90$).

ASSUMPTION 2:   Selecting high-volume purchasers from credit files can be represented as a Bernoulli process. The probability of selecting a high-volume purchaser does not change no matter how many high-volume purchasers have already been selected.

We can summarize the information we have as:

The random variable X = number of high-volume purchasers in a sample of four
Possible values $\{0, 1, 2, 3, 4\}$
Known quantities $n = 4, \quad p = .1, \quad x = 0$
Unknown quantity $P(X = 0)$

Substituting the known values into expression (5.6), we obtain

$$p(X = 0) = {}_4C_0(.10)^0(.90)^{4-0} = .6561$$

Thus, there is a .6561 probability that we would select no high-volume purchasers in a sample of four. The binomial probability is accurate if the two assumptions are valid.

Example: Meeting Customer Demand   A bakery has five ovens. At least four ovens must be working in order to meet customer demand on a given day. The probability of a particular oven working is .90. What is the probability of meeting customer demand?

Define success as a working oven and failure as a nonworking oven. The two assumptions underlying the binomial expression for this example are given here:

ASSUMPTION 1:   There is a .90 chance of an oven working (success, $p = .90$) and a .10 chance of an oven not working (failure, $1 - p = .10$).

ASSUMPTION 2:   Working ovens can be represented as a Bernoulli process. The probability of an oven working does not change no matter how many ovens are already working.

The given information can be summarized as:

The random variable X = the number of ovens working on a given day
Possible values $\{0, 1, 2, 3, 4, 5\}$
Known quantities $n = 5, \quad p = .9, \quad x = 4, 5$
Unknown quantity $P(X = 4) + P(X = 5)$

Since *at least* four ovens must be working in order to meet customer demand, we must compute the probabilities of four or five ovens working and add them:

$$P(X = 4) = {}_5C_4(.90)^4(.10)^{5-4} = .3280$$
$$P(X = 5) = {}_5C_5(.90)^5(.10)^{5-5} = \underline{.5905}$$
$$.9185$$

Thus, there is almost a 92% chance of meeting customer demand. The binomial probability is accurate if the two assumptions are valid.

The Binomial Table

Recall that a probability distribution for a discrete random variable consists of all possible numerical values of the random variable and their associated probabilities. We now compute the probability distribution for the random variable—the number of high-volume purchasers of Example 1:

$$P(X = 0) = {}_4C_0(.10)^0(.90)^{4-0} = .6561$$

$$P(X = 1) = {}_4C_1(.10)^1(.90)^{4-1} = .2916$$

$$P(X = 2) = {}_4C_2(.10)^2(.90)^{4-2} = .0486$$

$$P(X = 3) = {}_4C_3(.10)^3(.90)^{4-3} = .0036$$

$$P(X = 4) = {}_4C_4(.10)^4(.90)^{4-4} = \underline{.0001}$$
$$1.0000$$

We could also have determined the five probabilities using the binomial table in Appendix 1. To use the appendix, perform the following steps:

1. Find the correct sample size, n. Sample sizes from 1 to 20 are the major column headings of the table.
2. Find the appropriate probability of success, p. The success probabilities are shown in increments of .01 from .01 to .50 and form the column subheadings.
3. Find the number of successes for which you wish to calculate probabilities. These are the row headings located along the extreme left-hand side of the table.
4. The desired probability is at the intersection of the appropriate value of p and the value of x.

We can use Appendix 1 to determine the probability of getting exactly zero high-volume purchasers in a sample of four when the probability of success is .10:

$$P(X = 0 \text{ for } n = 4, p = .10) = .6561$$

| | | | | | $n = 4$ | | | | | |
x $\diagdown$ p	.01	.02	.03	.04	.05	.06	.07	.08	.09	.10
0	.9606	.9224	.8853	.8493	.8145	.7807	.7481	.7164	.6857	**.6561**
1	.0388	.0753	.1095	1416	.1715	.1993	.2252	.2492	.2713	.2916
2	.0006	.0023	.0051	.0088	.0135	.0191	.0254	.0325	.0402	.0486
3	.0000	.0000	.0001	.0002	.0005	.0008	.0013	.0019	.0027	.0036
4	.0000	.0000	.0000	.0000	.0000	.0000	.0000	.0000	.0001	.0001

We can use Appendix 1 even when the probability of a success is greater than .5. Suppose the probability of selecting a high-volume customer was .7. We wish to compute the probability of selecting three high-volume customers—$P(Y = 3 \text{ for } n = 4, p = .70)$. We cannot use Appendix 1 directly because it only goes up to a p value of .5. However, selecting three high-volume customers is the same as selecting one low-volume purchaser since there are only two types of credit customers. Thus,

$$P(Y = 3 \text{ for } n = 4, p = .7) = P(X = 1 \text{ for } n = 4, p = .3) = .4116$$

FIGURE 5.3   Binomial Probability Histogram: $n = 4$, $p = .10$

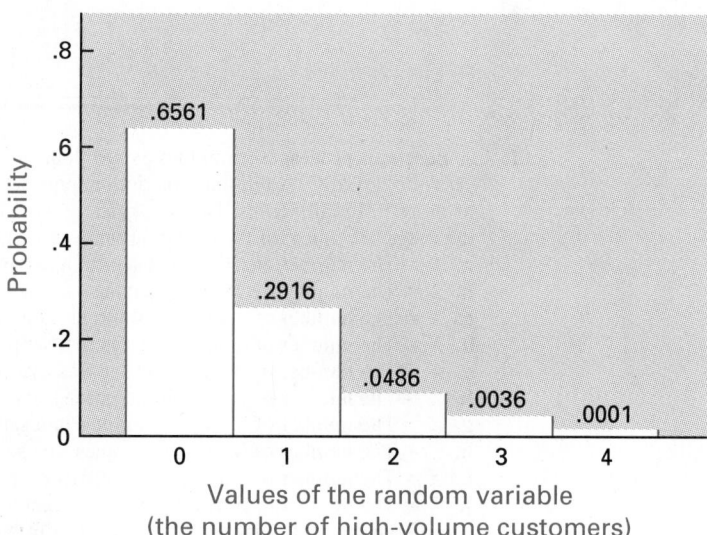

Mean and Standard Deviation of a
Binomial Distribution

Consider again the problem of credit classification in Example 1. Figure 5.3 shows a probability histogram for the number of high-volume purchasers in a sample of size four.

We could approximate the mean in this figure visually by placing a steel rod under the probability histogram and moving it back and forth until we balance the histogram. It would balance near the value of .5 high-volume purchaser.

We could also use expression (5.1) to compute the mean for the probability distribution shown in Figure 5.3. However, there is a simpler expression for binomial probabilities, given by

$$\text{Mean} = \mu = np \qquad (5.8)$$

Remember, the term n is the number of trials and p is the probability of a success on a single trial. Thus, for the credit classification problem,

$$\text{Mean number of high-volume purchasers} = 4(.1) = .4$$

This agrees with our approximation. To compute the standard deviation we could use expression (5.2). But again, there is a simpler expression for binomial probabilities:

$$\sigma = \sqrt{np(1 - p)}$$
$$= \sqrt{4(.1)(.9)} = .6 \text{ high-volume purchaser} \qquad (5.9)$$

The mean number of high-volume purchasers is .4 and the standard deviation is .6.

In summary, to use the binomial distribution, two assumptions must be true. First, only two outcomes can occur on a single trial. Second, the probability of any particular outcome must remain constant from trial to trial. If these assumptions are met, we can use the binomial expression or table to generate valid probabilities.

SECTION 5.3 EXERCISES

1. A Bernoulli process is a random experiment in which each trial results in either a "success" or "failure". A binomial random experiment consists of counting the results of one or more Bernouilli trials. Define (1) success and failure for each Bernoulli trial and (2) the range of values for the binomial random variable, X.
    a. X = The number of workers absent in a department of 10 employees on any day.
    b. X = The number of American-made cars in a parking lot of 30 spaces.
    c. X = The number of loans that are in default at a bank in a sample of 10 loans.
    d. X = The number of defective items in a sample of 10.
    e. X = The number of weeks an order was placed in the past 6 weeks.
    f. X = The number of high-volume purchasers in a sample of 4 buyers.
    g. X = The number of taxpayers audited in a sample of 10.
    h. X = The number of incorrect invoices in a sample of 40.
    i. X = The number of late arrivals for parcels in the past 20 deliveries.
    j. X = The number of times there was perfect agreement with the movement of January and annual Dow Jones Index values (up in both January and for the year or down in both January and for the year) for the past 30 years.
    k. X = Number of occupied beds in a university infirmary with 20 beds.

2. Assume the probability of striking oil in a West Texas oil field is .10. Wildcatters Inc. plans to drill 10 wells in the oil field. They are interested in computing the probability distribution of the number of wells in which they strike oil in the 10 wells they will drill. Assume that striking oil is a Bernoulli process.
    a. Define the random variable of interest and its possible outcomes or values.
    b. What is the probability of not striking oil in any of the 10 wells?
    c. What is the probability of striking oil in two or three wells?
    d. How would Wildcatters Inc. establish that the probability of finding oil in the West Texas oil field is .10?

3. The probability of being involved in an auto accident each year is .1. Assume that involvement in an auto accident is a Bernoulli process.
    a. What is the probability of being involved in an auto accident in each of the next three years?
    b. What is the probability of not being involved in an auto accident in any of the next three years?
    c. What is the probability of being involved in an accident exactly one of the next three years?
    d. What assumptions did you make in answering parts **a–c?**
    e. What data would we need to estimate that the probability of being involved in an accident is .1?

4. Assume that the probability of obtaining a home equity loan is .40. Let X = the number of applicants that get a loan in a sample of 10 applicants. Use the binomial table in Appendix 1 to determine the following probabilities.
    a. $P(X = 9)$
    b. $P(X > 7)$
    c. $P(X \leq 3)$
    d. $P(2 \leq X \leq 4)$
    e. $P(X < 4)$
    f. $P(X \geq 2)$
    g. $P(X = 4)$
    h. P(Exactly 10 will get a loan)
    i. P(Fewer than 6 will get a loan)
    j. Explain why the probability that 4 applicants obtain a loan should be higher than the probability that 10 applicants obtain a loan.

5. Define a discrete random variable as follows:

$$X = \text{the number of taxpayers audited in a sample of five returns}$$

$$p = .02 \text{ (from IRS published data)}$$

Translate the following three binomial probability statements into English and then compute and interpret their probabilities.

a. $P(X = 0)$

b. $P(X > 4)$

c. $P(X \le 2)$

d. Draw the binomial probability histogram for the number of taxpayers audited in a sample of five.

e. Use the histogram to approximate the mean or expected number of taxpayers audited.

f. Use expressions (5.8) and (5.9) to determine the expected number of taxpayers audited and the standard deviation.

g. If p were to equal .50 (not .02), the standard devation for the random variable would be larger than in part **f.** Verify this by using expression (5.9). What is the practical consequence of the larger standard deviation?.

6. Define a discrete random variable as follows:

$$Y = \text{the number of Yuppies (a market segment) in a sample of five consumers}$$

$$p = .24 \text{ (from the firm's market research data base)}$$

Select five consumers at random. What is the probability of selecting

a. One Yuppie?

b. At least four Yuppies?

c. At most two Yuppies?

d. Between one and three Yuppies, inclusive?

e. Draw the binomial probability histogram for the number of Yuppies in a sample of five.

f. Use the histogram to approximate the mean or expected number of Yuppies.

g. Use expressions (5.8) and (5.9) to determine the expected number of Yuppies and the standard deviation.

h. Given the probability of a success (selecting a Yuppie) is .24, why is the probability of selecting one Yuppie greater than the probability of selecting five Yuppies?

7. Without doing any computation, which of the following pairs of random variables have the larger expected value? Which of the following pairs of random variables have the smaller standard deviation?

a.

R1			
.10	.40	.40	.10
0	1	2	3

R2			
.25	.25	.25	.25
0	1	2	3

b.

S1			
.40	.10	.10	.40
0	1	2	3

S2			
.10	.40	.40	.10
0	1	2	3

c.

T1			
.60	.35	.03	.02
0	1	2	3

T2			
.02	.03	.35	.60
0	1	2	3

d.

U1			
.20	.40	.30	.10
0	1	2	3

U2			
.80	.15	.03	.02
0	1	2	3

8. Define a discrete random variable as follows:

X = the number of years there will be agreement in the January and annual Dow Jones Index movements over the next seven years

p = .85 (based on *Wall Street Journal* article, 2/1/84)

Translate the following three binomial probability statements into English and then compute and interpret their probabilities.
a. $P(X = 5)$
b. $P(X > 4)$
c. $P(X \le 3)$
d. Draw the binomial probability histogram for the number of years there will be agreement in the January and annual Dow Jones Index movements over the next seven years.
e. Use the histogram to approximate the mean or expected number of years there will be agreement.
f. Use expressions (5.8) and (5.9) to determine the expected number of years there will be agreement and the standard deviation.
g. If p were to equal .50 (not .85), the standard devation for the random variable would be larger than in part **f.** Verify this by using expression (5.9). Explain the logic behind the increasing standard deviation.

9. Define a discrete random variable as follows:

X = the number of class mean grades over 70 for the 10 quizzes during the semester

p = .90 (from the past 10 semesters)

Translate the following three binomial probability statements into English and then compute and interpret their probabilities.
a. $P(X = 10)$
b. $P(X \le 3)$
c. $P(X > 9)$
d. $P(2 < X < 5)$
e. $P(2 \le X \le 5)$
f. Draw the binomial probability histogram for the number of class mean grades over 70 for the 10 quizzes during the semester.
g. Use the histogram to approximate the mean or expected number of mean grades over 70.
h. Use expressions (5.8) and (5.9) to determine the expected number of class mean grades over 70 for the 10 quizzes and the standard deviation.
i. If p were to equal .50 (not .90), the standard devation for the random variable would be larger than in part **h**. Verify this by using expression (5.9). Explain the logic behind the increasing standard deviation.

10. Define a discrete random variable as follows:

Y = the number of incorrect invoices in a sample of 10

p = .03 (from past accounting data)

Translate the following statements into the correct mathematical notation. For example, $P(X = x)$.
a. The chances that in a sample of 10, 4 invoices will be incorrect.
b. The probability that in a sample of 10, at most 3 invoices will be incorrect.
c. The chances that in a sample of 10, at least 6 invoices will be incorrect.
d. The probability that in a sample of 10, between 4 and 6 invoices will be incorrect.
e. Calculate the expected number of incorrect invoices in a sample of 10.

11. Accident claims are checked for completeness by a branch office before they are sent to the regional office for payment. Suppose the probability that a claim is complete is .7. Use the binomial table to determine the following probabilities.
    a. Of the next 5 claims processed, all 5 will be complete.
    b. Only 1 of the next 5 claims processed will be complete.
    c. One of the next 5 claims processed will be incomplete.
    d. What are the mean and standard deviation for the number of complete claims in a sample of 5 claims?

12. A good sales representative expects to make a sale on 25% of her calls. She plans to make 10 calls over the next week. Assume that whether she makes a sale or not on each call is a Bernoulli process.
    a. Define a success and a failure.
    b. Define the random variable and its possible values.
    c. What are the mean and standard deviation of this random variable?
    d. What is the probability that over the next 10 calls, the sales representative will make more than 7 sales?
    e. What is the probability that the sales representative will make at least 2 sales, but not more than 6 sales?

13. A quality-control worker for Xcel selects a sample of 10 items from a shipment from Supplyall and inspects for defects. Each item will be classified as either acceptable or defective. Supplyall claims that its defect probability is .10, but Xcel suspects that it might be .30. In the next shipment, the quality-control worker finds 3 defective pieces in a sample of 10. Is Supplyall's claim or Xcel's claim more reasonable? Explain.

14. A market researcher plans to conduct a telephone survey of 100 customers to ask if they either favor or oppose a new customer policy. Suppose 70% of all customers favor the policy.
    a. Find the expected number of favorable responses in the sample of 100.
    b. Find the standard deviation.
    c. Explain the meaning of the mean and standard deviation in the context of this problem.

15. Define a discrete random variable as follows:

R = the return (value appreciation) on a stock portfolio for the years 1992–1995

    a. Can the expected, or mean, return on a stock portfolio be negative?
    b. What must be true for the expected return to be negative?
    c. Can the standard deviation in the stock portfolio return be negative? Why not?
    d. Can the standard deviation in the stock portfolio return be zero? Explain.

5.4 ▤ Problem Solving and the Binomial Distribution

In the previous section we presented the basics of the binomial distribution. Now we will demonstrate how the binomial distribution can improve problem solving and decision making. By the end of this section you should be able to:

1. use binomial probabilities to assess the consequences of decisions;
2. use binomial probabilities to sense emerging problems or opportunities; and
3. determine if real-world situations approximate a Bernoulli process.

Assessing Consequences

The following problem illustrates how binomially generated probabilities can help managers assess consequences of different strategies.

Example: Which Inspection Rule to Choose?   COMCEL buys electronic components from ZT Audio for its cellular phones. COMCEL requires that each lot of 1,000 components contain 10% or fewer defectives. Inspecting every component is not practical. Thus COMCEL selects and tests a sample of 10 components. It is considering two acceptance rules: Accept the lot of 1,000 if (1) one or no components of the sample of 10 are defective or (2) two or fewer components of the sample of 10 are defective. If COMCEL rejects a lot, ZT must replace it.

Assume that ZT Audio can consistently produce acceptable lots—that is, lots with at most 10% defectives. Even so, a sample of 10 taken from a lot that contains 10% defectives could have two or more defective components. Given the first acceptance rule, what percentage of ZT's future shipments will be rejected even though they contain at most 10% defectives? COMCEL is interested in computing the probability of getting one or no defects in a sample of size 10. Thus a success is finding a defective component. Given here are the assumptions and the random variable of interest:

ASSUMPTION 1:   There is a .10 chance that a component is defective (success, $p = .10$) and a .90 chance that a component is good (failure, $1 - p = .90$) in a sample of 10.

ASSUMPTION 2:   Inspecting components is a Bernoulli process. The probability that a component is defective does not change no matter how many defectives COMCEL finds during inspection. We will examine this assumption shortly.

The random variable X = the number of defectives in a sample of size 10
Possible values $\{0, 1, 2, 3, \ldots, 9, 10\}$
Known quantities $n = 10, \quad p = .10, \quad x = 0, 1$
Unknown quantity $P(X = 0) + P(X = 1)$

Using Appendix 1, we find

$$P(X = 0) + P(X = 1) = .3487 + .3874 = .7361$$

Assume all the lots of 1,000 contain 10% defectives. Remember, 10% defectives is acceptable, and so COMCEL should accept all of the lots. However, COMCEL's incoming component inspectors will find one or no defectives in a sample of 10 only about 74% of the time. Thus, COMCEL will actually accept only 74% of ZT's shipments even though 100% are good lots. Due to the sampling rule, $(1 - .7361)$, or approximately 26%, of acceptable lots will be rejected. This is called the *producer's risk*. The producer, ZT Audio, is at risk because although all the lots it has submitted are good lots, 26% of them will be rejected because of the sampling rule.

Now consider the second acceptance rule: Accept the lot if COMCEL finds *two or fewer* defectives. Now what is the producer's risk? Using Appendix 1, we determine that

$$P(X = 0) + P(X = 1) + P(X = 2) = .3487 + .3874 + .1937 = .9298$$

About 93% of the time, the COMCEL inspectors will find two or fewer defectives in a sample of 10. Thus, COMCEL will accept about 93% of the shipments from ZT. The producer's risk will drop to $1 - .93 = .07$. With only 7% of acceptable lots rejected by the second rule, ZT Audio would prefer rule (2), of course.

The second sampling rule reduces the producer's risk and is more agreeable for ZT, but what about COMCEL? It must be concerned about stopping lots that contain more than the acceptable 10% level of defectives. For example, suppose that ZT sends lots that all contain 20% defectives—twice the acceptable defective rate. These are all bad lots and should all be rejected. Analyze how successful the two acceptance rules are at stopping such lots from entering COMCEL. We have rewritten Assumption 1 to reflect the increased probability of a defective component, $p = .20$. Assumption 2 has not changed and so we have omitted it.

ASSUMPTION 1:   There is a .20 chance that a component is defective (success, $p = .20$) and an .80 chance that a component is good (failure, $1 - p = .80$) in a sample of 10.

Known quantities $n = 10, \quad p = .20, \quad x = 0, 1$

On the basis of rule (1) and using Appendix 1, we find that

$$P(X = 0) + P(X = 1) = .1074 + .2684 = .3758$$

On the basis of rule (2) and using Appendix 1, we find that

$$P(X = 0) + P(X = 1) + P(X = 2) = .1074 + .2684 + .3020 = .6778$$

Under rule (1), COMCEL inspectors will find one or no defectives in a sample of 10 in lots that actually contain 20% defectives about 38% of the time. Thus 38% of the time, COMCEL will accept lots that contain 20% defectives.

Under rule (2), COMCEL inspectors will find two or fewer defectives in a sample of 10 in lots that actually contain 20% defectives about 68% of the time. Thus 68% of the time, COMCEL will accept lots that contain 20% defectives. Of the two sampling rules, COMCEL prefers rule (1).

The probability of accepting a bad lot is called the *consumer's risk*. The consumer or customer is at risk since it will accept bad lots. As we reduce the producer's risk, we increase the consumer's risk. COMCEL wants a sampling rule with a low consumer's risk whereas ZT Audio wants a low producer's risk. Expect serious negotiations between the two parties.

Problem Sensing

Problem sensing is a crucial managerial capability, since a manager cannot solve a problem until he or she knows it exists. We have already used descriptive statistics to sense problems; now we will use binomial probabilities.

Example: Deviation from Past Performance?   ABC Inc. buys computer paper from Apex Stationery. From historical data, Apex knows that the probability that ABC will place an order in a given week is .40. There have been no orders from ABC in the last six weeks. Could Apex be facing a problem with a decline in orders from ABC Inc.?

Begin by stating the two assumptions and defining the random variable.

ASSUMPTION 1: In a particular week, there is a .40 chance that ABC Inc. will place an order (success, $p = .40$) and a .60 chance that ABC will not place an order (failure, $1 - p = .60$).

ASSUMPTION 2: Orders from ABC Inc. are a Bernoulli process. The probability of ABC placing an order in a week does not change no matter how many orders ABC Inc. has placed in previous weeks. We will discuss this assumption shortly.

The random variable X = the number of orders in the last six weeks
Possible values   {0, 1, 2, 3, 4, 5, 6}
Known quantities $n = 6$, $p = .40$, $x = 0$
Unknown quantity $P(X = 0)$

Using Appendix 1, we find that

$$P(X = 0) = .0467$$

The chance of ABC placing no orders in the last six weeks is only .047. Yet, that is what actually happened. What could account for it? Please think about it before reading on. There are three possible explanations:

1. The probability of ABC placing an order is still. 40, and there is *no problem.* The chance of getting no orders in the past six weeks is only .047. However, even though the probability is small, it is an event that could happen.
2. The probability of ABC placing an order has changed, and Apex does have *a problem* of declining sales. How does it know it has a problem? It is more likely to get no orders if the chance of getting an order dropped from the historic .40 to, say, .10. In that case, the chance of getting no orders in the last six weeks would have been .531 (a likely event) instead of .047. Please verify the .531 probability using Appendix 1.
3. Orders from ABC Inc. can no longer be modeled by a Bernoulli process. If this is true, then the .047 probability may not be meaningful. Apex *cannot tell* if it has a problem with declining orders.

If Apex believed that getting orders from ABC could still be modeled by a Bernoulli process, then it must choose one of the first two explanations. The chance of there being no problem is less than 1 in 20 (.047). The probability is so low that most managers would reject the "no problem" explanation. They would conclude that there is a declining order problem and would begin to diagnose its causes.

Assessing the Bernoulli Process Assumption

While we do not expect many real-world situations to be exactly a Bernoulli process, are they near-Bernoulli? Does the probability of a success remain *approximately* the same from trial to trial? If so, the binomial probabilities are meaningful and can be used in problem solving. We will examine whether the Bernoulli process assumption of independence is justified for the Apex Stationery and COMCEL inspection examples.

Apex Stationery Example   Does the probability of obtaining an order in a particular week from ABC Inc. remain the same no matter how many such orders ABC has recently placed?

To determine if this is a near-Bernoulli process, consider the two sets of time-ordered sales data shown in Table 5.6. Either ABC Inc. places an order in a week (O) or it does not place an order (NO). Both patterns show that in 40% of the weeks, ABC places an order. Yet one pattern is inconsistent with the requirements of a Bernoulli process. Can you tell which? Please think about it before reading on.

Table 5.6

Possible Patterns of ABC Placing Orders over Time

Week	Pattern A	Pattern B
1	O	O
2	O	NO
3	O	NO
4	O	NO
5	NO	O
6	NO	NO
7	NO	NO
8	NO	O
9	NO	NO
10	NO	O
11	O	NO
12	O	NO
13	O	NO
14	O	O
15	NO	O
16	NO	NO
17	NO	NO
18	NO	O
19	NO	NO
20	NO	O

$$P(\text{order}) = \frac{8}{20} = .40 \quad P(\text{order}) = \frac{8}{20} = .40$$

Pattern A is not representative of a Bernoulli process. Once ABC places an order, it does so for the next three weeks, and once ABC does not order in a week, it does not do so for the next five weeks. The trials are not independent.

Pattern B is consistent with a Bernoulli process. Orders are interspersed among no orders. The .40 probability holds for the first five weeks, the second five weeks, the third five weeks, and the last five weeks.

COMCEL Inspection Program Example   Is the probability that a component is defective the same no matter how many defectives COMCEL finds during inspection? That is, is the probability of a success, p, constant from trial to trial?

If lots of 1,000 are 10% defective, then COMCEL should expect about 100 defective components in each lot. Now ask the following questions:

1. What is the probability that the first component in a sample of 10 is defective?

$$p = \frac{100}{1,000} = .100$$

2. What is the probability that the second component is defective if the first component was defective?

$$p = \frac{99}{999} = .099$$

3. What is the probability that the tenth component is defective if the first nine components were defective?

$$p = \frac{91}{991} = .092$$

Since the three probabilities of success are very similar, we have a near-Bernoulli process. We may use the binomial expression or table to calculate meaningful probabilities. If the three probabilities of success varied greatly (a judgment call), we should not use the binomial expression or table to calculate probabilities.

SECTION 5.4 EXERCISES

1. COMCEL sells two phones—the standard and the deluxe. Historically, deluxe phones have accounted for 60% of sales. What is the probability that exactly 0 of the next 10 sales will be for deluxe phones? Suppose that in fact COMCEL does not sell any deluxe phones in its next 10 sales. What could that mean? Explain.

2. At every company-sponsored workshop, 15 workers sign up. However, most times, fewer than 10 workers actually attend. The manager of Human Resource Development is considering two strategies to improve actual attendance: (1) send constant reminders to registered workers and (2) have supervisors encourage their workers to attend programs. The manager estimates the following personal probabilities of workers actually attending a workshop for which they have registered:

$$P(\text{attend} \mid \text{reminders}) = .50$$

$$P(\text{attend} \mid \text{encourage}) = .70$$

What is the probability that the next workshop will have 10 or more workers attend if the manager uses the first strategy? the second strategy? Other things being equal, which strategy should the manager use?

3. Suppose that Joel Associates offers to buy each lot of 1,000 units from Gail Industries only if none of a sample of 5 units is defective. If Gail Industries expects 5% of the units to be defective, what percentage of the lots will Joel Associates reject over the long run?

4. A manufacturer claims that no more than 5% of its items are defective. You adopt the following decision rule: Reject a shipment of 500 items if more than 1 of the 10 sampled items is defective. Otherwise, you accept the shipment.
    a. What is the probability of rejecting the lot when in fact only 5% are defective? Is this a consumer risk or a producer risk?
    b. Suppose that 10% of the 500 items are actually defective. What is the probability of accepting the lot when it should be rejected? Is this a consumer risk or a producer risk?

5. A manufacturer claims that no more than 5% of its items are defective. You adopt the following decision rule: Reject a shipment of 500 items if more than 1 of the 20 sampled items is defective. Otherwise, you accept the shipment.
    a. What is the probability of rejecting the lot when in fact only 5% are defective? Is this a consumer risk or a producer risk?
    b. Suppose that 10% of the 500 items are actually defective. What is the probability of accepting the lot when it should be rejected? Is this a consumer risk or a producer risk?
    c. Compare the results of this exercise with those of Exercise 4. What is the effect of increasing the sample size on producer and consumer risk, everything else held constant?

6. A major appliance manufacturer conducts phone surveys each quarter to check customer satisfaction. One district has 100,000 customers. Suppose that 10% of its customers are dissatisfied. The company selects 50 customers from the district to check the number that are dissatisfied. Should the company use the binomial model to analyze the data for the district? Explain.

7. Assuming no other changes, would your answer change in Exercise 6 if the district has 100 customers? Explain.

8. Suppose there are 20 beads in a bowl—15 are blue and five are red.
   a. Selecting without replacement, what is the probability of selecting the first red bead? The second red bead given a red bead was selected on the first draw? The third red bead given that two red beads were selected? The fourth red bead given the three red beads were selected?
   b. Is the bead selection process near-Bernoulli?
   c. Selecting with replacement, what is the probability of selecting the first red bead? The second red bead given a red bead was selected? The third red bead given that two red beads were selected? The fourth red bead given that three red beads were selected?
   d. Is the bead selection process near-Bernoulli?

9. In acceptance sampling, a receiving firm evaluates a portion of each incoming lot of switches and based on the test results, accepts or rejects it. Suppose a vendor ships a lot that has 950 acceptable switches and 50 defective switches to a receiving firm.
   a. What is the probability of selecting one acceptable switch from the lot?
   b. Without replacing the switch, what is the probability of selecting a second acceptable switch from the lot?
   c. Without replacing the first two switches, what is the probability of selecting a third acceptable switch from the lot?
   d. Does the probability of a success vary much from trial to trial (sample to sample)?
   e. Is the sampling process near-Bernoulli and can we compute meaningful binomial probabilities?

10. In acceptance sampling, COMCEL evaluates a portion of each incoming lot (of size 1,000 components) and based on the test results, accepts or rejects it. The acceptable quality level, AQL, is the maximum percentage of incoming defective components that COMCEL can tolerate. Assume that COMCEL and its vendor (Superior Electronics) have agreed to a 5% ($p = .05$) AQL. A random sample of 20 is selected from each incoming lot. It will be accepted only if zero or one defectives are found—20·.05 or less. Define a binomial random variable as follows: the number of defective pieces in a sample of 20.
   a. Suppose that Superior Electronics ships a lot that is excellent; that is, the actual percent defective is 3% ($p = .03$)—well below the negotiated AQL. What is the probability that COMCEL will accept a lot?
   b. Given that the probability of accepting a good lot of 1,000 pieces is .88, does this seem fair to Superior Electronics? *Note:* Superior is sending lots to COMCEL whose percentage defective is below the negotiated AQL and yet COMCEL will accept only 88% of the lots. Discuss.
   c. Suppose that Superior Electronics ships a lot that is terrible; that is, the actual percent defective is 10% ($p = .10$)—well above the negotiated AQL. What is the probability that COMCEL will accept a lot?
   d. Given that the probability of accepting a horrible lot of 1,000 pieces is .39, does this seem fair to COMCEL? *Note:* The percentage defective is well above the negotiated AQL and yet COMCEL will accept 39% of these lots. Discuss.
   e. Professor Deming, a leading quality expert, has said that acceptance sampling is a waste of time. Given your responses to the above questions, is acceptance sampling effective? Do good incoming lots always get accepted? Do horrible incoming lots always get rejected?

11. In this exercise we examine the impact of increasing the number of pieces inspected and its impact on accepting good and horrible lots. Recall that the AQL is 5%. In Exercise 10 we computed the probabilities of accepting the following lots.

Good lot, .03 defective $P(X = 0) + P(X = 1) = .88$

Horrible lot, .10 defective $P(X = 0) + P(X = 1) = .39$

A random sample of 40 (rather then 20) is selected from each incoming lot. It will be accepted only if zero, one, or two defectives are found—40·.05 or less.

a. Compute the probability of accepting a lot that has 3% ($p = .03$) defectives—that is, a good lot.

b. Compute the probability of accepting a lot that has 10% ($p = .10$) defectives—that is, a horrible lot.

c. Compare your answers to Exercise 10, parts **a** and **c.** What is the impact of increasing the number of pieces sampled at incoming inspection while maintaining the same AQL?

12. Refer to Exercise 10. Compute the following probabilities.

a. P(accepting a lot) $[P(X = 0) + P(X = 1)]$ if Superior lots contain 0% defectives.

b. P(accepting a lot) $[P(X = 0) + P(X = 1)]$ if Superior lots contain 3% defectives.

c. P(accepting a lot) $[P(X = 0) + P(X = 1)]$ if Superior lots contain 6% defectives.

d. P(accepting a lot) $[P(X = 0) + P(X = 1)]$ if Superior lots contain 9% defectives.

e. P(accepting a lot) $[P(X = 0) + P(X = 1)]$ if Superior lots contain 12% defectives.

f. P(accepting a lot) $[P(X = 0) + P(X = 1)]$ if Superior lots contain 15% defectives.

g. P(accepting a lot) $[P(X = 0) + P(X = 1)]$ if Superior lots contain 18% defectives.

h. P(accepting a lot) $[P(X = 0) + P(X = 1)]$ if Superior lots contain 21% defectives.

i. Draw a scatter plot (Chapter 3) of the probability of accepting a lot (vertical axis) and the percent defectives (horizontal axis). You have just constructed an operating characteristics (*OC*) curve. Explain what the curve indicates to a nontechnical operating manager.

13. At the Ford Motor Company, production workers maintain quality control charts (see Chapter 15) on weld strengths of Escort door frames. The operators record the shift on the horizontal axis and the weld strength of one door selected from the shift's production on the vertical axis. Control charts (line graphs from Chapter 2) are used to monitor the welding process and take corrective action if the process is out of statistical control. When a process is out-of-control, there is an assignable cause which must be determined by the operators.

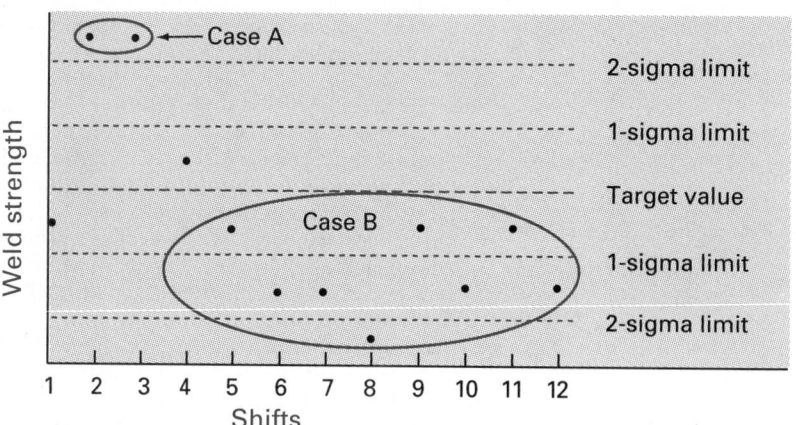

Quality experts have developed the following rules to detect "out-of-control" situations that must be fixed. These are called freak patterns.

1. Two out of three successive data points that fall beyond the two sigma limits on the same side of the centerline (case A).
2. Eight successive data points lie on one side of the centerline or target value (case B).
3. Four out of five successive data points fall beyond the one-sigma limits above the centerline.

a. If the probability of success (data point more than 2 sigma above the centerline) is .023, what is the probability that 2 out of 3 successive data points will fall beyond 2 sigma above the centerline or target value of a control chart?

b. If the probability of falling below the centerline or target value is .50, what is probability that 8 successive data points will lie below the centerline or target value?

c. If the probability of success (data point more than 1 sigma below the centerline) is .16, what is the probability that 4 out of 5 successive data points fall more than 1 sigma below the centerline?

d. Note that the three probabilities in parts **a–c** are very small—.001 – .004 range. Why do these probabilities suggest that the welding process is "out-of-control"?

e. What should the operator do if she obtains one of the above data patterns?

f. Would three (not eight) successive points on one side of the centerline indicate the need to take corrective action? That is, is the variation random or is it due to an assignable cause? Compute the probability of getting three successive data points above the centerline in a control chart. Explain.

5.5 ▤ The Poisson Distribution

Like the binomial distribution, the Poisson distribution provides probability values and is an alternative approach to obtaining probabilities through surveys or personal assessments. The Poisson distribution is a discrete probability distribution where the values of a random experiment may take on only whole numbers. By the end of this section you should be able to:

1. state the conditions for using the Poisson distribution;
2. calculate and interpret Poisson probabilities;
3. use the Poisson probability table in Appendix 2; and
4. compute and interpret the mean and standard deviation for a Poisson random variable.

Here are some examples of Poisson random variables:

Random Variable	Area of Opportunity
Number of accidents in a factory	per minute, hour, week, year
Number of defects	per foot, yard of cable
Number of errors	per line, page, ten pages

A single trial is some fixed *area of opportunity* such as a fixed length of time (a day) or space (a page). The outcome on a single trial is a count of occurrences per area of opportunity, such as accidents per week. The possible values of each of these random variables are $\{0, 1, 2, 3, 4, \ldots\}$—any non-negative integer value.

For a variable to be Poisson distributed, three conditions must hold:

1. An event, such as an accident, has many opportunities to occur, but the probability that the event will occur at any opportunity is extremely small.

For example, there are many hours in a year, and most go by without an accident in a single work place. There are many pages in a book, but very few have a typo.

2. The probability of an event is proportional to the size of the area of opportunity.

For example, the probability that an accident will happen in a COMCEL plant is greater over a period of one month than over a period of one week.

3. The events must be statistically independent.

The third condition requires that events do not occur in clusters. For example, if an accident occurs on Monday, this has no effect on the probability that other accidents will occur in the same week. If a spelling error is found on one page, it does not affect the probability of finding other errors on the same page.

The Poisson Expression

Use expression (5.10) for computing Poisson probabilities:

$$P(X = x) = \frac{e^{-\lambda}\lambda^x}{x!} \tag{5.10}$$

λ (read as lambda) is the *average number* of occurrences over a given area of opportunity. The constant e equals 2.71828.

Consider the following problem, which involves a Poisson random variable.

Example: Defects per Standard Phone Unit   Inspectors have kept careful records of the number of defects (scratches, paint flaws, etc.) over the last 500 standard car phones produced at COMCEL. The area of opportunity is a standard phone unit. One phone can have more than one defect. The inspectors recorded a total of 125 defects on the 500 sets, for an average of .25 defect (125/500) per phone; $\lambda = .25$. What is the probability of finding no defects on the next phone inspected? What is the probability that the next phone will have exactly one defect?

Begin by defining the random variable of interest.

The random variable X = number of defects per standard phone
Possible values   { 0, 1, 2, 3, 4, 5, ... }
Known quantities $\lambda = .25$, $x = 0$, $x = 1$
Unknown quantities $P(X = 0)$, $P(X = 1)$

From expression (5.10):

$$P(X = 0) = \frac{e^{-.25}(.25)^0}{0!} = .779$$

Note that $0! = 1$, $.25^0 = 1$, and that $e^{-.25} = 1/e^{.25}$. There is a .779 probability that the next standard phone examined will have no defects.

$$P(X = 1) = \frac{e^{-.25}(.25)^1}{1!} = .195$$

There is a .195 probability that the next standard phone examined will have exactly one defect. Both probabilities are accurate if (1) the average number of defects per phone is .25 and (2) the defects are Poisson distributed; that is, the three conditions have been met.

The Poisson Table

We could also have determined the two probabilities using the cumulative Poisson table in Appendix 2. To use the table, find the average number of occurrences, λ. Values of λ are column headers. Values of x are the row headers. The intersection of a value of x and a value of λ is the cumulative probability, $P(X \leq x)$.

Use Appendix 2 to find the probability of finding no defects on a standard phone unit if the average number of defects per phone is .25.

$$P(X = 0 \text{ when } \lambda = .25) = .779$$

How do we find the probability of finding exactly one defect on a standard phone? The number at the intersection of λ equal to .25 and the row labelled 1 is .974. The tabled number, .974, is a cumulative probability—the probability of observing one *or fewer* defects on a single standard phone. It is $P(X \leq 1$ when $\lambda = .25)$. Note that

$$P(X \leq 1) = P(X = 0) + P(X = 1)$$

Therefore,

$$P(X \leq 1) - P(X = 0) = P(X = 1)$$

$$.974 - .779 = .195$$

λ x	.02	.04	.06	.08	.10	.15	.20	.25
0	.980	.961	.942	.923	.905	.861	.819	.779
1	1.000	.999	.998	.997	.995	.990	.982	.974
2		1.000	1.000	1.000	1.000	.999	.999	.998
3						1.000	1.000	1.000

That is, to find the probability of exactly one defect, we subtract the probability of finding exactly zero defects from the probability of finding either zero or one defect. In general, the way to find the probability of x defects is to subtract the cumulative probability of finding $x - 1$ defects from the cumulative probability of finding x defects.

Problem Sensing and the Poisson Distribution

In Section 5.4 we illustrated how the binomial distribution could be used to sense problems. We now demonstrate how the Poisson distribution can also be used to sense problems.

Example: Accidents at the Dallas Plant   The manager of COMCEL's Dallas plant notes that there have been 27 accidents within the plant over the past 36 months. Table 5.7 contains a breakdown of how many of the 36 months had 0, 1, 2, 3, 4, and 5 accidents. What is the probability that more than 3 accidents will occur next month?

Table 5.7

Breakdown of the Past 36 Months
According to Number of Accidents

Accidents per Month	Number of Months
0	18
1	12
2	4
3	1
4	1
5	0
	36

Before using the Poisson probability table we must list the assumptions. If they are not reasonable, then calculated probabilities may not be meaningful.

ASSUMPTION 1:   The average number of accidents per month is .75. There were no accidents in 18 of the months. There was 1 accident in 12 of the months. The total number of accidents for the past 36 months is 0(18) + 1(12) + 2(4) + 3(1) + 4(1) + 5(0), or 27. Therefore, the average number of accidents per month, λ, is 27/36, or .75 accident per month.

ASSUMPTION 2:   The probability of an accident occurring at any point in time is very small. The probability increases as the length of time increases. The area of opportunity is 1 month.

ASSUMPTION 3:   The probability that another accident will occur is the same, no matter how many accidents have already occurred in that month.

Begin by defining the random variable of interest.

The random variable X = the number of accidents in a month
Possible values $\{0, 1, 2, 3, 4, 5, \ldots\}$
Known quantity λ = .75 accident per month
Unknown quantity $P(X > 3)$

From Appendix 2,

$$P(X > 3) = 1 - P(X \le 3) = 1 - .993 = .007$$

The probability that the Dallas plant will experience more than 3 accidents next month is .007. This probability assessment will be accurate if the actual accident distribution is Poisson distributed with a mean of .75 accident per month.

Now suppose that next month there are more than 3 accidents at the Dallas plant. What could that mean? One possibility is that there is no increasing accident problem in Dallas. However, the computed probability of more than 3 accidents is only .007— a highly unlikely event. On the other hand, the high number of accidents could suggest that the Dallas plant has an increasing accident problem. Most managers would choose the increasing accident rate explanation.

What should the manager do? He should investigate and seek possible root causes. He could ask: What changes occurred in Dallas this month? What is unique about this month in comparison to other months? For example, suppose that COMCEL installed new equipment. That might account for the higher-than-normal number of accidents. Perhaps new personnel have been assigned to the plant. That too might account for the problem. Effective managers, once they sense problems, investigate them.

Assessing the Poisson Process Assumptions

Suppose the number of accidents in a month in the Dallas plant is Poisson distributed. Then how many of the 36 months should have had exactly zero accidents? How many months should have had exactly one accident, two accidents, etc.?

Table 5.8 contains the plant accident data and the Poisson probabilities of having exactly 0, 1, 2, 3, 4, or 5 accidents. For example, from Appendix 2, the probability of having exactly one accident next month is .827 − .472 = .355. Please verify the other probabilities shown.

Table 5.8

Accidents at the Dallas Plant over 36 Consecutive Months

Accidents per Month	Actual Number of Months	Poisson Probability	Expected Number of Months
0	18	.472	36(.472) = 16.99
1	12	.355	36(.355) = 12.78
2	4	.132	36(.132) = 4.75
3	1	.034	36(.034) = 1.22
4	1	.006	36(.006) = .22
5	0	.001	36(.001) = .04
	36	1.000	36.00

The last column in the table contains the expected number of months that should have had 0, 1, 2, 3, 4, and 5 accidents if the number of accidents is Poisson distributed. For example, we would expect no accidents in 16.99 of the 36 months—that is, 36 months times the Poisson probability of .472. There were 18 months when there were no accidents. Note that all the actual and expected frequencies agree very well. It appears that the number of accidents at the Dallas plant is Poisson distributed.

Mean and Standard Deviation of a Poisson Distribution

The mean of a probability distribution is the long-run average value. The mean for any Poisson distribution is λ, the average number of occurrences per area of opportunity. To see that λ is the mean, use Table 5.8 to develop a probability histogram for the number of accidents. The histogram will balance at about .75 accident per month.

We could use expression (5.2) to compute the standard deviation, but there is a simpler one for a Poisson distribution:

$$\sigma = \sqrt{\lambda} \tag{5.11}$$

The standard deviation for a Poisson random variable is simply the square root of its mean. For the Dallas plant's accident study, the standard deviation is $\sqrt{.75} = .87$ accident per month.

In summary, we use the Poisson distribution when we must calculate probabilities for the number of events—an error, an accident—over a given area of opportunity—a page, a week, etc. A critical assumption is that the events must be statistically independent. The mean and standard deviation for a Poisson distributed random variable are λ and $\sqrt{\lambda}$, respectively.

SECTION 5.5 EXERCISES

1. Explain how you could estimate lambda(λ) for the following Poisson random variables?
   a. The average number of defects per 1,000 pieces.
   b. The average number of misspelled words on a page.
   c. The average number of people arriving at a bank teller station during lunch hour.
   d. The average number of deaths per 1,000 operations at a single hospital.
   e. The average number of power failures in a city in a year.

2. State the conditions that must be true in parts **a–e** of Exercise 1 to use the Poisson expression or Appendix 2 to determine probabilities.

3. Use Appendix 2 to determine the Poisson probabilities.
  a. $P(X \leq 3$ for lambda $= 1.2)$
  b. $P(X < 3$ for lambda $= 1.2)$
  c. $P(X = 3$ for lambda $= 0.7)$
  d. $P(X \geq 7$ for lambda $= 3.6)$
  e. $P(2 \leq X \leq 4$ for lambda $= 2.4)$
  f. The probability that there are less than or equal to 3 defects in a yard of cable if the average number of defects per yard is .55.
  g. The probability that there are 4 accidents in a week if the average number of accidents per week is 4.
  h. The probability that there are more than 3 errors in a book if the average number of errors in a book is 1.2.
  i. The probability that there are 3 or more errors in a book if the average number of errors in a book is 1.2.
  j. The chances of between 2 and 4, inclusive, errors in a book if the average number of errors in a book is 3.

4. Define a discrete random variable as follows:

$$X = \text{the number of DUI traffic accidents in a week}$$

$$\lambda = 3.0 \text{ DUI accidents per week (from police arrest reports)}$$

Translate the following three Poisson probability statements into English and using Appendix 2, determine and interpret their probabilities.
  a. $P(X = 5)$
  b. $P(X > 4)$
  c. $P(X \leq 3)$
  d. What is the average number of DUI accidents per week? Use expression 5.11 to determine the standard deviation.
  e. Suppose that Mothers Against Drunk Driving (MADD) has just completed a reduce DUI campaign. Suppose in the following week no DUI accidents happened. If lambda were still 3.0 (MADD campaign not effective), are no accidents likely? Is the probability large or small? If small, what does that mean in terms of the MADD program success? Explain.

5. Define a discrete random variable as follows:

$$X = \text{the number of defects per 1,000 yards of electrical cable}$$

$$\lambda = 3 \text{ defects per 1,000 yards (from past quality inspection data)}$$

Translate the following statements into the correct mathematical notation; for example, $P(X = x$ for a given $\lambda)$.
  a. The chances that in 1,000 yards of cable, 3 defects will be found.
  b. The probability that in 1,000 yards of cable, at most 5 defects will be found.
  c. The chances that in 1,000 yards of cable, at least 3 defects will be found.
  d. The probability that in 100 yards of cable, 1 or 2 defects will be found.
  e. How could Apex Cable Inc. estimate the value of lambda?

6. Define a discrete random variable as follows:

$$X = \text{the number of DUI accidents per week}$$

$$\lambda = 1.50 \text{ DUI accidents per week (from police arrest reports)}$$

Translate the following statements into the correct mathematical notation; for example, $P(X = x$ for a given $\lambda)$.
  a. The chances that in one week there will be three DUI accidents.

     b. The probability that in one week there will be at most two DUI accidents.

     c. The chances that in one week, there will be at least three DUI accidents.

     d. The probability that in one month there will be between four and six, inclusive, DUI accidents.

     e. How could the police department estimate the value of lambda.

7. A book editor expects to find 1 error per 5 pages of text. What is the probability that over the next 5 pages the editor will find:

     a. At least 1 error?

     b. More than 1 error?

     c. Exactly 1 error?

     d. What is the mean number of errors over the next 15 pages?

     e. How could the editor estimate λ?

8. Suppose that the number of persons per car arriving at the entrance to One Flag over Guam amusement park is Poisson distributed with $\lambda = 3.2$. What is the probability that a car arriving at the entrance contains:

     a. One person?

     b. Fewer than four persons?

     c. What are the mean and standard deviation for the number of persons per car?

     d. How could the amusement park estimate λ?

9. A retailer sells office copiers. The problem facing the store manager is knowing how much inventory to stock. Large inventories tie up capital and increase insurance premiums. Alternatively, stockouts can result in lost sales. The store manager knows that it takes 5 business days from placing an order to delivery of a new supply of copiers. After an analysis of sales data she finds that she sold an average of 5 copiers per 5-day period.

     a. List the assumptions you must make before using the Poisson probability table. Be sure to define the Poisson random variable and describe its possible values.

     b. What is the area of opportunity?

     c. If she waits until 5 copiers remain in inventory before reordering, what is the probability that she will experience a stockout while she is waiting for new copiers to arrive?

     d. If she reorders when 12 remain in inventory, what is the probability that she will experience a stockout while she is waiting for new copiers to arrive?

     e. What should be her reorder point if she wants no more than a 5% chance of stockout?

10. The factory has experienced an average of four accidents per month over the last three years. The manager decided to require each employee to attend an accident prevention workshop.

     a. Assuming that the workshop has no effect on the accident rate, what is the probability that next month there will be at least four accidents? at least two accidents?

     b. Suppose that next month there is only one accident. Would you conclude that the workshop was successful? Defend your answer.

11. Car phones are shipped in boxes of four. The average number of defects per phone is .5. Define the Poisson random variable, X, as the number of defects in a box of four phones.

     a. What are the mean and standard deviation of this random variable?

     b. Construct a probability histogram to display the distribution.

     c. Suppose that the next box of four phones contained six defects. Could this suggest that something is wrong? Explain.

12. In an office the number of employees smoking in any 15-minute interval is Poisson distributed with a standard deviation of 3. What is the mean number of employees smoking in any 15-minute interval? What is the probability that during a 15-minute time period exactly three employees will be smoking?

13. Define a discrete random variable as follows:

$$X = \text{the number of defects per 1,000 yards of electrical cable}$$

$$\lambda = 3 \text{ defects per 1,000 yards (from past quality inspection data)}$$

     a. Use Appendix 2 to determine the probability distribution for the discrete random variable, X.

     b. Draw the Poisson probability histogram for the number of defects per 1,000 yards.

  c. Use the histogram to approximate the expected number of defects per 1,000 yards.
  d. What is the average number of defects per 1,000 yards?
  e. Use expression (5.11) to determine the standard deviation in the number of defects.
  f. Suppose that the firm implements a Total Quality Management (TQM) program. It should reduce the number of defects in their cable. After the program has been introduced, the firm finds zero defects per 1,000 yards in their next shipment. If lambda has not changed, what is the probability of getting zero defects? Is the probability large or small? If small, what does that mean in terms of the TQM program success?

14. Define a discrete random variable as follows:

$$X = \text{the number of rejects in a lot of 200}$$

$$\lambda = 1.2 \text{ rejects per lot (from past quality inspection data)}$$

  a. Use Appendix 2 to determine the probability distribution for the discrete random variable, X.
  b. Draw the Poisson probability histogram for the number of rejects per lot of 200.
  c. Use the histogram to approximate the expected number of rejects per lot of 200.
  d. What is the average number of rejects per lot?
  e. Use expression (5.11) to determine the standard deviation in the number of rejects.
  f. Suppose that the firm implements a Total Quality Management (TQM) program which it believes will reduce the number of rejects. After the program has been introduced, the firm finds zero defects in a lot of 200 in their next production run. If λ has not changed, what is the probability of getting zero defects? Is the probability large or small? If relatively large, what does that mean in terms of the TQM program success?
  g. Suppose that the firms finds zero defects in the next three lots. That probability can be determined as follows:

$$P(\text{no defects}) \cdot P(\text{no defects}) \cdot P(\text{no defects})$$

Compute the above probability. If λ has not changed, what is the probability of getting zero defects in the next three lots? Is the probability large or small? If small, what does that mean in terms of the TQM program success?

5.6 The Normal Distribution

While the binomial and Poisson distributions are useful, many business problems involve continuous random variables. Continuous random variables can take on an infinite, or uncountable, number of values. For these cases, we will need a new probability distribution for problem solving—the normal distribution. By the end of this section, you should be able to:

1. explain the importance of the normal distribution;
2. describe the characteristics of the normal distribution;
3. explain what z-scores are;
4. compute normal probabilities;
5. use the normal distribution to help sense emerging problems and make decisions; and
6. explain why the mean and standard deviation of the normal distribution are not known *with certainty* except in statistics books.

Why Is the Normal Distribution So Useful?

There are many continuous probability distributions. Why single out the normal distribution? There are two reasons.

FIGURE 5.4   Probability Histogram for 100 Tosses of a Fair Coin

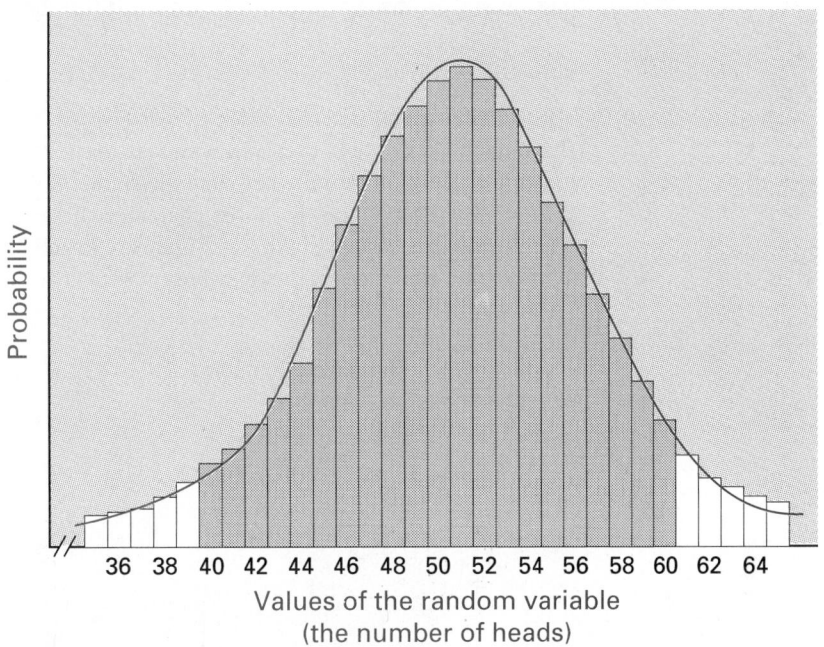

Values of the random variable
(the number of heads)

First, the normal distribution is an *approximation* to many probability distributions. For instance, we can use the normal distribution to approximate the binomial distribution when the number of binomial trials, *n,* is very large. The normal distribution involves much less computation.

To illustrate this idea, consider tossing a fair coin 100 times and counting the number of heads. The discrete random variable—the number of heads in 100 flips—can take on any of 101 values (0, 1, 2, 3, . . . , 100). Figure 5.4 is a probability histogram of the 101 probabilities. We have drawn a smooth curve through the top of each rectangle. The probability histogram for 100 tosses is very close to the bell-shaped curve that we discussed in Chapter 2.

Now, we have two ways to compute the probability of getting between 40 and 60 heads:

1. Treat the random variable as discrete, use the binomial distribution, and determine the *exact* probability. This is the sum of the 21 shaded rectangles in Figure 5.4.
2. Treat the random variable as continuous, use the normal distribution, and *approximate* the probability. This is the area underneath the curve between 40 and 60 heads.

The binomial distribution requires that we compute factorials such as 100!. The normal distribution is a quick probability calculator for the binomial distribution.

The normal distribution is also used to *approximate* the distributions for variables such as IQ, height, grade point average, blood pressure, and the diameter of machined parts. All these variables share one thing in common: They are affected by a large number of independent factors. For example, blood pressure is influenced by genetic factors, diet, weight, lifestyle, aerobic conditioning, and other factors. A frequency histogram of the blood pressures of 1,000 people would be nearly bell-shaped. In summary, when many independent factors affect a continuous random variable, its behavior can often be described by the normal distribution.

Second, the normal distribution plays a key role in market research and quality management procedures where sample statistics, such as a sample mean or sample percentage, are used to draw valid conclusions about target populations of interest.

Characteristics of the Normal Distribution

The normal distribution is a *family* of bell-shaped curves. All have the same basic bell shape and differ only in their mean and standard deviation. The mean determines the location of the center of the bell, and the standard deviation determines the spread of the bell. Figure 5.5 presents three characteristic shapes. As the mean increases, the distribution shifts to the right. See Figures 5.5a and 5.5b for comparison. As the standard deviation increases, the distribution spreads out or flattens about the mean; see Figures 5.5b and 5.5c.

FIGURE 5.5   Three Normal Curves

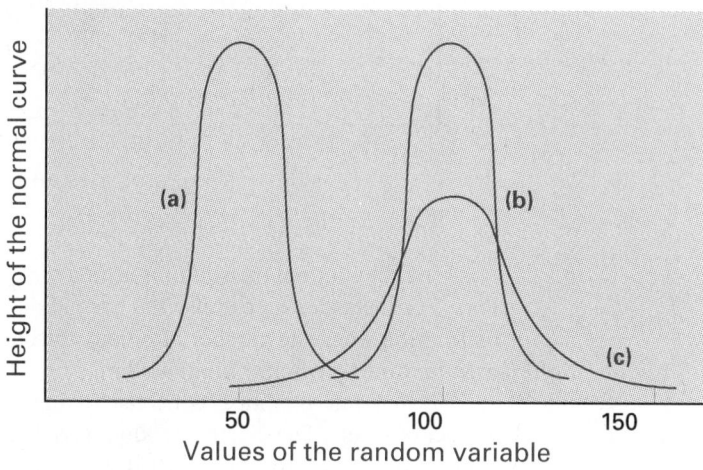

All normal curves have the following characteristics:

1. They are symmetric.
2. The total area under the curve is 1. Probabilities are the areas under the normal curve. Recall that the second rule of probability states that the sum of the probabilities of all possible nonoverlapping events is 1.0, and this idea extends to continuous probability distributions.
3. The values of x can range from $-\infty$ to $+\infty$. However, in practice, we rarely consider values of x lying at a distance beyond 3 standard deviations from the mean.
4. The normal curve is *asymptotic* to the horizontal axis. The curve gets closer to this axis as x gets very large or small, but never actually reaches the axis.
5. The probability that x will fall below (above) the mean is .5.
6. The probability that x lies within a distance of 1 standard deviation from the mean is .6826. The probability that x lies within a distance of 2 standard deviations from the mean is .9544. The probability that x lies within a distance of 3 standard deviations from the mean is .9974.

In Chapter 2 we used the Empirical rule to identify outliers. When a frequency histogram is *approximately* bell-shaped, about 68% of all data values fall within a distance of 1 standard deviation from the mean. Nearly all the observations fall within a distance of 3 standard deviations from the mean. When the histogram represents a perfect normal distribution, the exact percentages are 68.26% and 99.74%, respectively.

z-Scores and Finding Probabilities

Probabilities are the areas under normal curves, as shown in Figure 5.4. Because computing these areas requires calculus, statisticians have done the integration for us. However, instead of having one probability table for each normal curve (for each possible combination of a mean and standard deviation), we use only one table—the standard normal, or z, table. See Appendix 3.

The following example demonstrates how to use Appendix 3. Assume that a histogram for the weights of 1,000 female students is normally distributed. The mean and standard deviation are 120 pounds and 10 pounds. We wish to compute the probability that a female student weighs between 120 and 132 pounds, or $P(120 < \text{weight} < 132)$.

To determine the probability, we first convert the weights of 120 pounds and 132 pounds into z-scores using expression (5.12) and then use Appendix 3. A z-score for a value—say, 132 pounds—is simply **the number of standard deviations that the value is from the mean:**

$$z\text{-score} = \frac{\text{Value of normal random variable } - \text{ Mean}}{\text{Standard deviation}}$$

$$= \frac{x - \mu}{\sigma} \tag{5.12}$$

$$\text{Converting a 120-pound weight into a } z\text{-score: } \frac{120 - 120}{10} = 0.0$$

$$\text{Converting a 132-pound weight into a } z\text{-score: } \frac{132 - 120}{10} = +1.2$$

To find $P(120 < \text{weight} < 132)$, we must find the area under the standard normal curve, $P(0 < z < +1.2)$, in Appendix 3.

In Appendix 3, the column labelled z contains values from 0.0 to 3.0 in increments of .10. The ten column headings indicate z-scores in increments of .01. These permit finding probabilities for z-scores to two decimal places. The numbers in the table body are areas under the standard normal curve (probabilities) between z-scores of 0.00 and 3.09.

z	.00	.01	.02	.03	.04	.05	.06	.07	.08	.09
0.0	.0000	.0040	.0080	.0120	.0160	.0199	.0239	.0279	.0319	.0359
0.1	.0398	.0438	.0478	.0517	.0557	.0596	.0636	.0675	.0714	.0753
0.2	.0793	.0832	.0871	.0910	.0948	.0987	.1026	.1064	.1103	.1141
0.3	.1179	.1217	.1255	.1293	.1331	.1368	.1406	.1443	.1480	.1517
0.4	.1554	.1591	.1628	.1664	.1700	.1736	.1772	.1808	.1844	.1879
0.5	.1915	.1950	.1985	.2019	.2054	.2088	.2123	.2157	.2190	.2224

To determine $P(0 < z < +1.2)$, find the row z value of 1.2 and the column labelled .00. The value at the intersection is the area under the standard normal curve that lies between the mean of 0 and a z-score of +1.2, or .3849. The probability that a female student weighs between 120 and 132 pounds is thus .3849.

Compute the probability of selecting a female student who weighs between 92.4 pounds and 130 pounds, $P(92.4 < \text{weight} < 130)$. We again use expression (5.12) to convert weights into z-scores:

$$\text{Converting a 92.4-pound weight into a } z\text{-score: } \frac{92.4 - 120}{10} = -2.76$$

$$\text{Converting a 130-pound weight into a } z\text{-score: } \frac{130 - 120}{10} = +1.00$$

To find $P(92.4 < \text{weight} < 130)$, we must find the area under the standard normal curve, $P(-2.76 < z < +1.00)$ in Appendix 3. We find the area from 0 to -2.76 and the area from 0 to $+1.00$, and then add the two probabilities.

Since the normal curve is symmetric, areas under the curve are the same for positive and negative z-scores of the same magnitude. Find the row z value of 2.7 and the column labelled .06. The value at the intersection is the area under the normal curve that lies between the z-score of 0 and -2.76, or .4971. Find the z value of 1.0 and the column labelled .00. The tabled value at the intersection is .3413. Thus the desired probability is the sum of the two probabilities, $.4971 + .3413$, or .8384. The probability of selecting a female student who weighs between 92.4 and 130 pounds is .8384.

In summary, to find normal probabilities, we must find the areas under the standard normal curve. Thus, it makes no sense to talk about $P(\text{weight} = 125 \text{ pounds})$. There is no area over a point. There is area only over an interval, say between 105 and 106 pounds.

The Normal Distribution and Decision Making

Normal probabilities are often used to help managers make decisions among alternative actions. Consider the courier service problem presented at the beginning of the chapter.

Example: Courier Service Problem   Federal Service advertises that its mean delivery time is 30 hours, while United Express claims that its mean delivery time is 34 hours. However, United Express's arrival times are more consistent because the standard deviation of its delivery times is only 2 hours, whereas the standard deviation of Federal's delivery times is 5 hours. Which service should we use if our document must arrive within 36 hours?

We recommend the following three-step process when using the normal distribution to solve business problems:

1. State the Assumptions and Define Random Variables

ASSUMPTION 1:   If we drew a frequency histogram of document arrival times for both courier services for the past several months, the histograms would be nearly bell-shaped.

ASSUMPTION 2:   The mean arrival times for the past several months are indicative of mean arrival times in the future. The mean arrival time for Federal Service is 30 hours and for United Express is 34 hours.

ASSUMPTION 3:   The standard deviations in arrival times for the past several months are indicative of the standard deviations in the future. The standard deviation for Federal Service is 5 hours and for United Express is 2 hours.

The random variables X = Arrival time for Federal Service
                            Y = Arrival time for United Express
Possible values X, Y: an uncountable number of values
Unknown quantities $P(X < 36$ hours$)$, $P(Y < 36$ hours$)$

2.   Sketch the Normal Curve(s)   This will help to visualize the probability we are trying to determine. The Federal Service curve is centered at the mean of 30 hours. The United Express curve is centered at the mean of 34 hours. The curves extend about 3 standard deviations on each side of their means. Figure 5.6 depicts two such curves. We shade those areas that represent the desired probabilities. The figure indicates that Federal Service appears to have a higher probability of meeting the 36-hour maximum deadline.

3.   Convert to z-Scores and Find Probabilities   *Computation for Federal Service*   The probability that the arrival time is less than 36 hours is made up of two

FIGURE 5.6   **Distributions for Federal Service and United Express**

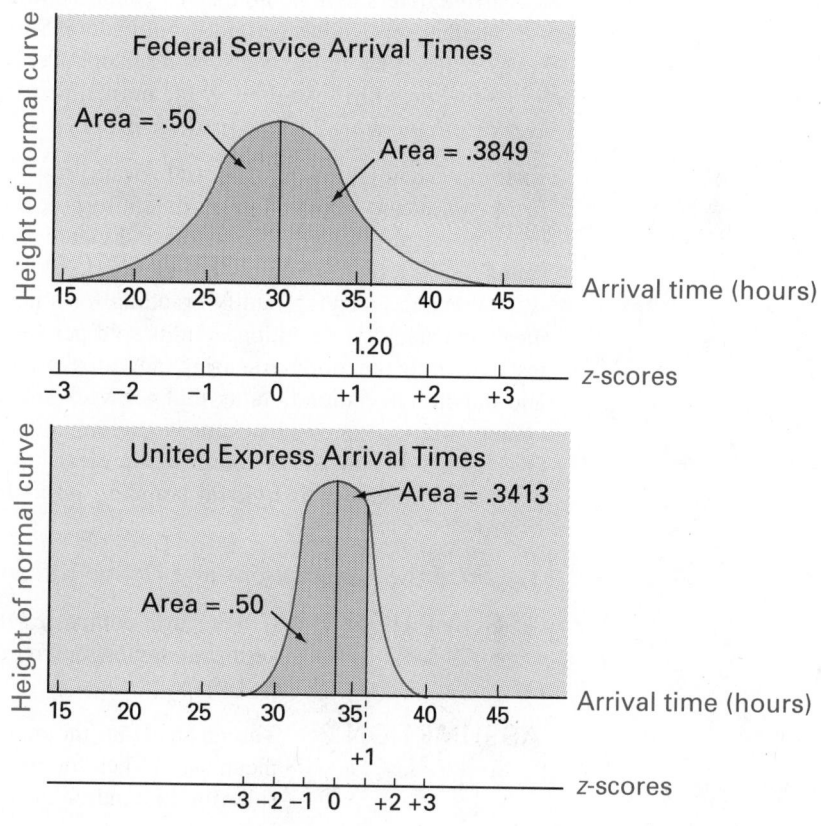

areas in the upper graph of Figure 5.6—the area below the mean and the area between the mean and 36 hours. The area below the mean is .50. The probability that the arrival time is between 30 and 36 hours is determined as

$$P(30 < X < 36) = \text{Probability that the } z\text{-score is between } \frac{30 - 30}{5} \text{ and } \frac{36 - 30}{5}$$

$$= \text{Probability that the } z\text{-score is between } 0 \text{ and } +1.2$$

$$= .3849 \text{ (from Appendix 3)}$$

Thus, $P(X < 36) = .50 + .3849 = .8849$. The documents delivered by Federal Service will arrive in less than 36 hours 88.49% of the time.

Computation for United Express   The probability that the arrival time is less than 36 hours is made up of two areas in the lower graph of Figure 5.6—the area below the mean and the area between the mean and 36 hours. The area below the mean is .50. The probability that the arrival time is between 34 and 36 hours is determined as

$$P(34 < Y < 36) = \text{Probability that the } z\text{-score is between } \frac{34 - 34}{2} \text{ and } \frac{36 - 34}{2}$$

$$= \text{Probability that the } z\text{-score is between } 0 \text{ and } +1.0$$

$$= .3413 \text{ (from Appendix 3)}$$

Thus, $P(Y < 36) = .50 + .3413 = .8413$. The documents delivered by United Express will arrive in less than 36 hours 84.13% of the time.

Neither service is a certainty, but Federal Service is more likely to meet the 36-hour deadline. Therefore, we should select Federal Service as our courier.

Now we will illustrate how the normal distribution can help a marketing manager determine which of two marketing strategies to use in selling a product.

Example: Family vs. Individual Branding   Family branding occurs when a firm applies one brand name to its entire product line, such as Levi's. Individual branding occurs when a firm uses individual brand names for its products—for example, Procter & Gamble's Pringles, Crisco, and Tide.

GSP, Inc. is trying family branding for a new toothpaste in 20 test cities. The mean and standard deviation in units sold per week are 2,250 and 250. GSP is also test marketing the toothpaste using individual branding in 20 similar cities. The mean and standard deviation in units sold per week are 2,250 and 500. GSP will select the strategy that maximizes its chance of selling at least 2,350 units per week. This will ensure that it meets its return on project investment goal. Which marketing approach—family or individual branding—should GSP select for mass-marketing its product?

1. State the Assumptions and Define Random Variables

ASSUMPTION 1:   If we record toothpaste sales in units per week for both marketing strategies, the frequency histograms would be nearly bell-shaped.

ASSUMPTION 2:   The means from the marketing study are indicative of the mean sales when the product is mass-marketed. The mean sales for both individual and family branding are 2,250 units per week.

ASSUMPTION 3:   The standard deviations are indicative of the variability in sales when the product is mass-marketed. The standard deviation for family branding is 250 units per week. The standard deviation for individual branding is 500 units per week.

The random variables	FB = Sales per week using family branding
	IB = Sales per week using individual branding
Possible values	FB, IB: several thousand values each
Unknown quantities	$P(FB > 2{,}350)$, $P(IB > 2{,}350)$

2.   Sketch the Normal Curve(s)   Figure 5.7 presents the normal probability distribution curves for the two marketing approaches.

3.   Convert to z-Scores and Find Probabilities   *Computation for family branding*   The probability that weekly sales exceed 2,350 units is the shaded area in the upper graph of Figure 5.7. The area between 2,250 and 2,350 and the area above 2,350 total 0.5. Thus the desired area or probability is the area between 2,250 and 2,350 subtracted from .5.

FIGURE 5.7   Weekly Sales Distributions for Family and Individual Branding

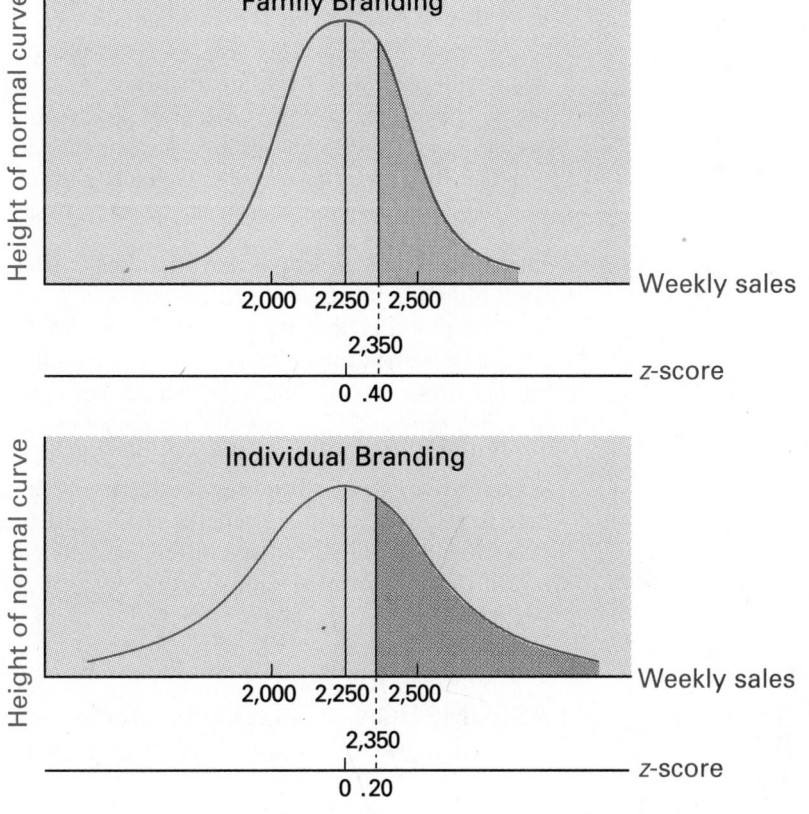

The probability that weekly sales are between 2,250 and 2,350 is obtained as

$P(2{,}250 < FB < 2{,}350)$

$=$ Probability that the z-score is between $\dfrac{2{,}250 - 2{,}250}{250}$ and $\dfrac{2{,}350 - 2{,}250}{250}$

$=$ Probability that the z-score is between 0 and $+.4$

$= .1554$ (from Appendix 3)

Thus, $P(FB > 2{,}350) = .50 - .1554 = .3446$. There is a .3446 probability of selling more than 2,350 units per week using family branding.

Computation for individual branding   The probability that weekly sales exceed 2,350 units is the shaded area in the lower graph of Figure 5.7. The desired area or probability is the area between 2,250 and 2,350 subtracted from .5.

The probability that weekly sales are between 2,250 and 2,350 is computed as

$P(2{,}250 < IB < 2{,}350)$

$=$ Probability that the z-score is between $\dfrac{2{,}250 - 2{,}250}{500}$ and $\dfrac{2{,}350 - 2{,}250}{500}$

$=$ Probability that the z-score is between 0 and $+.2$

$= .0793$ (from Appendix 3)

Thus, $P(IB > 2{,}350) = .50 - .0793 = .4207$. There is a .4207 probability of selling more than 2,350 units per week using individual branding.

With family branding, there is a .34 chance of meeting the minimum sales target, while with individual branding, there is a .42 chance of meeting the minimum sales target. Other things being equal, GSP should go with individual branding, unless it decides not to enter the market because neither probability is greater than .5.

Our final case illustrates how quality control personnel can use the normal distribution to determine if a firm can begin full-scale production.

Example: Process Capability Studies   Before full-scale production begins, firms often run process capability studies to determine if the production process can produce products that meet engineering specifications. COMCEL's Engineering Design Group determines that the shatter strength for the cellular phone plastic handset must be between 4,600 and 4,900 pounds per square inch (ppsi). The *lower specification limit* (LSL) is 4,600 ppsi and the *upper specification limit* (USL) is 4,900 ppsi.

The Quality Control Department conducts a process capability study by selecting five handsets from each of the first 15 production shifts. The mean and standard deviation of shatter strengths of the 75 handsets are 4,750 ppsi and 70 ppsi, respectively. What percentage of the handsets produced will have shatter strengths within the specification limits, between 4,600 and 4,900 ppsi? Should COMCEL begin full-scale production?

1. State the Assumptions and Define Random Variables

ASSUMPTION 1:   The histogram of 75 shatter strengths from the process capability study is nearly bell-shaped.

ASSUMPTION 2:   The mean shatter strength will be the same for the process capability study and full-scale production. The mean shatter strength is 4,750 ppsi.

ASSUMPTION 3:   The standard deviation of shatter strength will be the same for the process capability study and full-scale production. The standard deviation is 70 ppsi.

The random variable	SS = Shatter strength of handset
Possible values	An uncountable number of values
Unknown quantity	$P(4{,}600 < SS < 4{,}900)$

2. Sketch the Normal Curve(s)   Figure 5.8 shows the normal probability distribution curve for the process capability study.

3. Convert to z-Scores and Find Probabilities   The desired probability is the shaded area in Figure 5.8. It consists of two parts—the area between a z-score of -2.14 and the mean, and the area between the mean and a z-score of $+2.14$. These two parts have the same area. Thus we need to find only one area or probability and double it. The probability that shatter strength is between 4,750 and 4,900 ppsi is

$P(4{,}750 < SS < 4{,}900)$

$\quad$ = Probability that the z-score is between $\dfrac{4{,}750 - 4{,}750}{70}$ and $\dfrac{4{,}900 - 4{,}750}{70}$

$\quad$ = Probability that the z-score is between 0 and $+2.14$

$\quad$ = .4838 (from Appendix 3)

Thus, $P(4{,}600 < SS < 4{,}900) = .4838 + .4838 = .9676$. Therefore, 96.76% of the handsets will have shatter strengths within the specification limits. If COMCEL finds the 97% figure acceptable, it will start full-scale production. If this percentage is too low, COMCEL has two choices:

FIGURE 5.8   **Process Capability Study Data**

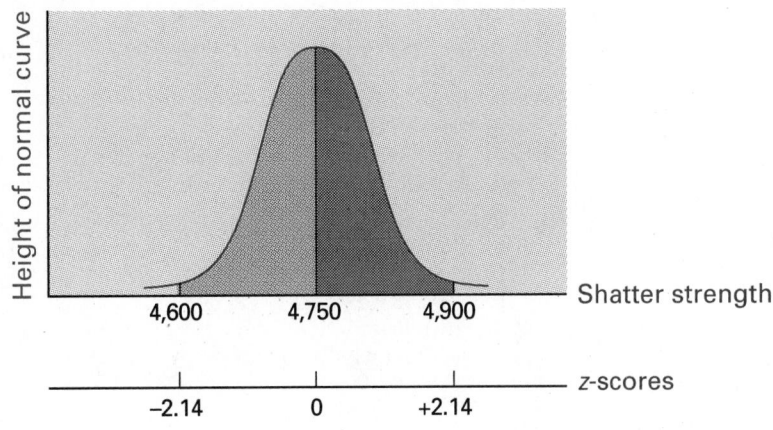

1. Widen the specification limits from 4,600–4,900 ppsi to 4,500–5,000 ppsi. Please verify that almost 100% of the handsets will then have acceptable shatter strengths. However, potential customers may not like the new specification limits. If customers do not care, then widening the limits makes sense.
2. Reduce the standard deviation of the process. Suppose that COMCEL reduces the standard deviation from 70 ppsi to 50 ppsi. Please verify that then almost 100% of its handsets will meet the 4,600 to 4,900 ppsi specification limits. This strategy can require extensive capital investment in new machinery or process improvements, but it is usually the better approach.

Validity of the Normal Distribution Assumptions

To use the z-tables of Appendix 3 we must know the normal distribution's mean and standard deviation. How do we know these values? For example, how would we know the mean shatter strength of *all* plastic phone handsets—that is, the population of handsets?

The only way to know with certainty the population's mean and standard deviation is to test the entire population. With a few exceptions, this is not practical. Generally speaking then, we never know the population mean and standard deviation. However, there are two ways to *estimate* these values. First, we can assume that the sample and population have the same mean and standard deviation. That was our assumption in the process capability study. We took a sample of 75 handsets and assumed that its mean and standard deviation were equal to the corresponding population values. Second, we can estimate the population mean and standard deviation using methods of formal statistical reasoning. The latter approach is better. Formal statistical reasoning will be our topic for the remainder of the book.

In summary, using normal probabilities to make decisions assumes that the probabilities are meaningful. Computed normal probabilities will be meaningful only when the following three assumptions are true:

1. The random variable's frequency histogram is nearly bell-shaped.
2. The mean of the sample data is a good estimate of the mean of the population.
3. The standard deviation of the sample data is a good estimate of the standard deviation of the population.

SECTION 5.6 EXERCISES

1. Under what general conditions would you expect that a distribution will be normally distributed?

2. Refer to the standard normal table, Appendix 3. How much of the area under the curve lies:
    a. To the left of the mean of 0?
    b. Between 0 and 1 standard deviation above the mean?
    c. To the left of a point 1 standard deviation below the mean?
    d. To the right of a point 1 standard deviation below the mean?

3. Refer to the standard normal table. Find the following probabilities:
    a. $P(-1 < z < 1)$
    b. $P(-2.33 < z < 2.33)$
    c. $P(-2.58 < z < 2.58)$
    d. $P(-1.96 < z < 1.96)$
    e. $P(-3.00 < z < 3.00)$
    f. $P(z < -3.00)$
    g. $P(z > -3.00)$
    h. $P(1.2 < z < 2.3)$
    n. $P(1.46 < z < 2.45)$
    o. $P(-1.34 < z < -.098)$
    p. $P(z > 3.00)$
    q. $P(z > 3.00) + P(z < -3.00)$
    r. $P(z < -1.00)$
    s. $P(z > 2.00)$
    t. $P(z > 0)$
    u. $P(z = -1.23)$

    i. $P(.2 < z < 1.3)$ **v.** $P(-2.45 < z < -.69)$
    j. $P(z = 1.3)$ **w.** $P(z < -2)$
    k. $P(z > -1.55)$ **x.** $P(0 < z < 1.89)$
    l. $P(z < 2.65)$ **y.** $P(-3.00 < z < 1.00)$
    m. $P(-1.56 < z < 1.07)$ **z.** $P(z = 0.0)$

4. Use the standard normal table. Draw a probability histogram and determine the value of k for the following probabilities:

    a. $P(z < k) = .50$ **h.** $P(z > k) = .7257$
    b. $P(0 < z < k) = .3413$ **i.** $P(z < k) = .0062$
    c. $P(-k < z < k) = .6828$ **j.** $P(k < z < 2) = .1359$
    d. $P(0 < z < k) = .4772$ **k.** $P(-1 < z < k) = .8185$
    e. $P(-k < z < k) = .9554$ **l.** $P(-2 < z < k) = .6860$
    f. $P(z < k) = .8413$ **m.** $P(1 < z < k) = .1528$
    g. $P(z > k) = .1357$

5. Convert the following z-scores into hours to complete a project. The mean is 1,000 hours and the standard deviation is 200 hours.

    a. z-score of   1.00   **i.** z-score of   1.645
    b. z-score of -0.65 **j.** z-score of -1.96
    c. z-score of -2.50 **k.** z-score of   1.05
    d. z-score of   0.00   **l.** z-score of   2.49
    e. z-score of -3.00 **m.** z-score of -1.76
    f. z-score of   3.00   **n.** z-score of   0.05
    g. z-score of   2.00   **o.** z-score of -0.21
    h. z-score of -1.00

6. Convert the following parcel delivery times into z-scores. The mean delivery time is 36 hours and the standard deviation is 2 hours.

    a. 36 hours   **i.** 39.7 hours
    b. 32 hours   **j.** 32.4 hours
    c. 38.5 hours   **k.** 29.5 hours
    d. 28 hours   **l.** 31.3 hours
    e. 37 hours   **m.** 36.5 hours
    f. 42 hours   **n.** 30.56 hours
    g. 44 hours   **o.** 40.23 hours
    h. 34.6 hours

7. Consider a normal distribution centered around a mean of 10.0 cm with a standard deviation of 1.0 cm. You are given the following set of observations: {7.5 cm, 8.2 cm, 10.0 cm, 12.0 cm}.

    a. Draw a picture of the normal distribution and place the observations on the graph.
    b. Place a standard normal, z-score, scale below the scale of the distribution in part **a** so the standard deviation units of the standardized normal scale correspond to the standard deviation distances of the original population.
    c. How far is each measurement from the mean of 10.0 cm as measured in standard deviation units?

8. The hours-to-burnout of fuses are normally distributed with a mean of 500 hours and a standard deviation of 25 hours. If a new fuse is installed, find the probability that it will last

    a. at least 450 hours.
    b. more than 550 hours.
    c. between 425 hours and 575 hours.
    d. less than 425 hours.
    e. between 425 and 450 hours.
    For each part above: (1) Draw and label the normal distribution. (2) Place the standard normal scale below the hours scale. (3) Shade the area corresponding to the desired probability.

9. Two companies are bidding to supply your company with computer chips. The first company claims the mean life of its chips is 1,000 hours and the standard deviation is 200 hours. The second company claims the mean life of its chips is 1,200 hours and the standard deviation is 300 hours. Assume chip life is normally distributed. Which company would you buy from if a chip should last at least 800 hours? At least 400 hours?

10. Suppose the scores on a mechanical aptitude test are normally distributed with a mean of 50 and a variance of 25.
    a. What score would you have to make so that fewer than 1% of the scores are higher than yours?
    b. If a counselor told you that your z-score on the test was $+1.4$, what was your actual score?
    c. The counselor tells you that the company only hires applicants who score 60 or above. What percentage of the applicants will qualify for a job with the company?

11. The admissions office of a university had a policy of not considering an applicant who scores below 475 on the verbal portion of the SAT exam. Suppose verbal scores are normally distributed with a mean of 500 and a standard deviation of 100. Because of declining enrollment, in 1991 the administration lowered the cutoff score to 450. If the university has 10,000 applicants for the class of 1996, how many more will be accepted because of the revised policy?

12. A vending machine sells coffee in 6-ounce cups. If the machine is set to dispense 5 ounces of coffee, the amount of coffee dispensed per cup is normally distributed with a mean of 5 ounces and a standard deviation of .25 ounce. Assume that the standard deviation is .25 regardless of the mean amount dispensed.
    a. If the machine is set to dispense a mean of 5.75 ounces, what is the probability the dispensed coffee will overflow the 6-ounce cup?
    b. If the machine is set to dispense a mean of 5 ounces, what percentage of the customers will get only 4.5 ounces or less?
    c. Where would we set the mean amount dispensed so that only 2.5% of cups would overflow?
    d. Suppose you decide that overflows of hot coffee are worse for business than giving the customer a short cup. You set the machine to dispense a mean of 5.0 ounces and the next cup overflows. Would you conclude that the machine isn't working properly? Why?

13. Document arrival times are normally distributed with a mean of 30 hours and a standard deviation of 3 hours.
    a. What is the first quartile of document arrival times? *Hint:* Draw a curve and cross-hatch the lowest 25% of the normal curve. Find the z-score and convert to hours.
    b. What is the third quartile?
    c. Find the interquartile range.

14. Weight loss experienced in the Jenny Krag program method averages about 10 pounds in the first month with a 1.5 pound standard deviation. Determine the following probabilities:
    a. A weight loss of at least 8.5 pounds.
    b. A weight loss of at most 13 pounds.
    c. A weight loss of between 7.6 and 11.4 pounds.
    d. A weight loss of at most 7.55 pounds.
    e. A weight loss of more than 8 pounds.
    f. A weight loss of more than 11.64 pounds.
    g. A weight loss of 7.655 pounds.
    For each part above: (1) Draw and label the normal distribution, (2) Place the standard normal scale below the weight-loss scale, (3) Shade the area corresponding to the desired probability.

15. Manufacturing firms must conduct a process capability study before starting full-scale production. COMCEL records the tensile strengths of its phone handsets. The mean tensile strength is 4,750 pounds per square inch (ppsi) and equals the desired target value. The standard deviation is presently 150 ppsi. The lower and upper specification limits are the minimum and maximum tensile strengths that the public wants. The limits set by the engineering department are 4,500 and 5,000 ppsi.
    a. What percentage of the phone handsets will be out-of-specification—that is, below the lower specification limit or above the upper limit?

    Since the percentage is too high, COMCEL must attempt to reduce process variation before starting full-scale production.

    b. Suppose COMCEL reduces its process standard deviation from 150 ppsi to 50 ppsi. Now what percentage of the phone handsets will be out-of-specification?

c. Given your answers in parts **a–b,** comment on the following statement.

Excessive variation is the major battle manufacturers have today in achieving high product quality.

d. Suggest several ways that management could reduce tensile strength process variation.

e. In quality control, the process capability index is used to assess a process's capability of producing good parts.

$$C_{pk} = |\text{ nearest specification limit } - \text{ mean }| \, 3 \cdot \text{standard deviation}$$

Compute the index for the original manufacturing process and then for the improved process.

Today American firms want indices above 2.00 before starting production. Ten years ago indices above 1.33 were acceptable.

16. Service industry firms must conduct a process capability study before starting full-scale service. Apex Credit Report Inc. records the amount of time to prepare a credit report. The mean time is 6.5 hours and equals the desired target value. The standard deviation is presently 1.5 hours. The lower and upper specification limits are the minimum and max-imum report times that Apex's clients want (and are willing to pay Apex's price). The limits are 4 to 9 hours.

a. What percentage of the credit reports preparation times will be out-of-specification? That is, below the lower specification limit or above the upper limit.

Since the percentage is too high, APEX must attempt to reduce process variation before starting full-scale service.

b. Suppose Apex reduces its process standard deviation from 1.5 hours to .75 hour. Now what percentage of the credit report times will be out-of-specification?

c. Given your answers in parts **a–b,** comment on the following statement.

Excessive variation is the major battle service industries have today in achieving high service quality.

d. In quality control, the process capability index is used to assess a process's capability of producing good service.

$$C_{pk} = |\text{ nearest specification limit } - \text{ mean }| \, 3 \cdot \text{standard deviation}$$

Compute the index for the original preparation time process and then for the improved process.

Today American firms want indices above 2.00 before starting a production line. Ten years ago indices above 1.33 were acceptable.

17. Refer to the quality control chart example in Exercise 13 in Section 5.4. We have repro-duced the control chart.

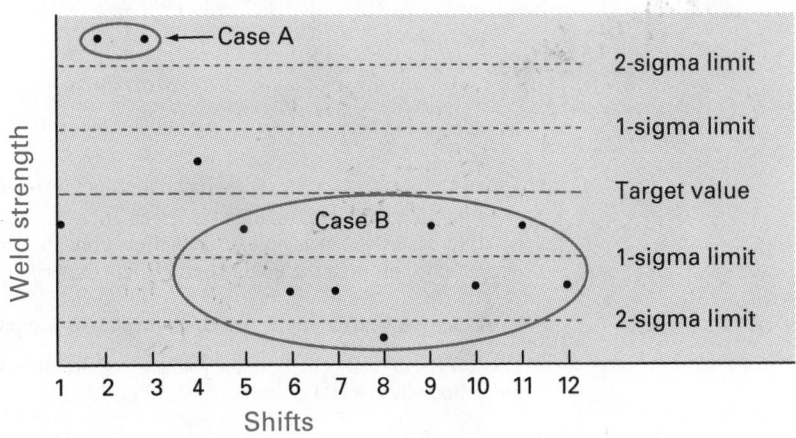

We stated that the probability of a data point falling outside the 2 sigma limits above the centerline is .0228.

a. Please verify this using the standard normal table.

We stated that the probability of a data point falling outside the 1 sigma limits above the centerline is .1587.

b. Please verify this using the standard normal table.
c. What is the probability of a data point falling outside the 3 sigma limits below the centerline?
d. What is the probability of a data point falling between the 1 and 2 sigma limits below the centerline? above the centerline?

18. The project completion time is normally distributed with a mean of 100 hours and standard deviation of 10 hours.

a. Determine the completion time that is equivalent to the 10th percentile. That is, how many hours must elapse so that 10% of the projects will be completed.
b. Determine the completion time that is equivalent to the 25th percentile, the first quartile.
c. Determine the completion time that is equivalent to the 50th percentile, the median.
d. Determine the completion time that is equivalent to the 75th percentile, the third quartile.
e. Determine the completion time that is equivalent to the 90th percentile.
f. Determine the interquartile range and compare its magnitude to the standard deviation.

19. Refer to the hours-to-burnout-of-fuses example is this section. What assumptions must you make in order to use the standard normal table for computing probabilities? How would you verify these assumptions? *Hint:* recall charting techniques and descriptive statistics from Chapter 2.

20. Travel time to the Atlanta airport from the north side of town is normally distributed and depends on which route you take:

I-75 route	I-285 route
Mean time is 30 minutes	Mean time is 35 minutes
Standard deviation is 10 minutes	Standard deviation is 5 minutes

a. If you have 35 minutes to reach the airport, which route is best? Why?
b. If you have 40 minutes to reach the airport, which route is best? Why?
c. If you have 45 minutes to reach the airport, which route is best? Why?

21. In quality control, operators use precontrol charts to monitor a manufacturing process that has been brought under control and improved to an acceptable level. A product (Taurus axle shaft diameters measured in inches) within the lower and upper specification limits (LSL, USL) is acceptable, and a product outside the limits is a reject. Four zones are defined in precontrol charts.

Red zone	Yellow zone	Green zone	Green zone	Yellow zone	Red zone

LSL   USL

9.7495 inches   9.7500 inches   9.7505 inches

Diameter shaft in inches

The operator selects one axle shaft and measure its diameter. The following rules are used:

- If the first shaft measures in the green zone, he lets the process run.
- If the first shaft measures in the yellow zone, he checks a second shaft. If the second shaft is in the green zone, he lets the process run. If not, he adjusts the process.
- If the first shaft is in the red zone, he adjusts the process.

The left (right) red zone boundary is at a z-score of -3.41 (3.41). The left (right) yellow-green boundary is at a z-score of -1.70 (1.70).

a. Given the above information, determine the process standard deviation using the z-score expression, 5.12.

b. Determine in inches the boundary of the right and left yellow-green zones.

22. To use the standard normal tables, we must know (or be able to estimate accurately) the mean and standard deviation. For time-ordered data (Chapter 2), recall that mean and standard deviation are only meaningful if the data are stationary. Which of the following time-ordered data sets are stable.

Day	Process 1 Tensile Strength	Process 2 Billing Accuracy	Process 3 Service Time
1	4,750 ppsi	92%	10 min.
2	4,775	90	9
3	4,790	91	11
4	4,810	93	8
5	4,840	90	12
6	4,830	88	7
7	4,905	91	12
8	4,900	92	6
9	4,925	89	14
10	4,925	92	4

For which process can we compute a meaningful mean and standard deviation? Explain.

23. Rogers, a leading authority in the product diffusion process, notes that consumers can be subdivided into five class. Innovators are the first to purchase new goods or services. Early adopters are next to buy new goods, followed by the early majority, late majority, and lastly, the laggards. The following normal product diffusion curve is taken from his writings.

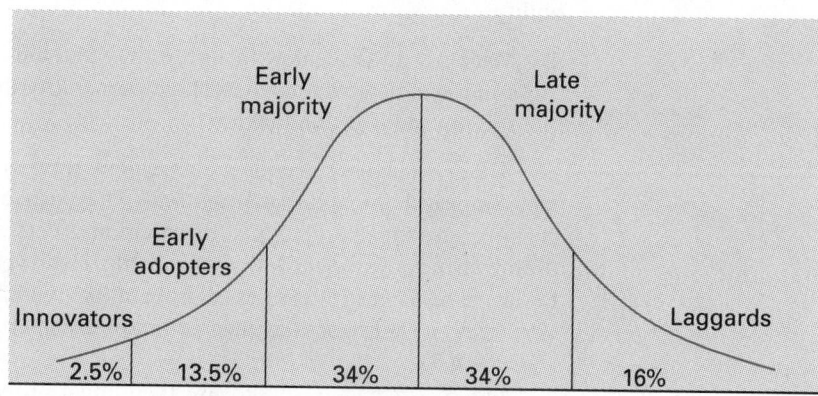

Time to adopt a new product

If the average time to adopt a new product was 15 weeks and the standard deviation was 3 weeks, compute the time in weeks that separates the

a. innovator and early adopter consumers.

b. early adopter and early majority consumers.

c. early majority and late majority consumers.

d. late majority and laggard consumers.

24. A stock portfolio's yearly rate of return (capital appreciation plus dividends) is normally distributed with a mean of 11.5% and a standard deviation of 1.5%. Complete the following sentences by filling in the blank.

    a. The probability that the rate of return is less than _____ % is .8413.
    b. The probability that the rate of return is more than _____ % is .46.
    c. The probability that the rate of return is less than _____ % is .1587.
    d. The probability that the rate of return is more than _____ % is .9772.
    e. The probability that the rate of return equals _____ % is .1587.
    f. The probability that the rate of return is between 11.5% and _____ % is .45.

25. A stock portfolio's yearly rate of return (capital appreciation plus dividends) is normally distributed with a mean of $X\%$ and a standard deviation of 1.5%.

    a. Determine the mean ($X\%$) if the probability of the rate of return exceeding 11.5% is .1587.

    b. Determine the mean ($X\%$) if the probability of the rate of return being less than 10% is .0668.

    c. Determine the mean ($X\%$) if the probability of the rate of return exceeding 12% is .0228.

    d. Determine the mean ($X\%$) if the probability of the rate of return being less than 15.2% is .1154.

    e. Determine the mean ($X\%$) if the probability of the rate of return exceeding 12% is .9772.

    f. Determine the mean ($X\%$) if the probability of the rate of return being less than 21% is .9987.

5.7 ≡ Integrating Framework and Key Ideas

Managers build mental models of their firm's operations by collecting, organizing, and summarizing descriptive data, and by using probability distributions. Mental models help managers sense unusual occurrences, detect emerging problems, find relationships between variables, evaluate alternatives, and make decisions. Table 5.11 summarizes some tools for improving problem solving.

    We conclude with two key ideas which emerge from the two chapters on probability:

1. Managers must deal with uncertainty through probabilities. They should use empirical, personal, or theoretical probability distributions to improve problem solving and decision making.

    Often managers can collect data, calculate relative frequencies, and thereby estimate empirical probability distributions. They also rely on intuition and judgment and construct personal probability distributions. Personal probabilities are especially useful when no historical data are available. However, personal probabilities can lead to flawed decisions if the rules of probability are violated. We have shown how decision trees can help guard against common managerial information processing errors (Section 4.7).

    Finally, managers should use theoretical probability distributions to generate probabilities. We have presented three types of distributions—the binomial, the Poisson, and the normal.

2. Underlying the theoretical probability distributions are sets of assumptions. These assumptions must be reasonable if the calculated probabilities are to be meaningful. When properly used, theoretical probability distributions improve decision making.

    In considering either the binomial or Poisson distribution, check for a near-Bernoulli or Poisson process. When considering the normal distribution, check that the data frequency histogram is almost bell-shaped.

Table 5.11

Using Chapters 2–5 to Improve Problem Solving

A.   Sensing unusual occurrences—outliers

Cross-Sectional Data   Use descriptive statistics, stem-and-leaf displays, and box plots. Outliers are data points that are more than 3 standard deviations from the mean or are outside the fences of a box plot.

Time-Ordered Data   Use moving average and residual line graphs. Outliers are extremely large positive or negative residuals.

Probability   Use personal, empirical, or theoretical probability distributions. Outliers are events with low probabilities that actually happen.

B.   Looking for relationships between variables

Cross-Sectional Data   Use cross-tabs tables or scatter diagrams. Compute row or column percentages. Variables are related when all the row (or column) percentages are not the same.

Time-Ordered Data   Use scatter diagrams, multiple line graphs, and cross-correlations. Two time series are related if $r(k) \sqrt{n - k} > 2$.

Probability   Compute conditional probabilities. Events are related if the conditional and unconditional probabilities are not the same.

C.   Evaluating alternatives and making decisions

Cross-Sectional Data   Use one-way tables or multiple box plots to summarize impacts of alternatives. Select the alternative that has the highest mean or median or the lowest standard deviation or interquartile range.

Time-Ordered Data   Use moving averages to assess impacts. Select the alternative that has the fastest increasing or decreasing moving average.

Probability   Use probabilities to predict impacts. Select the alternative that has the highest probability of accomplishing the goals.

If managers are subject to using theoretical probability distributions improperly, why not rely on empirical or personal distributions? Empirical distributions are based on sample data and are only estimates of probabilities. In contrast, if a theoretical distribution accurately describes a population, then a manager can proceed to act with confidence that he knows the composition of the entire population and can predict the relative frequency of all possible outcomes. For example, the normal distribution will provide more meaningful probabilities than an empirical distribution.

Furthermore, collecting empirical probabilities on many events can be time-consuming. To use the normal probability distribution, all we need to know or estimate are the mean and standard deviation. We need to know only the probability of a success and the sample size to compute binomial probabilities, and the mean to compute Poisson probabilities.

COMCEL

Date: February 17, 1994
From: Sang Kim, Quality Assurance
To: Howard Bright, Plant Manager
Re: Quality of circuit breakers

The Department of Quality Assurance does continuous monitoring of our circuit breakers. The defect rate has been approximately 5% for some time. Unfortunately, three or more defective items in a box of 25 must be expected at times. The fact that our customer found three defective circuit breakers does not suggest that the defect rate has increased.

We claim an *average* defect rate of 5% per sample of 25 circuit breakers. This means that, in the long run, our customers can expect an average of 1.25 defective circuit breakers in boxes con-taining 25 units. The average is 1.25 because most boxes will have no defective units or one defective unit. But some boxes will have two or more defective units due to chance.

If the underlying causes of the defects remain stable, and the defect rate remains constant at 5%, then approximately 13% of all boxes of 25 items will contain three or more defective units. On the other hand, only 3.4% of the boxes will contain four or more defective items in the long run. Since the cost of examining the whole manufacturing process is substantial, this department would examine the system only when the sampling process shows four or more defective items in a box of 25. We would reason that it is possible, but not very likely, to find four defective items in a box of 25 when the defect rate is 5%. In that case, something could be wrong, and we would examine the system. However, even if a box has four defective units, it isn't certain that the defect rate has increased.

We continue to look for ways—better materials, improved manufacturing methods—to reduce the average defective rate from 5%. Even if the rate could be reduced to 2% and the average number of defectives per box of 25 reduced to .5, some boxes (1.3%) would still contain three or more defective units over the long run.

CHAPTER 5 QUESTIONS

1. Can you change a continuous random variable into a discrete random variable? If so, provide an example.

2. Let X = the number of engines found in a standard passenger car. Is X a random variable? Why?

3. How are probability and relative frequency histograms similar and how are they different?

4. Correct, if necessary, the following statement:

   If two stock portfolios have the same *expected return,* but portfolio A has a larger standard deviation, then A is a *less-risky* stock portfolio.

5. Explain what a Bernoulli process is.

6. When the standard deviation for a binomial distribution is very close to zero, what would the binomial distribution look like? Why?

7. Suppose that the binomial probability of an event happening is very low—.005. Yet the event does happen. From a problem-sensing perspective, what can you conclude?

8. Referring to Question 7, what are two other possible explanations for an event that happens even though it had a low probability of happening?

9. Under what real-world conditions would you consider applying the Poisson distribution for problem solving?

10. The insurance industry knows that .005% of the population will die of a particular disease this year. Let X = number of people who die from the disease per 100,000 population. Is X a Poisson random variable? Why?

11. What happens to the shape of a Poisson histogram as the mean gets larger?

12. Compare the binomial and Poisson distributions. How are they alike and how are they different?

13. Explain what a z-score is.

14. Suggest a random variable from the business world not presented in the text that should be normally distributed. Explain your reason(s).

15. What is the probability that a normal random variable takes on a single specific value equal to 0?

16. If a process capability study indicates that the 3σ limits are inside the lower and upper specification limits, what can you conclude about the process? Explain.

17. Suppose the normal curve indicates that the chance of a project being completed in less than 40 days is .001. Yet your team actually completes its next project in less than 40 days. What should you conclude? Explain.

CHAPTER 5 APPLICATION PROBLEMS

1. A real estate salesperson can sell a home in Midtown about 25% of the time, a home in Buckhead about 50% of the time, and a home in West End about 10% of the time. In five attempted sales in a given section of the city, the salesperson sells exactly one home. Assuming a Bernoulli process, what is the probability of selling exactly one home in five attempts if:
   a. The home is in Midtown (all attempts are in Midtown)?
   b. The home is in Buckhead (all attempts are in Buckhead)?
   c. The home is in West End (all attempts are in West End)?
   d. What does it mean to say that selling a home can be modeled as a Bernoulli process?

2. Which of two approaches should we use to implement the installation of a new computer system? Approach A requires that *systems developers* manage the installation. Approach B requires that *system users* manage the installation. Based on previous installations, with systems developers the mean installation time is 20 weeks and the standard deviation is 2 weeks. With system users, the mean time is 16 weeks and the standard deviation is 4 weeks. Installation times are nearly bell-shaped for both approaches.
   a. What approach should we use to maximize the chance of completing the installation within 22 weeks? Explain.

b. Explain how we could verify that the installation times for both approaches are nearly bell-shaped.

 3. Maky's department store has determined that demand for compact disk players is Poisson distributed with a mean of three per day.
a. Construct the probability distribution for the daily demand for compact disk players.
b. If the store stocks six players on a particular day, what is the probability that demand will be greater than supply?
c. Explain what must be true if demand is Poisson distributed.

 4. A franchise is planning to add as many as five additional outlets next year. The CEO has made the following six personal probability estimates.

Number of New Outlets	Personal Probability
0	.02
1	.13
2	.40
3	.30
4	.10
5	.05

a. Compute the expected number of new outlets.
b. Compute the standard deviation in the number of new outlets.
c. Suppose that the firm makes $150,000 net profit from each outlet. What is the expected net profit from the new outlets for next year?

 5. An operations manager is considering two machines to fill 1-pound bags of coffee. She has received the following fill data from two vendors. Apex machine fills are close to normally distributed with a mean of 16.5 oz. and a standard deviation of 1 oz. Zenith machine fills are close to normally distributed with a mean of 15.5 oz. and a standard deviation of .25 oz.
a. Which of the two machines has less variability in fills? Why?
b. Suppose that a "1-pound bag" must have *at least* 16 ounces. Which machine has a greater probability of meeting that goal?
c. Suppose that a "1-pound bag" must have *at least* 15 ounces. Which machine has a greater probability of meeting that goal?
d. Explain why the best machine changed as we changed the minimum number of ounces in the bag.

 6. A new laptop microcomputer breaks down on the average once a month. During the past month the laptop has broken down three times. Assume breakdowns can be represented by a Poisson process.
a. What is the probability of having three or more breakdowns in a month?
b. This month the laptop did break down three times. From a problem-sensing perspective, what might you conclude? Explain.

 7. There are five stages in the consumer adoption decision—awareness, interest, evaluation, trial, and adoption. The chance of adopting a product increases, the more stages the consumer goes through. Here are relative frequency probability estimates:

$$P(\text{adopting} \mid \text{awareness stage only}) = .10$$

$$P(\text{adopting} \mid \text{awareness through trial stage}) = .80$$

We select five consumers. We are interested in computing probabilities that different numbers of consumers will adopt a product.
a. Define the two random variables of interest and their possible values.
b. Assume a Bernoulli process. What is the probability that *at least* four consumers will adopt the product if all five went only through the awareness stage? if all five went through the awareness through the trial stages?

c. Given the two probabilities, what should you, the marketing manager, attempt to do? Explain.

8. Outel Corporation produces 80486 computer chips. Based on historical data, Outel knows that chip life (time to failure in hours) is near normally distributed with a mean of 2,000 hours and a standard deviation of 200 hours.

a. What percentage of the chips will have times to failure below 1,550 hours?

b. Now suppose that in the past month, more than 20% of the chips have failed in under 1,550 hours in Outel's final inspection. From a problem-solving perspective, what might that suggest? Explain.

c. How could Outel check whether time to failure is really normally distributed?

9. Cars arrive at a bank drive-in window at the rate of 10 per hour. Assume the arrivals are Poisson distributed.

a. Calculate the probability that one car arrives during a 6-minute period.

b. If more than three cars arrive during a 6-minute period, the customers will have to wait for service and may become annoyed. What is the probability that more than three cars arrive during a 6-minute period?

10. A stock analyst claims that he can accurately predict whether a company's return on investment (ROI) will increase from the previous year. He receives ten different company reports and is asked to determine which of the ten firms' ROIs will increase and which will decrease in the following year. Assume that none of the firms' ROIs stays the same. He predicts nine correctly.

a. If he were merely guessing, what is the probability that he would have made nine or more correct predictions?

b. Based on your answer, is the stock analyst an accurate predictor? Explain.

11. A vice-president of finance must decide which of two projects to implement. Shown are their net profits and personal probabilities.

Project A		Project B	
Net Profit	Probability	Net Profit	Probability
−$30k	.25	$0	.4
$0	.25	$10k	.3
$20k	.25	$30k	.2
$75k	.25	$50k	.1

a. Find the expected net profit and standard deviation for the two projects.

b. Which project is riskier? Why?

12. Based on historical data, accidents on a certain highway occur at a rate of five per month. About three months ago the Highway Patrol began a driver awareness program to reduce accidents. Over the past month there was one accident. Has there been any reduction in accidents? Assume that accidents are Poisson distributed.

a. Compare the probability of having one or fewer accidents in a month if the average rate were still five per month.

b. What can you conclude about the effectiveness of the Highway Patrol program? Explain.

13. Savings and loan associations (S&Ls) were created to provide home mortgages for borrowers and long-term savings for individual investors. In the 1970s S&Ls were allowed to engage in riskier loans. By 1986 S&Ls started to collapse at an alarming rate. In 1988 the government dealt with 205 insolvent S&Ls. Suppose that an economist for the Federal Home Loan Bank System, which regulates federally chartered S&Ls, estimates that the mean number of remaining insolvent S&Ls is 350 and the standard deviation is 25. Assume that the number of insolvent S&Ls is normally distributed.

a. What is the probability that more than 300 S&Ls will fail in the upcoming years?

b. If the cost of bailing out each insolvent S&L is $500 million, what is the probability that the federal government will have to spend more than $175 billion in the upcoming years?

14. An owner of a small motel with ten rooms is considering buying VCRs to rent to his customers. He estimates that half of his customers would be willing to rent a VCR. Therefore, he buys five sets. Define the random variable as the number of requests for a VCR in an evening. Assume 100% occupancy and only one request per room.
  a. What is the probability of meeting possible customer demand for VCRs?
  b. If the owner increases the number of VCRs to seven, what is the probability of meeting possible customer demand?
  c. If he increases the number of VCRs to nine, what is the probability of meeting possible customer demand?
  d. What other information would you need before you could decide whether to increase the number of VCRs from five to seven or nine?

15. A university economic forecasting unit indicates that next year's discount rate most likely will be 9%. The discount rate is the interest rate that the Federal Reserve banks charge their commercial bank customers to borrow money. Assume that the uncertainty about the discount rate can be represented by a normal distribution with a standard deviation of 1%. Assume that the forecast turns out to be accurate.
  a. Find the probability that the actual rate will be between 8% and 10%.
  b. Find the probability that the actual rate will be no higher than 10.5%.
  c. Suppose the forecasting unit changes its estimate of the standard deviation from 1% to some other figure. If the probability that the actual rate is less than 11% is .8413, what is the new estimate of the standard deviation?

16. A firm evaluates two different ways to manage a new product: (1) through a new product committee and (2) by a product manager. Shown are some comparative data on past attempts to use these approaches. Define the random variable of interest as sales performance.

Possible Outcomes		Committee	Product Manager
2% below target	−2	.05	.20
1% below target	−1	.10	.20
Meet target	0	.70	.20
1% above target	+1	.10	.20
2% above target	+2	.05	.20

  a. What are the mean sales performances for both strategies?
  b. What are the standard deviations of sales performance for both strategies?
  c. Which strategy is less risky? Why?

17. Telephone sales operators make on the average 1 call every 10 minutes. Assume that the number of calls made can be represented by a Poisson distribution. Recently, operators have become upset with their working conditions and you wonder if they are slowing down to retaliate. You observe one operator who has made no calls in the past 50 minutes. Assume that the average of 1 call every 10 minutes has not changed.
  a. What is the probability that no calls would have been made in the past 50 minutes?
  b. Given your answer in part **a,** what can you conclude?

18. Based on past records, National Telephone has bought at least 20 computers in 80% of its previous orders. However, in the past 5 orders, National has bought at least 20 computers only once. Does this mean that National is cutting back on the number of computers it purchases?
  a. What are the chances of 1 or fewer orders for at least 20 computers in the past 5 sales to National?
  b. Is National cutting back on the number of computers it purchases? Explain.

19. The number of hours before a battery must be replaced in Wellbuilt watches is normally distributed with a mean of 1,900 hours and a standard deviation of 145 hours.
  a. What proportion of watches will fail before 1,600 hours?
  b. Suppose that during the next 6 months, more than 50% fail before 1,600 hours. From a problem-sensing perspective, what might you conclude? Explain.

20. How would you determine the root causes of the increased failures of Wellbuilt watches in Problem 19? What questions might you ask to help understand and solve the problem? Suggest several changes that might explain the onset of the problem.

 21. According to the New York Stock Exchange, in 1985, the mean number of daily shares traded was about 110 million and the standard deviation was about 20 million. Assume that daily volume is near normally distributed. In 1988 we noted that the daily volumes were running at about 162 million shares.

a. What is the probability that the daily volume will exceed 162 million shares if the mean and standard deviation are still 110 million and 20 million shares, respectively?

b. How can you explain the 162 million shares a day in 1988?

 22. Based on the 1987 *Bureau of the Census Current Population Reports,* an economist believes that the percentage of all races below the poverty level will most likely be 13% in 1992. She also believes that the probability that the percentage below the poverty level will exceed 14% is .20. Assume that the economist's subjective beliefs can be represented by a normal curve. Given this information, what is the economist's estimate of the standard deviation for the 1992 percentage below the poverty level?

 23. The inventory manager at a retail farmer's market has just checked 100 50-pound bags from PacNorWest Potato Company.

Number of Rotten Potatoes in Bag	Number of Bags
0	45
1	37
2	13
3	4
4	1
	100

The manager believes that the number of rotten potatoes per bag is Poisson distributed with a mean of .8. Assume that the manager is correct.

a. Calculate the probability of finding 0, 1, 2, 3, or 4 rotten potatoes per bag.

b. How many bags would you expect to have 0, 1, 2, 3, or 4 rotten potatoes if the manager's assumption of a Poisson distribution is true? Compare the expected number to the actual number of rotten potatoes per bag. What can you conclude?

c. Assume that the manager can live with a mean of .8 rotten potato per bag. How can the manager use the knowledge that the number of rotten potatoes is Poisson distributed to set a policy for inspecting and accepting 50-pound bags from PacNorWest? Assume that each bag will be inspected before the manager accepts it.

 24. Consider the following three binomial probability distributions:

$$\text{Distribution 1:} \quad n = 5, \quad p = .5$$
$$\text{Distribution 2:} \quad n = 10, \quad p = .5$$
$$\text{Distribution 3:} \quad n = 20, \quad p = .5$$

Using Appendix 1, graph the three probability distributions. What can you conclude about the relationship between the binomial and normal distributions?

 25. A CEO is considering several major strategic alternatives with respect to the product line. The firm can:

1. Choose to stay with its present products in its present markets.
2. Expand its line into either related or unrelated products.
3. Choose to expand its present line into new markets (international).

The CEO has developed the following personal probabilities for each strategy and its impact on net profit after taxes over the next several years.

	Strategy 1	Strategy 2	Strategy 3
Increase net profit by $10 million	.20	.40	.50
No change in net profit	.60	.20	.40
Decrease net profit by $10 million	.20	.40	.10

a. Which strategy gives the highest mean increase in net profit for the firm?

b. One measure of a strategy's risk is the coefficient of variation, which is the standard deviation divided by the mean. The lower the coefficient of variation, the lower the risk. Compute the coefficient of variation for the three strategies. Which strategy is least risky?

6.1 Data and managerial performance
6.2 Sampling principles and statistical inferences
   Sample size
   Level of confidence
   Variation of the target population
6.3 Basic sampling terminology
6.4 Planning and conducting a survey: An
   overview
   Margin of error
6.5 Simple random sampling design
   Selecting a simple random sample
   A note of caution
6.6 Stratified random sampling design
   When to consider stratified random sampling
   Selecting a stratified random sample
   A note of caution
   Other designs: Systematic and cluster
   designs
6.7 Selecting a survey method
   Obtaining a representative sample

   Questionnaire length and flexibility
   Obtaining accurate answers
   Administrative issues
6.8 General principles for writing questions
   Determining information needs: Diagnosing
   the problem
   Choosing the question format
   Avoiding wording errors
   A final thought
6.9 Basic principles of experimental design
   Basic terminology
   Experiments vs. nonexperiments
   The importance of randomization
6.10 Avoiding problems in experimental design
   The history effect
   Diffusion of treatment
   Compensatory rivalry
   Trivial changes
   Random error
6.11 Key ideas of data collection

Date: October 1, 1994
To: Ann Tabor, President
From: Howard Bright, Norcross Plant Manager
Re: Proposed Employee Morale Survey

BACKGROUND

I have been monitoring the employee morale survey results to detect any sudden changes or downward trends. Because we give this test weekly to a random sample of employees, we can identify morale problems that inevitably affect productivity. I am happy to report that averages have remained stable for the past year.

I was discussing our morale scores with a friend of mine who works for a competitor that gives the same test. His firm's average scores are one point higher, which he attributes to the high level of employee participation in decision making.

AUTHORIZATION REQUEST

We should survey our employees to learn how many think there is not enough employee input into production decisions. We will develop a questionnaire and interview a random sample of our production employees in the Norcross plant. If low participation is the problem, we can hire a quality circle expert to help increase employee participation. Since employees would be interviewed on company time, I need your approval to proceed. Should we proceed if the project cost is under $50,000?

6.1 ≡ Data and Managerial Performance

Managers use data to understand their organization and its environment. Successful managers develop simple mental models of their departments. They ask themselves: "How is my department doing? How has it done in the past? At what levels could we perform?" Using these models, they sense when problem-solving action is needed and when it is not.

As disturbance handlers, managers use data to determine what factors cause a significant deviation from historic or budgeted performance levels. For example, for the past two years the company's reject rate varied between 1% and 2%. This past quarter it jumped to 6%. Data help determine the root causes of such deviations.

As entrepreneurs, managers seek to improve departmental performance. They use data in evaluating planned improvements. For example, managers want to know: "Which of three material handling systems best reduces our level of inventory?" Without data, managers cannot evaluate the systems' costs and benefits, and will be unable to decide which to install.

How do managers obtain data? They have three sources. They already have it within their organization, create it themselves, or buy it from firms that specialize in selling data. Their firm's management information system (MIS) provides the first type of data in the form of routine structured reports. These reports contain financial, accounting, marketing, and operations data and describe the state of the firm. Managers should use these data to sense disturbance problems—gaps between actual and historical or budgeted performance.

Managers can create data by conducting *surveys* and *planned change studies.* A survey is a representative sampling of facts or opinions that is used to approximate what a complete collection and analysis might reveal. Typical business examples include attitude surveys and marketing research studies. Managers also seek ways to improve departmental performance by running small-scale planned-change experiments or pilot projects and studying the results. If the planned change is an improvement, managers implement it permanently.

Finally, managers can either buy data from outside sources or use data published by public agencies. Often their own management information systems do not contain external data on industrywide sales or local or national economic data. Thus firms purchase data from bureaus that sell specialized data bases. For example, Information Resources Inc. tracks every TV commercial played in the homes of its panelists and every purchase they make at the supermarket. Marketing managers find this information crucial in managing their products.

In this chapter we discuss survey sampling designs and methods, questionnaire design, and experimentation to obtain valid data. Statistics is a collection of powerful tools for data analysis, but these tools are not magic. If we collect invalid data, no analysis can make the results meaningful.

6.2 ≡ Sampling Principles and Statistical Inferences

Several days before the 1992 presidential election, most polling organizations were 95% confident that Govenor Clinton would receive 44% ± 3% of the vote. He actually received about 44%. How can polling organizations be so accurate and confident when they interview fewer than 1,500 voters out of the target population of 90,000,000 voters? Sampling principles allow us to make *precise* and *highly confident* inferences from a sample to a target population. By the end of this section you should be able to:

1. explain what margin of error is;
2. explain how sample size affects the margin of error;
3. explain why increasing the level of confidence will increase the margin of error; and
4. explain why greater variation in the target population produces greater margins of error.

The margin of error is the possible difference we allow between the sample result and the result we would obtain if we sampled the entire population.

Precise inferences have small **margins of error.** In the 1992 polling example, the margin of error was plus or minus 3%. That meant that the population percentage of voters supporting Clinton could vary by as much as ±3% from the sample result of 44%—from 41% to 47% of the votes. Pollsters were 95% confident in their prediction.

Meaningful inferences require small margins of error. What would be the value of knowing that a candidate will receive 59% ±30% of the votes? The margin of error would be too wide to draw useful conclusions.

The level of confidence in an inference is also important. Higher levels of confidence are more meaningful. For example, it is not very informative to be only 20% confident that a candidate will receive 59% ± 3% of the votes. No one will listen to an organization that is not very confident in its inferences. Many organizations prefer to operate at a 95% level of confidence. They can accept a 5% chance that their inferences are wrong, but there is nothing sacred about a 95% level of confidence.

In summary, our goal is to show how to obtain highly confident inferences with small margins of error. Sample size, level of confidence, and variability of the target population affect the margin of error.

Sample Size

We will consider first the influence of sample size on the margin of error. We can reduce the margin of error by increasing the sample size. We illustrate this idea by considering a population with only five students. Suppose the problem is to estimate the mean age of the five students using the mean age of a single sample of three. How different could any sample mean be from the population mean?

Student	Age
A	18
B	19
C	20
D	21
E	22

The students' ages range from 18 to 22, with a mean age of 20. This is the population mean. Suppose we write each student's age on a piece of paper, mix the papers well, and select three pieces of paper. We do not replace a slip of paper once it is drawn. This is *sampling without replacement.* Table 6.1 shows the ten possible sample means we could get if we selected a single random sample of three names. The mean age of the three youngest students is 19.0 years; the mean age of the three oldest students is 21.0 years. Since the population mean age of all five students is 20 years, the maximum margin of error is 1 year—the maximum difference between a sample result and the result that we would get if we sampled everyone in the population.

We could reduce the maximum margin of error by taking a sample of size four. There are five possible samples of size four—ABCD, ABCE, ABDE, ACDE, BCDE.

The mean age of the four youngest students is 19.5 years, sample ABCD, and the mean age of the four oldest students is 20.5 years, sample BCDE. Thus, the maximum margin of error drops from 1 year to .5 year. Please verify our calculations before reading on.

LESSON 1:   Increasing the sample size reduces the margin of error.

However, the disadvantage of larger sample sizes is that they increase the cost of the survey or planned change study.

Table 6.1

All Possible Samples of Size Three and Sample Means Drawn from a Population of Five

Possible Sample	Sample Values			Mean
A, B, C	18	19	20	19.0
A, B, D	18	19	21	19.3
A, B, E	18	19	22	19.7
A, C, D	18	20	21	19.7
A, C, E	18	20	22	20.0
A, D, E	18	21	22	20.3
B, C, D	19	20	21	20.0
B, C, E	19	20	22	20.3
B, D, E	19	21	22	20.7
C, D, E	20	21	22	21.0

Level of Confidence

Suppose we draw a sample from Table 6.1, compute the mean, and insert it in the statement below.

> The mean age of the class is within the interval _____ years plus or minus a margin of error of .5 year.

The statement is true when the interval includes the population mean of 20. For example, if we obtain a sample mean of 19.7 (from sample ABE or ACD), then the statement is true since the interval includes 20 (it extends from $19.7 - .5 = 19.2$ years to $19.7 + .5 = 20.2$ years).

What is the probability that the statement will be true? That is, from Table 6.1, what percentage of the sample means plus or minus .5 year contains the population mean of 20 years? Since 6 of the 10 intervals include 20 years, we are 60% confident that any interval would contain the population mean of 20 years.

Suppose we want to have 80% confidence that any interval would contain the population mean of 20 years. The interval will have to be wider than plus or minus .5 year. But how wide? An interval width of plus or minus .7 year will ensure that 8 of 10 intervals would contain the population mean of 20 years. Please verify this.

LESSON 2:   If we increase the level of confidence in an inference, the price we pay is an increase in the margin of error.

We face a dilemma. We want a high level of confidence and a small margin of error. There is a solution: We could increase our sample size as we increase the desired level of confidence. However, that solution, as we have stated before, is costly.

Variation of the Target Population

The third factor that affects the margin of error is variation in the target population. Larger population variation produces greater margins of error. Consider another class of five students. Table 6.2 displays the age data for both classes.

Table 6.2

Two Populations with Different Variations

Class 1		Class 2	
Student	Age	Student	Age
A	18	F	18
B	19	G	21
C	20	H	24
D	21	I	27
E	22	J	30

The ages in the second class range from 18 to 30, and the mean age is 24. There is greater variation in ages in the second class. How does this affect the maximum margin of error?

As an exercise, construct a table like Table 6.1 for the second population. Write down all the possible samples of size three without replacement—samples FGH, FGI, FGJ, . . . , HIJ—and compute the sample means. The smallest sample mean is 21 years (FGH). The largest sample mean is 27 years (HIJ). The maximum margin of error is 3 years, 27 − 24 or 24 − 21. This compares with 1 year for the first population, which has less variation in the five students' ages.

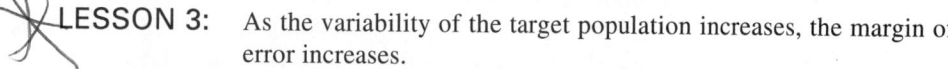

LESSON 3:   As the variability of the target population increases, the margin of error increases.

In summary, managers need to have small margins of error. Realistically, they cannot reduce the variability of the target population. Reducing the level of confidence is not effective because it raises doubts about our assertions. The most effective way to reduce margin of error is to increase the sample size.

SECTION 6.2 EXERCISES

1. A telephone survey showed that 40% of a sample prefers brand X. The margin of error was ± 5%. Explain what that means.

2. A political consultant proudly tells his client that a poll he conducted shows she will win the election with 53% of the vote. "What was the margin of error?" she asked. He said ± 8%. She fired the consultant. Why?

3. An economist reports: "I am 95% confident that the sales revenue for the coming year will be $150 million ± $10 million." If the forecaster wanted a higher level of confidence, would the margin of error increase or decrease?

4. A population consists of the numbers {2, 4, 6}.
    a. Find the mean of these numbers.
    b. List all possible samples of size two without replacement.
    c. Find the sample mean for each of these samples.
    d. Find the mean of the sample means.
    e. If you selected one of the sample means as an estimate of the population mean, how far off could you be?

       f. State the relationship between the mean of the population and the mean of the sample means.

5. Consider the following population of numbers: $\{2, 4, 6, 8, 10\}$.
   a. List all possible samples of two, without replacement, and the mean of each sample.
   b. If your goal was to estimate the population mean and you selected one sample of size two, by how much could your sample mean differ from the population mean?
   c. List all possible samples of size four, without replacement, and the mean of each sample.
   d. If your goal was to estimate the population mean and you selected one sample of size four, by how much could your sample mean vary from the population mean?
   e. What happened to the maximum margin of error when you doubled the sample size?

6.3 ≣ Basic Sampling Terminology

The field of sampling has its own set of terminology. Once you have mastered it, you can communicate intelligently with survey designers. By the end of this section, you should be able to:

1. explain sampling terminology; and
2. illustrate these terms with your own examples.

    Consider three situations where sampling plays an important problem-solving role. Each situation requires a different data source.

Sampling From the MIS   An auditor wishes to determine if the monthly business expense reports in the management information system are accurate. The auditor will select a sample from last month's 1,500 business expense reports and compare the computer data to the actual expense reports. If the computer values are inaccurate, the auditor will conduct a more complete investigation.

Obtaining Data Through Surveys   The Director of Automotive Safety at Alliance Motors is considering installing air bags in all the cars. There are no data on drivers' attitudes toward air bags. He will conduct a market research survey on a sample of drivers.

Obtaining Data Through Planned Change Studies   Compared to published industry figures, work teams at COMCEL's Norcross plant have not been as successful in reducing unit labor costs as have other firms. The manufacturing manager will test two possible methods of reducing labor costs:

1. Teaching work group members each other's jobs—job-switching
2. Teaching work group members creative methods

She will select a sample of work groups for the study. If either workshop significantly reduces unit labor costs, she will require that all work groups attend the more effective workshop.

    We will use these three examples to illustrate the following sampling terminology: element, target population, sampling unit, frame, and sampling design.

An element is an object for which we take a measurement. When the objects are people, we call them subjects.

    In the MIS study, an **element** is a single monthly business expense report. The measurement of interest is its dollar value. In the air bag study, an element is a registered driver. The measurement of interest is the driver's attitude toward air bags in cars. In the planned change study, an element is a work group. The measurement of interest is the reduction in unit labor costs.

A target population is a collection of elements about which we wish to make an inference.

    In the MIS study, the **target population** consists of the monthly business expense reports for all 1,500 salespeople. In the air bag study, the target population is the group of all registered drivers in the country. (Note that we have ignored adults who do not drive a car, although they may be passengers.) In the planned change study, the target population is all the work groups in the Norcross plant.

Sampling units are non-overlapping collections of elements from the target population. A sampling unit can be an individual element.

In the MIS study, **sampling units** would be individual monthly business expense reports filed by the 1,500-member sales force. Each expense statement is unique; they do not overlap. Each statement covers one salesperson's monthly expenses.

Joe Smith, Sr., Mary Smith, and Joe Smith, Jr. are sampling units in the air bag study. They are different people. However, we could group the three Smiths into the Smith household. This would make sense if we plan to interview households. Often, grouping by household is more practical because it could be too costly to sample individual elements. Other possible groupings are all residents of a city block or of a political district.

When households are sampling units, we must define them so that no individual element can be sampled more than once. If Joe Smith, Jr. lives in a college dorm in town, is he a member of the dorm household or the Smith household? We must define household so that Joe Smith, Jr. cannot be selected more than once in the study. Double sampling would bias the findings.

The work groups within the Norcross plant are the sampling units in the planned change study. Work group membership must be unique. That is, the same worker cannot be in more than one group.

A frame is a list of sampling units.

In the MIS study, the sampling **frame** is the list of 1,500 salespeople. If we specify the individual driver as a sampling unit, lists of registered drivers from the 50 states and the District of Columbia serve as a sampling frame. In the planned change study, the sampling frame is the list of work groups in the Norcross plant.

Sometimes we use *multiple* sampling frames. In sampling voters we could start with city blocks as sampling units and then sample voters within those blocks. Our first sampling frame is a list of city blocks, and the second frame is a list of voters within each block.

The sampling design specifies the method of selecting the sample.

Later we will discuss the four most common **survey sampling designs**—simple random sampling, stratified random sampling, systematic sampling, and cluster sampling.

SECTION 6.3 EXERCISES

1. What is the difference between a target population and a sampling frame?

2. We want to estimate the proportion of registered voters who favor a proposed amendment to the state constitution. The frame for the study is the 36 books of registered voters from the 36 counties in the state. What is the sampling unit? Is the sampling unit the same as an element of the population?

3. The target population is all females in a city over the age of 40 years. The frame is a list of street addresses used by the Census Bureau. What is the sampling unit?

4. A company wishes to survey its employees concerning the choice of medical plans. A list of all employees is generated. What is the sampling unit? What is the element?

5. You work for a large bank that has 100 branch offices. You want to survey the opinions of employees about staying open longer on Saturdays. What would you use for a frame? What would be the sampling unit and element for the survey?

6.4 ≡ Planning and Conducting a Survey: An Overview

Conducting surveys involves more than selecting a survey sampling design. It requires planning. By the end of this section, you should be able to:

1. describe the nine-step procedure for planning a survey;
2. differentiate between selection, response, and nonresponse errors; and
3. differentiate between these errors and margin of error.

Scheaffer, Mendenhall, and Ott (1986) suggest the following nine-step procedure in planning a survey.

1. State the Objectives   In order to state the objectives, we often need to ask questions, such as: What is the survey's exact purpose? What specifically don't we know? What inferences do we need to draw? Begin by developing a specific list of information needs. Then write focused survey questions.

2. Identify the Target Population   Whom are we interested in drawing conclusions about? all adults? only adults aged 18–49?

3. Select a Sampling Frame   After identifying the target population, obtain a sampling frame. Three problems can occur at this stage.

First, it may not be possible to find a perfect sampling frame. For example, in the air bag study lists of drivers from the 50 states and the District of Columbia could serve as a sampling frame. However, driver registration lists may not be complete because the states do not update them daily. Also, some people on the lists have died. Even good sampling frames may have omissions. With this knowledge it may be possible to improve the sampling frame.

A second problem is called selection error. For example, we are interested in determining filmgoers' attitudes toward horror films. Suppose that our sampling frame is households that have purchased a VCR. We have just made a **selection error.** Many filmgoers do not own VCRs and thus our sampling frame is not a complete listing of the target population.

Increasing the sample size will not solve the problem. The problem is not the sample size, but who is included in the sampling frame.

A third problem is called the **nonresponse error.** This occurs when a large percentage of the sampling frame does not respond to the survey. Suppose that in the air bag study we ask respondents to call a 900 number to be interviewed. Because a 900 call costs $2 per minute, many drivers may not respond. Thus the final sample of respondents may not even represent the sampling frame.

Lower-income and upper-income families often do not answer mailed surveys. Thus middle-income families are usually overrepresented in the final responses. Nonresponse error occurs even in face-to-face interviews. Those people who are not at home when the interviewer stops by may be systematically different from those who are at home. An example might be families with two wage earners vs. families with one wage earner. Families with two wage earners dine out more often and thus may be underrepresented in the final responses.

Selection and nonresponse errors are different. Selection error occurs when the sampling frame does not reflect the target population. Nonresponse error occurs when the respondents do not reflect the sampling frame.

In contrast to the selection error, increasing the sample size by resampling those who did not initially respond will reduce the nonresponse error. Furthermore, we should determine whether respondents and nonrespondents differ systematically in terms of age, race, or socioeconomic status. To do this, we compare the composition of respondents to census figures for the sampling frame. If they differ, we cannot draw inferences from the data.

Selection error occurs when the sampling frame is not a complete listing of the target population because some members of the target population are excluded from the sample.

Nonresponse error occurs when the respondents do not reflect the sampling frame.

4. Select a Sample Design   Decide how to select the respondents from the sampling frame and determine the sample size. In Sections 6.5 and 6.6 we will discuss four plans: simple random sampling, stratified random sampling, systematic sampling, and cluster sampling.

5. Select a Survey Method   Decide how to collect the data. In Section 6.7 we will discuss personal interviews, telephone interviews, and mailed questionnaires.

6. Develop the Questionnaire   Write the questionnaire. Decide on the wording, the type of questions, and other issues discussed later in this chapter.

Response error occurs when respondents do not understand the question, are influenced by word variations, do not have enough information and guess, or do not want to give out information.

    Response errors often occur in public opinion surveys. Roll and Cantril (1972) illustrate this error. They asked some citizens if they favored "adding to" the Constitution a one-term limit for the president. Others were asked if they favored "changing" the Constitution to include a one-term limit. Fifty percent were in favor when Roll and Cantril used the first wording, and 65% were in favor when they used the second wording.

    The order in which the candidates' names appear in a survey questionnaire can also affect a person's response. The name that is placed first can often pick up five percentage points more than if it were placed at the end of the list.

    Race is another factor that can make a difference. A white interviewer of a black respondent may obtain a different response than a black interviewer would of a black respondent. This is especially true when the questions deal with black-white relations. Increasing the sample size will not eliminate response error. The problem lies not in the sample size, but with other factors such as questionnaire wording or the method of administering the questionnaire. Using valid survey sampling designs will not help either, for the problem is not how we selected the sample but how we worded or presented the questions.

7. Pretest the Questionnaire   Select a very small sample from the sampling frame. Conduct the survey and see what goes wrong. Correct any problems before carrying out the full-scale study.

8. Conduct the Survey   Monitor the interviewers to ensure consistent interviewing skills.

9. Analyze the Data   Even before conducting the survey, determine how the data will be analyzed once collected. We will learn in future chapters how to use statistical analysis to draw valid inferences from the sample data to the target population.

Margin of Error

Selection, response, and nonresponse errors are mistakes made in conducting a survey. They are correctable. The margin of error is not a mistake. It is the possible difference we allow between the sample result and the result that would be obtained if we sampled the entire population. Table 6.1 included sample means that varied between 19 and 21. Most sample means were very close to the population mean of 20 years in this simple example. However, in a real-world study, a mean based on a small sample might vary considerably from the population mean. When drawing inferences about a large population, we must live with a margin of error. At this point, the most effective way to reduce the margin of error is to increase the sample size.

    Choosing the appropriate sampling design can also reduce the margin of error. In the next two sections we cover simple random sampling, stratified random sampling, systematic sampling, and cluster sampling. Each sampling design differs in the method of selecting the sample, the ease of selecting the sample, and the accuracy of the inferences about the target population.

SECTION 6.4 EXERCISES

1. List the nine steps involved in planning a survey.

2. The first step in planning a survey is to get a group together and start hammering out a questionnaire. Do you agree?

3. When asked what his sampling method would be in an upcoming survey, the manager said, "We will use stratified sampling." Did the manager answer the question? Explain.

4. Suppose you want to test market a new safety razor by having prospective customers actually use the razor. What is the target population? What could you use as a frame?

5. What do we mean by response error? How is this type of error different from a nonresponse error?

6. For the following statements, state whether each involves a selection error (S), a response error (R), a nonresponse error (N), or some combination of these errors (C).
   a. Respondent misunderstands the question.
   b. Respondent wants to look good to the interviewer and lies about his income.
   c. Fearing for their safety, interviewers substitute high-income areas for low-income areas.
   d. Interviews are conducted at a supermarket only during the day on Saturday.
   e. Respondents hang up the phone when they realize it is another bothersome surveyor.
   f. The secretaries of company executives always complete mail questionnaires for their bosses.
   g. The telephone directory is used as a frame in a survey of all families in a county.
   h. The interviewer smiles whenever she gets a response she agrees with.
   i. The sampling frame bears only a slight resemblance to the target population.

7. A group of college students conducts interviews in an older part of a city where apartment buildings have no elevators. When instructed to go to the sixth floor of an apartment building, some students substitute apartments on the first floor rather than walk the stairs. The students argue that because the intended and substitute respondents live in the same building, this practice will not introduce error into the survey results. Do you agree? Discuss.

8. Television talk shows feature an author who claims that over half of all married women are dissatisfied with their marriages. This claim is based on the results of 3,500 responses obtained from 100,000 mailed questionnaires. What type of error might affect the conclusions from this survey?

9. A market research firm wants to survey the U.S. Hispanic population through a telephone survey. The firm uses the Miami telephone directory as its frame. List any errors of selection, response, or nonresponse that might be associated with the survey.

10. How is the margin of error different from selection, response, and nonresponse errors? Which error is easiest for managers to control?

6.5 Simple Random Sampling Design

Simple random sampling occurs when every possible sample of size n elements has the same chance of being selected from a target population of N elements. The sample is a simple random sample.

The goal in obtaining data through survey sampling is to use a sample to make precise inferences about the target population. Moreover, we want to be highly confident of our inferences. We begin with the basic *probability* sampling design—**simple random sampling**. Other designs build upon it. By the end of this section, you should be able to:

1. select a simple random sample using a table of random numbers;
2. explain why simple random sampling can sometimes produce poor estimates of the target population; and
3. explain the problems with using nonprobability samples.

Consider the following scenario. An auditor wishes to determine whether the monthly business expense reports for the 1,500-member sales force are accurate. If they are inaccurate, she will conduct a more complete investigation.

There are 1,500 monthly business expense reports in the target population. Examining every account would take too long and be too costly. The sampling frame is the list of 1,500 sales representatives. The auditor selects a **simple random sample** of size 10 from the sampling frame. Based on the 10 accounts, she can then estimate the total business expenses for the 1,500-member sales force.

Selecting a Simple Random Sample

To select a random sample, we need to know how to use a random numbers table. Think of the 1,500 business expense reports as being numbered 0001, 0002, 0003, ..., 1499, 1500. The number 0001 represents the first sales representative's report, the number 0002 represents the second report, and the number 1500 represents the 1,500th report. Now start at the upper left corner of the random numbers table (see Appendix 4) and select the first 30 five-digit numbers from the first column. See Table 6.3.

Table 6.3

Table of 30 Random Numbers

10480	22368	24130	42167	37570	77921
99562	96301	89579	85475	28918	63553
09429	10365	07119	51085	02368	01011
52162	07056	48663	54164	32639	29334
02448	81525	29676	00742	05366	91921

Since we are interested in numbers 0001 to 1500, eliminate the last digit in each group of five digits. If a random number occurs twice, ignore the second occurrence and select another random number. If the first four digits exceed 1500, go to the next number. Reading across the rows, we select accounts 1048, 942, 1036, 711, 236, 101, 705, 244, 74, and 536. These 10 reports are a simple random sample.

What is the idea behind the random numbers table? Imagine we wrote the five-digit numbers 00000 to 99999 on 100,000 slips of paper, one number to a slip. We place them in a large barrel and rotate the barrel. Next we select one slip at a time, record its value, replace the slip in the barrel, and then select another slip until we record 100,000 numbers. We have just constructed a table of random numbers similar to Appendix 4—the hard way. Using a prepared table of random numbers is easier.

A Note of Caution

Probability sampling, such as simple random sampling, is more effective than nonprobability sampling designs. For example, in *convenience sampling* we select the first *n* customers who enter a store. Although such a sampling scheme would be easy

Table 6.4

Years of Schooling Data Based on a Simple Random Sample of 10 Army People

	Enlisted Personnel	Officers
n	5	5
Grades Completed	10.0	16.0

to carry out, we cannot legitimately calculate the probable margin of error. There is no guarantee that the first *n* customers represent the target population of all customers. The statistical expressions in the remainder of the book apply only to probability sampling.

A simple random sampling design can also produce very poor estimates. Suppose we want to estimate the mean grade level completed by army personnel. We select a simple random sample of 10 people and obtain the results given in Table 6.4.

Our sample includes 5 enlisted personnel and 5 officers. The enlistees, on average, completed 10th grade. The officers, on average, completed college—16th grade. The mean grade level for the 10 army people is 13th grade. Common sense tells us that this mean is too high for the army overall. Why might that figure be a poor estimate for the mean grade completed by people in the army? Please think about it before reading on.

Look at the target population. It has many more enlisted personnel than officers. Yet the sample has the same number of officers and enlisted personnel. As the sample does not mirror the target population, our estimate is not accurate. Nonrepresentative samples can occur in simple random sampling because each sample has the same chance of selection. Even rare samples, such as those composed of all enlisted personnel or all officers can (but are not likely to) occur.

In summary, probability sampling is superior to nonprobability sampling. For some situations, simple random sampling is not the best type of probability sampling. We need additional survey sampling designs.

SECTION 6.5 EXERCISES

1. You want to draw a simple random sample of 10 people from a list of 520 people. You decide to use the last three digits of each group of five digits and read down each column. List the numbers of the 10 people selected.

10480✓	22368	24130	43167
37570	77921	99562	96301
89579	85475	28918	63553
09429✓	10365	07119	51085
02368	01011	52162	04056

2. What do you see as the major drawback of the simple random sampling design?

3. An appliance manufacturer has hired you to survey customers who have had a service call over the past two years. The frame is a list of names and addresses of service calls made. Some customers have had more than one call and are listed more than once. The list also includes calls made more than two years ago. What problems does this frame present to a sampler in selecting a simple random sample?

6.6 ≡ Stratified Random Sampling Design

The goal in obtaining data through survey sampling is to use a sample to make precise inferences about the target population. Properly done, *stratified random sampling* can produce more accurate inferences than simple random sampling. By the end of this section, you should be able to:

1. explain *when* to stratify a target population;
2. explain *how* to stratify a target population to obtain the most accurate inferences;
3. explain how to select a stratified random sample; and
4. explain when stratified random sampling can produce poor estimates of the target population.

When to Consider Stratified Random Sampling

We saw how a sample of 10 enlisted personnel and officers produced an inaccurate estimate of the mean years of schooling. The sample obviously did not reflect the true percentages of enlistees and officers in the army. How should we have selected the sample to ensure that it represented the target population? First, we should separate the target population into enlistees and officers. Then we should select a random sample from each group or *stratum.*

Why do we group the target population into the two strata? Not merely because enlistees and officers differ, but because they differ especially on what we wish to measure—years of schooling. Officers tend to have about 15–17 years of schooling. On the other hand, enlistees tend to have about 9–12 years of schooling.

Stratifying by military rank may not be useful if we are interested in determining attitudes toward increased pay. If the attitudes of officers and enlistees do not differ, then we can take a simple random sample.

Consider another problem. Howard Bright, manager at COMCEL's Norcross plant, plans to determine the employees' attitudes toward the firm. (See Table 1.2 for the nine questions in the climate survey.) He wants to know if the employee attitudes have worsened since last year's survey. If so, he will then determine the root causes and take corrective action. Although the total population is only 300 people, he decides to take a sample.

The plant consists of three groups—blue-collar, management or professional, and hourly support staff. Bright expects that job attitudes are similar within each group but different among groups. Thus, he divides the target population of 300 employees into three strata—blue-collar, management or professional, and hourly support staff. He will then select a simple random sample from each stratum.

Consider **stratified random sampling** when there are subgroups within a target population that are likely to have similarities—job attitudes or years of schooling—within a stratum but differences among strata.

> A stratified random sample is one obtained by separating the target population into nonoverlapping groups, or strata, and then selecting a simple random sample from each stratum.

Selecting a Stratified Random Sample

We begin the process of selecting a stratified random sample by determining the total sample size. Larger samples have smaller margins of error but are more costly. Thus, balancing precision and cost calls for managerial judgment.

After determining the total sample size, we must decide on the sample size per stratum. There are many ways to allocate the total sample among the strata or groups.

Each allocation method may result in a different margin of error. Three factors affect the allocation:

1. the total number of elements in each stratum;
2. the variation in the measurements within each stratum; and
3. the cost of obtaining observations from each stratum.

Considering only the first factor, base the sample size on the number of elements in each stratum. Select larger size samples from strata with many elements. The logic is simple. A sample of size 50 from a target population of 500 is more likely to be representative than a sample of size 50 from a population of 50,000, so the margin of error will be smaller.

Considering only the second factor, select larger size samples from strata that have greater variability. Suppose that army enlistees have between 11 and 12 years (total range of 1 year) of schooling. To obtain an accurate estimate of enlistees' mean years of schooling, we need only a very small sample. If officers had between 16 and 20 years (total range of 4 years) of schooling, we must take a larger sample to get an accurate estimate. Remember Lesson 3: As the variability of the target population increases, the margin of error increases. Taking larger samples will reduce the margin of error.

Considering only the third factor, select smaller size samples from strata when the cost of sampling is high. If one stratum is a large election district extending over 400 square miles, the travel costs for personal interviews will be high. Therefore, reduce the sample size in this stratum. Of course, if you use telephone interviewing, sampling costs for the large geographic stratum will be similar to the costs of sampling other strata.

In proportional allocation sampling, the percentage of each stratum in the sample mirrors its percentage in the population.

Use **proportional allocation sampling** when sampling costs are the same for all strata and when all strata exhibit the same variability. We will illustrate proportional allocation sampling for the job attitude study.

Howard Bright selects a total sample size of 10. There are 30 managers or professionals, 60 support staff, and 210 blue-collar workers. Since 10% of the plant population are managers or professionals, 10% of the sample will come from this group. Of the 10 people in the sample, one must be a manager or professional. Since 70% of the plant population are blue-collar workers, 70% of the sample will be blue-collar workers. Of the 10 people in the sample, 7 must be blue-collar workers. Similarly, 2 support staff will be randomly selected. Thus the sample should include 1 manager or professional, 7 blue-collar workers, and 2 support staff.

Now Bright can select a simple random sample from each stratum of employees using a random numbers table, Appendix 4. He assigns the numbers 001–030 to the 30 managers or professionals, the numbers 031–090 to the 60 support staff, and the numbers 091–300 to the 210 blue-collar workers. Then he selects a random starting point in Appendix 4—say, line 21, column 4—and reads across the row. The study participants are worker 143, worker 91, staffer 47, worker 221, worker 224, worker 253, worker 263, staffer 66, worker 215, and manager 002.

A Note of Caution

Properly used, stratified random sampling provides more precise estimates than simple random sampling. However, stratifying may produce worse results than simple random sampling if we stratify the target population incorrectly.

Consider the following problem. We want to estimate potential sales of a new product. We can test it in eight stores for one month. Since we sell to three retail chains, we choose to stratify the sample. The first chain has 20 stores, and there are 10 stores in each of the other two chains. Using proportional allocation sampling, we randomly select four stores from the first chain and two each from the other two chains. Do not be surprised if the monthly sales estimate is inferior to that obtained by a simple random sample. Why? Please think about it before reading on.

Stratifying by chains may not be meaningful. Stratifying works best when the variability of the variable of interest is low within each stratum and high between different strata. Are sales of the 20 stores within the first chain very similar and are they different from sales of the other two chains? If not, then stratifying by chains is inappropriate.

Other Designs: Systematic and Cluster Designs

Two other commonly used survey sampling designs are *systematic* and *cluster sampling*. Systematic sampling occurs when we select one element at random from the first k elements in a sampling frame, and then select every kth element thereafter. This is a **1-in-k** systematic sample. Systematic sampling simplifies the selection process. This design is especially useful when we do not know the target population's size, and so simple random sampling is not possible.

Industrial quality control (QC) departments often use systematic sampling. These departments approve vendors, evaluate raw material component selection, do quality planning, analyze customer returns, and measure and report compliance with quality policies. In the compliance role, they select items from production lines or service centers and take measurements on variables such as product weight or the number of complaints. They compare the mean value of the measurements with the company standards to determine if quality is being maintained.

QC departments often use systematic sampling designs such as 1-in-100 items or one item per half-hour. These samples will include items from the beginning to the end of the shift. Thus if rejects increase over the shift as workers tire, the sample will reflect the target population. This target population is *ordered*. A simple random sample may not contain elements over the entire shift. The first hour of the shift may be overrepresented in the sample and the last hour may be underrepresented. Systematic sampling is useful for ordered populations.

Systematic sampling can sometimes produce poor estimates. For example, we must estimate a department store's weekly sales. Using a 1-in-7 systematic sampling design, we could select a day at random where $k = 1$ means Sunday and $k = 7$ means Saturday, and then sample the sales figures every 7 days thereafter. If we randomly select Saturday, we will overestimate the weekly sales since Saturday and Sunday are by far the busiest shopping days. If we randomly select Wednesday, we will underestimate weekly sales. This target population is *periodic*. The variable of interest varies in a predictable pattern. Therefore, do not use systematic sampling for periodic populations.

Cluster sampling occurs when we randomly select a set of m clusters from a target population and then examine or interview every element within each selected cluster. For example, we could divide a city into clusters of sampling units such as city blocks, groups of city blocks, or political districts. The sampling frame would then be lists of city blocks or political districts. Select a random sample of clusters and then interview *everyone* in the cluster.

The merit of cluster sampling is that it is cost-effective. By sampling all households within a cluster, we reduce travel costs. Consider cluster sampling when (1) a sampling frame listing population elements is not available or is costly to obtain, or (2) travel costs are very high for other survey designs.

Clustering and stratifying are two different methods for grouping a target population. The elements within an ideal stratum should have similar measurements on the variable of interest, but there should be large differences on the variable of interest among strata. In contrast, the elements within an ideal cluster should have widely different measurements on the variable of interest, but there should be small differences in the variable of interest *among* clusters.

In summary, Table 6.5 compares the four survey sampling designs.

Table 6.5

A Comparison of Four Survey Sampling Designs

Design	How to Select Sample	Strengths/Weaknesses
Simple random	Assign numbers to elements in sampling frame. Use random numbers table in Appendix 4 to select sample.	The basic building block. Simple, but often costly. Cannot use unless we can assign a number to each element in the target population.
Stratified	Divide population into groups that are similar within and different between on the variable of interest. Use Appendix 4 to select the sample from each stratum.	With proper strata, can produce very accurate estimates. Less costly than simple random sampling. Must stratify target population correctly.
Systematic	Select every *k*th element from a list after a random start.	Produces very accurate estimates when elements in a population exhibit *order*. Used when simple random or stratified sampling is impractical: e.g., the population size is not known. Simplifies the selection process. Do not use with periodic populations.
Cluster	Randomly choose clusters and sample all elements within each cluster.	With proper clusters, can produce very accurate estimates. Useful when sampling frame unavailable or travel costs high. Must cluster target population correctly.

SECTION 6.6 EXERCISES

1. List the circumstances when you would prefer stratified random sampling over simple random sampling.

2. List the factors that determine the division of the total sample among strata.

3. What do we mean by proportional allocation of the total sample among the strata? Under what circumstances is this method the best one to use?

4. The federal government is planning to survey the 50 states and thinks that the measurement of interest will vary by the population of the state. They divide the states into three strata: five large states, 15 medium-sized states, and 30 small states. Budgetary restrictions limit the sample to a size of 10.
   a. How many states should be drawn from each stratum if the proportional allocation method is used?
   b. Why not use simple random sampling?

5. A company has divided a county into three strata of equal population size. The estimated income standard deviation for each stratum is $225. The standard deviation for the whole county is also $225. Should the firm use proportional allocation stratified sampling?

6. The IRS uses stratified sampling to audit tax returns. Suppose there are 120 million individual returns in any tax year and that the returns are stratified by adjusted gross income as follows.

$0–34,999	60 million
$35,000–49,999	40 million
$50,000–74,999	15 million
$75,000 and above	5 million

   a. How many returns should be audited from each stratum if only 2% of the returns can be audited and the sample is allocated according to the size of the strata?
   b. If you were making audit policy for the IRS, would you use proportional allocation to determine the composition of the total sample? Explain.

7. List the reasons for the popularity of systematic random sampling.

8. Distinguish between a random and a periodic population. Why might systematic sampling be a poor choice of a sampling plan when the population is periodic?

9. "My sampling frame is an alphabetized list of all my employees. Therefore, the frame isn't random." Comment.

10. Suppose the sampling frame consists of 10,000 residences listed by zip code. You are studying purchasing patterns of households and want to interview 250 families. Suppose you selected the 20th address, then the 70th, 120th, 170th, and so on over the entire list of 10,000 residences. What is the sampling constant, k, and what sample size would result?

11. Suppose your sampling frame is the white pages of the telephone directory. You are studying purchasing behavior of households. If the kth name in the directory is a business and is therefore ineligible, should you take the name listed right after the name of the business? Why?

12. List the conditions when you would consider using cluster sampling.

13. A company has 20 factories located in different parts of the country. It wants to survey its employees consisting of white-collar and blue-collar workers. Suggest a sampling plan (a) if the measurement of interest is expected to vary more by factory than by type of worker and (b) if the measurement of interest varies more by worker than by factory.

14. The target population consists of 200 stores numbered from 001 to 200, from which 5 stores have been selected. Based on the numbers of the stores, indicate whether the sampling design was most likely to be a simple random sample, systematic sample, cluster sample, or a convenience (nonrandom) sample (one set of numbers represents each design).
    a. 110 111 112 113 114   c. 037 063 110 139 181
    b. 098 099 156 157 158   d. 025 065 105 145 185

6.7 ≣ Selecting a Survey Method

We have identified our sampling frame and selected a survey sampling design. Next we must decide which of three survey methods to use: personal interview, telephone interview, or mail questionnaire. There is no one best method for all situations. By the end of this section you should be able to:

1. compare and contrast the three methods; and
2. decide which method to use for a particular study.

Dillman (1978) points out how the three survey methods affect (1) obtaining a representative sample, (2) questionnaire length and flexibility, (3) obtaining accurate answers, and (4) administrative issues, such as how quickly we need the answers and how much we are willing to spend to get them. We will elaborate on these issues next.

Obtaining a Representative Sample

We must select samples based on chance and not personal bias. When we pick a specific individual or household from the sampling frame using a table of random numbers, that person or household should be interviewed. However, if that person is not available, we will need to select an appropriate substitute person or household. This is costly and time-consuming. Which of the three survey methods is best at avoiding substitutions?

Personal interviews.   The advantage of personal interviews is that if the interviewee can be located, we are likely to get the interview. The interviewee will find it difficult to ask the interviewer to leave, whereas hanging up the telephone receiver or tearing up the mail questionnaire is easier to do. If we cannot locate the interviewee, then we can easily select a house three doors down the street. This should not present problems since people on the same street usually have similar social and economic characteristics. If the person is located but refuses to be interviewed, we should note the reason for refusal or the person's demographic characteristics.

The disadvantage of personal interviews is that locating a specific person may be difficult if the study covers a wide geographic area or the person is simply difficult to reach. Moreover, people who work during the day are difficult to locate. While they can be reached in the evening, many respondents are less willing to be personally interviewed after dark or after a hard day's work.

Telephone interviews.   Telephone interviews are almost as useful as the personal interview in locating specific persons. They may even be better for locating persons who are geographically dispersed. Moreover, a telephone interview may require fewer substitutions than the personal interview because callbacks are much less expensive than return visits. Finally, people who work are more easily reached by telephone than by personal interview at night.

Unfortunately, not all people have telephones, and of those who do, some have unlisted numbers. Random-digit dialing reduces the latter problem as all possible numbers are randomly generated. For example, if the exchange number is 633-XXXX, we can program a computer to generate all possible sets of the last four numbers. Any unlisted number then has the same chance of selection as any other number with a 633 prefix.

Mail questionnaires.   Even if busy schedules preclude a personal or telephone interview, people eventually pick up their mail. In surveys of homogeneous populations such as professional associations, the mail questionnaire may do as well as other methods in getting a representative sample. However, a mail questionnaire addressed to the "Director of Information Systems" or "Resident" may never reach the intended person. Even if it does, there is no guarantee that the recipient will complete the questionnaire. Often, unless we provide other incentives—money or a promise of sharing the survey results—the response rate may be significantly below that of personal or telephone interviews.

When the target population is the general public, the personal interview is the best method for getting a representative sample. Personal and telephone interviews are superior to the mail questionnaire in controlling selection of respondents, in response rates, and in avoiding unknown bias from refusals. With a homogeneous target population, such as a professional association, the mail questionnaire is almost as effective as the other two methods in obtaining a representative sample.

Questionnaire Length and Flexibility

The most difficult part of any survey is knowing what to ask and how to ask it. Later in this chapter, we will discuss the actual writing of the questions. Here we discuss how the survey methods affect the length and type of questions.

Personal interviews. Personal interviews permit more complex and open-ended (short essay) questions since we can prompt the respondent. The structuring of questions is less important than with the other two methods. *Screening questions,* which make some questions inapplicable to some respondents, are less likely to cause problems in the personal interview. For example, the following question can cause difficulty if it is part of a mail questionnaire, but should cause no difficulty for a trained interviewer:

Do you rent or own your place of residence?

1.   RENT
2.   OWN
IF RENT, GO TO QUESTION 12.

Telephone interviews. Telephone interviews should be shorter than the two other methods. As boredom or impatience sets in, respondents answer less carefully and may hang up. The telephone interview also requires the least complex questions. For example, a respondent asked to rank several items must retain the list in his head before ranking. In a personal interview, we can show the list to the respondent.

Mail questionnaires. The mail questionnaire requires the most careful construction. It must sell itself, be pleasing to the eye, and be constructed so responses can be given easily. Otherwise, the questionnaire will be discarded. Using open-ended questions is risky since respondents vary considerably in their writing skills. Many may answer in short and generally uninterpretable phrases when there is no interviewer present to probe for a fuller response. Use of screening questions, which requires bypassing some questions, can also lead to response errors. Finally, a higher nonresponse rate is more likely, since no interviewer is present to probe for answers or explain difficult questions.

The personal interview permits the longest and most detailed questionnaire, while the telephone method allows the shortest and least detailed questions. Personal and telephone interviews are both better than mail questionnaires at controlling the sequence of questions and are more successful in the use of screening questions. With respect to questionnaire flexibility and length, the personal interview is the best, the telephone interview a close second, and the mail questionnaire third.

Obtaining Accurate Answers

A successful study requires that we survey the right person, that the person have the information, and that he or she be willing to give it. How well do the three methods elicit a respondent's true attitudes, behaviors, and demographic characteristics?

Personal interviews.   An interviewer who is helpful in guiding a respondent through complex and open-ended questions may also introduce serious bias. A disapproving facial expression or change in tone of voice can suggest the "correct" or socially desirable answer. In general, the socioeconomic status and race of the interviewer should not be too different from the respondent's or the respondent may distort answers to mislead the interviewer. Interviewers can be trained to minimize these problems, but it is expensive to do so.

Telephone interviews.   Voice inflections from the interviewer can inadvertently bias responses. The problem is not as serious as in personal interviews since the interviewer's body language is not visible.

Mail questionnaires.   Since no interviewer is involved, the respondent's willingness to provide true answers depends almost entirely on how the questions are presented. We say *almost* because the respondent may discuss the questionnaire with others before answering. This outside interference is most difficult to control in the mail survey, more easily controlled in the telephone interview, and most easily controlled in the personal interview.

Briefly, the mail questionnaire ranks highest in obtaining honest and unbiased answers, followed by the telephone interview, and then the personal interview. The opportunity for interviewer distortion is greatest in the personal interview.

Administrative Issues

The final issues to consider in selecting a survey method involve, of course, time and money. *When* do we need the information? *How much* is the budget? If we need the information in two weeks or a month, the best choice is a telephone interview. If potential respondents are spread over the world, the best choice is a mail questionnaire especially if the project budget is small. Here we discuss cost and other administrative issues related to the three survey methods.

Personal interviews.   This is the most expensive method because of personnel costs, which include interviewers' salaries, travel, lodging, and meals. Finding and supervising qualified interviewers are difficult. They must be trained not to bias answers. We must verify that the interviews were completed as planned, and that the interviewer did not fill in the answers in the comfort of a hotel room.

Market research firms that have existing survey instruments will often allow their clients to add additional questions. *"Piggy-backing"* reduces client survey costs and allows several firms to survey the same target population with just one trip to a respondent. The interviewers should be professional, since the research firms offer steady employment and continual training.

Telephone interviews.   This method is less expensive than personal interviews because fewer interviewers can call more people from one central location. In addition, the interviewers can be closely monitored, thus reducing the cost of recruiting, training, and supervision. WATS line technology reduces the cost per call even over great distances. Thus, larger samples can be taken in comparison with the personal interview.

Mail questionnaires.   This is the least expensive method since it avoids the cost of training, supporting, and supervising interviewers. Mailing costs are uniform throughout the United States. Although the increasing use of facsimile machines may increase the cost of mail questionnaires, it will also reduce the time it takes to obtain the survey information.

In summary, the telephone is the fastest method and the personal interview is the slowest method. The least expensive method is the mail questionnaire and the most expensive is the personal interview. Considering speed and cost only, the personal interview should be avoided. Whether to telephone or mail the questionnaire depends on the trade-off between cost and time.

SECTION 6.7 EXERCISES

1. Which is the best survey method—personal interview, telephone interview, or mail questionnaire—for achieving each of the following objectives?
    a. Obtaining a representative sample
    b. Ease of questionnaire construction
    c. Obtaining accurate answers
    d. Minimum time and cost

2. Which is the worst survey method for achieving each of the four objectives in Exercise 1?

3. Your firm writes computer programs to help store and summarize residential sales data. You want to improve your current product to boost sales of the product and maintain customer loyalty. You want to survey current users and identify what they like and dislike about the current system. You have a list of names and phone numbers of all 1,500 licensed brokers in the target population. Considering all four of the general criteria for selecting a survey method, which method would you use?

4. Given each of the following characteristics of a proposed survey, which method would you think best to use?
    a. You need the information within a month.
    b. You are surveying the incidence of crime among new immigrants.
    c. Product usage survey
    d. Survey of attitudes of the members of the American Accounting Association
    e. Attitude survey with many complicated questions
    f. Asks many personal or potentially embarrassing questions
    g. Identifying the correct person to interview is not possible until after the sampling unit is selected.
    h. Budget is very tight.

5. Explain the meaning of interviewer bias. How does it affect the results of surveys? How can you measure its effects?

6.8 ≡ General Principles for Writing Questions

Constructing the questionnaire is the most difficult part of any study since the wording of questions is more of an art than a science. We will cover how to determine the information needed, the type of questions to be written, and how to word the questions. After completing this section, you should be able to:

1. relate problem diagnosis to questionnaire construction;
2. determine what question format to use in a particular study; and
3. write questions that overcome the most common wording errors.

Determining Information Needs: Diagnosing the Problem

Companies do not conduct surveys merely to get data. They want to have important questions answered. They use surveys when diagnosing a problem. For example, suppose the firm must determine why sales of a recently introduced product are less than expected—a deviation from expected performance. Why aren't consumers buying the new product as rapidly as projected? What factors caused the deviation from expected sales?

Managers often focus too narrowly on the cause of a problem. They view a problem from the perspective of their own discipline. Marketers focus on consumer-oriented root causes. Engineers focus on poor product design root causes. To overcome a narrow view of a problem, we recommend using the "Alternative Worldview Method" to expose possible root causes (Ramakrishna and Brightman, 1986). This creative method requires that we brainstorm for multiple root causes in two distinct areas: internal to the firm and external to the firm. Internal root causes are those that originate inside the firm and over which we have control. External root causes are those that originate outside the firm and over which we have little or no control.

The root causes are explored at a brainstorming session, where no one criticizes any ideas. Participants just call out possible root causes in the two areas as fast as they can and list them on an easel pad. Afterwards, they can group similar causes together, identify the likely causes, and then address them in the survey. Shown here are the results of a brainstorming session for the sales deviation problem.

> *Internal factors*:   Poor product features, distribution channel failures, lack of product service support, poor product quality, or ineffective distribution.

> *External factors*:   Fierce competition, lack of consumer motivation to learn about the product, reduction in discretionary income, or fear of economic downturn.

Possible questions to ask include: Is the cause of lower-than-expected sales the consumers' lack of knowledge about the product? Does the product have the features they want? Is the service department at fault? Is the perceived quality lower than that of our competition? Before writing the first question, we must have a list of possible areas to investigate.

Surveys provide four types of information: (1) respondent behaviors, or what they say they do; (2) levels of knowledge, or what they know; (3) attitudes and opinions, or what they believe; and (4) socioeconomic characteristics, or who they are. These four types of information capture most of what we would need to know about an element in the target population.

Choosing the Question Format

Once the firm determines the information needed, what question format should it use? The choice depends on which survey method it selects—the personal interview, the telephone interview, or the mail questionnaire.

Most surveys consist of a combination of open-ended and closed-ended questions. Consider the questions in Table 6.6. From the table, we see examples of two basic formats for questions—open-ended and closed-ended.

Open-ended questions. Use open-ended questions when the list of all responses is very long or not obvious. For example, asking the question "What cigarette brand do you smoke?" would require too many alternatives for a complete list. Consider open-ended questions also for a pretest questionnaire (Step 7 in planning a survey). In a pretest telephone interview, ask respondents to name all the radio stations they listen to. Use their responses in the major study as choices for a closed-ended question.

A disadvantage of open-ended questions is that answers depend on respondents' ability to write or speak as much as on their knowledge. Two respondents might have

Table 6.6

Types of Question Formats in Surveys

Question	Format
Which country makes the best cars?	Open-ended
Which country makes the best cars? 1. USA 2. JAPAN 3. GERMANY	Closed-ended: Unordered alternatives
Which country makes the best cars? 1. USA 2. JAPAN 3. GERMANY 4. OTHER _____ (Please specify)	Partially closed-ended
If you own a Ford, how satisfied are you with its performance? 1. VERY SATISFIED 2. SATISFIED 3. UNSATISFIED	Closed-ended: Ordered alternatives
If you own a Ford, are you satisfied with it? YES ____ NO ____	Closed-ended: Binary alternatives

the same knowledge and opinions, but their answers may seem different because of their varying abilities. In interview surveys, the response accuracy also depends on the interviewer's ability to faithfully record everything the respondent says. Thus, considerable interviewer bias or error is possible. Finally, responses to open-ended questions are more difficult to interpret and analyze than are those to closed-ended questions.

Closed-ended questions. Use closed-ended questions when the full range of choices is known, when the list of questions is not too long, and when the questionnaires must be analyzed quickly.

However, there are several problems with closed-ended questions. First, we cannot determine the reasons behind a selection. A respondent could answer NO to the question "Do you intend to remodel your home this year?" for several reasons. He might not want to remodel his house or he is considering remodelling but he cannot afford it. Second, even when the DON'T KNOW option is offered, respondents will usually select from the other choices. They want to avoid the appearance of having no opinion. This is especially true when the wording of the question implies that they *should* know the answer.

Finally, the position of a choice affects the chances that it will be selected. This is called the *position bias*. For example, asked the amount of money spent each week for soft drinks, respondents will often pick the middle selection when they do not know the answer. Alternatively, where a long list of choices is *read* to respondents, they often select the last alternative. When the same choices are *visually* presented to the respondents, they will often select the first choice. Therefore, consider two approaches for minimizing the position bias. In mail questionnaires, print questionnaires with the choices in different sequences. In personal and telephone interviews, choose a different starting place every time you read the choices to a new respondent.

Avoiding Wording Errors

Suppose we know our information needs and have selected the question formats. Now we must write the actual questions. Remember that the respondent must (1) understand the question, (2) have the information, and (3) be willing to give it.

Table 6.7

General Principles for Writing Questions

Understanding the Question

Match wording to the respondent's intelligence level or needs.
Avoid vague questions.
Avoid double questions.
Make the answers mutually exclusive.

Having the Information

Write questions that people can answer.
Write questions that people can answer without too much effort.

Willing to Give Information

Avoid questions that invade people's privacy.
Phrase questions so that social desirability does not play a role in selecting a response.
Never ask embarrassing questions.
Avoid questions that direct the respondent to select one answer over the others.

Table 6.7 provides general guidelines for writing questions.

Understanding the question. Will the words have the same meaning to all potential respondents? Tailor the wording to the vocabulary of the potential respondents. If surveying a homogeneous population of doctors or lawyers, use technical language so that respondents will take the survey seriously. If the potential respondents are general public consumers, do not use specialized vocabulary.

A question such as "Do you attend church regularly?" is vague. Respondents may define *regularly* differently. Rephrase the question this way:

How often did you attend church services in the past month?

1. NOT AT ALL
2. LESS THAN ONCE A WEEK
3. ONCE A WEEK
4. MORE THAN ONCE A WEEK

Ask only one question at a time. For example, "Do you own a second home or vacation home?" asks two questions.

Do not overlap answers in such a way that respondents could check two answers.

Where do you learn about sales in grocery stores?

1. FLYERS
2. NEWSPAPERS
3. RADIO
4. TELEVISION
5. FRIENDS AND NEIGHBORS

Since newspapers often contain insert flyers, choices 1 and 2 overlap.

Having the information.   Have you assumed that respondents are more knowledgeable than they actually are or have greater access to information than they do? Respondents who do not possess the information requested, but who believe they should, will guess rather than admit they do not know. People often claim to subscribe to magazines that do not exist. Consider the following question.

Has your spouse read this issue of *Time?*

1. YES
2. NO

Trying to answer this question could pose one or several problems for some respondents. First of all, it assumes the respondent is married, which may not be the case. Second, it assumes that, if married, the person would know whether the spouse has read the magazine. Finally, it also assumes that the respondent knows what the term "spouse" means.

Even if respondents have the information, will it be "at their fingertips" and if not, will they be able and willing to find the information? For example, most people could not name the brand of tires on their car unless they went out and looked. But would they? Asking cigarette smokers to state the number of packs of cigarettes smoked last month will produce significant guessing since very few smokers are likely to know the exact number. Furthermore, they may not be willing to admit to themselves that they don't know the number!

Willing to give the information.   Respondents will often lie when a truthful answer would adversely affect their prestige or invade their privacy. Personal questions may have higher rates of nonresponse and should be placed at the end of the questionnaire. Once the respondent has developed a rapport with the interviewer, he may provide truthful answers to prestige-laden or personal questions.

Unfortunately, it is not always obvious which questions are prestige laden. In one study, beer drinkers said they preferred light to regular beer but sales figures disagreed. Respondents lied because they perceived people who drank light beer as more discriminating and they wanted to be a part of that group.

People may also lie when the correct response would be embarrassing or make them appear to be members of an undesirable group, such as shoplifters, alcoholics, or drugs users. The following question might prompt the respondent to give answer 2 or 3 rather than admit to consuming the greatest quantity on the scale.

Approximately how many cans of beer do you consume each week, on average?

1. NONE
2. 1 TO 3   ,
3. 4 TO 6
4. MORE THAN 6

Consider extending the range of choices far beyond what is expected. Then the respondent can select an answer closer to the middle and feel more in the "normal" range.

Avoid biased questions. When a question or the list of responses seems to suggest a desired answer, respondents may give inaccurate information rather than disagree with the investigator's opinions. Suppose we handed out a questionnaire in a department store and one of the items was the following:

This store's merchandise is reasonably priced.

1. YES
2. NO

The item is heavily biased toward a YES response. It is clear how the researcher wants the shopper to respond. Revise the question as follows:

In comparison with other stores selling similar merchandise, would you say that our prices are higher, lower, or about the same?

1. HIGHER
2. LOWER
3. ABOUT THE SAME

A Final Thought

Managers are problem solvers. Surveys can help diagnose problem causes, identify current and future respondent needs, desires, and wants, and determine the effectiveness of managerial policies and actions.

Statisticians think of surveys in terms of survey sampling designs and sample size. Sampling designs and sample size affect the size of the margin of error and are crucial to the results obtained. In order to obtain true responses, managers must also consider question wording and format. Studies have shown that when the same people are reinterviewed, responses can change dramatically with a different interviewer or with a slightly different question wording. Therefore, it is very important to always pretest a questionnaire on a sample of respondents that have the same intellectual ability and knowledge of the topic area as the target population. We conduct the pretest as if it were the full study, and thereby we can discover question wording or format problems. There are two common ways of detecting wording problems. First, have respondents complete the questionnaire and then have them explain their answers. Second, ask respondents to think out loud as they answer each question. Finally, pretesting helps us find additional problems with questionnaire layout, question sequence, and branching instructions. Branching instructions direct respondents to answer certain questions depending on their responses to previous questions.

In addition, pretesting allows us to estimate response rates and the time needed to complete an interview. We can then compare this information with budgeted estimates to see if adjustments are needed.

Having followed our guidelines on (1) analyzing the problem before writing the questions, (2) selecting the proper survey sampling design, (3) selecting the best survey method, (4) choosing the proper question format, and (5) writing effective questions, we are now ready to obtain data through survey sampling.

For a more complete discussion of survey methods, question formats, and question wording, we recommend the work of Dillman (1978).

SECTION 6.8 EXERCISES

1. In order to give accurate responses, the respondent must (1) understand the question, (2) have the information, and (3) be willing to give it. With these criteria in mind, identify the flaws in the following questions.
   a. How many times did you visit a shopping mall in the past month?
   b. Do you use hairspray?

      c. Which is more important to you in purchasing foods, the caloric content or the levels of polyunsaturates?

      d. Have you been satisfied with the service provided by Rich's department store?

      e. Which car do you consider faster and more reliable, Porsche or BMW?

      f. Are you a frequent user of headache remedies?

      g. Listed below are stores generally considered to be upscale. Please check the ones you have shopped.

2. For each of the questions below, list the general source of error as not understanding the question (U), not having the information (I), or being unwilling to give the information (W).

      a. What is your income?

      b. Do you think that smoking ads should be banned or do you think that American businesses should have the right to advertise?

        1. YES   2. NO   3. NO OPINION

      c. How far would you drive to attend a cultural event?

      d. About how many alcoholic drinks do you consume on a weeknight?

      e. How many novels have you read in the last month?

      f. What percentage of your yearly income do you contribute to charitable causes?

3. Consider two forms of the same question shown here.

    (1) Which brands did you consider before you bought your last television?

    (2) Which of the following brands did you consider before you bought your last television?

      _____a. ADMIRAL _____b. RCA _____c. MAGNAVOX

      _____d. SONY ____e. OTHER

The first version is referred to as unaided recall and the second is aided recall. What are the pros and cons of each form of this question?

6.9 Basic Principles of Experimental Design

Besides survey sampling, managers can obtain data by conducting *planned change studies*. Managers should continually seek ways to improve their workers' and their own performance, service, or product quality when needed. Unfortunately, they sometimes do not seek improvements. Some reasons are:

1. They have no time because they are always putting out brush fires—dealing with minor details and problems.
2. They assume that present performance, service, or quality cannot be improved. They are not innovators.
3. They are dissatisfied with present performance but do not have the courage to improve it. They fear that improving a system makes those who developed it appear incompetent—including themselves.
4. They are lazy or are looking for the easy way out.

To be innovative, managers need to continually ask questions, such as:

1. How can we improve production methods or service?
2. How can we train management and employees better?
3. How can we reduce marketing costs?
4. Will the customer use the product? How can we improve its present usage or make it more useful?

Once managers identify potential improvements, they should run planned change studies, preferably on a small scale, to determine if a potential improvement actually does improve performance or service. They should study the results. If the planned change is an improvement, they should implement it permanently. By the end of this section you should be able to:

1. define experimental design terms;
2. distinguish between an experiment and a nonexperiment; and
3. explain how randomization helps rule out alternative explanations and why that is important.

Basic Terminology

What is an experiment, or planned change study? The "scientist image" represents experimentation in chemistry, physics, or psychology. However, managers also must run experiments to determine if planned changes do improve performance, service, or quality. So, what is an experiment? It's simply a *controlled study* in which a manager varies one or more factors and then measures the effects on the dependent variable.

Experimental factor.   In business, factors, or treatments, are the planned changes that managers believe will improve performance, service, or quality. Factors could include different advertising approaches, production machine speeds, methods of cooking food, types of bonus systems, and so forth.

Level.   Each variation of a planned change factor is a factor level. A marketing manager may try two different advertising approaches—two levels. A production manager may try three different speeds—three levels. We present some examples here.

Factor	Levels
Advertising approaches	Man-on-the-Street or Big Name Star
Polishing speeds	600 revolutions per min. (rpm), 1,200 rpm, or 1,800 rpm
Cooking burgers	Broil or grill
Bonus systems	Individual or group bonus

Experimental unit.   The entities that experience the planned change, or factor level, are the experimental units. They can be people, groups of people, or items on a production line. When the units are people, we call them subjects. Examples of possible experimental units for factors are the following:

Factor	Experimental Units
Advertising approaches	Customers
Polishing speeds	Eyeglass lenses
Cooking burgers	Burgers
Bonus systems	Workers

Dependent variable.   Dependent variables are quantities that the manager measures to determine if the planned change has had any impact. We will limit our discussion to experiments that have only one dependent variable. Examples of possible dependent variables include:

Factor	Dependent Variable
Advertising approaches	Customer sales volume
Polishing speeds	Number of scratches on eyeglasses
Cooking burgers	Tastiness of burgers
Bonus systems	Number of units produced by workers

Experiments vs. Nonexperiments

To run an experiment, the manager must meet two requirements:

1. assign experimental units to different factor levels, introduce a planned change, and measure the impact; and
2. control for extraneous factors.

We will illustrate both requirements in the following three scenarios.

Scenario 1   Max Drucker owns a rental car agency that provides four types of cars: Buick Regal, Oldsmobile Cutlass, Chevrolet Caprice, and Pontiac Grand Am. Max's major expense is unscheduled maintenance, which includes all repair work except routine oil changes, lubrication, etc.

Last year, Max asked himself if the cost of unscheduled maintenance was different for the four types of rental cars. He plans to drop those cars that have the highest costs. Max collected the unscheduled maintenance records for the past five years and then computed the total cost for each of the four types of cars. Since he owned an equal number of each type, Max compared the costs directly. Here are the results.

Buick Regal	Oldsmobile Cutlass	Chevrolet Caprice	Pontiac Grand Am
$3,950	$5,100	$5,300	$4,500

Question: Has Max run an experiment? Think about it before reading on.

He has not because he did not assign experimental units to factor levels, introduce a planned change, and measure the effects. First, there is no experimental factor since Max did not vary anything. Second, since there was no experimental factor, Max could not assign his cars (experimental units) to different factor levels. All he did was examine historical records. This is an *observational study* in which the manager collects data on an event that has already happened. Four types of cars have been used for five years, and Max has merely collected the historical maintenance cost data.

Observational studies are not experiments and are difficult to interpret. The observational study suggests that the Buick Regal has the lowest unscheduled maintenance cost. If Max were naive, he would purchase only Buick Regals to reduce his maintenance costs. However, that may be an incorrect strategy! The Buick's low maintenance cost may be due to *extraneous factors,* factors beyond the car itself. Possible extraneous factors include:

1. Miles driven per year for each car type
2. Driver differences (abusive drivers, fast drivers, etc.)
3. Road surface differences (dirt, asphalt, concrete, etc.)
4. Operating environment differences (city, highway, etc.)
5. Type of gas and quality of oil differences
6. Customer neglect
7. Wrecks

On the basis of the cost data he has collected, Max cannot determine *why* the Buick Regal had the lowest cost. It may be that the Buick is indeed the least expensive car to maintain. On the other hand, its low cost may be due to at least seven other reasonable alternative explanations. For example, his Buick Regals may have been driven less than the other cars and thus lower mileage may explain the low maintenance costs. Max may *confuse* the effect of car manufacturer with mileage differences. Perhaps the Buicks may have been driven only on the highways and that accounts for their reduced maintenance cost. Again Max may confuse the car manufacturer and the operating conditions. In short, extraneous factors are possible alternative explanations to the factor under study—car type—that might account for the differences in the dependent variable—unscheduled maintenance cost.

If a manager does not introduce a planned change, there may be many alternative explanations to observed findings. Choose experiments over observational studies whenever possible as observational studies cannot control extraneous variation. However, simply introducing a planned change and measuring its effects do not control extraneous variation either.

Scenario 2   A university professor compares two teaching methods, lecture vs. case (the planned change), for an advanced business law course. Since he now teaches two sections, he uses the lecture method in the first section and the case method in the second section. After six weeks, he gives a different version of a chapter test to each section. The mean score in the lecture class is 83, as compared with a mean of 65 for the case method. *Question:* Has the professor run an experiment? Think about it before reading on!

The professor has introduced a planned change and measured the effects. He has taught sections using the case and lecture methods. He has measured the impact of different teaching methods by an examination. Therefore, he has met the first requirement of an experiment. However, his study is not an experiment. An experiment ensures that the measured effects result from the planned change and not extraneous factors, factors outside the experiment. The professor has not controlled for *any* potential extraneous factors. Therefore, he has not conducted an experiment.

Before reading on, generate a small list of potential extraneous factors that could explain why the lecture method produced better results, which may not be due to the method itself. This is difficult, so take your time.

Following is a list of potential extraneous factors that could have invalidated the experiment.

1. The professor may be a better lecturer than case teacher.
2. Students in the lecture class were smarter, more alert, or more motivated than students in the case method class.
3. The final exam in the lecture class was easier.
4. The lecture class met in the late morning and the case class met in the late evening. Students cannot think as clearly in the late evening.

Now compare this study with Scenario 3.

Scenario 3   Using *simple random sampling,* the professor selects two sections of business law from the five sections being taught at 10 A.M. The sections are scheduled in different buildings on campus. Students are not allowed to register for an individual class, merely the 10 A.M. class time. The professor selects a colleague who, like himself, is equally effective in both teaching approaches. The professor determines randomly which section his colleague will teach and which section he will teach. The professor then randomly assigns students to the two sections by using a random numbers table and the following assignment scheme:

First Two Digits of Random Numbers	Assignment
00–49	Lecture method
50–99	Case method

During the first class the instructors give students in both sections the same pretest on business law fundamentals to determine their entry-level knowledge. After six weeks, the instructors give the same posttest to both sections. Here are the results.

	Section 1: Case Method			Section 2: Lecture Method		
	Pretest	Posttest	Difference	Pretest	Posttest	Difference
Class Mean	48	76	+28	45	95	+50

This is an experiment. The instructor has controlled for the four previously mentioned possible extraneous factors. He used two different approaches: (1) eliminating potential extraneous factors and (2) randomization. Examples of the former approach are his use of the same pretest and posttest and selecting sections taught at the same time of day. The professor used randomization when he selected the two 10 A.M. sections, subdivided the students into two groups, assigned them to the two sections, and assigned the two instructors.

Students in the lecture method class appear to do better. And it is unlikely that the lecture method class's superior performance is due to experimenter preferences, class section, test version, or time of day differences. Now there is no confusion as to why the lecture method students did better. All things being equal, lecturing is superior to the case method.

The Importance of Randomization

Randomization is essential to running a valid planned change study. Randomization minimizes the chance that two groups of students will systematically differ due to extraneous factors. In other words, randomization tends to equalize the groups on most potential extraneous factors. For example, randomization minimizes the chances that most of the better-prepared, highly motivated, or smarter students are in the lecture method course. Thus, if we find a difference in the groups' performances, it is due to the planned change, not extraneous factors.

Randomize to the fullest extent possible in a planned change study. Use randomization to (1) select experimental units, (2) subdivide them into groups, and (3) assign the groups to the factor levels.

We conclude with several basic experimental design principles:

PRINCIPLE 1: Choose experiments over observational studies whenever possible. Observational studies collect past data and do not generate new data. They are after-the-fact studies and are not experiments.

PRINCIPLE 2: Conduct an experiment by assigning experimental units to different treatment levels, introducing a planned change, and measuring the impact. You must also control for extraneous factors.

PRINCIPLE 3: Control extraneous factors by using randomization and eliminating possible extraneous factors from the experiment. Both approaches ensure that the experimental factors caused the improvement in the product or service, and not some extraneous factor. We call this the *RO* **principle**—*R*uling *O*ut extraneous factors.

SECTION 6.9 EXERCISES

1. List the differences between an observational study and an experiment.

2. What is a factor? Is it a suspected cause or a symptom of the problem?

3. In order to solve a problem, a manager must first diagnose the causes. Explain how a properly conducted experiment helps to identify the real causes of a problem.

4. Explain how you would use a table of random numbers to assign 30 people to three equal-sized groups.

5. What is the purpose of randomization? Wouldn't it be better for a knowledgeable experimenter to place people in each group so the groups are equal except for the difference in treatment level? Explain.

6. In a recent telephone survey, a random sample of 400 respondents showed that men are more likely than women to vote for a Republican candidate. Is this an experiment? Explain. no

7. A company wishes to study the relationship between job satisfaction and length of service with the company. The company decides to divide the length of service into two categories, under 5 years and 5 years and above. It randomly selects 20 employees from each of these two groups for testing and interviews.
   a. Is this an experiment or observational study? Explain.
   b. If the firm finds that people with longer tenure are more satisfied, can the company conclude that people who are new hires will automatically become more satisfied as time goes on? Why?

8. A consumer products testing laboratory wants to compare the wear on three brands of tires. The lab randomly assigns a different set of tires to each of three cars of the same make and randomly assigns one of three drivers to drive each car. After being driven around a test track for 10,000 miles, brand A has the smallest mean wear, and the lab concludes that brand A is the best tire. Do you think this conclusion is warranted? If not, what factors could have confounded the experiment, and how would you rule them out on the next experiment?

6.10 ≣ Avoiding Problems in Experimental Design

While the RO principle is essential for an experiment, it alone does not eliminate all planned change study problems. Next we consider several other serious problems and how to overcome them. By the end of this section you should be able to:

1. illustrate each potential experimental problem; and
2. correct each experimental problem.

Example: COMCEL's Study of Reduction in Labor Costs   According to published industry figures, work teams at COMCEL's Norcross plant have not been as successful in reducing labor costs as have other firms. Recently, the plant manager asked Sarah Teman, Manager of Manufacturing, to design a plantwide cost-reduction program. First, Teman will conduct a small-scale study. Below are the two variations of her planned change:

1. Job switching within groups (JS workshop)
2. Teaching work groups creativity methods (CM workshop)

Teman identifies many teams in the plant that have a similar number of years of experience and prior success in implementing cost-saving ideas. From this pool, she randomly selects ten work teams of five workers each. She randomly assigns the ten teams to two groups of five teams each. She then randomly assigns one group of five teams to the JS workshop and the other group of five teams to the CM workshop. The dependent variable is the reduction in unit labor cost of producing a mobile telephone six months after the workshops. Table 6.8 presents the hypothetical data for the one-factor, two-level planned change study.

While Teman has ruled out some extraneous factors by eliminating them (similar years of experience and prior cost-savings idea success) and by using randomization, she can still improve her study. We will discuss some potential major problems that can spoil an experiment's findings.

Table 6.8

One-Factor, Two-Level Planned Change Study

Factor: Type of Workshop

JS Workshop	CM Workshop
$1.30	$1.25
$1.35	$1.26
$1.10	$1.43
$1.15	$1.03
$1.02	$1.10

Dependent variable: Reduction in unit labor cost from January to June

The History Effect

Illustrating History   Both the JS and CM groups had similar reductions in unit labor costs. However, suppose that during the six-month experiment the JS groups were given major bonuses for reasons that had nothing to do with the planned change study. Now we cannot be sure what their reductions in labor costs would have been had the JS groups received no bonuses during the experiment. The longer it takes to complete the study, the more likely it is that the **history effect** may occur.

The history effect occurs when a change in the dependent variable is not due to the experimental factor, but an unplanned change that happened during the experimental period.

Minimizing History   The first way to minimize the history effect is to use randomization. Second, we should keep experiments as short as possible. Third, we should avoid running experiments during a period when there will be other major changes. For example, do not start a cost-reduction study when the plant is switching to new production equipment. Finally, we should take frequent measurements on the dependent variable. Instead of just one measurement six months after the workshops, we should take measurements every week or month after introducing the planned change. Then if an unplanned major change does occur, we can determine whether the factor we varied appeared to be having any effect before the unplanned change happened. Showing that the JS groups' unit labor costs were already decreasing before they received their bonuses would probably rule out the bonus as the reason.

We can also determine whether there was a history effect by including *control groups* in the study. Control groups are work groups that receive no treatment—workshop, in this case. We would expect the control groups to experience no change in unit labor cost since they did not receive a planned change. However, if they showed a large reduction in unit labor cost, then history has affected the results. The experiment is flawed!

Diffusion of Treatment

Illustrating Diffusion of Treatment   Suppose that members of the JS and CM groups tell each other what they have learned in their workshops. Now both groups have received the same factor level, or treatment. That may explain why the JS and

CM groups had similar reductions in unit labor costs. **Diffusion of treatment** has ruined the experiment!

Minimizing Diffusion of Treatment   Ask members of the experimental groups not to talk with one another. Explain to them the need to maintain the purity of each factor level. If that does not work, physically separate the groups so they cannot talk to one another. It is critical that the differences between factor levels not be blurred.

Compensatory Rivalry

Illustrating Compensatory Rivalry   Suppose that the JS group members feel that they have been slighted. They wonder why they were not allowed to learn creative methods. In retaliation, they work extra hard to reduce labor costs. Now, the two groups differ in two ways: (1) different treatments and (2) different levels of motivation. We have a flawed experiment! Due to **compensatory rivalry**, the slighted groups may strive to outperform the CM groups. This confounds the impact of the factor level with the level of the groups' motivation.

Minimizing Compensatory Rivalry   First, do not make a public announcement about which groups are assigned to which factor levels. Second, assure all groups that all factor levels are equally worthwhile. Do not allow the groups to view one factor level as inferior. This may be difficult if one factor level really is inferior.

Trivial Changes

Illustrating Trivial Changes   In the COMCEL study the two treatment levels differ significantly from one another. The premise of the JS workshop is that cost savings are achieved through job switching. The premise of the CM workshop is that creativity will help uncover new and innovative cost-saving ideas.

The following example illustrates a trivial change. We are varying car speed (factor) to determine its impact on gas mileage (dependent variable). We set the two factor levels at 20 mph and 21 mph—a **trivial change**. Since the difference is small, we cannot expect major changes in gas mileage. Consider running cars at 20 mph and at 50 mph.

Minimizing Trivial Changes   Be sure to make significant changes between factor levels to give the factor a reasonable chance to show its impact. "Pull apart" the levels of the experimental factor.

However, if we pull apart too far, we run into other problems. Suppose we randomly select people with IQs of 60 and 180 for a study on learning. We certainly have pulled apart the levels of the IQ factor. However, now we have two new problems: (1) finding people with such low and high IQ levels and (2) such people do not represent students in general, whose IQs vary between 110 and 140. Pull apart, but be mindful of the two problems.

Random Error

Illustrating Random Error   From Table 6.8, the reduction in unit labor costs varies among the five teams within the JS treatment level (also among the five teams within the CM workshop). Random error or variation accounts for these differences since all five groups received the same JS treatment. The five values differ because of other factors not included in the study. These include level of worker motivation,

Diffusion of treatment occurs when experimental groups that have received different treatments communicate with one another and thus the differences between factor levels become blurred.

Compensatory rivalry occurs when assignment of subjects to factor levels is made public, and subjects under one factor level believe they have received a second-class treatment.

Trivial changes are differences in the factor levels that are so small that we cannot detect a difference in the dependent variable.

Random error causes the values of the dependent variable to differ within a factor level. Random error is due to the impact of all potential factors not included in the planned change study.

skill level, and differences in workers' ages. There are many other differences among team members. Their net effect accounts for **random error**.

Minimizing Random Error   Randomization tends to *equalize* the impact of extraneous factors over the factor levels. We will demonstrate in Chapter 10 that a multifactor design can reduce the impact of extraneous factors.

Multifactor designs have two or more experimental factors, each at two or more levels. Table 6.9 illustrates the design of a two-factor study with 12 work groups: (1) JS vs. CM workshop and (2) level of worker motivation—low and high. To run this study, Teman must first determine the level of motivation for all groups within the Norcross plant. She would then randomly select six groups with low motivation and six groups with high motivation. She would randomly subdivide each group of six into two sets of three work groups each and randomly assign each set of three low-motivation teams to either the JS or CM treatment. She would do likewise for the two groups of high-motivation teams. The dependent variable remains the reduction in unit labor cost from January to June.

Table 6.9

A Two-Factor Design

Motivation Level	JS Workshop Group	CM Workshop Group
Low	1	3
	5	6
	9	12
High	4	2
	7	8
	11	10

In summary, we must use randomization in planned change studies. Moreover, we must take steps to minimize the history effect, diffusion of treatment, compensatory rivalry, and trivial changes. Such actions result in first-rate planned change studies.

SECTION 6.10 EXERCISES

1. Explain the *pull-apart* principle.

2. Explain what the history effect is. Why is it a threat to the interpretability of an experiment? As a manager how can you control for history?

3. What is random error? Does randomization help to reduce random error?

4. A company is planning to purchase a single word processing package for the entire office. The office manager wants a package that is easy to learn and decides to compare two packages by means of an experiment. The manager selects 20 secretaries from the secretarial pool and randomly assigns ten to learn each package for a period of four hours. At the end of that time all are required to perform the same common word processing functions.
   a. List some factors, other than differences in the word-processing packages, that might affect the outcome of this experiment.
   b. Would these factors ruin the validity of the experiment?
   c. Suggest ways to improve this experiment.

5. A State Patrol identifies ten high-accident locations each month. The patrol wants to demonstrate that a program of selective enforcement is an effective way to reduce accidents. Under this program, a police car is placed at each location. Motorists see the patrol

car and reduce speed. To show the effectiveness of selective enforcement, the total number of accidents from the 10 high-accident locations will be compared before and after the selective enforcement. Evaluate this experiment and suggest ways to improve it.

6.11 ≡ Key Ideas of Data Collection

We conclude this chapter with a set of important data collection ideas.

1. In drawing inferences, we must allow for a margin of error. However, we try to make it as small as practical. Margin of error decreases as sample size increases.
2. For the same level of confidence, different survey sampling designs may produce different margins of error.
3. There is no one best survey sampling *design*. Evaluate the four designs—simple random, stratified random, systematic, and cluster sampling. Select the one with the most advantages and the fewest disadvantages in a given situation.
4. There is no one best survey *method*. Evaluate the three methods—personal interview, telephone interview, and mail questionnaire. Select the most advantageous method.
5. There is no one best *question format*. Select the one that will provide the needed responses.
6. Avoid the most common wording errors (see Section 6.8).
7. Observational studies collect past data and do not generate new data. They are after-the-fact studies and are not experiments.
8. Conducting an experiment means randomly assigning experimental units to different treatment levels, introducing a planned change, and measuring the impact. We must also control for extraneous factors.
9. Control extraneous factors by using randomization and eliminating possible extraneous factors from the experiment. Both approaches ensure that the factor we varied caused the improvement in the product or service, and not some extraneous factor. We call this the RO principle—Ruling Out extraneous factors.
10. We should maximize the potential impact of a factor by pulling apart its levels.
11. We should minimize random error by using multifactor designs.
12. We should control for the history effect, diffusion of treatment, compensatory rivalry, and trivial changes.

COMCEL

Date: October 6, 1994
To: Howard Bright, Norcross Plant Manager
From: Ann Tabor, President
Re: Proposed Employee Morale Survey

I agree that raising the employees' morale is worth doing. But do we have a problem? Is there really a difference between this other company's average morale and ours? Our numbers are based on samples and therefore subject to a margin of error. Calculate the margin of error on past samples to see if our average plus the margin of error meets or exceeds their average morale score. There may be no problem.

SCOPE OF PROBLEM

You suggest interviewing a sample of production workers at the Norcross plant. What about our managerial staff and salaried workers? If we do have a morale problem, does it exist at all plants, among all shifts, and among all employees? Morale scores should be broken down by plant, shift, and employee type to see where we have a problem and where we don't.

PROBLEM CAUSES

If morale scores are lower than they should be, are you sure that the cause is too little participation in decision making? Maybe we give them too much decision-making responsibility, and not enough task support. Aren't there other explanations also, such as differences in training and experience, or physical working conditions?

SURVEY SAMPLING ISSUES

I discussed your memo with Cherian Jain, who is knowledgeable about different sampling designs. Since the morale gap might differ among departments and by type of worker, he recommends using stratified sampling instead of simple random sampling. Stratified sampling is effective when some subgroups are small and might be missed entirely, or when we want to draw a conclusion about a specific subgroup. Also, since we are trying to get honest feelings, perhaps we should use an outside consultant to ensure impartiality. You should also consider a questionnaire mailed to each employee's home by a consulting firm. People often answer sensitive questions more honestly when they are in the privacy of their own homes and no interviewer is present.

THE NEXT STEP

Prepare a final set of recommendations for my review by October 14.

CHAPTER 6 QUESTIONS

1. What are three ways that managers obtain data?

2. Why do managers conduct surveys and run planned change studies? Why aren't all their information needs met by the management information system?

3. Explain margin of error and why it should be as small as possible.

4. Why does margin of error decrease as we increase sample size? Why does margin of error decrease as the variation in the target population decreases?

5. Suggest and defend a sampling frame for a job climate survey for COMCEL's Dallas manufacturing plant. The plant contains hourly, professional, and management personnel.

6. For a touchy subject such as attitude toward the job, what survey method should we use?

7. How are selection and nonresponse errors different?

8. Why doesn't increasing the sample size reduce the chances of selection error?

9. How does using a table of random numbers ensure that we will select a simple random sample?

10. What is wrong with convenience sampling?

11. In your own words, what is stratified random sampling?

12. Explain the logic behind the three rules for selecting the strata sample sizes.

13. When can stratified random sampling produce larger margins of error than simple random sampling?

14. How can a preliminary problem diagnosis help in designing your survey questionnaire?

15. How can the survey results help your final problem diagnosis?

16. What is the purpose of creating data through planned change studies?

17. How do experiments differ from observational studies?

18. Why can't managers always run experiments? That is, why must they resort to observational studies?

19. How can we accomplish the RO principle in planned change studies?

20. Why is the history effect more likely as the length of the planned change study increases?

21. What are the dangers in "pulling apart" an experimental factor—such as a personality or socioeconomic factor—too much?

22. Is compensatory rivalry likely when all treatment groups view their treatments as equally desirable?

23. Why is diffusion of treatment a serious problem in planned change studies?

CHAPTER 6 APPLICATION PROBLEMS

1. A business polling group recently reported that 51% of the respondents favored retaliatory trade barriers for those nations that do not open their countries to American products. The findings are based on a telephone survey with 1,000 senior managers of multinational firms. The margin of error is ±3% and the level of confidence is 95%. Can we conclude at the 95% level of confidence that a majority of senior managers in multinational firms across the United States favor retaliatory trade barriers? Discuss.

2. A marketing manager in charge of telemarketing—phone sales—wants to know the mean number of phone calls her operators make each month. While there is little variation within a month, there is much month-to-month variation. What sampling design would you recommend to estimate the overall mean number of calls made monthly? Explain.

3. Identify the sample and the population in the following situations:
   a. Goal: to study the problem of noise at major airports. You set up monitoring equipment at 10 randomly selected airports in the United States.
   b. Goal: to assess compliance with the revised tax code. You perform detailed tax audits on selected taxpayers' returns.
   c. Goal: to assess how a firm's hourly staff, support personnel, and professionals feel about a flexible benefits package. You send out a survey to selected workers.

4. Do soft-drink consumers prefer Pepsi or Coke? You are to design a one-factor planned change study. Describe the (1) experimental factor, (2) levels, (3) dependent variable, and (4) experimental units.

5. You want to select a simple random sample of eight states for a survey. Below are listed the abbreviations of 50 states in alphabetical order.

AL	AK	AR	AZ	CA	CO	CT	DE	FL	GA
HI	ID	IL	IN	IA	KS	KY	LA	ME	MD
MA	MI	MN	MS	MO	MT	NE	NV	NH	NJ
NM	NY	NC	ND	OH	OK	OR	PA	RI	SC
SD	TN	TX	UT	VT	VA	WA	WV	WI	WY

Let AL = 1, AK = 2, . . . , WY = 50. Select eight states starting with the fifth entry in row 26 of the random numbers table and move across the rows (see Appendix 4).

Use two-digit random numbers; eliminate the last three digits in each group of five digits. What states will be included in your survey?

6. About six months ago a firm installed a computerized inventory management system. The goal was to reduce inventory costs. The manager measured the reduction of inventory costs since the system was installed. Has the manager conducted a planned change study? Why or why not?

 7. A multinational firm has divisions in the United States, Great Britain, Canada, Japan, and Egypt. The CEO wants to survey his workers on a proposed retirement plan. What would you suggest he use as a survey sampling design? What survey method would you recommend? Explain.

 8. Shown are the before-treatment and after-treatment sample means of a study to improve consumer awareness of the attributes of a product such as mineral water. Different groups of consumers were given either the present advertising approach (control group) or the new advertising approach (treatment). The dependent variable is the number of product attributes that a consumer can correctly recall one week after the treatment. Do the study results indicate diffusion of treatment as a potential problem?

Group	Before Measure	After Measure
Control	2	2
Experimental	2	5

 9. A marketing research firm wishes to estimate the number of New Yorkers who prefer the clarity of a new phone to that of a phone made by a major manufacturer. One hundred curious people enter a marketing research booth in a shopping mall and 65 prefer the new phone.
   a. What is the target population in this study?
   b. Did the marketing firm select a simple random sample?
   c. What problems are there in using this type of sampling?

 10. You want to estimate the percentage of defects in a manufacturing plant that has four different production lines. You believe that the percentage varies greatly among the four lines. There is, however, little day-to-day variation within each of the four lines.
   a. What problem might you have if you use simple random sampling?
   b. What survey sampling design is appropriate for this study? Explain.

 11. One hundred thousand families live in the two towns in a county. Town A has 70,000 families and town B has 30,000 families. The chairman of the county commission wants to determine the perceived need for additional fire and police services in the county. He plans to use stratified random sampling with each city as a stratum.
   a. Using stratified sampling means that he believes that each city has very different perceived needs for additional fire safety. Suggest several reasons why this might be so.
   b. The total sample size will be 1,000 families. What size sample should he take from each city? Assume that the variability of perceived need for additional fire and police services is similar in both towns. Explain.

 12. You are running a planned change study on the impact of two leadership styles on worker productivity. Explain how you should use randomization in your study.

 13. You take a simple random sample of 10 people from a population. Your goal is to estimate the mean weight of the population from the sample data listed below.

	Men	Women
Sample Size	2	8
Weight (pounds)	170	120

The mean weight (weighted average) of the sample is 130 pounds. That seems too low for the target population. What might account for the simple random sample average weight being very different from the average weight of the population?

14. Shown are the before and after sample means from a study to improve consumer awareness of the attributes of a product such as mineral water. Different groups of consumers were given either the present advertising approach (control group) or the new advertising approach (treatment). The dependent variable is the number of product attributes that a consumer can correctly recall one week after the treatment. Do the study results indicate that the history effect is a potential problem?

Group	Before Measure	After Measure
Control	2	4.5
Experimental	2	5

15. You wish to estimate the number of coding errors made by a new data entry clerk. You suspect that at first he will make many mistakes, but over time, he will improve. The target population is 5,000 data entries. You cannot check them all, so you decide to take a sample.
   a. Why could simple random sampling generate a very poor estimate? Explain.
   b. What survey sampling design of the four presented is best at accurately estimating the number of data entry errors made by the clerk since he started?

16. An auditor selects a simple random sample from 500 accounts to check for compliance with audit control procedures and to verify the actual dollar amount in the accounts. Below are the data.

Account	Amount ($)	Compliance	Account	Amount ($)	Compliance
10	248	Yes	111	413	Yes
34	94	Yes	234	66	Yes
66	168	No	345	134	Yes
67	233	Yes	377	170	No
99	45	No	455	100	Yes

   a. Compute the sample mean dollar amount and the sample proportion of accounts in compliance.
   b. Why aren't the sample and population means expected to be the same, and why aren't the sample and population proportions expected to be the same?

17. In the legal case of *Amstar Corp. v. Domino's Pizza Inc.* (5th Circuit, 1980), Amstar Corp., producers of Domino sugar, attempted to show that the public might believe that Domino's Pizza was related to their product line. They wanted Domino's Pizza to change its name.
   Amstar Corp. interviewed females who were responsible for making food purchases for their households. Each respondent was shown a Domino's Pizza box and asked if she believed the company that made the pizza made any other products. If she answered yes, she was asked what other products were made by the company. Seventy-one percent of those answering the second question said sugar.
   The 5th Circuit rejected Amstar's survey and said that it was seriously flawed. From a target population and sampling frame perspective, what is one major flaw in the study?

18. The five most common reasons why firms acquire other firms are:

Synergy	To increase the value of the combined enterprises
Tax considerations	To shelter the income of the acquiring firm
Assets	To obtain assets whose replacement value is higher than their market value
Diversification	To stabilize a firm's earning stream
Control	To gain control of the firm

You wish to determine which reasons have been the prime motivators for acquisitions that cost at least $100 million in the past five years. Discuss how you would select a simple random sample.

 19. Does providing customer feedback on car service improve a car dealer's level of service? You are to design a one-factor planned change study. Describe the (1) experimental factor, (2) levels, (3) dependent variable, and (4) experimental units.

 20. In the case of *Brooks Shoe Manufacturing Co. v. Suave Shoe Corp.* (S.D. Fla., 1981), Brooks sued Suave Shoe for infringement of its common law trademark—a **V** logo on its high-performance track shoes. Brooks shoes, a major brand name, sold for $25 and Suave shoes, a no-brand name, sold for $8. Brooks conducted a survey of track shoe owners and asked a series of questions to determine whether Suave's **V** logo had caused consumers to think the shoes they were buying were Brooks running shoes. The Court rejected Brooks's argument, in part, because of improperly worded survey questions.

a. Below are two forms of the same question. Version 2 is properly written and version 1 is improperly written. Why?

1. I am going to hand you a shoe. Please tell me what brand you think it is.
2. I am going to hand you a shoe. Do you know who makes or sells it?

b. Later in the survey, the following question was asked. What is improper about this question?

How long have you known about Brooks running shoes?

REFERENCES

Dillman, Don A. *Mail and Telephone Surveys: The Total Design Method.* New York: John Wiley & Sons, 1978.

Ramakrishna, H., and H. Brightman. "The Fact Net Model: A Diagnostic Approach." *Interfaces* 16, no. 6 (November–December 1986): 86–94.

Roll, C., Jr., and A. Cantril. *Polls—Their Use and Misuses in Politics.* New York: Basic Books, 1972.

Scheaffer, Richard, William Mendenhall, and Lyman Ott. *Elementary Survey Sampling.* Boston: Duxbury Press, 1986.

MAKING INFERENCES ABOUT ONE POPULATION

7.1   Problem solving and statistical inferences
7.2   The distribution of the sample mean
        Mean and standard error of a sampling
          distribution of $\bar{x}$
        The Central Limit Theorem
7.3   Confidence intervals on an unknown
        population mean
        t-based confidence intervals
        Setting the level of confidence
        The finite population correction factor
        Confidence intervals and time-ordered data
7.4   One-sided confidence intervals on an unknown
        population mean
7.5   Stratified random sampling
        Impact of using simple random sampling
7.6   Confidence intervals on an unknown
        population proportion
        Distribution of the sample proportion
        Estimated standard error of the proportion

7.7   Determining the sample size
        Two-sided interval on an unknown
          population mean
        Two-sided interval on an unknown
          population proportion
7.8   Sign test-based nonparametric confidence
        interval for an unknown population median
        Constructing approximate 95% confidence
          intervals
        Assumptions for confidence intervals on the
          population mean and median
        Confidence intervals on the mean in the
          presence of outliers
7.9   Confidence intervals on an unknown
        population variance and standard deviation
        The chi-square distribution
7.10 Key ideas and overview
Appendix: Statistical Software

CHAPTER OUTLINE

COMCEL   INTEROFFICE
         COMMUNICATION

Date: July 21, 1994
  To: Nat Gordon, V.P. of Manufacturing
From: Ann Tabor, CEO
  Re: Improving Quality and Reducing Breakdowns

The quality-control department notified me that our mobile
phones, on the average, experience a breakdown after 2,000
hours of service. According to published industry reports,
the mean time-to-failure for phones from all manufacturers
is 2,500 hours. I am not satisfied with our phones' performance.

I am authorizing you to set up a project team to improve
phone performance. The project team will report directly to
you. I want personnel from quality control, engineering, and
manufacturing on the team. Improving time-to-failure has
the highest priority, so assign your best people to the team.
I won't be satisfied unless our time-to-failure exceeds 2,750
hours. If you need additional support personnel, let me
know. I want the team's report by the end of March.

7.1 Problem Solving and Statistical Inferences

Managers use descriptive statistics to build mental models, sense and understand problems and opportunities, seek root causes, make decisions, and assess potential impacts. They do this by asking the right questions. For example:

What is our customers' mean income level?

What is the median number of days for parts to arrive from a vendor?

What proportion of the firm's employees favor a flex-time system?

What is the variability in the impact resistances of plastic TV cabinets made in the Springfield plant?

Managers realize it would be too costly to survey all customers, review all shipping records, interview all employees, or test all TV cabinets in order to answer their questions. As we learned from Chapter 6, cost is a key factor in survey considerations. We can, however, take a simple random sample from each target population and compute descriptive statistics. However, the sample mean, median, proportion, or standard deviation is not target population's mean, median, proportion, or standard deviation. In this chapter we will use descriptive statistics and the method of confidence intervals to *estimate* target population parameters. In short, we will make *statistical inferences*. By the end of the section you should be able to:

1. distinguish between a target population and a sample;
2. distinguish between a population parameter and a sample statistic; and
3. explain what the population standard deviation really measures.

We begin with some very important definitions.

A *target population* is the entire group of elements about which we want information. An element is an object or subject on which we take a measurement. For example, all the employees in a firm and the television cabinets produced in a plant are target populations. An element would be a *particular* employee (subject) or TV cabinet.*

A *sample* is a part of the target population. We gain knowledge about the population from the sample. For example, a sample might be the salaries of 100 randomly selected employees or impact resistance measurements of 50 randomly selected TV cabinets.

A *population parameter* is a numerical measure that describes the target population. It could be the mean, median, proportion, or variance. Population parameters are fixed, or constant, values and are generally unknown. For example, population parameters would be the actual proportion of all employees who favor flex-time or the variance in impact resistances of all plastic TV cabinets.

---

* The term *population* is often used to refer to the set of measurements themselves, in addition to the entire set of elements on which the measurements are taken. When we think of a population as a set of measurements, we can refer to a population distribution of ages or a population distribution of salaries for the same target population of employees (elements).

A *sample statistic* is computed after obtaining the sample data. We use a sample statistic to *estimate* an unknown population parameter. While the population parameter is a constant value, a sample statistic will vary from sample to sample. For example, sample statistics are the sample proportion of the 100 employees who favor flex-time or the sample standard deviation of impact resistances of 50 TV cabinets. A different random sample of 100 employees or a different sample of 50 TV sets would most likely produce a different sample proportion and a different sample standard deviation.

It is important to remember the distinction that statistics describe samples and parameters describe populations. We estimate population parameters from sample statistics using statistical inference methods.

Statistical inferences permit us to assign a level of confidence that the inference is correct and to compute a margin of error. For example, we might be 95% confident that the mean income level of all our customers (target population) is $35,500 ± $5,000. The $5,000 figure is the margin of error (see Chapter 6). Margin of error measures the possible difference between the sample statistic and the population parameter.

Managers want small margins of error. Two effective methods are (1) to increase the sample size and (2) to select the proper sampling design. Recall from Chapter 6 that increasing a population standard deviation increases the margin of error. Unfortunately, there is little we can do to reduce a population standard deviation in the short run.

The population standard deviation measures the spread in the values within a population. The spread is not due to sampling mistakes made during data collection. Rather, it is due to inherent variability. Suppose we tested the impact resistance of every plastic TV cabinet. Should we expect all cabinets to have the same impact resistance? Since there are many production factors that the firm cannot totally control, impact resistances will vary. For example, different assemblers worked on the cabinets at different times of the day. Some assemblers may have tired, and that affected the impact resistance. The raw material may have varied slightly among cabinets. If we could eliminate all sources of variability, the population standard deviation would be zero. In practice, this is impossible.

In summary, sample statistics describe a sample and population parameters describe a population. We use descriptive statistics and statistical inference methods to estimate unknown population parameters.

SECTION 7.1 EXERCISES

1. Explain the difference between a statistic and a parameter.

2. Consider a population of four data values, {1, 2, 3, 4}. The mean of these values is 2.5. The mean of a single sample of size two consisting of {2, 4} is 3. Which of these two means is a parameter and which is a statistic?

3. A marketing research group is hired by a soft drink company to sample the preferences of consumers. The research company selects a random sample of 1,000 members of the general public and finds that 400 preferred brand A.
   a. What is the target population?
   b. What is the population parameter of interest?
   c. What is the sample statistic?

4. A manufacturer wants to estimate the mean dollar loss from breakage resulting from shipping a product from New York to Detroit. As boxes are delivered, one in every 10 boxes is opened, and the dollar value of broken contents is measured. In a sample of 50 boxes the mean dollar loss per box is $10.23.
   a. What is the target population?

   b. What is the population parameter of interest?
   c. What is the sample statistic?

5. List the factors that affect the margin of error.

6. Explain why it is necessary to state a margin of error when estimating a population parameter.

7. An insurance company is about to do a planned change study. From a large group of experienced claims checkers, two groups of 15 are selected. One group will continue checking claims as usual. The other group will work in teams of three and specialize in some part of the claim form. After a period of three weeks, the claims manager intends to compare the mean number of claims checked per day between the two groups to see if specialization improves productivity.
   a. What are the target populations?
   b. What are the population parameters of interest?
   c. What are the sample statistics?

8. You place four new and identical light bulbs into a light fixture. Why is it unlikely that all the bulbs burn out at the same time? What statistical measure would tell you how far apart the burnouts might be?

9. Federal Express wants to estimate the mean delivery time for its overnight parcel delivery. It selects a simple random sample of 100 parcels and finds that the mean delivery time is 15.5 hours.
   a. What is the target population?
   b. What is the population parameter of interest?
   c. What is the sample?
   d. What is the sample statistic?

10. In acceptance sampling a firm selects a random sample from an incoming lot and inspects it. If the sample has fewer than a predetermined number of defective pieces, the firm accepts the lot, otherwise it rejects it. The vendor must then supply a replacement shipment. The purpose of acceptance sampling is to keep lots with high percentages of defective pieces from entering the plant.

    COMCEL uses MIL-STD-105D acceptance sampling plans (see Chapter 15). For lot sizes of between 1,201 and 3,200 it selects 125 pieces, and if 3 or less are found to be defective, they accept the lot. That is, the percentage of defective pieces in the sample is acceptably low.
    a. What is the target population?
    b. What is the population parameter of interest?
    c. What is the sample?
    d. What is the sample statistic?
    e. Why are the sample statistic and the population parameter likely to differ?

11. In control charting a COMCEL operator selects a sample of five handsets during the shift and records their mean tensile strength (pressure needed to crack phone) in pounds per square inch. She then plots the mean on a line graph that records the shift on the horizontal axis and the mean tensile strength on the vertical axis (see Chapter 15). When a sample mean falls outside the 3-sigma limits, she must stop the production process and correct the causes for the outlier observation.
    a. What is the target population?
    b. What is the population parameter of interest?
    c. What is the sample?
    d. What is the sample statistic?
    e. Why are the sample statistic and the population parameter likely to differ?

12. Practor and Gimble wants to know the percentage of the target audience that will purchase its new snack treat priced at $1.09. In a market research study, they select 1,500 potential customers and find that 300 would purchase the product.
    a. What is the population parameter of interest?
    b. What is the sample statistic?
    c. Why are the sample statistic and the population parameter likely to differ?

13. Brand insistence means the customer considers only one brand of a product category acceptable. Ads such as the following seek to create brand insistence—"If it doesn't say

Fiskars on the blade, it doesn't say much for the scissors." Fiskars Manufacturing conducts a survey of 500 buyers and finds that 150 insist on purchasing a Fiskars scissor.
   a. What is the target population?
   b. What is the population parameter of interest?
   c. What is the sample?
   d. What is the sample statistic?
   e. Why are the sample statistic and the population parameter likely to differ?

14. Engel's law states that as income increases, the percentage spent on (1) food will decrease, (2) housing will remain constant, and (3) all other categories, including amount saved, will increase. A sample of 500 families was selected from each income group shown below, and the average percentage spent on food, housing, and other items was determined.

	Under $20,000	$20,000–$39,999	$40,000–$60,000
Food	15.6%	9.9%	7.1%
Housing	24.0%	24.5%	23.7%
Other	60.4%	65.6%	69.2%

   a. How many populations are suggested by this data?
   b. What are the population parameters of interest?
   c. What are the sample statistics?
   d. Why are the sample statistics and the population parameters likely to differ?

15. Marketers are interested in market density which is the number of people per square mile who are potential customers for the marketer's offering. Coca-Cola wants to know the market density of Hispanics in San Antonio. They divide San Antonio into square-mile tracts on a map and randomly select five of these tracts. They find a total of 10,000 Hispanics in the five square-mile tracts. Thus the sample market density is 2,000 Hispanics per square mile.
   a. What is the population parameter of interest?
   b. What is the sample statistic?
   c. Why are the sample statistic and the population parameter likely to differ?

16. Consider a target population of 10,000 phone handsets. COMCEL has set a desired mean tensile strength (pressure needed to crack phone) of 4,750 pounds per square inch (ppsi). This has been achieved; the mean tensile strength of the population is very close to 4,750 ppsi.
   a. If the population standard deviation were zero, what would this mean in terms of the tensile strengths of the 10,000 phones?
   b. Explain how one could actually compute the standard deviation in tensile strength of the 10,000 phones.
   c. Is it likely that the population standard deviation would equal zero? Explain.
   d. Why would COMCEL want to reduce the population standard deviation (also called process variation) in tensile strength?
   e. Suggest several ways that COMCEL could reduce the population standard deviation in the long run. Are they costly?

17. Consider a target population of 300,000 Goodyear Eagle radial tires. Goodyear wants to know the mean tire life before the tire tread is below Federal safety standards.
   a. Describe how you would compute the population standard deviation in tire life.
   b. Is it likely to equal zero? Why?
   c. Why might Goodyear want to increase the population mean tire life and reduce its population standard deviation?
   d. Explain why it is not practical to determine with absolute certainty the population mean and standard deviation in tire life.
   e. To estimate both the population mean and standard deviation, Goodyear will take a sample of 1,500 tires and run them until failure. What are the population parameters of interest?
   f. What are the sample statistics?
   g. Why are the sample statistics and population parameters likely to differ?

7.2 The Distribution of the Sample Mean

Suppose we take a random sample of 10 families and determine the sample mean income. Because this is one of many possible samples, the sample mean, $\bar{x}$ will probably not equal the population mean, μ. The two means will differ because of variation within the population and because the composition of samples varies. However, most sample means will be close to the population mean because of the properties of the *distribution of the sample mean* (sampling distribution of $\bar{x}$).

By the end of this section you should be able to:

1. distinguish between a population distribution, a sample distribution, and a sampling distribution;
2. construct a sampling distribution for the mean and explain what it means;
3. distinguish between the mean and standard deviation of (1) a population distribution, (2) a sample distribution, and (3) the distribution of the sample mean;
4. explain why the standard deviation of the sampling distribution, or standard error, must be smaller than the standard deviation of the population; and
5. explain how the parameters of the sampling distribution—the mean and especially the standard error—are useful in estimating an unknown population mean;
6. explain why the distribution of the sample mean will be nearly normally distributed, provided the sample size is sufficiently large.

Mean and Standard Error of a Sampling Distribution of $\bar{x}$

Table 7.1 contains income data for a population of three families. Although the population size is unrealistically small, it will help accomplish objectives 1–5.

Table 7.1

Annual Incomes for a Population of Three Families (in tens of thousands)

$4.0	$3.0	$8.0

We begin by computing the population mean and standard deviation. The population mean income is

$$\mu = \frac{\sum_i x_i}{N} \tag{7.1}$$

where x_i represents *all* the family incomes in the population
N represents the population size.

For the population data in Table 7.1, we calculate

$$\mu = \frac{(\$4 + \$3 + \$8)}{3} = \$5 \text{ or } \$50{,}000$$

The population standard deviation is

$$\sigma = \sqrt{\frac{\sum_i (x_i - \mu)^2}{N}} \tag{7.2}$$

where x_i represents *all* the family incomes in the population

N represents the population size

μ represents the population mean.

Note that the denominator in expression (7.2) is N. When computing the *sample* standard deviation, the denominator is $n - 1$, where n represents the sample size taken from the population. For the population data in Table 7.1, we calculate

$$\sigma = \sqrt{\frac{(4 - 5)^2 + (3 - 5)^2 + (8 - 5)^2}{3}}$$

$$= \$2.16 \text{ or } \$21,600$$

Next we compute a sample mean and standard deviation based on one sample of size two families—#1 and #3—from the population in Table 7.1. The sample mean income for the two families is

$$\bar{x} = \frac{\sum_i x_i}{n} \tag{7.3}$$

where x_i represents the family incomes in the *sample*

n represents the sample size or number of observations.

For the sample data, we calculate

$$\bar{x} = \frac{(\$4 + \$8)}{2} = \$6 \text{ or } \$60,000$$

Note that the sample mean, $\bar{x}$, does not equal the population mean, μ. But the two means are close.

In Chapter 2 we used expression (2.2) to compute the sample standard deviation. We reproduce it here. The sample standard deviation is

$$s = \sqrt{\frac{\sum_i (x_i - \bar{x})^2}{(n - 1)}} \tag{7.4}$$

where x_i represents the family incomes in the *sample*

n represents the sample size

$\bar{x}$ represents the sample mean.

For the sample data, we calculate

$$s = \sqrt{\frac{(4 - 6)^2 + (8 - 6)^2}{(2 - 1)}} = \$2.828 \text{ or } \$28,280$$

Note that the sample standard deviation, s, does not equal the population standard deviation, σ. But the two standard deviations are close.

Instead of taking one sample of size two, suppose we took *all possible samples of size two with replacement* from the population and computed the sample means. That would give us a distribution of the sample mean for samples of size 2. Sampling with replacement produces a sampling distribution that has the same properties as those computed from large populations. Table 7.2 displays all the possible sample means, the sampling distribution.

The sampling distribution consists of nine sample means. The *overall* mean of the nine sample means is the mean of the sampling distribution, $\mu_{\bar{x}}$.

We can now compute the mean of the sampling distribution in Table 7.2. Do you think it will be smaller, larger, or the same as the population mean, μ, for the three families? Please think about it before reading on.

Table 7.2
List of Sample Means for Samples of Size Two

Sample	Sample Means
4,3	3.5
4,8	6.0
3,8	5.5
4,4	4.0
3,3	3.0
8,8	8.0
3,4	3.5
8,4	6.0
8,3	5.5

We use expression (7.5) to compute the mean of the distribution of the sample mean for samples of size two.

$$\mu_{\bar{x}} = \frac{\sum_i \bar{x}_i}{K} \tag{7.5}$$

where $\bar{x}_i$ represents *all possible* sample mean incomes
K represents the number of possible sample means in the sampling distribution.

For the sampling distribution data in Table 7.2, we calculate

$$\mu_{\bar{x}} = \frac{(3.5 + 6.0 + 5.5 + \cdots + 3.5 + 6.0 + 5.5)}{9} = \$5$$

Note the denominator is the total number of possible samples—not the population size, $N = 3$.

LESSON 1   The mean of any distribution of the sample mean is the same as the mean of the population from which it was derived. That is,

$$\mu_{\bar{x}} = \mu$$

The standard deviation of the sampling distribution, $\sigma_{\bar{x}}$ (sigma sub-$\bar{x}$), measures the spread of the nine sample means around its mean, the mean of the sampling distribution. It is called the *standard error of the mean.* Will the standard error be larger, smaller, or the same as the population standard deviation of $\$2.16$ (or $\$21,600$)? This brings us to the second lesson, which holds true for all sampling distributions.

LESSON 2   The standard error of the mean, $\sigma_{\bar{x}}$, is smaller than the standard deviation of the population, σ.

Now we compute the standard error of the mean, the standard deviation of the sampling distribution, for the sample means found in Table 7.2. The standard error of the mean is

$$\sigma_{\bar{x}} = \sqrt{\frac{\sum_i (\bar{x}_i - \mu_{\bar{x}})^2}{K}} \tag{7.6}$$

where $\bar{x}_i$ represents *all possible* sample mean incomes
K represents the number of possible sample means in the sampling distribution.
$\mu_{\bar{x}}$ represents the mean of the sampling distribution.

For the sampling distribution data in Table 7.2, we calculate

$$\sigma_{\bar{x}} = \sqrt{\frac{(3.5 - 5.0)^2 + (6.0 - 5.0)^2 + \cdots + (5.5 - 5.0)^2}{9}} = \$1.527$$

Note that the standard error is smaller than the standard deviation of the population, $\sigma = \$2.16$. What does this mean?

The variation among the three family incomes is greater than the variation among the nine sample mean incomes. In short, the nine sample mean incomes are relatively close to one another and to the population mean. Remember, if the standard error were zero, then all nine sample means would be the same and would equal the mean of the sampling distribution.

Expression (7.7) represents the relationship between the population standard deviation and the standard error.

$$\sigma_{\bar{x}} = \frac{\sigma}{\sqrt{n}} \tag{7.7}$$

where n is the sample size taken from the population
σ is the population standard deviation.

For the sampling distribution in Table 7.2, we can use expression (7.7) to compute the standard error. It will be the same as computed earlier from expression (7.6)—namely, $\$1.527$.

$$\sigma_{\bar{x}} = \frac{\$2.16}{\sqrt{2}} = \$1.527$$

This brings us to the third lesson.

LESSON 3   The standard error of the mean decreases as the sample size, n, increases.

The sample size, n, is in the denominator of expression (7.7). One way to reduce the size of the standard error is to increase the sample size. As n increases, the standard error decreases. As the standard error decreases, all sample means tend to move closer to the population mean.

Let us be clear on one point! Managers *never* construct a sampling distribution. This would require taking all possible samples of size "n" from a population. For a realistic population size, there would be an extremely large number of possible samples. Yet knowing the properties of the sampling distribution will help us estimate an unknown population mean.

To estimate an unknown population mean, suppose you have the following two choices.

1. Take *one* sample of size 3 or
2. Take *one* sample of size 300.

Cost considerations aside, you would take the larger sample. How does this choice relate to the properties of the sampling distribution? These focused questions will help:

1. If you did take all possible samples of size three and all possible samples of size 300, what would the means of the two sampling distributions equal?

   From Lesson 1, they would both equal the unknown population mean, the parameter you are trying to estimate.

2. Why is a sample mean based on 300 observations *more likely* to be closer to the unknown population mean? How can this be explained in terms of the standard error of the mean?

   From Lesson 3, the standard error decreases as you increase the sample size from 3 to 300. Most sample means based on samples of size 300 will be close to the unknown population mean. A sample mean based on only three observations could still be very far from the unknown population mean.

   In summary, we should take the largest sample size we can afford. We first learned that larger samples reduce the margin of error (see Section 6.2). Now we know the reason. As we increase the sample size, the standard error gets smaller.

The Central Limit Theorem

We know the mean and standard deviation of the distribution of sample means. We must also know the shape of the distribution in order to calculate probabilities and margins of error. The shape of a sampling distribution depends on the shape of the population and the size of the sample selected.

(1) If the population is normally distributed, then the distribution of the sample mean is normally distributed, regardless of the size of the sample selected.

(2) If the population is not normally distributed, then the *central limit theorem* tells us that the distribution of the sample mean will be near-normal as long as the size of the sample drawn is sufficiently large.

The importance of the central limit theorem cannot be overstated. It provides the foundation for literally the remainder of the statistical methods in this text.

We demonstrate this theorem with a small population, the income of 100 families in an apartment complex. Table 7.3 contains the 100 family incomes. The incomes range between $20,000 and $60,000. Based on the COMSTAT UNGROUPED tool, the population mean income, μ, is $37,711 and the population standard deviation, σ, is $11,485.

The population histogram for the 100 family incomes appears in Figure 7.1. One thing is clear—the distribution is not normal-shaped.

Table 7.3

Incomes for a Population of 100 Families
(in thousands)

1	$43.48	26	$40.89	51	$57.17	76	$43.68
2	28.53	27	32.33	52	45.70	77	42.88
3	29.06	28	39.80	53	28.76	78	24.54
4	33.57	29	24.92	54	44.18	79	48.69
5	52.08	30	44.39	55	30.20	80	27.61
6	58.51	31	47.93	56	22.82	81	34.20
7	36.30	32	26.74	57	52.26	82	29.07
8	20.83	33	53.49	58	20.08	83	43.48
9	30.88	34	31.16	59	21.41	84	34.13
10	51.72	35	57.86	60	37.98	85	31.66
11	59.03	36	38.06	61	35.31	86	26.79
12	24.77	37	49.61	62	21.90	87	47.96
13	28.34	38	59.74	63	26.53	88	41.41
14	50.96	39	39.29	64	30.57	89	54.60
15	39.58	40	52.40	65	25.54	90	24.98
16	38.29	41	28.02	66	26.31	91	25.62
17	24.28	42	20.98	67	40.56	92	32.04
18	40.30	43	32.72	68	22.74	93	51.62
19	50.62	44	30.06	69	24.57	94	40.96
20	50.25	45	43.51	70	58.43	95	30.02
21	27.85	46	25.94	71	30.02	96	28.32
22	41.38	47	42.03	72	32.45	97	35.72
23	47.82	48	20.26	73	53.92	98	57.06
24	22.56	49	51.93	74	22.27	99	57.33
25	39.52	50	36.84	75	55.25	100	48.34

FIGURE 7.1   Histogram for a Population of 100 Family Incomes

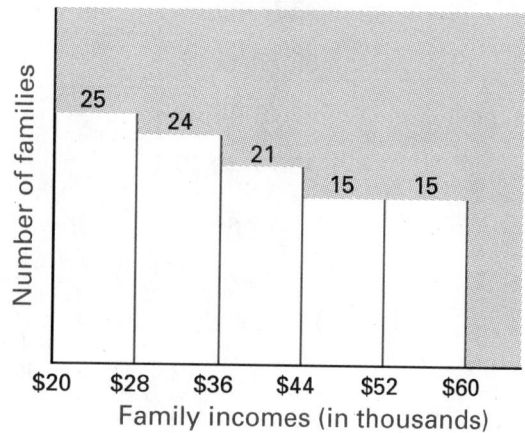

Figure 7.2 is a histogram of several hundred sample means for samples of size 3 from the population of 100 families. We used the CENTRAL LIMIT THEOREM Tool of the COMSTAT software package to develop the histogram. The exercises at the section's end illustrate the input screens for this tool.

Figure 7.2 illustrates an approximate distribution of the sample mean for samples of size 3.[*] It is a sampling distribution because we took several hundred samples of size 3 from the population of 100 families and computed the sample means. It is a distribution because Figure 7.2 shows the values obtained for the sample means, $\bar{x}$, together with their associated probabilities.

We again used the CENTRAL LIMIT THEOREM tool to take several hundred samples of size 15 (rather than of size 3) and computed the sample means. Before displaying the distribution of the sample mean, we present the data for one of the sample means. This will illustrate the difference between a *sample distribution* (a distribution of one sample of size 15) and the *distribution of the sample mean* for samples of size 15. The former is a distribution of 15 observations. The latter is theoretically a distribution of the sample means for all possible samples of size 15.

$25,565	$58,506	$37,824
51,010	42,213	38,500
34,600	47,810	54,490
45,500	22,143	30,654
26,746	29,789	22,546

The sample mean and standard deviation are

$$\bar{x} = \$37,859$$
$$s = \$11,760$$

FIGURE 7.2   Approximate Distribution of the Sample Mean for $n = 3$

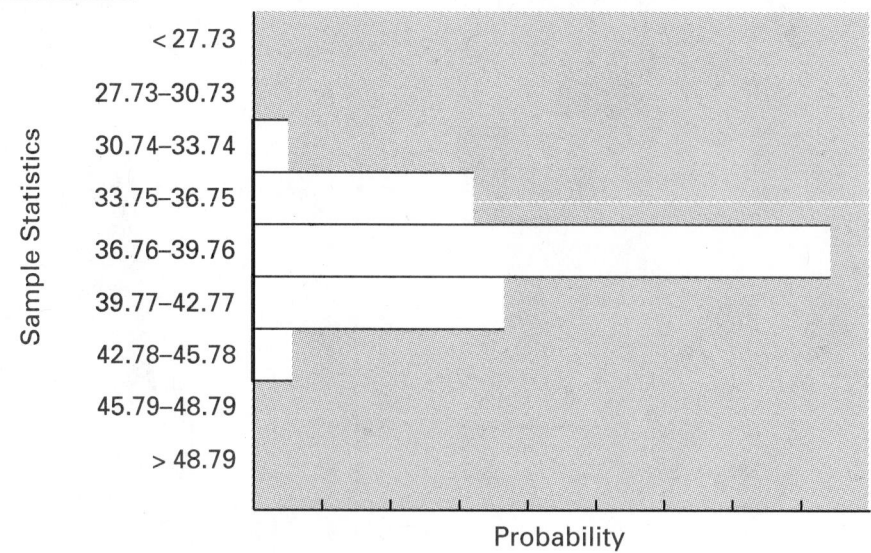

---

[*] To be a true sampling distribution of the mean, *all* possible samples of size 3 must be taken. Due to computer and time constraints, COMSTAT only takes several hundred samples. Thus Figure 7.2 is an *approximate* sampling distribution of the mean.

FIGURE 7.3   Histogram for a Sample of 15 Family Incomes

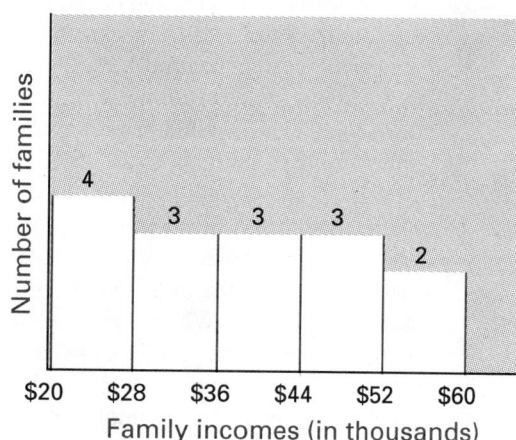

Figure 7.3 shows the histogram of the 15 observations. The shape of the histogram resembles that of the population and is *not* bell-shaped. Yet the distribution of the sample mean will be nearly bell-shaped.

Figure 7.4 shows the histogram for the approximate distribution of the sample mean for samples of size 15.

How do the shapes of the approximate sampling distributions of the mean in Figures 7.2 and 7.4 compare to the population distribution in Figure 7.1? The population histogram is definitely not a normal curve. Yet notice how the shape of the approximate sampling distributions of the mean become more normal as the sample size increases from 3 to 15. For samples of size 30 or more, the distribution of the sample mean will become more normal-shaped.

FIGURE 7.4   Approximate Distribution of the Sample Mean for $n = 15$

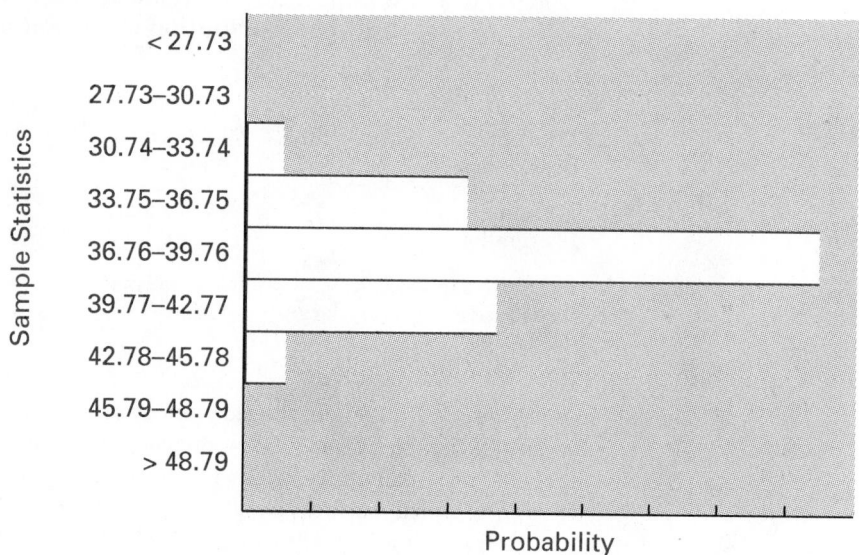

The central limit theorem is central because it deals with the sample mean, which is a measure of the center. It is a limit theorem because it describes what happens to the shape of the distribution of sample means as the sample size increases (from samples of size 3 to 15 to 30 or more).

Why does the central limit theorem work? Why does the shape of the distribution of the sample mean become more normal as we increase the sample size from three to 15 and beyond? From Figure 7.4, a sample of size 15 is unlikely to include only families with incomes in the $20,000 to $28,000 class. A sample of size 15 that contains families with incomes in the $20,000 to $28,000 range is also likely to have several families with incomes in the $52,000 to $60,000 range. This was certainly true for the sample distribution of 15 income values shown above. Thus, many sample means will be in the mid- to upper-$30,000 range (note that $\bar{x}$ was $37,859 for one sample of size 15). We call this the "averaging effect." High incomes tend to balance out low incomes, and a sample mean falls in the middle of the two income extremes. The further we move away in either direction from the population mean, the fewer the sample means. For a sample mean to equal $32,000, all 15 families must have relatively low incomes. But this will only rarely happen (see the one star in the $30,730 to $33,739 class in Figure 7.4).

In other words, as we increase the sample size, most of the sample means will fall near the center of the distribution of the sample mean. The further we move above or below the center, the fewer the sample means. That is a description of a near-normal curve. The central limit theorem works because of the "averaging effect."

This brings us to the fourth lesson.

LESSON 4   If the population is normal or the sample size is sufficiently large, say greater than 30, the distribution of the sample mean will be near-normal. We will be able to use the standard normal table to compute normal probabilities for sample means.

We conclude this section with Table 7.4, which summarizes the important lessons. We constructed the table using the population of 100 family incomes.

Table 7.4

Properties of a Population Distribution, a Distribution of a Sample, and the Distribution of the Sample Mean

	Size	Shape	Mean	Standard Deviation
The Population Distribution	$N = 100$	Not normal (Figure 7.1)	$\mu = \$37,711$	$\sigma = \$11,485$
A Sample Distribution	$n = 15$	Not normal (Figure 7.3)	$\bar{x} = \$37,859$	$s = \$11,760$
The Sampling Distribution for $n = 15$	$K =$ very large	Near-normal (Figure 7.4)	$\mu_{\bar{x}} = \$37,711$	$\sigma_{\bar{x}} = \sigma/\sqrt{n}$ $11,485/\sqrt{15}$ $= \$2,965$

For the last time, note that the standard error of $2,965 is less than the population standard deviation, $11,485. What this means is that *any* sample mean based on 15 observations is likely to be relatively close to the population mean which is always unknown in typical business populations. We could further reduce the standard error to $1,624 by taking a sample of size 50, $11,485/ \sqrt{50}$. We will use the properties of the distribution of the sample mean in the next section when the population mean and standard deviation are *not* known.

SECTION 7.2 EXERCISES

1. Consider the population of data values {2, 4, 6}. Suppose we select one item, write down the number, and replace it so it can be drawn again. The list of all possible samples of size $n = 2$ with replacement is shown here:

2,2	4,2	6,2
2,4	4,4	6,4
2,6	4,6	6,6

    a. Find the population mean, μ.
    b. Find the population standard deviation, σ.
    c. Find the means of the nine samples and the mean of the means, $\mu_{\bar{x}}$.
    d. Find the standard deviation of the sample means.
    e. What is the relationship between the population mean and the mean of the means?
    f. Show that the standard error of the sample mean is found by dividing the population standard deviation by the square root of the sample size.

2. Three distributions are involved in any inference. Refer to Exercise 1 and state the sizes of the population, the sampling distribution, and any sample distribution.

3. All distributions have means, and most distributions have standard deviations. Complete the table below by writing the symbol for each (please do not refer to the book).

	Mean	Standard Deviation
The Population Distribution	_____	_____
The Sampling Distribution	_____	_____
A Sample Distribution	_____	_____

4. A population consists of 100,000 consumers whose income we wish to estimate. Explain to a marketing manager:
    a. How to compute the mean and standard deviation of the population. How costly and time consuming would it be to determine the population mean and standard deviation? What the symbols are for the population parameters.
    b. How to compute a sample mean and standard deviation. What are the sample statistics' symbols?
    c. How to construct a distribution of the sample mean for samples of size 30. How costly and time consuming would it be to construct a sampling distribution? What are the symbols that represent the mean and standard error of the sampling distribution?

5. Time to complete a project is normally distributed with a mean time of 40 hours and a standard deviation of 16 hours. Using Lessons 1–4:
    a. Determine the mean of the distribution of the sample mean for samples of size 30.
    b. Determine the standard error.
    c. Would the standard error be smaller if a sample of 100 were taken? Why?
    d. Is the distribution of the sample mean normal-shaped? Why?

6. Time to complete a project is not normally distributed with a mean time of 100 hours and a standard deviation of 10 hours. Using Lessons 1–4:
    a. Determine the mean of the distribution of the sample mean for samples of size 40.
    b. Determine the standard error.
    c. Would the standard error be smaller if a sample of 400 were taken? Why?
    d. Is the distribution of the sample mean normal-shaped? Why?

7. Do managers construct a distribution of the sample mean? If not, what use is the sampling distribution concept? That is, what useful information does it provide?

8. Consider a population of phone handsets whose tensile strength measurements in pounds per square inch (ppsi) is not normally distributed. The population mean and standard deviation are known to be 4,750 ppsi and 150 ppsi, respectively.

  a. What are the symbols for the population parameters—mean and standard deviation?

  b. Suppose we took one sample of size 30 and computed the sample mean and standard deviation. Explain how to do this. What are the symbols for the sample mean and standard deviation?

  c. Suppose we conducted a hypothetical, or imaginary, study by taking 100,000 repeated samples of size 30 and computing the sample means. If we plotted the distribution of these sample means, would the distribution be near bell-shaped?

  d. Suppose we computed the mean of the 100,000 sample means. This is the mean of the sampling distribution. What is its symbol? Determine the mean of the sampling distribution.

  e. Would all 100,000 sample means be the same? Why?

  f. What is the symbol for the standard error?

  g. Use expression (7.7) to determine the standard error.

  h. Explain without resorting to expression (7.7) why the standard error must be less than the population standard deviation.

  i. In the real world would we ever know for sure the population mean and standard deviation? Discuss.

9. As the sample size increases, the spread of the sampling distribution, as measured by the standard error, gets smaller. Suppose you selected a simple random sample of size 25 from a population and found that your standard error was too large to suit your needs. What size sample would you have to take the next time in order to cut the standard error in half?

10. The measurements taken on items from an assembly line are normally distributed with a mean of 50.0 cm. Consider the distribution of means based on all samples of size $n = 36$. If the population standard deviation is .5 cm, describe the distribution of the sample mean in terms of shape, measure of central tendency, and measure of dispersion. Draw a picture and label all parts.

11. Refer to Exercise 10. According to the Empirical rule, 68% of all sample means will fall between what two numbers? Approximately 95% of the sample means will fall between what two numbers?

12. A distribution of the sample mean is normally distributed with a mean of 20 pounds and a standard error of 4 pounds. Refer to Section 5.6 (normal distribution) to find:

  a. $P(\bar{x} > 24 \text{ pounds})$

  b. $P(\bar{x} < 19 \text{ pounds})$

  c. the probability that a sample mean selected at random will differ from the population mean by more than 6 pounds in either direction.

13. A radial tire's mileage population distribution is normally distributed with a mean of 52,000 miles and a standard deviation of 3,000 miles. Take one tire from the population. Draw upon Section 5.6 to find:

  a. $P(x > 49,000 \text{ miles})$

  b. $P(x < 47,500 \text{ miles})$

  c. If the population of tire mileage were not normally distributed, could you use the standard normal tables to solve for the probabilities in parts **a–b?** Explain.

  d. We hypothetically take repeated samples of size 900 and plot the sample mean tire mileage. Determine the mean of the sampling distribution.

  e. Determine the standard error.

  Use the information in parts **d–e** to find:

  f. $P(\bar{x} > 52,500 \text{ miles})$

  g. $P(\bar{x} < 50,450 \text{ miles})$

  h. If the population of tire mileage were not normally distributed, could you use the standard normal tables to solve for the probabilities in parts **f–g?** Explain.

14. A parcel weight population distribution is normally distributed with a mean of 35 pounds and a standard deviation of 10 pounds. Take one parcel from the population. Draw upon Section 5.6 to find:

  a. $P(x > 44 \text{ pounds})$

  b. $P(x < 35 \text{ pounds})$

c. If the population of parcel weights were not normally distributed, could you use the standard normal tables to solve for the probabilities in parts **a–b?** Explain.

d. We hypothetically take repeated samples of size 36 and plot the sample mean parcel weights. Determine the mean of the sampling distribution.

e. Determine the standard error.

Use the information in parts **d–e** to find:

f. $P(\bar{x} > 44 \text{ pounds})$

g. $P(\bar{x} < 22.5 \text{ pounds})$

h. If the population of parcel weights were not normally distributed, could you use the standard normal tables to solve for the probabilities in parts **f–g?** Explain.

15. Family incomes in Akron, Ohio, are not normally distributed. The population mean income is \$35,500 and the standard deviation is \$5,000. We select one sample of 100 families and determine the sample mean. Use your knowledge of the normal curve to find:

a. $P(\bar{x} > \$36,500)$

b. $P(\bar{x} < \$34,000)$

c. $P(\$35,000 < \bar{x} < \$35,750)$

d. $P(\bar{x} > \$35,100)$

e. $P(\$35,600 < \bar{x} < \$35,900)$

f. $P(\bar{x} = \$36,112)$

g. If you selected one family, could you compute the following probability? Why? $P(x > \$36,000)$

h. What permits you to use the standard normal table to answer parts **a–e?**

16. Using standard methods, a trained worker can complete a task in 12.0 minutes with a standard deviation of 2.1 minutes. An industrial engineer specializing in time and method studies suggests a new way of completing the task. A sample of 49 trained workers complete the task using the new system in an average of 11.4 minutes.

a. If the new method is no better than the standard method, what is the probability of obtaining a sample mean of 11.4 minutes or less?

b. As manager in charge, would you conclude that the new method is better than the existing method? Explain.

17. Consider a small population of 100 people whose family incomes we wish to know. We select 100 people and record their incomes. We will simulate this using the COMSTAT software to illustrate the properties (shape, mean, dispersion) of the distribution of the sample mean. Do the following steps:

a. Insert software and obtain initial worksheet screen.

b. Type in INCOME in the column A header.

c. Select the RANDOM VARIABLE option.

Insert the following information in the input screen:

DESTINATION	column A
TYPE	Uniform distribution
FIRST	1
NUMBER OF OBS	100
MINIMUM	20000
MAXIMUM	60000

The numbers in column A represent the family incomes of 100 people. Everyone in this population has a family income between \$20,000 and \$60,000.

d. Select the UNGROUPED DATA option.

Insert the following information in the input screen:

SUMMARIZE	column A

Question: Record the population mean and standard deviation in family incomes for the 100 people. Explain what these two terms represent to a nontechnical person. What are the symbols for the two population parameters?

e. Select the GRAPHS option.

Insert the following information in the input screen:

OPTION	frequency histogram
GRAPH	column A
CLASSES	5
WIDTH	10000
LOWER LIMIT	20000

Question: Note the shape of the population of 100 data values. Are the data near bell-shaped?

f. Select the CENTRAL LIMIT THEOREM option.
Insert the following information in the input screen:

POPULATION	column A
NUMBER-POP	100
NUMBER-SAMPLE	30

Note: Each star in the histogram represents a sample mean based on 30 observations taken *without replacement* from the population of 100 family incomes. That means once a family is selected it is removed from the population.

1. Find the mean of the approximate sampling distribution from the output screen.
2. Is it the same as the population mean?
3. What are the symbols for the mean and the standard error of the approximate sampling distribution?
4. Find the standard error from the output screen.
5. Is the standard error the same as the population standard deviation? Why should it be less than the population standard deviation? *Note:* Expression (7.7) does not hold for the example. The expression assumes sampling with replacement.
6. What is the shape of the distribution of the sample mean? Explain in terms of the Central Limit Theorem.

18. Consider a small population of 99 tires that Firerock Tire has tested until the tires have failed to meet Federal mileage safety standards. Firerock records the tire mileage at failure. We will now simulate this with the COMSTAT software to illustrate the properties (shape, mean, dispersion) of the distribution of the sample mean. Do the following steps:
   a. Insert software and obtain initial worksheet screen.
   b. Type in MILES-FAIL in the column A header.
   c. Select the RANDOM VARIABLE option.
   Insert the following information in the input screen:

DESTINATION	column A
TYPE	Uniform distribution
FIRST	1
NUMBER OF OBS	99
MINIMUM	45000
MAXIMUM	49999

The numbers in column A represent the tire life of 99 Firerock tires. All tires failed between 45,000 and 49,999 miles.
   d. Select the UNGROUPED DATA option.
   Insert the following information in the input screen:

SUMMARIZE	column A

Question: Record the mean and standard deviation in mileage for the *population* of 99 tires. Explain what these two terms represent to a nontechnical manager. What are the symbols for the two population parameters?
   e. Select the GRAPHS option.

Insert the following information in the input screen:

OPTION	frequency histogram
GRAPH	column A
CLASSES	5
WIDTH	1000
LOWER LIMIT	45000

Question: Note the shape of the population of 99 data values. Are the data near bell-shaped?

f. Select the CENTRAL LIMIT THEOREM option.
Insert the following information in the input screen:

POPULATION	column A
NUMBER-POP	99
NUMBER-SAMPLE	30

Note: Each star in the histogram represents a sample mean based on 30 data values taken *without replacement* from the population of 99 tires. That means once a tire is selected it is removed from the population.

1. Find the mean of the approximate sampling distribution from the output screen.
2. Is it the same as the population mean?
3. What are the symbols for the mean and the standard error of the approximate sampling distribution?
4. Find the standard error from the output screen.
5. Is the standard error the same as the population standard deviation? Why should it be less than the population standard deviation? *Note:* Expression 7.7 does not hold for the example. The expression assumes sampling with replacement.
6. What is the shape of the distribution of the sample mean? Explain in terms of the Central Limit Theorem.

7.3 ≡ Confidence Intervals on an Unknown Population Mean

While we should always select the largest possible sample size, we cannot sample the entire target population because it would be too costly and too time-consuming. Rather we will use descriptive statistics and the method of confidence intervals to estimate an unknown population mean. By the end of this section you should be able to:

1. explain what a confidence interval is and how it is derived from the distribution of the sample mean;
2. explain the need for, and the impact of, using the *t*-table in constructing confidence intervals;
3. construct confidence intervals using the *t*-table;
4. make decisions based on interpreting confidence intervals;
5. distinguish between the degree of certainty and meaningfulness in constructing confidence intervals;
6. explain why it is impossible to construct a meaningful 100% confidence interval; and
7. explain why confidence intervals are inappropriate for nonstationary time-ordered data.

Consider the following situation of a tire manufacturer. The company will shortly announce a new Milemaster tire. The company must know the mean tire life so that it can set the limits for its treadwear warranty. If the warranty is set too low, the company may lose its competitive advantage. If it is too high, the company will have to replace too many tires.

Knowing the mean tire life with absolute certainty would require testing each and every Milemaster tire. Clearly this is not a practical approach. It takes too long, is too costly, and there would be no tires left to sell. A practical alternative is to take a simple random sample from the population of tires. We can then compute the sample statistics, $\bar{x}$ and s, and use them to estimate the population parameters, μ and σ.

The boss asks how we will arrive at an estimate. We tell him that we will take one simple random sample of size 900 from the population of tires in the warehouse. In a simple random sample, each possible collection of 900 tires has an equal chance of being selected. The boss nods his head in agreement.

We test the sample of 900 tires in a laboratory until the tread thickness is below federal standards. Here are the sample data:

$$\bar{x} = 47{,}500 \text{ miles}$$

$$s = 3{,}000 \text{ miles}$$

The unknown population mean is not 47,500 miles. That is, if we took another simple random sample of 900 tires, we would probably not get a sample mean of 47,500 miles again. The sample means will vary from one sample to another. The standard error reflects the sample-to-sample variation.

We tell the boss to imagine that instead of taking one sample of 900, we take all possible samples of 900 from the population and test the tires. When he complains that this is impractical, we respond that we aren't really going to do this; just imagine it.

We then tell him that from the central limit theorem, the distribution of the sample mean based on 900 observations will be normally distributed and that the mean of the sampling distribution is the same as the unknown population mean. He is not impressed. He says that if he does not know the mean of the population, then he does not know the mean of the sampling distribution either.

Next we tell the boss that the standard error of the mean is much smaller than the population standard deviation. But since we do not know σ, we do not know the standard error either. However, we can use the *estimated standard error*, $s/\sqrt{n}$, to estimate the standard error, $\sigma_{\bar{x}}$. We will substitute the standard deviation for the one sample of 900 tires for the unknown population standard deviation. The estimated standard error, $s_{\bar{x}}$, is

$$\frac{s}{\sqrt{n}} = \frac{3{,}000}{\sqrt{900}} = 100 \text{ miles}$$

Figure 7.5 shows an approximate sampling distribution for the sample mean[*] tire life based on a sample of 900. Note that 47.5% of the area lies in the shaded area below the mean and in the shaded area above the mean. From Appendix 3, the .475 area is equivalent to a z-value of 1.96.

The boss says that is a lovely picture, but he still does not know the population mean, so what good is it? We present the following arguments, which are based on the normal distribution:

---

[*] The sampling distribution shown is not the true sampling distribution because σ is unknown.

FIGURE 7.5   Sampling Distribution of the Sample Means for $n = 900$

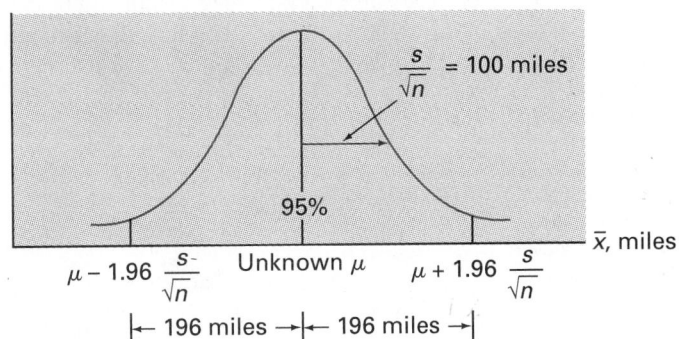

1. Theoretically, 95% of all sample means will be within 1.96 estimated standard errors [1.96(100) = 196 miles] of the unknown population mean.
2. The probability is .95 that any sample mean will be within 196 miles of the unknown population mean.
3. We are 95% confident that our sample mean of 47,500 miles will be within 196 miles of the unknown population mean.
4. We are 95% confident that the interval 47,500 ± 196 miles contains the unknown population mean.

What does a 95% confidence level mean? If we constructed 1,000 confidence intervals based on 1,000 different samples we would expect that about 950 of these confidence intervals would contain the unknown population mean and 50 would not. We show this idea in Figure 7.6.

Assume that the population mean is 47,600 miles. Each of the 1,000 confidence intervals is centered at its sample mean, shown as a dot in Figure 7.6. 95% of the intervals would contain the value 47,600 miles. Thus, 950 intervals will contain the

FIGURE 7.6   1,000 Confidence Intervals for Tire Life Study

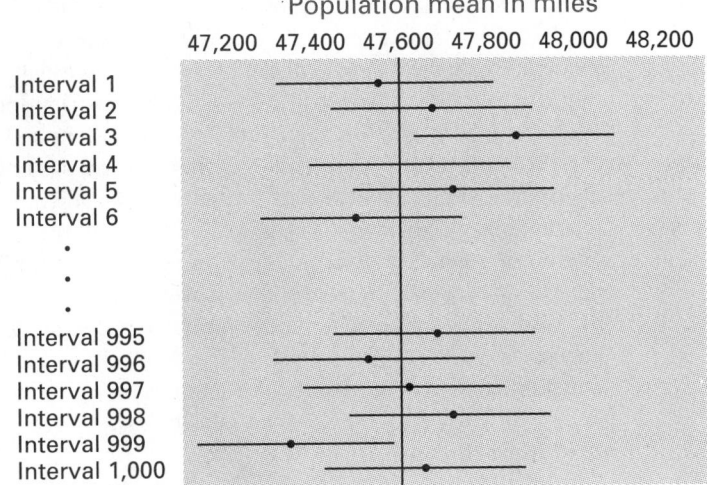

population mean. Notice that any sample mean that is beyond 1.96 estimated standard errors, or 196 miles in our example, from the population mean results in a confidence interval that does not contain the population mean. For example, see intervals 3 and 999 in Figure 7.6. Thus, the **confidence interval** will not contain the population mean approximately 5% of the time, or 50 out of 1,000 times.

A confidence interval is a range estimate of an unknown population parameter. The level of confidence associated with an interval estimate is the percentage of intervals that will include the unknown population parameter over a large number of similarly constructed intervals.

t-Based Confidence Intervals

We use the following expression to construct a two-sided ($\pm$) confidence interval for an unknown population mean:

$$\bar{x} \pm \text{Margin of error}$$

$$\bar{x} \pm (\text{reliability coefficient})(estimated \text{ standard error})$$

$$\bar{x} \pm t(\text{two-sided confidence \%}, n-1)\left(\frac{s}{\sqrt{n}}\right) \tag{7.8}$$

We already know how to compute the sample mean and the estimated standard error. That leaves only the reliability coefficient to discuss.

Reliability Coefficient   Use Appendix 5 to determine the reliability coefficient for expression (7.8). Appendix 5 is called the t-table. Theoretically, two conditions must be true to use the t-table. First, the population standard deviation, σ, is unknown. This is almost always true in the business world. We use the sample standard deviation, s, to estimate σ. Second, the population is normally distributed. If the population is normally distributed and the population size is infinite, then tabled t-values provide exact confidence intervals.

As a practical matter, statisticians use the t-table to obtain *approximate* confidence intervals when either of the following conditions are met:

1. For samples of size 30 or more, the population is symmetric or only moderately skewed.
2. For samples under 30, a stem-and-leaf display or histogram of the data should be nearly bell-shaped.

In practice a manager rarely knows the shape of the population distribution. However, for samples of 30 or more, the central limit theorem assures us that the distribution of the sample mean will be nearly bell-shaped, provided the population is only moderately skewed. For small samples ($n < 30$), we cannot depend on the central limit theorem to ensure normality of the sampling distribution. To determine if the population may be normal, we suggest drawing a stem-and-leaf display for the sample data. If the display is reasonably normal-shaped, assume the population is normally distributed. If the display is not normally shaped, do not use Appendix 5 to determine the reliability coefficient. Fortunately, business professionals often take samples of size 30 or greater, so we can depend on the central limit theorem. This was true for the Milemaster study where 900 tires were selected.

Table 7.5 is a portion of the t-table. To use it, we select a desired level of confidence and determine the degrees of freedom (df), which equals the sample size minus one. For example, the t-value for a sample size of 5 and a two-sided 90% confidence interval is 2.132 (the intersection of the 90% two-sided column and $5 - 1$ or 4 degrees of freedom row).

Table 7.5

A Short Table of *t*-Values

Degrees of Freedom	Desired Level of Confidence for Two-Sided Intervals			
	80%	**90%**	**95%**	**99%**
4	1.533	2.132	2.776	4.604
9	1.383	1.833	2.262	3.250
16	1.337	1.746	2.120	2.921
25	1.316	1.708	2.060	2.787
29	1.311	1.699	2.045	2.756
Infinity	1.282	1.645	1.960	2.576

The *t*- and *z*-values are identical for an infinite number of degrees of freedom. Based on Figure 7.5, for a 95% confidence interval, 47.5% of the area would be below and above the mean of the sampling distribution curve. From Appendix 3, the *z*-value for a two-sided 95% confidence interval is 1.96.

$$P(-1.96 < z < +1.96) = .95$$

The *t*-value for a 95% confidence interval and an infinite number of degrees of freedom is also 1.96. We discuss why this is so shortly.

Figure 7.7 contains *t*-distribution curves for 4 and 16 degrees of freedom. It also contains the normal, or *z*, curve. Two comments are worth making.

1. Each *t*-distribution curve is flatter than the normal curve.
2. As the number of degrees of freedom increases, the *t*-distribution curves look more like the normal curve.

What is the impact of the first comment? For small sample sizes, *t*-table values are appreciably larger than *z*-table values. Thus, from expression (7.8), the margin of error increases beyond what it would have been if we could have used the normal

FIGURE 7.7   Selected Distributions from the *t*-Table

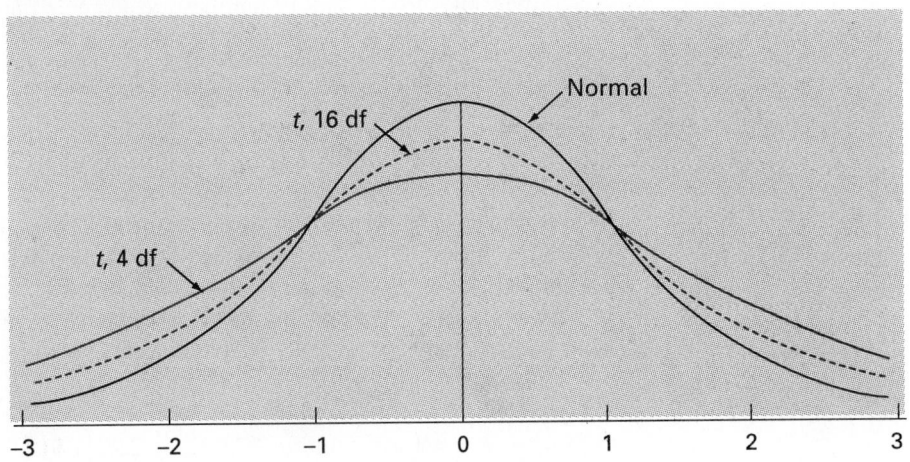

table value for the reliability coefficient. But from Chapter 5, to use the normal curve we must know σ, the population standard deviation. And that we never know. Wider margins of error are the price we pay for not knowing σ and for using the sample standard deviation to estimate it. As we shall see shortly, wider margins of error provide less meaningful information.

What is the impact of the second comment? The sample standard deviation, s, is likely to be a more accurate estimate of σ as we increase the sample size. Thus, as the sample size increases, the t-distribution approaches the normal distribution. Hence, the t-values for an infinite number of degrees of freedom are identical to z-values obtained from Appendix 3, the normal table.

For 29 or more degrees of freedom ($n \geq 30$), z-values and t-values are reasonably close. For example, t(two-sided 95%, 29 df) = 2.045, whereas $z = 1.960$. So in practice, for 29 or more degrees of freedom, analysts often substitute the z-value for the exact t-value.

Example: Eligibility for Federal Aid

Is a census tract containing 5,000 families eligible for aid under Federal Program HR 247? Suppose that program eligibility requires that the mean income for a family of size four must be between $7,500 and $8,500. There are other programs for poorer families. Only during a census year would the population mean income be known. In other years the program administrator must determine eligibility by estimating the population mean income using confidence intervals.

We begin by taking a simple random sample of 12 families of size four from the census tract. The sample data are cross-sectional. Recall that cross-sectional data are measurements from *one time period* taken on different persons, places, or things. Let's set up a 95% confidence interval on the population mean income. Table 7.6 contains the raw data.

First we compute the sample mean, $7,983, and sample standard deviation for the 12 observations, $441. The sample standard deviation is an estimate of the population standard deviation.

We must distinguish between the standard deviation of a single sample and the estimated standard error of the mean. We know the latter must be smaller. The sample standard deviation is $441, and the estimated standard error of the mean is $441/\sqrt{12}$ or $127.

The confidence interval will be valid only if the following assumptions hold:

ASSUMPTION 1:   The 12 families are a simple random sample taken from the census tract population.

ASSUMPTION 2:   The population distribution of incomes is near-normal shaped.

Assumption 1 is valid since we did use simple random sampling to select the sample. Assumption 2 is necessary because, when the sample size is small, we can use the t-table only when the population is near-normal. We check the normality assumption by constructing a stem-and-leaf display for the 12 sample data values, as shown in Figure 7.8. Since Figure 7.8 shows that the sample data are near-normal shaped, the population may be also near-normal shaped.

Now we can substitute the descriptive statistics and the correct t-value into expression (7.8):

$$\bar{x} \pm t(\text{two-sided } 95\%, 11\text{df})(\text{estimated standard error})$$

Lower limit: $7,983 - (2.201)(\$127) = \$7,703$
Upper limit: $7,983 + (2.201)(\$127) = \$8,263$

Table 7.6

Incomes of 12 Randomly Selected Families

$7,300	$7,700	$8,100	$8,400
$7,400	$7,800	$8,300	$8,500
$7,600	$7,800	$8,300	$8,600

FIGURE 7.8   Stem-and-Leaf Display for Sample Income Data

		800	400	
		800	300	
	400	700	300	600
	300	600	100	500
$7,	$7,	$8,	$8,

Interpretation: We are 95% confident that the unknown mean income is between $7,703 and $8,263. Alternatively, this confidence interval could be one of the 5 in every 100 that does not contain the unknown population mean.

Is the tract eligible for the program? It is, because we are 95% confident that the mean income for families of size four is between $7,703 and $8,263. Since every value within that range is between the program limits of $7,500 and $8,500, the tract is eligible.

Suppose we had obtained either of the following two intervals; what could we have concluded about the tract's eligibility? Please think it through before answering.

95% confidence interval   ($6,810 to $7,390)
95% confidence interval   ($7,310 to $7,890)

Since the upper limit of the first confidence interval is below $7,500, the tract is not eligible for this program. The second interval includes incomes less than and greater than $7,500. Thus, we *cannot* tell if the tract is eligible. If the population mean were below $7,500, the tract would not be eligible; otherwise it would.

If we obtained the second confidence interval, what should we do to determine if the tract is eligible? One possibility would be to increase the sample size. That would reduce the estimated standard error and therefore the margin of error. Eventually the margin of error would become so small that the upper and lower limits of the confidence interval would be either less than $7,500 (not eligible), between $7,500 and $8,500 (eligible), or greater than $8,500 (not eligible). Remember, we reduce the estimated standard error by increasing the sample size.

The next problem illustrates how we can use confidence intervals to detect changes from past performance levels—an important problem-solving skill.

Example: The Tenure Discount Problem

Length-of-tenure discounts are the differences between the rents charged long-time apartment renters and newer tenants. Discounts keep good tenants and minimize turnover. The American Housing Group wants to construct a 99% confidence interval on the population mean discount for renters who have lived in their present apartment for more than five years. The mean discount was 12% five years ago. Has it changed?

They select a simple random sample of 400 apartment dwellers from across the United States who have lived at their current addresses for more than five years.

Given here are the sample mean and standard deviation for the cross-sectional discount data:

$$\bar{x} = 8\%$$

$$s = 2\%$$

$$\text{Estimated standard error of the mean} = \frac{2}{\sqrt{400}} = .1\%$$

The confidence interval will be valid only if the following assumption holds:

ASSUMPTION 1: The 400 apartment dwellers are a simple random sample from the target population.

ASSUMPTION 2: The population distribution of discounts is near-normal shaped.

Assumption 1 is valid since we used simple random sampling. Although the population may not be normal, with the sample of 400, the central limit theorem ensures that the sampling distribution will be near normal. Thus, we can use the t-table for determining the reliability coefficient. Because the degrees of freedom ($400 - 1 = 399$) are greater than 29, we use the infinity row to determine the coefficient.

Now we can substitute the descriptive statistics and the t-value into expression (7.8)

$$\bar{x} \pm t(\text{two-sided } 99\%, \, 399 \text{ or infinite df})(\text{estimated standard error})$$

Lower limit: $8\% - (2.576)(.1\%) = 7.74\%$
Upper limit: $8\% + (2.576)(.1\%) = 8.26\%$

Interpretation: We are 99% confident that the unknown population mean discount is between 7.74% and 8.26%. There is a 1 in 100 chance that the interval does not contain the unknown population mean.

The tenure discount has dropped in the past five years. Five years ago it was 12%. Now we are 99% confident that it is between 7.74% and 8.26%. What might account for the drop? Is there greater demand for apartments? Is the perception that long-term renters should be rewarded with major discounts no longer valid? The American Housing Group must diagnose the possible causes for the discount drop.

Setting the Level of Confidence

Is it better to be 99% confident than 95% confident? Is it better to be 95% confident than 80% confident that an interval will contain the unknown population mean? Maybe not!

We have constructed 80%, 95%, and 99% confidence intervals for the following data:

$$\bar{x} = 100$$

$$n = 31 \text{ (degrees of freedom} = 30)$$

$$\frac{s}{\sqrt{n}} = 30$$

80% confidence interval: $100 \pm 1.310(30)$ (60.7 to 139.3)
95% confidence interval: $100 \pm 2.042(30)$ (38.7 to 161.3)
99% confidence interval: $100 \pm 2.750(30)$ (17.5 to 182.5)

The confidence interval gets wider as the level of confidence increases. Thus, the wider confidence intervals provide less meaningful information.

We have two choices in constructing a confidence interval. *Keeping the sample size constant,* we can construct either a narrower interval with a low level of confidence or a wider interval with a high level of confidence. Ninety or 95% confidence levels are often used by companies. However, there is no magic number to use. Each of us must decide upon the trade-offs between level of confidence and the width of the confidence interval.

The Finite Population Correction Factor

Up to now, our sample sizes, *n,* have been very small in comparison to the population size, *N.* When the sample size is more than 5% of the population, we can use the finite population correction factor in calculating the estimated standard error of the mean. The estimated standard error is then given by

$$s_{\bar{x}} = \frac{s}{\sqrt{n^x}} \sqrt{\frac{(N - n)}{(N - 1)}} \qquad (7.9)$$

The expression under the radical, $(N - n)/(N - 1)$, is the finite population correction factor. Note that as the sample size *n* increases, the finite population correction factor gets smaller. This reduces the estimated standard error and ultimately the margin of error.

Confidence Intervals and Time-Ordered Data

In Chapter 2 we learned that the mean and standard deviation summarize cross-sectional and stationary time-ordered data. A line graph for stationary time-ordered data will show no upward or downward pattern over time. Sample values fluctuate around a *constant* mean. Since the population mean is constant, we can construct confidence intervals to estimate it. Nonstationary data do not have a constant mean. The data increase or decrease over time. There is no constant population mean to estimate. Thus confidence intervals are valid only for cross-sectional and stationary time-ordered data.

SECTION 7.3 EXERCISES

1. What conditions must hold in order to construct valid confidence intervals?

2. This exercise focuses on distinguishing between the standard error of the mean, the sample standard deviation, and the estimated standard error of the mean.
    a. Which two terms refer to the distribution of the sample mean?
    b. Which two terms are based on sample data?
    c. Which term is smaller—the estimated standard error or the sample standard deviation?
    d. Which term estimates the population standard deviation?

3. Correct, if necessary, the following statements: As the sample size increases from $n = 10$ to $n = 1000$,
    a. the estimated standard error decreases.
    b. the sample standard deviation decreases.
    c. the reliability coefficient decreases.
    d. the sample mean decreases.
    e. the margin of error increases.

4. Explain in managerial terms why using the correction factor should reduce the standard error of the mean.

5. Consider a sample of 64 people taken from a population of 250. The sample standard deviation in height is 4.5 inches.
   a. Without using the population correction factor, compute the estimated standard error.
   b. Use the population correction factor and compute the estimated standard error.
   c. What is the impact of using the population correction factor on the estimated standard error?
   d. If the sample size equalled the population size, what would be the size of the estimated standard error? Explain in terms a business professional could understand.

6. The margin of error equals the product of the t-value and the estimated standard error. Consider an estimated standard error of $100 based on a sample size of 25 selected from a normal population of incomes.
   a. Find the margin of error for a two-sided 80% confidence interval on the population mean income.
   b. Find the margin of error for a two-sided 90% confidence interval on the population mean income.
   c. Find the margin of error for a two-sided 95% confidence interval on the population mean income.
   d. Find the margin of error for a two-sided 99% confidence interval on the population mean income.
   e. Based on your answers to parts a–d, what is the relationship between increasing the level of confidence and the width of the margin of error?

7. This exercise illustrates the impact of increasing the sample size on the sample standard deviation and the estimated standard error of the mean.
   a. Below is a random sample of five weekly wages for union plumbers in the St. Louis area. Compute the sample standard deviation and the estimated standard error.

$454 $470 $516 $524 $476

   b. Below is a random sample of ten weekly wages for union plumbers in the St. Louis area. Compute the sample standard deviation and the estimated standard error.

$475 $519 $518 $527 $500
459   453   530   516   466

   c. Below is a random sample of 15 weekly wages for union plumbers in the St. Louis area. Compute the sample standard deviation and the estimated standard error.

$476 $540 $509 $502 $479
537   473   457   450   480
463   544   524   504   469

   d. As the sample size increased, what happened to the size of the sample standard deviation? The estimated standard error?
   e. Why didn't the sample standard deviation systematically change? Why did the estimated standard error become smaller?

8. Suppose a random sample of 10 observations was selected from a normal population of N = 1,000. The sample mean is 45, and the sample standard deviation is 15.
   a. Construct a 90% confidence interval for the population mean.
   b. Construct a 95% confidence interval for the population mean.
   c. Construct a 99% confidence interval for the population mean.

9. Repeat Exercise 8, but assume that the sample size was n = 500. Explain why the confidence intervals in Exercise 8 are wider than the confidence intervals in this exercise.

10. A sample of n = 9 observations is selected from a normal population. The results are shown here:

{2, 6, 7, 1, 4, 2, 5, 6, 3}

   a. Find the sample mean and the sample standard deviation.

b. What number will you use for an estimate of the population standard deviation?

c. Construct a 90% confidence interval for the mean of the population from which the sample was drawn.

d. State the assumptions you made in constructing the confidence interval in part **c.**

11. Koca Kola wants to estimate the mean income of its blue-collar market segment. It selects 10 families from the segment and obtains the following income data.

$24,500	$30,500
26,700	32,400
31,000	30,675
21,500	20,550
28,500	25,500

a. Compute the family income sample mean and standard deviation.

b. Determine the estimated standard error.

c. Construct and interpret a two-sided 99% confidence interval on the mean income.

d. The marketing manager believes that the population mean income for the blue-collar segment is above $21,500. Is the manager correct in her assessment? Explain.

e. What must be true about blue-collar incomes to use expression (7.8) to construct a confidence interval?

12. A manufacturing process is supposed to produce an item that measures 10 cm in diameter. The diameter measurements are normally distributed. In order to check that the process is working properly, a quality-control expert selects 25 items from the assembly line and measures the diameters of these items. The sample mean is 10.3 cm and $s = 0.5$ cm.

a. Construct a 95% confidence interval for the population mean.

b. On the basis of this interval, do you conclude that the manufacturing process is working as it should? Explain.

13. A company purchases transistors from a large distributor. The distributor claims that the mean life of the transistors is 2,000 hours and the population standard deviation is 150 hours.

a. Consider the distribution of all possible means of $n = 400$ transistors. If the distributor's claim is correct, what is the mean of the sampling distribution? What is its standard error?

b. You select a sample of 400 transistors and calculate the mean life of these units. If you then constructed a 95% confidence interval based on this sample mean, why would you expect the interval to contain the unknown population mean life?

c. Suppose the upper and lower bounds of a 95% confidence interval were 1,965 hours and 1,990 hours respectively. Does this confidence interval confirm the distributor's claim? Explain.

14. A random sample of 100 union plumbers in a large city showed that the mean weekly income was $525.75 with a standard deviation of $52.50. You want to estimate the mean weekly income of unionized plumbers.

a. What is the target population?

b. What is the parameter of interest?

c. What assumptions do you have to make in order to construct a confidence interval for this population mean? Sample size large

d. Estimate the mean weekly income of all unionized plumbers in the city using a 95% reliability coefficient.

15. The Federal Trade Commission tests cigarettes to determine whether the level of nicotine agrees with the claims made by the manufacturer. Suppose a sample of 20 cigarettes of brand A showed that the mean level of nicotine was .5 mg per cigarette with a standard deviation of .01 mg. The FTC wants to estimate the mean level of nicotine per cigarette in brand A.

a. What is the target population?

b. What is the parameter of interest?

c. What assumptions do you have to make in order to construct a confidence interval for this population mean?

d. Construct a 99% confidence interval for the mean level of nicotine per cigarette for brand A.

16. A telemarketing manager wants to estimate the mean time his operators spend in making their sales pitch to customers. He selects 15 operators and records their calls without their knowledge. Below are the data on call talk time to the nearest ten seconds.

Seconds	Seconds	Seconds
200	210	200
150	230	200
170	180	160
250	150	170
100	170	190

a. Compute the call talk time sample mean and standard deviation.
b. Determine the estimated standard error.
c. Construct and interpret a two-sided 80% confidence interval on the mean talk time.
d. The manager has implemented several programs to increase the operator-customer talk time. Last year the mean time for the year was 140 seconds. Based on part **c,** has talk time increased—has his objective been accomplished?
e. What must be true about call talk times to use expression (7.8) to construct a confidence interval?

17. A manager wants to estimate the mean weekly downtime of photocopy machines within the firm. Below are the weekly downtime data for eight randomly selected machines to the nearest minute.

Downtime Minutes	Downtime Minutes
5	12
8	9
10	8
7	7

a. Compute the downtime sample mean and standard deviation.
b. Determine the estimated standard error.
c. Construct and interpret a two-sided 98% confidence interval on the mean downtime.
d. The photocopying administrator has set a maximum average downtime of 11 minutes per week. Has the goal been achieved?
e. What must be true about photocopy machine downtime to use expression (7.8) to construct a confidence interval?

18. COMCEL wants to estimate the mean reduction in unit labor cost that is produced by providing one week of team-building training to its autonomous work groups in its Dallas plant. Two months after a sample of 10 work groups received their training, COMCEL determines their unit labor cost reductions. Below are the data.

$1.09	$1.22
1.34	1.19
1.24	1.65
0.98	0.85
1.56	1.05

a. Compute the unit labor-cost-reduction sample mean and standard deviation.
b. Determine the estimated standard error.
c. Construct and interpret a two-sided 95% confidence interval on the mean unit labor-cost reduction.
d. COMCEL had hoped to achieve a plantwide reduction of $.90 or more. Has the target been achieved?

e. What must be true about reduction in unit labor cost to use expression (7.8) to construct a confidence interval?

19. The margin of error for a tire life study is 349 miles. The sample standard deviation is 3,000 miles and the sample size is 400. What is the level of confidence for the two-sided confidence interval on mean tire life?

20. The margin of error for intent-to-purchase scores is 2.48 points (on a 100-point scale). The sample variance is 64 points and the sample size is 30. What is the level of confidence for a two-sided confidence interval on mean intent-to-purchase score?

21. American Optical Company has constructed a two-sided 95% confidence interval on the mean hardness of its Executive series eyeglass temples (the part that attaches the eyeglass frame to one's ear). The sample standard deviation is 150 pounds per square inch (ppsi). The margin of error is 9.80 ppsi. What size sample did American Optical use to construct the confidence interval? Initially assume the sample size will exceed 120.

22. In the past, the administrative office of a large military installation received a mean of 45 complaints a week. Four weeks ago the installation implemented Deming's quality management methods to reduce the number of complaints. The officer in charge plotted the total number of complaints per week. The graph is shown here.

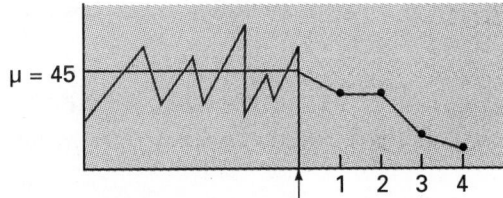

a. Would you characterize the time series before the quality program as stationary or non-stationary?
b. Would you use a confidence interval to estimate the mean number of complaints before implementation of the quality program? Why?
c. How would you characterize the series after implementation of the quality program?
d. Would you use a confidence interval to estimate the mean number of complaints after the implementation of the quality program? Why?

23. In *single-observation quality-control charting,* the operator records one measurement per shift or day. After 15 shifts, the operator can construct a line graph, provided the process data are stable. The operator can then construct a 99% confidence interval on the measurement. Subsequent observations outside these limits signal assignable cause, not random variation. The operator must then stop the process and fix it. Below are the power usages (kwh) for 15 successive days.

September	Power Usage (kwh)	September	Power Usage (kwh)
12	30.4	20	31.4
13	32.4	21	29.4
14	28.7	22	28.5
15	30.4	23	31.2
16	29.5	24	30.5
17	33.2	25	29.6
18	29.8	26	31.5
19	28.6		

a. Construct a line graph for the time-ordered data.
b. Are the data stationary?
c. Can a meaningful confidence interval on the population mean daily power usage be constructed for the above data? Discuss.
d. Construct and interpret a 99% confidence interval on the mean daily power usage.

24. Refer to the single observation quality control charting idea discussed in Exercise 23. Below are the journal diameters of a rear-wheel tractor axle to dimensions between 44.950 to 44.990 mm for 15 consecutive shifts.

Shift	Journal Diameters	Shift	Journal Diameters
1	.989	9	.969
2	.987	10	.970
3	.985	11	.964
4	.986	12	.966
5	.980	13	.960
6	.975	14	.955
7	.978	15	.956
8	.974		

a. Construct a line graph for the time-ordered data.
b. Are the data stationary?
c. Can a meaningful confidence interval on the population mean journal diameter be constructed for the above data? Discuss.

7.4 ▤ One-Sided Confidence Intervals on an Unknown Population Mean

Up to now, all confidence intervals have been two-sided; they extended an equal amount on each side of the sample mean (see expression (7.8)). Two-sided intervals have a lower and an upper limit. Sometimes we want to make statements such as: "I am 95% confident that the mean amount of personal time taken per week is *at most* 1.5 hours" or "I am 90% confident that the mean work group productivity is *at least* 30 units per hour." These are examples of one-sided confidence intervals; they do not extend an equal amount on each side of the sample mean. They do not have a lower and upper limit. By the end of this section you should be able to:

1. explain when to use a one-sided confidence interval; and
2. construct and interpret a one-sided interval.

We use the following expressions to construct a one-sided confidence interval for an unknown population mean. An "at least" interval has no upper limit; we use expression (7.10) to compute its lower limit. An "at most" interval has no lower limit; we use expression (7.11) to compute its upper limit.

$$\text{At least: } \bar{x} - t(\text{one-sided confidence \%}, n - 1)\left(\frac{s}{\sqrt{n}}\right) \qquad (7.10)$$

$$\text{At most: } \bar{x} + t(\text{one-sided confidence \%}, n - 1)\left(\frac{s}{\sqrt{n}}\right) \qquad (7.11)$$

We use different *t*-table values to construct one-sided and two-sided intervals. The column headers in Appendix 5 indicate which *t*-values to use for varying confidence levels for both types of intervals.

Figure 7.9 shows that the *t*-value for a two-sided 90% confidence interval for 20 degrees of freedom (Figure 7.9a) is the same as the *t*-value for a one-sided 95% confidence interval (Figure 7.9b). The *t*-value in expression (7.8) is based on the area between the mean and the lower limit and between the mean and the upper limit of

FIGURE 7.9   One- and Two-Sided Intervals

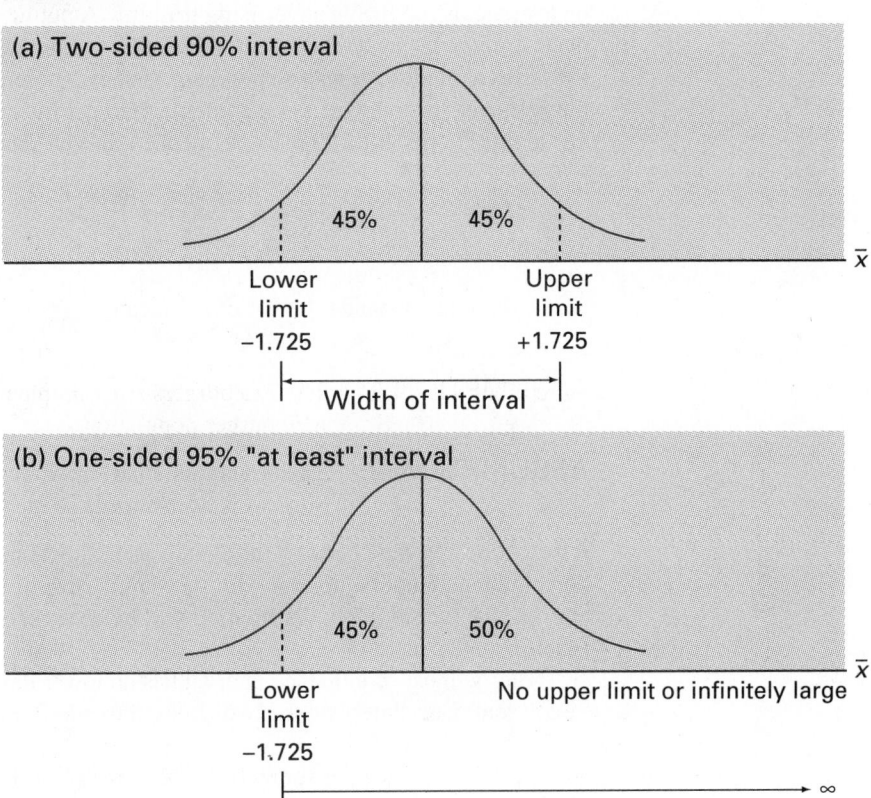

(a) Two-sided 90% interval

45%   45%

Lower   Upper
limit   limit
−1.725   +1.725

$\bar{x}$

Width of interval

(b) One-sided 95% "at least" interval

45%   50%

Lower   No upper limit or infinitely large
limit
−1.725

$\bar{x}$

Width of interval   ∞

the interval. Forty-five percent of the area is in each tail. Thus the limits of a two-sided 90% confidence interval for 20 degrees of freedom are

Lower limit: $\bar{x}$ − 1.725(estimated standard error)
Upper limit: $\bar{x}$ + 1.725(estimated standard error)

A one-sided "at least" interval has no upper limit. The lack of an upper limit is represented by the 50% area in the upper tail of the distribution in Figure 7.9b. To obtain a one-sided 95% confidence interval, the lower tail of this distribution must contain 45% of the area. To find the lower limit for this interval, we must look up the t-value that represents 45% of the area shown. This is the same as the t-value for a two-sided 90% confidence interval. Thus, the lower limit of an (at least) one-sided 95% confidence interval is

Lower limit: $\bar{x}$ − 1.725(estimated standard error)

We have demonstrated that a one-sided 95% interval has the same t-value as a two-sided 90% interval. Thus, a one-sided $(100 - x)\%$ interval has the same t-value for its limit as a two-sided $(100 - 2x)\%$ interval. The column headers in Appendix 5 reflect this fact.

Next we construct and interpret a one-sided interval to determine whether a firm's advertising is truthful.

Example: Truth in Advertising   Howdy Burger is a local chain in St. Louis. Recently it introduced a new burger, which it claims has *no more than* 120 calories on average. Is the firm's advertising truthful? A public policy watchdog agency conducts a study. Using a random numbers table, agency workers enter Howdy Burger's six stores at random times and purchase the new burger. They collect a sample of 225 burgers over several weeks and compute their caloric content. The agency will set up an "at most" one-sided 99.5% confidence interval. The descriptive statistics follow:

$$\bar{x} = 108 \text{ calories}$$

$$s = 60 \text{ calories}$$

$$\text{Estimated standard error of the mean } \frac{60}{\sqrt{225}} = 4 \text{ calories}$$

ASSUMPTION 1:   The 225 burgers are a simple random sample taken from the new burger population.

ASSUMPTION 2:   The population distribution for the number of calories in the burgers is near-normal shaped.

Assumption 1 is valid because the agency used simple random sampling. Although the population may not be normal with the sample size of 225, the central limit theorem ensures that the sampling distribution will be near normal. Therefore, we can use the *t*-table.

The "at most" confidence interval has no lower limit. The *t*-value for a one-sided 99.5% confidence interval for 224 degrees of freedom is 2.576. From expression (7.11):

Upper limit: $108 + 2.576(4) = 118.3$ calories

Interpretation: We are 99.5% confident—virtually certain—that the population mean number of calories for the new burger is at most 118.3. Howdy Burger has been truthful in its advertising.

In summary, we use one-sided confidence intervals to make "at least" or "at most" statements. "At least" means the population mean is at least some number, and "at most" means that the population mean is at most some number. When we are interested in making statements that the population mean is between two numbers, we construct two-sided confidence intervals.

SECTION 7.4 EXERCISES

1. We use expressions (7.8), (7.10), and (7.11) to construct confidence intervals on a population mean. Which expression should be used to estimate the following:
   a. The mean time to complete a project is at least . . . .
   b. The greatest amount of mean fat per serving (in grams) in a snack treat is . . . .
   c. The mean photocopier downtime is between . . . .
   d. The smallest reduction in mean unit labor cost is . . . .
   e. The mean wait time in a clinic is at most . . . .
   f. The mean length of tenure discount is from . . . .

2. Ten items are selected from a normally distributed population. The mean of a sample is 15 and the standard deviation is 5.
   a. Construct a two-sided 95% confidence interval for the population mean.
   b. Construct a 95% "at most" confidence interval to establish an upper limit for the population mean.
   c. Construct a 90% "at least" confidence interval to establish a lower limit for the population mean.

3. A sample of 250 bank loans was selected from 1,000 loans made during a given month. The mean loan made was $650 with a standard deviation of $450.
   a. Is the distribution of bank loans normally distributed? Why? [*Hint:* Can loan size take on negative values?]
   b. If the distribution of bank loans is not normal, then how can we estimate the mean loan size for the 1,000 loans?
   c. Estimate the standard error of the mean both with and without using the finite population correction. How much is the standard error reduced by including the finite population correction factor?
   d. Construct a 95% confidence interval for the mean loan amount using the correction.
   e. Construct a 95% one-sided confidence interval to establish a lower limit on the mean loan amount.
   f. Construct a 99% one-sided confidence interval to establish an upper limit on the mean amount of the 1,000 loans.

4. A soft-drink machine is set to dispense a mean of 6.5 ounces of fill excluding ice. A sample of nine cups had a mean of 6.0 ounces with a standard deviation of .6 ounce. Construct a 99% one-sided confidence interval that will establish a lower limit on the mean amount actually dispensed.

5. A random sample of 100 bank depositors reveals a mean checking balance of $590 with a standard deviation of $720. Construct a 90% confidence interval that establishes an upper limit on the mean checking balance.

6. All employees of a company are required to take a battery of skills tests. The mean dexterity score is 70. An industrial psychologist believes that the mean score made by assembly line employees is higher than 70. A random sample of records of 25 assemblers showed a mean score of 77 with a standard deviation of 6.
   a. Construct a 90% confidence interval that will establish a lower limit on the mean dexterity score of assembly line workers.
   b. Based on your confidence interval, would you conclude that the psychologist is correct?

7. To be eligible for a particular Federal aid program, the mean family income in a census tract must be at most $12,500. A random sample of 400 families in tract 2145 are interviewed, and the following data are obtained.

$$\bar{x} = \$12,150$$

$$s = \$5,700$$

Use a 95% level of confidence. Is tract 2145 eligible for the program? Why?

8. United Parcel will consider a quality management program successful if there has been a reduction of at least 10 customer complaints per month. Below are cross-sectional data taken from a sample of ten customer service representatives over a one-month period. The data represent the reduction in the number of complaints from the base period (the same month last year).

Reduction in Complaints	Reduction in Complaints
14	15
12	14
15	16
14	14
10	14

   a. Construct a 95% confidence interval and determine if the quality management program has been successful.
   b. What must be true about the number of complaints data to construct a meaningful confidence interval?

9. A product may advertise that it has no fat if it contains at most .1 gram per serving. Can Know-Fat cheese advertise that it contains "no" fat? Use a 90% level of confidence.

$$\bar{x} = 0.06 \text{ gram per serving}$$

$$s^2 = 0.16$$

$$n = 400 \text{ cheese square servings}$$

10. A goal of the Division of Tuberculosis Elimination (DTBE) of the National Center for Prevention Services in Atlanta is to reduce patient waiting time in TB clinics to at most an average of 75 minutes. They collect data on a random sample of clinics in 10 cities and obtain the following data.

City	Minutes	City	Minutes
Hartford	53	Columbia, SC	58
Birmingham	65	Madison, WI	51
Denver	57	Columbus, OH	72
Seattle	65	San Francisco	68
San Antonio	57	New York City	77

Use a 95% level of confidence. Has DTBE been successful? Discuss.

11. The second stage in the marketing adoption decision is product interest. The consumer searches for information about the new product. Kinsu Knives wants to know if an innovative ad has helped potential consumers obtain correct information on the product's (deluxe steak knife) attributes. Kinsu Knives interviews 225 people who have seen the ad at least four times in the past month and records the number of product attributes correctly identified.

$$\bar{x} = 2.15 \text{ attributes}$$

$$s^2 = .75$$

$$n = 225$$

Kinsu Knives will consider the ad successful if consumers, on average, can recall at least 2.20 attributes. Using a 95% level of confidence, has the ad been successful?

12. Federal Express wants to estimate the maximum mean number of shocks greater than 3 Gs that a package encounters along a 500-foot conveyor belt as the package is loaded into a truck for shipment. Excessive shock can cause breakage, and Federal Express is financially liable. They use a test package that records any shock beyond 3 Gs. They slip the test package on the conveyor belt without the operator's knowledge. They record the following hourly data.

Time	Shocks Greater than 3 Gs
8:00 A.M.	3
9:00 A.M.	5
10:00 A.M.	4
11:00 A.M.	6
12:00 A.M.	6
1:00 P.M.	7
2:00 P.M.	8
3:00 P.M.	10
4:00 P.M.	12
5:00 P.M.	11

    a. Are the time-ordered data stationary?
    b. Can a meaningful one-sided confidence interval be constructed?
    c. What is the important lesson that part **b** illustrates?

7.5 Stratified Random Sampling

Recall from Chapter 6 that we consider stratified random sampling when there are subgroups within a target population that are likely to have similarities on the variable of interest within a stratum but differences between strata. A stratified random sample is one obtained by separating the target population into nonoverlapping groups, or strata, and then selecting a simple random sample from each stratum. It can produce confidence intervals with smaller margins of error than simple random sampling. By the end of this section you should be able to:

1. construct confidence intervals on the population mean using stratified random sampling; and
2. explain the impact of using stratified random sampling on the width of the confidence interval.

When using stratified random sampling, we use expressions (7.12) and (7.13) to compute the sample statistics. Expression (7.12) assumes that the finite population correction factor is not needed.

$$\bar{x}_{ST} = \frac{N_1}{N}\,\bar{x}_1 + \frac{N_2}{N}\,\bar{x}_2 + \cdots + \frac{N_L}{N}\,\bar{x}_L \tag{7.12}$$

$$\text{Est } SE_{ST} = \sqrt{\left(\frac{N_1}{N}\right)^2 \frac{s_1^2}{n_1} + \cdots + \left(\frac{N_L}{N}\right)^2 \frac{s_L^2}{n_L}} \tag{7.13}$$

N_i is the number of sampling units in each stratum. N is the population size. n_i is the sample size drawn from each stratum.

The estimate of the population mean is a weighted average of the sample means from the strata. While expression (7.13) is complex, it bears some similarity to the estimated standard error in simple random sampling. Note that the sample variances for each stratum are divided by their respective sample sizes.

We can substitute the above descriptive statistics into expression (7.14) to construct a two-sided confidence interval on an unknown population mean using stratified random sampling:

$$\bar{x}_{ST} \pm t(\text{two-sided confidence \%}, n_{total} - 1) \cdot \text{Estimated } SE_{ST} \tag{7.14}$$

where n_{total} is the total sample from all strata.

Consider the following example.

Example: Mean Number of Sick Days   A recent report noted that firms within the mobile phone industry average 5.05 sick days per employee per year. COMCEL's Southern Region wants to estimate the mean number of sick days taken per employee last year. The region has 1,500 hourly workers, 200 managers, and 200 administrative support staffers. COMCEL believes that the three groups will differ greatly on the number of sick days taken. Hence, it uses stratified random sampling. COMCEL selects a 4% sample from each stratum of employees. The sample includes 60 workers, eight managers, and eight support staff—n_{total} = 76 people. Within each stratum, a simple random sample is selected. COMCEL wants a two-sided 95% confidence interval on the mean number of sick days taken within the past year for all 1,900 employees.

Table 7.7 presents the descriptive statistics for the 76 participants in the study (raw data not shown). Since the degrees of freedom exceed 30, we use the z-value of 1.96 found in the infinity row of Appendix 5.

$$\bar{x}_{ST} \pm t(\text{two-sided confidence 95\%, infinity})(\text{Est } SE_{ST})$$

Table 7.7

Descriptive Statistics for Number of Sick Days Taken

Statistic	Hourly Employees	Management	Support Staff
n_i	60	8	8
$\bar{x}_i$	4.85	8.88	6.63
s_i^2	.57	.41	.27
N_i	1,500	200	200

$$\bar{x}_{ST} = \frac{1,500}{1,900}(4.85) + \frac{200}{1,900}(8.88) + \frac{200}{1,900}(6.63) = 5.46$$

$$\text{Est } SE_{ST} = \sqrt{\left(\frac{1,500}{1,900}\right)^2 \frac{.57}{60} + \left(\frac{200}{1,900}\right)^2 \frac{.41}{8} + \left(\frac{200}{1,900}\right)^2 \frac{.27}{8}} = .083$$

Lower limit: $5.46 - (1.96)(.083) = 5.29$ days
Upper limit: $5.46 + (1.96)(.083) = 5.63$ days

Interpretation: We are 95% confident that the mean number of sick days taken for all Southern Region personnel is between 5.29 and 5.63.

COMCEL's mean number of sick days is above the industry mean. How can COMCEL reduce it? Table 7.7 indicates that both managers and support staff are taking more sick days than hourly employees. If the overall mean is to be brought down, COMCEL must focus on the manager and support staff strata. It should ask the following diagnostic questions:

1. Have there been *any changes* lately that might account for the difference between the mean numbers of sick days taken by hourly employees and by management and the support staff?
2. What (beyond the mean number of sick days) is *unique or distinctive* about hourly employees vs. management and the support staff?

For example, suppose that for the past year, COMCEL's administrative offices have been undergoing extensive renovation. The noise levels, the erratic behavior of the heating and cooling equipment, and the constant departmental relocations may have caused managers and support staff to take sick days. If the renovation was the cause, the number of sick days should now drop as the renovation has been completed.

Impact of Using Simple Random Sampling

Suppose that stratified random sampling is called for in a study. What is the impact of using simple random sampling instead? Imagine that COMCEL had taken a simple random sample instead of a stratified random sample. Suppose that the same 76 people had been selected. Thus the 76 observations would be the same as those obtained by a stratified random sample. However, the sample standard deviation for the 76 employees would have been 1.51 days and the estimated standard error of the mean would have been .173 day (calculations not shown). This is more than twice as large as the estimated standard error using stratified random sampling. Using stratified random sampling when it was appropriate reduced the estimated standard error by more than 50%. This cuts the margin of error for the confidence interval in half.

In summary, we use stratified random sampling when there are subgroups within a target population that are likely to have similarities on the variable of interest within a stratum but differences between strata. Stratified random sampling can produce narrower, and thus more meaningful, confidence intervals than simple random sampling.

SECTION 7.5 EXERCISES

1. You must decide between a simple random and a stratified random sampling plan. List the conditions under which you would prefer a stratified random sampling plan.

2. Using stratified random sampling, a manager took a simple random sample from two plants and determined the mean number of minutes to assemble a VCR. The results are shown here:

	Plant 1	Plant 2
Sample mean (minutes)	120	135
Sample variance	25	144
Stratum size (N_i)	3,000	7,000
Sample size (n_i)	30	70

   a. What is the sample mean for the stratified random sample?
   b. What weight should you give to the sample mean from plant 1? from plant 2?
   c. Estimate the variance of the sample mean for the stratified random sample in part a.
   d. Construct a 90% confidence interval for the population mean of the two plants.

3. A marketing research firm wishes to estimate the mean number of hours a week spent watching television. The firm believes that the mean will vary significantly by household income. Using census data, it divides a county into three income classes—low, medium, and high. A proportional sample from each stratum shows the following:

	Income Class		
	Low	Medium	High
Sample mean (hours)	56	40.5	26.7
Sample variance	7.2	8.1	7.3
Proportion of the total population	.5	.3	.2
Sample size	300	180	120

   Construct a 95% confidence interval to estimate the mean number of hours of television watched over the total population.

4. An auditor wants to estimate the mean age of the accounts receivable. He subdivides the population into three strata by size of account. He selects a simple random sample from each stratum. Here are the data:

| | Account Size | | |
	Small	Medium	Large
Sample mean (days)	33.9	25.1	19
Sample variance	35.4	232	87.6
Stratum size	1,000	360	540
Sample size	40	13	23

Construct a 99% confidence interval to estimate the mean age of accounts receivable.

7.6 ≡ Confidence Intervals on an Unknown Population Proportion

We have been dealing with quantitative data up to this point. In this section we focus on yes/no data—data often used to code responses to questionnaires. Typical yes/no questions include:

1. Do you use the firm's aerobic facilities?
2. Do you plan to vote for candidate A?
3. Is your department planning to purchase additional computers?

In Chapter 2, we organized and summarized yes/no data. Now we will estimate population proportions from sample yes/no data, or sample proportions. By the end of this section, you should be able to:

1. describe the distribution of the sample proportion and explain why it is as a special case of the distribution of the sample mean; and
2. construct and interpret confidence intervals on population proportions using simple random sampling.

Distribution of the Sample Proportion

Suppose a target population can be divided into two categories—yes and no.

Let p = the proportion of the population that is classified as yes

$q = 1 - p$ = the proportion of the population that is classified as no

Assign a 1 to each element in the yes group and a 0 to each element in the no group. That is, let

$$x_i = 1 \quad \text{if person responded yes}$$
$$0 \quad \text{if person responded no}$$

Since the population proportion, p, is usually unknown, we will estimate p using a sample proportion $\hat{p}$ (read p-hat). As shown below, $\hat{p}$ is the sample mean for yes/no or 1,0 data.

$$\text{Sample proportion} = \hat{p} = \frac{\sum_i x_i}{n} = \frac{X}{n} \tag{7.15}$$

where X = the number of people who respond yes, assigned as the 1s
   n = sample size

Since $\hat{p}$ is a sample mean of 1,0 data, the distribution of the sample proportion, $\hat{p}$, is a special case of the distribution of the sample mean. It follows that

$$\mu_{\bar{x}} = \mu_{\hat{p}} = p \tag{7.16}$$

That is, the mean of the distribution of the sample proportion is equal to the population proportion, p. The standard error of the sample proportion is

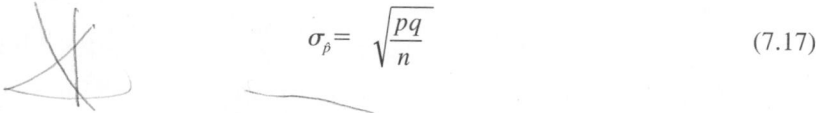

$$\sigma_{\hat{p}} = \sqrt{\frac{pq}{n}} \tag{7.17}$$

Estimated Standard Error of the Proportion

Since the standard error of the proportion involves the unknown population proportion, p, it must be estimated using sample data.
Use $\hat{p}$ and $\hat{q} = 1 - \hat{p}$ in place of p and q.

$$\text{Estimated standard error of the sample proportion} = \sqrt{\frac{\hat{p}\hat{q}}{n}} \tag{7.18}$$

We can use expression (7.19) to construct two-sided confidence intervals on the population proportion:

$$\frac{X}{n} \pm \text{Margin of error}$$

$$\hat{p} \pm z(\text{estimated standard error of sample proportion}) \tag{7.19}$$

$$\hat{p} \pm z\sqrt{\frac{\hat{p}\hat{q}}{n}}$$

where z-values are from the standard normal table. These are the same as the tabled values in the bottom row (infinite degrees of freedom) of Appendix 5.
   The following problem illustrates constructing a two-sided confidence interval on an unknown population proportion.

Example: Japan—The Leading Economic Power?   An international business council wants to estimate the population proportion of Californians who believe that Japan is the leading economic power. The council takes a simple random sample of 200 Californians. One hundred sixteen of those sampled said they believe Japan is the leading economic power. The council wants to construct a two-sided 90% confidence interval on the unknown population proportion.

Here are the assumptions:

ASSUMPTION 1:   The sample of 200 Californians is a simple random sample from the population.

ASSUMPTION 2:   The shape of the distribution of the sample proportion of Californians who rank Japan as the leading economic power is normally distributed.

Assumption 1 is realistic because we used simple random sampling. According to Cochran (1977), our second assumption is also realistic. Cochran provides the following rules on the normality of the distribution of the sample proportion, as given in Table 7.8. Since $\hat{p} = 116/200 = .58$, the necessary sample size is 50. The distribution of the sample proportion will be normal and we can use Appendix 5 or the normal table to obtain the standard normal values, z.

Table 7.8

Cochran's Rules for Normality of the Distribution of the Sample Proportion

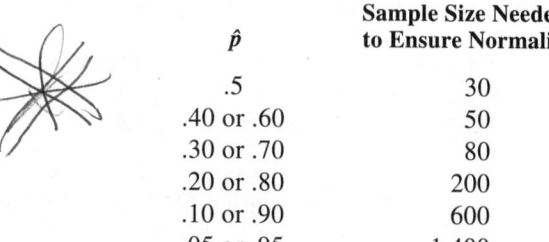

$\hat{p}$	Sample Size Needed to Ensure Normality
.5	30
.40 or .60	50
.30 or .70	80
.20 or .80	200
.10 or .90	600
.05 or .95	1,400

Here are the descriptive statistics from the survey:

$$\hat{p} = \frac{116}{200} = .58$$

$$\text{Estimated standard error} = \sqrt{\frac{(.58)(.42)}{200}} = .035$$

From expression (7.19), the two-sided 90% confidence interval on the population proportion is

$$.58 \pm t(90\%, \text{infinite})(\text{estimated standard error of sample proportion})$$

Lower limit: $.58 - (1.645)(.035) = .523$
Upper limit: $.58 + (1.645)(.035) = .637$

Interpretation: We are 90% confident that between 52.3% and 63.7% of Californians believe that Japan is the leading economic power.

In summary, just as we use the sample mean to estimate the population mean, we use the sample proportion to estimate the population proportion.

SECTION 7.6 EXERCISES

1. You believe that no more than 5% of a population prefer brand A, but want to confirm this belief by a telephone survey. If you are correct in your belief, would a sample of 40 respondents allow you to construct an at most confidence interval? Explain.

2. A marketing research study of 400 members of the general public indicated that only 86 respondents preferred brand A. Estimate the proportion of the population that prefers brand A. Use a two-sided 95% confidence interval.

3. A manufacturer claims that 90% of his electrical parts are defect-free. A sample of 600 parts showed that 78 were defective.
   a. Construct a two-sided 90% confidence interval.
   b. Based on your confidence interval, does it appear that the manufacturer's claim is justified? Explain.

4. An insurance agency that processed 40,000 claims last year wants to know the percentage of these claims that were processed incorrectly. A sample of 1,500 claims showed that 93 had at least one error.
   a. The office manager wants to know how bad the error rate could be. Construct a 99% "at most" confidence interval for the percentage error rate for the population of 40,000 claims.
   b. What error rate would you expect to find if you did reexamine all 40,000 claims? Explain.
   c. Construct a 95% "at least" confidence interval to establish a lower limit on the error rate.

5. Just-in-Time Inc. is a stock market timing service. It is interested in knowing the percentage of business economists who believe there will be a recession next year. Using the membership list of 4,500 members in the American Association of Business Economists as a sampling frame, the service calls 150 randomly selected members. Forty-three believe the country will experience a recession next year.
   a. Construct a 95% confidence interval to estimate the proportion of business economists who believe there will be a recession next year.
   b. Would this confidence interval apply to all economists? Explain.

6. According to a survey in *New Venture* magazine, 62% of 350 CEOs interviewed used company profitability as the most important factor in determining bonuses and perks. Assuming that the 350 CEOs constitute a simple random sample of the population of all CEOs, construct a 90% confidence interval for the proportion of CEOs who use profitability as the most important factor in determining bonuses and perks.

7. COMCEL inspects a sample of 1,500 handsets per day. If a handset has a surface blemish, it is a defective and the blemishes must be corrected before shipment. Consider the following data over the past 10 days.

Day	Sample	Proportion Defective
1	1,500	.08
2	1,500	.06
3	1,500	.09
4	1,500	.08
5	1,500	.08
6	1,500	.09
7	1,500	.08
8	1,500	.06
9	1,500	.08
10	1,500	.09

   a. Are the daily proportion defective time-ordered data stationary? Plot the data.

b. If the data are stationary, determine the average proportion defective by summing the ten proportion defectives and dividing by 10.

c. Insert the average proportion defective into expression (7.19). Construct and interpret a two-sided 99.74% confidence interval (*z*-value = 3.00). In control charting the lower and upper limits are called the *lower and upper control limits.* When the daily proportion defective is above the upper control limit or below the lower control limit, the operator investigates the causes. Data values outside the control limits are considered outliers, and the operator must seek assignable causes.

d. When the daily proportion defective exceeds the upper control limit, this is clearly bad and the operator must investigate the problem. Why must the operator investigate when the daily proportion defective is less than the lower control limit? After all, isn't an exceptional low proportion defectives good?

8. An article reported that 60% of 500 potential record customers sampled preferred compact disks over digital tapes. We wish to construct a two-sided 95% confidence interval on the proportion of people who prefer compact disks over digital tapes. Below are three possible confidence intervals; only one is correct. Identify the correct and incorrect intervals and defend.

$$.60 \pm 1.96 \sqrt{\frac{(.60)(.40)}{500}}$$

$$60 \pm 1.96 \sqrt{\frac{(.60)(.40)}{500}}$$

$$.40 \pm 1.96 \sqrt{\frac{(.60)(.40)}{500}}$$

9. A presidential voting survey just released states that the polling firm is 95% confident that the proportion of voters favoring Candidate X is 52% with a margin of error of ± 4%.

a. Given the wide margin of error, does it appear that if the election were held today Candidate X would win? Discuss.

b. If your answer is "cannot yet tell", what can the polling firm do to reduce the margin of error while maintaining a 95% level of confidence? *increase sample size*

10. Construct and interpret a 95% confidence interval on the unknown population proportion of homeless people in a city. Of 1,000 people interviewed, 98 responded that they were homeless.

7.7 ═ Determining the Sample Size

Early in a sample survey or planned change study, a project manager must *determine* the sample size. Up to now we have assumed that we knew the desired sample size. In this section we discuss how to determine the sample size so that we can be confident that the sample statistic will differ from the population parameter by no more than an amount that we specify. We want the margin of error to be as small as our budget and time allow. Observations cost time and money. Thus we try to keep the sample size small. On the other hand, if the sample size is too small, we will not get useful information and the entire survey or study will be for naught. We can reduce the margin of error by increasing the sample size. But larger size samples increase the study's cost. There are no easy solutions. By the end of this section you should be able to:

1. determine the sample size for simple random sampling to limit the margin of error to some maximum value in estimating an unknown population mean;

2. determine the sample size for simple random sampling to limit the margin of error to some maximum value in estimating an unknown population proportion; and
3. explain without using formulas how to determine the sample size.

Two-Sided Interval on an Unknown Population Mean

To set up a confidence interval on an unknown population mean we have used the following expression:

$$\bar{x} \pm t(\text{estimated standard error of the mean})$$

Since in most business applications the sample size exceeds 30, we can substitute the z-value for the t-value. The expression then becomes

$$\bar{x} \pm z\sqrt{\frac{s^2}{n}} \qquad (7.20)$$

However, $z\sqrt{s^2/n}$ is simply the margin of error. To determine the necessary sample size, we set $z\sqrt{s^2/n}$ equal to the desired margin of error and solve for n:

$$\text{Margin of error (ME)} = z\sqrt{\frac{s^2}{n}} \qquad (7.21)$$

The term s^2 is the sample variance. We will not know what it is until we have taken our sample. At this point, we do not even know our sample size, so we must estimate s^2. Three common approaches are to:

1. use the sample variance from a small *pilot* study;
2. use the sample variance from similar studies; or
3. estimate the range, which equals the estimated maximum value minus the estimated minimum value. Then divide the range by 6 and square that value to obtain the estimated sample variance.

We now illustrate how expression (7.21) can determine the sample size.

Example: Milemaster Tire Study   The population mean tire life of Milemaster tires must be estimated. Based on a small pilot study of 20 tires, the sample *standard deviation* is 800 miles. What must be the sample size to be 95% confident that the sample mean will be within 100 miles of the unknown population mean? In other words, what sample size provides 95% confidence that the margin of error will be ±100 miles?

Begin by substituting what we know into expression (7.21). Remember that the z-value for a 95% two-sided confidence interval can be found in Appendix 5 and is 1.96. Now solve for n, the unknown sample size:

$$\text{Margin of error (ME)} = z\sqrt{\frac{s^2}{n}}$$

$$100 \text{ miles} = 1.96\sqrt{\frac{640,000}{n}}$$

In terms of a formula:

$$n = \frac{z^2 s^2}{\text{ME}^2} = \frac{(3.8416)(640,000)}{10,000} \tag{7.21}$$

$$= 245.86 \text{ or } 246 \text{ tires (always round up when determining sample size)}$$

A simple random sample of 246 tires will allow us to be 95% confident that the sample mean will be within 100 miles of the unknown population mean tire life. The margin of error will be 100 miles. The pilot study sample size counts toward the 246 observations. Thus, we will need only an additional 226 tires to complete the study.

Now think about what the previous paragraph tells us. The population of Milemaster tires is very large. Yet if we take a simple random sample of 246 tires we are 95% confident that our sample mean will be within 100 miles of the unknown population mean. This demonstrates the power of statistical inference.

We can extend sample size determination to one-sided confidence intervals. Expressions (7.20) and (7.21) will not change, but we do need to adjust the z-value to reflect a one-sided confidence interval. For example, for a one-sided 95% confidence interval the z-value would be 1.645, not 1.96.

Two-Sided Interval on an Unknown Population Proportion

To set up a confidence interval on an unknown population proportion we have used the following expression:

$$\hat{p} \pm z \sqrt{\frac{\hat{p}\hat{q}}{n}}$$

However, $z\sqrt{\hat{p}\hat{q}/n}$ simply the margin of error. To determine the necessary sample size, set $z\sqrt{\hat{p}\hat{q}/n}$ equal to the desired margin of error and solve for the sample size, n:

$$\text{Margin of error} = z \sqrt{\frac{\hat{p}\hat{q}}{n}} \tag{7.22}$$

In this situation, the problem is that we do not know what $\hat{p}$ is and we will not know it until we take our sample. So we must estimate $\hat{p}$. Four common approaches are to:

1. use the sample proportion from a small pilot study;
2. use the sample proportion from similar studies;
3. estimate the minimum and maximum possible values of $\hat{p}$ using managerial judgment or intuition. Use both estimates to determine sample sizes. To be on the safe side, select the larger sample size; or
4. use a $\hat{p}$ of .5, which will avoid underestimating the sample size. However, if $\hat{p}$ turns out to be very small (i.e., .01–.10) or very large (i.e., .90–.99) we will have significantly overestimated the sample size. This increases the study cost.

Now we can use expression (7.22) to determine the sample size.

Example: Ambulance Service Study   We want to estimate the unknown population proportion of voters who favor improved ambulance service in the county. Based on a pilot study of size $n = 50$, we estimate $\hat{p}$ to be .40. What sample size is needed to be 99% confident that the sample proportion will be within .04 of the unknown population proportion? That is, we desire a margin of error of ±.04.

Begin by substituting what we know into expression (7.22). Then solve for *n*, the unknown sample size:

$$ME = .04 = 2.576 \sqrt{\frac{(.4)(.6)}{n}}$$

In terms of a formula:

$$n = \frac{z^2 \hat{p}\hat{q}}{ME^2} = \frac{(6.636)(.4)(.6)}{.04^2} \qquad (7.23)$$

$$= 995.4 \text{ or } 996 \text{ people}$$

Thus, a simple random sample of 996 people provides 99% confidence that our sample proportion will be within .04 of the unknown population proportion. In other words, the margin of error will be ±.04. The pilot study of sample size 50 counts toward the overall sample of 996 people.

Again with a relatively small sample from a large population we can estimate the unknown population proportion quite accurately. That explains how the Gallup Organization can draw accurate inferences about all voters while interviewing only about 1,500 people.

We can also extend sample size determination to one-sided confidence intervals. Expressions (7.22) and (7.23) do not change, and we simply adjust the *z*-value to reflect a one-sided confidence interval.

In summary, once we set the maximum margin of error that we can tolerate—a manager's prerogative—and the desired level of confidence, we can determine the sample size to estimate the population mean or proportion.

SECTION 7.7 EXERCISES

1. List the factors that should be considered in calculating the required sample size.

2. A manager wants to estimate a population mean and asks your help. Here is the information at hand:

Population size (*N*)	50,000
Estimated population variance	2,500
Required margin of error	5
Required confidence level	95%

   a. Calculate the necessary sample size.
   b. Some people believe that a *good* sample size is about 10% of the population. Do you agree?

3. Tenure discounts are the difference between the rents charged long-time tenants and newer tenants. Landlords give discounts to keep good tenants and minimize turnover. The American Housing Group wishes to estimate the mean tenure discount in Dallas, Texas. They desire a margin of error of ±2% and a two-sided 95% level of confidence. Based upon previous studies in other cities, the tenure discount estimated standard deviation is 6%.
   a. Determine the necessary sample size.
   b. Given your answer in part **a**, determine the estimated standard error of the mean.

    c. Suppose The American Housing Group wishes to reduce the margin of error to $\pm 1\%$ (reduce by 1/2 from the present $\pm 2\%$). What must the new sample size be?

    d. Based on parts **a** and **c,** describe the exact relationship between sample size and margin of error.

    e. After determining the desired sample size in part **a,** The American Housing Group selects a sample of apartment dwellers and determines that the sample mean tenure discount is 3.5%. Construct and interpret a two-sided 95% confidence interval.

4. Refer to Exercise 3. Compare the answers to the following questions with your answer in part **a** of Exercise 3.

    a. Redo for a one-sided 95% confidence interval.

    b. How does constructing a one-sided confidence interval affect the necessary sample size?

    c. Redo for a two-sided 99% confidence interval.

    d. How does increasing the level of confidence affect the necessary sample size?

    e. Redo for two-sided 95% confidence interval where the tenure discount estimated standard deviation is 3%, not 6%.

    f. How does reducing the estimated standard deviation by 1/2 affect the necessary sample size?

5. The First National Bank of Minneapolis wishes to estimate the mean customer service inquiry resolution time—the time needed to resolve a customer question or complaint on banking services. The resolution time is known to be stationary over time, but its mean is unknown. They desire a margin of error of ± 5 minutes and a two-sided 90% confidence interval. Based on industrywide data, the estimated resolution time variance is 600 minutes.

    a. Determine the necessary sample size.

    b. Suppose that the customer resolution time data were not stationary. Does determining the sample size make sense? *Hint:* Review Sections 2.4 and 2.9 before answering the question.

6. A marketing research firm wishes to estimate the percentage of homeowners who are dissatisfied with their present homeowner's insurance policy. The firm has no feel for what the percentage might be, but it wants to be within 2% of the true proportion with 95% confidence. Calculate the required sample size if the firm plans to use simple random sampling.

7. A major appliance dealer surveys its customers every quarter to determine whether its service department is doing a good job. The company wants to estimate the proportion of its customers who are dissatisfied with its service. The company wants to be 90% confident that the estimate will be within 1.5% of the true proportion. In previous studies the company found that approximately 10% of its customers were dissatisfied.

8. COMCEL inspects a sample of phone handsets for blemishes or scratches. A handset with a blemish or scratch is a defective product and must be refinished. The daily proportion of defectives is known to be stationary over time, but COMCEL has not yet estimated the population proportion defective. They desire a two-sided 99.54% confidence interval (z-value $= 3.00$) and a margin of error of $\pm.0186$. Based upon previous studies, the estimated sample proportion defective is .02. Determine the necessary sample size.

7.8 ≡ Sign Test-Based Nonparametric Confidence Interval for an Unknown Population Median

In the examples we have covered, we assumed that either the population or distribution of the sample mean was normal. This is a good assumption for most data. However, when there are outliers or the population is highly skewed, neither the population nor the sampling distribution may be normal. How then can we construct confidence intervals?

To do so, we will set up a *nonparametric* confidence interval on the *median. Nonparametric* refers to a set of statistical inference methods that do not require a normal population. By the end of this section you should be able to:

1. explain when to construct a confidence interval for the median;
2. construct a confidence interval for the median; and
3. explain the impact of constructing a confidence interval on the mean when an interval on the median should be constructed.

Constructing Approximate 95% Confidence Intervals

Constructing a confidence interval on a population median is relatively simple. The procedure uses ranks and guarantees that the level of confidence will be approximately 95%. This is the procedure:

1. Rank order the data from the smallest to the largest values.
2. Determine the sample median.
3. If there are data values that equal the sample median, delete them. Reduce the sample size by the number of deletions.
4. Look up the sample size in Table 7.9. Determine the *number of values* associated with the sample size.
5. Count up that many data values from the smallest value. This is the lower limit of the confidence interval for the population median.
6. Count down that many data values from the largest value. This is the upper limit of the confidence interval for the population median.

For larger samples—more than 50—determine the number of values as follows. Divide the sample size by 4, take the square root of that number, and multiply by 1.96. Then subtract the result from one-half of the sample size. Use the closest integer.

Table 7.9

Determining Limits of an Approximate 95% Two-Sided Confidence Interval on the Population Median

Sample Size	Number of Values
6–8	1
9–11	2
12–14	3
15–16	4
17–19	5
20–22	6
23–24	7
25–27	8
28–29	9
30–32	10
33–34	11
35–36	12
37–39	13
40–41	14
42–43	15
44–46	16
47–48	17
49–50	18

For example: For $n = 100$, $(100/2) - 1.96\sqrt{100/4}) = 40.2$ or 40. The lower limit of the confidence interval will be the 40th value counting up from the smallest value, and the upper limit will be the 40th largest value, counting down from the largest.

Next we illustrate the nonparametric method for constructing a two-sided 95% confidence interval on an unknown population median.

Example: COMCEL Worker Attitude Study   COMCEL conducts a monthly worker attitude, or job climate, survey. Each month a simple random sample of 20 workers anonymously rate the job climate along the following 10-point scale. COMCEL wishes to construct a two-sided 95% confidence interval estimate on the unknown population median.

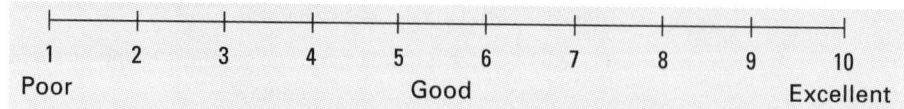

Table 7.10 contains the rank-ordered data for the latest month. Figure 7.10 shows that the attitudes of workers B, N, and Q are outliers; they have very poor attitudes in comparison to everyone else. The outliers suggest that the population from which the sample was taken may be long-tailed or nonnormal. Given that there are outliers, we should construct a confidence interval on the population median.

From Chapter 2 we know that the rank of the sample median is (1 + number of data values)/2. Given 20 data values, the median is halfway between the 10th and 11th ranked data values, or 8.5 (see Table 7.10). Since no sample value equals the sample median, the sample size remains 20. The tabled value (see Table 7.9) for a sample size of 20 is 6. Thus the lower limit of the confidence interval is observation 6 in the column labelled "Count from the Smallest Data Value," or 8. The upper limit is observation 6 in the column labelled "Count from the Largest Data Value," or 9.

Interpretation: We are about 95% confident that the unknown population median job climate attitude at COMCEL is between 8 and 9 on the 10-point scale. This is excellent!

We have the same interpretation for confidence intervals on the mean and median. If we collected 1,000 samples of 20 workers' attitudes, approximately 950 of the confidence intervals would contain the unknown population median. About 50 intervals would not. Therefore, we are about 95% confident that the interval we did construct does contain the unknown population median.

Assumptions for Confidence Intervals on the Population Mean and Median

We must make two assumptions in constructing confidence intervals on the population mean. First, the sample must be a simple random sample from the population. Second, the population must be normally distributed. Only the former assumption is necessary for constructing confidence intervals on the population median. That is, every subgroup of size *n* from the target population must have an equal chance of being selected for the sample.

Confidence Intervals on the Mean in the Presence of Outliers

When the population has outliers, the size of the confidence intervals on the mean and median will differ. What effect will outliers have on the mean? What effect will

FIGURE 7.10   Stem-and-Leaf Display and Box Plot for Job Climate Data

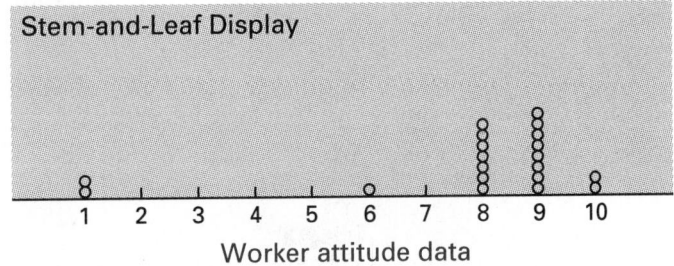

Worker attitude data

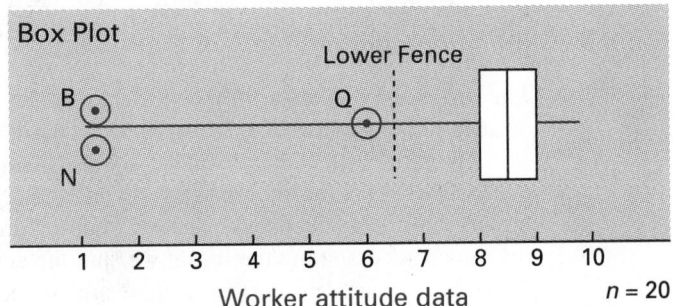

Worker attitude data $n = 20$

Table 7.10

Ranked Worker Attitude Data

Worker	Data	Count from the Smallest Data Value	Count from the Largest Data Value
B	1	1	20
N	1	2	19
Q	6	3	18
C	8	4	17
E	8	5	16
G	8	6	15
L	8	7	14
T	8	8	13
A	8	9	12
D	8	10	11
F	9	11	10
H	9	12	9
J	9	13	8
K	9	14	7
M	9	15	6
O	9	16	5
P	9	17	4
S	9	18	3
I	10	19	2
R	10	20	1

they have on the standard error of the mean? Will a confidence interval for the mean be wider than for the median? Why? Please think about it before reading on.

Construct an approximate 95% two-sided confidence interval on the mean for the COMCEL worker-attitude data.

$$\bar{x} = 7.80$$

$$s = 2.48$$

$$\frac{s}{\sqrt{n}} = \frac{2.48}{\sqrt{20}} = .55$$

$$\bar{x} \pm t(\text{two-sided 95\%, 19})(\text{estimated standard error})$$

Lower limit: $7.80 - (2.093)(.55) = 6.65$
Upper limit: $7.80 + (2.093)(.55) = 8.95$

Interpretation: We are 95% confident that the unknown population mean worker attitude rating is between 6.65 and 8.95 on the 10-point scale.

The results show that the mean—7.8—is smaller than the median—8.5. This is due to the effect of the three outliers—workers B, N, and Q. In determining the median, we are concerned only that the number of observations above and below the median be the same. In computing the mean, we sum the actual values of the observations and divide by the sample size. Thus if there are outliers, the median and mean may differ. Notice how the outliers—in this case, all very low values—*pulled* the mean toward them. Outliers will not affect the median. Remember, when we have outliers, the median is a better measure of the center for it is robust, or insensitive, to outliers.

Even more important to note is that the confidence interval for the mean is wider than that for the median. The outliers produce a relatively large estimated standard error. Even one or two outliers can significantly increase the sample standard deviation because we take the *squared* deviations around the mean. This yields a wider confidence interval for the mean, and wider confidence intervals are less meaningful.

In summary, when sample data contain outliers, construct confidence intervals for the population median using the nonparametric approach. However, when the population or the sampling distribution is near normal, confidence intervals for the mean will be narrower than when using the nonparametric method.

SECTION 7.8 EXERCISES

1.   Explain when you should construct a confidence interval for the median rather than a confidence interval for the mean.

2.   Consider the following sample of data points: {1, 2, 4, 6, 7, 50}.
      a. Find the sample median.
      b. Construct an approximate 95% confidence interval for the population median.

3.   Refer to Exercise 2.
      a. Construct a 95% confidence interval for the population mean.
      b. Which interval is wider? Why?
      c. Which interval—on the population median or mean—is more appropriate? Why?

4.   Participants in a training class are asked to rate a new instructor. The rating scale ranges from 0 = poor to 10 = outstanding. The following scores were obtained from 13 trainees:

{1, 4, 5, 5, 6, 6, 6, 7, 7, 7, 7, 8, 9}

a. Find the sample median.

b. What is the resulting sample size after adjustment for the repeating values of the median?

c. Construct an approximate 95% confidence interval for the population median.

d. What practical meaning could the director of training assign to this confidence interval?

5. A shop steward wants to estimate the mean number of days of sick leave taken by the workers in a large plant. He selects a random sample of 50 employees and records the following numbers of days over the past month:

0	0	0	1	1	2	3	3	3	5
0	0	0	1	1	2	3	3	4	6
0	0	1	1	1	2	3	3	4	7
0	0	1	1	1	2	3	3	4	14
0	0	1	1	1	2	3	3	4	18

After seeing the sample data, the steward decides to estimate the population median rather than the population mean. Do you agree with his choice? Explain.

6. Below are profit margins on sales—net income after taxes divided by sales—for 10 firms. Construct an approximate 95% confidence interval on the population median.

5%   5.1%   5.5%   5.9%   6%   6.3%   6.6%   6.8%   7.7%   13.4%

7. Quality circles are small groups of employees who meet on a regular basis to identify and solve problems that keep them from doing their jobs right. Quality circles use the Ishikawa Diagram (see Chapter 15) to brainstorm many ideas. The circle coordinator wishes to estimate the "average" number of ideas generated by the circles. Her goal is for every circle to generate over 50 separate solutions per problem. Consider the following sample data on the number of solutions generated for a materials problem in 15 quality circles that used Ishikawa diagrams.

5	49	52	55	57
58	59	60	61	62
63	70	121	123	124

a. Construct a box plot for the data.

b. Construct and interpret an approximate 95% two-sided interval on the population median. Has the coordinator's goal been achieved? Discuss.

c. Why did the circle coordinator construct an interval on the population median, and not the population mean number of solutions per group.

8. Fine Foods Inc. wishes to estimate the "average" income of its most affluent consumer market segment. It suspects that income within this segment is not normally distributed. Below is a random sample of 20 families taken from the affluent market segment.

$75,750	$77,050	$80,750	$82,450
85,675	91,000	96,000	97,750
150,000	155,750	157,250	160,500
165,500	175,000	190,500	495,500
510,000	650,000	750,500	1,250,500

a. Construct a box plot for the data. Do the income data have outliers?

b. Construct and interpret an approximate 95% two-sided interval on the population median.

c. Construct and interpret a 95% two-sided interval on the population mean.

d. Which interval is more meaningful and why?

7.9 ▦ Confidence Intervals on an Unknown Population Variance and Standard Deviation

Up to this point, we have drawn inferences about the center of the population. For qualitative yes/no data we constructed confidence intervals on the population proportion. For quantitative data we constructed confidence intervals on either the population mean or median. However, sometimes we will be interested in making inferences about the population's standard deviation rather than its mean value. By the end of this section you should be able to:

1. explain the characteristics of the chi-square distribution; and
2. construct and interpret confidence intervals on the population standard deviation.

  The following problem illustrates why constructing confidence intervals on an unknown population standard deviation is necessary.

Example: Just-in-Time Manufacturing Systems COMCEL has recently installed a just-in-time (JIT) manufacturing system. COMCEL does not stockpile the materials needed to manufacture its mobile phones. Instead it relies on vendors to deliver the materials needed for daily production at noon every day. COMCEL's vendors have agreed to a delivery schedule with a maximum standard deviation in delivery times of 2 hours. Assuming a normal distribution, 95% of the time material should arrive within ±4 hours of noon (± two standard deviations). COMCEL collects the delivery times for the 10 most recent working days. Are its vendors able to meet the maximum 2-hour standard deviation around noon? COMCEL wants to construct a 90% confidence interval on the population standard deviation in delivery times.

  How can COMCEL estimate the population standard deviation in delivery times? All inferences made in this chapter depend on prior knowledge of the distribution of the sample statistic used to make the inference. We can construct confidence intervals for a population mean because we know that the distribution of the sample mean is normally distributed. What would happen if we took repeated samples from a normal population and calculated the sample variance, s^2, for each sample? What is the distribution of the sample variance?

  Consider the following ratio: $(n-1)s^2/\sigma^2$. This ratio is a sample variance multiplied by the sample size minus 1, then divided by the population variance. Since the population variance is a fixed, but unknown, value, the ratio will vary as the sample variance varies. If we take repeated samples of size n and calculate the ratio, what would the resulting histogram look like? Would it be normal or skewed?

  The answer is that it would be skewed toward higher values and here is why. The smallest value for the ratio is zero, which happens when all the sample observations are the same and therefore s^2 is zero. Since the variance cannot be negative, the ratio cannot be negative. The ratio can take on very large values when the sample data are very different from one another. Since the ratio's lower bound is zero and it has no theoretical upper bound, the histogram must be skewed toward higher values.

The Chi-Square Distribution

The histogram of this ratio is called a chi-square distribution. The chi-square distribution is a family of curves. While the curves vary in shape, all values of chi-square have a lower bound of zero and are skewed toward higher values. If we took repeated samples of size 10 from a population with variance σ^2 and calculated the ratio, $(n-1)s^2/\sigma^2$, the distribution of ratios is chi-square distributed with $(n-1)$, or 9 degrees of freedom.

Please look at Appendix 6. Each row represents a different distribution within the chi-square family. Find the row labelled 9 degrees of freedom and the chi-square column labelled .025. The tabled number is 2.70. If we took repeated samples from the population and computed the ratios, $9s^2/\sigma^2$, 2.5% of them will have values between 0 and 2.70. Moving over to the chi-square column labelled .975, the tabled number is 19.02. Thus, 97.5% of the ratios will be less than 19.02. Since we have identified the 2.5 percentile and the 97.5 percentile, the middle 95% of all ratios will fall between 2.70 and 19.02. Figure 7.11 displays this chi-square distribution with 9 degrees of freedom. [*Note:* Chi-square is also written as χ^2.]

Thus, the lower and upper limits of a 95% confidence interval on a ratio are

$$2.70 \leq \frac{(n-1)s^2}{\sigma^2} \leq 19.02$$

Generalizing, the lower and upper limits of a confidence interval on a ratio are

$$\chi^2_{x/2} \leq \frac{(n-1)s^2}{\sigma^2} \leq \chi^2_{1-x/2}$$

where $x = 1 -$ desired level of confidence expressed as a number between 0 and 1.

Rearranging terms, we obtain the following expression for constructing confidence intervals on the population variance:

$$\frac{(n-1)s^2}{\chi^2_{1-x/2}} \leq \sigma^2 \leq \frac{(n-1)s^2}{\chi^2_{x/2}} \tag{7.24}$$

Expression (7.24) says we can construct a confidence interval for any population variance by multiplying the degrees of freedom by the sample variance and dividing by the appropriate percentile values from the chi-square table. To obtain a confidence interval on the population standard deviation, we simply take the square root of the lower and upper limits.

Now we can construct a 90% confidence interval on the unknown population standard deviation in delivery times. Before doing so, we state our assumptions:

ASSUMPTION 1:   The 10 days for which we collected data are representative of vendors' typical delivery times.

ASSUMPTION 2:   In the population, vendor arrival times are normally distributed.

FIGURE 7.11 χ^2 Distribution with 9 Degrees of Freedom

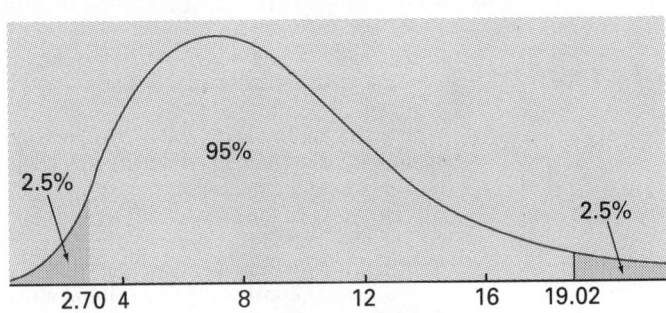

To test the first assumption, COMCEL could compare these 10 arrivals with deliveries from other weeks. Assumption 1 would be met if there was no discernible difference. Assumption 2 is realistic since a stem-and-leaf display for the 10 delivery times is near-normal shaped. This suggests that the population may well be normal shaped. The raw data and corresponding statistics are presented here:

Day	1	2	3	4	5	6	7	8	9	10
Arrival time	Noon	Noon	1:00	11:00	Noon	11:00	1:00	2:00	Noon	Noon
Hours off target	0	0	1	−1	0	−1	+1	+2	0	0

$$\bar{x} = .2 \text{ hour off noon target}$$

$$s^2 = .84$$

$$s = .92 \text{ hour off noon target}$$

To construct a 90% interval, we need the chi-square values for 9 degrees of freedom at the 5th percentile (.05) and at the 95th percentile (.95). Now substitute the sample variance and sample size into expression (7.24):

$$\frac{(10-1)(.84)}{16.92} \le \sigma^2 \le \frac{(10-1)(.84)}{3.33}$$

$$.45 \le \sigma^2 \le 2.27$$

To obtain a 90% confidence interval on the population standard deviation, σ, we take the square root of the lower and upper limits:

$$.67 \text{ hour} \le \sigma \le 1.51 \text{ hours}$$

Interpretation: We are 90% confident that the population standard deviation in vendor delivery about the noon target time is between .67 hour and 1.51 hours.

What can COMCEL conclude about the variability in delivery times? Since the confidence interval's upper limit is less than 2 hours, COMCEL's vendors are more than meeting the 2-hour standard deviation requirement.

Suppose that the lower and upper limits of the interval had been greater than 2 hours. What could COMCEL have concluded? Please think about it before reading on.

COMCEL could have concluded that it had sufficient reason to complain that its vendors are not meeting the agreed-upon reliability standards (standard deviation) in delivery schedules.

In summary, when we are interested in performance variability rather than mean performance, we construct confidence intervals on the population standard deviation. We use the chi-square distribution to construct the limits of the confidence interval.

SECTION 7.9 EXERCISES

1. For each of the following statements, indicate whether the z, t, or chi-square distribution applies. (One or more distributions may apply to each statement.)
   a. The area under the curve equals 1.
   b. The choice of the exact curve depends on the degrees of freedom.
   c. The distribution is symmetric about zero.
   d. The distribution is skewed to the right.
   e. The graph describes the distribution of the sample mean.
   f. The distribution is used to estimate a population proportion.
   g. The distribution is used to estimate a population variance.

2. Complete the following table by finding the chi-square values for each of the sample sizes listed.

Sample Size	Degrees of Freedom	2.5 Percentile	97.5 Percentile
4	_____	_____	_____
8	_____	_____	_____
12	_____	_____	_____

3. Determine the two appropriate chi-square values for expression (7.24) for the following business studies.

Sample Size	Level of Confidence
25	80%
10	90%
17	95%
121	98%
31	99%

4. A quality-control inspector wishes to estimate the population standard deviation of a set of measurements. A sample variance of 25 squared cm was calculated based on a sample of size 9. Construct a 95% confidence interval for the population standard deviation.

5. Consider the following set of data values selected from a normal population: {1, 4, 3, 2, 5}.
    a. Calculate the sample mean and sample variance.
    b. Estimate the population mean using a 90% reliability coefficient.
    c. Construct a 90% confidence interval for the population standard deviation.

6. A manufacturer makes a machine that injects a specified amount of heart stimulant into a patient's bloodstream. The manufacturer claims that the standard deviation of the amount injected is less than .05 milliliter. If the standard deviation is greater than .05, the patient may not get enough stimulant or get too much stimulant and die. The variance in a sample of 10 injections was .00587.
    a. Construct an 80% confidence interval to estimate the standard deviation of the amount injected.
    b. Construct a 99% confidence interval to estimate the standard deviation of the amount injected.
    c. Keeping in mind that people's lives depend on your decision, would you conclude that the machine is safe to use? Defend your position.

7. A parcel delivery service wants to reduce the amount of time that it takes to deliver parcels within a city. Should the firm construct a confidence interval on the population mean or population standard deviation?

8. A parcel delivery service wants to increase delivery time consistency for parcels within a city. Should the firm construct a confidence interval on the population mean or population standard deviation?

9. Excessive variation is the major battle manufacturing industries have today in achieving high product quality. At the B&L Optical Company, the process standard deviation in the tensile strength of its eyeglass frames has been 150 pounds per square inch (ppsi). Based on suggestions from its hourly production workers, B&L has made what it thinks are major process improvements. First B&L ensures that the new process has been stabilized—the standard deviation over 15 successive shifts is neither increasing or decreasing over time. Then it takes a random sample of 121 eyeglass frames from a production shift and determines that the process standard deviation is now 123 ppsi.
    a. Construct and interpret a 95% interval on the population standard deviation
    b. Have these improvements reduced the process standard deviation from the historical 150-ppsi level?

10. Six months ago, the standard deviation in strength of phones was 50 pounds per square inch. COMCEL engineers have installed new equipment which they believe will reduce the process variation. Here are 10 phones' tensile strengths after the new equipment has been installed. Construct a 95% confidence interval on the standard deviation. Has COMCEL's quality-improvement program been successful?

4,750	4,775
4,775	4,745
4,755	4,760
4,730	4,865
4,750	4,756

11. Consistently superior service in the parcel delivery business means (1) achieving the desired target mean delivery time and (2) achieving it with little parcel-to-parcel delivery time variation. Based on customer wants and desires, United Parcel has set a mean target delivery time of 180 minutes for an intracounty delivery and a standard deviation in delivery time of 10 minutes. After the delivery time process has been stabilized (both the mean and standard deviation are neither increasing nor decreasing over time), United Parcel conducts a *process capability study*. It tracks a random sample of 25 intracounty packages and records the following delivery times (in minutes to the nearest five minutes).

170	160	170	180	185
180	190	170	175	195
190	185	175	170	185
175	180	170	190	170
175	190	190	170	190

a. Determine the sample mean and standard deviation.
b. Construct and interpret a 99% confidence interval on the mean and standard deviation.
c. Has United Parcel met its established twin goals? Discuss.

7.10 Key Ideas and Overview

We summarize Chapter 7 with the following four key ideas:

IDEA 1: We use sample statistics to estimate population parameters.

Population parameters are fixed but unknown values for which we obtain estimates by using:

1. the sample mean to construct a confidence interval on the population mean;
2. the sample proportion to construct a confidence interval on the population proportion;
3. the sample median to construct a confidence interval on the population median; and
4. the sample standard deviation to construct a confidence interval on the population standard deviation.

We use confidence intervals to estimate population parameters of cross-sectional and stationary time-ordered data.

IDEA 2: As the sample size increases the sample statistics tend to get closer to the unknown population parameters.

The estimated standard error of the mean and proportion are $s/\sqrt{n}$ and $\sqrt{\hat{p}\hat{q}/n}$, respectively. As we increase the sample size, the estimated standard error gets smaller. Thus the sample mean (or proportion) tends to move closer to the unknown population mean (or proportion).

As the sample size increases, the sample variance also gets closer to the population variance. We can see this from expression (7.24). Set up two 95% confidence intervals for the population variance—one for 2 degrees of freedom and one for 120.

<table>
<tr><td></td><td style="text-align:center">2 Degrees of Freedom</td><td style="text-align:center">120 Degrees of Freedom</td></tr>
<tr><td>Lower Limit</td><td style="text-align:center">$\dfrac{2s^2}{\chi^2_{.975}} = \dfrac{2s^2}{7.38}$</td><td style="text-align:center">$\dfrac{120s^2}{\chi^2_{.975}} = \dfrac{120s^2}{152.21}$</td></tr>
<tr><td></td><td style="text-align:center">$= .27s^2$</td><td style="text-align:center">$= .79s^2$</td></tr>
<tr><td>Upper Limit</td><td style="text-align:center">$\dfrac{2s^2}{\chi^2_{.025}} = \dfrac{2s^2}{.0506}$</td><td style="text-align:center">$\dfrac{120s^2}{\chi^2_{.025}} = \dfrac{120s^2}{91.58}$</td></tr>
<tr><td></td><td style="text-align:center">$= 39.53s^2$</td><td style="text-align:center">$= 1.31s^2$</td></tr>
</table>

For a sample size of 3 (2 degrees of freedom), the confidence interval is very wide. It ranges from .27 to 39.53 times the sample variance. For a sample size of 121, the confidence interval shrinks. It ranges from .79 to 1.31 times the sample variance. Idea 2 holds for all sample statistics.

Table 7.11

Overview of Types of Confidence Intervals

Unknown Population Parameter	Survey Design	Assumptions	Sample Statistic	Two-Sided Confidence Interval (Correction Factor Omitted)
Population mean	Simple random	Population distribution is near normal.	$\dfrac{\sum_i x_i}{n}$	Lower limit: $\bar{x} - t\left(\dfrac{s}{\sqrt{n}}\right)$ Upper limit: $\bar{x} + t\left(\dfrac{s}{\sqrt{n}}\right)$
Population median	Simple random		Sample median	Lower limit: see Table 7.9 Upper limit: see Table 7.9
Population mean	Stratified random	Population distribution is near normal.	Strata means $\bar{x}_1, \bar{x}_2, \ldots,$ overall sample mean $\bar{x}_{ST}$ see (7.12)	Lower limit: $\bar{x}_{ST} - t(\text{Est } SE_{ST})$ Upper limit: $\bar{x}_{ST} + t(\text{Est } SE_{ST})$
Population proportion	Simple random	Sampling distribution of sample proportion is near normal. Use Cochran's rules. _table 7.8_	$\hat{p} = X/n$ $\hat{q} = 1 - \hat{p}$ X = number of "yes" responses n = sample size	Lower Limit: $\hat{p} - z\sqrt{\dfrac{\hat{p}\hat{q}}{n}}$ Upper Limit: $\hat{p} + z\sqrt{\dfrac{\hat{p}\hat{q}}{n}}$
Population standard deviation	Simple random	Population is normal. _Appendix 6_	Sample standard deviation	Lower limit: $\dfrac{(n-1)s^2}{\chi^2_{1-x/2}}$ Upper limit: $\dfrac{(n-1)s^2}{\chi^2_{x/2}}$

IDEA 3:   Confidence intervals provide a probable range within which the population parameter will fall.

Table 7.11 contains a summary of the types of confidence intervals covered in this chapter.

Regardless of whether we select a simple random sample or a stratified random sample, the general expression for any confidence interval involving means or proportions is simply

$$\text{Sample statistic} \pm (\text{reliability coefficient})(\text{estimated standard error})$$

We cannot use the above expression for estimating the population median and standard deviation. When the population is highly skewed and the sample size is small, use the nonparametric confidence interval method. To estimate the population standard deviation, use expression (7.24) and the chi-square distribution.

IDEA 4:   Confidence intervals measure only the effects of sampling error. They provide accurate and useful information only when the manager avoids the selection, response, and nonresponse errors discussed in Chapter 6.

COMCEL

Date: March 9, 1995
To: Ann Tabor, CEO
From: Nat Gordon, V.P. of Manufacturing
Re: Project Team Report: Improving Time-to-Failure

SUMMARY
In November, the team installed new robotic manufacturing equipment to improve time-to-failure. We have just completed our final tests and the project team has achieved its goal. The mean time-to-failure is at least 2,813 hours.

SUPPORTING ANALYSIS
The team first reviewed all the causes of breakdowns for our phones. It appeared that improper welding was the major cause. Thus the team chose to install additional robotics in the spot welding operation. By late January we were producing phones with the new equipment. Shortly thereafter we began running our time-to-failure tests. Two days ago we completed the final accelerated life testing. We selected a simple random sample of 61 phones from the over 3000 phones produced on the new equipment. The sample mean and the standard deviation for the 61 phones were 2,855 hours and 200 hours, respectively. Given these data, we constructed a one-sided "at least" 95% confidence interval. The lower limit is 2,813 hours. Thus we are 95% confident that the population mean time-to-failure is at least 2,813 hours. There is a 5% chance that the population mean is not greater than 2,813 hours.

CHAPTER 7 QUESTIONS

1. You are interested in whether certified public accountants favor a recent change in the tax laws. What are the target population, the unknown population parameter, and the sample statistic for this study?

2. What does the population standard deviation measure?

3. Under what conditions must the sample statistic equal the corresponding population parameter?

4. Explain why the variance of a distribution of the sample mean must be less than the variance of the population from which it was constructed.

5. You do not know either the mean of the population or the sampling distribution. Yet the distribution of the sample mean is useful in drawing inferences about the unknown population mean. Why?

6. Suppose the central limit theorem did not exist. What impact, if any, would this have on constructing confidence intervals on μ?

7. You select the first 20 people who exit a theater and ask them to rate the movie on a scale from 1 to 10. You wish to draw inferences from these 20 people to the theater-going population. Why will your confidence interval not be meaningful?

8. What information does a confidence interval provide that the sample mean does not?

9. The margin of error for estimating a population mean is $t \cdot s/\sqrt{n}$. Without changing the level of confidence, what is a practical way to reduce the margin of error?

10. Why would you want to reduce the margin of error?

11. Why is a t-based confidence interval larger than an equivalent z-based interval?

12. What would the limits be for a 100% confidence interval?

13. What is a one-sided confidence interval? When is it necessary?

14. Provide an example different from those in the book where you would recommend using a stratified random sample rather than a simple random sample. Discuss.

15. If a stratified sample is required but you select a simple random sample, what impact, if any, will this have on the confidence interval's margin of error?

16. Why does increasing the confidence level increase the margin of error?

17. Why do outliers or highly skewed populations require confidence intervals on the median rather than the mean?

18. Suppose you compute a confidence interval on the mean when there are outliers. What impact will this have on the sample mean, the estimated standard error, and the width of the confidence interval?

19. Provide an example different from those in the book where it would be important to estimate an unknown population standard deviation.

20. Even if the population is not normal-shaped, you can use the z- or t-tables to construct confidence intervals. Why?

21. How are sample means and proportions similar and how are they different?

CHAPTER 7 APPLICATION PROBLEMS

1. An attempted hostile takeover occurs when the target firm's management resists acquisition. Maximizing share price is the most effective way to resist. Then the acquiring firm may have to pay too steep a price for the acquisition. Other less effective approaches are taking a *poison pill* or using *greenmail.*

   An investment banking house wants to estimate the proportion of firms that use the strategy to maximize share price. It takes a simple random sample of 1,000 firms. Eight hundred indicate that they use the strategy to maximize share price.

   a. Set up and interpret a 90% confidence interval on the population proportion that uses this strategy.

   b. What two assumptions must be true for the statistical inference to be meaningful?

2. The American Housing Association wants to estimate the mean length-of-tenure discount after five years across the United States. It selects a simple random sample of 900 tenants and finds that the mean discount after five years is 8% and the sample standard deviation is 5%. That is, tenants who have lived at an apartment for five years pay about 92% of the rent that new tenants pay at the same apartment complex. Set up and interpret a 95% confidence interval on the mean discount after five years.

3. Historically, the mean age of accounts payable has been 22 days. For the past six months the firm has tried several ways to reduce the age of accounts payable. The accounting supervisor selects a simple random sample of 225 accounts payable. The sample mean age is 20.5 days and the sample standard deviation is 7.5 days.
   a. Set up the appropriate 90% confidence interval.
   b. Based on the confidence interval, has the firm been successful in reducing the mean age of accounts payable?

4. A health care firm is considering introducing a home plaque removal system that is almost as effective as a dental cleaning. The systems will retail for $89. The firm will introduce the product only if the population proportion of potential customers who would buy the product is at least .22 (or 22%). The firm selects a simple random sample of 900 potential customers, and 234 indicate a willingness to buy the product.
   a. Set up and interpret the appropriate 95% confidence interval.
   b. Based on the confidence interval, should the firm introduce the product nationwide?

5. A firm is presently using family branding on a consumer product and selling about 1,750 cartons per store per week in the southeast United States. The marketing group has developed a new media campaign that it believes will increase sales substantially. It convinces management to try individual branding for six months. After the test period the firm selects a random sample of 400 stores and finds that these stores have sold a mean of 1,760 cartons per store per week; the sample standard deviation is 2,000 cartons per week.
   a. Set up and interpret the appropriate 95% confidence interval.
   b. Based on the confidence interval, do you conclude that the individual branding has increased the mean level of sales.

6. The quality-control department takes a simple random sample of 2,000 TV cabinets each week (400 per day). They check for the presence of scratches or surface blemishes. If more than 5% of the production line's TVs have scratches or blemishes, the product does not conform to specifications, and the week's production is 100% inspected.
   Shown below are the daily defect figures for this week's production run:

Day	Number of Defects	Sample	Sample Proportion
Monday	13	400	.0325
Tuesday	11	400	.0275
Wednesday	14	400	.0350
Thursday	10	400	.0250
Friday	12	400	.0300
For week	60	2,000	.0300

   a. Plot the daily sample proportions. Place the days of the week on the horizontal axis and the daily sample proportions on the vertical axis. Do the daily sample proportions appear to be stable in the mean? [*Hint:* See Chapter 2 for line graphing.]
   b. What is the maximum proportion of nonconforming products for the week's production run? Set up and interpret an appropriate 90% confidence interval.
   c. Should the firm 100% inspect last week's production run? Discuss.

7. One hundred economic forecasters are interviewed and asked to make predictions as to whether the budget deficit will be reduced next year. The 95% confidence interval on the population proportion of forecasters who predict that the budget deficit will be reduced is .49 to .53.
   a. Can we say at a 95% level of confidence that a majority of the economic forecasters in the United States believe that the deficit will be reduced next year? Explain.

b. Suppose the answer in part **a** does not allow you to say that a majority of forecasters believe that the deficit will be reduced next year. Would reducing the margin of error help, and, if so, how can it be reduced? Explain.

8. Industrial psychologists believe that stress is curvilinearly related to performance. That is, too little stress produces no drive to excel. Too much stress causes anxiety, which reduces performance. From 1989 to 1991, a firm worked to optimize the level of stress within a plant. At the beginning of the period, the level of stress was at 5 (on a scale of 1 to 10)—the optimal level. However, in the past nine months several things have happened that may have caused a change in the stress level.

   The firm's psychologist selects a simple random sample of 50 workers from the 2,000 employees and administers a stress test. The mean level of stress is 5.35 with a sample variance of .36.
   a. Construct a 99% confidence interval for the mean stress level for the plant.
   b. Does it appear that mean stress level has changed from the optimum of 5?

9. The manager of a service center must estimate the mean time it takes for her telephone operators to handle a customer complaint over the phone. She has 50 operators in her department. She takes a simple random sample of 10 operators on a randomly selected day and obtains the following data on the time (in minutes) spent per call:

$$2 \quad 3 \quad 2 \quad 3 \quad 3 \quad 3 \quad 2 \quad 2 \quad 2 \quad 3$$

   a. Set up and interpret an appropriate 90% confidence interval.
   b. Last year the mean time was 3.2 minutes. Has the time to handle calls changed? Explain.

10. The manager of a repair center must estimate the mean travel time between customers for an 800-person repair force. From other repair firms' data, she estimates the standard deviation in travel times will be about 20 minutes. What size sample must she take so that she can be 90% confident that the sample mean will not vary from the population mean by more than 6 minutes?

11. A human resources manager wants to know the proportion of firms in the United States that have daycare facilities on their premises. His pilot study of 30 plants indicates that .20 have day care facilities. What is the sample size needed to be 95% confident that the sample proportion will be within .05 of the unknown population proportion?

12. An arbitrator wishes to estimate the mean number of grievances per week in all plants with 1,000—5,000 hourly employees. He selects a simple random sample of 25 firms and obtains the following data:

$$\bar{x} = 9$$

$$s = 5$$

Set up and interpret an appropriate 80% confidence interval.

13. A vice president of a large manufacturing firm wants to estimate the median productivity rate of his 2,000 work teams. He selects a simple random sample of 9 teams and obtains the following productivity data as percentage of standard:

$$92\% \quad 95\% \quad 89\% \quad 96\% \quad 104\% \quad 138\% \quad 99\% \quad 92\% \quad 101\%$$

   a. Set up and interpret an appropriate 95% confidence interval.
   b. What must the vice president have assumed about the 2,000 work groups' productivities that made him think that a confidence interval on the median, and not the mean, was appropriate?
   c. Are the sample data consistent with his thinking?

14. Howard Bright, plant manager at COMCEL, wants to estimate how much variability there is in job climate among all blue-collar workers. He selects a simple random sample of 12 workers and obtains the following data on a 10-point job climate scale (higher numbers mean a more positive attitude toward the firm).

5   6   6   7   6   5   7   6   6   5   7   6

a. Set up and interpret an appropriate 90% confidence interval on the standard deviation in job climate among all blue-collar workers.

b. Why must he set up a confidence interval? After all, he knows the sample standard deviation of the 12 blue-collar workers. Explain.

15. A firm wishes to estimate the mean weekly sales in cartons per week. The marketer selects a stratified sample of 25 stores from the low monthly sales stratum and 25 stores from the high monthly sales stratum. Each stratum has 1,000 stores. Shown below are the statistics for the weekly sales data (in cartons) for a randomly selected week.

	Stratum 1	Stratum 2
$\bar{x}_i$	45	100
s_i^2	60	150
n_i	25	25

Set up and interpret an appropriate 90% confidence interval on the mean weekly sales over all stores.

16. A quality-control group checks the weight of automobile batteries. One major shipment contained the last two months' production. Since the group believes there is much month-to-month variation, the members select a stratified random sample using each month as a stratum. In January the firm produced 1,000 batteries, and in February it produced 800 batteries. Here are the sample statistics:

	January	February
$\bar{x}_i$	15.0 lb	16.0 lb
s_i^2	.75	.90
n_i	30	24

a. Set up and interpret an appropriate 95% confidence interval on the mean weight of the batteries.

b. The engineering specification states that the mean weight of this battery is 15.6 pounds. Has the shipment met weight specification? Explain.

17. COMCEL's quality-control department has set the mean impact resistance standard for plastic headphones at 4,660 pounds per square inch (ppsi). It has set the standard deviation in impact resistances at 22 pounds per square inch. During each shift the quality control department takes a sample of 10 phones (about one every 45 minutes) and tests their impact resistance. Shown below are the data for one shift:

Time	Impact Resistances (ppsi)
1	4,650
2	4,650
3	4,600
4	4,700
5	4,650
6	4,650
7	4,700
8	4,650
9	4,600
10	4,650

a. Plot the 10 time-ordered impact resistance data values. Place time into shift on the horizontal axis and impact resistance on the vertical axis. Is the production process stationary?
b. Set up and interpret an appropriate 95% confidence interval on the population mean.
c. Set up and interpret an appropriate 95% confidence interval on the standard deviation.
d. Are both manufacturing standards being met on this shift? Explain.
e. As a manager, what problem-solving action should you take?

 18. The U.S. Park Service takes a random sample of tourists entering a federal park to determine the mean length of stay (in days) of all tourists. It obtains the following responses:

$$2 \quad 3 \quad 4 \quad 2 \quad 40 \quad 3 \quad 4 \quad 5 \quad 4 \quad 3$$

a. Set up and interpret an appropriate 95% confidence interval on the population mean.
b. Set up and interpret an appropriate 95% confidence interval on the population median.
c. Given the raw data, which approach makes more sense? Explain.

 19. The engineering manager has been testing a new brake pad. Because of its cost, the pad must last, on average, at least 50,000 miles before replacement. The manager selects a simple random sample of 10 cars and fits them with 10 randomly selected new brake pads. The cars are tested in simulated city and highway driving until the pads need replacement. Here are the sample statistics:

$$n = 10$$

$$\bar{x} = 54{,}000 \text{ miles}$$

$$s = 3{,}162 \text{ miles}$$

a. Set up and interpret an appropriate 99% confidence interval.
b. What action should the manager take? Should he or she stay with the present brake pads or switch to the new pads? Explain.
c. Why did you need to construct a confidence interval? After all, the sample mean was much larger than 50,000 miles.

 20. A food distributor claims that its frozen diet meals contain no more than a mean of 200 calories per serving. As head of a consumer watchdog group, you question this claim. You select a sample of 20 meals and determine the sample mean and standard deviation for the number of calories in a meal. Following are the sample statistics:

$$n = 20$$

$$\bar{x} = 195 \text{ calories}$$

$$s = 44.72 \text{ calories}$$

a. Set up and interpret an appropriate 95% confidence interval.
b. Is the food distributor's claim justified? Explain.

 21. In *Swain v. Alabama,* the U.S. Supreme Court compared the fraction of grand jurors who are black (about 12%) with their fraction in the community (about 26%). The Court decided that the difference in percentages was insufficient to create a *prima facie* case. *Prima facie* means that the evidence appears to indicate that discrimination is occurring. If the plaintiffs demonstrate a *prima facie* case, then the burden of proof shifts to the defendant to explain or justify the apparent discrimination.
   Assume that blacks formed 12% of the 2,000 jurors over the past 10 years.
a. Assume for the moment that the population proportion of blacks in the community is unknown. Set up an "at most" 95% confidence interval on the unknown population proportion of blacks in the community based on the 12% figure.
b. Relying on census data, the court knew that the population proportion of blacks in the community was 26%. Given your answer in part **a,** what could the court have concluded about the potential for racial discrimination in selecting juries?

22. The Securities and Exchange Commission (SEC) requires companies to file annual reports concerning their financial status. Firms cannot audit every account receivable, so the SEC permits firms to estimate the true mean. Suppose the SEC requires that a reported mean be within $5 of the true mean with 95% confidence. Given a small sample of 20, firm Y estimates the standard deviation to be $50. What must the total sample size be so that the firm can be 95% confident that the sample mean will be within $5 of the true mean?

23. In *Sears, Roebuck and Co. v. City of Ingelwood,* Sears claimed that it had overpaid its sales tax because of an erroneous definition of what constituted an out-of-city sale. The law read that sales made to persons in the city limits were not subject to the tax. To support its claim, Sears selected a random sample of 900 sales slips and found that 330 of them were for sales to persons within the city and thus not subject to the sales tax. Set up a two-sided 95% confidence interval on the population proportion of sales to persons within the city.

24. In an antitrust case, *U.S. v. United Shoe Machinery Corp.,* the government estimated the market share United Shoe held on a variety of machines for the shoe industry. Using a simple random sample of 41 firms, United Shoe's sample proportion of fitting room machines was .41. Set up and interpret a 95% two-sided confidence interval on the population proportion (market dominance) of United Shoe's fitting room machines.

25.

Date: March 17, 1992
To: Cherian Jain, Manager of Marketing Research
From: Bill O'Hara, Vice-President of Marketing
Re: Partial Harrid Survey Data for Four Sales Regions

As you recall, COMCEL commissioned the Harrid Survey Group to conduct a survey in our four sales regions. Harrid took several different random samples from our four sales regions. Among other questions, the firm determined the importance that consumers place on the need to buy American-made phones and the need for FAX capability in mobile car phones. The Harrid Survey Group has sent me some preliminary data. I would like your people to review the data and answer the following questions:

1. How important is buying American-made phone sets to our customers nationally?
2. What proportion of all our customers desire FAX capability?
3. How much variation is there within the Southern Region customers in terms of their desire to *buy American?*

There is no rush since we will be receiving additional data from Harrid in several weeks. I would like to see your report within a month.

Use Data Base III in Appendix 9 for your analysis. Your response to Bill O'Hara should include a brief memo and your analysis.

REFERENCES

Cochran, William G. *Sampling Techniques, 3rd edition.* New York: John Wiley & Sons, 1977.

Marascuilo, Leonard A., and Maryellen McSweeney. *Nonparametric and Distribution-Free Methods for the Social Sciences.* Pacific Grove, California: Brooks/Cole, 1977.

APPENDIX Statistical Software

Example 1: The first example shows how to use MINITAB, Release 8, to construct a *t*-based confidence interval for the income data in Table 7.6 of the text.

Input

```
01    MTB > SET C1
02    DATA> 7300 7400 7600 7700 7800 7800
03    DATA> 8100 8300 8300 8400 8500 8600
04    DATA> END
05    MTB > TINTERVAL 95 C1
```

Explanation of Input

01   MINITAB commands operate on a worksheet of rows and columns, like COM-STAT and spreadsheet programs. Each column is assigned to a different variable and the rows contain observations on each variable. The SET command typed by the user at the MTB prompt tells MINITAB that data on a single variable will be entered. This data should be entered into Column 1.

02–04   After reading the SET command MINITAB issues a DATA prompt. Data can be entered all in one row or in several rows. MINITAB knows that all of the data for the single variable have been entered when the user types the END statement.

05   TINTERVAL is the MINITAB command used to construct the confidence interval. The statement tells MINITAB to construct a user-specified 95% confidence interval using the data found in Column 1.

Output

	N	MEAN	STDEV	SE MEAN	95.0 PERCENT C.I.
C1	12	7983.33	440.73	127.23	(7703.23, 8263.43)

Interpretation of Output

MINITAB calculates the estimated standard error of the mean in addition to the sample mean and standard deviation. The confidence interval shown is the same as in the text.

EXAMPLE 2: This example shows how to use MINITAB, Release 8, to construct a confidence interval for a population based on a sample of worker attitude data shown in Table 7.10.

Input

```
01    MTB > SET C2
02    DATA> 1 1 6 8 8 8 8 8 8 8 9 9 9 9 9 9 9 9 9 10 10
03    DATA> END
04    MTB > SINTERVAL C2
```

Input Interpretation

04   MINITAB refers to the confidence interval for the median as the sign confidence
            interval, so the command is SINTERVAL. The name refers to the fact that the value
            in Table 7.9 of the text depends on the number of sample values that fall above (+)
            or below (−) the sample median.

Output

```
SIGN CONFIDENCE INTERVAL FOR MEDIAN
                              ACHIEVED
        N    MEDIAN    CONFIDENCE    CONFIDENCE INTERVAL POSITION
C2     20    8.500      0.8847      (   8.000,    9.000)     7
                         0.9500      (   8.000,    9.000)    NLI
                         0.9586      (   8.000,    9.000)     6
```

Interpretation of Output

MINITAB presents three confidence intervals for the population median. The first confidence
interval is based on using the 7th smallest and 7th largest observation as the lower and upper
limits of the confidence interval. This confidence interval has an exact confidence level of
88.47%. The third confidence interval uses the 6th smallest and 6th largest values as the lower
and upper limits of the confidence interval. It has an exact confidence level of 95.86%.
MINITAB uses nonlinear interpolation (NLI) to estimate what an exact 95% confidence interval
would be. Table 7.11 in the text is intended to provide *approximate* 95% confidence intervals, and
will provide value (POSITION) numbers that are closest to 95% confidence without
interpolation. Note that the example suggests that the 6th smallest and largest value be used.

MAKING INFERENCES ABOUT TWO POPULATIONS

8.1   Improving departmental performance
8.2   Comparing two populations of data
   Are both populations normal?
   Do both populations have the same mean?
   Transforming the data
   Do both populations have the same variance?
   Summary of data exploration principles
8.3   Inferences on the difference between two
     population means
   Distribution of the difference between two
   sample means
   Estimated standard error of the difference
   between two sample means
   A two-sample t-based confidence interval
   Reducing the margin of error
   Beyond the normality and equal variance
   assumptions
8.4   Inferences on the difference between two
     population proportions

8.5   The Mann-Whitney nonparametric confidence
     interval for the difference between two
     population medians
   Confidence interval on the difference
   between two population medians
   Interpretation of Mann-Whitney confidence
   intervals
   Logic behind the Mann-Whitney method
8.6   Inferences on two population variances for
     normal populations
   Distribution of the variance ratio
   Constructing a confidence interval for the
   variance ratio
8.7   A nonparametric method for comparing two
     population variabilities
   Steps in the Mood test
8.8   Key ideas and overview
Appendix: Statistical Software

CHAPTER OUTLINE

 **INTEROFFICE COMMUNICATION**

Date: November 14, 1994
To: Sarah Teman, Manager of Operations
From: Howard Bright, Plant Manager
Re: Results of labor cost study at Norcross plant

In a conversation we had some months ago, you mentioned a study you were conducting to reduce unit labor costs. I believe you said that ten work groups were assigned to a team-building workshop and ten to a creative methods workshop. You said you would measure the success by comparing the cost of producing mobile phones six months after the workshops. I am anxious to know the results of your study. Please send an update on its progress.

I know you have training in statistics, but sample sizes of only ten teams seem pretty small. Are you going to be able to make a judgment on the value of the two methods based on these small samples? And, if one method reduces labor costs more than another, how can you be sure that the difference is due to the difference between the workshops and not some other factor that has nothing to do with the study?

I look forward to receiving your update.

8.1≣ Improving Departmental Performance

Effective managers not only solve disturbance problems but initiate improvement projects. We showed how descriptive statistics (see Chapters 2 and 3) and probability models (see Chapter 5) are important in sensing and solving disturbance problems. A disturbance problem is a gap between a department's previous, expected, or budgeted performance levels and its present performance levels. Managers must eliminate the gap. For example, if a department experiences a sudden and dramatic decrease in productivity, a manager must diagnose the problem's causes and take corrective action to solve the problem permanently. Managers must put out brush fires whenever they occur.

However, a manager's ability to solve disturbance problems does not improve the firm's performance levels. It only restores service or productivity levels to previous levels. Consider this analogy. A hotel manager sees smoke, gets a fire extinguisher, and puts out the fire. Extinguishing the fire is important, but it does not improve the hotel's service.

In order to be able to identify potential improvement projects, managers must be innovative and vigilant. One effective way is to use Pounds's *extraorganizational strategy* (see Chapter 1). Trade journals, competitors, other divisions within the firm, or professional conferences can sometimes suggest potential improvement projects. Questions regarding performance should be asked regularly. Is there a difference between our performance and that of our East Coast operations? Should we adopt competitors' practices? Should we adopt a new procedure seen at a trade show? How do we compare with published industrywide performance levels?

When groups differ, the natural follow-up question is *why.* Asking that question is an essential step in identifying possible improvement projects. In this chapter we will compare the population means, medians, proportions, and variances of two groups. By comparing differences between groups statistically, we should be able to answer many of these questions.

8.2≣ Comparing Two Populations of Data

How should we compare two populations of data? How different are they? Are there differences between their shapes, means, or variances? In short, what is different?

Begin by exploring sample data. Draw stem-and-leaf displays or box plots. Graph the data before doing statistical analysis. Let the data speak. Look for outliers or different patterns in the two samples of data. Then apply confidence interval methods. By the end of this section you should be able to:

1. use stem-and-leaf displays to explore differences between the shapes, means, or variances of two samples of data;
2. transform the two samples of data to normalize the distributions and to equalize the variances; and
3. explain why the square root and logarithmic transformations may make a highly skewed sample distribution more normal-shaped.

Are Both Populations Normal?

To compare two populations of data, we start by drawing stem-and-leaf displays. Figure 8.1 shows a sample of quick ratios—current assets minus inventories divided by current liabilities—for manufacturing firms from two regions of the country. The quick ratios vary from 1.1 to 3.7. Are there any differences in the two regions?

The data are not perfectly bell-shaped, nor should we expect them to be. Remember that the data are only samples from two populations. Even if both populations were

FIGURE 8.1 **Stem-and-Leaf Displays of Quick Ratios from Firms in Two Regions**

Northeast

	9	
	8	
9	7	
3	5	7
1	2	4
1.	2.	3.

Southeast

	7	
	5	
	4	4
6	3	3
4	1	2
1.	2.	3.

normal, we would not expect each sample distribution to be *perfectly* bell-shaped. However, the sample distributions should be near normal, as they are.

What can we conclude from Figure. 8.1? Subject to statistical verification, there are no differences between the quick ratios of firms in the Northeast and firms in the Southeast.

Figure. 8.2 shows a sample of list prices for ballpoint pens in two cities. Note that the two data sets have similar shapes, means, and variances. However, neither sample is normally distributed; both have outliers.

Why is it important that the population distributions be near normal? Recall that in constructing confidence intervals on the mean, we assume that

1. the population distribution is normal or
2. the distribution of the sample mean is normal.

For sample sizes greater than 30, the latter will be true because of the central limit theorem. For sample sizes under 30 from highly skewed distributions, consider using *nonparametric* methods to compare population medians (Section 8.5) and population variabilities (Section 8.7). Remember first to construct stem-and-leaf displays of samples to check the population shapes before analyzing the data.

FIGURE 8.2 **Two Similar Highly Skewed Groups**

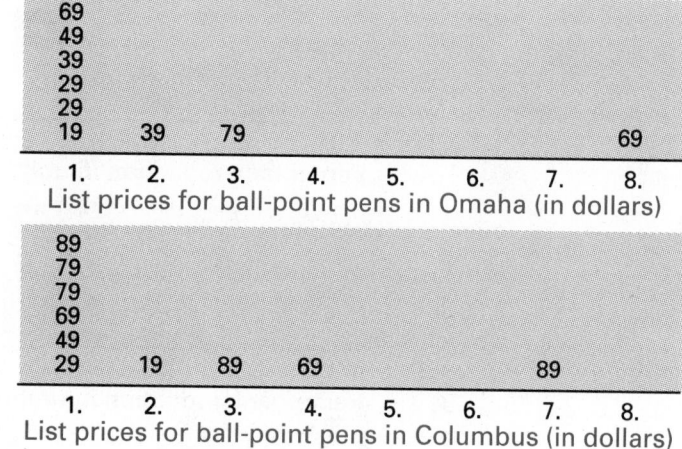

69							
49							
39							
29							
29							
19	39	79					69
1.	2.	3.	4.	5.	6.	7.	8.

List prices for ball-point pens in Omaha (in dollars)

89							
79							
79							
69							
49							
29	19	89	69			89	
1.	2.	3.	4.	5.	6.	7.	8.

List prices for ball-point pens in Columbus (in dollars)

Do Both Populations Have the Same Mean?

Potential improvement projects are often initiated by asking comparative questions, such as:

1. Do the mean performances of the two groups differ?
2. If so, which group does better and why?

One of the confidence interval methods that compares two population means assumes that these populations have the same variances and are normally distributed. Figure. 8.3 illustrates two sample data sets where these assumptions are valid. Both data sets have the same near-normal shape and variance. Thus we can use the method developed in Section 8.3 to determine whether the mean population performance levels differ.

Consider the two data sets in Figure. 8.4. The data are the percentages sales increase from the previous year for two regions. The data vary from 1.2% to 8.5%. The stem-and-leaf displays show that the samples differ markedly. We conclude that probably neither population distribution is normal. Also, the population variances are probably different.

What should we do when sample data suggest that the population shapes are not normal and the variances differ? First, we can ignore the assumptions and apply the method described in Section 8.3. For highly skewed data (and for sample sizes of less than 30 per group) this is risky since our inferences may not be valid. We do not recommend this approach. Second, there are two other approaches to consider:

1. We could *transform* the data sets to make the shapes more normal and the variances more equal. Then we could use the first confidence interval method developed in Section 8.3.
2. If a transformation fails, we can use the *nonparametric* method developed in Section 8.5 to compare two population medians.

Remember, if the sample sizes are 30 or more per group, the central limit theorem tells us that the two distributions of the sample means will be normal. And we may use the confidence interval method developed in Section 8.3. The need for a stem-and-leaf display to assess normality arises only for sample sizes under 30 per group.

FIGURE 8.3   Two Normally Distributed Groups with Different Means

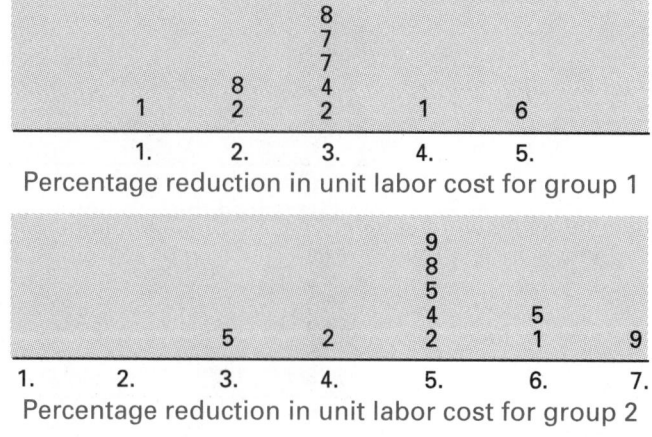

Percentage reduction in unit labor cost for group 1

Percentage reduction in unit labor cost for group 2

FIGURE 8.4   Two Nonnormally Distributed Groups with Different Means and Variances

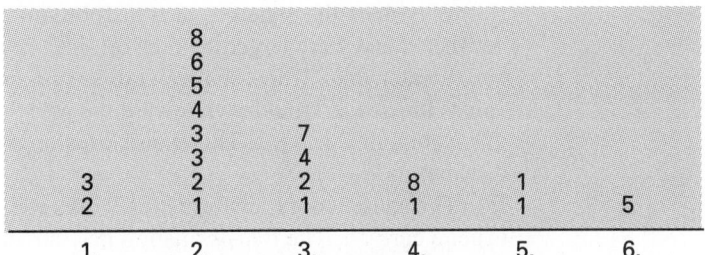

Percentage sales increase from previous year for group 1

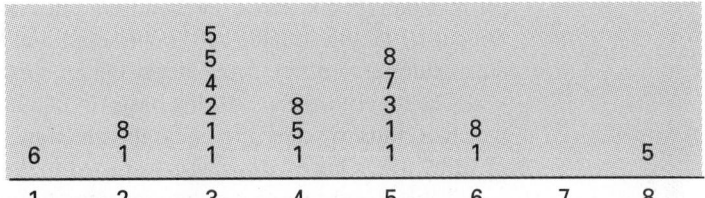

Percentage sales increase from previous year for group 2

Transforming the Data

Transforming the data simply means changing the scale of measurement. Just as dividing each number by 12 in changing from feet to inches is a transformation, so is adding 100 to each data value a transformation. However, neither transformation will make a distribution more normal. Both transformations simply shift the distribution, but do not change its shape or its variance. This is seen readily in Figure 8.5.

In order to make the shapes more normal and help equalize their variances, we can use the square root and logarithmic transformations. Consider these transformations when the data are highly skewed and consist only of positive numbers.*

In Table 8.1 we have used the square root transformation to rescale the two sets of sample data on percentage sales increase in Figure. 8.4. Figure. 8.6 presents the stem-and-leaf displays for the transformed data sets. Compare these with the displays in Figure 8.4. Note that both sample distributions are *more* normal. Also the variances

FIGURE 8.5   Transformation by Adding 100

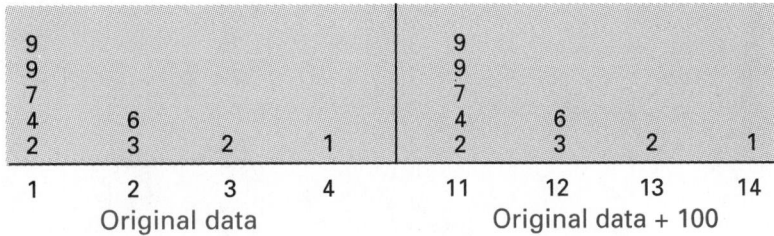

Original data   Original data + 100

---

* The logarithm or the square root of a negative number is undefined.

are *more* alike. Now we will be able to use the confidence interval method (8.3) in Section 8.3 on the *transformed* data to determine whether the means of the two transformed populations differ.

Why does the square root transformation work? The square roots of numbers between 0 and 1 are larger than the original raw values, and the square roots of numbers greater than 1 are smaller than the original raw values. In other words, data values in each tail are drawn toward the mean of the transformed data. We illustrate this feature in Table 8.2. This transformation results in a more symmetrically shaped distribution.

The square root transformation works well when a distribution is skewed, but it is not a cure-all. The transformation may not normalize the data when there are outliers. Consider the size of contract award data in Table 8.3. Note that contracts 1 and 6 are outliers. Contract 1 is only about one-hundredth as large as the middle four contracts. Contract 6 is about one hundred times larger than the middle four data values. Even after taking square roots, contracts 1 and 6 are still outliers. When one or more data values are outliers, consider using a *logarithmic base 10* transformation.

The logarithm base 10 (log base 10) of a number is the exponent or the power to which 10 must be raised to equal the given number. For example, 3 is the logarithm of 1,000 to the base 10 because 10 raised to the power 3 equals 1,000.

Table 8.3 shows that a data set transformed by the log base 10 has no outliers. While the log base 10 transformation is generally effective, there may be times when other transformations should be considered. A readable source for other transformations is Siegel's *Statistics and Data Analysis* (1988).

Table 8.1

Square Root Transformation

Upper Stem-and-Leaf Display		Lower Stem-and-Leaf Display	
Original Data	**Square Root Transformed**	**Original Data**	**Square Root Transformed**
1.2	1.10	1.6	1.26
1.3	1.14	2.1	1.45
2.1	1.45	2.8	1.67
2.2	1.48	3.1	1.76
2.3	1.52	3.1	1.76
2.3	1.52	3.2	1.79
2.4	1.55	3.4	1.84
2.5	1.58	3.5	1.87
2.6	1.61	3.5	1.87
2.8	1.67	4.1	2.02
3.1	1.76	4.5	2.12
3.2	1.79	4.8	2.19
3.4	1.84	5.1	2.26
3.7	1.92	5.1	2.26
4.1	2.02	5.3	2.30
4.8	2.19	5.7	2.39
5.1	2.26	5.8	2.41
5.1	2.26	6.1	2.47
6.1	2.47	6.8	2.61
6.5	2.55	8.5	2.92

FIGURE 8.6   Stem-and-Leaf Displays After Square Root Transformation

```
                  Group 1                                   Group 2
            92
            84                                                    47
            79                                                    41
            76                                        87          39
            67                                        87          30
            61    47                                  84          26
   48       58    26                                  79          26
   45       55    26                                  76          19
   14       52    19                       45         76    12          92
   10       52    02         55            26         67    02          61

   1.        1.    2.         2.            1.         1.    2.          2.
```
Square root of the percentage sales increase from previous year

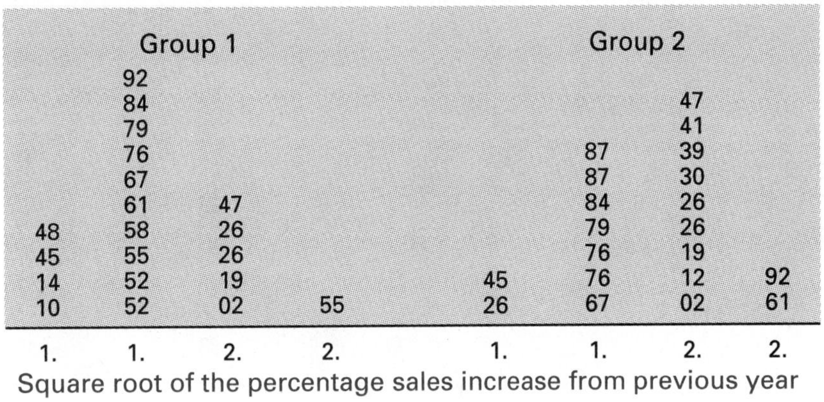

Table 8.2

Impact of Square Root Transformation on Data Distribution

Original Data	Square Root	Transformed Data
.25	.50	Shift upward
1.85	1.36	
2.50	1.58	
3.50	1.87	
8.00	2.83	Shift downward

Table 8.3

Size of Contracts Awarded to COMCEL

Contract	Size	Square Root	Log Base 10
1	1,000	31.62	3.00
2	75,000	273.86	4.88
3	75,000	273.86	4.88
4	100,000	316.23	5.00
5	150,000	387.30	5.18
6	10,000,000	3,162.28	7.00

Do Both Populations Have the Same Variance?

Managers are most often concerned about mean performance. However, when two groups or products have the same mean performance, managers want to know:

1. Do the two groups' variances differ?
2. If so, which group has the more consistent or less variable performance?
3. What accounts for a group's smaller variance?

Chapter 8 Making Inferences About Two Populations

Table 8.4

Data Sets with the Same Mean but Different Variances

	Industry A	Industry B
	11	22
	22	31
	24	31
	32	32
	33	**33**
	34	33
	35	35
	36	35
	43	36
	47	38
	51	41
Mean	33.5 days	33.4 days

Table 8.4 contains the average collection period—receivables divided by mean sales per day—for a sample of firms from two industries. Both industries have about the same average collection period—33.4 days. However, industry A firms exhibit more variance, with the average collection period varying from 11 to 51 days. The average collection period for industry B firms varies from 22 to 41 days. Figure 8.7 highlights the differences between the variances for the two industries.

If the sample data are near normal (as in Figure 8.7), we use the method of constructing confidence intervals in Section 8.6 to determine if the variances of the two populations differ. When the sample data are highly skewed and a square root or log base 10 transformation does not work, we use the nonparametric method in Section 8.7.

FIGURE 8.7   Two Normally Distributed Data Sets with Different Variances

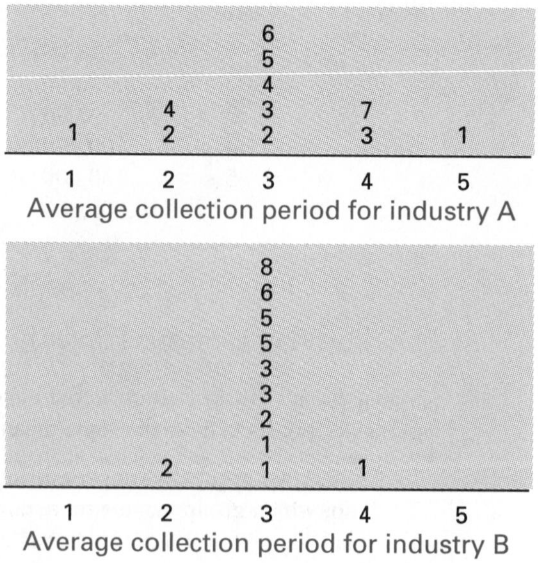

Average collection period for industry A

Average collection period for industry B

Summary of Data Exploration Principles

We summarize the data exploration principles:

1. Underlying confidence interval methods on population means (Section 8.3), proportions (Section 8.4), or variances (Section 8.6) is the assumption of normality of either the population or the distribution of the sample means. The central limit theorem justifies the latter assumption for sample sizes of 30 or more per group.

2. For sample sizes of under 30 per group, use stem-and-leaf displays to compare two sample data sets visually. Are the two samples normally distributed? If so, the populations are probably normally distributed. If one or both stem-and-leaf displays are highly skewed or contain outliers, apply a square root or log base 10 transformation. Transformations often normalize the data.

3. Underlying the confidence interval method on population means is the assumption of equal population variances. Use stem-and-leaf displays to compare two sample data sets visually. Do the two samples have near equal variances? If so, the two population variances are probably equal. If the two samples do not have near equal variances, apply a square root or log base 10 transformation. Transformations often equalize variances.

4. When transformations do not normalize the data sets or equalize the variances, consider (1) constructing Mann-Whitney confidence intervals on the difference between two population medians and (2) using Mood's test to compare two population dispersions. We discuss these methods later in this chapter.

SECTION 8.2 EXERCISES

1. In comparing two data sets, managers compare their shapes, centers, and spreads. Give examples of each of these three distribution characteristics.

2. Explain the purpose of transforming data.

3. Suppose the following values were typical of a data set: $\{1.2, .5, 0, -.5, -1\}$.
    a. Would the log transform be useful for these data? Why?
    b. Would the square root transform be useful? Why?

4. Explain why it is important to explore the data with stem-and-leaf displays before selecting an estimation method.

5. You wish to construct a confidence interval on the mean population size of loans for used cars at the Jax Federal Savings and Loan. Here is a random sample of used-car loans from the Jax Federal loan portfolio.

$3,000	$4,200	$4,800	$6,000
3,350	4,500	5,450	6,500
3,500	4,500	5,700	8,000
3,500	4,800	5,800	13,500
4,050	4,800	5,850	15,500

   a. Why is it necessary to transform the data set before constructing a confidence interval for the mean?
   b. Use a square root transform and a log base 10 transform. Which transform appears to be better at normalizing the data?

6. Several years ago Motorola, Inc. won the Malcolm Baldrige National Quality Award. One major factor was its attention to product development control. It developed a "six sigma" manufacturing target which, if attained, would ensure a defect rate of no more than a *few parts per million.* Sigma (standard deviation) describes the variation about the mean of the manufacturing process. The American Society for Quality Control determines the sigma levels for ten American-owned firms in the computer chip industry.

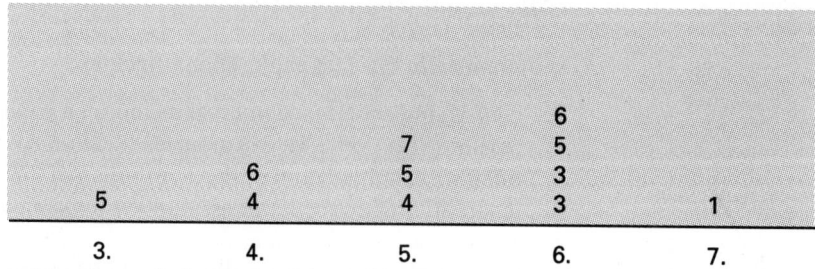

		7	6	
	6	5	5	
5	4	4	3	
			3	1
3.	4.	5.	6.	7.

Number of sigmas achieved in manufacturing computer chips

a. Are the "sigma" data near normal? Could the data have been drawn from a normal population?

b. Are these ten firms consistently achieving at Motorola's "six sigma" limit? Compute the appropriate descriptive statistics.

c. If the survey firm wishes to draw inferences to all computer chip manufacturers it will have to use the statistical methods in Chapter 7. Thus it is necessary to "normalize" the data because the sample size (10) is too small to use the Central Limit Theorem. Square-root transform and log base 10 transform the data. Which transform appears to be better at normalizing the data?

7. Shown are loan portfolios of two savings and loans in Kansas City. Without computing descriptive statistics, do there appear to be any differences between the distribution shapes, means, or variances of the two portfolios?

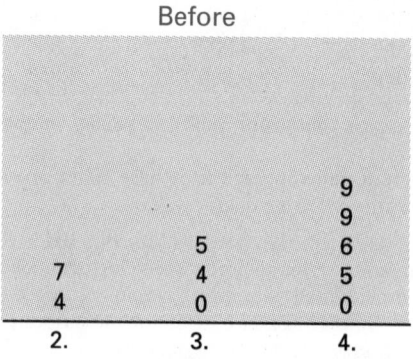

950		
900		
875		
650		
500	350	
450	150	900
250	100	250
3	4	5

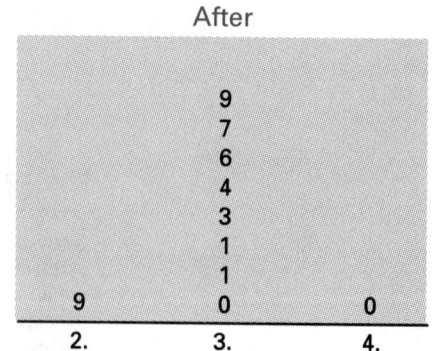

810		960
800		900
400		400
275	800	175
100	200	150
3	4	5

8. Shown are money transfer processing times at the Second National Bank of Las Vegas before and after the bank implemented a Total Quality Management program. The CEO wanted to reduce processing time and obtain more consistent telephone processing times. Both data sets were obtained after the money transfer processing times had stabilized—were stationary—over time.

Before

		9
		9
	5	6
7	4	5
4	0	0
2.	3.	4.

After

	9	
	7	
	6	
	4	
	3	
	1	
	1	
9	0	0
2.	3.	4.

Telephone processing transaction time in minutes

a. Without computing descriptive statistics, do the two processes have similar shapes, means, or dispersions?

b. Has the CEO achieved his twin goals.

c. Customers seriously want a consistent telephone processing time of under 3 minutes. Make up 10 telephone processing times that represent customers' desires, and then develop a stem-and-leaf display for your hypothetical data.

d. Should the bank strive to further reduce the mean and standard deviation in telephone processing time? Why?

8.3≣ Inferences on the Difference Between Two Population Means

When managers look at two groups or two products, they compare differences in performance, service level, or quality. For example, a manager asks: "Which group has a better mean performance—Los Angeles or Minneapolis?" or, "Does our product have, on average, fewer breakdowns than that of our major competitor?" Remember, managers must compare the present level of performance, service, or quality to previous levels or to the levels of others. Major deviations signal the onset of a problem or an opportunity.

Sometimes we are interested only in whether two *sample* means differ. Here exploratory data analysis provides us with all the information. More often, we are interested in the populations from which the samples were taken. Drawing upon Chapter 7, we will set up a confidence interval on the difference between two population means. Even here, exploratory data analysis helps to assess the underlying assumptions of the confidence interval method. By the end of this section you should be able to:

1. set up a confidence interval on the difference between two population means;
2. interpret the confidence interval and determine if two population means differ beyond mere sampling variability; and
3. explain how a confidence interval on the difference between two population means is an extension of a confidence interval on one population mean.

We introduce confidence intervals on the difference between two population means in the following example.

Example: COMCEL Study of Reducing Unit Labor Costs   According to published industry figures, work teams at COMCEL's Norcross plant have not been as successful in reducing unit labor costs as have other companies. Recently the manufacturing manager designed two cost-reduction programs. Given here are her planned changes.

1. Improve team building to reduce labor costs—TB workshop.
2. Teach creativity methods that will help work groups to reduce labor costs—CM workshop.

At the 95% level of confidence, the manager wants to determine which method is more effective at reducing unit labor costs.

Following the planned change methods discussed in Chapter 6, she selected 20 teams that had about the same amount of experience working together and had about the same success in implementing cost-saving ideas. Then she randomly assigned 10 teams to each of the two workshops. The manager recorded the unit labor cost of each

Table 8.5

Results of Planned Change Study to Reduce Unit Labor Costs

Factor: Type of Workshop

TB Workshop	CM Workshop
$3.05	$4.12
3.10	4.13
3.13	4.21
3.14	4.21
3.18	4.22
3.22	4.24
3.22	4.26
3.24	4.27
3.29	4.27
3.32	4.36

	TB Workshop	CM Workshop
$\bar{x}$	$3.19	$4.23
s	$ .085	$ .070
s^2	.0072	.0049

Dependent variable: Reduction in unit labor cost from January to June

team in January and then in June to measure the reduction in unit labor cost resulting from the workshops. Recall from Chapter 6 that this study is a one-factor, two-level design. The factor is the type of workshop. The levels of the factor are the TB workshop and the CM workshop. Table 8.5 shows the results of the study.

While the two groups clearly have different sample means, do the two population means differ? A formal statistical analysis begins by determining how different the two sample means are since we use the sample means to estimate the population means. The difference between the sample means is

$$\$4.23 - \$3.19 = \$1.04$$

Based on only 10 observations per workshop, does a difference of $1.04 between the sample means suggest that the two population means differ? Or, is the $1.04 difference so small that it can be attributed to sampling variability?

Distribution of the Difference Between Two Sample Means

Figure 8.8 is essential to understanding this section. The left-most distribution in panel (a) represents the possible labor cost reductions from team-building training for a single team. The right-most distribution represents the possible labor cost reductions from creativity training for a single team. We make two assumptions about the two populations:

ASSUMPTION 1:   Both populations are normally distributed.

ASSUMPTION 2:   The variances of the two populations are equal.

Panel (b) shows the two distributions of the sample means. The left-most distribution represents all possible average labor cost reductions based on random samples

FIGURE 8.8   Distribution of the Difference Between Two Sample Means

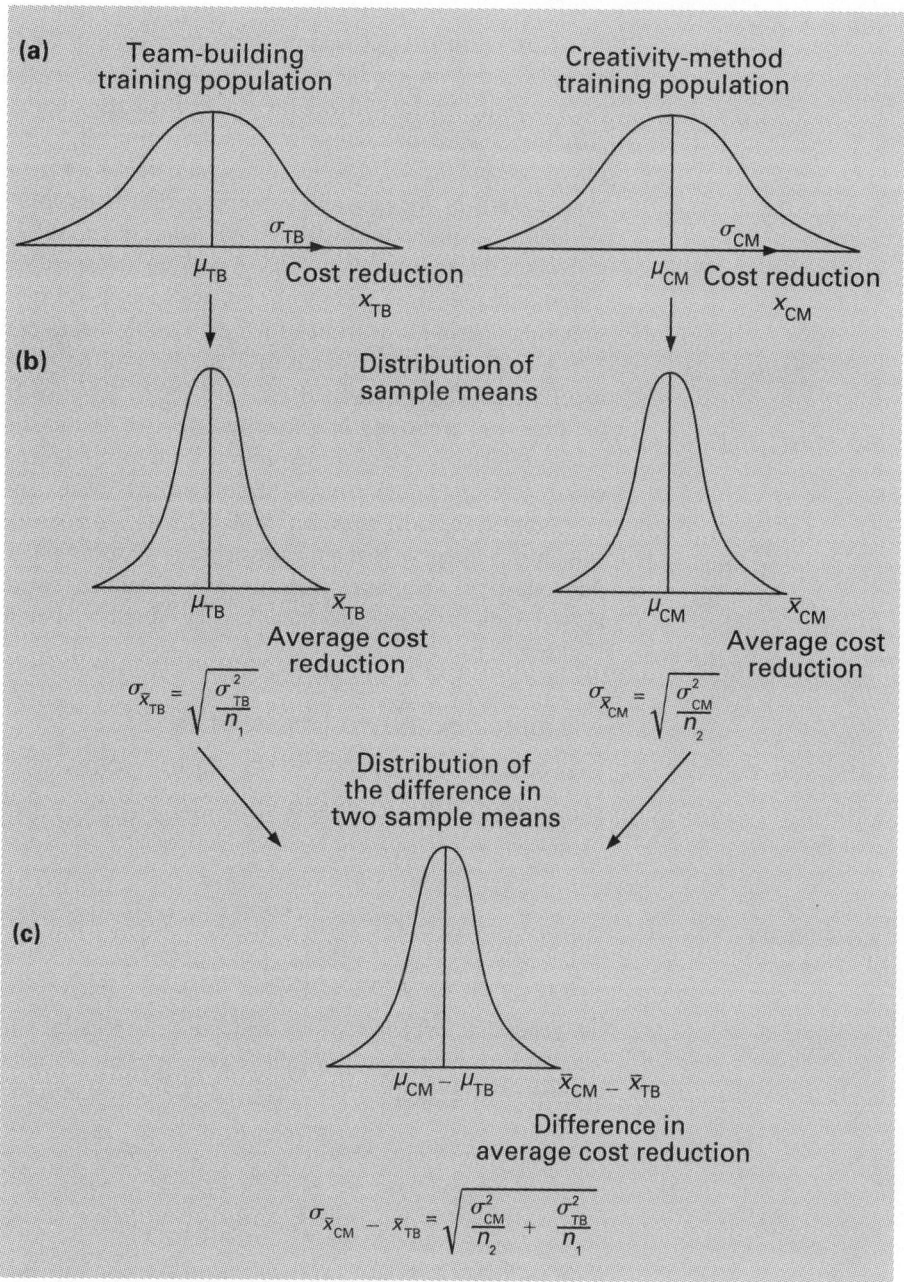

of size n_1 teams taken from the population located above it in panel (a). The right-most distribution represents all possible average labor cost reductions based on random samples of size n_2 teams taken from the population located above it in panel (a). Both sampling distributions in panel (b) are normally distributed. The standard error for each sampling distribution is $\sqrt{(\sigma_{TB}^2/n_1)}$ and $\sqrt{(\sigma_{CM}^2/n_2)}$, respectively. In taking samples from each population in panel (a) we make the following assumption.

ASSUMPTION 3:   The random samples drawn from each population are independent, or not related to one another.

Now we select one sample mean from each of the two sampling distributions in panel (b) and compute the difference, $\bar{x}_{CM} - \bar{x}_{TB}$. Now imagine we select all possible pairs of sample means (rerun the planned change study many times) and compute the differences. This produces the distribution of all possible *differences* between two sample means shown in panel (c). In fact, the $1.04 figure from COMCEL's planned change study is one possible value from this distribution.

Panel (c) shows the distribution's shape, mean, and spread. The distribution is normally distributed. Its mean is $\mu_{CM} - \mu_{TB}$, and its standard error is $\sqrt{(\sigma_{CM}^2/n_2 + \sigma_{TB}^2/n_1)}$. The standard error is merely the square root of the *sum of the variances* of the two sampling distributions from which the samples were drawn.

The distribution in panel (c) represents all possible outcomes, $\bar{x}_{CM} - \bar{x}_{TB}$, from the TB versus CM planned change study. Suppose that in the population, team building and creativity are equally effective in reducing unit labor costs. Equally effective means no difference in reducing unit labor cost. What would $\mu_{CM} - \mu_{TB}$ equal? It would equal zero, as a value of zero means no difference.

Now the critical question is: How likely is an observed difference of $1.04—the sample difference—when the mean of the distribution in panel (c) is zero? To answer that question we must determine the estimated standard error of the difference between the two sample means—the standard deviation of the distribution in Figure 8.8(c).

Estimated Standard Error of the Difference Between Two Sample Means

From Figure 8.8(c) we know the standard error of the differences between sample means is

$$\sigma_{\bar{x}_1 - \bar{x}_2} = \sqrt{\frac{\sigma_1^2}{n_1} + \frac{\sigma_2^2}{n_2}}$$

To generalize our discussion, we have substituted a 1 for TB and a 2 for CM in the standard error expression. We have already assumed that the two population variances, σ_1^2 and σ_2^2, are equal—Assumption 2. Thus we can rewrite the above expression.

$$\sigma_{\bar{x}_1 - \bar{x}_2} = \sqrt{\frac{\sigma^2}{n_1} + \frac{\sigma^2}{n_2}}$$

In Table 8.5, we computed two sample variances, .0072 and .0049, in the planned change study. Which should we use to estimate σ^2? Let's use both. Doesn't it make sense that we should "pool" or combine the sample variances? After all, an estimate of σ^2 based on a sample of 20 values should be better than an estimate based on a sample of 10 values. Expression (8.1) is the pooled variance, s_p^2.

$$s_p^2 = \frac{(n_1 - 1)s_1^2 + (n_2 - 1)s_2^2}{(n_1 + n_2 - 2)} \tag{8.1}$$

For equal sample sizes, expression (8.1) is simply the mean of the two sample variances. Expression (8.2) is the estimated standard error of the difference between two sample means.

$$\sqrt{\frac{s_{\mathrm{p}}^2}{n_1} + \frac{s_{\mathrm{p}}^2}{n_2}} = s_{\mathrm{p}}\sqrt{\frac{1}{n_1} + \frac{1}{n_2}} \tag{8.2}$$

For the COMCEL data, the pooled variance is

$$s_{\mathrm{p}}^2 = \frac{(10 - 1)(.0072) + (10 - 1)(.0049)}{18} = .0061$$

which is simply the mean of the two sample variances. From expression (8.2), the estimated standard error is

$$\sqrt{\frac{.0061}{10} + \frac{.0061}{10}} = .078\sqrt{\frac{1}{10} + \frac{1}{10}} = \$.035$$

A Two-Sample t-Based Confidence Interval

Again, we build on what we already know from Chapter 7. We lay out, side by side, confidence intervals on one and two population means. We can use expression (8.3) to construct two-sided confidence intervals on the difference between two population means.

On One Population Mean	**On Two Population Means**
$\bar{x} \pm$ Margin of error	$\bar{x}_2 - \bar{x}_1 \pm$ Margin of error
$\bar{x} \pm ts\sqrt{\dfrac{1}{n}}$	$\bar{x}_2 - \bar{x}_1 \pm ts_{\mathrm{p}}\sqrt{\dfrac{1}{n_1} + \dfrac{1}{n_2}}$

$$\bar{x}_2 - \bar{x}_1 \pm t(\text{two-sided confidence \%, df})s_{\mathrm{p}}\sqrt{\frac{1}{n_1} + \frac{1}{n_2}} \tag{8.3}$$

$$s_{\mathrm{p}}^2 = \frac{(n_1 - 1)s_1^2 + (n_2 - 1)s_2^2}{(n_1 + n_2 - 2)}$$

$$\text{df} = n_1 + n_2 - 2$$

Again, the margin of error is simply the t-value times the estimated standard error. In Chapter 7 the degrees of freedom for the t-value were $(n - 1)$. When we pooled the sample variances, we also pooled the degrees of freedom. The degrees of freedom are $(n_1 - 1) + (n_2 - 1) = n_1 + n_2 - 2$.

Next, we construct a two-sided 95% confidence interval for the difference between the two population means. Of such intervals, 95% will contain the true difference between the two population means.

Before constructing the interval, we must state and check the validity of our assumptions.

ASSUMPTION 1:   The two population distributions are normally distributed.

ASSUMPTION 2:   The variances of the two populations are equal (or nearly so).

ASSUMPTION 3:   The random samples drawn from each population are independent, or not related to one another.

We cannot use the central limit theorem to ensure normality of the sampling distribution because of the small sample sizes. Thus we must verify that the populations from which the samples were taken are normal. Figure 8.9 indicates that sample data are near-normal shaped. Thus the populations are probably near-normally distributed. The sample variances (see Table 8.5), .0072 and .0049, verify Assumption 2. Section 8.6 will explain how to determine if two population variances are equal. Assumption 3 is met because the project manager randomly assigned the 20 groups to the two workshops.

For ease of interpretation, always subtract the smaller sample mean from the larger sample mean when computing the difference. Thus, the two-sided 95% confidence interval is obtained from expression (8.3):

$$(\$4.23 - \$3.19) \pm t(\text{two-sided } 95\%, 18 \text{ df})(\text{estimated standard error})$$

Lower limit: $\$1.04 - (2.101)(\$.035) = \$ .97$
Upper limit: $\$1.04 + (2.101)(\$.035) = \$1.11$

There are two important things to notice about the confidence interval. First, since it does not include zero, there is a difference between the two population means, indicating that one training method is more effective in reducing unit labor costs. Second, it is the creative method workshop that is better. We are 95% confident that the creative training population mean labor cost reduction minus the team-building training labor cost reduction is between $.97 and $1.11. In other words, creativity training reduces unit labor cost by between $.97 and $1.11 *more than* team-building training.

A second way to draw the same conclusion is to look at the estimated standard error of $.035. It measures the impact of all factors except training on the reduction in unit labor cost. Think of $.035 or 3.5 cents as the sampling error or variability. The difference between the means for the two training methods is $1.04, which is almost 30 times as large as the sampling variability. Thus we are 95% confident that there is a difference between the two population mean unit labor cost reductions.

There is yet a third way to draw the same conclusion. If the training methods were equally effective, then from Figure 8.8(c), the mean of the sampling distribution should be zero. From the empirical rule in Chapter 2, approximately 95% of all differences between the two sample means should be within ±2 standard deviations of zero. Two standard deviations equal 2 × $.035 or $.07. But the difference between sample means is $1.04, which is well outside the two standard deviations range. In short, we are 95% confident that there is a difference between the two population means.

In short:

1. If the confidence interval does not include zero, then we can detect a difference in the two population means at the desired confidence level. An interval does not include zero when the difference in sample means is larger than the margin of error.

2. If the confidence interval does include zero, then we cannot detect a difference in the two population means at the desired confidence level. An interval does include zero when the difference in sample means is less than the margin of error.

Reducing the Margin of Error

Increasing the sample sizes reduces the estimated standard error, as we can see from expression (8.2). Increasing the sample sizes also reduces the t-value, due to the increasing degrees of freedom. The net effect is to reduce the margin of error. As the margin of error shrinks, the confidence interval shrinks, making it less likely that zero will be in the interval. Thus we are more likely to detect a difference between two population means. In summary, increasing the sample sizes makes it more likely to find statistically significant differences between two population means if the means are different.

Beyond the Normality and Equal Variance Assumptions

The assumption of population normality is not critical, provided both samples sizes are less than 30. In Figure 8.8(b) the sampling distributions were normal because the populations from which they were derived were normal. But the central limit theorem assures us that these sampling distributions will be approximately normal if n_1 and n_2 are at least 30, even if the populations are not normally distributed. *Note:* If both sample sizes are at least 30, then the degrees of freedom for the two samples would be large enough to use the infinity row of the t-table, the z-distribution, to construct confidence intervals.

The assumption of population normality is critical when both sample sizes are less than 30. Then we must construct two stem-and-leaf displays. If both displays suggest that the populations from which the samples were taken are normally distributed,

---

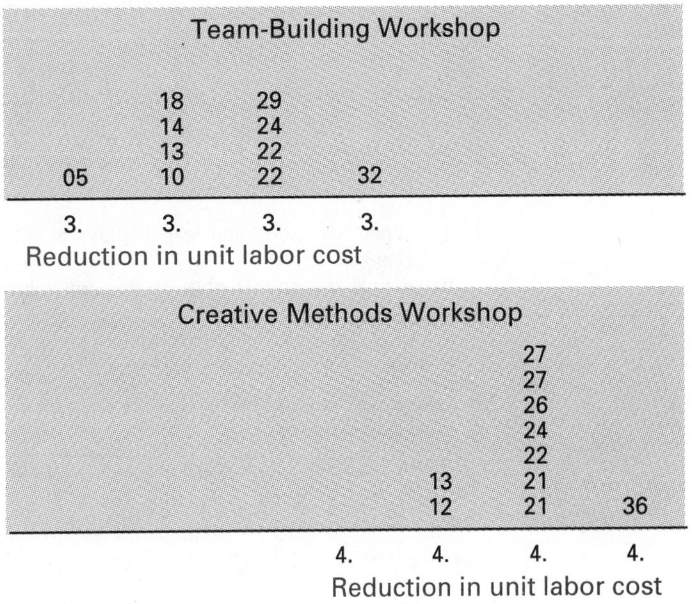

FIGURE 8.9   Stem-and-Leaf Displays for Sample Data for Team-Building and Creative Methods Workshops

we can use expression (8.3). If the stem-and-leaf displays indicate that the data are skewed, we can do the following:

1. Transform the raw data by taking the square root or log base 10. If both stem-and-leaf displays become more symmetric and the variances are nearly equal, use expression (8.3) on the transformed data to construct a confidence interval.
2. If the transformation does not normalize the data and equalize the variances, use the nonparametric method in Section 8.5.

When the population variances are not equal, we cannot "pool" the sample variances, and thus we cannot use expression (8.3). Without using a statistical method, managers often use the following rule of thumb to determine if two population variances differ: For samples of size 30 or more, the population variances probably differ when one sample variance is more than twice the other (see Section 8.6 for a statistical method).

When the population variances are not equal, and provided the sample sizes exceed 30, use expression (8.4) to construct confidence intervals on the difference in two population means.

$$\bar{x}_1 - \bar{x}_2 \pm z\sqrt{\frac{s_1^2}{n_1} + \frac{s_2^2}{n_2}} \qquad (8.4)$$

Provided both sample sizes exceed 30, each sample variance provides a reasonably good estimate of its corresponding population variance. *Note:* In expression (8.4), the two sample variances are *not* pooled.

SECTION 8.3 EXERCISES

1. *t*-Based confidence intervals on the difference between two population means are based on the assumption that the populations are normally distributed. Explain how a stem-and-leaf display can be used to judge whether this assumption holds.

2. The following data sets are the result of an experiment in which 15 subjects were randomly selected to serve in the experimental group. An additional 15 subjects were randomly selected to serve in the control group.

Experimental Group	Control Group
17, 17, 18, 22, 23, 25,	12, 22, 22, 32, 33, 38,
26, 28, 30, 30, 31, 33,	42, 43, 43, 44, 53, 54,
41, 52, 65	55, 56, 68

   a. Prepare two stem-and-leaf displays to determine the characteristics of the two data sets.
   b. Does it appear that both groups could have been drawn from normal populations? Explain.
   c. Apply a square root transformation to the data and construct new displays for the transformed data. Does the transformation make the data more normal-shaped?

3. Determine the appropriate *t*- or *z*-values for computing confidence interval limits for the following situations.

   Assume that the samples are independent random samples.

   a. $n_1 = 10$ $n_2 = 15$ 95% two-sided interval
       $s_1^2 = 20$ $s_2^2 = 25$

b. $n_1 = 100$ $\quad n_2 = 400$ $\qquad$ 99% two-sided interval

$\quad\;\; s_1 = 80$ $\qquad s_2 = 78$

c. $n_1 = 26$ $\quad n_2 = 26$ $\qquad$ 90% two-sided interval

$\quad\;\; s_1^2 = 40$ $\qquad s_2^2 = 60$

d. $n_1 = 6$ $\qquad n_2 = 8$ $\qquad$ 80% two-sided interval

$\quad\;\; s_1 = 8.4$ $\qquad s_2 = 10.6$

4. Under what circumstances should you pool the variances of two samples when estimating the difference between two population means?

5. For each of the four data sets in Exercise 3, compute a pooled estimate of the common population variance and an estimate of the standard error of the difference of means.

6. A marketing manager wishes to determine if competitive product advertising is more effective than retentive product advertising. The former highlights advantages over competing brands; the latter highlights major benefits. The dependent variable is the number of product attributes consumers can recall one month after viewing an ad four times within a week. Shown is a 95% confidence interval on the difference in the population mean number of attributes recalled for competitive advertising minus retentive advertising.

$$\text{Interval:} \qquad 4.00 - 3.44 \pm 1 \text{ attribute}$$
$$0.56 \pm 1 \text{ attribute}$$

Lower Limit: $\quad -0.44$ attribute

Upper Limit: $\quad +1.56$ attributes

a. At the 95% confidence level, is there a statistically significant difference in the two advertising approaches? Or is the difference in sample means (0.56) so small that it can be attributed to sampling variability?
b. What is the margin of error?
c. Given that we cannot conclude that one advertising approach is more effective than the other, what can be done to reduce the margin of error while maintaining the present 95% confidence level?
d. Suppose the firm obtained the following confidence interval on the difference between the population mean number of attributes recalled for competitive advertising and retentive advertising.

$$+.56 \pm .20 \text{ attribute}$$

What conclusion could be drawn?

7. Refer to Exercise 3. Determine the margin of error for each of the four data sets.

8. Degree of financial leverage (DFL) is the percentage change in earnings per share (EPS) that is associated with a given percentage change in earnings before interest and taxes (EBIT). A DFL of 1.43 means that a 100% increase in EBIT would result in a 143% increase in EPS. Do similar firms in two different countries have different DFLs? Given are descriptive data for 10 firms in each of two countries.

Descriptive Data	USA	European Community (EC)
n	10	10
$\bar{x}$	2.40	1.20
s	0.30	0.40

    a. Compute a pooled estimate of the common population variance. Compute the difference in the sample mean DFLs for the USA minus the EC.

    b. Construct and interpret a two-sided 95% confidence interval on the difference between the population mean DFLs for the USA and the EC.

9. An experiment was performed using an experimental (e) group and a control (c) group. The results are shown below.

$$n_e = 12 \qquad\qquad n_c = 8$$

$$\bar{x}_e = 14 \qquad\qquad \bar{x}_c = 10$$

$$s_e^2 = 25 \qquad\qquad s_c^2 = 36$$

    a. Pool the sample variances to estimate the common population variance.

    b. How many degrees of freedom are there for the pooled sample variance?

    c. Use the results of part **a** to compute the estimated standard error.

    d. Construct a 95% confidence interval on the difference between the two population means.

    e. Does it appear from your confidence interval that there is a difference between the population means of the experimental and the control groups? Explain.

    f. What assumptions did you make in constructing your confidence interval?

10. Refer to Exercise 2. The square root transformed data for the experimental and control groups appear near-normal.

    a. Compute the mean and standard deviation for the transformed data for the experimental and control groups.

    b. Estimate the common population variance for the transformed data.

    c. Compute the estimated standard error for the transformed data.

    d. Construct and interpret a 95% confidence interval on the difference between the population means for the experimental group and the control group for the transformed data.

11. A company decides to compare the mean lives of 2 brands of transistors. The company randomly selects 50 transistors of each brand and measures the life in hours. The results are shown below.

$$\bar{x}_1 = 26.5 \qquad\qquad \bar{x}_2 = 32.5$$

$$s_1^2 = 136 \qquad\qquad s_2^2 = 144$$

    a. Construct a 95% confidence interval on the difference between the two population means.

    b. Based on the confidence interval, does it appear that one brand of transistor lasts longer than the other?

12. An overnight package express service wants to determine if there is any significant difference in the numbers of packages delivered per day between experienced and novice drivers. It randomly selects one experienced driver and one novice driver. For each driver, the firm selects a random sample of 10 days over the past quarter. Given are the descriptive data for the 10 days.

Experienced Driver	Novice Driver
$n_1 = 10$	$n_2 = 10$
$\bar{x}_1 = 35$ packages	$\bar{x}_2 = 31$ packages
$s_1^2 = 17$	$s_2^2 = 19$

At the 99% level of confidence can we find a statistically significant difference between experienced and novice drivers in the number of packages delivered per day? Explain.

13. The Environmental Protection Agency (EPA) routinely checks to ensure that Anderson Metals is treating its toxic waste before discharging it into the Ohio River. The EPA collects six samples of water upstream from the plant and six samples of water downstream from the plant. It runs a bacteria count on the 12 independent random samples. Here are the data.

Downstream Data	Upstream Data
30	30
28	29
30	29
30	30
32	30
30	31

    a. Construct a 90% confidence interval on the difference in the population mean bacteria counts.

    b. Does the confidence interval indicate that Anderson Metals is still treating its toxic waste?

14. Do firms with sales under 25 million dollars that do strategic planning have higher returns on total assets—net income after taxes divided by total assets—than firms that do not do strategic planning? We select a random sample of 10 firms and obtain the following descriptive data:

Strategic Planning	No Strategic Planning
$n_1 = 5$	$n_2 = 5$
$\bar{x}_1 = 10\%$	$\bar{x}_2 = 6\%$
$s_1^2 = 1.2$	$s_2^2 = 1.0$

    a. Construct a 95% confidence interval on the difference between the two population means.

    b. Do firms that do strategic planning have higher returns on assets than firms that do not do strategic planning? Explain.

15. COMCEL runs a planned change study to determine if the creative method called analogy is superior to brainstorming. Superior means that more ideas are generated within a specified period of time. Both methods require groups of size 3–4. Five groups are trained in brainstorming, and 5 groups are trained in the analogy method. The 10 groups are given a never-before-seen problem, and the number of nonduplicate ideas generated within a 30-minute session are recorded. Here are the data.

Analogy	65	81	70	75	78
Brainstorming	68	55	65	72	61

    a. Prepare stem-and-leaf displays (with three leaves each). Does it appear that both groups could have been drawn from a normal population?

    b. Construct and interpret a 99% confidence interval on the difference between the population mean number of ideas for the analogy method and the brainstorming method. Is there a statistically significant difference, or is the difference in sample means so small that it can be attributed to sampling variability?

8.4 ≣ Inferences on the Difference Between Two Population Proportions

In Section 7.6 we constructed confidence intervals on an unknown population proportion. We extend that idea to intervals on the difference between two population proportions. Such confidence intervals are useful in answering questions such as: "Is the proportion of highly motivated workers the same in two plants?" or "Has our program to equalize the proportions of highly motivated workers in the two plants been successful?" Such questions are essential in problem sensing, diagnosis, and decision making.

Recall that sample proportions are similar to sample means. Both are measures of the center of a data set. While sample means can take on all possible negative and positive values, sample proportions are numbers between 0 and 1. By the end of this section you should be able to construct and interpret confidence intervals on the difference between two population proportions.

We introduce confidence intervals on the difference between two population proportions in the following example.

Example: Demographic Study: Are Multiple Advertisements Necessary?

An advertising agency surveys the demographic differences between subscribers to two magazines. It randomly selects 1,000 subscribers of *American Business* and asks: "Is your family income over $60,000?" Five hundred fifty subscribers respond yes. The agency randomly selects 500 subscribers of *The Entrepreneur* and finds that only 200 have family incomes over $60,000.

Is there a difference between the proportions of the two magazines' subscribers who have incomes over $60,000? If there is no difference, the agency can use similar advertisements for its product for both target audiences. If there is a difference, the agency must create different campaign strategies for each magazine; that is, it must segment the market.

The agency wants a 99% confidence interval on the difference between the two population proportions of subscribers with annual incomes over $60,000.

Expression (8.5) is the estimated standard error of the difference between the two sample proportions. We assign $\hat{p}$ to be the proportion of people who respond yes and $\hat{q}$ to be the proportion of people who respond no. The subscripts refer to the two data sets. We use expression (8.6) to construct a two-sided confidence interval on the difference between two population proportions.

$$\sqrt{\frac{\hat{p}_1 \hat{q}_1}{n_1} + \frac{\hat{p}_2 \hat{q}_2}{n_2}} \tag{8.5}$$

$$\hat{p}_1 - \hat{p}_2 \pm z\sqrt{\frac{\hat{p}_1 \hat{q}_1}{n_1} + \frac{\hat{p}_2 \hat{q}_2}{n_2}} \tag{8.6}$$

Table 8.6 shows the computation of the estimated standard error for the market segment study data. Before constructing a confidence interval, we state the assumptions:

ASSUMPTION 1:   The two data sets are indendent simple random samples taken from the *American Business* and *The Entrepreneur* subscriber populations.

ASSUMPTION 2: The distribution of the difference between two sample proportions is normal.

The two assumptions are realistic. The agency took a simple random sample, and Assumption 1 is met. Cochran's rules for normality (Table 7.8) assure us that the sample sizes are sufficiently large to ensure normality.

Again, for ease of interpretation, always subtract the smaller sample proportion from the larger sample proportion when computing the difference.

Table 8.6

Hypothetical Data for Demographic Study

	American Business	*The Entrepreneur*
n	1,000	500
$\hat{p}$	$\dfrac{550}{1,000} = .55$	$\dfrac{200}{500} = .40$
$\hat{q}$	$\dfrac{450}{1,000} = .45$	$\dfrac{300}{500} = .60$

$$\text{Estimated standard error} = \sqrt{\frac{(.55)(.45)}{1,000} + \frac{(.40)(.60)}{500}}$$

$$= .027$$

Shown here is a two-sided 99% confidence interval:

$$.55 - .40 \pm (2.576)(.027)$$

Lower limit: $.15 - .07 = .08$
Upper limit: $.15 + .07 = .22$

Since the interval does not include 0, the two population proportions differ. We are 99% confident that the difference between the two population proportions is between 8% and 22%. In other words, we are 99% confident that *American Business* magazine has between 8% and 22% more subscribers making over $60,000 per year.

The conclusion should not be surprising. While the estimated standard error is only .027, the difference between the two sample proportions of .15 is over five times as large as the estimated standard error. That indicates that there is a statistically significant difference between the two population proportions.

In summary, we construct confidence intervals on the difference between two population means or proportions in the same way. The center point of each interval is the difference between the two sample statistics (subtracting the smaller from the larger sample value). The margin of error is simply the t-value or z-value times the estimated standard error. We also interpret confidence intervals on the difference between two population means or proportions in the same way. If 0 is in the interval, we conclude that the two population parameters do not differ at the desired level of confidence. If 0 is not in the interval, we conclude that there is a statistically significant difference between the two population parameters at the desired level of confidence.

SECTION 8.4 EXERCISES

1. Consider the following situations. Should the manager construct a confidence interval on the difference between two population means or two population proportions? Explain.
    a. Which of two production processes has a higher tensile strength?
    b. Which of two candidates will win an upcoming election?
    c. Has there been a drop in the proportion of people who wait more than one minute for teller service after implementing quality circles within the bank?
    d. Has there been a reduction in unit labor cost after providing team-building training?

2. A marketing manager wishes to determine if competitive product advertising is more effective than retentive product advertising. The former highlights advantages over competing brands; the latter highlights major benefits. The dependent variable is the proportion of potential consumers who have bought the product in the past month. Shown is a 95% confidence interval on the difference between two population proportions. For ease of interpretation, we have subtracted the smaller sample proportion (retentive advertising) from the larger proportion (competitive advertising).

$$\text{Interval:} \qquad .35 - .28 \pm .08$$
$$0.07 \pm .08$$

    a. What conclusion can be drawn from the above interval? Is there a statistically significant difference, or is the difference in sample proportions (0.07) so small that it can be attributed to sampling variability?
    b. What is the margin of error?
    c. Given that we cannot conclude that one advertising approach is more effective than the other, what can be done to reduce the margin of error while maintaining the present 95% level of confidence?
    d. Suppose the firm obtained the following confidence interval on the difference between two population proportions: $+0.07 \pm .04$. What conclusion could be drawn?

3. For the following data sets, compute the estimated standard error and the margin of error.
    a. $\hat{p}_1 = .60$ $\hat{p}_2 = .40$ 95% interval
        $n_1 = 100$ $n_2 = 400$
    b. $\hat{p}_1 = .55$ $\hat{p}_2 = .53$ 99% interval
        $n_1 = 1,000$ $n_2 = 1,000$
    c. $\hat{p}_1 = .05$ $\hat{p}_2 = .02$ 90% interval
        $n_1 = 2,000$ $n_2 = 2,500$

4. Refer to Exercise 3. Construct and interpret confidence intervals for the three data sets. Is there a significant difference between population proportions in each data set? Explain.

5. In a recent survey of managers of Japanese-owned firms located in the United States, 68% of the 500 respondents rated Japanese workers' desire to produce high-quality products as excellent. In the same survey, 37% of the 500 managers of American-owned firms rated American workers' desire to produce high-quality products as excellent.
    a. What, if anything, is wrong with the following confidence interval on the difference between two population proportions?

$$68 - 37 \pm \text{estimated standard error}$$

    b. Compute the correct estimated standard error.
    c. Construct a correct 95% confidence interval on the difference between the two population proportions. For ease of interpretation, subtract the smaller sample proportion from the larger proportion.
    d. Interpret the interval. Is there a statistically significant difference, or is the difference in sample proportions (0.31) so small that it can be attributed to sampling variability?

6. Suppose you conducted a study of 50 men and 100 women to estimate the difference between the sexes in percentages who prefer brand A to its competitors. The results are shown here.

	Men	Women
Sample size	50	100
Number who prefer A	20	50
Sample proportion	.4	.5

Construct a 95% confidence interval for the difference between the two population proportions. Interpret your confidence interval.

7. In preparing a defense against a hostile takeover, a firm's management wants to know if there is a difference between owners of common and preferred stock in attitudes toward the current management. The poll taken shows that 200 of 400 common stockholders surveyed were in favor of a change in management, while 130 of 200 preferred shareholders favored the change.

   a. Construct a 90% confidence interval for the difference between population proportions.

   b. Does it appear that there is a difference between the population proportions of common and preferred shareholders who favor a change in management? Explain.

8. A new drug is being compared to an existing drug for its effectiveness in curing an illness. Of 100 patients treated with the new drug, 63 were cured. Of the 60 patients treated with the existing drug, 33 were cured.

   a. Explain in managerial terms what population proportions would mean here; that is, what are the populations we are studying?

   b. Construct a 90% confidence interval for the difference between population proportions. Would you conclude that the new drug is more or less effective than the existing drug?

9. You want to compare the population proportion of Business majors and Arts and Sciences majors who are intuitive according to the Myers-Briggs Type Indicator (MBTI). You randomly select ten students each from the two majors at a large university and administer the MBTI. Eight Arts and Sciences majors are intuitive and three Business majors are intuitive. Although you have used randomization, you cannot construct a confidence interval on the difference between the two population proportions. Why?

10. Are the proportions of whites and blacks unemployed the same? The U.S. Bureau of Labor selects a random sample of 5,000 people from each race. Below are the descriptive statistics.

	Black	White
Sample size	5,000	5,000
Number of people employed	4,350	4,735

   a. Use a 90% confidence interval to estimate the difference between the population proportions of the races that are employed.

   b. Interpret the confidence interval.

11. After buying a product, the consumer may have post-purchase doubt. A consumer asks, "Did I make the right buying decision?" This doubt is called cognitive dissonance. A national tire dealer wants to estimate the difference between the proportions of consumers who experience cognitive dissonance after purchasing tires in two large retail outlets, one in Albany, New York, and one in Reno, Nevada. It asks 50 customers in succession (at both stores) on a Saturday, "Are you satisfied with your tire purchase?" Why shouldn't you set up a confidence interval on the difference between population proportions?

12. Within a few years, American firms that sell their products to European firms will have to conform to a new quality standard called ISO-9000. This will require significant investments. As of 1994, is there a difference in the proportion of firms in the hardware and software industries that have implemented the ISO-9000 quality standards?

	Hardware	Software
Sample Size	200	200
$\hat{p}$	.69	.51

Construct and interpret a 90% confidence interval on the difference between the two population proportions of firms that have implemented ISO-9000.

13. Firms must seek to reduce the percent of defective products. Defective products increase scrap and rework and thus reduce gross margin. COMCEL records the proportion defective over two ten-day periods—before and after making process changes. Based on 2,000 phone handsets each for the before and after groups, they obtain the following proportion defective data. At the 95% level of confidence, has COMCEL reduced the proportion defective after instituting a number of process improvements suggested by their hourly employees?

$$\hat{p} \text{ before} \quad .056$$
$$\hat{p} \text{ after} \quad .021$$

14. This exercise illustrates the impact of the sample proportion on the margin of error. Consider:

99% confidence interval: $Z = 2.576$ $n_1 = 1,000$ $n_2 = 1,000$

a. Compute the margin of error when both sample proportions ($\hat{p}_1$ and $\hat{p}_2$) equal .50.
b. Compute the margin of error when both sample proportions equal .90.
c. Compute the margin of error when both sample proportions equal .01.
d. What value of the sample proportions maximizes the margin of error? What value of the sample proportions minimizes the margin of error?

8.5 The Mann-Whitney Nonparametric Confidence Interval for the Difference Between Two Population Medians

Thus far, we have assumed in the data analysis that either the population was normal, the sampling distribution was normal, or the transformed data were normal. These are reasonable assumptions for most data. However, when the sample sizes are less than 30 per group and there are outliers, square root or log base 10 transformations may not make the data near normal. And when the sample sizes are small, we cannot rely on the central limit theorem. Consider the Mann-Whitney nonparametric approach. Nonparametric methods do not assume normal populations or normal sampling distributions.

We use the Mann-Whitney method to construct confidence intervals on the difference between two population *medians*. Recall that in the presence of outliers, we use the median, not the mean, as a measure of a population's center. By the end of this section you should be able to:

1. explain when to construct a Mann-Whitney confidence interval on the difference between two population medians;
2. construct and interpret a nonparametric confidence interval; and
3. explain the logic behind the method.

To construct a Mann-Whitney nonparametric interval we must make two assumptions:

ASSUMPTION 1:   The data sets are two random and independent samples taken from two populations.

ASSUMPTION 2:   The two population distributions have similar shapes—they need not be normal—and spreads.

Using simple random sampling ensures that the first assumption will be met. Construct box plots to confirm the second assumption.

We introduce confidence intervals on the difference between two population medians in the following example.

Example: COMCEL's Wellness Study   Last year, as part of a physical fitness program, all plant personnel had their cholesterol levels checked. About 30% of the workers had high levels, in excess of 275 mg/dl. A medical consulting team suggested two approaches to reduce cholesterol levels—a diet program and a diet/exercise regimen. The team conducted a one-factor, two-level completely random study. It randomly selected 20 workers who had high cholesterol levels and randomly assigned them to one of two test groups. After 90 days, test subjects had their cholesterol levels checked. The dependent variable is the drop in cholesterol level. Is one approach better in reducing cholesterol levels?

Table 8.7 contains the raw data, and Figure 8.10 contains the box plots.

Both groups have few observations ($n = 10$), as well as outliers. However, the box plots suggest that the two samples have similar shapes and equal interquartile ranges. Thus, we will use the Mann-Whitney nonparametric method for constructing a confidence interval on the difference between two population medians.

Table 8.7
Drop in Cholesterol Level (mg/dl) Data

	Diet-Only Subjects	Diet/ExerciseSubjects
	11	14
	12	16
	13	17
	15	18
	16	18
	17	19
	18	20
	20	24
	24	25
	70	54
$\bar{x}$	21.60	22.5
s	17.44	11.57
Sample median	16.50	18.50

FIGURE 8.10   Multiple Box Plots for Cholesterol Data

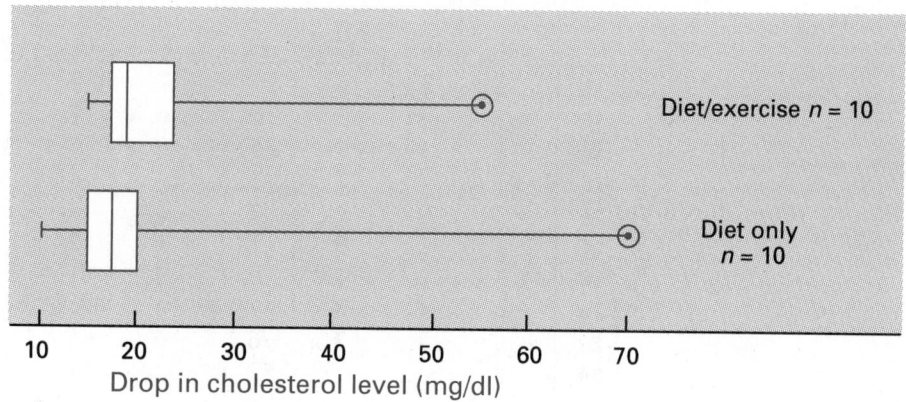

Drop in cholesterol level (mg/dl)

Confidence Intervals on the Difference Between Two Population Medians

1. Rank order each sample separately from the smallest to largest values.
2. Compute all possible differences between the data values in the two samples. For n observations per sample, there will be n^2 computed differences.
3. Look up the sample size in Table 8.8 and determine the *count* value. Call it K.
4. The Kth largest negative difference is the lower limit of the confidence interval for the difference between the two population medians.
5. The Kth largest positive difference is the upper limit of the confidence interval for the difference between the two population medians.

Table 8.9 contains the 100 computed differences for the wellness study data. To construct Table 8.9, we placed in ascending order the 10 data values for the diet-only sample in the left-most column. We placed in ascending order the 10 data values for the diet/exercise sample in the top row. We then computed all 100 differences; that is, we subtracted the drop in cholesterol levels of those who only dieted from those who used diet and exercise.

Table 8.8

Constructing a 95% Two-Sided Confidence Interval on the Difference Between Two Population Medians

Sample Size per Group*	Number of Largest and Smallest Differences	Sample Size per Group*	Number of Largest and Smallest Differences
5	3	13	46
6	6	14	56
7	9	15	65
8	14	16	76
9	18	17	88
10	24	18	100
11	31	19	124
12	38	20	128

* We assume equal sample sizes. For unequal sample sizes or sample sizes above 20, consult the tables in an applied nonparametric book.

Table 8.9

Table of Differences
Diet/Exercise

Diet Only	14	16	17	18	18	19	20	24	25	54
11	3	5	6	7	7	8	9	13	14	43
12	2	4	5	6	6	7	8	12	13	42
13	1	3	4	5	5	6	7	11	12	41
15	−1	1	2	3	3	4	5	9	10	39
16	−2	0	1	2	2	3	4	8	9	38
17	−3	−1	0	1	1	2	3	7	8	37
18	−4	−2	−1	0	0	1	2	6	7	36
20	−6	−4	−3	−2	−2	−1	0	4	5	34
24	−10	−8	−7	−6	−6	−5	−4	0	1	30
70	−56	−54	−53	−52	−52	−51	−50	−46	−45	−16

With a sample size of 10 in each group, $K = 24$ from Table 8.8. First we find the 24 largest positive differences in Table 8.9 (see upper right-hand corner values). These are in descending order: 43, 42, 41, 39, 38, 37, 36, 34, 30, 14, 13, 13, 12, 12, 11, 10, 9, 9, 9, 8, 8, 8, 8, and 7. The value +7 is the 24th largest positive difference, and so it is the upper limit of the confidence interval. Second, we find the 24 largest negative differences in Table 8.9 (see lower left-hand corner values). These are in ascending order: −56, −54, −53, −52, −52, −51, −50, −46, −45, −16, −10, −8, −7, −6, −6, −6, −5, −4, −4, −4, −3, −3, −2, and −2. The value −2 is the 24th largest negative difference, and so it is the lower limit of the confidence interval.

In summary, the limits of the confidence interval on the difference between the two population medians is

$$\text{Lower limit:} \quad -2 \text{ mg/dl}$$

$$\text{Upper limit:} \quad +7 \text{ mg/dl}$$

Interpretation of Mann-Whitney Confidence Intervals

We interpret a Mann-Whitney nonparametric confidence interval just as we have other intervals. We are 95% confident that the difference between the two population medians is between −2 and +7 mg/dl. Since the interval includes 0, we conclude that there is *no statistically significant* difference between the population medians. Although the difference between sample medians was $18.5 - 16.5 = 2$, we cannot conclude that the two population medians differ.

If both the upper and lower limits were positive, then we would be 95% confident that the median drop in cholesterol was larger for the diet and exercise plan than for the diet plan alone. Remember, we computed the drop in cholesterol for the diet/exercise group minus the diet-only group. If both the upper and lower limits were negative, we would be 95% confident that the median drop in cholesterol was smaller for diet/exercise than for diet only.

Logic Behind the Mann-Whitney Method

The Mann-Whitney method compares medians by determining the degree of overlap between *all the data values* of the two samples. Consider the two small data sets in Table 8.10. Clearly, the two samples in data set 1 have no overlap, while the two samples in data set 2 have complete overlap. Now we compute the two tables of differences and present the results in Table 8.11.

Table 8.10

Illustrating the Overlap Idea
for Two Small Data Sets

	Data Set 1		Data Set 2	
	Group 1	Group 2	Group 1	Group 2
	11	16	11	11
	12	18	12	12
	13	19	13	13
Median	12	18	12	12

Table 8.11

Tables of Differences for Two Small Data Sets

Data Set 1				Data Set 2		
	16	18	19		11	12	13
11	5	7	8	11	0	1	2
12	4	6	7	12	−1	0	1
13	3	5	6	13	−2	−1	0

When there is no overlap, the differences will be all positive or all negative. This suggests that the two population medians must be different. When there is considerable overlap, about 50% of the differences will be positive and 50% negative. This suggests that the two population medians will be the same. It is in this sense that the Mann-Whitney method uses the percentage of positive differences to determine whether the two population medians are different. Is the percentage closer to 50% (no difference) or 100% (a difference)?

Returning to the wellness study, we count 70 positive (70%) and 30 negative differences in Table 8.9. That was not quite enough for us to conclude, at the 95% confidence level, that the two population medians differ.

In summary, consider using the Mann-Whitney confidence interval method when the sample sizes are small and the data contain outliers. If the confidence interval includes the value of 0, we conclude, at the 95% level of confidence, that we cannot detect any difference between the two population medians. In short, there is no statistically significant difference.

SECTION 8.5 EXERCISES

1. You are a manager looking for the best way to compare the centers of two populations based on two sample data sets. You have two choices—the t-test and the Mann-Whitney alternative. Under what circumstances would you construct a confidence interval on the difference between population medians rather than on the difference between population means?

2. We are comparing population median incomes of two market segments for General Motors—Basics and Sporties. Consider the following output from the Mann-Whitney Method module (NONPARAMETRIC—option #2) in COMSTAT. The table of difference is constructed by subtracting the incomes of Basics from the income of Sporties. Is there a statistically significant difference between the two population median incomes? Explain.

   Lower limit of the 95% confidence interval is $21,000.

   Upper limit of the 95% confidence interval is $110,000.

3. We are comparing population median incomes of two market segments for Sony VCR buyers—Yuppies and Blue Collars. Consider the following output from the Mann-Whitney Method module (NONPARAMETRIC—option #2) in COMSTAT. The table of difference is constructed by subtracting the incomes of Blue Collars from the incomes of Yuppies. Is there a statistically significant difference between the two population median incomes? Explain.

   Lower limit of the 95% confidence interval is −$17,000.

   Upper limit of the 95% confidence interval is +$23,000.

4. Has creativity training led to a reduction in unit labor cost? Would it be appropriate to construct Mann-Whitney confidence intervals for the following data to answer the above question? If not, what analysis method is correct?

a. Dependent Variable: Reduction in unit labor cost

Creativity Training	$.78	.64	.73	.70	.62	.69
Control Group	$.05	−.04	.03	−.02	−.06	11

b. Dependent Variable: Reduction in unit labor cost

Creativity Training	$−.78	.64	.73	.70	.62	1.69
Control Group	$−.95	−.04	.03	−.02	.01	1.02

5. Consider the following sets of data points.

Group 1:	1	3	5	10	3	4
Group 2:	10	11	14	12	25	42

a. Find the medians of the two groups and construct a table of differences between the two groups. Based on the percentage of the positive differences, would you say that the population medians of the two groups are different at the 95% level of confidence?

b. Construct a 95% confidence interval on the difference between population medians using the Mann-Whitney method. Interpret this confidence interval.

6. Consider the results of an experiment that compared the time needed (in minutes) to produce an item under the current method with the time needed under a new method.

Current:	68	70	72	73	77	85
New:	60	63	64	65	70	79

a. Find the medians of the two groups and construct a table of differences for the two groups. Based on the percentage of the positive differences, would you say that the population median time needed to produce an item is less under the new method at the 95% level of confidence?

b. Construct a 95% confidence interval on the difference between population medians using the Mann-Whitney method. Does it appear that the new method reduces the median time to produce the item?

7. Consider the results of another experiment that compared the time (in minutes) needed to produce an item under the current method with the time needed under a new method.

Current:	68	70	72	73	74	75	77	85
New:	63	65	65	67	70	71	72	72

a. Find the medians of the two groups and construct a table of differences for the two groups. Based on the percentage of the positive differences, would you say that the population median time needed to produce an item is less under the new method at the 95% level of confidence?

b. Construct a 95% confidence interval on the difference between population medians using the Mann-Whitney method. Does it appear that the new method reduces the median time to produce the item?

8. You want to compare students' average grades for two different teaching methods, lecture vs. the case method. Assume that all students will obtain a grade between 70 and 100.

a. Construct a data set that would suggest that you should set up a confidence interval on the difference between two population means.

b. Construct a data set that would suggest that you should set up a confidence interval on the difference between two population medians.

9. Below are samples of student SAT scores from two public universities. At the 95% level of confidence, can we say that there is a difference between the population median SAT scores at the two universities?

University A	University B
800	850
900	875
950	910
975	950
1,150	1,050

10. Determine a 95% confidence interval on the difference in median incomes between Los Angles and New Haven. Interpret the interval. Also determine the sample median incomes for the two cities.

Income—Los Angeles	Income—New Haven
$ 8,500	$ 7,500
9,500	12,000
15,600	23,000
45,000	34,500
56,000	41,500
125,000	45,500
275,000	55,500
750,000	65,500
1,200,000	90,500
1,750,000	175,000

8.6 Inferences on Two Population Variances for Normal Populations

Thus far, we have drawn inferences about differences in measures of the center—mean, median, and proportion. Now we ask whether two population variances are equal.

Why is it important to know whether population variances are equal? First, in constructing confidence intervals on two population means, we assume that the two population variances are equal or nearly so. It is time to verify statistically that assumption. Second, given that two groups have the same mean performance, managers want to know:

1. Do the two groups' variances differ?
2. If so, which group has the more consistent or less variable performance?
3. What accounts for a group's smaller variance?

Consistent (or near-zero variance) performance is an important managerial goal. Highly variable performance can cause great concern for a manager. Some days performance is excellent; other days it is not. Consistent performance minimizes uncertainty and makes a manager's job easier.

Consistent product performance is important from the consumer's perspective. If product workmanship varies greatly, consumers will look to other brands. Consumers want consistently good product workmanship and performance. By the end of this section you should be able to:

1. construct and interpret confidence intervals on the ratio of two population variances; and
2. explain what the F-distribution is and what it represents.

We introduce confidence intervals on the ratio of two population variances in the following example.

Example: Productivity Study in Baltimore and Dallas Plants   COMCEL's

Dallas and Baltimore plants produce electronics for the mobile telephones. Management believes that Baltimore's weekly productivity is less variable (more consistent) than the Dallas plant. If correct, management will investigate the causes and attempt to reduce Dallas' weekly productivity variance.

COMCEL randomly selects 21 workers from each plant and records their weekly productivity. Table 8.12 contains the descriptive data. The sample variance in the Dallas plant is 5 times as large as that in the Baltimore plant. Are the two *sample* variances so different that we should conclude that the two *population* variances differ? Before answering that question, we must introduce the distribution of the ratio of two sample variances, or the *variance ratio*.

Table 8.12

Descriptive Data in Units per Hour (uph) for Two COMCEL Plants

	Dallas Plant	Baltimore Plant
Sample size (n)	21	21
Sample mean productivity ($\bar{x}$)	50.2 uph	50.3 uph
Sample productivity variance (s^2)	20	4
Sample standard deviation (s)	4.47 uph	2.00 uph

Distribution of the Variance Ratio

Assume that the workers' productivities in each plant are nearly normally distributed. Now run the productivity study and compute the following ratio of two sample variances:

$$\text{Variance ratio} = \frac{s_D^2}{s_B^2}$$

Assume that the *population* variances are the same for the two plants. What should the value of the variance ratio be? Please think about it before reading on.

If the *population* variances are the same, most sample variance ratios should be close to 1. After all, if the two population variances are equal, the two sample variances should be similar and their ratio should be close to 1.

Now imagine taking another random sample from each plant and computing the ratio of the two sample variances. Continue to rerun the study and compute the sample variance ratios. We will obtain a sampling distribution of the variance ratios, which has a shape shown in Figure 8.11. The sampling distribution is called an F-distribution.

If the two population variances are equal, the mean of the sampling distribution is about 1 because most variance ratios should be close to 1. The sampling distribution shape is skewed toward higher values because when the numerator of the variance ratio is much smaller than the denominator, the ratio approaches zero. It cannot

FIGURE 8.11   *F*-Distribution for 20 Degrees of Freedom in the Numerator and 20 Degrees of Freedom in the Denominator. *Assumption:* Two Population Variances Are Equal

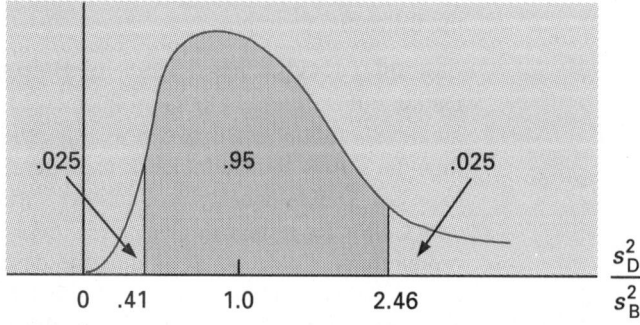

be negative since variances can never be negative! When the numerator is much larger than the denominator, the variance ratio becomes very large. That accounts for the skewed distribution.

The *F*-distribution is really a family of curves. The actual shape depends on the degrees of freedom for the sample variances in the numerator and the denominator. These are $(n_1 - 1)$ and $(n_2 - 1)$, respectively; n_1 is the sample size for one sample (for example, the Dallas plant), and n_2 is the sample size for the other sample (the Baltimore plant).

In the COMCEL study, the sample size from each plant was 21. Figure 8.11 represents an *F*-distribution that has 20 degrees of freedom for the numerator and 20 for the denominator. The total area underneath the curve is, of course, 100%. The curve shows that 2½% of the variance ratios will have values below .41. How do we know this? Refer to Table 8.13. Find the intersection of 20 degrees of freedom for the numerator and 20 for the denominator in the .025 row. The value is .41. Likewise, the table indicates that 97.5% of the variance ratios will have values below 2.46. (See the intersection of 20 degrees of freedom for the numerator and 20 for the denominator in the .975 row.) Thus, 95% (97.5% − 2.5%) of the sample variance ratios will have values between .41 and 2.46 *if the two population variances are equal* (see shaded area of Figure 8.11). Also, since the total area is 100%, 2½% of the variance ratios will have values above 2.46.

Table 8.13

An Abbreviated *F*-Table from Appendix 7

df for Denominator	Percentiles of the *F*-curve	df for Numerator		
		10	20	30
10	.025	.27	.36	.40
	.050	.34	.43	.46
	.950	2.98	2.77	2.70
	.975	3.72	3.42	3.31
20	.025	.29	.41	.45
	.050	.36	.47	.52
	.950	2.35	2.12	2.04
	.975	2.77	2.46	2.35

If the population productivity variances for both plants were the same, 95% of the time we would obtain a variance ratio between .41 and 2.46. However, the actual sample variance ratio in the COMCEL study was 5.* From Figure 8.11, that is a very rare happening—far out in the distribution's right tail. Yet that is what happened in the COMCEL study. What could account for such a large variance ratio? Think about it before reading on.

There are two possible explanations:

1. This is one of those very rare happenings. *Conclusion:* The two population variances are equal.
2. This is not one of those very rare happenings. *Conclusion:* The two population variances are not equal.

Although we could be wrong, we assume the latter is true. When the actual variance ratio falls above the upper *F*-value, we conclude that the two population variances are not the same.

Exactly how much greater is the productivity variance in the Dallas plant? The sample variance ratio is 5. However, if we took another sample we would probably not obtain the same sample variance ratio. Therefore we must construct a confidence interval on the sample variance ratio that incorporates the idea of the margin of error.

Before constructing the confidence interval, we state the assumptions:

ASSUMPTION 1:   The two data sets are simple random samples taken from the Baltimore and Dallas plants.

ASSUMPTION 2:   Worker productivities in both Baltimore and Dallas are normally distributed.

Assumption 1 will be met if we randomly select workers from the two plants. We can use two stem-and-leaf displays to check the second assumption.

Constructing a Confidence Interval for the Variance Ratio

We use expression (8.9) to construct a confidence interval for the variance ratio. The steps are presented here, along with their application to the COMCEL study.

General Procedure	For COMCEL Study
Set a desired confidence level.	We want a 90% confidence interval. The confidence level determines the percentiles from the *F*-curve. Percentile for the lower tail is $(1 - .90)/2$ or .05. Percentile for the upper tail is $.90 + (1 - .90)/2$ or .95. The area between the tails is $.95 - .05$ or .90, the desired level of confidence.

*The common practice is to place the larger sample variance in the numerator of the variance ratio.

Compute the sample variance ratio.	Place the larger sample variance in the numerator.

$$VR = \frac{s_1^2}{s_2^2}$$

$$VR = \frac{20}{4} = 5$$

The lower limit of the confidence interval is	Both data sets have sample sizes of 21. Locate the F-value for 20 degrees of freedom for the numerator and 20 degrees of freedom for the denominator and the percentile for the upper tail, .95. The F-value is 2.12 (see Appendix 7).

$$\frac{VR}{F\text{-value from the upper tail}}$$

$$\text{Lower limit} = \frac{5}{2.12} = 2.36$$

Dividing the variance ratio by a number greater than 1 reduces its value and thus defines the confidence interval's lower limit.

The upper limit of the confidence interval is	Locate the F-value for 20 degrees of freedom for the numerator and 20 degrees of freedom for the denominator and the percentile for the lower tail. The F-value is .47.

$$\frac{VR}{F\text{-value from the lower tail}}$$

$$\text{Upper limit} = \frac{5}{.47} = 10.64$$

Dividing the variance ratio by a number less than 1 increases its value and thus defines the confidence interval's upper limit.

Expressions (8.7) and (8.8) summarize the computations for the lower and upper limits of the confidence interval.

$$\text{Lower Limit:} \quad \frac{VR}{F_{1-x/2;n_1-1,n_2-1}} \tag{8.7}$$

$$\text{Upper Limit:} \quad \frac{VR}{F_{x/2;n_1-1,n_2-1}} \tag{8.8}$$

$$\frac{VR}{F_{1-x/2;n_1-1,n_2-1}} \leq \frac{\sigma_1^2}{\sigma_2^2} \leq \frac{VR}{F_{x/2;n_1-1,n_2-1}} \tag{8.9}$$

where VR is the variance ratio (place larger variance in numerator)
F-value is found in Appendix 7
x is 1-confidence level expressed as a number between 0 and 1.0
n_i are the sample sizes for the two groups

Conclusion. We are 90% confident that the ratio of the two population variances is between 2.36 and 10.64. Simply put, Dallas' variance is between 2.36 and 10.64 *times as large* as Baltimore's variance, or Dallas' standard deviation in units per hour is between 1.54 and 3.26 times that of Baltimore.

So what does that mean? What sample variance ratio value would we expect to see *within* the confidence interval if the two population variances were the same? When looking for differences between population means, we checked whether zero was in the interval. If so, it meant that managers could not conclude that the population means differed. What number should be in the interval if the two population variances could be the same? Please give it some thought before continuing.

A value of 1 indicates that the two population variances could be the same. Remember, we constructed a *ratio,* not a *difference.* Thus, if the confidence interval includes 1, we cannot conclude that at the desired level of confidence, the two population variances differ. If the interval does not include 1, then the two population variances differ.

Based on the *F*-distribution, we are 90% confident that the Dallas workers' productivities exhibit more variance than their Baltimore counterparts. An effective manager now asks why and begins seeking possible reasons. Why are the Baltimore plant workers more consistent? What can we do to reduce the Dallas plant workers' variability?

In summary, we construct a confidence interval on the ratio of two population variances either to determine which of two performances, products, or services exhibits less variability or to verify an assumption underlying the confidence intervals on the difference between two population means.

SECTION 8.6 EXERCISES

1. Look up the following *F*-values.

    $F_{.95;\,10,\,10}$

    $F_{.05;\,5,\,10}$

    $F_{.99;\,20,\,24}$

2. Determine the appropriate *F*-values for the following four data sets.

    a. $s_1^2 = 65$ $s_2^2 = 10$ 90% confidence

         $n_1 = 10$ $n_2 = 10$

    b. $s_1^2 = 35$ $s_2^2 = 30$ 95% confidence

         $n_1 = 5$ $n_2 = 16$

    c. $s_1^2 = 30$ $s_2^2 = 60$ 90% confidence

         $n_1 = 400$ $n_2 = 600$

    d. $s_1^2 = 20$ $s_2^2 = 40$ 95% confidence

         $n_1 = 25$ $n_2 = 11$

3. We wish to determine if two population variances are similar. One assumption underlying variance ratio confidence intervals is that both populations are normally distributed.

Group 1	9.6	7.8	12.1	11.5	8.7	8.8	9.6	10.1	10.6	9.7	11.3	10.6	10.6	9.2
Group 2	7.8	8.6	10.6	9.4	8.9	6.7	9.3	9.5	8.6	11.4	7.6	8.5	10.7	9.9

    a. Does it appear that both groups might have been drawn from normal populations? Draw two stem-and-leaf displays.

    b. From your stem-and-leaf displays, does it appear that the two population variances are similar?

4. Refer to Exercise 2. Do construct confidence intervals on the population variance ratios for the four data sets. Do the two population variances for each data set differ? Explain.

5. Refer to Exercise 3. Construct and interpret a 95% confidence interval on the variance ratio.

6. If the variance ratio confidence interval includes the value of one, we say there is no statistically significant difference in the two population variances. Explain.

7. The purpose of an experiment is to compare two population variances. Six observations are drawn from population 1 and nine observations from population 2. The variance of the first sample is 82.5, and the variance of the second sample is 26.5. Assuming that the populations are normally distributed, construct both a 90% confidence interval for the ratio of the population variances and a 95% confidence interval.

8. Apex, Inc. is considering purchasing thermostats from two different companies, A and B. The quality of a thermostat is measured by the amount of variation between the actual temperature and the reading of the thermostat. Apex selects eight different thermostats from each vendor and puts them into a test chamber where the temperature is controlled at 70°. The recorded temperatures are shown.

Company A:	68.5	69.0	70.0	70.1	70.4	70.6	70.9	71.5
Company B:	68.9	69.5	69.9	70.1	70.1	70.1	70.2	70.8

a. Assuming that the populations of measurements are normally distributed, construct a 90% confidence interval to estimate the variance ratio.

b. Does one company produce thermostats that are less variable than the other? Explain.

9. What role do confidence intervals for variance ratios play in comparing the population means of two distributions?

10. Suppose that the monthly rates of return on stocks X and Y are normally distributed and stationary. From 60 months of data, random samples of six months of stock X and six months of stock Y showed the following percentage returns:

Stock X:	1	7	6	−5	−1	10
Stock Y:	4	3	2	3	8	10

a. Construct a 90% confidence interval to estimate the ratio of the population variances.

b. Does it appear that the variances in returns of the two stocks are different? Explain.

11. A pharmaceutical company purchases the same raw material from two different suppliers. The company is concerned that the level of impurities could vary considerably among shipments and could affect the quality of the end product. To compare the percentage levels of impurities between the two suppliers, the company selects nine shipments from each supplier and measures the percentage impurities in each shipment. The results are shown here.

	Supplier 1	Supplier 2
$\bar{x}$	1.72	1.79
s^2	.156	.082
n	16	16

Construct a 90% confidence interval for the ratio of population variances. Does it appear that variation in impurities differs between the two suppliers? Explain.

12. Refer to Exercise 11. Suppose that the percentage of impurities are as shown below. Should you construct a confidence interval on the population variance ratio? Explain.

Supplier 1:	.30	.35	.37	.39	.40	.75	3.00	6.15	17.10
Supplier 2:	.20	.25	.26	.27	.30	5.05	7.10	10.19	15.12

13. A firm's quality-assurance function seeks to reduce process or service variation. For example, in a just-in-time delivery system, vendors' parts arrive at a plant just before production. This reduces a firm's inventory storage costs. But vendors' parts must arrive at or very near the scheduled time, otherwise production is stopped. Consistent (low variance) delivery times are preferred to inconsistent (high variance) delivery times. COMCEL has arranged with Hiteck Inc. that electronic parts should arrive daily at noon for a particular production line. For over six months, Hiteck had trouble meeting the schedule. A joint problem-solving team made several recommendations. Below are arrival data for two 10-day periods before and after the joint problem-solving effort. COMCEL records the number of hours off the noon target (*Note:* a +2 means that a shipment arrived at 2:00 P.M.).

Day	1	2	3	4	5	6	7	8	9	10
Before	+3	+2	−3	0	+3	−4	−1	+2	+2	−4
After	−1	0	+1	−1	+1	0	+1	−1	0	0

a. Line graph the before and after delivery process data. Are both data sets stationary?
b. Compute the mean, standard deviation, and variance for the two data sets.
c. Construct a 90% confidence interval on the population variance ratio. Has the COMCEL-Hiteck problem-solving team significantly reduced the variance in arrival times? Explain.

14. Management seeks to reduce process variation by investing in improved machinery, methods, materials, training, and supervision. Has COMCEL reduced the process variation in tensile strength (in pounds per square inch) of phone handsets in its Norcross, Georgia, plant? It collects production data before and after the investment in new machinery.

Day	Before	After
1	4,875	4,770
2	4,625	4,800
3	4,750	4,675
4	4,900	4,800
5	4,700	4,775
6	4,550	4,700
7	4,800	4,780
8	4,775	4,650
9	4,500	4,750
10	4,975	4,800

a. Line graph the before and after tensile strength process data. Are both processes stationary?
b. Compute descriptive statistics for the two processes.
c. Construct a 95% confidence interval on the population variance ratio. Has the investment in new machinery helped COMCEL reduce process variation? Explain.

8.7 ≡ A Nonparametric Method for Comparing Two Population Variabilities

When constructing confidence intervals on the variance ratio using the F-tables, we must assume that the two population distributions are near normal. When the data have outliers or when the distributions are highly skewed, we must use a nonparametric approach to compare population variability. Here, we choose the Mood (1964)

FIGURE 8.12   Multiple Box Plot for COMCEL Sick Leave Data

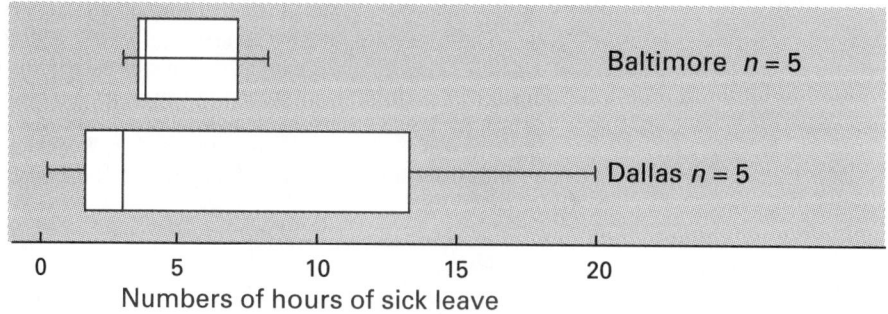

test. Mood's test compares the dispersion (not variances) of two populations. By the end of this section you should be able to:

1. use Mood's test to determine if the dispersions in two populations are the same; and
2. explain why either very small or large test values indicate that two populations have different dispersions.

We illustrate the Mood test in the following example.

Example: COMCEL Sick Leave in Baltimore and Dallas Plants   Are the dispersions in sick leave (hours) taken in the two plants the same? COMCEL randomly selects the personnel records of five workers from each plant and obtains the descriptive data given in Table 8.14.

Table 8.14

Hours of Sick Leave Taken Last Quarter

	Dallas Plant	Baltimore Plant
	.2	3.5
	1.2	3.6
	3.4	3.7
	14	6.9
	20	7.6
Sample size	5	5
Sample median	3.4 hours	3.7 hours

To use the Mood test, we must make two assumptions:

ASSUMPTION 1:   The two data sets are independent random samples.

ASSUMPTION 2:   The two populations have similar medians but may have different dispersions.

The first assumption is true because COMCEL used simple random sampling. Draw a multiple box plot to verify Assumption 2. The box plot in Figure 8.12 suggests that the two data sets have similar sample medians but different sample dispersions. Do the population dispersions differ?

Testing for equality of population dispersions begins by ranking the 10 data values. The ranked values are presented in Table 8.15, with B for Baltimore and D for Dallas. The Baltimore sample data have less dispersion than the Dallas data. The five values in the middle belong to the Baltimore workers, while the first three and last two data values belong to the Dallas workers.

Since we are dealing with ranked data, the second step is to find the rank of the median value. Given 10 data values, the *rank* of the median value is $(n + 1)/2$, or $(10 + 1)/2 = 5.5$th largest value.

Table 8.15

Rank Ordering of Sample Sick Leave Data

Rank-Ordered Data		Rank
.2	D	1
1.2	D	2
3.4	D	3
3.5	B	4
3.6	B	5
3.7	B	6
6.9	B	7
7.6	B	8
14	D	9
20	D	10

The third step is to measure the dispersion of the ranked data. We cannot use the variance since we are using ranked data. However, we can make an analogy to the variance by computing the sum of the squared differences between the *rank* of each Baltimore data point (and each Dallas data point) and the *rank* of the median. Denote the sum of the squared differences as the computed M-value. Table 8.16 contains the computations for $M_{Baltimore}$ and M_{Dallas}. Although both M-value calculations are shown here, you need only calculate one M-value (Dallas *or* Baltimore).

Table 8.16

Computation of Sum of Squares for COMCEL Data Set

	Data Set Computation for Baltimore				Data Set Computation for Dallas		
	[R]ank	R − 5.5	(R − 5.5)²		[R]ank	R − 5.5	(R − 5.5)²
D	1			D	1	−4.5	20.25
D	2			D	2	−3.5	12.25
D	3			D	3	−2.5	6.25
B	4	−1.5	2.25	B	4		
B	5	−.5	.25	B	5		
B	6	.5	.25	B	6		
B	7	1.5	2.25	B	7		
B	8	2.5	6.25	B	8		
D	9			D	9	3.5	12.25
D	10			D	10	4.5	20.25
		$M_B = 11.25$				$M_D = 71.25$	

Next we compare the computed M-value with the values in Table 8.17. If the computed M-value is less than the lower limit, then the population from which the sample was taken has less dispersion than the other population at the 95% level of confidence. If the computed M-value is greater than the upper limit, the population from which the sample was taken has more dispersion than the other population at the 95% level of confidence. If the computed M-value is between the lower and upper limits, we cannot detect any difference in the populations' dispersions at the 95% level of confidence.

The computed M-value for Baltimore is 11.25. Since it is less than the tabled M-value for a sample size of 5 (15.25), we are 95% confident that the population of workers in Baltimore has less dispersion in the number of sick days taken than their Dallas counterparts. Alternatively, we could reach the same conclusion by comparing the computed M-value for Dallas (71.25) to the tabled M-value in Table 8.17.

Table 8.17

Tabled M-Values for an Approximate 95% Level of Confidence*

Sample Size per Group	Lower Limit	Upper Limit
5	15.25	65.25
10	198.50	464.50
15	758.50	1,489.00
20	1,917.60	3,412.40
25	3,903.18	6,509.31
30	6,944.84	11,050.10
40	17,123.90	25,536.00
50	34,323.00	49,002.00

*For other sample sizes, see any book on applied nonparametric statistics.

Table 8.18

Computation of Sum of Squares for Second Data Set

Data Set Computation for Baltimore				Data Set Computation for Dallas			
	R	R − 5.5	(R − 5.5)²		R	R − 5.5	(R − 5.5)²
D	1				1	−4.5	20.25
B	2	−3.5	12.25		2		
D	3				3	−2.5	6.25
B	4	−1.5	2.25		4		
D	5				5	−.5	.25
B	6	.5	.25		6		
D	7				7	1.5	2.25
B	8	2.5	6.25		8		
D	9				9	3.5	12.25
B	10	4.5	20.25		10		
		$M_B = 41.25$				$M_D = 41.25$	

For a sample of size 5, computed M-values between 15.25 and 65.25 indicate that the two population dispersions could be the same. We illustrate this with the following ranked data set:

D,   B,   D,   B,   D,   B,   D,   B,   D,   B

The Dallas and Baltimore data values alternate; the Dallas data values range from the first to the ninth observations while the Baltimore data range from the second to the tenth data values. That suggests that both populations have the same dispersion.

Now we will show that the computed M-values fall between 15.25 and 65.25. Table 8.18 shows the sum of squared differences between the ranks of the Baltimore data (or Dallas data) and the rank of the median. The median is still the 5.5th—$(10 + 1)/2$—largest data value. Both computed M-values are 41.25.

We summarize the Mood test procedure.

Steps in the Mood Test

1. Combine the two samples and rank order the data. Be able to identify which data values belong to which samples.
2. Determine the rank of the median value. This is $(n + 1)/2$, where n is the total sample size.
3. Select one sample and compute the sum of squares (M) between the rank of its data values and the rank of the median value.
4. Compare the computed M-value to the upper and lower limits from Table 8.17.
5. If the computed M-value is less than the lower limit, then the population from which the sample was taken has less dispersion than the other population, at the 95% level of confidence.
6. If the computed M-value is greater than the upper limit, then the population from which the sample was taken has more dispersion than the other population, at the 95% level of confidence.
7. If the computed M-value is between the lower and upper limits, the two populations may have the same dispersion at the 95% level of confidence.

Note that in analyzing two population dispersions, it is not necessary to compute both M-values. If one M-value is below the lower limit, the other M-value will be above the upper limit.

In summary, when the data have outliers or are highly skewed, use the Mann-Whitney confidence interval method for comparing two population medians and the Mood test for comparing two population dispersions.

SECTION 8.7 EXERCISES

1. What are the assumptions behind the Mood method? When would you choose this method over the variance ratio method described in the previous section?

2. One assumption underlying the Mood test is that both populations have similar medians. Construct a multiple box plot to verify this assumption for the following data.

Group A	10	15	26	40	45	54	65	78	90	100
Group B	40	42	45	48	49	53	54	56	58	61

3. Consider the following output obtained from the COMSTAT-NONPARAMETRIC tool (F7). Do the two population variabilities differ? Explain.

M statistic for column A	546.00
M statistic for column B	118.00
Lower limit from Table 8.17	198.50
Upper limit from Table 8.17	464.50

4. Consider the following data sets:

Group 1	Group 2
3	7
6	9
14	16
42	19
43	24

    a. Rank the observations from the two groups and find the sum of the squared differences between the rank of each observation and the rank of the median for both groups.

    b. Compare the sums you found in part **a** to Table 8.17 in the text. What do you conclude from the table about the dispersions of the two populations from which the samples were drawn?

5. A cigarette manufacturer has produced two new brands of cigarettes—Clouds and Springs—with reduced tar and nicotine. Tests have shown that both brands have about the same average tar and nicotine content, so the manufacturer is interested in the variation in tar and nicotine of these two brands. They will market the brand with the smaller variation. They select 10 cigarettes of each brand and determine the tar and nicotine content in milligrams. The results are shown here.

Clouds		Springs	
19.0	21.3	19.3	21.0
19.1	21.4	19.9	21.6
19.2	22.4	20.0	21.9
19.6	23.2	20.3	22.1
20.6	23.9	20.4	22.9

    a. Find the sample medians for the two brands.

    b. Suppose you were not willing to assume that the samples were drawn from normal populations. Use the Mood procedure to determine if the variation in tar and nicotine differs between the two brands. State your conclusion.

    c. Suppose that you were willing to assume that the samples were drawn from normal populations. Construct a 95% confidence interval for the variance ratio. Does this confidence interval suggest that the population variances are different? Explain.

6. An investor wishes to compare the risks associated with different stocks. Risk is measured by the variation in daily price changes. She selects a random sample of five daily price changes for two stocks. Below are the data.

Stock 1	Stock 2
0	.625
.125	−.50
−.25	−.75
.50	.25
.75	1.50

Can we say with 95% confidence that there is a difference between the two stocks in the risk associated with them?

7. Proktor & Gimble wants to know if two market segments—Yuppies and Dinks (Double Income, No Kids)—have similar population income variabilities.

Yuppies		Dinks	
$23,550	$32,000	$21,000	$ 32,500
23,750	34,500	22,500	41,000
24,000	35,000	23,000	56,000
29,500	36,500	29,000	78,000
30,000	39,500	31,000	114,000

8.8 ≡ Key Ideas and Overview

Managers must know when and how to improve departmental performance. They begin by conducting surveys to find potential improvement projects. Then they design potential improvements and run small-scale planned change studies to determine if they really improve performance or service. Finally, they analyze the data and study the results. They ask: What did we learn? If the planned change is effective, they implement it permanently.

Confidence intervals play an important role in improving departmental performance. Table 8.19 provides an overview of the confidence interval methods presented in the last two chapters. In Table 8.19 we have listed the chapter sections for constructing confidence intervals on the mean, median, proportion, variance, and dispersion for one or two data sets. It also shows the expressions for constructing confidence intervals on the various population parameters.

Table 8.19

Overview of Inference Methods

	Center	
	One Group	**Two Groups**
Normal Distribution	Mean Section 7.3 t-based interval $\bar{x} \pm t(\%, \text{df}) \cdot \dfrac{s}{\sqrt{n}}$	Means Section 8.3 t-based interval $\bar{x}_2 - \bar{x}_1 \pm t(\%, \text{df})s_p\sqrt{\dfrac{1}{n_1} + \dfrac{1}{n_2}}$
	Proportion Section 7.6 z-based interval $\hat{p} \pm z\sqrt{\dfrac{\hat{p}\hat{q}}{n}}$	Proportions Section 8.4 z-based interval $\hat{p}_1 - \hat{p}_2 \pm z\sqrt{\dfrac{\hat{p}_1\hat{q}_1}{n_1} + \dfrac{\hat{p}_2\hat{q}_2}{n_2}}$
Nonparametric	Median Section 7.8 Rank-based interval Rank data. Determine the rank of the lower and upper limits from Table 7.9	Medians Section 8.5 Mann–Whitney-based interval Compute table of differences. Determine the rank of the lower and upper limits from Table 8.8.

	Dispersion	
	One Group	**Two Groups**
Normal Distribution	Variance Section 7.8 Chi-square-based interval	Variances Section 8.6 F-distribution-based interval

$$\frac{(n-1)s^2}{\chi^2_{1-x/2}} \le \sigma^2 \le \frac{(n-1)s^2}{\chi^2_{x/2}} \qquad \frac{s_1^2/s_2^2}{F_{1-x/2}} \le \frac{\sigma_1^2}{\sigma_2^2} \le \frac{s_1^2/s_2^2}{F_{x/2}}$$

Nonparametric		Dispersions Section 8.7 Mood test Rank data. Compute the sum of squares of the ranks about the rank of the median value. Compare the sum of squares to the tabled values from Table 8.17.

COMCEL

Date: November 22, 1994
To: Howard Bright, Plant Manager
From: Sarah Teman, Manager of Operations
Re: Report on labor cost reduction study in the Norcross plant

SUMMARY
Over the 6-month period, the 10 work groups that had teambuilding training reduced unit labor cost by an average of $3.19. The 10 groups that had creativity training reduced unit labor cost by an average of $4.23. The difference of $1.04 is too big to attribute to sampling variability, so the results are statistically significant. I recommend that we provide creativity training for all work groups.

SUPPORTING ANALYSES
You asked how I could be sure that the results were due to the differences in the workshops and not some other factors. I can't be absolutely sure, but I did everything feasible to protect against the common threats to the study's validity.

I selected 20 teams that had about the same experience working together and had about the same success in implementing cost-saving ideas. The teams were randomly assigned to the two workshops. This method of assignment prevented my biases from affecting the assignments. We chose only 20 groups because the workshops are expensive, in terms of both lost production and direct cost.

One problem I did have was convincing the participants not to discuss the training with members of the other treatment groups. Otherwise we would not get a clear picture of the impact of each training method. I told the 20 teams that when the study was completed, all groups would be given the workshop that resulted in the greater cost reductions. They agreed not to discuss the ideas they learned in the workshops for a period of 6 months. I also made it clear that both workshops were effective in reducing costs and that neither method was inferior. I told them how they were selected for the study and how I assigned them to the two workshops by a flip of a coin. I made it clear that the study would be invalid if they assigned themselves to the workshops.

My biggest concern was that other cost-saving methods might be discovered by other work groups, vendors, or other divisions of the company and implemented during the study. This could make it difficult to determine the cost reductions due to the two training methods. Thus I took biweekly cost measurements rather than waiting until the end of the study.

In summary, I ran a valid study. The statistically significant differences in cost reduction between the two workshops is due to the type of training, and not other factors.

CHAPTER 8 QUESTIONS

1. In comparing two sets of data, what are we interested in? Why?

2. If two groups of data come from nonnormal populations with different variances, what can be done to make the data more normal and to make the variances more equal?

3. What assumptions are necessary in constructing confidence intervals on the difference between two population means?

4. If two sample means differ, must the two population means also differ?

5. What does the estimated standard error of the difference between sample means measure?

6. If the confidence interval on the difference between two population means does not include 0, what can we conclude?

7. Are you likely to conclude that two population means differ when the difference between their sample means is much larger than the estimated standard error?

8. Provide an example (different from those in the book) where we would need to draw inferences about two population proportions.

9. Correct, if necessary, the following statement: If the confidence interval on the difference in two population proportions includes the value of 0, we conclude that the two sample proportions are not different.

10. If the sample proportion is greater than 1, what can we conclude?

11. When should we use the Mann-Whitney confidence interval method?

12. Explain the logic of the Mann-Whitney method.

13. Why is consistent performance, product, or service desirable?

14. If the confidence interval on two population variances includes the value of 1, why would managers conclude that the two population variances do not differ?

15. What are the differences between the assumptions underlying confidence intervals on the variance ratio and the Mood test?

16. When the computed M-value is either larger or smaller than the tabled values (Table 8.17), the population dispersions of the two groups differ. Explain the logic.

17. What role do stem-and-leaf displays and box plots play in constructing confidence intervals?

18. Why won't a square root or log base 10 transformation work on negative data values, such as dollar loss?

19. Why is it important to identify potential improvement projects?

20. What role can confidence intervals play in identifying potential improvement projects?

CHAPTER 8 APPLICATION PROBLEMS

1. Best Dairy Inc. has segmented its market into eight groups. Among these separate markets are the Machos and Status Seekers. Machos are young males, blue-collar workers with high-school degrees who live in the city. Status Seekers are young males, white-collar workers with college degrees who live in the suburbs. Best Dairy Inc. takes a sample of 10 from both market segments and asks each person his annual income. Below are the data. Is there a difference between the population mean incomes of the Machos and Status Seekers?

Machos		Status Seekers	
$22,500	$22,900	$29,000	$29,000
22,000	20,000	28,500	27,500
22,700	22,500	28,000	28,000
22,000	23,500	27,500	28,000
23,000	21,500	28,500	28,000

a. Draw stem-and-leaf displays for both market segments. Do the shapes appear normal? Do the variances appear to be the same?

b. Set up and interpret an 80% confidence interval on the difference between the two population means.

2. The Vice-President for Human Resource Development wishes to determine if the proportion of hourly employees who believe that senior management is open to their ideas is the same in two plants. He randomly selects 100 workers in each plant and asks them if senior management is open to their ideas. Shown are the sample proportions that respond yes.

	Plant	
	Hartford, CT	Austin, TX
n	100	100
$\hat{p}$	.56	.48

a. Set up and interpret a 95% confidence interval on the difference between the two population proportions.

b. Why can you assume that the sampling distribution for the difference between two sample proportions is near normal? Explain.

3. COMCEL buys the plastic for its mobile phone housings from two suppliers. It wonders if both suppliers' plastics have the same mean impact resistance. It takes a simple random sample of 10 phones made from each vendor's material and runs impact tests. Here are the data.

Impact Resistance in Pounds per Square Inch

Vendor A	Vendor B
4,600	4,700
4,650	4,750
4,700	4,600
4,650	4,650
4,750	4,650
4,850	4,675
4,600	4,800
4,900	4,625
4,650	4,675
4,600	4,690

a. What is the appropriate confidence interval to construct for this problem? [*Hint:* Drawing a stem-and-leaf display or box plot may be helpful in answering the question.]
b. Set up and interpret a 95% confidence interval.

 4. A manager tests interacting and nominal group structures. The former is run by a directed leader who closely controls the meeting. Members speak when they have something to say; otherwise, they remain quiet. The nominal group provides time for all to think about the problem, the opportunity to share ideas with others, and to compare and contrast ideas and reach a consensus. The manager compares 10 groups with each group structure using the Moon Survival game. Groups must identify the top five items (from a list of 15) to help them travel from a crash site to the mother ship some 200 miles away. The groups' results are compared to those of NASA survival experts. Below are the number of correct items each group identified.

Interacting	2	3	2	5	2	3	4	4	3	4
Nominal	3	4	4	4	5	5	4	5	5	4

a. Draw two stem-and-leaf displays for the number of correct items selected. Which group structure appears to produce more correct items and less variability in the number of correct items?
b. Which group structure yields better mean results? Set up a 90% confidence interval on the difference between the two population means.
c. Which group has less variance in the number of correct items? Set up a 90% confidence interval on the ratio of the two population variances.

 5. Shown are the number of months required for American firms to negotiate major contracts with firms in Europe and the Far East.

Europe	Far East
3	2
4	6
5	10
7	20
8	48

At the 95% level of confidence, are the dispersions in negotiating times the same for Europe and the Far East?

6. The American Housing Association (AHA) believes that the size of an apartment complex affects the length-of-tenure discount size. AHA takes a simple random sample of 10 small and 10 large apartment complexes and determines the mean discount within each complex for renters who have lived there five or more years. Here are the data:

Discount as Percentage of Normal Starting Rent

	Small Complex	Large Complex
$\bar{x}$	7.9	2.5
s^2	.8	.5
s	.89	.71
Sample size	10	10

a. Set up and interpret a 95% confidence interval on the difference between the two population mean discounts.

b. Set up and interpret a 95% confidence interval on the ratio of the two population variances. Are discounts in large complexes more consistent than discounts in small complexes?

7. When team members learn to do each other's jobs, is the proportion of defects produced by the team reduced? An operations manager runs a planned change study in which she randomly selects 3,000 groups. Of these groups, 1,500 are given cross-job training and 1,500 are not. Several weeks after the training, she assesses the proportion of defects for both the study and control groups. Here are the data.

	Control Groups	Cross-Trained Groups
n	1500	1500
$\hat{p}$	.04	.01

a. Set up and interpret a 95% confidence interval on the difference between the two population proportions.

b. Has the cross training been successful in reducing the proportion of defects?

8. A nutritionist determines the impact of bran on reducing cholesterol levels. He randomly selects ten people who have the same level of elevated cholesterol and randomly assigns them to one of two groups—the bran group and the control group. Each person in the bran group eats a bowl of bran every day for six weeks. The control group eats the same foods as the bran group except for the bran. After six weeks the researcher measures the drop in cholesterol levels of individuals in both groups.

Bran group:	10	15	20	10	80
Control group:	0	5	0	0	5

a. Set up and interpret a 95% confidence interval on the difference between the two population medians (drop in cholesterol level).

b. Does bran appear to reduce cholesterol levels? Explain.

c. Why couldn't you set up a confidence interval on the difference between two population means? Explain.

9. FarWestern Power wants to even out commercial power usage during the day. Typically, power usage is very high during the day and very low in the evening hours. This forces FarWestern Power to use old and inefficient coal-burning plants to generate the necessary power to meet peak demand. FarWestern launches a new campaign to get commercial users to postpone some of their power needs until the evening hours. Have they been successful in reducing the variability in daily consumption? Below are day and evening power usages before and after the campaign for two randomly selected weeks. Assume that the "before" and "after" populations are normally distributed.

Data in Thousands of Kilowatts for 12-Hour Periods

	Before Campaign	After Campaign
Monday A.M.	2,000	1,500
Monday P.M.	300	900
Tuesday A.M.	2,100	1,400
Tuesday P.M.	500	1,000
Wednesday A.M.	1,500	1,200
Wednesday P.M.	100	400
Thursday A.M.	2,500	1,700
Thursday P.M.	700	1,500
Friday A.M.	2,000	1,500
Friday P.M.	500	1,000

Set up and interpret a 90% confidence interval on the ratio of the population variances in power consumption. Has the campaign to even out daily power consumption been successful?

10. Apex must reduce its mean age of accounts receivable (A/R) from over 30 days. It tries a program of inducements—discounts for prompt payment in Hartford and no inducements in New Haven. It then randomly selects 10 accounts from both cities. Does the program appear to be successful?

Age of A/R in Days

With Inducement	No Inducement
20	30
21	28
20	31
16	35
19	30
24	30
21	29
22	34
25	32
21	32

a. Draw stem-and-leaf displays for the two data sets. Do the data sets look normal and appear to have the same variance?

b. Set up an appropriate 99% confidence interval.

11. An ad firm evaluates which of two approaches is more successful in helping potential consumers remember the advertising message. It tries a man-in-the-street approach using real customers talking about the product. The other approach uses movie stars and sports heroes talking about the product. The firm tries each approach in one city for one month. Two weeks later, it selects a simple random sample of 500 potential customers who have seen the ads and asks them what the ad's message was. Below are the proportions of consumers who correctly identified the ad's message.

	Man in the Street	Stars and Sports Figures
n	500	500
$\hat{p}$	.40	.60

a. Is there any difference between the two approaches at the 95% level of confidence?

b. Why can we be reasonably sure that the sampling distribution of the difference in sample proportions is normal? Explain.

12. Are the average earnings per share for firms in the high-tech and heavy-industry market segments the same? Given are seven firms, selected at random from each segment, and their last year's earnings per share.

High-Tech	.50	2.00	2.10	2.50	2.75	3.50	7.00
Heavy-Industry	2.00	2.90	3.10	3.30	3.50	4.00	14.00

Set up and interpret a 95% confidence interval on the difference between the two population medians.

13. Which of two courier services has more consistent delivery times? Based on a sample of 21 days, Reliable Delivery's sample standard deviation is 1.0 hour and United Delivery's sample standard deviation is 1.20 hours. Set up and interpret a 95% confidence interval on the two population variances.

14. A poison pill is an action that a firm takes to make it unattractive to potential hostile takeovers. We wish to determine whether the proportion of firms that use a poison pill changed in the decade of the 1980s. Shown are hypothetical data for 1980 and 1990 surveys.

1980	1990
$n = 1000$	$n = 1000$
$\hat{p} = .11$	$\hat{p} = .06$

At the 99% level of confidence, can we say that there has been a drop in the proportion of firms that have used the poison pill strategy from 1980 to 1990?

15. A firm tries two different leadership styles in two plants to determine their impact on productivity. Two plants are randomly selected. The project manager randomly selects 15 groups in plant A to be led by an autocratic leader and 15 groups in plant B to be led by a participative leader. Below are productivity data six months later.

Productivity as Percentage of Standard

	Participative Leadership	Autocratic Leadership
n	15	15
$\bar{x}$	105	98
s	1.5	1

a. Set up and interpret a 90% confidence interval. Which leadership style has the higher mean worker productivity? Explain.

b. The data are in percentages. Why did we set up confidence intervals on the population means and not the population proportions?

16. Given are daily outputs from two production lines. Which production line is more consistent? Assume the two populations are normally distributed.

Production in Units per Hour

Line A	Line B
50	47
53	55
60	57
61	62
65	66

Set up a 95% confidence interval on the ratio of the two population variances.

17. Which fixed disk lasts longer? We have time-to-failure data in hours for two vendors' fixed disks. Which vendor has a higher average time-to-failure? Set up and interpret an 80% confidence interval on the difference between the two population means.

Time-to-Failure in Hours

	Vendor A	Vendor B
n	50	50
$\bar{x}$	1,000	800
s	50	40

18. Two universities wish to compare median Graduate Management Aptitude Test (GMAT) scores for their incoming graduate classes. Below are randomly selected samples from both universities.

University A: 400 510 540 560 600 610 610 650 780
University B: 410 500 550 560 600 600 610 630 680

    a. Draw box plots for the data sets.
    b. Set up and interpret a 95% confidence interval on the difference between two population medians.

19. In *Eison v. City of Knoxville*, a female candidate at the Knoxville Police Academy claimed that the physical qualification tests tended to reject female applicants. If Eison could show this, she would have established a prima facie case for discrimination. Then the city of Knoxville would have to demonstrate that the physical qualification test is crucial to on-the-job performance. Below are the data.

	Pass	Fail	Total
Female	32	9	41
Male	84	9	93

    a. Compute the sample proportions of both genders that passed the physical qualification tests.
    b. Set up a 95% confidence interval on the difference between the two population proportions. What can you conclude?

20. Two years ago, Alliance Motors launched the Luxor, a $50,000 two-door sedan, to compete with the BMW 733. Alliance had targeted consumers who are 35–49 years old. Luxor car sales have been disappointing. Alliance suspects that the car is attracting older buyers, a market segment that is generally unwilling to spend $50,000 for a car. Alliance Motors randomly selects 100 Luxor owners and 100 BMW 733 owners. Shown are the descriptive data on owners' ages.

	Luxor	BMW 733
Sample size	100	100
$\bar{x}$	52.5 years	41.5 years
s	2.1 years	2.3 years

    a. Construct a 99% confidence interval on the difference between the two population mean ages.
    b. Is the Luxor attracting the same age buyers as the BMW 733? Explain.

21. In *Boykin v. Georgia Pacific Corporation*, two black plaintiffs complained that blacks were primarily assigned to low-level utility jobs. They presented the following data to support their position.

Race	Assigned to Nonutility Job	Assigned to Utility Job	Total
Black	22	295	317
White	90	354	444

a. Compute the sample proportions of blacks and whites assigned to nonutility jobs.

b. Set up a 90% confidence interval on the difference between the two population proportions. What can you conclude?

 22. Do stocks in different industries have the same variance in their beta coefficients? The beta coefficient is a measure of the extent to which the returns on a given stock move with the stock market. A stock with a beta of 1 means that if the market rises (or falls) by 10%, the stock price will rise (or fall) by 10%. Below are hypothetical beta coefficients for stocks for two industries.

Computer	Public Utility
1.70	.55
1.20	.65
1.00	.60
2.10	.65
1.95	.62

Set up a 95% confidence interval on the ratio of the two population variances. What can you conclude?

 23. Suppose we take two random samples of five male and five female full professors from state universities and we obtain the following nine-month salary information.

Males	Females
$47,000	$39,000
53,000	44,000
59,000	49,000
65,000	56,000
79,000	67,000

a. Set up a 95% confidence interval on the difference between the two population median incomes.

b. If your answer to part **a** indicates that there is a difference, does this mean that there is gender discrimination in salaries? Discuss.

 24. Marketers who use price lining offer products in set price lines and target each line to a particular market segment. For example, a national retailer advertises car batteries as good or excellent. Below are hypothetical data on the number of seconds of cranking power for the good and the excellent brands.

Good Brand	Excellent Brand
65	140
78	146
85	148
85	148
88	148
94	149
100	155

    a. Construct multiple box plots to compare the locations and dispersions of the two samples. What do you conclude?

    b. Explain why it is unnecessary to construct a confidence interval for the difference between the population medians.

    c. Explain why the Mood test for the difference of dispersions is inappropriate.

 25. We randomly select ten families in each of two cities and determine their family incomes. Are the dispersions in incomes the same in the two cities?

Eugene, OR	Akron, OH
$ 9,000	$11,000
19,000	14,000
22,500	19,500
25,000	24,500
29,900	27,500
30,000	35,000
32,500	37,000
45,000	47,500
60,000	55,500
79,000	82,000

Use Mood's method. Do the two population dispersions differ? Explain.

26.

Date: September 7, 1994
To: Howard Bright, Norcross Plant Manager
From: Sarah Teman, Manager of Operations
Re: Comparison of Dallas and Norcross Plants

I received a copy of Martin Young's analysis of the overall job attitude and the level of perceived task support within the Dallas plant. That got me to thinking that it would be informative to compare our performance with the Dallas plant's. In a couple of days I will be sending you my report. I'm looking forward to seeing how we compare to the Dallas operation. If you have any questions after receiving my analysis, please contact me.

    Use Data Base I in Appendix 9, and develop a report that compares the Dallas and Norcross plants on overall job attitude and level of perceived task support. Write a memo summarizing the major findings to Howard Bright.

27.

Date: April 15, 1995
To: Bill O'Hara, Vice-President of Marketing
From: Cherian Jain, Manager of Marketing Research
Re: Additional Analysis of Harrid Survey Data

Having completed the initial analysis requested in your March 17 memo, I thought of some additional analyses we might do. It occurred to me that we should make comparisons among the various regions. I am especially interested in answering the following questions:

1.   What is the buy-American attitude across the four regions? Is the pro buy-American attitude in the South found elsewhere?

2.   Is the desire for FAX machines in the Northeast and West the same as in the South and Midwest regions?

3. Is the age of the accounts receivable the same in the South as in the other three regions?
4. Is the variation in the age of accounts receivable the same in the South as in the other three regions?

I'll have the additional report by the week of the 21st. Perhaps then we can discuss the marketing implications. Let's have several people from Peter Miangi's finance group sit in, for they may find the aging of the accounts receivable information informative.

Use Data Base III in Appendix 9 to analyze the data. Write a short memo to Bill O'Hara summarizing your response to the four questions. Include your statistical analyses to support your findings.

REFERENCES

Mood, Alexander. "On the Asymptotic Efficiency of Certain Nonparametric Two-Sample Tests." *Ann. Math. Statist.* 25 (1964): 514–522.

Siegel, Andrew. *Statistics and Data Analysis.* New York: Wiley, 1988.

APPENDIX: Statistical Software

Example 1: This example shows how to use MINITAB, Release 8, to construct stem-and-leaf displays. The data set consists of list prices of ballpoint pens in Omaha, and are shown in the top panel of Figure 8.2.

Input

```
01 MTB > SET C1
02 DATA> 1.19 1.29 1.29 1.39 1.49 1.69 2.39 3.79 8.69
03 DATA> END
04 MTB > STEM AND LEAF C1;
05 SUBC> INCREMENT K=1.
```

Explanation of Input

01–03   See Software Appendix of Chapter 7.

04   STEM AND LEAF tells MINITAB to construct a stem-and-leaf display for the data entered in column 1.

05   Many MINITAB commands have SUBCommands. MINITAB expects a subcommand when the previous command ends with a semicolon. The last subcommand ends with a period. The INCREMENT subcommand, K=1, tells MINITAB that stems should be 1 unit apart, or that the "class width" should be 1, or $1.00.

Output

```
Stem-and-leaf of C1        N  = 9
01     Leaf Unit = 0.10
02     6)    1 122346
03     3     2 3
       2     3 7
       1     4
       1     5
       1     6
       1     7
       1     8 6
```

Interpretation of Output

01   There is a difference between the stem-and-leaf display shown in Figure 8.2 of the text and the stem-and-leaf display produced by MINITAB. Even though the data are in dollars and cents, the MINITAB display shows no decimal points. "Leaf Unit=0.10" tells us where to place the decimal point. Since it is .10, we know that the decimal point goes between the stem of 1 and the leaf of 1 shown in the first row. The first number is $1.1. If the Leaf unit had been 1.0, then the first number would have been $11. We show the decimal points in our stem-and-leaf displays for ease of interpretation.

02   Another difference between the stem-and-leaf displays in the text and the
        MINITAB version is that MINITAB only shows one-digit leaves. The two-digit
        leaves are "truncated," meaning that the last digit is simply dropped, rather than
        rounded. So, even though the leaves are in 10-cent units, the data have not been
        rounded to the nearest 10 cents.
            The parentheses around the 6 in the first column tells us two things: (1) there
        are 6 leaves in the row and (2) the median is contained within the row.

03   With the exception of the row containing the median, the numbers in the first
        column tell us how many observations are in its row or beyond. The 3 indicates that
        the total number of observations in the second row and beyond is 3, namely, 2.3,
        3.7, and 8.6.

Example 2: This example shows how to use MINITAB, Release 8, to construct a confidence
interval for the difference between two population means for the unit labor cost data shown in
Table 8.5.

Input

```
01  MTB > NAME C3 ='TBW'
02  MTB > SET 'TBW'
DATA> 3.05 3.10 3.13 3.14 3.18 3.22 3.22 3.24 3.29 3.32
DATA> END
03  MTB > NAME C4 ='CMW'
MTB > SET 'CMW'
DATA> 4.12 4.13 4.21 4.21 4.22 4.24 4.26 4.27 4.27 4.36
DATA> END
04  MTB > TWOSAMPLE 'CMW' 'TBW';
05  SUBC> POOLED.
```

Explanation of Input

01–03   The NAME command can be used to name a column or variable. TBW refers to the
        group that received the TB Workshop. See Table 8.5. The name reference must
        always be enclosed in single quotes. "CMW" refers to the group that received the
        CM workshop.

04–05   TWOSAMPLE produces a two-sided confidence interval to estimate the difference
        between two population means. The SUBCommand, POOLED, tells MINITAB to
        pool the sample variances to obtain the estimated standard error.

Output

```
    TWOSAMPLE T FOR CMW VS TBW
        N      MEAN     STDEV    SE MEAN
    CMW  10    4.2290   0.0700    0.022
    TBW  10    3.1890   0.0850    0.027
01  95 PCT CI FOR MU CMW - MU TBW: (0.967, 1.113)
02  TTEST MU CMW = MU TBW (VS NE): T= 29.86  P=0.0000  DF=  18
    POOLED STDEV =       0.0779
```

Interpretation of Output

01	MINITAB produces the same 95% confidence interval as the text.
02	The TWOSAMPLE command also performs a statistical test for the difference between population means. See Section 9.4 for a discussion of the use of hypothesis testing to compare two population means.

HYPOTHESIS TESTING

9.1 Introduction to hypothesis testing

9.2 Hypothesis testing on one population mean
State hypotheses and managerial actions
Determine the costs of the decision-making
errors
Set a significance level and determine a
sample size
Data collection
Test the null hypothesis and make a decision
p-value
State hypotheses and managerial actions
Determine the costs of the decision-making
errors
Set a significance level and determine a
sample size
Data collection
Test the null hypothesis and make a decision
p-value

9.3 Hypothesis testing on one population
proportion
State hypotheses and managerial actions
Determine the costs of errors, set α level and
sample size
Data collection
Test the null hypothesis and make a decision
p-value

9.4 Hypothesis testing on the difference between
two population means
State hypotheses and managerial actions
Determine the costs of errors, set α level and
sample size
Data collection
Test the null hypothesis and make a decision
The paired comparison, or paired difference,
test
State hypotheses
Determine the costs of errors, set α level and
sample size
Data collection
Test the null hypothesis and make a decision

9.5 Hypothesis testing on the difference between
two population proportions
State hypotheses and managerial actions
Determine the costs of errors, set α level and
sample size
Data collection
Test the null hypothesis and make a decision

9.6 Key ideas and overview

Appendix A: Relationships between Type I and
Type II errors

Appendix B: Statistical software

INTEROFFICE COMMUNICATION

Date: July 21, 1994
To: Sang Kim, Quality-Assurance Manager
From: Nat Gordon, V.P. Manufacturing
Re: Investigation of Injection Molding Problems

As you know, our engineering group set the process mean target strength on telephone handsets at 4,750 pounds per square inch (ppsi) and set the process standard deviation at 25 ppsi. It also set the upper and lower acceptable strength limits at 4,900 ppsi and 4,600 ppsi, respectively. For the past several months we achieved our process mean target value. Recently the operators expressed concern that the mean strength has dropped. Engineering believes that the strength has actually drifted upwards. In either case, if the mean has substantially shifted from the target value, we will increase the chances of producing handsets outside the 4,600 to 4,900 ppsi limits.

Please investigate the injection molding process. On the average, is it still producing at the target value? If not, we must determine the problems and correct them. But I don't want us to go tinkering with the molding process if it is still producing at the target value of 4,750 ppsi. Because of the concerns raised, I am inspecting every handset and will continue to do so until you complete your analysis. As 100% inspection is expensive (and frankly, not always effective), I want your analysis by tomorrow.

9.1 Introduction to Hypothesis Testing

The confidence interval methods presented in Chapters 7 and 8 help estimate population parameters and ultimately help us make decisions. Hypothesis testing is an alternative approach to making decisions.

Hypothesis testing has four advantages over confidence intervals. Hypothesis testing

1. makes you aware that there are two different types of errors in decision making.
2. requires that you determine the costs of making these errors.
3. is decision oriented. It tests if a population parameter is less than, equal to, or greater than a specific value that is important in making a decision.
4. introduces the p-value.

In Chapters 7 and 8 we assumed that we either had a sample from a normal population or the sample size was sufficiently large that the central limit theorem applied. This permitted us to use the t-distribution table in constructing confidence intervals. The same assumptions will permit us to use the t-distribution table in testing hypotheses in this chapter.

We first introduce hypothesis testing on one population mean. It is useful when a manager must make a decision in which the best action depends on the value of an unknown population mean.

9.2 Hypothesis Testing on One Population Mean

We begin this section with a product manager who has to make a decision about introducing a new product. By the end of this unit you should be able to:

1. formulate hypotheses and their associated managerial actions;
2. explain the idea of Type I and Type II errors;
3. determine the costs associated with the two decision-making errors;
4. test the null hypothesis and make a decision;
5. compute and interpret p-values; and
6. explain the need for additional assumptions for time-ordered process data.

Example: Milemaster Product Introduction Decision   Based on a competitive market analysis, Milemaster Inc. will market a new tire recently developed by the engineering group only if the population mean tire life exceeds 47,000 miles. That is, unless the new tire's average life exceeds 47,000 miles, it is not worth marketing. The engineering group believes that the mean tire life exceeds 47,000 miles. It should. After all, it developed the tire. However, the product manager is unsure if the population mean tire life is less than, equal to, or greater than 47,000 miles. The uncertainty makes his marketing decision difficult.

We now apply a five-step hypothesis testing approach to make the Milemaster tire decision.

1. State hypotheses and associated actions.
2. Determine the costs associated with the two types of decision-making errors.
3. Set a significance level, α, and determine a sample size.
4. Collect the data and compute the sample mean and the estimated standard error.
5. Test the null hypothesis, make a decision, and compute a p-value.

State Hypotheses and Managerial Actions

The first step is to develop two hypotheses about an unknown population mean tire life, μ_{tire}. These are called the null and alternative hypotheses. A hypothesis is simply a testable claim or statement about a population parameter such as a population mean.

The null hypothesis is always the opposite of the claim made by others who wish to influence a decision. A vendor claims its product is better than what your firm is currently using; the decision maker's null hypothesis is that the product is not better. A prosecuting attorney claims a defendant is guilty; the jury's null hypothesis is that the defendant is not guilty. In short, the decision maker's null hypothesis is always the "I-don't-believe-your-claim" hypothesis.

Here is the logic behind the "I-don't-believe-your-claim" null hypothesis. Decision makers are always bombarded by others inside and outside the firm who make claims and who want to influence the decision. The decision maker must be skeptical of these claims. After all, have you ever heard anyone claim that their product or service is worse than what is currently being used? The null hypothesis reflects the decision maker's skepticism about claims made by others.

The decision maker assumes that the null hypothesis is true until proven otherwise. This idea is already familiar to you. In a jury trial, the judge tells the jury that it must assume the defendant is not guilty. The jury may only reject this hypothesis when the evidence proves beyond a reasonable doubt that the defendant is guilty.

For the Milemaster product decision, the engineering group claims that the population mean tire life, denoted as μ_{tire}, is more than 47,000 miles. But the product manager must be skeptical of this claim. Therefore, the null hypothesis is that the population mean tire life is *not* more than 47,000 miles. Rather, it is at most 47,000 miles.

The alternative hypothesis is almost always the claim made by others. In the Milemaster product decision, the alternative hypothesis is based on the engineering group's claim. That is, the population mean tire life is more than 47,000 miles.

Together the null and alternative hypotheses take into account all possible values of the population mean tire life, μ_{tire}. It is either at most 47,000 miles or it is greater than 47,000 miles.

The product manager should also state what business actions he will take if he rejects the null hypothesis or if he fails to reject it.

In summary, here is a procedure for developing the null and alternative hypotheses. First, engineering claims that the population mean is more than 47,000 miles. This is the alternative hypothesis, called H_1. Second, the null hypothesis, H_0, represents all other possible values for the population mean tire life. That is, μ_{tire} is at most 47,000 miles (47,000 miles or less).

	Hypotheses	Action
H_0	The unknown population mean tire life is less than or equal to 47,000 miles—or, at most 47,000 miles. $\mu_{\text{tire}} \leq 47,000$ miles	Failure to reject the null hypothesis means Milemaster *will not* market the tire.
H_1	The unknown population mean tire life is greater than 47,000 miles. $\mu_{\text{tire}} > 47,000$ miles	If Milemaster rejects the null hypothesis, it *will* market the tire.

H₁ = usually what they're claiming

Note several important features of the two hypotheses. First, the product manager has stated what action he will take if he fails to reject or if he rejects the null hypothesis. Clearly, hypothesis testing is decision oriented. Second, the two hypotheses are mutually exclusive and exhaustive. Either the unknown population mean tire life is at most 47,000 miles, or it is more than 47,000 miles. Both hypotheses cannot be true, but one must be true. Third, both hypotheses make claims about an unknown (and unknowable) population mean. Unless Milemaster Inc. checks every tire in the population (which is not practical), it must rely on sample data either to test hypotheses or to construct confidence intervals before making the product introduction decision.

In conclusion, upon completing this step, you will develop one of the following three sets of hypotheses.

Set I: $H_0 \quad \mu \le \mu_0$

                                                        $H_1 \quad \mu > \mu_0$

This is a one-sided, upper-tailed test. We use it to test someone else's claim that the population mean is greater than a hypothesized value, μ_0 (i.e., 47,000 miles). The Milemaster product decision is a one-sided, upper-tailed test.

Set II: $H_0 \quad \mu \ge \mu_0$

                                                        $H_1 \quad \mu < \mu_0$

This is a one-sided, lower-tailed test. We use it to test someone else's claim that the population mean is less than a hypothesized value.

Set III: $H_0 \quad \mu = \mu_0$

                                                        $H_1 \quad \mu \ne \mu_0$

This is a two-sided, or two-tailed, test. We use it to test someone else's claim that the population mean has changed or differs from a hypothesized value.

Determine the Costs of the Decision-Making Errors

The second step is to determine the two types of possible errors and their associated costs.

We can be either right or wrong when we test a hypothesis about an unknown population mean. Table 9.1 shows that there are two ways to be right and two possible errors.

Table 9.1

Two Types of Errors in the Milemaster Decision

Based on the Sample Data the Manager:	Null Is True ($\mu \le 47{,}000$ miles)	Null Is False ($\mu > 47{,}000$ miles)
1. Does not reject null (doesn't market tire)	Correct decision	Type II error
2. Rejects null (markets the tire)	Type I error	Correct decision

Table 9.1 tells us that if the product manager does not reject the null hypothesis, he has made either (1) a correct decision or (2) a Type II error. If the product manager rejects the null hypothesis, he has made either (1) a Type I error or (2) a correct decision.

Here we present the formal definitions of the two errors. Note how we translate the formal definitions into the Milemaster product introduction decision setting.

Type I error: Reject the null hypothesis when the null hypothesis is true.

Translation of Type I Error	1. "Reject the null" means that Milemaster will market the tire.
	2. "Null is true" means the population mean is at most 47,000 miles and the tire should not be marketed.
Description of Type I Error	Milemaster markets the tire when it should not have marketed it.

Type II error: Do not reject the null hypothesis when the null is false.

Translation of Type II Error	1. "Do not reject" the null means that Milemaster will not market the tire.
	2. "Null is false" means population mean is greater than 47,000 miles and the tire should be marketed.
Description of Type II Error	Milemaster does not market the tire when it should have marketed it. A lost marketing opportunity.

Business errors are almost always costly. The product manager would make a Type I error if he marketed the tire when μ_{tire} was actually 47,000 miles or less. He would make a Type II error if he did not market the tire when μ_{tire} was actually more than 47,000 miles. What costs are associated with the Type I and Type II errors in the Milemaster tire study?

Costs of a Type I Error   If it markets the tire, Milemaster will claim that, on average, the tire will last more than 47,000 miles. Suppose that, in fact, the tire wears out, on average, before reaching 47,000 miles. Milemaster will not discover this overnight, but only after a large number of tires have been sold. Then problems will begin. Possible costs include reduced consumer confidence in the company, expensive tire replacements under the tread warranty, and possible class action suits filed by irate consumers. A Type I error would be very costly for Milemaster Inc.

Costs of a Type II Error   Suppose Milemaster does not market the tire when in fact μ_{tire} is greater than 47,000 miles. In failing to market a superior tire, Milemaster would lose a major marketing opportunity. The potential loss depends on how good the new tire really is. If the population mean tire life is only 48,000 miles (only slightly better than currently available competitors' brands), its losses might be small. But if μ_{tire} is 75,000 miles, then failure to market this superior tire would be very costly in terms of lost profit.

While there is a single Type I error cost, the cost of a Type II error depends on how far above 47,000 miles μ_{tire} is. Suppose that Engineering believes that the mean tire life could be as high as 52,000 miles. The project manager should use the 52,000-

mile figure to determine the *most likely* Type II error cost. That is, he could determine the lost profit of not marketing a tire with a mean tire life of 52,000 miles. For this study, the cost in lost profits is moderate.

In summary, for the Milemaster study, the Type I error cost is very high and the cost of the most likely Type II error is moderate.

Set a Significance Level and Determine a Sample Size

The third step requires setting a significance level, α. It should be based on the relative costs of making Type I or Type II errors.

No one likes making errors. However, when testing hypotheses, there is always the chance of making an incorrect decision—a Type I or Type II error. The **significance level,** α, addresses the probability of making a Type I error. Decision makers rely on judgment to set the α level. How should they do it?

As shown in Appendix A, the probabilities of making Type I and Type II errors are related. For a given sample size, as we reduce the α level, the probability of making a Type II error increases. This inverse relationship leads to the following three guidelines:

> The significance level is the *maximum* probability of making a Type I error that the decision maker can accept. It is called the α (alpha) level.

PRINCIPLE 1:   If a Type I error is costly (or serious) and the most likely Type II error is not costly, set a low significance level—an α of .01 or less. A low α level protects the decision maker from making a costly Type I error. Do not worry about making a Type II error if it is not costly or serious.

PRINCIPLE 2:   If the most likely Type II error is costly and a Type I error is not as serious, set α higher—at .20 or above. This reduces the probability of making a costly Type II error.

PRINCIPLE 3:   When both errors are costly, set the significance level, α, at .05 or .01. Reduce the probability of making a costly Type II error by increasing the sample size of the study.[*]

The product manager concluded that a Type I error was more costly than the most likely Type II error. Therefore, he set the significance level very low, an α of .01. If he rejects the null hypothesis, the *maximum* probability of making a Type I error is only 1 in 100. Thus he can be at least $100(1 - \alpha)\%$, or 99%, confident of having made a correct decision.

The product manager must also determine the sample size for the study. How should this be done? We recommend the largest sample size that the initial project budget and time will allow. If this does not reduce sufficiently the probability of making the most likely Type II error, then ask for a larger budget and larger sample. In the tire study, the product manager chose a sample size of 1,000 tires.

Data Collection

This step involves obtaining the sample data and computing the sample statistics.

How do we obtain the data for testing the null hypothesis? We use data that already exist in the firm's information system, we run studies, or we purchase the data. Chapter 6 discussed how to conduct valid survey sampling or planned change studies.

---

[*] Appendix A shows that, for a given α level, increasing the sample size reduces the probability of making a Type II error. For a more complete explanation, see an advanced statistics text such as B. J. Winer's *Statistical Principles of Experimental Design*.

The product manager ran a study. He *randomly* selected 1,000 tires and mounted them on 250 *randomly* selected cars. Randomization is a critical assumption underlying hypothesis testing (see Section 6.9). He recorded the mileage at which each tire failed to meet federal standards for tread wear. Here are the study's sample statistics:

Sample mean	$\bar{x} = 47{,}300$ miles
Sample standard deviation	$s = 3{,}162$ miles
Sample size	$n = 1{,}000$ tires
Estimated standard error of the mean	$\dfrac{s}{\sqrt{n}} = \dfrac{3{,}162}{\sqrt{1{,}000}} = 100$ miles

Given that the sample mean of 47,300 miles is larger than 47,000 miles (the null hypothesis), you may be asking yourself if we should automatically reject the null hypothesis. The answer is no, and we present the reason in the next section.

Test the Null Hypothesis and Make a Decision

The final step involves determining the *rejection region*—the values of the sample mean that will cause the decision maker to reject the null hypothesis.

Suppose the *sample* mean, $\bar{x}$, had been 22,000 miles instead of 47,300 miles. Should the product manager reject the null hypothesis that the population mean, μ_{tire}, is 47,000 miles or less? That is, given a sample mean, $\bar{x}$, of 22,000 miles, would it be more likely that (1) the unknown population mean tire life is 47,000 miles or less or (2) the population mean is greater than 47,000 miles? Please think about it before reading on.

The product manager should not reject the null hypothesis. A sample mean of 22,000 miles is more likely to occur when the unknown population mean is less than or equal to 47,000 miles than when it is greater than 47,000 miles.

Suppose the *sample* mean, $\bar{x}$, had been 72,000 miles instead of 47,300 miles. In that case, should the product manager reject the null hypothesis that the population mean, μ_{tire}, is 47,000 miles or less? That is, given a sample mean, $\bar{x}$, of 72,000 miles, would it be more likely that (1) the unknown population mean tire life is 47,000 miles or less or (2) the population mean is greater than 47,000 miles? Please think about it before reading on.

The product manager should now reject the null hypothesis. A sample mean of 72,000 miles is more likely to occur when the unknown population mean is greater than 47,000 miles than when it is 47,000 miles or less.

From the above two thought questions, the product manager should only reject the null hypothesis when the sample mean is *significantly (or much)* larger than 47,000 miles. How far above 47,000 miles must the sample mean be before the product manager should reject the null hypothesis?

To answer this question, let's briefly review the sampling distribution of the mean presented in Section 7.2. Begin by assuming that the null hypothesis is true; μ_{tire} is at most 47,000 miles. The product manager has selected only one sample of size 1,000 tires. But if he took repeated samples of size 1,000 and computed the sample means he could construct a sampling distribution. Even if the tire life population was not normally distributed, given samples of size 1,000, the sampling distribution of the mean would be normal because of the central limit theorem.

FIGURE 9.1   Sampling Distribution of $\bar{x}$ for the Milemaster Study

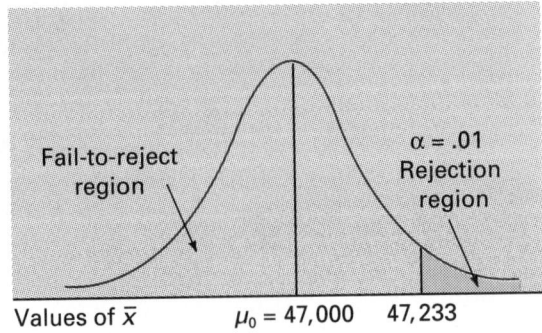

Figure 9.1 shows the sampling distribution of the mean for the Milemaster study. It is normal if (1) the population from which the one sample of 1,000 is taken is normal or (2) the sample size is 30 or more (from the central limit theorem). Please note several important features of the curve.

1. The mean of the sampling distribution is 47,000 miles.

   Reason: We initially assume that the null hypothesis is true. The population mean is at most 47,000 miles.

2. The rejection region, the values of the sample mean that will cause the decision maker to reject the null hypothesis, is in the upper tail of the curve.

   Reason: 1. Given our two thought questions, the product manager would only reject the null hypothesis if the sample mean is *significantly (or much)* larger than 47,000 miles. Sample means larger than 47,000 miles are found in the upper tail of the curve.
   2. A mechanical procedure: The alternative hypothesis is upper-tailed, $\mu_{tire} > 47,000$ miles. So the rejection region is in the upper tail.

We must now determine how far above 47,000 miles the sample mean must be before we reject the null hypothesis. It might seem that the following rule is logical, but as we will demonstrate, it is not!

Reject the null hypothesis if the sample mean is greater than 47,000 miles.

Here is why the rule doesn't work. From Figure 9.1, what is the probability of obtaining a sample mean above 47,000 miles if the null hypothesis is true? It is the area under the curve to the right of the mean that represents a probability of .50. Thus, the probability of rejecting the null hypothesis when the null is true, a Type I error, would then be .50. But in step 3, the product manager set the significance level at .01, not .50. Thus, the above rule is unacceptable.

The rejection region must equal the upper .01 of the area under the curve, the α level. This leads to the following idea:

3. *The rejection region equals the significance level, α.*

   Reason: Only 1% of the time would a sample mean fall in the shaded region if the null hypothesis were true. So if the sample mean falls in the shaded region, it is unlikely that the null is true. That is, we reject the null hypothesis. Thus, the shaded area is called the rejection region.

Given Figure 9.1, the product manager's *decision rule* is:

Only if the sample mean based on 1,000 tires falls in the shaded rejection region should the product manager reject the null hypothesis and market the tire.

Next the product manager must determine the *critical value* that separates the fail-to-reject and rejection regions in Figure 9.1. Use expression (9.2) to determine the critical value for a *one-sided, upper-tailed* alternative hypothesis.

$$\mu_0 + t[\text{one-sided}, 100(1 - \alpha)\%, n - 1](\text{estimated standard error}) \qquad (9.2)$$

We explain the notation in computing the critical value for the Milemaster product introduction decision.

1. μ_0 is the population mean tire life under the null hypothesis. It equals 47,000 miles. (See Figure 9.1.)
2. From Appendix 5, the *t*-value for a one-sided, 99%, $100[1 - (\alpha = .01)]\%$, test with an infinite number of degrees of freedom (999 df) is 2.326. Recall from Section 7.3 that we use the infinity row for sample sizes greater than 30.
3. The estimated standard error of the mean, $s/\sqrt{n}$, from the study data is 100 miles.

The critical value for the Milemaster decision is

$$47,000 + 2.326(100) = 47,233 \text{ miles}$$

The Milemaster decision rule tells us to reject the null hypothesis only if the sample mean based on 1,000 tires is greater than 47,233 miles.

Since the sample mean of 47,300 miles falls in the rejection region, the product manager rejects the null hypothesis and will market the Milemaster tire.

General Principles for Determining Critical Values   Determining the critical value involves two steps. First, locating the rejection region. Is it in the upper tail, the lower tail, or both tails? Second, selecting the correct expression to determine the critical value.

The rejection region under the sampling distribution curve depends on the nature of the alternative hypothesis. A one-sided, upper-tailed alternative hypothesis (the Milemaster decision) has the rejection region in the upper tail of the curve. From our two thought questions, we should reject H_0 only if $\bar{x}$ is *significantly far above* the hypothesized value of μ ($\mu_{\text{tire}} \leq 47,000$ miles in the Milemaster decision). Similarly, a one-sided, lower-tailed alternative hypothesis has the rejection region in the lower tail of the curve. That is, we should reject H_0 only if $\bar{x}$ is *significantly far below* the hypothesized value of μ, μ_0. A two-tailed alternative hypothesis has two rejection regions—one in the lower tail and one in the upper tail. That is, we should reject H_0 for values of $\bar{x}$ *significantly far* from the hypothesized value of μ *in either direction.* Extremely small or large values of $\bar{x}$ should cause us to reject the null hypothesis.

Expressions 9.1 to 9.3 define the term "significantly far" for us.

• Use expression (9.1) to determine the critical value for a *one-sided, lower-tailed* alternative hypothesis.

$$\mu_0 - t[\text{one-sided}, 100(1 - \alpha)\%, n - 1] \frac{s}{\sqrt{n}} \qquad (9.1)$$

- Use expression (9.2) to determine the critical value for a *one-sided, upper-tailed* alternative hypothesis.

$$\mu_0 + t[\text{one-sided, } 100(1 - \alpha)\%, n - 1]\frac{s}{\sqrt{n}} \qquad (9.2)$$

- Use expression (9.3) for a *two-tailed* alternative hypothesis.

$$\mu_0 \pm t[\text{two-sided, } 100(1 - \alpha)\%, n - 1]\frac{s}{\sqrt{n}} \qquad (9.3)$$

The population mean, μ_0, in the above expressions is always based on the null hypothesis, H_0. The t-value can be found in Appendix 5.

p-Value

A *p*-value is the probability of obtaining a value of the sample mean equal to or more extreme than actually obtained given the null hypothesis is true. It can be determined only after the data have been collected. ▪

The product manager has rejected the null hypothesis and marketed the tire. From Table 9.1, either he has made a correct decision or he has rejected the null hypothesis when he should not have—a Type I error. He cannot have made a Type II error. The **p-value** is the *actual* probability that the product manager made a Type I error. The lower the *p*-value, the more certain the manager can be that he made a correct decision in rejecting the null hypothesis.

In the Milemaster study, the *p*-value is the probability of getting a sample mean of 47,300 miles *or larger (or more extreme)* if the null hypothesis is true—if μ_{tire} is at most 47,000 miles. Figure 9.2 illustrates the *p*-value. Note that the mean of the sampling distribution is 47,000 miles (based on H_0), and the critical value is 47,233 miles. The *p*-value is the shaded area to the right of the actual sample mean, $\bar{x} = 47,300$ miles. It is less than .01 because the area to the right of the critical value of 47,233 miles is .01.

We now show how to compute the *p*-value for an $\bar{x}$ of 47,300 miles.

$P(\bar{x} > 47,300 \text{ miles})$	The shaded area in Figure 9.2 is the probability of obtaining a value of the sample mean equal to or greater (or more extreme) than actually obtained, given the null hypothesis is true.
$P\left(t > \dfrac{47,300 - 47,000}{100}\right)$	To find the shaded area under the curve, compute the sample mean minus the population mean, divided by the estimated standard error.
$P(t > +3.00) < .005$	The explanation follows.

To determine the approximate *p*-value, turn to Appendix 5. Now move across the infinite degrees of freedom row (sample size of 1,000) until you find the *t*-value closest to +3.00. It is 2.576, which is in the column labelled 1-sided 99.5% CI. We use the one-sided confidence level column because the alternative hypothesis is one-sided. What does the 99.5% column mean? It means that .995 of the area under the *t*-curve lies below +2.576. Therefore, the area under the *t*-distribution curve above +2.576 is $1 - .995$, or .005. That is, for a *t*-value of 2.576, the *p*-value would be exactly .005. Since the *t*-value of 3.00 is greater than 2.576, the *p*-value must be less than .005.*

---

* Since we used the infinity row of Appendix 5, the t and normal distributions are identical. We could use Appendix 3 to determine the exact p-value. From Appendix 3, $P(z > +3.00) = .50 - .4987 = .0013$.

FIGURE 9.2   Graphical Approximation of *p*-Value for the Milemaster Study

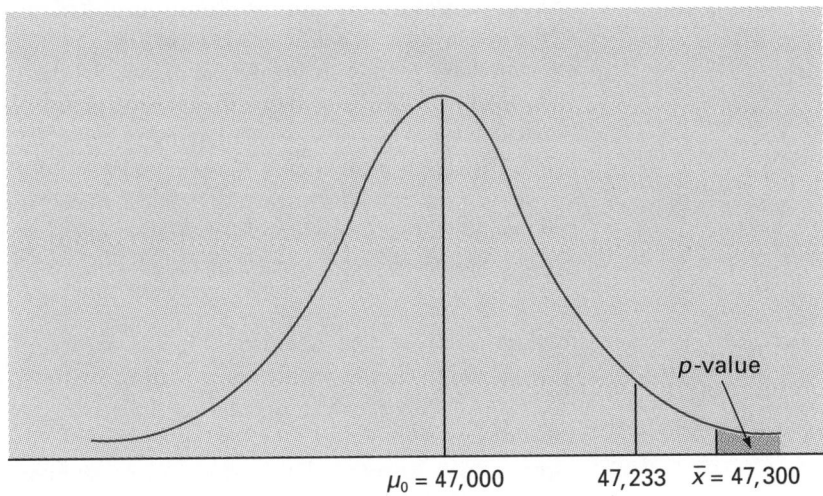

$\mu_0 = 47{,}000$ $47{,}233$ $\bar{x} = 47{,}300$

Often the *p*-value is reported in the following format:

$$t > +3.00, \qquad p < .005$$

In plain English, the notation means that the sample mean of 47,300 miles was 3 estimated standard errors above (+ sign) the mean, assuming the null hypothesis is true; namely, $\mu_{\text{tire}} = 47{,}000$ miles. The probability of obtaining a sample mean of 47,300 *or larger,* the *p*-value, is less than .005.

The actual probability of making a Type I error is less than 5 in 1,000. The product manager can be very certain that he made a correct decision when he rejected the null hypothesis.

The *p*-value and the significance level are different. A decision maker *sets* the significance level, α, *before* running the study. It is the maximum probability of making a Type I error that the decision maker can tolerate, given its costs. The *p*-value can be *determined* only *after* computing the sample mean for the study data. It is the probability of getting a sample result or more extreme if the null hypothesis is true.

Some managers prefer computing a *p*-value to setting a significance level. That is, they do not set an α level before the study. Rather, after computing the sample mean, $\bar{x}$, they determine the approximate or exact *p*-value. Then, based on the size of the *p*-value, they either reject or fail to reject the null hypothesis.

Whether using a *p*-value or significance level, a decision maker must always determine the costs of Type I and Type II errors. These costs should dictate either the setting of the significance level or the size of the *p*-value that will cause the decision maker to reject the null hypothesis. This concludes the five-step hypothesis-testing approach.

Assumptions Underlying Hypothesis Testing   To do hypothesis testing, the following assumptions must be true:

1. The decision maker must select a simple random sample from the population.
2. The sample either must be (1) taken from a normal population or (2) larger than 30 to use the central limit theorem.

Randomization is essential in hypothesis testing. Please review Sections 6.5 and 6.9.

When samples under size 30 are taken, the sampling distribution of the mean (Figure 9.1) may not be normal. Now we must determine if the population from which the sample was taken is normal. Construct a stem-and-leaf display of the sample data. If the display is near bell-shaped, assume the population is normally distributed, and do hypothesis testing. If the display is not near bell-shaped, you may normalize the data. Section 8.2 presented two transformations, the square root and logarithmic base 10, which can make nonnormal data more bell-shaped. If the transformations do not work, then ask a professional statistician for help.

A second example, presented in the chapter's opening memo, describes a potential manufacturing process problem. It illustrates two-sided, or two-tailed, hypothesis testing on time-ordered process data.

Example: Must the Molding Operation Be Adjusted?   COMCEL's engineering group set the process mean target strength on telephone handsets at 4,750 pounds per square inch (ppsi) and set the process standard deviation at 25 ppsi. For the past several months COMCEL achieved its process mean and standard deviation target values. Recently the operators expressed concern that the mean strength has dropped. Engineering believes that the strength has actually drifted upwards. If the mean strength has substantially shifted from the target value in *either* direction, COMCEL's probability of producing defective handsets increases.

The quality monitoring team randomly selects one phone handset about every 15 minutes for a 7.5-hour period (30 observations) and determines its durability or strength. Table 9.2 displays the time-ordered data. For example, the first column in Table 9.2 shows the data for the first 10 time periods (150-minute period).

Table 9.2

Time-Ordered Strength Data (in ppsi)

4,744	4,723	4,724
4,728	4,749	4,734
4,738	4,789	4,773
4,797	4,780	4,763
4,744	4,725	4,753
4,779	4,732	4,746
4,790	4,747	4,761
4,750	4,745	4,730
4,759	4,738	4,735
4,710	4,705	4,761

Figure 9.3 displays the time-ordered strength data. It appears that the data are stationary. From Section 2.3, this means that the general data level remains nearly constant over the entire 7.5-hour time period. The values randomly fluctuate around a constant mean value. Since the data are stationary, COMCEL can compute a meaningful sample mean and estimated standard error of the mean.

Both engineering and the workers claim that the mean has shifted from 4,750 ppsi. If so, the process has stabilized and the process data are again stationary. If the process data had not been stationary over the 7.5-hour test period, COMCEL's quality team would have had to stabilize the process before doing hypothesis testing.

The quality team will use the five-step hypothesis testing approach to determine if $\mu_{strength}$ has shifted upward *or* downward from the target value of 4,750 ppsi.

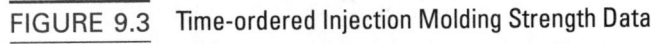

FIGURE 9.3   Time-ordered Injection Molding Strength Data

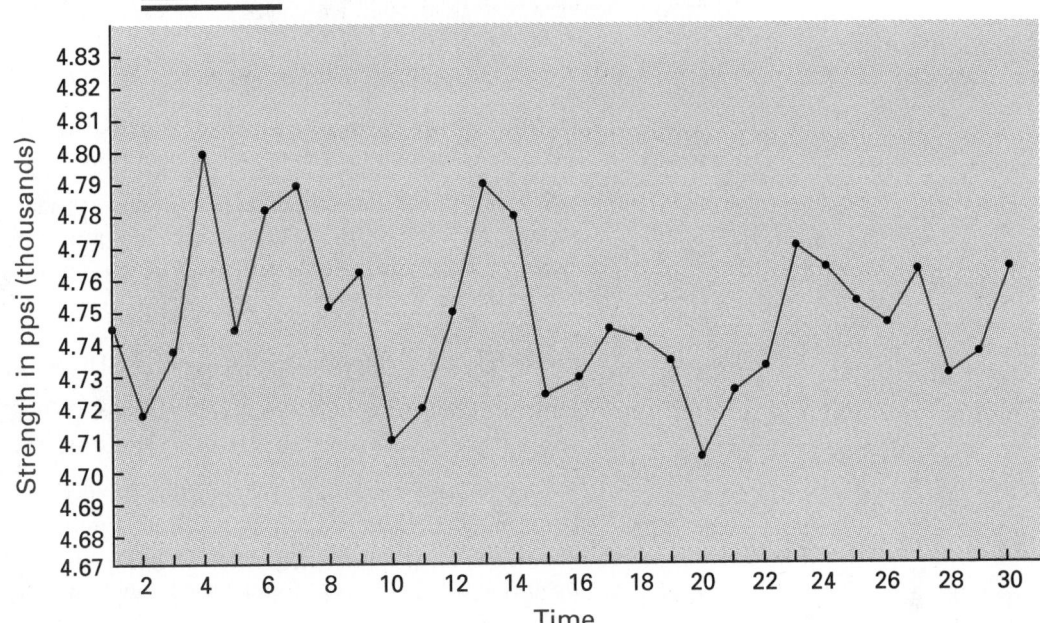

State Hypotheses and Managerial Actions

Engineering and the operators claim or suspect that the unknown process mean, $\mu_{strength}$, has changed from its target value of 4,750 ppsi. Their claims are the alternative hypothesis:

$$H_1: \mu_{strength} < 4{,}750 \text{ ppsi} \quad \text{or} \quad \mu_{strength} > 4{,}750 \text{ ppsi.}$$

$$\text{or} \quad H_1: \mu_{strength} \neq 4{,}750 \text{ ppsi}$$

Since the null and alternative hypotheses are mutually exclusive and exhaustive,

$$H_0: \mu_{strength} = 4{,}750 \text{ ppsi.}$$

Also note that the null is the "I-don't-believe-your-claims" hypothesis.

The alternative hypothesis is two-tailed. COMCEL is testing whether the mean has shifted—either upwards or downwards. That is, COMCEL is testing if $\mu_{strength}$ differs from 4,750 ppsi. There will be two rejection regions—one in the lower tail and one in the upper tail of the sampling distribution curve.

	Hypotheses	Action
H_0	The unknown population mean strength is still 4,750 ppsi. $\mu_{strength} = 4{,}750$ ppsi	Failure to reject the null hypothesis means the process does not have to be adjusted.
H_1	The unknown population mean strength is not 4,750 ppsi. $\mu_{strength} \neq 4{,}750$ ppsi	Rejecting the null hypothesis means the process must be adjusted and causes of the process shift have to be investigated.

Determine the Costs of the Decision-Making Errors

As before, there are costs associated with Type I and Type II errors.

Type I   Reject the null hypothesis when the null hypothesis is true.

Rejecting the null hypothesis means COMCEL will adjust the process. If the null is true, no adjustment is necessary.

After an unnecessary adjustment, the process may start producing rejects. Once the team finds no problems with the process, it will readjust the process. The costs of a Type I error are moderate and involve rejects and two process adjustments.

Type II   Fail to reject the null hypothesis when the null hypothesis is false.

Failure to reject the null hypothesis means COMCEL will not adjust the process. If the null is false, an adjustment is necessary.

Failure to make necessary process adjustments could result in a large number of defective phones. Both Engineering and the workers believe that the process mean has shifted by at least 10 ppsi. A shift of this size, if undetected, would be very costly.

Set a Significance Level and Determine a Sample Size

In this example, the most likely Type II error is more costly than the Type I error. Balancing the costs of the Type I and II errors, COMCEL sets α at .20. This is the maximum probability of making a Type I error that COMCEL is willing to tolerate.

Data Collection

Table 9.2 contains the time-ordered data for the study. The sample statistics are

Sample mean	$\bar{x} = 4{,}748.40$ ppsi
Sample standard deviation	$s = 23.33$ ppsi
Sample size	$n = 30$ periods
Estimated standard error of the mean	$\dfrac{s}{\sqrt{n}} = \dfrac{23.33}{\sqrt{30}} = 4.26$ ppsi.

Test the Null Hypothesis and Make a Decision

Figure 9.4 shows the sampling distribution for the injection molding study. Please note several important features of the curve.

1. The mean of the sampling distribution is 4,750 ppsi.

   Reason: This is the value under the null hypothesis. Remember, we initially assume the null hypothesis is true.

2. There are rejection regions in both tails of the curve.

Reason: COMCEL would reject the null hypothesis if the sample mean is either *significantly smaller or significantly larger* than 4,750 ppsi. The alternative hypothesis is two-tailed. Therefore there are two rejection regions.

3. The rejection region in each tail equals one-half of the significance level, α.

Reason: Since the alternative hypothesis is two-tailed, we divide the significance level, α, by 2. Each rejection region contains .10 of the area. Thus the total probability of making a Type I error is .20.

Given Figure 9.4, COMCEL's *decision rule* is:

Only if the sample mean based on 30 time periods falls within either shaded rejection region should COMCEL reject the null hypothesis and investigate and correct the process mean shift.

Next COMCEL uses expression (9.3)—reproduced below—to determine the lower and upper critical values in Figure 9.4. The sample size, *n*, is 30 observations.

$$\text{Lower critical value: } \mu_0 - t[\text{two-sided, } 100\,(1 - \alpha)\%, \; n - 1]\frac{s}{\sqrt{n}}$$

$$\text{Upper critical value: } \mu_0 + t[\text{two-sided, } 100\,(1 - \alpha)\%, \; n - 1]\frac{s}{\sqrt{n}}$$

1. μ_0 is the population mean process strength under the null hypothesis. It equals 4,750 ppsi. (See Figure 9.4.)
2. The *t*-value for a two-sided, 80%, $100(1 - .20)\%$ test with $30 - 1 = 29$ degrees of freedom is 1.311.
3. The estimated standard error of the mean from the study data is 4.26 ppsi.

The critical values that separate the fail-to-reject region from the rejection regions in Figure 9.4 are

$$\text{Lower critical value: } 4,750 - 1.311(4.26) = 4,744.42 \text{ ppsi}$$

$$\text{Upper critical value: } 4,750 + 1.311(4.26) = 4,755.58 \text{ ppsi}$$

FIGURE 9.4   Sampling Distribution of $\bar{x}$ for the Strength Study

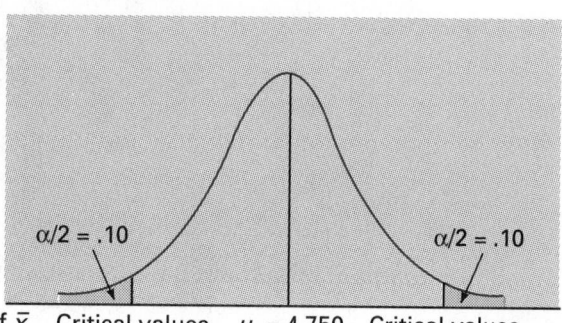

Values of $\bar{x}$ Critical values $\mu_0 = 4,750$ Critical values

Since the sample mean, 4,748.40 ppsi, does not fall in either rejection region, COMCEL does not reject the null hypothesis. It will not adjust the process because the sample data do not suggest that the process population mean has changed from the target value of 4,750 ppsi. From Table 9.1, failure to reject the null hypothesis means that COMCEL has either made (1) a correct decision or (2) a Type II error.

p-Value

The shaded area in Figure 9.5 is one-half of the p-value. The shaded area is the probability of obtaining a sample mean of 4,748.40 ppsi or less. The p-value is *twice* the shaded area because we have a two-tailed alternative hypothesis. The significance level is twice the area of the lower rejection region—.10. Likewise, the p-value is twice the area to the left of 4,748.40 ppsi in Figure 9.5.

Here is how to compute the approximate p-value for an $\bar{x}$ of 4,748.40 ppsi.

$P(\bar{x} < 4{,}748.40 \text{ ppsi})$

The shaded area in Figure 9.5 is *one-half* of the p-value. It is the probability of obtaining a value of the sample mean or less than actually obtained, given that the null hypothesis is true.

$$P\left(t < \frac{4{,}748.40 - 4{,}750}{4.26}\right)$$

$P(t < -.3756)$

To find the shaded area under the curve to the left of 4,748.40 ppsi, we compute the sample mean minus the population mean divided by the estimated standard error.

$.60 < p < .80$

The explanation follows.

To determine the approximate p-value, turn to Appendix 5. Now move across the 29 degrees of freedom (sample size of 30) row until you find a t-value closest to .3756 (ignore the minus sign because the t-distribution is symmetrical). The two closest t-values are .256 and .530, which are in the columns labelled "2-sided 20%" and "2-sided 40% CI," respectively. We use the two-sided confidence level column because

---

FIGURE 9.5   Graphical Determination of p-Value for the Strength Study

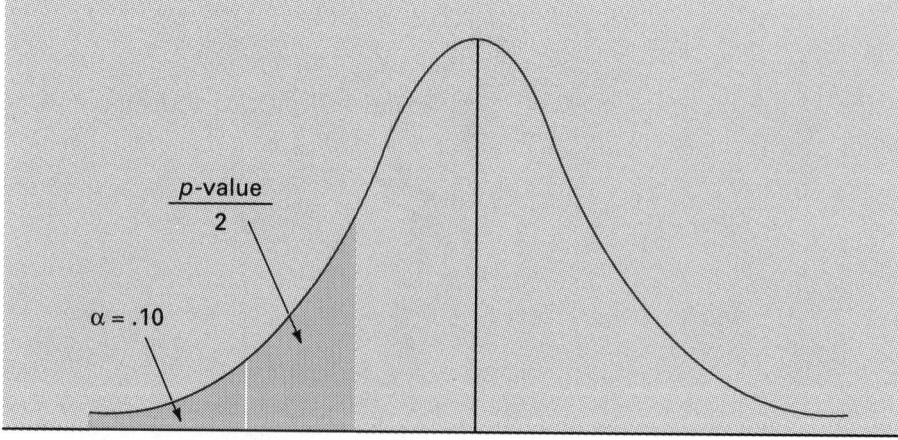

4,744.42   4,748.40   4,750 ppsi

the alternative hypothesis is two-tailed. For a t-value of $-.256$, the p-value would be exactly $1 - .20$ or $.80$. For a t-value of $-.530$, the p-value would be exactly $1 - .40$ or $.60$. Thus the p-value is between $.60$ and $.80$. Or, the p-value is in the interval

$$.60 < p < .80$$

Since COMCEL had set the maximum probability of making a Type I error at $.20$ (the α level), COMCEL did not reject the null hypothesis, because the p-value is between $.60$ and $.80$, which is greater than $.20$.

Assumptions for Time-Ordered Process Data   There are two additional assumptions for doing hypothesis testing on time-ordered process data.

1. The time-ordered process data must be stationary.
2. The sample standard deviation must be at (or near) the process population standard deviation target value set by the process designers.

Figure 9.3 confirmed the first assumption. Regarding the second assumption, COMCEL's engineering department had set a 25 ppsi target for the process population standard deviation. The sample standard deviation of 23.33 ppsi was consistent with the target value. The second assumption was also justified.

In Chapter 2 you learned that time-ordered data must be stationary if meaningful sample statistics ($\bar{x}$, s) are to be computed. Why is the second assumption necessary? Suppose that the sample standard deviation had been 50 ppsi—significantly more than the process target value of 25 ppsi. First, the process already has a known excessive variation problem that must be corrected. Second, a large standard deviation increases the estimated standard error of the mean. From expression (9.3), this will shift the critical values further away from 4,750 ppsi. It will take more extreme sample data to reject the null hypothesis. These two reasons make the second assumption necessary.

In summary, when analyzing time-ordered data, construct a line graph to ensure that the process data are stationary and to determine if the sample standard deviation is at (or near) the process population standard deviation target value.

Hypothesis testing and confidence interval approaches are similar. Researchers and scientists prefer the hypothesis testing approach. Managers and business professionals tend to favor the more intuitive confidence interval methods. Both approaches are useful.

SECTION 9.2 EXERCISES

1. What, if anything, is wrong with the following pairs of null and alternative hypotheses?
    a. $\bar{x} \leq 2$ **d.** $\mu < 2$
        $\bar{x} > 2$ $\mu > 2$
    b. $\mu > 10$ **e.** $\bar{x} < 20$
        $\mu < 9$ $\bar{x} \geq 20$
    c. $\mu = 250$ **f.** $\mu = \bar{x}$
        $\mu \neq 250$ $\mu \neq \bar{x}$

2. Consumers who have seen a particular advertising approach can recall two or fewer product attributes one month later. The marketing group has developed a new approach that it believes will increase the number of product attributes consumers can recall. Set up the null and alternative hypotheses and actions.

3. Over the past several years, car salesmen who worked on commission had take-home pay that averaged $3,500 per month. This past year two things have happened that could change the mean take-home pay: (1) a slowdown in the economy and (2) car manufacturers

bundling more expensive options in the base price. Has the mean take-home pay changed? The manager plans to take a simple random sample of car salesmen. Set up the null and alternative hypotheses.

4. Until this year the mean braking distance of a Nikton automobile moving at 60 mph was 175 feet. Nikton engineers have developed what they consider a better braking system. They plan to test the new brake system on 100 cars and determine the braking distance at 60 mph. Set up the null and alternative hypotheses and actions.

5. Determine the correct t-value for expressions (9.1)–(9.3) under the following conditions:
    a. One-tailed alternative hypothesis $\alpha = .05$ $n = 10$
    b. Two-tailed alternative hypothesis $\alpha = .01$ $n = 400$
    c. One-tailed alternative hypothesis $\alpha = .01$ $n = 700$
    d. Two-tailed alternative hypothesis $\alpha = .05$ $n = 22$

6. Consider the three alternative hypotheses and rejection regions shown below. Which hypothesis is related to which rejection region? That is, relate the direction and type of alternative hypothesis to the number (one or two) of rejection regions and their location (upper-, lower-, or two-tailed). Explain the connection.

Alternative Hypothesis   Rejection Region(s)

H_1 $\mu < 100$ Two-tailed
H_1 $\mu > 100$ Lower-tailed
H_1 $\mu \neq 100$ Upper-tailed

7. Given the four sets of null and alternative hypotheses, correct, if necessary, the mean (μ_0) of the hypothesized sampling distribution and the location of the rejection region(s).
    a. Given: H_0 $\mu = 10$ days
                H_1 $\mu \neq 10$ days
                        $\bar{x} = 11.2$ days

        1. The mean of the sampling distribution is 11.2 days.
        2. The sampling distribution has a two-tailed rejection region.

    b. Given: H_0 $\mu \leq \$100$
                H_1 $\mu > \$100$
                        $\bar{x} = \$109.56$

        1. The mean of the sampling distribution is $100.
        2. The sampling distribution has a lower-tailed rejection region.

    c. Given: H_0 $\mu \geq 180$ feet
                H_1 $\mu < 180$ feet
                        $\bar{x} = 181.67$ feet

        1. The mean of the sampling distribution is 181.67 feet.
        2. The sampling distribution has an upper-tailed rejection region.

    d. Given: H_0 $\mu \geq 4$ errors
                H_1 $\mu < 4$ errors
                        $\bar{x} = 3.76$ errors

        1. The mean of the sampling distribution is 4 errors.
        2. The sampling distribution has a lower-tailed rejection region.

8. Use the hypotheses in Exercise 2. The α level is .05. You take a sample of 100 consumers and obtain the following sample data:

$$\bar{x} = 2.8 \text{ attributes}$$
$$s = 5.0 \text{ attributes}$$

Based on your data, should you reject or fail to reject the null hypothesis? What managerial action would you take?

9. Use the hypotheses in Exercise 3. The significance level is .10. You take a sample of 36 car salesmen and obtain the following data:

$$\bar{x} = \$3{,}250$$
$$s = \$600$$

Based on your sample data, should you reject or fail to reject the null hypothesis?

10. Use the hypotheses in Exercise 4. The significance level is .01. You test 81 sets of brakes and obtain the following data:

$$\bar{x} = 173 \text{ feet}$$
$$s = 27 \text{ feet}$$

Given these sample data, should you reject or fail to reject the null hypothesis?

11. Suppose you are a mountain climber. Your life depends on the strength of your rope. The mean strength of the rope must be at least 350 pounds per square inch. You plan to cut 10 pieces of rope from a long roll, test the breaking strength of each piece, and find the mean breaking strength for the sample.
    a. Set up the null and alternative hypotheses and actions.
    b. List the consequences of making Type I or Type II errors.
    c. With these consequences in mind, should your significance level be .01 or .20? Explain.

12. Every jury trial is a test of the null hypothesis that the defendant is innocent against the alternative hypothesis that the defendant is guilty.
    a. What kind of error has the jury made if it convicts an innocent defendant? If they let Al Capone, the Chicago mobster, go free?
    b. Reducing the probability of making a Type I error increases the probability of making a Type II error. Thomas Jefferson said, "It is better for ten guilty men to go free than for one innocent man to be convicted." Would this statement translate to a small or large significance level if jury trials could be translated to statistical tests?
    c. If the jury arrives at the verdict of not guilty, has the trial proven the innocence of the defendant?

13. Determine the approximate p-value for the following exercises:
    a. t-value = 2.09 $n = 21$ H_1 is one-tailed
    b. t-value = -1.92 $n = 10$ H_1 is two-tailed
    c. t-value = 1.23 $n = 18$ H_1 is one-tailed
    d. t-value = -2.96 $n = 31$ H_1 is two-tailed

14. The National Optical Company presently uses A-1 polishing pads to polish eyeglass lenses. Pad life is critical, as National spends \$15,000 per day on pad cost. B-2 vendor argues that its pad will have a longer polishing life. The present A-1 pads last, on average, 25 minutes before they must be replaced. Given that both vendors are noted for their quality and both pads cost the same, National will switch to B-2 if its pad lasts longer than 25 minutes. The decision facing National Optical Company is whether to switch or not to switch to the B-2 vendor.
    a. You are manager of polishing at National. Set up the null and alternative hypotheses and the associated managerial actions.
    b. In nontechnical language, describe the Type I and Type II errors and their associated costs.
    c. If the Type I error were costly, would National Optical Company want to set a .01 or .20 significance level? Explain.

    Suppose National uses 200 B-2 polishing pads. The sample mean number of minutes before failure is 26.1, and the sample standard deviation is 3.5 minutes.
    d. Compute the estimated standard error of the mean.
    e. Using a .05 α level, determine the rejection region.
    f. Based on the sample evidence, should National reject the null hypothesis that the population mean minutes before pad failure is less than or equal to 25?

g. Having rejected the null hypothesis, what is the probability of now making a Type II error? Explain.

h. Compute the approximate p-value for a sample mean of 26.1 minutes, assuming the null hypothesis is true.

15. Consider the following data.

$$H_0 \qquad \mu = 10$$
$$H_1 \qquad \mu \neq 10$$
$$\alpha = .01, \qquad n = 10$$

Assume the sample of 10 is taken from a normal population.

Sample Data

8	11
9	9
10	10
9	10
10	9

a. Compute the sample statistics, $\bar{x}$ and s.

b. Should the null hypothesis be rejected?

c. Compute the approximate p-value.

16. Determine the approximate p-values in the form $(a < p < b)$ or $(p < c)$ for the following exercises:

a. One-sided test	$n = 10$	t-value =	1.98
b. Two-sided test	$n = 400$	t-value =	1.52
c. One-sided test	$n = 20$	t-value =	-2.74
d. Two-sided test	$n = 15$	t-value =	-0.74

17. A Ford Motor Company quality-improvement team believes that its recently completed defect-reduction program has reduced the mean number of defects per 100 cars built. Defects range from rattling windows to engine failures. Prior to the start of the defect-reduction program, the number of defects had averaged 71 per 100 cars and had been stationary for the past six months. Has the recently completed program been successful in reducing the mean number of defects per 100 cars?

a. Set up the null and alternative hypotheses and the associated managerial actions. Consider yourself a member of the Ford senior management team.

b. In nontechnical language, describe the Type I and Type II errors and their associated costs.

c. The Type I error is very costly. Should senior management at Ford set a .01 or .20 significance level? Explain.

Ford selects 200 cars built after the completion of the defect-reduction program. The sample mean number of defects per 100 cars is 61, and the sample standard deviation is 30 defects.

d. Based on the sample evidence, should Ford reject the null hypothesis that the population mean number of defects per 100 cars is still 71 or more? Let $\alpha = .01$.

e. Compute the approximate p-value for a sample mean of 61 defects, assuming H_0 is true.

18. The Environmental Protection Agency (EPA) has ordered Chemdump Inc. to reduce the mean level of a toxic chemical in its wastewater to less than 20 parts per million (ppm). Chemdump Inc., which has a poor track record of meeting the EPA's standard, has recently developed a new waste treatment process that it says will now meet that standard. Below are 20 samples of Chemdump Inc.'s wastewater taken by the EPA over a four-week period. Assume that the population from which the samples are taken is normally distributed.

	Day 1	Day 2	Day 3	Day 4	Day 5
Week 1	19.5	20.0	18.5	18.7	19.5
Week 2	20.7	18.5	19.4	20.5	19.8
Week 3	19.1	20.3	20.1	19.6	20.3
Week 4	18.7	19.5	19.7	19.1	18.3

a. Are the time-ordered process data stationary?
b. Compute the sample statistics, $\bar{x}$ and s.
c. Suppose the EPA has set a target value for the wastewater process standard deviation of 0.7 ppm. Does it appear that Chemdump Inc. is meeting this target value?
d. Given your answers in parts **a** and **c,** can Chemdump Inc. continue with hypothesis testing on the population-mean pollution level in its wastewater? Explain.
e. Should the null hypothesis on the population mean pollution level be rejected? Let $\alpha = .05$.
f. Compute the approximate p-value for the sample mean.

19. The Smooth and Creamy Ice Cream plant in Abilene, Texas, sells 32-ounce cartons of Fudge Delite low-fat ice cream. The production process is highly automated. The filling machine for the 32-ounce carton is good but not perfect. It can go out of adjustment and put either less than or more than 32 ounces in a carton. At the end of each shift, several samples of 32-ounce cartons are tested to determine the actual number of ounces in the cartons. Based on that finding, the machine is adjusted prior to the next shift. A line graph indicates that the filling process (in ounces per carton) has been stationary for the past six months. Assume that the population is normally distributed.
a. You are the production supervisor. Set up the null and alternative hypotheses and the associated managerial actions.
b. In nontechnical language, describe the Type I and Type II errors and their associated costs.

You select $n = 10$ 32-ounce cartons. The process data are stationary. The sample mean number of ounces per carton is 31.67, and the sample standard deviation is 0.66 ounces.
c. Based on the sample evidence, should you reject the null hypothesis that the population mean is still 32 ounces? Let $\alpha = .01$.
d. Suppose that the mean filling-weight data (time-ordered) for the past six shifts had not been stationary. Would it make sense to do hypothesis testing? Explain.

20. Amerhosp Inc. records the total number of surgical complications in its ten Midwest hospitals. Amerhosp claims that it has reduced the mean number of surgical complications per day to less than 4.0. Below are the time-ordered data on the number of complications over a two-week period. Assume that the population is normally distributed.

Day	Complications	Day	Complications
1	4	8	3
2	2	9	5
3	3	10	2
4	4	11	4
5	1	12	3
6	3	13	2
7	4	14	4

a. Are the time-ordered process data stationary?
b. Compute the sample statistics, $\bar{x}$ and s.
c. Should the null hypothesis on the population mean number of surgical complications be rejected? The significance level is .05.
d. Compute the approximate p-value for the sample mean.

21. Consider the following data.

$$H_0 \qquad \mu \leq 15 \text{ minutes}$$
$$H_1 \qquad \mu > 15 \text{ minutes}$$
$$\alpha = .05, \qquad n = 500$$
$$\text{Estimated standard error of the mean} = 2.0$$

   a. Verify that the critical value is 18.29.
   b. Suppose the sample mean is 19.76. The p-value will be less than .05. Draw a graph similar to Figure 9.2. to verify that $p < .05$.
   c. Suppose the sample mean is 20.02. Compute the approximate p-value. Given the significance level, should we reject the null hypothesis?
   d. Suppose the sample mean is 17.5. Compute the approximate p-value. Given the significance level, should we reject the null hypothesis?

22. Consider the following data.

$$H_0 \qquad \mu = 15 \text{ pounds}$$
$$H_1 \qquad \mu \neq 15 \text{ pounds}$$
$$\alpha = .05, \qquad n = 500$$
$$\text{Estimated standard error of the mean} = 2.0$$

   a. Verify that the critical values are 11.08 and 18.92.
   b. Suppose the sample mean is 19.76. The p-value will be less than .05. Draw a graph similar to Figure 9.5 to verify that $p < .05$.
   c. Suppose the sample mean is 20.02. Compute the approximate p-value. Given the significance level, should we reject the null hypothesis?
   d. Suppose the sample mean is 17.5. Compute the approximate p-value. Given the significance level, should we reject the null hypothesis?

23. A branch clinic director claims that through new procedures she has reduced patient waiting time (elapsed time from patient entering clinic to patient receiving treatment) from the present 55 minutes. Before implementing her procedures nationwide, the clinic owner runs a small-scale study. Here are the data.

$$n = 30 \text{ randomly selected patients}$$
$$\bar{x} = 54.5 \text{ minutes}$$
$$s = 10 \text{ minutes}$$

   a. Set up the null and alternative hypotheses and the associated managerial actions.
   b. In nontechnical language, describe the Type I and II errors and their associated costs. Set $\alpha = .10$.
   c. Compute the estimated standard error of the mean.
   d. Using a .10 α level, determine the rejection region.
   e. Based on the sample evidence, should the clinic owner reject the null hypothesis that the population mean waiting time is greater than or equal to 55 minutes?
   f. Compute the approximate p-value.

24. *Research exercise:* Find an article in the *Wall Street Journal, Business Week,* or a similar business publication that discusses the mean of an important economic-variable. Develop the null and alternative hypotheses implied by the author.

9.3 ▤ Hypothesis Testing on One Population Proportion

In Section 7.6 we used confidence intervals to estimate an unknown population proportion. Recall that we computed a proportion, a number between 0 and 1, from yes/no qualitative data. We call the sample mean for yes/no data the *sample proportion*.

Here we present the five-step hypothesis-testing approach on one population proportion. All the ideas you learned in Section 9.2—stating hypotheses, determining Type I and Type II errors and their costs, determining the rejection region(s), and computing p-values—apply here too. The only difference is that we replace the sample mean and its estimated standard error with the sample proportion and its hypothesized standard error.

Hypothesis testing on one population proportion is useful when a manager must make a decision in which the best action depends on the value of an unknown population proportion. By the end of this unit you should be able to:

1. formulate hypotheses and their associated managerial actions;
2. determine the costs associated with Type I and Type II errors;
3. test the null hypothesis and make a decision;
4. compute and interpret p-values; and
5. distinguish between the sample mean and sample proportion.

Example: Has the Proportion of Rooms Uncleaned by 3:00 P.M. Declined?   For the past several years, room service has cleaned 5% (.05) of the guest rooms at the Holton Hotel after 3:00 P.M. Customer satisfaction surveys have indicated that room availability before 3:00 P.M. would be a big plus for the hotel. Recently the executive director took steps to reduce the proportion of rooms uncleaned by 3:00 P.M. Has her program succeeded?

State Hypotheses and Managerial Actions

Here we are testing a claim about the population proportion, p.*

Begin by writing the hypotheses. The executive director believes that her program has reduced the population proportion of uncleaned rooms below .05. This is the alternative hypothesis, $p_0 < .05$. The null hypothesis is that the population proportion, p_0, takes on any other possible value, $p_0 \geq .05$. In short, the null hypothesis reflects an "I-don't-believe-your-claim" attitude.

Hypotheses	Action
H_0 The unknown population proportion of uncleaned rooms is still .05 or more. $p_0 \geq .05$	Failure to reject the null hypothesis means the room service improvement program has not been successful. Another program must be developed.
H_1 The unknown population proportion of uncleaned rooms is less than .05. $p_0 < .05$	Rejecting the null hypothesis means that the program has been successful. Holton can advertise the increased room availability in its brochure.

Note that we use proportions (numbers between 0 and 1) and not percentages (numbers between 0 and 100%) in stating the hypotheses.

---

* Do not confuse the population proportion, p, with the p-value presented in Section 9.2. While the symbol "p" is used for both concepts, a p-value is not a population proportion. When referring to a population proportion we will use a subscript such as p_0.

Determine the Costs of Errors, Set α Level and Sample Size

We have combined hypothesis testing steps 2 and 3. Based on the costs of the Type I and Type II errors, the director sets the α level at .10 and the sample size at 1,400 rooms (approximately two weeks of work).

Data Collection

The director records the number of rooms uncleaned after 3:00 P.M. over a two-week period. Of the 1,400 rooms, 46 were cleaned after 3:00 P.M. Here are the study's sample statistics:

Number of uncleaned rooms	46
Sample size	$n = 1,400$
Sample proportion	$\hat{p} = 46/1,400 = .0329$

Test the Null Hypothesis and Make a Decision

Figure 9.6 shows the sampling distribution of the *proportion*. By Cochran's rule on page 378 the sampling distribution is approximately normally distributed, or z-distributed. Note several important features of the curve.

1.   The mean of the sampling distribution is .05.

     Reason: This is the smallest value possible under the null hypothesis. Remember, we initially assume the null hypothesis is true.

2.   The hypothesized standard error of the proportion is computed using expression (9.4).

$$\sqrt{\frac{p_0(1 - p_0)}{n}} \tag{9.4}$$

where p_0 is the *population* proportion based on the null hypothesis, H_0, and n is the sample size.*

FIGURE 9.6   Sampling Distribution of $\hat{p}$ for Holton Hotel Study

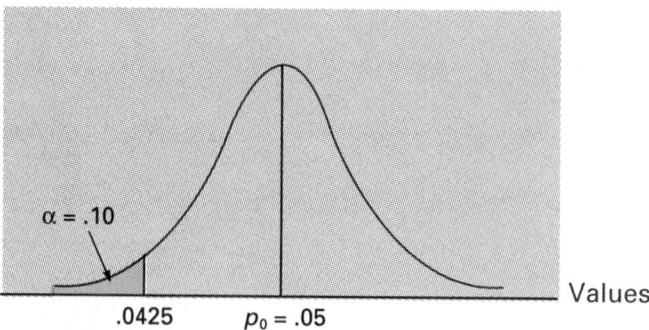

* In constructing confidence intervals on the population proportion, we used the sample proportion, not the population proportion, to estimate the standard error. The reason was that we had no knowledge of the population proportion prior to constructing the confidence interval. In hypothesis testing, we have knowledge of the population proportion; this is the null hypothesis.

In this example, the null hypothesis was that the *population* proportion is still .05 (or more). Therefore, we used $p_0 = .05$ in expression (9.4). We do *not* use the sample proportion, .0329. The hypothesized standard error is

$$\sqrt{\frac{(.05)(.95)}{1,400}} = .0058.$$

3. The rejection region is in the lower tail of the curve.

   Reason: The director would only reject the null hypothesis if the sample proportion was *significantly* smaller than .05. Also, the alternative hypothesis is lower-tailed. Therefore, the rejection region is in the lower tail.

4. The rejection region equals the significance level, α.

   Reason: Only 10% of the time would a sample proportion fall in the shaded region, if p_0 is .05. If the sample proportion falls in the shaded region, we reject the null hypothesis.

Use expression (9.5) to determine the critical value for a one-sided, lower-tailed alternative hypothesis:

$$p_0 - z[\text{one-sided, } 100(1 - \alpha)\%]\sqrt{\frac{p_0(1 - p_0)}{n}} \qquad (9.5)$$

1. p_0 is the assumed population proportion of uncleaned rooms under the null hypothesis. It equals .05. (See Figure 9.6.)
2. Use the infinity degrees of freedom row of Appendix 5 (or use Appendix 3) to obtain the z-value. The z-value for a one-sided, 90%, $100[1 - (\alpha = .10)]\%$ test is 1.282.
3. The hypothesized standard error is .0058.

The critical value for the Holton Hotel study is

$$.05 - 1.282(.0058) = .0425.$$

Given Figure 9.6, the director's decision rule is:

Only if the sample proportion based on 1,400 rooms falls in the shaded rejection region—less than .0425—should she reject the null hypothesis.

Since the sample proportion, $\hat{p}$, of .0329 falls in the rejection region, the executive director rejects the null hypothesis and concludes that her room service improvement program has been successful.

In conclusion, use the following expressions to determine the critical values for a lower-tailed, upper-tailed, and two-tailed alternative hypothesis, respectively.

Lower-tailed: $p_0 - z[\text{one-sided, } 100(1 - \alpha)\%]\sqrt{p_0(1 - p_0)/n}$ (9.5)

Upper-tailed: $p_0 + z[\text{one-sided, } 100(1 - \alpha)\%]\sqrt{p_0(1 - p_0)/n}$ (9.6)

Two-tailed: $p_0 \pm z[\text{two-sided, } 100(1 - \alpha)\%]\sqrt{p_0(1 - p_0)/n}$ (9.7)

The population proportion, p_0, in these expressions is always based on the null hypothesis.

FIGURE 9.7   Graphical Representation of *p*-Value for the Holton Hotel Study

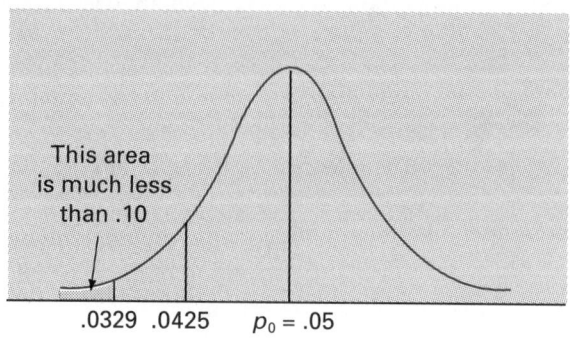

.0329 .0425 $p_0 = .05$

p-Value

Graphically, the *p*-value is the shaded area in Figure 9.7. It is much less than .10 because the area to the left of .0425 is .10. We now compute the approximate *p*-value for a $\hat{p}$ of .0329.

$P(\hat{p} < .0329)$

The shaded area in Figure 9.7 is the probability of obtaining a sample proportion equal to or less than actually obtained given the null hypothesis is true.

$$P\left(\hat{p} < \frac{.0329 - .05}{.0058}\right)$$

To find the shaded area under the curve, compute the sample proportion minus the population proportion divided by the hypothesized standard error.

$P(z < -2.95) < .005$

To determine the approximate *p*-value, turn to Appendix 5. Now move across the bottom row (since $n = 1,400$) until you find the closest value to 2.95 (you may ignore the negative sign since the distribution is symmetrical). The closest value is 2.576, which is in the column labelled 1-sided 99.5% CI. Use the one-sided confidence level because the alternative hypothesis is one-tailed. For a value of 2.576, the *p*-value would be exactly $1 - .995$, or .005. Since 2.95 is greater than 2.576, the *p*-value must be slightly less than .005. Or, in shorthand notation: $[z < -2.95, p < .005]$. The actual probability of making a Type I error is less than 5 in 1,000.

Hypothesis testing on one population mean and one population proportion are similar, but the applications differ. Use hypothesis testing on a population mean when the variable of interest is quantitative and its values are not restricted to numbers between 0 and 1—distance, speed, tensile strength, number of complaints etc. Use hypothesis testing on a population proportion when the variable of interest is qualitative (yes/no data) and its values are numbers between 0 and 1.

SECTION 9.3 EXERCISES

1. What, if anything, is wrong with the following pairs of null and alternative hypotheses?

    a. $\hat{p} \leq .04$
        $\hat{p} > .04$
    b. $p_0 > .10$
        $p_0 \leq .10$
    c. $p_0 = .25$
        $p_0 \neq .30$

    d. $p_0 < \hat{p}$
        $p_0 \geq \hat{p}$
    e. $p_0 < .70$
        $p_0 \geq .30$

2. Which type of hypothesis testing—on μ or p—should be done for the following problems? We wish to draw conclusions about the
   a. stopping distance of a brake.
   b. percentage of voters who favor candidate X.
   c. fraction of defective pieces.
   d. time needed to complete a project.

3. Formulate the null and alternative hypotheses for the following situations:
   a. An operations manager claims that the fraction of defectives on a production line has changed from the historical level of .05.
   b. A financial manager claims that more than 20% of the firms in the electronics industry have current ratios in excess of 2.5.
   c. A marketing manager claims that the proportion of customer complaints has dropped from the historical level of .02.
   d. A real estate manager claims that the percentage of vacant apartments in Houston has recently dropped below 10%.

4. Given the four sets of null and alternative hypotheses, correct, if necessary, the mean of the hypothesized sampling distribution and the location of the rejection region(s).
   a. Given: H_0 $p_0 = .50$
             H_1 $p_0 \neq .50$
                       $\hat{p} = .476$

   1. The sampling distribution has a two-tailed rejection region.
   2. The mean of the sampling distribution is .50.

   b. Given: H_0 $p_0 \leq .245$
             H_1 $p_0 > .245$
                       $\hat{p} = .261$

   1. The sampling distribution has a lower-tailed rejection region.
   2. The mean of the sampling distribution is .261.

   c. Given: H_0 $p_0 \geq .75$
             H_1 $p_0 < .75$
                       $\hat{p} = .761$

   1. The sampling distribution has an upper-tailed rejection region.
   2. The mean of the sampling distribution is .75.

   d. Given: H_0 $p_0 \geq .04$
             H_1 $p_0 < .04$
                       $\hat{p} = .0376$

   1. The sampling distribution has a lower-tailed rejection region.
   2. The mean of the sampling distribution is 4.

5. Test the following hypotheses. Also compute the approximate p-values.
   a. H_0 $p_0 \leq .45$
      H_1 $p_0 > .45$
               $\alpha = .01$ $\hat{p} = .46$ $n = 100$

   b. H_0 $p_0 = .24$
      H_1 $p_0 \neq .24$
               $\alpha = .05$ $\hat{p} = .256$ $n = 700$

   c. H_0 $p_0 \geq .57$
      H_1 $p_0 < .57$
               $\alpha = .10$ $\hat{p} = .58$ $n = 500$

6. A Ford Motor Company quality improvement team believes that its recently completed defect-reduction program has reduced the proportion of paint defects. Prior to the program, the proportion of paint defects was .03, and had been stationary for the past six months. Has the recently completed program been successful in reducing the proportion of paint defects?
   a. Set up the null and alternative hypotheses and the associated managerial actions. Consider yourself a member of the Ford senior management team.
   b. In nontechnical language, describe the Type I and Type II errors and their associated costs.

Ford selects 2,000 cars built after the completion of the defect-reduction program. There are 20 cars with paint defects.

  c. Compute the sample proportion.
  d. Using a .05 α level, determine the rejection region.
  e. Based on the sample evidence, should Ford reject the null hypothesis that the population proportion is still .03 or more?
  f. Compute the approximate p-value for a $\hat{p}$ of .01. Explain what the p-value measures.

7. Apex Inc. will build a health club within its plant if over 60% of the employees want it. One year ago management did a survey, and less than 60% were in favor of the health club. They wonder if the proportion is now over 60%. They are planning to conduct another survey shortly.

  a. Set up the null and alternative hypotheses and the associated managerial actions.

Apex randomly selects 150 employees, and 100 now want a health club on the facilities.

  b. Compute the sample proportion in favor of the health club and the hypothesized standard error.
  c. Using a .10 significance level, determine the rejection region.
  d. Based on the sample evidence, should Apex reject the null hypothesis that the population proportion is still .60 or less?
  e. Compute the approximate p-value for a $\hat{p}$ of .666. Explain what the p-value measures.

8. The manager of accounts receivable believes that more than 10% of the invoices have at least one error. In a random sample of 400 invoices, 51 invoices contain one or more errors. Do the data support the manager's claim? Let $\alpha = .05$.

9. A financial analyst claims that more than 60% of the firms in the electronics industry have a current ratio (current assets divided by current liabilities) of over 2.5. In a random sample of 100 firms, 61 have a current ratio of over 2.5. Do the data support the manager's claim? Let $\alpha = .01$.

10. The American Civil Liberties Union (ACLU) claims that the proportion of blacks in jury pools in Richmond County is below the proportion of blacks in the county, namely, 23%. In a random sample of 500 potential jurors, 97 are black. Do the data support the ACLU's claim? Let $\alpha = .05$. Compute the approximate p-value.

11. A product manager claims that the proportion of customers with incomes over $75,000 is more than .30. In a random sample of 400 customers, 140 have incomes over $75,000. Do the data support the product manager's claim? Let $\alpha = .10$. Compute the approximate p-value.

12. An operations manager claims that the fraction of defective items on a production line has changed from the historical level of .02. In a random sample of 1,000 items, 12 are defective. Do the data support the operations manager's claim? Let $\alpha = .05$.

13. *Research exercise:* Find an article in the *Wall Street Journal, Business Week,* or a similar publication that discusses the proportion of an important economic variable. Develop the null and alternative hypotheses implied by the author.

9.4 ≡ Hypothesis Testing on the Difference Between Two Population Means

In Section 8.3 we presented confidence intervals on the difference between two population means. These helped us compare two groups, processes, or products. For example, which plant has a better mean performance—Norcross or Dallas? Does our product receive, on average, fewer customer complaints than the competitors' brands? Is the mean strength of phone handsets on two production lines similar?

Hypothesis testing on the difference between two population means can answer these questions. All the ideas you learned in Section 9.2 apply here, too. The only difference is that we replace the sample mean and its estimated standard error with the difference between two sample means and its estimated standard error. By the end of this unit you should be able to:

1. formulate hypotheses and their associated managerial actions;
2. determine the costs associated with Type I and Type II errors;
3. test the null hypothesis and make a decision;
4. compute and interpret p-values; and
5. analyze data from a paired difference test.

Example: Productivity Comparison for Two Plants   For some time, Howard Bright, COMCEL's Norcross plant manager, has believed that the Dallas plant workers, who produce the same mobile phone as his own plant, have a higher mean productivity. If correct, he will determine the differences between the two plants (leadership, personnel, production methods, machinery, etc.) and then make the necessary changes and improvements in his own plant. He uses the five-step hypothesis-testing approach to assess his claim.

State Hypotheses and Managerial Actions

First, Bright develops his alternative hypothesis based on his claim that Dallas' mean population productivity, μ_D, exceeds his plant's productivity, μ_N. In our notation,

$$H_1: \qquad \mu_D > \mu_N \qquad \text{or}$$

$$H_1: \qquad \mu_D - \mu_N > 0.$$

Therefore the null hypothesis is that the productivity in Dallas is *not* greater than (i.e., is equal to or less than) that in Norcross. In our notation,

$$H_0: \qquad \mu_D \leq \mu_N \qquad \text{or}$$

$$H_0: \qquad \mu_D - \mu_N \leq 0.$$

	Hypotheses	**Action**
H_0	The difference between the two population means is less than or equal to 0. $\mu_D - \mu_N \leq 0$	Failure to reject the null hypothesis means that Bright will not investigate Dallas' operations.
H_1	The difference between the two population means is greater than zero. $\mu_D - \mu_N > 0$	Rejecting the null hypothesis means that Dallas has a higher productivity. Bright will investigate Dallas' operations.

In summary, we first develop the alternative hypothesis, and then the null hypothesis. Remember, the two hypotheses are mutually exclusive and exhaustive.

Determine the Costs of Errors, Set α Level and Sample Size

We have combined hypothesis-testing steps 2 and 3. There are different costs associated with Type I and Type II errors.

Type I error   Investigate Dallas' operations when, in fact, its produc-
                      tivity is not higher than Norcross'. Costs of unproductive
                      problem-solving efforts are relatively low.

Type II error   Failure to investigate Dallas' operations when, in fact, its
                      productivity is higher than Norcross'. Bright has lost an
                      opportunity to improve his plant's productivity.

A Type II error is more serious; it represents a lost opportunity to make process
improvements in the Norcross plant. Based on the relative costs, Bright sets the α
level at .20 and decides to use a sample size of 62 workers, 31 from each plant.

Data Collection

Bright selects two random samples of workers from each plant and records their
productivity data. From Section 6.9, this is called *a one-factor, two-level completely
random* study. The factor is COMCEL's plant location and the two levels are the
Norcross, Georgia, and Dallas, Texas, plants. The productivity data are measured in
units per hour (uph). Here are the study's sample statistics:

Norcross	Dallas
$\bar{x}_N = 100.45$ uph	$\bar{x}_D = 103.68$ uph
$s_N = 6.51$ uph	$s_D = 5.96$ uph
$s_N^2 = 42.38$	$s_D^2 = 35.52$
$n_N = 31$ workers	$n_D = 31$ workers

Since the alternative hypothesis states that Dallas' productivity exceeds Norcross',
Bright computes the Dallas sample mean productivity minus the Norcross sample
mean productivity.

$$\bar{x}_D - \bar{x}_N = 103.68 - 100.45 = +3.23 \text{ uph}$$

Does a sample difference of +3.23 units per hour indicate that Bright should reject
the null hypothesis?

Next we compute the pooled variance, s_p^2, using expression (8.1), which is reproduced here.

$$s_p^2 = \frac{(n_N - 1)s_N^2 + (n_D - 1)s_D^2}{n_N + n_D - 2}$$

When the two sample sizes are equal, the pooled variance, s_p^2, is simply the average
of the two sample variances. For the present study the pooled, or average, sample
variance equals:

$$s_p^2 = \frac{(31 - 1)42.38 + (31 - 1)35.52}{31 + 31 - 2}$$

$$s_p^2 = 38.95$$

When computing a pooled variance, we assume that the productivity variances for the
Norcross and Dallas populations are equal. Given how close the two sample variances
are—42.38 and 35.52—the assumption seems reasonable.

Next we compute the estimated standard error of the difference in the two sample means using expression (8.2), which is reproduced here.

$$\sqrt{\frac{s_p^2}{n_N} + \frac{s_p^2}{n_D}}$$

The terms n_N and n_D are the sample sizes from the two populations. Note how similar the expression is to the estimated standard error of the mean, $\sqrt{s^2/n}$, from Section 9.2. From the expression above, the estimated standard error for the Norcross-Dallas study is:

$$\sqrt{\frac{38.95}{31} + \frac{38.95}{31}} = 1.59 \text{ units per hour}$$

Test the Null Hypothesis and Make a Decision

Figure 9.8 shows the sampling distribution of the difference between two means for the productivity study. It is normal if (1) the two populations from which the samples are taken are normal or (2) the sample sizes include at least 30 observations from each population (from the central limit theorem). Please note several important features of the curve.

1. The mean of the sampling distribution is 0.

    Reason: We initially assume the null hypothesis is true.

2. The rejection region is in the upper tail of the curve.

    Reason: Bright would reject the null hypothesis only if the difference between the two sample means is *significantly* larger than zero. Also the alternative hypothesis is upper-tailed. Therefore, the rejection region is in the upper tail.

3. The rejection region equals the significance level, α.

    Reason: Only 20% of the time would the difference between the two sample means fall in the shaded region if $\mu_D - \mu_N$ is zero. So if the difference between the two sample means falls in the shaded region, Bright rejects the null hypothesis.

FIGURE 9.8   **Sampling Distribution of $\bar{x}_D - \bar{x}_N$ for the Productivity Study**

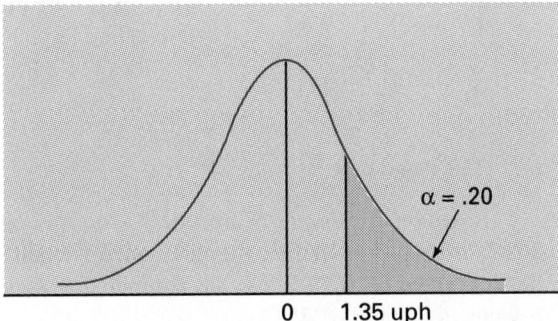

Use expression (9.9) to determine the critical value for a one-sided, upper-tailed alternative hypothesis.

$$\mu_D - \mu_N + t[\text{one-sided}, 100(1 - \alpha)\%, n_D + n_N - 2]\sqrt{\frac{s_p^2}{n_N} + \frac{s_p^2}{n_D}} \tag{9.9}$$

1. $\mu_D - \mu_N$ is the population mean under the null hypothesis. It equals 0. (See Figure 9.8.)
2. From Appendix 5, the t-value for a one-sided 80% test for $31 + 31 - 2$ or 60 degrees of freedom is .848. Or use the t-value for an infinite number of degrees of freedom, .842.
3. The estimated standard error, $\sqrt{s_p^2/n_N + s_p^2/n_D}$, is 1.59 units per hour.

The critical value for the Dallas-Norcross study is

$$0 + .848(1.59) = 1.35 \text{ units per hour.}$$

Given Figure 9.8, Bright's decision rule is:

Only if the difference between the two sample means falls in the shaded rejection region—greater than 1.35 uph—should he reject the null hypothesis.

Since $103.68 - 100.45 = 3.23$ units per hour does fall in the rejection region, Bright rejects the null hypothesis. He should investigate possible reasons why Dallas' productivity is higher than his own plant. He can then determine how to increase productivity in his plant. Having rejected the null hypothesis, he has made either a correct decision or a Type I error.

In conclusion, use the following expressions for a lower-tailed, upper-tailed, and two-tailed alternative hypothesis, respectively.

Lower-tailed: $\quad \mu_1 - \mu_2 - t[\text{one-sided}, 100(1 - \alpha)\%, n_1 + n_2 - 2]\sqrt{s_p^2/n_1 + s_p^2/n_2}$ $\qquad$ (9.8)

Upper-tailed: $\quad \mu_1 - \mu_2 + t[\text{one-sided}, 100(1 - \alpha)\%, n_1 + n_2 - 2]\sqrt{s_p^2/n_1 + s_p^2/n_2}$ $\qquad$ (9.9)

Two-tailed: $\quad \mu_1 - \mu_2 \pm t[\text{two-sided}, 100(1 - \alpha)\%, n_1 + n_2 - 2]\sqrt{s_p^2/n_1 + s_p^2/n_2}$ $\qquad$ (9.10)

The difference between population means in these expressions is always based on the null hypothesis.

Bright will now determine the approximate p-value for the sample difference in means of 3.23 units per hour.

$P(\bar{x}_D - \bar{x}_N > 3.23 \text{ uph})$ $\qquad$ From Figure 9.8, this area is much less than .20. It equals the area underneath the curve to the right of 3.23 uph.

$$P\left(t > \frac{3.23 - 0}{1.59}\right)$$

$$P(t > +2.03) < .025$$

Based on 60 degrees of freedom in the study, the closest t-value from Appendix 5 is 2.000, which is in the column labelled 1-sided 97.5% CI. Thus, a t-score of 2.000 has a p-value of .025. Since the computed t-score of 2.03 is larger than 2.000, the p-value is less than .025.

In summary, hypothesis testing on the difference between two population means can detect significant differences between two groups, processes, or products. Business judgment and creativity are necessary to determine what factors caused the significant differences. Both steps are essential to making continuous process or product improvements, which are now accepted quality improvement principles of American managers.

The Paired Comparison, or Paired Difference, Test

We want to determine which of two creativity-training methods is best for first-line supervisors. We could run a one-factor, two-level study. That is, we could select two random samples from the population and randomly assign one sample to each of the two training methods. However, one sample might include all highly motivated supervisors with prior creativity training, and the other sample might include all unmotivated supervisors with no prior creativity training. This would clearly weaken the study's validity.

To ensure that the two groups are similar, the manager could use a *matched-pair design* rather than a one-factor, two-level design. The manager *randomly* selects n pairs of supervisors, who are matched (are similar) in terms of motivation level and amount of prior training in creativity. One member of each pair is *randomly* assigned to Method A, and the other is *randomly* assigned to Method B. If a pair of members' scores differ, it cannot be due to differences in motivation level or prior training because the two members are similar on these characteristics. Score differences can only be due to the impact of the creativity training. The matched-pair design is used because it can detect significant differences between two treatment levels more effectively than the one-factor, two-level design.

Example: Which Creativity Training Is Superior?   Ten pairs of supervisors are matched in terms of motivation level and amount of prior creativity training. One member of each pair is randomly assigned to the Brainstorming method; the other is assigned to the Analogy method. After the training, all supervisors are given a problem, and the trainer records the number of nonduplicate solutions produced. The trainer believes that the Brainstorming method generates more solutions than the Analogy method.

Table 9.3 shows the number of nonduplicate solutions produced by the $n = 10$ pairs of supervisors. Note that there are major differences among pairs of supervisors. The two supervisors of pair 7 generated 79 and 90 solutions, while the two supervisors of pair 6 generated only 11 and 20 solutions. The manager anticipated this difference, and thus chose the matched-pair design.

Since the trainer believes that Brainstorming is superior to Analogy, in column 4 we have computed the number of solutions using Brainstorming minus the number of solutions using Analogy, and have labelled it the difference. If the two creativity methods were equally effective, we would expect in the long run to find an equal number of differences (column 4) above and below zero. Also we would expect the true, or population difference, μ_{diff}, to be zero. If Brainstorming is better than Analogy, we would expect the difference scores to be greater than zero, and μ_{diff} to be greater than zero.

Since we will only test a small number of pairs of supervisors, we must use the hypothesis-testing approach to assess the trainer's claim that Brainstorming is better (generates more solutions) than Analogy.

Table 9.3

Number of Nonduplicate Solutions Generated by Ten Pairs of Supervisors

Pair	Brainstorming	Analogy	Difference Brainstorm minus Analogy
1	50	46	4
2	40	27	13
3	60	50	10
4	35	28	7
5	56	49	7
6	20	11	9
7	90	79	11
8	70	71	−1
9	60	45	15
10	45	31	14
			$\bar{d} = 8.9$

State Hypotheses

Given the trainer's claim, we have the following hypotheses:

H_0:   Brainstorming does not generate more $\mu_{\text{diff}} \leq 0$
solutions than Analogy.

H_1:   Brainstorming does generate more solutions $\mu_{\text{diff}} > 0$
than Analogy.

Determine the Costs of Errors, Set α Level and Sample Size

Because the Type I error was relatively costly, the manager set $\alpha = .05$. The manager also decided to select $n = 10$ pairs of supervisors for the study.

Data Collection

For each pair of supervisors, we have computed the sample difference, $x_{\text{BRAIN}} - x_{\text{ANALOGY}}$, in Table 9.3. From this we can compute the sample mean difference for the 10 pairs, the sample standard deviation, and the estimated standard error of the difference.

Sample mean difference $\bar{d}$ = 8.9 solutions

$$\bar{d} = \frac{\sum_i d_i}{n}$$

where d_i = the difference in the measurements between
the ith pair of subjects
n = the number of pairs of subjects

Sample standard deviation s_d = 4.90 solutions

$$s_d = \sqrt{\frac{\sum_i (d_i - \bar{d})^2}{n - 1}}$$

$$\text{Estimated standard error of} \quad \frac{s_d}{\sqrt{10}} = 1.55 \text{ solutions}$$
$$\text{the difference}$$

Test the Null Hypothesis and Make a Decision

We use one of three expressions, (9.11)–(9.13), to determine the critical value. For the creativity study we use expression (9.12) because the alternative hypothesis, H_1, is upper-tailed, $\mu_{\text{diff}} > 0$.

The three expressions *assume* that the population from which the pairs were taken is normally distributed. You can test this assumption by developing a stem-and-leaf display for the 10 sample difference data values.

Lower-tailed: $\mu_{\text{diff}} - t[\text{one-sided}, 100(1 - \alpha)\%, n - 1]s_d/\sqrt{n}$ (9.11)

Upper-tailed: $\mu_{\text{diff}} + t[\text{one-sided}, 100(1 - \alpha)\%, n - 1]s_d/\sqrt{n}$ (9.12)

Two-tailed: $\mu_{\text{diff}} \pm t[\text{two-sided}, 100(1 - \alpha)\%, n - 1]s_d/\sqrt{n}$ (9.13)

where n is the number of pairs taken from the population
μ_{diff} is based on the value from the null hypothesis (and is often zero)

We used expression (9.12) to determine the critical value.

$$0 + t(\text{one-sided}, 95\%, 9 \text{ df})(1.55)$$
$$0 + 1.833(1.55) = 2.84 \text{ solutions}$$

DECISION RULE   If the sample difference, $\bar{d}$, is greater than 2.84, reject the null hypothesis.

Since $\bar{d}$ equals 8.9 solutions for the ten pairs of supervisors, we reject the null hypothesis. We are at least 95% confident that Brainstorming generates more solutions than Analogy.

In summary, there are two types of studies managers can run when they wish to determine the difference between two population means. These are the one-factor, two-level study and the matched-pair design. To use the matched pair design, the manager must be able to (1) identify characteristics of the population elements (people, cars, etc.) to match on and (2) find elements within the population with the matching characteristics.

How can a manager identify what characteristics to match on? An important criterion is:

Match on characteristics that are known (or believed) to have an effect on the dependent variable in the study.

In the creativity study, the manager suspected that motivation level and prior training in creativity could affect the number of solutions generated. Highly motivated supervisors with prior training might generate a large number of solutions. He was right (see pair 7). Nonmotivated supervisors with no prior training might generate a small number of solutions. He was right (see pair 6). These personal characteristic differences did not interfere with his ability to detect a significant difference between the two types of creativity training.

SECTION 9.4 EXERCISES

1. What, if anything, is wrong with the following pairs of null and alternative hypotheses?

a. $\mu_1 - \mu_2 \le 0$ **c.** $\bar{x}_1 - \bar{x}_2 \le 0$
$\mu_1 - \mu_2 > 0$ $\bar{x}_1 - \bar{x}_2 > 0$

b. $\mu_1 - \mu_2 < 0$ **d.** $\mu_1 - \mu_2 = \bar{x}_1 - \bar{x}_2$
$\mu_1 - \mu_2 > 0$ $\mu_1 - \mu_2 \ge \bar{x}_1 - \bar{x}_2$

2. Which type of hypothesis testing—on one population mean or on the difference between two population means—should be done for the following problems? We wish to draw conclusions about:

a. the amount of pollutants in a river.
b. which product has superior reliability.
c. the number of hours to computer chip failure.
d. which plant has the lowest number of lost man-hours per quarter.

3. Formulate the null and alternative hypotheses for the following situations:

a. A plant manager claims that, on average, the Buffalo plant has more absenteeism than the Chicago plant.
b. A financial manager claims that the mean current ratios in the electronics and manufacturing industries differ.
c. A marketing manager claims that, on average, product X has fewer customer complaints than product Y.
d. A real estate manager claims that the average rental cost is higher in the suburbs than in the city center.

4. Given the four sets of null and alternative hypotheses, correct, if necessary, the mean of the hypothesized sampling distribution and the location of the rejection region(s).

a. Given: H_0 $\mu_1 - \mu_2 \le \$0$
         H_1 $\mu_1 - \mu_2 > \$0$

             $\bar{x}_1 - \bar{x}_2 = \$1.06$

1. The sampling distribution has an upper-tailed rejection region.
2. The mean of the sampling distribution is $1.06.

b. Given: H_0 $\mu_1 - \mu_2 = 6$ days
         H_1 $\mu_1 - \mu_2 \ne 6$ days

             $\bar{x}_1 - \bar{x}_2 = 7$ days

1. The sampling distribution has a two-tailed rejection region.
2. The mean of the sampling distribution is 0.

c. Given: H_0 $\mu_1 - \mu_2 \ge 0$
         H_1 $\mu_1 - \mu_2 < 0$

             $\bar{x}_1 - \bar{x}_2 = -1.7$ units per hour (uph)

1. The sampling distribution has a lower-tailed rejection region.
2. The mean of the sampling distribution is 0.

d. Given: H_0 $\mu_1 - \mu_2 = 0$ pounds per square inch (ppsi)
         H_1 $\mu_1 - \mu_2 \ne 0$ ppsi

             $\bar{x}_1 - \bar{x}_2 = 1.5$ ppsi

1. The sampling distribution has a two-tailed rejection region.
2. The mean of the sampling distribution is 1.5 ppsi.

5. Test the following hypotheses. Also compute the approximate *p*-values.

a. H_0 $\mu_1 - \mu_2 = 6$ days
    H_1 $\mu_1 - \mu_2 \ne 6$ days
           $\alpha = .01$

$$\bar{x}_1 = 21.5 \text{ days} \qquad s_1^2 = 10 \qquad n_1 = 100$$

$$\bar{x}_2 = 14.5 \text{ days} \qquad s_2^2 = 15 \qquad n_2 = 100$$

b. H_0 $\mu_1 - \mu_2 \geq 0$ uph

   H_1 $\mu_1 - \mu_2 < 0$ uph

   $\alpha = .05$

   $\bar{x}_1 = 60.5$ uph $s_1^2 = 10$ $n_1 = 50$

   $\bar{x}_2 = 62.2$ uph $s_2^2 = 15$ $n_2 = 100$

c. H_0 $\mu_1 - \mu_2 \leq \$0$

   H_1 $\mu_1 - \mu_2 > \$0$

   $\alpha = .10$

   $\bar{x}_1 = \$18.06$ $s_1^2 = 50$ $n_1 = 100$

   $\bar{x}_2 = \$17.00$ $s_2^2 = 40$ $n_2 = 300$

6. A financial analyst wants to determine if the average collection periods (value of accounts receivable divided by average sales per day) are different for two industries. She randomly selects two samples of firms, one from each industry, and obtains the following data:

   $\bar{x}_A = 36$ days $s_A^2 = 7.5$ $n_A = 25$

   $\bar{x}_B = 38.3$ days $s_B^2 = 9.4$ $n_B = 20$

   Do these data support her claim that the mean average collection periods differ between the two industries? Let $\alpha = .05$.

7. The manager of Quik Speed bicycle messenger service claims that his service can deliver a letter faster than his major competitor, Velocity Inc. We must now evaluate the claim. We give both services 61 letters to deliver that require a similar mix of distances, times of day, and street conditions. Below are the data.

   $\bar{x}_{QS} = 36$ minutes $s_{QS}^2 = 14.5$ $n_{QS} = 61$

   $\bar{x}_{VI} = 40.6$ minutes $s_{VI}^2 = 19.4$ $n_{VI} = 61$

   Do these data support the claim that Quik Speed's mean delivery time is faster than Velocity Inc.'s? Let $\alpha = .01$.

8. A quality-improvement team is seeking to increase a product's strength in pounds per square inch (ppsi). They believe that their latest efforts have resulted in an increase of more than 200 ppsi at no additional cost to the customer. In testing their claim, they obtain the following data:

   $\bar{x}_{OLD} = 700$ ppsi $s_{OLD}^2 = 1,750$ $n_{OLD} = 100$

   $\bar{x}_{NEW} = 918$ ppsi $s_{NEW}^2 = 1,900$ $n_{NEW} = 100$

   Do these data support the claim that the quality-improvement team has increased the product's strength by more than 200 ppsi? Let $\alpha = .10$.

9. A management consultant believes that, within the same industry, firms that do formal strategic planning obtain higher returns on total assets (net income after taxes, divided by total assets) than firms that do not do formal planning. To test his hypothesis, he selects two random samples of firms that do and do not do formal planning and obtains the following data:

   $\bar{x}_{PLAN} = 11.4\%$ $s_{PLAN}^2 = 5.5$ $n_{PLAN} = 21$

   $\bar{x}_{NOPL} = 9.8\%$ $s_{NOPL}^2 = 5.9$ $n_{NOPL} = 21$

Do these data support the claim that firms that do formal strategic planning obtain higher returns on total assets than firms that do not do formal planning? Let $\alpha = .05$.

10. A manager uses a matched-pair design to test two different advertising approaches. She selects $n = 10$ pairs of consumers between the ages of 21 and 35 matched in terms of gender and socioeconomic class. For each pair, she randomly assigns one consumer to an MTV-style advertising presentation and the other consumer to a traditional advertising presentation. She records the number of product features each consumer can recall one week later (see data below). Assume that recall of product features is normally distributed in the population. The manager believes that the MTV ad will be more effective (recall more attributes) for 21–35-year-old consumers. Let $\alpha = .01$.

Pair	1	2	3	4	5	6	7	8	9	10
MTV	4	3	4	5	4	2	4	4	5	4
Traditional	1	0	2	1	0	2	1	0	2	0

a. Since the manager believes that the MTV ad will be more effective, let the difference $= x_{MTV} - x_{TRAD}$. Compute the 10 difference scores.
b. Compute the sample mean difference score and the estimated standard error of the difference.
c. Determine the critical value. Can the manager reject the null hypothesis?

11. A manager wishes to test a gas additive that he believes will improve mileage. He selects $n = 8$ pairs of cars matched in terms of horsepower, weight, and type of transmission. For each pair, he randomly assigns one car to the gasoline without the additive and one car to the gasoline with the additive. He runs each car and determines the miles per gallon (see data below). Assume that miles per gallon is normally distributed in the population. Let $\alpha = .05$. Do the sample data indicate that he can reject the null hypothesis?

Pair	1	2	3	4	5	6	7	8
Without Additive	20	14	26	34	34	49	15	24
With Additive	21	13	24	37	34	47	18	24

a. Since the manager believes that the additive will improve mileage, let the difference $= x_{ADD} - x_{NOADD}$. Compute the eight difference scores.
b. Compute the sample mean difference score and the estimated standard error of the difference.
c. Determine the critical value. Can the manager reject the null hypothesis?

12. A firm that conducts SAT review courses claims that students will improve their SAT scores by taking the half-day course. To prove this, they take $n = 10$ students and record their SAT scores before and after taking the course. Each student is paired with himself. This form of the matched pair design is called a *repeated measures design*. Assume that SAT scores are normally distributed in the population. Let $\alpha = .05$. Do the sample data indicate that we can reject the null hypothesis?

Student	1	2	3	4	5	6	7	8	9	10
Before	700	1,140	900	940	1,000	890	1,100	790	1,050	1,100
After	740	1,130	970	1,000	1,010	890	1,120	820	1,040	1,150

a. Since the manager believes that the workshop will improve SAT scores, let the difference $= x_{AFTER} - x_{BEFORE}$. Compute the 10 difference scores.
b. Compute the sample mean difference score and the estimated standard error of the difference.
c. Determine the critical value. Can the manager reject the null hypothesis?

13. A Koger senior manager claims that Koger has *lower* prices than Cab Foods. He selects $n = 6$ pairs of products and then determines the prices of these products at both food chains. Let $\alpha = .05$. Do the sample data indicate that we can reject the null hypothesis that Koger does not have lower prices?

Product	Cab Foods	Koger
Jam	$1.34	$1.31
Milk	1.89	1.74
Juice	1.50	1.47
Ice cream	4.59	4.23
Oranges	1.00	.97
Lettuce	.99	.99

a. Since the manager believes that Koger has a lower price, let the difference $= x_{\text{KOGER}} - x_{\text{CAB}}$. Compute the six difference scores.
b. Compute the sample mean difference score and the estimated standard error of the difference.
c. Determine the critical value. Can the manager reject the null hypothesis?

14. Given the following data, can we reject the null hypothesis that the population mean difference is greater than or equal to zero? Let $\alpha = .05$. Assume that $n = 11$ pairs of data were taken from a normal population.

Sample Differences Scores

$$-4 \quad -6 \quad -3 \quad -4 \quad -6 \quad 0 \quad -1 \quad -4 \quad 5 \quad -5 \quad -6$$

a. Compute the sample mean difference, standard deviation, and the estimated standard error of the difference.
b. Compare the sample mean difference to the critical value. Can we reject the null hypothesis?

9.5 Hypothesis Testing on the Difference Between Two Population Proportions

In Section 8.4 we presented confidence intervals on the difference between two population proportions. They helped us compare two groups, processes, or products. Hypothesis testing on the difference between two population proportions can also be used to compare two groups, processes, or products.

All the ideas you learned in Section 9.3 apply here, too. The only difference is that we replace the sample proportion and its hypothesized standard error with the difference between two sample proportions and its hypothesized standard error. By the end of this unit you should be able to:

1. formulate hypotheses and their associated managerial actions;
2. determine the cost associated with Type I and Type II errors;
3. test the null hypothesis and make a decision; and
4. compute and interpret p-values.

Example: Demographic Study: Are Multiple Advertisements Necessary?

An account manager at an advertising agency believes that the proportion of subscribers with family incomes more than $60,000 differs between two magazines, *American Business* and *The Entrepreneur*. If true, the account manager must create different campaign strategies for one of her products in each magazine; that is, she must segment the market. If there is no difference, the account manager can use a similar advertisement for both target audiences. Let us evaluate the account manager's claim.

State Hypotheses and Managerial Actions

First, we develop the alternative hypothesis based on the manager's claim that the two population proportions differ. In our notation,

$$p_{AB} \neq p_{TE} \qquad \text{or}$$

$$p_{AB} - p_{TE} \neq 0.$$

Second, since the null and alternative hypotheses must be mutually exclusive and exhaustive, we can now state the hypotheses.

Hypotheses		Action
H_0	The is no difference between the two population proportions. $p_{AB} - p_{TE} = 0$	Failure to reject the null hypothesis means that the same ad campaign will be developed for both target audiences. The account manager will not segment the market.
H_1	There is a difference between the two population proportions. $p_{AB} - p_{TE} \neq 0$	Rejecting the null hypothesis means that the manager will develop two different ad campaigns. She will segment the market.

Determine the Costs of Errors, Set α Level and Sample Size

There are costs associated with both errors.

Type I error   Using different campaign strategies when, in fact, two different strategies were not necessary. Costs include campaign development costs and possible failure to obtain desired market share.

Type II error   Not using two different campaign strategies when, in fact, two different strategies were necessary. Costs include possible failure to obtain desired market share. The cost depends on how different the two population proportions really are. As stated before, there is not a single Type II error cost.

Both errors are very costly. Thus, we set the α level at .01 and select large samples of 1,000 families each.

Data Collection

Of $n_{AB} = 1,000$ randomly selected subscribers to *American Business*, 550 respond that their family income is more than \$60,000. Of $n_{TE} = 1,000$ randomly selected subscribers to *The Entrepreneur*, 500 respond that their family income is more than \$60,000. Here are the study's sample statistics:

American Business	*The Entrepreneur*
Number of families with incomes over $60,000 = 550	Number of families with incomes over $60,000 = 500
$n_{AB} = 1{,}000$	$n_{TE} = 1{,}000$
$\hat{p}_{AB} = .55$	$\hat{p}_{TE} = .50$
$\hat{q}_{AB} = 1 - \hat{p}_{AB} = .45$	$\hat{q}_{TE} = 1 - \hat{p}_{TE} = .50$

Since the alternative hypothesis is two-tailed, the manager may compute either of the following two statistics:

$$.55 - .50 = .05 \qquad \text{or}$$
$$.50 - .55 = -.05$$

Does a sample difference of .05 (or $-.05$) indicate that the manager should reject the null hypothesis? Is the sample difference of .05 *significantly* above zero that we must reject the null hypothesis?

Before determining the decision rule, we must compute the estimated hypothesized standard error. Which of the two sample proportions, .55 or .50, will we use to compute it? Since the null hypothesis assumes that the two population proportions are the same, we compute a *pooled* estimate using expression (9.14).

$$\hat{p}_{pooled} = \frac{(n_1\hat{p}_1 + n_2\hat{p}_2)}{(n_1 + n_2)} \qquad (9.14)$$

For the advertising study, the pooled estimate of the sample proportion is

$$\hat{p}_{pooled} = \frac{1{,}000(.55) + 1{,}000(.50)}{1{,}000 + 1{,}000} = .525$$

When the two sample sizes are the same (as they are in the example), $\hat{p}_{pooled}$ is simply the mean of the two sample proportions. We then use expression (9.15) to compute the estimated hypothesized standard error for the advertising study.

$$\sqrt{\frac{\hat{p}_{pooled}(1 - \hat{p}_{pooled})}{n_1} + \frac{\hat{p}_{pooled}(1 - \hat{p}_{pooled})}{n_2}} \qquad (9.15)$$

For the advertising study, the estimated hypothesized standard error is

$$\sqrt{\frac{525(.475)}{1{,}000} + \frac{525(.475)}{1{,}000}} = .022$$

Test the Null Hypothesis and Make a Decision

Figure 9.9 shows the sampling distribution of the difference between two proportions. Given sample sizes of 1,000, the distribution is approximately normal. Note several important features of the curve.

1. The mean of the sampling distribution is 0.

   Reason: This is the value under the null hypothesis. Remember, we initially assume that the null hypothesis is true.

FIGURE 9.9   Sampling Distribution of $\hat{p}_{AB} - \hat{p}_{TE}$ for the Marketing Study

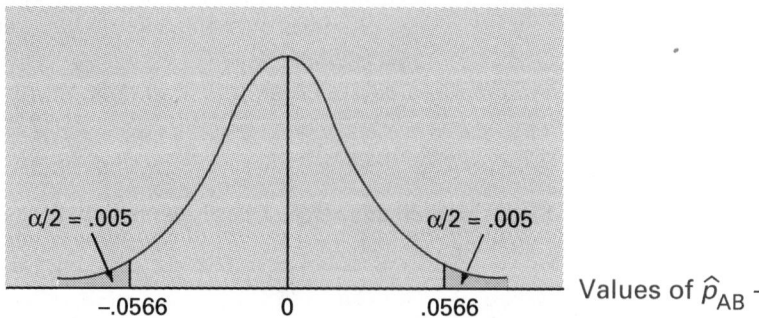

2. There are two rejection regions.

   Reason: The manager is looking for a difference. She will reject the null hypothesis if the difference between the two sample proportions was either *significantly* larger or smaller than zero. Also, the alternative hypothesis is two-tailed. Therefore, there are two rejection regions.

3. The rejection region equals the significance level, α.

   Reason: Since the alternative hypothesis is two-tailed (greater than or less than), we divide the significance level, α, by 2. Each rejection region contains .005 of the area. Thus, the total probability of making a Type I error is .01.

Use expression (9.18) to determine the critical value for a two-sided alternative hypothesis.

$$p_{AB} - p_{TE} \pm z[\text{two-sided, } 100(1 - \alpha)\%]\sqrt{\frac{\hat{p}_{\text{pooled}}(1 - \hat{p}_{\text{pooled}})}{n_{AB}} + \frac{\hat{p}_{\text{pooled}}(1 - \hat{p}_{\text{pooled}})}{n_{TE}}}$$

1. $p_{AB} - p_{TE}$ is the population mean under the null hypothesis. It equals 0. (See Figure 9.9.)
2. From Appendix 5, the z-value for a two-sided, 99% test (use bottom row) is 2.576.
3. The estimated hypothesized standard error is .022.

The critical values for the advertising study are
$$.00 - 2.576(.022) = -.0566$$
$$.00 + 2.576(.022) = +.0566$$

Given Figure 9.9, the manager's decision rule is:

   Only if the difference between the two sample proportions falls in either shaded rejection region—less than $-.0566$ or greater than .0566—should she reject the null hypothesis.

Since the difference between the two sample proportions, $.55 - .50 = .05$, does not fall in the rejection region, the account manager does not reject the null hypothesis. She concludes that there is no significant difference between the two population proportions. Two different advertising campaigns will not be needed. Having failed to reject the null hypothesis, she has made either a correct decision or a Type II error.

In conclusion, use the following expressions for a lower-tailed, upper-tailed, and two-tailed alternative hypothesis, respectively.

Lower-tailed: $p_1 - p_2 - z[\text{one-sided, } 100(1 - \alpha)\%]\sqrt{\dfrac{\hat{p}_{\text{pooled}}(1 - \hat{p}_{\text{pooled}})}{n_1} + \dfrac{\hat{p}_{\text{pooled}}(1 - \hat{p}_{\text{pooled}})}{n_2}}$ (9.16)

Upper-tailed: $p_1 - p_2 + z[\text{one-sided, } 100(1 - \alpha)\%]\sqrt{\dfrac{\hat{p}_{\text{pooled}}(1 - \hat{p}_{\text{pooled}})}{n_1} + \dfrac{\hat{p}_{\text{pooled}}(1 - \hat{p}_{\text{pooled}})}{n_2}}$ (9.17)

Two-tailed: $p_1 - p_2 \pm z[\text{two-sided, } 100(1 - \alpha)\%]\sqrt{\dfrac{\hat{p}_{\text{pooled}}(1 - \hat{p}_{\text{pooled}})}{n_1} + \dfrac{\hat{p}_{\text{pooled}}(1 - \hat{p}_{\text{pooled}})}{n_2}}$ (9.18)

The difference between population proportions in the above expressions is always based on the null hypothesis.

As in the previous three sections, we could now determine the p-value for the study. We have omitted a p-value presentation because the computation has already been thoroughly covered.

To determine the estimated hypothesized standard error, we do not always compute the pooled estimate of the sample proportion. This is only done when the null hypothesis states that the two population proportions are equal. Sometimes the hypothesized difference in the population proportions is not zero. For example,

$$H_0: \quad p_1 - p_2 = .05.$$

To compute the estimated hypothesized standard error we insert the two sample proportions into expression (9.19).

$$\sqrt{\dfrac{\hat{p}_1(1 - \hat{p}_1)}{n_1} + \dfrac{\hat{p}_2(1 - \hat{p}_2)}{n_2}} \qquad (9.19)$$

SECTION 9.5 EXERCISES

1. What, if anything, is wrong with the following pairs of null and alternative hypotheses?
    a. $p_1 - p_2 \le .05$
       $p_1 - p_2 > 0$
    b. $\hat{p}_1 - \hat{p}_2 < 0$
       $\hat{p}_1 - \hat{p}_2 > 0$
    c. $p_1 - p_2 = 0$
       $p_1 - p_2 > 0$

2. Formulate the null and alternative hypotheses for the following situations:
    a. The Reno plant manager claims that, on average, the Buffalo plant produces a greater fraction of defects than his plant.
    b. A financial manager claims that the percentage of insolvent S&Ls differs in two regions of the country.
    c. A quality manager claims that, of the total customer complaints with new cars, the proportion of brake problems is less than the proportion of squeaks and rattles.

3. Correct, if necessary, the following four sets of hypotheses.
    a. Given: H_0 $p_1 - p_2 \le \$0$
              H_1 $p_1 - p_2 > \$0$
                       $\hat{p}_1 - \hat{p}_2 = \$1.06$

       1. The sampling distribution has an upper-tailed rejection region.

       2. The mean of the sampling distribution is $0.

b. Given: $H_0 \quad p_1 - p_2 = .30$
$H_1 \quad p_1 - p_2 \neq .30$
$\hat{p}_1 - \hat{p}_2 = .14$

1. The sampling distribution has a two-tailed rejection region.

2. The mean of the sampling distribution is .30.

c. Given: $H_0 \quad p_1 - p_2 \geq .05$
$H_1 \quad p_1 - p_2 < .05$
$\hat{p}_1 - \hat{p}_2 = .025$

1. The sampling distribution has a lower-tailed rejection region.

2. The mean of the sampling distribution is .05.

d. Given: $H_0 \quad p_1 - p_2 = 0$
$H_1 \quad p_1 - p_2 \neq 0$
$\hat{p}_1 - \hat{p}_2 = .056$

1. The sampling distribution has an upper-tailed rejection region.

2. The mean of the sampling distribution is 0.

4. Test the following hypotheses:

a. $H_0 \quad p_1 - p_2 = 0$
$H_1 \quad p_1 - p_2 \neq 0$
$\alpha = .01$
$\hat{p}_1 = .765 \qquad n_1 = 500$
$\hat{p}_2 = .785 \qquad n_2 = 1{,}000$

b. $H_0 \quad p_1 - p_2 \geq 0$
$H_1 \quad p_1 - p_2 < 0$
$\alpha = .05$
$\hat{p}_1 = .150 \qquad n_1 = 1{,}500$
$\hat{p}_2 = .165 \qquad n_2 = 3{,}000$

c. $H_0 \quad p_1 - p_2 \leq 0$
$H_1 \quad p_1 - p_2 > 0$
$\alpha = .10$
$\hat{p}_1 = .51 \qquad n_1 = 500$
$\hat{p}_2 = .47 \qquad n_2 = 500$

5. Vendor A claims that it produces a superior product to COMCEL's present material vendor, vendor P. Both vendors charge the same price and are reputable suppliers. As the purchasing manager at COMCEL you must evaluate Vendor A's claim. You ask both vendors to send 1,000 pieces of raw material. You find 10 defective pieces from Vendor P and 8 defective pieces from Vendor A. Do the data support Vendor A's claim? Let $\alpha = .01$.

6. To attract older people to her community, the city manager of St. Petersburg claims that her city has a higher proportion of retirees than Boca Raton. Do the following data support her claim? Let $\alpha = .05$.

St. Petersburg	Boca Raton
Number of retirees = 714	Number of retirees = 689
Sample size = 1,000	Sample size = 1,000

7. A human resource manager claims that the proportion of extroverted managers in the U.S. division is at least 15% greater than in the European division. He selects two random samples of 100 managers and has them take the Myers-Briggs Type Indicator. Do the following data support his claim? Let $\alpha = .10$.

U.S. Division	European Division
Number of extroverts = 65	Number of extroverts = 45
Sample size = 100	Sample size = 100

8. A stockbroker believes that a greater proportion of upper-income families purchase municipal bonds than do middle-income families. Upper-income families are in the highest tax bracket and can avoid paying taxes by buying tax-exempt municipal bonds. Do the following randomly selected data support his claim? Let $\alpha = .05$.

Middle Income	Upper Income
Number of families that have purchased municipal bonds = 90	Number of families that have purchased municipal bonds = 120
Sample size = 200	Sample size = 200

9. Construct a word problem from a business area not previously mentioned in the text for the following two hypotheses:

$$H_0 \qquad p_1 - p_2 \leq .15$$
$$H_1 \qquad p_1 - p_2 > .15$$

10. *Research exercise:* Find an article in the *Wall Street Journal, Businessweek,* or a similar business publication that discusses the difference between two population proportions. Develop the null and alternative hypotheses implied by the author.

9.6 Key Ideas and Overview

Managers and students often have difficulty in formulating hypotheses and determining the rejection region(s). Here we summarize several ideas to help overcome these problems.

IDEA 1: Based on the pending decision, determine the population parameter of interest—μ, $\mu_1 - \mu_2$, p, or $p_1 - p_2$.

IDEA 2: Develop the alternative hypothesis first. Base it on the claim to be tested.

IDEA 3: Develop the null hypothesis. Together, the null and alternative hypotheses must be mutually exclusive and exhaustive.

IDEA 4: Determine the rejection region(s) from the alternative hypothesis. For example, an upper-tailed alternative hypothesis requires a rejection region in the upper tail.

Hypothesis testing and confidence intervals are alternative approaches to drawing conclusions about one or more population parameters. We conclude this chapter with two tables that connect Chapters 7–9.

Table 9.4

The Hypothesis Testing and Confidence Interval Connection

Population Parameter		Confidence Intervals	Hypothesis Testing
Mean	μ	7.3, 7.4	9.2
Two means	$\mu_1 - \mu_2$	8.3	9.4
Proportion	p	7.6	9.3
Two proportions	$p_1 - p_2$	8.4	9.5

Two-sided confidence intervals are similar to two-tailed hypothesis tests. One-sided confidence intervals are similar to one-tailed hypothesis tests.

Table 9.5 contains the formulas for constructing two-sided confidence intervals and determining the critical values for two-tailed hypotheses for the four population parameters. Note the similarities and differences between the two sets of expressions. In all cases, we multiply the *t*- or *z*-scores by the estimated or hypothesized standard error of the sample statistic. The center of the confidence intervals always equals the value of the sample statistic. In determining the critical values, the four population parameters—μ, $\mu_1 - \mu_2$, p, $p_1 - p_2$—are based on the value from the null hypothesis. Remember, we assume the null hypothesis is true until proven otherwise.

Table 9.5

Formulas for Constructing Two-Sided Confidence Intervals and Determining the Two Rejection Regions for Two-Tailed Tests

Parameter	Confidence Intervals	Critical Values
μ	$\bar{x} \pm t\,\dfrac{s}{\sqrt{n}}$	$\mu_0 \pm t\,\dfrac{s}{\sqrt{n}}$
$\mu_1 - \mu_2$	$\bar{x}_1 - \bar{x}_2 \pm t\sqrt{\dfrac{s_p^2}{n_1} + \dfrac{s_p^2}{n_2}}$	$\mu_1 - \mu_2 \pm t\sqrt{\dfrac{s_p^2}{n_1} + \dfrac{s_p^2}{n_2}}$
p	$\hat{p} \pm z\sqrt{\dfrac{\hat{p}(1-\hat{p})}{n}}$	$p_0 \pm z\sqrt{\dfrac{p_0(1-p_0)}{n}}$
$p_1 - p_2$	$\hat{p}_1 - \hat{p}_2 \pm z\sqrt{\dfrac{\hat{p}_1(1-\hat{p}_1)}{n_1} + \dfrac{\hat{p}_2(1-\hat{p}_2)}{n_2}}$	$p_1 - p_2 \pm z\sqrt{\dfrac{\hat{p}_{POOLED}(1-\hat{p}_{POOLED})}{n_1} + \dfrac{\hat{p}_{POOLED}(1-\hat{p}_{POOLED})}{n_2}}$ *

* The estimated hypothesized standard error is correct when the null hypothesis is
$$H_0:\ p_1 - p_2 = 0$$
$$p_1 - p_2 \leq 0$$
$$p_1 - p_2 \geq 0$$
otherwise, use expression (9.19) to compute the estimated hypothesized standard error.

COMCEL

Date: July 22, 1994
  To: Nat Gordon, V. P. Manufacturing
From: Sang Kim, Quality-Assurance Manager
  Re: Investigation of Injection Molding Problems

SUMMARY
On average, the process appears to be producing phone handsets at the target value of 4,750 ppsi. We recommend eliminating the 100% inspection.

SUPPORTING ANALYSIS
A quality monitoring team randomly selected one phone handset about every 15 minutes for a 7.5-hour period (30 observations) and determined its strength. The sample mean and standard deviation

were 4,748.40 ppsi and 23.33 ppsi, respectively. The estimated standard error was 4.26 ppsi.

The team then used the hypothesis testing approach to determine if the process needed adjustment. Based on the relative costs of the Type I and Type II errors, we set an α level of .20. The team concluded that the process was producing handsets at the target value of 4,750 ppsi, $[t < -.36, p > .60]$.

**CHAPTER 9
QUESTIONS**

1. What are the advantages of hypothesis testing over the confidence interval method?

2. How are $\bar{x}$ and μ different? How are $\hat{p}$ and p different?

3. Explain the difference between the sample standard deviation and the estimated standard error.

4. What is wrong with the following hypotheses?

$$H_0 \qquad \bar{x} \le 4.7 \text{ hours}$$

$$H_1 \qquad \bar{x} > 4.7 \text{ hours}$$

5. Why is it possible to make either a Type I or Type II error before a study, but only one type of error after the study?

6. If a Type II error is costly but a Type I error is not, why would you set the significance level, α, at .20 or higher?

7. Correct if necessary, the following statement: Hypotheses are claims about *sample statistics*.

8. What does the p-value tell you?

9. Suppose you set the α level at .05. You obtain the following p-value—$[t > 2.03, p = .0212]$. Should you reject the null hypothesis? Why?

10. What is the relationship between the type of the alternative hypothesis (one- or two-tailed) and the location of the rejection region(s)?

11. Why must time-ordered data be stationary and the sample standard deviation be at or near the target value before conducting hypothesis testing on a population mean?

12. Suppose H_1: $\mu > 30$ minutes and the computed $\bar{x}$ is 35 minutes. Why is it necessary to do hypothesis testing? After all, an $\bar{x}$ of 35 minutes is greater than 30 minutes.

13. Develop a business decision-making example different from those mentioned in the text where hypothesis testing on one population mean would be useful. Develop the null and alternative hypotheses.

14. How are the sample mean and proportion similar, and how are they different?

15. What can you conclude if the sample proportion equals 1.45?

16. Develop a business decision-making example different from those mentioned in the text where hypothesis testing on one population proportion would be useful. Develop the null and alternative hypotheses.

17. Suppose H_1: $p < .05$ and the computed $\hat{p}$ is .03. Why is it necessary to do hypothesis testing? After all, a $\hat{p}$ of .03 is less than .05.

18. Given the following hypotheses, describe your subordinate's claim about the proportion defective in a process.

$$H_0 \qquad p \ge .10$$

$$H_1 \qquad p < .10$$

19. Why would a manager be interested in doing hypothesis testing on the difference between two population means?

20. Why would a manager be interested in doing hypothesis testing on the difference between two population proportions?

21. Suppose you reject the null hypothesis that two groups have the same mean number of days lost due to accidents. Does hypothesis testing tell you why the two groups significantly differ? Explain.

22. Is it possible for a *p*-value to be greater than 1? Explain.

23. Develop a business decision-making example different from those mentioned in the text where hypothesis testing on the difference between two population means would be useful. Develop the null and alternative hypotheses.

24. Develop a business decision-making example different from those mentioned in the text where hypothesis testing on the difference between two population proportions would be useful. Develop the null and alternative hypotheses.

25. Throughout the chapter we have assumed either that we take samples from normal populations or that the sample sizes are sufficiently large that the central limit theorem applies. Why was this necessary?

CHAPTER 9 APPLICATION PROBLEMS

1. Historically, the mean age of accounts payable has been 22 days. For the past six months the firm has tried several ways to reduce the age of accounts payable.
   a. Set up the appropriate null and alternative hypotheses.
   b. In the problem context, what are the Type I and Type II errors?

   The accounting supervisor selects a simple random sample of 225 accounts payable. The sample mean age is 20.5 days and the sample standard deviation is 7.5 days. Given an α of .05, what can the accounting supervisor conclude?
   c. Show the rejection region and indicate what action to take.
   d. Based on part **c**, is it now possible to make a Type II error? Explain.
   e. Determine the approximate *p*-value.

2. A firm is presently using family branding on a consumer product and selling about 1,750 cartons per week in the southeast United States. The marketing group has developed a new media campaign that it believes will increase sales substantially. It convinces management to try individual branding for six months.
   a. Set up the appropriate null and alternative hypotheses.
   b. In the problem context, what are the Type I and Type II errors?
   c. Identify one cost associated with each error.

   After the test period the firm selects a random sample of 400 and finds that these stores have sold a mean of 1,760 cartons per week; the sample standard deviation is 2,000 cartons per week. Given an α level of .10, what can the firm conclude from its test?
   d. Show the rejection region and indicate what action to take.
   e. Why didn't you reject the null hypothesis? After all, the sample mean was greater than 1,750 cartons per week.
   f. Is it now possible to make a Type II error? Explain?
   g. Determine the approximate *p*-value.

3. Industrial psychologists believe that stress is curvilinearly related to performance. That is, too little stress produces no drive to excel. Too much stress causes anxiety, which reduces performance. From 1989 to 1991, a firm worked to optimize the level of stress within a plant. At the beginning of the period, the level of stress was at 5 (on a scale of 1 to 10)—the optimal level. However, in the past nine months several things have happened that may have caused a change in the stress level.
   a. Set up the appropriate null and alternative hypotheses.
   b. In the problem context, what are the Type I and Type II errors?

   The firm's psychologist selects a simple random sample of 50 workers from the 1,000 employees and administers a stress test. The mean level of stress is 5.35 with a sample variance of .36. Given an α of .01, what can the psychologist conclude?
   c. Given the sample evidence, what action should the firm take?
   d. Determine the approximate *p*-value.

4. A medical consumer watchdog agency believes that the average cost per day in hospitals in Alabama is greater than in the neighboring state of Mississippi. It randomly selects 50 hospitals (the same mix of not-for-profit and profit hospitals) in both states and obtains the following daily cost data.

	Alabama	Mississippi
	$\bar{x} = \$616$	$\bar{x} = \$501$
	$s = 95.50$	$s = 88.59$
	$n = 50$	$n = 50$

At an α level of .01, evaluate the agency's claim.

5. Attorneys within a criminal justice division believe that the proportion of nonviolent white criminals is different from the proportion of violent white criminals. Of 200 randomly selected nonviolent prisoners, 122 are white. Of 200 randomly selected violent prisoners, 100 are white. Given the data and a significance level of .05, evaluate the claim. The sample proportions are based on data taken from the *Sourcebook of Criminal Justice Statistics, 1988.*

6. An operations manager believes that the efficiency of a just-in-time (JIT) delivery system has recently slipped. Just-in-time means that subassemblies arrive at the plant as they are needed in the production process. JIT almost eliminates the need for inventorying subassemblies. In the past, parts have been delivered late only 2% of the time. Due to personnel changes at the vendor, the operations manager believes that the percentage of late deliveries has recently increased. He does not want to talk to the vendor until he has more evidence.

a. Set up the null and alternative hypotheses and the associated managerial actions.

b. Describe the Type I and Type II errors and their associated costs.

The operations manager obtains data. Of the next 100 deliveries over a several-day period, 5 deliveries are late.

c. At the .05 significance level, evaluate the manager's claim. What action should he take now?

7. Recently Atlantic Airlines offered coupons worth $50 off air flights between Dallas and Chicago. The firm thought the sales promotion strategy would increase its market share for this route beyond its present 10%.

a. Set up the null and alternative hypotheses and the associated managerial actions.

b. Describe the Type I and Type II errors and their associated costs.

Several weeks later their new market share is 10.8%. Assume the number of travelers between Dallas and Chicago was 10,000 for the period under study.

c. At a .05 α level, has Atlantic Airlines significantly increased its market share?

8. The comptroller wants to know how his firm compares with others on the fixed-asset utilization ratio. This ratio is sales divided by net fixed assets, and indicates how effectively a firm is using its fixed assets. If his firm's ratio is low compared to the industry's, he will probably deny funds for new capital equipment in the next planning cycle. The comptroller believes that the industry average fixed-asset ratio is now greater than 3. But he is not sure. He needs to estimate the industry average fixed asset ratio.

a. Set up the null and alternative hypotheses.

The comptroller selects 30 firms at random and, based on the Compustat data base financial reports, obtains the following data.

$$\bar{x} = 3.12 \text{ times}$$

$$s = 1.56 \text{ times}$$

$$n = 30$$

b. Given the data, evaluate the comptroller's claim. Let $\alpha = .01$.

c. Compute the approximate *p*-value for the study.

...

9. A group of recently retired human resource managers are considering opening a consulting group. It would provide human resource services to small firms that do not have their own departments. In a 1993 study of the industry, 15% of small firms had no human resource departments. The group believes that with such a high percentage they can be successful. They wonder if the percentage has recently dropped for, if it has, they may not start their consulting firm.

 a. Set up the null and alternative hypotheses and the associated managerial actions.

 b. Describe the Type I and Type II errors and their associated costs.

 They select a random sample of 200 small firms in the state and find that 28 do not have human resource departments.

 c. Given an α level of .01, should the group reject the null hypothesis? Based solely on the study, should the group go into business? Explain.

 d. Compute the approximate p-value for the study.

10. An economist believes that the proportion of consumers with a favorable attitude toward the economy's growth differs between two regions of the country. Of 1,500 randomly selected adult consumers in the Southeast, 750 believe the economy will improve within the next year. Of 1,500 randomly selected adult consumers in the Northeast, only 500 believe the economy will improve within the next year. Given a significance level of .01, evaluate the economist's claim.

11. For the past several months the proportion of quality-circle ideas that were implemented by senior management has been .65. Recently the Director of Quality has taught the circle members new problem-solving techniques that should increase the proportion of ideas implemented by senior management. Have the new tools raised the proportion of implemented ideas?

 a. Set up the null and alternative hypotheses and the associated managerial actions.

 b. Describe the Type I and Type II errors and their associated costs.

 Of the next 150 ideas developed by the quality circles, senior management implements 110 of them (*Note:* not a random sample).

 c. Given an α level of .10, have the new tools been successful in raising the proportion of implemented ideas above .65? Explain.

 d. Compute the approximate p-value for the study.

12. The St. Louis engineering division manager believes that his staff takes longer to document engineering changes in a product than the Dayton division personnel. If correct, he will determine why Dayton division personnel are faster, and then implement their practices in St. Louis.

 a. Set up the null and alternative hypotheses and the associated managerial actions.

 b. Describe the Type I and Type II errors and their associated costs.

 He randomly selects 50 similar engineering change requests in the two divisions and records the time to document them. Below are the data:

St. Louis	Dayton
$\bar{x} = 6.40$ hours	$\bar{x} = 5.55$ hours
$s = 2.56$ hours	$s = 2.12$ hours
$n = 50$ changes	$n = 50$ changes

 c. At the .01 significance level, evaluate the St. Louis manager's claim. What action should he now take?

13. Over the past year, 95% of the guests at the Hilmark Hotel have indicated that they are satisfied with the hotel service and their stay. The executive director wants to increase the percentage of satisfied guests. Based upon guest feedback surveys, she has increased the number of nonsmoking rooms, reduced the delays at check-in, and offered low-fat entree alternatives in the restaurant. Based on a random sample of 2000 recent guests, 1960 indicated they were satisfied with the hotel service and their stay. Let $\alpha = .05$.

 a. Have her efforts been successful in raising the proportion of satisfied customers above .95?

 b. Compute the approximate p-value for the study.

14. The chamber of commerce knows that over the past two years, conference attenders spent, on average, about $135 per day (excluding hotel room charges). Recently the city and local businesses attempted to make the downtown more attractive to out-of-town visitors by creating pedestrian walkways, outdoor cafes, and "green" areas. Have these additions led to increased spending by conference attenders?

a. Set up the null and alternative hypotheses and the associated managerial actions.

b. Describe the Type I and Type II errors and their associated costs.

After implementing the changes, the chamber randomly selected 250 conference attenders and asked them to record their daily expenditures. Here are the data.

$$\bar{x} = \$178.34$$

$$s = \$156.50$$

$$n = 250$$

c. At a .10 significance level, have the city's efforts to increase daily spending above $135 been successful? Explain.

d. Compute the approximate p-value for the study.

15. Personnel in the operations and research/development groups have always had difficulty talking to each other. A senior manager believes that one reason is that operating-group personnel are detail- and fact-oriented, whereas the research personnel are theory- and "big picture"-oriented. When the two groups get together it sounds like the day workers at the Tower of Babel. The manager believes that the proportion of detail-oriented people in the operating group is higher than in the research group. She gives the Myers-Briggs Type Indicator to a random sample of 50 workers in each group. Sixty-five% of the operations personnel are detail-oriented, but only 45% of the research personnel are detail-oriented. Let $\alpha = .05$. Evaluate the manager's claim.

16. A marketing manager believes that magazine and newspaper coupons are more effective than proof-of-purchase refund offers in stimulating spending on a product. Based on 2 samples of 25 randomly selected customers, the manager obtains the following data on the weekly dollar amount of purchases of a product, using the two sales promotion methods.

Coupons	Refund Offers
$\bar{x} = \$9.45$	$\bar{x} = \$9.14$
$s = \$8.59$	$s = \$8.89$
$n = 25$ customers	$n = 25$ customers

a. Set up the null and alternative hypotheses and the associated managerial actions.

b. Describe the Type I and Type II errors and their associated costs.

c. Let $\alpha = .01$. Evaluate the manager's claim that coupons are more effective than refunds in stimulating spending.

17. Firms such as NameLab Inc. develop and test brand names. For example, NameLab invented the COMPAQ personal computer brand name. Suppose NameLab Inc. has suggested "CLIMTECK" for a new mountain-climbing and day-hiking boot. It claims that over 75% of potential customers will like the new name. The boot manufacturer evaluates the new name. It asks 100 potential customers to react to the "CLIMTECK" brand name. Seventy-five customers report that they like the new name. Let $\alpha = .10$. Evaluate NameLab's claim.

18. In 1988 Arthur Anderson Worldwide Organization announced a five-year, $5 million commitment to assist and encourage the teaching of business ethics in business schools. A researcher wishes to determine the program's impact on the number of hours of ethics training in undergraduate schools of business. He believes that over 20 hours are now devoted to ethics in the undergraduate curriculum. To test his claim, he selects a random sample of 50 accredited business schools and obtains the following data. Let $\alpha = .05$.

$$\bar{x} = 24.5 \text{ hours}$$

$$s = 20.50 \text{ hours}$$

$$n = 50$$

    a. Evaluate the researcher's claim
    b. Compute the approximate p-value for the study.

 19. According to Philip Crosby, an expert in the quality field, an essential ingredient in a total quality-management program is that information about the progress of quality-improvement actions is continually supplied to all employees. COMCEL's Director of Quality believes that the firm has recently improved communications. Historically, the average communication score was 70 on a 0 to 100-point scale instrument. The director randomly selects 100 workers and asks them to rate the internal communications within the firm. Here are the data:

$$\bar{x} = 74.5$$

$$s = 36.5$$

$$n = 100$$

    Let $\alpha = .10$.
    a. Evaluate the director's claim
    b. Compute the approximate p-value for the study.

 20. Little Rock's division manager claims that a greater proportion of her employees believe the policies on quality are clear and unambiguous than do Salt Lake City employees. To assess her claim, she randomly selects 100 employees in both divisions and asks them, "Are the policies on quality clear?" Here are the data.

Little Rock	Salt Lake City
Number of yes responses = 91	Number of yes responses = 82
Sample size = 100	Sample size = 100

    a. Set up the null and alternative hypotheses.
    b. Let $\alpha = .01$. Evaluate the manager's claim.
    c. Compute the approximate p-value for the study.

 21. First Bancorp of Tulsa has been attempting to reduce the amount of time needed to provide mortgage information to its customers. For several years the mean time was 20 minutes. First Bancorp has implemented several programs to reduce the time to under 10 minutes. Have they been successful? Here are the time-ordered data over the most recent 21 customers.

Customer	Time (minutes)	Customer	Time (minutes)	Customer	Time (minutes)
1	8.5	8	8.6	15	8.2
2	8.7	9	7.9	16	8.8
3	9.4	10	9.3	17	7.9
4	9.3	11	8.5	18	8.9
5	8.5	12	8.7	19	9.1
6	8.7	13	8.1	20	8.3
7	8.2	14	9.3	21	8.7

    a. Are the time-ordered process data stationary?
    b. Compute the sample statistics, $\bar{x}$ and s.

   c. Should the null hypothesis on the population mean amount of time be rejected? Let $\alpha = .05$.

   d. Compute the approximate p-value for the sample mean.

 22. An economist believes that a greater proportion of professional employees systematically plan their retirement finances than do blue-collar workers. The economist randomly selects two samples of 500 workers each in the 50–55 age bracket and asks them, "Have you done systematic financial planning for your retirement?" Here are the data:

Professionals	Blue-Collar
$\hat{p} = .17$	$\hat{p} = .09$

Let $\alpha = .05$. Evaluate the economist's claim.

 23. An educational researcher believes that student performance on a common final examination will improve if an instructor uses in-class, small-group exercises. To test his claim, he teaches two sections of statistics. In one section, he uses a straight lecture method. In the other section, he uses small groups. Both classes follow the same course syllabus and take the same common final. Assume that the students in the two classes are random samples. Here are the data on performance on the common final:

Lecture Class	Small-Group Class
$\bar{x} = 75.6$	$\bar{x} = 80.4$
$s = 5.78$	$s = 7.90$
$n = 41$	$n = 45$

   a. Set up the null and alternative hypotheses and the associated managerial actions.

   b. Let $\alpha = .10$. Evaluate the researcher's claim.

   c. Compute the approximate p-value for the study.

 24. Benchmarking is the continuous process of measuring products, processes, and services against the companies recognized as industry leaders. Through benchmarking, firms learn from the best, copy or modify their practices, and then implement these practices. The American Society for Quality Control (ASQC) believes that over 42% of the firms within the electronics industry are doing benchmarking. To test its claim, ASQC conducts a study and obtains the following data:

$$\text{Number of firms doing benchmarking} = 113$$

$$\text{Sample size} = 250$$

Let $\alpha = .05$. Evaluate the ASQC's claim.

 25. An accounting firm wants to compare two CPA training methods. They use a matched-pair design. They select 10 pairs of accountants matched in terms of years of experience and grade-point average in upper-division accounting courses. Each member of each pair is randomly assigned to one of the two training methods—videotape or live classroom lecture. After completing the training, all 20 accountants take a common exam. Here are their scores:

Pair	1	2	3	4	5	6	7	8	9	10
Videotape	75	90	40	80	70	90	87	45	78	94
Live Classroom	84	95	50	85	76	92	92	52	81	100

   a. Based on previous experience, the accounting firm believed that the live classroom was superior to the videotape training. At the $\alpha = .05$ level, evaluate the firm's belief.

b. Look at the ten pairs of scores. Does it appear that matching on experience and GPA was necessary? *Hint:* Look at pair 3's scores versus pair 10's scores. What do these two pairs of scores suggest to you? Was matching appropriate?

c. *Optional:* Assume we did not match on years of experience and grade-point average; instead we ran a one-factor, two-level design. However, we obtained the same data as above for the one-factor, two-level design.

    1. Compute the sample mean score for the live classroom training and the sample mean score for the video training. Now compute the difference in sample means, Live scores – Video scores.

    2. Compute two sample variances—the sample variances for the 10 videotape scores and the 10 live classroom scores.

    3. Use expression (8.1) to compute the pooled variance. Note the size of the pooled variance versus the sample variance of the difference scores for the matched pair design that you computed in part **a.** Which is larger?

    4. Use expression (8.2) to compute the estimated standard error of the difference in two sample means.

    5. Use expression (9.9) to determine the critical value for the one-factor, two-level study. Given the difference in sample means, can we conclude that live instruction is superior at the $\alpha = .05$ level of significance? Compare this answer to the answer in part **a.**

APPENDIX A: Relationship Between Type I and Type II Errors

Figure 9.10a (upper curve) shows the sampling distribution of the mean for the Milemaster study when the null hypothesis is true–that is, when the population mean is 47,000 miles or less. The α level is .01. Figure 9.10b (lower curve) shows one of many possible sampling distributions when the alternative hypothesis is true and the population mean is greater than 47,000 miles. We have assumed the population mean is 47,300 miles, and thus we have shifted the lower curve to the right, centered at 47,300 miles.

Suppose the population mean is really 47,300 miles but the sample mean is less than 47,233 miles. According to the upper curve, we should fail to reject the null hypothesis. But the null hypothesis is false–the population mean is really 47,300 miles. The shaded area in the lower curve represents the chance of making a Type II error if the population mean is 47,300 miles.

Now suppose we increase the probability of making a Type I error. This will shift the critical value in the upper curve to the left. This will also reduce the shaded area in the lower curve. Thus the chance of making a Type II error becomes smaller. Figure 9.11 shows the chance of making a Type II error for an α level of .10.

This is the logic. As we increase the rejection region in the upper curve (Figure 9.11), we increase the chance of rejecting the null hypothesis. However, the only way to make a Type II error is *not* to reject the hypothesis. Thus, by increasing the chance of rejecting the null hypothesis, we reduce the probability of making a Type II error.

Alternatively, as we increase the chance of making a Type I error, the critical value drops from 47,233 miles to 47,128 miles. The critical value shifts to the left. This reduces the fail-to-reject region in the upper curve (Figure 9.11), thereby reducing the probability of making a Type II error.

FIGURE 9.10   Type II Error for $\alpha = .01$

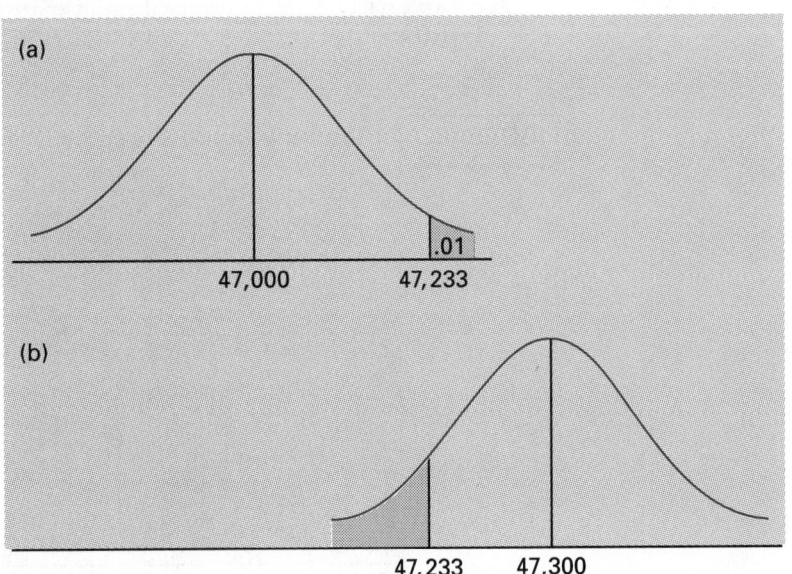

FIGURE 9.11   Type II Error for $\alpha = .10$

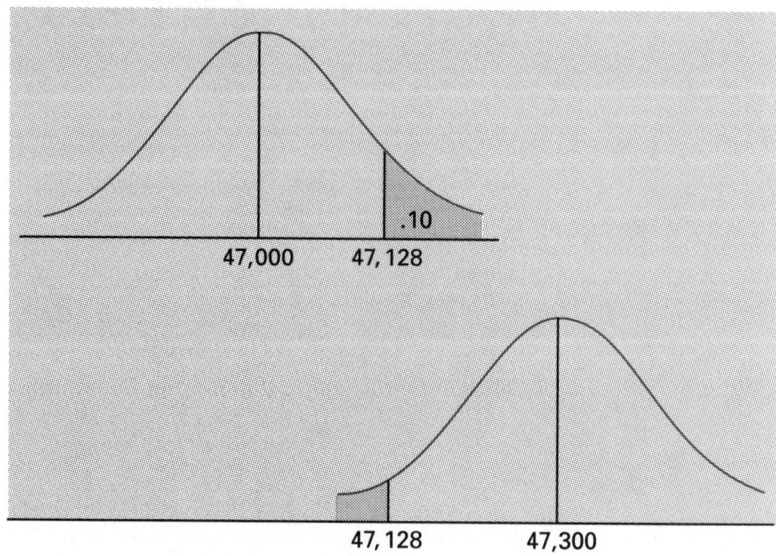

We can also reduce the chance of making a Type II error by increasing the sample size. Figure 9.12 shows the sampling distribution for the Milemaster study when the null hypothesis is true for samples of size 1,000 and 5,000 tires. The rejection region has an area of .01 for both sampling distributions. However, the sampling distribution for samples of 5,000 tires has the smaller estimated standard error. Thus its critical value will be less than the sampling distribution for samples of 1,000.

Now assume that the population mean is still 47,300 miles. By shifting the critical value in the $n = 5,000$ curve to the left, we decrease the probability of making a Type II error.

In summary:

1. Increasing the probability of making a Type I error reduces the probability of making a Type II error.
2. For a constant α level, increasing the sample size reduces the probability of making a Type II error.

FIGURE 9.12   Impact of a Sample Size on the Type II Error

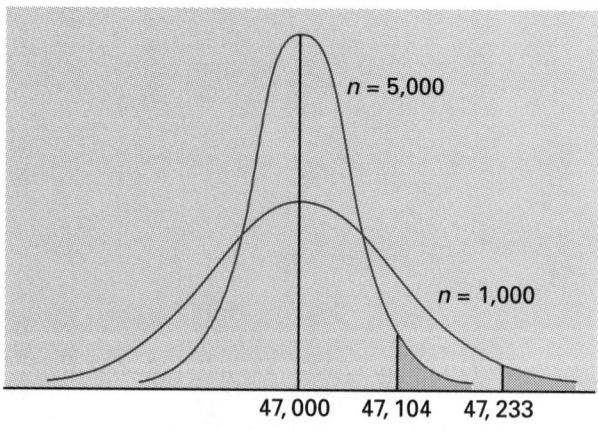

APPENDIX B: Statistical Software

Example 1: This example shows how to use MINITAB, Release 8, to perform a test of hypothesis. The data are the breaking strengths in pounds per square inch (ppsi). Table 9.2 contains the data. The process mean target strength for a telephone handset is 4,750 ppsi. A test of significance is performed to determine whether the process mean has changed from 4,750 ppsi.

Input

```
     MTB  > SET C1
     DATA > 4744 4728 4738 4797 4744 4779 4790 4750 4759
     DATA > 4710 4723 4749 4789 4780 4725 4732 4747 4745 4738 4705
     DATA > 4724 4734 4773 4763 4753 4746 4761 4730 4735 4761
     DATA > END
01   MTB  > TTEST 4750 C1
```

Explanation of Input

01   TTEST is the MINITAB command used to perform a test of hypothesis for a single population mean. The only number that must be specified to perform a two-tailed test is the hypothesized mean of 4750. To perform a one-tailed test, the SUBCommand, ALTERNATIVE=K, must be typed, where K is -1 for a "less than" alternative and $K=+1$ for a "greater than" alternative.

Output

```
01      TEST OF MU = 4750.000 VS MU N.E. 4750.000
```

		N	MEAN	STDEV	SE MEAN	T	P VALUE
02	C1	30	4748.400	23.326	4.259	-0.38	0.71

Interpretation of Output

01   MINITAB states the null and alternative hypotheses tested.

02   MINITAB computes the p-value, rather than determining the critical value. The program calculates the exact p-value associated with the sample mean. Using the methods described in the text, we concluded that $.60 < p < .80.$, whereas the exact two-tailed p-value is .71. This is the smallest significance level for which the null hypothesis can be rejected. In other words, if the null hypothesis were rejected, there is a .71 probability of making a Type I error.

Example 2: This example shows how to use the TTEST command to perform a test for paired comparisons. The data are the number of solutions generated by matched pairs of supervisors using Brainstorming or Analogy. (See Table 9.3.)

Input

```
01    MTB > READ C2 C3
      DATA> 50 46
      DATA> 40 27
      DATA> 60 50
      DATA> 35 28
      DATA> 56 49
      DATA> 20 11
      DATA> 90 79
      DATA> 70 71
      DATA> 60 45
      DATA> 45 31
      DATA> END
02    MTB > LET C4=C2-C3
03    MTB > TTEST 0 C4
```

Explanation of Input

01   The READ command tells MINITAB that data for more than one variable will be entered, or that the data will be entered by rows. Two variables will be entered, C2 in column 2 and C3 in column 3.

02   This line instructs MINITAB to perform row-by-row subtraction of the elements of C3 from C2 and put the difference in column C4.

03   The null hypothesis tested is that the mean difference is 0 for the data in C4.

Output

```
      TEST OF MU = 0.000 VS MU N.E. 0.000

                 N      MEAN    STDEV   SE MEAN      T    P VALUE
01    C4        10     8.900    4.886    1.545     5.76    0.0003
```

Explanation of Output

01   The p-value indicates that the null hypothesis can be rejected for any significance level greater than $\alpha = .0003$.

ANALYSIS OF VARIANCE

10.1 The role of experimentation in problem
    solving
    Problem definition
    Problem diagnosis and solving
10.2 Exploratory data analysis
    Null and alternative hypotheses
    Spread charts
    Guidelines for interpreting spread charts
10.3 Analysis of variance for a one-factor, k-level
    study
    Total sum of squares and its components
    Degrees of freedom
    Hypothesis testing and the analysis of
    variance
10.4 Testing for significant differences between
    pairs of population means
    The problem of multiple comparisons
    Tukey HSD confidence intervals
    How Tukey HSD confidence intervals
    provide 95% or 99% experimentwise level
    of confidence

10.5 The Kruskal–Wallis nonparametric analysis of
    variance
    Statistical hypotheses
    Logic behind the test
    Kruskal–Wallis test statistic
    Dunn's multiple comparisons
    Construction and interpretation of Dunn's
    multiple comparisons
10.6 The two-factor, completely random factorial
    study
    Designing a factorial study
    Exploratory data analysis: graphing profiles
    Total sum of squares
    Sum of squares within
    Degrees of freedom
    Hypotheses
10.7 Key ideas and overview
Appendix: Statistical Software

 **INTEROFFICE COMMUNICATION**

Date: November 15, 1994
To: Bill Katz, Production Testing
From: Sarah Teman, Manager of Operations
Re: Problem at Apex Plastics and Metals

Our Apex Plastics and Metals Inc. subsidiary is experiencing an excessive number of defects in its desk drawers. Over the last several years, Apex has been able to hold the percentage of defective cracked drawers to just 1%. Yesterday, the defect rate jumped to 6%, and they can't figure out why.

This has top priority as Apex has shut down its main production line. Please provide daily status reports.

10.1 ≡ The Role of Experimentation in Problem Solving

Planned change studies or experiments are essential to determining root causes of disturbance problems. A disturbance problem is a sudden and significant deviation from historical or planned performance levels, such as a sudden increase in rejects or a major drop in service levels. Faced with a disturbance problem, the manager must be able to:

1. separate the symptoms from the facts—problem definition;
2. identify potential root causes—problem diagnosis; and
3. determine which are the true root causes—problem solving.

The first activity uncovers what happened. The last two activities seek to reveal why the problem happened.

The following example illustrates the role of experimentation in determining root causes.

Example: The Case of the Cracked Typing Table Drawers   Apex Plastics and Metals, a COMCEL subsidiary, makes the housing for COMCEL's mobile phones. Apex also produces three sizes of drawers or compartments for typing tables sold by Contemporary Office Furniture, Inc. Model A is a 4-inch-deep drawer, model B is a 7-inch-deep drawer, and model C is a 10-inch-deep drawer.

There are three steps in manufacturing drawers. At blanking, workers cut the raw material to the approximate drawer size. Next, workers use stamping presses that bend the blanked metal to form the drawer. Stamping press 3 makes the 4-inch drawer, presses 1 and 4 make the 7-inch drawer, and press 2 makes the 10-inch drawer. Finally, workers inspect for cracks and other damage. Defect-free drawers are then packaged for shipment to Contemporary. During stamping, cracking sometimes occurs at the lower corners of the drawer where the metal undergoes the maximum deformation and therefore stress. Over the past several years, the reject rate due to cracking has been about 1%.

At 8:00 A.M. on Tuesday, stamping press 2 started producing about 6% cracks. The line supervisor had Engineering check the press, but no problems were found. After the morning break (10:00 A.M.), stamping press 1 started producing about 4% rejects. Finally at 11:00 A.M., stamping press 4 started producing about 4% rejects. At noon, only stamping press 3 was still producing 1% rejects.

Apex has a severe disturbance problem. Why have there been fourfold and sixfold increases in reject rates on three of the four stamping presses? What is going on?

Before we can take corrective action we must understand the disturbance problem. The Kepner–Tregoe method is an effective tool for understanding disturbance problems.*

Problem Definition

The Kepner–Tregoe method (1988) transforms ambiguous symptoms, facts, and assumptions into a clear statement of the disturbance problem. To define the problem, start by asking and answering the following questions:

What is the deviation (vs. what isn't it)?

When did the deviation occur (vs. when didn't it occur)?

---

* We present several other diagnostic tools including the Pareto chart and Ishikawa method in Chapter 15.

Where did the deviation occur (vs. where didn't it occur)?

How much, how many, and to what extent did the deviation occur (vs. to what extent didn't it occur)?

Reject vague phrases. "Something is wrong" is an unacceptable answer to a "what is" question. Also avoid useless adjectives such as "We have *a lot of* defects." Be specific. Be precise. If the information is vague or imprecise, we need to do more detective work before entering the data into a problem definition worksheet, such as that in Table 10.1.

Table 10.1

Problem Definition for the Cracked Typing Table Drawer Problem

	The Deviation Is	The Deviation Is Not
WHAT	4%–6% cracks on 7″ and 10″ drawers	Excessive scratches Bent drawers 4%–6% for 4″ drawers
WHEN	8:00 A.M. on press 2 10:00 A.M. on press 1 11:00 A.M. on press 4	No problems on press 3 On press 2 before 8:00 A.M. On press 1 before 10:00 A.M. On press 4 before 11:00 A.M.
WHERE	Presses 1, 2, 4 Lower four corners of drawers	Press 3 Cracks randomly distributed at blanking operation
EXTENT	Press 2: 6% Presses 1, 4: 4%	Press 3: normal 1%

Problem Diagnosis and Solving

Diagnosing a problem begins with developing *problem-solving hypotheses*. A problem-solving hypothesis is a tentative statement of the cause of a problem that can be disproved. It is an informed guess that has a reasonable chance of being correct. It is an unproved assumption, a plan of attack. It is an alternative route to the solution.

We recommend the following problem diagnosis guidelines and demonstrate their application to the Apex drawer problem.

RULE 1:   Generate many problem-solving hypotheses.

Yesterday, 1% of Apex's typing table drawers had cracks. Today three presses are producing 4%–6% rejects. Something must have changed recently to cause the sudden increase in rejects.

The more hypotheses we generate, the more likely we are to solve the problem, because hypotheses point out directions in which to seek data to identify the real causes. Ultimately, we must select one or two hypotheses for serious analysis.

Think in terms of the following root cause areas: (1) *changes* in workers' or supervisors' motivations, likes/dislikes, etc., (2) *changes* in technology, processes, raw materials, or methods, and (3) *changes* in organizational structures or the external environment.

Table 10.2

Possible Root Causes

Root Cause Areas	Recent Change at Apex
People	Yesterday the company disciplined a worker who failed a random drug test. Perhaps a drug problem is the root cause.
Technology or methods	Today, Apex switched to a new raw material supplier. The new raw material is less costly. Perhaps the raw material is the root cause.
Organization or environment	Because of a drop in market share, Apex has recently laid off workers. Those still employed know that there will be more layoffs. Perhaps excessive worker stress is the root cause.

Apply this threefold strategy to Apex's problem. Table 10.2 presents a breakdown of possible root cause areas, along with possible explanations.

RULE 2:   Suspend judgment about the hypotheses until most of the facts are in. Keep an open mind.

Keeping an open mind is difficult. Many managers jump to conclusions about the root causes of a problem. A manager who had a recent problem with workers might jump to the conclusion that workers' stress or sabotage caused the cracked drawers. A manager who recently had a problem with raw material might jump to the conclusion that the raw material caused the cracked drawers. We must suspend judgment until we have collected Kepner–Tregoe problem definition data and have looked at all changes.

RULE 3:   If possible, rigorously test hypotheses.

Testing runs the gamut from casual observation to formal studies or experiments. Casual observation is the weakest form of testing. Managers use casual observation when they say, "If event A and event B occur together frequently, then A is the cause of B." All of us use this form of "testing," but it is inconclusive. For example, alcoholics often have cirrhosis of the liver. Thus, we might conclude that excessive alcohol causes cirrhosis, but it does not. Rather, certain vitamin deficiencies cause cirrhosis. The problem is that alcoholics do not eat well-balanced meals. Casual observation is useful in generating problem-solving hypotheses, not *testing* them.

Sometimes all we can use is casual observation. How else could we test the sabotage or stress hypotheses? We could make observation more rigorous by generating other possible root causes. Then, *compare and contrast* the root causes and determine which one better explains the known facts.

Conducting formal planned change studies is the best way to test problem-solving hypotheses. Suppose that, based on the Kepner–Tregoe analysis, the plant manager believed that there were two root causes of excessive cracked drawers—(1) the new material and (2) the drawer depth. The drawer depth could be a cause since the excessive cracking did not occur on the 4-inch-deep drawers, but did occur on the deeper 7- and 10-inch drawers. The manager could then run a two-factor planned change study. The factors would be material supplier and drawer depth. The raw material factor has two levels—old and new material supplier. The drawer depth factor has three levels—4-inch, 7-inch, and 10-inch drawer depth. In Section 10.6 we will analyze the results of a two-factor study to determine the root causes of the excessive cracking of desk drawers.

Experimentation also plays an important role in evaluating potential management improvements in product, service, performance, or quality. For example, a manager believes that training in creativity or training in team building can reduce unit labor costs. The manager should run a planned change study and test three training variations—creativity training, team-building training, and no training (control groups). In Section 10.3 we will analyze the results of a one-factor, three-level unit labor cost-reduction study.

In summary, experimentation plays a crucial role in evaluating possible root causes to disturbance problems, and improving performance. In this chapter we will learn how to analyze experimental data. However, if we improperly design our studies, no analysis in the world can correct them. Please review the experimental design principles and terminology in Chapter 6.

SECTION 10.1 EXERCISES

1. According to Kepner and Tregoe, "A problem is a deviation from planned or expected performance," and "A problem is always caused by a change."
    a. What was the expected reject rate due to cracking at Apex Plastics and Metals?
    b. What was the problem?
    c. List some possible changes that may have occurred to produce the deviation.

2. Why is it as important to know where the problem does not exist as where it does exist? Refer to Table 10.1 in answering the question.

3. Refer to the Apex Plastics example again. Suppose we learned that only press 4 started using raw material from a new vendor. Press 2, which makes 10-inch drawers, is still using the old material. How should we respond to someone who quickly concludes, "We made a mistake in changing vendors. The new vendor's material is defective."

4. What is the connection between managerial problem solving and design of experiments?

5. Why is it important to seek changes to explain a disturbance problem?

6. In the Kepner–Tregoe method we must not use vague phrases, such as "It is not working right," in defining a problem. Explain.

10.2 ≡ Exploratory Data Analysis

A central theme of this book is to use graphical tools to explore the data before analyzing them. Previously we have used stem-and-leaf displays and box plots for cross-sectional data. Here we introduce the *spread chart* as a graphical tool. By the end of this section you should be able to:

1. develop null and alternative hypotheses;
2. draw spread charts for a one-factor, k-level experimental data set;
3. visually determine if you are *likely* to reject (or fail to reject) the null hypothesis of no difference among the k-levels; and
4. explain when you are likely to reject (or fail to reject) the null hypothesis using the concept of spread both within and between levels.

Null and Alternative Hypotheses

From Section 9.2, we know that a statistical hypothesis is a testable claim or statement about one or more population parameters. The null hypothesis is a statement of "no difference," "no change," "no improvement," or "I don't believe you." We also define a second hypothesis—alternative hypothesis—that we hope or suspect is true.

Table 10.3

Null and Alternative Hypotheses for Cost-Reduction Study

Hypotheses	Action
H_0 The unknown population mean unit labor cost reductions are the same for the three treatment levels. $$\mu_{TB} = \mu_{CR} = \mu_{CG}$$	Failure to reject the null hypothesis means that creativity or team building is no more effective than no training. Do not implement either team building or creativity training throughout the plant.
H_1 The unknown population mean unit labor cost reductions are not the same for the three levels. Not all μ the same	One (or more) workshop reduces unit labor cost more than the others. Determine which workshop is best and implement it throughout the plant.

We should also state what actions we will take if we reject the null hypothesis and what we will do if we fail to reject it.

Table 10.3 presents the null and alternative hypotheses for the unit labor cost-reduction study mentioned in the previous section. The *no difference* null hypothesis states that the *population* unit labor cost reductions *are the same* for the three workshops—creativity training, team-building training, and no training (control groups). Because the null and alternative hypotheses are mutually exclusive and exhaustive, the alternative hypothesis is the population unit labor cost reductions *are not all the same* for the three workshops.

Table 10.4 shows two possible data sets, as a result of the cost-reduction study. When we complete our statistical analysis, we will reject the null hypothesis for one of the data sets. After drawing spread charts we will be able to make an educated guess as to which data set will cause rejection of the null hypothesis.

The hypothetical data sets have some similarities and some differences. Both data sets have the same sample means. However, note that the spread in the values within each workshop, or treatment, level in data set 1 is much less than in data set 2.

Table 10.4

Two Sets of Hypothetical Data for Reduction in Unit Labor Costs

	Data Set 1 Workshop			Data Set 2 Workshop		
	Team-Building	Creativity	Control	Team-Building	Creativity	Control
	$3.05	$4.12	$.15	$-1.81	$8.23	$.10
	3.10	4.13	.07	10.19	-1.77	-3.90
	3.13	4.21	.30	9.19	7.23	10.10
	3.14	4.21	.05	.19	.23	-7.90
	3.18	4.22	.15	11.19	9.23	-1.90
	3.22	4.24	.02	-2.81	-2.77	.10
	3.22	4.26	.08	2.19	.23	7.10
	3.24	4.27	.03	.19	13.23	-7.90
	3.29	4.27	.05	3.19	.23	.10
	3.32	4.36	.10	.19	8.23	5.10
$\bar{x}$	$3.189	$4.229	$.10	$\bar{x}$ $3.189	$4.229	$.10

Spread Charts

We begin a visual exploration of the data by translating each column of numbers into a spread chart. We do this in the following way:

1. Draw a horizontal line and scale it in the units of the dependent variable. In this case, the dependent variable is the dollar reduction in unit labor costs.
2. Place a "1" above the horizontal line for each observation of the first treatment level—TB workshop. The actual height above the line is not important. Place a "2" above the horizontal line for each observation of the second treatment level and a "3" above the horizontal line for each observation of the third treatment level.
3. Place a labelled "$\bar{x}$" symbol at each of the three sample mean values, in this case, $\bar{x}_{TB}$, at \$3.189, $\bar{x}_{CR}$ at \$4.229, and $\bar{x}_{CG}$ at \$.10 for data set 1.

From Figure 10.1, we see that the data values for each workshop for data set 1 cluster together. There is very little spread in the data values within a treatment level. Also, the three sample means are quite different. What are the small spread of values within each treatment level and the large spread *between* sample means trying to tell us?

The large spread between sample means suggests that the dollar reductions in unit labor costs for the three types of training may be different. The small spread within each treatment level suggests that the data are *unchanging*. Even if we ran each treatment level 10 more times, the three sample means would not change very much from the present values. Thus the sample means in data set 1 will tend to maintain their rank order—lowest reduction for control groups, highest reduction for the creative methods workshop. Thus we will *probably* conclude that all population mean unit labor cost reductions are not the same at the three treatment levels. Remember that we are making inferences from this one study to the population. Statistically speaking, we will reject the null hypothesis for data set 1.

For data set 2, note the large spread among the data values within each treatment level. Suppose we ran each treatment level 10 more times and recomputed the

---

FIGURE 10.1   Spread Charts for Unit Labor Cost Study

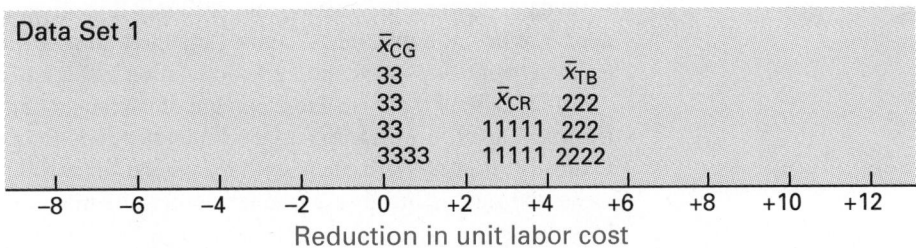

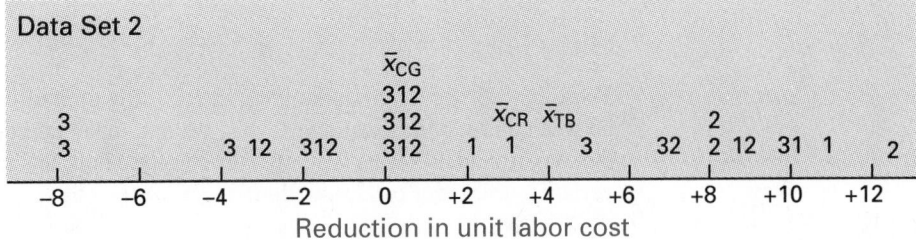

three sample means. Would we expect them to be very close to the present values of $3.19, $4.23, and $.10? It is quite likely that the next 10 numbers within each level would be very different from the first 10 numbers. The three sample means could dramatically change. Thus, we cannot be sure whether the differences among the three sample means indicate real differences in the population mean unit labor cost reductions. We will probably conclude that the type of workshop has no impact on reducing unit labor costs. Statistically speaking, we cannot reject the null hypothesis for data set 2.

We use a spread chart or box plot and plot the data before beginning formal analysis; that is, to get a feel for the data. Remember, however, that charting is not a substitute for a formal statistical analysis.

Table 10.5 contains two additional data sets. For which data set are we likely to reject a null hypothesis of no difference among population means? Again, we draw the spread charts.

Table 10.5

Two Data Sets for Spread Charting

	Data Set 3 Type of Training Workshop				Data Set 4 Type of Sales Display		
	1	2	3		1	2	3
	$.50	$.60	$.70		$180	$218	$210
	.52	.58	.69		200	178	215
	.50	.62	.71		200	200	170
	.48	.60	.70		220	196	213
$\bar{x}$	$.50	$.60	$.70	$\bar{x}$	$200	$198	$202

Dependent variable: unit labor cost reduction in dollars

Dependent variable: daily sales volume in dollars

The spread charts in Figure 10.2 suggest that we would probably reject the null hypothesis for data set 3. Note that the spread in the unit labor cost data values *within* each treatment level is very small. The data are unchanging. Even if we collected more data, the sample means would probably remain quite constant. Moreover, there appear to be large differences among the three sample means. This suggests that not all three workshops have the same population mean unit labor cost reduction.

In data set 4 there is a large amount of spread among the data values *within* each treatment level. If we continued the study, the three sample means could change dramatically. Furthermore, there is little spread *among* the three sample means. The closer the sample means are to one another, the more difficult it is to reject the null hypothesis.

Guidelines for Interpreting Spread Charts

Table 10.6 presents guidelines for interpreting spread charts. Based on the spread between and within treatment levels, we can make an educated guess as to whether the experimental factor, type of training workshop, has an impact on the dependent variable, unit labor cost reduction.

FIGURE 10.2   Additional Spread Charts

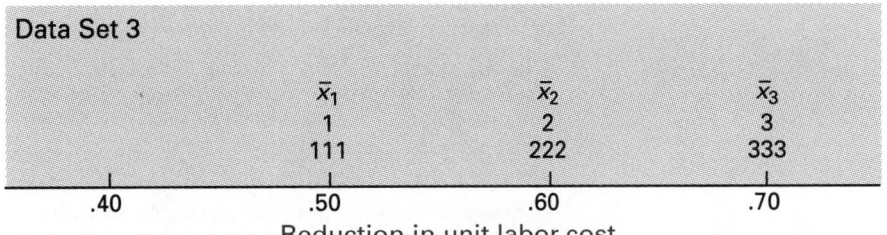

Data Set 3

Reduction in unit labor cost

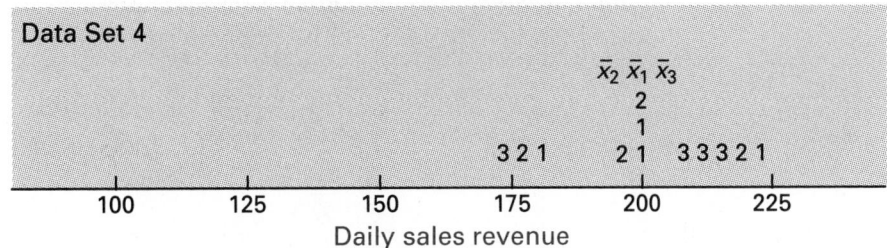

Data Set 4

Daily sales revenue

Data sets 1 and 3 illustrate the third guideline. There is little spread within each level and much spread among the three sample means. Data set 2 illustrates the fourth possibility. There is much spread both within and among the three treatment levels. Data set 4 typifies the second situation. There is much spread within each treatment level and little spread among the three sample means.

In summary, spread charting will provide a feel for the data. As an alternative, you may also construct multiple stem-and-leaf displays or box plots (see Section 3.3) to explore the data. However, graphical data exploration is not a substitute for a formal statistical analysis. We still need to quantify the terms *little* and *much spread,* which is our next topic.

Table 10.6

Guidelines for Interpreting Spread Charts

When the spread between sample means is	and the spread within the levels is	then:
1. small	small	it is hard to tell if the factor has an impact.
2. small	large	the factor probably has no impact; do not reject the null hypothesis.
3. large	small	the factor probably has an impact; reject the null hypothesis.
4. large	large	it is hard to tell if the factor has an impact.

SECTION 10.2 EXERCISES

1. A grocery chain wants to test the appeal of three different sales promotion strategies—contest, free sample, and point-of-purchase display—on soft drink sales. Set up the null and alternative hypotheses and the accompanying managerial actions.

2. A faculty member wishes to evaluate four teaching methods to determine which one is best for teaching an introductory accounting course. The four methods are (1) lecture, (2) lecture/recitation, (3) case, and (4) business game simulation. Set up the null and alternative hypotheses and accompanying faculty actions.

3. COMCEL wants to determine which of three injection molding temperatures—500°, 550°, or 600° Celsius—produces the fewest scratches on phone handsets. Set up the null and alternative hypotheses and the accompanying managerial actions.

4. A grocery chain wants to test the appeal of three different sales promotions on soft drink sales. It selects three different stores in similar neighborhoods and randomly assigns one of the promotions to each store. Sales (in tens of bottles) are recorded over a period of five days.

	Type of Sales Promotion		
Day	Contest	Free Sample	Point-of-Purchase Display
1	8	12	16
2	8	15	18
3	9	11	18
4	10	13	19
5	10	12	20

a. Plot a spread chart for this experiment.
b. Does it appear that the three displays will produce the same population mean sales? Explain your answer in terms of the relationship of the spread between to the spread within.
c. If your graph suggests that one display is better than the others, which appears to be the best at producing sales?

5. Develop a box plot for each of the three sales promotion approaches in Exercise 4. Does it appear that the three displays will produce the same median sales over the long run? Use the three interquartile ranges to represent the spreads within the types of sales promotion and the difference in the three medians to approximate the spread between.

6. COMCEL managers believe that all employees need to learn problem-solving skills. It experiments with three different methods of teaching these skills. Five employees are randomly assigned to each method. After a specified period of instruction, each person is presented with the same set of problems. The employees' scores (coded) are shown below. Higher scores indicate greater problem-solving ability.

Teaching Method		
Lecture	Case	Role Playing
14	15	21
14	17	20
16	19	21
15	17	22
19	17	22

a. Plot a spread chart for this experiment.
b. Does it appear that any of the methods is more or less effective than the others in teaching problem solving? Explain your answer in terms of the relationship of the spread between to the spread within.
c. Does the spread chart suggest which method would produce the highest population mean problem-solving score? Explain.

7. A telephone market research company has experienced a substantial rate of nonresponse on a question that is asked routinely. It experiments with three different forms of the question to try to improve response rates. The research firm records the nonresponse rates (in percent) for a five-day period. Below are the results.

Question Format

Day	Open-Ended	Closed-Ended	Partially Closed-Ended
1	14	15	15
2	14	17	19
3	15	19	21
4	19	20	22
5	22	23	25

a. Plot a spread chart for this experiment.
b. Does it appear that any of the question formats is best at reducing the population non-response rates?

8. The Hi-Stereo chain selects 15 customers who recently purchased a compact disk player. They are asked to rate the sound quality of three brands of speakers (one customer to a brand of speakers) on a scale from 0 (poor) to 100 (outstanding). Below are the results.

Brand of Speakers

Polk	Fisher	Pioneer
95	95	90
55	95	50
75	85	85
60	70	95
90	75	85

a. Compute the three sample means and construct a spread chart.
b. Does it appear that Hi-Stereo will be able to reject the "no difference in sound quality" null hypothesis? Explain your answer in terms of spread within and spread between.

9. Below are data from a planned change study conducted by COMCEL. The dependent variable is the number of scratches (only seen under magnification) on a phone handset after injection molding.

Injection Molding Temperature (Celsius)

500°	550°	600°
5	2	6
4	0	7
6	1	8
7	1	6
5	0	8
6	1	7
7	0	8

a. Compute the three sample means and construct a spread chart.
b. Does it appear that COMCEL will be able to reject the "no difference in the number of scratches" null hypothesis? Explain your answer in terms of spread within and spread between.

10. Explain why we had to use the word *appear* in Exercises 4 and 6–9.

11. Construct a data set for a one-factor, four-level study that would cause us to conclude that there is probably no difference among the four treatment levels. Defend.

12. Construct a data set for a one-factor, four-level study that would cause us to conclude that there is probably a difference among the four treatment levels. Defend.

13. Construct a data set for a one-factor, four-level study that would make it difficult to tell if there is a difference among the four treatment levels. Defend.

10.3 Analysis of Variance for a One-Factor, k-Level Study

The one-factor, k-level study is an important experimental design. The manager varies one factor or treatment and determines its impact on the dependent variable. The manager will implement the treatment permanently if it improves performance.

To determine if performance has improved, we conduct an analysis of variance (ANOVA). The analysis of variance compares two variances to determine whether k population means are the same. The ANOVA is an extension of material covered in Section 8.6. By the end of this section you should be able to:

1. explain why there are only two sources of variation that account for the total sum of squares in a one-factor, completely randomized study;
2. see the connection between the variance-within and variance-between terms and the spread charts;
3. explain the computation for the sums of squares;
4. explain why degrees of freedom equal the relevant sample size minus 1;
5. solve and interpret analysis of variance problems using statistical software; and
6. explain the use of the F-table in testing hypotheses.

To illustrate an ANOVA, we will analyze the cost-reduction data for data set 1 in Table 10.4. The spread chart for these data in Figure 10.1 suggested that we would reject the null hypothesis of no differences among population mean unit labor-cost reductions. Before beginning the analysis, we restate the null and alternative hypotheses. We also present the assumptions underlying the analysis.

H_0:   The population mean unit labor cost reductions for the three treatment levels are the same. The experimental factor, type of workshop, has no effect on the population means.

$$\mu_{TB} = \mu_{CR} = \mu_{CG}$$

H_1:   The population means for the three workshops are not the same. At least one treatment level produces a different population mean unit labor cost reduction.

Not all μ the same

ASSUMPTION 1:   The observations within each of the three treatment levels are independent random samples.

ASSUMPTION 2:   The observations within each of the three treatment levels are near-normally distributed.

ASSUMPTION 3:   The variances within each of the treatment levels are the same or nearly so.

The first assumption is true because we ran a one-factor, completely randomized study. We randomly selected the 30 teams from the population. We randomly divided the 30 teams into three groups of 10 teams each. We randomly assigned each group of 10 teams to a workshop (or no workshop in the case of control groups). The stem-and-leaf displays in Figure 10.3 indicate that assumptions 2 and 3 are reasonable for the creativity and team-building workshops. However, the data for the control group may not be normal.

If either of the last two assumptions is seriously in question, consider transforming the raw data by a square root or log base 10 transformation. Alternatively, use the Kruskal–Wallis nonparametric test (Section 10.5). Serious doubts about these assumptions occur when:

1. outliers exist at one or more treatment levels; or
2. the largest range within a treatment level is more than five times the smallest range within a treatment level.

Applying Tukey's rule to the unit labor-cost-reduction data, there are no outliers in any workshop, including the control group. The data ranges for the three treatment levels are:

Team-building training	$3.32 − $3.05 = $.27
Creativity training	$4.36 − $4.12 = $.24
Control groups	$.30 − $.02 = $.28

FIGURE 10.3   Stem-and-Leaf Displays

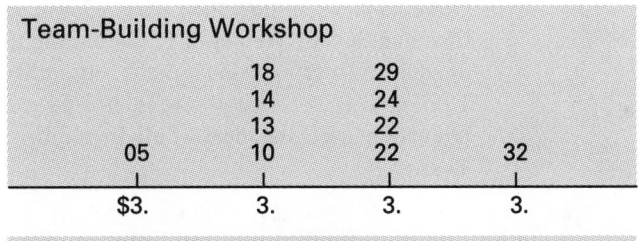

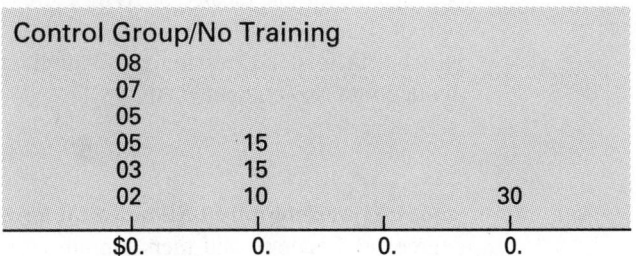

$$\frac{\text{Largest range}}{\text{Smallest range}} = \frac{.28}{.24} = 1.17$$

Therefore, we have no reason to doubt the validity of assumptions 2 and 3. We may continue the formal statistical analysis.

With spread charts, we compared the spread between the sample means to the spread within the treatment levels. If the former is much larger than the latter, we probably will reject the null hypothesis. In the formal analysis of variance we compute a ratio of two variances—the *variance between* the sample means divided by the *variance within* the treatment levels. The larger the ratio, the more likely we are to reject the null hypothesis.

Expression (10.1) is the equation for the variance. The numerator is called the sum of squares (SS) and the denominator is called the degrees of freedom (df). Because we divide the sum of squares by the denominator, the variance is also known as the *mean square (MS)*. It is close to the average sum of squares.

$$s^2 = \frac{\sum_i (x_i - \bar{x})^2}{n - 1} \qquad (10.1)$$

The sum of squares always equals the sum of the squared differences between the *relevant* observations and their mean. The degrees of freedom equal the *relevant* sample size minus 1. We will soon explain the term *relevant*.

Total Sum of Squares and Its Components

The total sum of squares (SST) is the sum of the squared differences between each observation and the overall mean, the mean of all the observations.

Our goal is to compute the variance between treatment levels and the variance within treatment levels. We begin by computing the **total sum of squares**. The total sum of squares determines how much variability there is in the 30 data values of data set 1 in Table 10.4. Since we are interested in the sum of squares of all 30 numbers, the relevant mean is the mean of all 30 numbers or the overall mean, which equals 2.506. Thus,

$$SST = (3.05 - 2.506)^2 + (3.10 - 2.506)^2 + \cdots$$
$$+ (.05 - + (.10 - 2.506)^2$$
$$= 92.41 \text{ units of variability}$$

What accounts for the 92.41 units of variability? Why aren't all the 30 data values the same? Or, why isn't SST equal to zero? In a one-factor, completely randomized study there are two sources that account for the total sum of squares. Variability is due either to the factor we varied (the experimental factor) or to all other possible factors that we might have varied but chose not to. The sum of squares between the sample means (SSB) measures the impact of the experimental factor. The sum of squares within the treatment levels (SSW) measures the impact of all other possible factors. Expression (10.2) indicates that the total sum of squares can be divided into two components:

$$SST = SSB + SSW \qquad (10.2)$$

Next we determine SSB and SSW, divide each component by its corresponding degrees of freedom, and then compute a ratio of the two variances to test the null hypothesis.

The sum of squares within the treatment levels (SSW) is the sum of the squared differences between each observation within a treatment and the mean for that treatment, or column, summed over all the treatment levels.

First, consider the **sum of squares within treatment levels (SSW)**. How should we compute it? Why aren't the 10 data values for the team-building workshop (in Table 10.4, data set 1) the same? Since all 10 teams received the team-building training, any variation must be due to the impact of all other factors except type of training workshop. Table 10.7 shows the calculations for computing SSW. Note that the SSW term consists of three terms in this study, one for each level.

Table 10.7

Computation of SSW for Unit Labor Cost Study

Team-Building Workshop	Creativity Workshop	Control Groups
$(3.05 - 3.189)^2$	$(4.12 - 4.229)^2$	$(.15 - .10)^2$
$(3.10 - 3.189)^2$	$(4.13 - 4.229)^2$	$(.07 - .10)^2$
⋮	⋮	⋮
$(3.32 - 3.189)^2$	$(4.36 - 4.229)^2$	$(.10 - .10)^2$
$SS_1 = .065$	$SS_2 = .044$	$SS_3 = .063$

$$SSW = .065 + .044 + .063 = .17 \text{ unit of variability}$$

The sum of squares between sample means (SSB) is the sum of the squared differences between each sample mean and the overall mean, each weighted by the treatment sample size.

The sum of squares within (SSW) accounts for .17 of the 92.41 units of the total sum of squares. Since there are only two sources of variation for a one-factor study, the **sum of squares between sample means (SSB)** must equal $92.41 - .17 = 92.24$. There is a more informative way to calculate SSB, which we will consider next.

The three sample means best represent the mean reductions in unit labor cost for the three treatment levels. These become the relevant observations in the sum of squares between calculation. The mean of these three numbers is the overall mean of 2.506. (This is true only when the number of observations under each treatment level is the same.) The following expression for SSB is almost correct, but it disregards the sample size:

$$SSB \neq (3.189 - 2.506)^2 + (4.229 - 2.506)^2 + (.10 - 2.506)^2$$

The three sample means in the study are based on only 10 observations each. Suppose we obtained the same sample means for 5,000 observations. Which case would provide more impressive evidence about whether the population means really differ?

A study based on 5,000 observations provides more impressive evidence, of course. Larger samples give us a better indication of the population than do smaller samples. Think about it. Which is more accurate—a Gallup Poll based on a sample of 10 or 5,000 people? Clearly, the latter. The point is that the SSB expression ignores the number of observations used to calculate the three sample means. Therefore, we must multiply each term of the previous expression by the number of data values used to compute each sample mean:

$$SSB = 10(3.189 - 2.506)^2 + 10(4.229 - 2.506)^2 + 10(.10 - 2.506)^2$$
$$= 10[(3.189 - 2.506)^2 + (4.229 - 2.506)^2 + (.10 - 2.506)^2]$$
$$= 92.24 \text{ units of variability}$$

Since there are 10 observations at each treatment level, the 10 in each term is called a *weighting constant*. If we had assigned 5,000 teams to each of the three types of training, the weighting constant would have been 5,000.

As the sum of squares computations are tedious, use the ANOVA tool in a statistical software package.

Degrees of Freedom

According to expression (10.1), to obtain the variance terms we must divide SSB and SSW by their corresponding degrees of freedom. The degrees of freedom for each sum of squares component equal the relevant sample size minus 1. Why? Suppose we must compute the SSB for three sample means whose overall mean is 3. Could you correctly guess the three sample means if we told you that one sample mean was 1? No, you could not do it. However, if we told you that two of the sample means were 1 and 4, you would know that the third sample mean must be 4. This is because only $1 + 4 + 4$ equals 9, and thus the overall mean is 3. Thus, when two of the three numbers and the overall mean are known, the third sample mean is known. Once we know the first two sample means, the third number is automatically determined—thus, the loss of freedom.

The degrees of freedom are always the relevant sample size minus 1. What are the degrees of freedom for SST? Since there are 30 numbers in the calculation, the relevant sample size is 30. The degrees of freedom are 29. In general, the total degrees of freedom are the total sample size minus 1.

What are the degrees of freedom for SSB? This term measures the differences in sample means between the treatment levels. Therefore the relevant sample size is the number of levels (3) minus 1. In our example there are then 2 degrees of freedom.

In determining the degrees of freedom for SSW, note that there are 10 observations for each treatment level. That produces 9 degrees of freedom for each level. Thus, there are 27 degrees of freedom for SSW. In general, the degrees of freedom for SSW equal the number of observations within a treatment level minus 1, times the number of treatment levels.

Table 10.8 is the analysis of variance (ANOVA) table for the reduction in unit labor cost study.

Table 10.8

ANOVA Table for Reduction of Unit Labor Cost Study

Source of Variation	Sum of Squares	df	MS	Variance Ratio
Between	92.24	2	46.12	7,249
Within	.17	27	.0063	
Total	92.41	29		

The variance between (MSB)—impact of training workshop factor—is much greater than the variance within (MSW)—impact of all other possible factors. The ANOVA table quantifies what we already knew from the spread chart in Figure 10.1 (the upper panel)—namely, the data exhibit a large spread between sample means and a small spread within treatment levels.

The variance ratio, MSB/MSW, is the variance between divided by the variance within. In our example the variance ratio equals 46.12/.0063, or 7,249. The variance due to the training workshops is 7,249 times larger than the variance generated by all other possible factors. The large value of the variance ratio suggests that the type of workshop affects the reduction in unit labor costs. In short, we should reject the null hypothesis.

While we recommend using a software package to do the analysis of variance, here are the formulas for computing the total sum of squares, sum of squares between, and sum of squares within and their corresponding degrees of freedom.

$$SST = \sum_i \sum_j (x_{ij} - \bar{\bar{x}})^2 \qquad (10.3)$$

$$df_{TOTAL} = kn - 1$$

where the x_{ij} are the data values for the $i = 1, 2, \ldots, k$ treatment
levels and $j = 1, 2, 3, \ldots, n$ observations per level

$\bar{\bar{x}}$ is the overall mean, or the mean of all the data values
k is the number of treatment levels
n is the number of observations per treatment level
df   are the degrees of freedom

$$SSB = n\left[\sum_i (\bar{x}_i - \bar{\bar{x}})^2\right] \qquad (10.4)$$

$$df_{BETWEEN} = k - 1$$

$$SSW = \sum SS_i \qquad (10.5)$$

$$SS_i = \sum_j (x_{ij} - \bar{x}_i)^2$$

$$df_{WITHIN} = k(n - 1)$$

$$VR = \frac{MSB}{MSW} \qquad (10.6)$$

Hypothesis Testing and the Analysis of Variance

Recall what the two variance or MS terms measure. Variance within (MSW) measures the impact of all other possible factors. Variance between (MSB) measures the impact of all other possible factors *plus* the impact of the experimental factor, type of training. If the null hypothesis were true, then, except for sampling error, the numerator and denominator of the variance ratio should be the same. The ratio should be close to 1.

Consistent with the hypothesis testing approach, we determine whether the variance ratio falls in the rejection region under the *F*-curve. When the variance ratio does not fall in the rejection region, we do not reject the null hypothesis. When the variance ratio falls in the rejection region, we reject the null hypothesis.

Here is how to determine the rejection region. From Section 8.6, we know that if the null hypothesis is true, the sampling distribution of the variance ratio is *F*-distributed. For the unit labor cost-reduction study, the variance ratio is *F*-distributed with 2 and 27 degrees of freedom. These are the degrees of freedom for the numerator and denominator of the variance ratio.

To determine the critical value that separates the acceptance from the rejection region, we must set the level of significance. Recall from Section 9.2 that the level of significance is the *maximum* probability we are willing to accept in making a *Type I error*. It is called the alpha (α) level. A .05 α level is commonly used when the Type I error is costly.* Thus, in the COMCEL study, the critical value is the *F*-value for 2

---

*For a complete discussion of Type I and II errors and their costs, please review Section 9.2 and the Appendix of Chapter 9.

FIGURE 10.4   *F*-Distribution for 2 and 27 Degrees of Freedom

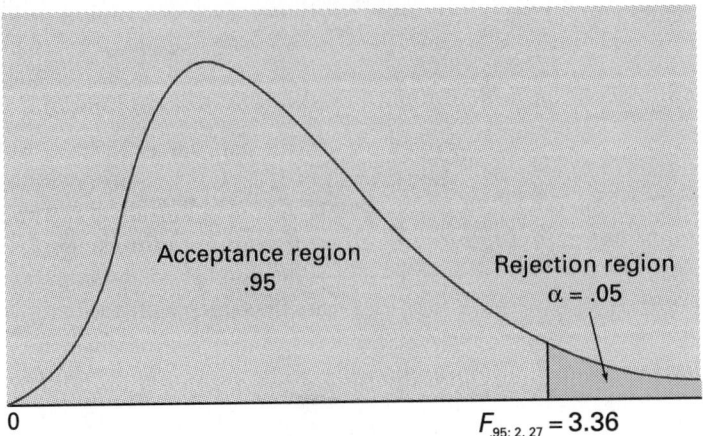

and 27 degrees of freedom and a percentile value equal to $(1 - \alpha)$, or .95. The critical *F*-value is 3.36 (interpolated from Appendix 7)*. The area to the right of 3.36 in Figure 10.4 contains .05 of the area and is the rejection region.

Given Figure 10.4, the decision rule is:

> Only if the VR (variance ratio) is greater than the critical *F*-value should COMCEL reject the null hypothesis.

From Appendix 7, the critical value is:

$$\text{Critical value} = F(1 - \alpha \text{ percentile value; } df_{\text{BETWEEN}}, df_{\text{WITHIN}})$$

Since the variance ratio of 7,249 falls in the rejection region, we reject the null hypothesis. We conclude that the type of workshop does affect the unit labor cost reduction. The ANOVA has confirmed our spread chart analysis.

What is the logic behind rejecting the null hypothesis when the variance ratio falls in the rejection region? There are only two possible explanations for a variance ratio as large as 7,249:

1. The null hypothesis is *true*. The chance of getting a variance ratio of 7,249 or larger is the area under the curve in Figure 10.4 that lies to the right of 7,249. From Section 9.2, the area is called the *p-value* and is almost zero.
2. The null hypothesis is *false*. A variance ratio of 7,249 or larger almost never happens if the null hypothesis is true. Therefore, the null hypothesis must not be true, and that is why we obtained such a large variance ratio.

The second explanation is the more reasonable one. After all, the *p*-value is almost zero.

Next we will analyze the unit labor-cost reduction data for data set 2 in Table 10.4, reproduced here in Table 10.9. The spread chart in Figure 10.1 (the lower panel) suggested that we would not reject the null hypothesis of no difference.

Table 10.10 contains the ANOVA table for data set 2. The variance ratio is 46.12/31.11, or 1.48. From Appendix 7, for 2 and 27 degrees of freedom and a .95 percentile value, the critical value is 3.36. The variance ratio falls in the acceptance

---

*From Appendix 7: $F_{.95; 2, 24} = 3.40$ and $F_{.95; 2, 30} = 3.32$

Table 10.9

Reduction in Unit Labor Costs—Data Set 2

	Team-Building Workshop	Creativity Workshop	Control Groups
	$-1.81	$8.23	$.10
	10.19	-1.77	-3.90
	9.19	7.23	10.10
	.19	.23	-7.90
	11.19	9.23	-1.90
	-2.81	-2.77	.10
	2.19	.23	7.10
	.19	13.23	-7.90
	3.19	.23	.10
	.19	8.23	5.10
$\bar{x}$	$3.189	$4.229	$.10

Using expressions (10.3), (10.4), and (10.5):

$$\text{SST} = (-1.81 - 2.506)^2 + (10.19 - 2.506)^2 + \cdots + (5.10 - 2.506)^2$$
$$= 932.24$$

$$\text{SSB} = 10[(3.189 - 2.506)^2 + (4.229 - 2.506)^2 + (.10 - 2.506)^2]$$
$$= 92.24$$

$$\begin{aligned}
\text{SSW} =\ & (-1.81 - 3.189)^2 + \cdots + (.19 - 3.189)^2 && \text{Team-building workshop} \\
& + (8.23 - 4.229)^2 + \cdots + (8.23 - 4.229)^2 && \text{Creativity workshop} \\
& + (.10 - .10)^2 + \cdots + (5.10 - .10)^2 && \text{Control groups} \\
=\ & 840
\end{aligned}$$

Table 10.10

ANOVA Table for Reduction of Unit Labor Cost Study—Data Set 2

Source of Variation	Sum of Squares	df	MS	Variance Ratio
Between	92.24	2	46.12	1.48
Within	840.00	27	31.11	
Total	932.24	29		

region. Therefore we do not have sufficient evidence to reject the null hypothesis. We conclude that the type of workshop has no impact on unit labor cost reductions. The exploratory data analysis for data set 2 has been verified.

In summary, we use the analysis of variance to determine whether k population means are the same. If we reject the null hypothesis and conclude that the population means differ, then we are interested in determining the best of the k treatment levels. That is our next topic.

SECTION 10.3 EXERCISES

1. Distinguish between sum of squares and variance.

2. What are the two sources of variation that explain the total sum of squares in a one-factor, k-level study? Explain.

3. Determine the total degrees of freedom, the within degrees of freedom, and the between degrees of freedom for the following one-factor, k-level studies.
    a. Four-level study with five observations per treatment level
    b. Three-level study with ten observations per treatment level
    c. Two-level study with one observation per treatment level
    d. Based on the answer to part c, what is the minimum sample size per treatment level? Explain.

4. Determine the critical F-values that separate the acceptance from the rejection region for each of the studies described in Exercises 3a–b for the following α values:
    a. .05
    b. .01
    c. .10
    Draw the F-distribution for each α level and label the acceptance and rejection regions.

5. COMCEL provides creative problem-solving training to its quality circles. COMCEL seeks the best method—the one that maximizes the quantity of solutions for a given problem. COMCEL will include it in their quality-circle training curriculum. COMCEL selects at random 21 quality-circle members. Each member receives training in one of three creative methods. The workers then work on a common and difficult problem. Below are the number of solutions generated for the common problem.

Brainstorming	Analogy	Visualizing
15	34	10
7	10	4
45	5	6
21	23	12
34	25	13
56	40	10
17	11	9

    a. Use software to construct multiple box plots and determine descriptive statistics for the three treatment levels.
    b. Does it appear that assumptions 2 and 3 underlying the analysis of variance are justified? Discuss.

6. A manager of a car service center wants to reduce the number of complaints about improperly made repairs. She tries two approaches: (1) a more detailed write-up of the car's problem and (2) a callback in which the repair person calls the customer two days after making the repairs to determine if the customer is satisfied. Given are the percentages of complaints over a three-week period. Assume an equal number of customers under each treatment. The manager sets an α level of .05.

Week	Detailed Write-up	Callback	Control Group
1	1	6	8
2	5	2	10
3	3	4	12

    a. Find the overall mean and the mean of each treatment level.
    b. Find the total sum of squares for this data set.
    c. Compute the sum of squares between and the sum of squares within.
    d. How many degrees of freedom are there for the total sum of squares, the between sum of squares, and the within sum of squares?
    e. Complete the following analysis of variance table.

Source of Variation	Sum of Squares	df	MS	Variance Ratio
Between	_____	_____	_____	_____
Within	_____	_____	_____	
Total	_____	_____		

f. Based on an α level of .05, can we conclude that the population mean percentage of complaints under the three methods differ? Explain.

7. Consider the following data from a planned change study.

Treatment A	Treatment B	Treatment C
1	1	7
2	2	8
3	3	9

a. Find the overall mean and the mean for each treatment level.
b. Find the total sum of squares.
c. Compute the sum of squares within and between.
d. Determine the degrees of freedom total, within, and between.
e. Develop an analysis of variance table.
f. Given an α level of .01, can we reject the "no difference in population treatment means" null hypothesis?

8. This problem illustrates why the rejection region is in the upper tail of the F-distribution curve (see Figure 10.4). The variance ratio is MSB/MSW.

1. MSW measures the impact of all factors except the treatment on the dependent variable. For the cost-reduction study, "all" factors include differences in the age, seniority, motivation of workers, etc.
2. MSB also measures variance-within *plus* the impact of the experimental factor-type of workshop.

If the workshop experimental factor affects the unit labor cost,
a. should the MSB term be larger or smaller than the MSW term?
b. as the MSB term becomes larger than the MSW term, what should happen to the magnitude of the variance ratio?
c. Given your answers in parts **a** and **b**, explain why there is no rejection region in the lower tail of the F-distribution.

9. Conduct an analysis of variance for the sales promotion study data in Exercise 4 of Section 10.2 Exercises. Use an α level of .01. Do your results confirm the conclusions you made based on the spread chart alone?

10. Conduct an analysis of variance for the problem-solving study data in Exercise 6 of Section 10.2 Exercises. Use an α level of .10. Do your results confirm the conclusions you made based on the spread chart alone?

11. Conduct an analysis of variance for the telemarketing data in Exercise 7 of Section 10.2 Exercises. Use an α level of .05. Do your results confirm the conclusions you made based on the spread chart alone?

12. A marketing report shows the prices of the same items charged by department stores and boutiques. Shown are the prices for the same bottle of perfume at four department stores and four boutiques. Assume that the prices are representative samples from their respective populations.

Department Stores	Boutiques
$13.50	$14.75
14.00	15.50
15.25	15.50
13.50	16.00

a. Based on Section 6.10, is the above study an experiment? Why?
b. State the null and alternative hypotheses.
c. State the assumptions we must make before using the ANOVA.
d. At an α level of .01, can we conclude that the population mean price for the bottle of perfume differs between department stores and boutiques?

13. COMCEL wants to reduce the unit labor-cost of producing its mobile phones. It conducts a one-factor, three-level study. Below are the unit labor-cost reductions for 12 work groups. Four groups attended either the team-building workshop, the creativity workshop, or both workshops.

	TB	CM	TB and CM
	$.50	$.60	$.70
	.52	.58	.69
	.50	.62	.71
	.48	.60	.70
$\bar{x}$	$.50	$.60	$.70

a. State the null and alternative hypotheses.
b. Are the assumptions underlying the ANOVA realistic for the data in the study?
c. Given an α level of .01, should COMCEL fail to reject or reject the null hypothesis? Explain.
d. If COMCEL rejects the null hypothesis, what action should it take?

14. A company is looking for a new chief executive. Each candidate must be evaluated by four committees of six members each. Each committee member independently rates the candidate's qualifications from 1 (unqualified) to 10 (highly qualified). Here are the evaluation scores on the first candidate.

Committee 1	Committee 2	Committee 3	Committee 4
5	4	6	8
2	6	4	9
3	8	5	5
4	5	5	7
4	7	7	7
4	6	8	8

a. Based on Section 6.10, is this an experiment? Why?
b. State the null and alternative hypotheses.
c. Are the assumptions underlying the ANOVA realistic for the data in the study?
d. Perform an analysis of variance.
e. Given an α level of .05, does it appear that the four committees are rating the candidate differently?

15. This exercise illustrates how the p-value idea learned in Section 9.2 can be applied to the analysis of variance. Consider the following computer output. The α level for the study was .05—$F(.95; 2, 12) = 3.89$.

Source of Variation	Sum of Squares	df	MS	Variance Ratio	F-value Critical
Between	19.73	2	9.87	8.71	3.89
Within	13.60	12	1.13		
Total	33.33	14			

a. Since the variance ratio exceeds the critical value, we reject the "no difference in population means" null hypothesis. The p-value is the area to the right of 8.71 under the F-distribution curve. Graphically, is the area much less than .05?

b. Use Appendix 7. Find the F-value (.975; 2, 12). Is the variance ratio larger than this value? If so, the p-value is less than $1 - .975 = .025$.

c. Again use Appendix 7. Find the F-value (.99; 2, 12). Is the variance ratio larger than this value? If so, the p-value is less than $1 - .99 = .01$.

d. Again use Appendix 7. Find the F-value (.995; 2, 12). Is the variance ratio larger than this value? If so, the p-value is less than $1 - .995 = .005$.

e. Is the p-value less than .001? Explain.

16. This exercise illustrates the connection between the variance-within (MSW) and the variance-between (MSB) and spread charts. Consider the following two data sets. Both have the same treatment sample means.

Data Set A

Treatment 1	Treatment 2	Treatment 3
50	90	70
48	92	70
52	88	72
50	90	68
50	90	70

Data Set B

Treatment 1	Treatment 2	Treatment 3
50	100	70
30	80	60
70	110	80
40	70	50
60	90	90

a. Construct and interpret spread charts for the two data sets. Which variance-within (MSW) will be larger? Which variance-between (MSB) will be larger?

b. Use a software package to construct two ANOVA tables to check your answers in part **a.** Use $\alpha = .05$.

17. During the product development cycle, firms often ask potential customers to rate product features at various costs. The firms can then include product features that consumers want at a price they are willing to pay. An important feature of coffee makers is the brew capacity. Thirty potential consumers rate their intent to purchase the following three coffee makers along a scale ranging from 0 (absolutely certain not to buy) to 100 (absolutely certain to buy).

1. 4-cup capacity for $19.99
2. 6-cup capacity for $25.99
3. 8-cup capacity for $34.99

4-cup	6-cup	8-cup
50	70	35
45	75	30
50	80	40
40	85	40
55	90	30
40	80	50
45	75	30
45	80	35
50	80	35
45	75	35

a. State the null and alternative hypotheses.

b. Given a .05 α level, use a software package to analyze the data.

10.4 ≡ Testing for Significant Differences Between Pairs of Population Means

The analysis of variance (ANOVA) does not always provide the answers that managers need. For example, someone asks: "Is the team-building workshop more effective than the creativity training workshop?" Remember, the alternative hypothesis says only that all k population means are not the same. If we reject the null hypothesis, it does not follow that all k means are different. A variance ratio that falls in the rejection region *signals* that we must conduct follow-up comparisons to determine which population means are different from each other. In managerial terms, we must know which treatment level is best, which is second best, etc. By the end of this section you should be able to:

1. explain the need for testing beyond the analysis of variance;
2. explain the need for an *experimentwise* protection level;
3. explain how the Studentized range statistic provides an experimentwise protection level; and
4. construct and interpret Tukey HSD confidence intervals.

We use COMCEL's one-factor, three-level, cost-reduction study to illustrate how to construct Tukey confidence intervals, which are based on comparisons of pairs of population means. In that study, there are three possible comparisons we can make, namely,

1. Team-building workshop vs. control group
2. Creativity workshop vs. control group
3. Team-building vs. creativity workshop

The Problem of Multiple Comparisons

In comparing the team-building group vs. the control group, we can control the probability of making a Type I error by using a .05 α level. This is equivalent to a $100(1 - \alpha)\%$, or 95%, confidence level. The error for a single comparison is called the *per comparison error rate* and equals the α level. We could also use a .05 α level for comparing the team-building vs. creativity workshops. However, the probability of making a Type I error in one or both comparisons is not .05; it is larger.

Keppel (1973) shows that for α levels of .05 or less, and for six or fewer comparisons, the *experimentwise error rate* is roughly

$$\text{Experimentwise error rate (EER)} = c \cdot \alpha \text{ level}$$

$$\text{Experimentwise level of confidence} = 100(1 - \text{EER})\% \qquad (10.7)$$

The α level is the per comparison error rate and c is the number of comparisons. The experimentwise error rate is the probability of making one or more Type I errors in a set of comparisons.

Expression (10.7) says that the experimentwise error rate increases as we increase the number of treatment levels and thus the number of comparisons of pairs of population means. As the experimentwise error rate increases, the experimentwise level of confidence decreases.

When comparing three pairs of population means, each at a .05 α level, the probability of making one or more Type I errors increases from .05 to about .15 $(= 3 \cdot .05)$.

This is equivalent to a 100(1 − .15)%, or 85%, confidence level for all three comparisons. The experimentwise error rate increases to roughly .30 (= 6 · .05) when making six comparisons. This is equivalent to a 70% confidence level for all six comparisons. Most managers would consider 70% and 85% confidence levels too low.

Tukey HSD Confidence Intervals

John Tukey's (1953) honestly significant difference (HSD) method constructs confidence intervals for all possible pairs of population means. It sets the experimentwise error rate (or confidence level) constant at whatever level we desire no matter how many pairwise comparisons we make.

Shown in expression (10.8) is the Tukey HSD confidence interval for an equal sample size per treatment level:

$$\bar{x}_1 - \bar{x}_2 \pm \text{Margin of error}$$

$$\bar{x}_1 - \bar{x}_2 \pm q(\text{confidence level, df}_{\text{WITHIN}}, \text{number of treatment levels}) \sqrt{\frac{\text{MSW}}{n}} \qquad (10.8)$$

The MSW term and the degrees of freedom within come from the analysis of variance table for the study. The value of n is the common sample size of each treatment level. Instead of the t-table, we use another table—the Studentized range distribution, symbolized by the letter q. An abbreviated portion is presented in Table 10.11 (See Appendix 8).

Table 10.11

A Short Table for the Studentized Range Values

Within df	Experimentwise Confidence Level	Number of Treatment Levels 2	3	4
10	95%	3.15	3.88	4.33
	99%	4.48	5.27	5.77
20	95%	2.95	3.58	3.96
	99%	4.02	4.64	5.02
27	95%	2.90	3.50	3.86
	99%	3.91	4.49	4.85

Here is how to interpret a Tukey confidence interval. First, determine if the confidence interval constructed using expression (10.8) contains the value of zero. A value of zero within the confidence interval indicates *no difference* in the two population means. If the interval does not contain zero, then one population mean is different from the other. Second, from the lower and upper limits of the confidence interval you can determine how different the two population means are (and which treatment level is better from a managerial viewpoint).

Table 10.12 contains Tukey HSD 95% confidence intervals for the unit labor cost-reduction study applied to data set 1. We selected a 95% experimentwise confidence level since the α level for the original study had been set at .05. For ease of interpretation, we placed the largest sample mean first in using expression (10.8).

The Tukey HSD intervals tell us that creativity training is better than team-building training in reducing unit labor costs and that both are better than no training. Therefore, COMCEL should consider implementing creativity training throughout the plant.

Table 10.12

Summary Table of Three Tukey HSD Comparisons for the Unit Labor-Cost-Reduction Study

MSW (see Table 10.8)	.0063
df_{WITHIN} (see Table 10.8)	27
Desired *experimentwise* confidence level ($\alpha = .05$)	95%
Number of treatment levels	3
Studentized range value (see Table 10.11 for q)	3.50
Sample size per treatment level (n)	10

Comparison	Tukey CI	Interpretation
TB vs. Control	$(3.19 - .10) \pm 3.50 \sqrt{\dfrac{.0063}{10}}$ $\$3.09 \pm \$.09$ lower limit = \$3.00 upper limit = \$3.18	Interval does not include zero. Team-building training is more effective than the control group in reducing unit labor cost (by between \$3.00 and \$3.18).
CM vs. Control	$(4.23 - .10) \pm .09$ $\$4.13 \pm \$.09$ lower limit = \$4.04 upper limit = \$4.22	Interval does not include zero. Creativity training is more effective than the control group in reducing unit labor cost (by between \$4.04 and \$4.22).
CM vs. TB	$(4.23 - 3.19) \pm .09$ $\$1.04 \pm \$.09$ lower limit = \$0.95 upper limit = \$1.13	Interval does not include zero. Creativity training is more effective than team building in reducing unit labor cost (by between \$0.95 and \$1.13).

The next example illustrates the application of the Tukey HSD method to a one-factor study with four treatment levels.

Example: Which Regimen Is Most Effective in Reducing Cholesterol?

A health maintenance organization (HMO) tests three ways to reduce cholesterol levels: (1) diet, (2) diet and exercise, and (3) medication. They include a fourth treatment level—a control group, consisting of people who receive no treatment. The project manager randomly selects 20 people and randomly assigns $n = 5$ people each to the four treatment levels. The dependent variable is the drop in cholesterol level after three months. The HMO sets α at .01.

The resulting treatment level sample means are as follows:

Diet (D)	$\bar{x}_D$ = 30-point drop
Diet and exercise (D/E)	$\bar{x}_{D/E}$ = 31-point drop
Medication (M)	$\bar{x}_M$ = 40-point drop
Control group (C)	$\bar{x}_C$ = 5-point drop

Table 10.13 presents the analysis of variance for this study based on the COMSTAT ANOVA tool. Since the variance ratio, 82.8, is larger than the critical F-value, we reject the null hypothesis.

Table 10.13

ANOVA Table for Cholesterol Study

Source of Variation	Sum of Squares	df	MS	Variance Ratio	F-value Critical
Between	3,385	3	1,128	82.8	5.29
Within	218	16	13.63		
Total	3,603	19			

As there are four treatment levels, there are six possible comparisons. Table 10.14 contains the six 99% experimentwise confidence intervals. For ease of interpretation, we have placed the largest sample mean first in using expression (10.8).

These results show that medication is the most effective treatment. Diet and diet with exercise are equally effective, but both are less effective than medication. No treatment is the least effective way. Tukey's HSD method allows the family of six comparisons to be made at the 99% level of confidence.

In summary, when we reject the null hypothesis, we should construct Tukey HSD confidence intervals on the difference between all pairs of population treatment level means. When we reject the null hypothesis, we will find at least one significant difference between pairs of population means. From the Tukey confidence intervals we can determine which treatment level is best and implement it.

In conclusion, we need Tukey HSD confidence intervals because as the number of comparisons increases, t-based confidence intervals would provide too low experimentwise protection levels (See expression 10.7).

How Tukey HSD Confidence Intervals Provide 95% or 99% Experimentwise Level of Confidence

Ninety-five% (or 99%) experimentwise protection is achieved at the expense of having larger margins of error than for equivalent t-based confidence intervals. Widened confidence intervals are more likely to include the value of zero. In short, we are less likely to find a significant difference between population means using Tukey intervals vs. t-based intervals. However, if zero is not in the confidence interval, we can be 95% or 99% confident that there is a real difference, *no matter how many pairwise comparisons of population means we make.*

Why are the margins of error wider for Tukey vs. t-based confidence intervals? The q-values from Appendix 8 are larger than the equivalent t-values from Appendix 5. Moreover, from Appendix 8, the q-values (and thus the margins of error) increase as the number of treatment levels increases. The large q-values account for the wider margins of error. But they also provide us with a high, 95% or 99%, experimentwise confidence levels.

Table 10.14

Summary Table of Six Tukey HSD Comparisons for the Cholesterol Study

MSW (see Table 10.13)	13.63
df_{WITHIN} (see Table 10.13)	16
Desired *experimentwise* confidence level ($\alpha = .01$)	99%
Number of treatment levels	4
Studentized range value (see Appendix 8 for q)	5.19
Sample size per treatment level (n)	5

Table 10.14 (Continued)

Comparison	Tukey CI	Interpretation
D/E vs. D	$(31 - 30) \pm 5.19 \sqrt{\dfrac{13.63}{5}}$ 1 ± 8.57 lower limit $= -7.57$ upper limit $= +9.57$	Interval includes zero. No difference between diet and diet/exercise.
M vs. D	$(40 - 30) \pm 8.57$ 10 ± 8.57 lower limit $=$ 1.43 upper limit $= 18.57$	Interval does not include zero. Medication is more effective than diet in reducing cholesterol by 1.43 to 18.57 units.
D vs. C	$(30 - 5) \pm 8.57$ 25 ± 8.57 lower limit $= 16.43$ upper limit $= 33.57$	Interval does not include zero. Diet is more effective than control (no treatment) in reducing cholesterol by between 16.43 and 33.57 units.
M vs. D/E	$(40 - 31) \pm 8.57$ 9 ± 8.57 lower limit $=$ 0.43 upper limit $= 17.57$	Interval does not include zero Medication is more effective than diet/exercise in reducing cholesterol by between .43 and 17.57 units.
D/E vs. C	$(31 - 5) \pm 8.57$ 26 ± 8.57 lower limit $= 17.43$ upper limit $= 34.57$	Interval does not include zero. Diet/exercise is more effective than no treatment in reducing cholesterol by between 17.43 and 34.57 units.
M vs. C	$(40 - 5) \pm 8.57$ 35 ± 8.57 lower limit $= 26.43$ upper limit $= 43.57$	Interval does not include zero. Medication is more effective than no treatment in reducing cholesterol by between 26.43 and 43.57 units.

SECTION 10.4 EXERCISES

1. Explain why we cannot rely on the analysis of variance to tell us which population means are different for a one-factor, three-level study.

2. Explain why we can rely on the analysis of variance to tell us which population mean is different for a one-factor, two-level study.

3. Whenever we make more than one inference from the same data set, the probability of making at least one Type I error increases. How does the Tukey confidence interval correct this problem?

4. Consider a study that has four treatment levels. The manager sets an α level of .05. If Tukey HSD confidence intervals are not used, what is the approximate experimentwise error rate and the experimentwise level of confidence? What would the experimentwise error rate and the experimentwise level of confidence be for Tukey HSD confidence intervals?

5. Explain why it is unnecessary to use the Tukey procedure if we do not reject the null hypothesis based on the analysis of variance table.

6. Determine the correct q values from Appendix 8 for the following studies:

	Experimentwise Confidence Level	Number of Treatment Levels	df_{WITHIN}
a.	95%	3	12
b.	95%	4	12
c.	99%	3	20
d.	99%	4	20

e. Based on the experimentwise confidence levels, determine the α levels for the four studies.

f. What happens to the margin of error for the Tukey confidence interval as the q values increase?

g. If other things are held constant as the margin of error increases, what happens to the probability that the value of zero will fall between the lower and upper limits of the confidence interval?

h. If the value of zero is in the interval, can we detect a significant difference between two population means?

7. Here is computer output for a one-factor, three-level study. The experimental factor is type of sales display and the dependent variable is daily sales revenue. Interpret the output and determine which display produces the highest population mean daily sales revenue.

		Confidence Interval	
Comparison	Difference in Means	Lower	Upper
DISPLAY1 − DISPLAY2	$20	$14	$26
DISPLAY1 − DISPLAY3	25	19	31
DISPLAY2 − DISPLAY3	5	−1	11

8. Use the Tukey procedure to make all pairwise comparisons for Exercise 6 in Section 10.3 Exercises. Which population means are different? Set a 95% experimentwise level of confidence.

9. Use the Tukey procedure to make all pairwise comparisons for Exercise 9 in Section 10.3 Exercises. Which population means are different? Set a 99% experimentwise level of confidence.

10. Use the Tukey procedure to make all pairwise comparisons for Exercise 11 in Section 10.3 Exercises. Which population means are different? Set a 95% experimentwise level of confidence.

11. Use the Tukey procedure to make all pairwise comparisons for Exercise 13 in Section 10.3 Exercises. Which population means are different? Set a 99% experimentwise level of confidence.

12. The Tukey procedure controls the experimentwise Type I error rate by increasing the width of the confidence interval. How does increasing the confidence interval's width affect the probability of concluding that pairs of population means are different?

10.5 ≣ The Kruskal–Wallis Nonparametric Analysis of Variance

Now suppose that we have completed a one-factor, k-level, completely randomized experiment. Before analyzing the data, we test the following underlying assumptions:

The observations within each of the k treatment levels are near-normally distributed.

The variances within each treatment level are the same, or nearly so.

We construct k stem-and-leaf displays to assess the assumptions. Suppose that the data are highly skewed with one or more outliers or that the range in the data at one treatment level is 5 times or more greater than the range at other treatment levels. What course do we follow?

We could transform the raw data using a square root or log base 10 transformation. If that makes the data more normal-shaped and equalizes the variances, we can apply the F-based analysis of variance from Section 10.3. Otherwise, we use the Kruskal–Wallis *nonparametric* analysis of variance. By the end of this section you should be able to:

1. explain when to use the Kruskal–Wallis test;
2. explain the logic of the Kruskal–Wallis test statistic;
3. apply the Kruskal–Wallis test; and
4. apply and interpret Dunn's follow-up test of differences between pairs of population medians.

We illustrate the Kruskal–Wallis test with the following planned change study.

Example: Determining the Best Advertising Approach   Soky Inc. is considering three approaches for advertising its digital tape players: informative advertising, persuasive advertising, and retentive advertising. Soky randomly selects 28 people from its target population. It randomly assigns seven people to each of the three advertising methods. The remaining seven people will serve as a control group. Except for the control group subjects, each subject will be shown a tape player ad (developed using one of the three strategies) four times over a one-week period. Afterward, each person (including those in the control group) will indicate his or her intent to buy a digital tape player on a scale from 0 (definitely will not buy) to 100 (definitely will buy). Soky Inc. has set a .05 α level. Table 10.15 contains the data for the advertising study.

The box plots in Figure 10.5 indicate that each treatment level contains an outlier. The presence of outliers requires us to use the Kruskal–Wallis nonparametric analysis of variance method.

Statistical Hypotheses

We begin by stating the null and alternative hypotheses:

H_0:   The four population *median* purchase intentions are the same.

H_1:   Not all the population *median* purchase intentions are the same.

Note that the Kruskal–Wallis method tests population medians, not means. That is reasonable as we use the median as the measure of the center when the data have outliers.

<u>**Table 10.15**</u>

Data for One-Factor, Four-Level Marketing Study

Informative	Persuasive	Retentive	Control Group
55	42	56	0
60	45	62	8
61	48	63	8
68	50	65	10
71	51	66	11
72	52	73	12
100	70	99	30

Experimental Factor: Type of Advertising[*]

[*]Values represent intent to purchase on a 0–100 scale, where 100 indicates a definite intent to purchase.

Next, we rank all the observations, as shown in Table 10.16, by assigning a 1 to the smallest of the 28 values, a 2 to the next higher value, and so forth. If two or more values are the same, assign each of them the mean of the two or more ranks. The numbers in parentheses in Table 10.16 are the data ranks.

Logic Behind the Test

Before proceeding with the logic behind the test, examine Table 10.16. If the four population medians are the same (the null hypothesis is true), the ranks should be randomly distributed among the four treatment levels. All the low ranks or high ranks would not be concentrated in one treatment level. However, notice that the control group contains all the low ranks while the informative and retentive approaches contain most of the highest ranks. This indicates that we probably will reject the null hypothesis.

FIGURE 10.5   Box Plots for Four-Level Planned Change Study

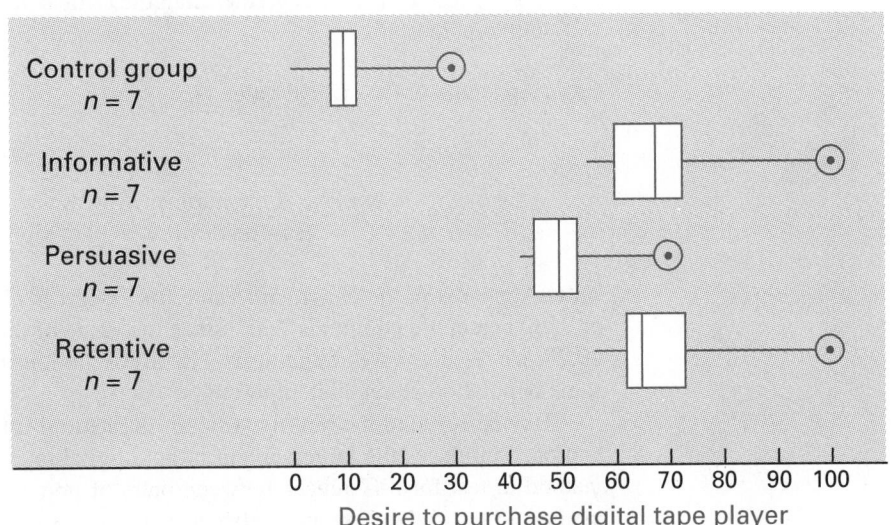

Desire to purchase digital tape player

Table 10.16

Advertising Data Rank-Ordered

Informative	Persuasive	Retentive	Control Group
55 (14)	42 (8)	56 (15)	0 (1)
60 (16)	45 (9)	62 (18)	8 (2.5)
61 (17)	48 (10)	63 (19)	8 (2.5)
68 (22)	50 (11)	65 (20)	10 (4)
71 (24)	51 (12)	66 (21)	11 (5)
72 (25)	52 (13)	73 (26)	12 (6)
100 (28)	70 (23)	99 (27)	30 (7)

Kruskal–Wallis Test Statistic

Instead of computing a variance ratio, we compute the following Kruskal–Wallis test statistic, H:

$$H = \frac{12}{N(N + 1)} \sum_j \frac{R_j^2}{n_j} - 3(N + 1) \qquad (10.9)$$

where N is the total sample size

R_j is the sum of the ranks for treatment level j

n_j is the sample size for treatment level j

Warning: This expression is valid only if less than one-fourth of the observations are ties.

Table 10.17 shows the calculations for the Kruskal–Wallis test statistic. For sample sizes of 5 or more within each treatment level, if the null hypothesis is true, the H statistic is chi-square distributed with $k - 1$ (the number of treatment levels less 1) degrees of freedom. We first encountered the chi-square family of curves in Section 7.9.

As in the F-test in Section 10.3, we must find the acceptance and rejection regions. The decision rule is:

Only if the H statistic is greater than the critical value should we reject the null hypothesis.

From Appendix 6, the critical value is:

Critical value = chi-square[$k - 1$ df, $(1 - \alpha)$ percentile value]

where k is the number of treatment levels

α is the desired level of significance.

From Appendix 6, the chi-square value for 3 degrees of freedom and the $(1 - .05)$, or 95th, percentile column is 7.81. Since the value of the Kruskal–Wallis statistic is 20.27, we reject the null hypothesis. Not all of the four treatment levels produce the same population median intent to buy.

Having rejected the null hypothesis, the natural follow-up question is, "Which approach produces the largest intent to buy digital tape players?" We used Tukey's method to test for differences between pairs of population means. We use Dunn's method to test for differences between pairs of population medians. Both methods provide an experimentwise protection level.

Table 10.17

Computation of Kruskal–Wallis Test Statistic

Treatment	Rank Sums	Sample Size, n_j
Informative	$14 + 16 + 17 + 22 + 24 + 25 + 28 = 146$	7
Persuasive	$8 + 9 + 10 + 11 + 12 + 13 + 23 = 86$	7
Retentive	$15 + 18 + 19 + 20 + 21 + 26 + 27 = 146$	7
Control group	$1 + 2.5 + 2.5 + 4 + 5 + 6 + 7 = 28$	7

$$H = \frac{12}{28(29)}\left(\frac{146^2}{7} + \frac{86^2}{7} + \frac{146^2}{7} + \frac{28^2}{7}\right) - 3(28 + 1)$$

$$= 20.27$$

Dunn's Multiple Comparisons

Use expression (10.10) to construct either 90% or 95% experimentwise multiple pairwise comparisons of medians (Dunn, 1964):

$$\bar{R}_i - \bar{R}_j \pm D\sqrt{\frac{N(N + 1)}{12}\left(\frac{1}{n_i} + \frac{1}{n_j}\right)} \tag{10.10}$$

where N is the total sample size
$\bar{R}_i$ is the mean rank for treatment level i
n_i is the sample size for treatment level i
D is the appropriate value from the following table

Experimentwise Level of Confidence	Number of Treatment Levels		
	3	4	5
90%	2.13	2.39	2.58
95%	2.39	2.64	2.81

Note: Always place the higher mean rank first in expression (10.10). It makes interpreting the results simpler.

The term following the $\pm$ sign in expression (10.10) is the margin of error. As always, the margin of error is simply the reliability factor for the confidence level, D, times the estimated standard error, the remainder of the expression.

For the one-factor, four-level advertising study (Table 10.15), there are six possible pairwise comparisons:

1. Informative vs. control group
2. Persuasive vs. control group
3. Retentive vs. control group
4. Informative vs. persuasive
5. Informative vs. retentive
6. Persuasive vs. retentive

Given here are the mean ranks for the four treatment levels that we will need for expression (10.10).

Treatment Level	Mean Rank	
Informative	$\bar{R}_i$	$\dfrac{146}{7} = 20.86$
Persuasive	$\bar{R}_p$	$\dfrac{86}{7} = 12.29$
Retentive	$\bar{R}_r$	$\dfrac{146}{7} = 20.86$
Control group	$\bar{R}_c$	$\dfrac{28}{7} = 4.00$

Construction and Interpretation of Dunn's Multiple Comparisons

Using expression (10.10)—Dunn's method—we can construct a 90% confidence interval on the difference between the informative strategy and the control group:

$$(20.86 - 4.00) \pm 2.39 \sqrt{\frac{(28)(29)}{12}\left(\frac{1}{7} + \frac{1}{7}\right)}$$

$$= 16.86 \pm 2.39(4.40)$$

$$= 16.86 \pm 10.5$$

Lower limit: $16.86 - 10.5 = 6.36$
Upper limit: $16.86 + 10.5 = 27.36$

Note that the interval does *not* include the value of zero. Thus, we are 90% confident that the informative strategy produces a higher population median intent to buy digital tape players than no advertising—the control group.

Table 10.18 presents a summary of the six pairwise comparisons.

Table 10.18

Summary Table of Six Dunn Comparisons and Interpretations at a 90% Experimentwise Level of Confidence for the Marketing Study

Comparison	Dunn CI	Interpretation
Informative vs. control	$(20.86 - 4) \pm 10.5$ 16.86 ± 10.5 lower limit $= 6.36$ upper limit $= 27.36$	Interval does not include zero. The informative strategy produces a higher median intent to buy than the control group.
Persuasive vs. control	$(12.29 - 4) \pm 10.5$ 8.29 ± 10.5 lower limit $= -2.21$ upper limit $= 18.79$	Interval does include zero. Cannot detect any statistical difference.
Retentive vs. control	$(20.86 - 4) \pm 10.5$ 16.86 ± 10.5 lower limit $= 6.36$ upper limit $= 27.36$	Interval does not include zero. The retentive strategy produces a higher median intent to buy than the control group.
Informative vs. persuasive	$(20.86 - 12.29) \pm 10.5$ 8.57 ± 10.5 lower limit $= -1.93$ upper limit $= 19.07$	Interval does include zero. Cannot detect any statistical difference.

Informative vs. retentive	$(20.86 - 20.86) \pm 10.5$ 0 ± 10.5 lower limit $= -10.5$ upper limit $= +10.5$	Interval does include zero. Cannot detect any statistical difference.
Retentive vs. persuasive	$(20.86 - 12.29) \pm 10.5$ 8.57 ± 10.5 lower limit $= -1.93$ upper limit $= 19.07$	Interval does include zero. Cannot detect any statistical difference.

The informative and retentive strategies are each more effective than the control group. There are no other significant differences at the 90% experimentwise confidence level.

In summary, when there are outliers at some or all of the treatment levels, we use the Kruskal–Wallis nonparametric method and Dunn's multiple comparisons to compare k population medians. If we reject the null hypothesis, we will find at least one significant difference between pairs of population medians in Dunn's follow-up method.

SECTION 10.5 EXERCISES

1. Explain when we should consider using the Kruskal–Wallis nonparametric procedure instead of the F-based analysis of variance.

2. Explain the logic of the Kruskal–Wallis test.

3. Use Appendix 6 to determine the critical value that separates the acceptance and rejection regions for the following studies. State the conditions under which we should reject the "no difference in population medians" null hypothesis for each study.

Level of Significance	.01	.10	.05	.005
Number of Treatment Levels	4	5	2	3

4. To use the F-based analysis of variance, the data within each treatment level must not be highly skewed or contain outliers. A manager investigates the impact of quality circles and top management support on the number of defects per 100 cars in three plants that produce the Ford Tempo. Below are the weekly number of defects per 100 cars data for 21 work groups six months after the start of the study.

No Quality Circles	QC—No Top Support	QC—Top Support
80	79	56
81	83	67
89	84	69
105	90	71
106	91	73
107	92	78
167	137	80

   a. Develop box plots for the three treatment levels. Are assumptions 2 and 3 (see page 538) underlying the F-based analysis of variance reasonable for the study data? Also determine the three sample median number of defects per 100 cars.
   b. Assign ranks to the 21 observations. Are more than one-fourth of the observations ties?
   c. Sum the ranks for the three treatment levels. Are the sums similar? If not, what does that *suggest*?

5. Here are data from a one-factor, three-level study:

| | Level | |
1	2	3
26	12	22
28	14	42
30	18	42
31	20	46
46	40	47
27	15	44

   a. Why would we select the Kruskal–Wallis procedure over the F-based analysis of variance?
   b. State and test the null and alternative hypotheses.
   c. If we reject the null hypothesis at an α level of .10, use Dunn's procedure to determine which population medians are different at an experimentwise 90% confidence level.

6. A coffee producer hires an expert taster to sample four new blends of coffee. The firm will market the best blend. Sixteen samples are placed before the taster, who is asked to rank the samples from 1 (best) to 16 (worst). The 16 samples actually contain the four different blends of coffee, four cups of each blend. The rankings are shown here.

Blend 1	Blend 2	Blend 3	Blend 4
1	4	6	12
2	7	8	14
3	9	11	15
5	10	13	16

   a. What is the null hypothesis being tested?
   b. For an α level of .05, does there appear to be a difference in the blends of coffee? If so, rank the blends of coffee for the company. Use an experimentwise 95% level of confidence. Which coffee blend should the company introduce? Explain.

7. A manager wants to know whether there is a difference in the median number of days of sick leave taken by the employees in three different departments. It is well known that the distribution of sick leave days is skewed to the right. Based on the given data, does it appear that the median number of sick leave days varies by department? Set the α level at .05.

Dept. A	0	1	3	6	9	14	16	19	25	38
Dept. B	0	1	4	6	11	15	18	22	26	34
Dept. C	0	2	5	8	10	12	16	20	27	31

8. Refer to Exercise 4 in this section. Which treatment level produces the minimum number of defects per 100 cars? Set an experimentwise 95% level of confidence.

9. Consider the following study to reduce cholesterol level (mg/dl). The researcher randomly selects 24 patients with cholesterol levels above 300. She randomly assigns the patients to one of three treatment levels. After six months of treatment, she determines each patient's drop in cholesterol level.

Diet/Exercise	Exercise	Diet
34	4	7
35	10	17
45	11	18
60	12	21
70	15	22
80	18	28
81	19	29
130	20	30

Which treatment level produces the largest reduction in cholesterol levels? Set an experimentwise 90% level of confidence.

10. A manager investigates the impact of job switching on the amount of rework (%) at a plant. Below are the weekly rework data for 24 work groups one month after the start of the study.

Job Switch—Daily	Job Switch—Weekly	No Job Switch
1.83	2.06	4.44
1.64	1.67	2.42
1.54	1.56	2.15
1.27	1.25	2.13
1.19	1.19	2.07
0.90	0.85	2.00
0.79	0.65	1.85
0.09	0.41	1.80

a. Use software to develop box plots for the three treatment levels. Are assumptions 2 and 3 underlying the F-based analysis of variance reasonable for the study data? Also determine the three sample median rework percentages.

b. Which treatment level produces the minimum rework percentage? Set an experimentwise 90% level of confidence.

10.6 The Two-Factor, Completely Random Factorial Study

We have focused up to this point on one-factor, k-level studies. Sometimes managers run planned change studies that have two or more experimental factors. We now turn to these multifactor, or factorial, experiments. By the end of this section you should be able to:

1. draw a set of profiles for a factorial study and determine whether there is likely to be a significant interaction effect;
2. analyze a factorial experiment; and
3. explain what an interaction is and what are its decision making implications.

Return to the case of the cracked table drawers discussed in Section 10.1. Using the Kepner–Tregoe diagnostic method (Table 10.1), Apex suspected that the combination of new raw material and the 10-inch-deep drawers had caused excessive cracking. This called for a two-factor study. Factor A, material vendor, has two levels and factor B, stamping depth, has three levels. Apex chose an α level of .01 for the 2 (levels of Factor A) $\times$ 3 (levels of Factor B) completely randomized factorial study, which is outlined here.

Factor A	Factor B
Material vendor	Stamping depth
Original vendor—old material	4 inches
New vendor—new material	7 inches
	10 inches

Apex tested all six (2 $\times$ 3) combinations of material and stamping depth. It ran each combination, or experimental cell, five times for one hour each. Apex randomly selected enough old raw material to make 15 one-hour runs and randomly assigned the old material to the three stamping depths. Next, the team randomly selected enough new raw material to make 15 one-hour runs and randomly assigned the new material to the three stamping depths. The team randomly determined the sequence of the six combinations of runs and recorded the percentage of cracks for each one-hour run. Table 10.19 contains the results.

A factorial study has at least two experimental factors. Experimental factors are simply what managers vary in hopes of improving the product, service, performance, or quality. In a factorial study, every level of one factor is run in combination with every level of all other factors. Thus, each type of material will be tested at all three stamping depths. For example, the upper left-hand cell represents five one-hour runs using old material and stamping 4-inch-deep drawers.

Table 10.19

Data for Two-Factor Cracked Drawer Study

| | Stamping Depth (inches) | | | |
	4	7	10	Means
Old Material	1	1	0	
	0	0	0	
	0	1	2	1
	2	2	1	
	2	1	2	
New Material	0	4	6	
	2	5	5	
	0	3	7	3.667
	2	4	6	
	1	4	6	
Means	1	2.5	3.5	2.333 overall mean

Dependent variable: Percentage of drawers cracked over a one-hour run. For example, using the old material to produce 4-inch-deep drawers generated 1%, 0%, 0%, 2%, and 2% cracked drawers. The cell mean is 1%.

Designing a Factorial Study

In designing a factorial experiment, we must make decisions about the following:

1. the number of experimental factors or treatments
2. the number of levels of each factor or treatment
3. the sample size in each experimental cell
4. the design and execution of the study

With regard to the number of experimental factors, we need to include all treatments that we believe affect the dependent variable. However, the study size increases very rapidly as we increase the number of experimental factors. For example, a study with five factors, each at two levels, has 32 cells,* while adding one more factor with two levels doubles the number of cells. *A good rule of thumb*: Keep the number of factors to four or less.

---

*To determine the number of experimental cells, multiply the numbers of levels of all the factors.

Similarly, the study size increases as we increase the number of levels per factor. A five-factor study, each at four levels, has 1,024 cells. Unless there is a compelling need, we should consider only two levels for each factor. In the cracked drawer study, the compelling need is that three depths of drawers are produced. *A good rule of thumb:* Limit to two, or at most three, the number of levels of each experimental factor, unless the manager can make a strong argument as to why there should be more.

A factorial study should have at least two observations in each of its experimental cells in order to get a measure of the sum of squares within variation. Without it, we cannot compute a variance ratio. While large sample sizes in each experimental cell are desirable, they also increase the cost of the study.

To design and execute a valid study, we know, from Chapter 6, that we must control for history, diffusion of treatment, and compensatory rivalry, and use randomization whenever possible. The analysis of variance is meaningful only when the study is valid.

We consider a factorial study when we think that two or more factors, or treatments, affect the dependent variable of interest or when we suspect an interaction effect. We discuss interaction effects next.

Exploratory Data Analysis: Graphing Profiles

The factorial study introduces a new concept—the interaction effect. We will use Table 10.20 to illustrate the interaction effect for the cracked drawer factorial study. The tabled values are the mean percentages of cracked drawers over five one-hour runs.

Table 10.20

Data Sets to Illustrate the Absence and Presence of an Interaction Effect

	Data Set 1			Data Set 2		
	4 inches	7 inches	10 inches	4 inches	7 inches	10 inches
Old	1%	2%	1%	7%	5%	1%
New	4%	5%	4%	1%	6%	8%

Profile graphs are an effective way of seeing (but not testing for) an interaction effect. To construct a profile graph, place one experimental factor on the horizontal axis. In Figure 10.6 we have selected the stamping depth factor. The vertical axis represents the dependent variable—percentage cracking. Plot the cell mean values for each level of the second experimental factor (type of material). Figure 10.6 is called a *material vendor* profile graph. It is a graph of the two types of materials.

Figure 10.6 (next page) shows that the profiles are parallel. Irrespective of the stamping depth, the old material produces fewer percentage defects than the new material. In short, the old material *appears* to be better. We say appears because we have only plotted profiles and not done the formal statistical analysis.

Figure 10.7 (next page) shows the material vendor profile graph for data set 2. In this case, the profiles are *not* parallel. That is, *it appears* that the better material *depends* on the stamping depth. The old material works best for the 10-inch drawers, and the new material works best for the 4-inch drawers.

FIGURE 10.6   Material Vendor Profile for Data Set 1

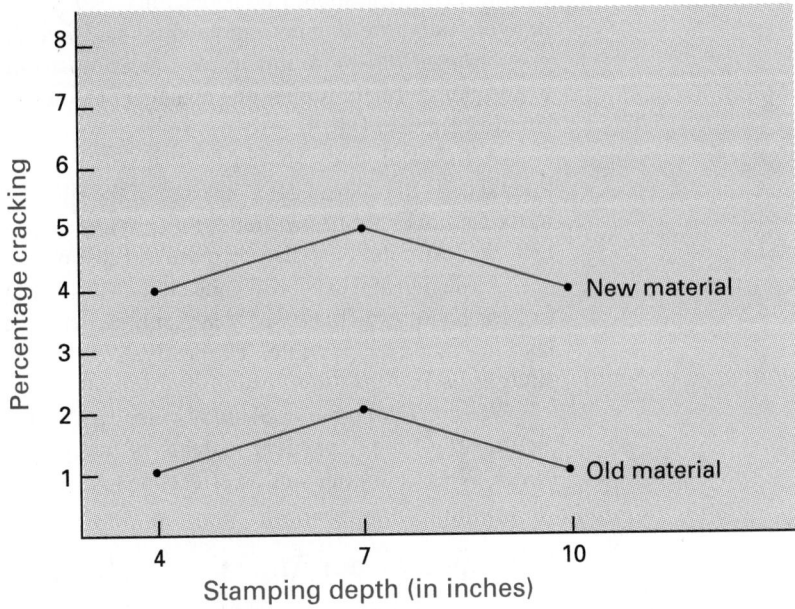

Two factors exhibit an
interaction effect when the
effect of one factor changes
at different levels of the
other factor(s).▪

Figure 10.7 *suggests* an **interaction effect,** while Figure 10.6 does not. When an interaction is present, the best level of one factor depends on the level of the other factor(s). We cannot make general statements such as "one material is best overall." The best material depends on the stamping depth.

FIGURE 10.7   Material Vendor Profile for Data Set 2

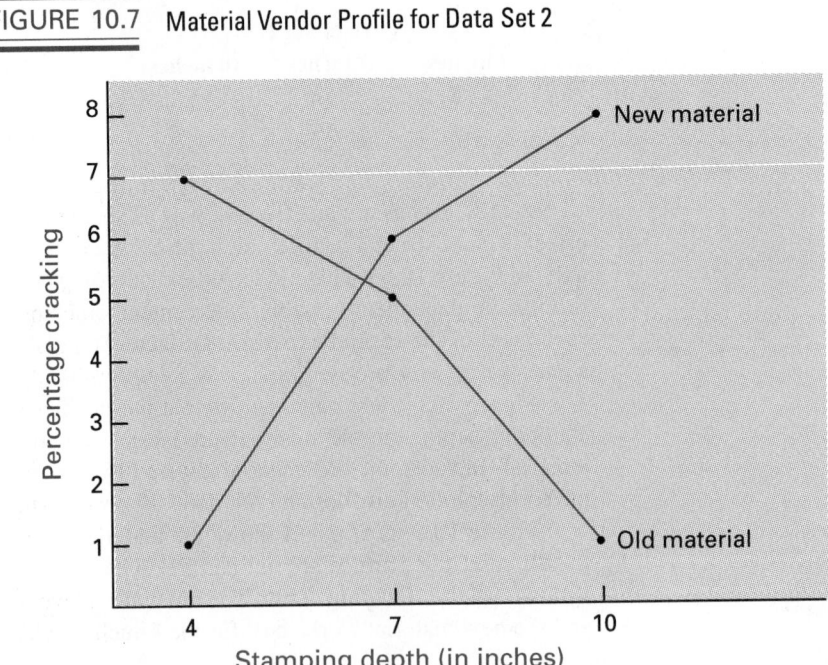

FIGURE 10.8   Material Vendor Profile for Apex Study

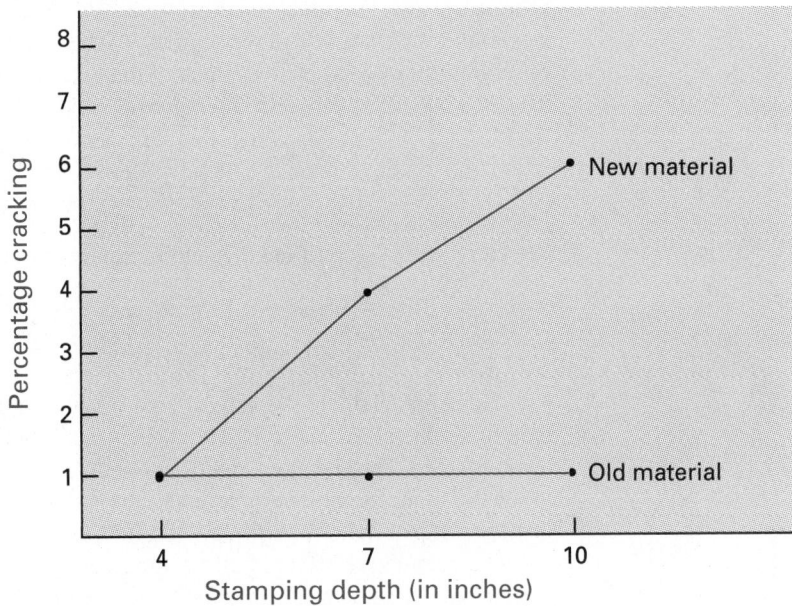

It makes no difference which factor we graph. In Figures 10.6 and 10.7, we drew *material vendor* profiles. We would have drawn the same tentative conclusions had we drawn *stamping depth* profiles—that is, where we assign type of material to the horizontal axis and the profiles reflect the three different stamping depths.

Now return to the actual study. Table 10.19 suggests that there is an interaction between the material vendor and the stamping depth. Figure 10.8 shows the profile plots for the six cell means in Table 10.19. The old material vendor profile is horizontal, while the new material vendor profile slopes upward to the right. Clearly, we have nonparallel profiles. Now we must do the analysis of variance to confirm the interaction effect.

Total Sum of Squares

As in the one-factor design, we begin by computing the total sum of squares. This represents the total variation in all 30 observations in Table 10.19 about the overall mean of 2.333%. It is given by

$$\text{SST} = (1 - 2.333)^2 + (0 - 2.333)^2 + \cdots + (6 - 2.333)^2 + (6 - 2.333)^2$$

$$= 134.67 \text{ units of variation}$$

What accounts for the 134.67 units of variation? It is due to four sources:

1. the *main effect* of factor A (material vendor treatment)
2. the *main effect* of factor B (stamping depth treatment)
3. the *interaction effect* between material vendor and stamping depth, and
4. all other possible factors that we might have varied but chose not to—the *within effect*.

Let's compute the first two sources of variation. Although we are analyzing a new design, we can use our basic definitions for the sum of squares terms.

Sum of Squares for Main Effects

What two numbers best represent the main effect of the material vendor? The row sample means. The mean of these two row means is the overall mean of 2.333%. Remember that we will have to weight the squared differences by the number of observations used to calculate each of the two sample means, the weighting constant. Thus the sum of squares for the material vendor factor is

$$SSA = 15\,[(1 - 2.333)^2 + (3.667 - 2.333)^2]$$

$$= 53.33 \text{ units of variation}$$

We can likewise determine the sum of squares for the stamping depth factor:

$$SSB = 10[(1 - 2.333)^2 + (2.5 - 2.333)^2 + (3.5 - 2.333)^2]$$

$$= 31.67 \text{ units of variation}$$

Next we calculate the sum of squares within term. Look at the upper left-hand experimental cell in Table 10.19 where Apex ran old material and produced 4-inch-deep drawers. The five data values are not all the same. The differences must be due to all the other factors we ignored in the study. These include stamping operators' levels of experience or skill, age of stamping equipment, closeness of supervision, etc. The cumulative effect of all the ignored factors causes variation within an experimental cell. Given this, how should we calculate the within sum of squares? Please think about it before reading on.

Sum of Squares Within

We compute the sum of the squared differences between each cell value and its cell mean. The six cell means are 1%, 1%, 1%, 1%, 4%, and 6%. The calculation contains 30 terms, since there are five observations in each of six experimental cells. This approach is identical to the way we calculated the within sum of squares for a one-factor, completely randomized design. The sums of the squared differences, along with their corresponding cell factors, are given by

Within Sum of Squares	Cell
$(1 - 1)^2 + \cdots + (2 - 1)^2$	old material and 4-inch drawers
$+(1 - 1)^2 + \cdots + (1 - 1)^2$	old material and 7-inch drawers
$+(0 - 1)^2 + \cdots + (2 - 1)^2$	old material and 10-inch drawers
$+(0 - 1)^2 + \cdots + (1 - 1)^2$	new material and 4-inch drawers
$+(4 - 4)^2 + \cdots + (4 - 4)^2$	new material and 7-inch drawers
$+(6 - 6)^2 + \cdots + (6 - 6)^2$	new material and 10-inch drawers

$$SSW = 18 \text{ units of variation}$$

SSA, SSB, and the within sum of squares have accounted for 103.00 of the 134.67 units of total variation. The remainder, or 31.67 units of variation, must be due to the possible interaction effect of factors A and B, the AB interaction. In general, the AB interaction effect equals

$$SSAB = SST - (SSA + SSB + SSW) \qquad (10.11)$$

Because the sums of squares computations for a factorial study can be time-consuming, we recommend using statistical software.

Degrees of Freedom

For the data in Table 10.19, the total number of degrees of freedom is the total sample size minus 1, or 29. The degrees of freedom for factor A is the number of levels minus 1, or 1. The degrees of freedom for factor B is $3 - 1 = 2$. The degrees of freedom for the within term is 24. Since there are five observations per cell, there must be $5 - 1 = 4$ degrees of freedom for each cell. There are six cells and therefore there are 24 degrees of freedom. The remaining 2 degrees of freedom belong to the interaction sum of squares term. Another way to compute the degrees of freedom for the AB interaction term is to multiply the degrees of freedom for factors A and B ($1 \cdot 2 = 2$).

Now it becomes clear why it is necessary to have at least two data values per experimental cell. With only one observation, there would be no degrees of freedom for the within term and we could not compute the variance-within term. Without the variance-within term, we could not compute a variance ratio.

Table 10.21 is the analysis of variance table for the cracked drawer study. The three variance ratios are simply the variances due to factors A, B, and AB, each divided by the variance-within (MSW) term, .75. Now we can determine whether either the main effects or the interaction effect affects the dependent variable, the percentage of cracked drawers.

Table 10.21

ANOVA for the Cracked Drawer Study

Source of Variation	Sum of Squares	df	MS	Variance Ratio
Treat-A Material	53.33	1	53.33	71.11
Treat-B Depth	31.67	2	15.83	21.11
Treat-AB	31.67	2	15.83	21.11
Within	18.00	24	75	
Total	134.67	29		

Hypotheses

For a two-factor factorial study, there are three sets of null and alternative hypotheses to test:

1. H_0: Material vendor and stamping depth do not interact to affect the population mean percentage of cracked drawers. There is no interaction effect
   H_1: There is an interaction effect.

2. H_0: Stamping depth (treatment B) has no effect on the population mean percentage of cracked drawers.
   H_1: Stamping depth has an effect.

3. H_0: Material vendor (treatment A) has no effect on the population mean percentage of cracked drawers.
   H_1: Material vendor has an effect.

   $\alpha = .01$

As in the one-factor design, the denominator of the variance ratio is the within-cell variance (MSW). We begin by testing for an interaction effect. If there is a significant interaction, then we know that the percentage of cracking depends on the combination of material and drawer depth. If there is no interaction, then we can determine if either factor has an impact on the dependent variable.

Test for Interaction Effect   Here is the decision rule for the interaction effect:

Only if the variance ratio for the AB INTERACTION is greater than the critical F-value should Apex reject the interaction null hypothesis.

From Appendix 7, the critical value is:

Critical value $= F(1 - \alpha$ percentile value; $\mathrm{df}_{AB}, \mathrm{df}_{WITHIN})$

We will reject the interaction null hypothesis if its variance ratio is greater than 5.61, $F(.99; 2, 24)$. Since the variance ratio of 21.11 falls in the rejection region, there is a material vendor–stamping depth interaction effect.

The statistically significant interaction tells us that the percentage of cracks depends on the material vendor and the stamping depth. The material vendor profile graph presented earlier in Figure 10.8 helps us understand the managerial implications of the significant interaction.

The profiles in Figure 10.8 suggest that

1. with the old material, the percentage of cracks is 1% for all stamping depths; and
2. with the new material, the percentage of cracks increases with increasing stamping depth.

The two-factor study has verified that the root cause of the cracked drawers is the new material in combination with the 7-inch and 10-inch stamping depths. That is, the new material works well for the 4-inch drawers, but the metal cracks when used for the deeper drawers. Now Apex must take corrective action. They have two options:

1. Switch back to the original material vendor. Note that the percentage cracking is constant at 1% over all stamping depths with that vendor's material.
2. Ask the new vendor to adjust the composition of its material so that there will not be an increase in cracking at the 7-inch and 10-inch stamping depths.

Given a significant interaction effect, there is no need to test the remaining hypotheses—treatment A or treatment B. We already know the two factors interact to affect the dependent variable.

However, suppose that the variance ratio for the interaction effect had fallen in the acceptance region—that is, it was less than 5.61. Then we would have compared the variance ratio for each main effect against its corresponding critical value.

Tests for Main Effects   Here are the decision rules for testing the main effects when no significant interaction effect is found:

Factor B

Only if the variance ratio for the TREAT-B is greater than the critical F-value should a manager reject the factor B null hypothesis.

Critical value $= F(1 - \alpha$ percentile value; $\mathrm{df}_B, \mathrm{df}_{WITHIN})$

Factor A

Only if the variance ratio for the TREAT-A is greater than the critical F-value should a manager reject the factor A null hypothesis.

Critical value $= F(1 - \alpha$ percentile value; $\mathrm{df}_A, \mathrm{df}_{WITHIN})$

In summary, consider a factorial study when you think that two or more factors affect the dependent variable of interest or when you suspect an interaction effect. Always draw profile graphs before doing the analysis of variance. The profiles are necessary also to understand the managerial implications of a significant interaction.

SECTION 10.6 EXERCISES

1. How many experimental factors are there in a 2×2 factorial experiment? How many levels of each experimental factor are there?

2. How many experimental cells would a 2×3 factorial design have? How many experimental units would be needed if we wanted 10 observations per cell?

3. What are the main effects for a 2×2 factorial design?

4. What is an interaction? Why is it important to test for an interaction before testing the main effects?

5. Determine the critical F-values for the following four data sets. Are the main effects or interactions significant?

   a. $MSA = 65$ $MSW = 10$ $\alpha = .05$
       $df_A = 1$ $df_{WITHIN} = 15$

   b. $MSB = 35$ $MSW = 30$ $\alpha = .01$
       $df_B = 2$ $df_{WITHIN} = 24$

   c. $MSAB = 230$ $MSW = 30$ $\alpha = .025$
       $df_{AB} = 1$ $df_{WITHIN} = 24$

   d. $MSAB = 20$ $MSW = 9.4$ $\alpha = .005$
       $df_{AB} = 3$ $df_{WITHIN} = 60$

6. Suppose that COMCEL tries two different promotions in two different market segments (income levels) to induce customers to increase car phone usage. The results of the analysis for the promotion—market segment factorial experiment are shown here.

Source of Variation	Sum of Squares	df	MS	Variance Ratio
Treat-A: Promotion	2,530	1	2,530.00	_____
Treat-B: Income	1,050	1	1,050.00	_____
Treat-AB	15	1	15.00	_____
Within	160	16	10.00	
Total	3,755	19		

   a. Complete the table by filling in the variance ratios.
   b. For an α level of .05, is there an interaction between promotion and income?
   c. For an α level of .05, is there a difference between the mean responses to the two different types of promotion?
   d. For an α level of .05, is there a difference between the mean responses to the two different levels of income?

7. A firm seeks to maximize consumer awareness (on a 0–100 scale) for a new breakfast cereal. Cereal box designers will vary two factors, or treatments: (1) package size— $8\frac{1}{2}''$ by $12''$ vs. $10''$ by $14''$ and (2) package color—brown/red vs. green/blue.
   a. Consider the following size of package profile. What conclusion can be drawn? Does there appear to be an interaction?

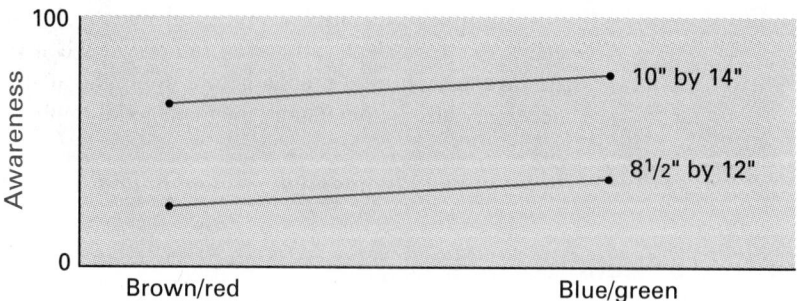

b. Consider the following box color profile. What conclusion can be drawn? Does there appear to be an interaction? If the package must be 8½" by 12" (to fit on grocery shelves), what package color would you recommend?

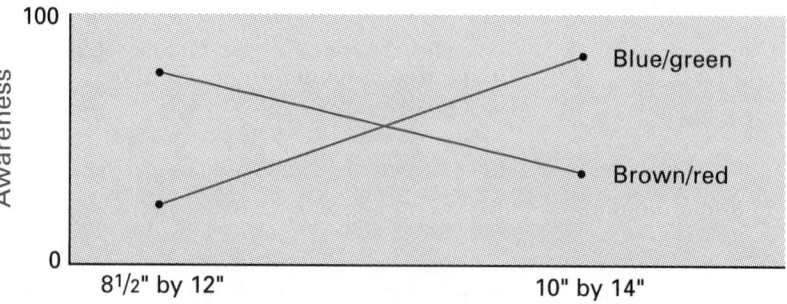

8. We have conducted a 2 × 2 factorial study on the effect of teaching method and students' SAT scores on test scores in a freshman history class. Here are the data.

| | | Factor A | | |
		Lecture	Discovery	Means
	Less than 900	70	85	77.5
Factor B	More than 1100	80	95	87.5
	Means	75	90	82.5

a. Plot a profile graph for this study. Assign type of teaching—lecture and discovery—to the horizontal axis. Assign test scores to the vertical axis. Plot the SAT level profile. Does there appear to be an interaction?

b. Plot a profile graph for this study. Assign the SAT score—less than 900 and more than 1,100—to the horizontal axis. Assign test scores to the vertical axis. Plot the type of teaching profile. Does there appear to be an interaction?
  Note: The two profile graphs provide the same information. Thus, the choice of which factor to assign to the horizontal axis is purely a personal choice.

c. It appears that mean performance under discovery teaching is greater than the mean performance under the lecture method. If this difference in means is statistically significant, can we conclude that discovery teaching is best overall? Explain.

9. We have conducted a 2 × 2 factorial study on the effect of teaching method and students' SAT scores on test scores in a freshman history class. Here are the data.

	Factor A		
	Lecture	Discovery	Means
Less than 900	80	50	65
Factor B More than 1100	70	100	85
Means	75	75	75

a. Plot either an SAT-level or type-of-teaching profile graph for this experiment. Does there appear to be an interaction?

b. Does there appear to be one best teaching method? Explain.

10. We conduct a study to determine the number of trials needed to learn two different tasks by two methods of training. Four employees were randomly assigned to each task-method combination. The results are shown.

	Task 1	Task 2
Method 1	2, 3, 3, 2	4, 6, 6, 8
Method 2	5, 7, 6, 8	3, 2, 2, 3

a. Compute the cell means and plot the profiles for the two factors. What can we conclude from the profiles?

b. Perform an analysis of variance on these data. Let $\alpha = .01$.

c. Does it appear that one task takes fewer trials to learn than the other or that one method requires fewer trials to learn the two tasks? Explain.

11. Consider the following data from a small scale 2×2 factorial study. The dependent variable is the number of lost bags per 10,000 passengers over two successive weeks. Present practice at Allegheny Airlines is that counter personnel receive 20 hours of check-in training and manually tag baggage. The airlines' goal is zero lost bags per 10,000 passengers.

	Factor A	
	Manual Tag	Computer Tag
20 Hours	10	8
	8	6
Factor B		
40 Hours	9	0
	9	2

a. Compute the cell means and plot (1) tag method and (2) hours of training profiles.

b. Perform an analysis of variance. Use a .05 α level.

c. What tag method and training hours combination should Allegheny Airlines institute? Explain.

12. Complete the following ANOVA table and answer the questions relating to it.

Source of Variation	Sum of Squares	df	MS	Variance Ratio
Treat-A	170	___	___	___
Treat-B	450	1	___	___
Treat-AB	14	2	___	___
Within	___	24	___	
Total	950	29		

a. How many levels does factor A have?

b. How many observations per cell were there, assuming an equal number per cell?

c. Can the hypothesis of no interaction be rejected at the $\alpha = .05$ level? Explain.

d. Is there a difference in the treatment means of factor A at the $\alpha = .05$ level? Explain.

e. Is there a difference in the means of factor B at the $\alpha = .05$ level? Explain.

13. We run a study to determine which type of clothes dryer, gas or electric, is better at drying clothes. At the same time, the purpose of the experiment was to determine which brand of dryer, A, B, or C, was most effective. The effectiveness of each dryer was measured by the percentage moisture that remained in the test clothing after 30 minutes. Here are the data.

		Brand		
		A	B	C
Type	Gas	17, 13, 21, 19, 15	7, 10, 6, 5, 7	12, 9, 13, 11, 15
	Electric	15, 11, 18, 12, 19	8, 12, 5, 8, 7	11, 8, 15, 10, 11

a. Plot a profile graph. Does it appear that there is an interaction between the type of dryer and brand? Explain what an interaction would mean in practical terms.
b. Use a software package to perform an analysis of variance on these data. Use a .01 level of significance.
c. Is there a significant interaction between type of dryer and brand?
d. Is one type of dryer better than the other?
e. Is there a difference among the three brands?

14. Mr. Koffee is in the product development phase for its new coffee maker. It wants to know which product attributes consumers want and the price they are willing to pay for these attributes. Two important attributes are (1) brew capacity and (2) brew time. Mr. Koffee selects a random sample of 18 potential consumers. Two consumers each will be given one of the nine prototype coffee makers described below. They must indicate the likelihood of purchasing the prototype. This method is a simplified version of what in marketing is called **conjoint analysis.**

Prototype	Brew Capacity (cups)	Brew Time (minutes)	Cost
1	4	3	$24.99
2	4	5	27.99
3	4	7	33.99
4	6	3	26.99
5	6	5	29.99
6	6	7	35.99
7	8	3	29.99
8	8	5	32.99
9	8	7	38.99

Consider the data for the product feature-cost study. The dependent variable is intent to purchase on a 0–100 scale.

		Factor A		
		4-cup	6-cup	8-cup
Factor B	3 minutes	55 65	40 50	50 45
	5 minutes	50 70	80 90	30 40
	7 minutes	55 65	10 30	50 70

a. Compute the cell means and plot (1) brew capacity and (2) brew time profiles.

b. Use a software package to conduct an ANOVA. Use the ANOVA results and the computed cell means to determine the combination of brew capacity and brew time that consumers most desire. Use a .05 α level.

15. Process improvements are critical for maintaining or obtaining a competitive edge. This example illustrates a simplified version of *evolutionary operations,* a method used to improve manufacturing processes. COMCEL seeks to increase the tensile strength of its phone handsets by varying the injection molding temperature and pressure. Presently COMCEL is achieving a mean tensile strength between 4,750 and 4,800 pounds per square inch (ppsi). Shown are the results of a 2 $\times$ 2 factorial study. Present manufacturing conditions are 1,200 degrees and 500 kilograms (kg).

	Study 1	
	1,200 degrees	1,250 degrees
500 kg	4,750	4,725
	4,775	4,750
	4,800	4,800
600 kg	4,525	4,925
	4,500	4,950
	4,550	4,950

a. Compute the cell means and plot (1) injection temperature and (2) pressure profiles.
b. Use a software package to conduct an ANOVA. Use the ANOVA results and the computed cell means to determine the best combination of injection temperature and pressure. Use $\alpha = .05$.

COMCEL obtained the highest tensile strength at 1,250 degrees and 600 kg of pressure. COMCEL wonders if increasing the temperature and pressure further will yield even greater tensile strengths. It uses the 1,250 degrees and 600 kg settings as a base and runs the following 2 $\times$ 2 factorial study.

	Study 2	
	1,250 degrees	1,300 degrees
600 kg	4,925	4,825
	4,930	4,850
	4,940	4,825
650 kg	4,805	4,780
	4,800	4,750
	4,825	4,760

c. Compute the cell means and plot (1) injection temperature and (2) pressure profiles.
d. Use a software package to conduct an ANOVA. Use the ANOVA results and the computed cell means to determine the best combination of injection temperature and pressure. Use $\alpha = .05$.

10.7 Key Ideas and Overview

In this chapter we have discussed the two most commonly used experimental designs, the one-factor and factorial designs. Both are alternatives to the survey-based random or stratified sampling data collection methods that were used in Chapters 6, 7, 8, and 9. When designing *planned change* studies, use these two rules in deciding between the one-factor and factorial studies:

RULE 1:   Design and run a one-factor study when there is reason to believe that only one factor, or treatment, will have a major impact on the dependent variable. You are assuming that all other factors do not have much impact on the dependent variable.

RULE 2:   Design and run a factorial study when there is reason to believe that two or more factors will have a major impact on the dependent variable, or when there is reason to suspect an interaction (nonparallel profiles) between two or more factors.

Good management has the capability to ask the right questions. In the last four chapters, we have learned the proper questions to ask when solving problems and making decisions. Tables 10.22 and 10.23 summarize those questions and review the exploratory and analytical tools available to answer them. After all, good questions deserve good answers.

Table 10.22

Asking the Right Questions

Typical Managerial Questions	Statistical Questions
1. What is our customers' mean income?	What is the population mean, median, or proportion?
2. What is the median service time?	
3. What percentage of employees favor a flex-hours system?	
4. Which group has better mean performance—Chicago or Denver?	Are two population means, medians, or proportions the same?
5. Which plant has a higher median level of job satisfaction?	
6. Is the proportion of high-income car phone users the same in two regions?	
7. Which group's productivity shows less fluctuation?	Are two population variances or dispersions the same?
8. Does the Seattle plant have greater dispersion in sick leave taken than the Philadelphia plant?	
9. Which of three sales displays generates the highest income?	Are the factors significant?
10. Do all employees respond best to one approach for improving morale? Or, does the best approach differ for hourly, professional, and management personnel?	Is there an interaction effect between two or more factors?

Table 10.23

Statistical Tools to Answer Managerial Questions

Statistical Questions	Exploratory Tools	Analytical Methods
What is the population mean, median, or proportion?	Stem-and-leaf displays Box plots	Confidence interval or hypothesis testing on one population parameter—Chapters 7 and 9.
Are two population means, medians, or proportions the same? Are two population variances or dispersions the same?	Multiple stem-and-leaf displays Multiple box plots	Confidence interval or hypothesis testing on the difference between two population parameters—Chapters 8 and 9.
Are the factors significant? Is there an interaction effect?	Spread charts Interaction profiles	F-based or Kruskal–Wallis analyses of variance and Tukey or Dunn confidence intervals on differences between population means or medians—Chapter 10.

COMCEL

Date: November 17, 1994
To: Sarah Teman, Manager of Operations
From: Bill Katz, Production Testing
Re: Resolution of Apex Material Cracking Problem

SUMMARY
Substandard material purchased from a new supplier caused the cracking problem. The new material cracked when drawers were stamped at a depth of greater than 4 inches. Apex has returned to its former supplier and the problem has not returned.

SUPPORTING ANALYSIS
A Kepner–Tregoe problem definition worksheet indicated that material from a new vendor had probably caused the increase in cracking. Since we suspected the new material, we ran a 2 × 3 factorial study to compare

percentage cracking rates for the new and old materials for stamping 4-, 7-, and 10-inch drawers.

We conducted the study in the following manner. We used one operator and one machine. We randomly selected panels from stock and randomly assigned the panels to the six experimental cells. We then made five 1-hour production runs for each combination of material and drawer depth. We randomly determined the run sequence.

The statistical analysis indicated that the 7-inch- and 10-inch-deep drawers made with panels of the new material had cracking rates well beyond 1%. The 4-inch-, 7-inch-, and 10-inch-deep drawers made with the old material had cracking rates of 1%. In short, the new material caused the excessive cracking.

CHAPTER 10 QUESTIONS

1. In the Apex Plastics and Metals case study, suggest several other possible causes for the increased cracking rate.

2. Why isn't it always possible to conduct planned change studies when testing problem-solving hypotheses?

3. Explain why "no treatment effect" is the null hypothesis.

4. Why is it necessary to use the Kepner–Tregoe method in problem solving?

5. What source of variation does the spread within reflect?

6. What source of variation does the spread between reflect?

7. When the spread between is much larger than the spread within, we are likely to reject the null hypothesis of no treatment effect. Why?

8. Why must we do the analysis of variance? Can't spread chart exploratory data analysis replace the analysis of variance?

9. What do the sum of squares total, between, and within measure?

10. In a one-factor, k-level design, why are there only two sources of variation?

11. Why is a large variance ratio necessary to reject the "no treatment effect" null hypothesis?

12. What assumptions must we make about the data in order to use the analysis of variance?

13. If we reject the null hypothesis in an analysis of variance, why is it necessary to run Tukey's HSD comparisons?

14. Correct if necessary:

    If an HSD confidence interval contains the value of 1, we conclude that two sample means do not differ.

15. What is an experimentwise error rate?

16. If an exploratory data analysis indicates excessive outliers in a one-factor design study, what analysis should we do?

17. If we reject the null hypothesis of no difference in population medians, must we find differences in all the pairwise comparisons in Dunn's follow-up analysis?

18. Provide a business example where you would suspect an interaction between two factors.

19. What problems might we have if we ran a five-factor factorial study with each factor, or treatment, at three levels?

20. What does the expression, "there is no one best way," mean in a statistical sense?

CHAPTER 10 APPLICATION PROBLEMS

1. A firm wishes to compare three training methods to determine which is best in improving problem-solving skills: lecture (L), role play (R), and case method (C). The spread chart shows the results on a common examination given to the 15 participants in the study.

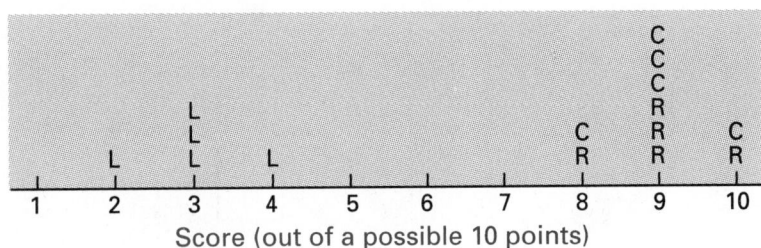

Score (out of a possible 10 points)

    a. Describe how the firm should have selected participants and assigned them to the three treatment levels.
    b. Does the spread chart suggest that the three teaching methods are equally effective?

2. Firms often use the Watson–Glaser Critical Thinking Appraisal to measure problem-solving ability. The instrument measures the ability to make inferences, assess assumptions, draw conclusions, and evaluate arguments. Below are data from a study to determine whether the level of critical thinking affects the time to solve a complex disturbance problem.

Time in Minutes to Solve the Problem

High Critical	Medium Critical	Low Critical
10	18	39
20	100	118
35	126	139
47	149	157
379	565	784

    a. Draw a multiple box plot for the three treatment levels.
    b. What analysis is appropriate? Why?
    c. Analyze the data using an α level of .05.

3. You believe that different types of managers learn problem solving best by different teaching methods. You will classify managers according to the Sensing–Intuition dimension of the Myers–Briggs Type Indicator. Sensing managers like presentations that are detailed and organized, while intuitive managers prefer to discover the important principles in a presentation. Thus you believe that sensing managers will prefer the lecture method, while intuitive managers will prefer the case method. You wish to test your beliefs.
    a. What type of experiment should you design?
    b. Construct a data table for the two-factor study that agrees with your beliefs. Show cell mean scores on the common final—from 0 to 100.
    c. Draw type-of-manager profile graphs for your data. That is, assign type of teaching method to the horizontal axis. Plot how sensing and intuitive managers perform when taught by the two methods.

4. You wish to reduce the time customers must wait to get their equipment repaired. You test three different strategies and include a control group—the present repair method. Shown is a multiple box plot of the results. What are you likely to conclude? Explain.

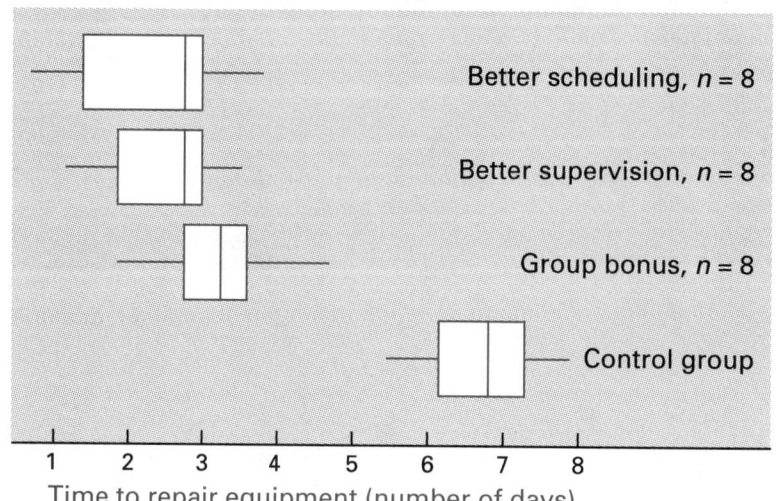

5. You believe that workers with both high and low need for independence work best under a participative style leader, and not an autocratic leader.

   a. How many factors should you have in your study to test your assertion? Why?
   b. How many levels of the leadership factor should there be?
   c. If you believe that workers with low need for independence work best under an autocratic leader and workers with high need for independence work best under a participative leader, which experimental design is best? Why?
   d. Construct a data table for the two-factor study that agrees with your beliefs. Show cell mean scores (in productivity per hour).

6. Shown are two spread charts for a one-factor, three-level study conducted by a foundation on the effect of three types of TV ads on increasing awareness of sickle cell anemia. The three strategies are informative (I), persuasive (P), and emotional (E). Given the hypothetical data, for which study does it appear that we would reject the null hypothesis of no treatment effect? Defend your answer.

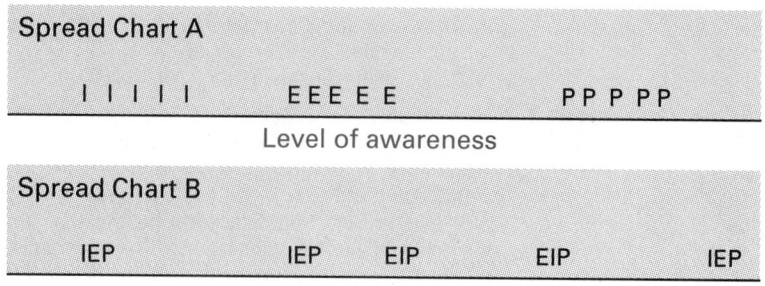

7. Which of three sales displays generates the largest revenue? Shown are the data from a one-factor, three-level planned change study.

Daily Revenue

Display A	Display B	Display C
$1,300	$150	$1,450
1,400	250	1,700
1,800	450	1,850
1,900	800	2,400
5,000	900	4,960

a. Draw a multiple box plot.
b. Are the three population median revenues the same for the displays? Use a .05 level of significance.
c. Set up 95% Dunn multiple comparisons on the differences among all pairs of population medians.

 8. Which computer has the longest time to failure? Shown are data on 15 randomly selected computers that have been tested until failure.

Time to Failure in Hours

Model A	Model B	Model C
105	35	143
4	2	66
65	110	15
197	145	99
56	76	80

a. Draw a multiple box plot for the data.
b. Is there any difference in the median time to failure among the three models? Use an α level of .05.

 9. You consider two possible improvements for razor blades that could increase the number of smooth shaves. The accompanying data are the results of a planned change study. The dependent variable is the number of shaves before the blade is no longer usable.

Plastic Coating on Blade	Lubricant on Blade	Standard Blade
15	15	7
13	17	9
11	15	8
13	11	8
13	12	8

a. Are the three sample mean numbers of shaves different?
b. Do you need an analysis of variance to answer part a?
c. Are the three population mean numbers of shaves different? If we set α at .05, can we reject the null hypothesis?
d. Which type of improvement extends the life of blades the most? Use a 95% experimentwise confidence level.

 10. A capstone course for an undergraduate Decision Science major uses a business simulation game. Student teams make a set of decisions in a hypothetical, but competitive, environment. Final stock price is the measure of decision effectiveness. Is there any difference in the performance among teams that do not use decision aids, those that use manual aids, and those that use computer-based decision aids? Here are the final stock prices of 15 teams under the three conditions.

No Aids	Manual Aids	Computer Aids
$ .12	$ .15	$1.00
1.59	3.16	4.10
3.50	3.60	6.20
3.52	4.70	6.30
13.55	16.25	22.40

   a. Draw a multiple box plot of the data.
   b. What analysis does the box plot suggest?
   c. Complete the suggested analysis. Set α at .05.

 11. Shown are data for a 2 × 2 factorial study on type of manager and teaching method first discussed in Exercise 3. The dependent variable is performance on the final exam.

Score on Final Exam
(Out of a Possible 10 Points)

	Lecture	Case Method
Sensing	9	3
	9	5
	9	4
Intuitive	2	9
	5	10
	5	8

   a. Draw a type-of-manager profile graph.
   b. Having set an α level of .05, is there a significant interaction effect?
   c. If you were in charge of training, what would the interaction effect mean for the way you run your training classes?

 12. Groupthink is the tendency of groups to reach a quick consensus and generate poor decisions. Groupthink happens to groups under high stress that have poor leadership. Shown is a factorial study that tests for the necessity of both conditions—high stress and poor leadership. The dependent variable is the number of symptoms of groupthink that each group exhibits as it solves a complex business case.

Number of Groupthink Symptoms

	Poor Leadership	Good Leadership
Low Stress	2	1
	3	1
	3	1
	4	1
High Stress	7	1
	7	1
	7	2
	7	0

   a. Draw the type-of-leadership-style profile graph.
   b. Draw the level-of-stress profile graph.
   c. Do an analysis of variance. Use a .05 level of significance.
   d. In simple terms, what does the interaction mean in terms of groupthink?

 13. Which creativity method—brainstorming or analogy—is better? Fifteen managers are randomly selected and are randomly divided into three groups of five each. Each group is randomly assigned to one of two creative methods or the control group. After learning the assigned creative method (managers in the control group receive no creativity training), each manager is given a minicase. At the end of 30 minutes we record the number of different ideas each manager has generated. Here are the data.

Control Group	Brainstorming	Analogy
1	7	9
2	11	9
3	12	11
5	12	12
7	13	14

   a. Draw a spread chart.
   b. Determine whether the three population mean numbers of alternative solutions are the same. Use a .01 alpha level.
   c. Which method (or methods) is best at generating the largest number of different ideas? Set up 99% experimentwise confidence intervals.

 14. Shown are the productivity cell means (units per hour) for a 2 × 5 factorial study.

	<1	1–3	4–6	7–9	10 or More
		Length of Time Employed in the Firm (years)			
Individual Bonus	100	100	95	90	85
Group Bonus	85	90	95	100	110

   a. Draw a length-of-time employed profile graph.
   b. Draw a type-of-bonus profile graph.
   c. Without doing a formal statistical analysis, does it appear that there is an interaction? Explain.

 15. A firm is considering three different strategies to collect accounts receivable. All three strategies are effective in collecting overdue accounts. However, the firm wants to determine which strategy maintains the accountholders' goodwill. Eighteen accounts that are 20 days past due are selected and subdivided randomly into three groups. Each group of accounts is randomly assigned to one strategy. The firm asks each accountholder after it has received its treatment to indicate the level of goodwill on a 10-point scale (1 = poor goodwill to 10 = excellent goodwill). Here are the data.

Letter	Phone Call	Letter and Phone Call
7	5	2
8	5	2
7	6	3
9	7	4
9	6	3
8	6	3

   a. Draw a spread chart.
   b. Which strategy (or strategies) is best at maintaining goodwill? Use a 95% experimentwise level of confidence.
   c. Explain why the letter and phone call strategy might have the lowest goodwill scores.

 16. Three new drugs are tested for effectiveness at two different hospitals by two independent teams of doctors. Suppose both teams found the same variance ratio. Yet, one team rejected the null hypothesis and concluded that at least one drug's effectiveness is different

from the other two. The other team, using the same level of significance, fails to reject the null hypothesis.
  a. Explain how this is possible.
  b. Construct a numerical example to support your explanation.

17. COMCEL is considering two promotion strategies to increase customer phone usage. The inverse rate promotion reduces the cost per minute with increasing phone usage. The free gifts promotion provides different gifts for different usage levels. COMCEL believes that the free gifts will work better with middle income users and the inverse rate promotion will work better with high income users.
  a. How many factors are there in the study?
  b. Assume COMCEL desires 50 subjects per cell. What is the total sample size for the study?
  c. Explain how COMCEL should select subjects for the factorial study and how they will be assigned to the experimental cells. Provide a detailed description.

18. Cola International wants to taste-test proposed reformulations of its major soft drink. It will try three types of sweeteners: sugar, saccharin, and aspartame. Twenty subjects rate each of the three formulations for tastiness on a scale from 0 = awful to 100 = very good.
  a. Shown are three 95% experimentwise confidence intervals for the difference between all pairs of treatment population means. What can you conclude?

Sugar – Saccharin	$(78-65) \pm 7$
Sugar – Aspartame	$(78-63) \pm 7$
Saccharin – Aspartame	$(65-63) \pm 7$

  b. Describe how Cola International should have conducted the study—that is, how it should have selected its sample, assigned the subjects to the three treatment levels, etc.

19. Refer to Exercise 18. Shown is a portion of the data in the cola reformulation study.

Sugar	Saccharin	Aspartame
80	65	65
75	66	70
81	61	62
78	65	65
75	60	63

  a. What factors might account for the fact that all the observations within each treatment level are not the same?
  b. Draw a spread chart. Which cola formulation do customers seem to prefer? Explain.

20. Does a stock's risk vary among industries? A stock analyst randomly selects five stocks from three industries—utilities, telecommunications, and computer technology—and records the historic beta coefficients. A beta coefficient measures a stock's volatility. Beta coefficients under 1.0 indicate stocks with very little risk; beta coefficients over 1.0 indicate risky stocks.
  Given are the three 95% Tukey confidence intervals on the difference in population mean beta coefficients. What can you conclude?

Technology – Utilities	$(1.80-.56) \pm .32$
Technology – Telecommunications	$(1.80-1.10) \pm .32$
Telecommunications – Utilities	$(1.10-.56) \pm .32$

21. Is the infant mortality rate in the United States lower than in other Western countries? We collect data from five randomly selected cities in the United States (U), West Germany (W), and France (F). We record the number of infant deaths per 1,000 births. The data, which are based on a UN Department of International Economic and Social Affairs report, are shown in the accompanying spread chart. What tentative conclusions can you draw from the spread chart? Discuss.

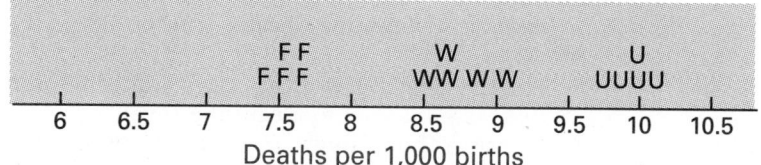

Deaths per 1,000 births

22. Does the mean indebtedness of delinquent card holders differ among the following three income classes?

Less than $20,000	$30,000–$50,000	Over $75,000
$146	$210	$585
124	156	708
178	112	606
156	165	647
145	110	578

a. Use statistical software to compute the variance ratio. What can you conclude about the mean level of indebtedness and level of annual income? Use $\alpha = .05$.
b. Does the mean level of indebtedness differ among all income classes? Use an experimentwise error rate of .05.

23. Suppose you believe that the mean level of indebtedness is affected not only by the credit card holder's annual income level (see Exercise 22) but also by his or her need for material goods—low or high need. Each factor affects the mean level of indebtedness. However, you suspect that high-income card holders with a high need for material possessions will have extraordinarily high mean levels of indebtedness.
a. What type of study should you consider running?
b. Develop hypothetical data that would support your position. Defend without doing the analysis of variance.

24. Do all states have the same mean cost per day for a hospital stay? A public policy watchdog group chooses three states—Alaska, South Dakota, and Georgia. It randomly selects six community hospitals and determines their mean cost per day. The data taken from the 1987 report of *Health Statistics* are shown here.

Alaska	South Dakota	Georgia
$892	$318	$456
808	350	500
980	370	425
880	280	450
901	325	460
870	300	470

a. Using the spread within and spread between ideas, does it appear that the population mean costs per day at community hospitals in the three states differ? Discuss.
b. If we are interested in drawing inferences only about the 18 hospitals in the study, do we need to conduct a formal analysis of variance?

25.

Date: October 21, 1995
To: Bill Katz, Supervisor of Testing
From: Sarah Teman, Manager of Operations
Re: Results of Planned Change Study

For the past 36 working days (since September 7), we have been testing two new microchip circuits as well as the present circuit. Our goal is to increase the number of hours of operation for our telephone units to over 1,100 hours before failure. Bill O'Hara tells me that this is absolutely essential to maintain our share of market. It will also reestablish us as a leading technology firm in the industry.

Specifically I want the answers to the following questions:

1. Is either circuit better than our present one?
2. Which microchip circuit is better in terms of accomplishing our 1,100-hour goal?

I will need your analysis by the end of the week.

Use Data Base IV in Appendix 9 for your analysis. Your response to Sarah Teman should include a brief memo and your analysis.

REFERENCES

Box, George; Hunter, W. G.; and J. S. Hunter. *Statistics for Experimenters.* New York: John Wiley, 1978.

Dunn, Olive J. "Multiple Comparisons Using Rank Sums." *Technometrics* 6(1964): 241–255.

Kepner, Benjamin, and Charles Tregoe. *The New Rational Manager.* Princeton, New Jersey: Princeton Research Press, 1988.

Keppel, Geoffrey. *Design and Analysis: A Researcher's Handbook.* Englewood Cliffs, New Jersey: Prentice-Hall, 1973.

Kirk, Roger. *Experimental Design: Procedures for the Behavioral Sciences.* Pacific Grove, CA: Brooks/Cole, 1982.

Montgomery, Douglas. *Design and Analysis of Experiments.* New York: John Wiley, 1992.

Tukey, John. "The Problem of Multiple Comparisons." Unpublished manuscript. Princeton, New Jersey, 1953.

APPENDIX: Statistical Software

Example: Here we use SAS to perform an analysis of variance. We compare the reductions in unit labor cost resulting from three different types of treatments: (1) team-building workshop; (2) creativity workshop; (3) control group (no workshop). The data are shown in Table 10.4, Data Set 1.

Input

```
01    DATA TEST;
02    INPUT TREAT $ COST; @@;
03    CARDS;
04    TB 3.05   TB 3.10 TB 3.13 TB 3.14 TB 3.18
      TB 3.22   TB 3.22 TB 3.24 TB 3.29 TB 3.32
05    CM 4.12   CM 4.13 CM 4.21 CM 4.21 CM 4.22
      CM 4.24   CM 4.26 CM 4.27 CM 4.27 CM 4.36
06    C    .15  C   .07 C   .30 C    .05 C    .15
      C    .02  C   .08 C   .03 C    .05 C    .10
07    ;

08    PROC ANOVA;
09    CLASS TREAT;
10    MODEL COST=TREAT;
11    MEANS TREAT/TUKEY CLDIFF;
12    ALPHA=.05;
```

Explanation of Input

01–07	See explanation in Software Appendix at the end of Chapter 2. The only added feature in this input is the $ after the TREAT variable. It tells SAS that the variable, TREAT, is nonnumeric.
08	Instructs SAS to perform the analysis of variance PROCess.
09	Tells SAS which of the variables entered is the qualitative or treatment variable. The variable TREAT represents the TB, CM, and C workshops.
10	Tells SAS that COST, the quantitative dependent variable, is dependent on (meaning of = sign) the TREATment level, the qualitative independent variable.
11	Tells SAS to construct Tukey confidence intervals between all pairs of population means.
12	SAS allows the user to specify the ALPHA level used for all pairwise comparisons. The options are .01, .05, and .1.

Output

```
Analysis of Variance Procedure
          Class Level Information
          Class    Levels    Values
01        TREAT    3         TB CM  C
          Number of observations in data set = 30
          Analysis of Variance Procedure
          Dependent Variable: COST
```

	Source	DF	Sum of Squares	Mean Square	F Value	Pr > F
02	Model	2	92.24054000	46.12027000	7249.08	0.0001
03	Error	27	0.17178000	0.00636222		
04	Corrected Total	29	92.41232000			

	R-Square	CV	Root MSE	COST Mean
05	0.998141	3.182903	0.079764	2.506000

	Source	DF	Anova SS	Mean Square	F Value	Pr > F
06						
07	TREAT	2	92.24054000	46.12027000	7249.08	0.0001

```
     Analysis of Variance Procedure
     Tukey's Studentized Range (HSD) Test for variable: COST

NOTE: This test controls the type I experimentwise error rate.


08   Alpha= 0.05  Confidence= 0.95  df= 27  MSE= 0.006362

       Critical Value of Studentized Range= 3.506  (See Appendix 8)


09   Minimum Significant Difference= 0.0884

10   Comparisons significant at the 0.05 level are indicated by '***'.
```

	Comparison		TREAT	Simultaneous Lower Confidence Limit	Difference Between Means	Simultaneous Upper Confidence Limit	
11	CM	-	TB	0.95156	1.04000	1.12844	***
	CM	-	C	4.04056	4.12900	4.21744	***
	TB	-	CM	-1.12844	-1.04000	-0.95156	***
	TB	-	C	3.00056	3.08900	3.17744	***
	C	-	CM	-4.21744	-4.12900	-4.04056	***
	C	-	TB	-3.17744	-3.08900	-3.00056	***

Interpretation of Output

01	Names the treatment levels (TB, CM, C)
02–04	The ANOVA program handles more than one factor. SAS begins by testing whether any factor is related to the dependent variable. For example, the two-factor design presented in section 10.5 would be modelled by ANOVA as

$$\%CRACKS = f(DEPTH, MATERIAL, DEPTH \times MATERIAL)$$

The Model SS would be the portion of the total sum of squares due to these three factors. The "Corrected Total" is the technical term for Total Sum of Squares. When there is only one factor or treatment, the Model sum of squares is the Between treatment sum of squares, SSB, we discussed in this chapter. The Error sum of squares is the Within treatment sum of squares, SSW.

05	The R-square is the ratio of the model sum of squares to the Corrected Total sum of squares. It indicates the proportion of the total variation in the dependent variable due to all the factors included in the model. (See Chapter 11 for more on this ratio.)
06–07	Tests the significance of each factor (treatment) included in the model. When there is only one factor, the test of the model is the same as the test for the single factor. Note that the degrees of freedom and the F-values are the same for the test of the Model and the test of TREAT variable.
08	MSE is the pooled variance within the treatments which we call MSW. Unless otherwise specified by the SAS user, $\alpha = .05$.
09	The minimum significant difference, .0884 (in dollars), is the margin of error we add to the difference of means to construct Tukey confidence intervals. (See text). Recall the margin of error is the same for all confidence intervals. The margin of error is called the minimum significant difference because when the absolute difference between any pair of sample means exceeds this amount, we conclude that the means of the populations from which the samples were drawn are different.
10	If a confidence interval has "***" next to it then we would conclude, with 95% confidence, that the population means are different.
11	SAS first ranks the sample means in descending order, and then compares each sample mean with every other sample mean. Thus, there are two confidence intervals for each pair of means. Note that the confidence interval for CM –TB is the same confidence interval as TB–CM, except that the signs are reversed. Since there are three asterisks next to all of the confidence intervals, we can conclude that all population means are different.

Furthermore, the creativity workshop produces greater population mean unit labor cost reductions (between $.95 and $1.12) than the team-building workshop. Both produce greater population mean unit labor cost reductions than the control groups that received no training.

REGRESSION ANALYSIS

11.1 Looking for relationships among variables
       Relating two categorical variables
       Relating a quantitative dependent variable to
         categorical predictor variables
       Regression analysis: relating a quantitative
         dependent variable to quantitative or
         categorical predictor variables
11.2 Collecting data for a regression study
       Running experimental studies
       Running correlational studies
11.3 Plotting scatter diagrams and measuring the
         strength of relationships
       The simple correlation matrix
11.4 Curve fitting: estimating conditional means
       Simple linear regression
       The method of least squares
       Multiple regression
11.5 Evaluating the regression model
       The need for statistical testing
       Testing the entire regression model: analysis
         of variance
       The standard error of the estimate
       The coefficient of multiple determination

       Removing nonsignificant predictor variables
         from the model
       Assessing the significance of a single
         predictor variable
11.6 Evaluating the regression model assumptions:
         residual analysis
       Assumptions underlying regression models
       Examining residual plots
       Nonlinearity of regression line
       Unequal variance
       Nonnormality
       Outliers
       Autocorrelation
11.7 Using regression models for prediction
       Prediction versus extrapolation
       Differences between prediction and
         confidence intervals
       Reducing the width of confidence or
         prediction intervals
11.8 Integrating framework
Appendix A: COMCEL job satisfaction and salary
         data
Appendix B: Statistical software

 INTEROFFICE
COMMUNICATION

Date: September 6, 1994
To: Cherian Jain, V.P. Marketing Research
From: Ann Tabor, CEO
Re: Increasing Retail Sales of Model 76 Car Phones

The sales and inventory reports over the last two months
show that sales of the Model 76 car phone have been flat,
and that inventory has been increasing. Perhaps we should
lower the price or increase advertising or both to move this
inventory. Are car phone sales sensitive to price changes?
Do sales increase with increases in advertising? We do not
want to lower prices if sales are relatively insensitive to
price changes, and we do not want to waste money on
ineffective advertising.

Please look into this and report back as soon as possible.

11.1 ≣ Looking for Relationships Among Variables

A dependent variable is a variable we wish to explain, predict, or control.

An independent or pre-dictor variable is a variable thought to affect a dependent variable.

A categorical variable is not measured on a numer-ical scale.

A quantitative variable is measured on a numerical scale.

Measuring relationships among variables is critical to business success. Managers want to explain, predict, or control important business variables such as unit sales, worker productivity, or brand recognition. These variables are called **dependent variables**. Managers then search for **predictor variables**, variables that they believe affect a dependent variable. Perhaps price or amount of advertising affects unit sales. Perhaps type of training or leadership style affects worker productivity. Perhaps race or gender affects brand recognition. By determining which predictor variables affect important dependent variables, managers can improve their firms' performance.

Managers can use three "relationship-detection" tools. Which tool is appropriate depends, in part, on whether the dependent and predictor variables are categorical or quantitative. From Chapter 3, a **categorical variable** is *not* measurable on a numer-ical scale. Race and gender are categorical variables. Race is White, Black, Hispanic, Asian, or Other. Gender is either Male or Female. These scales are not quantitative. **Quantitative variables** are measured on a quantitative scale. Sales can be mea-sured in units sold or dollars of revenue—both are quantitative scales. We begin the regression analysis chapter by comparing the three "relationship-detection" tools. By the end of this section you should be able to:

1. distinguish between dependent and predictor variables;
2. distinguish between quantitative and categorical variables;
3. determine when each of the three relationship detection tools is most appropriate;
4. explain a positive and inverse relationship in words and pictures; and
5. explain why prediction, explanation, and control are important to managers.

Relating Two Categorical Variables

A product manager wants to know if a customer's race affects brand recognition for her product. Brand recognition is the dependent variable and race is a predictor vari-able. Both variables are categorical—brand recognition (Yes or No) and race (White, Black, or Other). She interviews a random sample of 600 potential customers and dis-plays the data in a *cross-tabs table* (See Section 3.4). Table 11.1 presents the data as *frequency counts*. A frequency count is the number of people that fall into a partic-ular cell of the cross-tabs table. For example, 95 potential customers were white and recognized the brand name.

It appears that race may be related to brand recognition. Of the 200 White customers, 95, or 47.5%, recognized the brand. Of the 200 Black customers, 65, or 32.5%, recognized the brand. Of the 200 Other customers, only 25, or 12.5%, recog-nized the brand.

The chi-square test of independence is a formal statistical method used to deter-mine if two categorical variables are related in the population of potential customers, not merely the sample of 600 selected for the study. We present the test of indepen-

Table 11.1

Cross-Tabs Table on Race and Brand Recognition

	White	Black	Other	Total
Recognized	95	65	25	185
Not recognized	105	135	175	415
Total	200	200	200	600

dence in Chapter 14. It expands on the idea of statistical independence and row and column percentages first presented in Chapter 3.

Relating a Quantitative Dependent Variable to Categorical Predictor Variables

An operations manager wants to know if the type of training workshop affects worker productivity. Worker productivity is the dependent variable and type of training is a predictor variable. Worker productivity is a quantitative variable (measured in units per hour) and type of training is a categorical variable (Team Building/Creativity/ Control Group.

He runs the planned change study shown in Table 11.2. The operations manager is interested in determining which type of training yields the highest population mean productivity. That is, what type of training yields the highest productivity for all workers in the population, not merely the 15 workers selected for the study.

Table 11.2

Improving Productivity Study

Team Building (units per hour)	Creativity (units per hour)	Control Group (units per hour)	
22.5	34.4	15.5	
22.4	32.4	17.6	
21.4	34.3	14.6	
25.4	31.5	16.5	
24.4	30.6	15.5	
23.22	32.64	15.94	$\bar{x}$

Sections 6.9–6.10 and Chapter 10 explained how to conduct planned change studies and analyze the results using the analysis of variance (ANOVA) to determine if one or more categorical predictor variables affected a quantitative dependent variable.

Regression Analysis: Relating a Quantitative Dependent Variable to Quantitative or Categorical Predictor Variables

Managers use regression analysis when they want to know how variables affect one another, not merely whether they do or do not. We develop a regression model, or equation, that

1. *predicts* the dependent variable. For example, we wish to predict units sold from two predictor variables—price and numbers of advertisements (ads);
2. *explains* how each predictor variable affects a dependent variable. For example, we wish to explain how price and number of ads individually affect units sold; and
3. *controls* departmental or individual performance by setting performance standards. For example, a store that sells phones for $85 and runs three ads per day should sell 22.47 ± 5.1 phones.

Regression analysis is a mathematical technique for determining and measuring relationships among variables. It can be used whether the predictor variables are

Table 11.3

Three Statistical Tools for Detecting Relationships Among Variables

Tool	Dependent Variable	Predictor, or Independent, Variable
ANOVA	Quantitative	Categorical
Chi-square	Categorical	Categorical
Regression	Quantitative	Quantitative
		Categorical

quantitative or categorical. Categorical variables may be converted to "dummy" or indicator variables so they can be treated like quantitative variables (see Chapter 12).

Table 11.3 points out that the choice of which "relationship-detection" tool to use depends, in part, on how we measure the dependent variable and the predictor variables.

We introduce regression analysis, this chapter's topic, with the following example.

Example: Increasing Car Phone Sales   COMCEL sells its entire line of car phones directly to the public through 60 retail outlets in shopping malls around the country. Recently, sales of the Model 76 have been flat, and inventory has been increasing. COMCEL is considering both price cuts and radio ads to boost sales. However, it doesn't want to lower prices if sales are relatively insensitive to price reductions. It also does not want to waste money on ineffective advertising.

COMCEL selects 24 outlets with comparable sales from different cities across the country. It will study the impact of four different prices and three different numbers of ads on sales in the 24 outlets. It will test market each price and ad combination in two randomly selected stores for one week. The ads will be run during morning drive time on the highest rated radio station in the test city. COMCEL will record the number of Model 76 phones sold during the test week. Based on the marketing study, COMCEL will apply the best price and number of radio ads strategy to all 60 stores.

Table 11.4 contains the data for the marketing regression study. Since price and number of ads will be used to predict units sold, and not the other way around, the number of Model 76 units sold is the dependent variable. Price and number of ads are the predictor variables. Regression studies have only one dependent variable, but can have one or more predictor variables. Note that the dependent variable and the two predictor variables are measured on a quantitative scale.

Prediction is the most often cited reason for using regression analysis. To understand the idea of prediction, note that outlets 1 and 2 each charged $100 and ran one ad per day, yet sales differed (9 and 11 units). What sales level would you predict if all 60 outlets charged a price of $100 and ran one ad per day? Please think about it before reading on.

Your prediction should be that all 60 outlets that charged $100 and ran one ad per day would sell the *mean* value for the two outlets, namely, 10 units. Regression analysis develops a mathematical equation to predict the mean value of the dependent variable for different values of the predictor variable(s).

Using regression software, the marketing research group obtained the following equation based on the sample of 24 outlets for one week.*

---

* We discuss how to develop the regression equation, or model, in Section 11.4.

Table 11.4

COMCEL Marketing Study Data

Outlet	Predictor Variables Price (dollars)	Number of Ads per Day	Dependent Variable Units Sold
1	100	1	9
2	100	1	11
3	100	3	19
4	100	3	15
5	100	5	26
6	100	5	24
7	90	1	14
8	90	1	19
9	90	3	24
10	90	3	28
11	90	5	31
12	90	5	32
13	85	1	17
14	85	1	19
15	85	3	29
16	85	3	25
17	85	5	30
18	85	5	30
19	80	1	26
20	80	1	23
21	80	3	26
22	80	3	24
23	80	5	37
24	80	5	34

$$\text{UNITS SOLD-PRED} = 60.891 - .530\text{PRICE} + 3.313\text{ADS} \qquad (11.1)$$

UNITS SOLD-PRED is the predicted mean number of units sold for particular values of PRICE and ADS (number of ads per day). COMCEL will use equation (11.1) for predicting units sold, explaining the effect of each predictor variable on units sold, and controlling sales of their 60 retail outlets.

Prediction: Equation (11.1) says that if we set price at $85 and run two radio ads per day, COMCEL predicts that its stores should sell, on the average, 22.47 phones per week. We simply "plugged" those particular values of the predictor variables into equation (11.1) and predicted the value of the dependent variable.

$$\text{UNITS SOLD-PRED} = 60.891 - .530(85) + 3.313(2)$$

$$= 60.891 - 45.05 + 6.626$$

$$= 22.47$$

Explanation: To understand the numerical weights or *sample regression coefficients* attached to the two predictor variables, suppose COMCEL restricts the number of ads to one per day.

$$\text{UNITS SOLD-PRED} = 60.891 - .530\text{PRICE} + 3.313(1)$$
$$= 60.891 + 3.313 - .530\text{PRICE}$$
$$= 64.204 - .530\text{PRICE} \qquad (11.2)$$

When holding the number of ads constant at any level, we estimate that each dollar increase in price reduces the mean number of units sold by .530 phones.

Figure 11.1 is a graph of equation (11.2). The straight line has an intercept of 64.204 and a slope of −.530. When the price is zero, the straight line crosses the vertical axis, units sold, at 64.204 units. Note what happens when we increase price by one dollar from $80 to $81.

At $80: $\text{UNITS SOLD-PRED} = 64.204 - .530(80) = 21.804$

At $81: $\text{UNITS SOLD-PRED} = 64.204 - .530(81) = 21.274$

Price change = +$1   Change in units sold = −.530 phones

Since the regression coefficient for the price variable is negative, price and units sold are *inversely* related. When price goes up, the mean number of units sold goes down. An inverse relationship is represented by a *negative sign* in equation (11.2) and by a negative slope in Figure 11.1.

Referring again to equation (11.1), suppose we charge $90 for the Model 76 car phone.

FIGURE 11.1   Phones Sold versus Price for One Ad Per Day

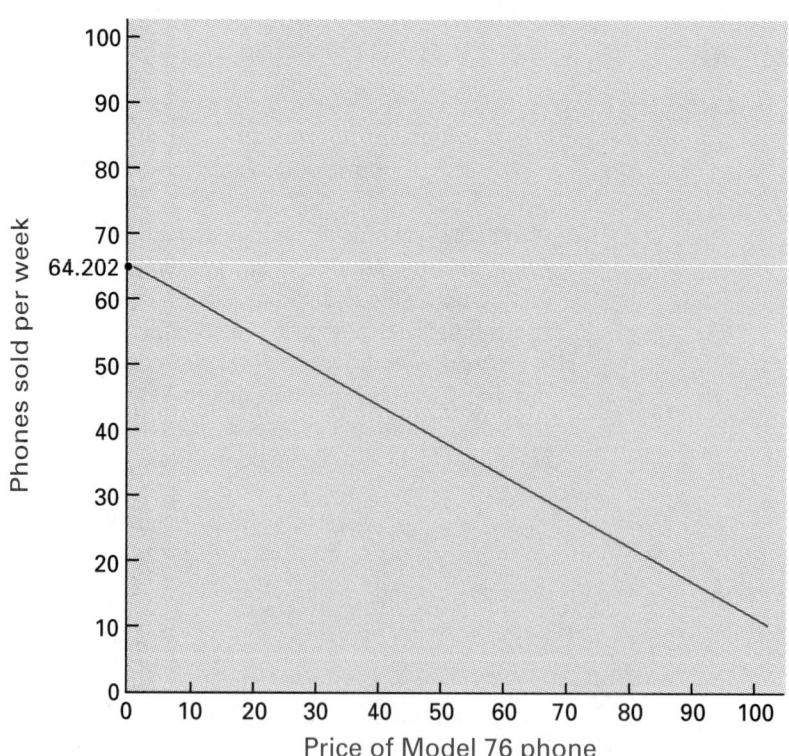

$$\text{UNITS SOLD-PRED} = 60.891 - .530(90) + 3.313\text{ADS}$$

$$= 60.891 - 47.70 + 3.313\text{ADS}$$

$$= 13.191 + 3.313\text{ADS} \qquad (11.3)$$

Holding the price constant at any level, we estimate that each additional ad per day increases the mean number of sales by 3.313 units.

The straight line in Figure 11.2 has an intercept of 13.191 and a slope of $+3.313$. When no ads are aired, the straight line crosses the vertical axis, units sold, at 13.191 units. Units sold increase from this point by 3.313 phones for each additional ad. There is a *positive* relationship between number of ads and number of units sold.

Thus, we interpret each sample regression coefficient ($-.530$ or 3.313) as the effect on the dependent variable for a one-unit change in a predictor variable *when all the other predictor variables in the equation are held constant.*

To this point we have explained the sample regression coefficients attached to the two predictor variables. We must also discuss the sample intercept of 60.891 in expression (11.1). What does it represent? In mathematical terms, the intercept of a linear equation is the value of the dependent variable when the value of the predictor variables in the equation are equal to zero. In business terms, the sample intercept in expression (11.1) has no meaning since we have no information about purchasing behavior outside the range of the sample. Specifically, we don't know how many units would be purchased if price and the number of ads were zero. As a case in point, the intercept of (11.1) is *not* saying that approximately 60.891 units will be "sold" if the price and the number of ads were zero!

Control: COMCEL can use equation (11.1) to control sales. If a store charges $85 and runs two radio ads per day, equation (11.1) predicts that it will sell 22.47 phones per week. The store manager realizes that the actual units sold may differ from 22.47 phones. However, if the actual units sold are either very far above or below 22.47

FIGURE 11.2   Phones Sold versus Number of Ads for a $90 Price

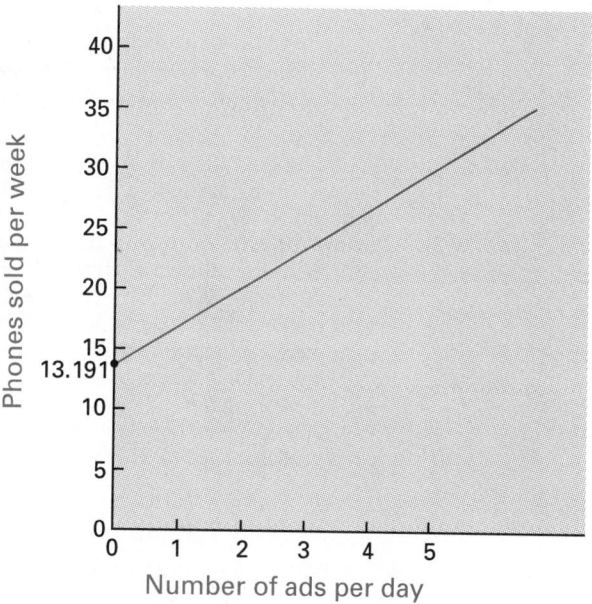

phones, the store manager will want to know why.* This is a deviation from expected performance and *may* signal the onset of a disturbance problem or opportunity.

In summary, we can use a regression equation, or model, such as expression (11.1) to predict mean values of a quantitative dependent variable based on the values of one or more predictor variables. We can measure the effects of each predictor variable on the dependent variable by the sample regression coefficient attached to that predictor variable. Each regression coefficient measures the effect on the dependent variable of a one-unit change in a predictor variable when all the other predictor variables in the equation are held constant. Finally, we can use a regression model to set performance standards for the dependent variable. Failure to meet performance standards may signal the onset of a disturbance problem or opportunity.

SECTION 11.1 EXERCISES

1. A TV ratings firm sends a diary to a sample of people and asks them to record the stations and programs they watch over a one-week period. The ratings firm also places an electronic monitoring device on the TV to record the number of hours the TV is on each day. The firm also obtains demographic information on the head of household. Here are some of the variables obtained from the diary and monitoring device.

Head of household gender	Male, female
Head of household age	Under 30 years
	30–54 years
	Over 54 years
Head of household education level	Did not finish high school
	Completed high school
	Did not finish college
	Completed college
	Some graduate work
Network watched the most	CBS
	ABC
	NBC
	Cable
	Other
Number of hours the TV was on	
Number of people (over 3 years old) in the household	

In each of the following questions, identify (1) the dependent variable and whether it is categorical or quantitative, (2) the predictor variable(s) and whether they are categorical or quantitative, and (3) which of the following relationship detection tools—chi-square, analysis of variance, regression—is most appropriate for answering the question.

a. Is there a relationship between the number of hours the TV was on and the age of the head of household?
b. Is there a relationship between the age and education level of the head of household?
c. Is there a relationship between the number of hours the TV was on and the number of people in the household?
d. Is there a relationship between the number of hours the TV was on and the number of people in the household and the education level of the head of household?
e. Is gender related to which network was watched the most during the week?

* Section 11.7 will explain how to determine how far away the actual sales should be from the predicted sales for the manager to investigate.

2. The purpose of regression analysis is to relate *changes* in predictor variables to corresponding changes in the dependent variable. When there is only one predictor variable, the change in the dependent variable is measured by the slope of a linear equation. The slope is defined as the change in the dependent variable per unit change in the predictor variable. The intercept of a linear equation is the value of the dependent variable when the predictor variable is zero.

  a. Plot each of the following equations and identify the slope and intercept.
    (1) $y = 10 + 2x$ (2) $y = 5x$ (3) $y = 10 - 2x$
  b. For each equation, predict the value of y when $x = 2$.
  c. Determine which of the equations passes through the points $(x_1, y_1) = (1, 8)$ and $(x_2, y_2) = (3, 4)$ by calculating the slope of the line connecting these points. Use the relationship

$$\text{Slope} = \frac{\text{Change in } y}{\text{Change in } x} = \frac{y_2 - y_1}{x_2 - x_1}$$

  d. When asked to provide an English interpretation of the slope of equation (1), a student said: For a one-unit increase in y, x goes up by 2 units. Do you agree?

3. Most colleges and universities use regression models to predict the academic success of their applicants. Suppose the College of Fine Arts uses only the verbal part of the SAT examination, VSAT, and has found that it can predict sophomore GPA from the model

$$\text{SOPHGPA-PRED} = 1.1 + 0.0035\text{VSAT}$$

  a. Predict the mean GPA for all sophomores in the College of Fine Arts who scored 500 on the verbal portion of the SAT.
  b. Would you expect each sophomore in the College of Fine Arts who scored 500 on the verbal portion of the SAT to have exactly a 2.85 GPA? Why?
  c. Explain the meaning of the sample regression coefficient for the VSAT variable without using the word "slope." That is, complete the following sentence: "For each one-point increase in VSAT, . . ."
  d. Sketch a graph relating SOPHGPA-PRED and VSAT.
  e. Interpret the intercept of 1.1. What does it tell you?

4. Suppose the College of Business uses the verbal SAT score, VSAT, and the math SAT score, MSAT, to predict GPA at the end of the sophomore year. Here is the regression model.

$$\text{SOPHGPA-PRED} = 1.0 + .0015\text{VSAT} + .0020\text{MSAT}$$

  a. Use the model to predict the mean GPA of all sophomore business students who scored 400 on verbal portion of the SAT and 700 on the math portion of the SAT.
  b. Would you expect each sophomore in the College of Business who scored 400 on the verbal portion of the SAT and 700 on the math portion to have a 3.00 GPA? Why?
  c. If a business student who scored 400 on VSAT and 700 on MSAT has a sophomore GPA of 2.90, based on the regression model, would you consider this performance unusual? Explain.
  d. Sketch a graph relating SOPHGPA-PRED and VSAT for all business students who scored 600 on the math portion of the SAT. Is the relationship between VSAT and SOPHGPA-PRED positive or negative?
  e. Sketch a graph relating SOPHGPA-PRED and MSAT for all business students who scored 500 on the verbal portion of the SAT. Is the relationship between MSAT and SOPHGPA-PRED positive or negative?
  f. Explain the meaning of the sample regression coefficients for the VSAT and MSAT variables without using the word *slope*.
  g. Explain why the intercept (by itself) has no practical meaning in the above regression model.

5. You wish to predict the number of sick days taken by COMCEL workers during the winter months.
  a. Suggest four predictor variables—two categorical and two quantitative—that could be related to the number of sick days taken.

   b. Explain why you believe the predictor variables are related to the number of sick days.
   c. Discuss whether you believe each predictor variable will be positively or inversely related to the dependent variable.

6. Suppose a realtor selected a sample of 100 recent residential sales and developed the following regression equation relating selling price of the home to the number of square feet of living space in the home. The homes in the sample ranged from 1,100 square feet to 3,200 square feet.

$$\text{PRICE-PRED} = 35,000 + 47.8\text{SQFT}$$

   a. Predict the mean selling PRICE for all homes with 2,000 square feet of living space.
   b. Would you expect all homes with 2,000 square feet of living space to sell for this price?
   c. Explain the meaning of the sample regression coefficient for the SQFT variable without using the word *slope*.
   d. Sketch a graph relating PRICE and SQFT.
   e. Can we interpret the intercept of $35,000 as the mean price of an unimproved lot? Explain.

11.2 ≡ Collecting Data for a Regression Study

Managers must make a series of decisions in designing a regression study. First, they must decide on the type of study—either experimental or correlational. Then they must identify critical predictor and dependent variables, select a data source, determine the levels of the predictor variables (for an experimental study), and obtain the data. By the end of this section you should be able to:

1. explain what an observation is in a regression study;
2. explain the meaning of a unit of association;
3. distinguish between two types of regression studies—experimental and correlational; and
4. select appropriate predictor variables and the proper number of levels for each variable in an experimental study.

Running Experimental Studies

In order to understand the decision-making process behind running an experimental study, return to the COMCEL study. Recall that it was designed to measure the relationship of price and the number of ads per day to the number of phones sold.

Identifying Predictor Variables   COMCEL wants to predict and explain units sold, a quantitative dependent variable. It chose price and number of radio ads per day as the predictor variables because it believed that these variables affect units sold. The choice of predictor variables is not always so obvious. We must always establish a *logical* connection between the dependent variable and each predictor variable.

Selecting the Unit of Association   COMCEL chose an individual store as the experimental unit or *unit of association*. The unit of association is the person, place, or thing on which we collect our data. Refer to Table 11.4. COMCEL collected 24 observations, one for each of the 24 selected stores. Each row of the table is a new observation. *Each observation consists of the value of the dependent variable for that store and the values of the two predictor variables for that store.* For example, the observation values for store 1 were (9 units, $100, 1 ad). COMCEL selected one store in each of 24 cities that had comparable sales in order to control for variables other than price and number of ads that might affect units sold.

Determining the Levels of the Predictor Variables   The levels of the independent variables must be far enough apart so that potential effects on the dependent variables can be measured. The present price of the Model 76 phone is $100. COMCEL needed to know how much it could charge and still make an acceptable profit. Eighty dollars was the lower limit according to the accountants. For the ADS variable, COMCEL determined that commuters generally hear five or fewer ads while driving to work. It decided to vary price between $80 to $100 and the number of ads between one to five.

In selecting the actual prices and number of ads, COMCEL used the following two principles:

1. Use at least three equally spaced levels for each predictor variable.
2. Have the same number of observations for every combination of predictor variables.

COMCEL had originally considered three price levels—$100, $90, and $80. However, one manager was interested in studying the effects of a 15% discount, so COMCEL added a fourth price level—$85.

Note that in Table 11.4, each price was paired twice with each number of ads. Having an equal number of observations for every combination of predictor variables is called a balanced design. In Chapter 12 we will learn that a balanced design eliminates multicollinearity, a potentially serious problem in regression studies.

Running Correlational Studies

In experimental studies, the manager can determine the levels of the predictor variables and ensure a balanced design. In correlational studies, the manager cannot do either of these things. The manager merely *records* the data from historical records or sample surveys. We first discussed correlational studies in Chapter 6.

Many times it is either impractical or unethical to conduct experimental studies. Suppose we wanted to measure the effect of price and number of ads per day for all firms selling car phones. We could *record* the prices charged by our competitors and their number of daily radio ads, but we could not ask them to vary their prices or number of ads so that we could obtain a balanced design. Due to the impracticality of experimental studies, correlational regression studies are more common.

In correlational studies, managers must still select their predictor variables and choose the unit of association. However, they cannot determine the levels of the predictor variables, nor can they obtain balanced designs. They simply collect whatever data are available.

In correlational studies often the predictor variables are highly correlated with each other. When predictor variables are highly correlated we have trouble measuring the affect of individual predictor variables. This is the problem of multicollinearity. Consider a correlational study to predict worker job satisfaction in a large corporation. Management considers three predictor variables—salary, years of experience, and job level within the firm. Clearly the three predictor variables are positively related. Salary tends to increase with years of experience and job level. We discuss the multicollinearity problems associated with correlational studies in Chapter 12.

SECTION 11.2 EXERCISES

1. A human resources manager wants to determine whether age, salary level, and years on the job are related to job performance. He will randomly select 100 workers' records and determine whether the variables are related.
   a. What is the dependent variable?
   b. What are the predictor variables?
   c. What is the unit of association?
   d. What is an observation in the study?
   e. Is this an experimental or correlational study?

2. A marketing manager wants to determine what affects share of market. She believes that relative price and relative level of advertising are critical variables. Relative price is the ratio of our price to the average of all our competitors' prices. The manager collects data on the three variables for the past 16 quarters.
   a. What is the dependent variable?
   b. What are the independent variables?
   c. What is the unit of association?
   d. What is an observation in the study?
   e. Is this an experimental or correlational study?

3. An operations manager wants to determine whether the amount of plastic filler used to produce TV cabinets affects the percentage of cabinets rejected due to scratches or nicks. She plans to vary the amount of filler from 2% to 8% in 1% increments.
   a. What is the dependent variable?
   b. What is the predictor variable?
   c. What is the unit of association?
   d. What is an observation in the study?
   e. Is this an experimental or correlational study?

4. Does advertising lead sales by one quarter? Does advertising in one quarter affect sales in the next quarter? The manager plans to collect data for 24 months to determine whether there is a relationship.
   a. What is the dependent variable?
   b. What is the predictor variable?
   c. What is the unit of association?
   d. What is an observation in the study?
   e. Is this an experimental or correlational study?

5. You want to determine what quantitative factors affect grade point average (GPA) of students in accounting. Generate two variables that should explain GPA.
   a. What is the dependent variable?
   b. What are the predictor variables?
   c. Discuss why you believe there is a relationship between these variables and the dependent variable.

6. An operations manager wants to know if the production run size and age of equipment affect cost per unit of molded phone sets. He plans to vary production run size from 333 to 667 to 1,000 units and to use equipment from 1 to 3 to 5 years of age.
   a. What is the dependent variable?
   b. What are the predictor variables?
   c. Suppose we decide on the above three levels of production run size and three levels of age of equipment. What values of each predictor variable must we run to achieve a balanced design? Why?

11.3 ≡ Plotting Scatter Diagrams and Measuring the Strength of Relationships

Regression analysis produces a mathematical expression relating the dependent variable to one or more predictor variables. Equation (11.1) for the COMCEL study, relating units sold to price and number of ads per day, is called a *multiple regression.* Multiple means that there is more than one predictor variable. By contrast, in a *simple linear regression,* there is only one predictor variable. *Linear* means that if we plotted the single predictor variable against the dependent variable the graph, called a *scatter plot* (see Chapter 3), would indicate a straight-line relationship.

Before computing regression equations like (11.1), plot each predictor variable against the dependent variable and generate a simple correlation matrix. These two tools provide insights into the relationships among the dependent and predictor variables. By the end of this section, you should be able to:

1. plot scatter diagrams and detect obvious departures from linearity in the predictor variables;
2. use simple correlation coefficients from a correlation matrix to assess the strength of a linear relationship between the dependent variable and each predictor variable;
3. identify clusters in a scatter diagram; and
4. interpret clusters accurately.

Return to the COMCEL regression study. Figures 11.3 and 11.4 are plots or *scatter diagrams* of each predictor variable against the dependent variable. In Figure 11.3, as price increases, sales tend to drop. This negative relationship is reflected in the negative sign of the PRICE regression coefficient, −.530, in expression (11.1). In Figure 11.4, as number of ads increases, sales tend to increase, and the sign of the regression coefficient for the ADS variable is positive, 3.313.

Recall from Chapter 3 that if we can enclose the data points of a scatter diagram with an upward-sloping or downward-sloping ellipse, then the relationship between the two variables could be linear. But a scatter diagram can be influenced by the scaling of the variables, and thus can be misleading. To supplement the scatter diagram, in Chapter 3 we introduced the correlation coefficient, *r*.

FIGURE 11.3   Price versus Phones Sold*

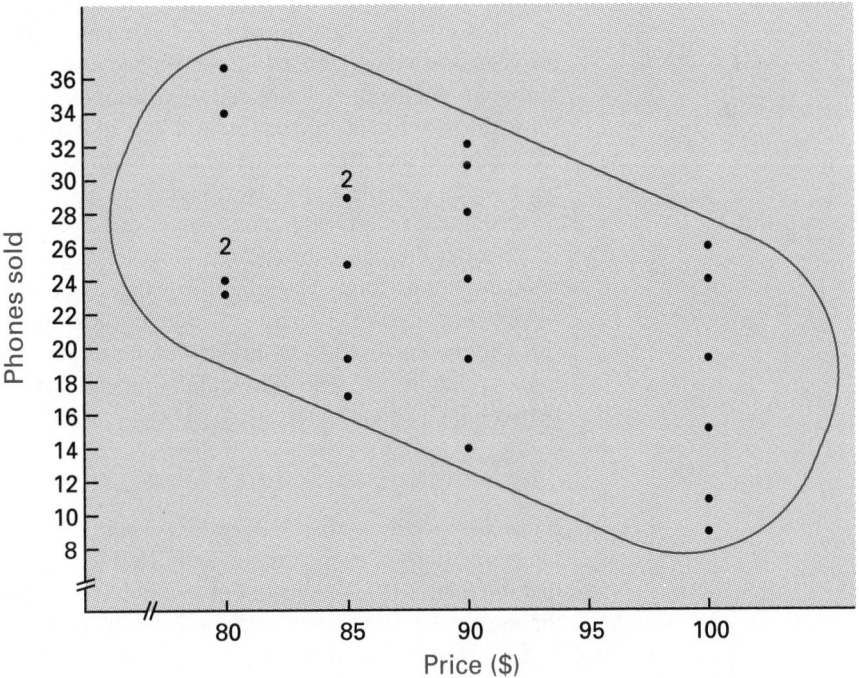

* The symbol "2" indicates two observations.

FIGURE 11.4   Phones Sold versus Number of Ads Per Day

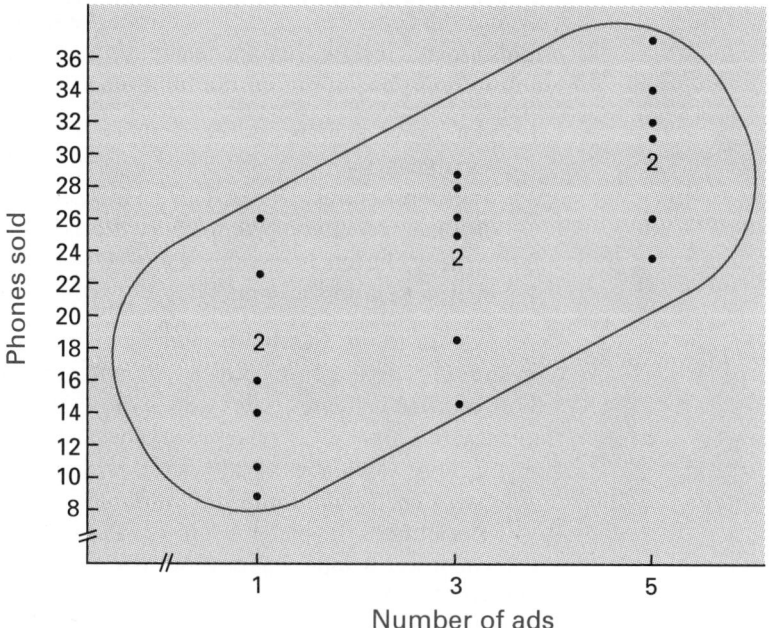

The correlation coefficient is a descriptive numerical measure of how closely a scatter of points fit a straight line. Recall that correlation coefficients can vary from -1 to $+1$. The graphs in Figure 3.14, reproduced on page 605, show different degrees of linear associations and their r values.

In scatter diagram (a), $r = +1$. There is a perfect positive linear relationship between the two variables. It is perfect because r equals 1 and positive because of the plus sign. All the data points fall on a straight line. The relationship is perfect in the sense that if we knew the equation of the straight line and the value of the variable x, we could predict the y value with perfect certainty. The relationship is positive because, as variable x increases, variable y also increases. Graph (e) shows a perfect inverse linear relationship, and r has a value of -1.

Scatter diagrams (b) and (d) show lines that fit the pattern of data points quite well, but not perfectly. A tight ellipse can enclose the data points. Correlation coefficients are close to $+1$ and -1. Scatter diagram (c) shows a pattern of points that can only be enclosed by a circle. The correlation coefficient is zero, indicating *no linear* relationship. The horizontal line reflects the lack of a linear relationship between the two variables.

The Simple Correlation Matrix

Table 11.5 shows a *simple correlation matrix* produced by COMSTAT. It contains the correlations of each variable with itself and with every other variable. Please note that the matrix is symmetric. For example, the correlation of UNITS SOLD and ADS is the same as ADS and UNITS SOLD—.7627. In Table 11.5 we have boxed the important correlations. These are the $r_{\text{UNITS SOLD, PRICE}}$, $r_{\text{UNITS SOLD, ADS}}$, and $r_{\text{PRICE, ADS}}$.

The correlation matrix supports the conclusions drawn from Figures 11.3 and 11.4. That is, PRICE is negatively related to UNITS SOLD $(-.5521)$ and the number of ADS per day is positively related to UNITS SOLD $(+.7627)$.

FIGURE 3.14   Examples of the Range of Correlation Coefficients

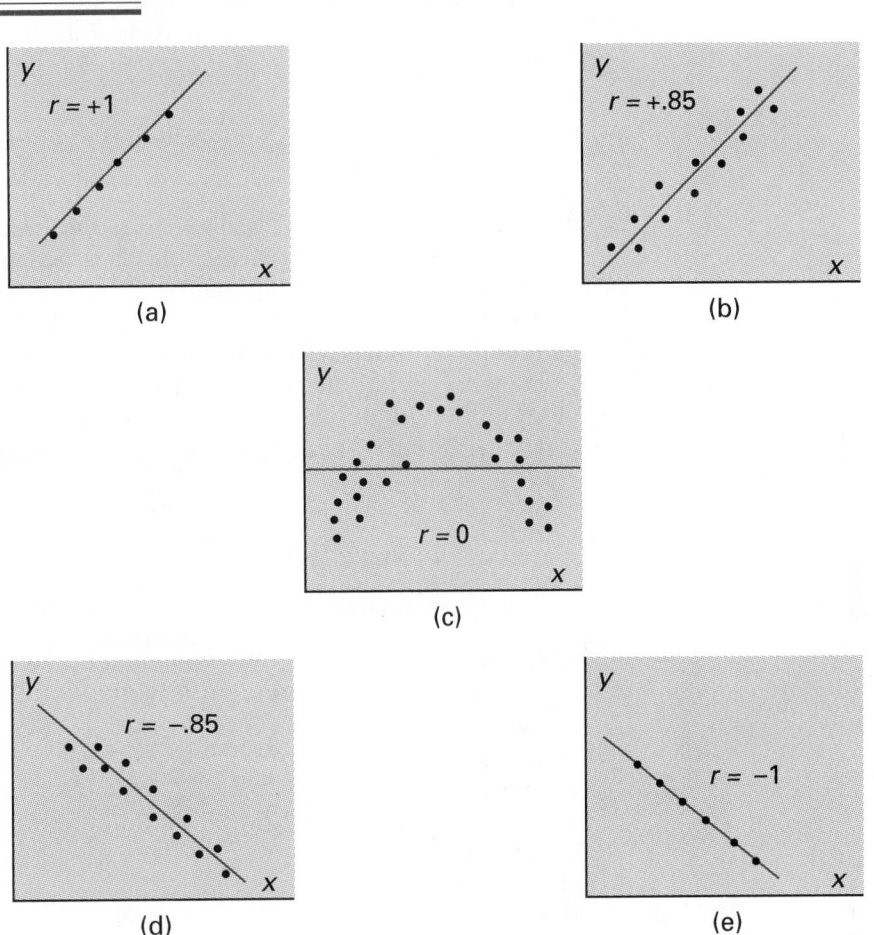

(a)

(b)

(c)

(d)

(e)

But the correlation matrix provides more information than Figures 11.3 and 11.4 do. First, it tells us that ADS is a stronger linear predictor of UNITS SOLD than PRICE, because $|r_{\text{UNITS SOLD, ADS}}|$ is greater than $|r_{\text{UNITS SOLD, PRICE}}|$. Second, a correlation matrix also measures the correlation(s) between all pairs of predictor variables. There is a zero correlation between PRICE and ADS, $r_{\text{PRICE, ADS}}$, because COMCEL used a balanced design in the study. In correlational studies, the predictor variables are often correlated and this can produce *multicollinearity* problems that we discuss in Chapter 12.

Table 11.5

A Simple Correlation Matrix

	UNITS SOLD	PRICE	ADS
UNITS SOLD	1.0000	−0.5521	0.7627
PRICE	−0.5521	1.0000	0.0000
ADS	0.7627	0.0000	1.0000

Finally, the correlation matrix helps us understand the coefficient of determination which we present in Section 11.4.

The expression used to calculate each of the three key simple correlations in Table 11.5 is

$$r_{xy} = \frac{\sum_i x_i y_i - n\bar{x}\bar{y}}{\sqrt{\sum_i x_i^2 - n\bar{x}^2}\sqrt{\sum_i y_i^2 - n\bar{y}^2}} \tag{11.4}$$

where x represents one variable and y represents the second variable. We have omitted an example of numerical computation because we recommend using computer software to generate the simple correlation matrix.

We still recommend plotting each predictor variable against the dependent variable because the correlation matrix can only detect *linear relationships* between pairs of variables. Consider the marketing data first presented in Chapter 3 and again in Table 11.6. It illustrates two limitations of the correlation matrix. A correlation coefficient cannot detect (1) a nonlinear relationship or (2) the presence of clusters.

Table 11.6

Marketing Data for 12 COMCEL Regions

Region (%)	Dependent Variable	Predictor Variables		
	Market Share	Advertising (thousands of dollars)	Average Years of Sales Experience	Relative Price
Atlanta	20	13	3	1.50
Birmingham	50	28	12	.60
Charlotte	30	17	15	1.00
Jacksonville	10	8	1	1.75
New Orleans	25	16	18	1.30
Orlando	30	18	7	.90
Miami	35	21	8	2.00
Washington	5	6	23	2.90
Baltimore	45	25	9	1.50
Dallas	55	32	11	1.10
Houston	20	11	20	2.50
Austin	28	16	17	2.25

Note: The predictor variable, relative price, is the ratio between COMCEL's price for its least expensive phone and the average price of its competitors' least expensive phones.

Departures from Linearity   Figure 11.5 is a scatter diagram of market share versus average years of sales experience. It shows a *nonlinear relationship* that can be represented by an inverted U. That is, as years of sales experience increases, market share increases initially. It peaks between 11 and 13 years, and then drops off. And the nonlinear relationship makes sense. As the sales force gains more experience, it grabs more market share from the competition. However, after 13 years, salespersons may begin to experience burnout—they lose enthusiasm, and market share decreases. Other explanations, such as increase in the number or strength of competitors, are also possible.

The simple correlation coefficient between these two variables (computation not shown) is only −.155, suggesting little or no linear relationship between the two variables. Yet from Figure 11.5, the two variables show a strong nonlinear relationship.

FIGURE 11.5   Market Share versus Average Years of Experience

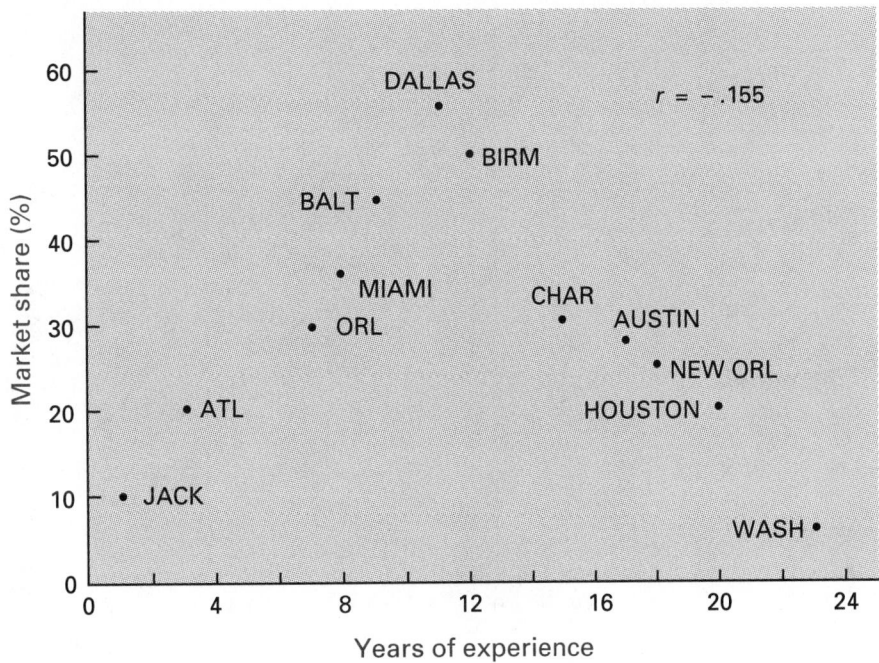

Clusters   Figure 11.6, which relates market share and relative price, illustrates *clusters*. There appears to be an overall inverse relationship between market share and relative price; we can enclose the data with an ellipse that slopes downward to the right. This is consistent with a simple correlation of −.65 (computation not shown). However, upon closer examination, there are two distinct clusters of data points, each consisting of six cities. The cluster closer to the origin (cluster 1) includes the Atlanta, Birmingham, Charlotte, Jacksonville, New Orleans, and Orlando regions. The other cluster lies further from the origin.

What do the clusters mean? Both slope downward to the right. Within each cluster, the higher COMCEL's price is compared to the competition's average price, the lower its market share. That makes economic sense. Now compare two cities—one in each cluster—that have the same relative price. In cluster 1, Atlanta has a 1.5 relative price. In cluster 2, Baltimore has the same 1.5 relative price. In both regions, COMCEL charges 50% more than the competition's average price. Then why does Baltimore have a 45% market share and Atlanta only a 20% market share? There must be other predictor variables that explain the significant difference in market shares for the same relative price. We should call a meeting to brainstorm for additional predictor variables.

In summary, begin every regression analysis by plotting each predictor variable against the dependent variable to detect linear relationships, nonlinear relationships, and clusters. If the scatter diagram reveals clusters, we must seek additional predictor variables that explain the clusters. If the pattern of points appears to be linear, generate a simple correlation matrix to measure the strength of the linear relationships and to assess the importance of each predictor variable.

FIGURE 11.6   Market Share versus Relative Price

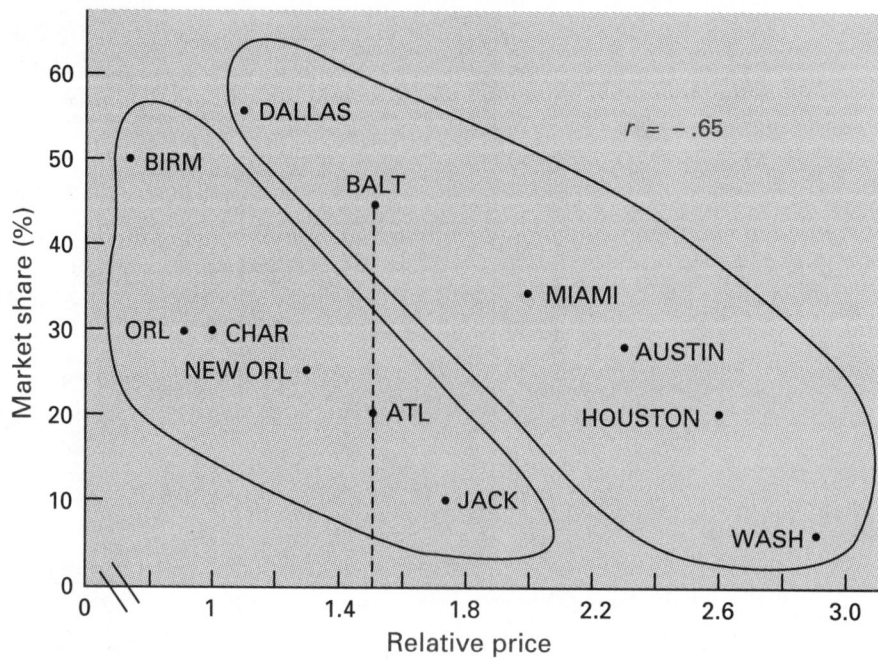

SECTION 11.3 EXERCISES

1. Shown is a small data set on productivity in number of sales for over $100,000 made in a year and annual salary in thousands of dollars.

PROD	15	17	15	18	24	22	28	34	33	38
SALARY	20	22	26	30	32	35	35	40	45	47

a. Plot a scatter diagram between PROD and SALARY.
b. Does SALARY appear to be linearly related to PROD? Explain.
c. Use software to determine the simple correlation matrix. Relate the $r_{\text{PROD, SALARY}}$ correlation coefficient to the scatter diagram.

2. Given the following observations:

x	0	1	2
y	4	5	6

a. Plot the points.
b. Calculate the simple correlation between x and y.
c. Explain why the correlation coefficient is +1 in terms of your graph.

3. Shown is a small data set on amount of study time (STUDYTIME in minutes) and test performance (TESTPERF).

STUDYTIME	30	60	75	90	100	135	160	200	240	300
TESTPERF	65	67	66	72	78	77	82	83	84	82

a. Plot a scatter diagram between TESTPERF and STUDYTIME.
b. Does STUDYTIME appear to be linearly related to TESTPERF? Explain.
c. Use software to determine the simple correlation matrix. Relate the $r_{\text{STUDYTIME, TESTPERF}}$ correlation coefficient to the scatter diagram.

4. Given is a time-ordered data set that includes quarterly sales, inventory, and net plant and equipment expenditures. The corporate economist believes that inventory and net plant and equipment expenditures can explain the level of sales.

Quarter	SALES	INVENTORY	NPEE
1	32,900	2,011	65
2	38,200	2,100	57
3	32,500	2,160	58
4	33,800	2,225	67
5	45,700	2,300	82
6	44,500	2,325	79
7	42,000	2,400	80
8	44,750	2,450	86
9	38,000	2,575	65
10	41,000	2,550	80
11	26,000	2,200	64
12	30,000	2,150	54

SALES	Quarterly sales of capital equipment in millions of dollars
INVENT	Mean level of inventory during quarter
NPEE	Net plant and equipment expenditures in thousands of dollars

   a. Plot a scatter diagram between SALES and each predictor variable.
   b. Does it appear that either (or both) predictor variable(s) is (are) linearly related to the dependent variable? Explain.
   c. Use software to determine the simple correlation matrix. Relate the $r_{SALES,\ INVENT}$ and $r_{SALES,\ NPEE}$ correlation coefficients to the scatter diagrams.
   d. Are the two predictor variables related to one another? That is, what is $r_{INVENT,\ NPEE}$?
   e. Is this an experimental or correlational study?

5. Given is a cross-sectional data set for 18 managers. It is a random sample of monthly salaries of managers at the same level within a major firm. The three predictor variables are months on the job, level of interpersonal communication skill along a 1 (poor) to 10 (good) scale, and the manager's gender. The firm wishes to predict monthly salary.

	Monthly Salary	Months on the Job	Level of Communication Skill	Gender of Manager
1	2,000	14	3	Female
2	2,100	14	2	Female
3	2,150	12	3	Female
4	2,200	25	4	Female
5	2,300	27	6	Female
6	2,200	30	5	Female
7	2,400	32	7	Female
8	2,300	36	8	Female
9	2,500	40	9	Female
10	2,700	15	1	Male
11	2,800	16	3	Male
12	2,900	22	4	Male
13	3,200	27	5	Male
14	3,200	26	5	Male
15	3,100	30	6	Male
16	3,400	34	8	Male
17	3,600	32	7	Male
18	3,900	38	9	Male

a. Plot monthly salary versus months on the job. Does there appear to be a linear relationship between the two variables?

b. Plot monthly salary versus level of communication skill. Does there appear to be a linear relationship between the two variables?

c. Label each of the data points in the scatter diagram in part **b** as male or female (the gender variable). Are there distinct clusters when we include the gender variable?

d. What can we conclude about the impact of gender on monthly salary?

e. Recode gender as follows: Code Female = 1 and Male = 0. Use software to determine the simple correlation matrix for the four variables. Relate the correlation coefficients—$r_{SALARY, MONTHS}$, $r_{SALARY, COMM}$, and $r_{SALARY, GENDER}$ to the scatter diagrams in parts **a–c.**

6. Shown is a random sample of data on 12 physicians in the 45–50-year-old group. We have recorded their amount of life insurance, their annual income for the past year, and their marital status. We wish to predict amount of life insurance.

Physician	Amount of Life Insurance (thousands of dollars)	Annual Income (thousands of dollars)	Marital Status
1	250	60	Single
2	350	75	Single
3	450	85	Single
4	500	110	Single
5	650	130	Single
6	800	160	Single
7	790	60	Married
8	950	80	Married
9	1,200	90	Married
10	1,300	120	Married
11	1,400	140	Married
12	1,350	150	Married

a. Plot a scatter diagram between amount of life insurance and annual income. Does there appear to be a linear relationship between the two variables?

b. Label each point in the scatter diagram with the marital status of the physician—single or married. Are there distinct clusters? What can we conclude about the impact of marital status on the amount of life insurance purchased?

c. Code single as 1 and married as 0. Use software to determine the simple correlation matrix for the three variables. Relate the correlation coefficients—$r_{AMOUNT, INCOME}$, $r_{AMOUNT, STATUS}$ —to the scatter diagrams in parts **a–b.**

7. Here is a set of data showing the historic rates of return for stock Y (the dependent variable) and the New York Stock Exchange (NYSE)—the predictor variable.

Year	Stock Y	NYSE
1	3.0%	5.0%
2	8.2%	13.5%
3	−6.0%	−12.5%
4	−9.5%	−20.2%
5	13.5%	17.5%
6	7.5%	14.5%

a. Plot a scatter diagram between the rates of return for stock Y and the NYSE.

b. Does rate of return for stock Y appear to be linearly related to the rate of return for the entire NYSE? Interpret.

c. Use software to determine the simple correlation matrix. Relate the correlation coefficient to the scatter diagram.

8. Here are data on amount of stress and worker productivity. We wish to predict worker productivity.

Stress Level	Worker Productivity
10 (low)	15 pieces per hour
20	22
30	27
40	32
50	32
60	28
70	24
80 (high)	17

  a Use software to determine the simple correlation matrix. Interpret the correlation coefficient, $r_{STRESS, PROD}$.

  b. Plot a scatter diagram between stress level and worker productivity. Does there appear to be a linear relationship? Does there appear to be any relationship?

9. This exercise illustrates multicollinearity—where two predictor variables are highly correlated with one another. Here are data on the final exam scores in a sophomore statistics class. There are two predictor variables: (1) MATHSAT—score on math portion of the SAT, (2) GRADECAL—final grade in freshman calculus.

FINAL	MATHSAT	GRADECAL
72	475	68
79	550	79
65	450	65
89	600	84
95	610	89
78	500	74
75	490	70
73	480	71

  a. Use software to determine the simple correlation matrix. Does it appear that the two predictor variables—MATHSAT and GRADECAL—are linearly related? If $r_{MATHSAT, GRADECAL}$ is near 1 or −1 we have multicollinearity, and this presents problems that we discuss in Chapter 12.

  b. Draw a scatter diagram of MATHSAT against GRADECAL. Does it appear that the two predictor variables are linearly related?

  c. You should not be surprised that the two predictor variables are highly related. Explain why using only common sense.

11.4 Curve Fitting: Estimating Conditional Means

We have plotted scatter diagrams to check for nonlinearity or clusters. We have also computed the simple correlation matrix. Now we are ready to compute a regression equation, or model, (for example, see expression (11.1)) with one or more predictor variables. In this chapter we will limit our discussion to regression equations in which the predictor variables are raised to the first power. By the end of this section you should be able to:

1. explain what subpopulations and what population conditional means are;
2. explain how by estimating the population regression line we can estimate the population conditional means;
3. explain what is meant by the term *least squares;* and
4. calculate a least squares equation for the one-predictor variable case.

Simple Linear Regression

Refer again to the scatter diagram in Figure 11.4. Suppose we want to develop an equation to predict sales based on number of ads alone. Eight different stores ran one ad, but only outlets 8 and 14 sold the same number of units, namely 19. This is a typical situation in which there is randomness in the outcomes. The scatter diagram shows that for any particular number of ads, a *probability distribution* of units sold is likely. The probability distribution of the dependent variable (UNITS SOLD, or *y* in general) for each value of a predictor variable (ADS, or *x* in general) is called a *subpopulation.* The scatter diagram thus represents eight observations drawn from each of the ADS = 1, 3, and 5 subpopulations. The shape, mean, and standard deviation of the three subpopulations are unknown, and we must make assumptions about these distributions in regression analysis.

   The simple linear regression method *assumes* that all subpopulations:

1. are normally distributed;
2. have the same variance or standard deviation; and
3. have means that fall on the same straight line.* The subpopulation means are called *population conditional means* because the mean of each subpopulation depends, or is conditional, upon the value of the ADS predictor variable.

   Figure 11.7 is Figure 11.4 redrawn to show the three regression assumptions. Figure 11.7 shows the 24 sample values as observations from three subpopulations— ADS = 1, 3, and 5.

FIGURE 11.7   The Simple Linear Regression model

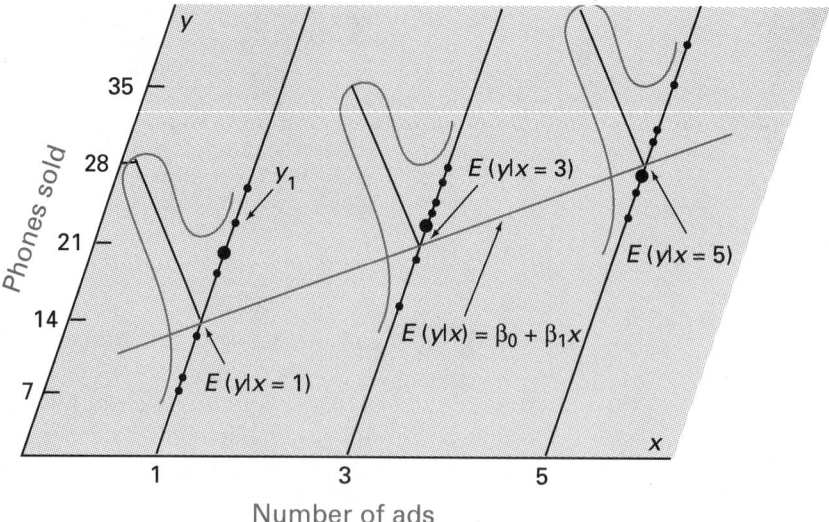

*We present one additional assumption underlying regression analysis in Section 11.6.

Recall from Chapter 5 that the mean of a probability distribution is called its expected value. The population conditional mean of the first subpopulation is $E(y \mid x = 1)$. This reads as "the expected number of units sold *given* that ADS is one per day."

The problem we address in this section is how to estimate these three unknown population conditional means from the sample data. The problem is simplified because we assume that all the population conditional means lie on a straight line. Thus estimating them requires only estimating the intercept, β_0, and the slope, β_1, of the population regression equation shown in Figure 11.7. We use the method of least squares to estimate β_0 and β_1.

The Method of Least Squares

The method of least squares is used for fitting regression models, or equations, to sample data. Since the method requires considerable calculation even when there is only one predictor variable, a software package is essential. We provide an example below to illustrate the calculations for a single predictor variable—simple regression.

Consider the following set of five observations:

Data Set A

Predictor Variable x	Dependent Variable y
1	5
2	7
3	6
4	8
5	10

Suppose that for data set A, we believe that the population conditional means of y for the five values of x lie on a straight line. The *population* regression equation for the straight line (see Figure 11.7) has the following form:

$$E(y \mid x) = \beta_0 + \beta_1 x \qquad (11.5)$$

$E(y \mid x)$ represents the population conditional means of y, given different values of x. β_0 and β_1 are unknown population parameters, or constants. These could only be determined with certainty if our sample included not five observations, but the entire population.

We must estimate β_0 and β_1 based on information from only one sample of size five. The *sample* regression equation has the following form:

$$y\text{-pred} = b_0 + b_1 x \qquad (11.6)$$

The term "y-pred" represents the predicted value of y and is an *estimate* of the population conditional mean of y for any value of x. The terms b_0 and b_1 are called *sample regression coefficients* and are estimates of β_0 and β_1. The sample intercept is b_0 and the sample slope is b_1.

If we find values for b_0 and b_1 that best fit the sample data, these will also be our best estimates of β_0 and β_1.

A *prediction error* is the difference between the actual value of the dependent variable, y, and the value predicted by equation (11.6). Prediction errors are also called residuals.

$$\text{Prediction error}_i = \text{residual}_i = y_i - y_i\text{-pred} \qquad (11.7)$$

The method of least squares minimizes the sum of the squared prediction errors. It determines the values of b_0 and b_1 that minimize

$$\sum_i (y_i - y_i\text{-pred})^2 \qquad (11.8)$$

Based upon the least squares equation presented shortly, the regression equation fitted to data set A is

$$y\text{-pred} = 3.9 + 1.1x \qquad (11.9)$$

Table 11.7 illustrates the predictions and prediction errors.

Table 11.7

Prediction and Prediction Errors for Data Set A

x	y	y-pred	Prediction Error	Squared Prediction Error
1	5	$3.9 + 1.1(1) = 5.0$	.0	.00
2	7	$3.9 + 1.1(2) = 6.1$	.9	.81
3	6	$3.9 + 1.1(3) = 7.2$	-1.2	1.44
4	8	$3.9 + 1.1(4) = 8.3$	$-.3$	.09
5	10	$3.9 + 1.1(5) = 9.4$	.6	.36
Sums			0.0	2.70

Figure 11.8 also shows the prediction errors. For example, when x is 3, the actual value of y was 6 and the predicted value of y based on the regression equation (11.9) was $3.9 + 1.1(3)$ or 7.2. Thus, the prediction error is $6 - 7.2$, or -1.2.

The sum of the squared prediction errors is 2.70, the smallest quantity possible for the sample data. If we changed the sample intercept, b_0, or sample slope, b_1, even slightly, the sum of the squared prediction errors would increase. We illustrate this in Table 11.8. For a sample slope of 1.1, when we vary the intercept around the least squares solution of 3.9, the sum of the squared prediction errors increases. For an intercept of 3.9, when we vary the slope around the least squares solution of 1.1, the sum of the squared prediction errors increases.

Table 11.8

Impact of Changing Least Squares Sample Regression Coefficients

Intercept, b_0	Slope, b_1	Sum of Squared Prediction Errors
3.8	1.1	2.75
3.9	1.1	2.70←Smallest
4.0	1.1	2.75
3.9	1.0	3.25
3.9	1.1	2.70←Smallest
3.9	1.2	3.25

FIGURE 11.8   Illustrating Residuals or Prediction Errors

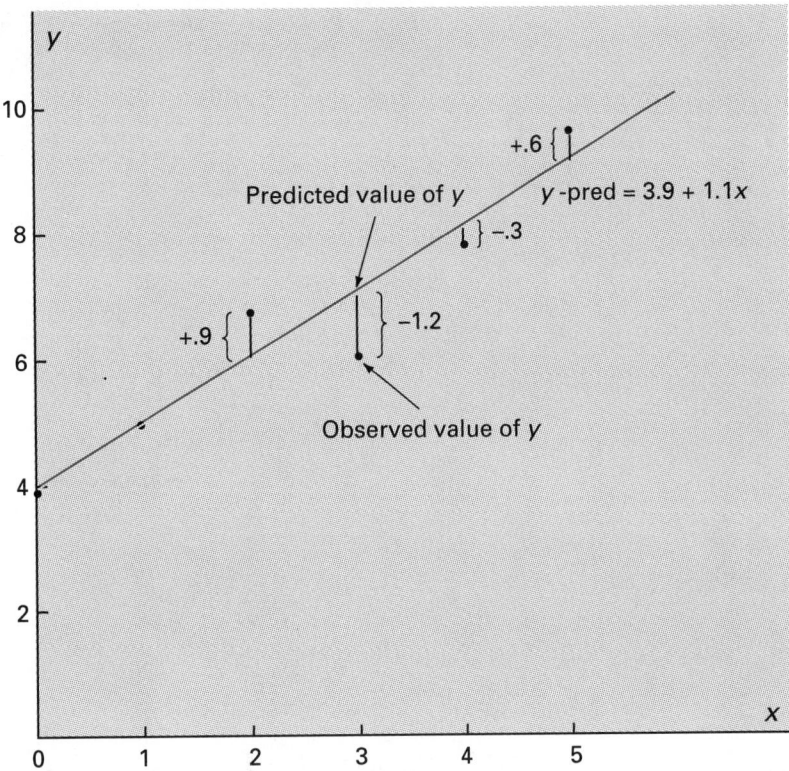

The method of least squares finds the sample regression coefficients, b_0 and b_1, that minimize the sum of the *squared* prediction errors. Hence the method is called the method of least squares.

Here are the equations for the two-variable case:

$$b_1 = \frac{\sum_i x_i y_i - n\bar{x}\bar{y}}{\sum_i x_i^2 - n(\bar{x})^2} \tag{11.10}$$

$$b_0 = \bar{y} - b_1\bar{x} \tag{11.11}$$

Note that the denominator of 11.10 is always positive. So the sign of b_1 is determined by the numerator. But the numerator is the same as the numerator of the correlation coefficient, r, (11.4). Therefore, the sign of the correlation coefficient will always be the same as the sign of b_1. Moreover, if $r = 0$ (no correlation between x and y), then $b_1 = 0$, meaning that the best-fitting line is parallel to the x, or horizontal, axis.

Table 11.9 shows the calculations for determining the sample intercept and slope. To calculate b_0 and b_1 we need to compute the product of each pair of x and y values and the square of each x value.

Table 11.9

Calculations of Least Squares Sample Intercept and Sample Slope

	Predictor Variable x	Dependent Variable y	Product of Variables xy	Square of x x^2
	1	5	5	1
	2	7	14	4
	3	6	18	9
	4	8	32	16
	5	10	50	25
Sums	15	36	119	55

$$\bar{x} = \frac{15}{5} = 3, \quad \bar{y} = \frac{36}{5} = 7.2, \quad n = 5$$

$$b_1 = \frac{\sum_i x_i y_i - n\,\bar{x}\bar{y}}{\sum_i x_i^2 - n\,(\bar{x})^2}$$

$$= \frac{119 - 5(3)(7.2)}{55 - 5(3)^2} = 1.1$$

$$b_0 = \bar{y} - b_1 \bar{x}$$

$$= 7.2 - 1.1(3) = 3.9$$

$$y\text{-pred} = 3.9 + 1.1x$$

Why is the best-fitting straight line not the line that minimizes the *sum* of the prediction errors? That is, why must we use the least *squares* method? See Figure 11.9. We have drawn two lines that each minimize the sum of the prediction errors, or residuals. Neither line is a "best-fitting line." The two lines are not even close to the actual data values.

The problem with minimizing the sum of the residuals is that positive residuals cancel out negative residuals. The sum is zero even though the two lines are not close to the actual data values. One way to solve the problem is to square the residuals, and that is why we use the least squares method.

Multiple Regression

The assumptions of simple regression and the least squares method can be extended to the case of two or more predictor variables. The probability distribution of the dependent variable (UNITS SOLD, or y in general) for each combination of predictor variables (PRICE and ADS, or x_1 and x_2 in general) is called a *subpopulation*. The first two outlets in Table 11.4 charged $100 and ran one ad per day. The first outlet sold 9 phones and the second sold 11 phones. The two observations represent a sample from the PRICE = 100 and ADS = 1 subpopulation.

The multiple regression method *assumes* that all subpopulations:

1. are normally distributed;
2. have the same variance or standard deviation; and
3. have means that fall on the same *plane*. With two or more predictor variables we are beyond two-dimensional space and the line becomes a plane.

FIGURE 11.9   Graph Illustrating the Problem of Minimizing the Sum of the Prediction Errors

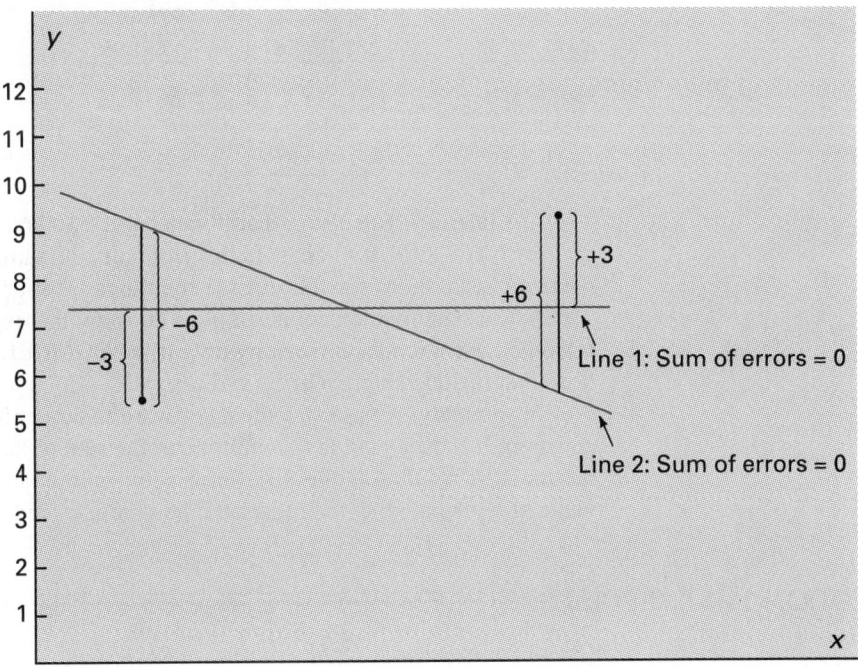

For the two predictor variable case, expression (11.12) represents the population regression plane.

$$E(y \mid x_1, x_2) = \beta_0 + \beta_1 x_1 + \beta_2 x_2 \qquad (11.12)$$

For the COMCEL marketing study, the population regression equation is

$$E(\text{UNITS SOLD} \mid \text{PRICE, ADS}) = \beta_0 + \beta_1 \text{ PRICE} + \beta_2 \text{ ADS} \qquad (11.13)$$

$E(\text{UNITS SOLD} \mid \text{PRICE, ADS})$ is the mean number of phones sold *given* any specific values of the PRICE and ADS predictor variables. The problem is how to estimate these unknown *population* conditional means from the sample data. But since we assume that all population conditional means lie on same plane, estimating them is equivalent to estimating β_0, β_1, and β_2 in expression (11.13).

Because the computation is burdensome, we omit the least squares equations for two or more predictor variables. Use a statistical software package to determine the sample regression coefficients, b_i for $i = 0, 1, 2, \ldots$

Interpreting Computer Output   Table 11.10 shows the computer output for the data in Table 11.4. Units sold is the dependent variable and price and ads are the two predictor variables. Since we must estimate the parameters β_0, β_1, and β_2 of the population regression equation, in Table 11.10 we look under the heading PARAMETER ESTIMATE for the sample regression coefficients. The sample intercept, b_0, is 60.891, the sample regression coefficient for price, b_1, is $-.530$, and the sample re gression coefficient for number of ads, b_2, is 3.313. Thus, the least squares equation is

$$\text{UNITS SOLD-PRED} = 60.891 - .530\text{PRICE} + 3.313\text{ADS}$$

Table 11.10

Parameter Estimation for COMCEL Data

VARIABLE	PARAMETER ESTIMATE	STANDARD ERROR	t-VALUE	TWO-TAILED p-VALUE
INTERCEPT	60.891	—	—	—
PRICE	-.530	.07	-7.51	$p < .001$
ADS	3.313	.32	10.37	$p < .001$

The intercept value says that if we charged \$0 and ran no ads we would sell (or give away) 60.891 car phones. In this example, the sample intercept has no practical meaning because \$0 was far outside the range of prices COMCEL has tried (\$80 – \$100). The sample intercept is simply a constant that is needed to make predictions. It would have a practical meaning only if the COMCEL data had contained observations that included a price of \$0 and zero ads.

In summary, we use statistical software to determine the best-fitting regression equation. It is the equation that minimizes the sum of the squared prediction errors or residuals. A residual is the difference between the actual sample value, *y,* and the value of *y* predicted by the regression equation, *y*-pred.

SECTION 11.4 EXERCISES

Use a software package for all problems in this section.

1. Refer to the data set in Exercise 1 of Section 11.3. Estimate the linear regression equation between SALARY (dependent variable) and PROD. Interpret the sample intercept and sample slope. Draw the best-fitting line in your scatter diagram of the data.

2. Refer to the data set in Exercise 3 of Section 11.3. Estimate the linear regression equation between TESTPERF (dependent variable) and STUDYTIME. Interpret the sample intercept and sample slope. Draw the best-fitting line in your scatter diagram of the data.

3. Refer to the data set in Exercise 5 of Section 11.3. Estimate the linear regression equation between MONTHLY SALARY (dependent variable) and MONTHS ON THE JOB for men. Then determine the linear regression equation between MONTHLY SALARY (dependent variable) and MONTHS ON THE JOB for women. Draw both best-fitting lines in your scatter diagram of the data. Given the two sample intercepts and sample slopes, does there appear to be a difference in the salaries of men and women?

4. Refer to the data set in Exercise 6 of Section 11.3. Estimate the linear regression equation between AMOUNT OF INSURANCE (dependent variable) and INCOME for single physicians. Then determine the linear regression equation between AMOUNT OF INSURANCE and INCOME for married physicians. Draw both best-fitting lines in your scatter diagram of the data. Given the two sample intercepts and sample slopes, does marital status appear to affect the amount of life insurance a doctor buys?

5. Refer to the data set in Exercise 7 of Section 11.3. Estimate the linear regression equation between the historic returns on stock Y (the dependent variable) and the returns on the NYSE, or market. Plot a scatter diagram.

   In finance, the slope estimate is called the beta coefficient. It measures the extent to which returns of a given stock move with the stock market. Beta coefficients less than 1 indicate low-volatility stocks (such as utility companies); beta coefficients greater than 1 indicate highly volatile stocks (high-technology companies). Interpret the beta coefficient for stock Y.

6. Shown are the results of an experimental regression study first discussed in Exercise 6 of Section 11.2 Exercises. The dependent variable is cost per unit. The two predictor variables are the size of the production run and age of the equipment.

Cost per Unit	Size of Production Run	Age of Equipment (years)
$1.50	1,000	1
1.60	1,000	1
1.75	1,000	3
1.75	1,000	3
2.10	1,000	5
2.00	1,000	5
1.70	670	1
1.70	670	1
1.85	670	3
1.95	670	3
2.30	670	5
2.40	670	5
2.00	333	1
2.10	333	1
2.25	333	3
2.35	333	3
2.50	333	5
2.50	333	5

    a. Obtain the correlation matrix for this data. Which variable is a stronger predictor of cost?

    b. Estimate the least squares linear regression model. The dependent variable is COST per unit and the two predictor variables are size of production RUN and AGE of equipment. Interpret the sample intercept and sample slopes of the multiple linear regression equation.

    c. Use the regression equation from part **b** to predict the COST for a RUN of 1,000 units using 5-year-old AGE equipment.

    d. Does COST-PRED from part **b** equal $E(\text{COST} \mid \text{RUN} = 1,000, \text{AGE} = 5)$? Why not?

7. Shown are the results of an experimental regression study. The dependent variable is job PERFORMance and the two predictor variables are SKILL level and MOTIVation level.

Job Performance (1 to 10)	Skill Level (0 to 100)	Motivation Level (0 to 100)
1	20	30
2	20	30
2	20	30
3	20	30
5	80	30
5	80	30
6	80	30
6	80	30
6	20	80
6	20	80
6	20	80
6	20	80
9	80	80
10	80	80
9	80	80
8	80	80

    a. Obtain the correlation matrix for this data. Which variable is a stronger predictor of job performance?

b. Estimate the least squares linear regression equation. The dependent variable is job PERFormance and the two predictor variables are SKILL and MOTIV. Interpret the sample intercept and sample slopes of the multiple linear regression equation.

c. Use the regression equation from part **b** to predict the job PERFormance for a worker with a SKILL level of 80 and a MOTIVation level of 80.

d. Does PERF-PRED from part **b** equal $E(\text{PERF} \mid \text{SKILL} = 80, \text{MOTIV} = 80)$? Why not?

11.5 ≡ Evaluating the Regression Model

Before COMCEL can use regression model (11.1) for prediction, explanation, or control it must evaluate the model. What does evaluation mean and why must we do it? Since Chapter 7 we have used samples to draw conclusions about populations. For example, in Chapter 7 we constructed confidence intervals to estimate population means. In this section we estimate population regression coefficients—β_i for $i = 1$, $2, \ldots, k$. That is, based on one sample we determine if some or all of the k predictor variables are *statistically significant,* or *statistically related* to the dependent variable in the *population.* We evaluate, or test for, statistical relationships using confidence intervals and the analysis of variance (ANOVA).

In this section we discuss several statistical tests and measures of fit that will address questions such as:

1. Is the regression model worth using at all?
2. Are all the predictor variables needed in the model?
3. How well does the regression model predict?
4. Is a single predictor variable statistically related to the dependent variable after controlling for the other predictor variables in the model?

By the end of this section you should be able to:

1. explain the decomposition, or partitioning, principle;
2. explain the role of analysis of variance in determining whether a regression model is worth using at all;
3. define the coefficient of multiple determination and explain why it is a measure of fit;
4. explain how we use a confidence interval to determine the significance of a single predictor variable; and
5. explain the role of the standard error of the estimate in evaluating a regression model.

The Need for Statistical Testing

One major reason for building a regression model is to predict a dependent variable. COMCEL wished to predict the mean units sold for individual outlets. There are two ways to do this:

1. Compute the mean number of units sold for all 24 stores in the sample.
2. Use expression (11.1) reproduced here containing two predictor variables to predict mean units sold.

$$\text{UNITS SOLD-PRED} = 60.891 - .530\text{PRICE} + 3.313\text{ADS}$$

Which method provides better predictions? It depends on whether the dependent variable is *statistically* related to one or more predictor variables. If it is, then using the regression model provides better and more precise predictions.

Strategy 1 uses $\bar{y}$ to make predictions. Here are the mean and standard deviation for the units sold data in Table 11.4.

$$\bar{y} = \frac{9 + 11 + 19 + \cdots + 24 + 37 + 34}{24}$$

$$= 23.83 \text{ phones}$$

$$s_{\text{UNITS SOLD}} = \sqrt{\frac{(9 - 23.83)^2 + (11 - 23.83)^2 + \cdots + (34 - 23.83)^2}{23}}$$

$$= 7.25 \text{ phones}$$

The Empirical rule from Chapter 2 says that roughly 95% of the stores will sell the mean number of phones plus or minus two standard deviations, i.e., $23.83 \pm 2(7.25)$ phones, or between 9.33 and 38.33 phones. This is a wide interval and makes sales forecasting and inventory control difficult. Is there a way to reduce uncertainty—to narrow the wide interval—by reducing the standard deviation of units sold?

Strategy 2 uses the regression model (11.1) to make predictions. It will reduce the standard deviation of units sold *if* one or more of its predictor variables are statistically related to the dependent variable. When we conclude the analysis, the regression model will turn out to be statistically significant. The standard deviation will then only be 2.55 phones, not 7.25 phones.

If none of the predictor variables are statistically related to the dependent variable, COMCEL must use $\bar{y}$ and accept a large standard deviation, s_y. Or it can brainstorm for additional predictor variables and develop and evaluate a new regression model.

We begin our statistical tests by determining if the regression model is worth using at all for making predictions.

Testing the Entire Regression Model: Analysis of Variance

We cannot determine if the variables are related in the *population* by merely looking at the values of the sample regression coefficients. Even if the population regression coefficients, β_i, were equal to zero (no relationship), we would not expect the sample regression coefficients, b_i, to equal zero because of sampling variability. The analysis of variance is the formal way of determining whether one or more of the predictor variables and the dependent variable are related in the population.

Stating Hypotheses   We begin by stating the null and alternative hypotheses for the COMCEL marketing study. From Section 9.2, we know that the null hypothesis is a statement of "no difference," "no change," or "no improvement." In regression analysis, the null is the "no relationship" hypothesis.

<table>
<tr><th>Hypotheses</th><th>Actions</th></tr>
</table>

H_0 None of the predictor variables are *statistically* related to the dependent variable.

Seek statistically significant predictor variables.

$\beta_1 = 0$ and $\beta_2 = 0$*

Or, use mean units sold in all stores to predict sales in an outlet.

H_1 At least one of the predictor variables is *statistically* related to the dependent variable.

Use the regression model to predict the dependent variable *if* the standard deviation for the dependent variable is sufficiently small.

Not both β_1 and β_2 equal 0.

Based on the costs of making a Type I error, COMCEL set the significance level, α, at .05.

Decomposition of the Total Sum of Squares   The analysis of variance begins with a decomposition of the total sum of squares. Refer to the data in Table 11.4. Note that the dependent variable, units sold, varies among the 24 stores. How much variation is there about the mean number of phones sold, of 23.83? This variation is measured by the total sum of squares, SST. The general form of SST for any dependent variable, y, is:

$$SST = \sum_i (y_i - \bar{y})^2 \tag{11.14}$$

For our data,

$$SST = (9 - 23.83)^2 + (11 - 23.83)^2 + \cdots + (37 - 23.83)^2 + (34 - 23.83)^2$$

$$= 1{,}207.33 \text{ units of variation}$$

What accounts for the 1,207.33 units of variation? There are two sources. The total variation is either due to the two predictor variables in the model or it is not. The two sources that are represented by the right-side terms in expression (11.15) account for the total sum of squares:

$$\sum_i (y_i - \bar{y})^2 = \sum_i (y_i\text{-pred} - \bar{y})^2 + \sum_i (y_i - y_i\text{-pred})^2 \tag{11.15}$$

The first right-side term is called the regression sum of squares (SSR). It measures the variation in y due to the two predictor variables, price and number of ads. The second term is the familiar sum of the squared prediction errors. Prediction errors are due to the many other predictor variables we could have included in the model but did not. In the COMCEL marketing study, this includes every potential predictor variable except price and number of ads. This source of variation is called the error sum of squares (SSE). Thus,

$$SST = SSR + SSE \tag{11.16}$$

*β_1 is the population regression coefficient that measures the relationship between price and units sold. β_2 is the population regression coefficient that measures the relationship between number of ads and units sold. Note that we are not interested in β_0, the population intercept.

In summary, we partition the total sum of squares into two components that reflect the impact of (1) the predictor variables in the model and (2) all other possible predictor variables not included in the model. We recommend using a statistical software package rather then expression (11.15) to compute the three sum of squares terms.

Computing the Variance Ratio   After completing the decomposition, we must convert the three sum of squares to *mean squares,* or variances. Remember, the statistical method is called the analysis of *variance.* (See Section 10.3 for a complete discussion of the analysis of variance.).

1. The *total* degrees of freedom is $n - 1$. In the COMCEL study, $24 - 1 = 23$.
2. The *regression* degrees of freedom equals the number of predictor variables, k. In the COMCEL study, $k = 2$.
3. The *error* degrees of freedom is the remainder, $n - k - 1$. In the COMCEL study, $24 - 2 - 1 = 21$.

Next we compute the mean square regression (MSR) and mean square error (MSE). We divide each sum of squares term by its appropriate degrees of freedom. MSR equals the SSR divided by k. MSE equals SSE divided by $n - k - 1$.

Finally, we compute the variance ratio. It is the mean square regression (MSR) divided by the mean square error (MSE).

$$VR = \frac{MSR}{MSE} \tag{11.17}$$

The variance ratio measures the size of MSR in comparison to MSE. MSE measures the impact on the dependent variable of all potential predictor variables other than those in the model. MSR measures the impact of all potential predictor variables— those in the model (price and number of ads) *plus* those not included.

We use the VR to test the null hypothesis that none of the predictor variables in the model are statistically related to the dependent variable.

Table 11.11 shows a computer-generated ANOVA table for the COMCEL marketing study. It shows that the MSR is almost 82 times as large as the MSE. Can we reject the null hypothesis?

Hypothesis Testing   Does a variance ratio of 81.989 favor the null or the alternative hypothesis? MSE measures the impact of all potential predictor variables other than those in the study. MSR measures MSE *plus* the impact of price and number of ads. If the null hypothesis is true and price and number of ads are not statistically related to the dependent variable, then, except for sampling error, the numerator and denominator of the variance ratio should be the same. If H_0 is true, the ratio should

Table 11.11

ANOVA Table for COMCEL Marketing Data

Source of Variation	Sum of Squares	df	Mean Square	Variance Ratio
Regression	1,070.27	2	535.13	81.989
Error	137.06	21	6.53	
Total	1,207.33	23		

Standard error	2.555	
Coefficient of determination	88.647%	
F-value critical (.05)		3.470

be close to 1, but it is not. MSR is almost 82 times as large as MSE. Is this sufficiently large to reject the null hypothesis? To answer this question we must re-introduce the sampling distribution of the variance ratio.

Assume that price and number of ads are not statistically related to units sold. Suppose we ran many studies on price, number of ads, and units sold in the 24 outlets, and for each study we computed the variance ratio. The variance ratios would differ and thus form a distribution. As explained above, the distribution's mean would be approximately 1. The smallest variance ratio would be zero (variances cannot be negative). Occasionally, a variance ratio would be large.

Figure 11.10 illustrates the distribution of variance ratios. As in Chapter 9, hypothesis testing, we must now determine the critical value and the decision rule for rejecting the null hypothesis.

The sampling distribution of the variance ratio is F-distributed (see Appendix 7). The critical value that separates the fail to reject from the rejection region is:

$$\text{Critical value} = F_{1-\alpha;\ \text{df: numerator, df: denominator}}$$

where α is the significance level.

DECISION RULE   Reject the null hypothesis if the variance ratio is greater than the critical value. Otherwise do not reject the null hypothesis.

For the COMCEL marketing study, the critical value is $F_{.95;\ 2,\ 21}$. From Appendix 7, the two closest F-values are $F_{.95;\ 2,\ 20} = 3.49$ and $F_{.95;\ 2,\ 24} = 3.40$. The interpolated F-value is 3.47 and is denoted in the computer-generated analysis of variance output as *F-value critical*.

Since the variance ratio of 81.989 is greater than the critical value, we reject the null hypothesis. We can say that the model has "passed" the ANOVA test, or that the regression model is significant.

In conclusion, we are more than 95% confident that at least one of the predictor variables affects units sold. COMCEL can generalize these findings to all 60 stores

---

FIGURE 11.10 *F*-Distribution When Null Hypothesis Is True

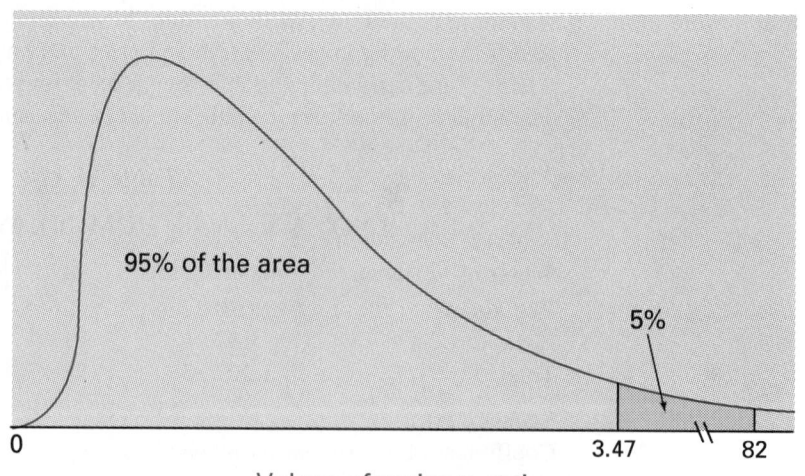

Values of variance ratio

in its chain. If COMCEL had failed to reject the null hypothesis, then the regression model would not be worth using. COMCEL should then consider seeking additional predictor variables to evaluate.

p-Value   If price and number of ads had no impact on units sold, the probability of getting a variance ratio of 82 or larger is much less than .05 (see cross-hatched area). Recall from Section 9.2 that this area or probability is called the *p*-value. So the *p*-value for the COMCEL study is much less than .05. We can estimate the *p*-value by using Appendix 7.

Here are interpolated *F*-values for 2 and 21 degrees of freedom for percentiles ranging from .950 to .999:

$$F_{.95} = 3.47$$

$$F_{.975} = 4.43$$

$$F_{.990} = 5.80$$

$$F_{.995} = 6.92$$

$$F_{.999} = 9.83$$

Since the VR of 81.989 is larger than $F_{.999} = 9.83$, the *p*-value is less than $1 - .999$, or $p < .001$.*

Managers often reject the null hypothesis when the *p*-value is .05 or less. However the *p*-value necessary for rejecting the null hypothesis depends on the costs of a Type I error. The more costly the Type I error, the lower the *p*-value should be before rejecting the null hypothesis.

Having rejected the null hypothesis, COMCEL can now consider using the regression model for making predictions provided the assumptions underlying the model are valid (see Section 11.6). Even if the assumptions are valid, a regression model for making predictions is useful only if it generates precise predictions. Recall that when we used $\bar{y} = 23.83$ phones to estimate units sold in an outlet, the standard error, $s_{\text{UNITS SOLD}}$, was 7.25 phones. The Empirical rule indicated that 95% of the stores will sell $23.83 \pm 2 (7.25)$ phones, or ± 14.5 phones. The prediction interval was too wide and therefore meaningless. What is the standard deviation in sales when we use regression model (11.1), which we just concluded is statistically related to units sold?

The Standard Error of the Estimate

One of the assumptions of the regression model is that all subpopulations have the same standard deviation. This common standard deviation is unknown and must be estimated from sample data. The estimated standard deviation of the dependent variable in the regression model is called the *standard error of the estimate,* and is denoted as $s_{y|1,2,3,\ldots,k}$ where the $1, 2, 3, \ldots, k$ represent the k predictor variables in the model. The standard error of the estimate is

$$s_{y|1,2,3,\ldots,k} = \sqrt{\text{MSE}} = \sqrt{\frac{\sum_i (y_i - y_i\text{-pred})^2}{n - k - 1}}$$

---

* Suppose the VR = 6.04. Since it falls between the .990 and .995 percentile values, the *p*-value $< 1 - .990$, or $p < .010$.

The standard error of the estimate is determined by the size of the prediction errors and is denoted in the computer-generated analysis of variance output as the *standard error*. For the COMCEL study $s_{\text{UNITS SOLD|PRICE, ADS}}$ is $\sqrt{6.53}$, or 2.555 phones (see Table 11.11). Using the Empirical rule, our prediction interval—2(2.555) or $\pm$ 5.10 phones—is now approximately only one-third as wide as when we used $\bar{y}$ to predict sales.

Table 11.12 provides insight as to what the standard error of the estimate actually measures. UNITS represent the actual units sold. UNITS SOLD-PRED represents the predicted, or estimated, units sold based on the regression model (11.1). For example, store #1 charged $100 and ran 1 ad per day (see Table 11.4). Its actual sales were 9 phones. Predicted sales were $60.891 - .530(100) + 3.313(1) = 11.251$ phones. The residual is -2.251 phones.

The sum of the squared residuals in Table 11.12 is SSE from the ANOVA table. It is the smallest possible sum of the squared prediction errors because the least squares equations were used to calculate the sample regression coefficients.

Table 11.12

Table of Residual Values

UNITS SOLD-PRED $= 60.891 - .530$PRICE $+ 3.313$ADS

OBS	UNITS	UNITS SOLD-PRED	RESIDUAL
1	9	11.251	-2.251
2	11	11.251	-0.251
3	19	17.876	1.124
4	15	17.876	-2.876
5	26	24.501	1.499
6	24	24.501	-0.501
7	14	16.546	-2.546
8	19	16.546	2.454
9	24	23.171	0.829
10	28	23.171	4.829
11	31	29.796	1.204
12	32	29.796	2.204
13	17	19.194	-2.194
14	19	19.194	-0.194
15	29	25.819	3.181
16	25	25.819	-0.819
17	30	32.444	-2.444
18	30	32.444	-2.444
19	26	21.842	4.158
20	23	21.842	1.158
21	26	28.467	-2.467
22	24	28.467	-4.467
23	37	35.092	1.908
24	34	35.092	-1.092

$$s_{\text{UNITS SOLD|PRICE,ADS}} = \sqrt{\frac{(-2.251)^2 + (-.251)^2 + \cdots + (-1.092)^2}{24 - 2 - 1}}$$

$$= 2.555 \text{ phones}$$

Note that the denominator for the standard error of the estimate is the degrees of freedom for the error source of variation from the ANOVA table.

The standard error of the estimate is much smaller than $s_{\text{UNITS SOLD}} = 7.25$ phones. However, it may still be too large to produce meaningful, or precise, prediction intervals.

There are two ways to reduce the standard error of the estimate.

1. Add statistically significant predictor variables to the regression model.
2. Remove nonsignificant predictor variables from a regression model that has passed the ANOVA test. Remember, in rejecting the null hypothesis, at least one predictor variable must be significant. But all the predictor variables may not be significant.

The coefficient of multiple determination measures the percentage of the variation in the dependent variable accounted for by the pre- dictor variables.

The first strategy requires understanding the **coefficient of multiple determination**. The second strategy requires understanding the parameter estimate section of the computer-generated output.

The Coefficient of Multiple Determination

The variance ratio does not indicate how much of the dependent variable's total variation is accounted for by the two predictor variables. In short, how much of the variation in units sold do price and number of ads explain? For that we compute the coefficient of multiple determination. It is given by

$$R^2 = \frac{\text{SSR}}{\text{SST}} \tag{11.18}$$

and is denoted as Coefficient of Determination in the computer-generated analysis of variance output.*

The coefficient of multiple determination is the ratio of the regression sum of squares to the total sum of squares. The coefficient of multiple determination measures the percentage of the variation in the dependent variable accounted for by the predictor variables in the model. The possible range of values for the coefficient of multiple determination is between 0 and 1 (or 0% to 100%).

The coefficient of multiple determination for the COMCEL data shown in the ANOVA table, Table 11.11, is

$$R^2 = \frac{\text{SSR(PRICE,ADS)}}{\text{SST}}$$

$$= \frac{1{,}070.27}{1{,}207.33} = .88647 \text{ or } 88.647\%$$

PRICE and ADS together account for 88.647% of the variation in the 24 stores' sales figures. The remaining variation in units sold, 11.353%, is due to all predictor variables other than price and number of ads, and is still unaccounted for.

If COMCEL could add statistically significant predictor variables to the regression model, the coefficient of multiple determination would increase and the standard error of the estimate would decrease.

---

*When we have only one predictor variable, the symbol is r^2—the simple coefficient of determination. However, it still equals SSR/SST, which can be obtained from the analysis of variance table. For one predictor variable, the simple coefficient of determination is the square of the simple correlation coefficient, $r_{y,x}$ first discussed in Section 11.3.

Removing Nonsignificant Predictor Variables From the Model

We have reproduced the parameter estimate section from the computer-generated output in Table 11.10.

Table 11.10

Parameter Estimate Section for COMCEL Data

VARIABLE	PARAMETER ESTIMATE	STANDARD ERROR	t-VALUE	TWO-TAILED p-VALUE
INTERCEPT	60.891	—	—	—
PRICE	−.530	.07	−7.51	$p <$ .001
ADS	3.313	.32	10.37	$p <$ .001

The column labelled "Standard Error" contains the *standard errors of the regression coefficients* and are denoted as $s(b_i)$. These measure the amount of uncertainty in the parameter estimates.* For example, if COMCEL repeated the marketing study again, it would obtain different units sold data. The parameter estimates displayed above would change. The standard errors indicate by how much the parameter estimates are likely to change. A large standard error of the regression coefficient (in comparison to the size of the parameter estimate) means that the parameter estimate would change greatly from study to study. A small standard error of the regression coefficient means that the parameter estimate would change little from study to study.

Consider the standard errors of the regression c628oefficients for the PRICE and ADS predictor variables. The parameter estimate for the ADS variable is 3.313 with a standard error of the regression coefficient of .32. The .32 is small relative to the parameter estimate. Thus, the parameter estimate, 3.313, is stable and would not change much if the study were repeated. The parameter estimate for PRICE is also very stable.

We use the t-value column output to determine the significance of the parameter estimates. The larger the t-value, the more significant (as measured by the p-value) the parameter estimate. The t-value is simply the ratio of a parameter estimate to the standard error of its regression coefficient.

For the COMCEL study, the t-values are:

1. t-value for PRICE   −.530/.07 = −7.57
2. t-value for ADS   3.313/.32 = +10.35

Rounding errors cause the results not to coincide precisely with Table 11.10.

Maddala (1992) suggests a *screening procedure* to remove nonsignificant predictor variables from a regression model that has passed the ANOVA test. The procedure uses the t-values described above. Use the screening procedure when the purpose of the regression analysis is prediction and the goal is to reduce the standard error of the estimate, $s_{y|1,2,3,\ldots,k}$.

---

*Note: The standard errors of the regression coefficients and the standard error of the estimate differ. However, they are related to one another. The standard errors of the regression coefficients decrease (increase) as the standard error of the estimate decreases (increases).

Here are the steps to the screening procedure:

1. Take the absolute value of the t-values found in the parameter estimate section of your computer output.
2. Delete the predictor variable with the smallest t-value provided it is less than 1.
3. Use your software to re-estimate the regression model with the remaining predictor variables.
4. Repeat steps 2 and 3, one predictor variable at a time, until all the remaining predictor variables have $|t| \geq 1$.

This procedure does not guarantee that all the predictor variables in the final regression model are statistically significant at the .05 level. However, it minimizes the standard error of the estimate. This will reduce the width of prediction intervals we discuss in Section 11.7.

Using the screening procedure, none of the predictor variables in the COMCEL regression model

$$\text{UNITS SOLD-PRED} = 60.891 - .530\text{PRICE} + 3.313\text{ADS}$$

should be removed. The absolute t-values of 7.51 and 10.37 are much larger than the cutoff value of one. That is, we cannot reduce the standard error of the estimate below 2.555 by removing either predictor variable from the regression model.

Why does this screening method work? First recall that the standard error of the estimate is

$$s_{y|1,\,2\,3,\dots,k} = \sqrt{\text{MSE}} = \sqrt{\frac{\text{SSE}}{n-k-1}}$$

SSE (sum of squares-error) measures the impact of all potential predictor variables not yet in the model. As we add predictor variables to a regression model, SSE must become smaller. Thus, the numerator of $s_{y|1,\,2,\,3,\dots,k}$ gets smaller. However, each additional predictor variable also increases k and reduces the number of degrees of freedom by one. Thus, the denominator of $s_{y|1,\,2,\,3,\dots,k}$ also gets smaller. Whether the two reductions lead to an increase or decrease in the standard error of the estimate depends on the relative reductions in the numerator and denominator.

Maddala shows that

$$\frac{\text{MSE}_{k \text{ variables}}}{\text{MSE}_{k+1 \text{ variables}}} = \frac{\text{df} + t^2}{\text{df} + 1}$$

where $\text{df} = n - k - 1$. Thus, $\text{MSE}_{k \text{ variables}} < \text{MSE}_{k+1 \text{ variables}}$ if $|t| < 1$.

Adding a predictor variable with an absolute t-value of less than 1 produces a reduction in SSE that is smaller than the relative reduction in degrees of freedom. So MSE and thus, $s_{y|1,\,2,\,3,\dots,k}$ will increase. Thus, we can reduce the standard error of the estimate by removing predictor variables from the model whose absolute t-values are less than 1.

In summary, to reduce the standard error of the estimate:

1. Remove predictor variables, one at a time, from the model whose $|t|$ values are less than 1, or
2. Add predictor variables to the model whose $|t|$ values are greater than 1.

Assessing the Significance of a Single Predictor Variable

Managers use regression models for more than prediction and control. Explanation is also important. For example, managers want to know if price and units sold are related after controlling for the impact of number of ads. Are salary and gender related after controlling for the impact of education level? Students want to know if grades and hours studied are related after controlling for the impact of SAT scores.

Interval Estimation Method   The interval estimation method allows us to determine if a single regression coefficient, β_k, is different from zero. Recall that if β_k is zero, the two variables are not statistically related to one another. We use the sample regression coefficient, b_k, and expression (11.19) to estimate the population regression coefficient, β_k.

$b_k \pm$ reliability coefficient $\cdot$ standard error of the regression coefficient

$$b_k \pm t[\text{two-sided } 100(1 - \alpha)\% \ n - k - 1 \text{ df}] \cdot s(b_k) \tag{11.19}$$

where the t-value is found in Appendix 5,
α is the significance level, and
$n - k - 1$ are the degrees of freedom for MSE

Return to the COMCEL marketing study. Is price related to units sold after controlling for the impact of number of ads? That is, does β_1 not equal zero?

Once again we have reproduced the parameter estimate section from the computer-generated output from Table 11.10 to help construct the confidence interval.

Table 11.10

Parameter Estimate Section for COMCEL Data

VARIABLE	PARAMETER ESTIMATE	STANDARD ERROR	t-VALUE	TWO-TAILED p-VALUE
INTERCEPT	60.891	—	—	—
PRICE	−.530	.07	−7.51	$p < .001$
ADS	3.313	.32	10.37	$p < .001$

Given $\alpha = .05$, a two-sided 95% confidence interval on the price predictor variable is

$-.530 \pm t[\text{two-sided } 100(1 -.05)\% = 95\%, 21 \text{ df}] \cdot .07$

$-.530 \pm 2.080(.07)$

$-.530 \pm .15$

$-.38 \le \beta_1 \le -.68$

We are 95% confident that β_1 is between $-.38$ and $-.68$. That is, mean units sold will decrease by between .38 and .68 phones for each additional \$1 increase in price within the range of \$80 to \$100 after controlling for number of ads.

Since the confidence interval does not contain zero, we are 95% confident that the population regression coefficient for the price variable is not zero. COMCEL can conclude that price negatively affects units sold after controlling for number of ads.

Alternatively, we could determine if the number of ads is related to units sold after controlling for the impact of price. That is, does β_2 not equal zero? Again we use expression (11.19).

$$3.313 \pm 2.080(.32)$$

$$3.313 \pm .67$$

$$2.64 \leq \beta_2 \leq 3.98$$

We are 95% confident that β_2 is between 2.64 and 3.98. That is, mean units sold will increase by between 2.64 and 3.98 phones for each additional ad within the range of 1 to 5 ads after controlling for price. Since the interval does not contain zero, we are 95% confident that the population regression coefficient for the number of ads variable is not zero. COMCEL can conclude that the number of ads positively affects units sold after controlling for price.

Warning: Expression (11.19) is useful for determining if a single predictor variable is statistically related to the dependent variable after controlling for the other predictor variables in the model. Managers abuse the confidence interval method if they use it to determine whether *all* the predictor variables are statistically related to the dependent variable. Suppose a manager develops a regression model with five predictor variables and constructs five confidence intervals using expression (11.19). It would be improper to use the intervals to estimate all five population regression coefficients due to the problem of multiple comparisons discussed in Section 10.4.

Suppose we construct a 95% confidence interval for each of the five predictor variables. The probability of making an incorrect conclusion for each confidence interval is $1 - .95 = .05$. However, the probability of making one or more incorrect conclusions for all five confidence intervals is not .05, it is larger.

In Section 10.4 we noted that when constructing five confidence intervals, the probability of making one or more incorrect conclusions increases from .05 to about .25 ($5 \cdot .05$). This is equivalent to a $100(1 - .25)\%$, or 75%, confidence level for all five intervals. As the number of confidence intervals increases, so too does the probability of making one or more incorrect conclusions.

In Section 10.4, we presented the Tukey procedure for protecting against this increasing probability. This idea can be extended to regression analysis. There are methods for constructing *joint confidence intervals* that maintain the probability of making one or more incorrect conclusions at α, the chosen significance level. For a full discussion of these methods see Neter, Wasserman, and Kutner (1985).

In summary, use expression (11.19) only for estimating a single population regression coefficient. You will want to do this when your goal is to determine if a single predictor variable is statistically related to the dependent variable after controlling for all the other predictor variables in the model.

SECTION 11.5 EXERCISES

Use software for the problems that require extensive calculation.

1. We run a regression study with one dependent variable and three predictor variables. The total sample size is 24. The model is

$$E(y \mid x_1, x_2, x_3) = \beta_0 + \beta_1 x_1 + \beta_2 x_2 + \beta_3 x_3$$

a. Write the null and alternative hypotheses tested by ANOVA.
b. What are the degrees of freedom for the numerator of the variance ratio? Explain.
c. What are the degrees of freedom for the denominator of the variance ratio? Explain.
d. What is the critical F-value from Appendix 7 for the appropriate degrees of freedom if $\alpha = .05$?

2. A variance ratio for 3 degrees of freedom in the numerator and 30 degrees of freedom in the denominator equals 4.52.
a. Use Appendix 7 to determine the p-value for a variance ratio of 4.52. Assuming the level of significance is $\alpha = .05$, should we reject the null hypothesis?
b. Interpret the p-value.

3. The numerator of the variance ratio in Exercise 2 is 1,200 and the denominator is 265.50. Compute and interpret the coefficient of multiple determination.

4. Suppose that the variance ratio has a p-value of .10. Many managers use the .05 p-value rule and would not reject the null hypothesis. Make an argument about when a p-value of .10 could cause a manager to reject the null hypothesis.

5. A credit scoring regression model evaluates the creditworthiness of loan applicants. The predictor variables considered are salary, number of years living at present address, marital status, and number of years at present job. Set up the null and alternative hypotheses for a regression model using all the predictor variables.

6. Shown is a cross-sectional data set for 16 skilled laborers. Job satisfaction is the dependent variable and is measured on a 1–10 scale. There are two predictor variables. Closeness of supervision is the degree to which workers are constantly watched and supervised. A score of 10 indicates very close supervision. Salary is the annual salary in thousands of dollars.

Job Satisfaction	Closeness of Supervision	Salary (thousands of dollars)
1	10	22
2	9	20
3	7	38
3	9	36
5	7	27
4	7	25
6	5	30
6	6	31
7	4	28
7	5	32
8	4	34
9	3	25
8	4	36
9	2	24
10	2	38
10	1	39

a. Set up the null and alternative hypotheses.
b. Estimate the multiple regression model.
c. Develop an ANOVA table. Is the p-value for the variance ratio less than .05?
d. Compute and interpret the coefficient of multiple determination.
e. What is the standard error of the estimate.

f. Predict the mean job satisfaction of workers for a closeness of supervision score of 3 and a salary of $27(000).

g. Use the Empirical rule and standard error of the estimate to set up an interval around your predicted mean job satisfaction score.

7. In Exercise 5 of Section 11.3 there is a cross-sectional data base for 18 managers. Two of the predictor variables are months on the job and the manager's gender. In Exercise 3 of Section 11.4, you developed two regression models—one for males and one for females.

a. Develop two ANOVA tables to evaluate both models. Are the two p-values for the variance ratios each less than .01?

b. Interpret the two simple coefficients of determination.

c. What are the two respective standard errors of the estimate?

8. In Exercise 4 of Section 11.3 there is a time-ordered data set for 12 quarters of data. SALES is the dependent variable and INVENTORY and NPEE are the predictor variables.

a. Set up the null and alternative hypotheses.

b. Estimate the multiple regression model.

c. Develop an ANOVA table. Is the regression significant at the $\alpha = .01$ level? Is the p-value less than .01?

d. Interpret the coefficient of multiple determination.

e. Obtain the standard error of the estimate.

f. Use the absolute t-value screening procedure. Can you remove any predictor variables from the model to improve prediction?

9. Shown is a time-ordered data set on company sales (dependent variable) and disposable personal income.

Year and Quarter		Sales (millions of dollars)	Disposable Personal Income (billions of dollars)
1990	1	35.2	133.5
	2	35.5	135.5
	3	35.9	137.7
	4	36.7	140.0
1991	1	37.7	143.9
	2	38.4	147.2
	3	39.2	148.9
	4	39.3	149.0
1992	1	41.2	153.2
	2	41.4	155.6
	3	42.3	160.9
	4	43.1	163.5

a. Estimate the simple linear regression model.

b. Develop an ANOVA table. Test the significance of the regression model if $\alpha = .10$. Is the p-value < .10?

c. Interpret the simple coefficient of determination.

d. Obtain the standard error of the estimate.

e. Predict mean sales for a disposable personal income level of 150.

10. Refer to Exercise 7 in Section 11.3 and Exercise 5 in Section 11.4 in which we computed the beta coefficient for stock Y.

a. Set up the null and alternative hypotheses.

b. Develop an ANOVA table.

c. Is the p-value for the variance ratio less than .05?

d. Obtain the standard error of the estimate.

11. Is YEARS on the job (predictor variable) related to SALARY (dependent variable) after controlling for the impact of AGE? Here are data from a correlational regression study.

EMPLOYEE	AGE	YEARS	SALARY
1	23	5	35.98
2	64	30	59.09
3	46	12	34.48
4	39	7	41.56
5	31	4	18.10
6	26	2	15.41
7	18	1	10.31
8	21	4	13.36
9	26	7	21.19
10	25	1	30.74
11	40	6	59.86
12	30	4	10.94
13	61	22	33.21
14	22	2	19.93
15	18	1	19.69
16	22	2	11.37
17	36	5	41.75
18	37	14	40.96
19	26	5	10.70
20	43	7	41.48
21	27	2	27.58
22	70	6	50.55
23	30	9	19.91
24	31	5	19.40
25	25	4	14.00
26	20	3	17.71
27	46	7	49.56
28	62	7	30.66
29	34	4	15.21
30	48	24	43.93

  a. Plot AGE and YEARS against SALARY and develop a correlation matrix for this data. Do AGE and YEARS appear to be linearly related to SALARY?

  b. Construct and interpret a 95% confidence interval for the regression coefficient of the YEARS variable, after controlling for AGE.

  c. Based on your confidence interval, does it appear that YEARS with the company is related to SALARY after AGE has been controlled for?

12. A real estate appraiser collected the following data for a random sample of 30 apartment rental units. He wants to use this information to predict rents. The appraiser believes that monthly RENT is affected by the number of BEDROOMS, the size of the complex measured by the number of UNITS, the AGE of the unit, whether all UTILities are included (no = 0; yes = 1), and whether COVered PARKing is provided (no = 0; yes = 1).

OBS	RENT	BEDROOM	UNITS	AGE	UTIL	COVPARK
1	135	1	4	30	0	0
2	135	1	5	32	0	0
3	145	1	4	24	0	0
4	150	1	5	18	0	0
5	150	1	8	15	0	0
6	175	1	12	15	0	0
7	180	1	15	12	0	0
8	200	1	15	15	0	1
9	200	1	20	13	0	0
10	210	1	20	15	1	0
11	230	2	5	32	0	0
12	235	1	20	10	0	0
13	260	1	20	8	0	1
14	285	2	15	24	0	0
15	300	2	20	18	0	0
16	305	1	60	10	1	1
17	315	2	20	15	0	1
18	325	1	80	10	0	1
19	350	2	30	12	0	0
20	375	2	20	15	1	0
21	395	1	80	5	1	1
22	405	2	45	8	0	0
23	415	2	45	10	0	1
24	445	3	30	25	0	0
25	480	2	75	10	0	1
26	530	2	80	15	1	1
27	585	3	30	20	1	1
28	610	3	60	22	0	0
29	675	3	45	5	1	0
30	680	3	80	8	0	1

a. Estimate a regression model that can be used to predict rent.

b. Develop an ANOVA table. Is the regression significant at the $\alpha = .05$ level? Is the p-value less than .05?

c. Use the absolute t-value screening procedure to minimize the standard error of the estimate.

d. Record the values of the standard error of the estimate as you delete variables with $|t|$-values less than 1. How would you describe the change(s)?

11.6 ≡ Evaluating the Regression Model Assumptions: Residual Analysis

Before using regression model (11.1) to make predictions or to establish controls, COMCEL must verify the model's assumptions. If the assumptions are not valid, we must adjust the model before using it to make predictions.

In this section, we discuss how an examination of sample prediction errors, or *residuals,* helps us test the assumptions. By the end of this section you should be able to:

1. explain the symptoms of an inadequate model that are revealed by examining the residuals;

2. explain autocorrelation and why it suggests an inadequate model;
3. explain homoscedasticity; and
4. suggest remedies for problems identified by a residual analysis.

Assumptions Underlying Regression Models

Figure 11.7, which we have reproduced here, illustrates three assumptions—linearity, normality, and equal variances. We first mentioned these assumptions in Section 11.4.

Linearity   We assume that the population regression line or plane connecting the means of the subpopulations (the conditional probability distributions of the dependent variable) is linear in the parameters.*

Normality   We assume that each subpopulation is normally distributed.

Equal Variances   We assume that the variances of the conditional probability distributions of the dependent variable are equal. This is called the assumption of *homoscedasticity*.

We need to add one more assumption to complete the description of the regression model, the assumption of independence.

Independence   We assume that a *y*-value from any subpopulation is unrelated to *y*-values from the same or other subpopulations. For example, in Figure 11.7, if actual units sold for one ad (y_1) is above the mean of its conditional distribution, actual units sold for three ads or five ads may be above or below their respective means. Units sold by any store that runs one ad is unrelated to units sold by any other store.

FIGURE 11.7   The Simple Linear Regression model

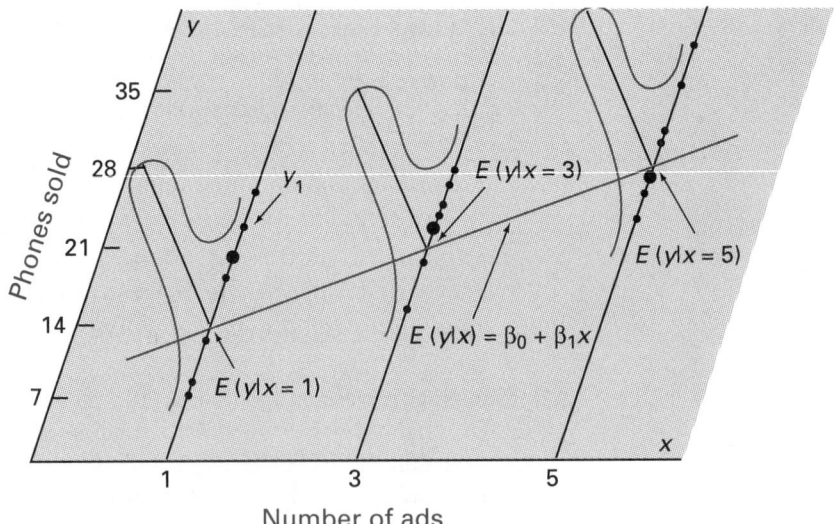

Number of ads

---

*See Chapter 12.

The independence assumption would not be valid if two stores were located in the same small town and the town's major employer closed its doors. Sales of both stores would fall because of the town's drop in purchasing power.

Examining Residual Plots

A residual plot is a graph showing the residuals on the vertical axis and y-pred, a predictor variable, or time on the horizontal axis.

We use **residual plots** to determine whether a regression model meets the four assumptions. A prediction error or residual is the difference between the actual value of y and the value of y predicted by the regression model. There is one residual for each observation in the sample:

$$\text{Residual}_i = y_i - y_i\text{-pred}$$

We plot residuals against each predictor variable and against y-pred for cross-sectional data. We plot residuals against time for time-ordered data.

Figure 11.11 shows how a sample residual plot might look when all four regression assumptions are met. The residuals oscillate within an equal-width horizontal band centered on zero and should display no systematic pattern of positive or negative residuals.

If each subpopulation is normally distributed as in Figure 11.7, then the residuals should be centered around zero. Why? Because y-pred is an estimate of the population conditional mean of each subpopulation, $E(y \mid x = 1)$, $E(y \mid x = 3)$, $E(y \mid x = 5)$. For a normal distribution, 50% of the values lie above and 50% lie below the mean. Thus, about half of the residuals should be positive and half should be negative.

If the assumption of equal variances is realistic, then the size of the residuals above the mean should equal the size of those below the mean. Thus, the residuals should oscillate within a band of constant width around a horizontal line at a mean of zero.

We use residual plots to determine whether any of the following five problems exist for our regression model:

1. The population regression line or plane is not linear.
2. The subpopulations do not have equal variances.
3. The subpopulations are not normally distributed.
4. The subpopulations contain outliers.
5. The model does not exhibit independence; the data exhibit autocorrelation.

FIGURE 11.11   Residual Plot When All Regression Assumptions are Met

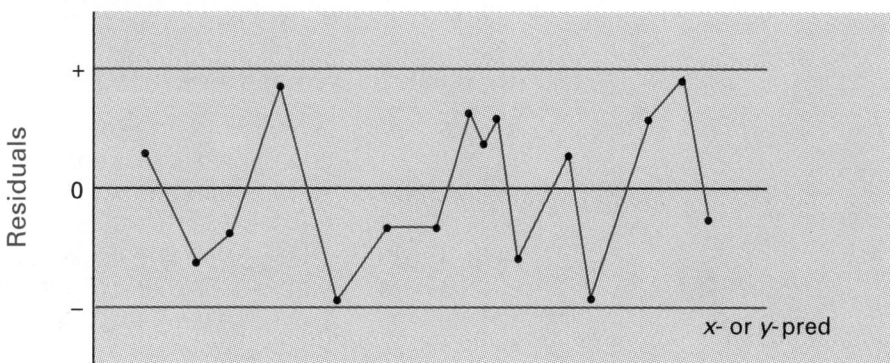

Nonlinearity of Regression Line

Nonlinearity means that the relationship between the dependent variable and the predictor variables cannot be described by a straight line or plane. Table 11.13 contains nonlinear data for which we used software to compute a linear regression line.

$$y\text{-pred} = -12.714 + 8.25x$$

Table 11.13

Residuals for a Linear Curve Fitted to Nonlinear Data Set

y	x	y-pred	Residual
1	1	$-12.714 + 8.25(1) = -4.464$	5.464
5	2	$-12.714 + 8.25(2) = 3.786$	1.214
8	3	$-12.714 + 8.25(3) = 12.046$	-4.046
14	4	$-12.714 + 8.25(4) = 20.286$	-6.286
26	5	$-12.714 + 8.25(5) = 28.546$	-2.546
38	6	$-12.714 + 8.25(6) = 36.786$	1.214
50	7	$-12.714 + 8.25(7) = 45.036$	4.964

Figure 11.12 shows a plot of the residuals against the predictor variable, x. The residual plot shows a systematic pattern of positive and negative residuals. The residuals are first positive, then negative, and then positive again. The curvilinear pattern tells us that the regression model is not linear.

How can we correct the nonlinearity problem? We used software to fit a *curvilinear* regression model to the data in Table 11.13. First, we generated a second predictor variable, x^2, by squaring each value of the predictor variable. Second, we fit a multiple regression model with two predictor variables, x, x^2. Expression (11.20) is a nonlinear regression model. Note that the predictor variable, x, is raised to the second power, so the equation is nonlinear in the variable x. We will discuss nonlinear relationships in Chapter 12.

$$y\text{-pred} = 1.143 - .988x + 1.155x^2 \tag{11.20}$$

Table 11.14 contains the residuals for the curvilinear regression model. Now a residual plot would reveal an equal-width horizontal band centered on zero with no systematic pattern of positive or negative residuals.

Table 11.14

Residuals for a Nonlinear Curve Fitted to Nonlinear Data

y	x	x^2	y-pred	Residual
1	1	1	$1.143 - .988(1) + 1.155(1) = 1.310$	-.310
5	2	4	$1.143 - .988(2) + 1.155(4) = 3.786$	1.214
8	3	9	$1.143 - .988(3) + 1.155(9) = 8.551$	-.551
14	4	16	$1.143 - .988(4) + 1.155(16) = 15.617$	-1.617
26	5	25	$1.143 - .988(5) + 1.155(25) = 25.071$	.929
38	6	36	$1.143 - .988(6) + 1.155(36) = 36.786$	1.214
50	7	49	$1.143 - .988(7) + 1.155(49) = 50.810$	-.810

FIGURE 11.12   Residual Plot for Nonlinear Datas are Met

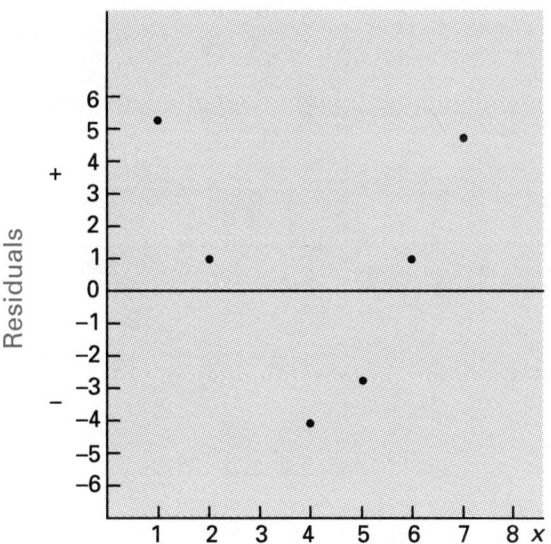

Unequal Variances

When the variances of the subpopulations in Figure 11.7 are not the same, the residuals do not form an equal-width horizontal band. Rather, the residuals increase or decrease as the values of y-pred or the values of a predictor variable increase. Under these conditions, the statistical tests presented in the previous section and prediction intervals covered in the next section are invalid.

Table 11.15 contains a data set that violates the assumption of equal variances. We used software to develop the least squares regression model, y-pred = 2.286 + 2.679x, for the seven data values. Figure 11.13 shows a plot of the residuals versus x, the predictor variable. Notice that as x increases, the residuals become larger.

How can we fix the problem of unequal variances? One possibility, for data values that are positive, is to transform the dependent variable using the square root or log base 10 transformation. (See Section 8.2 for a review of transformations.) Use software to take the square root of each value of the dependent variable. Calculate the

Table 11.15

Data Set with Increasing Variances

y	x	y-pred	Residual
4	1	2.286 + 2.679(1) = 4.954	−.9548
8	2	2.286 + 2.679(2) = 7.643	.357
9	3	2.286 + 2.679(3) = 10.321	−1.321
16	4	2.286 + 2.679(4) = 13.00	3.000
13	5	2.286 + 2.679(5) = 15.679	−2.679
24	6	2.286 + 2.679(6) = 18.357	5.643
17	7	2.286 + 2.679(7) = 21.036	−4.036

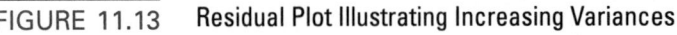

FIGURE 11.13   Residual Plot Illustrating Increasing Variances

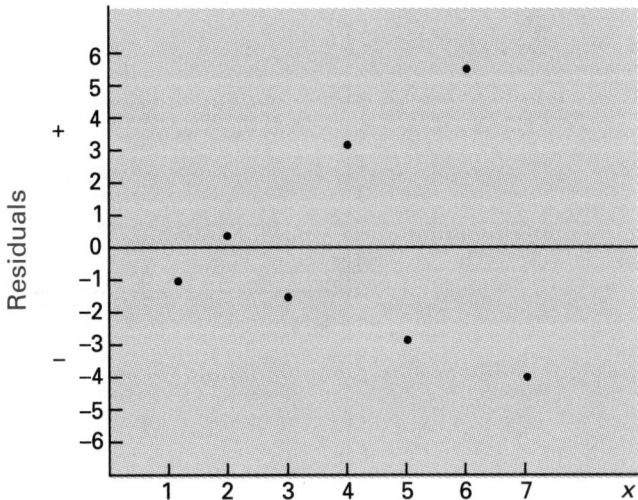

least squares regression model with the transformed dependent variable. Check the residual pattern again.

We have taken the square root of the y-values in Table 11.15 and recalculated the best-fitting linear equation. The transformed regression equation is now $\sqrt{y}\text{-pred} = 1.906 + .397x$. Note that the residuals in Table 11.16 now form an equal-width horizontal band.

Table 11.16

Square Root Transformed Data Set

$\sqrt{y}$	x	$\sqrt{y}$-pred	Residual
2.000	1	$1.906 + .397(1) = 2.303$	−.303
2.828	2	$1.906 + .397(2) = 2.700$	.128
3.000	3	$1.906 + .397(3) = 3.097$	−.097
4.000	4	$1.906 + .397(4) = 3.493$	.507
3.605	5	$1.906 + .397(5) = 3.890$	−.285
4.898	6	$1.906 + .397(6) = 4.287$	.611
4.123	7	$1.906 + .397(7) = 4.684$	−.561

Of course, we still want to estimate y, not its square root. To do this, substitute a value of x into the transformed regression model and determine the square root of y. Then square this value to get an estimate of y. For example, to estimate y when $x = 1.5$:

$$\sqrt{y}\text{-pred} = 1.906 + .397(1.5) = 2.502$$

$$y\text{-pred} = (2.502)^2 = 6.258$$

Nonnormality

Check for normality of the subpopulations in Figure 11.7 by computing *standardized residuals:*

$$\text{Standardized residual}_i = \frac{\text{Residual}_i}{\sqrt{\text{MSE}}} \qquad (11.21)$$

The numerator is the residual and can be found in the software-generated table of residuals (see Table 11.12). The denominator is the standard error of the estimate, 2.555, and can be found in the software-generated ANOVA output (see Table 11.11).

If the data are normal, about 68% of the standardized residuals should lie between -1 and $+1$. About 95% should lie between -1.96 and $+1.96$. If the data violate the normality assumption, try transforming the dependent variable using the square root or log base 10 transformation. These transformations, which often equalize the variances, also tend to normalize the data.

Outliers

Outliers (see Section 2.6) will draw the computed regression model away from the main body of data points and distort the value of the sample regression coefficients. Thus, the sample regression coefficients, b_i, will be poor estimates of the population regression coefficients, β_i. Use standardized residuals to check for outliers. Neter, Wasserman, and Kutner (1985) define an outlier as any value whose standardized residual lies outside the range of -4 to $+4$. If the standardized residuals indicate outliers, the ANOVA discussed in the previous section will not be applicable.

How can we correct for the problem of outliers? First, check to make sure that they are not the result of a clerical error or an administrative decision, such as a one-time-only price clearance. If the observation is definitely in error or uncharacteristic of the population we want to describe with the regression model, then eliminate the data point and recompute the model. If we cannot discard the outlier, use a log base 10 transformation on the dependent variable, fit the new model, and check the residuals again. If that does not work, seek expert statistical help.

Autocorrelation

Nonindependence means that the residuals are related. They do *not* exhibit a random pattern when plotted against y-pred, a predictor variable, or time. Nonindependence often occurs in time-ordered data. Thus, for time-ordered data, we should plot the residuals against time and check for a nonrandom pattern.

Consider the 16 quarters of firm and industry sales data in Table 11.17. We used software to compute the residuals from the best-fitting line, y-pred $= -1.502 + .177$IND. Figure 11.14 shows the residual plot versus time.

The plot of residuals versus time shows long strings of positive and then negative residuals. The independence assumption is not satisfied. When there are long strings of positive and negative residuals, we have the problem of positive *autocorrelation.* If residuals bounce back and forth predictably between positive and negative values (a sawtooth pattern), we have negative autocorrelation. In either case the regression model is invalid and should not be used.

Table 11.17

Data Set Illustrating Nonindependence

Year	Quarter	y Firm Sales (millions of dollars)	IND Industry Sales (millions of dollars)	y-pred	Residual
1992	1	20.96	127.3	20.981	−.021
	2	21.40	130.0	21.458	−.058
	3	21.96	132.7	21.935	.025
	4	21.52	129.4	21.352	.168
1993	1	22.39	135.0	22.341	.049
	2	22.76	137.1	22.712	.048
	3	23.48	141.2	23.436	.044
	4	23.66	142.8	23.719	−.059
1994	1	24.10	145.5	24.196	−.096
	2	24.01	145.3	24.160	−.150
	3	24.54	148.3	24.690	−.150
	4	24.30	146.4	24.355	−.055
1995	1	25.00	150.2	25.026	−.026
	2	25.64	153.1	25.538	.102
	3	26.36	157.3	26.280	.080
	4	26.98	160.7	26.880	.100

FIGURE 11.14   Residuals versus Time

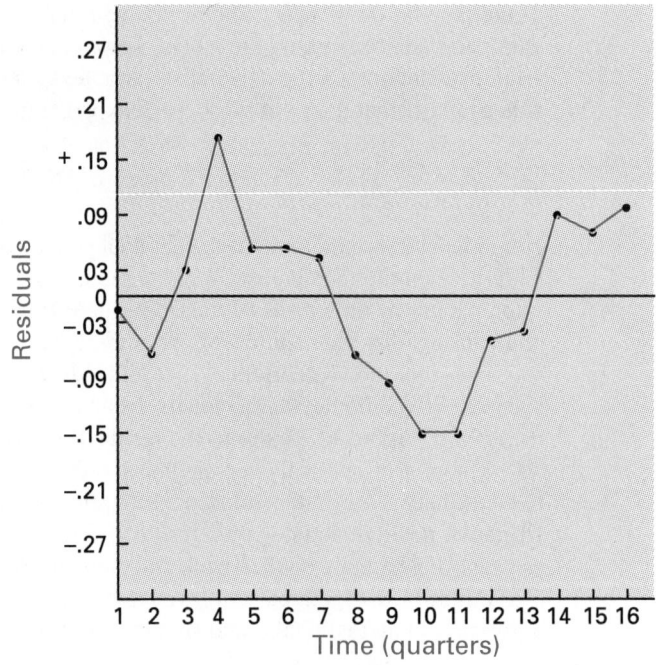

How can we remedy this violation? We have three choices:

1. We can fit a curvilinear model such as expression (11.20) to the data. Then we reexamine the residual pattern.
2. We can brainstorm for additional predictor variables. We then include these predictor variables in the model and reexamine the residual pattern.
3. We can develop an *autoregressive* model. Autoregressive models use previous values of the dependent variable as the predictor variable. Equation (11.22) is an autoregressive model which says that sales for a period depend on sales from one period earlier:

$$\text{SALES-PRED}_t = b_0 + b_1 \text{ SALES}_{t-1} \tag{11.22}$$

We discuss autoregressive models in Section 13.3. After developing an autoregressive model, we reexamine the residual pattern.

In summary, never use a regression model, even though it has passed the ANOVA test, without first checking the underlying assumptions. Begin by plotting the residuals against y-pred and against each of the predictor variables and, in the case of time-ordered data, against time. The residuals should be random, centered around zero, and should not contain outliers.

If there is an increasing pattern (Figure 11.13) or a decreasing pattern to the residuals, use a square root or log base 10 transformation on the dependent variable's values. This will help also to normalize the data and minimize the impact of outliers. If there are long strings of positive and negative residuals, the data are autocorrelated. We have either the wrong form of the regression function—e.g., linear when it should be nonlinear; or we are missing one or more important predictor variables—or we should consider an autoregressive model. Statisticians use the Durbin–Watson test to assess autocorrelation. Neter, Wasserman, and Kutner's text (1985) presents a very readable discussion of this test.

Residual Analysis of COMCEL Marketing Study Data

Table 11.18 shows the table of residuals and standardized residuals for the COMCEL study. For example, store 1, which charged a PRICE of $100 and ran one ad per day (ADS), sold 9 units. The predicted value derived from the regression model (11.1), UNITS SOLD-PRED, is 11.251. The residual is -2.251, which appears in the RESIDUAL column. The last column contains the standardized residuals. Each residual is divided by the standard error of the estimate, which is 2.555 phones for the COMCEL data.

We plotted the residuals against UNITS SOLD-PRED and each predictor variable in Figure 11.15. We see that the residual plots contain no systematic patterns.

Table 11.18 shows that all the standardized residuals are between -2 and $+2$. Therefore, there are no outliers.

The normality assumption is probably met. We expect about 68% of the standardized residuals to lie between -1 and $+1$. Actually, there are 79% in that range. We expect 95% of the standardized residuals to lie between -1.96 and $+1.96$. We see that 100% fall in this range. Furthermore, the histogram of standardized residuals in Figure 11.16 appears to be bell-shaped. Therefore, we conclude that our model has met the normality assumption.

In summary, residual plots are diagnostic indicators. They suggest whether our regression model is in good shape or is in need of correction. The residual analyses presented above indicate that model (11.1) is valid and can be used for prediction, explanation, and control.

Table 11.18

Table of Residual and Standardized Residual Values[*]

UNITS SOLD-PRED $= 60.891 - .530$PRICE $+ 3.313$ADS

OBS	UNITS	UNITS SOLD-PRED	RESIDUAL	STD. RESIDUAL RESIDUAL/$\sqrt{\text{MSE}}$
1	9	11.251	−2.251	−0.881 = −2.251/2.555
2	11	11.251	0.251	−0.098
3	19	17.876	1.124	0.440
4	15	17.876	−2.876	−1.126
5	26	24.501	1.499	0.587
6	24	24.501	−0.501	−0.196
7	14	16.546	−2.546	−0.996
8	19	16.546	2.454	0.960
9	24	23.171	0.829	0.324
10	28	23.171	4.829	1.890
11	31	29.796	1.204	0.471
12	32	29.796	2.204	0.863
13	17	19.194	−2.194	−0.859
14	19	19.194	−0.194	−0.076
15	29	25.819	3.181	1.245
16	25	25.819	−0.819	−0.321
17	30	32.444	−2.444	−0.957
18	30	32.444	−2.444	−0.957
19	26	21.842	4.158	1.627
20	23	21.842	1.158	0.453
21	26	28.467	−2.467	−0.966
22	24	28.467	−4.467	−1.748
23	37	35.092	1.908	0.747
24	34	35.092	−1.092	−0.427

* COMSTAT only provides a table of residuals. You will need to calculate the standardized residuals.

FIGURE 11.15   Residual Plots for Expression (11.1)

(a) Residuals vs. Price

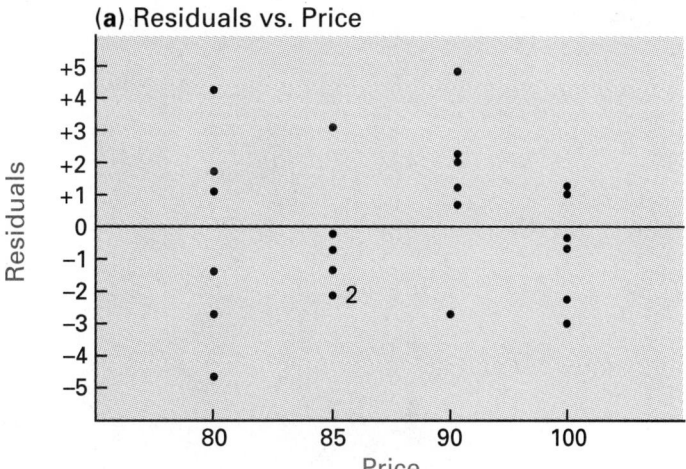

(b) Residuals vs. Number of ads

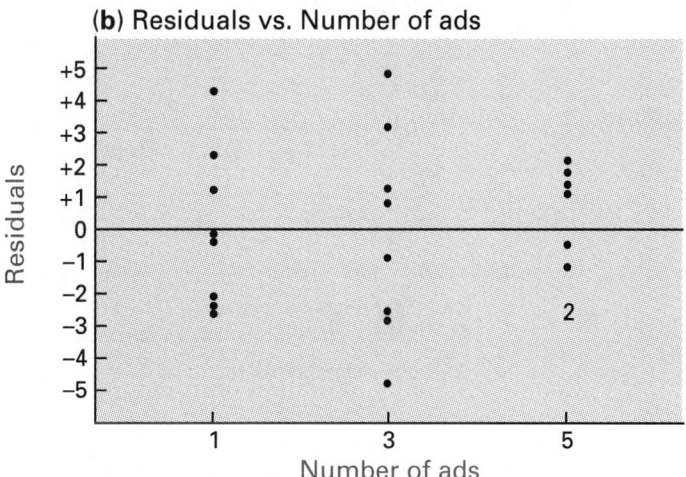

(c) Residuals vs. y-pred

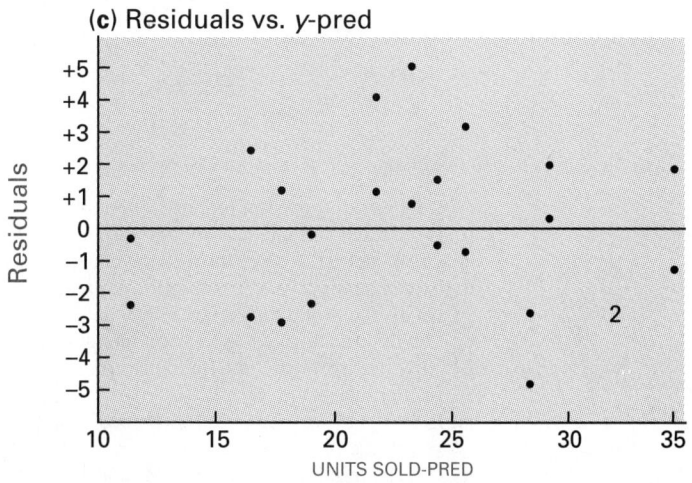

FIGURE 11.16   Histogram of Standardized Residuals

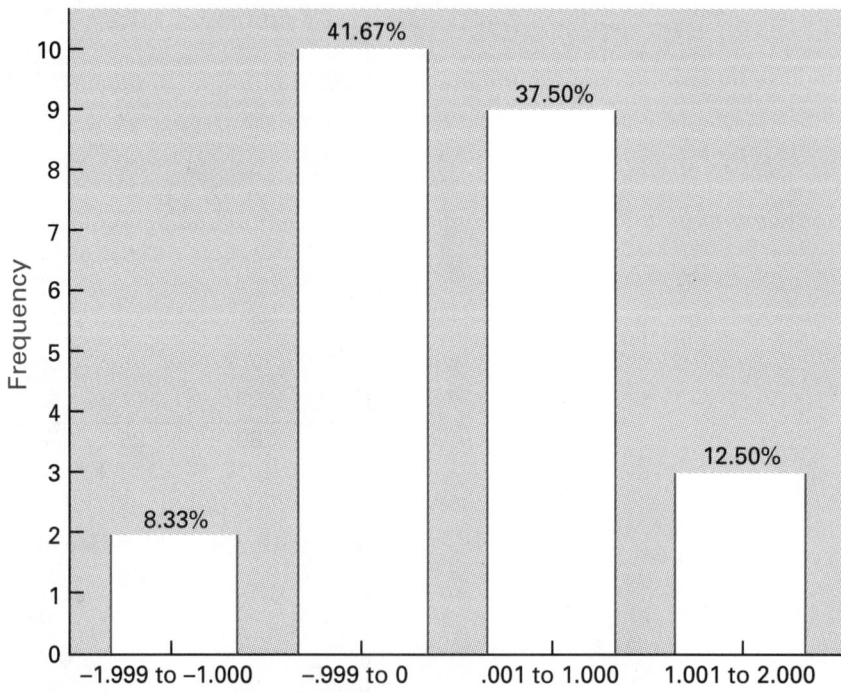

SECTION 11.6 EXERCISES

Use computer software for all problems that require calculations in this section.

1. If all the residuals from a best-fitting line are zero, do any predictor variables beyond those now in the regression model affect the dependent variable?

2. Shown is a small cross-sectional data set.

y	x
5	1
6	2
10	3
14	4
9	5
21	6
12	7
28	8

a. Develop a regression model and obtain a table of residuals.
b. Is the equal variance assumption reasonable? Plot residuals versus the predictor variable.
c. Use a log base 10 transform on the dependent variable, *y*. Recompute the best-fitting line.
d. Is the equal variance assumption reasonable for the transformed model? Plot residuals versus the predictor variable.
e. Use the transformed regression model to predict the value of *y* for $x = 5.5$.
f. Now use a square root transform on the dependent variable, *y*. Recompute the best-fitting line.
g. Is the equal variance assumption reasonable for the transformed model? Plot residuals versus the predictor variable.
h. Use the transformed regression model to predict the value of *y* for $x = 5.5$.

3. Explain how to use standardized residuals to check for violations of the normality assumption.

4. Shown is a small cross-sectional data set.

y	x	x^2
3	1	1
10	2	4
20	3	9
31	4	16
51	5	25

   a. Develop a simple linear regression model with x as the predictor variable. Obtain a table of residuals.
   b. Is the linearity assumption reasonable? Plot residuals versus the predictor variable. Draw a scatter diagram of y versus x also.
   c. Draw a freehand nonlinear curve that is a good-fitting line.
   d. Develop a curvilinear regression model for the above data. Use two predictor variables—x and x^2.
   e. Plot the residuals versus the predictor variable x. Does the residual plot reveal an equal-width horizontal band centered on zero with no systematic pattern of positive and negative residuals?

5. Fit a multiple regression model to the job satisfaction, closeness of supervision, and salary cross-sectional data set in Exercise 6 of Section 11.5.
   a. Are the linearity and equal variance assumptions reasonable? Plot residuals versus both predictor variables.
   b. Is the normality assumption reasonable? Compute standardized residuals and construct a frequency distribution of the standardized residuals.
   c. Is autocorrelation likely to be a problem?

6. Fit a model to the time-ordered data set in Exercise 9 of Section 11.5 on company sales in millions of dollars and disposable personal income in billions of dollars.
   a. Are the linearity and equal variance assumptions reasonable? Plot residuals versus the predictor variable.
   b. Is the normality assumption reasonable? Compute standardized residuals.
   c. Is the independence assumption reasonable?

7. Shown is a small cross-sectional data set.

Division	Proportion defects	Hours of quality training/ employee/year
1	.020	8
2	.010	16
3	.005	30
4	.016	10
5	.002	45
6	.019	7
7	.034	4
8	.008	26
9	.019	8
10	.001	45
11	.024	7
12	.033	5
13	.025	6
14	.009	16
15	.003	40
16	.041	2

a. Fit a linear regression model to the data using proportion defects as the dependent variable.

b. Are the linearity, equal variance, and normality assumptions reasonable?

8. Shown is a small cross-sectional data set.

y	x
1	1
5	2
9	3
17	4
27	5
35	6
48	7
66	8
80	9
104	10

a. Fit a linear regression model to the data.

b. Is the linearity assumption reasonable?

c. Plot y versus x. Does a linear model seem reasonable from a scatter plot?

d. Fit a curvilinear model to the data using x and x^2 as predictor variables.

11.7 ≡ Using Regression Models for Prediction

In regression analysis we use statistically significant (ANOVA) models that have met all the assumptions to make predictions about the dependent variable. By the end of this section you should be able to:

1. distinguish between prediction and extrapolation;
2. explain the dangers of extrapolation;
3. explain the difference between a confidence interval and a prediction interval;
4. interpret prediction and confidence intervals; and
5. explain how to reduce the widths of prediction or confidence intervals.

Prediction versus Extrapolation

Regression models help us estimate values of the dependent variable. There are two types of estimation, which we will explain in the context of the COMCEL marketing study. **Prediction** means estimating units sold for prices between $80 and $100 and numbers of ads between 1 and 5. Note the predictor variables' values are within the range of the original study. **Extrapolation** means estimating units sold for prices below $80 or above $100 and numbers of ads less than one or more than five. Note the predictor variables' values are outside the range of the original study.

> Prediction means estimating values of the dependent variable for values of the predictor variables within the range of the original study.

> Extrapolation means estimating values of the dependent variable for values of the predictor variables outside the range of the original study.

Figure 11.17 shows the danger of extrapolation. It illustrates a nonlinear relationship between two variables in the population. If we fit a linear model to data values between **a** and **b**, we see that the linear equation is a reasonably good fit within this range. However, the model would generate an inaccurate estimate of y for $x = c$. We have assumed that the linear relationship extends outside the range of data values, but it *may* not.

Extrapolation is risky. When extrapolating, be prepared to explain why the regression model can provide meaningful estimates outside the range of the original data. If good arguments cannot be made, do not use the model for extrapolation.

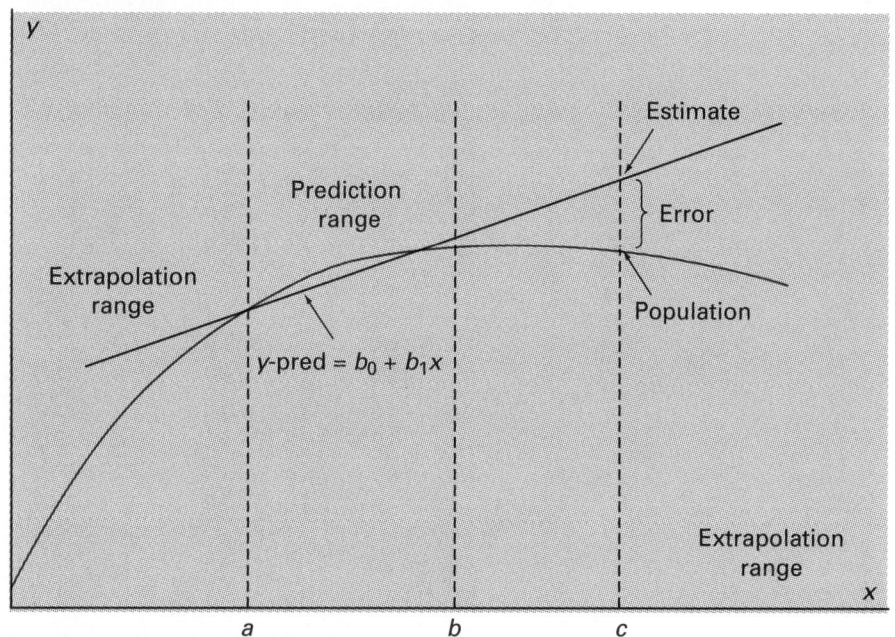

FIGURE 11.17   Comparing Prediction and Extrapolation

Differences Between Prediction and Confidence Intervals

Which would be easier to do: Predict the mean class grade or predict a single student's score? Predicting the class mean is easier because it usually ranges between 70 and 80. A student's score could range anywhere from 0 to 100. Thus, estimation intervals for the class mean should be narrower than for a single student.

In regression analysis, we use *confidence intervals* to predict mean values of y. Here we estimate $E(y \mid x)$, the population conditional means in Figure 11.7. We use *prediction intervals* to predict a single value of y. Using the test grade example for insight, we recognize that confidence intervals must be narrower than prediction intervals.

Confidence Interval   Table 11.19 contains prediction and confidence intervals generated by a software package. The first row of Table 11.19 tells us that COMCEL is 95% confident that the *mean* sales for *all* stores that charge $100 and run one ad will be between 8.87 (L95MEAN) and 13.63 (U95MEAN) phones per week. L95MEAN and U95MEAN are the symbols for the lower and upper limits of a 95% confidence interval on the population conditional mean.

Prediction Interval   Table 11.19 also shows 95% prediction intervals for sales by a single store. For example, we are 95% confident that a single store that charges $100 and runs one ad will sell between 5.43 (L95) and 17.07 (U95) phones per week. L95 and U95 are the symbols for the lower and upper limits for a 95% prediction interval for a single value of y.

Note that the prediction interval for sales of an individual store is wider than the confidence interval for the mean sales of all stores.

Table 11.19

95% Confidence Intervals and Prediction Intervals for COMCEL Data

OBS	PRICE	ADS	UNITS SOLD	UNITS SOLD-PRED	L95MEAN	U95MEAN	L95	U95
1	100	1	11	11.2512	8.8717	13.6307	5.4298	17.0726
2	100	1	9	11.2512	8.8717	13.6307	5.4298	17.0726
3	100	3	19	17.8762	15.9019	19.8505	12.2083	23.5441
4	100	3	15	17.8762	15.9019	19.8505	12.2083	23.5441
5	100	5	26	24.5012	22.1217	26.8807	18.6798	30.3226
6	100	5	24	24.5012	22.1217	26.8807	18.6798	30.3226
7	90	1	14	16.5464	14.8219	18.2709	10.9607	22.1322
8	90	1	19	16.5464	14.8219	18.2709	10.9607	22.1322
9	90	3	24	23.1714	22.0716	24.2713	17.7459	28.5970
10	90	3	28	23.1714	22.0716	24.2713	17.7459	28.5970
11	90	5	31	29.7964	28.0719	31.5209	24.2107	35.3822
12	90	5	32	29.7964	28.0719	31.5209	24.2107	35.3822
13	85	1	17	19.1940	17.3933	20.9948	13.5843	24.8038
14	85	1	19	19.1940	17.3933	20.9948	13.5843	24.8038
15	85	3	29	25.8190	24.6031	27.0350	20.3688	31.2693
16	85	3	25	25.8190	24.6031	27.0350	20.3688	31.2693
17	85	5	30	32.4440	30.6433	34.2448	26.8343	38.0538
18	85	5	30	32.4440	30.6433	34.2448	26.8343	38.0538
19	80	1	26	21.8417	19.7000	23.9834	16.1133	27.5700
20	80	1	23	21.8417	19.7000	23.9834	16.1133	27.5700
21	80	3	26	28.4667	26.7866	30.1468	22.8944	34.0389
22	80	3	24	28.4667	26.7866	30.1468	22.8944	34.0389
23	80	5	37	35.0917	32.9500	37.2334	29.3633	40.8200
24	80	5	34	35.0917	32.9500	37.2334	29.3633	40.8200

Prediction or confidence intervals—when does each make sense? That depends on the purpose of the study. Is the goal to explain, predict, or control the performance of a single store, person, production run, etc.? If so, construct prediction intervals. Or is the goal to explain, predict, or control the mean performance of all stores, persons, production runs, etc.? If so, construct confidence intervals.

Reducing the Width of Confidence or Prediction Intervals

We build regression models to predict values of the dependent variable. Since a wide confidence or prediction interval does not provide meaningful information, how do we reduce the width?

The expressions for confidence and prediction intervals for *simple* linear regression models are shown in equations (11.23) and (11.24), respectively, for a specified value of the predictor variable, x_p. We present these expressions because they show us how to reduce an interval's width.

Confidence interval:

$$y\text{-pred} \pm t(n - k - 1)s_{y|1,2,3,\ldots,k} \sqrt{\frac{1}{n} + \frac{(x_p - \bar{x})^2}{\sum_i (x_i - \bar{x})^2}} \tag{11.23}$$

Prediction interval:

$$y\text{-pred} \pm t(n - k - 1)s_{y|1,2,3,\ldots,k} \sqrt{1 + \frac{1}{n} + \frac{(x_p - \bar{x})^2}{\sum_i (x_i - \bar{x})^2}} \tag{11.24}$$

There are three strategies to reduce a prediction or confidence interval's width:

1. *Increase the sample size.*
   Note that as n increases (1) $1/n$ and (2) $(x_p - \bar{x})^2/\sum(x_i - \bar{x})^2$ in expressions (11.23) and (11.24) become smaller. Thus the width of the intervals becomes smaller.

2. *Spread out the values of the predictor variables. This strategy can be done only for experimental regression studies.*
   The second strategy increases the $\sum(x_i - \bar{x})^2$ term and thus reduces the width of the interval. Consider two different sets of predictor variables, x, as shown below. Note that the values of x in the second column are further apart than those in the first column. The pulled apart values of x cause $\sum(x_i - \bar{x})^2$ to increase, which causes the interval to shrink.

$\underline{x}$	$\underline{x}$
1	1
2	5
3	9
$\sum_i (x_i - \bar{x})^2$ = 2	32

3. *Reduce the size of the standard error of the estimate.*
   The standard error of the estimate, $s_{y|1,2,3,\ldots,k}$ measures variation of the dependent variable due to all significant predictor variables not in the regression model. As we saw above, we can reduce the size of $s_{y|1,2,3,\ldots,k}$ by

   1. *adding* predictor variables with $|t|$ values >1, or
   2. *removing* predictor variables from the regression model with $|t|$ values <1.

For example, suppose that COMCEL believes that sales are affected by the size of the shopping centers where its stores are located. Larger centers generate more shopper traffic and therefore more phone sales. COMCEL could enter a SIZE of shopping center predictor variable into the regression equation and evaluate the model.

In summary, we use prediction and confidence intervals to predict values of the dependent variable. Extrapolation is risky and should be done only when we can explain why the relationship between the variables should extend outside the range of the original study. Finally, we can increase sample size, pull apart the values of the predictor variables, or seek or remove predictor variables to reduce the width of a prediction or confidence interval. Remember, narrow intervals are more meaningful than wide intervals.

SECTION 11.7 EXERCISES

Use a software package for all the problems in this section that require calculation.

1. Refer to Exercise 6 in Section 11.5.
   a. Set up a 95% prediction interval on job satisfaction for a closeness-of-supervision score of 6.5 and a salary of $30,000. Interpret the prediction interval.
   b. Set up a 95% confidence interval on the mean job satisfaction for a closeness-of-supervision score of 6.5 and a salary of $30,000. Interpret the confidence interval.
   c. When would constructing each interval make sense? Discuss.

2. Refer to Exercise 9 in Section 11.5. We expect the disposable personal income (DPI) in the first quarter of 1993 to be $165.2 billion. Set up a 95% prediction interval on sales for a DPI of 165.2. Interpret the prediction interval.

3. Refer to Exercise 5 in Section 11.3. Develop a simple regression model for female employees using months on the job as the predictor variable.
   a. Set up a 95% prediction interval on monthly salary for a woman with 26 months of job experience. Interpret the prediction interval.
   b. Set up a 95% confidence interval on the mean monthly salary for all women with 26 months of job experience. Interpret the confidence interval.
   c. Is there any risk in using the regression model to construct a prediction interval on salary for 50 months on the job? Discuss.

4. Refer to Exercise 3 above. Develop a simple regression model for male employees using months on the job as the predictor variable.
   a. Set up a 95% prediction interval on monthly salary for a man with 26 months of job experience. Interpret the prediction interval.
   b. Set up a 95% confidence interval on the mean monthly salary for all men with 26 months of job experience. Interpret the confidence interval.
   c. Is there any risk in using the regression model to construct a confidence interval on salary for 5 months on the job? Discuss.

5. Refer to Exercise 3 above. Develop a simple regression model for female employees using months on the job as the predictor variable.
   a. Set up a 95% confidence interval on the mean monthly salary for all women with 14 months of job experience. Interpret the confidence interval.
   b. Set up a 95% confidence interval on the mean monthly salary for all women with 26 months of job experience. Interpret the confidence interval.
   c. Set up a 95% confidence interval on the mean monthly salary for all women with 40 months of job experience. Interpret the confidence interval.
   d. Look at the widths of the three confidence intervals. Are the widths different? When do you get the smallest width? When do you get the largest width? What practical problems do you foresee in using the regression model to make predictions for either 14 or 40 months on the job? (*Hint:* How does confidence interval width affect the interval's meaningfulness?)

11.8 ≡ Integrating Framework

Managers solve problems, forecast and plan for the future, and control and allocate resources. To be effective in these roles, they must build mental models of how their departments or firms operate. Good mental models require an understanding of relationships between crucial business and economic variables.

Regression analysis is an essential tool for detecting and measuring relationships among variables. Figure 11.18 is a flowchart that describes the steps in analyzing data from a regression study.

FIGURE 11.18   A Flowchart for Analyzing Regression Data

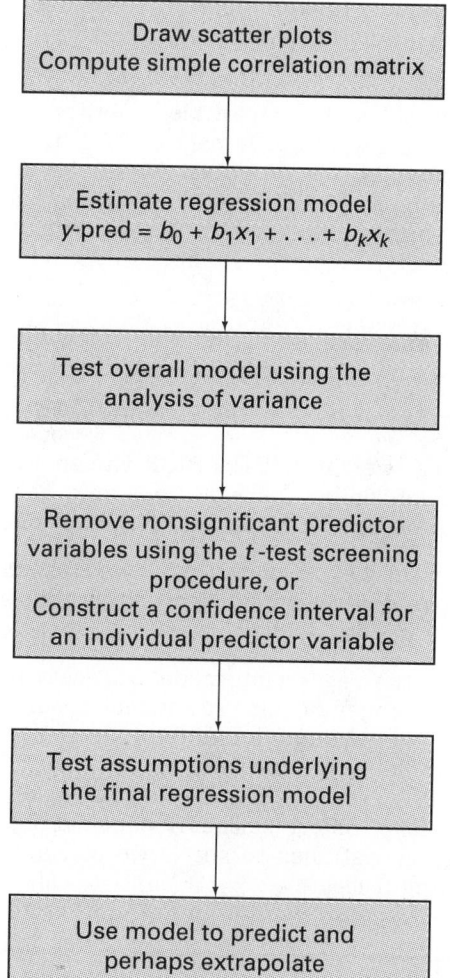

Helps understand the meaning of the sample regression coefficients, identifies clusters and departures from linearity, and assesses the strength of the linear relationships among the variables.

From Parameter Estimate section of computer output.

If the overall model is not significant, seek additional predictor variables.

Will reduce $s_{y|1,2,3, ..., k}$ and produce narrower prediction or confidence intervals.

Useful for testing if one predictor variable is related to a dependent variable after controling for all other predictor variables in the model.

If residual plots suggest violations, fix the model.

The flowchart boxes read:

- Draw scatter plots / Compute simple correlation matrix
- Estimate regression model / $y\text{-pred} = b_0 + b_1 x_1 + \ldots + b_k x_k$
- Test overall model using the analysis of variance
- Remove nonsignificant predictor variables using the t-test screening procedure, or / Construct a confidence interval for an individual predictor variable
- Test assumptions underlying the final regression model
- Use model to predict and perhaps extrapolate

COMCEL

Date: October 10, 1994
To: Ann Tabor, CEO
From: Cherian Jain, V.P., Marketing Research
Re: Analysis of Market Research Study to Improve Sales of Model 76 Phones

SUMMARY

We should reduce the price of the Model 76 phone to $80 and run five ads per day on the most highly rated radio station in those cities where our retail stores are located. These actions will increase sales to about 35 units per store per week and will reduce our inventory.

SUPPORTING ANALYSIS

We selected 24 outlets with comparable sales from different cities across the country. We then tested the impact of four different prices and three different frequencies of ads on sales. We assigned each combination of price and advertising to two different outlets for one week. The ads were aired on the most highly rated station in each test city during the morning drive time. We then recorded the number of Model 76 phones sold during the test week.

Using regression analysis, we found the following relationship between sales versus price and the number of radio ads aired per day:

$$\text{UNITS SOLD-PRED} = 60.891 - .530\text{PRICE} + 3.313\text{ADS}$$

The .530 numerical weight of the PRICE variable measures the effect of price on sales. Each dollar increase in price (between $80 and $100) reduces the mean number of units sold by about one-half phone.

The 3.313 numerical weight of the ADS variable measures the effect of number of ads per day on sales. Each additional ad results in a mean increase of over 3 phones sold per week.

To increase sales, the regression model suggests that we drop the price and increase the number of ads. The model predicts that our stores will sell 35.13 units per week at an $80 price and with five ads per day. Dropping the price below $80 or running more than five ads might further increase sales. However, we would be extrapolating the model, and extrapolation is risky. Before seriously considering prices under $80, we should run additional studies to see if we continue to obtain increasing sales with dropping prices.

CHAPTER 11 QUESTIONS

1. Why is it important for managers to predict, explain, and control?

2. Develop a words-only mental model based on the regression equation (11.1).

3. Distinguish between experimental and correlation regression studies.

4. Does lack of a linear relationship mean that two variables are completely unrelated?

5. What does the simple correlation matrix provide that scatter plots for all pairs of variables do not?

6. Explain what clusters are and why a simple correlation matrix may fail to detect them.

7. During the introduction phase of a product, sales are initially very slow and then increase at an increasing rate. If we have time-ordered data, sales versus time, would we expect a straight line to represent the data accurately?

8. In simple terms, what is a subpopulation?

9. Explain how b_0 and b_1 differ from β_0 and β_1. If we sampled the entire population, would b_1 equal the β_1?

10. What does "minimizing the sum of squared residuals" mean?

11. What must be true in order for the sum of squared errors (SSE) term to be zero?

12. If the variance ratio is greater than the critical value from the F-table, can we conclude that each predictor variable is statistically related to the dependent variable?

13. Suppose the sample regression coefficients are not zero. Why can't we conclude that the predictor variables are statistically related to the dependent variable? Why must we do an ANOVA?

14. Why is the standard error of the estimate smaller than the standard deviation of the dependent variable when the predictor variables are significantly related to the dependent variable?

15. Explain the purpose of the *t*-value screening procedure.

16. Explain when you should consider constructing a confidence interval on a single predictor variable regression coefficient.

17. How do we calculate residuals?

18. If all the assumptions of the linear regression model are met, what should the residual plots look like?

19. If the original data are nonlinear and we fit a straight line regression, what should the plot of the residuals versus the predictor variable look like?

20. If the plot of residuals versus time follows a recurring up-down pattern, what does that pattern suggest?

21. If a confidence interval on β_i includes zero, we say that the predictor variable is not statistically related to the dependent variable. Why?

22. Logically, why must prediction intervals be wider than confidence intervals?

23. When should we use prediction intervals and when should we use confidence intervals?

24. Why should we reduce the width of either confidence or prediction intervals?

25. We fit a regression model and find a set of significant predictor variables. Even if the model meets the four assumptions underlying regression analysis, does this guarantee that management will want to use the model for making predictions?

CHAPTER 11 APPLICATION PROBLEMS

Problems 1–9 use the following data set.

Shown is a data set for 16 skilled workers. DAYS (the number of days a worker exceeded quota during last quarter) is the dependent variable. There are five predictor variables. AGE is a proxy variable for experience in the labor force. A proxy variable is a substitute for a variable that we cannot directly measure. CLOSENESS of supervision is the degree to which workers are constantly watched and supervised. A score of 10 indicates very close supervision. SALARY is a worker's annual salary in thousands of dollars. TRAINING is the number of hours of skill training in the past quarter. EQUIP is the age in years of the equipment that a worker uses.

WORKER	DAYS	AGE	CLOSENESS	SALARY	TRAINING	EQUIP
1	6	25	5	22	15	6
2	3	28	9	28	25	8
3	3	24	10	25	30	2
4	7	26	4	24	10	3
5	13	30	1	29	5	1
6	7	32	6	32	15	1
7	11	35	2	38	15	2
8	3	35	7	32	3	2
9	8	38	3	36	10	3
10	4	40	9	35	20	4
11	4	41	10	39	15	1
12	7	42	2	43	0	8
13	3	43	8	30	5	6
14	10	44	3	30	23	3
15	3	50	7	32	8	5
16	9	52	2	41	5	1

1. What is the unit of association? What type of study is it, experimental or correlational?

2. Draw a scatter diagram between DAYS and each predictor variable. Do the predictor variables appear to be related to DAYS?

3. Generate the simple correlation matrix. Interpret the simple correlations by squaring the coefficients and then interpreting the simple coefficients of determination.

4. Use software to compute the multiple regression model with all five predictor variables. Write the null and alternative hypotheses for testing the significance of the regression model, and test the model using $\alpha = .05$.

5. Use software and the t-value screening procedure to produce a final regression model that minimizes the standard error of the estimate. Explain the meaning of the standard error of the estimate in practical terms.

6. Interpret the meaning of the coefficient of multiple determination in the context of this problem.

7. Compute the residuals from the final regression model. Draw residual plots against each remaining predictor variable in the model. Have the linearity, equal variances, normality, and independence assumptions been met?

8. Explain how you could now use the new model to explain, predict, and control.

9. Suppose that, instead of prediction, the purpose of the regression was to estimate the effect of CLOSENESS of supervision on DAYS, after controlling for AGE, SALARY, TRAINING, and EQUIPMENT. Construct a 95% confidence interval for the population regression coefficient for the CLOSENESS variable. Interpret your confidence interval to shed light on the question: Should workers be closely supervised?

 Problems 10–18 use the data set in the Appendix A of this chapter.

Job satisfaction and salary data and seven biographical variables were collected for a random sample of 50 COMCEL employees. For the purpose of these exercises assume that job SATISfaction is the dependent variable. The predictor variables for these exercises are: (1) SALARY, measured in thousands of dollars; (2) YEARS with the company; (3) AGE; (4) years of formal EDUCation; (5) years of EXPERience in a related field before joining COMCEL; and (6) MANAGment, an indicator variable that is equal to 1 if the employee has management responsibility, and 0 if the employee has no management responsibility. Do *not* include the indicator variables for GENDER and RACE.

10. What is the unit of association? What type of study is it, experimental or correlational?

11. Plot a scatter diagram between SATISfaction and each of the six predictor variables listed above. Do the predictor variables appear to be related to SATISfaction?

12. Generate the simple correlation matrix. Interpret the simple correlations of the dependent variable with each predictor variable. To do this, square the coefficients and then interpret the simple coefficients of determination.

13. Use software to compute the multiple regression model with all six predictor variables. Write the null and alternative hypotheses for testing the significance of the regression model and test the model using $\alpha = .05$.

14. Use software and the t-value screening procedure to produce a final regression model that minimizes the standard error of the estimate. Explain the meaning of the standard error of the estimate in practical terms.

15. Interpret the meaning of the coefficient of multiple determination of the final model in the context of this problem.

16. Compute the residuals from the final regression model. Draw residual plots against each remaining predictor variable in the model. Have the linearity, equal variances, normality, and independence assumptions been met?

17. Explain how you could now use the new model to explain, predict, and control.

18. Suppose that, instead of prediction, the purpose of the regression was to determine whether personnel with MANAGement responsibility are more SATISfied than nonmanagers, after controlling for SALARY, YEARS, AGE, EDUCation and EXPERience. Remember that

MANAG is an indicator variable where 1 = Management responsibility and 0 = No management responsibility. Construct a 90% confidence interval for the population regression coefficient for the MANAG variable. Does it appear from your confidence interval that managers are more satisfied with their jobs?

 Problems 19−27 use the following data set.

A staff manager runs a planned change study to determine whether the size of the problem-solving group and the amount of group problem-solving training are related to performance on a group task. He selects four groups of two, four, and six workers for a total of 12 groups. For each set of four groups, he provides two groups with four hours of training and two groups with no training. Shown are the data.

GROUP	PERF	GROUPSIZE	TRAIN
1	50	2	0
2	52	2	0
3	68	2	4
4	72	2	4
5	57	4	0
6	63	4	0
7	79	4	4
8	83	4	4
9	70	6	0
10	69	6	0
11	88	6	4
12	92	6	4

19. What is the unit of association? What type of study is it, experimental or correlational?

20. Draw a scatter diagram between PERFormance and each predictor variable. Do the predictor variables appear to be related to PERFormance?

21. Generate the simple correlation matrix. Interpret the simple correlations of the dependent variable with each predictor variable. To do this, square the coefficients and then interpret the simple coefficients of determination. Explain why the two predictor variables are not correlated.

22. Use software to compute the multiple regression model with all predictor variables. Write the null and alternative hypotheses for testing the significance of the regression model, and test the model using $\alpha = .05$.

23. Use software and the t-value screening procedure to produce a final regression model that minimizes the standard error of the estimate. Explain the meaning of the standard error of the estimate in practical terms.

24. Interpret the meaning of the coefficient of multiple determination of the final model in the context of this problem.

25. Compute the residuals from the final regression model. Draw residual plots against each remaining predictor variable in the model. Have the linearity, equal variances, normality, and independence assumptions been met?

26. Use software to obtain a confidence interval on the mean task performance for a group of size three and with two hours of training. Obtain a prediction interval on the task performance for a single group of size three with two hours of training. Explain the difference between the two intervals in managerial terms.

27. Suppose that, instead of prediction, the purpose of the regression was to estimate the effectiveness of each additional hour of TRAINing, after controlling for GROUPSIZE. Construct and interpret a 95% confidence interval for the population regression coefficient for the TRAINing variable.

Problems 28–35 use the following data set.

All publicly traded firms are required to have their financial statements audited by an independent CPA firm. When planning for the year's end, the comptroller is concerned about two things: the cost of the audit (in dollars) and the length of time the audit will take. The audit contract is negotiated by the Board of Directors. The comptroller, however, might be able to take steps to reduce audit time, and therefore the disruption to normal activities.

An organization of 30 comptrollers has pooled data to measure the effects of three variables on the amount of time needed (in hours) to complete an audit. The first variable is sales (in millions $)—the larger the company, the more time an audit is likely to require. The second is the number of hours spent on internal audit—a function carried out within the firm by the company's own employees. The feeling is that the more work done by the company's employees, the less time an outside auditor will need to spend. The third is the strength of internal controls—how tightly the accounting process is controlled on a day-to-day basis. For this study, controls were categorized as either strong (= 1) or weak (= 0).

The following data were collected (sales are in millions of dollars).

FIRM	HOURS	SALES	IN-AUDIT	CONTROL
1	78.5	5.8	3,695.9	0
2	574.2	12.3	3,221.4	1
3	972.7	16.3	2,686.6	0
4	1,220.7	21.7	3,062.6	1
5	1,061.7	19.9	3,296.1	1
6	866.3	15.9	2,770.0	1
7	782.2	16.6	2,584.2	1
8	687.6	13.1	2,712.0	0
9	665.0	14.2	3,167.3	1
10	704.8	13.8	3,482.1	1
11	545.9	11.9	3,109.8	1
12	709.1	14.9	3,594.0	1
13	1,030.4	17.3	2,247.6	1
14	598.9	10.0	2,429.8	0
15	701.9	13.4	2,846.6	1
16	459.8	7.9	2,898.6	1
17	999.2	18.7	3,945.6	1
18	473.2	9.4	2,264.5	0
19	786.4	15.1	2,024.0	1
20	896.1	15.5	2,947.3	1
21	1,157.9	18.3	3,380.9	0
22	1,021.3	19.3	3,363.4	1
23	1,423.4	22.9	3,027.0	1
24	357.8	11.5	2,974.1	1
25	1,123.4	20.4	3,541.1	1
26	531.1	11.1	3,757.7	1
27	533.0	12.7	2,789.2	1
28	903.4	16.8	2,458.8	1
29	731.1	14.4	3,200.6	1
30	909.7	17.6	2,563.0	1

28. What is the unit of association? What type of study is it, experimental or correlational?

29. Draw a scatter diagram between HOURS and each predictor variable. Do the predictor variables appear to be related to HOURS?

30. Generate the simple correlation matrix. Interpret the simple correlations of the dependent variable with each predictor variable. To do this, square the coefficients and then interpret the simple coefficients of determination.

31. Use software to compute the multiple regression model with all predictor variables. Write the null and alternative hypotheses for testing the significance of the regression model, and test the model using $\alpha = .05$.

32. Use software and the t-value screening procedure to produce a final regression model that minimizes the standard error of the estimate. Explain the meaning of the standard error of the estimate in practical terms.

33. Interpret the meaning of the coefficient of multiple determination of the final model in the context of this problem.

34. Compute the residuals from the final regression model. Draw residual plots against each remaining predictor variable in the model. Have the linearity, equal variances, normality, and independence assumptions been met?

35. Suppose that, instead of prediction, the purpose of the regression was to estimate the effectiveness of IN-house AUDIT on reducing the total number of HOURS needed to complete an audit, after controlling for SALES and strength of CONTROLS. Construct and interpret a 95% confidence interval for the population regression coefficient for the IN-AUDIT variable.

36. Lenders who offer mortgages on single-family homes can usually get protection against borrower default by requiring mortgage guarantee insurance. One source of insurance is the Federal Housing Administration (FHA). The premium on such insurance becomes part of the purchaser's monthly payment.

   In forecasting demand for loans, the FHA believes the number of loans (in thousands) insured (the dependent variable) varies directly with the loan-to-value ratio (the amount borrowed divided by the market value of the house), the length of the loan in years (TERM), and the interest rate of the loan. In addition, FHA expects to insure fewer loans as the price of the insurance rises. The price of insurance is a fixed percentage of the loan.

   Data are collected over a number of quarters, and the following model* is developed to predict the number of mortgages that will require insurance:

Variable	Parameter Estimate	Standard Error	t-Value
INTERCEPT	−79.21	16.85	−4.70
LOAN-VALUE	.58	.24	2.45
TERM	1.72	.69	2.51
INTEREST-RATE	2.37	.53	4.51
INSURE-PRICE	−94.54	15.19	−6.22

Number of observations = 58 $R^2 = .82$

   a. If the purpose of the regression was prediction, could we reduce the standard error of the estimate by dropping any of the four variables? Why?
   b. Interpret each of the regression coefficients in terms a manager would understand.
   c. Interpret the meaning of the coefficient of multiple determination in the context of this problem.

37. Banks, like other firms, can follow a strategy of growth through acquisition. An important consideration in any acquisition is, of course, the price. The purchase price of an acquired bank can be above, equal to, or below the acquired bank's net asset value—the market value of the acquired bank's assets less the market value of its liabilities. If the purchase price is above the net asset value, then the acquired bank is selling at a premium. If the price is below net asset value, then the bank is selling at a discount.

   Bankers believe that the growth rate of the bank to be acquired, as measured by the growth rate in deposits, has some influence on the purchase premium/discount. Another variable is profitability. In banking circles, one measure of profitability is the net interest

---

*David L. Kasserman, "Default Risk and the Home Mortgage Insurance Industry," *Quarterly Review of Economics and Business* 18, no. 4 (Winter 1978): 59–68.

spread (the difference between the rates paid depositors, and the rates charged to borrowers). Finally, the tax status of the transaction (taxable = 0, nontaxable = 1) should
also have some influence, since shareholders of the acquired bank should demand a higher
price to compensate for the additional taxes they will have to pay.

Data have been collected for a number of bank acquisitions,* and the following model
developed to predict the dependent variable—premium or discount—measured in percent:

Variable	Parameter Estimate	Standard Error	t-Value
INTERCEPT	−42.95	20.26	−2.12
DEPOSIT GROWTH%	4.03	.85	4.72
NET INTEREST SPREAD%	11.21	3.96	2.83
TAX STATUS	−16.37	7.78	−2.10

Variance ratio = 12.57 R^2 = .53

Number of observations = 64

a. Write the null and alternative hypotheses for testing the significance of the regression
model and test the model using $\alpha = .05$.

b. If the purpose of the regression was prediction, could we reduce the standard error of
the estimate by dropping any of the four variables? Why?

c. Interpret each of the regression coefficients in terms a manager would understand.

38. The IRS is always concerned about taxpayers' compliance with the tax laws. The tax code
requires that when services are bartered (exchanged for other services), the fair value of
those services should be reported as income. A staff member proposed that a predictive
model could be developed from the data collected on past taxpayer audits. The proposed
model would be used to predict which taxpayers were underreporting taxable income and
should be audited.

The dependent variable is the dollar amount of taxable barter income not reported by
the taxpayer. The independent variables were (1) the amount of income from wages
reported on form W-2, (2) the amount of self-employment income reported on Schedule
C, and (3) the type of business engaged in by the taxpayer: professional = 1 and nonprofessional = 0.

Variable	Parameter Estimate	Standard Error
INTERCEPT	−12,231.2	
W-2	.237	.063
SCHEDULE C	.122	.015
BUSINESS TYPE	1.572	709.797

Degrees of freedom: 96

a. Interpret the regression coefficients in managerial terms.

b. Is W-2 income related to the dependent variable after controlling for SCHEDULE-C and
BUSINESS-TYPE? Set a 95% confidence interval for the W-2 population regression
coefficient.

c. Does the intercept value of −12,231.2 mean that taxpayers, who report no W-2 income
and no Schedule C income and are not professionals, overpay their income taxes by
$12,231.20? Explain.

---

* Adapted from: Randolph P. Beatty, John F. Reim, and Robert F. Schapperle, "The Effect of
Barriers to Entry on Bank Shareholder Wealth: Implications for Interstate Banking," *Journal of
Bank Research* 16, no. 1 (Spring 1985): 8–13.

39.

Date: June 12, 1995
To: Bill O'Hara, Vice-President of Marketing
From: Cherian Jain, Manager of Marketing Research
Subject: Regression Analysis on Share of Market Data

I just reviewed the latest market share report for our 30 sales territories. Our overall market share nationally is 39%. While very good, there is much variation over our 30 sales territories. For example, we have only 10%–11% SOM in Albany, NY, and Chicago but over 70% in Dallas and New York. I have been wondering why there is so much variation. I will be reviewing our market-share database to see if I can draw some conclusions. I will forward my results to you when I have completed my regression analysis.

Use Data Base III in Appendix 9 and develop a memo along with your attached analysis.

40.

Date: February 3, 1995
To: Bill O'Hara, Vice-President of Marketing
From: Pam Ascher, National Sales Manager
Subject: Regression Analysis of Forces Affecting Atlanta Sales

In your January 24 memo, you asked me to review what factors affect sales in the Atlanta market. I have already sent you a preliminary analysis that indicated those factors that I believe affect sales.

I think a more complete analysis is warranted. Accordingly, I will be sending you a more formal report that uses proven and sound statistical methods for drawing conclusions from the data. It will support my quick analysis and allow us to determine more exactly the impact of the various factors on sales. It will also allow us to make accurate predictions of future sales in the territory. What especially excites me is the possibility of taking what we learn in Atlanta and applying it throughout the Southern region and perhaps nationally. I look forward to your comments on my analysis.

Use Data Base II in Appendix 9 and develop a memo along with your attached analysis.

REFERENCES

Maddala, G. S. *Introduction to Econometrics.* 2nd ed. New York: Macmillan Publishing Co., 1992.

Mosteller, F., and J. Tukey. *Data Analysis and Regression Analysis.* Reading, Mass.: Addison-Wesley Publishing Co., 1977.

Neter, J., W. Wasserman, and M. Kutner. *Applied Linear Statistical Models.* 2nd ed. Homewood, Ill.: Richard D. Irwin, 1985.

Roberts, H. *Data Analysis for Managers with Minitab.* Redwood City, Calif.: The Scientific Press, 1988.

APPENDIX A: COMCEL Job Satisfaction and Salary Data

OBS	SATIS	SALARY	YEARS	AGE	EDUC	EXPER	GENDER	RACE	MANAG
1	9.9	39.78	7	26	17	0	1	1	0
2	7.8	32.22	13	34	14	0	0	0	0
3	11.0	62.89	32	65	16	8	1	1	1
4	9.3	38.28	14	49	16	11	1	1	0
5	9.2	27.78	14	37	15	1	1	0	0
6	8.3	45.36	9	42	17	5	0	1	0
7	5.2	21.90	6	34	15	9	1	0	0
8	7.0	22.31	3	22	15	0	0	1	0
9	3.9	16.96	4	36	14	4	0	0	0
10	5.0	19.21	4	29	14	1	0	1	0
11	11.9	61.06	29	65	16	10	1	1	0
12	5.2	14.11	3	21	13	0	0	0	0
13	9.6	17.16	6	24	13	0	1	0	0
14	7.4	41.57	18	63	16	12	1	1	0
15	5.5	24.99	9	29	16	0	1	1	0
16	6.2	34.54	3	28	16	0	0	1	0
17	3.8	14.25	3	21	12	0	0	0	0
18	11.1	63.66	8	43	19	6	1	1	1
19	4.4	14.74	6	33	13	5	1	0	0
20	11.2	23.57	4	23	15	0	1	1	1
21	8.1	37.01	24	64	15	4	0	1	0
22	5.2	23.73	4	25	16	2	0	1	0
23	9.8	50.42	7	38	17	3	1	1	1
24	9.9	23.49	3	21	13	0	0	0	0
25	5.6	15.17	4	25	12	1	0	1	0
26	5.9	45.55	7	39	18	5	1	1	0
27	8.1	25.10	23	65	13	6	0	0	0
28	5.1	16.34	4	27	13	0	0	1	1
29	11.9	44.76	16	40	16	0	1	1	1
30	5.4	14.50	7	29	12	2	0	0	0
31	8.8	22.70	20	46	13	5	1	0	0
32	5.2	42.40	11	43	16	4	1	1	0
33	10.1	45.28	9	46	16	5	0	0	1
34	9.0	31.38	4	30	16	3	0	1	0
35	8.7	54.35	8	65	16	15	0	0	1
36	6.8	59.32	18	40	19	0	1	1	1
37	5.6	15.80	7	35	12	6	0	0	0
38	10.2	23.71	11	33	13	0	0	1	1
39	8.1	21.02	6	32	13	3	0	0	0
40	6.5	21.28	11	39	12	3	0	1	0
41	9.6	23.20	7	34	14	5	0	0	0
42	8.3	22.28	4	23	15	0	1	1	0
43	10.0	39.79	13	49	14	12	1	0	0
44	9.0	21.51	5	23	14	0	1	1	0
45	7.7	53.36	9	49	18	9	1	1	0
46	7.9	34.46	9	65	16	18	0	0	0
47	3.7	19.01	6	37	15	6	0	1	0

48	10.2	47.73	24	51	16	3	1	0	0
49	8.9	43.44	14	37	16	0	1	1	0
50	13.1	29.50	15	32	13	0	1	1	1

GENDER: 1 if male, 0 if not.
RACE: 1 if white, 0 if not.
MANAGEment: 1 if management responsibility, 0 if not.

APPENDIX B: Statistical Software

Example: Here we use SAS to perform a multiple regression analysis. We regress unit sales on price and number of radio ads for COMCEL's 24-outlets. The data are shown in Table 11.4.

Input

```
01  DATA TEST;
02  INPUT PRICE ADS SALES;
03  CARDS
04 1    100    1       9
   2    100    1      11
   3    100    3      19
   4    100    3      15

   . . . . . . . . . . . . . . . . . .

   22    80    3      24
   23    80    5      37
   24    80    5      34
   ;
05  PROC REG;
06     MODEL SALES=PRICE ADS;
07     OUTPUT OUT=OUTPUT
08          P=PRED
09          R=RESID
10       L95M=L95MEAN
11       U95M=U95MEAN
12        L95=L95
13        U95=U95;
14     PROC PLOT; PLOT RESID*PRICE='*'/HAXIS=80 TO 100 BY 5;
15             PLOT RESID*ADS='*'/HAXIS=0 TO 5 BY 1;
16             PLOT RESID*PRED='*';
17     PROC PRINT;
```

Explanation of Input

01   Creates a temporary data set called TEST.

02   Tells SAS to read three variables per observation(outlet) in the following order: PRICE, ADS, SALES.

03   Tells SAS that data follow immediately and that the end of the data file will be signaled by a semicolon.

04   The first of 24 observations from Table 11.4.

05   Performs a REGression analysis.

06   Names SALES as the dependent variable and PRICE and ADS as the predictor variables.

07   Tells SAS to write the variables listed on lines 8–13 to a file called OUTPUT.

08   SAS allows specific variables to be written to an output file. The SAS names for
            these variables are on the left side of the equal sign, and the user-supplied name is
            on the right side. The single letter P is the SAS name for the predicted value of the
            dependent variable, SALES, given the values of each predictor variable for each
            observation. The user-supplied name is PRED, but any eight-charater name begin-
            ning with a letter could be used.

09   Writes to the OUTPUT file the residual, SAS-name R, user-supplied name RESID,
            for each observation.

10–11   Writes to the OUTPUT file the lower and upper limits for 95% confidence inter-
            vals for the conditional means, L95MEAN and U95MEAN, for each PRICE-ADS
            combination in Table 11.4.

12–13   Writes to the OUTPUT file 95% prediction limits for an individual value of the
            dependent variable, SALES, for each PRICE-ADS combination in Table 11.4.

14   PLOTs the RESIDuals on the vertical axis and the values of the predictor variable,
            PRICE, on the horizontal axis. Scales the Horizontal AXIS from $80 to $100 in
            increments of $5.

15–16   Plots RESIDuals against ADS and against the PREDicted values of the dependent
            variable, SALES.

17   PRINTs all variables in the data set OUTPUT, which includes the input variables
            on line 02, and the requested output variables on lines 8–13.

Output

```
Model: MODEL1
Dependent Variable: SALES

Analysis of Variance
```

	Source	DF	Sum of Squares	Mean Square	F-Value	Prob>F
01	Model	2	1070.26905	535.13452	81.989	0.0001
02	Error	21	137.06429	6.52687		
03	C Total	23	1207.33333			

04	Root MSE	2.55477	R-square	0.8865
05	Dep Mean	23.83333	Adj R-sq	0.8757
06	C.V.	10.71933		

```
   Parameter Estimates
```

	Variable	DF	Parameter Estimate	Standard Error	T for H0: Parameter=0	Prob >|T|
07	INTERCEP	1	60.891071	6.35285674	9.585	0.0001
08	PRICE	1	-0.529524	0.07051846	-7.509	0.0001
09	ADS	1	3.312500	0.31934676	10.373	0.0001

10   Plot of RESID*PRICE.   Symbol used is '*'.

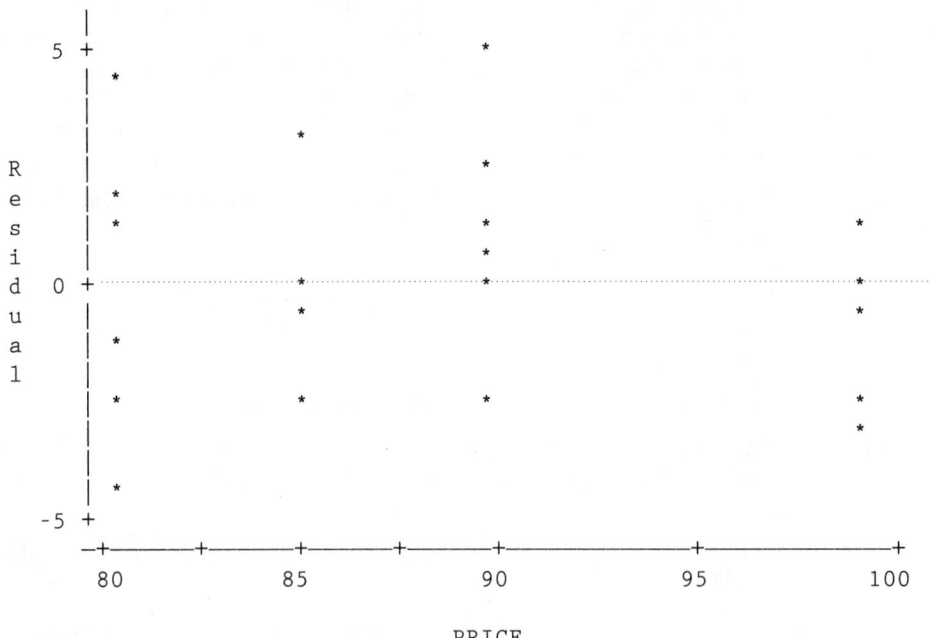

PRICE

NOTE: 4 obs hidden.

11   Plot of RESID*ADS.   Symbol used is '*'.

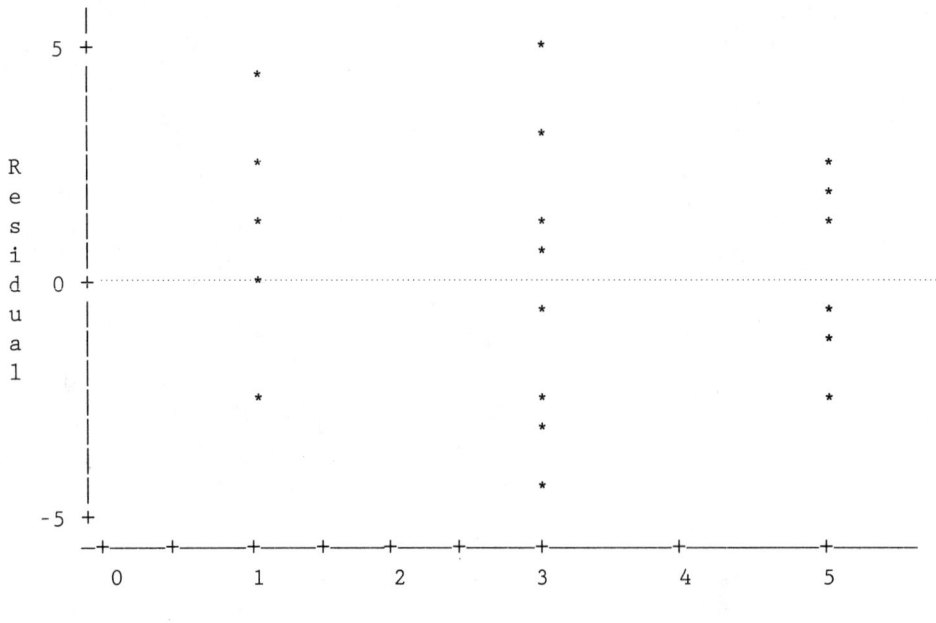

ADS

NOTE: 5 obs hidden.

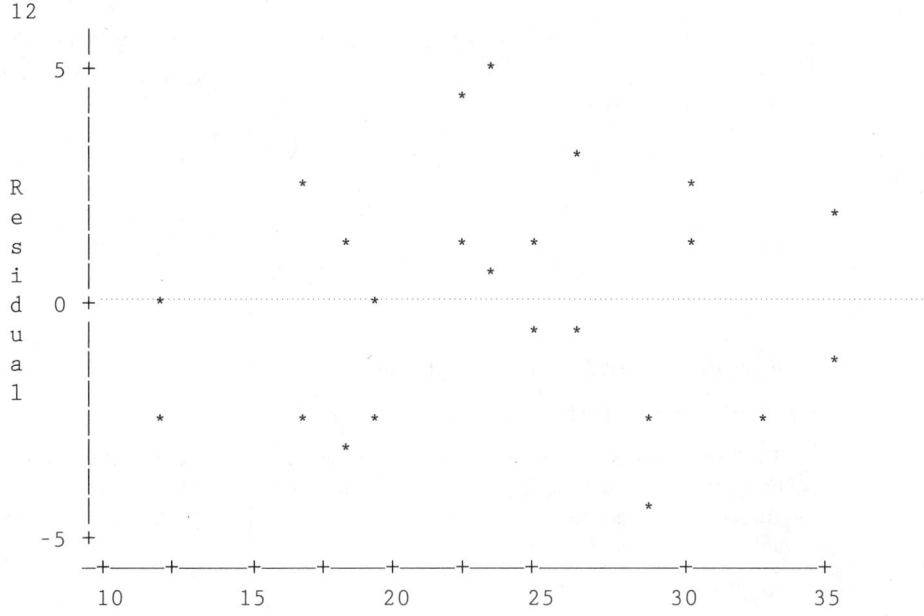

Plot of RESID*PRED.   Symbol used is '*'.

Predicted Value of SALES

NOTE: 1 obs hidden.

OBS	PRICE	ADS	SALES	13 PRED	14 L95MEAN	15 U95MEAN	16 L95	17 U95	18 RESID
1	100	1	9	11.2512	8.8716	13.6307	5.4297	17.0727	-2.25119
2	100	1	11	11.2512	8.8716	13.6307	5.4297	17.0727	-0.25119
3	100	3	19	17.8762	15.9018	19.8505	12.2083	23.5441	1.12381
4	100	3	15	17.8762	15.9018	19.8505	12.2083	23.5441	-2.87619
5	100	5	26	24.5012	22.1216	26.8807	18.6797	30.3227	1.49881
6	100	5	24	24.5012	22.1216	26.8807	18.6797	30.3227	-0.50119
7	90	1	14	16.5464	14.8219	18.2709	10.9606	22.1322	-2.54643
8	90	1	19	16.5464	14.8219	18.2709	10.9606	22.1322	2.45357
9	90	3	24	23.1714	22.0715	24.2713	17.7458	28.5970	0.82857
10	90	3	28	23.1714	22.0715	24.2713	17.7458	28.5970	4.82857
11	90	5	31	29.7964	28.0719	31.5209	24.2106	35.3822	1.20357
12	90	5	32	29.7964	28.0719	31.5209	24.2106	35.3822	2.20357
13	85	1	17	19.1940	17.3933	20.9948	13.5842	24.8039	-2.19405
14	85	1	19	19.1940	17.3933	20.9948	13.5842	24.8039	-0.19405
15	85	3	29	25.8190	24.6031	27.0350	20.3687	31.2694	3.18095
16	85	3	25	25.8190	24.6031	27.0350	20.3687	31.2694	-0.81905
17	85	5	30	32.4440	30.6433	34.2448	26.8342	38.0539	-2.44405
18	85	5	30	32.4440	30.6433	34.2448	26.8342	38.0539	-2.44405
19	80	1	26	21.8417	19.7000	23.9834	16.1133	27.5700	4.15833
20	80	1	23	21.8417	19.7000	23.9834	16.1133	27.5700	1.15833
21	80	3	26	28.4667	26.7866	30.1468	22.8944	34.0389	-2.46667
22	80	3	24	28.4667	26.7866	30.1468	22.8944	34.0389	-4.46667
23	80	5	37	35.0917	32.9500	37.2334	29.3633	40.8200	1.90833
24	80	5	34	35.0917	32.9500	37.2334	29.3633	40.8200	-1.09167

Interpretation of Output

01   SAS uses the term "Model" to refer to the regression sum of squares, which the text calls SSR. Since the estimated equation contains two predictor variables, PRICE and ADS, the degrees of freedom (DF) associated with the regression sum of squares is 2.

02   Error refers to the error sum of squares, SSE.

03   "C Total" is the total sum of squares, SST. SST is referred to as the "C(orrected total) sum of squares" because the mean is subtracted from each value of the dependent variable before squaring.

04   Root MSE is the standard error of the estimate, or $\sqrt{MSE}$.

      R-square is the coefficient of multiple determination.

05   "Dep Mean" is $\bar{y}$, the mean value of the multiple dependent variable, SALES.

      The "Adj(usted) R-square" is an alternative measure of fit to the coefficient of multiple determination, R-square. R-square will always increase as predictor variables are added to the equation, even if the variables are unrelated to the dependent variable. The adjusted R-square is

      Adj R-square $= 1 - (SSE/n - k - 1)/(SST/n - 1)$

      and, like MSE, will go down if the percent reduction in SSE resulting from adding a variable is less than the percent increase in the error degrees of freedom, $n - k - 1$. Note that the adjusted R-square contains MSE, $(SSE/n - k - 1)$. Maximizing the adjusted R-square is equivalent to minimizing MSE.

06   C.V. stands for coefficient of variation, and is the ratio of the Root MSE (the standard deviation of the residuals) to the dependent mean, $\bar{y}$, times 100. Root MSE measures prediction error and is measured in the same units as the dependent variable. The coefficient of variation measures prediction error in relative terms, that is, as a percentage of the mean value of the dependent variable.

07–09 The "Parameter Estimates" section is identical to the output discussed in the text.

10–12 The residual plots are the same as those in the text.

13–17 Discussed in the text in Table 11.19.

18   RESIDuals for each of the 24 values. These are shown in Table 11.12.

ADVANCED TOPICS IN REGRESSION ANALYSIS

12.1 Introduction
12.2 Indicator variables
    Representing categorical variables
    Hypothesis test on a population regression
    coefficient
    Interaction
    Categorical variables with three or more
    classes
    Summary
12.3 Nonlinear regression
    Scatter diagramming and the need for
    nonlinear models
    Building and evaluating nonlinear models

12.4 The extra sum of squares principle and the
    general linear test
    The extra sum of squares principle
    Tests that some population regression
    coefficients equal zero
12.5 Multicollinearity
    What is multicollinearity?
    Why is multicollinearity a problem?
    Detecting multicollinearity
    Procedures for coping with multicollinearity
    Summary
Appendix A: COMCEL Personnel data
Appendix B: HICOMM Job satisfaction data

Date: September 6, 1995
To: Marvin Elrod, Manager of Human Resources
From: Ann Tabor, CEO
Re: Salary Determinant Study

I want you to conduct a salary determinant study to ensure that males/females and whites/nonwhites who have the same qualifications are receiving the same compensation within our firm. If there is unintentional discrimination, you are to correct the problem immediately.

I want your final report within two **weeks**.

12.1 ≡ Introduction

Chapter 12 introduces four advanced regression analysis topics: (1) using categorical variables in regression models, (2) building nonlinear regression models, (3) building and evaluating models using the general linear test, and (4) detecting and minimizing multicollinearity.

Many business applications of regression analysis involve categorical, or qualitative, predictor variables. For example, managers' salaries may depend on categorical variables—gender and race—in addition to quantitative variables—education and experience. In this chapter we show how to include and interpret categorical predictor variables in a regression model.

In Chapter 11 we presented linear regression models. Often one or more predictor variables are nonlinearly related to a dependent variable. In this chapter we show how to develop and interpret nonlinear regression models that include the quadratic terms (x_1^2, x_2^2) and the interaction term $(x_1 x_2)$ in model (12.1).

$$E(y) = \beta_0 + \beta_1 x_1 + \beta_{11} x_1^2 + \beta_2 x_2 + \beta_{22} x_2^2 + \beta_{12} x_1 x_2 \qquad (12.1)$$

In Chapter 11 we used a confidence interval approach to test for the significance of a single predictor variable. We warned you not to use this method to test the significance of several predictor variables simultaneously, because the probability of making at least one Type I error increases with each additional test. So how do we determine whether a *group* of predictor variables is related to the dependent variable after controlling for the other predictor variables in the model? In this chapter, we use the general linear test to build regression models. Model building addresses the following two questions:

1. Which predictor variables should be included in the model?
2. Should the model have linear terms, quadratic terms, and interaction terms?

In Chapter 11, COMCEL conducted an experimental regression study. The predictor variables, PRICE and ADS, were not correlated with one another. When predictor variables are highly correlated, we have the problem of *multicollinearity*. Multicollinearity presents problems in interpreting the sample regression coefficients and in model building. In this chapter we discuss how to detect and minimize multicollinearity.

12.2 ≡ Indicator Variables

In Chapter 11 we informally introduced the idea of including categorical predictor variables such as gender (male, female) in a regression model. We now formally cover the topic and extend it to deal with categorical predictor variables with more than two categories, such as department type (operations, accounting, marketing), or degree (BBA, MBA, Ph.D). We also provide a graphical interpretation of categorical variables. By the end of this section you should be able to:

1. represent categorical variables by creating one or more indicator variables;
2. interpret the regression coefficient of an indicator variable in a regression model;
3. explain the meaning of an interaction term; and
4. use indicator variables to compare regression equations for differences in intercepts and slopes.

In the first example, we explain how to code, or represent, a categorical variable with two classes and how to interpret a regression model with a coded indicator variable.

Example: Smith-Jones Account Executives Data   We want to estimate the effect of gender on annual salary (dependent variable) after controlling for months of service. We have included the gender variable because we want to learn how the salaries of the company's female account executives compare with those of their male counterparts. We select a stratified (by gender) random sample of 40 personnel records of account executives and record the annual SALARY (measured in thousands of dollars), the number of MONTHS with the company, and the GENDER of each employee.

Representing Categorical Variables

The GENDER variable is a categorical variable with two classes, males and females. We represent it as follows:

$$\text{GENDER} = \begin{cases} 1 & \text{if the employee is female} \\ 0 & \text{if the employee is male} \end{cases}$$

In general:

> We represent a categorical variable with c classes by $c - 1$ indicator variables, each taking on a value of 0 or 1.

Table 12.1 contains the data for the Smith-Jones study. Once we code an employee's gender as a 0 or 1, we treat the gender variable the same as any other predictor variable in the regression model.

Table 12.1

Smith-Jones Salary Data for Account Executives

Males			Females		
SALARY	MONTHS	GENDER	SALARY	MONTHS	GENDER
48.0	39	0	38.5	80	1
63.5	80	0	45.9	78	1
49.1	45	0	40.2	84	1
46.7	36	0	29.7	24	1
49.6	47	0	44.3	84	1
37.2	6	0	32.3	35	1
64.5	84	0	31.2	38	1
43.1	56	0	22.5	12	1
51.6	60	0	38.8	65	1
47.8	21	0	46.8	73	1
57.4	84	0	37.8	65	1
54.6	73	0	21.1	10	1
56.9	67	0	34.0	45	1
33.2	7	0	41.1	54	1
58.3	84	0	40.2	73	1
40.7	18	0	29.5	24	1
61.5	72	0	20.4	5	1
35.9	2	0	25.2	8	1
42.7	27	0			
35.0	12	0			
57.1	74	0			
43.8	36	0			

FIGURE 12.1   **Salary versus Months of Service**

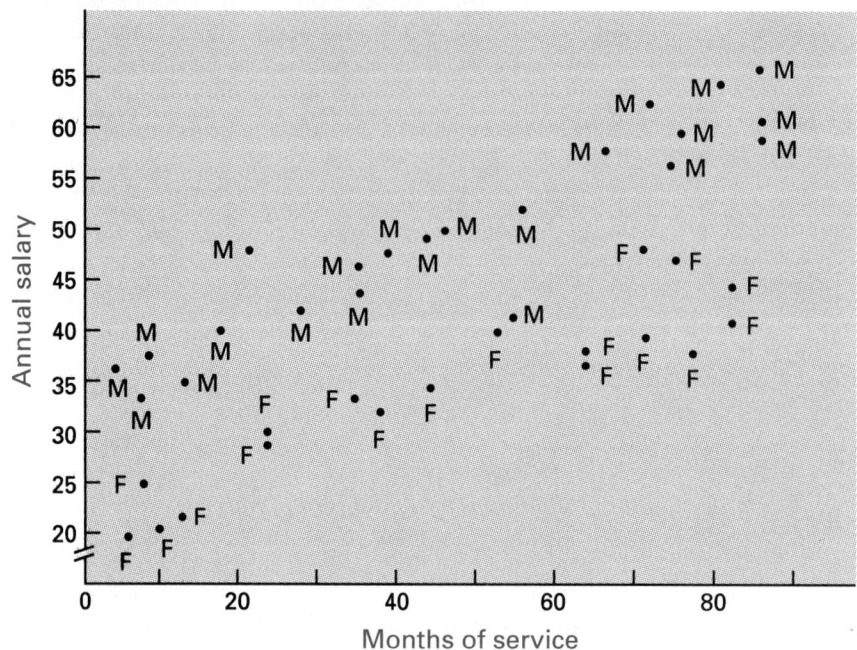

Before computing a regression model, we plot SALARY versus the number of MONTHS for both males and females in Figure 12.1. The relationship between MONTHS and SALARY appears to be linear, but male (M) executives' salaries appear to be systematically higher than female (F) executives' salaries, suggesting that GENDER is a significant predictor of SALARY.

$$E(\text{SALARY}) = \beta_0 + \beta_1 \text{MONTHS} + \beta_2 \text{GENDER} \tag{12.2}$$

We wish to estimate the parameters in (12.2) using the method of least squares, and test the significance of the GENDER variable, because it answers the question: "Are male and female salaries the same for people with the same number of months of service?"

Table 12.2

Parameter Estimate Section

VARIABLE	PARAMETER ESTIMATE	STANDARD ERROR	t-VALUE	TWO-TAILED p-VALUE
INTERCEPT	35.145	—	—	—
MONTHS	.296	.02	16.10	$p < .001$
GENDER	-14.827	1.02	-14.50	$p < .001$

From Table 12.2, we obtained the parameter estimates for regression model (12.3):

$$\text{SALARY-PRED} = 35.145 + .296\text{MONTHS} - 14.827\text{GENDER} \qquad (12.3)$$

The ANOVA table (not shown) indicated that the overall model was significant ($VR = 231.467 > F_{.99; 2,37}$; $p < .001$). We conclude that at least one of the two independent variables is a significant predictor of salary.

We constructed a confidence interval on β_2 to determine if the GENDER variable is significant after controlling for MONTHS. From expression (11.19), a 95% confidence interval on the gender indicator variable is

$$b_2 - t(\text{2-sided 95\%, df}_{\text{error}})s(b_2) \leq \beta_2 \leq b_2 + t(\text{2-sided 95\%, df}_{\text{error}})s(b_2)$$

where $\text{df}_{\text{error}} = n - k - 1$
$n = $ sample size
$k = $ number of predictor variables

$$-14.827 - t(\text{2-sided 95\%, 37})(1.02) \leq \beta_2 \leq -14.827 + t(\text{2-sided 95\%, 37})(1.02)$$

$$-14.827 - 2.027(1.02) \leq \beta_2 \leq -14.827 + 2.027(1.02)$$

$$-16.895 \leq \beta_2 \leq -12.759$$

Since this interval does not contain zero, we conclude that GENDER is statistically related to salary, after controlling for MONTHS.

Hypothesis Test on a Population Regression Coefficient

Table 12.2 provides the data for an alternative approach to constructing confidence intervals on a population regression coefficient, such as β_2. The alternative approach is hypothesis testing. To test

$$H_0: \quad \beta_2 = 0$$

$$H_1: \quad \beta_2 \neq 0$$

we use the t-value column. The computed t-values in column 4 are simply the ratios of the parameter estimates in column 2 to the standard errors of these estimates in column 3. The computer software then compares the absolute value of the computed t-value against the t-table values for the error degrees of freedom (from Appendix 5) and determines the p-value (column 5). If the p-value is less than α, the desired significance level, we reject the null hypothesis and conclude that β_2 does not equal zero.

From Appendix 5, the interpolated t-values for 37 degrees of freedom are:

t(2-sided 95% CI)	2.027
t(2-sided 98% CI)	2.433
t(2-sided 99% CI)	2.718

Since $|-14.50| > 2.718$, the p-value is less than .01 (see Table 12.2). We conclude that β_2 does not equal zero.*

The confidence interval approach from Chapter 11 and the hypothesis test method shown above are equivalent. We will use the hypothesis test for testing the significance of a single predictor variable for the remainder of this chapter.

Conclusion   The statistically significant GENDER variable means that there is a pay differential for men and women with the same length of service.

To find the mean salary of males or females with a given length of service, we simply insert a 1 for female employees or a 0 for male employees for the GENDER variable and the appropriate number of MONTHS of service into model (12.3). For example, the mean salary of females with 36 months of service is

$$\text{SALARY-PRED}_{(F)} = 35.145 + .296(36) - 14.827(1)$$
$$= 20.318 + .296(36)$$
$$= 30.974 \quad \text{or} \quad \$30,974$$

The mean salary for males with 36 months of service is

$$\text{SALARY-PRED}_{(M)} = 35.145 + .296(36) - 14.827(0)$$
$$= 35.145 + .296(36)$$
$$= 45.801 \quad \text{or} \quad \$45,801$$

The interpretation of the GENDER variable sample regression coefficient is that after controlling for length of service, the mean salary of females is $45,801 - $30,974 or $14,827 lower than that of males. This is simply the sample regression coefficient for the GENDER predictor variable. Thus, the regression coefficient of an indicator variable is the difference between the mean values of the dependent variable for the two groups represented by that variable.

This difference in mean salaries does not depend on how we coded the GENDER variable. If we represented GENDER as male = 1 and female = 0, the regression equation would have been

$$\text{SALARY-PRED} = 20.318 + .296\text{MONTHS} + 14.827\text{GENDER}$$

The predicted mean salary for males with 36 months of service would be $20.318 + .296(36) + 14.827(1) = 45.801$ or $45,801—the same result we obtained above. The predicted mean salary for females with 36 months of service would still be $20.318 + .296(36) + 14.827(0) = 30.974$ or $30,974. In fact, we could use any two numbers to represent a categorical variable with two classes, but 1 and 0 are the easiest to interpret.

Figure 12.2 shows the sample linear regression lines for males and females considered separately. The two lines are parallel, crossing the SALARY, or vertical, axis at different points. When MONTHS is zero, the graph for females (GENDER coded as 1)

---

*Suppose the computed t-value was 2.350. Then, since 2.350 is greater than 2.027 but less than 2.433, the p-value would be between .02 and .05.

FIGURE 12.2 Parallel Lines for Male and Female Executives

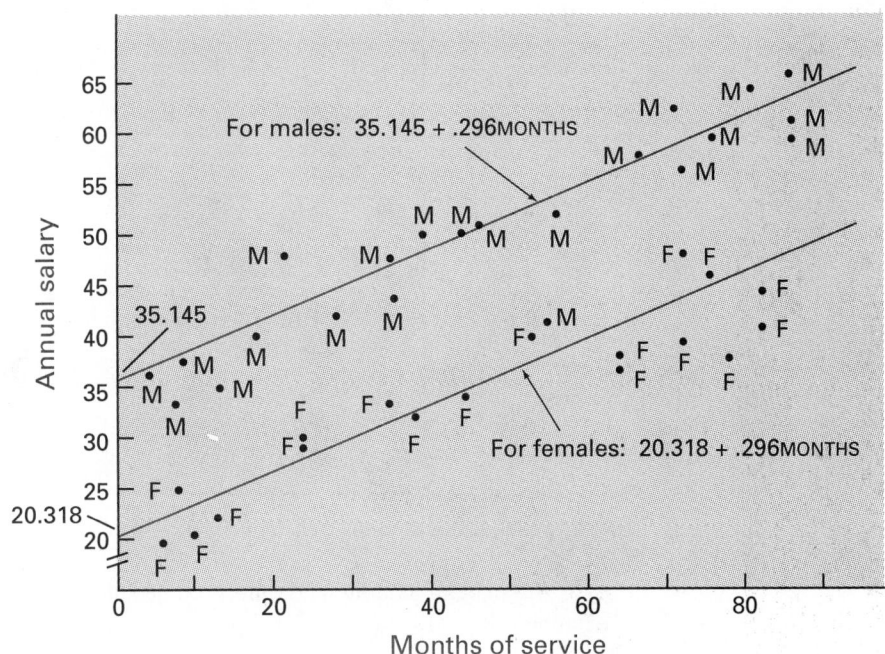

crosses the SALARY axis at \$20,318. The graph for males (GENDER coded as 0) crosses the SALARY axis at \$35,145. Smith-Jones pays female account executives lower starting salaries than males. However, since the lines are parallel, the \$14,827 difference in salaries is maintained over the next several years. That is, the mean salary increase per month is the same. Salaries of males and females have increased at a mean rate of .296 thousand, or \$296, per month.

Interaction

Suppose that male account executives at Smith-Jones not only had higher starting salaries (intercept), but also received salary increases at a higher mean rate than females. How would the parallel lines in Figure 12.2 change? Please think about it before reading on.

Figure 12.3 shows the lines in the case where the salaries of the males increase at the rate of \$900 per month, while those of the females increase at \$296 per month. The two regression lines are no longer parallel. The slope of the equation for male account executives is steeper than that of females. The salaries of the males not only start off higher but also increase more rapidly.

We used a GENDER indicator variable to determine whether starting salaries (the intercepts) differed between males and females. We will use an **interaction variable** to determine whether the two slopes, the rates of salary increases, are the same. We say that an interaction occurs when the regression lines for different levels of the indicator variable are not parallel. We first discussed the interaction concept in factorial experiments in Chapter 10.

An interaction occurs when the rate of change (the slope) of y versus one predictor variable depends on the level of another predictor variable.

FIGURE 12.3   Nonparallel Lines for Male and Female Executives

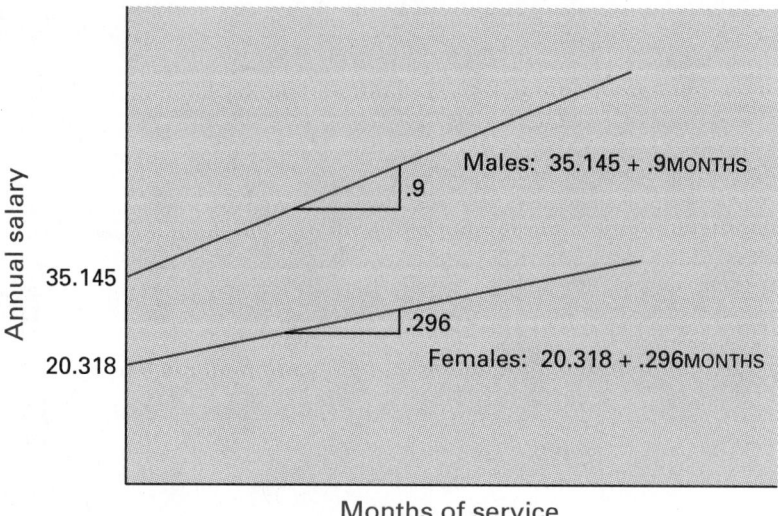

We explain coding and interpreting interaction variables in the following example.

Example: Smith-Jones Creative Staff Data   We select a stratified (by gender) random sample of creative staff personnel records. Figure 12.4 is the scatter plot.

FIGURE 12.4   Salary versus Months of Service

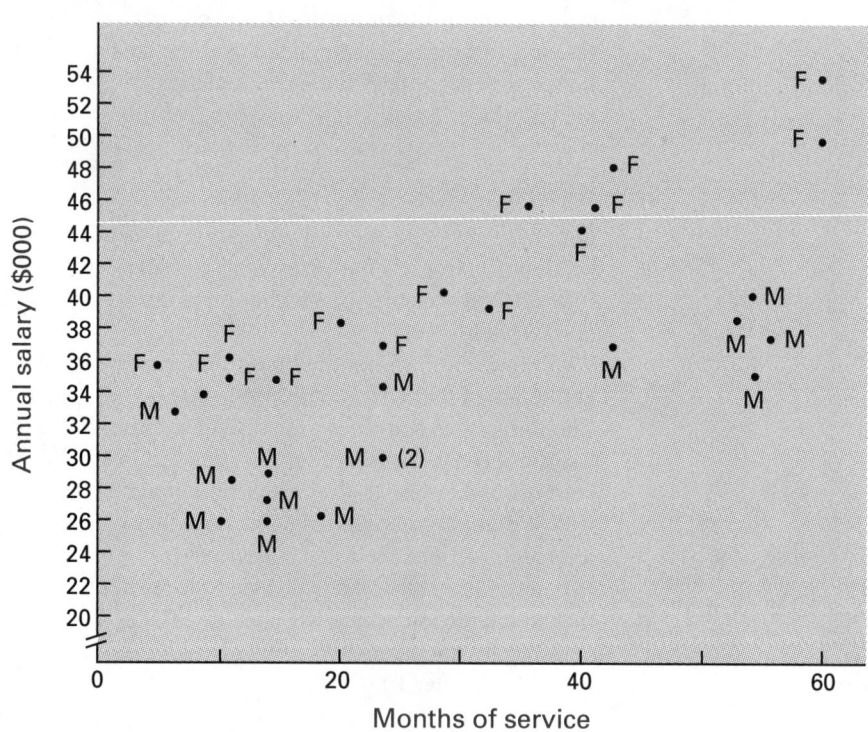

Note that females (F) appear to have higher starting salaries, and their salaries increase faster than those of their male counterparts. The former comment suggests that we should include a gender variable in the model. The latter comment suggests that we should include an interaction variable in the model. That is, we should evaluate the following regression model:

$$E(\text{SALARY}) = \beta_0 + \beta_1 \text{MONTHS} + \beta_2 \text{GENDER} + \beta_{12} \text{GENDER} \times \text{MONTHS}$$

We create the interaction variable, GENDER × MONTHS, by *multiplying* the value of the MONTHS variable by the value of the GENDER variable for each observation in the sample. Table 12.3 shows the values for the two original predictor variables and the created interaction predictor variable.

Table 12.3

Smith-Jones Salary Data for Creative Staff

Males				Females			
SALARY	MONTHS	GENDER	GENDER × MONTHS	SALARY	MONTHS	GENDER	GENDER × MONTHS
26.4	10	0	0	35.0	15	1	15
26.4	18	0	0	39.8	32	1	32
32.2	7	0	0	35.7	6	1	6
35.5	54	0	0	40.2	28	1	28
37.2	42	0	0	32.7	9	1	9
29.3	14	0	0	37.0	24	1	24
34.3	24	0	0	38.0	19	1	19
27.8	14	0	0	36.0	12	1	12
30.0	24	0	0	50.4	60	1	60
37.5	55	0	0	54.0	60	1	60
30.0	24	0	0	46.4	40	1	40
26.2	14	0	0	46.5	36	1	36
28.9	12	0	0	44.1	39	1	39
40.0	53	0	0	35.0	12	1	12
41.5	54	0	0	48.3	43	1	43

Equation (12.4) is the estimated multiple regression model for the creative staff salary data.

$$\text{SALARY-PRED} = 25.340 + .246\text{MONTHS} + 5.423\text{GENDER} + .116\text{GENDER} \times \text{MONTHS} \qquad (12.4)$$

Smith-Jones then conducted an ANOVA and a hypothesis test on the β_{12}, GENDER × MONTHS, population regression coefficient (neither analysis shown). The GENDER × MONTHS predictor variable was statistically significant.

Let us explore the significant interaction predictor variable. Since females are coded GENDER = 1, the regression equation for annual salary versus number of months of service for females is

$$\text{SALARY-PRED}_{(F)} = 25.340 + .246\text{MONTHS} + 5.423\text{GENDER} + .116\text{GENDER} \times \text{MONTHS}$$

$$= 25.340 + .246\text{MONTHS} + 5.423(1) + .116(1) \times \text{MONTHS}$$

$$= 30.763 + .362\text{MONTHS} \qquad (12.5)$$

FIGURE 12.5 Two Nonparallel Regression Lines

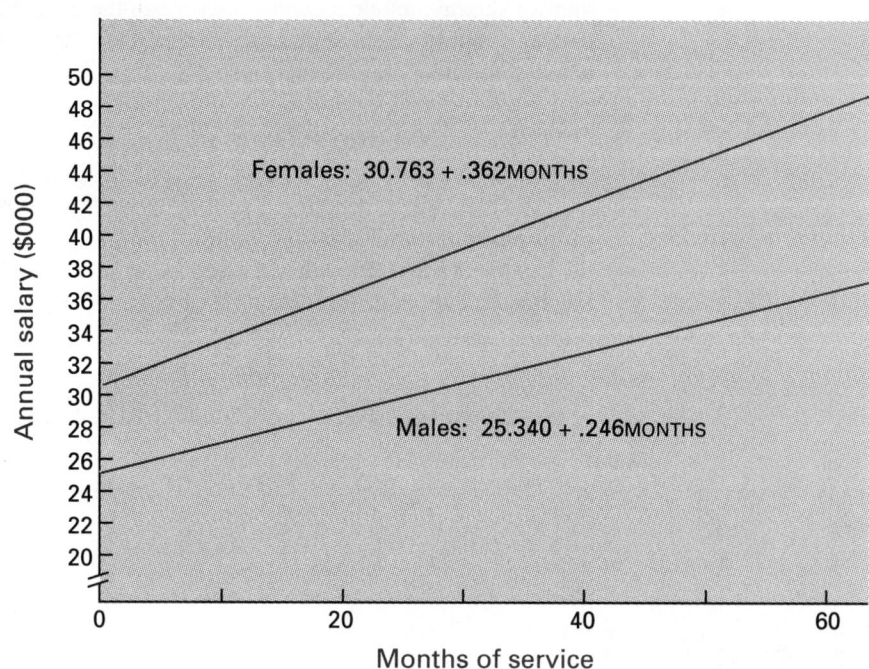

The regression equation for annual salary versus number of months of service for males is

$$\text{SALARY-PRED}_{(M)} = 25.340 + .246\text{MONTHS} + 5.423\text{GENDER} + .116\text{GENDER} \times \text{MONTHS}$$

$$= 25.340 + .246\text{MONTHS} + 5.423(0) + .116(0) \times \text{MONTHS}$$

$$= 25.340 + .246\text{MONTHS} \qquad (12.6)$$

The intercept for the regression line for the female creative staff is 30.763 ($30,763), as compared with 25.340 ($25,340) for the male staff. The difference in intercepts of 5.423 results from adding the value of the GENDER regression coefficient to the intercept for the female staff, but not for the male staff.

The slope of the equation for females is .362 as compared with .246 for males. The difference in slopes of .116 results from adding the value of the GENDER × MONTHS regression coefficient to the slope for females, but not for males. Figure 12.5 shows the graphs of equations (12.5) and (12.6).

Model (12.4) can be used to make predictions. For example, to predict the annual salary of a female with 40 months of service, we substitute GENDER = 1 and MONTHS = 40 into model (12.4).

$$\text{SALARY-PRED}_{(F)} = 25.340 + .246\text{MONTHS} + 5.423\text{GENDER} + .116\text{GENDER} \times \text{MONTHS}$$

$$\text{SALARY-PRED}_{(F)} = 25.340 + .246(40) + 5.423(1) + .116(1 \cdot 40)$$
$$= 45.243 \quad \text{or} \quad \$45,243 \qquad (12.4)$$

In summary, the statistical significance of the GENDER $\times$ MONTHS variable indicates that the mean salaries of females have increased at a rate different from the mean salaries of males. The significant GENDER $\times$ MONTHS variable means that the relationship between salary and months on the job *depends* on an employee's gender. Or, in short, there is a gender-months interaction.

Categorical Variables with Three or More Classes

Up to now, we have considered only categorical variables with two classes, male and female. However, categorical variables often have three or more classes. This will require adding additional indicator variables to the regression model.

In our next example, we explain how to code a categorical variable with three classes. The example is taken from the health care industry, which accounted for approximately 14% of the U.S. gross domestic product in 1992.

Example: Predicting the Number of X-Rays   Our goal is to predict the number of x-ray exposures taken per month (dependent variable). The two predictor variables are (1) mean daily patient load per month and (2) type of hospital: private (for profit), public, and teaching. Mean daily patient load is the hospital's total number of inpatients and outpatients divided by the number of days in a month. Table 12.4 contains hypothetical data for a stratified sample of five hospitals from each of the three hospital type categories.

Table 12.4

X-Ray and Patient Load Data by Hospital Type

Hospital	Number of X-Rays Taken per Month	Mean Daily Patient Load	Hospital Type
1	2,105	15.5	Private
2	9,700	50.5	Private
3	17,800	100.5	Private
4	30,600	150	Private
5	61,600	300	Private
6	1,800	18.7	Public
7	7,000	45	Public
8	16,250	90.5	Public
9	48,950	250	Public
10	79,000	400	Public
11	26,000	50	Teaching
12	35,000	100.5	Teaching
13	56,500	200	Teaching
14	89,200	350.5	Teaching
15	118,100	500	Teaching

The hospital type variable is a categorical variable with three classes. Thus we must create two indicator variables. For example, one way to represent the hospital type categorical variable is as follows:

$$\text{PRIVATE} = \begin{cases} 1 & \text{if the hospital is private} \\ 0 & \text{otherwise} \end{cases}$$

$$\text{TEACHING} = \begin{cases} 1 & \text{if the hospital is a teaching hospital} \\ 0 & \text{otherwise} \end{cases}$$

We have created two new indicator variables, PRIVATE and TEACHING, from the single categorical variable, hospital type, as shown in Table 12.5. *Note:* We have not created interaction variables because we do *not* believe that the relationship between mean daily patient load and number of x-ray exposures *depends* on the type of hospital.

We need only two indicator variables, even though the categorical variable, hospital type, has three classes. For example, using the above coding scheme, we represent a

private hospital as PRIVATE $= 1$ and TEACHING $= 0$,

teaching hospital as PRIVATE $= 0$ and TEACHING $= 1$,

public hospital as PRIVATE $= 0$ and TEACHING $= 0$.

A public hospital is neither a private hospital (PRIVATE $= 0$) nor a teaching hospital (TEACHING $= 0$). Thus, public hospitals are represented by assigning the value 0 to each indicator variable. In other words, once we know a hospital is not a private or teaching hospital, we know that it must be a public hospital. Thus, we need only two indicator variables to represent a categorical variable with three classes.

Table 12.5

X-Ray and Patient Load Data by Type of Hospital

Hospital	Number of X-Rays Taken per Month (XRAY)	Mean Daily Patient Load (LOAD)	PRIVATE	TEACHING	Hospital Type
1	2,105	15.5	1	0	Private
2	9,700	50.5	1	0	Private
3	17,800	100.5	1	0	Private
4	30,600	150	1	0	Private
5	61,600	300	1	0	Private
6	1,800	18.7	0	0	Public
7	7,000	45	0	0	Public
8	16,250	90.5	0	0	Public
9	48,950	250	0	0	Public
10	79,000	400	0	0	Public
11	26,000	50	0	1	Teaching
12	35,000	100.5	0	1	Teaching
13	56,500	200	0	1	Teaching
14	89,200	350.5	0	1	Teaching
15	118,100	500	0	1	Teaching

Using the boxed data, we obtained the following regression model.

$$\text{XRAY-PRED} = -2{,}357 + 204.9\text{LOAD} + 2{,}488.9\text{PRIVATE} + 18{,}098.3\text{TEACHING} \quad (12.7)$$

The ANOVA indicated that regression model (12.7) is statistically significant. Shown are the three equations used to estimate the mean number of x-rays for each hospital type:

For public hospitals, PRIVATE = 0 and TEACHING = 0:

$$\text{XRAY-PRED}_{(PU)} = -2{,}357 + 204.9\text{LOAD} + 2{,}488.9\text{PRIVATE} + 18{,}098.3\text{TEACHING}$$
$$= -2{,}357 + 204.9\text{LOAD} + 2{,}488.9(0) + 18{,}098.3(0)$$
$$= -2{,}357 + 204.9\text{LOAD} \tag{12.8}$$

For private hospitals, PRIVATE = 1 and TEACHING = 0:

$$\text{XRAY-PRED}_{(PR)} = -2{,}357 + 204.9\text{LOAD} + 2{,}488.9\text{PRIVATE} + 18{,}098.3\text{TEACHING}$$
$$= -2{,}357 + 204.9\text{LOAD} + 2{,}488.9(1) + 18{,}098.3(0)$$
$$= 131.9 + 204.9\text{LOAD} \tag{12.9}$$

For teaching hospitals, PRIVATE = 0 and TEACHING = 1:

$$\text{XRAY-PRED}_{(T)} = -2{,}357 + 204.9\text{LOAD} + 2{,}488.9\text{PRIVATE} + 18{,}098.3\text{TEACHING}$$
$$= -2{,}357 + 204.9\text{LOAD} + 2{,}488.9(0) + 18{,}098.3(1)$$
$$= 15{,}741.3 + 204.9\text{LOAD} \tag{12.10}$$

Models (12.8), (12.9), and (12.10) differ only in their intercepts. Private hospitals take, on average, 2,488.9 more x-rays per month than public hospitals after controlling for daily patient load. The term 2,488.9 is the difference between the intercepts in models (12.8) and (12.9). It is also the sample regression coefficient for the PRIVATE indicator variable in the model.

$$131.9 - (-2{,}357) = 2{,}488.9$$

Teaching hospitals take, on average, 18,098.3 more x-rays per month than public hospitals after controlling for daily patient load. The term 18,098.3 is the difference between the intercepts in equations (12.8) and (12.10). It is also the sample regression coefficient for the TEACHING indicator variable in the model.

$$15{,}741.3 - (-2{,}357) = 18{,}098.3$$

The differences in the mean numbers of x-rays taken would not change if we had used either of the following two possible codes to represent the categorical variable, hospital type:

$$\text{PRIVATE} = \begin{cases} 1 & \text{if the hospital is private} \\ 0 & \text{otherwise} \end{cases}$$

$$\text{PUBLIC} = \begin{cases} 1 & \text{if the hospital is public} \\ 0 & \text{otherwise} \end{cases}$$

$$\text{PUBLIC} = \begin{cases} 1 & \text{if the hospital is public} \\ 0 & \text{otherwise} \end{cases}$$

$$\text{TEACHING} = \begin{cases} 1 & \text{if the hospital is a teaching hospital} \\ 0 & \text{otherwise} \end{cases}$$

We should conduct follow-up studies to determine why both private and teaching hospitals take more x-rays per month than public hospitals, after controlling for the mean number of patients treated. The greater number of x-rays may be due to the differing levels of care, the type and severity of diseases treated, or the profit orientations of each hospital type.

Summary

Recognizing when to include an interaction term in a regression model is important. Consider developing a regression equation to model the following beliefs:

1. Performance on a common final exam (dependent variable) depends on a student's level of critical thinking as measured by the Watson–Glaser Critical Thinking Appraisal (quantitative predictor variable) and the type of instruction, lecture versus case method (categorical predictor variable). Students taught by the lecture method will outperform students taught by the case method by a constant amount irrespective of their level of critical thinking.

   Since we do not believe there is an interaction between the two predictor variables, the following regression model should be evaluated:

$$E(\text{PERF}) = \beta_0 + \beta_1\text{CRIT} + \beta_2\text{LECTURE}$$

   A significant indicator variable—LECTURE—means that the two types of instruction affect the dependent variable. Graphically, the intercepts of the two regression lines are different, but the slopes are the same.

   Now consider developing a regression equation to model the following beliefs:

2. Performance on a common final exam depends on a student's level of critical thinking and type of instruction. Students with low critical thinking skills will do better when taught by the lecture method. Students with high critical thinking skills will do better when taught by the case method.

   In the second situation the belief is that level of critical thinking and type of teaching interact. That is, the relationship between performance and type of teaching depends on the level of critical thinking. We should include an interaction variable, CRIT × LECTURE:

$$E(\text{PERF}) = \beta_0 + \beta_1\text{CRIT} + \beta_2\text{LECTURE} + \beta_{12}\text{CRIT} \times \text{LECTURE}$$

   A significant interaction variable means that the two regression lines are not parallel. Their slopes differ.

SECTION 12.2 EXERCISES

Use a statistical software package for all problems in this section that require calculation.

1. We believe that the number of product innovations for firms in the insurance industry is related to the firm's asset size and whether the firm is a mutual or stock company. Show two ways to code the categorical variable, type of insurance company—mutual or stock.

2. Shown are the data for a study of product innovations in the insurance industry. Code the type of insurance company as FIRM = 1 if stock company and 0 otherwise.

Firm	Number of Product Innovations Over a 3-Year Period	Asset Size	Type of Firm
1	10	500	Mutual
2	13	600	Mutual
3	14	575	Mutual
4	17	800	Mutual
5	20	1,100	Mutual
6	19	950	Mutual
7	4	400	Stock
8	7	500	Stock
9	8	700	Stock
10	10	650	Stock
11	13	950	Stock
12	14	1,000	Stock

    a. Plot asset size versus number of product innovations. Use different symbols for stock and mutual firms. Does it appear that type of firm affects the number of innovations? Does it appear that asset size affects the number of innovations?

    b. Compute and interpret a multiple regression model predicting the number of innovations using the above data (assuming no interaction term).

    c. Use the ANOVA table to determine if the overall model is significant at a .05 level. Use the hypothesis testing (computed t-value) approach to determine if the indicator predictor variable is statistically significant.

    d. Interpret the indicator variable sample regression coefficient. What does it mean? Explain it in terms that an insurance executive could understand.

3. Suppose we suspect an interaction between type of firm and asset size on the number of product innovations. Insert an interaction term into the model. That is, include an ASSET × FIRM column in the input data for the multiple regression model. Test for the presence of an interaction term using the hypothesis testing (computed t-value) approach. Use $\alpha = .05$. Explain the lack of a significant interaction term in terms that an insurance executive could understand.

4. We believe that the qualitative variable, season of the year, affects air conditioner sales. Since there are four seasons, we will need three indicator variables. We use the following indicator variables:

$$x_1 = \begin{cases} 1 & \text{if the season is winter} \\ 0 & \text{otherwise} \end{cases}$$

$$x_2 = \begin{cases} 1 & \text{if the season is spring} \\ 0 & \text{otherwise} \end{cases}$$

$$x_3 = \begin{cases} 1 & \text{if the season is fall} \\ 0 & \text{otherwise} \end{cases}$$

    a. How would we code an observation for the summer season?

    b. Suppose the population regression coefficient for the intercept is not zero, but all three other population regression coefficients are zero. Are there any seasonal effects?

5. Auto firms use two different market segmentation approaches: (1) a concentration approach and (2) a multisegment approach. Rolls Royce uses the former strategy. It sells exclusively to the super-luxury market segment. Nissan uses the multisegment approach. It sells the Sentra to the economy-minded market, the Ultima to the mainstream family market, the 300ZX to the affluent sports car enthusiasts market, and the Infinity to the luxury market segment. Show two different ways to code the market segmentation approach.

6. We believe that dollar sales volume in dress departments, SALES, depends on square footage, FEET, of the department. Larger departments tend to produce more dollar sales volume. Sales volume also depends on whether the salespeople are on commission. The presence of commission is thought to be positively related to dollar sales volume. Represent the categorical variable commission, COMM, as follows:

$$\text{COMM} = \{1 \quad \text{if the salesperson is on commission}$$
$$\{0 \quad \text{otherwise}$$

Does the following model represent our beliefs? If not, correct the model.

$$E(\text{SALES}) = \beta_0 + \beta_1 \text{FEET} + \beta_2 \text{COMM} \qquad \beta_1; \beta_2 > 0$$

7. Refer to Exercise 6. Suppose we believe that SALES depends not only on FEET and COMM but also on the interactive, or joint, effect of the two variables. Develop a proposed model that now reflects this belief. Describe the interaction term in words that a department manager could understand.

8. Draw a scatter plot that would suggest a significant interaction.

9. Here is an estimated multiple regression model.
The categorical variable, INSTRUCT, was coded as follows:

$$\text{INSTRUCT} = 1 \text{ if the case method was used, otherwise } 0$$

The quantitative predictor variable is

$$\text{CRIT} = \text{the score on a test for critical thinking}$$

$$\text{PERF-PRED} = 50 + .30\text{CRIT} + 8\text{INSTRUCT}$$

a. Predict the performance of a student who scored an 80 on the critical thinking test and whose instructor used the lecture method.
b. Predict the performance of a student who scored an 80 on the critical thinking test and whose instructor used the case method.
c. Graph critical thinking versus performance for the lecture and case method classes. Explain the graph.

10. Here is an estimated multiple regression model.
The categorical variable, INSTRUCT, was coded as follows:

$$\text{INSTRUCT} = 1 \text{ if the case method was used, otherwise } 0$$

The quantitative predictor variable is

$$\text{CRIT} = \text{the score on a test for critical thinking}$$

The interaction variable is

$$\text{CRIT} \times \text{INSTRUCT}$$

$$\text{PERF-PRED} = 50 + .30\text{CRIT} + 8\text{INSTRUCT} + .15\text{CRIT} \times \text{INSTRUCT}$$

a. Predict the performance of a student who scored an 80 on the critical thinking test and whose instructor used the lecture method.
b. Predict the performance of a student who scored an 80 on the critical thinking test and whose instructor used the case method.
c. Graph critical thinking versus performance for the lecture and case method classes and explain the graph.

11. Exercise 6 in Section 11.3 presented life insurance data for a random sample of 12 physicians in the 45–50-year-old group. The data are reproduced below for your convenience. We wish to predict amount of life insurance purchased.

Physician	Amount of Life Insurance (thousands of dollars)	Annual Income (thousands of dollars)	Marital Status
1	250	60	Single
2	350	75	Single
3	450	85	Single
4	500	110	Single
5	650	130	Single
6	800	160	Single
7	790	60	Married
8	950	80	Married
9	1,200	90	Married
10	1,300	120	Married
11	1,400	140	Married
12	1,350	150	Married

a. Develop a scatter diagram between amount of life insurance and annual income. Label each point with the marital status of the physician. Does there appear to be an interaction between the two variables, income and marital status? Explain in your own words what an interaction would mean in the context of this problem.

b. Code STATUS = 1 if single, otherwise 0. Estimate the regression model and predict

$$E(\text{AMOUNT}) = \beta_0 + \beta_1 \text{INCOME} + \beta_2 \text{STATUS} + \beta_{12} \text{INCOME} \times \text{STATUS}$$

the mean amount of insurance that will be purchased by a married physician with an annual income of $100,000. A single physician with an annual income of $100,000.

c. Test the significance of the interaction term and state your conclusions. Use $\alpha = .05$.

12.3 ≣ Nonlinear Regression

In Section 11.3, we stressed plotting each predictor variable against the dependent variable. In Section 11.6 we stressed plotting the residuals against y-pred and each predictor variable. One reason for both types of plots was to detect obvious departures from a linear relationship. In this section we consider building models similar to model (12.1)—a *second-order model* with two predictor variables—reproduced from page 672.

$$E(y) = \beta_0 + \beta_1 x_1 + \beta_{11} x_1^2 + \beta_2 x_2 + \beta_{22} x_2^2 + \beta_{12} x_1 x_2 \qquad (12.1)$$

Model (12.1) is called a second-order model because the exponents for the predictor variables are raised to the second power. The last term is called an interaction term and was discussed in the previous section. Of course, we can extend model (12.1) to include more predictor variables, x_3, x_4, ... We can also develop cubic models by including predictor variables whose exponents are raised to the third power.

Consider building a second-order model when you believe that (1) one or more predictor variables are nonlinearly related to the dependent variable or (2) the predictor variables interact to affect the dependent variable. By the end of this section, you should be able to:

1. distinguish between linear in the variables and linear in the parameters;

2. determine when quadratic terms (second-power terms) should be included in the model;
3. determine when an interaction term should be included in the model; and
4. build and interpret regression models that are nonlinear in the variables.

Scatter Diagramming and the Need for Nonlinear Models

In Chapter 11 we developed the following regression model to predict SALES (in units sold) using two predictor variables—PRICE, ADS.

$$\text{SALES-PRED} = 60.891 - .530\text{PRICE} + 3.313\text{ADS} \qquad (12.11)$$

Recall that the sample regression coefficients, 60.891, −.530, and 3.313, are estimates of the unknown population parameters—β_0, β_1, and β_2. Expression (12.11) is

1. linear in the variables,
2. linear in the parameters, and
3. additive.

It is *linear in the variables* because the implied exponent of each predictor variable is 1. It is *linear in the parameters* because no parameter estimate appears as an exponent and no exponent is multiplied or divided by another exponent. It is *additive* because the effect of ADS on SALES, β_2, does not depend on the level of the PRICE variable, and the effect of the PRICE variable on SALES, β_1, does not depend on the level of the ADS variable.

When should a model builder consider developing and evaluating a second-order model that can include PRICE^2 or ADS^2 terms or a PRICE $\times$ ADS interaction term?

Including Second-Order Terms   Consider including second-order terms— PRICE^2 or ADS^2—when common sense or scatter diagrams suggest that the relationship between a predictor and dependent variable is not linear. Panel (a) in Figure 12.6 shows that as PRICE increases, SALES drop rapidly at first and then level off. Panel (b) in Figure 12.6 shows that as ADS increase, SALES increase rapidly at first and then level off. These scatter diagrams suggest that PRICE^2 and ADS^2 terms should be added to regression model (12.11). Later we discuss how to determine if the quadratic terms are necessary; that is, how to evaluate the model statistically.

Including an Interaction Term   Consider including an interaction term—PRICE $\times$ ADS—when common sense suggests that the effect of one predictor variable on the dependent variable *depends* on the level of at least one other predictor variable. For example, suppose we believe

1. increasing the number of ads will increase SALES rapidly for high PRICE levels, and
2. increasing the number of ads will increase SALES moderately or not at all for low PRICE levels.

The effect of ADS on SALES *depends* on the level of PRICE. This suggests a PRICE $\times$ ADS interaction term should be added to model (12.11). Later we discuss how to test if the interaction term is statistically significant.

Also consider including an interaction term when a scatter diagram suggests an interaction. The data in Table 12.6 illustrate the graphical method.

FIGURE 12.6   Inclusion of Quadratic Terms

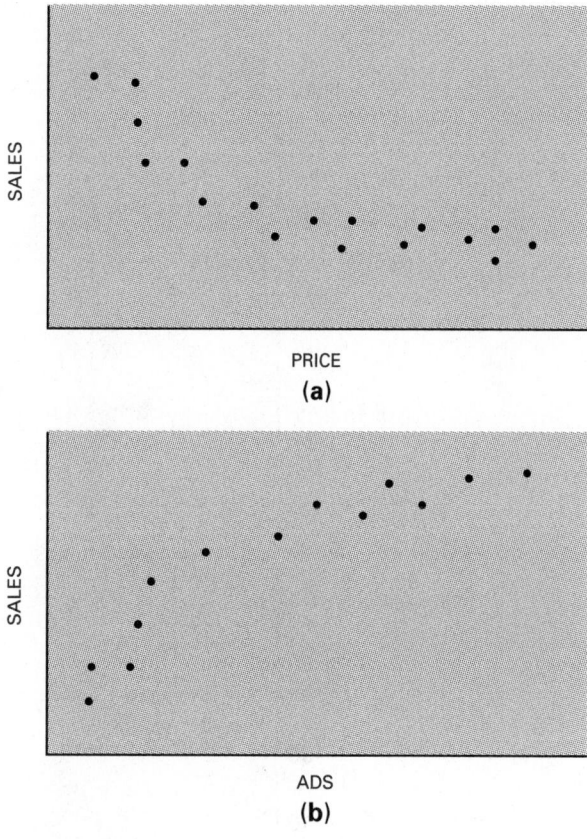

Table 12.6

Data Set to Illustrate Interaction between
Predictor Variables, PRICE and ADS

SALES	PRICE	ADS
100	$70	1
90	80	2
110	90	3
120	50	3
160	75	4
130	45	5

Begin by plotting one predictor variable against the dependent variable. Panel (a) of Figure 12.7 shows ADS versus SALES. Then determine the median value for the second predictor variable, PRICE. The median value for the six price values is halfway between $70 and $75, or $72.50. For each data point in panel (a), determine if the price level was less than or greater than the median price value of $72.50. If the price was less than the median, replace the dot symbol in panel (a) with a minus sign. If the price was more than the median, replace the dot symbol in panel (a) with a plus sign.

FIGURE 12.7   Inclusion of Interaction Term

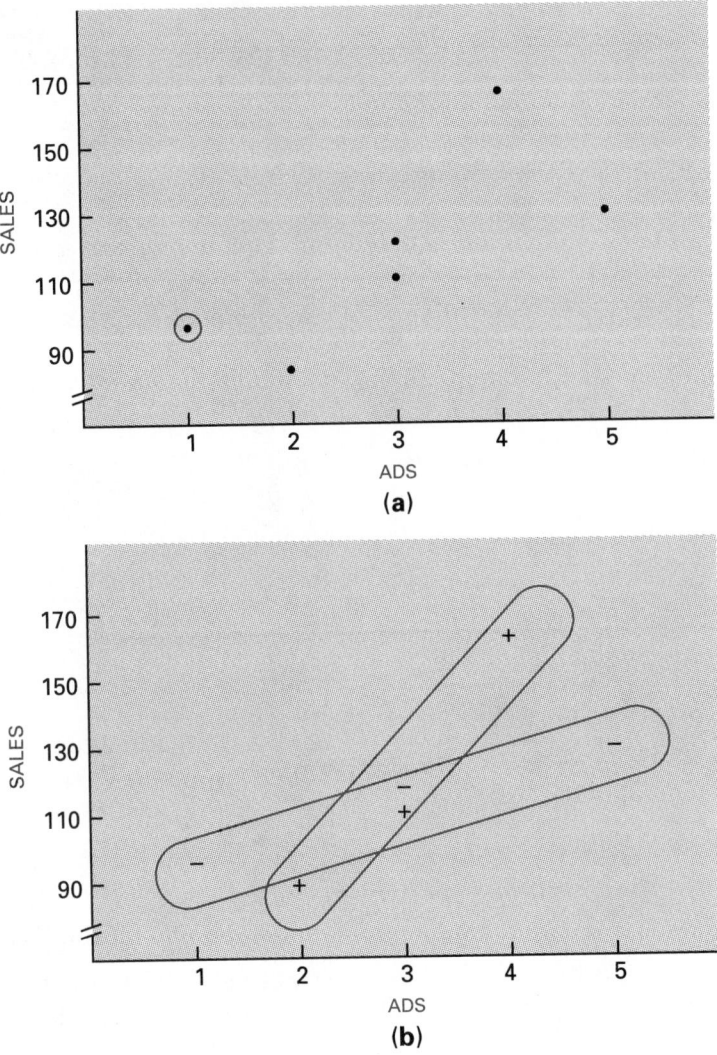

(a)

(b)

For example, the circled data point in panel (a) represents the ADS-SALES observation (1,100). The PRICE value for this observation was $70, which is below the median value of $72.50. Replace the dot symbol with a minus sign.

Now see panel (b) in Figure 12.7. Note for high (+) PRICE values, increasing the number of ads has a dramatic effect on SALES; note the steep slope. For low (−) PRICE values, increasing the number of ads has only a moderate effect on SALES; note the gradual slope. The slopes of the two clusters are different. And as you learned in the previous section, this suggests that we should include a PRICE × ADS interaction term for model (12.11).

Warning: Scatter diagrams can be misleading, especially when squared terms are also in the model. Thus, consider quadratic or interaction terms when the combination of scatter diagrams and your knowledge of the subject area suggest the presence of at least one of the higher-order terms.

Building and Evaluating Nonlinear Models

Here we discuss how to build and evaluate a second-order model with two predictor variables.

Example: COMCEL Car Phone Study (Revisited)   Since the introduction of its car phone, COMCEL has experienced increased competition from retail chains and outlets selling competing brands. COMCEL managers want to assess the effect of price and advertising spending on unit sales. They believe that the number of units sold depends on the price they set relative to their competitors' average price. Since they can't ask their competitors to vary their prices, COMCEL must perform a correlational study rather than an experimental study. COMCEL has kept records of its price, its advertising expenditures, and the average price of its competitors in 30 different market areas for the latest quarter of the year. COMCEL sets a .05 significance level. The data appear in Table 12.7.

Table 12.7

COMCEL Car Phone Sales Correlational Study

MKT	DEMAND (thousands of units)	PRICE	AVGPRICE	PDIFF	ADV (thousands of dollars)	ADV^2	PDIFF $\times$ ADV
1	80	65	75	10	85	7225	850
2	150	80	100	20	130	16900	2600
3	115	110	110	0	130	16900	0
4	91	75	95	20	70	4900	1400
5	50	80	90	10	50	2500	500
6	140	70	60	−10	153	23409	−1530
7	135	75	77	2	130	16900	260
8	40	100	89	−11	90	8100	−990
9	150	75	85	10	140	19600	1400
10	90	80	69	−11	125	15625	−1375
11	160	70	90	20	150	22500	3000
12	170	65	75	10	150	22500	1500
13	70	75	73	−2	90	8100	−180
14	95	75	95	20	90	8100	1800
15	35	75	66	−9	70	4900	−630
16	170	65	55	−10	155	24025	−1550
17	65	50	60	10	70	4900	700
18	59	60	51	−9	110	12100	−990
19	79	60	80	20	50	2500	1000
20	160	70	70	0	150	22500	0
21	120	80	70	−10	140	19600	−1400
22	131	60	80	20	115	13225	2300
23	91	80	80	0	110	12100	0
24	185	85	90	5	165	27225	825
25	180	89	90	1	165	27225	165
26	140	88	88	0	142	20164	0
27	51	88	90	2	75	5625	150
28	110	90	100	10	110	12100	1100
29	39	95	95	0	55	3025	0
30	15	100	90	−10	50	2500	−500

The dependent variable is DEMAND, and COMCEL selects the following four predictor variables.

1. PDIFF, which represents the competitions' average price minus COMCEL's price for the equivalent phone. COMCEL believes that DEMAND depends on the *difference* between its price and its competitors' average price.
2. ADV, which represents advertising expenditures.
3. ADV^2, which represents the quadratic term for the ADV predictor variable. A scatter plot of ADV (not shown) suggested including this quadratic term.
4. PDIFF × ADV, which represents the interaction term between the two predictor variables. COMCEL believes that the effectiveness of advertising dollars depends on the difference between its price and those of its competitors. Thus, an interaction term was added.
5. COMCEL did not include a PDIFFSQ predictor variable because there did not appear to be a nonlinear relationship between PDIFF and DEMAND.

COMCEL thus decided to fit the following model, using the boxed data in Table 12.7. The goal was to test the significance of the PDIFF × ADV interaction term.

$$E(\text{DEMAND}) = \beta_0 + \beta_1 \text{PDIFF} + \beta_2 \text{ADV} + \beta_{22} \text{ADV}^2 + \beta_{12} \text{PDIFF} \times \text{ADV} \qquad (12.12)$$

Expression (12.12) is a second-order model. It *is not* linear in the predictor variables (the exponent for the ADV variable is raised to the second power), but *it is* linear in the parameters. The linear in the parameters property allows us to use the least squares method to estimate the β_0, β_1, β_2, β_{22}, and β_{12} coefficients in model (12.12).

Table 12.8 shows the parameter estimates. The best estimate of model (12.12) is

$$\begin{aligned} \text{DEMAND-PRED} = {} & 23.969 + 2.879\text{PDIFF} - .141\text{ADV} \\ & + .007\text{ADV}^2 - .012\text{PDIFF} \times \text{ADV} \end{aligned} \qquad (12.13)$$

The variance ratio of 270.204 from the ANOVA table (not shown) has a p-value of much less than .001. The coefficient of multiple determination is 97.74%, and the standard error of the estimate is 7.923, or 7,923 units.

The PDIFF × ADV interaction term is statistically significant. From Table 12.8, its computed t-value has a p-value of .0046. Since the p-value is less than $\alpha = .05$, we conclude that β_{12} is not zero.

Table 12.8

Parameter Estimate Section for COMCEL Data

VARIABLE	PARAMETER ESTIMATE	STANDARD ERROR	t-VALUE	TWO-TAILED p-VALUE
INTERCEPT	23.969	—	—	—
PDIFF	2.879	.4292	6.71	$p < .001$
ADV	-.141	.2821	-.50	$p > .30$
ADV2	.007	.0013	5.14	$p < .001$
PDIFF × ADV	-.012	.0038	-3.14	$p = .0046$

FIGURE 12.8   Effect of Advertising on Demand at Two Levels of Price Difference

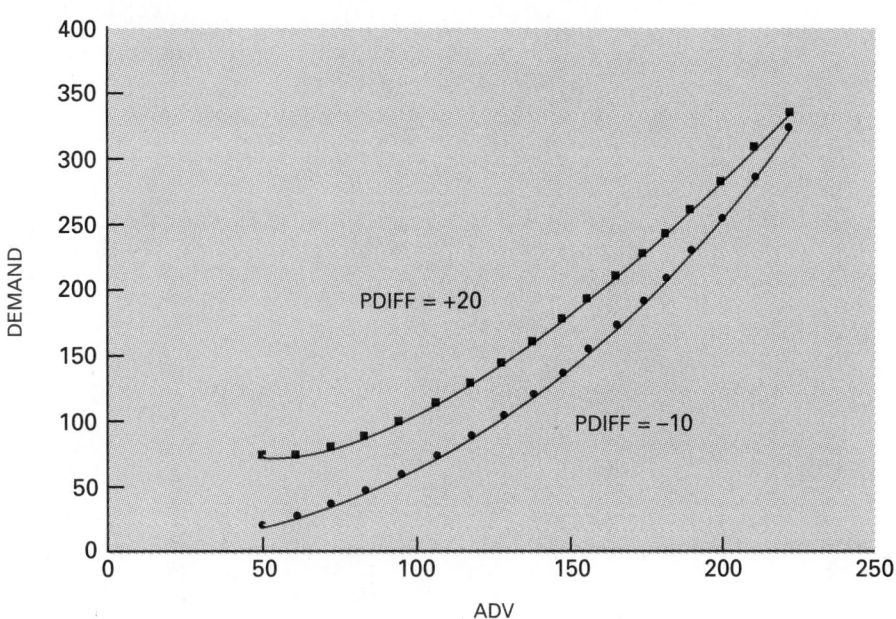

When PDIFF is negative, COMCEL's price is higher than its competitors'.

What does the statistically significant interaction mean? Figure 12.8 is a graph of ADV versus DEMAND when PDIFF = −$10 and when PDIFF = $20. We obtained Figure 12.8 as follows:

1. We inserted PDIFF = +20 into expression (12.13). Then we plotted DEMAND versus ADV for values of advertising from 50 to 220. See the upper curve in Figure 12.8.
2. We inserted PDIFF = −10 into expression (12.13). Then we plotted DEMAND versus ADV for values of advertising from 50 to 220. See the lower curve in Figure 12.8.

Recall that PDIFF = AVGPRICE − PRICE. So when PDIFF = −$10, COMCEL's price is 10 dollars higher than its competitors' average price. When PDIFF = $20, COMCEL's price is 20 dollars lower than its competitors' average price.

From Figure 12.8, when COMCEL's price is higher than the average competitors' price, advertising is more effective at increasing demand (note the steepness of the curve) than when COMCEL's price is lower than the average price. As advertising increases, demand increases faster than when PDIFF = 20. When COMCEL is $20 below the average price of its competitors, purchasers do not need further convincing to purchase from COMCEL, rather than its competitors.

In summary, consider including for evaluation quadratic or interaction terms into a regression model. Base your decision on either common sense or scatter diagrams. Sometimes your knowledge of the field alone suggests that one or more predictor variables are nonlinearly related to a dependent variable. Nevertheless, always plot each predictor variable against the dependent variable and look for departures from linearity.

SECTION 12.3 EXERCISES

Use a statistical software package for all problems in this section that require calculation.

1. Are the following models linear in the variables, linear in the parameters, neither or both?
   a. $E(y) = \beta_0 + \beta_1 x_1 + \beta_2 x_2$
   b. $E(y) = \beta_0 + \beta_1 x_1 + \beta_2 x_2 + \beta_{11} x_1^2$
   c. $E(y) = \beta_0 e^{\beta_1 x_1} + \beta_2 x_2$
   d. $E(y) = \beta_0 + \beta_1 x_1 + \beta_2 x_2 + \beta_{12} x_1 x_2$

2. Check each data set below to determine if quadratic or interaction terms are reasonable and should be added to a first-order model. Draw two graphs similar to Figure 12.7 to examine for a possible interaction. Plot a scatter diagram of x_1 versus y and develop the plus and minus signs based on the x_2 variable.

a. y	x_1	x_2		b. y	x_1	x_2		c. y	x_1	x_2
1	1	10		1	1	3		4	1	3
10	1	25		0	1	5		6	2	5
3	2	13		9	3	9		11	4	9
9	2	30		10	3	31		10	3	14
5	3	11		24	5	27		17	5	20
5.5	3	21		26	5	28		26	7	28
8	4	16		48	7	50		20	6	30
2	4	24		50	7	60		19	6	17
10	5	17		78	9	14		25	8	32
1	5	29		81	9	81		30	9	35

3. What is a major disadvantage of relying solely on scatter diagrams to assess whether quadratic or interaction terms should be included in a model for evaluation?

4. Shown is a small data set on test performance and study time for a sample of 12 students.

TIME	30	35	60	70	120	130	180	195	240	250	300	290

PERF	40	50	45	65	65	75	85	83	88	92	80	95

   a. Is there any theoretical reason to suggest that a curvilinear model is appropriate? Plot the data to check your reasoning.
   b. Estimate the model

   $$E(\text{PERF}) = \beta_0 + \beta_1 \text{TIME} + \beta_{11} \text{TIME}^2$$

   and test the significance of the quadratic term. Use $\alpha = .10$.

5. Recall from Chapter 11 that a model should not be used if any of the assumptions of the regression model are violated. Suppose that you did not plot the data in Exercise 4, and fit a linear instead of a quadratic model to the data.
   a. How would a residual analysis tell you that a curvilinear model was more appropriate?
   b. Verify your answer in **a** by fitting a linear model to the data in Exercise 4 and by performing a residual analysis.

6. Shown are the results of an experimental regression study to study the effect of closeness of supervision on different levels of salaried employees. The dependent variable is job SATISfaction measured from 1 (low) to 10 (high), and the two predictor variables are SALARY and CLOSEness of supervision measured from 1 (low) to 10 (high).

SATIS (1 to 10)	SALARY (thousands of dollars)	CLOSE (1 to 10)
1	20	1
2.5	20	5
3.5	20	10
1.5	25	1
3.5	25	5
4.5	25	10
5.1	30	1
5.0	30	5
5.2	30	10
7.5	35	1
6.5	35	5
5.5	35	10
9.5	40	1
8.5	40	5
7.5	40	10

a. Plot SALARY against SATISfaction. Plot CLOSEness against SATISfaction. Does there appear to be a curvilinear relationship between either predictor variables and SATISfaction?

b. Estimate the regression model

$$E(\text{SATIS}) = \beta_0 + \beta_1\text{SALARY} + \beta_{11}\text{SALARY}^2 + \beta_2\text{CLOSE} + \beta_{12}\text{SALARY} \times \text{CLOSE}$$

and test the significance of the interaction term implied by the manager's hypothesis. Use $\alpha = .01$.

c. Plot the estimated regression equation by setting CLOSEness of supervision = 1 and varying SALARY.

d. Plot the estimated regression equation setting CLOSEness of supervision = 10 and varying SALARY.

e. Explain what the interaction means in managerial terms.

12.4 ≣ The Extra Sum of Squares Principle and the General Linear Test

Model building is a process of determining (1) which predictor variables to include in a regression equation and (2) whether to include first-order, quadratic, and interaction terms.

Model building determines which predictor variables to include in a regression equation. For example, we want to predict managers' salaries. We already know that education level and years on the job affect salaries and thus should be included in the model. Should race and gender *also* be included? That is: Are salary, race, and gender related after controlling for the impact of education level and years on the job?

Model building also involves choosing the functional form of a regression equation. For example, a model contains only first-order terms. Should quadratic and interaction terms *also* be included? Are quadratic and interaction terms necessary after controlling for the impact of the first-order terms?

The analysis of variance cannot answer these two questions. It tests if an overall model is significant, or worth using. The hypothesis test (Section 12.2) on a single predictor variable cannot answer the questions. It can test if salary or race are related after controlling for the impact of education and years on the job. Or it can test if one quadratic term should be included in a model. But to answer both questions a model builder would have to perform multiple tests. And you learned in Section 11.5 that performing repeated tests using a constant significance level increases the probability of making at least one Type I error, i.e, concluding that a variable is significant when it is not.

In this section we present a third, and very powerful, test procedure called the *general linear test*. Managers use it to test whether one predictor variable or a *group of predictor variables* is statistically significant. The general linear test can determine if *both* race and gender or if the *group* of quadratic and interaction terms are statistically significant. By the end of this section, you should be able to:

1. explain what extra sum of squares measures;
2. compute extra sum of squares;
3. develop the null and alternative hypotheses to test if one or more predictor variables are related to a dependent variable after controlling for the impact of other predictor variables already in the model; and
4. test the significance of portions of a regression model, using the general linear test.

We illustrate the extra sum of squares principle and the general linear test in the following example.

Example: Salary Determinant Study   COMCEL conducts an annual sample survey to determine the factors that affect salary. COMCEL also seeks to ensure that males/females and whites/nonwhites who have the same qualifications are receiving the same compensation.

COMCEL selects a random sample of 50 employees and matches the salary of each employee with biographical factors, other than gender and race, that should be related to the employee's salary. Table 12.9 lists the dependent variable and potential predictor variables.

Table 12.9

Dependent and Predictor Variables

Predictor Variable	How Measured
YEARS	Number of years at COMCEL
EDUC	Years of formal education
GENDER	Indicator variable: 1 if male, 0 if female
RACE	Indicator variable: 1 if white, 0 if nonwhite

Dependent Variable	
SALARY	Yearly compensation, in thousands of dollars

Unlike the marketing study presented in Chapter 11, COMCEL cannot vary the predictor variables to study their effects on SALARY. COMCEL must conduct a correlational study using available data within the firm. See the Appendix of Chapter 11 for the data set.

The Extra Sum of Squares Principle

We illustrate the extra sum of squares principle by computing three regression models using the variables described above.

Model A:	SALARY $= f$(EDUC)	50 observations with EDUC as the only predictor variable
Model B:	SALARY $= f$(YEARS, EDUC)	50 observations with two predictor variables
Model C:	SALARY $= f$(YEARS)	50 observations with YEARS as the only predictor variable

Table 12.10 shows the decomposition of the total sum of squares for the three separate regression analyses. Recall that the regression sum of squares, SSR, is the portion of the total variation of the dependent variable, SST, that is accounted for or "explained by" the predictor variables in the model. This definition is essential to understanding the extra sum of squares idea.

Table 12.10

Results of Three Separate Regressions on the Salary Data

	Model	SSR	SSE	SST
A	EDUC	6,863.05	3,467.32	10,330.37
B	EDUC, YEARS	8,572.34	1,758.03	10,330.37
C	YEARS	3,232.43	7,097.94	10,330.37

In model A, we regressed SALARY on EDUCation alone. The regression sum of squares was 6,863.05, and the error sum of squares was 3,467.32.

When SALARY was regressed on EDUC and YEARS (model B), the regression sum of squares increased to 8,572.34. The difference between 6,863.05 and 8,572.34, or 1,709.29, measures the impact of adding the YEARS predictor variable to a regression model that already included the EDUC variable. We use the following notation to represent the additional regression sum of squares.

$$\text{SSR(YEARS}|\text{EDUC)} = \text{SSR(EDUC, YEARS)} - \text{SSR(EDUC)}$$

$$= 8{,}572.34 - 6{,}863.05$$

$$= 1{,}709.29 \text{ units of variation}$$

SSR(YEARS|EDUC) is called the *extra sum of squares* due to the YEARS predictor variable. It is the *marginal effect* of introducing the YEARS predictor variable into the model after the EDUC predictor variable was in the model and has been controlled for. In other words, after EDUC was in the model, YEARS accounts for an *additional* 1,709.29 units of variation. Computing extra sums of squares is essential to the general linear test.

In general, to compute the extra sum of squares, $\text{SSR}(x_1, x_2 \ldots | x_k, x_{k+1} \ldots)$, you must compute two regression sums of squares:

1. $\text{SSR}(x_1, x_2, \ldots, x_k, x_{k+1}, \ldots)$ A model with all the predictor variables

2. $\text{SSR}(x_k, x_{k+1}, \ldots)$ A model with only the $x_k, x_{k+1}, \ldots$
                                                          predictor variables.

$$\text{SSR}(x_1, x_2, \ldots | x_k, x_{k+1}, \ldots) = \text{SSR}(x_1, x_2, \ldots, x_k, x_{k+1}, \ldots)$$
$$- \text{SSR}(x_k, x_{k+1}, \ldots) \qquad (12.14)$$

where the left-hand term is the *extra sum of squares due to the $x_1, x_2, \ldots$ predictor variables.*

Note one thing more. Compare the extra sum of squares due to YEARS against the regression sum of squares when SALARY was regressed on YEARS alone (model C). Please note that

$$\text{SSR}(\text{YEARS} | \text{EDUC}) < \text{SSR}(\text{YEARS})$$

$$1{,}709.29 < 3{,}232.43.$$

With EDUC already in the model, YEARS explains only 1,709 units of variation. Without EDUC in the model, YEARS explains 3,232 units of variation. The regression sum of squares for YEARS after EDUC is controlled for accounts for much less of the total variation than it did when SALARY was regressed on YEARS alone. Thus, the explanatory power of the YEARS predictor variable depends on whether the EDUC predictor variable is already in the model.

Key Lesson: The extra sum of squares principle tells us that the explanatory power of a predictor variable depends on which other predictor variables are already in the model and thus have been controlled for.

Why aren't SSR(YEARS|EDUC) and SSR(YEARS) the same? Here is the reason. The two predictor variables, EDUC and YEARS, are correlated (Use a statistical software package to verify that the simple correlation, $r_{\text{EDUC, YEARS}}$, is .197). In model A, where we regressed SALARY on EDUC, some of the impact of YEARS on SALARY was already accounted for because EDUC and YEARS are related.

Although we will not illustrate the principle until the next section, the greater the correlation among pairs of predictor variables, the smaller the extra sum of squares will be. That is, if YEARS and EDUC had been highly correlated, say $r_{\text{EDUC, YEARS}}$ = .80, then SSR(YEARS|EDUC) would have been much less than SSR(YEARS). If the two predictor variables had not been related at all, then

$$\text{SSR}(\text{YEARS} | \text{EDUC}) = \text{SSR}(\text{YEARS})$$

In summary, the extra sum of squares measures the *marginal effect* of introducing one or more predictor variables into a model after one or more different predictor variables are already in the model. The extra sum of squares principle tells us that the explanatory power of one or more predictor variables depends on which other predictor variables are already in the model and thus have been controlled for.

Tests that Some Population Regression Coefficients Equal Zero

We return now to the COMCEL salary study. Remember, the goal was to determine if there is evidence of gender or race discrimination in compensation. Common sense tells us to include the EDUC and YEARS predictor variables in the salary determination model. Irrespective of a person's race or gender, education and number of years with a firm generally affect salary.

The key question is: With EDUC and YEARS already in the model, does adding GENDER and RACE to the model significantly improve its explanatory power?

Thus, we will compare the SSR for a model with only EDUC and YEARS to a model with all four predictor variables. The model with all four predictor variables is called the *full model*. The model with a subset of predictor variables is called the *restricted model*. Both are shown here:

Full model $\qquad \beta_0 + \beta_1\text{YEARS} + \beta_2\text{EDUC} + \beta_3\text{GENDER} + \beta_4\text{RACE}$

Restricted model $\qquad \beta_0 + \beta_1\text{YEARS} + \beta_2\text{EDUC}$

The goal is to determine if there is evidence of gender or race discrimination in compensation. This translates into a test of the following null and alternative hypotheses (in symbols and words):

H_0: $\beta_3 = \beta_4 = 0$ — GENDER and RACE are not statistically related to SALARY after controlling for EDUC and YEARS. Do not change salary administration policies.

H_1: Not both β_3 and β_4 equal 0 — Gender and/or race are statistically related to SALARY after controlling for YEARS and EDUC. COMCEL should examine its salary administration policies. It may be violating the law.

The significance level, α, equals .05.

COMCEL generated two ANOVA tables—one for the full model and one for the restricted model—using the appropriate data from Chapter 11, Appendix A. Shown below are abbreviated ANOVA outputs for both models. We have included only the information necessary to test the null hypothesis that $\beta_3 = \beta_4 = 0$.

The test of the null hypothesis follows the sequence underlying the analysis of variance. The analysis involves:

1. computing the appropriate extra sum of squares,
2. converting the extra sum of squares into the extra mean square,
3. computing a variance ratio, and
4. comparing the computed variance ratio against the critical value found in Appendix 7.

Begin by computing the extra sum of squares due to the GENDER and RACE predictor variables. For the salary study, expression (12.14) becomes:

SSR(GENDER, RACE | EDUC, YEARS) = SSR(GENDER, RACE, EDUC, YEARS) − SSR(EDUC, YEARS)

SSR(GENDER, RACE | EDUC, YEARS) = 8,601.53 − 8,572.34 = 29.19

That is, after controlling for EDUC and YEARS, adding RACE and GENDER to the model only increased the regression sum of squares by 29.19 units.

Table 12.11

ANOVA Outputs for Full and Restricted Models

Full Model: EDUC, YEARS, GENDER, RACE

Source of Variation	Sum of Squares	df	Mean Square	Variance Ratio
Regression (SSR)	8,601.53	4		
Error	1,728.84	45	38.42	
Total	10,330.37	49		

Restricted Model: EDUC, YEARS

Source of Variation	Sum of Squares	df	Mean Square	Variance Ratio
Regression (SSR)	8,572.34	2		
Error		47		
Total	10,330.37	49		

To compute the extra mean square, we must divide the extra sum of squares by its degrees of freedom. Going from the restricted to the full model gained 29.19 units. However, we lost 2 degrees of freedom, $47 - 45$. Thus the extra MSR is simply

$$\text{MSR}(\text{GENDER, RACE} | \text{EDUC, YEARS}) = 29.19/2 = 14.595.$$

Next we compare the extra MSR with the variance due to all other predictor variables not yet included in the full model. From Table 12.11, MSE for the full model is 38.42.

The variance ratio, or F^* as it is more commonly known, is simply

$$F^* = \frac{14.595}{38.42} = .38$$

Finally, we compare F^* to the F-values found in Appendix 7. Recall from Chapter 11 that to reject the null hypothesis, the test statistic must be significantly larger than one. The decision rule specifies the size of the test statistic, the *critical value,* that will cause us to reject the null hypothesis.

The *decision rule for the general linear test* is

If F^* is greater than $F[(1 - \alpha); \text{df}(R) - \text{df}(F), \text{df}(F)]$ reject the null hypothesis.

where   df (R) = the error degrees of freedom associated with the restricted model

df (F) = the error degrees of freedom associated with the full model

α is the significance level

$F[(1 - \alpha); \text{df}(R) - \text{df}(F), \text{df}(F)$ is the critical value

Since $.38 < F[.95; 2, 45] = 3.24$ (interpolated from Appendix 7), we cannot reject the null hypothesis. We do not have enough evidence to conclude that GENDER and RACE affect SALARY after controlling for EDUC and YEARS.

To summarize, there are four steps in the general linear test.

1. Fit the *full* model and record the regression sum of squares, SSR(F) and mean square error, MSE(F).
2. Fit the *restricted* model and record the regression sum of squares, SSR(R)
3. Compute the F^* statistic

$$F^* = \frac{\dfrac{SSR(F) - SSR(R)}{df(R) - df(F)}}{MSE(F)} \tag{12.15}$$

4. Use the decision rule to evaluate the null hypothesis.

Logic of the F^* Test   Adding predictor variables to a regression model will always increase the regression sum of squares, SSR, and decrease the error sum of squares, SSE. How big is the increase in SSR? Is the increase in the resulting MSR greater than merely chance variation? The MSE from the full model is the best estimate of chance variation. That is why in expression (12.15) we compare the extra mean square to the MSE from the full model.

1. If the additional predictor variables are unrelated to the dependent variable, the F^* will be less than the critical value.
2. If one or more of the additional predictor variables are related to the dependent variable after controlling for the variables already in the model, the F^* will be greater than the critical value.

We conclude this section by illustrating how to use the general linear test to determine if the quadratic terms and the interaction term are necessary in a regression model with two predictor variables. The full model for two predictor variables is

$$\text{Full model: } E(y) = \beta_0 + \beta_1 x_1 + \beta_{11} x_1^2 + \beta_2 x_2 + \beta_{22} x_2^2 + \beta_{12} x_1 x_2$$

Are the x_1^2, x_2^2, and $x_1 x_2$ terms needed in the model? The null and alternative hypotheses are:

$$H_0: \beta_{11} = \beta_{22} = \beta_{12} = 0$$

$$H_1: \text{Not all three } \beta_{ij} \text{ equal } 0$$

Thus, the restricted model is

$$\text{Restricted model: } E(y) = \beta_0 + \beta_1 x_1 + \beta_2 x_2$$

Then we use expression (12.15) to determine the F^* test statistic and compare it to the critical value from Appendix 7. If we reject the null hypothesis, the restricted model should not be used for prediction. At least one of the second-order terms should be included in the model.

The confidence interval on a single predictor variable (Section 11.5) and the hypothesis testing approach (Section 12.2) are special cases of the general linear test*. What this practically means is this. To test if a single predictor variable should be in the model, you have three approaches:

1. Use the hypothesis test approach. If the t-value's associated p-value is greater than α, delete the predictor variable from the model.
2. Use the confidence interval method. Construct a confidence interval on β_i using expression (11.19). If the confidence interval includes zero, delete the predictor variable from the model.
3. Use the general linear test and evaluate two models:

Full   Includes all predictor variables

Restricted   Includes all predictor variables except the variable you wish to test.

If $F^* < F[(1 - \alpha); \text{df (R)} - \text{df (F)}, \text{df (F)}]$, delete the predictor variable from the full model.

The three approaches are equivalent; all are *marginal approaches.* All assess the impact of one predictor variable on a dependent variable after controlling for all the other predictor variables already in the model. However, the general linear test can also test if a *group of predictor variables* is statistically related to the dependent variable.

The general linear test is a powerful model-building approach. It helps determine the model's predictor variables and functional form. Use the general linear test to test if one or a group of predictor variables can be eliminated from a model.

SECTION 12.4 EXERCISES

Use a statistical software package for all problems in this section that require calculation.

1. Refer to the data set in Appendix A, Chapter 11. Compute the SSR for the following seven models.

   a. $E(\text{SALARY}) = \beta_0 + \beta_1\text{EDUC}$

   b. $E(\text{SALARY}) = \beta_0 + \beta_1\text{YEARS}$

   c. $E(\text{SALARY}) = \beta_0 + \beta_1\text{GENDER}$

   d. $E(\text{SALARY}) = \beta_0 + \beta_1\text{RACE}$

   e. $E(\text{SALARY}) = \beta_0 + \beta_1\text{EDUC} + \beta_2\text{GENDER}$

   f. $E(\text{SALARY}) = \beta_0 + \beta_1\text{YEARS} + \beta_2\text{EDUC} + \beta_3\text{GENDER}$

   g. $E(\text{SALARY}) = \beta_0 + \beta_1\text{YEARS} + \beta_2\text{EDUC} + \beta_3\text{GENDER} + \beta_4\text{RACE}$

2. Refer to Exercise 1. Compute the following extra sum of squares.
   a. (1) SSR(RACE|EDUC, YEARS, GENDER)
   (2) SSR(YEARS|EDUC, GENDER)
   (3) SSR(GENDER|EDUC)
   (4) SSR(EDUC|GENDER)
   (5) SSR(EDUC, GENDER|RACE)

* See Neter, Wasserman, and Kutner (1990) for the proof.

b. Given the regression sums of squares in Exercise 1, can you compute the following extra sums of squares? Why not?

$$SSR(\text{EDUC, GENDER}|\text{RACE, YEARS})$$

$$SSR(\text{YEARS, GENDER}|\text{RACE, EDUC})$$

3. Refer to Exercise 2, part **a.** Explain in nontechnical language what the five extra sum of squares represent.

4. Refer to Exercise 1 and Exercise 2, part **a.**
   a. Note that SSR(GENDER|EDUC) does not equal SSR(GENDER). Compute the simple correlation between GENDER and EDUC. Are the two predictor variable related? Explain why the two regression sum of squares given above are different.
   b. Note that SSR(YEARS|EDUC, GENDER) does not equal SSR(YEARS). Compute the three simple correlations among EDUC, GENDER, and YEARS. Are the three predictor variables related? Explain why the two regression sum of squares given above are different.

5. Shown here are two small data sets. Data set A contains two predictor variables that are not correlated. Data set B contains two predictor variables that are highly correlated. This exercise will demonstrate the impact of highly correlated predictor variables on the extra sum of squares.

<table>
<tr><td colspan="3">Data Set A
Uncorrelated Data Set</td><td colspan="3">Data Set B
Correlated Data Set</td></tr>
<tr><th>SALES</th><th>PRICE</th><th>ADS</th><th>SALES</th><th>PRICE</th><th>ADS</th></tr>
<tr><td>8</td><td>1</td><td>2</td><td>8</td><td>1</td><td>2</td></tr>
<tr><td>10</td><td>1</td><td>6</td><td>10</td><td>2</td><td>4</td></tr>
<tr><td>13</td><td>3</td><td>4</td><td>11</td><td>3</td><td>3</td></tr>
<tr><td>11</td><td>5</td><td>2</td><td>13</td><td>4</td><td>6</td></tr>
<tr><td>17</td><td>5</td><td>6</td><td>17</td><td>5</td><td>8</td></tr>
</table>

   a. Verify that PRICE and ADS in data set A are not correlated by computing the simple correlation coefficient.
   b. Compute SSR(PRICE, ADS), SSR(PRICE), and SSR(ADS).
   c. Compute SSR(PRICE|ADS), the extra sum of squares due to PRICE.
   d. Compare SSR(PRICE|ADS) to SSR(PRICE). Are they equal?
   e. Verify that PRICE and ADS in data set B are highly correlated by computing the simple correlation coefficient.
   f. Compute SSR(PRICE, ADS), SSR(PRICE), and SSR(ADS).
   g. Compute SSR(PRICE|ADS), the extra sum of squares due to PRICE.
   h. Compare SSR(PRICE|ADS) to SSR(PRICE). Are they equal?
   i. Based on your answers to parts **d** and **h,** what can you conclude?

6. **a.** You wish to determine the impact of RACE on SALARY after controlling for EDUC, YEARS, and GENDER. In words only, state the null and alternative hypotheses. What terms must the full and restricted models include to test the null hypothesis?
   b. You wish to determine the impact of FIRMSIZE on MONTHS needed to implement new administrative practices after controlling for FIRMTYPE. In words only, state the null and alternative hypotheses. What terms will the full and restricted models include to test the null hypothesis?
   c. You wish to determine the impact of the quadratic terms for two predictor variables, ADV and SPACE, on DEMAND after including first-order terms in the model. In words only, state the null and alternative hypotheses. What terms will the full and restricted models include to test the null hypothesis?

7. Determine the critical value for the following general linear tests:
   a. Sample size equals 20
   FULL model contains four predictor variables
   RESTRICTED model contains two predictor variables
   $\alpha = .05$

b. Sample size equals 30
  FULL model contains five predictor variables
  RESTRICTED model contains two predictor variables
  $\alpha = .005$

c. Sample size equals 70
  FULL model contains nine predictor variables
  RESTRICTED model contains four predictor variables
  $\alpha = .01$

8. Refer to Appendix A, Chapter 11, for data. Use the general linear test to determine if RACE and GENDER affect SALARY after controlling for EDUC and YEARS. Let $\alpha = .05$.

9. Refer to Appendix A, Chapter 11, for data. Let $\alpha = .05$.
  a. Use the hypothesis test to determine if RACE affects SALARY after controlling for GENDER, EDUC, YEARS, EXPER, and MANAG.
  b. Use expression (11.19) to construct a confidence interval on the population regression coefficient for the RACE predictor variable.
  c. Use the general linear test to determine if RACE affects SALARY after controlling for GENDER, EDUC, YEARS, EXPER, and MANAG.
  d. Show that the F^* test statistic from part **c** equals the square of the t-test statistic from part **a.**

10. An experimental study was conducted to determine the effects of size of product run and age of equipment on unit cost.

Cost per Unit	Size of Production Run (thousands)	Age of Equipment (years)
$1.50	10	1
1.60	10	1
1.75	10	3
1.75	10	3
2.10	10	5
2.00	10	5
1.50	6.7	1
1.50	6.7	1
1.65	6.7	3
1.75	6.7	3
2.10	6.7	5
2.20	6.7	5
2.25	3.3	1
2.35	3.3	1
2.50	3.3	3
2.60	3.3	3
2.75	3.3	5
2.75	3.3	5

  a. Plot each independent variable against the dependent variable. Do either of the independent variables, RUNSIZE or AGE, appear to be related to the dependent variable, UNITCOST? If so, are the relationships linear?
  b. Estimate the regression model

$$E(\text{UNITCOST}) = \beta_0 + \beta_1\text{RUNSIZE} + \beta_{11}\text{RUNSIZE}^2 + \beta_2\text{AGE} + \beta_{22}\text{AGE}^2$$

  and test the significance of the age variables, AGE and AGE^2, using the general linear test. Use $\alpha = .05$. What conclusion can you draw from conducting the test?
  c. In Chapter 11 we presented the absolute t-value method for building a predictive model. We stated that only one variable with $|t| < 1$ can be deleted at a time. Suppose you deleted both age variables because both have $|t| < 1$. Do the results of the general linear test in **b** indicate that this would be unwise? Explain.

d. We can extend the absolute t-method as follows:

> If the F^* resulting from the general linear test is less than 1 for any *group* of variables, then MSE can be reduced by deleting these variables from the regression model. The converse of this is that if F^* is greater than 1, then deleting the group of variables will increase MSE.

Since F^* in the test in **b** was > 1, use the absolute t-value method to decide which of the age variables to delete from the model.

12.5 Multicollinearity

Managers use regression analysis to predict a dependent variable and/or to explain what predictor variables affect it. No problems arise in using regression analysis for prediction or explanation when predictor variables are uncorrelated or only slightly correlated. Unfortunately in business and economics, predictor variables are sometimes highly correlated. For example, we use AGE and YEARS with a company to predict JOBSATISFACTION. The two predictor variables will be positively and, perhaps, highly correlated. That is, younger workers will have few years on the job; older workers will have many years on the job. Even though there may be some older employees who recently joined the company, the two predictor variables may be highly correlated.

Highly correlated predictor variables do not jeopardize prediction but do hamper explanation. Highly correlated predictor variables make it difficult to estimate the size and importance of population regression coefficients, β_i. This, in turn, makes it difficult to answer questions such as (1) What is the effect of one predictor variable on the dependent variable? or (2) Is one variable a significant predictor of the dependent variable after controlling for other predictor variables?

By the end of this section you should be able to:

1. explain what multicollinearity is;
2. explain why multicollinearity poses problems in correlational regression studies, but not in experimental regression studies;
3. explain why multicollinearity causes a problem in determining the relative importance of individual predictor variables;
4. detect multicollinearity; and
5. reduce the impact of multicollinearity.

What Is Multicollinearity?

In Chapter 11, COMCEL conducted an experimental regression study that assessed the effect of PRICE and number of ADS on UNITS SOLD. We continue that example here and reproduce Table 11.4 on page 706 for your convenience.

The following three models show what happens when we compute regression equations for: UNITS SOLD versus ADS, UNITS SOLD versus PRICE, and then UNITS SOLD versus PRICE and ADS.

$$\text{UNITS SOLD-PRED} = 13.854 \qquad\qquad + 3.313\text{ADS} \qquad (12.16)$$

$$\text{UNITS SOLD-PRED} = 70.830 - .530\text{PRICE} \qquad\qquad (12.17)$$

$$\text{UNITS SOLD-PRED} = 60.891 - .530\text{PRICE} + 3.313\text{ADS} \qquad (12.18)$$

Models (12.16)–(12.18) exhibit a very important property—the sample regression coefficients remain the same as additional predictor variables are added to the regression model.

Compare models (12.17) and (12.18). Sales drop by .530 units for every one-dollar increase in price *regardless of whether we include the* ADS *variable in the regression equation.* We get a clear measure of the effect of price on the number of units sold.

Compare models (12.16) and (12.18). Sales increase by 3.313 units for every additional ad run *regardless of whether we include the* PRICE *variable in the regression equation.* We get a clear measure of the effect of the number of ads on the number of units sold.

Table 11.4

COMCEL Marketing Study Data

	Predictor Variables		Dependent Variable
Outlet	Price	Number of Ads per Day	Units Sold
1	100	1	9
2	100	1	11
3	100	3	19
4	100	3	15
5	100	5	26
6	100	5	24
7	90	1	14
8	90	1	19
9	90	3	24
10	90	3	28
11	90	5	31
12	90	5	32
13	85	1	17
14	85	1	19
15	85	3	29
16	85	3	25
17	85	5	30
18	85	5	30
19	80	1	26
20	80	1	23
21	80	3	26
22	80	3	24
23	80	5	37
24	80	5	34

From Table 11.4, note that COMCEL ran one, three, and five ads for every price level. This is a balanced design study. In experimental regression studies, the manager exerts experimental control and achieves a balanced design. The balanced design ensures that the predictor variables are not correlated. This, in turn, ensures that the sample regression coefficients will not change as we add or remove predictor variables from the model.

Balanced designs are rare in business and economics. Instead, managers often run correlational studies. In correlational studies, the manager cannot exert control or achieve a balanced design. As a result, the predictor variables are correlated to some degree, and the sample regression coefficients change as predictor variables are added to the regression equation.

To see the effect of an unbalanced design, suppose that stores 5, 6, 19, and 20 close due to poor weather. Then observations (100, 5, 26), (100, 5, 24), (80, 1, 26), and (80, 1, 23) would be deleted from Table 11.4. The regression design is no longer balanced. We computed regression equations for the remaining 20 observations for: UNITS SOLD versus ADS, UNITS SOLD versus PRICE, and then UNITS SOLD versus PRICE and ADS.

$$\text{UNITS SOLD-PRED} = 10.52 \qquad\qquad + 4.38\text{ADS} \qquad (12.19)$$

$$\text{UNITS SOLD-PRED} = 93.13 - .79\text{PRICE} \qquad (12.20)$$

$$\text{UNITS SOLD-PRED} = 54.21 - .48\text{PRICE} + 3.60\text{ADS} \qquad (12.21)$$

The effect of removing four observations is dramatic. The PRICE coefficient changes from $-.79$ to $-.48$ when ADS is included in the equation. The ADS coefficient changes from 4.38 to 3.60 when PRICE is included. *Adding or removing any predictor variable affects the size of the other sample regression coefficients.* We do not obtain a clear measure now of the effect of price or number of ads on the number of units sold. For example, as we increase the price by $1, how much does the number of units sold drop? Equation (12.20) says by .79, while equation (12.21) says by .48.

When the regression design is balanced, the predictor variables are *not* linearly related to each other. Figure 12.9 is a scatter diagram of the *predictor variables,* PRICE and ADS, for all the data in Table 11.4. It shows a balanced design. We can see that the best-fitting line for the two predictor variables appears to be horizontal—a slope of zero. Graphically, the data can be enclosed only by a circle or a horizontal ellipse. Thus, the two predictor variables are not linearly related to one another.

When the regression design is not balanced, the predictor variables are linearly related to one another. Look at Figure 12.10, from which we have deleted the four data values previously mentioned. The best-fitting line no longer appears to be horizontal. Rather, it has a negative slope. An ellipse that is slightly downward sloping to the right does a better job of enclosing the points than a circle does. When there is a linear relationship between the predictor variables, they are *correlated.* When predictor variables are highly correlated, we can enclose the scatter plots of pairs of predictor variables by tight ellipses sloping upward or downward. This indicates **multicollinearity**, which can occur in correlational regression studies. And as we demonstrated in models (12.19)–(12.21), highly correlated predictor variables can cause problems in estimating regression parameters.

> Multicollinearity means that some or all of the predictor variables are highly correlated with one another.

FIGURE 12.9   Scatter Diagram for PRICE versus ADS: Balanced Design
(Each * represents two observations.)

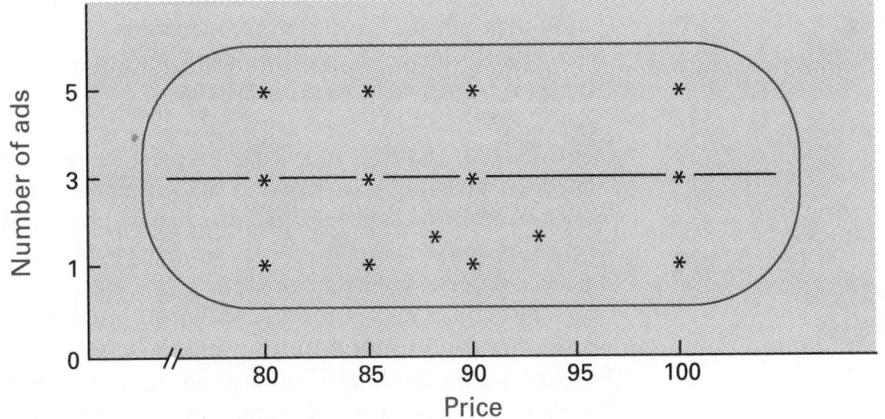

FIGURE 12.10   Scatter Diagram for PRICE versus ADS: Correlated Predictor Variables (Each * represents two observations.)

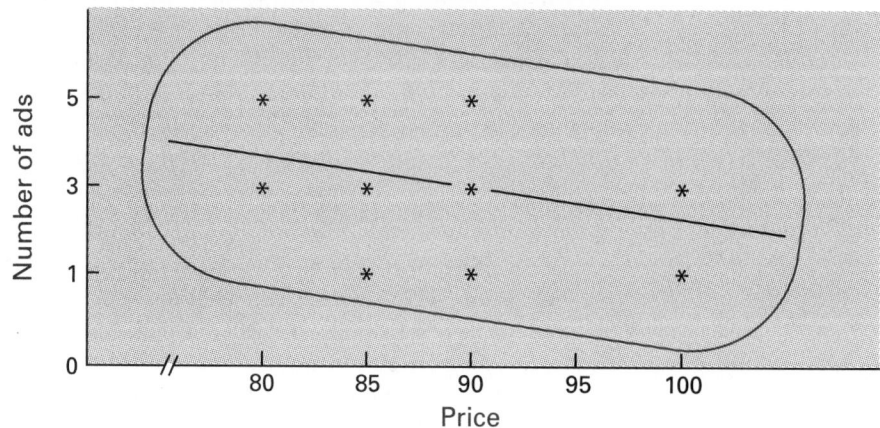

Why Is Multicollinearity a Problem?

When the predictor variables are highly correlated, four problems can occur:

1. The values of the sample regression coefficients vary dramatically as predictor variables or observations are added or deleted.
2. The signs (+ or −) of some sample regression coefficients may be the reverse of what logic suggests. This makes interpreting a regression coefficient difficult.
3. The general linear test may produce puzzling results.
4. The concept of measuring the effect of one predictor variable on a dependent variable while holding the other predictor variables constant loses its meaning.

Varying Regression Coefficients   Models (12.19)–(12.21) show that the magnitude of the sample regression coefficients changed as we added another predictor variable to the model. Thus, when predictor variables are highly correlated, it is difficult to estimate the effect of one predictor variable on a dependent variable.

We must emphasize that the term multicollinearity refers to *highly* correlated predictor variables. Except for experimental studies, pairs of predictor variables will always be correlated. The sample regression coefficients will always change somewhat when predictor variables or observations are added or deleted. The problem is one of the amount of change in the regression coefficients brought on by the degree of correlation among the predictor variables. Later in the section we will suggest two strategies for detecting multicollinearity.

Unexpected Signs   Logically, UNITS SOLD in the COMCEL marketing study should be inversely related to the PRICE variable. The higher the price, the fewer phones sold. Be concerned if you run a regression analysis and obtain a positive price regression coefficient. The unexpected sign could occur because price is highly correlated with other predictor variables.

The signs of the regression coefficients provide valuable information. They tell us whether the dependent variable is positively or negatively related to a predictor variable. Unexpected signs can cause problems in understanding, and thus explaining to others, the relationship between a predictor and a dependent variable.

Unusual General Linear Test Results   When multicollinearity is present we can obtain the following contradictory results: (1) the ANOVA indicates we have a good predictive model and (2) the hypothesis test approach indicates that there are no significant predictor variables. We now use the extra sum of squares principle to demonstrate how this can happen.

Consider the two hypothetical data sets in Table 12.12. One set contains uncorrelated predictor variables and the other contains highly correlated predictor variables.

Table 12.12

Correlated and Uncorrelated Data Sets

Correlated Data Set			Uncorrelated Data Set		
SALES	PRICE	ADS	SALES	PRICE	ADS
8	1	2	8	1	2
10	2	4	10	1	6
11	3	3	13	3	4
13	4	6	11	5	2
17	5	8	17	5	6

$$r_{\text{PRICE, ADS}} = .9191 \qquad\qquad r_{\text{PRICE, ADS}} = .0000$$

In the correlated data set, PRICE and ADS are positively related, $+.9191$. As PRICE increases, ADS also tends to increase. In the uncorrelated data set, PRICE and ADS are not related.

We developed a regression model for SALES versus PRICE and ADS for the correlated data set. The variance ratio of 33 (computer output not shown) has a p-value less than .005. Assuming an α level of .05, the ANOVA indicates that at least one predictor variable is significantly related to SALES.

However, the hypothesis tests on the two predictor variables in Table 12.13 show that neither predictor variable has a p-value of less than .05*. Thus, for the correlated data set, we reach a strange conclusion:

1. the ANOVA indicates we have a good predictive model and
2. the hypothesis tests indicate that there are no significant predictor variables

To show how these strange results occurred, we will determine the sums of squares and regression models for both data sets in Table 12.12 for:

1. both predictor variables—PRICE and ADS—in a multiple regression model,
2. PRICE only in a simple regression model, and
3. ADS only in a simple regression model.

Table 12.13

PARAMETER ESTIMATES SECTION
Output for Correlated Data Set

VARIABLE	PARAMETER ESTIMATE	STANDARD ERROR	t-VALUE	TWO-TAILED p-VALUE
INTERCEPT	5.256	—	—	—
PRICE	1.244	.66	1.88	.2006
ADS	.611	.43	1.41	.2955

---

*Recall that a hypothesis test on a population regression coefficient using the computed t-value is equivalent to the general linear test using the F^* test statistic.

The results are given in Table 12.14.

Table 12.14

Sums of Squares and Models for Data Sets in Table 12.12

Data Set	SSR	SSE	SST	Regression Model
Correlated				
PRICE, ADS	45.44	1.36	46.80	5.256 + 1.244PRICE + .611ADS
PRICE only	44.10	2.70	46.80	5.500 + 2.100PRICE
ADS only	43.04	3.76	46.80	5.534 + 1.362ADS

*Note the instability of the PRICE and ADS sample regression coefficients.

Data Set	SSR	SSE	SST	Regression Model
Uncorrelated				
PRICE, ADS	41.00	5.80	46.80	4.050 + 1.250PRICE + 1.000ADS
PRICE only	25.00	21.80	46.80	8.050 + 1.250PRICE
ADS only	16.00	30.80	46.80	7.800 + 1.000ADS

*Note the stability of the PRICE and ADS sample regression coefficients.

Correlated Data Set   The regression sum of squares for the PRICE-only model is 44.10. When we include the ADS variable, the regression sum of squares increases to 45.44. Including the ADS variable increases the regression sum of squares by 45.44 − 44.10 = 1.34 units. The extra sum of squares for ADS when PRICE is already in the model is

$$\text{SSR(ADS|PRICE)} = 1.34 \text{ units}$$

It is the marginal effect of introducing the ADS variable *given* the PRICE variable was already in the model.

The regression sum of squares for the ADS-only model is 43.04. When we include the PRICE variable, the regression sum of squares increases to 45.44. Adding the PRICE variable increases the regression sum of squares by 45.44 − 43.04 = 2.40 units. The extra sum of squares for PRICE when ADS is already in the model is

$$\text{SSR(PRICE|ADS)} = 2.40 \text{ units}$$

It is the marginal effect of introducing the PRICE variable *given* the ADS variable was already in the model.

Why are both SSR(PRICE|ADS) and SSR(ADS|PRICE) small for the correlated data set? Consider the model with the ADS variable only. When we include the PRICE variable, its impact on the dependent variable is small, (SSR(PRICE|ADS) = 2.40 units), because the ADS variable was already in the model and the ADS and PRICE variables are highly correlated. Thus, much of the PRICE variable's impact on the dependent variable is already in the model even before we include it. A similar argument can be made for adding the ADS variable to a model that already contains the PRICE variable.

To summarize, although SSR for the full model is large—45.44—the two extra sum of squares terms are small.

Now we can explain the two paradoxical findings. The ANOVA uses the SSR of 45.44 units. Since it is large (in relation to SST), the mean square regression will be large and the variance ratio test statistic will be larger than its critical value. Thus, the ANOVA will indicate that we have a good predictive model. However, the general linear test uses the extra sum of squares for computing the F^* test statistic. Since both extra sum of squares are small—2.40 and 1.34—the test statistics, F^*, will be smaller than the critical value. Thus, neither predictor variable will be significant.

Uncorrelated Data Set   The paradoxical findings cannot occur for uncorrelated predictor variables. The regression sum of squares for the PRICE-only model is SSR(PRICE) = 25.00. When we include the ADS variable, the regression sum of squares, SSR(PRICE, ADS), increases to 41.00. Thus, including the ADS variable increases the regression sum of squares by $41.00 - 25.00 = 16$ units.

$$SSR(ADS|PRICE) = 16$$

The regression sum of squares for the ADS-only model is SSR(ADS) = 16.00. When we include the PRICE variable, the regression sum of squares SSR(ADS, PRICE) increases to 41.00. Adding the PRICE variable increases the regression sum of squares by $41.00 - 16.00 = 25$ units.

$$SSR(PRICE|ADS) = 25$$

Note that

FULL MODEL   RESTRICTED MODELS

$$SSR(PRICE, ADS) = SSR(PRICE|ADS) + SSR(ADS|PRICE) \qquad (12.22)$$

$$41 \text{ units} = 25 \text{ units} \qquad + 16 \text{ units}$$

The regression sum of squares for the full model equals the sum of the extra sum of squares contributed by each predictor variable in the model.

So what are the implications? For uncorrelated data, if SSR(PRICE, ADS) is large, at least one of the extra sum of squares terms on the right-hand side of expression (12.22) must also be large. Since the general linear test uses the extra sum of squares in its calculations, at least one of the predictor variables must be significant. Thus, we cannot have a good predictive model with no significant predictor variables.

For correlated data, expression (12.22) is not true. Even if SSR(PRICE, ADS) is large, both extra sum of squares terms may be very small. Thus, we can have a good predictive model with no significant predictor variables.

In summary:

1. For uncorrelated predictor variables, the full-model SSR is the sum of the unique extra sum of squares contributed by each predictor variable. A significant variance ratio means that there will be at least one significant predictor variable.
2. For highly correlated predictor variables, the full-model SSR is not equal to the sum of the extra sums of squares of the predictor variables. A significant variance ratio may not mean that there will be at least one significant predictor variable.

Holding One Variable Constant?   When the data exhibit multicollinearity, the concept of measuring the effect of one predictor variable while holding the others constant is meaningless. We interpret each regression coefficient as the effect on the dependent variable of a one-unit change in a predictor variable while holding the other predictor variables in the equation constant. However, if two predictor variables are highly correlated, then we cannot hold one predictor variable at a constant level and vary the others. In short, the regression coefficients lose their meaning.

In summary, multicollinearity may cause wide swings in the values of the sample regression coefficients, including sign changes, as observations or predictor variables are added or deleted. It may also cause the general linear test to produce contradictory results.

Next we present a realistic correlational regression study that illustrates how to detect and minimize multicollinearity.

Example: Predicting Hospital Workload   Table 12.15 lists the variables for a U.S. Navy study to predict hospital workload. Table 12.16 contains data collected from 17 U.S. Naval hospitals.

Table 12.15

Hospital Workload Study Variables

Variable Name	How Measured
Predictor variables	
LOAD	Average daily patient load
XRAY	Monthly X-ray exposures
BEDDAY	Monthly occupied bed days
POP	Eligible population in the area/1,000
STAY	Average length of patient's stay in days
Dependent variable	
HOURS	Monthly man-hours

Table 12.16

U.S. Naval Hospital Manpower Data

	Predictor Variables					Dependent Variable
SITE	LOAD	XRAY	BEDDAY	POP	STAY	HOURS
1	15.57	2463	472.9	18.0	4.45	566.5
2	44.02	2048	1339.8	9.5	6.92	696.8
3	20.42	3940	620.3	12.8	4.28	1033.1
4	18.74	6505	568.3	36.7	3.90	1603.6
5	49.20	5723	1497.6	35.7	5.50	1611.4
6	44.92	11520	1365.8	24.0	4.60	1613.3
7	55.48	5779	1687.0	43.3	5.62	1854.2
8	59.28	5969	1639.9	46.7	5.15	2160.5
9	94.39	8461	2872.3	78.7	6.18	2305.6
10	128.02	20106	3655.1	180.5	6.15	3503.9
11	96.00	13313	2912.0	60.9	5.88	3571.9
12	131.42	10771	3921.0	103.7	4.88	3741.4
13	127.21	15543	3865.7	126.8	5.50	4026.5
14	252.90	36194	7684.1	157.7	7.00	10343.8
15	409.20	34703	12446.3	169.4	10.78	11732.2
16	463.70	39204	14098.4	331.4	7.05	15414.9
17	510.22	86533	15524.0	371.6	6.35	18854.4

Source: Procedures and Analysis for Staffing Standards Development; Data/Regression Analysis Handbook: San Diego, Calif: Navy Manpower and Material Analysis Center, 1979.

The variance ratio of 237.79 (computer output not shown)* has a p-value less than .0001. Thus, at least one of the five predictor variables is significantly related to HOURS. The parameter estimate section output provides the following regression model.

$$\text{HOURS-PRED} = 1962.95 - 15.85\text{LOAD} + .056\text{XRAY} + 1.59\text{BEDDAY} \qquad (12.23)$$
$$- 4.22\text{POP} - 394.31\text{STAY}$$

Since the hospital manpower study is correlational, we need to determine whether we have a multicollinearity problem. How can we detect it?

Detecting Multicollinearity

We will discuss two methods for detecting multicollinearity—the R^2 (multiple coefficient determination) method and the sign reversal method.

The R^2 Method   Table 12.17 shows the upper portion of the correlation matrix for the hospital manpower data. The HOURS column shows the relationship between the dependent variable and each predictor variable. As expected, all the predictor variables are positively correlated with HOURS.

The remaining correlations represent the relationships between pairs of predictor variables. For example, the correlation between patient LOAD and monthly occupied BEDDAY is .99990. The two predictor variables are nearly measuring the same thing. In fact, the only predictor variable that is not very highly correlated with the others is length of STAY.

Here is the R^2 method and its accompanying rule of thumb for assessing multicollinearity:

Step 1:   Regress the dependent variable on the full set of predictor variables. Record the coefficient of multiple determination, R^2.

Step 2:   Regress each predictor variable on the remaining predictor variables. Record the R^2 for each model. This requires developing k models, where k is the number of predictor variables.

Step 3:   Apply the following rule of thumb: If an R^2 for any model involving only predictor variables is greater than the R^2 for the model with the dependent variable and the full set of predictor variables, multicollinearity is present.

Table 12.17

Correlation Matrix for Hospital Manpower Study

	LOAD	XRAY	BEDDAY	POP	STAY	HOURS
LOAD	1.00000	0.90738	0.99990	0.93569	0.67120	0.98565
XRAY		1.00000	0.90715	0.91047	0.44665	0.94517
BEDDAY			1.00000	0.93317	0.67111	0.98599
POP				1.00000	0.46286	0.94036
STAY					1.00000	0.57858
HOURS						1.00000

*For the remainder of this section we will use SAS, a commercially available statistical software package.

We apply the R^2 method to the naval hospital manpower data.

Step 1:   The R^2 for model (12.23) is .9908. Here we used LOAD, XRAY, BEDDAY, POP, and STAY, to predict HOURS.

Step 2:   We estimated k = five models and determined their R^2s.

Model 1	Use XRAY, BEDDAY, POP, STAY to predict LOAD.	$R^2 = .9999$
Model 2	Use LOAD, BEDDAY, POP, STAY to predict XRAY.	$R^2 = .8741$
Model 3	Use LOAD, XRAY, POP, STAY to predict BEDDAY.	$R^2 = .9999$
Model 4	Use LOAD, XRAY, BEDDAY, STAY to predict POP.	$R^2 = .9571$
Model 5	Use LOAD, XRAY, BEDDAY, POP to predict STAY.	$R^2 = .7663$

Step 3:   The R^2 values for models 1 and 3 are larger than the R^2 when the full set of predictor variables is used to predict the dependent variable. For example, when XRAY, BEDDAY, POP, and STAY are used to predict LOAD, the four variables account for 99.99% of the variation in patient LOAD. Patient LOAD and the four other predictor variables are measuring virtually same thing.

In conclusion, based on the rule of thumb, the data set exhibits multicollinearity.

The Sign-Reversal Method   If any sample regression coefficient sign differs from what we would expect from logic or from the correlation matrix, we may have multicollinearity. Regression coefficient signs that are inconsistent with logic or theory do not always signal multicollinearity. Our logic or theory may be wrong, but generally a sign reversal is likely to be evidence of multicollinearity.

Regression coefficient signs that are inconsistent with their correlation coefficient signs can also signal multicollinearity. See the correlation matrix in Table 12.17. Note that the dependent variable, HOURS, is positively related to the five predictor variables. Thus, we should expect that the five sample regression coefficients in model (12.23) should also be positive. And yet the LOAD, POP, and STAY regression coefficients are negative. This is a clear sign that multicollinearity is present.

There are other methods for detecting multicollinearity, but for our purposes here we have limited the discussion to the R^2 and sign-reversal methods. We next consider what can be done about multicollinearity.

Procedures for Coping with Multicollinearity

Highly correlated predictor variables do not jeopardize prediction but do hamper explanation. That is, we cannot determine the effect of a predictor variable on a dependent variable after controlling for the impact of all predictor variables already in the model. If your sole goal is explanation, you must obtain additional data to break the pattern of the highly correlated predictor variables. If your goal is prediction, you can either ignore multicollinearity or drop one or more highly correlated predictor variables from the model to improve its "face validity." We explore these ideas next.

Getting More Data   The correlation matrix in Table 12.17 indicates that XRAY is highly correlated with BEDDAY, about +.91. Figure 12.11 shows a scatter diagram of

FIGURE 12.11   Scatter Diagram of XRAY and BEDDAY for Hospital Manpower Study

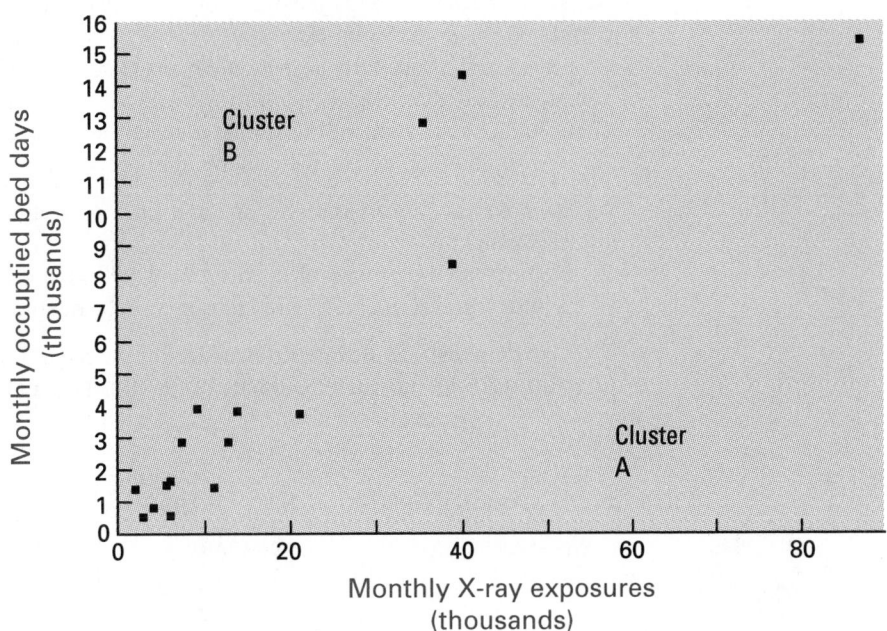

the XRAY versus BEDDAY predictor variables. The points can be encircled by a tight ellipse that slopes upward to the right.

For the study we should seek additional observations (hospitals) that have high XRAY usage, but low BEDDAY values (cluster A) and that have high BEDDAY values but low XRAY usage (cluster B). The extra observations break the linear pattern between the XRAY and BEDDAY predictor variables. By turning the ellipse into a circle, we can reduce the extent of correlation.

Breaking the pattern is not always feasible. There may not be any hospitals that are in clusters A or B. Patients with longer hospital stays are there for more serious illnesses, and usually require more XRAYS. In general, finding data to break the pattern may be difficult. And what is worse, multicollinearity may involve more than two predictor variables.

Discard Highly Correlated Predictor Variables   Mosteller and Tukey (1977) demonstrate that a model with highly correlated predictor variables can produce good predictions, provided the values of the predictor variables are within the range of the original data.

$$\text{HOURS-PRED} = 1962.95 - 15.85\text{LOAD} + .056\text{XRAY} + 1.59\text{BEDDAY}$$
$$- 4.22\text{POP} - 394.31\text{STAY} \qquad (12.23)$$

Then why not use model (12.23)? That is, why not ignore multicollinearity? A problem with model (12.23) is that it simply does not make sense. LOAD, POP, and STAY cannot be negatively related to HOURS. A model user could be discouraged from using the model by the unreasonable signs. So managers often use screening procedures to discard highly correlated predictor variables. This approach improves a model's "face validity."

In Chapter 11 we presented a screening procedure that minimizes the standard error of the estimate. We removed predictor variables, one at a time, from the model whose |t| values were less than one. You may use this procedure to also discard highly correlated predictor variables.

A second procedure is to remove predictor variables, one at time, whose |t| values are less than one *or* whose regression coefficient signs (+ or −) contradict either logic or the signs of the simple correlation coefficients.

To summarize, consider two screening procedures:

1. Remove predictor variables, one at a time, from the model whose |t| values are less than one.
2. Remove predictor variables, one at time, whose |t| values are less than one *and/or* whose regression coefficient signs are unreasonable.

We demonstrate the latter procedure for the naval manpower study. Table 12.18 contains the SAS parameter estimate output for model (12.23).

Table 12.18

Parameter Estimates Section of SAS Output—FULL MODEL

VARIABLE	DF	PARAMETER ESTIMATE	STANDARD ERROR	T FOR H_0: PARAMETER = 0	PROB > $|T|$
INTERCEPT	1	1962.94816	1071.36170	1.832	0.0941
LOAD	1	-15.85167473	97.65299018	-0.162	0.8740
XRAY	1	0.05593038	0.02125828	2.631	0.0234
BEDDAY	1	1.58962370	3.09208349	0.514	0.6174
POP	1	-4.21866799	7.17655737	-0.588	0.5685
STAY	1	-394.31412	209.63954	-1.881	0.0867

Also the ROOT MSE (read as the square root of the mean square error) was 642.0884 hours. COMSTAT represents ROOT MSE as the Standard Error (of the estimate).

Patient LOAD is the first predictor variable dropped, since it has the smallest |t| value under one and has an illogical sign. That is, logic and $r_{HOURS, LOAD}$ from Table 12.17 tell us that HOURS should be positively related to LOAD. But the LOAD regression coefficient in model (12.23) has a negative sign.

We dropped LOAD from the model and developed a second regression model of HOURS against the remaining predictor variables. Table 12.19 contains the SAS output for the second model.

Table 12.19

Parameter Estimates Section of SAS Output—LOAD not in Model

VARIABLE	DF	PARAMETER ESTIMATE	STANDARD ERROR	T FOR H_0: PARAMETER = 0	PROB > $|T|$
INTERCEPT	1	2032.18806	942.07483	2.157	.0520
XRAY	1	0.05607934	0.02035863	2.755	.0175
BEDDAY	1	1.08836904	0.15339754	7.095	.0001
POP	1	-5.00406579	5.08071295	-0.985	.3441
STAY	1	-410.08296	178.07810	-2.303	.0400

ROOT MSE = 615.4887 hours

Note that the standard error of the estimate dropped from 642 to 615 hours.

After dropping patient LOAD, we dropped the POP variable because it had the smallest $|t|$ value under one, and an unreasonable sign. We next fitted a regression model of HOURS against the three remaining predictor variables. Table 12.20 contains the SAS output for the third model.

Table 12.20

Parameter Estimates Section of SAS Output—LOAD and POP not in Model

VARIABLE	DF	PARAMETER ESTIMATE	STANDARD ERROR	T FOR H_0: PARAMETER = 0	PROB > $|T|$
INTERCEPT	1	1523.38924	786.89772	1.936	.0749
XRAY	1	0.05298733	0.02009194	2.637	.0205
BEDDAY	1	0.97848162	0.10515362	9.305	.0001
STAY	1	-320.95083	153.19222	-2.095	.0563

ROOT MSE = 614.7794 hours

Note that the standard error of the estimate dropped from 615.5 to 614.8 hours.

At this point all the absolute t-values are greater than one. According to the first screening procedure, this completes our model building. However, the sign of the STAY predictor variable is negative, which defies both logic and $r_{\text{HOURS, STAY}}$ from Table 12.17. According to the second screening procedure, we should remove the STAY predictor variable from the model. The question is, should we delete the STAY variable?

Two opposing arguments can be made.

1. Delete the STAY predictor variable.

   If the STAY predictor variable is not deleted, the model will lose "face validity." Other model users may question the negative coefficient for the STAY predictor variable. As a result, they may not "buy into" the model and may not use it.

2. Keep the STAY predictor variable.

   None of the $|t|$ values in Table 12.20 are less than one. Thus, if we drop the STAY predictor variable, the standard error of the estimate will *increase* to 685 hours (SAS computer output not shown). This is an increase of 70.4 hours, and will widen our prediction and confidence intervals.

   It is a judgment call. Keeping the STAY variable minimizes the standard error of the estimate. The downside is having a model with a sample regression coefficient that calls into question the model's face validity. Deleting the STAY variable maximizes the model's face validity. The downside is having a model with a larger standard error of the estimate.

   Therefore, should the STAY predictor variable be deleted? While it is a judgment call, it might be worth the relatively small increase in prediction errors to have a model that everyone can "buy into." We would delete the STAY predictor variable. Thus, the regression model for the naval hospital study data becomes

$$\text{HOURS-PRED} = -68.314 + .0748\text{XRAY} + .823\text{BEDDAY} \qquad (12.24)$$

Note that the two predictor variables have plus signs, which is consistent with logic and the $r_{\text{HOURS, XRAY}}$ and $r_{\text{HOURS, BEDDAY}}$ correlation coefficients in Table 12.17.

Summary

Unless we run a balanced experimental regression study, the predictor variables will always be correlated to some degree. When the predictor variables are highly correlated (multicollinearity), sample regression coefficients are unstable and may be uninterpretable, due to sign reversals. However, prediction is not affected by multicollinearity.

Multicollinearity may be a problem if (1) the signs of sample regression coefficients are different from expected and (2) an R^2 relating predictors with other predictor variables is greater than the R^2 relating the dependent variable to the full set of predictor variables.

Partial remedies for multicollinearity include (1) obtaining additional data to break the pattern, (2) dropping highly correlated predictor variables from the equation—especially when the goal is prediction, or (3) ignoring it.

SECTION 12.5 EXERCISES

Use a statistical software package for all problems in this section that require calculation.

1. Suppose a plot of a pair of predictor variables shows linearity. Describe what the scatter diagram would look like for the following correlation coefficients:
   a. $r = +1.0$
   b. $r = +.5$
   c. $r = 0$
   d. $r = -.5$
   e. $r = 1.0$

2. Shown is a small data set.

y	x_1	x_2
4	1	2
6	2	4
8	3	3
12	4	5
10	5	7

   a. Plot the predictor variables. Does the data set exhibit multicollinearity?
   b. Plot y versus x_1. Plot y versus x_2.
   c. Compute the multiple regression equation for y on x_1, for y on x_2, and for y on x_1 and x_2.
   d. Why is the sign of the x_2 regression coefficient negative ($-.666$) in the regression model of y versus x_1 and x_2 when the plot of y versus x_2 shows a positive relationship?
   e. What conclusion can you draw about the meaningfulness of the regression coefficients when the data exhibit multicollinearity?
   f. Use the multiple regression model to predict y for $x_1 = 3$ and $x_2 = 3$.
   g. Is the predicted value of y close to the actual value of y? If so, what conclusion can you draw about the impact of multicollinearity on prediction?
   h. Use the correlation matrix output to show why the data exhibit multicollinearity.

3. Shown is a small data set.

y	x_1	x_2
4	1	1
6	6	2
7	4	4
8	2	7
12	7	7

a. Plot the predictor variables. Do the data exhibit multicollinearity?

b. Plot y versus x_1. Plot y versus x_2.

c. Compute the regression equation for y on x_1, for y on x_2, and for y on x_1 and x_2.

d. Why do the signs of the regression coefficients not change? For example, the x_1 coefficient is $+.526$ with x_2 in the model. It is $+.769$ without x_2 in the model.

e. Use the correlation matrix output and show why the data do not exhibit multicollinearity.

4. Refer to Exercise 2 in this set. What (x_1, x_2) observations should you seek to break the pattern?

5. If the dependent variable and one of the predictor variables has a correlation of $+.95$, can we conclude that the data exhibit multicollinearity? Discuss.

6. Refer to Exercise 6 in Section 12.3. Use the data to fit the full model shown below.

$$E(\text{SATIS}) = \beta_0 + \beta_1 \text{SALARY} + \beta_{11} \text{SALARY}^2 + \beta_2 \text{CLOSE} + \beta_{12} \text{SALARY} \times \text{CLOSE}$$

a. Determine the ANOVA and parameter estimate section output for the full model. Test the full model using $\alpha = .01$.

b. Use the R^2 method to determine the presence of multicollinearity.

c. Now use screening procedure 2 to discard predictor variables from the full model.

7. Here are two small data sets.

	Data Set A			Data Set B	
SALES	PRICE	ADS	SALES	PRICE	ADS
800	500	200	800	500	200
1000	400	400	1000	500	600
1100	300	300	1300	300	400
1300	200	600	1100	100	200
1700	100	800	1700	100	600

a. Plot a scatter diagram of the predictor variables for both data sets.

b. Compute the correlation between the two predictor variables for both data sets.

c. For data set A, compute the following models.

$$E(\text{SALES}) = \beta_0 + \beta_1 \text{PRICE}$$

$$E(\text{SALES}) = \beta_0 + \beta_1 \text{ADS}$$

$$E(\text{SALES}) = \beta_0 + \beta_1 \text{PRICE} + \beta_2 \text{ADS}$$

Use the three sample regression equations to show that the sample regression coefficients are unstable.

d. For data set B, compute the following models.

$$E(\text{SALES}) = \beta_0 + \beta_1 \text{PRICE}$$

$$E(\text{SALES}) = \beta_0 + \beta_1 \text{ADS}$$

$$E(\text{SALES}) = \beta_0 + \beta_1 \text{PRICE} + \beta_2 \text{ADS}$$

Use the three sample regression equations to show that the sample regression coefficients are stable.

e. Explain what you have learned about the impact of multicollinearity on the stability of the sample regression coefficients.

8. Consider the following regression model.

$$\text{EXAMGRADE-PRED} = 60 - 2.5\text{STUDYHRS} + 1.5\text{MATERDIFF}$$

EXAMGRADE   is the exam grade on a statistics chapter
STUDYHRS   is the number of hours studied for the exam
MATERDIFF   is an indicator variable; 1 if material is difficult, 0 otherwise

a. Would the model have high face validity?
b. What might cause the signs of the regression coefficients to be the reverse of logic?
c. Using logic alone, would you expect the two predictor variables to exhibit multicollinearity?

9. Shown here is a small data set.

y	x_1	x_2
200	10	20
325	20	31
499	30	38
578	50	57
678	70	81
878	90	99

a. Use the R^2 method to determine whether the predictor variables exhibit multicollinearity.
b. Determine the least squares regression equation.
c. Make predictions on y for the following three pairs of values of the two predictor variables.

x_1	40	20	69
x_2	40	30	78

d. Does a model developed from highly correlated predictor variables generate reasonable predictions on y?

COMCEL

Date: September 16, 1995
To: Ann Tabor, CEO
From: Marvin Elrod, Manager of Human Resources
Re: Salary Determinant Study

SUMMARY
Based on a regression analysis, we do not find evidence of race or gender discrimination in our salary structure.

SUPPORTING ANALYSIS
We selected a random sample of 50 employees and matched the salary of each employee with biographical factors that should be related to the

employee's salary. These included years of formal education, number of years at COMCEL, gender, and race.

Common sense told us to include education and years with the company in the salary determination model. Irrespective of a person's race or gender, education and years generally affect salary. The key question was: With education and years already in the model, does adding gender and race to the model significantly improve its explanatory power?

The null hypothesis was that gender and race are not statistically related to salary. We compared the full model with all four predictor variables to the restricted model with the education and years variables. The extra sum of squares due to gender and race was only 29.18 units.

We formally tested the null hypothesis by computing the F^* statistic. Since $F^* = .38 < F[.95; 2, 45] = 3.24$, we cannot reject the null hypothesis. We do not have enough evidence to conclude that gender and race affect salary after controlling for education and years with the company.

CHAPTER 12 QUESTIONS

1. Why do we need only $c - 1$ indicator variables to represent c categorical variables?

2. If an indicator variable is significant, what impact does it have on the best-fitting lines for the two levels of the categorical variable?

3. Explain in nontechnical terms what is meant by an interaction.

4. Provide an example different from those in the text in which you would suspect an interaction between a categorical and quantitative variable.

5. Explain why different intercepts and different slopes suggest that a categorical and quantitative variable interact.

6. Distinguish between linear in the variables and linear in the parameters.

7. When should quadratic terms (second-power terms) be considered for a model?

8. When should an interaction term be considered for a model?

9. Distinguish between interaction and quadratic terms.

10. Explain what the extra sum of squares measures.

11. Given the following regression sums of squares, what can you conclude about the relationship between the two predictor variables?

$$SSR(ADS) \neq SSR(ADS|PRICE)$$

12. Given the following regression sums of squares, what can you conclude about the relationship between the two predictor variables?

$$SSR(ADS) = SSR(ADS|PRICE)$$

13. You wish to determine if hours studied and course difficulty are related to test performance given that math SAT score and grade in freshman calculus are already in the model. In words, set up the null and alternative hypotheses.

14. The two-tailed p-value is less than .05 for the computed t-value for a population regression coefficient. Would a 95% confidence interval on the population regression coefficient include zero?

15. When should the general linear test be used?

16. Under what conditions, if any, can the extra sum of squares be less than zero?

17. Explain why multicollinearity poses problems in correlational regression studies, but not in experimental regression studies.

18. What impact does multicollinearity have on the stability of the sample regression coefficients?

19. Explain why when multicollinearity is present it is hard to estimate the impact of one predictor variable on the dependent variable while holding the other predictor variables already in the model constant.

20. Explain how establishing a model's face validity can increase the standard error of the estimate. Why is an increased standard error of the estimate bad?

CHAPTER 12 APPLICATION PROBLEMS

1. Suppose that a particular cancer is indicated by a test using a count of chromosome effects, COUNT. There are two predictor variables: CIG is the number of cigarettes an individual smokes each day; ALCOH is the number of ounces of alcohol the individual drinks each day. The project manager has proposed the following regression model:

$$E(\text{COUNT}) = \beta_0 + \beta_1\text{CIG} + \beta_2\text{ALCOH}$$

From previous studies, we know that the combined effect of heavy smoking and drinking produces a higher count of chromosome effects than would be predicted by each predictor variable singly.

a. Is the above model appropriate, given the known information?

b. Propose a more realistic model that incorporates the idea that the combined effect of heavy smoking and drinking produces a higher count of chromosome effects than would be predicted by each predictor variable singly.

2. We wish to study whether female union members are earning the same amount of money, SALARY, as comparably situated male union members. Thus, we include a GENDER variable in the model. According to Title VII of the 1964 Civil Rights Act and empirical studies of lifetime earnings, the only economically and legally justifiable factor explaining earnings differential is seniority. The plaintiffs use two measures of seniority: (1) years on job, YEARS, and (2) age in years, AGE. The plaintiffs propose the following regression model:

$$E(\text{SALARY}) = \beta_0 + \beta_1\text{AGE} + \beta_2\text{YEARS} + \beta_3\text{GENDER}$$

a. If females are represented as GENDER = 0 and males as GENDER = 1, and if females receive significantly lower salaries than comparably situated males, should the sign of the sample regression coefficient, β_3, be positive or negative? Discuss.

b. If females are represented as GENDER = 0 and males as GENDER = 1, and if females receive the same salaries as comparably situated males, what will the population regression coefficient for the GENDER variable equal? Discuss.

c. Suppose we wish to estimate the effect of YEARS on SALARY, after controlling for the impact of AGE and GENDER. Given the three predictor variables, is multicollinearity likely to be a problem? (*Hint:* Are AGE and YEARS likely to be related?)

3. In *Segar v. Smith*, the plaintiffs introduced four regression models of annual salary, using the following predictor variables: education, years of prior federal experience, years of prior nonfederal experience, and race. The RACE variable was coded as follows.

$$\text{RACE} = \begin{cases} 1 & \text{if the agent is a minority} \\ 0 & \text{otherwise} \end{cases}$$

The study included several hundred agents of the Drug Enforcement Agency. Shown are the parameter estimates for the race coefficients and their t-values in the four models.

Year	Race Coefficient	t-Value	Two-Tailed p-Value
1976	$-\$1,864$	-2.54	.015
1977	$-\$1,119$	-3.18	.005
1978	$-\$\ 866$	-2.07	.040
1979	$-\$1,026$	-2.30	.030

a. Have the plaintiffs shown that minority drug enforcement agents receive lower annual salaries than comparably situated white officers? Discuss.

b. The defendants argued that since the four multiple coefficients of determination, R^2, ranged between .42 and .52 (computations not shown above), the plaintiffs' case should be dismissed. The judge rejected this argument. Explain the judge's logic in arguing that the value of R^2 was not a critical factor in accepting the plaintiffs' four studies.

 4. A substantial portion of a large shipment of oil was damaged due to sedimentation in some of the tanks or holds of an oil tanker. Oil chemists thought that sedimentation could have been due to the shipper neglecting to make sure that a particular type of oil (type A) was not present in all the tanks. Type A oil is suspected of causing sedimentation. Alternatively, the temperature at which the oil is loaded into the tanker and discharged at the port also may cause sedimentation. Loading and discharge temperatures are the responsibility of the oil carrier. Thus, two different parties may have been responsible for the sedimentation and the damage. An arbitration panel had to decide which party should pay the major share of the damages. A third party provided regression analysis data to the arbitration panel. This study had the following variables:

Dependent variable: Percentage of sediment in the tanks, SEDIMENT

Predictor variables: Discharge temperature in Fahrenheit, DISCH
                        Loading temperature in Fahrenheit, LOAD
                        Presence of type A Oil, TYPEA = 1 if the type A
                        oil is absent from tanks, 0 if otherwise.

Shown is the regression model based on 13 tanks of an oil tanker:

$$\text{SEDIMENT-PRED} = -4.97 - 3.19\text{TYPEA} + .014\text{DISCH} + .038\text{LOAD}$$

Parameter Estimates

Variable	Parameter Estimate	t-Value	Two-Tailed p-Value
INTERCEPT	-4.97	—	
TYPEA	-3.19	-7.22	$<.001$
DISCH	$+.014$	$+1.02$	$>.300$
LOAD	$+.038$	$+1.36$	$>.100$

a. Explain in simple terms the meaning of the sample regression coefficients for the three predictor variables.

b. Given the above data, which predictor variable appears to have the most significant impact on percentage of sedimentation? Discuss.

c. Given the above data, what do you think the arbitration panel concluded? That is, who was more responsible for the sedimentation damage—the shipper whose job is to ensure that type A oil is not present or the oil carrier who is responsible for the loading and discharge? Discuss.

5. A critical step in auditing the financial statements of a firm involves assessing the strength of internal controls. One measure is compliance with established policies and procedures, e.g., having credit limits checked and authorized before processing a sales invoice. First, the auditor must make a judgment as to what the error rate is for the population of sales invoices that will be checked. This information is then used to determine the sample size, and later to test the hypothesis that the observed error rate is within acceptable bounds.

To assist in making the preliminary estimate of the population error rate, an auditing firm decides to construct a regression model based on a sample of 100 firms audited during the previous year. The dependent variable is the error rate *(in percent)*. The auditors believe that error rates are related to (1) the VOLUME of transactions processed during the accounting period, (2) the AVErage SIZE of a sales invoice—large transactions are more likely to be properly handled, (3) the number of TRANSactions per CLERICAL worker during the period—high volume is expected to lead to higher error rates, and (4) the number of TRANSactions per TEMPorary worker—error rates are expected to be higher for this group because temporaries are less experienced and less committed than permanent employees. The results of the regression analysis appear here.

Variable	Parameter Estimate	Standard Error	*t*-Value
INTERCEPT	.56763		
VOLUME	.00011	.00002	5.50
AVESIZE	−.00261	.00064	−4.08
TRANS/CLERICAL	.00075	.00146	.52
TRANS/TEMP	.00458	.00144	3.18

$R^2 = .352$

a. Can we say from these results that error rate is not related to the number of transactions per clerical worker? Explain.

b. If the volume of transactions rose by 1,000 over a previous period, would the error rate increase by .11% or by 11%, assuming that the other variables in the model stayed the same?

c. "Temporary employees are causing the greatest percentage of our errors in compliance." Evaluate, using the parameter estimate and R^2.

 6. The IRS is always concerned about taxpayers' compliance with the tax laws. The tax code requires that when services are bartered (exchanged for other services), the fair value of those services should be reported as income. A staff member proposed that a predictive model could be developed from the data collected on past taxpayer audits. The proposed model* would be used to predict which taxpayers were underreporting taxable income and should be audited.

The dependent variable is the dollar amount of taxable barter income not reported by the taxpayer. The independent variables are (1) the amount of income from wages reported on form W-2, (2) the amount of self-employment income reported on Schedule C, and (3) the type of business engaged in by the taxpayer: professional = 1 and nonprofessional = 0.

Variable	Parameter Estimate	Standard Error
Intercept	−12,231.2	
W-2	.237	.063
Schedule C	.122	.015
Business type	1,572	709.797

Degrees of freedom: 96

---

*Adapted from Randolph P. Beatty, John F. Reim, and Robert F. Schapperle, "The Effect of Barriers to Entry on Bank Shareholder Wealth: Implications for Interstate Banking," *Journal of Bank Research* 16, no. 1 (Spring 1985): 8–13.

a. Interpret the regression coefficients in managerial terms.
b. Which, if any, of the independent variables are linearly related to underreported barter income? Use a 1% significance level.
c. Does the intercept value of $-12,231.2$ mean that taxpayers who report no W-2 income and no Schedule C income and are not professionals overpay their income taxes by $12,231.20? Explain.

7. An appraiser wishes to develop a regression model that will predict the sales price of parcels of land of different sizes. The appraiser obtains information on comparable sales for 15 recently sold parcels.

Parcel	Sales PRICE (thousands of dollars)	ACRES
1	114.9	2.47
2	124.0	3.07
3	125.0	3.20
4	128.9	3.25
5	134.9	3.60
6	130.9	3.77
7	137.0	4.41
8	133.0	4.63
9	125.0	4.81
10	141.0	5.01
11	141.0	5.32
12	150.0	5.53
13	144.9	6.69
14	148.9	7.22
15	150.0	7.26

a. Plot sales PRICE (dependent) against ACRES. Based on the graphs, which of the following models appears to best describe the data?

Restricted model: $E(\text{PRICE}) = \beta_0 + \beta_1\text{ACRES}$

Full model: $E(\text{PRICE}) = \beta_0 + \beta_1\text{ACRES} + \beta_{11}\text{ACRES}^2$

b. Fit the full model and perform a t-test to determine the significance of the squared term. Use a .05 significance level.
c. Use the general linear test to determine whether the squared term can be dropped from the regression model.
d. Compare the results of **b** and **c**.

8. A experiment was conducted to determine the relationship between degree of brand PREFERENCE (dependent) and MOISTURE content and degree of SWEETNESS of a new product. The coded data are shown below.

MOISTURE:	4	4	4	6	6	6	8	8	8	10	10	10
SWEETNESS:	2	4	6	2	4	6	2	4	6	2	4	6
PREFERENCE:	15	38	20	18	55	40	18	75	60	15	60	17

a. Plot MOISTURE and SWEETNESS against brand PREFERENCE.
b. Fit model (12.1) and test whether the squared and interaction terms can be dropped from the model. Use $\alpha = .05$.
c. Plot MOISTURE against PREFERENCE for sweetness levels of 2, 4, and 6. Your scatter plot should contain three clusters. What level of moisture and sweetness appears to be optimal?

9. In 1992 the U.S. spent over 14 cents of every dollar of GNP on health care. One factor contributing to these health costs is medical malpractice law. Courts have awarded plaintiffs such large compensation for medical malpractice that many insurance companies no longer provide medical malpractice coverage or offer it at premiums that are not affordable for many physicians.

Both physician groups and the insurance industry currently are lobbying for legislation that limits the size of tort awards granted by the courts in an effort to make malpractice insurance more affordable. Most insurance companies differentiate among physician risks based on characteristics of various physicians' groups.

Following are New York physician malpractice claims data for the years 1980–1983 by field of practice. Medical specialties have been collapsed into three GROUPS: GROUP=NSG if nonsurgical general; GROUP=NSS if nonsurgical specialty; and GROUP=SUR if surgical. The size of each practice field is the number of physicians practicing in New York within a given field during 1980–1983. PDCLAIMS is the total number of malpractice claims arising from each field of practice that were paid during 1980–1983. PHWCLAIM represents the percent of physicians within a given practice that had at least one paid claim during this period. Finally, TOTAWARD equals the total malpractice awards made to claimants during this period arising from a particular field.

OBS	GROUP	SIZE	PDCLAIMS	PHWCLAIM	TOTAWARD (thousands)
1	NSS	1372	179	12.0	22615.9
2	NSS	520	38	6.1	1481.4
3	NSS	1923	109	5.1	9102.9
4	NSG	1815	850	29.2	49663.3
5	SUR	2255	638	23.1	43739.7
6	NSG	7744	514	5.7	43296.4
7	SUR	231	79	25.5	9187.3
8	SUR	2175	694	24.1	70301.9
9	NSS	1187	144	9.4	9833.0
10	SUR	1906	396	13.8	33261.6
11	NSS	516	101	14.7	7934.5
12	NSG	2822	158	4.9	15514.2
13	SUR	285	78	16.8	4048.2
14	NSS	4740	63	1.2	6028.9
15	NSS	1467	106	6.3	5202.9
16	NSS	613	78	10.9	5269.4
17	NSS	3981	80	1.9	6661.7

You wish to use regression analysis to determine whether there is a difference in the mean total awards paid to claimants among the three medical groups using indicator variables.
a. How many indicator variables would you need?
b. What null and alternative hypotheses would you test?
c. What statistic from your regression output would you use to test the hypotheses?
d. Create two indicator variables as follows:

$$\text{NSS} = 1 \quad \text{if GROUP} = \text{NSS; 0 otherwise}$$

$$\text{NSG} = 1 \quad \text{if GROUP} = \text{NSG; 0 otherwise}$$

Fit the following model and test if there is a difference in the mean TOTAWARDS among the three groups. Use $\alpha = .05$.

$$E(\text{TOTAWARD}) = \beta_0 + \beta_1 \text{NSS} + \beta_2 \text{NSG}$$

e. Estimate the mean TOTAWARD for each type of group: NSS, NSG, and SUR.

10. Refer to the data in Problem 9.
  a. Plot scatter diagrams of TOTAWARD against SIZE, PDCLAIMS, and PHWCLAIM. Do the predictor VARIABLES appear to be related to TOTAWARD?
  b. Estimate the regression model

$$E(\text{TOTAWARD}) = \beta_0 + \beta_1\text{SIZE} + \beta_2\text{PDCLAIMS} + \beta_3\text{PHWCLAIM} + \beta_4\text{NSS} + \beta_5\text{NSG}$$

where   NSS $= 1$ if the GROUP $=$ NSS and NSS $= 0$ otherwise

NSG $= 1$ if the GROUP $=$ NSG and NSG $= 0$ otherwise

Does the variance ratio indicate that the above model is significant? Use $\alpha = .05$.

c. It is reasonable to think that PDCLAIMS and PHWCLAIM might be highly correlated, since they are both measures of the amount of claims. Plot a scatter diagram of PDCLAIMS against PHWCLAIM to check for multicollinearity. Does this graph tell us anything about the results in part **b?**

d. Use the absolute t-value elimination procedure to develop a predictive model that minimizes MSE.

Problems 11–16 use the data set found in Appendix A of this chapter.

 The personnel department of COMCEL gives a battery of four tests to prospective employees of its professional staff. Since the company is highly selective, it tests many more applicants than it hires. The manager of the personnel department wishes to reduce the number of tests in order to cut cost, but without reducing the effectiveness of the screening process. The manager selects a random sample of 60 employees and obtains an average performance SCORE for each. She wishes to relate the performance scores of these employees to the scores made on these four tests.

The company also has a policy of offering higher salaries to candidates with advanced degrees. The personnel manager wishes to determine whether candidates with advanced degrees generally outperform other candidates with similar test scores. The manager records the highest degree earned by the employee and whether the advanced degree is related to the job applied for.

11. Compute a correlation matrix relating only the four test scores to the dependent variable, job performance SCORE. Interpret the correlation coefficient $r_{\text{TEST1, SCORE}}$.

12. Use the R^2 procedure to detect the presence of multicollinearity among the test scores. Does it appear that multicollinearity will present problems in interpreting the regression coefficients?

13. Create two indicator variables:

MA $= 1$ if the highest degree is MA

0 if MA is not the highest degree

PHD $= 1$ if the highest degree is PHD

0 if PHD is not the highest degree

Estimate the model

$$E(\text{SCORE}) = \beta_0 + \beta_1\text{MA} + \beta_2\text{PHD}$$

a. Predict the mean performance score made by employees whose highest degree is a BA. Whose highest degree is an MA. Whose highest degree is the Ph.D.

b. What statistic should you use to answer the question: Do holders of advanced degrees tend to perform differently from employees with bachelor's degrees?

c. What is the null hypothesis tested in **b,** and what is the alternative hypothesis?

d. Interpret the sample regression coefficients of the MA and PhD indicator variables.

e. Use a t-test to determine whether employees with master's degrees outperform employees with bachelor's degrees. Use $\alpha = .05$.

14. For candidates with advanced degrees the personnel manager creates an indicator variable RELATED $= 1$ if the candidate's advanced degree is related to the job applied for, RELATED $= 0$ if the advanced degree is unrelated to the job, or if the candidate has no advanced degree. Estimate the model

$$E(\text{SCORE}) = \beta_0 + \beta_1\text{MA} + \beta_2\text{PHD} + \beta_3\text{RELATED}$$

and test the significance of the RELATED variable using $\alpha = .05$. What policy conclusion can you draw from the results of this test?

15. Fit the full model

$$E(\text{SCORE}) = \beta_0 + \beta_1\text{TEST1} + \beta_2\text{TEST2} + \beta_3\text{TEST3} + \beta_4\text{TEST4} + \beta_5\text{MA} + \beta_6\text{PHD} + \beta_7\text{RELATED}$$

and the reduced model

$$E(\text{SCORE}) = \beta_0 + \beta_1\text{TEST1} + \beta_2\text{TEST2} + \beta_3\text{TEST3} + \beta_4\text{TEST4}$$

a. Compute the extra sum of squares contributed by the variables, MA, PHD, and RELATED.

b. We want to determine whether the MA, PHD, and RELATED variables contribute significantly to prediction after controlling for the scores made on the battery of tests. Write the null and alternative hypotheses that should be tested.

c. Test the significance of the extra sum of squares from **a,** using the general linear test. Use $\alpha = .05$. Does it appear that the MA, PHD, and RELATED variables are predictors of performance score after controlling for the battery of tests?

16. Fit the full model

$$E(\text{SCORE}) = \beta_0 + \beta_1\text{TEST1} + \beta_2\text{TEST2} + \beta_3\text{TEST3} + \beta_4\text{TEST4} + \beta_5\text{MA} + \beta_6\text{PHD} + \beta_7\text{RELATED}$$

a. Use the $|t|$ screening process outlined in Chapter 11 to select the tests and degree predictor variables that will minimize MSE.

b. Based on part **a,** how would you change the current personnel selection process at COMCEL?

 17. Exercise 5 in Section 11.3 showed cross-sectional monthly salary data for 18 managers at the same level within a major firm. The data are reproduced below for your convenience. The three predictor variables are MONTHS on the job, level of interpersonal COMMunication skill along a 1 (poor) to 10 (good) scale, and the manager's GENDER.

Suppose the firm wishes to predict monthly salary and believes that the prediction equation may be different between males and females. The firm then has two choices: (1) estimate each regression separately or (2) use indicator variables to capture any difference in intercepts and interaction terms to capture possible differences in slopes.

	Monthly (in hundreds) SALARY	MONTHS on the Job	Level of COMMunication Skill	GENDER of Manager
1	20.0	14	3	Female
2	21.0	14	2	Female
3	21.5	12	3	Female
4	22.0	25	4	Female
5	23.0	27	6	Female
6	22.0	30	5	Female
7	24.0	32	7	Female
8	23.0	36	8	Female
9	25.0	40	9	Female
10	27.0	15	1	Male
11	28.0	16	3	Male
12	29.0	22	4	Male
13	32.0	27	5	Male
14	32.0	26	5	Male
15	31.0	30	6	Male
16	34.0	34	8	Male
17	36.0	32	7	Male
18	39.0	38	9	Male

a. Plot MONTHS on the job and COMMunication skill against SALARY. Use different symbols for male and female. Does it appear that GENDER affects SALARY? Does it appear that MONTHS of service has a different effect on SALARY, depending on whether the employee is a female rather than a male? Does it appear that COMMunication skill has a different effect on SALARY, depending on whether the employee is a female rather than a male?

b. Recode GENDER as follows: Code Female = 1 and Male = 0. Estimate the regression model.

$$E(\text{SALARY}) = \beta_0 + \beta_1 \text{MONTHS} + \beta_2 \text{COMM} + \beta_3 \text{GENDER} + \beta_{13} \text{MONTHS} \times \text{GENDER}$$

$$+ \beta_{23} \text{COMM} \times \text{GENDER}$$

c. Write the null and alternative hypotheses you would test in order to determine whether there was *any* difference between the prediction equations for males and females. Use the general linear test to test these hypotheses. Let $\alpha = .05$. State your conclusions.

d. Write the null and alternative hypotheses you would test in order to determine whether there was a difference in the slope coefficients of the prediction equations for males and females. Test these hypotheses and state your conclusions. Let $\alpha = .05$.

e. Does it appear that multicollinearity is a problem? Why?

Problems 18–23 use the data set in Appendix B of this chapter.

 The data set consists of job satisfaction scores and biographical data recorded for 30 employees of HICOMM Inc., COMCEL's leading competitor. JOBSAT is the dependent variable. The predictor variables ‖are: (1) SALARY in thousands of dollars; (2) YEARS with HICOMM; (3) AGE; (4) years of formal EDUCation; (5) GENDER (1 = male, 0 = female); and (6) MANAGement (1 = yes, 0 = no).

18. Draw a scatter diagram between JOBSAT and each predictor variable. Do the predictor variables appear to be related to JOBSAT? Do any of the graphs suggest nonlinear relationships?

19. Compute the multiple regression model with all predictor variables entered as linear terms. Write the null and alternative hypotheses for testing the significance of the regression model, and test the model using $\alpha = .05$.

20. Use the t-value screening procedure from Chapter 11 to produce a final regression model that minimizes the standard error of the estimate.

21. Use the R^2 procedure to check for multicollinearity. Does it appear that multicollinearity has affected the "face validity" of the regression model by producing sample regression coefficients that are contrary to logic?.

22. Compute the residuals from the final regression model from Exercise 20. Draw residual plots against each remaining predictor variable in the model. Have the linearity, equal variances, normality, and independence assumptions been met? If not, add the appropriate squared and interaction terms, re-estimate the model, and check the residuals again. Interpret the sample regression coefficients of the final model in managerial terms.

23. Suppose that, instead of prediction, the purpose of the regression was to determine whether personnel with MANAGement responsibility are more satisfied than nonmanagers, after controlling for AGE, GENDER, SALARY, YEARS, and EDUC.

a. Why would the $|t|$-value screening procedure be the wrong approach for this purpose?.

b. Suppose the sample regression coefficient of the MANAGement variable was not significant, but the regression coefficient of the interaction variable, MANAG $\times$ GENDER, was positive and significant ($p < .001$). How would you interpret these results? Can you say that managers are more satisfied than nonmanagers?

REFERENCES

Maddala, G. S. *Introduction to Econometrics,* 2nd ed. New York: Macmillan, 1992.

Mosteller, F., and J. Tukey. *Data Analysis and Regression Analysis.* Reading, Mass.: Addison-Wesley, 1977.

Neter, J., W. Wasserman, and M. Kutner. *Applied Linear Statistical Models,* 3rd ed. Homewood, Ill: Richard D. Irwin, 1990.

Roberts, H. *Data Analysis for Managers with Minitab.* Redwood City, Calif.: The Scientific Press, 1988.

APPENDIX A: COMCEL Personnel Data

OBS	TEST1	TEST2	TEST3	TEST4	DEGREE	RELATED	SCORE
1	60	81	72	55	BA	0	58
2	67	70	76	78	BA	1	80
3	87	84	88	81	MA	0	66
4	67	64	68	63	BA	0	76
5	81	66	89	56	MA	0	50
6	55	66	66	52	BA	0	43
7	47	51	66	42	BA	0	28
8	69	87	67	83	PHD	1	94
9	59	86	64	65	BA	0	69
10	51	61	67	56	BA	0	34
11	91	67	87	57	MA	1	74
12	63	69	62	46	BA	0	41
13	82	90	76	87	PHD	1	99
14	99	83	88	86	PHD	1	99
15	53	81	70	80	MA	0	80
16	68	88	95	58	PHD	0	97
17	95	89	87	63	MA	0	69
18	64	66	73	58	BA	0	82
19	91	62	72	53	BA	0	67
20	64	65	68	81	MA	1	99
21	43	64	57	48	BA	0	48
22	91	66	62	82	PHD	0	65
23	99	68	92	51	BA	0	93
24	60	81	72	55	BA	0	58
25	67	70	76	78	BA	0	50
26	87	84	88	81	MA	1	76
27	67	64	68	63	BA	0	76
28	81	66	89	56	MA	1	60
29	55	66	66	52	BA	0	53
30	47	51	66	42	BA	0	38
31	92	67	69	80	PHD	1	80
32	69	87	67	83	PHD	1	84
33	59	86	64	65	BA	0	69
34	51	61	67	56	BA	0	34
35	90	64	88	86	PHD	0	96
36	91	67	87	57	MA	1	64
37	63	69	62	46	BA	0	41
38	82	90	76	87	PHD	0	61
39	99	83	88	86	PHD	1	89
40	53	81	70	80	MA	0	80
41	68	88	95	58	PHD	0	97
42	95	89	87	63	MA	0	69
43	64	66	73	58	BA	0	82
44	91	62	72	53	BA	0	67
45	64	65	68	81	MA	1	99
46	43	64	57	48	BA	0	48
47	91	66	62	82	PHD	0	65
48	99	68	92	51	BA	0	73

49	92	67	69	80	PHD	1	96
50	69	87	67	83	PHD	1	94
51	59	86	64	65	BA	0	69
52	51	61	67	56	BA	0	34
53	90	64	88	86	PHD	0	86
54	91	67	87	57	MA	1	74
55	63	69	62	46	BA	0	41
56	53	81	70	80	MA	0	80
57	95	89	87	63	MA	0	69
58	91	62	72	53	BA	0	67
59	64	65	68	81	MA	1	99
60	43	64	57	48	BA	0	48

APPENDIX B: HICOMM Job Satisfaction Data

OBS	JOBSAT	SALARY	YEARS	AGE	EDUC	GENDER	MANAG
1	58	52.4	1	22	16	1	1
2	51	49.7	13	53	16	1	0
3	76	100.5	17	43	14	1	1
4	45	37.9	17	36	18	1	1
5	64	65.9	15	34	17	1	1
6	49	43.2	6	48	17	0	1
7	40	29.4	5	29	14	1	1
8	62	95.1	13	53	16	0	1
9	29	25.8	1	22	12	1	0
10	66	76.0	4	43	18	0	0
11	45	45.5	8	50	14	1	0
12	61	98.8	14	62	16	1	1
13	43	37.0	4	43	16	1	0
14	36	51.9	17	62	16	0	1
15	69	90.3	10	52	17	1	1
16	43	47.1	10	52	14	0	0
17	58	80.2	6	48	19	1	0
18	59	75.0	8	50	18	0	0
19	36	36.0	15	34	16	0	1
20	38	40.0	2	38	17	0	0
21	80	90.9	12	46	19	1	1
22	41	27.3	3	25	14	0	0
23	68	75.6	2	38	16	1	0
24	67	70.9	17	36	14	0	1
25	33	31.3	9	30	12	0	0
26	42	33.4	12	32	16	1	0
27	57	58.4	5	29	17	0	0
28	54	53.2	3	25	14	1	0
29	54	60.1	9	30	16	1	0
30	68	62.9	12	32	16	0	0

FORECASTING

13.1 Data patterns and forecasting
13.2 Alternative forecasting approaches
13.3 Forecasting using regression analysis
    Autoregressive modeling
    Leading and coincident indicators
    Developing the model
    Analyzing residuals
    Mean absolute percentage error
    Limitations of regression models as
      forecasting tools
    Summary

13.4 Forecasting using the classical decomposition
     method
    Additive and multiplicative models
    Deseasonalized data
    The trend pattern
    The cycle pattern
    Short-term forecasting
13.5 Qualitative forecasting methods
    Expert panels
    Delphi method
Appendix: Statistical Software

CHAPTER OUTLINE

COMCEL INTEROFFICE COMMUNICATION

Date: August 13, 1994
To: Howard Bright, Manager, Norcross Plant
From: Ann Tabor, CEO
Re: Demand Forecasts for Car Phones in the Southern Region

I have seen your forecasts for the demand for our telephones in the Southern Region. If the forecasts materialize, we will be the industry leader. But, frankly, I have my doubts about your numbers. They seem too optimistic to me. Since our production schedule depends so heavily on these forecasts, we need to be sure of our numbers.

How did you generate these forecasts? Please provide me with a detailed description of the forecasting methodology. I will feel better when I can concur with your forecasts.

13.1 ≡ Data Patterns and Forecasting

Managers develop historical and forecasting models to predict the future and to detect significant deviations from expected behavior. Historical models look to the past. Under the assumption that the best estimate of the future is the recent past, managers expect continuity of performance. Whatever happened in the recent past should continue into the near future. If it does not, there may be a disturbance problem. Forecasting or planning models are forward looking. They serve two purposes. First, planning models set targets and goals for future performance. When actual future performance does not meet planned levels, managers may face a disturbance problem. Second, they provide basic input for developing production schedules and determining manpower, raw material, and capital equipment needs. In summary, accurate forecasts are essential in establishing, achieving, and monitoring progress toward business goals. Learning how to develop accurate forecasts is the goal of this chapter.

We will develop forecasts using time-ordered data. Time-ordered, or time series, data are data collected over time–data in chronological sequence. Forecasting begins by drawing a line graph of the historical data. The horizontal axis is time and the vertical axis is the level of the business or economic variable. Line graphs help managers see the systematic patterns underlying the data.

There are three common systematic patterns for time-ordered data: trend, seasonal, and cyclical. Time series data can include one or more of these patterns.

A *trend* pattern occurs when there is a long-term increase or decrease in the data. Figure 13.1 shows the product life cycle. Ignoring the roughness in the data, we see that, in Phase I, sales increase at an increasing rate—a nonlinear trend pattern. In Phase II, sales increase at a constant rate—a linear trend pattern. In Phase III, sales increase but at a decreasing rate. Sales begin to level off—a nonlinear pattern. In Phase IV, sales decrease at a nonlinear rate.

A *seasonal* pattern occurs when factors that are associated with a day of the week, a month, or quarter of the year influence the time-series data. The desire for long weekends may cause absenteeism to peak on Monday and Friday every week. High outdoor temperatures may cause sales of ice cream to peak during the summer months and to drop during the winter months every year. To qualify as seasonal, the data pattern must be repetitive—occurring the same day of every week, the same month or same quarter of every year.

FIGURE 13.1   Product Life Cycle—Trend Patterns

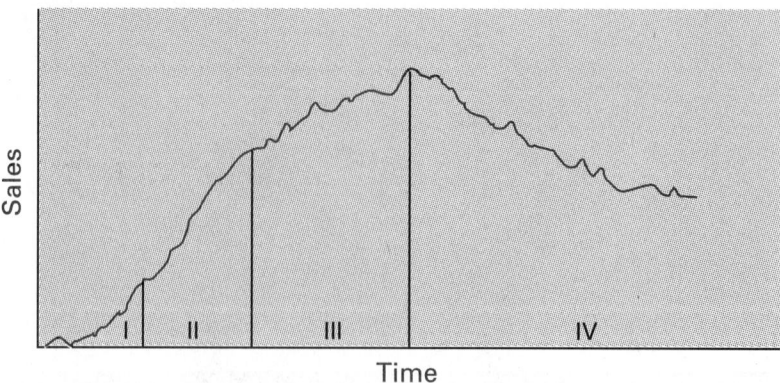

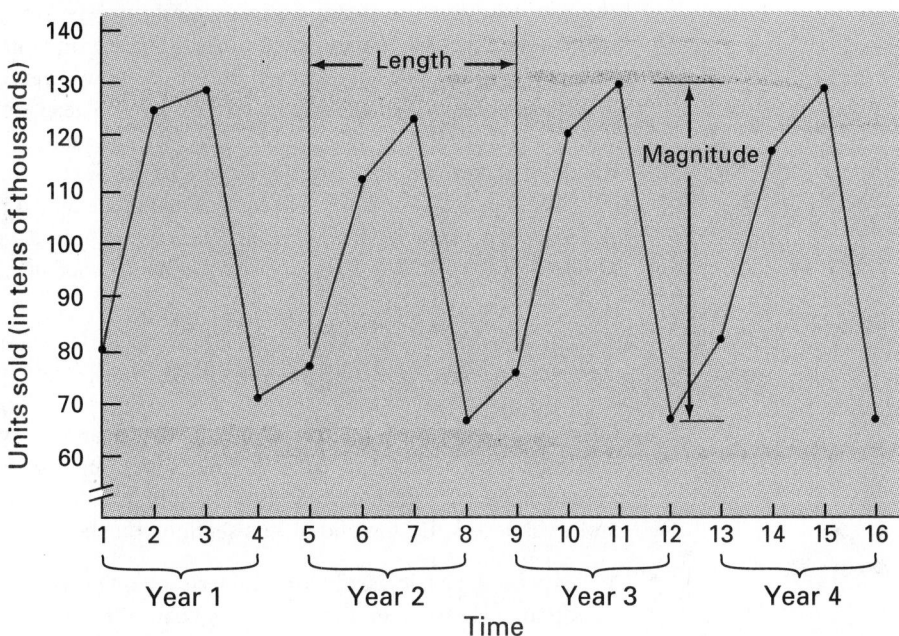

FIGURE 13.2 Seasonal Pattern

Figure 13.2 shows quarterly data with a seasonal pattern. The first and fourth quarters of every year are relatively weak sales periods. The second and third quarters are relatively strong sales periods. The pattern persists year after year. The magnitude of a seasonal pattern is measured as the peak (highest sales for the year) minus the trough (the lowest sales for the year). The length of the seasonal pattern is one year.

A *cyclical* pattern occurs when the data are influenced by business cycles that are longer than one year. Capital spending is an important determinant of the length

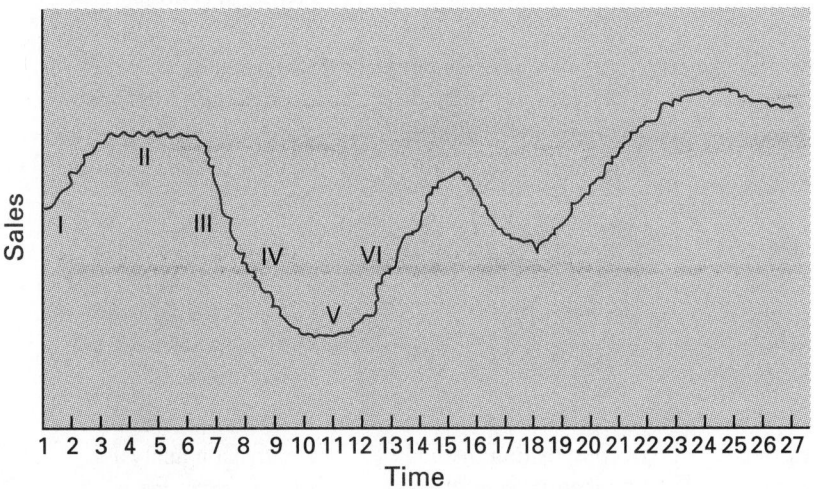

FIGURE 13.3 Cyclical Pattern

of business cycles. Thus, when managers anticipate a slowdown in the economy, they cut back their capital outlays. As they cut back, unemployment increases and the economy slows. Consumers are less willing to buy big-ticket items such as cars or major appliances when they fear layoffs. Soon we find ourselves in a recession. Business cycles affect sales of a firm. Figure 13.3 shows sales data with a cyclical pattern.

A business cycle can have up to six phases. These are growth (I), prosperity (II), warning (III), recession (IV), depression (V), and recovery (VI). The length and magnitude of cycles can vary from one cycle to the next.

The major distinction between seasonal and cyclical patterns is that the seasonal pattern is of constant length and recurs on a regular basis. Cycles vary in length and magnitude. Since World War II, business cycles have varied in length from 28 to 117 months.

13.2 ≡ Alternative Forecasting Approaches

Once we have graphed and reviewed the historical data, we develop forecasts. There are three forecasting approaches: time series, causal, and judgmental. The three approaches have different underlying assumptions, data requirements, and strengths and weaknesses. By the end of this section you should be able to:

1. explain the basic assumption underlying quantitative forecasting approaches;
2. distinguish between time series and causal forecasting approaches;
3. distinguish between quantitative and qualitative forecasting approaches; and
4. explain the major problem with qualitative approaches.

Table 13.1 summarizes the major forecasting approaches and lists some techniques that are used within each category.

Quantitative Forecasting Approaches

Quantitative approaches can provide accurate numerical short-term forecasts. Consider quantitative forecasting approaches when

Table 13.1

Forecasting Methods

| | Quantitative Data Available | | Qualitative Data Available Judgmental or Intuitive Methods |
	Time Series Methods	Causal Methods	
How Forecast Is Made	Forecasts the continuation of *patterns* into the future	Forecasts the continuation of *relationships* into the future	Management or expert groups *subjectively* assess the future
Examples	Predicting the growth of phone sales for the upcoming year	Predicting how our price versus competitors' prices and our advertising level affect car phone sales for the upcoming year	Predicting how car phones will look in the year 2000; predicting the percentage of car phones in the U.S. in the year 2010
Forecasting Methods	Decomposition method Exponential smoothing	Regression analysis Econometric models	Nominal group method Delphi method

1. you have past numerical data, and
2. you can assume that either the past data patterns or relationships among variables will continue into the near future.

This second condition, the *assumption of continuity,* is essential to all quantitative forecasting approaches. Continuity means that the recent past is a good guide to the near future. When sudden and major economic or political changes occur, quantitative forecasting approaches do not work well. For example, in 1973 forecasters severely overestimated gas consumption because they could not predict the Arab–Israeli war in June and the subsequent skyrocketing gas prices. Quantitative forecasting approaches seek to detect either (1) relationships among a set of business and economic variables—causal methods or (2) any of the three common data patterns discussed above—time series methods.

Relationship detection: In Chapters 11–12 we used regression analysis to detect relationships between a dependent variable and a set of predictor variables using cross-sectional data. In Section 13.3 we use regression analysis to develop forecasts using time-ordered data. For a valid forecast, the relationship based on the historical data must continue into the future.

Pattern detection: These quantitative forecasting methods help us identify the trend, seasonal, and cyclical patterns. We develop forecasts by projecting these patterns into the near future. Pattern detection methods include moving averages (see Chapter 2), exponential smoothing, and the classical decomposition method. We present the decomposition method in Section 13.4. For a valid forecast, the detected patterns based on historical data must continue into the future.

Which quantitative approach should we use? Both approaches can produce accurate predictions. If we wish only to make predictions, then time series models based on data patterns are easier to build and maintain. If we also want to identify the predictor variables that affect the forecasted dependent variable for explanation and control purposes, we use regression models. But regression models are often more costly (Makridakis, Wheelwright, and McGee, 1983).

Qualitative Approaches

Qualitative approaches draw upon intuitive thinking, judgment, and accumulated knowledge. We will consider only group-based methods that require more than a single person to generate forecasts. We will present the nominal group and Delphi methods in Section 13.5.

The nominal group and Delphi methods minimize many group interaction problems. When groups meet, they can make poor judgments. Ineffective group members rarely challenge one another and treat opinions as facts. Members often do not challenge questionable assumptions underlying their forecasts. Influential members stifle dissent and inhibit others from speaking. Ineffective group leaders interrupt colleagues, promote their own ideas early in the group discussion, and do not encourage and protect minority opinion.

The nominal group and Delphi methods still have problems because they both rely on judgments. In Chapter 4 we learned that judgments are often plagued by inconsistency and error. Business professionals have particular trouble in making judgments about the future. They may use rules of thumb that could result in poor forecasts. Table 13.2 provides examples of some poor forecasting rules of thumb. Robin Hogarth (1987) has catalogued over 20 rules that can produce poor intuitive forecasts.

Table 13.2

Some Poor Forecasting Rules of Thumb

Type	Description	Example
Availability	The ease with which specific instances are recalled affects judgment.	Frequencies of well-publicized events (e.g., earthquakes) are overestimated.
Anchor and adjust	Predictions are made by anchoring on a value and then making adjustments.	Make a sales forecast by taking last year's sales and adding 5%.
Wishful thinking	Managers' desires for outcomes affect their assessments.	Overestimate the likelihood of a cure for cancer by the year 2000.
Hindsight	Managers are not surprised about what happened in the past. They find plausible explanations.	Anyone could have foreseen the *Challenger* spacecraft disaster. After the crash some NASA officials said, "It was just a matter of time!" Why didn't they speak up before?
Selective perception	Managers look for information that is consistent with their own views.	If you think the stock market will drop, you seek out pessimistic forecasts and ignore optimistic ones.

SECTION 13.2 EXERCISES

1.   What is the basic assumption behind all quantitative forecasting methods? How can you be sure this assumption will hold?

2.   Distinguish between time series methods (pattern detection) and causal (relationship detection) forecasting methods.

3.   Distinguish between quantitative and qualitative forecasting methods. Provide examples of when each type of forecasting method might be used by a business organization.

4.   With which common systematic pattern for time-ordered data—trend, seasonal, or cycle—would you associate each of the following?
    a. The steady increase of foreign car sales from 1975 to 1990
    b. The drop in snow ski sales from October to April every year
    c. A decrease in sales due to a recession
    d. The drop in sales of consumer products in January of every year
    e. The explosive growth of personal computers in the late 1980s
    f. the peak in sales of wedding rings every year in June

5.   Suppose the date is December 1989. We wish to forecast the number of tourists to Eastern Europe for 1990. We have a data base for the period 1978–1988. If we used the data base to forecast, why might our forecast severely underestimate the number of tourists to Eastern Europe?

6.   From 1984 to 1990 the Atlanta Braves completed each baseball season near the bottom of the Western Division of the National League. Yet in 1991 and 1992 they won the Western Division. Why would a time series (pattern detection) method have failed to predict the Braves' success in 1991?

7.   Explain the major problems with qualitative forecasting approaches.

8. When the Soviet Union collapsed in 1991, political "experts" noted that it was not surprising. They had expected it. Yet none had made public predictions of the imminent collapse of the Soviet Union. What rule of thumb were these experts using?

9. You wish to predict the sales of a new product for your firm. What major problem will keep you from using quantitative forecasting methods?

13.3 Forecasting Using Regression Analysis

In regression analysis we seek predictor variables to forecast the dependent variable. Detected relationships are assumed to continue into the near future. This section extends regression analysis to time-ordered data. By the end of this section you should be able to:

1. explain the terms *lagging, autocorrelation, autoregressive model, coincident indicator, and leading indicator;*
2. develop, interpret, and use multiple regression models to make short-term forecasts;
3. explain the problem of using predictor variables that are coincident indicators in regression models based on time-ordered data; and
4. explain why the mean absolute percentage error (MAPE) is a useful measure of forecast accuracy.

Example: Forecasting Units Sold at COMCEL   Table 13.3 lists the units sold (in tens of thousands) of the deluxe mobile car phone for the past 16 quarters. It is now January 1, 1994. COMCEL wishes to forecast units sold for the first quarter of 1994.

Table 13.3

Units Sold Quarterly*

Year	QTR	TIME (t)	SALES$_t$ (tens of thousands)	SALES$_{t-1}$ (tens of thousands)	
1990	1	1	3.40	—	
	2	2	2.00	3.40	←Sales from Quarter 1
	3	3	1.90	2.00	←Sales from Quarter 2
	4	4	3.20	1.90	
1991	1	5	4.80	3.20	
	2	6	3.75	4.80	
	3	7	4.13	3.75	
	4	8	4.51	4.13	
1992	1	9	5.61	4.51	
	2	10	4.05	5.61	
	3	11	4.63	4.05	
	4	12	5.01	4.63	
1993	1	13	6.03	5.01	
	2	14	4.61	6.03	
	3	15	5.08	4.61	
	4	16	5.29	5.08	←Sales from Quarter 3

*We represent sales in a period as SALES$_t$ and sales in the previous time period as SALES$_{t-1}$. For example, sales in the second period was 20,000 units. This is SALES$_2$. Sales in the previous quarter was 34,000 units. This is SALES$_1$. Sales for period 16 is 52,900 units. This is SALES$_{16}$. Sales in the previous period is SALES$_{15}$, which is 50,800 units.

FIGURE 13.4   Line Graph of Sales

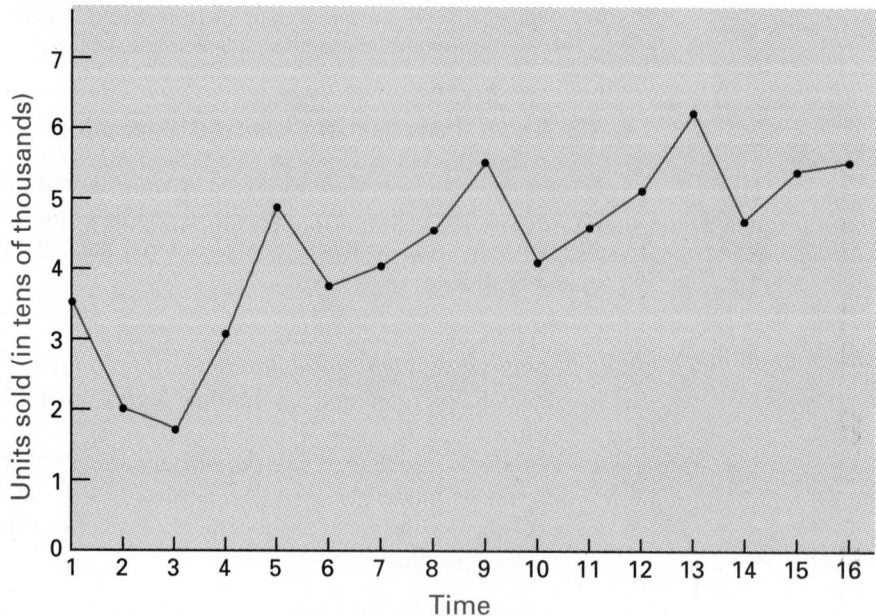

Figure 13.4 shows units sold over time. Units sold exhibit both a positive linear trend pattern and a seasonal pattern. Sales are relatively high in the first and fourth quarters and relatively low in the second and third quarters.

Regression analysis requires that we seek one or more predictor variables that explain the variation in units sold. An obvious first choice is sales from the previous quarter. Note that successive observations in Figure 13.4 are close to one another. Should our forecast of next quarter's sales be based, at least in part, on what we sold this quarter? We are asking: Is there a statistically significant relationship between sales in successive periods?

Autoregressive Modeling

We answer this question by creating a new predictor variable, $SALES_{t-1}$, where $SALES_{t-1}$ is the value of sales at the previous time period denoted as time period $t - 1$. We call this *one-quarter lagging*. (See the last column in Table 13.3.) To determine whether there is a relationship between $SALES_t$ and $SALES_{t-1}$, we draw a scatter plot. $SALES_t$, the dependent variable, is measured on the vertical axis, and $SALES_{t-1}$, a predictor variable, is measured on the horizontal axis.

We have labelled the data points in Figure 13.5. The data point for quarter 3 in 1990 represents $SALES_3 = 1.90$ (quarter 3) and $SALES_2 = 2.00$ (quarter 2). Figure 13.5 shows that the data points are upward sloping to the right, which suggests a positive linear relationship. That is, if sales in one quarter are low (high), sales in the following quarter will also be low (high). While the correlation is positive, it is not, however, perfect. All the data values do not lie on a straight line.

The term *autocorrelation* denotes the correlation between values of a variable and preceding values of the *same* variable. *Auto* means self or same. The data in

Figure 13.5 are positively autocorrelated. Again, all that means is that successive data points are close to one another.

Can we use the predictor variable, $sales_{t-1}$, to forecast $sales_t$? Is $sales_t$ related to $sales_{t-1}$? To find out, we fit a simple linear regression model to the boxed data in Table 13.3. $sales_t$ is the dependent variable, and $sales_{t-1}$ is the predictor variable. We have 15 observations from quarter 2, 1990, to quarter 4, 1993. We used the COMSTAT regression tool to develop the following simple linear regression model. Expression (13.1) is an **autoregressive model**.

An autoregressive model is one in which lagged values of the dependent variable are used to forecast the dependent variable.

$$\text{SALES}_t\text{-PRED} = 1.67 + .63\text{SALES}_{t-1} \tag{13.1}$$

We interpret the sample slope and intercept as we would in a typical regression model. Sales in any quarter are equal to a constant plus 63% of the sales the quarter before.

The variance ratio of 8.34 has a p-value of less than .05 [$F(.95; 1,13) = 4.67$]. Thus we can use expression (13.1) to forecast units sold for the first quarter of 1994. The first quarter of 1994 is time period, $t = 17$. We use 5.29, the actual sales for the fourth quarter of 1993 ($t = 16$), to forecast the sales for the first quarter of 1994:

$$\text{SALES}_{17}\text{-PRED} = 1.67 + .63(5.29) = 5.00, \quad \text{or } 50,000 \text{ phones}$$

Could we generate a more accurate forecast by bringing additional predictor variables into the model? The simple coefficient of determination provides an answer. From the COMSTAT REGRESSION tool output, the value of r^2 for this model is 39%. That is, 39% of the variation in units sold is explained by units sold in the preceding quarter. The relatively low r^2 value means that we should seek additional predictor variables.

FIGURE 13.5   Scatter Plot of Sales and Sales Lagged by One Quarter

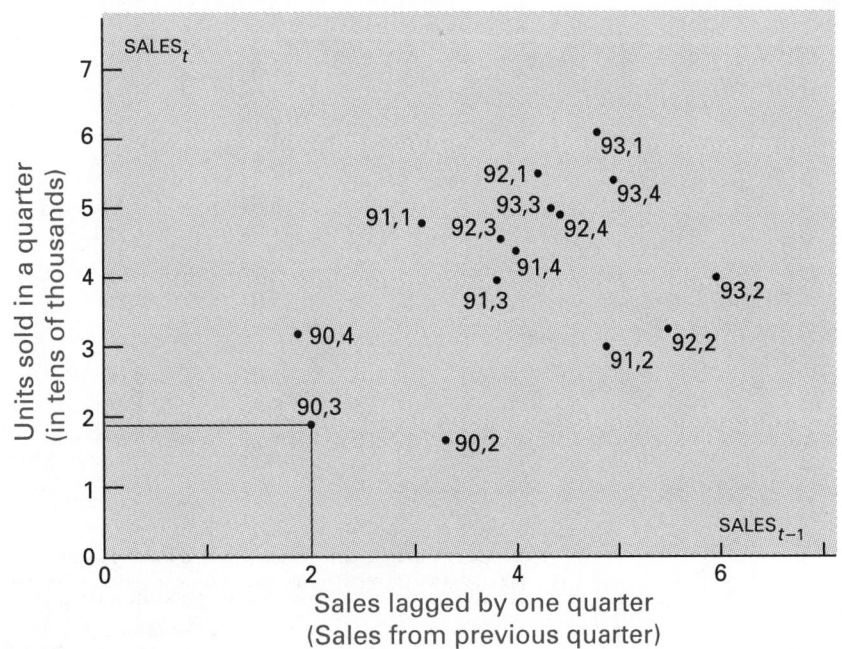

In summary, when forecasting any dependent variable Y_t, consider using lagged values of Y_t as predictor variables. This is autoregressive modeling. Plot Y_t versus one-period-lagged values of Y_{t-1} (denoted as the predictor variable). If the scatter plot indicates either a positive or negative autocorrelation, treat the lagged values of Y_t as a predictor variable. Also, consider variables with lags greater than one. Lagged values of two periods (denoted as the predictor variable Y_{t-2}) make sense if we believe that sales from two quarters ago also affect present-quarter sales. However, if the coefficient of determination is still relatively low for the final autoregressive model, seek predictor variables, X, other than lagged values of Y_t, to forecast Y_t. Examples include price, competitors' sales, and consumer income.

Leading and Coincident Indicators

We try to improve the forecasting power of the autoregressive model by adding another predictor variable—amount of advertising. We have also included lagged values of advertising, ADV_{t-1}, in Table 13.4. If lagged values of Y_t affect Y_t, doesn't it make sense that lagged values of X_t might also affect Y_t?

ADV_t, the level of advertising, in hundreds of thousands of dollars, is a *coincident indicator*. It represents the possibility that advertising in a quarter affects sales in the same quarter. ADV_{t-1} is a potential *leading indicator*.* ADV_{t-1} represents the possibility that advertising in one quarter affects sales in the next quarter.

Table 13.4

Quarterly Unit Sales and Predictor Variables

Year	QTR	TIME (t)	SALES$_t$	SALES$_{t-1}$	ADV$_t$	ADV$_{t-1}$
1990	1	1	3.40	—	1.10	—
	2	2	2.00	3.40	1.40	1.10
	3	3	1.90	2.00	3.30	1.40
	4	4	3.20	1.90	5.40	3.30
1991	1	5	4.80	3.20	1.50	5.40
	2	6	3.75	4.80	3.60	1.50
	3	7	4.13	3.75	3.70	3.60
	4	8	4.51	4.13	5.80	3.70
1992	1	9	5.61	4.51	1.90	5.80
	2	10	4.05	5.61	4.00	1.90
	3	11	4.63	4.05	4.10	4.00
	4	12	5.01	4.63	6.20	4.10
1993	1	13	6.03	5.01	2.50	6.20
	2	14	4.61	6.03	4.40	2.50
	3	15	5.08	4.61	4.50	4.40
	4	16	5.29	5.08	1.25	4.50

*Do not confuse the terms *coincident* and *leading indicators* with indicator variables from the previous two regression chapters. Indicator variables represent categorical variables with two or more classes.

Developing the Model

Are $SALES_{t-1}$, ADV_t, or ADV_{t-1} related to $SALES_t$?

We applied a software regression package to the boxed data in Table 13.4—quarter 2, 1990, to quarter 4, 1993. The t-tests shown in Table 13.5 indicate that ADV_t, ADV_{t-1}, and $SALES_{t-1}$ are significantly related to $SALES_t$ since the p-values are all less than .05 and all absolute t-values are greater than one.

Table 13.5

t-Tests for Predictor Variables

Variable	Parameter Estimate	t-Value	Two-Tailed p-Value
INTERCEPT	−.211	—	—
$SALES_{t-1}$	.508	13.89	$p < .001$
ADV_t	.086	3.17	.0092
ADV_{t-1}	.587	21.58	$p < .001$

Expression (13.2) is a multiple regression model of $SALES_t$ with three predictor variables: $SALES_{t-1}$, ADV_t, and ADV_{t-1}. The equation is

$$SALES_t\text{-PRED} = -.211 + .508SALES_{t-1} + .086ADV_t + .587ADV_{t-1} \quad (13.2)$$

The inclusion of ADV_t and ADV_{t-1} increases the multiple coefficient of determination to 98.6%. Thus, expression (13.2) accounts for almost all of the variation in SALES over the last 15 quarters.

Analyzing Residuals

Next we examine the residual plots to look for violations of the linear regression model assumptions (see Chapter 11). Because the data are time-ordered, plotting the residuals against time should be the first diagnostic check. Nonindependence occurs when the time sequence of residuals shows long strings of positive and negative values or when the residuals exhibit a sawtooth pattern.

The residuals in Table 13.6 were obtained from a software regression package. Figure 13.6, which plots residuals versus time, suggests that the model satisfies the independence assumption. If the model violates the independence assumption, we should seek professional statistical help.

Next we check for violations of the normality assumption and look for possible outliers. In Table 13.6 we standardize the residuals by dividing each one by the standard error of .160 (the square root of the mean square error term from the ANOVA output) obtained from the regression output. If the normality assumption is met, then by the Empirical rule, about 68% of the standardized residuals should lie between −1.00 and +1.00. About 95% should lie between −2.00 and +2.00. Almost all standardized residuals should fall between −3.00 and +3.00. If a standardized residual is beyond ±3, this data point should be considered a possible outlier.

Table 13.6

Residuals and Standardized Residuals

Year	QTR	TIME (t)	SALES$_t$	SALES$_t$-PRED from (13.2)	Standardized Residual	Residual
1990	2	2	2.00	2.281	−.281	−1.756
	3	3	1.90	1.909	−.009	−.056
	4	4	3.20	3.154	.046	.288
1991	1	5	4.80	4.710	.090	.563
	2	6	3.75	3.415	.335	2.094
	3	7	4.13	4.123	.007	.044
	4	8	4.51	4.555	−.045	−.281
1992	1	9	5.61	5.644	−.034	−.213
	2	10	4.05	4.095	−.045	−.281
	3	11	4.63	4.544	.086	.538
	4	12	5.01	5.078	−.068	−.425
1993	1	13	6.03	6.184	−.154	−.963
	2	14	4.61	4.695	−.085	−.531
	3	15	5.08	5.097	−.017	−.106
	4	16	5.29	5.115	.175	1.094

Table 13.6 indicates that there are no outliers. The normality assumption is difficult to check using the Empirical rule because percentages are very unstable when there are only 15 observations. However, 12 of 15 or 80.0% of the residuals are between −1 and +1, while 93.3% of the residuals are between −2.00 and +2.00. Although the

FIGURE 13.6   Residual$_t$ Plot versus Time

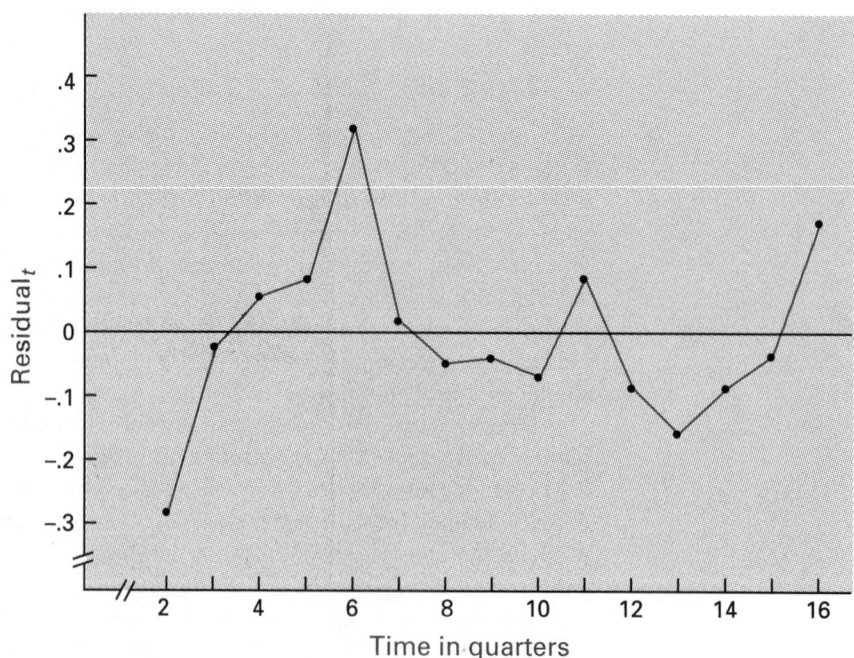

percentage of residuals lying between -1 and $+1$ is a bit high to meet the normality assumption, the departure from the expected percentage is not serious enough to require corrective action, such as a data transformation on the dependent variable.

We should also plot the residuals against SALES$_t$-PRED and the predictor variables. The residual plots (not shown) do not suggest serious violations. If serious violations occur (see Chapter 11), seek professional statistical help.

Finally, Table 13.7, a correlation matrix, shows that multicollinearity is not a serious problem. The correlations among the three predictor variables are low—.0048, .1538, and $-.1670$.

In summary, we have met to a large degree the assumptions underlying the linear regression model. Most importantly, we have met the independence assumption, which is commonly violated in time-ordered data. Multicollinearity is also not a serious problem. Therefore, we may use the model for explanation, prediction, and control.

Table 13.7

Correlation Matrix for COMCEL Sales Data

	SALES$_t$	SALES$_{t-1}$	ADV$_t$	ADV$_{t-1}$
SALES$_t$	1.0000	.6251	$-.0149$	.8502
SALES$_{t-1}$	.6251	1.0000	.0048	.1538
ADV$_t$	$-.0149$	.0048	1.0000	$-.1670$
ADV$_{t-1}$	.8502	.1538	$-.1670$	1.0000

Mean Absolute Percentage Error

We have repeated expression (13.2) below. The regression coefficients indicate the impact on units sold of each predictor variable, holding the other predictor variables constant.

$$\text{SALES}_t\text{-PRED} = -.211 + .508\text{SALES}_{t-1} + .086\text{ADV}_t + .587\text{ADV}_{t-1} \quad (13.2)$$

We can predict SALES$_{17}$ for the first quarter of 1994 by inserting into (13.2) the known sales level for the fourth quarter of 1993 (SALES$_{16}$ = 5.29; see Table 13.4), the known amount of advertising spent in the fourth quarter of 1993 (ADV$_{16}$ = 1.25; see Table 13.4), and the amount COMCEL plans to spend for advertising in the first quarter of 1994, (ADV$_{17}$ = 3.10 or $310,000). We obtain

$$\text{SALES}_{17}\text{-PRED} = -.211 + .508(5.29) + .086(3.10) + .587(1.25)$$
$$= 3.48, \quad \text{or } 34,800 \text{ phones}$$

How good is the forecast? Since the multiple coefficient of determination is 98.6%, the forecast should be accurate, provided the assumption of continuity holds. But how accurate is accurate? The *mean absolute percentage error,* or MAPE, is an excellent measure of forecasting accuracy. We compute the MAPE for expression (13.2). If the MAPE is small enough for our needs, we can then use the model for forecasting.

$$\text{Percentage error} = \text{PE}_t = \left(\frac{\text{Actual}_t - \text{Predicted}_t}{\text{Actual}_t} \right) 100 \qquad (13.3)$$

$$= \left(\frac{\text{Residual}_t}{\text{Actual}_t} \right) 100$$

$$\text{MAPE} = \frac{\sum |\text{PE}_t|}{n} \qquad (13.4)$$

where Actual_t are the actual values of the dependent variable for
$t = 1, 2, 3, \ldots, n$.
Predicted_t are the values of the dependent variable predicted
by the regression model for $t = 1, 2, 3, \ldots, n$, and
n is the number of periods of historical data.

Table 13.8 shows the MAPE calculations for the COMCEL sales data for the
past 15 quarters. Over the past 15 quarters, the model's predictions of sales differed
from the actual sales by a MAPE of 2.7%.

There are two reasons why the MAPE is useful. First, it is more informative than
the actual forecasting error. From Table 13.8, the actual forecasting error for the first
quarter of 1993 was $\text{residual}_{13} = -.154$ unit, or 1,540 phones. That is, expression
(13.2) overestimated actual sales by 1,540 phones. How far off is that? Well, it
depends on the actual sales for the period. An error of 1,540 units on actual sales of
2,000,000 car phones is trivial. An error of 1,540 units on actual sales of 1,500 units
is critical. Second, many business professionals think in terms of percentages. They
can tolerate small percentage errors, but must avoid large ones. The MAPE provides
the type of information that professionals need and will use. If the MAPE is

Table 13.8

Calculations of MAPE

Year	QTR	TIME (t)	ACTUAL SALES$_t$	SALES$_t$ -PRED from (13.2)	Residual$_t$	PE$_t$ (%)	|PE$_t$| (%)
1990	2	2	2.00	2.281	−.281	−14.1	14.1
	3	3	1.90	1.909	−.009	−.5	.5
	4	4	3.20	3.154	.046	1.4	1.4
1991	1	5	4.80	4.710	.090	1.9	1.9
	2	6	3.75	3.415	.335	8.9	8.9
	3	7	4.13	4.123	.007	.2	.2
	4	8	4.51	4.555	−.045	−1.0	1.0
1992	1	9	5.61	5.644	−.034	−.6	.6
	2	10	4.05	4.095	−.045	−1.1	1.1
	3	11	4.63	4.544	.086	1.9	1.9
	4	12	5.01	5.078	−.068	−1.4	1.4
1993	1	13	6.03	6.184	−.154	−2.6	2.6
	2	14	4.61	4.695	−.085	−1.8	1.8
	3	15	5.08	5.097	−.017	−.3	.3
	4	16	5.29	5.115	.175	3.3	3.3
							41.0

Mean absolute percentage error = (41.0/15) = 2.7%

sufficiently small, we can then use expression (13.2) for forecasting. In the COMCEL sales forecasting context: Is a mean forecasting error of 2.7% acceptable? Assume that the actual and predicted sales differed by as much as 2.7% for the first quarter of 1994. Could we then develop realistic production schedules, determine manpower and raw material needs, and the like given a MAPE of 2.7%? An answer of yes means using the forecasted sales values in planning. An answer of no means developing additional regression models or using other forecasting methods to obtain a forecast with a lower MAPE.

Limitations of Regression Models as Forecasting Tools

A hypothetical regression model relating a company's quarterly sales to quarterly gross national product (GNP) is shown below. Assume the model is statistically significant and meets all the assumptions of the linear regression model. Why would it be difficult to forecast sales for the upcoming quarter? Please think about it before reading on.

$$\text{SALES}_t\text{-PRED} = 15.5 + .111\text{GNP}_t \qquad\qquad (13.5)$$

GNP_t is a coincident indicator. To predict SALES_t, we must first predict the level of GNP_t. Experts often disagree on the forecasted GNP. Thus, forecasting by using a regression model with a coincident indicator is difficult. We must first forecast the value of the coincident indicator and then use it to forecast the value of the dependent variable. Using only lagged predictor variables reduces this problem. We use previous and already known values of the predictor variables to forecast future values of the dependent variable.

The coincident indicator, ADV_t, did not present a problem in model (13.2). Firms generally determine the amount of quarterly or monthly advertising for the upcoming year in their yearly budgets. Thus, the firm would know what it planned to spend over the next four quarters for advertising.

However, model (13.2) does have one limitation. We can forecast only one quarter ahead. We cannot predict sales for the second quarter of 1994 until we know the actual level of sales for the first quarter of 1994, which we will not know until the end of the quarter. Thus, model (13.2) is somewhat limited.

We could make forecasts for more than one quarter if our model had variables with lags longer than one period. Consider the following autoregressive model:

$$\text{SALES}_t\text{-PRED} = 12 + .80\text{SALES}_{t-4} \qquad\qquad (13.6)$$

With expression (13.6) we can develop forecasts for the four quarters of 1994. We use the sales of each quarter in 1993 to forecast sales in the corresponding quarter of 1994. See Table 13.9.

Table 13.9

Forecasting Using a Four-Quarter-Lag Model

TIME	1	2	3	4	5	6	7	8
QTR	1	2	3	4	1	2	3	4
1993	40	35	50	45				
1994					44*	40	52	48

*$\text{SALES}_5\text{-PRED} = 12 + .80(40) = 44$

In summary, a forecasting model with coincident indicators may be very good at explaining what affects any dependent variable, but it may not be very useful in forecasting. Including predictor variables with long lags increases the forecast horizon, the period of time over which we can use a model to make forecasts.

Summary

Managers often use time-ordered data to develop regression-based forecasting models. In this section, we have introduced three important extensions to the presentation of regression analysis in Chapters 11–12, namely,

1. Lagged values of Y to predict Y—autoregressive models
2. Lagged values of X to predict Y
3. MAPE as a measure of forecasting accuracy

How many lags should be included in a model? Roberts (1988) recommends that we include more, rather than fewer, lags. Then we can remove the lags that do not improve prediction using the absolute t-value method described in Chapter 11.

Once we have developed our model, check for multicollinearity and do a residual analysis. First plot the residuals against time to see if the independence assumption is violated. Then plot the residuals against Y_t-PRED and the predictor variables. Take corrective action or get professional statistical help if needed. We use the validated model to make short-run forecasts on Y_t provided the MAPE is sufficiently low for our planning needs.

SECTION 13.3 EXERCISES

Use statistical software, where appropriate, to solve the following exercises.

1. Shown are 20 quarters of sales data for ABC, Inc.

TIME (t)	1	2	3	4	5	6	7	8	9	10
SALES$_t$	41	57	63	72	89	98	101	112	129	137

TIME (t)	11	12	13	14	15	16	17	18	19	20
SALES$_t$	150	155	164	172	188	193	204	218	230	233

a. Plot SALES$_t$ versus TIME (in quarters) on a line graph. We always start the analysis by plotting a line graph.
b. We believe that SALES$_t$ are affected by SALES$_{t-1}$, sales from the previous quarter. Draw a scatter diagram of SALES$_t$ versus SALES$_{t-1}$.
c. Does the scatter diagram suggest positive autocorrelation, negative autocorrelation, or no autocorrelation?
d. Develop a regression model of SALES$_t$ versus SALES$_{t-1}$. The data for the autoregressive model are SALES$_t$ from periods 2–20 and SALES$_{t-1}$ from periods 1–19. There are 19 observations for fitting the regression model.
e. Compute the MAPE for the 19 quarters of historical data. Should we use the regression model given the size of the MAPE? Discuss.
f. Develop a sales forecast for time period 21.

2. Shown are 20 quarters of data on the number of grievances filed in an industry.

TIME	1	2	3	4	5	6	7	8	9	10
GRIEV$_t$	0	47	71	81	70	61	48	27	49	47

TIME	11	12	13	14	15	16	17	18	19	20
GRIEV$_t$	50	82	91	65	96	26	70	63	3	43

a. Plot GRIEV$_T$ versus TIME (in quarters) on a line graph.

b. We do not believe that GRIEV$_t$ is affected by GRIEV$_{t-1}$, the number of grievances in the previous quarter. Draw a scatter diagram of GRIEV$_t$ versus GRIEV$_{t-1}$ and verify.

c. Does the scatter diagram indicate positive autocorrelation, negative autocorrelation, or no autocorrelation?

3. Shown are 20 quarters of data on the ending inventory levels of mobile phones in the Southern Region. The actual inventory levels were divided by 10 to obtain the data.

TIME$_t$	1	2	3	4	5	6	7	8	9	10
INVEN$_t$	10	40	15	50	10	60	20	50	30	40

TIME$_t$	11	12	13	14	15	16	17	18	19	20
INVEN$_t$	25	35	20	45	30	60	10	50	15	55

a. Plot INVEN$_t$ versus TIME (in quarters) on a line graph.

b. We believe that INVEN$_t$ is affected by INVEN$_{t-1}$, inventory from the previous quarter. Draw a scatter diagram of INVEN$_t$ versus INVEN$_{t-1}$.

c. Does the scatter diagram indicate positive autocorrelation, negative autocorrelation, or no autocorrelation?

d. Develop a regression model of INVEN$_t$ versus INVEN$_{t-1}$. The data for the autoregressive model are INVEN$_t$ from periods 2–20 and INVEN$_{t-1}$ from periods 1–19.

e. Compute the MAPE for the 19 quarters of historical data. Should we use the regression model given the size of the MAPE?

f. Develop a forecast of INVEN$_t$ for time period 21.

4. Shown are 20 quarters of data on SALES and R&D expenditures (research and development). We believe that R&D expenditures in a quarter affect sales two quarters later.

TIME	SALES$_t$	R&D$_t$
1	40	10
2	37	20
3	50	20
4	70	15
5	60	20
6	60	30
7	72	35
8	88	25
9	101	25
10	80	35
11	81	40
12	97	30
13	110	35
14	89	45
15	103	50
16	117	35
17	131	40
18	98	50
19	112	55
20	134	25

a. Plot SALES$_t$ versus TIME (in quarters) on a line graph.

b. Draw a scatter diagram of SALES$_t$ versus R&D$_{t-2}$ (sales in a quarter and R&D expenditures two quarters earlier).

    c. Develop a regression model of SALES$_t$ versus R&D$_{t-2}$. The data for developing the regression model are R&D$_{t-2}$ from periods 1–18 and SALES$_t$ from periods 3–20.

    d. Compute the MAPE for the 18 quarters of historical data. Should we use the regression model given the size of the MAPE?

    e. Develop a sales forecast for time period 21.

5. Shown are 16 quarters of data. The dependent variable is SALES and a predictor variable is HS (housing starts). We believe that housing starts is a two-quarter leading indicator. We also believe that sales are affected by the previous quarter's sales.

TIME	SALES$_t$	HS$_t$
1	100	700
2	120	400
3	190	550
4	218	600
5	271	725
6	315	500
7	378	550
8	397	610
9	427	710
10	452	520
11	485	600
12	505	610
13	526	770
14	553	580
15	582	650
16	604	680

    a. Plot SALES$_t$ versus TIME (in quarters) on a line graph.

    b. Since we believe that SALES$_t$ is affected by SALES$_{t-1}$, draw a scatter diagram of SALES$_t$ versus SALES$_{t-1}$.

    c. Does the scatter diagram indicate positive autocorrelation, negative autocorrelation, or no autocorrelation?

    d. Draw a scatter diagram of SALES$_t$ (periods 3–16) versus HS$_{t-2}$ (periods 1–14). Do the two variables appear to be related?

    e. Develop a regression model of SALES$_t$ versus SALES$_{t-1}$ and HS$_{t-2}$. The data for the regression model are SALES$_t$ from periods 3–16, SALES$_{t-1}$ from periods 2–15, and HS$_{t-2}$ from periods 1–14.

    f. Do the absolute t-tests indicate that both predictor variables are needed?

    g. Compute the MAPE for the 14 quarters of historical data.

    h. Develop a sales forecast for time period 17.

6. In Exercise 1 there was a positive autocorrelation between SALES$_t$ and SALES$_{t-1}$. Compare successive values of the series. Put a plus sign (+) between two data values if the second value of each pair is greater than or equal to the first, and a minus sign if the second value is less than the first.

    a. How would you explain how to recognize positive autocorrelation by looking at these pairs of successive changes? Discuss.

    b. Could a graph have a downward trend and exhibit positive autocorrelation? If so, create a small series to support your answer.

7. In Exercise 2 there was no autocorrelation between GRIEV$_t$ and GRIEV$_{t-1}$. As in Exercise 6, identify the direction of pairwise changes (+ or −) from one period to the next. How would you characterize a series that has no autocorrelation in terms of these pairs of successive changes? Can you predict the direction of pairwise changes based on the pattern of pluses and minuses? Explain.

8. In Exercise 3 there was a negative autocorrelation between INVEN$_t$ and INVEN$_{t-1}$. As in Exercise 6, identify the direction of pairwise changes (+ or −) from one period to the next. How would you characterize a series that has negative autocorrelation in terms of these pairs of successive changes?

9. Interpret the following autoregressive model. EPS$_t$-PRED is the forecasted earnings per share for a firm for the upcoming quarter. Assuming the absolute t-values suggest keeping all the predictor variables in the model, explain in simple terms what the following model says about future earnings per share:

$$\text{EPS}_t\text{–PRED} = 1.75 + .5\text{EPS}_{t-1} + .4\text{EPS}_{t-2} + .1\text{EPS}_{t-3}$$

13.4 Forecasting Using the Classical Decomposition Method

In Section 13.3 we developed regression models to identify relationships between a dependent variable and a set of coincident and leading indicators. Regression models *explain* and *forecast* a dependent variable. In this section we use the decomposition method to identify the trend, seasonal, and cyclical patterns. Decomposition models do *not* contain predictor variables. Thus, they do not explain why the dependent variable varies. Decomposition models only provide forecasts. The forecasts are accurate provided that the assumption of continuity holds. The patterns found in the historical data must continue into the near future. By the end of this section you should be able to:

1. distinguish in pictures and words between an additive and a multiplicative decomposition model;
2. compute and explain raw seasonal indices;
3. compute and explain typical seasonal indices;
4. explain the differences among a seasonal pattern, no detectable seasonal pattern, and no seasonal pattern;
5. compute and explain deseasonalized data;
6. decide which trend expression should be used for forecasting;
7. compute and explain cyclical indices; and
8. make forecasts.

Additive and Multiplicative Models

Decomposition methods assume that actual values of the dependent variable, Y, are composed of up to four components: (1) trend, (2) seasonal, (3) cycle, and (4) random fluctuation:

Actual data values = Systematic pattern + Random fluctuation   (13.7)

$$Y_t = f[\text{trend } (T_t), \text{ seasonal } (S_t), \text{ cycle } (C_t), \text{ randomness } (RF_t)] \quad (13.8)$$

The function (f) in equation (13.8) could be additive or multiplicative. Before formally defining the terms, we illustrate a major difference between the two functions. Table 13.10 contains two data sets. One is an *additive* function of a trend and seasonal pattern. The other is a *multiplicative* function of a trend and seasonal pattern. For simplicity, we have omitted cycle and random fluctuation.

In Figure 13.7 we have superimposed a freehand linear trend line on the two data sets. The additive series has an upward linear trend and a seasonal pattern. Every year, quarters 1 and 2 are above the trend line and quarters 3 and 4 are below the trend line. The multiplicative series has the same upward linear trend and a seasonal pattern. Every year, quarters 1 and 2 are above the trend line and quarters 3 and 4 are below the trend line.

In the additive series, the magnitude (peak to trough, See Figure 13.2) of the seasonal pattern does *not* change over the 12 quarters of data. As the trend values increase, the magnitude of the seasonal pattern does *not* change. In an additive series,

Table 13.10

Time Series Data Sets with Additive and Multiplicative Functions of Trend and Seasonal Patterns

TIME	Additive Model $(T + S)$	Multiplicative Model $(T \times S)$
1	70	70
2	110	108
3	110	112
4	150	102
5	230	294
6	270	300
7	270	232
8	310	198
9	390	518
10	430	492
11	430	360
12	470	294

the time series components are not related. In a multiplicative series, the magnitude of the seasonal pattern does change over the 12 quarters. As the trend values increase, so does the magnitude of the seasonal pattern. There is a positive multiplicative relationship between the trend and seasonal patterns.

The multiplicative function represents most time series data in business and economics. Firms with $100,000,000 sales generally have greater seasonal sales

FIGURE 13.7   Additive and Multiplicative Time Series

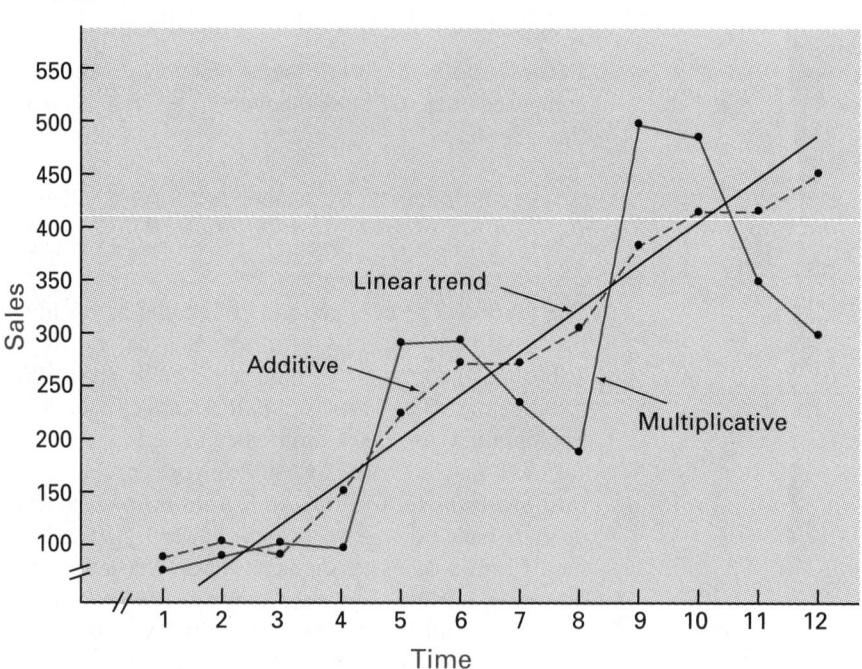

variation (peak to trough) than firms with only $100,000 sales. As sales increase, so does the magnitude of the seasonal variation around the trend line. Therefore, we will use the following multiplicative model in analyzing time series data:

$$Y_t = T_t \times S_t \times C_t \times RF_t \qquad (13.9)$$

Equation (13.9) says that we multiply the values of the trend, seasonal, cyclical, and random fluctuation components to obtain the Y-values.

The decomposition method identifies the trend, seasonal, and cyclical patterns underlying a time series, if these patterns exist. Random fluctuation does not exhibit a systematic pattern. Random fluctuation means that the data values are unpredictable.

We will apply the multiplicative decomposition model to the five years of data in Table 13.11. The data are the numbers of car phones (in hundreds) sold in COMCEL's Southern Region. Note that in Table 13.11 we have inserted a variable called TIME, which represents the 20 quarters of data. It is not a predictor variable in the sense of Chapters 11–12 or Section 13.3. It is a *proxy variable* that serves as a substitute for the predictor variable in regression-based forecasting models.

Figure 13.8 is a line graph of sales versus time. The graph suggests a distinct upward trend and seasonal pattern with a one-year length. There may also be a cyclical component.

We inserted the boxed data in Table 13.11 into the COMSTAT TIME SERIES ANALYSIS tool. It generated the outputs shown in the tables in the remainder of this section. We begin the analysis by identifying the seasonal pattern, if any.

Table 13.11

Car Phones Sold in Southern Region

Year	Quarter	TIME	Units, (hundreds)
1989	1	1	85
	2	2	133
	3	3	136
	4	4	94
1990	1	5	104
	2	6	154
	3	7	166
	4	8	115
1991	1	9	112
	2	10	184
	3	11	175
	4	12	140
1992	1	13	136
	2	14	205
	3	15	210
	4	16	144
1993	1	17	148
	2	18	229
	3	19	237
	4	20	170

FIGURE 13.8   Line Graph of Car Phone Sales in Southern Region

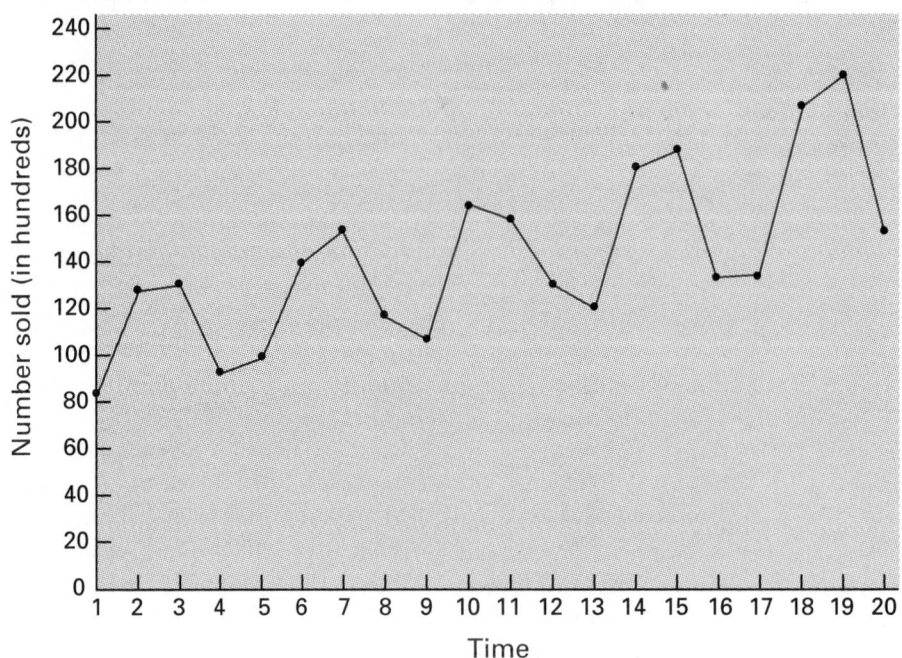

Ratio to Moving Average Method

We use the ratio to moving average method to determine the seasonal component. First, using the historical sales data, we compute a moving average that has the same length as the seasonal component in the data. For 1-year seasonal patterns, the length of the moving average should be 4 quarters (for quarterly data) or 12 months (for monthly data).

In Chapter 2 we first constructed moving averages. To compute a moving average of length four quarters (MA 4), take the first four values of the data set, add them, and compute the mean. Shown is the computation for the first value of the moving average for the COMCEL sales data in Table 13.11:

$$\text{First moving average value} = \frac{85 + 133 + 136 + 94}{4} = 112.00$$

COMCEL sold 85 units in quarter 1, as of March 31; 133 units in quarter 2, as of June 30; 136 units in quarter 3, as of September 30 and 94 units in quarter 4, as of December 31. March 31 is approximately the 90th day of the year, June 30 is the 180th day, September 30 is the 270th day, and December 31 is the 360th day. The mean of these four calendar dates is the 225th day of the year [(90 + 180 + 270 + 360)/4]. Thus, the moving average value of 112 units sold is the mean sales as of the 225th day, August 15. See the first entry under MA 4 in Table 13.12.

To compute the second moving average value, delete the first data value and add the fifth data value. Add the four terms and compute the mean.

Table 13.12

Calculating an MA 4 and a Centered Moving Average

Quarter		Calendar Date	Units$_t$	MA 4	Centered MA 4$_t$
1989	1	3/31/89	85	Cannot determine	
	2	6/30/89	133	Cannot determine	
		8/15/89		112.00	
	3	9/30/89	136		114.38
		11/15/89		116.75	
	4	12/31/89	94		119.38
		2/15/90		122.00	
1990	1	3/31/90	104		125.75
		5/15/90		129.50	
	2	6/30/90	154		132.13
		8/15/90		134.75	
	3	9/30/90	166		135.75
		11/15/90		136.75	
	4	12/31/90	115		140.50
		2/15/91		144.25	
1991	1	3/31/91	112		145.38
		5/15/91		146.50	
	2	6/30/91	184		149.63
		8/15/91		152.75	
	3	9/30/91	175		155.75
		11/15/91		158.75	
	4	12/31/91	140		161.38
		2/15/92		164.00	
1992	1	3/31/92	136		168.38
		5/15/92		172.75	
	2	6/30/92	205		173.25
		8/15/92		173.75	
	3	9/30/92	210		175.25
		11/15/92		176.75	
	4	12/31/92	144		179.75
		2/15/93		182.75	
1993	1	3/31/93	148		186.13
		5/15/93		189.50	
	2	6/30/93	229		192.75
		8/15/93		196.00	
	3	9/30/93	237	Cannot determine	
	4	12/31/93	170	Cannot determine	

$$\text{Second moving average value} = \frac{133 + 136 + 94 + 104}{4}$$

$$= 116.75$$

The moving average value of 116.75 is the mean sales as of the 315th day, November 15. This is one quarter later (3 months or 90 days) than the calendar date for the first

FIGURE 13.9   Original Data and MA 4 for Units Sold in the Southern Region

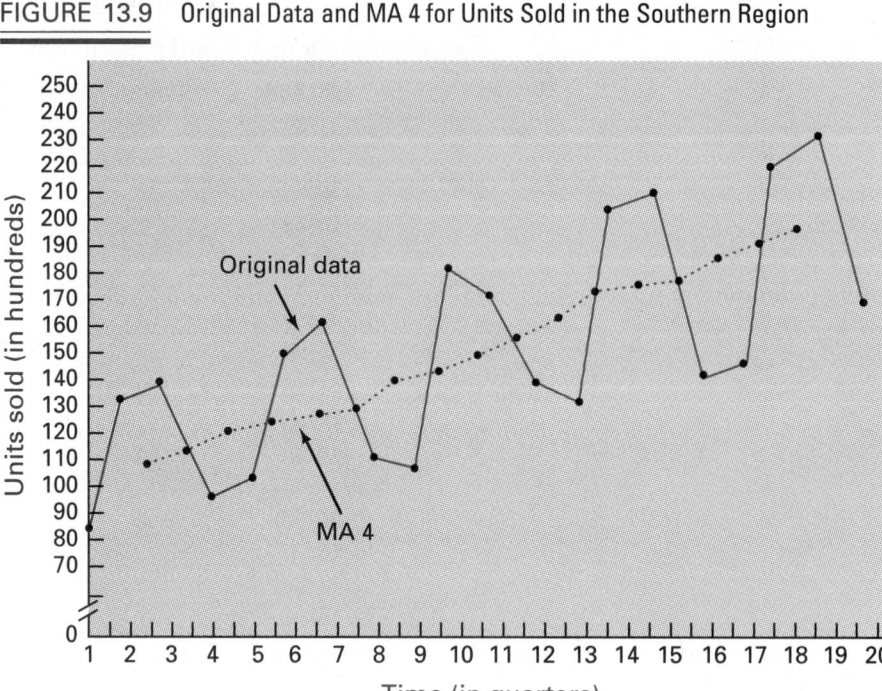

moving average value. See the second entry under MA 4 in Table 13.12. We computed the other 15 moving averages of length four quarters in the same way.

Figure 13.9 clearly shows that as a result of smoothing, the moving average of length four quarters contains no seasonal component. This is because the original data contain a seasonal pattern of length one year. Figure 13.9 also shows that as a result of averaging, the moving average has less random variation than the original data.

Of the original four components in model (13.9), the moving average contains only the T(rend) $-$ C(ycle) components; the seasonal and random components have been eliminated. To isolate the S(easonal) and random fluctuation components, we must divide the actual data by the moving average data. The resulting values are called *raw seasonal indices.* The raw seasonal indices contain only two components, S and RF:

$$\text{Raw seasonal indices} = \frac{\text{Actual data values}}{\text{Moving average values}}$$

$$\frac{T_t \times S_t \times C_t \times RF_t}{T_t \times C_t} = S_t \times RF_t \qquad (13.10)$$

Centered moving average: Expression (13.10) says to divide the original time series values by the moving average values. Now a problem arises. The original data are quarterly sales as of March 31, June 30, September 30, and December 31 over 5 years. The moving average is the mean sales as of August 15, November 15, February 15, and May 15 over the five years. We cannot divide the two time series because of the different calendar dates. However, by centering the moving average we can line up the moving average and original time series values. Only then is division meaningful.

We compute the mean of the first two moving average values of Table 13.12. The first value of the centered moving average is (112 + 116.75)/2, or 114.38. We place this value halfway between the August 15 and November 15 calendar dates—

that is, September 30. Now the first centered moving average value lines up with the September 30 calendar date of the original time series. Notice how all the values of the centered moving average line up with the data in the original data set. Now we can divide the two data sets as per expression (13.10).

Raw seasonal indices: Raw seasonal indices measure the level of activity of a specific period (day, quarter, or month) compared to the mean activity for that year. The raw seasonal indices include the seasonal and random fluctuation components, S_t and RF_t.

For the COMCEL data, the raw seasonal index for quarter 3 in 1989 is the actual data value for quarter 3 divided by the centered moving average data value for quarter 3:

$$\text{Raw seasonal index for 1989 quarter 3} = \frac{136}{114.38} = 1.189 \text{ or } 118.9\%$$

Thus, the actual sales were 18.9% higher than the centered moving average for the same quarter. The seasonal and random fluctuation components account for the 18.9% increase. If the random component is small, the seasonal impact explains most of the 18.9% sales increase over the trend and cycle. Simply put, sales were strong in the third quarter—almost 19% above the centered moving average.

The raw seasonal index for quarter 4 in 1989 is 94/119.38 = .7874 or 78.74%. Actual sales were only 78.74% of the centered moving average, or trend and cycle, value. Thus, sales were weak in the fourth quarter. Table 13.13 contains the raw seasonal index calculations. The format of Table 13.13 makes it difficult to see if there is a seasonal pattern. We transferred the raw seasonal indices of Table 13.13 into a year-by-quarter table. See Table 13.14.

Table 13.13

Calculating Raw Seasonal Indices—S and RF Components

Quarter		$Units_t$	$Centered\ MA_t$	Raw Seasonal $Indices_t$
1989	1	85	Cannot determine	
	2	133	Cannot determine	
	3	136	114.38	1.1891
	4	94	119.38	.7874
1990	1	104	125.75	.8270
	2	154	132.13	1.1656
	3	166	135.75	1.2228
	4	115	140.50	.8185
1991	1	112	145.38	.7704
	2	184	149.63	1.2297
	3	175	155.75	1.1236
	4	140	161.38	.8675
1992	1	136	168.38	.8077
	2	205	173.25	1.1833
	3	210	175.25	1.1983
	4	144	179.75	.8011
1993	1	148	186.13	.7952
	2	229	192.75	1.1881
	3	237	Cannot determine	
	4	170	Cannot determine	

Table 13.14

Year-by-Quarter Table of Raw Seasonal Indices

	Quarters			
Year	1	2	3	4
1989	Cannot determine		1.1891	.7874
1990	.8270	1.1656	1.2228	.8185
1991	.7704	1.2297	1.1236	.8675
1992	.8077	1.1833	1.1983	.8011
1993	.7952	1.1881	Cannot determine	

Table 13.15

Two Additional Year-by-Quarter Tables of Raw Seasonal Indices

Set A

	Quarters			
Year	1	2	3	4
1989	Cannot determine		1.4100	.4096
1990	1.1500	.8691	.9774	.3089
1991	1.3567	.7900	.8311	1.2100
1992	.1056	1.5023	1.5109	1.3451
1993	.4530	1.6789	Cannot determine	

Set B

	Quarters			
Year	1	2	3	4
1989	Cannot determine		1.0003	.9989
1990	1.0067	.9899	1.0001	1.0023
1991	.9999	1.0023	.9991	.9995
1992	1.0005	.9999	1.0100	1.0003
1993	.9995	1.0029	Cannot determine	

Before continuing with the seasonal analysis, please compare the two sets of raw seasonal indices in Table 13.15 with the indices in Table 13.14. Which set exhibits a seasonal pattern, which set exhibits wide variation but no seasonal pattern, and which set exhibits no seasonal pattern at all? Please think about it before reading on.

The raw seasonal indices in Table 13.14 exhibit a seasonal pattern. In each year, sales are low in the first and fourth quarters and high in the second and third quarters. The pattern is stable and repeatable. Note that there is much variation between quarters in each year, but little variation within each quarter between years. That variation pattern suggests a *seasonal* component.

In contrast, Set A has much variability but no repeatable pattern—no detectable seasonal component. There is much variation within each quarter between years. For example, the first-quarter raw seasonal indices varied from a low of .1056 to a high of 1.3567. There is no stable pattern from year to year. In short, there is much variation, but it is not a seasonal pattern. It is probably *random* fluctuation.

Set B also indicates a lack of any seasonal pattern. All indices are close to 1.0 in each quarter. The level of activity for each quarter is neither higher nor lower than the mean sales for the year. For example, the indices in Set B could represent sales of bread. As compared to ice cream or jewelry, bread sales are not affected by time of year—June weddings or Christmas—or temperature. Lack of variation within and between quarters over the five years indicates *no seasonality*.

Return to the COMCEL car phone study data. From Table 13.14 we have concluded that there is a seasonal pattern. Now we want to quantify it. Remember, each number in Table 13.14 consists of two components—seasonal and random fluctuation. Now we isolate the seasonal component by computing *typical seasonal indices*.

Typical seasonal indices: Raw seasonal indices measure the level of activity of a *specific period* compared to the mean activity for that year. We speak of the raw seasonal index for the third quarter of 1991 or 1992. Typical seasonal indices measure the level of activity of a *typical period* compared to the mean activity for a *typical year*. We speak of a typical seasonal index for the third quarter or the first quarter. The raw seasonal indices contain the seasonal and random fluctuation components, whereas the typical seasonal indices contain only the seasonal component.

To obtain the typical seasonal indices, we must eliminate random fluctuation from the raw seasonal indices. One way to do this is by computing *trimmed means*. Referring to Table 13.14, we eliminate the high and low raw seasonal indices for a quarter and then compute the mean of the remaining values. For example, to compute the trimmed mean for quarter 1, we eliminate the 1990 (the highest) and the 1991 (the lowest) quarter 1 raw seasonal indices. The trimmed mean is the mean of the remaining two indices, (.8077 + .7952)/2 = .8014. We would compute trimmed means in the same way for monthly data.

Here is the logic behind averaging. The differences among the raw seasonal indices for a given quarter over the five years are due to random fluctuation. By computing the trimmed means, we eliminate random fluctuation.

We must adjust the trimmed means to obtain the typical seasonal indices. The sum of the four trimmed means in Table 13.16 should be 4, for the following reason. Sales will be relatively strong in some quarters (or months) and the trimmed means will be greater than 1. Sales will be relatively weak in other quarters and the trimmed means will be less than 1. Strong quarters cancel out weak quarters and the mean of the four typical seasonal indices must be 1, or the sum must be 4. From Table 13.16, the sum of the four trimmed means is 3.9906. The reason the sum is not 4 (or 12 for monthly data) is that we eliminated the lowest and highest raw seasonal indices within each quarter before computing the trimmed means. To make the adjustment, multiply each trimmed mean by 1.0024 (i.e., 4.00/3.9906) to obtain the four typical seasonal indices.

Warning: Do not use the decomposition method unless you have five or more years of quarterly or monthly data. First, in computing the typical seasonal indices, we lose one year of data. We cannot determine the raw seasonal indices of the first two quarters of 1989 and the last two quarters of 1993 (see Table 13.16). Then we throw out two years of raw seasonal indices in computing the trimmed means. That leaves only two raw seasonal indices for each quarter (or month), which is barely enough to compute a meaningful typical seasonal index.

Table 13.16

Typical Seasonal Indices Calculations

Year	Quarters 1	2	3	4	
1989	Cannot determine		1.1890	.7874	
1990	.8270	1.1655	1.2228	.8185	
1991	.7704	1.2297	1.1236	.8675	
1992	.8077	1.1833	1.1983	.8011	
1993	.7951	1.1881	Cannot determine		
Trimmed means	.8014	1.1857	1.1937	.8098	3.9906
Typical seasonal indices	.8033	1.1885	1.1965	.8117	4.0000

Deseasonalized Data

Before determining the trend pattern, we *deseasonalize* the data by removing the seasonal pattern from the original time series values. Deseasonalized data are also known as seasonally adjusted data:

$$\text{Deseasonalized data} = \frac{T_t \times S_t \times C_t \times RF_t}{S_t} = T_t \times C_t \times RF_t \quad (13.11)$$

Equation (13.11) says to divide the original data values by the typical seasonal indices to obtain deseasonalized data. In the COMCEL data set (see Table 13.17), for example, the deseasonalized data value for period 1 is 85/.8033 = 105.81, or 10,581 phones.

In Figure 13.10 the graph of the deseasonalized data is *smoother* than that of the original data, because the deseasonalized data do not contain the seasonal pattern. In fact, the trend pattern literally jumps out at us from the deseasonalized data. We will perform the trend analysis next and it will quantify this observed trend pattern, just as the ratio to moving average method quantified the seasonal pattern.

Warning: Do not deseasonalize the data if there is no stable seasonal pattern (see Table 13.15, Set A) or if there is no seasonal pattern at all (see Table 13.15, Set B). Deseasonalizing does not make sense when there is no seasonal pattern. Instead of using deseasonalized data for the trend analysis, we would use the *original* data.

The Trend Pattern

Table 13.18 contains the data for determining the best-fitting trend line for the COMCEL data. The dependent variable is deseasonalized sales and the independent

Table 13.17

Deseasonalized, or Seasonally Adjusted, Data

TIME	Original Data Units$_t$	Typical Seasonal Indices	Deseasonalized Data Units$_t$
1	85	.8033	105.81
2	133	1.1885	111.91
3	136	1.1965	113.67
4	94	.8117	115.80
5	104	.8033	129.46
6	154	1.1885	129.58
7	166	1.1965	138.74
8	115	.8117	141.67
9	112	.8033	139.42
10	184	1.1885	154.82
11	175	1.1965	146.26
12	140	.8117	172.48
13	136	.8033	169.30
14	205	1.1885	172.49
15	210	1.1965	175.51
16	144	.8117	177.41
17	148	.8033	184.24
18	229	1.1885	192.68
19	237	1.1965	198.08
20	170	.8117	209.44

FIGURE 13.10   Original Data and Deseasonalized Data—Car Phone Sales in Southern Region

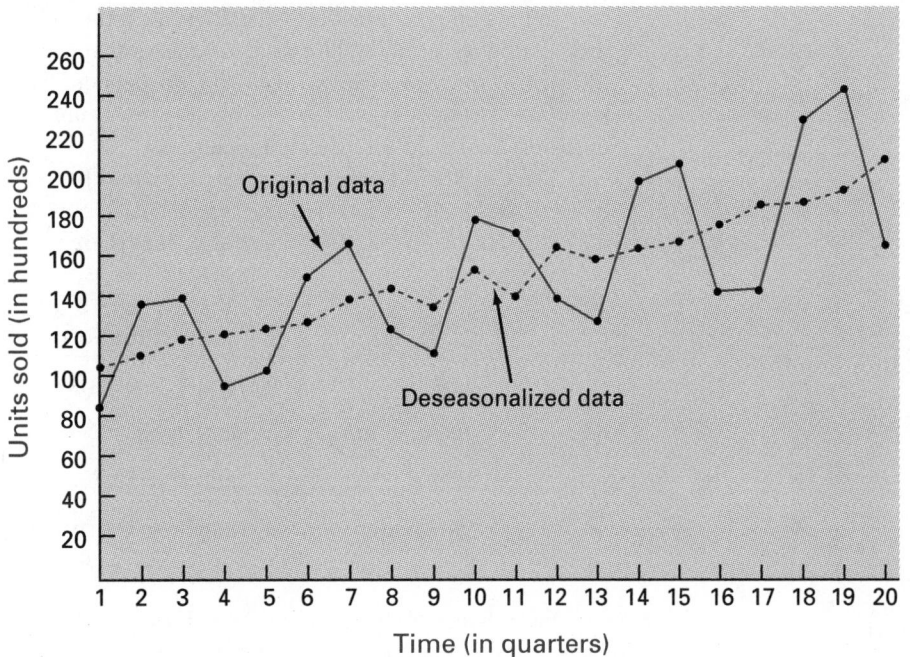

Table 13.18

COMCEL Sales Data for Trend Analysis

Period TIME	Deseasonalized Data Y_t
1	105.81
2	111.91
3	113.67
4	115.80
5	129.46
6	129.58
7	138.74
8	141.67
9	139.42
10	154.82
11	146.26
12	172.47
13	169.30
14	172.49
15	175.51
16	177.41
17	184.24
18	192.68
19	198.08
20	209.44

variable is TIME, 1, 2, 3, . . . , 20. The deseasonalized data are always the dependent variable for the trend analysis, except when there is no stable seasonal component or no seasonal component at all. Then we use the original data.

In the regression models of Section 13.3, the independent variables were legitimate predictor variables. "Legitimate" means that we believed the predictor variables affected Y_t. In trend analysis, TIME, the independent variable, is a proxy variable. We know that TIME does not affect Y_t. It serves as a substitute for the predictor variables in regression-based forecasting models.

The COMSTAT TIME SERIES ANALYSIS tool fits four best-fitting trend equations to the deseasonalized data—linear, exponential, power, and quadratic. Following are the equations of the four functions, as well as their graphs in Figures 13.11a–13.11d.

Trend	Equation	
Linear	$Y_t\text{-PRED} = a + b\text{TIME}$	(13.12)
Exponential	$Y_t\text{-PRED} = ae^{b\text{TIME}}$	(13.13)
Power	$Y_t\text{-PRED} = a\text{TIME}^b$	(13.14)
Quadratic	$Y_t\text{-PRED} = a + b\text{TIME} + c\text{TIME}^2$	(13.15)

For a linear trend equation, Y_t increases or decreases by a constant amount, b, each period. For an exponential trend, Y_t increases (or decreases) by an increasing (or decreasing) amount each period. A power trend equation is a very versatile curve. Its

FIGURE 13.11a   Linear Trend Patterns

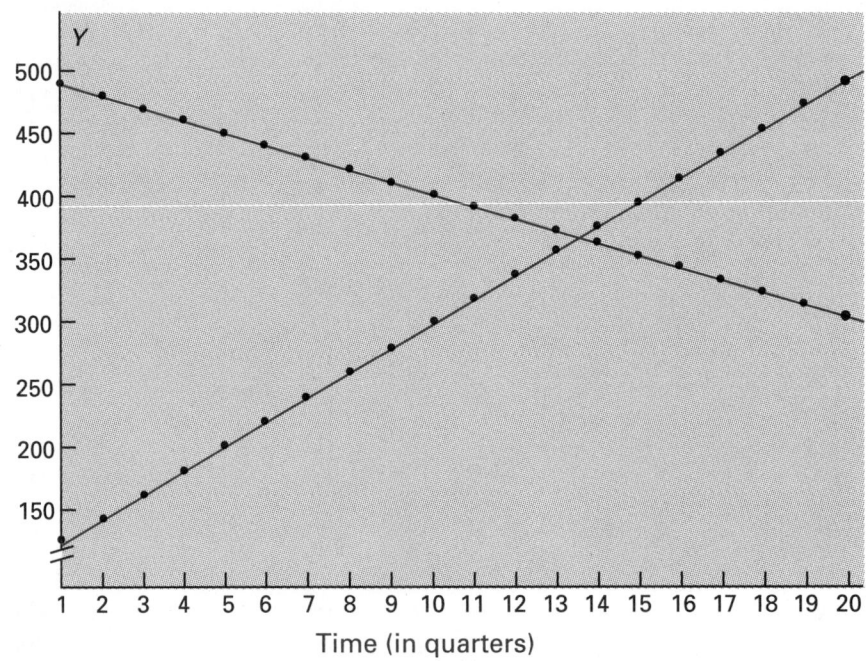

FIGURE 13.11b   Exponential Trend Patterns

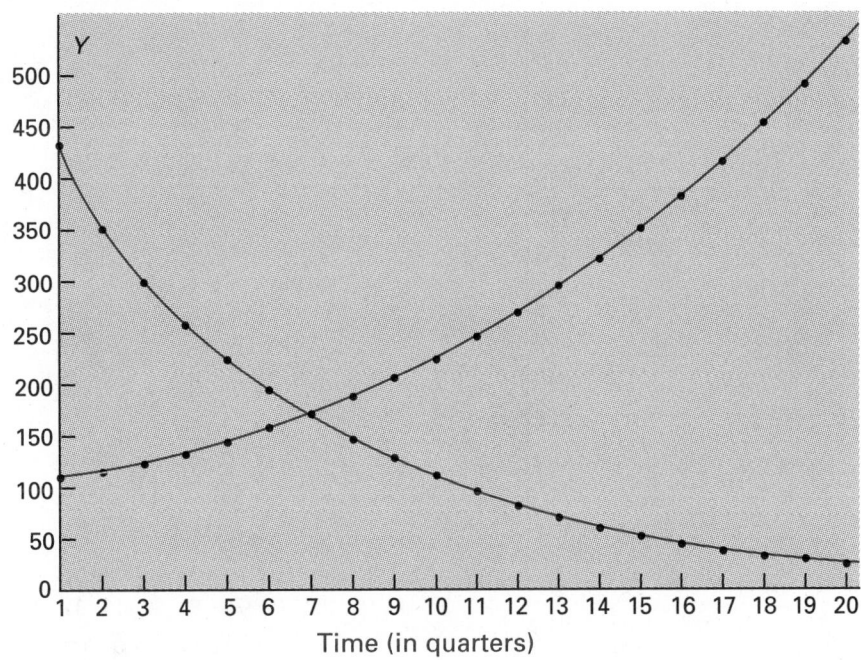

FIGURE 13.11c   Power Trend Patterns

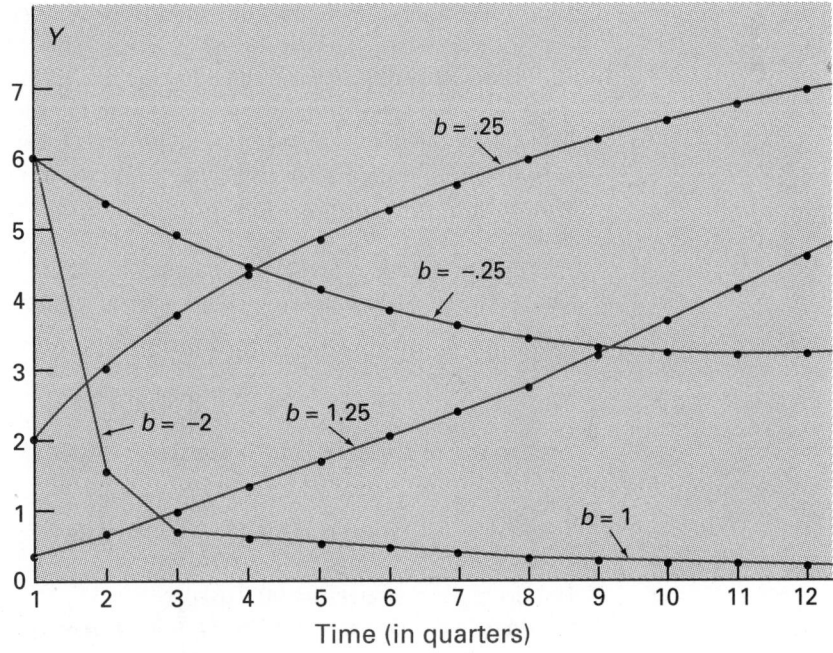

FIGURE 13.11d   Quadratic Trend Patterns

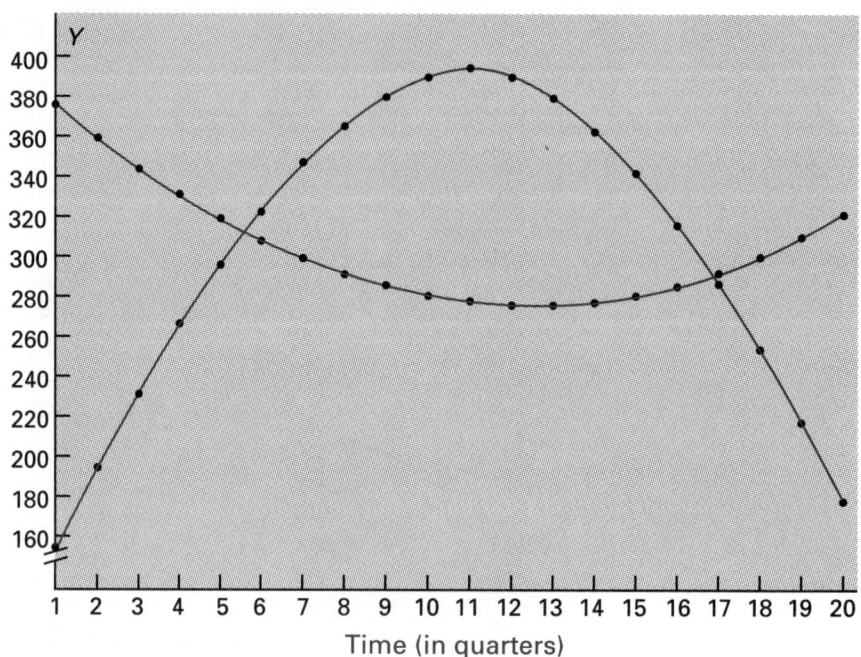

Time (in quarters)

shape depends on the value of b. See Figure 13.11c for some power curves. A quadratic trend equation is U-shaped—Y peaks or bottoms out.

Returning to the COMCEL sales data, the COMSTAT TIME SERIES ANALYSIS tool generated the four trend lines for the 20 quarters of deseasonalized data (see Table 13.18). The software provides the MAPE for Y_t versus Y_t-PRED for the 20 quarters of data for each curve. The results are given in Table 13.19.

The best-fitting linear trend equation has an intercept of 99.351 and a slope of 5.199. It is the best-fitting linear equation in the sense that it minimizes the sum of the squared deviations between Y_t and Y_t-PRED. The other three equations are likewise the best for their respective curves. Which trend equation should we select for forecasting? That is, which one is best overall? We recommend two strategies for making the selection.

Lowest MAPE: Select the equation that has the lowest MAPE. In the COMCEL study, it is the linear trend (or quadratic trend) equation. Over the past 20 quarters the

Table 13.19

Summary of Best-Fitting Equations for COMCEL Deseasonalized Data

Curve Type	Equation	MAPE	
Linear	Y_t-PRED $= 99.351 + 5.199$TIME	2.3%	(13.16)
Exponential	Y_t-PRED $= 105.092e^{.034\text{TIME}}$	2.6%	(13.17)
Power	Y_t-PRED $= 90.916$TIME$^{.239}$	5.5%	(13.18)
Quadratic	Y_t-PRED $= 101.024 + 4.742$TIME $+ .0220$TIME^2	2.3%	(13.19)

linear trend equation has proven to be the best with a mean forecasting error of only 2.3%. If the assumption of continuity holds, it should produce the smallest forecasting errors over the next several quarters.

We could also select the curve that produces the lowest MAPE for the most recent one or two years. As the recent past may be more relevant for forecasting than the distant past, we could select that curve with the best most recent, not overall, performance. You will need to hand-calculate the MAPE for the most recent one or two years of data for each curve as the COMSTAT TIME SERIES ANALYSIS tool does not provide it.

When we forecast sales of consumer products, consider using a second strategy for selecting the overall best equation.

Product life cycle: The product life cycle in Figure 13.1 reflects a consumer product's sales growth and decline. During phase I, Introduction, sales increase slowly at first and then increase rapidly. During phase II, Growth, sales increase at a steady rate. During phase III, Maturity, sales, while still increasing, slow down as consumers lose interest in the product. During phase IV, Decline, sales peak and begin to drop. Sales will continue to drop unless the firm revitalizes the product or its marketing campaign.

The best overall trend equation depends on where a consumer product is in its life cycle. Here are some recommendations:

Phase	Consider Using
Introduction	Exponential trend equation
Growth	Linear trend equation
Maturity	Power or quadratic trend equation
Decline	Quadratic or power trend equation

Since COMCEL has sold car phones for five years, sales are probably in the growth phase. Thus a linear trend equation is appropriate. In conclusion, use the linear trend equation as it is best according to both the MAPE and product life cycle strategies.

What should we do when the MAPE and product life cycle strategies recommend different trend equations? Select that trend equation that is easiest to explain to others. Usually, that will be the most straightforward. After all, if we cannot explain our forecast clearly, no one will listen. In explaining forecasts, use graphs. For example, do not try to explain a power curve in words. Graphs speak louder than words.

The Cycle Pattern

Before using the linear trend equation and the typical seasonal indices for forecasting, we can check for a cyclical pattern. If there is a cyclical pattern, our forecasts, which include only the trend and seasonal components, may be incorrect.

In the ratio to moving average method we constructed a centered moving average to determine the typical seasonal indices. The centered moving average contains the trend and cycle components. We can obtain the cycle component (if any) by dividing each centered moving average data value by the predicted trend value:

$$\frac{T_t \times C_t}{T_t} = C_t \tag{13.20}$$

Table 13.20

Isolating a Possible Cyclical Pattern

Period TIME	Centered Moving Average $(T_t \times C_t)$	99.351 + 5.199TIME (T_t)	Cyclical Indices (C_t)
1	Cannot determine	104.55	Cannot determine
2	Cannot determine	109.75	Cannot determine
3	114.38	114.95	.995
4	119.38	120.15	.994
5	125.75	125.35	1.003
6	132.13	130.55	1.012
7	135.75	135.74	1.000
8	140.50	140.94	.997
9	145.38	146.14	.995
10	149.63	151.34	.989
11	155.75	156.54	.995
12	161.38	161.74	.998
13	168.38	166.94	1.009
14	173.25	172.14	1.006
15	175.25	177.34	.988
16	179.75	182.54	.985
17	186.13	187.73	.991
18	192.75	192.93	.999
19	Cannot determine	198.13	Cannot determine
20	Cannot determine	203.33	Cannot determine

Table 13.20 shows the computations for identifying a possible cycle component for the COMCEL data. The second column contains the values of the centered moving average taken from Table 13.12, and the third column contains the predicted trend values calculated from the best trend equation, linear equation (13.16). The COMSTAT TIME SERIES ANALYSIS tool provided the data for columns 2 and 3. We then hand-calculated the cyclical indices by dividing the data in the second column by the corresponding values in the third column.

In economic terms, cyclical indices greater than 1 signify a booming economy. The economy is either in the growth (I), prosperity (II), or warning (III) phase (see Figure 13.3 on page 000). Cyclical indices less than 1 indicate a stagnant economy. The economy is either in the recession (IV), depression (V), or recovery (VI) phase.

Figure 13.12 is a plot of the cyclical indices for the COMCEL data. There does appear to be a cyclical pattern. The first cycle might have started in quarter 4 and concluded in quarter 10. A second cycle might have started in quarter 11 and concluded in quarter 18.

Warning: Since cycles do not have constant lengths or magnitudes, it is difficult to estimate future cyclical indices. If history is any guide, it appears from Figure 13.12 that the economy is about to enter a growth phase in quarter 19 or 20. However, around periods 21–23 the economy may go stagnant. We may wish to include the cycle component in our forecasts.

Estimating cyclical indices involves more than looking at historic patterns such as Figure 13.12. It requires knowledge of the level of economic or industry activity during the periods to be forecasted. Such knowledge is often judgmental, and perhaps the qualitative forecasting methods presented in Section 13.5 will be helpful.

FIGURE 13.12   Cyclical Pattern for COMCEL Data

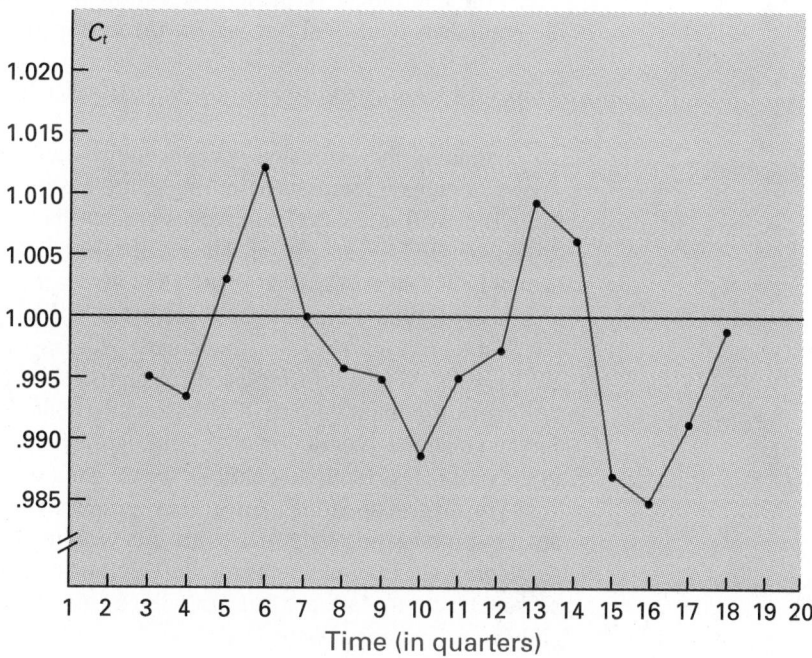

FIGURE 13.12   Cyclical Pattern for COMCEL Data

Short-Term Forecasting

We have isolated the trend and seasonal patterns and a possible cyclical pattern. We can now prepare a forecast for the upcoming four quarters of 1994, periods 21–24. We develop the initial forecasts by multiplying the trend value for each forecast period by the appropriate typical seasonal index. Remember, we are using a multiplicative—*not* additive—decomposition model. Table 13.21 illustrates the forecasts for the next four quarters. The first quarter of 1994 is quarter 21. Remember, the historical data in Table 13.10 cover periods 1–20.

To forecast quarter 1 of 1994 (period 21), we multiply the linear trend value (the best-fitting function) for the quarter from the second column by the typical seasonal index for the quarter in the third column. The forecast based on trend and seasonal index is 167.51, or 16,751 car phones. We generated the other three forecasts in the same way.

Table 13.21

Forecast Using Linear Trend Equation and Typical Seasonal Indices

TIME	Linear Trend Value $99.351 + 5.199$TIME	Typical Seasonal Index	Y_t Forecast
21	208.53	.8033	167.51
22	213.73	1.1885	254.01
23	218.93	1.1965	261.94
24	224.13	.8117	181.92

We can then incorporate the cycle into the forecast by *estimating* the cyclical indices for periods 21–24. Suppose we estimate 1.02, 1.01, .99, and .98, respectively. Given the multiplicative model, we multiply the forecast values in Table 13.21 by these numbers. Our final forecast for the first quarter of 1994 is

$$\text{Forecast for quarter 1, 1994} = Y_{21} = (167.51)(1.02) = 170.86, \quad \text{or 17,086 phones}$$

Including the estimated cyclical indices allows managers to do "what-ifing." They can prepare forecasts assuming that the economy will grow or that it will stagnate. They will select cyclical indices greater than 1 if they believe the economy will grow over the forecast period. They will select indices less than 1 if they believe the economy will stagnate. Making different assumptions about the economy or industry and incorporating them into the forecasts is called *"what-if"* analysis.

Table 13.21 provides a four-quarter forecast based on the trend and seasonal components. We could forecast more periods into the future, but that is risky. The decomposition method provides reasonably good forecasts for four to six quarters. Beyond that, the assumption of continuity may not hold. That is, whatever happened in the past is less likely to continue for the long term.

We suggest updating a forecast every quarter or as additional data become available, but forecasting only four to six quarters into the future.

One final reminder: If the data do not contain a stable seasonal pattern or a seasonal pattern at all, our forecast will consist of a trend component only—and possibly a cyclical component.

Summary of the Decomposition Method

Figure 13.13 summarizes the major steps in the decomposition method. We use the decomposition method to make short-term forecasts if there are at least five years of historical data. Our goal is to detect and quantify the trend, seasonal, and cyclical patterns if they exist. The decomposition method assumes that the recent past is a guide to the near future. That is, whatever happened recently will continue to happen. The decomposition method can produce accurate forecasts up to six quarters.

Begin with either monthly or quarterly data. Assume that the data are a multiplicative function of trend, seasonal, cycle, and random fluctuation.

First compute an MA 4 (quarterly data) or an MA 12 (monthly data). Center the moving average. The moving average contains only a trend and a cycle component.

Divide the original time series by the centered moving average. The resulting raw seasonal indices measure the level of activity in a specific period (quarter or month) compared to the mean activity for that year.

Check the stability of indices for each period. If stable, compute the typical seasonal indices. For each period eliminate the highest and lowest raw seasonal indices. Compute the trimmed mean and then determine the typical seasonal indices. These are used for forecasting.

Divide the original data by the typical seasonal indices. The resulting seasonally adjusted data contain only a trend, cycle, and random fluctuation component.

These are input data for the trend analysis. Use the original data if there is no stable seasonal pattern or if there is no seasonal pattern at all.

Many software packages provide the best linear, exponential, power, and quadratic trend equations. Base the selection on the lowest-MAPE trend equation or use the product life cycle strategy.

Divide the centered moving average by the trend values from the selected trend curve. Plot the cyclical indices.

FIGURE 13.13   Flowchart for the Decomposition Method

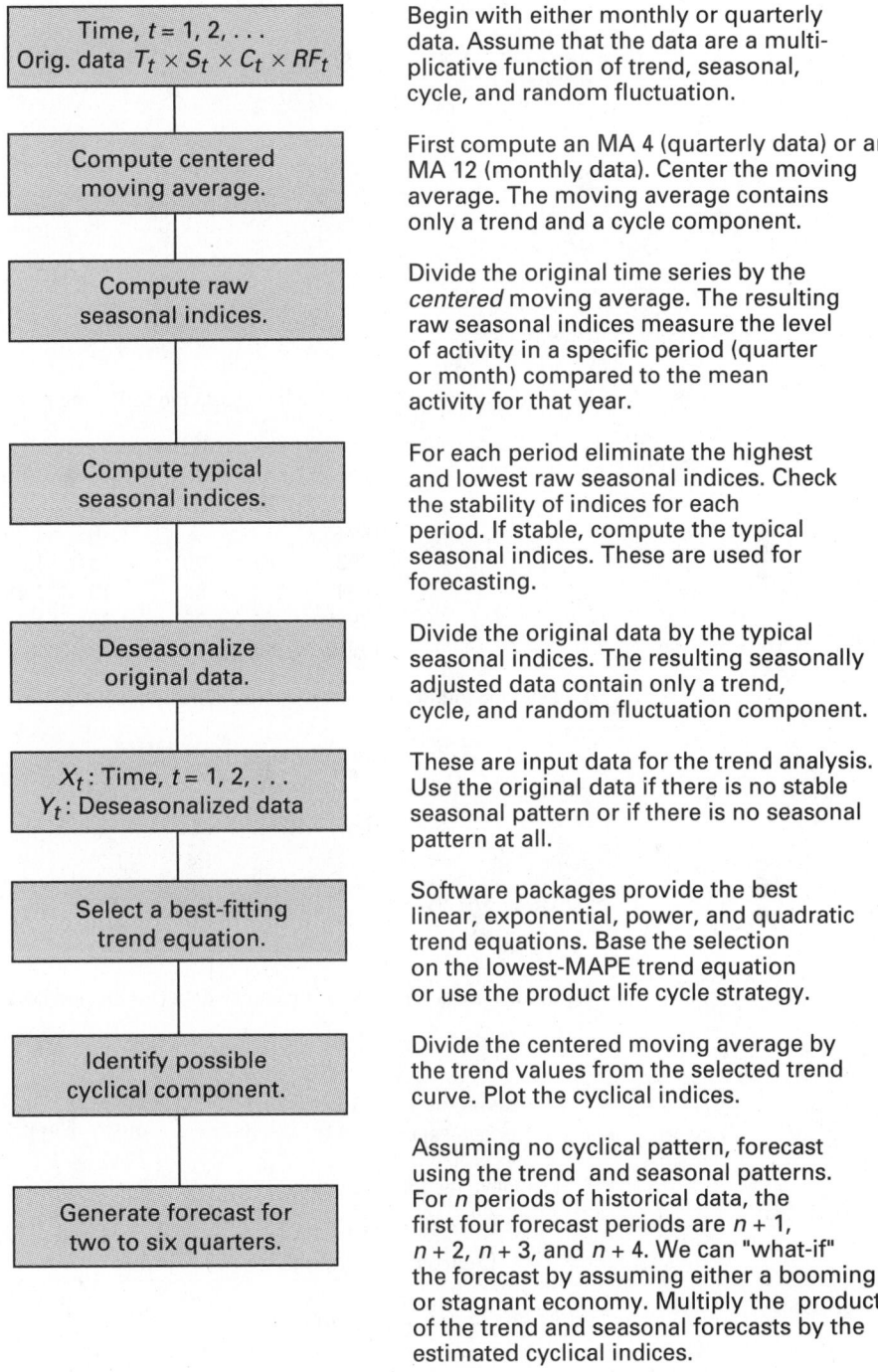

Flowchart box	Description
Time, $t = 1, 2, \ldots$ Orig. data $T_t \times S_t \times C_t \times RF_t$	Begin with either monthly or quarterly data. Assume that the data are a multiplicative function of trend, seasonal, cycle, and random fluctuation.
Compute centered moving average.	First compute an MA 4 (quarterly data) or an MA 12 (monthly data). Center the moving average. The moving average contains only a trend and a cycle component.
Compute raw seasonal indices.	Divide the original time series by the *centered* moving average. The resulting raw seasonal indices measure the level of activity in a specific period (quarter or month) compared to the mean activity for that year.
Compute typical seasonal indices.	For each period eliminate the highest and lowest raw seasonal indices. Check the stability of indices for each period. If stable, compute the typical seasonal indices. These are used for forecasting.
Deseasonalize original data.	Divide the original data by the typical seasonal indices. The resulting seasonally adjusted data contain only a trend, cycle, and random fluctuation component.
X_t: Time, $t = 1, 2, \ldots$ Y_t: Deseasonalized data	These are input data for the trend analysis. Use the original data if there is no stable seasonal pattern or if there is no seasonal pattern at all.
Select a best-fitting trend equation.	Software packages provide the best linear, exponential, power, and quadratic trend equations. Base the selection on the lowest-MAPE trend equation or use the product life cycle strategy.
Identify possible cyclical component.	Divide the centered moving average by the trend values from the selected trend curve. Plot the cyclical indices.
Generate forecast for two to six quarters.	Assuming no cyclical pattern, forecast using the trend and seasonal patterns. For n periods of historical data, the first four forecast periods are $n + 1$, $n + 2$, $n + 3$, and $n + 4$. We can "what-if" the forecast by assuming either a booming or stagnant economy. Multiply the product of the trend and seasonal forecasts by the estimated cyclical indices.

Assuming no cyclical pattern, forecast using the trend and seasonal patterns. For n periods of historical data, the first four forecast periods are $n + 1$, $n + 2$, $n + 3$, and $n + 4$. We can "what-if" the forecast by assuming either a booming or stagnant economy. Multiply the product of the trend and seasonal forecasts by the estimated cyclical indices.

SECTION 13.4 EXERCISES

1. Complete the following table. Put a dash if the value cannot be calculated.

Year	Quarter	Value	MA 4	Centered Moving Average
1	1	4		
	2	6		
	3	10	—	———
	4	12	—	———
2	1	17	—	———
	2	20	—	———
	3	22		
	4	26		

2. Find the typical seasonal indices from the following raw seasonal indices:

		Quarter		
Year	1	2	3	4
1991	—	—	1.10	1.20
1992	.85	.90	1.15	1.30
1993	.80	.88	1.13	1.18
1994	.84	.75	1.20	1.15
1995	.86	.85	—	—

3. Does the following year-by-quarter table indicate a stable seasonal pattern? If not, why not?

		Quarter		
Year	1	2	3	4
1991	—	—	.8	1.2
1992	.6	1.4	1.2	.8
1993	1.3	.5	.3	1.9
1994	.2	1.0	1.1	.6
1995	1.1	.7	—	—

4. Shown are six months of inventory data (INVEN$_t$ and INVEN$_t$-PRED). Compute the MAPE.

Period	Jan.	Feb.	March	April	May	June
INVEN$_t$	10	7	8	9	13	15
INVEN$_t$-PRED	8	6	9	11	13	14

5. Complete the following table:

Quarter	Original Value	Typical Seasonal Index	Deseasonalized Values
1	100	1.1	—
2	120	.9	—
3	140	1.2	—
4	150	.8	—

6. We fitted a linear equation to five years of deseasonalized quarterly sales data using the method of least squares. The resulting equation was

$$\text{SALES}_t - \text{PRED} = 15 + 3\text{TIME}$$

The typical seasonal indices for this series are

$S_1 = .95;$ $S_2 = .90;$ $S_3 = 1.05;$ $S_4 = 1.10$

Forecast the sales for quarters 21–24, which are quarters 1–4 of the sixth year.

7. Shown are the centered moving averages and the trend values for a time series. Compute and plot the cyclical indices.

Period	Trend	Centered Moving Average
1	50	60
2	61	68
3	52	59
4	65	66
5	54	53
6	65	60
7	58	56
8	70	70
9	63	66
10	72	77
11	66	70
12	77	80

8. Shown are eight years of data.

Year	1	2	3	4	5	6	7	8
Y_t	3	4	5	6	8	12	13	23

Use statistical software to generate the best-fitting linear and exponential trend curves.
a. Forecast the next three years with both curves.
b. Describe the differences between the forecasts for the linear and exponential trend equations.
c. Which curve would you use for forecasting years 9–11?

9. Shown are five years of quarterly data. Use statistical software to develop a forecast for periods 21–24.

		TIME	SALES$_t$
1990	1	1	4
	2	2	9
	3	3	10
	4	4	10
1991	1	5	10
	2	6	19
	3	7	18
	4	8	18
1992	1	9	19
	2	10	28
	3	11	29
	4	12	26
1993	1	13	23
	2	14	36
	3	15	37
	4	16	35
1994	1	17	30
	2	18	47
	3	19	45
	4	20	39

    a. Plot SALES$_t$ versus TIME. Do there appear to be trend and seasonal patterns?

    b. Use statistical software to determine the typical seasonal indices (if any) and the four best-fitting trend curves. Using the MAPE strategy, select a trend curve for forecasting.

    c. Forecast SALES$_t$ for the next four quarters based on the trend and seasonal patterns.

10. Shown are time-ordered data for eight periods.

TIME	1	2	3	4	5	6	7	8
Y_t	2	5	9	14	21	30	38	49

    a. Plot a line graph of Y_t versus TIME.

    b. Draw a freehand best-fitting line.

    c. Does it appear that a linear or power curve best represents the data? Describe in your own words the growth in sales.

11. *Research project.*   Obtain Dow Jones monthly closing data at the library for January 1987 to December 1991. Use statistical software to analyze the data.

    a. Prepare a forecast for the first four months of 1992 ($t = 61, 62, 63, 64$).

    b. How good was your forecast in comparison to the actual Dow Jones index monthly closings for January to April 1992? Compute the MAPE for the four forecasted months.

13.5 ≡ Qualitative Forecasting Methods

Time series and regression methods provide accurate short-term forecasts. Both are useful when we have past numerical data and we can assume that either the past data patterns or relationships among variables will continue into the near future. Qualitative approaches do not require numerical data and are often used for making rough long-term forecasts. They are useful for making short-term forecasts when quantitative data do not exist. Qualitative approaches are also useful when we do *not* expect the future to be like the recent past. By the end of this section you should be able to:

1. explain and run a nominal group expert panel; and
2. explain and run a Delphi study.

Expert Panels

In its most basic form, an expert panel is simply a group of executives or professionals sitting around a table making forecasts about the future. Generally, a company brings together panel members from various departments, thereby providing a broad base of experience and judgment. Whenever possible, the panel members are provided with background reports on the economy and specific information about the products of the firm. The expert panel is one of the simplest and most widely used qualitative forecasting methods in industry.

    An expert panel develops quick forecasts while pooling the best talent available from within or outside the firm. The major drawbacks of such panels are that they rely on judgment (see Table 13.2 for faulty rules of thumb), require costly executive time, and disperse forecasting responsibility. Moreover, groups can be ineffective.

    We recommend the *nominal group method* for running expert panels. It will minimize some of the problems of face-to-face expert panel meetings. Van de Ven and Delbecq's (1974) nominal group method (NGM) produces more accurate decisions or judgments, and stronger feelings of accomplishment than freeflowing, or interacting, expert panels. Interacting groups have no formal rules or structures to organize or control members' participation. People speak when they have something to say; otherwise, they remain quiet.

The assumption underlying the nominal group method is that difference of opinion is important at arriving at a good forecast. Disagreements force group members to explain their underlying beliefs. Group members can "reality test" their assumptions and beliefs and thereby produce more accurate forecasts.

Here are the four steps in the nominal group method:

STEP 1.   *Initial thoughts:* Group members *silently* and *independently* generate their forecasts. This can be done even before the meeting starts. Do not allow panel members to communicate during step 1.

STEP 2.   *Round robin:* Each member now presents his or her forecast. Do not discuss or criticize the presentations. Permit only questions of clarification. The panel leader can make a presentation, but should go last to avoid putting pressure on others to conform. Also ask panel members to write down and hand in their forecasts.

STEP 3.   *Discussion:* The panel explores and compares all the forecasts. Differences are examined, not ignored. The panel leader summarizes frequently and ensures that all forecasts are discussed, especially those suggested by junior team members. Panel members must make the assumptions behind their forecasts explicit. Assumptions are claims (not facts) about the future that support panel members' forecasts. Making assumptions explicit helps "reality test" the forecasts. The panel should strive for a synthesis that incorporates the best of each forecast.

STEP 4.   *Closure:* Seek a consensus forecast. If that is not possible, have each member write down a final forecast and submit it to the expert panel leader. Ensure anonymity. The panel leader can then either select the forecast he or she believes is most accurate or compute the mean of the final forecasts.

The nominal group method is superior to the typical expert panel. Brightman (1988) presents suggestions for improving the effectiveness of the nominal group method.

Delphi Method

The name Delphi comes from the site of an ancient Greek temple where the gods of Greek mythology gathered to make forecasts of the future. In its modern form, the Delphi method is a forum for reaching a group consensus about either values or "futures" forecasting (Helmer, 1977).

Unlike most group meetings, the Delphi group members do not meet face to face and may not even know who the others are. All communication is done through writing or electronic mail using computers. This minimizes the problems associated with interacting groups.

We illustrate the Delphi method in the following example. COMCEL wants to estimate the percentage of automobiles that will have telephones as standard equipment by the year 2010. Since they are forecasting many years into the future, quantitative forecasting methods will not work. Therefore, COMCEL tries the Delphi method, as follows.

PHASE 1: *Selection of experts.*   COMCEL selected 10 experts from a wide range of functional areas including research and development, marketing, and operations. This ensured a wide range of knowledge and perspective. It also selected 10 outside experts from the telecommunications industry, academe (marketing and sociology professors), and futurists (members of the World Future Society).

FIGURE 13.14   Results of Phase 2 of the Delphi Study on the Percentage of Cars
with Phones by the Year 2010

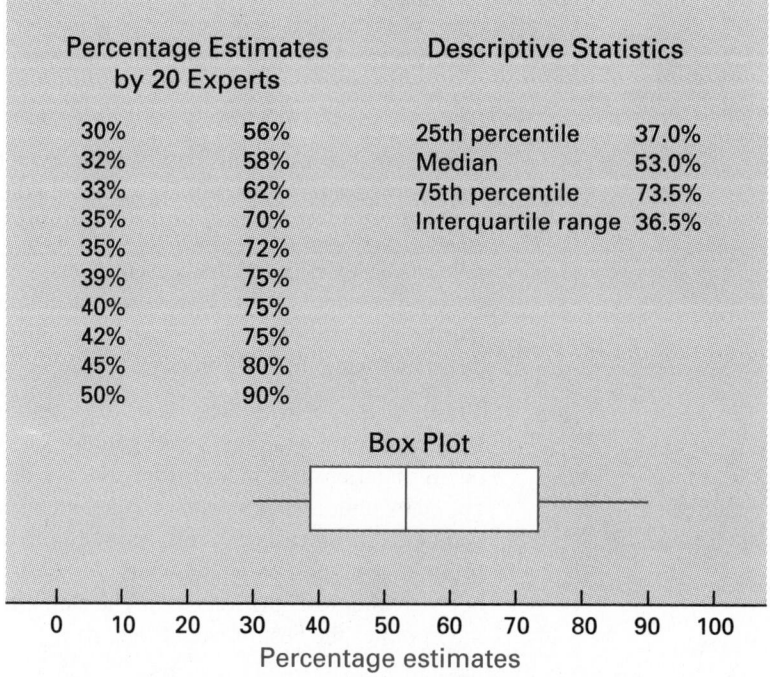

Percentage Estimates by 20 Experts		Descriptive Statistics	
30%	56%	25th percentile	37.0%
32%	58%	Median	53.0%
33%	62%	75th percentile	73.5%
35%	70%	Interquartile range	36.5%
35%	72%		
39%	75%		
40%	75%		
42%	75%		
45%	80%		
50%	90%		

PHASE 2: *First-round forecasts.*   The Delphi study team leader asked each member to estimate independently the percentage of automobiles with telephones as standard equipment by the year 2010. The group members returned their estimates to the team leader.

PHASE 3: *Summarize results and provide feedback.*   The leader summarized and displayed the initial forecasts using descriptive statistics—quartiles and the median—and a box plot, as shown in Figure 13.14.

The leader sent this information to the group members who could revise their estimates based on the summarized data. Experts who wished to maintain their initially widely divergent estimates—below the 25th or above the 75th percentile—were asked to provide reasons for doing so. The study leader returned the summarized data together with the reasons for any widely divergent forecasts.

PHASE 4: *Subsequent feedback.*   To further narrow the range of percentages, the leader repeated phase 3. The results are given in Figure 13.15. Note that the width of the interquartile range dropped from 36.5% in phase 2 to 9.0%. Had the group not reached a consensus (as evidenced by the small interquartile range), the team leader would have tried additional feedback sessions. Groups often can reach a consensus in three feedback sessions.

The Delphi method permits a spread of opinion to reflect group members' uncertainty. The goal is to narrow the interquartile range without pressuring the group members. Widely divergent views are still possible. However, members with widely divergent views must explain their positions in writing. In doing so, either they convince other members to change their positions or they move toward the median position.

The Delphi method has its strengths and weaknesses. It obtains estimates free of group power or political game playing. With the advent of electronic mail, it is quick and inexpensive. However, it can produce estimates with low reliability. Also, the study leader can influence the estimates by how he or she frames the questions and

FIGURE 13.15   Final Results of the Delphi Study on the Percentage of Cars with Phones by the Year 2010

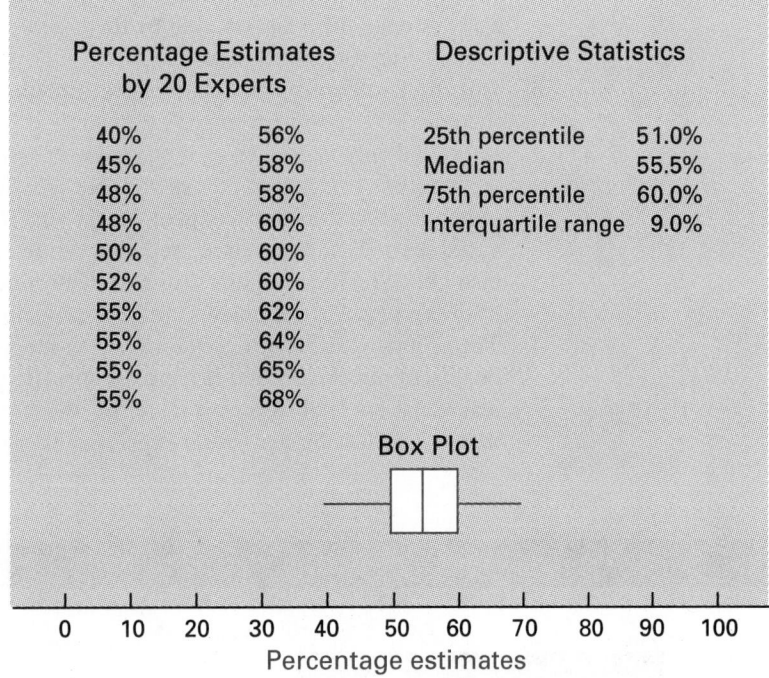

reports the findings from each round. Sachman (1975) evaluated the Delphi method and has suggested procedures to overcome its greatest shortcomings. In summary, the Delphi method is useful for reaching consensus on "futures" forecasting.

SECTION 13.5 EXERCISES

1. List the four steps of the nominal group method. Why is this method superior to an unstructured group approach for generating forecasts?

2. What is the Delphi technique? How does it differ from the nominal group technique?

3. A power-generating firm is using a nominal group expert panel to estimate the percentage of Columbus, Ohio, metro area homes with insulation at the R30 or higher level by the year 2005. Should we expect that the percentages developed during phase 1, the initial thoughts phase, will be similar? Discuss.

4. How might the group leader in a nominal group expert panel use descriptive statistics during the phase III discussion? Discuss.

5. What is the purpose of selecting participants from different functional fields to participate in a Delphi study? Could the strategy backfire? Discuss.

13.6≡ Key Ideas and Overview

We conclude this chapter on forecasting with the following key ideas:

1. Forecasting is an essential tool in planning. Managers cannot plan if they cannot forecast, nor can they detect deviations from plans if they have no plans. Predicting the future is akin to estimating a population parameter. Unfortunately, we cannot sample the future. In short, obtaining accurate forecasts can be difficult.

2. All quantitative forecasting approaches depend on the critical assumption that the past data patterns or relationships among variables will continue into the near future. If a major change takes place, quantitative models could become useless. For example, the equation used by the U.S. Army to forecast enlistments became useless after the abolition of the draft.

3. Quantitative forecasting approaches include time series methods and causal methods. We use the decomposition method (a time series method) when we are interested only in predicting Y_t and have at least five years of historical data. Time is a proxy (not a true predictor) variable. We use the regression method (a causal method) when we want to explain and predict future values of Y_t. Consider lagged variables of Y_t and X_t as true predictor variables. Check for multicollinearity and also check residuals against time to determine if the independence assumption has been met. Causal models are generally more costly to build and maintain.

4. The accuracy of quantitative forecasting methods depends on the existence and quality of historical data. If there are insufficient historical data or if the historical data are not representative of the future, use qualitative forecasting methods—the nominal group expert panel or the Delphi group method.

COMCEL

Date: August 17, 1994
To: Ann Tabor, CEO
From: Howard Bright, Manager, Norcross Plant
Re: Southern Region Forecasts

SUMMARY
We have reviewed our forecast and are still projecting that we will sell 86,533 units over the next year. The forecast is based on the assumption that the forecasted pattern will continue over the next four quarters. The forecast is in line with the sales growth of our product and in line with the product life cycle for the car phone market in general.

SUPPORTING ANALYSIS
We developed the forecast using the method of time series decomposition. The data for the first five years showed a stable seasonal pattern and an underlying linear trend.

Since there is no way to know what the correct trend model is, we fitted several models to the deseasonalized data. We evaluated each model in terms of how well it would have predicted past sales values. The linear model showed the lowest mean absolute percentage prediction error—a mean of 2.3% per quarter. Moreover, we believe that the car phone market is now in the growth phase of the product life cycle. The linear model has proven to be an appropriate description of growth during this phase.

The data provided strong evidence of a seasonal pattern. Over the past five years, we have sold approximately 80% of the trend in the first and fourth quarters and approximately 120% of the trend in the second and third quarters. I assume that these seasonal indices also will remain the same for the coming year.

We will, of course, monitor these forecasts and make adjustments as needed.

CHAPTER 13 QUESTIONS	

CHAPTER 13 QUESTIONS

1. How does forecasting help managers detect future disturbance problems?

2. Describe a product or service that had an upward trend in the late 1980s. Describe one that had a downward trend in the 1980s.

3. Describe a product or service that has a seasonal pattern. Describe one that has no seasonal pattern.

4. Distinguish between seasonal and cyclical components.

5. Why is the assumption of continuity important in quantitative forecasting methods?

6. A travel agent is preparing a qualitative forecast for next year's number of air fatalities. That day the worst airline disaster in history occurs. How might this affect her forecast and what rule of thumb may she have fallen prey to?

7. Distinguish between regression and autoregression.

8. Explain the problem of using coincident predictor variables in regression models based on time-ordered data.

9. Explain why the mean absolute percentage error (MAPE) is a useful measure of the forecast accuracy.

10. Which of the four linear regression model assumptions is most often violated in time-ordered data? How can we assess the validity of the assumption?

11. What is a major limitation in using regression models for forecasting?

12. What is a leading indicator?

13. Distinguish between additive and multiplicative models.

14. Why must we center the moving average?

15. Why do we lose two data points at the beginning and end of the centered moving average time series for quarterly data? How many points would we lose for monthly data? What is the general rule?

16. Why can't all the typical seasonal indices be greater than 1?

17. What problems will we have if we try the decomposition method on a data set that contains only three years of data?

18. When might the product life cycle method be better than the lowest-MAPE approach in selecting a curve type for the trend component? (*Hint:* In the product life cycle context, when might the recent past not be effective in predicting the short-term future?)

19. Why are quantitative forecasting methods not effective beyond 12 to 18 months into the future?

20. Distinguish between the decomposition method and the regression method as forecasting approaches.

21. How do the nominal group expert panel and the Delphi method overcome many of the problems that face-to-face groups encounter?

22. How do box plots or stem-and-leaf displays help Delphi participants reach a consensus?

**CHAPTER 13
APPLICATION
PROBLEMS**

1. Shown are 20 quarters of earnings per share (EPS) data for a *Fortune* 100 firm.

TIME	EPS$_t$	TIME	EPS$_t$
1	$1.50	11	$2.15
2	1.75	12	2.10
3	1.70	13	2.25
4	1.75	14	2.40
5	1.80	15	2.45
6	1.90	16	2.40
7	1.85	17	2.65
8	1.95	18	2.75
9	2.10	19	2.85
10	2.25	20	3.15

   a. Plot a line graph of the EPS data. Do there appear to be trend and seasonal components?
   b. Use regression analysis to develop a best-fitting straight line with EPS$_t$ as the dependent variable and the proxy variable, TIME, as the independent variable. Plot the best-fitting line on the graph from part **a**.
   c. Compute the MAPE for the linear equation in part **b**.
   d. Develop a forecast for quarters 21 and 22 using the equation from part **b**.
   e. TIME appears to be a reasonable proxy variable. For what is it a proxy? Could TIME be a proxy variable for the impact of previous quarters' earnings per share? That is, could one quarter's EPS data value depend on the EPS from the previous quarter? Plot EPS$_t$ versus EPS$_{t-1}$ (one quarter lag).
   f. Use regression analysis to develop a best-fitting line with EPS$_t$ as the dependent variable and EPS$_{t-1}$ as the independent variable for the following data:

$$\begin{array}{ll} \text{EPS}_t & \text{from periods } 2\text{--}20 \\ \text{EPS}_{t-1} & \text{from periods } 1\text{--}19 \end{array}$$

   g. Compute the MAPE for the autoregressive model.
   h. Can you develop a forecast for periods 21 and 22? If not, develop a forecast for period 21.
   i. Develop a line graph for the equations in parts **b** and **f**. Compare and contrast the two forecast equations. How are they similar and how are they different?

2. Shown are the number of grievances filed in a large firm for the past 20 quarters. The firm also records the ratio of the mean salary of skilled employees within the firm to the mean salary for the industry. A number less than 1 means that the firm pays its skilled workers less than the industry mean.

TIME	GRIEV$_t$	SALINDEX$_t$	TIME	GRIEV$_t$	SALINDEX$_t$
1	230	.90	11	190	1.18
2	290	.95	12	70	1.16
3	290	1.10	13	100	1.10
4	110	1.07	14	140	1.08
5	160	1.07	15	180	1.18
6	170	1.00	16	100	1.19
7	210	1.15	17	90	1.10
8	100	1.12	18	110	1.12
9	110	1.06	19	150	1.25
10	160	1.05	20	30	1.15

   a. Plot a line graph with time on the horizontal axis for the GRIEVance data. Do there appear to be trend and seasonal components?

b. Use statistical software to determine the typical seasonal indices and the best-fitting trend equation using the lowest-MAPE strategy. Plot the forecasted number of grievances for periods 1–20 on the line graph from part **a.**

c. Compute the MAPE for the forecasted number of grievances for periods 1–20.

d. Develop a forecast for quarter 21 using the trend and seasonal components.

e. Suppose we believe that the number of grievances is affected by the salary index. Moreover, we believe that SALINDEX is a one-period leading indicator. Use statistical software to regress GRIEV$_t$ as the dependent variable on SALINDEX$_{t-1}$ as the independent variable for the following data:

$$\text{GRIEV}_t \qquad \text{from periods } 2\text{--}20$$
$$\text{SALINDEX}_{t-1} \qquad \text{from periods } 1\text{--}19$$

Graph the regression model and original data.

f. Compute the MAPE for the regression model.

g. Use the regression (causal) model to develop a forecast for period 21.

3. Shown are 60 months of hypothetical data on the number of mobile car phones bought, in tens of thousands.

	Jan	Feb	Mar	Apr	May	June	July	Aug	Sept	Oct	Nov	Dec
1989	.9	1.1	1.1	1.2	1.3	1.3	1.4	1.6	1.8	1.8	1.9	1.9
1990	1.7	1.9	2.0	2.2	2.1	2.3	2.6	2.9	3.4	3.2	3.5	3.5
1991	3.1	3.7	3.7	3.9	3.8	4.1	4.7	5.2	6.0	5.7	6.5	6.4
1992	5.7	6.1	6.7	7.0	7.0	7.8	8.6	9.8	10.9	10.5	11.5	11.6
1993	10.4	11.4	12.2	12.8	12.7	14.7	15.6	17.3	19.9	19.1	19.0	21.1

a. Plot a line graph of the SALES data. Do there appear to be trend and seasonal components?

b. Use statistical software to determine the typical seasonal indices and the best-fitting trend equation using the lowest-MAPE strategy.

c. Compute the MAPE for the sales data for periods 1–60.

d. Develop a forecast for January to March of 1994 using the trend and seasonal components.

4. Shown are 24 quarters of sales data (in thousands of dollars) of a medium-size specialty women's clothing store. Sales are influenced by the timing of the sales promotions, including special one-day sales and other promotions.

TIME	SALES$_t$	TIME	SALES$_t$
1	80	13	110
2	91	14	81
3	121	15	90
4	110	16	120
5	81	17	111
6	89	18	81
7	119	19	89
8	111	20	119
9	80	21	112
10	90	22	79
11	122	23	90
12	109	24	122

a. Plot the data. Also use statistical software to compute the raw seasonal indices. Obtain a year-by-quarter table of raw seasonal indices. Does there appear to be a stable seasonal component?

b. Look at the raw seasonal indices closely. Can you detect a change in the pattern during the six years of data? Review your graph and the year-by-quarter table. When did a shift in the seasonal pattern happen?

c. What could account for the shift in the seasonal pattern?

5. Given are the total numbers of U.S. nuclear reactors built, being built, or planned (for power generation) between 1973 and 1982. *Source: U.S. Nuclear Regulatory Commission Reports.*

	TIME	NUC_t
1973	1	214
1974	2	233
1975	3	236
1976	4	235
1977	5	221
1978	6	207
1979	7	188
1980	8	163
1981	9	162
1982	10	146

a. Plot a line graph.

b. Regress the number of nuclear reactors on TIME using a regression software package. Use time as the predictor variable.

c. Forecast the numbers of nuclear reactors built, being built, or planned for 1983 to 1991 ($t = 11$ to $t = 19$).

d. What are the risks in using the regression equation to forecast nine years into the future?

6. A line graph of SALES_t for 16 quarters of data is shown in the figure. Without doing any calculations, would we obtain a lower MAPE on the historical data using an autoregressive model with a one-quarter lag (SALES_{t-1}) or a multiplicative time series decomposition model? Explain.

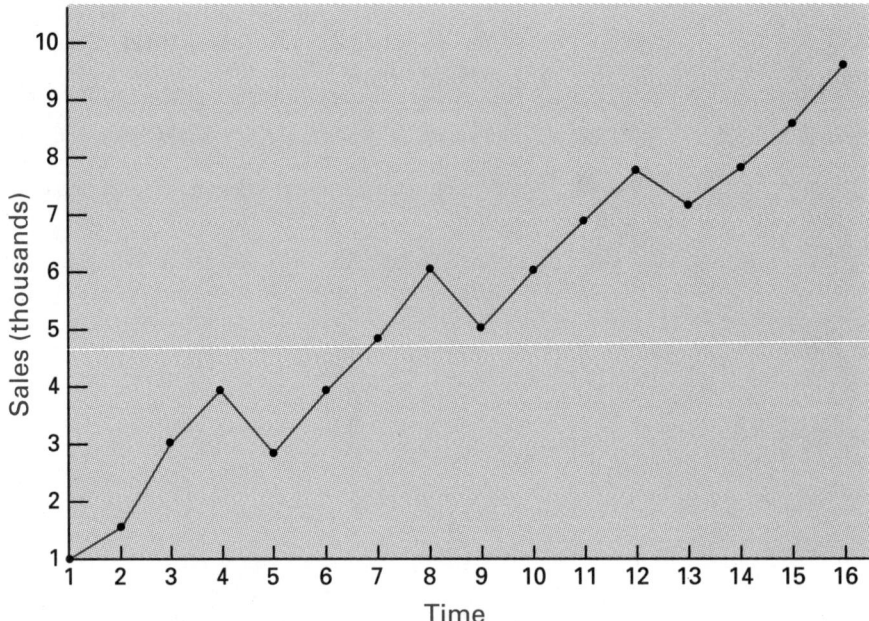

7. We have fitted the following autoregressive model to the monthly closing Dow Jones Industrial Index for the years 1976 to 1981. The market peaked in December 1976 at about 980 and bottomed out about two years later at under 800. By March 1981 the market again had climbed into the 960 range.

$$\text{DJ}_t\text{-PRED} = 101 + .886\text{DJ}_{t-1}$$

The analysis of variance indicated that the predictor and dependent variables are significantly related.

If we had plotted the monthly closing Dow-Jones Index (DJ_t) versus the Dow Jones Index for the previous month (DJ_{t-1}), how would the graph look? Explain.

8. A firm's quality control department takes measurements of the diameter of a part. For proper functioning, the diameter should be close to the target value of 40 (in hundredths of an inch). Below are data taken from 16 successive time periods over several days.

TIME	$DIAM_t$	TIME	$DIAM_t$
1	39	9	41
2	40	10	46
3	39	11	31
4	41	12	32
5	35	13	44
6	30	14	32
7	31	15	46
8	48	16	37

 a. Plot a line graph. Also draw a line representing the mean diameter over the 16 measurements.
 b. Does there appear to be a trend? Does there appear to be any systematic pattern?
 c. Given your answer in part **b,** if the production process continues to behave as it has for the past 16 observations, what would be your best prediction of future values of $DIAM_t$?
 d. From the graph in part **a,** the mean level of the process is constant, the variability of the process about the mean level is relatively constant, and there is no pattern in the observations around the mean level. What do we call such patternless behavior?
 e. Suppose we consider an autoregressive model between $DIAM_t$ and $DIAM_{t-1}$ (the diameter lagged by one period) for the given data. Without actually determining the model, would we expect a significant relationship between $DIAM_t$ and $DIAM_{t-1}$? Explain.
 f. Suppose that observations for time periods 17, 18, and 19 are 70, 71, and 65. What might that suggest in terms of the production process's ability to produce properly functioning parts? As manager of the production process, what should you do? Discuss.

9. Shown are quarterly data on the discount rate charged by the Federal Reserve Bank of New York. The discount rate is the interest rate that the Fed charges its commercial bank customers to borrow money and is one of several tools it uses in managing the overall economy. *Source: Federal Reserve Bulletin (Monthly).*

Quarter	TIME	$DISCOUNT_t$	Quarter	TIME	$DISCOUNT_t$
March 1980	1	13.00%	September 1983	15	8.75
June 1980	2	11.00	December 1983	16	8.75
September 1980	3	11.00	March 1984	17	9.00
December 1980	4	13.00	June 1984	18	9.00
March 1981	5	13.75	September 1984	19	8.50
June 1981	6	14.00	December 1984	20	8.00
September 1981	7	13.00	March 1985	21	7.75
December 1981	8	12.00	June 1985	22	7.50
March 1982	9	12.00	September 1985	23	7.50
June 1982	10	11.50	December 1985	24	7.00
September 1982	11	10.00	March 1986	25	7.00
December 1982	12	9.00	June 1986	26	6.00
March 1983	13	8.50	September 1986	27	5.50
June 1983	14	8.50	December 1986	28	5.50

a. Plot a line graph of the DISCOUNT data.
b. Develop an autoregressive model of DISCOUNT$_t$ versus DISCOUNT$_{t-1}$. Are the two variables significantly related?
c. Determine the MAPE for the autoregressive model.
d. Prepare a forecast for the March 1987 Federal Reserve Bank of New York discount rate.

10. Shown are the mean sales (in thousands of dollars) per employee of corporations, SALES$_t$, in the United States from 1980 to 1988. *Source: The Fortune Directory, Time, Inc.*

1980	1981	1982	1983	1984	1985	1986	1987	1988
71.1	75.9	91.0	92.2	100.6	106.0	110.7	124.4	137.9

a. Plot a line graph of mean sales per employee for 1980 to 1988.
b. Use software to regress SALES$_t$ as the dependent variable on SALES$_{t-1}$ as the independent variable.
c. Are the two variables significantly related?
d. Compute the MAPE for the historical data.
e. Develop a forecast for the mean sales per employee for 1989.

11. We wish to forecast the number of mergers or acquisitions (for more than $1 million) that will take place in 1989. We believe that GNP may be a coincident indicator. *Source: Statistical Abstracts of the United States, 1990.*

Year	NUMBER$_t$	GNP$_t$ (billions of 1982 dollars)
1980	1,560	3,187
1981	2,329	3,150
1982	2,298	3,166
1983	2,391	3,279
1984	3,164	3,501
1985	3,437	3,614
1986	4,381	3,717
1987	3,920	3,853
1988	3,487	4,024

a. Develop a scatter plot of the two variables.
b. Consider the following predictor variables, GNP$_t$ and NUMBER$_{t-1}$. Determine whether one or both predictor variables are significantly related to the dependent variable.
c. Do a residual analysis for the final regression model. Does it appear that the independence assumption has been met? Discuss.

12. We wish to forecast the percentage of eligible voters who will vote in the 1992 presidential election. Our data base includes data on two potential coincident indicators and the dependent variable for the last 15 presidential elections. The coincident indicators are (1) the indicator variable, presidential polls predicting a victory margin of 7.5% or more—yes or no, and (2) percentage of the civilian labor force unemployed. Code the indicator variable as: MARGIN = 1 if predicted victory margin is 7.5% or more, and 0 if otherwise. *Sources: Statistics of the Presidential and Congressional Elections, U.S. Congress; Employment and Earnings, U.S. Bureau of Labor Statistics.*

Election	TIME	PERCENT$_t$	MARGIN$_t$	UNEMPLOY$_t$
1932	1	52.4	Yes	23.6
1936	2	56.0	Yes	16.9
1940	3	58.9	Yes	14.6
1944	4	56.0	No	1.2
1948	5	51.1	No	3.8
1952	6	61.6	Yes	3.0
1956	7	59.3	Yes	4.1
1960	8	62.8	No	5.5
1964	9	61.9	Yes	5.2
1968	10	60.9	No	3.6
1972	11	55.2	Yes	3.3
1976	12	53.5	No	5.9
1980	13	52.6	Yes	5.1
1984	14	53.1	Yes	5.8
1988	15	50.2	Yes	4.3

a. Consider the following three predictor variables: PERCENT$_{t-1}$ (the percentage of voters in the previous election), MARGIN$_t$, and UNEMPLOY$_t$. Determine whether all the predictor variables are significantly related to the dependent variable, PERCENT$_t$.

b. Given the above data, can we make a prediction on the percentage of eligible voters who will vote in the 1992 presidential election? Discuss.

13. Given here are the daily attendance figures for five weeks for a movie theater in a mall.

Day	Week 1	Week 2	Week 3	Week 4	Week 5
Monday	150	135	155	175	125
Tuesday	175	165	165	135	145
Wednesday	135	150	150	165	145
Thursday	165	145	125	175	175
Friday	300	275	325	310	290
Saturday	600	650	700	600	610
Sunday	225	235	210	220	230

a. Plot a line graph of daily attendance.

b. Is there a 7-day seasonal pattern? Explain why such a 7-day seasonal pattern might exist.

c. Plot a moving average of length 3 days. Does the MA 3 still contain a seasonal pattern? Why or why not?

d. Plot a moving average of length 7 days. Does the MA 7 still contain a seasonal pattern? Why or why not?

e. Plot a moving average of length 21 days. Does the MA 21 still contain a seasonal pattern? Why or why not?

14. We believe that the number of people below the poverty level and the number of prisoners executed impact the number of violent crimes (murder, rape, aggravated assault, and robbery) committed each year. Our data include 1979–1988. *Sources: Crime in the United States,* U.S. Federal Bureau of Investigation; *Correctional Projections in the United States,* U.S. Bureau of Justice Statistics.

Year	VIOLENT$_t$ (millions)	POVERTY$_t$ (millions)	EXECUTE$_t$
1979	1.208	26.1	1
1980	1.345	29.3	1
1981	1.362	31.8	1
1982	1.322	34.4	2
1983	1.258	35.3	5
1984	1.273	33.7	21
1985	1.329	33.1	18
1986	1.489	32.4	18
1987	1.484	32.3	25
1988	1.566	31.9	11

a. Consider the following three predictor variables, VIOLENT$_{t-1}$ (the number of violent crimes in the prior year), POVERTY$_t$, and EXECUTE$_t$. Determine whether all the predictor variables are significantly related to the dependent variable, VIOLENT$_t$.

b. Does it appear that the independence assumption has been met for the final model? Discuss.

15.

Date: February 5, 1994
To: Pam Ascher, National Sales Manager
From: Bill O'Hara, Vice-President of Marketing
Subject: Forecast of Atlanta's Sales for Next Six Quarters

Your January 24 report generated more questions than it answered. You noted that sales have been steadily increasing and that the second and third quarters tend to be strong sales periods. Exactly how fast have sales been increasing? Exactly how strong are the second and third quarters? How weak are the first and fourth quarters?

I will also need for the upcoming planning meeting with Ann Tabor and the Senior Team a forecast for the Atlanta sales territory for the next six quarters. Keep the jargon and statistical "mumbo jumbo" to a minimum. You know how Ann likes straight talk. Please have the report on my desk by February 12.

Use Data Base II in Appendix 9 for your analysis. Your response to Bill O'Hara should include a brief memo and your analysis.

REFERENCES

Brightman, H. *Group Problem Solving: An Improved Managerial Approach.* Atlanta: Georgia State University Business Press, 1988.

Farnum, N., and L. Stanton. *Quantitative Forecasting Methods.* Boston: PWS/Kent, 1989.

Helmer, O. "Problems in Futures Research—Delphi and Causal Cross Impact Analysis." *Futures* 9 (1977).

Hogarth, R. *Judgment and Choice.* New York: John Wiley, 1987.

Makridakis, S., S. Wheelwright, and V. McGee. *Forecasting: Methods and Applications.* New York: John Wiley, 1983.

Newbold, P., and T. Bos. *Introductory Business Forecasting.* Cincinnati: South-Western, 1994.

Roberts, H. *Data Analysis for Managers.* Redwood City, Calif.: The Scientific Press, 1988.

Sachman, H. *Delphi Critique.* Lexington, Mass.: Lexington Books, 1975.

Van De Ven, A., and A. Delbecq. "The Effectiveness of Nominal, Delphi, and Interacting Group Decision Making Processes." *Academy of Management Journal* (December 1974): 605–621.

APPENDIX: Statistical Software

We use MINITAB, Release 8, to develop a regression model to predict sales in time period t, $SALES_t$, based on the values of advertising expenditures in the same period, ADV_t, and the values of sales and advertising expenditures in the previous time period, $SALES_{t-1}$ and ADV_{t-1}. The data are shown in Table 13.4.

Input

```
01    MTB > NAME C1='SALES'
02    MTB > NAME C2='ADV'
03    MTB > READ 'SALES' 'ADV'
      DATA > 3.40 1.10
      DATA > 2.00 1.40
      DATA > 1.90 3.30
      DATA > 3.20 5.40
      DATA > 4.80 1.50
      DATA > 3.75 3.60
      DATA > 4.13 3.70
      DATA > 4.51 5.80
      DATA > 5.61 1.90
      DATA > 4.05 4.00
      DATA > 4.63 4.10
      DATA > 5.01 6.20
      DATA > 6.03 2.50
      DATA > 4.61 4.40
      DATA > 5.08 4.50
      DATA > 5.29 1.25
      DATA > END
      16 ROWS READ
      MTB > NAME C3='SALES-1'
04    MTB > LAG 1 'SALES' 'SALES-1'
      MTB > NAME C4= 'ADV-1'
05    MTB > LAG 1 'ADV' 'ADV-1'
06    MTB > DELETE 1 'SALES' 'ADV' 'SALES-1' 'ADV-1'
07    MTB > REGRESS 'SALES' 3 'ADV' 'SALES-1''ADV-1'
```

Explanation of Input

01–03   See Statistical Software Appendix, Chapter 7

04–05   LAG the variable (column 1) SALES by 1 period and put the results in column 3, labelled SALES-1. LAG the variable (column 2) ADV by 1 period and put the results in column 4, labelled ADV-1. See Table 13.4.

06   DELETE row 1 in Table 13.4 because there are no values for SALES-1 and ADV-1 for the first period (TIME = 1). The result of the DELETE command is that 15 observations are available for the regression analysis.

07   Perform a least squares REGRESSION treating SALES as the dependent variable and include 3 predictor variables, namely, ADV, SALES-1, and ADV-1.

Output

The regression equation is

01   SALES = − 0.211 + 0.0860 ADV + 0.508 SALES-1 + 0.587 ADV-1

02 | Predictor | Coef | Stdev | t-ratio | p |
|---|---|---|---|---|
| Constant | -0.2108 | 0.2035 | -1.04 | 0.322 |
| ADV | 0.08598 | 0.02713 | 3.17 | 0.009 |
| SALES-1 | 0.50759 | 0.03654 | 13.89 | 0.000 |
| ADV-1 | 0.58664 | 0.02718 | 21.58 | 0.000 |

03    $s = 0.1596$ $R\text{-sq} = 98.6\%$ $R\text{-sq(adj)} = 98.2\%$

Analysis of Variance

SOURCE	DF	SS	MS	F	p
Regression	3	19.6736	6.5579	257.30	0.000
Error	11	0.2804	0.0255		
Total	14	19.9539			

04 | SOURCE | DF | SEQ SS |
|---|---|---|
| ADV | 1 | 0.0044 |
| SALES-1 | 1 | 7.7987 |
| ADV-1 | 1 | 11.8704 |

Unusual Observations

05 | Obs. | ADV | SALES | Fit | Stdev.Fit | Residual | St.Resid |
|---|---|---|---|---|---|---|
| 1 | 1.40 | 2.0000 | 2.2807 | 0.1053 | -0.2807 | -2.34R |
| 5 | 3.60 | 3.7500 | 3.4151 | 0.0757 | 0.3349 | 2.38R |

R denotes an obs. with a large st. resid.

Interpretation of Output

01–02   Shows the regression equation and the values of the sample regression coefficients. This is similar to COMSTAT's parameter estimate section found in the text.

03   s is the standard error of the estimate or $\sqrt{MSE}$. R-sq indicates that 98.6% of the variation in SALES is associated with the three predictor variables. The F-value of 257.30 in the ANOVA table indicates that we must reject the null hypothesis that none of the three predictor variables are related to SALES. The adjusted R-sq term is discussed in Chapter 11's software appendix.

04   SEQ SS is the marginal regression sum of squares contributed by each predictor variable as it enters the regression model. The first variable. ADV contributes only .0044 of the total Regression SS of 19.6736 in the ANOVA table. SALES-1 contributes an additional 7.7987 and ADV-1 contributes 11.8704.

05   This section indicates possible outliers in the data in Table 13.4. Minitab computes studentized residuals. Table 13.6 presents standardized residuals. The two residuals are different.

14.1 Introduction
14.2 The need for nonparametric methods
 Assumptions underlying the analysis
 Measurement scales
 Inferences beyond parameters
14.3 The chi-square goodness-of-fit test
 State hypotheses
 Compute expected frequencies
 Compute the calculated chi-square statistic
 Compare the calculated chi-square statistic to
  critical value
 Dangers of small expected frequencies
 Dunn confidence intervals on category
  probabilities
 Summary

14.4 The chi-square test of independence
 State hypotheses
 Compute expected frequencies for cross-tabs
  table cells
 Compute the calculated chi-square statistic
 Compare the calculated chi-square statistic to
  critical value
 Dangers of small expected frequencies
 Cramer's measure of association
 Summary
14.5 Key ideas and overview
Appendix: Statistical software

 **INTEROFFICE COMMUNICATION**

Date: September 13, 1994
To: Sang Kim, Quality-Assurance Manager
From: Ann Tabor, CEO
Re: Update on Progress of Quality-Improvement Team #25

Six months ago team #25 made a presentation on our top five warranty repair problems. At that time the executive group gave its permission to take corrective action. Our initial goal was to reduce the percentage of complaints about excessive static and volume fluctuations during telephone transmissions. Would you ask the team to have its follow-up report on my desk by the month's end?

Again, I want to thank you for leading the quality-improvement effort at COMCEL. You and your quality-improvement teams have made it possible to maintain our competitive edge.

14.1 ≣ Introduction

Effective business professionals must learn how to sense problems. Problem sensing is detecting differences or changes in one group (product or service) over time or among several groups at one point in time. Problem sensing is crucial, since we cannot solve a problem until we know it exists.

Problem diagnosis follows problem sensing. During problem diagnosis managers must ask "Why?" Why has there been a *change* from historical or expected performance? Why do two or more groups, products, or services *differ?* In answering the "why" questions, managers often seek variables or factors that might account for the changes or the differences. After completing the diagnosis, management can take corrective action.

In this book we have presented primarily *parametric* statistical methods to help professionals sense and diagnose problems. These methods shared three characteristics:

1. The data were quantitative, i.e., we had exact numerical measurements. We could add, subtract, multiply, or divide two numbers and the results made sense.
2. We assumed that the population distribution(s) were normally distributed.
3. We made inferences about the parameters, the mean or variance, of the population(s) from which the samples were taken.

In Chapters 7, 8, and 10 we presented several *nonparametric* methods when the assumption of normality was not met. In this chapter we present a goodness-of-fit test and a test of independence. We use these methods when we do not have numerical measurements on the variables of interest, or when the inference we wish to make does not concern the mean and variance of the population from which the sample was drawn.

14.2 ≣ The Need for Nonparametric Methods

A statistical method is nonparametric if it satisfies at least one of the following conditions:

1. The analysis requires only very general assumptions about the populations. It does not require that we select samples from normally distributed populations.
2. We measure or analyze data on either a nominal or ordinal measurement scale. The data are categorical (see Section 3.2).
3. We do not draw inferences about a population distribution parameter.

The second condition refers to the type of data used in the analysis. The first and third conditions refer to the type of analysis used on the data. In this section we will explain the three conditions fully. By the end of this section you should be able to:

1. determine if measurements are on a nominal, ordinal, interval, or ratio scale; and
2. explain when nonparametric methods are useful.

Assumptions Underlying the Analysis

Nonparametric methods require only very general assumptions about the populations from which the samples are taken. In Section 7.3, we constructed confidence intervals on an unknown population mean. We assumed that we selected a (1) random sample from (2) a normal population. Suppose that a stem-and-leaf data plot indicated an extremely skewed sample. It would be unlikely that it could have been taken from an underlying normal population. Unless the sample size was greater than 30 and we could apply the central limit theorem, we should not construct a confidence interval on the population mean.

To this point, the restrictive assumptions about the underlying population(s) have prompted the inclusion of nonparametric methods in the text. In Section 7.8 you learned how to construct a confidence interval on a population median. The non-parametric method only required that managers select a random sample from the population. The Mann–Whitney confidence interval (Section 8.5), the Mood test (Section 8.7), and the Kruskal–Wallis test (Section 10.5) also have fewer assumptions than their alternative parametric tests.

Should you use parametric or nonparametric methods? We recommend using a parametric method if the data meet its restrictive assumptions. Otherwise, we recommend using the *assumption-freer,* equivalent nonparametric method. But that is not the only reason for using nonparametric methods.

Measurement Scales

Managers must understand that the measurement scale also affects the type of analysis—parametric or nonparametric. Stevens (1946) proposed four levels of measurement scales. In increasing order of precision, these levels are nominal, ordinal, interval, and ratio.

Nominal Scale   When we *classify* people, products, or processes into categories, we are using a nominal measurement scale. We illustrate how tires may be measured on a nominal scale. A tire may be a blackwall or whitewall; a tire may be for a tractor, car, van, truck, or off-road vehicle. In short, a tire has or does not have a particular attribute. The word "nominal" means name; for example, we name or classify each tire as blackwall or whitewall. The classifications or categories must be mutually exclusive and exhaustive. When we measure data on a nominal scale, we often count the number of elements (or tires) in each classification. For example, how many tires are whitewalls?

The nominal scale is the weakest of the four measurement scales. We classify data into categories, but one category is not greater than or less than the others, or better or worse than the others. The categories are merely different. For nominal-scaled data, use nonparametric statistical methods.

Ordinal or Ranking Scale   When we rank people, products, or processes, we are using an ordinal or rank measurement scale. We can arrange the data is some meaningful order that corresponds to their relative value. For example, we can classify tires along the following ascending order of value: Economy, Standard, and Deluxe tire categories. In this sense, ordinal-scaled data are nominal data that we can arrange in some meaningful order.

Ordinal-scaled data are also called rank data. A sales manager ranks the effectiveness of her 30 salespeople. She assigns a rank of 1 to the most productive salesperson through a rank of 30 to her least productive salesperson. The ranks themselves cannot be treated as true numbers. That is, the lowest ranked salesperson (rank = 30) is not necessarily $\frac{1}{30}$th as effective as the highest ranked salesperson (rank = 1). Nor is the 20th-ranked person "five" better than the 25th-ranked person. Indeed, the sales manager could have assigned any 30 ascending numbers to represent her 30 salespeople—1, 4, 34, 67, 890, . . . 42,560. It is merely common practice to assign successive integers. You *cannot* meaningfully add, subtract, multiply, or divide ordinal scaled data. For ordinal-scaled data, use nonparametric statistical methods.

Interval Scale   An interval scale requires that (1) the data can be ranked (ordinal) and that (2) differences between data values are meaningful. Temperature is a familiar example of an interval-scale measure. Consider three temperatures: 30 degrees, 60 degrees, and 90 degrees. First, we can rank the three temperatures from coldest to warmest. Second, the difference in warmth between 30 and 60 degrees is the same as the difference between 60 and 90 degrees. However, 90 degrees is *not* three times as warm as 30 degrees.

Ratio Scale   If the data are measured on a ratio scale, the ratio of two numbers is meaningful. Height, weight, or distance are ratio-scale measures. A 180-pound person weighs twice as much as a 90-pound person. What makes height, weight, or distance ratio-scaled data is the possibility of having no (zero) height, weight, or distance. You can add, subtract, multiply, or divide ratio-scaled data.

In summary, we measure data on either an interval or ratio scale when we can say at least how much larger or better one person, product, or process is over another. It may even be possible to say that the ratio of two numbers is meaningful! For interval- or ratio-scaled data, use parametric statistical methods, provided the restrictive assumptions underlying the analysis are met.

Table 14.1 provides additional examples of variables measured on nominal, ordinal, interval, or ratio scales.

Table 14.1

Examples of Variables on Different Measurement Scales

Scale	Variable	Values
Nominal	Gender	Male or Female
	Financial institution	Bank, Savings and Loan, or Credit Union
	Retail structure	Independent, Chain, Association, or Franchise
Ordinal	Performance rating	Poor, Below Average, Average, Above Average, and Excellent
	Bond rating	AAA, AA, A, BBB, BB, B, CCC, D
	Rank order of cities by projected job increases by the year 2010	1 = Los Angeles 2 = New York City 3 = Chicago 4 = Washington, D.C. 5 = Philadelphia
Interval	SAT score	A person with a 1,500 SAT score is not twice as "smart" as a person with a 750 SAT score.
	Job climate	See Questionnaire in Table 1.2.
Ratio	Number of homes sold per week	0, 1, 2, 3, 4 . . .
	Fraction defectives in a sample	0 to 1.0

Inferences Beyond Parameters

A parameter is a measure that describes a population. Examples include the mean, variance, and regression coefficients. When we estimate these parameters we should use parametric methods, provided the data are measured on, at the least, an interval

FIGURE 14.1   Random Variation?

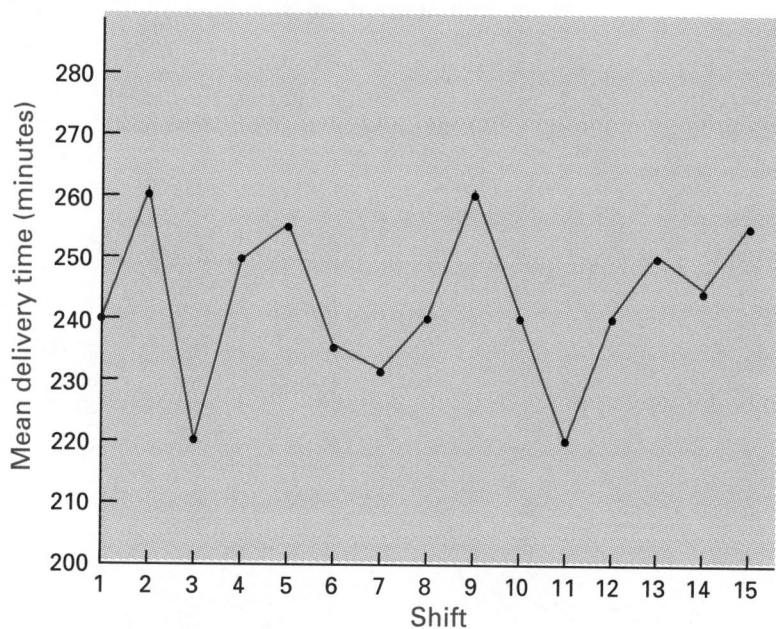

scale and the restrictive assumptions underlying the analysis have been met. Suppose we are not interested in estimating a population parameter. What methods should we now use? Nonparametric methods, of course.

Nonparametric inferences are important in statistics. In statistical process control (see Chapter 15), a firm must ensure that a manufacturing or service process exhibits only random variation before developing control charts. Random variation means that the time-ordered data do not exhibit an upward or downward trend, a widening or narrowing pattern, a cyclical pattern, or a shift-in-performance-level pattern.

Figure 14.1 illustrates the mean delivery time for five randomly selected packages over each of 15 shifts. Does the line graph exhibit only random variation? It may be difficult to tell by only graphing the data. Fortunately, there is a nonparametric statistical method —the *runs test*—to determine if the process exhibits only random variation. There is no equivalent parametric method because random variation is not a population parameter. Nonparametric methods provide a large number of tools to address important issues in statistics beyond estimating population parameters.

In summary, use nonparametric methods when at least one of the following conditions is true:

1. the study data are measured on a nominal or ordinal scale.
2. the study data do not meet the restrictive and specific assumptions about the populations from which you selected your samples.
3. you do not wish to draw inferences about population parameters.

SECTION 14.2 EXERCISES

1. Indicate the type of scale used to measure each variable.
    a. Mean shatter strength in pounds per square inch over a 15-day period
    b. Management level within a firm

    c. Number of nonconforming pieces produced per day
    d. IQ score
    e. Current ratio (from finance)
    f. Person's race
    g. Airlines' on-time rankings

2. Given the following three stem-and-leaf displays, is it likely that the populations from which the samples were taken are normal? Assuming you wish to estimate the population's center or spread, should you use nonparametric or parametric methods? Explain.

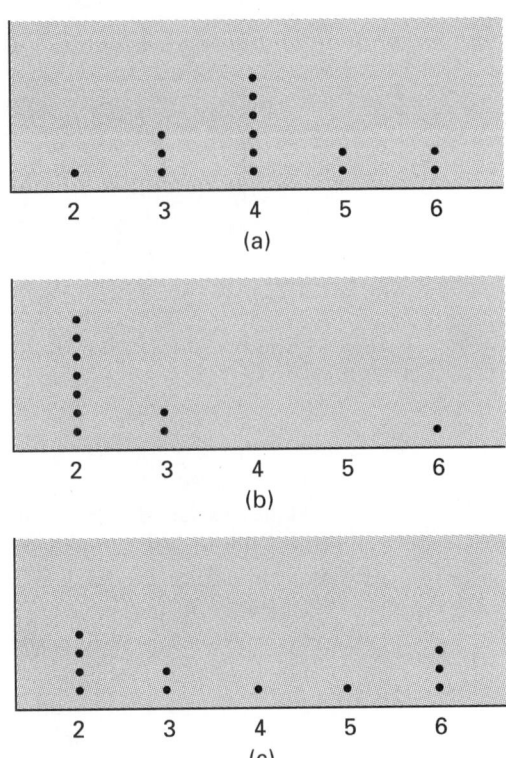

3. In 1992 a quality improvement team surveyed new car owners and reported the following customer problems within the first 30 days of car ownership. The data are presented here:

Type of Defect	Percentage Complaints
Squeaks	70%
Interior/exterior trim	22
Electrical problems	5
Transmission problems	2
Engine problems	1

    a. What type of measurement scale describes the variable, defect type?
    b. Suppose the quality-improvement team wanted to determine if the percentages of defect types had changed as a result of their improvement program. Should they use a parametric or nonparametric method of analysis?

4. A dairy wishes to determine if different market segments have different preferences for skim and whole milk. It selects 100 people from each market segment and determines their preferences. The dairy cross-classifies each person by market segment and milk preference. From Section 3.4, the dairy develops the following cross-tabs table.

	Macho Segment	Yuppie Segment	Total
Skim	30	90	120
Whole	70	10	80
Total	100	100	200

   a. What types of measurement scales describe the variables, market segments, and milk preference?

   b. Should the dairy use a parametric or nonparametric method to determine if milk preference is related to market segment?

5. A CEO wishes to know if each of his four vice presidents places the same relative importance on the firm's six mission statements as he does. He asks his VPs to rank order the six mission statements (5 = most important and 0 = least important).

	CEO	VP1	VP2	VP3	VP4
Customer Satisfaction	5	5	5	5	5
Teamwork	4	3	4	4	4
Performance Standards	3	4	1	2	3
Leadership	2	2	3	1	2
Accountability	1	1	2	0	1
Quality of Work Life	0	0	0	3	0

   a. What type of measurement scale has the CEO selected to measure mission statement priority preference?

   b. Should the CEO use a parametric or nonparametric method to determine if all six mission rankings are similar?

6. A quality-assurance consultant wants to know if firms in highly competitive industries are more likely to use total quality management (TQM) principles than firms in less competitive industries. He randomly selects 100 firms and cross-classifies them by level of competitiveness and use of TQM. The results are shown here.

	No TQM	TQM
Not Highly Competitive	35	15
Highly Competitive	40	10

   a. What types of measurement scales describe the variables, level of competitiveness, and use of total quality management?

   b. Should the consultant use a parametric or nonparametric method to determine if TQM usage is related to level of competitiveness within an industry?

7. Here is a ranking of large cities with the greatest number of jobs in 1985 and projected in the year 2010.

City	1985	2010
New York	2	2
Los Angeles	1	1
Washington, D.C.	6	4
Anaheim-Santa Ana	10	10
Houston	7	7
Atlanta	9	9
Philadelphia	4	5
Dallas	8	8
Boston	5	6
Chicago	3	3

Source: National Planning Association, 1987.

    a. What type of measurement scale has been used by the National Planning Association?

    b. Should we use a parametric or nonparametric method to determine if the rankings are similar?

8. Here are data on two variables—years on job and salary (in thousands)—of ten workers in a firm.

YEARS	1	3	5	5	6	7	7	7	9	12
SALARY	22	25	27	29	29	30	33	32	35	41

    a. What types of measurement scales describe the variables, YEARS and SALARY.

    b. Should we use a parametric or nonparametric method to determine if the two variables are related?

14.3 ≡ The Chi-Square Goodness-of-Fit Test

Problem sensing and diagnosis call for looking for changes or differences among persons, products, or processes and then determining the reasons. We have already presented three nonparametric methods for seeking differences:

Mann–Whitney method	Do two populations have the same median?
Mood test	Do two populations have the same variation?
Kruskal–Wallis test	Do three or more populations have the same median?

In this section we present the chi-square goodness-of-fit test. It examines how well a set of observed frequency data agree with expected frequency data from a specified probability distribution. We discuss two different uses for the goodness-of-fit test.

1. To determine if sample frequency data differ from an empirical distribution based on historical data. If so, a change has occurred. The change may signal that a problem is beginning or has been corrected.
2. To determine if a population is normally distributed (an assumption underlying many parametric tests).

By the end of this section you should be able to:

1. perform and interpret the chi-square goodness-of-fit test;
2. explain the need for, compute, and interpret confidence intervals on the proportion or probability in each category;
3. explain the logic underlying the goodness-of-fit test; and
4. explain when the goodness-of-fit test should be used.

Example: An Empirical Distribution   Quality-improvement teams use *Pareto* charts to determine what is wrong with a product or process and how to improve it. A basic chart shows the breakdown of problems by type and percentage. The horizontal axis displays problem type and the vertical axis measures the proportion occurrence of each problem. Figure 14.2 displays types of customer complaints and warranty work on COMCEL phones between October 1993 and March 1994.

    The quality-improvement team sought to reduce the two most frequent problems—static and volume fluctuation. After implementing their process improvements, they selected a random sample of 200 customers who required warranty work and recorded the number of complaints in the same five categories. Has COMCEL reduced the proportion of excessive static and volume fluctuation warranty problems? Has the empirical distribution of defect type (shown in Figure 14.2) changed?

FIGURE 14.2   Pareto Chart

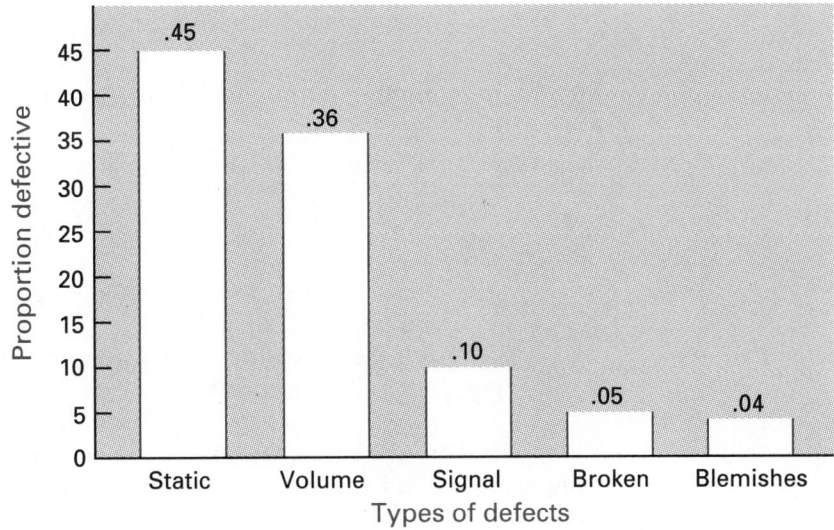

Table 14.2

**Observed Frequency of Types of Defects
After Process Improvements Were Implemented**

Defect Category	Observed Number of Defects
Excessive static	70
Volume fluctuation	50
Signal interference	35
Broken handset	25
Surface blemishes	20
	200

Next we apply the chi-square goodness-of-fit test to the process-improvement study data. We must do statistical testing for two reasons:

1. If we took another random sample of 200 customers, we would not obtain exactly the same frequency data as in Table 14.2. We must factor into our analysis the concept of margin of error first presented in Chapter 6.
2. We are interested in drawing conclusions about the distribution of complaint types for all customers, not merely the sample of 200 in the study.

State Hypotheses

From Section 9.2, the general rule is that a null hypothesis is the "no change" or "no difference" hypothesis. That is, the sample frequency data do not differ from the specified probability distribution shown in the Pareto chart.

H_0 The warranty defects are distributed as shown in Figure 14.2; namely, .45, .36, .10, .05, and .04 for the five warranty/defect categories. There has been *no* change in the distribution of defects.

H_1 The distribution of warranty defects differs from the specified empirical distribution in Figure 14.2. There has been a change.

The quality-improvement team set $\alpha = .05$.

Compute Expected Frequencies

If the null hypothesis is true, we can determine the number of each defect type we should *expect* in a sample of 200. This is simply

$$E_i = np_i \qquad (14.1)$$

where E_i is the expected frequency for category i
        n is the total sample size
        p_i is the probability, or proportion, for category i based on a specified distribution.

The specified distribution for this study is taken from the Pareto chart, Figure 14.2. Using expression (14.1), the expected frequencies for the quality-improvement study are:

Defect Category	Expected Frequency if H_0 is true
Excessive static	$200(.45) = 90$
Volume fluctuation	$200(.36) = 72$
Signal interference	$200(.10) = 20$
Broken handset	$200(.05) = 10$
Surface blemishes	$200(.04) = \underline{8}$
	200

Compute the Calculated Chi-Square Statistic

The calculated chi-square statistic measures the difference between the expected and observed frequencies over all the categories. If both sets of frequencies are very similar, we fail to reject the null hypothesis. If the expected and observed frequencies are very different, we reject the null hypothesis.

The size of the following statistic defines *very different:*

$$\text{Calculated } \chi^2 = \sum_i \frac{(O_i - E_i)^2}{E_i} \qquad (14.2)$$

where O_i is the observed frequency in category i
        E_i is the expected frequency in category i
                based on a specified probability distribution

Expression (14.2) says that for each category we should: (1) subtract the expected from the observed frequency and square the result; (2) divide the squared result by the expected frequency, then (3) add the results from (2) for all categories.

Table 14.3 shows the chi-square statistic calculations for the quality-improvement study data. The observed frequencies are taken directly from Table 14.2. We calculated the expected frequencies previously.

Table 14.3

Chi-Square Statistic Calculations for the Quality-Improvement Study

Category	O(bserved)	E(xpected)	$(O - E)^2$	$(O - E)^2/E$
Static	70	90	400	4.44
Fluctuation	50	72	484	6.72
Interference	35	20	225	11.25
Broken handset	25	10	225	22.50
Surface blemishes	20	8	144	18.00

Calculated $\chi^2 = 62.91$

The chi-square statistic's size affects the likelihood of rejecting the null hypothesis. If the observed and expected frequencies were identical, the calculated chi-square statistic would equal zero, and we should not reject the "no difference" null hypothesis. As the difference in the expected and observed frequencies increases, the calculated chi-square statistic gets larger, and we must consider rejecting the null hypothesis.

In the language of hypothesis testing, the goodness-of-fit test is always an *upper-tailed test*. That is, the rejection region will be in the upper tail of the chi-square distribution. But how large must the calculated chi-square statistic be before rejecting the null hypothesis?

Compare the Calculated Chi-Square Statistic to Critical Value

As in all hypothesis testing, we compare our test statistic (62.91 from Table 14.3) to the critical value. Appendix 6 contains the critical values for the goodness-of-fit test. The critical value is

$$\chi^2(k - 1 - m \text{ df}, 1 - \alpha) \tag{14.3}$$

where k is the number of categories
  α is the significance level
  m is the number of parameters (for example,
    μ or σ) that must be estimated to compute the
    expected frequencies.

Since the quality-improvement team did not need to estimate any parameters to calculate the expected frequencies shown in Table 14.3, $m = 0$. From Appendix 6, the critical value is $\chi^2 (5 - 1 - 0 \text{ df}, .95) = 9.49$ (the intersection of the 4-degrees-of-freedom row and the .95 column).

The decision rule for the quality-improvement study is:

Reject the null hypothesis if the calculated chi-square statistic is greater than 9.49.

Because the calculated chi-square statistic of 62.91 falls in the rejection region, we reject the null hypothesis. Because the calculated chi-square statistic of 62.91 is much greater than $\chi^2_{.995}$ (the largest value in the table for 4 degrees of freedom), the p-value is much less than .005 (see Figure 14.3). The proportion of defects in the five categories has *changed* from the empirical probability distribution shown in Figure 14.2.

FIGURE 14.3   Determination of Approximate p-Value

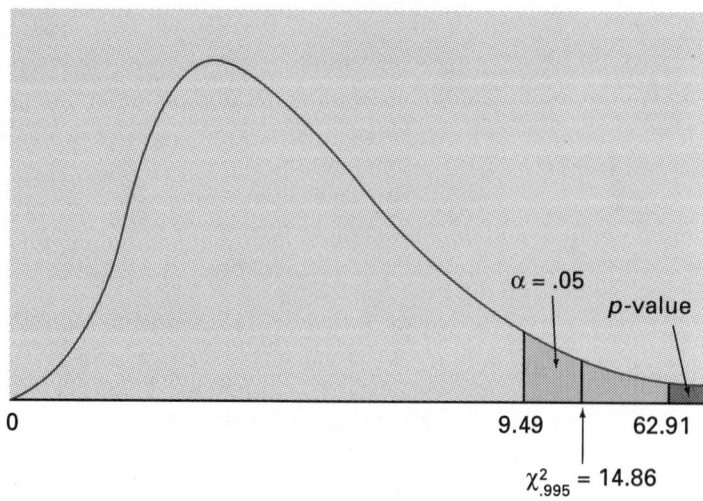

Dangers of Small Expected Frequencies

The test statistic (14.2) is chi-square distributed *only* for large expected frequencies. Use Appendix 6 to determine the p-value only when the *expected* frequency in each category is greater than one (Cochran, 1954). If one or more categories have expected frequencies of less than one, combine the categories in which they occur with adjacent categories until the minimum expected frequency requirement has been met. Of course, reducing the number of categories will also reduce the chi-square statistic's degrees of freedom.

Dunn Confidence Intervals on Category Probabilities

From a problem-solving perspective, the chi-square goodness-of-fit test has a limitation. In the quality-improvement study, COMCEL's CEO wanted to know if the proportion of static- and volume-fluctuation warranty complaints had dropped. In rejecting the null hypothesis, she was much more than 95%, or $100(1 - \alpha)\%$, confident that the observed frequency data differed from the expected frequency data based on the empirical distribution in Figure 14.2. But rejecting the null hypothesis does not mean that *each* observed category proportion, or probability, has changed. At least one proportion has changed, but has the proportion of static- and volume-fluctuation complaints dropped? We need a follow-up procedure to the goodness-of-fit test. We recommend the Dunn confidence interval method.*

The Dunn procedure uses expression (14.4) to compute a confidence interval for the proportion in each category.

$$\hat{p}_i \pm D \sqrt{\frac{\hat{p}_i \hat{q}_i}{n}}$$ (14.4)

---

*The first time we used a follow-up procedure was in Chapter 10. We used the Tukey procedure after conducting the analysis of variance.

where $\hat{p}_i$ is the *observed* proportion in category i

$\hat{q}_i$ is $1 - \hat{p}_i$

n is the total sample size

D is the appropriate Dunn value from the following table. The Dunn value depends on (1) k, the number of categories, (2) the total sample size, n, and (3) the desired confidence level, $100(1 - \alpha)\%$.

Number of Categories	Confidence Level	Total Sample Size			
		30	60	120	200 or more
3	95%	2.54	2.47	2.43	2.39
	99	3.19	3.06	2.99	2.94
4	95	2.66	2.58	2.54	2.50
	99	3.30	3.16	3.09	3.02
5	95	2.75	2.66	2.62	2.58
	99	3.39	3.24	3.16	3.09
6	95	2.83	2.73	2.68	2.64
	99	3.46	3.30	3.22	3.15

Table 14.4 presents the 95% Dunn confidence intervals for the five warranty proportions. Shown below is the calculation for the first category—excessive static—using expression (14.4). The D(unn) value for five categories of defects, a sample of 200, and a 95% confidence level is 2.58. The quality-improvement team chose a $100(1 - \alpha)\%$, or 95%, confidence level because it had set a .05 significance level for the study.

$$\hat{p}_{\text{static}} = \frac{70}{200} = .35$$

$$.35 \pm 2.58 \sqrt{\frac{(.35)\,(.65)}{200}}$$

$$.35 - .087 = .263$$

$$.35 + .087 = .437$$

Table 14.4

Dunn 95% Confidence Intervals for Quality-Improvement Study Data

Category	Observed Frequency	Observed Proportion	Lower Limit	Upper Limit
Static	70	70/200 = .350	.263	.437
Fluctuation	50	50/200 = .250	.171	.329
Interference	35	.175	.106	.244
Broken handset	25	.125	.065	.185
Blemishes	20	.100	.046	.154

COMCEL is 95% confident that the population proportion of static warranty complaints is now between .263 and .437. Or static now accounts for between 26.3% and 43.7% of the warranty complaints. Before the process improvements, static accounted for 45% of the complaints. Because the historical percentage—45%—lies above the confidence interval, COMCEL is 95% confident that the percentage has *statistically* dropped.

COMCEL is also 95% confident that the population proportion of volume-fluctuation warranty complaints is between .171 and .329. Or volume fluctuation now accounts for between 17.1% and 32.9% of the warranty complaints. Before the process improvements, volume fluctuation accounted for 36% of the complaints. The percentage has statistically dropped.

The drop in the proportion of excessive static- and volume-fluctuation complaints signals that action taken by COMCEL has been successful. COMCEL could continue to work on static- and volume-fluctuation complaints or turn its attention to other warranty problems.

Example: The Normal Distribution   When constructing confidence intervals in Chapters 7–8 and testing hypotheses in Chapters 9–10, we assumed that the sample(s) came from a normal population. We can now test that assumption using the goodness-of-fit test. That is, we can test if the population is normally distributed. If the population is not normally distributed and the sample size is less than 30, we must use nonparametric methods to construct confidence intervals or test hypotheses.

Table 14.5 contains a frequency distribution of the debt-to-total-asset ratio for 99 randomly selected firms. Could the sample of debt-to-total-asset ratios have been drawn from a normal distribution?

Table 14.5

**Frequency Distribution for
Debt-to-Total-Asset Ratios of 99 Firms**

Ratio Class	Observed Frequency
0 up to 20%	2
20 up to 40%	20
40 up to 60%	55
60 up to 80%	21
≥ 80%	1
	99

Even though the frequency distribution in Table 14.5 appears bell-shaped, we must use the goodness-of-fit test to test statistically for normality.

State Hypotheses

H_0 The debt-to-total-asset ratios of firms are normally distributed.

H_1 The distribution is not normally distributed.

We set α at .05.

Compute Expected Frequencies

Unlike the quality-improvement study where the proportions, or probabilities, from the specified distribution were already known, we must now use the normal curve to determine them. That is, we must convert the values of the debt-to-total-asset ratio classes into z-scores. Then we can use Appendix 3 to determine the class probabilities and use expression (14.1) to determine the expected frequencies.

1. *Estimate μ and σ*   To convert class limits to z-scores, we use the expression $z = (x - \mu)/\sigma$ first presented in Chapter 5. μ and σ are the mean and standard deviation of the debt-to-total-asset ratio for the entire industry, or population. Neither are known, but both can and must be estimated from the sample data. We used the COMSTAT GROUPED DATA tool and determined that the sample mean is 49.798% and the sample standard deviation is 14.707% for the frequency data in Table 14.5.

2. *Determine z-scores*   Now we convert the limits of the ratio classes—20, 40, 60, and 80—into equivalent z-scores. Because the total area under the normal curve must sum to 1.0, we can ignore the lower limit of the first class (and the upper limit of the last class). A class limit of 20% is equivalent to a z-score of -2.03, a class limit of 40% is equivalent to a z-score of -0.67, and so on.

$$z = \frac{20 - 49.798}{14.707} = -2.03$$

$$z = \frac{40 - 49.798}{14.707} = -0.67$$

$$z = \frac{60 - 49.798}{14.707} = +0.69$$

$$z = \frac{80 - 49.798}{14.707} = +2.05$$

3. *Determine Class Probabilities*   Figure 14.4 shows the probabilities for the five classes:

   The 0 up to 20% ratio class is equivalent to the area underneath the normal curve to the left of a z-score of -2.03.

   The 20 up to 40% class is equivalent to the area underneath the normal curve for z-scores between -2.03 and -0.67.

   The 40 up to 60% class is equivalent to the area underneath the normal curve for z-scores between -0.67 and $+0.69$.

   The 60 up to 80% class is equivalent to the area underneath the normal curve for z-scores between $+0.69$ and $+2.05$.

   The $\geq 80\%$ class is equivalent to the area underneath the normal curve to the right of a z-score of $+2.05$.

From Appendix 3, the expected probabilities are:

0 up to 20% class	$P(z < -2.03)$	$= .5000 - .4788 = .0212$
20 up to 40% class	$P(-2.03 < z < -0.67)$	$= .4788 - .2486 = .2302$
40 up to 60% class	$P(-0.67 < z < +0.69)$	$= .2486 + .2549 = .5035$
60 up to 80% class	$P(+0.69 < z < +2.05)$	$= .4798 - .2549 = .2249$
$\geq 80\%$ class	$P(z > +2.05)$	$= .5000 - .4798 = \underline{.0202}$
		1.0000

Please note that by the second law of probability the five expected probabilities sum to 1.0000.

FIGURE 14.4   Areas under Normal Curve Associated with Each Ratio Class

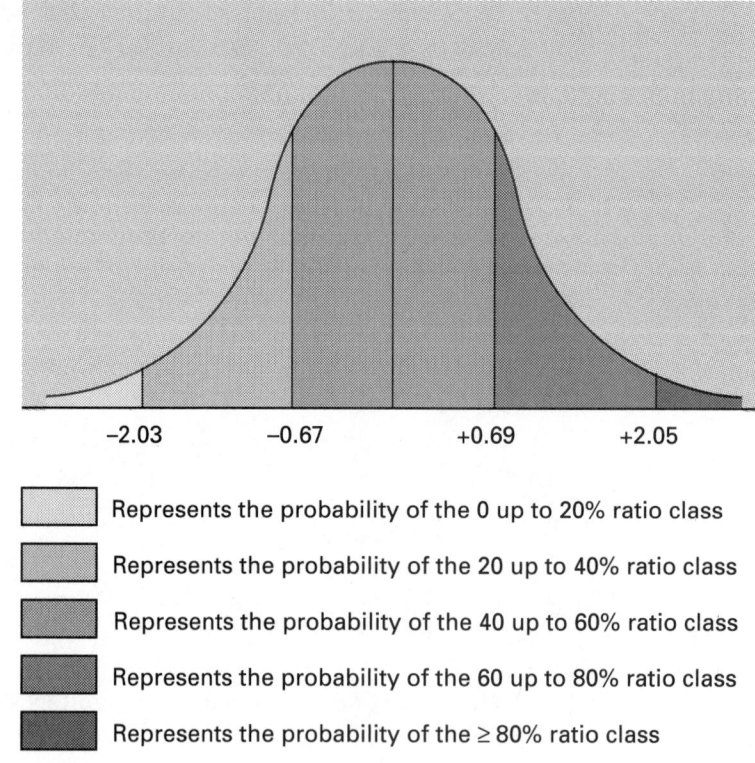

Table 14.6 displays the expected frequencies based on the expected probabilities given above and expression (14.1).

Table 14.6

Expected Frequencies, Assuming the Null Hypothesis Is True

Ratio Class	Probability	Expected Frequency
0 up to 20%	.0212	99(.0212) = 2.10
20 up to 40%	.2302	22.79
40 up to 60%	.5035	49.84
60 up to 80%	.2249	22.27
≥ 80%	.0202	2.00
	1.0000	99

Compute the Calculated Chi-Square Statistic

Table 14.7 shows the chi-square statistic calculations for the debt-to-total-asset data. The calculated chi-square statistic equals 1.453.

Table 14.7

Chi-Square Statistic Calculations
for the Debt-to-Total-Asset Data

Class	O(bserved)	E(xpected)	$(O - E)^2/E$
0 up to 20%	2	2.10	.005
20 up to 40%	20	22.79	.342
40 up to 60%	55	49.84	.534
60 up to 80%	21	22.27	.072
$\geq$ 80%	1	2.00	.500
		Calculated $\chi^2 =$	1.453

Compare the Calculated Chi-Square Statistic to the Critical Value

Unlike the first example, here we had to estimate two parameters (μ, σ) to determine z-scores for computing expected frequencies. Thus, $m = 2$. We compare the calculated chi-square statistic against χ^2 (5 $-$ 1 $-$ 2 df, .95) = 5.99 from Appendix 6. Because the calculated chi-square statistic of 1.453 is less than 5.99, we cannot reject the null hypothesis. The sample frequency data in Table 14.5 do not differ significantly from a normal distribution.

We can use the goodness-of-fit test to determine if sample frequency data could have been drawn from any specified probability distribution—binomial, Poisson, normal, empirical, and the like.

Summary

Use the chi-square goodness-of-fit test to determine how well a set of observed frequency, or count, data agree with expected frequency data from a specified probability distribution. Calculate expected frequencies based on the specified probability distribution. Remember, if one or more categories have expected frequencies of less than one, combine the categories in which they occur with adjacent categories until the minimum expected frequency requirement has been met. If the calculated χ^2 statistic, (14.2), is larger than the critical value from Appendix 6, conclude that the sample differs from the specified probability distribution. It may then be necessary to construct Dunn confidence intervals on the category proportions.

Finally, the assumptions underlying the chi-square goodness-of-fit test are:

1. The categories that define the variable of interest are mutually exclusive and exhaustive.
2. The frequency data are a random sample from a population.

SECTION 14.3 EXERCISES

1. Look up the critical value in Appendix 6 for the following studies (assuming no parameters are being estimated):
   a. Study 1: five categories, $\alpha = .05$
   b. Study 2: six categories, $\alpha = .10$
   c. Study 3: four categories, $\alpha = .01$

2. Determine the correct Dunn critical value for expression (14.4) for the following studies:
   a. Five categories, $\alpha = .05$, sample size $= 120$
   b. Six categories, $\alpha = .01$, sample size $= 400$

    c. Four categories, $\alpha = .01$, sample size $= 60$
    d. Three categories, $\alpha = .01$, sample size $= 30$

3. For the studies in Exercise 1, would you reject the null hypothesis for the following values of the calculated chi-square statistic?
    a. Study 1:   calculated $\chi^2 = 7.79$
    b. Study 2:   calculated $\chi^2 = 11.08$
    c. Study 3:   calculated $\chi^2 = 6.25$
    d. Determine the approximate p-value for each study.

4. A firm suspects that its African-American employees prefer to be mentored (guided) by a person of the same race and same gender. Eighty randomly selected African-American male employees choose their mentors within the firm.

Mentor Choice	Observed Frequency of Mentor Choice
African-American male (same race, same gender)	40
White male	15
African-American female	15
White female	10
	80

    a. What is the variable of interest and on what type of scale is it measured?
    b. Assume that the mentor's race and gender are not factors in the selection process. Thus, the specified distribution for the four categories is .25, .25, .25, and .25. Now set up the null and alternative hypotheses.
    c. Compute the expected frequencies using expression (14.1).
    d. Compute the calculated chi-square statistic using expression (14.2).
    e. Given $\alpha = .01$, what can you conclude? Explain.
    f. Construct and interpret 99% Dunn confidence intervals on the proportions for the four categories.

5. The First Federal Bank in Chicago classifies outstanding loans in the following repayment categories.

    A: Current
    B: Up to 30 days delinquent
    C: 31 to 60 days delinquent
    D: 61 to 90 days delinquent
    E: over 90 days delinquent

First Federal has established an internal standard that loans are "in control" when the percentage in each category is as follows:

    A: 80%   B: 14%   C: 3%   D: 2%   E: 1%

First Federal selects a random sample of 500 loans, and obtains the following data.

Repayment Category	Observed Frequency of Loan Repayments
Current	395
Up to 30 days	70
31 to 60 days	20
61 to 90 days	11
Over 90 days	4
	500

a. What is the variable of interest, and on what type of scale is it measured?
b. Why would First Federal be interested in knowing if loans are "in control"?
c. Assume that the loan repayment process is "in control." What are the expected proportions for the five categories; that is, what is the specified distribution?
d. Set up the null and alternative hypotheses.
e. Compute the expected frequencies.
f. Compute the calculated chi-square statistic.
g. Given $\alpha = .05$, what can you conclude? Explain.
h. Determine the approximate p-value.

6. A parcel-sort manager at United Express believes that the number of packages that operators mishandle varies over an 8-hour shift. She believes that operators mishandle four times as many packages in the second and fourth 2-hour periods—the periods nearest the lunch and shift breaks—as in the first and third 2-hour periods. She collects the following data from a randomly chosen 8-hour shift.

Shift Time	Observed Frequency of Mishandled Packages
First 2 hours	7
Second 2 hours	43
Third 2 hours	8
Fourth 2 hours	42
	100

a. What is the variable of interest, and on what type of scale is it measured?
b. Why would the manager run this study?
c. Assume that the manager's belief about the pattern of mishandled packages is correct. What are the four expected proportions? (*Hint:* let x = number of packages mishandled in the first or third 2-hour periods and $4x$ = number of packages mishandled in the second or fourth 2-hour periods. The sum of the four proportions is 1.00.)
d. Set up the null and alternative hypotheses.
e. Compute the expected frequencies.
f. Compute the calculated chi-square statistic.
g. Given $\alpha = .05$, what can you conclude? Explain.
h. Determine the approximate p-value.

7. World Motors has tracked the type and percentage of complaints that 30,000 new car owners report within the first 30 days of purchase for the past several years.

Complaint	Percentage
Squeaks	70%
Trim	22
Electrical	5
Transmission	2
Engine	1

They have attempted to reduce the percentage of engine and transmission problems. These are especially costly warranty repairs. After making process improvements, World Motors selects a random sample of customer complaints. The observed frequencies are shown below. Has World Motors been successful?

Complaint	Observed Fequency of Complaints
Squeaks	800
Trim	150
Electrical	46
Transmission	2
Engine	2

a. What is the variable of interest, and on what type of scale is it measured?
b. Why would World Motors run this study?
c. Assuming the process improvements have made no impact, what should the expected proportions for the five categories be?
d. Set up the null and alternative hypotheses.
e. Compute the expected frequencies.
f. Compute the calculated chi-square statistic.
g. Given $\alpha = .05$, what can you conclude? Explain.
h. Construct 95% Dunn confidence intervals on the proportion of transmission and the proportion of engine problems. Are these proportions now less than .02 and .01, respectively?

8. In 1981 McNeal and Zeren (*MSU Business Topics,* Spring 1981, p. 38) reported the following percentages of types of external firms used in selecting a brand name.

External Firm	Percentage
Ad agency	70.7%
Outside consultant	13.4
Trademark search firm	6.1
Package design firm	4.9
Other	4.9

Ten years later, other researchers conduct a brand-name selection study and obtain the results shown in the observed frequency column below. Has the proportion of different types of external firms changed from the 1981 study?

External Firm	Observed Frequency (1991)
Ad agency	146
Outside consultant	25
Trademark search firm	11
Package design firm	9
Other	9
	200

a. What is the variable of interest, and on what type of scale is it measured?
b. Set up the null and alternative hypotheses.
c. Compute the expected frequencies.
d. Compute the calculated chi-square statistic.
e. Given $\alpha = .05$, what can you conclude? Explain.
f. Compute 95% Dunn confidence intervals on the proportions for the five categories.

9. You want to construct a confidence interval on the mean number of claims processed per day. You select a random sample of 200 claim processors and record the number of completed claims. Could the following sample frequency data be drawn from a normal distribution?

Claims Processed	Observed Frequency
26 up to 30	10
30 up to 34	32
34 up to 38	57
38 up to 42	61
42 up to 46	35
46 up to 50	5

a. Develop a frequency histogram.
b. Use statistical software to estimate the sample mean and standard deviation.

c. Set up the null and alternative hypotheses.
d. Determine the z-scores for each class. Also draw a normal curve and shade in the areas that represent the expected probabilities for the six claims categories.
e. Determine the expected probability for each class.
f. Compute the calculated chi-square statistic.
g. Given $\alpha = .01$, what can you conclude? Explain.
h. Determine the approximate p-value.

10. You want to construct a confidence interval on the mean number of hours to complete a repetitive task. You select a random sample of 150 workers and record the number of hours it takes to complete the task. Could the following sample have been drawn from a normal distribution?

Hours to Complete the Project	Observed Frequency
0 up to 5	30
5 up to 10	60
10 up to 15	30
15 up to 20	20
20 up to 25	10

a. Develop a frequency histogram.
b. Use statistical software to estimate the sample mean and standard deviation.
c. Set up the null and alternative hypotheses.
d. Determine the z-scores for each class. Also draw a normal curve and shade in the areas that represent the expected probabilities for the hours to complete the project categories.
e. Determine the expected probability for each class.
f. Compute the calculated chi-square statistic.
g. Given $\alpha = .10$, what can you conclude? Explain.
h. Determine the approximate p-value.

11. You select a random sample of 225 burgers and determine the calories per burger. Could the following sample have been drawn from a normal distribution?

Number of Calories	Observed Frequency
95 up to 100	7
100 up to 105	12
105 up to 110	46
110 up to 115	97
115 up to 120	47
120 up to 125	10
125 up to 130	6

a. Develop a frequency histogram.
b. Use statistical software to estimate the sample mean and standard deviation.
c. Set up the null and alternative hypotheses.
d. Determine the z-scores for each class. Also draw a normal curve and shade in the areas that represent the expected probabilities for the seven number of calories categories.
e. Determine the expected probability for each class.
f. Compute the calculated chi-square statistic.
g. Given $\alpha = .05$, what can you conclude? Explain.

14.4 ≡ The Chi-Square Test of Independence

Problem diagnosis often requires looking for associations between variables. ANOVA studies (Chapter 10) and regression analysis (Chapters 11–12) are parametric methods to detect associations or relationships. Here we present the χ^2 test of independence. Use it when count or frequency data can be cross-classified according to two nominal or ordinal variables, and the goal is to detect associations between the two variables.

In Chapter 3 we discussed a discrimination suit in which women claimed to have a smaller probability of promotion than men. Table 14.8 shows a random sample of 200 employees, cross-tabulated by gender and promotion status. Is gender related to promotion status? If so, how strong is the association?

Table 14.8

2 × 2 Cross-Tabs Data* for Gender Discrimination Suit

	Male	Female	Total
Promoted	80	25	105
Not Promoted	30	65	95
Total	110	90	200

By the end of this section you should be able to:

1. perform and interpret a chi-square test of independence;
2. explain the need for statistical testing;
3. explain the need to measure the strength of association between two nominal or ordinal variables; and
4. compute and interpret the Cramer statistic.

Next we apply the chi-square test of independence to the gender discrimination suit data. We must do statistical testing for two reasons:

1. If we took another random sample of 200 employees, we would not obtain exactly the same cross-tabs data as in Table 14.8. We must factor into our analysis the concept of margin of error first presented in Chapter 6.
2. We are interested in drawing conclusions about the population of employees, not merely the sample of 200 in the study.

State Hypotheses

The null and alternative hypotheses for ANOVA studies, regression analysis, and the test of independence are similar. All null hypotheses assume that the two (or more) variables are not related.

H_0 Gender and promotion status are statistically independent, or not related, in the population.

H_1 Gender and promotion status are statistically dependent, or related, in the population.

The firm sets $\alpha = .05$.

Compute Expected Frequencies for Cross-Tabs Table Cells

If the null hypothesis is true, we can determine the *expected* number of people in each cell of the 2 × 2 cross-tabs table. From Chapter 4, if two events, A and B, are not

---

*See Chapter 3 for information on how to construct a cross-tabs table.

related, then the joint probability of A AND B equals the product of the marginal probabilities.

$$P(A \text{ AND } B) = P(A) \cdot P(B) \qquad (14.4)$$

Assume that gender and promotion status are not related. That is, assume the null hypothesis is true.

1. What is the joint probability of selecting an employee who is male and promoted?
2. How many employees would we expect in a sample of 200 to be male and promoted?

We use expression (14.4) on the data in Table 14.8 to answer the first question and expression (14.5) to answer the second question.

$$
\begin{aligned}
P(\text{Male AND Promoted}) &= P(\text{Male}) \cdot P(\text{Promoted}) \\
&= (110/200)(105/200) \\
&= .28875
\end{aligned}
$$

How many employees should have been males and promoted in the sample of 200 if the $P(\text{Male AND Promoted})$ is .28875? We can determine the expected frequency by using expression (14.5).

$$E(A \text{ AND } B) = n \cdot P(A \text{ AND } B) \qquad (14.5)$$

where E is the expected frequency of A AND B
n is the total sample size
$P(A \text{ AND } B)$ is the joint probability based on expression (14.4)

There should have been (200).28875, or 57.75 employees. Note that expected frequencies are rounded to two places after the decimal.

We compute the three remaining expected frequencies in a similar fashion:

$$
\begin{aligned}
E(\text{Male AND Promoted}) &= (200)(.55)(.525) &= 57.75 \\
E(\text{Male AND Not promoted}) &= (200)(.55)(.475) &= 52.25 \\
E(\text{Female AND Promoted}) &= (200)(.45)(.525) &= 47.25 \\
E(\text{Female AND Not promoted}) &= (200)(.45)(.475) &= 42.75
\end{aligned}
$$

Table 14.9 shows the observed and expected frequencies for the discrimination data. The observed frequencies are in the upper left corner of each cell; the expected frequencies are in the lower right corner.

Table 14.9

Observed and Expected Frequencies for Discrimination Study Data

	Male	Female	Total
Promoted	80 57.75	25 47.25	105
Not Promoted	30 52.25	65 42.75	95
Total	110	90	200

Compute the Calculated Chi-Square Statistic

The calculated chi-square statistic measures the difference between the expected and observed frequencies over all the cross-tabs table cells. If the expected and observed frequencies are very similar, we will fail to reject the null hypothesis. If the expected and observed frequencies are very different, we will reject the null hypothesis.

The size of the following statistic defines *very different:*

$$\text{Calculated } \chi^2 = \sum_i \sum_j \frac{(O_{ij} - E_{ij})^2}{E_{ij}} \tag{14.6}$$

where O_{ij} is the observed frequency in each cell of the cross-tabs table
            E_{ij} is the expected frequency in each cell of the cross-tabs table,
              based on expressions (14.4) and (14.5)

Expression (14.6) says that for each cross-tabs table cell we should: (1) subtract the expected from the observed frequency and square the result; (2) divide the squared result by the expected frequency; then (3) add the results from (2) for all cells.

Table 14.10 shows the calculation of the chi-square statistic for the discrimination data in Table 14.8.

Table 14.10

Calculated Chi-Square Test Statistic for Discrimination Data

Cell	(O)bserved	(E)xpected	$(O - E)^2$	$(O - E)^2/E$
Male AND Promoted	80	57.75	495.06	8.57
Male AND Not promoted	30	52.25	495.06	9.47
Female AND Promoted	25	47.25	495.06	10.48
Female AND Not promoted	65	42.75	495.06	11.58
			Calculated χ^2 =	40.10

Like the goodness-of-fit test, the test of independence is an upper-tailed test. The rejection region is in the upper tail of the chi-square distribution in Appendix 6. How large must the calculated χ^2 be before rejecting the null hypothesis?

Compare the Calculated Chi-Square Statistic to the Critical Value

As in Section 14.3, we use Appendix 6 to find the critical value. The critical value is

$$\chi^2[(r-1)\,(c-1)\text{ df, } 1-\alpha] \tag{14.7}$$

where r is the number of rows of the cross-tabs table
            c is the number of columns of the cross-tabs table
            α is the significance level

From Appendix 6, the critical value is χ^2 [(2−1)(2−1) df, .95] = 3.84. The decision rule for the discrimination suit data is:

Reject the null hypothesis if the calculated chi-square statistic is greater than 3.84.

Because the calculated chi-square = 40.10 falls in the rejection region, we reject the null hypothesis. Since 40.10 is greater than $\chi^2_{1,.995}$ = 7.88, the *p*-value is much less than .005. We conclude that promotion status and gender are statistically related in the population.

Is the firm guilty of discrimination? The fact that there is a significant association between gender and promotion status does not *necessarily* mean that gender is a cause of promotion status. There could be *intervening* variables. See Section 3.4 for a review of how to include intervening variables in the analysis.

We can use the chi-square test of independence when we have nominal or ordinal variables with more than two levels each. For example, is type of advertising (cooperative, comparative, or advocacy) related to level of product awareness (low, medium, or high)? Or is the level of a firm's social responsibility (low, medium, or high) related to its type of business organization (proprietorship, partnership, or corporation)?

Dangers of Small Expected Frequencies

The statistic, (14.6), is chi-square distributed *only* for large expected frequencies. *Do not* use the chi-square test of independence under the following conditions:

1. For a 2 × 2 cross-tabs table when:
   a. the total sample size, n, is less than 20.
   b. $20 \leq n \leq 40$ and any expected frequency is less than 5.
   c. $n > 40$ and any expected frequency is less than 1.

2. For a cross-tabs table with more than two rows or columns when:
   a. more than 20% of the cells have expected frequencies less than 5.
   b. any cell has an expected frequency less than 1.

Cramer's Measure of Association

When two nominal- or ordinal-scaled variables are related, a measure of the association's strength would be informative. In Chapters 3 and 11 we used the correlation coefficient to measure the association strength between two quantitative variables. Here we present Cramer's measure of association (Cramer, 1946).

Cramer defined his statistic as:

$$C = \sqrt{\frac{\chi^2}{n(t-1)}} \tag{14.8}$$

where calculated χ^2 is based on expression (14.6)
n is the total sample size for the study
t is the minimum of the number of the rows or columns of the cross-tabs table

For the gender discrimination study, the calculated chi-square statistic is 40.10, the total sample size is 200, and t equals 2. The Cramer association statistic equals

$$C = \sqrt{\frac{40.10}{200(2-1)}} = .447$$

Cramer's measure of association can vary from 0 to 1.* A value of zero means that the two nominal- or ordinal-scaled variables are not related. A value of 1 means that the two nominal- or ordinal-scaled variables are perfectly (positively or inversely) related. The .447 value for the gender discrimination study means that gender and promotion status are moderately related.

---

*In some software packages the Cramer statistic varies from −1 to +1.

Consider Table 14.11, a 2 × 2 cross-tabs table.

Table 14.11

New Cross-Tabs Data for Gender Discrimination Suit

	Male	Female	Total
Promoted	110	0	110
Not Promoted	0	90	90
Total	110	90	200

Note that the $P(\text{promoted}|\text{male}) = 110/110 = 1.00$ and the $P(\text{promoted}|\text{female}) = 0/90 = 0$. Clearly, gender and promotion status are related. These two conditional probabilities suggest that the two nominal-scaled variables are perfectly related, or $C = 1$.

In summary, the Cramer statistic measures the association strength between two nominal- or ordinal-scaled variables. It is a nonparametric alternative to the correlation coefficient.

Summary

Use the chi-square test of independence to test for an association between two nominal- or ordinal-scaled variables. Calculate expected frequencies, assuming that the two variables are statistically independent (unrelated). If the calculated chi-square statistic (14.6) is greater than the critical value from Appendix 6, reject the null hypothesis and conclude that the two variables are dependent (related).

The chi-square goodness-of-fit test and the test of independence are similar. Both tests compare expected and observed frequencies, and the two test statistics are similar. Both tests are used with nominal- or ordinal-scaled data. Moreover, both test statistics are chi-square distributed and we use Appendix 6 to determine the critical value.

While similar, the two chi-square tests have different purposes, and we collect the data and compute the expected frequencies differently. First, the goodness-of-fit test determines how well a set of observed frequency, or count, data agree with expected frequency data from a specified probability distribution such as the normal. The test of independence determines if two categorical variables are associated. Second, in the goodness-of-fit test we *classify* the nominal- or ordinal-scaled data into mutually exclusive and exhaustive categories. In the test of independence, we *cross-classify* the data into a $k \times r$ *cross-tabs table*. Third, in the goodness-of-fit test, we compute the expected frequencies based on a specified probability distribution. In the test of independence we compute expected frequencies based on the principle that the joint probability of two events is the product of its marginal probabilities. Do not be confused. The two chi-square tests have different purposes.

The assumptions underlying the test of independence are:

1. We cross-classify observations in the sample according to two nominal- or ordinal-scaled variables. Each variable must be divided into mutually exclusive and exhaustive categories.
2. The frequency data are a random sample from a population.

SECTION 14.4 EXERCISES

1. Determine the critical chi-square value from Appendix 6 for the following studies:
   Study 1: 2 × 2 cross-tabs table, $\alpha = .01$
   Study 2: 3 × 4 cross-tabs table, $\alpha = .05$
   Study 3: 4 × 5 cross-tabs table, $\alpha = .10$

2. A calculated chi-square statistic has a value of 5.78 for a 3 × 3 cross-tabs table.
    a. What are the degrees of freedom for a 3 × 3 table?
    b. Determine the *p*-value for the chi-square statistic.
    c. Would we reject the null hypothesis of statistical independence for $\alpha = .05$?

3. The larger the calculated chi-square statistic, the more likely we are to reject the null hypothesis. Why?

4. We interview 1,000 investors. Six hundred have an annual income of over $50,000. Of these, 400 have invested in at least one real estate limited partnership. Of the 400 investors with incomes of $50,000 or less, 200 have invested in at least one limited partnership.
    a. Identify the categorical variables and their levels.
    b. Construct a 2 × 2 cross-tabs table.

5. Perform the test of independence for the data in Exercise 4. Use a .01 significance level.

6. Shown is a 4 × 2 cross-tabs table on support for a balanced budget by region of the country. Two thousand registered voters are selected from the four regions.

	Strongly Support	Do Not Strongly Support	Total
Northeast	250	250	500
South	400	100	500
Midwest	300	200	500
West	250	250	500
	1,200	800	2,000

    a. Perform a chi-square test of independence. Use a .10 significance level.
    b. Compute Cramer's statistic.

7. Employees of a multinational firm believe that an overseas assignment reduces the chances of promotion at the corporate headquarters. The Human Resources manager randomly selects a sample of 100 managers and develops the following 2 × 2 cross-tabs table.

	No Overseas Assignment	Overseas Assignment	Total
Promoted	16	24	40
Not promoted	22	38	60
	38	62	100

    a. Perform the chi-square test of independence on the two categorical variables. Use a .05 significance level.
    b. Compute Cramer's statistic.

8. Is level of information systems technology related to bottom-line performance of firms? The American Computing Group (ACG) conducts a survey of 100 firms in the banking industry. Fifty banks are performing above the industry median; 50 are not. The ACG asks each firm to indicate the highest level of information systems technology it has achieved. Shown are the cross-tabs data.

	Level of Information Technology		
	Transaction Processing	Decision Support	Executive Support
Below median	30	10	10
Above median	10	15	25

    a. Perform the chi-square test of independence on the two categorical variables. Use a .10 sigificance level. What does the test tell you?

    b. Compute Cramer's statistic.

9. Is type of leadership related to level of worker job satisfaction? Shown are data for 50 workers.

	Autocratic Supervision	Participatory Supervision
Satisfied	11	26
Dissatisfied	9	4

    a. Perform the chi-square test of independence on the two categorical variables. Use a .05 significance level. What does the test tell you?

    b. Compute Cramer's statistic.

10. We study 1,000 customers to determine whether level of product satisfaction is related to income level categories. Of the 1,000 people interviewed, 815 people are satisfied with the product; 390 people earn less than $20,000 and are satified with the product.

	Less than $20,000	$20,000–$50,000	More than $50,000	Total
Satisfied	390	325	100	815
Dissatisfied	10	75	100	185
	400	400	200	1,000

    a. Perform the chi-square test of independence on the two categorical variables. Use a .005 significance level. What does the test tell you?

    b. Compute Cramer's statistic.

11. A quality-assurance consultant wants to know if firms in highly competitive industries are more likely to use total quality management (TQM) principles than firms in less competitive industries. He randomly selects 100 firms and cross-classifies them by level of competitiveness and use of TQM. The results are shown here:

	No TQM	TQM
Not Highly Competitive	35	15
Highly Competitive	40	10

    a. Set up the null and alternative hypotheses.

    b. Perform a chi-square test of independence. Use a .01 significance level.

    c. Determine the approximate p-value.

12. Zero coupon bonds (zeros) pay no annual interest but sell at a discount below par. This provides investors significant capital appreciation when the bond matures. Zeros are thought to be attractive because their yield is guaranteed even if interest rates drop. Thus, if investors believe interest rates will drop over the next five to ten years, they should be more interested in purchasing zeros. Is this true? A bond analyst selects 400 bond customers and cross-classifies them by their future interest rate prediction and type of bond preferred. The results are shown here.

	Not a Zero Coupon Bond	Zero Coupon Bond
Falling Interest	25	75
Steady or Increasing Interest	200	100

    a. Set up the null and alternative hypotheses.

    b. Perform a chi-square test of independence. Use $\alpha = .10$

    c. Determine the approximate p-value.

14.5 ≡ Key Ideas and Overview

Nonparametric methods play an important role in business problem solving. In fact, management and marketing specialists often use nonparametric methods more frequently than parametric methods. Consider using nonparametric methods when:

1. the variables are only measurable on a nominal or ordinal scale.
2. the study data do not meet the restrictive and specific assumptions—normality, etc.—about the populations from which you selected the samples.
3. you do not wish to draw inferences about population parameters.

We conclude this chapter by providing an overview of *all* the nonparametric methods presented in the text. Table 14.12 provides a quick index that should help you select the appropriate nonparametric tool.

Table 14.12

Quick Index for Selecting the Appropriate Nonparametric Tool

Statistical Question	Appropriate Nonparametric Tool	
What is the population median?	Confidence interval on median	(7.9)
Do two population medians differ?	Mann–Whitney method	(8.5)
Do two population variabilities differ?	Mood test	(8.7)
Do three or more population medians differ?	Kruskal–Wallis test	(10.5)
Do observed frequencies come from a specified probability distribution?	Goodness-of-fit test	(14.3)
Are two variables (generally nominal- or ordinal-scaled) associated?	Test of independence	(14.4)

COMCEL

Date: September 28, 1994
To: Ann Tabor, CEO
From: Sang Kim, Quality-Assurance Manager
Re: Quality-Improvement Team #25 Final Report

SUMMARY
Our process improvements have reduced the proportion of static and volume fluctuation complaints. Before the process improvements, static accounted for 45% of the complaints. It now accounts for approximately 35%. Before the process improvements, volume fluctuation accounted for 36% of the complaints. It now accounts for approximately 25%.

We will continue to develop additional process improvements to further reduce these two percentages.

SUPPORTING ANALYSIS

After developing our process improvements, we selected a random sample of customers who required warranty work. We then compared the observed frequencies of the five types of complaints against the expected frequencies using the Pareto chart historical proportions. The goodness-of-fit test and the follow-up Dunn confidence interval method indicated that we had significantly (at the 95% level of confidence) reduced the percentage of static and volume fluctuation complaints.

CHAPTER 14 QUESTIONS

1. What are the differences between parametric and nonparametric methods?

2. Consider a product such as a computer. Define a nominal-, an ordinal-, and a ratio-scaled variable that describes computers.

3. What type of scale measures the finish in a horse race? Can you meaningfully add, subtract, multiply, or divide the ranks of the finishers?

4. Why are Dunn confidence intervals useful when you reject the null hypothesis in the goodness-of-fit test?

5. Why is the Cramer measure of association useful when you reject the null hypothesis in the test of independence?

6. In Exercise 5 of Section 14.3, the observed frequency for the five categories of loan repayments were 395, 70, 20, 11, and 4, respectively. If the observed and expected frequencies (based on the bank's internal standard) were similar, we would probably fail to reject the null hypothesis in the goodness-of-fit test. Explain the logic.

7. You wish to determine if a data set consisting of 10 categories could be normally distributed. Which nonparametric test should you use? Why?

8. You wish to determine if firms that follow Deming's 14 quality principles have more satisfied employees. You develop two variables:

   Follow Deming's 14 principles   Yes or No
   Job satisfaction level   Low, Moderate, or High

   Which nonparametric test should you use? Why?

9. In the test of independence, you reject the null hypothesis of no association. The Cramer measure of association is .10. What can you conclude about the association between the two variables?

10. If the p-value for a data set is smaller than the study's significance level, you reject the null hypothesis. Why?

CHAPTER 14 APPLICATION PROBLEMS

1. Best Dairy Inc. knows that the Macho consumers have lower incomes than do the Status Seeker consumers. They wonder if Machos and Status Seekers also have different preferences for skim and whole milk. The marketing manager conducts a survey to determine if Machos and Status Seekers equally prefer skim and whole milk. He wants to verify that Best Dairy has meaningfully segmented its market. Best Dairy Inc. interviews 200 customers and cross-classifies them by the following two categorical variables. Use the .05 significance level to determine whether the two categorical variables are related.

	Machos	Status Seekers	Total
Skim	30	80	110
Whole	70	20	90
	100	100	200

2. Firms use an aging schedule to monitor their accounts receivable position. The schedule shows how long accounts receivable have been outstanding. National Inc.'s aging schedule as of December 31, 1994, is shown below.

Age of Account (Days)	Percentage of Accounts
0 up to 15	52%
15 up to 30	20
30 up to 45	13
45 up to 60	4
60 or more	11
	100%

Through its credit policies, National has attempted to reduce the percentages of accounts of 30 or more days. Has it been successful?

National selects a random sample of 400 accounts receivable in July 1995, and obtains the following data.

Age of Account (Days)	Observed Frequency
0 up to 15	265
15 up to 30	100
30 up to 45	25
45 up to 60	5
60 or more	5
	400

a. Set up the null and alternative hypotheses.
b. Compute the expected frequencies.
c. Compute the calculated chi-square statistic. Should H_0 be rejected if $\alpha = .05$?
d. Construct appropriate Dunn confidence intervals. Has National been successful in reducing the proportion of accounts from 30 up to 45 days, from 45 up to 60 days, and 60 or more days? Explain.

3. A stock analyst specializing in the retail industry wants to know if chain stores such as JC Penney stress the same focus—service or price—as do independents. She surveys 50 retail stores and cross-classifies them by type of store and price or service orientation. Here are the data. Use the .05 significance level to determine whether the two categorical variables are related.

	Service	Price	Total
Independents	25	5	30
Chains	4	16	20
	29	21	50

4. A firm records the percentage of type of defects in manufacturing car heaters over a six-month period. The data are shown here:

Type of Defect	Percentage
Cratered paint	50%
Bent fan	30
Bad motor	10
Frayed wires	5
Loose hose	5

For the past six months a quality-improvement team has sought ways to reduce the percentage of the cratered paint and bent fan problems. The team then installs their process improvements. They then collect a random sample of 200 heater problems for another six-month period.

Type of Defect	Observed Frequency
Cratered paint	60
Bent fan	40
Bad motor	35
Frayed wires	35
Loose hose	30

a. Set up the null and alternative hypotheses.
b. Compute the calculated chi-square statistic. Should H_0 be rejected? Use $\alpha = .05$.
c. Construct 95% Dunn confidence intervals for the cratered paint and bent fan proportions. Interpret the intervals and determine if the quality team has been successful in reducing the proportion of the cratered paint and bent fan problems.

5. A human resource development manager for a large firm wishes to know if the percentage of extraverts and introverts (as measured by the Myers–Briggs Type Indicator) varies by management level. She randomly selects 1,000 managers, and cross-classifies them by level and Myers–Briggs type. Here are the data. Use a .05 significance level to determine whether the two categorical variables are related.

	Extrovert	Introvert	Total
Upper	65	35	100
Mid	250	150	400
Lower	330	170	500
	645	355	1,000

6. In a 1983 article in *Marketing News,* October 28, p. 4, Steiber and Boscarino reported five market segments in the health care industry. They estimated the market segment shares as:

Market Segment	Percentage
"Doctor-knows-best" consumers	25%
Repeat consumers	15
Convenience consumers	25
High-technology consumers	10
Image consumers	25

Suppose that a recent health care survey found the following number of consumer types.

Market Segment	Observed Frequency
"Doctor-knows-best" consumers	5
Repeat consumers	5
Convenience consumers	10
High-technology consumers	30
Image consumers	50

Have the market segment proportions changed since 1983?
a. Set up the null and alternative hypotheses.
b. Compute the calculated chi-square statistic.

c. Overall, have the percentages of consumers in the five market segments changed? Why would this be useful to know? Let $\alpha = .10$.

d. Determine the approximate p-value for the study.

 7. A personnel manager of a large company wants to assess employees' desires for flex-time among four different divisions of a large factory. The personnel manager selects a random sample of 800 employees and cross-classifies them by division and opinion on flex-time. The results are shown.

	Division			
	1	2	3	4
Favor	146	150	142	84
Oppose	54	50	58	116
	200	200	200	200

a. Perform a chi-square analysis to determine whether the two categorical variables are related. Use $\alpha = .05$ to draw your conclusions.

b. Explain how the results of the chi-square test help the manager to draw policy conclusions. In simple terms, what does the manager know after performing the test that he or she did not know before?

 8. Assume that the four starting pitchers for the Atlanta Braves are equally effective. Suppose in the 1995 baseball season they each pitch the same number of games and collectively win a total of 80 games.

Starting Pitchers	Games Won
Tom Glavine	22
John Smoltz	21
Steve Avery	19
Greg Maddux	18
	80

Does the above data support the assumption that the pitchers are equally effective?

a. Set up the null and alternative hypotheses.

b. Determine the four proportions if the pitchers are equally effective.

c. Calculate the chi-square statistic.

d. Test the hypothesis that the pitchers are equally effective. Let $\alpha = .05$.

e. Determine the approximate p-value.

 9. Elizabeth Dole, former U.S. Secretary of Labor, referred to a "glass ceiling" that allegedly keeps women and minorities out of the top echelons of corporate management. The personnel manager of a large corporation wants to be sure that women and minorities are not discriminated against in promotion decisions in his corporation. He examines all of the promotion decisions made over the past two years. The results are shown.

	White Males	Women and Minorities	Total
Promoted	55	15	70
Not promoted	45	45	90
	100	60	160

a. Based on this sample of promotion decisions, does it appear that white males are favored in the promotion decision? Explain your conclusion in terms of the p-value of the test. Compute Cramer's statistic.

824

The personnel director repeated the study above, but this time he divided the sample into those that had an MBA degree and those that did not. The sample results are shown.

| | MBA Group | | No MBA Group | |
	White Males	Women and Minorities	White Males	Women and Minorities
Promoted	30	10	25	5
Not promoted	15	5	30	40

b. Does it appear that any difference in promotion rates is due to the education of the candidate and not minority status? Explain. Compute Cramer's statistics.

10. Is a census tract containing 5,000 families eligible for aid under Federal program HR 247? The government will select a random sample of families and construct a confidence interval on the population mean income. Before constructing the interval, they wish to determine if the population from which the sample will be taken is normally distributed. Here are the data:

Income Class	Observed Frequency
$5,000–5,999.99	3
6,000–6,999.99	23
7,000–7,999.99	49
8,000–8,999.99	22
9,000–9,999.99	3

a. Use statistical software to estimate the sample mean and standard deviation.
b. Set up the null and alternative hypotheses.
c. Determine the z-scores for each class. Also shade in the areas under a normal curve that represent the expected probabilities for the five income class categories.
d. Determine the expected probability for each class.
e. Compute the calculated chi-square statistic.
f. Given $\alpha = .01$, what can you conclude? Explain.

11. A store manager wonders if the number of customers is spread evenly over the six working days. She collects the following data.

Tuesday	45
Wednesday	40
Thursday	40
Friday	60
Saturday	65
Sunday	70

Given the above data, assess her claim. Let $\alpha = .05$.

12. Are homeowners better credit risks than renters? A bank manager randomly selects 200 personal loan borrowers and cross-classifies them by homeowner/renter and loan repayment performance. Here are the data:

Repayment	Homeowner	Renter
Always on time	90	75
Late one or more times	5	30

a. Set up the null and alternative hypotheses.
b. Given a .01 significance level, are the two variables related?
c. Compute and interpret the Cramer statistic.

13. In statistical process control, to construct control limits on the mean requires that the process data be normally distributed. Below are 100 data values from a manufacturing process:

Tensile Strength	Observed Frequency
4,500–4,599.99	12
4,600–4,699.99	30
4,700–4,799.99	40
4,800–4,899.99	15
4,900–4,999.99	3

Given $\alpha = .05$, was the sample data drawn from a normal distribution?

14. What must the cell values for the following 2×2 cross-tabs table be such that the Cramer statistic will be zero? Verify that your data set produces a zero Cramer statistic value by using statistical software. Explain why your data set generated a zero Cramer statistic value.

	Autocratic Leader	Nonautocratic Leader	Total
Low Satisfaction	—	—	75
High Satisfaction	—	—	225
Total	100	200	300

15. A software discount house manager currently offers four word processing packages. In determining how many to order for stock, the manager believes that Wordperfect is purchased five times as often as Multimate Advantage and Word and Lotus Ami Pro are purchased three times as often as Multimate Advantage. He tests his claim by selecting a random sample of 480 sales invoices.

Software Package	Observed Frequency
WordPerfect	195
Word	120
Ami Pro	130
Multimate Advantage	35

Given a significance level of .01, do the data refute the manager's claim?

REFERENCES

Cochran, William, G. "Some methods for strengthening the common X^2 tests." *Biometrics* 10 (1954): 417–451.

Cramer, H. *Mathematical Methods of Statistics.* Princeton: Princeton University Press, 1946.

Marasculio, Leonard, and M. McSweeney. *Nonparametric and Distribution-Free Methods for the Social Sciences,* Monterey, Calif.: Brooks/Cole, 1977.

Stevens, S. S.,"On the theory of scales of measurement," *Science* 161 (1946): 677–680.

APPENDIX: Statistical Software

We use MINITAB, Release 8, to perform a chi-square test of independence for the crosstabulation of gender and promotion status data shown in Table 14.8.

Input

```
01    MTB  >  NAME C1='MALE'
      MTB  >  NAME C2='FEMALE'
      MTB  >  SET 'MALE'
      DATA>  80 30
      DATA>  SET 'FEMALE'
      DATA>  25 65
      DATA>  END
02    MTB  >  CHISQUARE 'MALE' 'FEMALE'
```

Explanation of Input

01 The NAME command labels a column. The SET command tells MINITAB to enter data in the named column.

02 Perform a CHISQUARE test of independence on the count data in columns C1 and C2.

Output

```
Expected counts are printed below observed counts

               MALE       FEMALE     Total
01     1        80          25        105
02             57.75       47.25

       2        30          65         95
               52.25       42.75

       Total   110          90        200

03    ChiSq =  8.573 + 10.478 +
               9.475 + 11.580 = 40.105

      df  = 1
```

Interpretation of Output

01–02   Shows the observed and expected frequencies for each cell.

03   Shows the contribution to the chi-square statistic made by each cell of the cross-tabs table and the value of the calculated chi-square statistic. We must then compare 40.10 to the critical value which is χ^2 ([2 − 1][2 − 1] df, .95) = 3.84 (assume an α level of .05). Since 40.10 is larger than the critical value, we reject the no relationship null hypothesis.

QUALITY IMPROVEMENT

15.1 The strategic importance of quality
15.2 Types of quality
15.3 Control charting for variables
    Process control
    Process capability
    Basic control charts and problem solving
    Steps in building and using mean and
      standard deviation control charts
15.4 Control charts for attributes
    Process control
    Control limits for a proportion
      nonconforming, or p, chart
15.5 Tools for controlling and improving quality
    Control charts
    Pareto charts

    Kepner–Tregoe problem analysis
    Frequency histograms
    Fishbone diagrams
    Scatter diagrams
    Experimental design
15.6 Vendor certification and acceptance sampling
    Acceptance sampling basics
    The inability of acceptance sampling to
      completely eliminate nonconforming pieces
    Vendor certification
15.7 General principles
    General principles of quality
    General principles of statistical process
      control
Appendix: Statistical Software

COMCEL INTEROFFICE COMMUNICATION

Date: September 10, 1995
To: Sang Kim, Quality-Assurance Manager
From: Ann Tabor, CEO
Re: Capability Study for the Molding Process

According to your last report we are now ready to determine the process capability of our new molding operation for our Model 706 phone handset. While we need to implement the new molding process, I won't do it unless the process will produce less than two defective handsets per 100,000 phones. Otherwise, we cannot remain the quality leader in the industry.

Please have the process capability study results on my desk by next week.

15.1 ≡ The Strategic Importance of Quality

In 1980 NBC ran a program entitled "If Japan Can . . . Why Can't We?" The program compared Japanese and American business practices and concluded that one major reason for Japanese success was their attention to quality. That was a remarkable turnabout, for before World War II, Japanese products were poorly constructed and could not compete in world markets. The program told how Dr. W. Edwards Deming, a leading American quality consultant, had introduced statistical quality control to the Japanese in the early 1950s. The Japanese enthusiastically adopted Deming's recommendations and Japanese product quality became the envy of the world. The program asked why American manufacturers had ignored Deming. While quality has become more important, it was not until 1989 that the aerospace industry held its First National Total Quality Management Symposium.

While quality rarely makes the headlines, its absence does. Consider the following problems:

1. In 1985, General Motors recalls 100,000 cars with *blushing* paint.
2. In 1986, faulty O-rings cause the *Challenger* space shuttle disaster.
3. In 1986, the Chernobyl nuclear plant in the former USSR spews clouds of radiation that spread over several European countries.
4. In 1989, the Federal Aviation Administration cites recurring failures in maintenance at Eastern Airlines.
5. In 1990, a spacing error of 1.3 millimeters causes the $1.5 billion Hubble space telescope to send back blurry images. Its use will be limited until spacewalking astronauts can install a new camera in 1994.

Poor quality caused all these problems. The quality of the products or services of a firm is important to its financial success. Research by the Strategic Planning Institute (SPI) of Cambridge, Massachusetts, shows that firms that stress product quality have higher returns on investment (Gale, 1985). SPI asked 2,700 businesses to identify key product and service attributes (except price) and weight them in terms of customer importance. Each firm rated itself and its leading competitors on a scale from 1 to 10 on each attribute. SPI then compared the businesses' relative attribute scores against their return on investment (ROI). Relative quality was the only variable that always positively correlated with ROI. Figure 15.1 shows that the firms with the poorest relative quality product scores had a mean return on investment of about 12%. Firms with the highest relative quality product scores had a mean return on investment above 30%. Superior quality is a key to business success. As SPI noted, "Quality comes close to being a panacea (for business success)."

Dr. Deming (1986) uses the *Deming chain reaction* to explain the quality–ROI connection. Quality improvements reduce costs because there are fewer mistakes, less reworking, fewer delays, and better use of machines, people, and methods. The improved productivity helps capture a greater share of the market with better quality and lower prices.

15.2 ≡ Types of Quality

What is quality? Are there different types of quality? Whose responsibility is it to monitor quality? By the end of this section you should be able to distinguish between design and manufactured quality.

FIGURE 15.1   Relationship Between Relative Quality and ROI

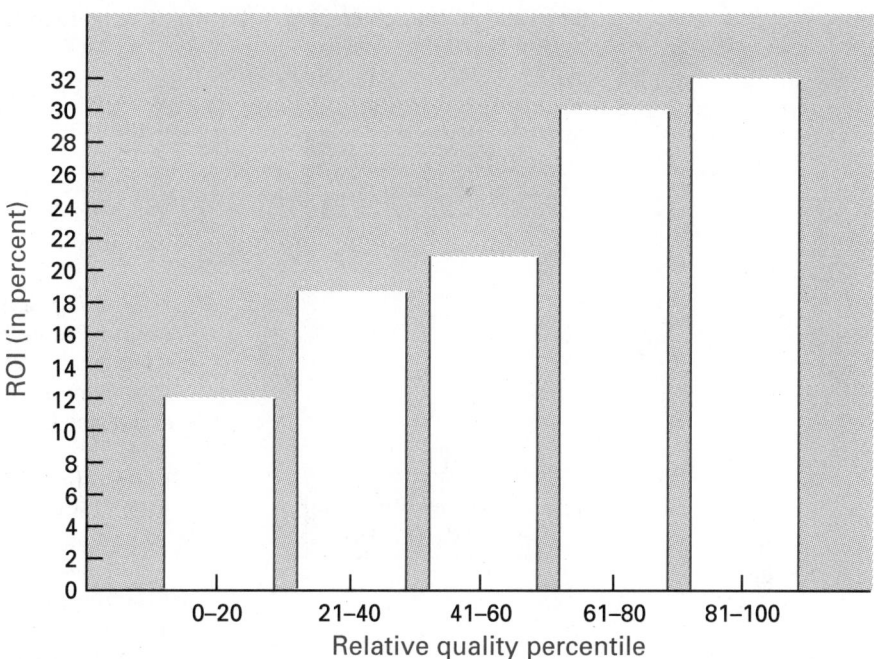

A dictionary definition of quality is the degree of excellence. In that sense, a BMW is a better-quality car than a Yugo. Professionals who deal with quality use two other definitions.

Dr. J. M. Juran, a pioneer in the field, defines quality as "fitness for use" (1974). Fitness for use is the *design quality* definition. Under this definition, producing 1-foot rulers with a tolerance of plus or minus 2 inches is unacceptable quality. Such rulers are not fit for use because of their inaccuracy. Design quality must be considered carefully in planning the design, manufacture, and marketing of a product or service. Marketing research and product design departments ensure (or improve) design quality during product conception. They determine what customers want (and are willing to pay) and translate customer wants into engineering specifications. After selling the product, the marketing and sales departments ensure product quality by tracking and correcting after-sales problems. Synonyms for design quality are performance, reliability, serviceability, durability, and safety. Higher design quality often means higher cost.

P. B. Crosby, a well-known consultant, defines quality as "conformance to requirements" (1979). If a Mercedes-Benz conforms to its engineering specification requirements, it is a quality car. If a Yugo conforms to its engineering specifications, it too is a quality car. Crosby warns not to talk of poor or good quality, but rather conformance or nonconformance. Conformance to requirements is *manufactured quality.* Under that definition, if a customer will accept a ruler with a tolerance of 1/32 inch for a cost of $.39, then manufactured quality is the ability to produce rulers to that design specification. Manufacturing and statistical quality control departments ensure (or improve) manufactured quality by purchasing and inspecting raw materials, renovating or purchasing equipment, and improving or monitoring the manufacturing process. Synonyms for manufactured quality are conformance with

FIGURE 15.2   Design and Manufactured Quality

The Design, Manufacturing,   Applied to COMCEL Car Phones
and Marketing Process

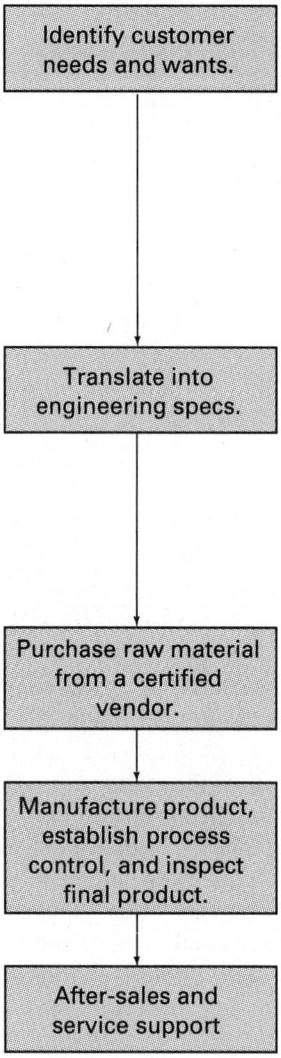

Customer Preferences
Lightweight
Attractive
Indestructible
Clear reception
Durable

Engineering Specifications
Weight: Phone handset unit weighs
   10 ounces ± 5%.
Attractiveness: Phone handset is free
   of surface blemishes to the naked
   eye.
Shatterproof: Phone handsets can with-
   stand between 4,600 and 4,900 pounds
   of pressure per square inch. The target
   value is 4,750 pounds per square inch.
Reception: The same standard as house
   phones.
Durable: Mean time between failures
   (MBTF) is 2,000 hours or more.

Manufacturing Process
Add fillers and dyes to raw material.
Mold the phone headpiece.
Test the installed electrical assemblies.
Install the electrical assembly into
   the phone headpiece.
Test the product at outgoing inspection
   for conformance to engineering
   specifications.

Implement a customer "800 hot-line"
   to handle after-sales and service
   support.
Open 1-day repair centers in all major
   markets.

Process boxes: Identify customer needs and wants. → Translate into engineering specs. → Purchase raw material from a certified vendor. → Manufacture product, establish process control, and inspect final product. → After-sales and service support

manufacturing standards, performance of all required manufacturing steps, and sub-jection to required inspection tests.

Firms can improve manufactured quality in two ways. Through *inspection,* they can detect and scrap nonconforming products (rejects). As Deming has noted, an excessive number of rejects increases manufacturing costs and sales price, which can reduce market share. Alternatively, firms can *improve* their manufacturing processes so that a greater percentage of products conform to the engineering specifications and thus will not be rejected during inspection. Remember, inspection only finds rejects, but process improvements reduce the number of rejects. Deming urges continuous process improvement as the key to higher manufactured quality, lower product cost, and more satisfied customers.

Customers expect and should receive quality goods and services. But who is the customer? From a quality viewpoint, a customer is anyone that uses your department's product or service. Thus customers can be members of one's own department, other departments within the firm, or traditional customers (consumers). Determining what all your "customers" want is essential to a successful companywide quality improvement effort.

Figure 15.2 illustrates the connections between design quality and manufactured quality in designing, manufacturing, and marketing the COMCEL car phone unit. COMCEL's original market research showed that customers wanted a lightweight, attractive, durable, and indestructible phone unit that had reception as clear as present home phones. Product design specialists translated these features into engineering specifications. The designers wanted longer durability (i.e., longer mean time between failures—MTBF), but settled for 2,000 hours to keep costs down. Once the engineering specifications (specs) were approved, the manufacturing department sought reputable raw materials suppliers and developed production processes to meet the specs. The statistical quality control group instituted work-in-progress inspections and a companywide quality improvement program to reduce costs and improve the manufactured quality. Finally, COMCEL developed after-sales support centers to ensure customer satisfaction.

Maintaining and improving quality must be a companywide effort involving all levels of management, quality professionals, and employees. Top management must develop quality targets and policies; middle management must implement them and monitor their progress. The quality control organization typically includes the following departments: procurement quality control, product inspection, and product testing and performance. Procurement handles inspection of incoming raw materials and subassemblies and approves suppliers. Product inspection directs work-in-progress inspection and process control and capabilities studies. Product testing directs functional testing (does the product do what the customer wants?), reliability testing (does it do it without failures or breakdowns?), and customer support. However, quality assurance is too important to be left to a few professionals. Besides, there are not enough quality-department personnel to do the job. The final responsibility for quality rests with those who produce the product or provide the service. Without their active participation, a companywide quality-control effort will fail.

SECTION 15.2 EXERCISES

1. How would a firm improve the design quality of its products?

2. How would a firm improve its manufactured quality?

3. According to retailer Sidney Marcus, of Neiman-Marcus, a BIC pen and a Rolex watch are both high-quality items. Explain how Marcus could put an item costing less than a dollar in the same class with an item costing thousands of dollars.

4. *Discuss the statement:* "Quality is not my job! That is what we pay inspectors for."

5. *Discuss the statement:* "The most effective way to improve quality is to continuously inspect the product during manufacturing."

6. *Discuss the statement:* "A high-quality service always costs more than a service of lower quality."

7. *Discuss the statement:* "Senior managers need not be as concerned with quality as hourly workers or lower level supervision."

15.3 ▤ Control Charting for Variables

Quality professionals have developed tools to help monitor, control, and improve manufacturing and service processes. A process is simply a repeated set of steps to accomplish a goal. Paying for merchandise by check at a store is a process. The steps include: (1) write a check for the amount, (2) salesperson asks for driver's license and credit card, (3) salesperson records license and credit card on check, (4) salesperson records check number on receipt and (5) salesperson places check into register. From the store's perspective, some key indicators of process success are (1) the time (mean and standard deviation) needed to complete the sales transaction and (2) the proportion of transactions in which the license and credit card information are correctly recorded.

Here we list some business processes and key quantitative indicators that could be monitored, controlled, and improved.

Process	Key Indicator of Process Success
1. Mold a handset	Mean shatter strength
2. Make a reservation by phone	Mean waiting time before being connected to an operator
3. Obtain a loan	Standard deviation of the time needed to process the loan
4. Obtain a loan	Mean cost of improperly completed loan application
5. Produce a part	Standard deviation of the product diameter
6. Repair a car	Mean customer satisfaction level

In this section we consider control charts when we use *quantitative data* to measure process success. Typical measurements are time, cost, width, satisfaction level, and diameter. Control charting techniques are useful in both manufacturing and service processes. Through control charting, firms reduce the number of defective items or services and become more competitive.

By the end of this section you should be able to:

1. produce mean and standard deviation control charts and explain how to use them to determine whether a process is under control;
2. distinguish between the natural tolerance of a process and the design specification limits;
3. compute and explain the C_p process capability index;
4. explain why there will be many rejected units when the natural tolerance of a process exceeds the design specification limits;
5. explain why reducing the process standard deviation is critical to business success;
6. explain why there may be problems even when the natural tolerance of a process is much less than the design specification limits;
7. compute upper and lower control limits for an $\bar{x}$ chart and an s-chart;
8. explain the difference between random and assignable cause variation; and
9. determine when a manufacturing (or service) process is temporarily out of control and corrective action is needed.

Process Control

Before initiating a manufacturing or service process, we must do a process control study. Process control studies determine whether a process is under statistical control. That is, whether the process is stable or predictable. A process that is under statistical control exhibits only random variation.

We illustrate the process control study idea. Before COMCEL started injection molding Model 706 car phone handsets, it chose the mean and standard deviation shatter strength in pounds per square inch (ppsi) as its key indicators of process success. For each of the first 10 shifts, COMCEL workers used a systematic 1-in-100 sampling procedure (see Section 6.6) to select five phone handsets. They then tested the phones for shatter strength. The two right-most columns of Table 15.1 contain the shift mean and shift standard deviation shatter strength based on the familiar equations:

$$\bar{x} = \frac{\Sigma x_i}{n} \qquad\qquad s = \sqrt{\frac{\Sigma(x_i - \bar{x})^2}{n-1}} \qquad\qquad (15.1)$$

Table 15.1

Process Control Study Data

Shift	\multicolumn{5}{Observations (in ppsi)}				$\bar{x}$	s
	1	2	3	4	5	$\bar{x}$	s
1	4,800	4,790	4,800	4,800	4,820	4,802	10.95
2	4,800	4,800	4,775	4,800	4,750	4,785	22.36
3	4,750	4,800	4,775	4,770	4,780	4,775	18.03
4	4,710	4,775	4,780	4,750	4,790	4,761	32.09
5	4,790	4,750	4,700	4,750	4,725	4,743	33.47
6	4,710	4,650	4,720	4,720	4,770	4,714	42.78
7	4,750	4,600	4,700	4,725	4,700	4,695	57.01
8	4,740	4,650	4,690	4,650	4,780	4,702	57.18
9	4,600	4,625	4,780	4,755	4,790	4,710	90.35
10	4,600	4,750	4,780	4,600	4,725	4,691	85.32

The sample size for each of the 10 shifts or subgroups, *n,* is 5. Generally, practitioners prefer to collect data on 20 or more subgroups in a process control study.

Figures 15.3 and 15.4 show line graphs for the means and standard deviations for the 10 shifts. Both line graphs indicate that the molding process is not yet under statistical control because the shift means and shift standard deviations are not stable, or stationary (using terminology of Chapter 2). Rather, we see that

1. the shift mean shatter strength is dropping over time; and
2. the shift standard deviation shatter strength is increasing over time.

COMCEL must look for *assignable* causes of the declining mean and the increasing standard deviation. Assignable causes explain the nonrandom patterns in Figures 15.3 and 15.4. Perhaps the molding equipment needs additional controls to maintain the proper shatter strength, or the molding supervisors need additional training. Once the operators identify the assignable causes, they must take corrective action, and rerun the process control study.

FIGURE 15.3   Example of a Process Not Under Control: Line Graph of Mean Shatter
                Strengths for Different Shifts

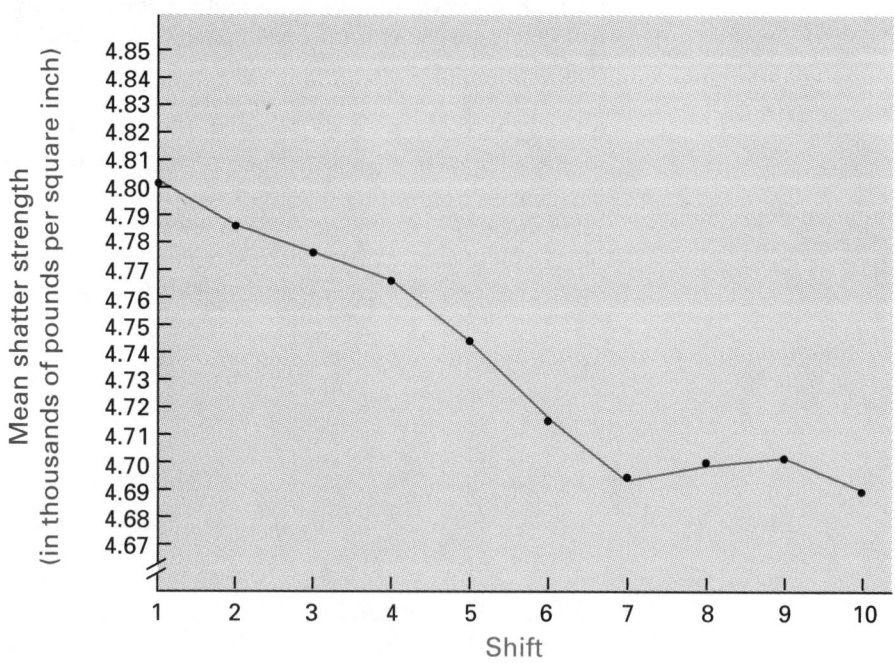

FIGURE 15.4   Example of a Process Not Under Control: Line Graph of Standard
                Deviation Shatter Strengths for Different Shifts

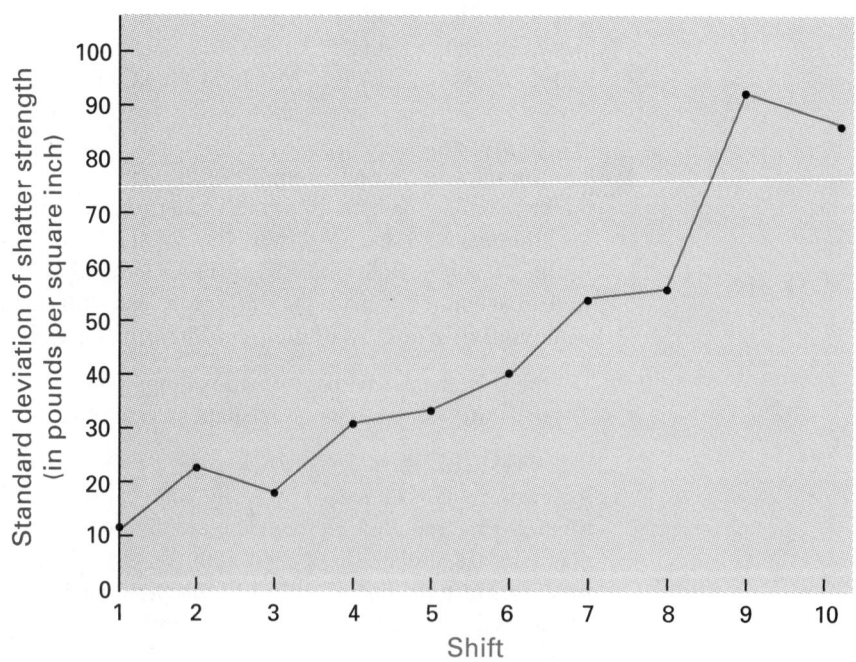

A process under statistical control exhibits only random variation. Random variation means:

1. The means and the standard deviations stay nearly constant from the start to the end of a process control study.
2. There are no systematic data patterns. The means and standard deviations do not exhibit an upward or downward trend, a cyclical pattern, a jump in the performance level pattern, a widening or narrowing pattern, etc. from the start to the end of a process control study.
3. Often, practitioners must go beyond visual checks to determine whether a process is under statistical control. They use control charts, which we will discuss shortly.

Process Capability

Assume that COMCEL has achieved process control of its molding operation. The graphs of the means and the standard deviations are stationary and exhibit only random variation. Now COMCEL must determine the molding operation's *process capability*.

Process capability determines to what extent a stable process can produce products within design specification limits set by the firm. If the process cannot meet the specifications, then the firm must either change its design specifications or, better yet, improve the manufacturing process by reducing the process variation. We discuss more on reducing process variation later.

Process control and process capability are different ideas. Process control determines whether a process is stable. Process capability determines whether the stable process can produce a sufficiently large number of parts within design specification limits. Alternatively, process capability determines the proportion of defective items (in manufacturing firms) or unacceptable services (in service firms) that the process will produce. We will illustrate the process capability study idea for COMCEL's molding process.

Setting Specification Limits   We begin by determining the specification limits of the molding process. First, based on the phone's probable cost, COMCEL determines the shatter strength that customers want. Second, the engineering design group translates customer wants into engineering specifications. For example, they determine that the handset shatter strength should be between 4,600 and 4,900 ppsi.

> The *lower specification limit* (LSL) is the lowest acceptable shatter strength—4,600 ppsi.

> The *upper specification limit* (USL) is the highest desired shatter strength (given the probable cost)—4,900 ppsi.

> The molding process *target value* is 4,750 ppsi—midway between the LSL and USL.

Determining the Process Standard Deviation   The process standard deviation, s, is the "natural" variation of the process. There is variation in all processes. For example, is your travel time to a mall precisely the same every trip? Of course not! It will depend on weather conditions, traffic conditions, etc. Similarly, a business process has a natural variation. Here we show how to estimate it.

Using systematic sampling, the workers select five handsets from each of 15 consecutive shifts or subgroups and determine the *shift* means and *shift* standard

Table 15.2

Process Capability Study Data

Observations (in ppsi)

Shift	1	2	3	4	5	$\bar{x}$	s
1	4,705	4,780	4,715	4,750	4,780	4,746	35.25
2	4,750	4,800	4,775	4,740	4,750	4,763	24.39
3	4,740	4,740	4,775	4,770	4,780	4,761	19.49
4	4,710	4,775	4,780	4,780	4,810	4,771	36.81
5	4,770	4,750	4,780	4,750	4,725	4,755	21.21
6	4,735	4,700	4,755	4,770	4,755	4,743	27.06
7	4,750	4,800	4,775	4,725	4,790	4,768	30.54
8	4,740	4,750	4,775	4,770	4,780	4,763	17.18
9	4,840	4,780	4,780	4,755	4,790	4,789	31.30
10	4,770	4,750	4,780	4,800	4,725	4,765	28.72
11	4,690	4,750	4,750	4,720	4,720	4,726	25.10
12	4,800	4,775	4,780	4,750	4,800	4,781	20.74
13	4,790	4,790	4,740	4,810	4,810	4,788	28.64
14	4,750	4,720	4,780	4,750	4,770	4,754	23.02
15	4,750	4,760	4,775	4,720	4,790	4,759	26.55

$$\bar{\bar{x}} = \frac{4{,}746 + 4{,}763 + \cdots + 4{,}754 + 4{,}759}{15} = 4{,}762.13 \text{ ppsi}$$

$$\bar{s} = \frac{35.25 + 24.39 + \cdots + 23.02 + 26.55}{15} = 26.40 \text{ ppsi}$$

deviations (see the two right-most columns in Table 15.2). They also determine the overall mean ($\bar{\bar{x}}$) and the average standard deviation ($\bar{s}$) using the following expressions:

$$\bar{\bar{x}} = \frac{\Sigma \bar{x}_i}{k} \qquad \bar{s} = \frac{\Sigma s_i}{k} \tag{15.2}$$

The term k is the number of subgroups (here, shifts) selected in the process capability study. In the COMCEL study, $k = 15$. The expressions of (15.2) assume that each of the k subgroups has the same sample size. In the COMCEL study, the sample size of each subgroup or shift is 5. A process capability study should have at least 15 subgroups and a sample size of 5 or more per subgroup. Walter Shewhart, the father of quality control, noted that in manufacturing, the population shapes are only mildly skewed. Therefore a sample of size five produces a nearly normal distribution of the sample mean. For highly skewed population shapes, samples of size 30 or more (central limit theorem) are required.

From the results in Table 15.2, we see that the overall mean of the 15 subgroup means, $\bar{\bar{x}}$, is 4,762 ppsi, which is close to the target value of 4,750 ppsi. If it were not, COMCEL must adjust the molding process until $\bar{\bar{x}}$ is at, or close to, the target value.

The average standard deviation, $\bar{s}$, does not equal the process standard deviation, s, but it is close. The process standard deviation, s, measures differences among products (or services):

1. within a shift due to variation in measuring equipment, material, people, the environment, etc., and
2. between shifts due to material, people, the environment, etc.

We compute $\bar{s}$ by taking the average of 15 standard deviations within each shift (see Table 15.2). Therefore $\bar{s}$ does not measure possible differences between shifts; it only measures the variation within each shift. Thus, $\bar{s}$ underestimates the process standard deviation, s.

We use expression (15.3) to estimate the process standard deviation, s.

$$s = \frac{\bar{s}}{c_4} \tag{15.3}$$

where the c_4 factor depends on the sample size per shift and can be found in Table 15.4 on page 725. Since the c_4 values are less than one, the process standard deviation, s, will be larger than the average standard deviation, $\bar{s}$. The estimated standard deviation for the molding process based on samples of size 5 is

$$s = \frac{26.40}{.9400} = 28.09 \text{ ppsi.}$$

When firms decrease the process standard deviation by investment in materials, equipment, and people, their product quality increases.

Determining the Natural Tolerance of a Process   The natural tolerance tells us how consistent a product or service the process can produce. Recall from the normal curve (Appendix 3), 99.74% of the observations will fall within ± 3 standard deviations of the mean. The natural tolerance of a process is defined as ± 3 process standard deviations, or 6 standard deviations. The natural tolerance of a process is simply what the process can produce 99.74% of the time.

$$\text{Natural Tolerance of Process} = 6 \cdot s \tag{15.4}$$

The natural tolerance of the molding process is

$$6 \cdot 28.09 \text{ ppsi} = 168.54 \text{ ppsi.}$$

Assuming the handset shatter strengths are normally distributed, the natural tolerance tells us that 99.74% of the individual handsets will have a shatter strength within $\pm$ 3 standard deviations ($\pm 3 \cdot 28.09 = \pm 84.27$ ppsi) of the actual process mean of 4,762 ppsi. Figure 15.5, a frequency histogram of the 75 individual observations in Table 15.2, assures us that shatter strength is reasonably normal-shaped.

The natural tolerance indicates that 99.74% of the handsets will have a shatter strength between 4,677.73 ppsi (4,762 − 84.27) and 4,846.27 ppsi (4,762 + 84.27). The difference between 4,846.27 and 4,677.73 equals the natural tolerance of 168.54 ppsi. Once we have computed the natural tolerance we can determine a process capability index.

Computing C_p, a Process Capability Index   The process capability index (C_p) is the ratio of the width of the design specification limits (what the customers want) to the natural tolerance of the process (what the process can produce 99.74% of the time). We use the C_p to determine whether a process is capable of producing products with an acceptably low number of defective items (ideally zero defective items). If so, full-scale production can begin.

FIGURE 15.5   Frequency Histogram of 75 Handset Shatter Strengths

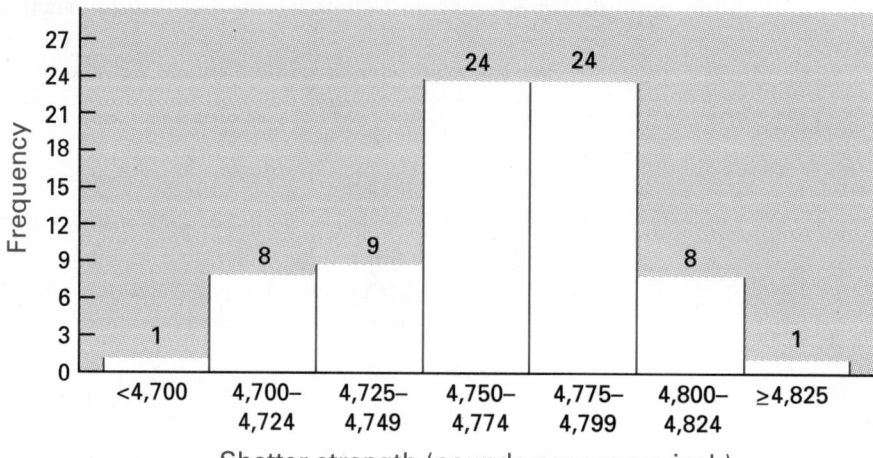

Shatter strength (pounds per square inch)

Expression (15.5) computes the C_p, process capability index.

$$C_p = \frac{\text{Design Specification Limits}}{\text{Natural Tolerance of Process}}$$

$$C_p = \frac{\text{USL} - \text{LSL}}{6s} \qquad (15.5)$$

The C_p for COMCEL's molding process is

$$\frac{4{,}900 - 4{,}600}{6 \cdot 28.09}, \text{ or } 1.78$$

The width of the design specification limits is 1.78 times as large as the natural tolerance of the molding process. Industry presently uses the following rule of thumb: If the C_p is greater than 1.33, generally begin full-scale production or service. We now explain why.

C_p and the Proportion of Defective Items   We will demonstrate the connection between the C_p value and the proportion of defective items produced (or unacceptable services provided). In general, the larger the C_p value, the smaller the proportion of defective items produced.

We can use the normal table in Appendix 3 to determine the proportion of defective items for the phone handset molding process with a C_p of 1.78. Refer to Figure 15.6. The C_p = 1.78 curve has a mean of 4,762 ppsi (see Table 15.2) and a process standard deviation of 28.09 ppsi. The proportion of defective items equals the area under the curve below LSL = 4,600 ppsi plus the area under the curve above USL = 4,900 ppsi. Remember, the LSL and USL are the limits of what customers will find acceptable, and thus be satisfied.

To determine the proportion of defective items, compute the following two probabilities.

$$P(x < 4{,}600) + P(x > 4{,}900) = P\left(z < \frac{4{,}600 - 4{,}762}{28.09}\right) + P\left(z > \frac{4{,}900 - 4{,}762}{28.09}\right)$$

$$P(z < -5.77) + P(z > +4.92) \sim 0.000$$

FIGURE 15.6   Relationship Between C_p and Proportion Defective

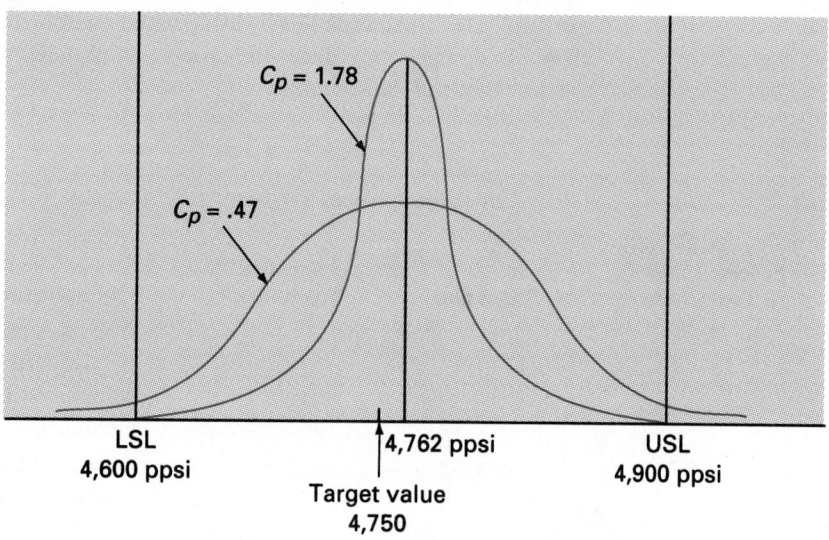

The sum of the two probabilities is almost zero as we cannot look up z-scores of -5.77 or $+4.92$ in Appendix 3. Thus, a process with a C_p of 1.78 will produce essentially no defective items (actually slightly more than one in 2 million). That is why COMCEL should begin full-scale production.

A process that has a C_p of much less than 1.33 will produce too many defective items. And as Deming has noted, rework (fixing defective items) leads to increased costs, lower market share, and lower profitability.

Let's suppose that the phone handset molding process mean remains 4,762 ppsi, but $\bar{s}$ is 100 ppsi, not 26.40 ppsi as per Table 15.2. In other words, suppose the process exhibited more variation. First, the process standard deviation would be 100/.9400, or 106.40 ppsi. Second, the C_p index would now equal 300/(6 · 106.40) = .47.

Note the areas below the LSL and above the USL for the C_p = .47 normal curve in Figure 15.6 are large. This means the proportion of defective items will be high, which is undesirable.

To determine the proportion of defective items, compute the following two probabilities.

$$P(x < 4,600) + P(x > 4,900) = P\left(z < \frac{4,600 - 4,762}{106.40}\right) +$$

$$P\left(z > \frac{4,900 - 4,762}{106.40}\right)$$

$$P(z < -1.52) + P(z > +1.30) = .0643 + .0968$$
$$= .1611 \text{ or about 161 defective items per thousand}$$

Today, quality-conscious American firms are trying to produce less than one defective item per one hundred thousand pieces, not 161 per thousand!

Ten years ago a C_p of 1.00 was considered acceptable. Given the recent emphasis on quality, firms now want a C_p process capability greater than 1.33. Some firms (for instance, Motorola) have achieved C_ps of 2.00 in their manufacturing processes.

If the C_p is much less than 1.33, a firm should not produce the product. The firm must reduce process variation, s, and this is management's responsibility, not the workers'. The firm can do this by using better equipment, methods, people, and supervision. In doing so, it reduces the proportion of defective items and can be competitive in today's global economy.

<u>Table 15.3</u>

Implications of Different C_p Values

Process Control: Process Under Statistical Control?	C_p Value	Satisfied Customer?	Implications
1. No	—	—	Process is unstable in either the mean or the standard deviation. Correct the problem before starting the process capability study.
2. Yes	> 1.33	Yes	Very few defective items will be produced. Process will meet specs and satisfy customers. Begin manufacturing but try to reduce process standard deviation. Continuous improvement is essential to remain competitive.
3. Yes	> 1.33	No	Customers are unhappy. The LSL and USL are too wide to meet customers' wants. Tighten the design specification limits.
4. Yes	< 1.33	No	The process produces many defective items and must be improved. May require capital expenditures. Ask workers for their ideas.

In summary, Table 15.3 indicates that the C_p process capability index provides useful information. In situation 1 the process is not under statistical control. Look for assignable causes, such as (1) gross blunders, (2) lack of training, (3) need for better equipment or processes, or (4) poor supervision. Do not run the process capability study! Situation 2 typifies a process that is under statistical control. Also, the process will produce very few defective items. Situation 3 represents a statistically controlled process in which design specification limits—USL and LSL—are too wide to meet customer wants. The product does not work well even though it is within specs. The solution is to tighten up the specs—increase the LSL and lower the USL—and ensure that the process can satisfy the new specs. In situation 4 we have a statistically controlled process that produces a high proportion of defective items. That is unacceptable, and the firm must reduce process variation, s, to remain competitive.

A Centered Process   The C_p index is an effective measure of process capability only when the process is *centered*. In a centered process, the actual process mean, $\bar{\bar{x}}$, is close to the target value. $\bar{\bar{x}}$ for the data in Table 15.2 was 4,762 ppsi. This is a centered process because $\bar{\bar{x}}$ is close to the 4,750 ppsi target value.

Figure 15.7 illustrates why C_p is not an effective process capability measure for a noncentered process. Suppose the actual process mean, $\bar{\bar{x}}$, is 4,630 ppsi—not close to the target value of 4,750 ppsi. The process standard deviation, s, is still 28.09 ppsi.

FIGURE 15.7   Why C_p Is Not an Effective Index for a Noncentered Process

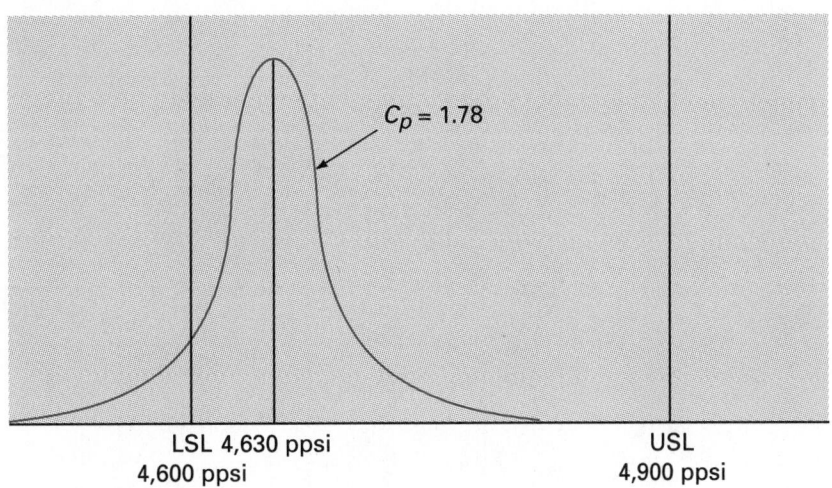

LSL 4,630 ppsi   USL
4,600 ppsi   4,900 ppsi

So C_p would still be 1.78, $(4,900 - 4,600)/(6 \cdot 28.09)$. However the proportion of defective items (area below the LSL) is now very high. We can see this by computing the proportion of defective items:

$$P(x < 4,600) + P(x > 4,900)$$

$$P\left(z < \frac{4,600 - 4,630}{28.09}\right) + P\left(z > \frac{4,900 - 4,630}{28.09}\right)$$

$$P(z < -1.07) + P(z > +9.61)$$

$$.1423 + .0000 = .1423 \text{ or about 142 defective items per thousand}$$

While there are process capability measures for noncentered processes, we recommend taking corrective action to center a process. Afterwards, the process capability can be determined using the C_p index.

Basic Control Charts and Problem Solving

Process control and capability studies ensure that a manufacturing or service process is under statistical control and capable of meeting the design specification limits. Then the firm can begin full-scale production or service. Occasionally, problems will crop up and the process may temporarily go out of control. Control charts warn an operator when this is happening so that he or she can take corrective action.

Basic Ideas   In 1926 Walter Shewhart introduced the control chart (Shewhart, 1926). It is a visual aid that provides information about the level of manufactured quality. The control chart in Figure 15.8 has three horizontal lines. The top line is the *upper control limit (UCL)* and the bottom line is the *lower control limit (LCL)*. The *centerline (CL)* is the average value of the key indicator of success measure or the target value set by the firm. The upper control limit is three standard deviations above the centerline, and the lower control limit is three standard deviations below the centerline. On each shift, or during each time period, an operator records a value (an $\bar{x}$ or s) in the control chart that indicates how well the process is doing.

FIGURE 15.8   The Basic Form of the Control Chart

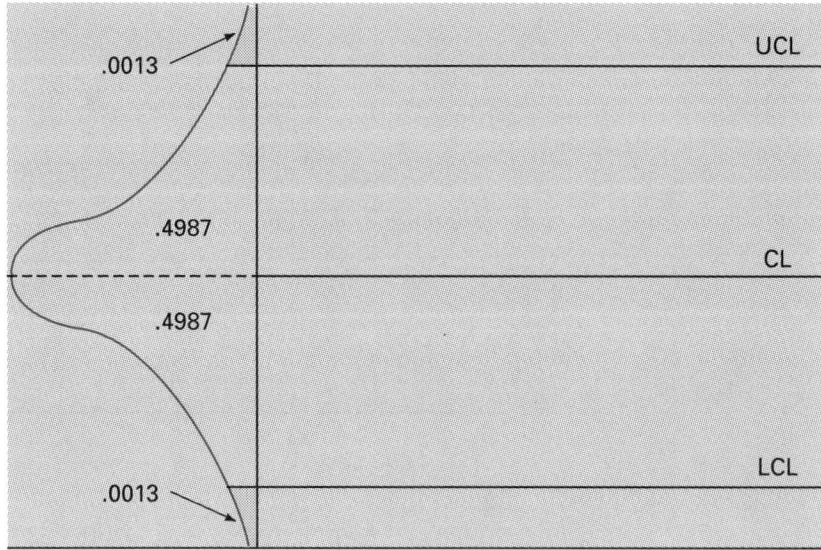

Shift or time period

A process under control will occasionally produce shift means or standard deviations outside of their 3-sigma limits. How often will this occur? If a process under control produces parts with measurements that are normally distributed (see Figure 15.8), the probability of a plotted data point lying outside the 3-sigma limits is only 26 in 10,000 (.0026 from Appendix 3). Thus, if a point lies outside the limits, Shewhart asserted that it signalled that the process is going out of control and the operator must determine why.

We use control charts to identify two important types of variation:

Random variation is due to many factors that are uncontrollable (in the short run). Their impact makes it impossible to produce parts or services that are exactly uniform. However, the mean and standard deviation are under control, and there is no need for immediate problem solving.

1.   Shift means or standard deviations within their 3-sigma limits merely signal **random variation,** or chance variation. When random variation is operating, the operator need not take corrective action. The process cannot be improved unless the firm undertakes a major investment in equipment, training, supervision, or materials.

2.   Shift means or standard deviations outside their 3-sigma limits signal assignable cause variation. The process is *temporarily* out of control, and it will continue to produce a high proportion of defective items. Therefore, the operator must *immediately* take corrective action. Later we will discuss several tools for troubleshooting **assignable cause variation.**

Assignable cause variation is due to a special cause(s) that must be corrected. In short, something is wrong, and the operators must take corrective action.

Others have developed additional rules (beyond the Shewhart 3-sigma rule) for determining when a process is out of control.* Any unusual data pattern—for example, 10 successive plotted points above (or below) the centerline—signals an out-of-control process. Always look for *unlikely* or *nonrandom* data patterns. As Deming (1951) has noted, "The control chart is no substitute for the brain."

Quality-control departments set up control charts, and workers on the production line or service operation maintain them. For that reason, control charts need to be simple to calculate and interpret. Two common control charts are those for the mean and standard deviation.

---

* In the 1950s, the Western Electric Company developed additional rules to warn an operator of an out-of-control process. Please see an advanced text on quality assurance for more details.

Control Limits for the Standard Deviation Chart   We begin by constructing a chart of the standard deviation—an s-chart—for the molding process data in Table 15.2. Expression (15.6) provides the centerline for the s chart.

$$\text{Centerline of } s\text{-chart (CL)} = \bar{s} = \frac{\Sigma s_i}{k} \qquad (15.6)$$

where s_i is the subgroup standard deviation
k is the number of subgroups

The centerline is merely the average standard deviation obtained from the process capability study, 26.40 ppsi (see Table 15.2). Once we have calculated the centerline, we can use Table 15.4 developed by quality-control professionals to determine the lower and upper control limits. Expressions (15.7) and (15.8) provide the lower and upper control limits for an s-chart.

$$\text{Upper control limit (UCL): } B_4\bar{s} \qquad (15.7)$$

$$\text{Lower control limit (LCL): } B_3\bar{s} \qquad (15.8)$$

The values of B_3 and B_4, found in Table 15.4, help us construct approximate* 99.74% confidence intervals on $\bar{s}$. About 99.74% of the standard deviations should fall between the LCL and UCL if the process is operating properly. How the B_3 and B_4 factor values were determined need not concern us.

The control limits for the s-chart for the molding operation data in Table 15.2 are shown here. The average standard deviation. $\bar{s} = 26.40$ ppsi, and the sample size per subgroup, or shift, was 5. From expressions (15.6)–(15.8):

Table 15.4

Quality-Control Factors

Sample Size per Subgroup	Factors for Constructing Mean and Standard Deviation Charts			Factor for Computing Process Standard Deviation
	Upper/Lower A_3	Lower B_3	Upper B_4	c_4
2	2.659	0	3.267	.7979
3	1.954	0	2.568	.8862
4	1.628	0	2.266	.9213
5	1.427	0	2.089	.9400
6	1.287	.030	1.970	.9515
7	1.182	.118	1.882	.9594
8	1.099	.185	1.815	.9650
9	1.032	.239	1.761	.9693
10	.975	.284	1.716	.9727
15	.789	.428	1.572	.9826
20	.680	.510	1.490	.9869
25	.606	.565	1.435	.9896

---

* The distribution of s is not normally distributed. Thus the probability of obtaining a standard deviation between the lower and upper control limits is not exactly .9974.

$$\text{LCL} = B_3 \cdot \bar{s} = 0 \cdot 26.40 \qquad = 0.00 \text{ ppsi}$$

$$\text{CL} = \bar{s} \qquad\qquad\qquad \doteq 26.40 \text{ ppsi}$$

$$\text{UCL} = B_4 \cdot \bar{s} = 2.089 \cdot 26.40 = 55.14 \text{ ppsi}$$

To complete the s-chart for the molding process, we plot the 15 standard deviation values in Table 15.2. The lower panel of Figure 15.9 shows the completed s-chart.

Control Limits for the Mean Chart Next we construct a control chart for the mean—the $\bar{x}$-chart—for the molding process data in Table 15.2.

Expression (15.9) provides the centerline for the $\bar{x}$-chart.

$$\text{Centerline of } \bar{x}\text{-chart (CL)} = \bar{\bar{x}} = \frac{\Sigma \bar{x}_i}{k} \tag{15.9}$$

where $\bar{x}_i$ is the sample mean for a subgroup
k is the number of subgroups

The centerline is merely the average process mean, $\bar{\bar{x}} = 4{,}762$ ppsi, obtained from the process capability study data in Table 15.2.

Expressions (15.10) and (15.11) provide the upper and lower control limits for an $\bar{x}$-chart. Table 15.4 provides the A_3 value.

$$\text{Upper control limit (UCL): } \bar{\bar{x}} + A_3 \bar{s} \tag{15.10}$$

$$\text{Lower control limit (LCL): } \bar{\bar{x}} - A_3 \bar{s} \tag{15.11}$$

99.74% of the $\bar{x}$ values should fall between the LCL and UCL when the process is operating properly.

The control limits for the $\bar{x}$-chart for the molding operation are shown here. Table 15.2 provided the process mean, $\bar{\bar{x}}$, of 4,762 ppsi, which is the centerline for the $\bar{x}$-chart. Also note that from Table 15.2, the sample size per subgroup, or shift, was 5. From expressions (15.9)–(15.11):

$$\text{LCL} = \bar{\bar{x}} - A_3 \cdot \bar{s} = 4{,}762 - (1.427) \cdot 26.40 = 4{,}724 \text{ ppsi}$$

$$\text{CL} = \bar{\bar{x}} \qquad\qquad\qquad\qquad = 4{,}762 \text{ ppsi}$$

$$\text{UCL} = \bar{\bar{x}} + A_3 \cdot \bar{s} = 4{,}762 + (1.427) \cdot 26.40 = 4{,}800 \text{ ppsi}$$

To complete the $\bar{x}$-chart for the molding process, we plot the 15 $\bar{x}$ values in Table 15.2. The upper panel of Figure 15.9 shows the completed $\bar{x}$-chart.

Figure 15.9 shows both control charts for the molding process. It is common practice to place the $\bar{x}$-chart above the s-chart. Line workers will now take samples from each shift, compute the mean and standard deviation, and plot these values on the appropriate control charts.

Using Control Charts Workers use control charts to monitor a process and initiate corrective problem-solving action. Under the Shewhart 3-sigma rule, neither the mean nor the standard deviation was temporarily out of control during the first 15 shifts in the COMCEL study (see Figure 15.9). That is, no point lies outside the 3-sigma control limits.

Figure 15.10 shows the means and standard deviations for the next 25 shifts—16–40. The means and standard deviations are based on samples of size 5 per subgroup taken during each shift.

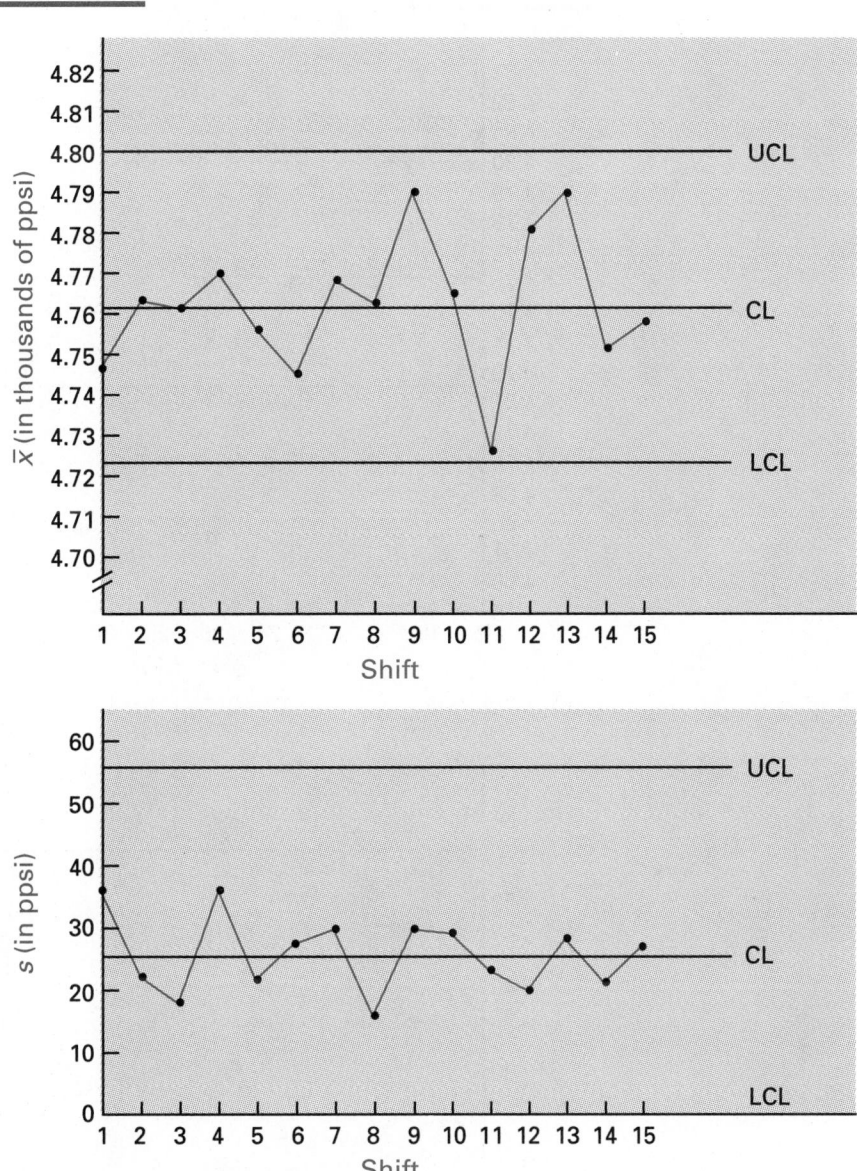

FIGURE 15.9   Control Chart for the Mean and Standard Deviation

On shift 28 the mean shatter strength dropped below the LCL. According to She-whart, the process has gone temporarily out of control because the very low value of $\bar{x}$ was unlikely to have happened by chance alone. Using problem-solving tools that we will discuss in Section 15.5, the operator determined the root causes. By the next shift, the mean was again within the 3-sigma control limits. On shift 33 the standard deviation was above the UCL. Again, the operator corrected the problem, and the next shift standard deviation was within the 3-sigma limits.

Control charts are useful in sensing changes in the process mean or standard deviation. As we know, problem sensing is essential to timely problem solving.

FIGURE 15.10   **Control Chart for the Mean and Standard Deviation: Shifts 16–40**

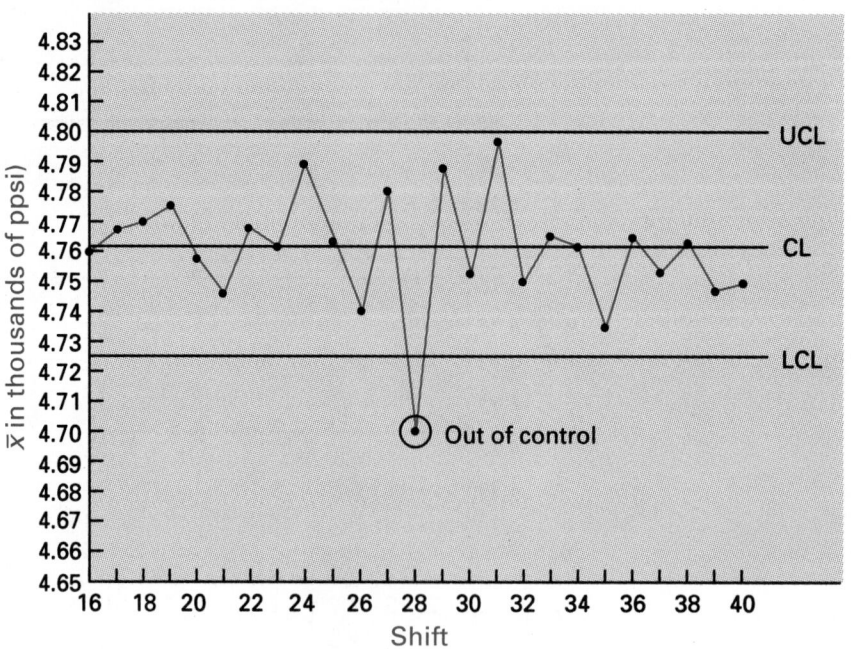

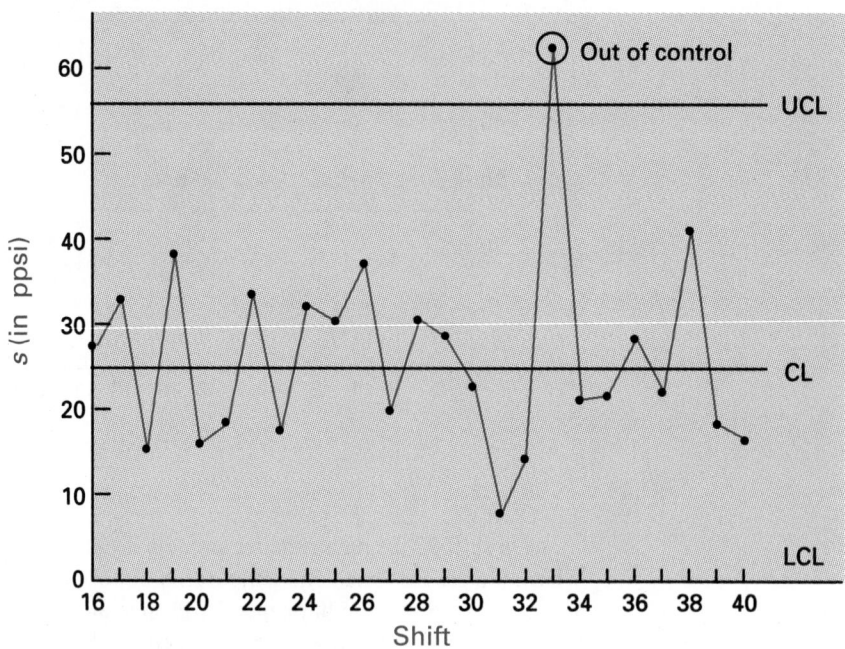

Delayed action can mean rework, extra cost, lost profitability, and lost market share. Quick detection and solution of quality problems are essential to a firm's success.

Steps in Building and Using Mean and Standard Deviation Control Charts

To summarize, here are the steps for building and using control charts:

1. Decide on a subgroup sample size. A sample size between 5 and 10 is common. Use systematic sampling during each shift (or appropriate time period) to select your observations.
2. Select 15 or more subgroups or consecutive time periods.
3. For each subgroup, compute the shift mean and standard deviation.
4. Compute the overall mean, $\bar{\bar{x}}$, and the average standard deviation, $\bar{s}$, using expression (15.2).
5. $\bar{\bar{x}}$ is the centerline on the $\bar{x}$-chart, and $\bar{s}$ is the centerline on the s-chart.
6. Calculate the control limits for the $\bar{x}$-chart using equations (15.10) and (15.11). Calculate the control limits for the s- chart using equations (15.7) and (15.8).
7. Draw the control charts. Place the s-chart below the $\bar{x}$-chart.
8. Use the control limits to monitor future shift subgroup means and standard deviations. If a subgroup mean or standard deviation lies within their 3-sigma limits, take no action. When a single plotted point falls outside either 3-sigma limit, determine the root causes and take corrective action.

   In summary, we first establish process control. We visually check for random variation and use control charts and apply the Shewhart 3-sigma rule. Once the process is under statistical control, we then determine whether the process can meet the design specs; we determine the process capability. If the centered process has a C_p greater than 1.33 (and we believe the customer will be satisfied with the product), we begin full-scale operation. Then we use control charts to monitor the process and to initiate problem solving to correct a process that is temporarily out of control. This is the joint responsibility of all employees.

SECTION 15.3 EXERCISES

1. Draw a line graph of a process under statistical control and a line graph of a process not under statistical control. Explain your graphs.

2. We select eight subgroups of five items each and weigh them. The subgroup means (in ounces) and standard deviations are shown here.

Shift	1	2	3	4	5	6	7	8
$\bar{x}$	5.1	5.3	4.8	5.1	5.2	5.0	4.9	5.3
s	.4	.5	.7	.8	.8	.9	1.2	1.5

   a. Construct a process control chart for the mean and the standard deviation.
   b. Is the process under statistical control? Explain.

3. Suppose the Mobile Phone Engineering Design group sets a target value for mean-time-to-failure at 2,000 hours, with a USL of 2,100 hours and an LSL of 1,900 hours. The firm runs a process capability study by taking 20 subgroups of five phones and running time-to-failure tests. Here are the sample mean data for the 20 subgroups.

Shift	Mean	Shift	Mean		Shift	Mean	Shift	Mean
1	2,105	6	2,117		11	2,038	16	2,124
2	2,145	7	2,049		12	2,061	17	2,040
3	2,071	8	2,001		13	2,131	18	2,036
4	2,039	9	2,018		14	2,051	19	2,116
5	2,106	10	2,017		15	2,081	20	2,102

    a. Plot the data. Do the data appear to exhibit only random variation?
    b. How close is $\bar{\bar{x}}$ to the target value?
    c. *Discuss the following statement:* A process can be in a state of statistical control and yet still be performing badly. Under what conditions is this true?

4. Which of the following four processes appear to be under statistical control? Discuss.

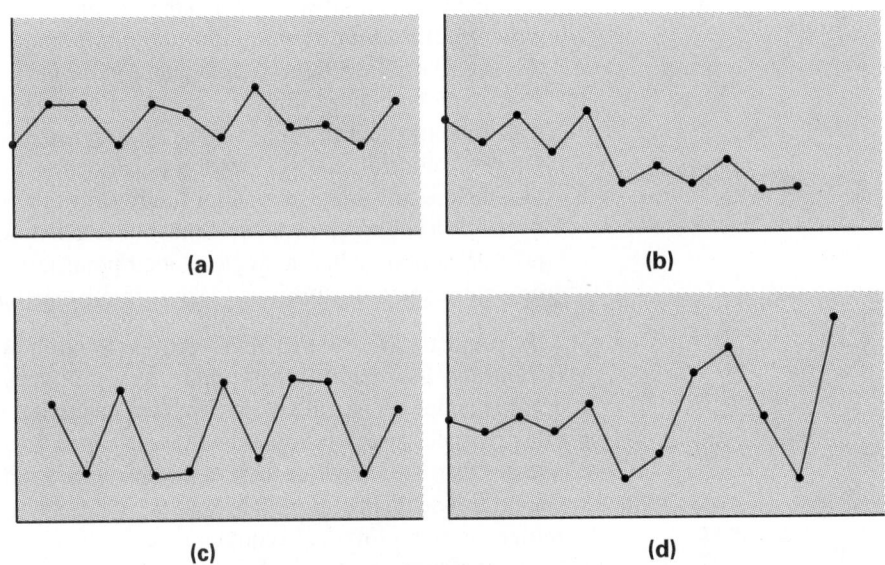

                    (a)   **(b)**

                    (c)   **(d)**

5. A sample of $n = 10$ items was selected each hour over an 8-hour period. Inspectors measured the shatter strength of the parts. The mean of the eight standard deviations was 100 pounds per square inch (ppsi). The mean of the eight sample means was 2,800 ppsi.
    a. Calculate the natural tolerance of the process.
    b. The lower and upper design specification limits are 2,400 ppsi and 3,200 ppsi. The target value was 2,800 ppsi. Calculate the process capability index, C_p.
    c. Is it necessary to know the target value to compute the C_p?
    d. Calculate the lower and upper control limits for the $\bar{x}$-chart.
    e. Calculate the lower and upper control limits for the s-chart.

6. Use Appendix 3 to verify that the probability of a plotted value in an $\bar{x}$-chart
    a. falling between the lower and upper control limits is .9974.
    b. falling outside the lower or upper control limits is .0026.

7. A sample $n =$ four items was selected each hour over a 5-hour period and the lengths were measured. The mean of the five sample standard deviations was 1.0 cm. The mean of the five sample means was 17.5 cm.
    a. Calculate the natural tolerance for the process.
    b. The lower and upper design specification limits are 15 and 20 cm, respectively. Calculate the process capability index, C_p.
    c. Given the value of the C_p, should a firm start producing the product?
    d. What would be the proportion of defective items produced by this process? Assume that the process is normally distributed.

8. This problem demonstrates that a C_p is valid only if the process is centered (or nearly so). Suppose the target value for a process is 50 seconds, with an LSL of 40 seconds and a USL of 60 seconds. Suppose that $\bar{x}$ is 50 seconds and the process standard deviation, s, is 1 second.
   a. Compute the C_p for the centered process.
   b. What proportion of parts would be defective? Discuss.

   Suppose that $\bar{x}$ is now 60 seconds but that the process standard deviation, s, is still 1 second.
   c. Compute the C_p for the noncentered process.
   d. What is the proportion of defective items produced by this process?
   e. Explain why C_p is valid only for centered processes.

9. A firm that makes batteries takes samples of $n = 5$ items per shift over $k = 10$ shifts. Inspectors measure the battery weight. The mean of the 10 standard deviations was .25 ounce. The mean of the 10 sample means was 20.5 ounces.
   a. Calculate the natural tolerance for the process.
   b. The lower and upper design specification limits are 19 ounces and 22 ounces. Calculate the process capability index, C_p.
   c. Compute the proportion of defective items in this process.
   d. Calculate the lower and upper control limits for the $\bar{x}$-chart.
   e. Calculate the lower and upper control limits for the s-chart.

10. This problem illustrates how we can use control charts to determine whether the process is under statistical control. Shown are sample means and standard deviations based on subgroups of size 5 each. The variable being measured is time in seconds.

	$\bar{x}$	s		$\bar{x}$	s
1	64.32	16.15	11	59.01	11.74
2	65.90	12.32	12	67.79	13.00
3	61.36	12.19	13	61.80	8.08
4	58.92	11.81	14	66.92	16.58
5	51.44	10.68	15	64.29	13.97
6	62.17	11.63	16	21.50	10.59
7	55.10	16.55	17	51.69	7.53
8	60.96	8.90	18	57.83	15.80
9	53.19	9.64	19	53.13	13.24
10	59.51	12.32	20	59.19	13.84

   a. Compute $\bar{\bar{x}}$ and $\bar{s}$.
   b. Set up *initial* control limits for the $\bar{x}$-chart. Are any of the first 20 subgroup means outside the limits?
   c. What action should you take for those sample means that are outside of the limits?
   d. Suppose you can determine an assignable cause for an out-of-control data point and you correct the problem. Now you eliminate that data point and recompute the *final* control limits. Do this for the data set above.
   e. Based on part **d**, is the process now under statistical control? Discuss.

11. Refer to Exercise 9. Given here are the means and standard deviations for the next 7 shifts, based on taking 5 items per shift. Is the process ever temporarily out of control? Use the 3-sigma rule. Explain.

Shift	11	12	13	14	15	16	17
$\bar{x}$	20.55	20.20	20.45	20.78	20.35	20.99	20.55
s	.10	.45	.25	.75	.15	.35	.15

12. Explain the difference between random and assignable cause variation.

13. Provide two explanations of how a manufacturing process with a C_p of 1.8 could still have problems satisfying customer wants. *Hint:* See Table 15.3 for one explanation.

14. The lower and upper design specification limits for a product's weight are 19 ounces and 21 ounces. What must the process standard deviation, s, be so that the C_p will equal 1.5? What could a firm do to reduce s?

15. Suppose a sample mean falls outside of the 3-sigma control limits. We must seek an assignable cause. What is the probability that such a point could occur without there being an assignable cause? Explain.

16. *Thought question:* Why not adopt a 1-sigma rule? That is, if *one* sample mean falls outside the 1-sigma limits, we look for an assignable cause.
    a. Use Appendix 3 to determine the probability of a plotted value above $\bar{\bar{x}} + 1$-sigma ($z > 1$) plus the probability of a plotted value below $\bar{\bar{x}} - 1$-sigma ($z < -1$).
    b. What problems do you foresee with such a rule?

17. Suppose that the C_p for a process is 1.4, and the customer is satisfied with the product. Does that mean that the firm need not attempt to improve the process? Discuss.

18. Based on general knowledge and from a student perspective, define one key *quantitative* indicator of success for each of the following processes:
    a. Students waiting in line to register for classes at a university.
    b. An instructor grading an exam and returning it.
    c. Students presenting case analysis in class for a grade.
    d. Married students seeking nearby day-care services.

19. Here are average customer satisfaction data for a car-repair shop over a period of 12 days. Is the process under statistical control?

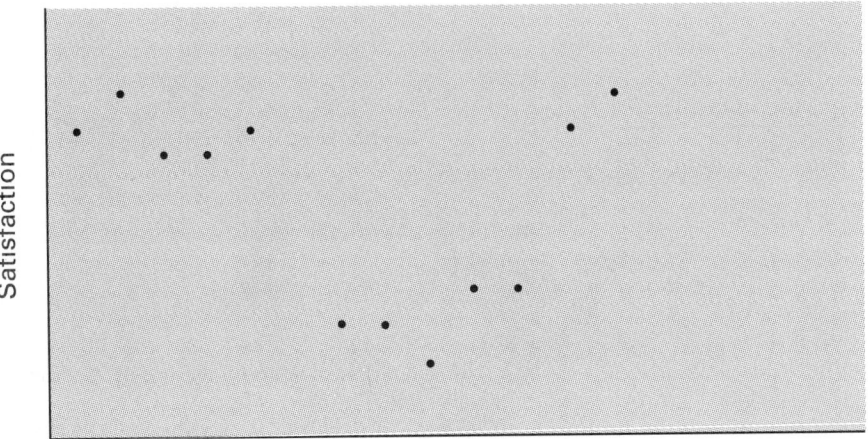

15.4 ≡ Control Charts for Attributes

We cannot always determine product or service quality by measuring length, time, cost, or shatter strength. For example, COMCEL's design specification for phone handset attractiveness is that "it should be free of surface blemishes to the naked eye" (see Figure 15.2). An inspection will conclude that either the surface is free of blemishes, or it is not. If the product is without a blemish, it conforms. If the product has blemishes, it is *nonconforming*. The attribute—free of surface blemishes—determines the quality. In the previous section we set up control charts on variables (quantitative data). We now turn to control charts for attributes; we use ***count, or yes/no data*** to assess process success.

Here are a few examples of business processes and key attribute indicators that we could monitor, control, and improve.

Process	Key Indicator of Process Success
1. Mold handset	Proportion of handsets that lack blemishes
2. Do surgery	Number of postsurgical complications
3. Obtain loan	Proportion of correctly completed loan applications

In this section we consider control charts when we use count data to measure process success. We could record the number or proportion of nonconforming products or services. The ultimate goal is to reduce the number or proportion of nonconforming products or services to zero. We will consider only the proportion nonconforming, or p, chart.

By the end of this section you should be able to:

1.   plot p (proportion nonconforming) charts; and
2.   determine the upper and lower control limits.

Process Control

COMCEL inspectors check each phone handset for surface blemishes before shipping to distributors. If they find one or more blemishes, the product is nonconforming. Finishers must then buff out the blemishes in a final polishing operation. COMCEL believes that blemished phones will alienate customers.

Table 15.5 shows the proportion of nonconforming handsets (one or more blemishes) for the first 10 production days. COMCEL inspects a sample of 500 handsets each day. Table 15.5 represents data for 10 subgroups, whereas practitioners would prefer about 20 subgroups.

Table 15.5

Initial Process Control Study Data

Day	Sample Size	Number Nonconforming	Proportion Nonconforming (p)
1	500	11	.022
2	500	14	.028
3	500	6	.012
4	500	8	.016
5	500	11	.022
6	500	7	.014
7	500	11	.022
8	500	6	.012
9	500	13	.026
10	500	11	.022

The line graph of proportion nonconforming in Figure 15.11 exhibits only random variation. That is, the data stay nearly constant from the start to the end of the process control study. The data also do not exhibit a trend, a cyclical pattern, a widening or narrowing pattern, a jump in the performance level pattern, etc. The process is under statistical control. As we begin full-scale production, we must develop control charts for the proportion nonconforming.

FIGURE 15.11   Proportion Nonconforming for Process Control Study

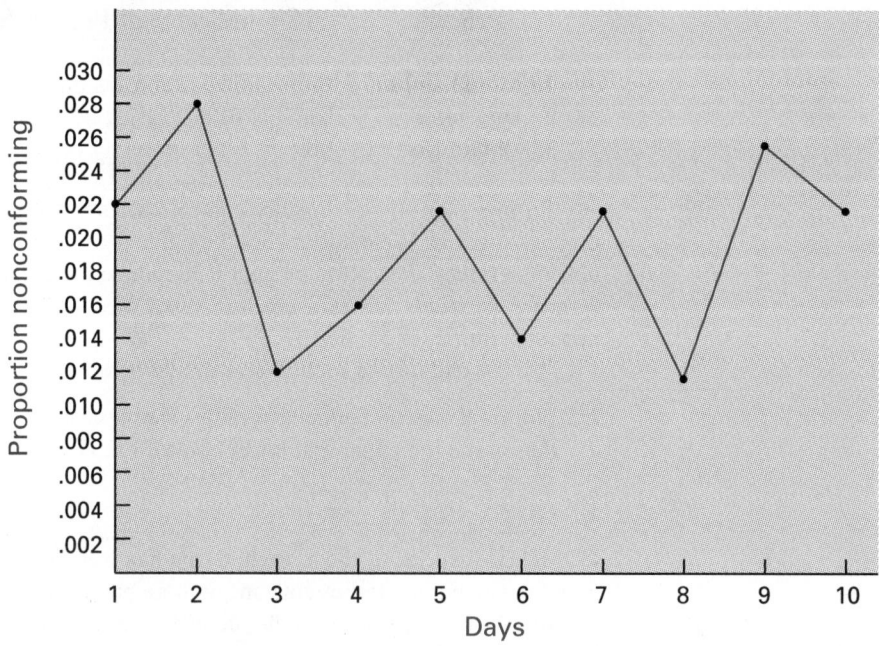

Control Limits for a Proportion Nonconforming, or p, Chart

When the sample size of each subgroup is the same, expression (15.12) provides the centerline for the p-chart.

$$\text{Centerline of } p\text{-chart} = \bar{p} = \frac{\Sigma p_i}{k} \tag{15.12}$$

where p_i = number of nonconforming in subgroup i/sample size in subgroup i
k = number of subgroups taken
$\bar{p}$ = average proportion nonconforming

The centerline is merely the average proportion of nonconforming items obtained from the process control study.

Expressions (15.13) and (15.14) provide the upper and lower control limits for a p-chart.

Control limits: $\bar{p} \pm 3$ Estimated standard errors of the proportion

$$\text{Upper control limit (UCL): } \bar{p} + 3 \sqrt{\frac{\bar{p}(1 - \bar{p})}{n}} \tag{15.13}$$

$$\text{Lower control limit (LCL): } \bar{p} - 3 \sqrt{\frac{\bar{p}(1 - \bar{p})}{n}} \tag{15.14}$$

where n is the sample size per period (shift, day, etc.)
$\bar{p}$ is the average proportion nonconforming

FIGURE 15.12   *p*-Chart for 15 Days of Operations

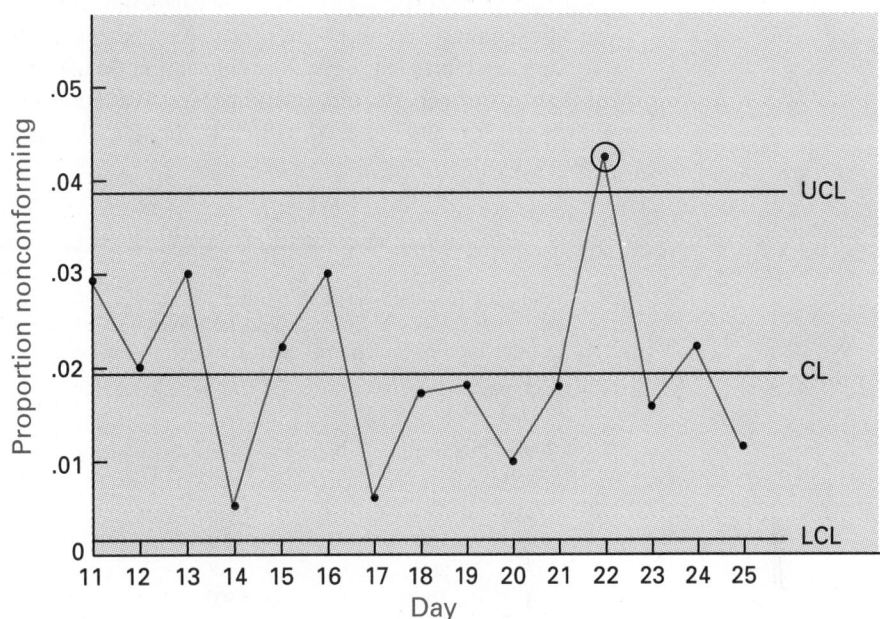

The control limits for the *p*-chart for the data in Table 15.5 are shown here.

$$\text{LCL} = .0196 - 3\sqrt{\frac{(.0196) \cdot (1 - .0196)}{500}} = .0100$$

$$\text{CL} = \bar{p} = \frac{.022 + .028 + \cdots + .026 + .022}{10} = .0196$$

$$\text{UCL} = .0196 + 3\sqrt{\frac{(.0196) \cdot (1 - .0196)}{500}} = .0382$$

As long as the proportion nonconforming falls between .0010 and .0382, the operators need not take corrective problem-solving action.

Figure 15.12 shows the proportion nonconforming based on samples of 500 handsets for each of the next 15 days—days 11–25. On day 22 the process produced an exceptionally high proportion of nonconforming handsets—a point above the upper control limit. This is a signal to look for an assignable cause. An analysis revealed that a new and improperly trained worker had run the molding operation. By the next day he had been properly trained and the proportion nonconforming again dropped between the LCL and UCL.

Here is a thought question. Why are we concerned if *p* falls below the lower control limit? After all, isn't that good? Why must we determine why the proportion nonconforming has dropped so low? Think about it before reading on!

A data point falling below the lower control limit means there may be an assignable cause for the very low proportion nonconforming pieces. If we can determine the causes, we may be able to permanently reduce the proportion nonconforming. For example, suppose the operator had incorrectly set the molding temperature that day.

He has accidentally discovered a way to reduce surface blemishes (assuming it does not reduce shatter strength). Now unless he had sought an assignable cause, he might have lost an opportunity to make a permanent process improvement.

In summary, control charts for variables and attributes help us determine when workers must initiate problem-solving action. Management and workers use a variety of tools to correct and improve processes. We have already presented some of them; others are new and are used mainly in the quality field. All will be discussed in the next section.

SECTION 15.4 EXERCISES

1. Inspector A selects an item from an assembly line and measures its width. Inspector B examines the item's finish and declares it to be either conforming or nonconforming. Suggest an appropriate control chart for each inspector.

2. A company selects a sample of 200 items each day for a 10-day period.

Day	Sample	Number Nonconforming	Proportion Nonconforming
1	200	7	.035
2	200	12	.060
3	200	8	.040
4	200	10	.050
5	200	13	.065
6	200	9	.045
7	200	11	.055
8	200	10	.050
9	200	14	.070
10	200	6	.030

   a. Compute $\bar{p}$ for the 10 days of data.
   b. Compute the lower and upper control limits for the process.
   c. Here is information on the firm's experience on days 11–15.

Day	11	12	13	14	15
Proportion Nonconforming	.055	.070	.040	.075	.105

   Construct a control chart for this attribute for days 11–15. Is the process ever out of control? What should you do?

3. The following are the results of the inspection of 10 samples of 100 units each.

Sample	Number Nonconforming
1	3
2	6
3	1
4	4
5	8
6	2
7	3
8	1
9	6
10	5

Set up the centerline and the upper and lower control limits for the proportion non-conforming for this process.

4. Is the following process under statistical control? Does the proportion nonconforming plot suggest only random variation?

Day	Sample	Proportion of Nonconforming Parts
1	100	.04
2	100	.06
3	100	.03
4	100	.07
5	100	.02
6	100	.08
7	100	.01
8	100	.09
9	100	.00
10	100	.10

5. What must the sample size be for each subgroup so that a process with a $\bar{p}$ of .02 will have a
   a. UCL of .05?
   b. UCL of .04?
   c. UCL of .03?

6. Do the two p-charts below suggest processes that are under statistical control? Discuss.

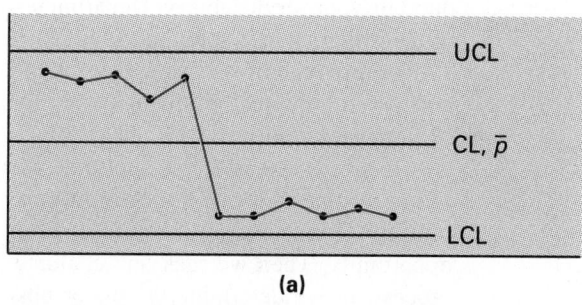

(a)

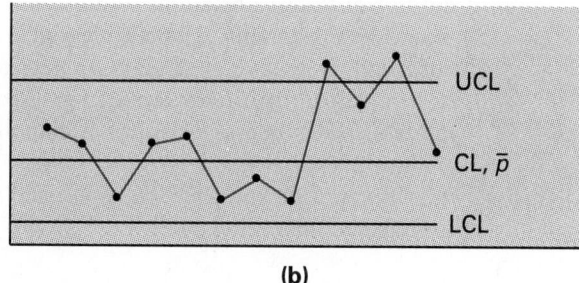

(b)

7. In an ideal process, what should the value of $\bar{p}$ be? Why?

8. The control limits for a p-chart are based on the assumption that p is approximately normally distributed. If this is so, then the probability of a plotted value falling outside the control limits is roughly .0026. Based on Table 7.8, if we expect the proportion nonconforming to be about .10 for a process, what size sample per subgroup must we take to ensure normality?

9. *Thought question:* If the computed LCL for a p-chart is less than zero, what should the operator use for the lower control limit in his chart?

10. Here are some processes. Suggest a key *attribute, or qualitative* (yes/no) indicator of process success for each.
  a. Flying between Dallas and Salt Lake City
  b. Registering for a course
  c. Mailing a package using an overnight express service
  d. Cleaning a hotel room by 3:00 P.M.

15.5 ≡ Tools for Controlling and Improving Quality

Companywide quality programs have two goals: (1) to control present manufactured quality and (2) to improve manufactured and design quality. Control charts for attributes and variables help with the first mission. They warn when a process is temporarily out of control and the operator must take corrective action. At that same time, management must continually seek to improve the manufacturing and service processes. Management does this by determining how to:

1. reduce the process variation, $s;$
2. increase the process mean, $\bar{x}$ (if an increased mean creates a superior product or service); and
3. reduce the proportion of nonconforming products or services.

Finally, improving design quality requires improving product performance, durability, or serviceability. Departments must seek out and respond to the concerns of their internal or external customers.

In this section we use our problem-solving model from Chapter 1 to illustrate how seven important problem-solving tools can help to control and improve quality. (Refer again to Figure 1.1 on page 2.)

In *problem sensing* we determine whether a process is out of control or is in need of improvement. We will show how control charts and Pareto charts aid in problem sensing. During *diagnosis and alternative generation* we clarify the problem or opportunity. Then we seek and evaluate possible root causes of the out-of-control process, or we determine the major obstacles to improving a process. Finally, we develop alternative solutions. We will show how Kepner–Tregoe problem analysis, frequency histograms, fishbone diagrams, and scatter diagrams aid in problem diagnosis and alternative generation. In *decision making and implementation* we select and implement an alternative action. Then we determine whether the action has reestablished process control or accomplished the desired improvement. We will show how experimental design can aid in the decision-making phase. By the end of this section you should be able to use and explain the following seven tools for controlling and improving quality:

Problem Sensing

1. Control charts
2. Pareto charts

Diagnosis and Alternative Generation

3. Kepner–Tregoe problem analysis
4. Frequency histograms (or stem-and-leaf displays)
5. Fishbone diagrams
6. Scatter diagrams

Decision Making and Implementation

7.   Experimental design and planned change studies

Among these, only the Pareto chart and fishbone diagram have not been presented elsewhere in the text.

Control Charts

Control charts are essential for monitoring and controlling the quality level. As long as $\bar{x}$, s, or p falls within its respective control limits, the process is under control. When a process goes out of control, workers should immediately determine the root causes and take corrective action.

Pareto Charts

Where should a firm concentrate its quality-improvement efforts? There may be hundreds of quality areas that need improvement. The Pareto chart helps sort out the "vital few" from the "trivial many." Named after an Italian economist, Pareto charts are among the most commonly used graphic techniques in quality-improvement programs. They organize problem-sensing data.

Pareto charts determine which quality problems occur most frequently, are most costly, or have the greatest impact on market share. We build a Pareto chart by (1) listing defect categories and (2) gathering data on the frequency of the different defects. The problem-solving team then selects the several most common or most expensive defects to correct or to improve first. Often, several defects account for over 80% of the problems. These are the vital few we must correct.

As an illustration of how to build a Pareto chart, consider the data for defects found during the manufacturing of heaters in Table 15.6. Figure 15.13 presents a **Pareto chart** of these results.

A basic Pareto chart shows the breakdown of problems by type and percentage. The horizontal axis displays problem type, and the vertical axis measures the percentage occurrence of each problem.

Table 15.6

Types of Defects in Manufacturing Heaters

Defect Category	Percent with Defects
Cratered paint	45%
Bent fan	36
Bad motor	10
Frayed wires	5
Loose hose	4
	100%

Cratered paint and bent fans are the major causes of nonconforming heaters. Together, they account for 81% of the defects. The next most common problem occurs only 10% of the time. Clearly, cratered paint and bent fans are the two vital areas that must be improved. It is not worthwhile at this point to spend time correcting loose hoses or frayed wires. They are not major defects.

The Pareto chart resembles the relative frequency histogram from Chapter 2. While they are similar, there is one major difference. In a relative frequency histogram, the horizontal axis displays values of a quantitative variable such as income, claims processed, days to complete a project, or group productivity. The horizontal axis for a Pareto chart displays problem type, a qualitative variable. The vertical axis for both graphical tools is percentage occurrence.

FIGURE 15.13   Pareto Chart

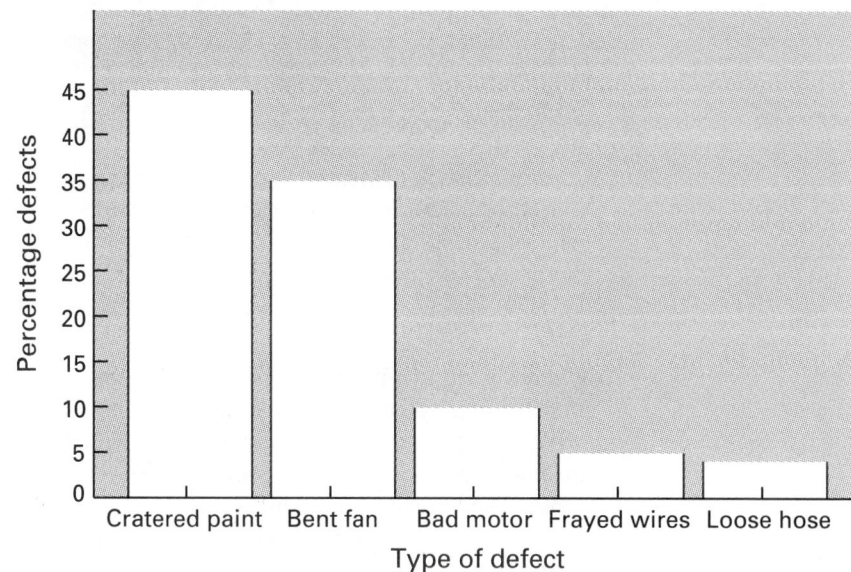

Table 15.7 presents after-sales warranty problems for COMCEL phones. The first two columns of Table 15.7 contain the data for a basic Pareto chart. Excessive static, volume fluctuation, and signal interference are the three most common warranty problems. The next most common problem happens only 3% of the time.

Should COMCEL focus its product redesign effort to eliminate these three problems? The answer is yes, but only if the firm's goal is to reduce the number of complaints.

Reducing excessive static, volume fluctuation, and signal interference may not help COMCEL reduce *annual warranty costs*. The third column of the table shows the costs of repairing the various warranty problems. Note that signal interference, limited channel usage, and total failures are the three most costly problems. While the latter two problems are rare (2% and 1% of the total), they are costly to correct.

Table 15.7

Types of Warranty Problems

Problem	Percent of All Problems	Annual Warranty Cost	Reason for Switching to Competitors
Excessive static	40%	$6,700	30%
Volume fluctuation	30	7,500	1
Signal interference	20	46,000	2
Broken handset	3	1,000	20
Limited channel usage	2	27,000	6
Surface blemishes	2	500	5
Total failures	1	15,500	35
Auto number recall failure	1	8,750	1
Sticky buttons	1	1,750	0
	100%		100%

Should COMCEL focus its product redesign efforts to eliminate these three problems? The answer is yes, but only if it wants to reduce the total warranty *costs*.

What types of problems cause COMCEL customers to switch to competitors' phones? Loss of customers will cause COMCEL to lose market share and profits. The fourth column shows the percentage of COMCEL customers who switched because of the nine problems. Note that excessive static, total failures, and broken handsets are the three major causes. Perhaps COMCEL should focus its product redesign effort in these three areas.

Basic (column 2) and dollar-based Pareto charts (columns 3 and 4) indicate which defects must be corrected. However, charts alone are useless unless we have clear goals (reduce complaints, minimize warranty cost, or minimize lost market share) and collect the required data.

Through control and Pareto charts we have identified areas to improve. Now we enter the diagnosis and alternative generation phase. We begin by specifying the problem clearly. The Kepner–Tregoe (1988) problem analysis method is particularly useful. Frequency histograms (or stem-and-leaf displays), fishbone diagrams, and scatter diagrams are also very useful in seeking and evaluating possible root causes.

Kepner–Tregoe Problem Analysis

We first discussed the Kepner–Tregoe (K–T) problem analysis method in Chapter 10. Through a series of specific questions, K–T transforms ambiguous symptoms, facts, and assumptions into a clear problem statement. It helps workers identify the root causes for a process that is temporarily out of control, or it helps workers and management to determine how to improve a process.

The general idea is that we must first define the problem before seeking its root causes. We define a problem by asking (and answering) four questions. We have illustrated these questions in the context of the cratered paint problem identified by the Pareto chart in Figure 15.13.

1. What is the deviation (versus what isn't it)?
    *   What exactly is *cratering?* Use more precise language to describe cratering. The term *cratering* is vague.

2. When did the deviation occur (versus when didn't it occur)?
    *   When (shift and day) did the cratering begin?

3. Where did the deviation occur (versus where didn't it occur)?
    *   Where is the cratering occurring on the heaters (on the top, bottom, or sides)?
    *   Where in the manufacturing process is the cratering occurring?
    *   Where is the cratering first noticed?
    *   Is the cratering occurring on heaters from all shifts?
    *   From all plants?

4. How much, how many, and to what extent did the deviation occur (versus to what extent didn't it occur)?
    *   Is the cratering problem increasing, decreasing, or remaining constant?
    *   Is cratering worse on the Monday and Friday shifts versus the other weekdays?
    *   How many paint craters are there on each heater?

Answering these questions will require additional data. In fact, a major value of the K–T method is that it identifies the data necessary to generate a clear problem statement. Having a clear problem statement increases the chance of identifying the causes of the paint cratering—the *why*.

The K–T method then aids in identifying the possible root causes. The problem solver looks for changes in equipment, processes, personnel, or suppliers that might explain the defined problem. For example, suppose the paint cratering happens on only one shift. What root cause might that suggest? Suppose the paint cratering happens only on the bottom of the heater. What root cause might that suggest?

In summary, the K–T method helps (1) define a problem and (2) determine its root causes. It involves answering four specific questions and then seeking changes that might explain the what, where, when, and the extent of the defined problem. The K–T method is one of the most commonly used diagnostic tools in industry today.

Frequency Histograms

Frequency histograms (or stem-and-leaf displays for small data sets) can help achieve process improvements. Consider the following example. Suppose that COMCEL's molding operation produces about 9% rejects. This is clearly unacceptable. The quality team undertakes a project to reduce process variation and thereby reduce the number of rejects. COMCEL is considering the following root causes areas.

People:	Improper supervision
Raw materials:	Too many plastics vendors of varying quality
Equipment:	Old or poorly maintained equipment. Too few controls on the present equipment
Methods:	Outdated manufacturing methods or too complex methods
Product design:	Too lenient design specification limits

Deming (1982) and Juran and Gryna (1980) suggest that about 85% of all quality problems can be corrected only by management. Note that all the above possible root causes are under management's control.

COMCEL suspects that raw material differences among its three plastics suppliers is the primary cause of the excessive process variation. The firm uses frequency histograms to compare plastic shatter strength for the last 260 lots of material from each of its three vendors.

Figure 15.14 shows that all three vendors' raw materials have roughly the same mean shatter strength, about 4,750 pounds per square inch. However, vendor B's raw material is the most consistent. Note the tightness of its frequency histogram. Since the excessive variation from vendors A and C may be causing the 9% reject rate, COMCEL should consider making vendor B its sole source. Alternatively, COMCEL can work with the two other vendors to help them reduce their shatter strength variation.

In general, first identify a quantitative success indicator of a process you wish to improve (reduce percent rejects). Second, brainstorm possible root cause factors that affect your process success measure (people, raw material, etc.). Third, select the most likely area for investigation (raw material). Fourth, draw appropriate histograms and answer one or more of the following questions:

1. Which process has the highest (or lowest) mean?
2. Which process has the smallest variation?
3. Which process is most bell-shaped?

Based on your answers, take corrective action to improve the process.

FIGURE 15.14   Shatter Strength of Plastic from Three Vendors

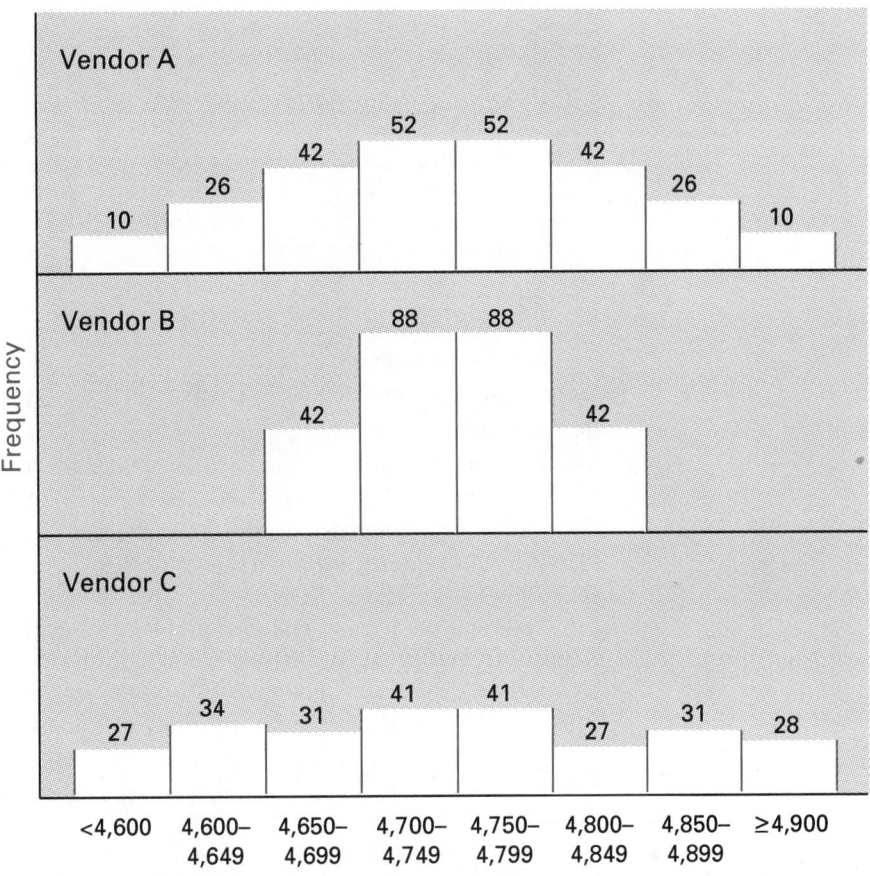

Fishbone Diagrams

Fishbone, or Ishikawa, diagrams are visual aids that help generate and evaluate the diagnosis of potential problem root causes or help in finding ways to make process or product improvements. We will illustrate how a fishbone diagram helped determine why the mean shatter strength at the COMCEL molding operation dropped below the LCL during shift 28 (see Figure 15.10).

A fishbone diagram begins with a goal box into which we write the goal of our investigation—in this case, to determine the reason why $\bar{x}$ was below the LCL on shift 28. Next, the quality team generates three or four potential major cause areas. These are shown as the "large bones" in the diagram in Figure 15.15. Good sources for major cause areas are the four M's: *methods, manpower, materials, and machines*. Alternatively, the group may generate its own list. Starting with each major bone, the group brainstorms two to six possible specific causes, or "small bones." Then it ranks the specific causes and investigates the most promising ones.

A brainstorming session produced the fishbone diagram in Figure 15.15. The quality team thought that either a new molding supervisor or a new plastics vendor was the most likely cause. Together with the purchasing and engineering depart-

FIGURE 15.15   Fishbone Diagram

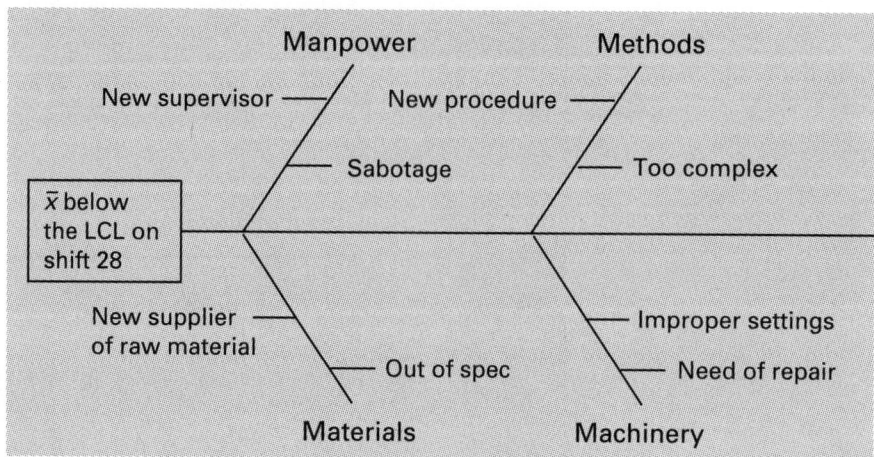

ments, they determined that the cause was the new vendor. When COMCEL returned to its previous supplier, the mean shatter strength rose to within the control limits (see shift 29 in Figure 15.10).

Returning to the paint-cratering problem, the quality improvement team used the Kepner–Tregoe problem analysis method to develop a clear problem statement. Assume that the goal box in Figure 15.16 is the result of this K–T analysis. The team generated five major cause areas—the four M's and a specification category. Then it

FIGURE 15.16   Fishbone Diagram for Cratered Paint Problem

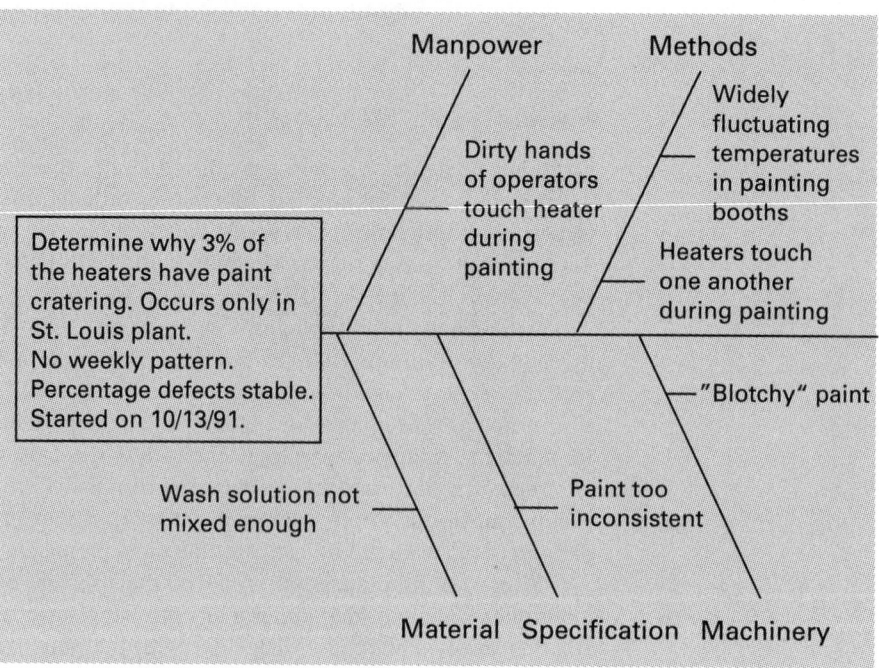

brainstormed possible specific causes within each of the five categories. The team believed that cratering was due to either (1) the heaters touching one another during painting or (2) wide daily temperature fluctuations in the painting booths. The team evaluated and rejected the touching hypothesis. **Fishbone diagrams** help quality teams focus on the problem, actively search for causes, suggest required data, and maintain and improve quality. Best of all, they are easily learned. However, do not develop fishbone diagrams until you have a clear understanding of the problem. Determining the root causes of a poorly defined problem is difficult.

A fishbone diagram is a visual aid that helps identify major problem cause areas or product improvement areas. Using brainstorming, specific causes or ways to improve the process or product are generated and then evaluated.

Scatter Diagrams

We encountered scatter diagrams in Chapter 3 and more recently in Chapter 11. Recall that they are useful in showing possible relationships between two quantitative variables. Place one variable on the vertical axis and the other variable on the horizontal axis. A data point is an (x, y) value.

Returning to the paint-cratering problem, the quality team next decided to use scatter diagrams in evaluating the temperature hypothesis. They recorded the daily mean temperature in the painting booth and the percentage of cratered heaters over each of 10 consecutive days. They then developed the accompanying scatter diagram.

Figure 15.17 clearly indicates that as the temperature drops below 68°F, the percentage of cratering increases. To eliminate cratering, the firm needs to keep temperature above 68°F in the painting booth.

Having determined the root causes of a problem, we then must select a corrective action and monitor its impact. Sometimes, as in the paint cratering problem, the best action is obvious. Increase the booth temperature. Other times, firms must use formal experiments to choose the best action to implement.

Experimental Design

Sometimes we must run formal experiments in order to improve processes or products. After testing a change, we study the results. What did we learn? If the planned

FIGURE 15.17   Scatter Diagram of Daily Mean Temperature and Percentage of Cratered Heaters

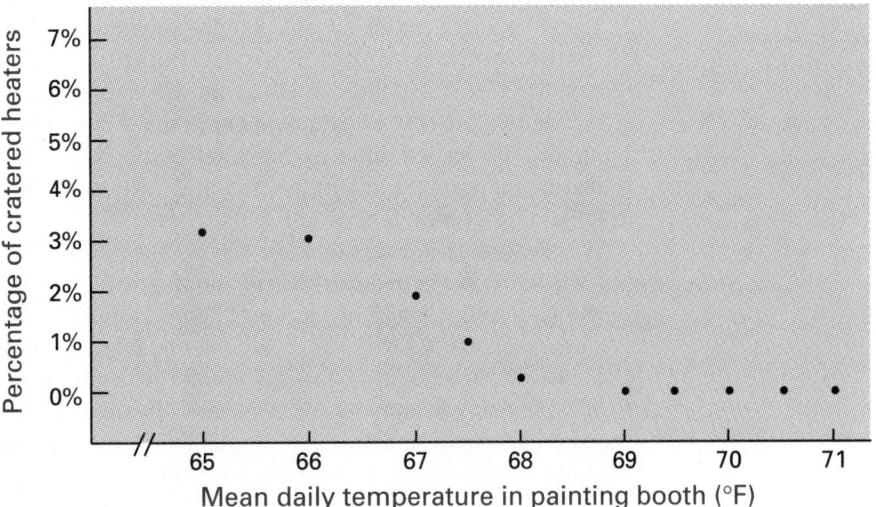

Table 15.8

Data for a One-Factor, Two-Level Experiment

	Original Vendor	New Vendor
	4,760	4,690
	4,800	4,650
	4,725	4,710
	4,775	4,730
	4,770	4,690
	4,700	4,630
	4,790	4,700
	4,750	4,660
	4,750	4,710
	4,760	4,680
$\bar{x}$	4,758 ppsi	4,685 ppsi
s	29.46 ppsi	30.64 ppsi

change was successful, we should implement it permanently. We first discussed how to conduct formal studies in Chapter 6 and more recently in Chapter 10.

We will illustrate how COMCEL used experimental design to determine that a new raw material supplier was the cause of the mean shatter strength dropping below the LCL on shift 28 (see Figure 15.10). The experiment also confirmed that COMCEL could solve the problem by returning to the original supplier.

COMCEL conducted a one-factor, two-level, experiment and set $\alpha = .01$. The factor was the raw material supplier. The original and new vendors were the two levels in the study. Both suppliers' manufacturing processes were under statistical control, and the material used in the study was representative of current production. COMCEL produced 10 phones each with raw material from the two suppliers. The firm then tested the shatter strength of the 20 phones. Table 15.8 contains the data for the formal study.

The variance ratio of 29.50 in Table 15.9 indicates that there is a significant difference between the two suppliers' raw materials ($p < .01$). The mean shatter strength for the new vendor's material, 4,685 ppsi, is below the LCL of 4,724 ppsi. The mean shatter strength for the original vendor's material, 4,758 ppsi, is in the middle of the control chart limits. COMCEL should return to its original supplier or require the new supplier to increase the shatter strength of its plastics.

Finally, COMCEL should monitor the corrective action to determine whether it has had the desired impacts. For example, the control chart in Figure 15.10 indicates that by returning to its original supplier, COMCEL did reestablish control over the molding process.

In summary, firms that use a systematic problem-solving model and the seven tools we've presented can control and improve both process and product. Managers can and do use many of the seven tools in more than one problem-solving phase. These tools reduce the chance that poor quality products will "make it out the door." However, no amount of process control and improvement can assure zero defects because many manufacturing companies purchase as much value in the form of raw material or subassemblies as they add in their own manufacturing. Thus, ensuring the quality of purchased items is crucial. In the next section we discuss several strategies for ensuring high quality of purchased items.

Table 15.9

ANOVA Table for Raw Material Study

Sources of Variation	Sum of Squares	df	MS	Variance Ratio	F-value Critical
Between	26,645	1	26,645	29.50	8.29
Within	16,260	18	903.33		
Total	42,905	19			

SECTION 15.5 EXERCISES

1. The Department of Decision Sciences gives a common final examination in basic statistics. Over the last 10 quarters the mean grade has been 75. This past quarter the mean grade was below 60, over three standard deviations below the historical mean. Draw a fishbone diagram to help identify possible root causes. Use the following major bones—final exam, students, and teachers—to brainstorm two possible subcauses for each major bone.

2. Refer to Table 15.7. Draw a Pareto chart for annual warranty cost and a Pareto chart for reasons for switching to competitors. Include only the top six causes for each chart.

3. Suppose you notice that your portable CD player sometimes does not work properly. Develop a list of questions that you should ask to develop a clear problem understanding. Use the Kepner–Tregoe problem analysis method to frame your questions.

4. A department store wishes to develop a Pareto chart on reasons for returning clothing. Develop five possible reasons that might account for returning clothing.

5. Refer to Exercise 3. Would asking why the portable CD player does not work be appropriate to developing a clear problem statement?

6. Why is a fishbone diagram ineffective unless we have a clear statement of the problem?

15.6 ▨ Vendor Certification and Acceptance Sampling

Given that purchased materials can run as high as 90% of manufactured cost, firms must establish effective supplier quality control systems. For many years, firms relied solely on incoming inspection. Inspectors tested samples from incoming lots and either accepted or rejected the lots. Firms are now relying less on incoming inspection for two reasons. First, incoming inspection cannot completely stop nonconforming raw materials or subassemblies from entering a plant. Second, the goal of effective supplier quality control is to obtain good parts, not merely to stop nonconforming parts. The strategy of finding and working with high-quality vendors is replacing, or at least complementing, incoming inspection. Perhaps in the near future, incoming inspection will become obsolete. By the end of this section you should be able to:

1. distinguish acceptance sampling from other inspection methods;
2. explain and demonstrate why an acceptance sampling plan cannot stop all nonconforming raw material or subassembly pieces from entering a firm; and
3. understand strategies to implement and maintain a vendor certification program.

Acceptance Sampling Basics

The degree to which a firm uses incoming inspection depends on the past quality performance history of its vendors, the importance of the part, and its intended use. There are several levels of incoming inspection.

No inspection.   Firms accept all incoming lots without inspecting them. A "no-inspection" policy is becoming the norm, but only with high-quality vendors. In lieu of testing, firms develop programs to certify high-quality vendors and work with them to improve their processes. We will cover more on this later.

100% inspection.   Firms inspect every piece of every lot they receive. However, this is costly and time-consuming. It is also impractical when testing destroys the product. A firm may have hundreds of vendors supplying thousands of parts. Furthermore, 100% inspection is not 100% effective at finding nonconforming parts. Fatigue and stress can cause inspectors to make mistakes. Despite these drawbacks, some purchasers still use 100% inspection. The National Aeronautics and Space Administration (NASA) relies on 100% inspection of incoming parts, since a nonconforming part can cause a shuttle disaster.

Acceptance sampling.   Acceptance sampling is a process that evaluates a portion of each incoming lot and, based on the test results, accepts or rejects the entire lot. Acceptance sampling is still used because of its low cost, although Deming and others argue that quality comes not from inspection but from process improvement.

There are several types of acceptance sampling plans. *Single-sampling plans* require inspectors to take one sample of size *n* from each incoming lot. Based on the test results, the firm accepts or rejects the lot. Vendors must then replace rejected lots. *Double-sampling plans* require that inspectors draw two samples, if needed, before making a yes/no decision. *Multiple-sampling plans* allow inspectors to select more than two samples if needed to make a decision.

Table 15.10

Some MIL-STD-105D Single-Sampling Plans for Normal Inspection*

| | | Acceptable Quality Levels | | | | | |
| | | 1.0% | | 2.5% | | 6.5% | |
Lot Size	Sample Size	Accept	Reject	Accept	Reject	Accept	Reject
51 to 90	13	0	1	1	2	2	3
91 to 150	20	0	1	1	2	3	4
151 to 280	32	1	2	2	3	5	6
281 to 500	50	1	2	3	4	7	8
501 to 1,200	80	2	3	5	6	10	11
1,201 to 3,200	125	3	4	7	8	14	15
3,201 to 10,000	200	5	6	10	11	21	22

*Taken from the master table, Table 11-A of MIL-STD-105D.

American firms use what is called MIL-STD-105D sampling plans. Table 15.10 illustrates some MIL-STD-105D single-sampling plans.

The acceptable quality level (AQL) is the maximum percent of incoming nonconforming pieces that a receiving firm will tolerate. Of course, receiving firms prefer lots with 0% nonconforming, but vendors argue that it is not possible. They say that the receiving firm should be satisfied if the maximum percentage of nonconforming is 1% or 2.5%. Vendors and receiving firms *negotiate* the AQLs.

Suppose that a receiving firm and its vendor have agreed to a 1% AQL. Further suppose that the vendor ships lots of 2,000 parts each. Using Table 15.10, the receiving firm will select a random sample of $n = 125$ pieces from each lot to inspect. If the receiving firm finds three or fewer nonconforming in the sample of 125, it accepts the lot. If it finds four or more nonconforming, it rejects the lot. This set of acceptance and rejection rules constitutes one MIL-STD-105D sampling plan. Each of the other 20 sets of acceptance and rejection rules in Table 15.10 constitutes a different MIL-STD-105D sampling plan.

Even low-AQL sampling plans will allow nonconforming pieces to enter a plant. Every nonconforming item that a firm receives from a vendor may cause serious problems. It makes no difference if a nonconforming piece comes from a lot that is .1% nonconforming or 1% nonconforming. Defects are defects! Acceptance sampling plans cannot keep all nonconforming pieces from entering a firm. We will illustrate this idea next.

The Inability of Acceptance Sampling to Completely Eliminate Nonconforming Pieces

Suppose that a firm using a 1% AQL sampling plan receives 100 lots of 2,000 parts each. The receiving firm takes a random sample of $n = 125$ pieces from each lot. The firm accepts the lot if it finds three or fewer nonconforming parts. How effective will acceptance sampling be in stopping nonconforming pieces from entering the firm? Assume that all lots contain exactly 1.0% nonconforming pieces, the negotiated AQL.

Incoming inspectors will randomly select and test 125 pieces from each lot, or 12,500 pieces in total [(125)(100 lots)]. Of the 12,500 pieces we expect to find 125 nonconforming pieces, or 1.0%. Moreover, we expect to accept about 96% of the incoming lots. Why? Because the Poisson distribution (see Chapter 5) tells us that for lots with a 1% (.01) nonconforming rate, inspectors will find three or fewer nonconforming pieces in the random sample of 125 pieces about 96% of the time. The .96 figure is based on the following Poisson probability:

$$P(D = d \text{ when } \lambda = np) \qquad (15.15)$$

where d = the number of nonconforming pieces that can be found and still accept the lot according to Table 15.10. That depends on the lot size and AQL.
n = the sample size from Table 15.10
p = the actual proportion nonconforming in the lot

For a lot size of 2,000 and an AQL of 1% (.01), expression (15.15) is

$$P(D \le 3 \text{ when } \lambda = 125(.01) = 1.25) = .96$$

Based on the Poisson distribution, about 96% of the lots will be accepted and 4% of the lots will be rejected. That is, samples from 96 lots will have three or fewer nonconforming pieces. Samples from 4 lots will have four or more nonconforming pieces. Consider the 100 lots in Table 15.11.

Given these data, how many nonconforming parts will enter the receiving firm? We have shown the calculations below:

Table 15.11

100 Hypothetical Lots of 2,000 Parts Each Containing 1% Nonconforming Pieces

Lot	Sample Size	Number of Nonconforming Pieces	Action
1	125	3	Accept
2	125	2	Accept
3	125	1	Accept
4	125	1	Accept
⋮	⋮	⋮	⋮
90	125	0	Accept
91	125	2	Accept
92	125	3	Accept
93	125	2	Accept
94	125	3	Accept
95	125	1	Accept
96	125	0	Accept
		106	
97	125	6	Reject
98	125	4	Reject
99	125	4	Reject
100	125	5	Reject
		125	

106 nonconforming parts found in lots 1–96
19 nonconforming parts found in lots 97–100

Number of accepted lots	96
Number of nonconforming pieces in accepted lots	$(96)(2{,}000 \text{ parts})(.01) = 1{,}920$
Number of nonconforming pieces found in accepted lots	106
Total number of nonconforming pieces entering plant	$1{,}920 - 106 = 1{,}814$

The 96 accepted lots contain 1% nonconforming parts. That accounts for 1,920 nonconforming parts. Inspectors found 106 nonconforming parts in the 96 lots they ultimately accepted. Therefore, 1,814 nonconforming parts got past incoming inspection. Had the firm accepted all 100 lots without testing, then $(100)(2{,}000)(.01) = 2{,}000$ nonconforming parts would have entered the firm. Thus, acceptance sampling kept *only* 186 nonconforming parts from entering the plant.

Acceptance sampling is not very effective at stopping nonconforming pieces from entering a plant when incoming lots consistently have a percentage of nonconforming parts at or near the AQL. Then why use acceptance sampling at all? Acceptance sampling plans are quite effective in rejecting lots with very high percentage of nonconforming parts. For example, suppose a lot actually contains 10% (.10) nonconforming parts. According to the Poisson distribution, the probability of finding three or fewer nonconforming parts in a random sample of $n = 125$ is only about .002. Thus few, if any, lots with 10% nonconforming parts will ever be accepted.

$$P(D \le 3 \text{ when } \lambda = (125)(.1) = 12.5) = .002$$

Even if incoming inspection were successful in stopping nonconforming parts, it does not ensure a continuous supply of good parts. Vendor certification programs can.

Vendor Certification

Most manufacturing companies buy as much value (raw material or subassemblies) as they add in manufacturing. The only way to ensure good quality of purchased items is to have good suppliers. *A company that wants to receive good parts and materials must buy from reputable suppliers.* Firms should not select vendors solely on the basis of cost. They must choose vendors who are competitive and who can provide evidence that they are using statistical process control principles in manufacturing their parts. If suppliers use statistical process control, there is generally less need to do incoming inspection.

Vendor certification programs identify and rank reputable vendors and seek long-term cooperative, nonadversarial, relationships. In his book, *The Chain of Quality* (1986), J. M. Groocock, a practicing quality professional at the TRW organization, discusses how to make vendor certification programs work. His suggestions include developing quality-of-purchased-items policy statements and joint vendor/firm quality-improvement activities.

Here are a few statements taken from TRW's quality-of-purchased-items policy:

1. The primary objective is progressively to reduce the proportion of purchased items that are nonconforming.
2. The division will purchase only from approved suppliers.
3. The division will establish a relationship of cooperation with its approved suppliers, with the purpose of helping them supply products conforming to the defined requirements.

Firms rank vendors through vendor surveys. Those vendors that score high are certified. Surveys generally include the following items:

1. Does the vendor have written statistical process control procedures?
2. How does the vendor handle its suppliers?
3. Is the vendor's information system for quality data adequate and used?
4. Are quality-control personnel competent and aggressive?
5. Is top management committed to the quality effort?
6. How do the vendor's engineering and quality-control personnel keep abreast of the customer's quality requirements?

The customer and vendor must have a successful "marriage." Suppliers must be viewed as team members, not adversaries. Quality will result when the receiving firm and vendor establish a sound and mutually profitable long-term relationship. Here are some ideas offered by Kenneth Kivenko, a quality professional (1984):

1. Explain the needed quality standards clearly to the vendor.
2. Get to know key vendor personnel. Build relationships.
3. Provide engineering support to vendors when they are having problems meeting your quality standards for incoming parts.
4. Hold "vendor days" at your plant. Show vendors how their products are used in your manufacturing process.

Acceptance sampling and vendor certification programs are useful. Acceptance sampling stops lots with a high percentage of nonconforming parts from entering the plant, but it will not improve the overall quality of incoming lots. Only a reputable vendor who will work with your company can do that. Vendor certification programs have greater success in ensuring a continuous stream of good parts and raw materials than do acceptance sampling plans.

SECTION 15.6 EXERCISES

1. A firm receives shipments of electronic components in lots of 1,000 units. The negotiated AQL is 1%.
    a. What size sample should the firm take at incoming inspection?
    b. Describe the acceptance and rejection rules using the sampling plan.
    c. The firm finds eight nonconforming components in a random sample of 80. What action should it take?

2. A firm receives shipments of subassemblies in lots of 7,500 units. The negotiated AQL is 6.5%.
    a. What size sample should the firm take at incoming inspection?
    b. Describe the acceptance and rejection rules using the sampling plan.
    c. The firm finds 18 nonconforming parts in a random sample of 200. What action should it take?

3. Dr. Deming noted in his 1986 book, *Out of the Crisis,* that "incredibly, courses and books in statistical methods still devote time and pages to acceptance sampling." What does he mean by that statement?

4. We made the statement that acceptance sampling is useful in stopping shipments with a very high percentage of nonconforming parts from entering a plant. Assume that 100 lots of size 1,000 are shipped to a plant. Assume that each lot contains 10% nonconforming parts. The negotiated AQL is 1%. Why would a very large percentage of these lots be rejected at incoming inspection?

5. Describe the major difference between vendor certification programs and acceptance sampling plans to control incoming quality of parts and subassemblies.

6. *Comment on the following statement:* Select the low-cost vendor for subassemblies even if it does not use statistical process control principles in its manufacturing.

15.7 General Principles

Our basic premise is that a high-quality product is a customer's right. For this to be more than a slogan, firms should adopt the philosophy that quality is more than just $\bar{x}$-, s-, p-charts, or vendor certification programs. It is more than techniques—Pareto charts, fishbone diagrams, and the like. It is an attitude. Quality occurs when workers and management commit themselves to controlling and improving quality. A commitment to quality should not be this month's pet project, but an ongoing and constant commitment.

We conclude the book with a set of principles to improve quality based on Deming's writings.

General Principles of Quality

PRINCIPLE 1:   Management should make workers feel secure in controlling and improving quality. Management should encourage workers to ask questions when they do not understand some aspect of operations and to report out-of-control processes, even if it means delaying schedules. Management should encourage workers to actively seek process improvements, rather than being passive operators.

PRINCIPLE 2:   Avoid purchasing from lowest-bid vendors, unless they are high-quality suppliers. Low cost may mean low-quality inputs, which will cause quality problems.

PRINCIPLE 3:   Institute quality circles or teams at all levels of the firm and train them. Quality circles are groups of 5 to 10 workers who periodically meet to control and improve quality. The leader may be a middle manager, foreman, or an hourly employee. Using the seven problem-solving techniques discussed in this chapter, quality circles can achieve significant results in quality improvement, cost reduction, productivity, and safety.

PRINCIPLE 4:   Instill pride of workmanship. Years ago, workers were craftsmen. Since automation, workers have taken less responsibility for their work. That must change. Managers and workers must regain pride of workmanship and service.

General Principles of Statistical Process Control

PRINCIPLE 5:   Variability is a fact of life. No two purchased items entering a plant are the same. No two finished products leaving a plant are the same. There are item-to-item, day-to-day, and week-to-week variations. Strive to minimize variation.

PRINCIPLE 6:   Use control charts to identify out-of-control processes.

PRINCIPLE 7:   Take quick and effective problem-solving action for an out-of-control process. Use the seven problem-solving tools to help identify root causes.

PRINCIPLE 8:   Strive to improve the product and the process. Use the seven problem-solving tools to help determine how.

PRINCIPLE 9:   Use vendor certification and acceptance sampling programs to improve the quality of purchased items or raw material.

A Final Thought

The Information Age is here. Each day, business professionals are swamped by data. Moreover, their day is highly fragmented. They have only a few minutes to review and digest the data before their next meeting or interruption. They can learn to do quick and simple analyses and to develop *mental models* on the state of their department or firm. Mental models suggest opportunities or emerging problems. These models need not be complex or mathematical. Rather, they can be simple, verbal, or visual.

Throughout this book we have intertwined quantitative statistical tools with qualitative problem-solving concepts. We believe that this unique combination can improve developing mental models. And better mental models make for better problem solvers, decision makers, and business professionals.

COMCEL

Date: September 17, 1995
To: Ann Tabor, CEO
From: Sang Kim, Quality-Assurance Manager
Re: Process Capability Study Results

SUMMARY

The process capability index, C_p, is 1.78. This is excellent and easily achieves our shatter strength durability goal. I recommend we implement the new molding process at once.

SUPPORTING ANALYSIS

Using systematic sampling, we selected five handsets from each of 15 consecutive shifts and determined the shift means and shift standard deviations. We then determined the overall shift mean and average standard deviation. These were 4,762 ppsi and 26.40 ppsi, respectively. The $\bar{x}$ of 4,762 ppsi is close to the target value of 4,750 ppsi, and therefore the process was centered. The process standard deviation was 26.40/.9400, or 28.09 ppsi.

The natural tolerance of the molding process is 6(28.09 ppsi) = 168.54 ppsi. The natural tolerance tells us that 99.74% of the individual handsets will have a shatter strength within 168.54/2 = 84.27 ppsi of the mean of 4,762 ppsi.

The process capability index (C_p) is the ratio of the width of the design specification limits (what the customers want) to the natural tolerance of the process (what the process can produce 99.74% of the time). The C_p for the molding process is

(4,900 – 4,600)/(6 · 28.09) or 1.78.

The width of the design specification limits is 1.78 times as large as the natural tolerance of the process. This guarantees that we will produce less than two nonconforming handset moldings per 100,000 phones.

CHAPTER 15 QUESTIONS

1. Distinguish between design and manufactured quality.

2. Should (or can) ensuring manufactured quality be the responsibility only of a quality-control department?

3. A Ford Company ad says that "Quality is job #1." What do you think that means?

4. What is the purpose of *process control* studies?

5. What is the problem with an increasing standard deviation in a process control study?

6. How does a *process capability* study differ from a *process control* study?

7. What information does the process capability index, C_p, provide?

8. A process with a C_p of 2.0 can still have two problems. Explain.

9. What remedies would you suggest for a process with a C_p of .5?

10. Distinguish the purpose of control charting versus process control studies and process capability studies.

11. If a data point ($\bar{x}$ or s) falls above or below the 3-sigma limit, is it possible that there is no problem? How often will this happen? What assumption must be true?

12. What problem might you have if you use a fishbone diagram without first clearly defining the problem?

13. How do basic Pareto charts differ from relative frequency histograms?

14. What advantage do dollar-based Pareto charts have over basic Pareto charts?

15. Why doesn't 100% incoming inspection of raw material and subassemblies stop all non-conforming parts from entering a plant?

16. What is the negotiated AQL and what does it mean?

17. What role does the Poisson distribution play in understanding sampling plans?

18. Can MIL-STD-105D sampling plans stop all nonconforming parts from entering a plant?

19. Acceptance sampling cannot stop nonconforming parts from entering a plant. Of what use, if any, is acceptance sampling?

20. Why are vendor certification programs and joint supplier/customer efforts needed to improve incoming quality?

CHAPTER 15 APPLICATION PROBLEMS

1. A firm produces car batteries. Each shift, inspectors use systematic sampling to select five batteries. They determine how long an engine will crank (in seconds) at 30° before needing to be recharged. The firm has set a lower specification limit of 85 seconds and an upper specification limit of 115 seconds. Shown are the process control and capability data based on the first 10 production shifts.

			Observation		
Shift	1	2	3	4	5
1	101	104	100	103	101
2	102	102	105	101	100
3	100	100	103	104	100
4	100	103	102	101	104
5	103	101	102	104	103
6	104	102	100	103	105
7	104	103	103	102	100
8	102	102	101	104	100
9	105	104	103	102	102
10	105	103	101	103	102

a. Are the process mean and standard deviation under control?

b. Compute $\bar{s}$. Is C_p greater than 1.33?

c. Compute $\bar{\bar{x}}$ and set up the LCL and UCL for the mean cranking time.

d. Set up the LCL and UCL for the standard deviation in cranking time.

2. Given are the cranking time data for the next 15 shifts for the battery manufacturer in the previous problem.

	Observation				
Shift	1	2	3	4	5
11	105	105	104	100	102
12	105	104	105	101	101
13	104	104	100	103	103
14	104	101	104	103	101
15	102	101	103	103	105
16	102	103	102	104	102
17	102	101	105	104	102
18	115	113	112	113	111
19	103	104	103	103	101
20	102	104	105	103	103
21	103	100	101	103	104
22	102	103	101	103	101
23	102	100	104	108	101
24	102	104	103	101	101
25	100	102	102	101	101

a. Is the process ever out of control according to the $\bar{x}$- and s-charts for the next 15 shifts?
b. If either statistic was out of control, was the firm able to correct the problem(s)? Explain.
c. Had you been the line manager, how would you have sought the root causes of the out-of-control production process?

3. Journal adjustments are made at the monthly closing only when there have been incorrect entries posted in the journal accounts. Shown are the number of adjusting entries made for the first 10 monthly closings for four major accounts. Each account has over 20,000 postings each month.

	Account			
Month	1	2	3	4
January	100	98	102	94
February	96	95	104	100
March	102	104	103	98
April	90	100	100	98
May	103	100	100	93
June	100	95	100	101
July	104	103	100	97
August	101	99	104	102
September	104	100	103	99
October	93	97	103	102

a. Is the journal adjustment process stable in the mean and standard deviation? Explain your reasoning.
b. If so, set up control limits for the mean and standard deviation.

4. Given are the number of adjusting entries for the four journal accounts for the next ten months.

	Account			
Month	1	2	3	4
November	96	95	103	96
December	100	96	105	99
January	102	101	100	105
February	101	95	102	104
March	110	85	103	91
April	104	97	101	102
May	99	99	98	99
June	102	104	102	99
July	95	102	96	104
August	98	96	98	96

a. Is the process ever out of control according to the $\bar{x}$- or s-charts?
b. Even if the process were under control, should the firm be satisfied with the number of adjusting entries needed each month?

5. A library at a major university employs 10 research librarians to help researchers locate articles and books. For the past 3 months the 10 librarians have kept records on the number of search requests per day. $\bar{x}$ is 18 requests per librarian per day. $\bar{s}$ is 4.
a. Determine the upper and lower control limits for the $\bar{x}$-chart ($n = 10$).
b. Using the Shewhart 3-sigma rule, was the process ever out of control in the mean number of requests per day over the next 10 days?

Day	Mean Number of Requests per Librarian
1	18.2
2	20.0
3	17.3
4	15.9
5	18.0
6	19.4
7	15.0
8	15.1
9	19.1
10	17.9

6. A firm produces wooden handles for umbrellas. The standard reads: *The handles shall be free of blemishes or rough spots.* Each shift, the inspector randomly selects $n = 500$ handles and inspects them for blemishes and rough spots. Shown are the data for the first 10 shifts.

Shift	Sample Size	Number of Nonconforming Handles
1	500	3
2	500	4
3	500	2
4	500	5
5	500	3
6	500	4
7	500	2
8	500	5
9	500	3
10	500	5

a. Determine the sample proportion nonconforming for the first 10 shifts. Is the manufacturing process in control?
b. Compute $\bar{p}$ for the first 10 shifts. Determine the LCL and UCL.

7. Shown are the numbers of nonconforming umbrella handles (see Problem 6) for the next 15 shifts — 11–25.

Shift	Sample Size	Number of Nonconforming Handles
11	500	3
12	500	4
13	500	3
14	500	2
15	500	3
16	500	4
17	500	10
18	500	11
19	500	10
20	500	4
21	500	3
22	500	5
23	500	2
24	500	3
25	500	2

a. Is the process ever out of control for the next 15 shifts?

b. If it was, was the firm able to correct the problem immediately? Explain.

8. Shown are data on the amount of time (in minutes) needed for a pill to enter or diffuse into the bloodstream. Each hour, an inspector randomly selects four pills and runs diffusion tests.

Hour	Observation 1	2	3	4
1	2.00	1.98	2.02	1.98
2	2.02	1.98	2.02	2.00
3	2.00	1.97	2.02	1.97
4	2.00	1.98	2.03	2.00
5	2.00	1.98	2.02	1.96
6	2.00	1.98	2.02	2.00
7	2.03	1.98	2.02	2.00
8	2.00	1.98	2.02	2.00
9	2.35	2.33	2.35	2.31
10	2.37	2.33	2.36	2.33
11	2.33	2.30	2.34	2.33
12	2.35	2.30	2.35	2.31
13	2.32	2.32	2.35	2.31
14	2.38	2.34	2.33	2.35
15	2.33	2.30	2.35	2.31

Are the mean and standard deviation of the process under control? Explain.

9. For the following problem, use the Kepner–Tregoe method to develop the *what, where, when,* and *extent* questions:

Electrodoor manufactures a line of garage door openers. Each of its three products is electronically triggered by a tiny transmitter in the car. The openers lower the garage door if it is raised and raise it if it is lowered. All three openers have a very short range so that one opener cannot open other garage doors on the same block. With the exception of the weight of the door that it will open, the three products in the line are identical.

Electrodoor introduced its line in the San Francisco area in April 1991. Until that time, it had sold its products exclusively in Arizona and New Mexico. At first, sales in the San Francisco area exceeded expectations. However, in September, complaints began to roll in. One customer complained that without touching the transmitter, his garage door opened. Another complained that the door came down in the middle of the car as she was backing out of her garage and almost took off her head. These were not isolated complaints. In the last quarter of 1991, over 40% of the door openers in the San Francisco area had exhibited the same problem. Only customers who lived in a wedge between the ocean and the bay were complaining. It appeared that the area of complaints was wider at the ocean end and narrower at the bay end. (Based on a case in *The Rational Manager,* by Kepner and Tregoe, McGraw-Hill, 1965.)

 10. Assume that each lot of size 75 entering a plant contains exactly 1% nonconforming parts. The firm uses a MIL-STD-105D plan with an AQL of 1%. Thus it takes a simple random sample of 13 and accepts the lot if it finds no nonconforming parts in the sample. Use the Poisson probability distribution from Chapter 5 to determine the probability of accepting lots that actually have 1% nonconforming parts. Interpret your results. *Hint:* Compute the following probability:

$$P[D = 0 \text{ nonconforming parts when } \lambda = (13)(.01) = .13]$$

 11. For the following problem, use the Kepner–Tregoe method to develop the *what, where, when,* and *extent* questions.

A plant makes two types of quarter panels for cars. Metal sheets are first cut into identical-size blanks and stacked 40 to a pallet. The pallets are then delivered to the stamping operation. Here stamping presses shape the blanks into hood panels. There is always a supply of blanks at 8 A.M., the beginning of the day shift, for the operators of the four stamping presses. The stamping operators use the starter supply while they wait for the morning shift to produce more blanks. The shallow draw (SD) and deep draw (DD) panels differ in only one respect—the depth of draw, or curvature of the quarter panels, after the stamping operation.

Lines 1 and 2 stamp 80 DD panels per hour. Line 4 stamps 50 DD panels per hour, and line 3 stamps 80 SD panels per hour. All except line 2 have four pallets of blanks at the beginning of the morning shift. Line 2 workers have complained that with only two stacks, they sometimes have to stop and wait for the morning shift to produce more blanks for stamping. They have demanded equal treatment with the other lines.

On Wednesday at 11:00 A.M., the plant manager calls an emergency meeting. This morning at about 9:30 A.M., the stamping press on line 2 started producing nearly 12% rejects. After the morning break at 10 A.M., the stamping press on line 1 also started producing about 12% rejects. The problem is excessive burrs and other rough spots. The normal rate is under 2%. The manager reports that engineering has not found anything wrong with the four presses.

Several supervisors argue that sabotage may be the problem. Everyone agrees that the workers could cause excessive burrs by mispositioning a blank in the press. Moreover, the supervisor on line 2 had sent a worker home for allegedly drinking on the job the day before. When he returned this morning the supervisor again confronted him and demanded an apology. For 30 minutes they argued while the workers on line 2 watched from the sidelines. Finally the supervisor sent the worker home again. The union has threatened to file a grievance. During the meeting the group learns that at 11:20 A.M. the stamping press on line 4 also started producing about 12% rejects. Only line 3, which is run by the most respected supervisor, is not yet experiencing any excessive rejects. (Based on the case entitled "Can You Analyze This Problem?" by P. Stryker in the *Harvard Business Review,* May–June 1965, 73–78.)

 12. Given an AQL of 1% (.01) and a lot size of 75, what percent of the lots will be accepted at incoming inspection if all lots actually have 1% defective? Given an AQL of 2.5% (.025) and a lot size of 75, what percent of the lots will be accepted at incoming inspection if all lots actually have 2.5% defective? Given an AQL of 6.5% (.065) and a lot size of 75, what percent of the lots will be accepted at incoming inspection if all lots actually have 6.5% defective? *Hint:* Use expression (15.15) to determine the desired Poisson probabilities.

13. The accompanying information (from which two Pareto charts could be constructed) illustrates the types of errors in typed documents in a major law firm. The Before column reflects the breakdown of errors before the firm began a quality improvement effort. The After column reflects the breakdown of errors after the quality-improvement effort.

	Before	After
Spelling errors	50%	
Missing words	35	
Improper punctuation	10	70%
Improper formatting	3	20
Additional words	1	5
Incorrect uppercase and lowercase lettering	1	5

a. What did the quality improvement program stress? Did it focus on the most important problems? Was it successful?

b. Has there been a drop in the overall number of typing errors?

c. Now what action should the firm take to improve the typing process?

14. The following data represent the numbers and types of problems for a production process that produces electronic circuits. Develop two Pareto charts, one for each week. What problem should the firm attempt to solve first? How should it go about solving the problem?

	Missing Component	Wrong Component	Failed Component
Week 1	10%	20%	70%
Week 2	11%	17%	72%

15. The traffic at a major shopping mall dropped about 20% between March 1993 and March 1994. Use a fishbone diagram and your general business knowledge to generate possible root causes. Identify four major bones and several subbones.

16. The College of Business does exit interviews with a random sample of undergraduates each year. The college wants to determine how to improve the education that students receive. Shown is a hypothetical data set based on 18 students. The symbol "x" represents each student's suggestion on how to improve undergraduate education.

Student	Eliminate Multiple-Choice Exams	Less Lecturing, More Cases	Less Theory, More Practice	More Internships
Joe K.			x	
Andrea T.		x		
Bob G.				x
Nat T.			x	
Jeanette T.			x	
Arlene B.			x	
Rebecca G.		x		
Lutfus S.	x			
Trisnadi I.			x	
Sang L.			x	
Carlos K.		x		
Pam B.				x
Ellen A.				x
Beth T.			x	
David A.		x		
Dwight T.			x	
Yezdi B.			x	
Juan S.	x			

Construct and interpret a Pareto chart on ways to improve the undergraduate training of business students at the college. $n = 18$ students.

17. Assume that lots of size 75 entering a plant contain 10% nonconforming parts. The firm uses an MIL-STD-105D plan with an AQL of 1%. Thus the firm takes a simple random sample of 13 and accepts the lot if it finds zero nonconforming parts in the sample. Use expression (15.15) to determine the probability of accepting lots that actually have 10% nonconforming parts.

18. An overnight parcel delivery service wishes to develop a control chart for the proportion of overnight parcels that are *not* delivered within the specified time limit. Shown are data for a small shipping center.

Day	Number of Overnight Parcels	Number Not Delivered on Time (Nonconforming)
1	10,000	10
2	9,000	7
3	9,000	10
4	11,000	10
5	13,000	12
6	12,000	14
7	9,000	9
8	10,000	8
9	15,000	16
10	12,000	9

a. Is the delivery process stable? Discuss.

b. In terms of late deliveries, the firm has set a desired target value proportion $\bar{p}$ of .002 or less. Has it met its target over the past 10 days? Calculate

$$\bar{p} = \frac{\text{Total number not delivered on time}}{\text{Total number of parcels delivered}}$$

c. Set up an LCL and UCL for the proportion of overnight parcels that fail to arrive within the specified time. Use 10,000 for the normal or typical sample size.

d. Suppose the firm wants to reduce late deliveries. What quality improvement tool should it use first? Discuss what analysis the firm should carry out.

19. The marketing director for a college continuing education program is tracking the proportion of people who sign up for one or more self-improvement courses each quarter. Using a mailing list of 10,000 names, the director has obtained the following results for the last 15 quarters.

Quarter	Number Signing Up for One or More Courses in a Quarter
1	405
2	505
3	599
4	705
5	610
6	500
7	415
8	521
9	605
10	735
11	620
12	570
13	455
14	535
15	635

    a. Is the proportion signing up for one or more courses stable? Discuss.

    b. Suppose the process were stable. Is a stable process desirable in this problem? From the director's viewpoint, what should the line graph look like? Discuss.

20.

Date:	October 21, 1994
To:	Sang Kim, Quality-Assurance Manager
From:	Howard Bright, Plant Manager
Subject:	Possible Ramifications of Ed Margate Dismissal

I was recently talking to Sarah Teman about the dismissal of Ed Margate for allegedly drinking on the job. You'll recall that Sarah dismissed him on Wednesday, September 30. I'm wondering if the work groups retaliated for his dismissal. If so, how did they do it? I keep hearing rumors of a slowdown, but that's all they are right now—rumors. I need some hard data. Your statistical process control charts may be helpful. If the work groups did take a job action, I may consider talking to the union as this is illegal under our present contract.

I need your report by the end of month.

> Use Data Base IV in Appendix 9 for your analysis. Your response to Howard Bright should include a brief memo and your analysis.

REFERENCES

Brightman, H. *Group Problem Solving: An Improved Managerial Problem Solving Approach.* Atlanta: Georgia State University Business Press, 1988.

Crosby, P. B. *Quality Is Free.* New York: McGraw-Hill, 1979.

Deming, W. E. *Elementary Principles of the Statistical Control of Quality.* Tokyo: Nippon Kagaku Gijutsu Remmei, 1951.

Deming, W. E. *Out of the Crisis.* Cambridge: Massachusetts Institute of Technology, Center for Advanced Engineering Studies, 1986.

Deming, W. E. *Quality, Productivity, and Competitive Position.* Cambridge: Massachusetts Institute of Technology, Center for Advanced Engineering Studies, 1982.

Gale, Bradley. *Quality as a Strategic Weapon.* Cambridge: The Strategic Planning Institute, 1985.

Groocock, J. M. *The Chain of Quality.* New York: John Wiley, 1986.

Juran, J. M., ed. *Quality Control Handbook.* 3rd ed. New York: McGraw-Hill, 1974.

Juran, J. M., and F. M. Gryna. *Quality Planning and Analysis.* New York: McGraw-Hill, 1980.

Kivenko, Kenneth. *Quality Control for Management.* Englewood Cliffs, New Jersey: Prentice-Hall, 1984.

Quality Problem Solving Summary. Princeton, New Jersey: Kepner–Tregoe, Inc., 1988.

Shewhart, W. "Quality Control Charts." *Bell Systems Technical Journal* (1926): 593–603.

Walton, Mary. *The Deming Management Method.* New York: Dodd, Mead, and Company, 1986.

APPENDIX: Statistical Software

Examples: Here we use MINITAB, Release 8, to create an $\bar{x}$ and s-chart for the shatter strength measurements for 15 samples of size $n = 5$ phone handsets. The data are shown in Table 15.2. The target value for phone handsets is 4,750 pounds per square inch (ppsi).

Input

```
01    MTB >  SET C1
      DATA>  4705     4780     4715     4750     4780
      DATA>  4750     4800     4775     4740     4750
      DATA>  4740     4740     4775     4770     4780
      DATA>  4710     4775     4780     4780     4810
      DATA>  4770     4750     4780     4750     4725
      DATA>  4735     4700     4755     4770     4755
      DATA>  4750     4800     4775     4725     4790
      DATA>  4740     4750     4775     4770     4780
      DATA>  4840     4780     4780     4755     4790
      DATA>  4770     4750     4780     4800     4725
      DATA>  4690     4750     4750     4720     4720
      DATA>  4800     4775     4780     4750     4800
      DATA>  4790     4790     4740     4810     4810
      DATA>  4750     4720     4780     4750     4770
      DATA>  4750     4760     4775     4720     4790
      DATA>  END
02    MTB >  XBARCHART C1 5;
03    SUBC>  SIGMA=28.09.
```

Explanation of Input

01 All 75 observations (15 periods of samples of size $n = 5$) are read into one column in order of occurrence (by row).

02 Produce an $\bar{x}$-chart using the data in column 1, and treat each 5 consecutive observations as a new sample (from a different shift).

03 Use 28.09 as an estimate of the process standard deviation. This is based on expression (15.3) in the text and equals 28.09 for the above data.

Output

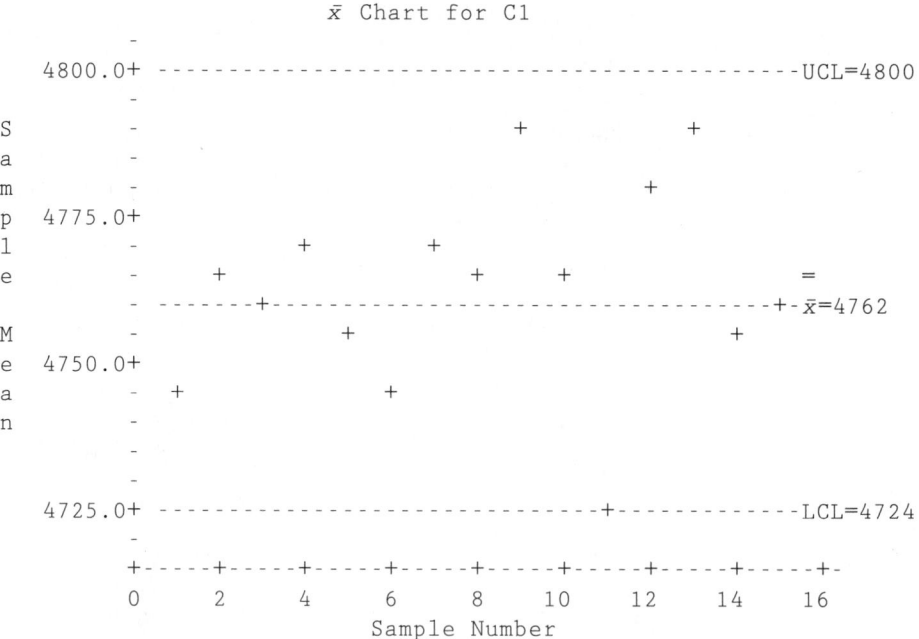

```
                          x̄  Chart  for  C1
          -
  4800.0+ - - - - - - - - - - - - - - - - - - - - - - - - - - - - - - - - - - UCL=4800
          -
S         -                                      +              +
a         -
m         -                                                +
p 4775.0+
l         -              +            +
e         -        +                       +        +                      =
          - - - - - - - - +- - - - - - - - - - - - - - - - - - - - - - - - - +- x̄=4762
M         -                     +                                  +
e 4750.0+
a         -  +                        +
n         -
          -
          -
  4725.0+ - - - - - - - - - - - - - - - - - - - - - - - - +- - - - - - - - - - - LCL=4724
          -
          +- - - - -+- - - - -+- - - - -+- - - - -+- - - - -+- - - - -+- - - - -+-
          0       2       4       6       8      10      12      14      16
                              Sample  Number
```

Interpretation of Output

The program calculates the process mean (CL) and the 3-sigma limits—the UCL and LCL.
1-sigma and 2-sigma limits can also be specified. The $\bar{x}$ chart is the same as shown in the text.

Input

```
MTB > SCHART C1 5;
SUBC> SIGMA=28.09.
                          S  Chart  for  C1
          -
          - - - - - - - - - - - - - - - - - - - - - - - - - - - - - - - - - - UCL=55.16
S   52.5+
a         -
m         -
p         -
l         -                  +
e   35.0+  +
          -                          +       +
S         - - - - - - - - - - - - - - +- - - - - - - - - - +- - - - - - - -+- - - - -+- S=26.40
t         -        +                                  +            +
d         -              +        +                          +
e   17.5+                               +
v         -
          -
          -
          -
   0.0+ - - - - - - - - - - - - - - - - - - - - - - - - - - - - - - - - - - - LCL=0.000
          +- - - - -+- - - - -+- - - - -+- - - - -+- - - - -+- - - - -+- - - - -+-
          0       2       4       6       8      10      12      14      16
                              Sample  Number
```

Interpretation of Output

With the exception of roundoff for the UCL value, the s-chart is the same as shown in the text. When the SIGMA command is not used, MINITAB calculates slightly different LCL, CL, and UCL values than found in the text.

1 APPENDIX The Binomial Table

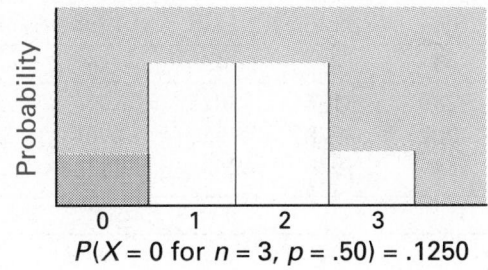

$P(X = 0$ for $n = 3$, $p = .50) = .1250$

$n = 1$

x \ p	.01	.02	.03	.04	.05	.06	.07	.08	.09	.10
0	.9900	.9800	.9700	.9600	.9500	.9400	.9300	.9200	.9100	.9000
1	.0100	.0200	.0300	.0400	.0500	.0600	.0700	.0800	.0900	.1000
	.11	.12	.13	.14	.15	.16	.17	.18	.19	.20
0	.8900	.8800	.8700	.8600	.8500	.8400	.8300	.8200	.8100	.8000
1	.1100	.1200	.1300	.1400	.1500	.1600	.1700	.1800	.1900	.2000
	.21	.22	.23	.24	.25	.26	.27	.28	.29	.30
0	.7900	.7800	.7700	.7600	.7500	.7400	.7300	.7200	.7100	.7000
1	.2100	.2200	.2300	.2400	.2500	.2600	.2700	.2800	.2900	.3000
	.31	.32	.33	.34	.35	.36	.37	.38	.39	.40
0	.6900	.6800	.6700	.6600	.6500	.6400	.6300	.6200	.6100	.6000
1	.3100	.3200	.3300	.3400	.3500	.3600	.3700	.3800	.3900	.4000
	.41	.42	.43	.44	.45	.46	.47	.48	.49	.50
0	.5900	.5800	.5700	.5600	.5500	.5400	.5300	.5200	.5100	.5000
1	.4100	.4200	.4300	.4400	.4500	.4600	.4700	.4800	.4900	.5000

$n = 2$

x \ p	.01	.02	.03	.04	.05	.06	.07	.08	.09	.10
0	.9801	.9604	.9409	.9216	.9025	.8836	.8649	.8464	.8281	.8100
1	.0198	.0392	.0582	.0768	.0950	.1128	.1302	.1472	.1638	.1800
2	.0001	.0004	.0009	.0016	.0025	.0036	.0049	.0064	.0081	.0100
	.11	.12	.13	.14	.15	.16	.17	.18	.19	.20
0	.7921	.7744	.7569	.7396	.7225	.7056	.6889	.6724	.6561	.6400
1	.1958	.2112	.2262	.2408	.2550	.2688	.2822	.2952	.3078	.3200
2	.0121	.0144	.0169	.0196	.0225	.0256	.0289	.0324	.0361	.0400

n = 2 (Continued)

x \ p	.21	.22	.23	.24	.25	.26	.27	.28	.29	.30
0	.6241	.6084	.5929	.5776	.5625	.5476	.5329	.5184	.5041	.4900
1	.3318	.3432	.3542	.3648	.3750	.3848	.3942	.4032	.4118	.4200
2	.0441	.0484	.0529	.0576	.0625	.0676	.0729	.0784	.0841	.0900
	.31	**.32**	**.33**	**.34**	**.35**	**.36**	**.37**	**.38**	**.39**	**.40**
0	.4761	.4624	.4489	.4356	.4225	.4096	.3969	.3844	.3721	.3600
1	.4278	.4352	.4422	.4488	.4550	.4608	.4662	.4712	.4758	.4800
2	.0961	.1024	.1089	.1156	.1225	.1296	.1369	.1444	.1521	.1600
	.41	**.42**	**.43**	**.44**	**.45**	**.46**	**.47**	**.48**	**.49**	**.50**
0	.3481	.3364	.3249	.3136	.3025	.2916	.2809	.2704	.2601	.2500
1	.4838	.4872	.4902	.4928	.4950	.4968	.4982	.4992	.4998	.5000
2	.1681	.1764	.1849	.1936	.2025	.2116	.2209	.2304	.2401	.2500

n = 3

x \ p	.01	.02	.03	.04	.05	.06	.07	.08	.09	.10
0	.9704	.9412	.9127	.8847	.8574	.8306	.8044	.7787	.7536	.7290
1	.0294	.0576	.0847	.1106	.1354	.1590	.1816	.2031	.2236	.2430
2	.0003	.0012	.0026	.0046	.0071	.0102	.0137	.0177	.0221	.0270
3	.0000	.0000	.0000	.0001	.0001	.0002	.0003	.0005	.0007	.0010
	.11	**.12**	**.13**	**.14**	**.15**	**.16**	**.17**	**.18**	**.19**	**.20**
0	.7050	.6815	.6585	.6361	.6141	.5927	.5718	.5514	.5314	.5120
1	.2614	.2788	.2952	.3106	.3251	.3387	.3513	.3631	.3740	.3840
2	.0323	.0380	.0441	.0506	.0574	.0645	.0720	.0797	.0877	.0960
3	.0013	.0017	.0022	.0027	.0034	.0041	.0049	.0058	.0069	.0080
	.21	**.22**	**.23**	**.24**	**.25**	**.26**	**.27**	**.28**	**.29**	**.30**
0	.4930	.4746	.4565	.4390	.4219	.4052	.3890	.3732	.3579	.3430
1	.3932	.4015	.4091	.4159	.4219	.4271	.4316	.4355	.4386	.4410
2	.1045	.1133	.1222	.1313	.1406	.1501	.1597	.1693	.1791	.1890
3	.0093	.0106	.0122	.0138	.0156	.0176	.0197	.0220	.0244	.0270
	.31	**.32**	**.33**	**.34**	**.35**	**.36**	**.37**	**.38**	**.39**	**.40**
0	.3285	.3144	.3008	.2875	.2746	.2621	.2500	.2383	.2270	.2160
1	.4428	.4439	.4444	.4443	.4436	.4424	.4406	.4382	.4354	.4320
2	.1989	.2089	.2189	.2289	.2389	.2488	.2587	.2686	.2783	.2880
3	.0298	.0328	.0359	.0393	.0429	.0467	.0507	.0549	.0593	.0640
	.41	**.42**	**.43**	**.44**	**.45**	**.46**	**.47**	**.48**	**.49**	**.50**
0	.2054	.1951	.1852	.1756	.1664	.1575	.1489	.1406	.1327	.1250
1	.4282	.4239	.4191	.4140	.4084	.4024	.3961	.3894	.3823	.3750
2	.2975	.3069	.3162	.3252	.3341	.3428	.3512	.3594	.3674	.3750
3	.0689	.0741	.0795	.0852	.0911	.0973	.1038	.1106	.1176	.1250

n = 4

x \ p	.01	.02	.03	.04	.05	.06	.07	.08	.09	.10
0	.9606	.9224	.8853	.8493	.8145	.7807	.7481	.7164	.6857	.6561
1	.0388	.0753	.1095	.1416	.1715	.1993	.2252	.2492	.2713	.2916
2	.0006	.0023	.0051	.0088	.0135	.0191	.0254	.0325	.0402	.0486
3	.0000	.0000	.0001	.0002	.0005	.0008	.0013	.0019	.0027	.0036
4	.0000	.0000	.0000	.0000	.0000	.0000	.0000	.0000	.0001	.0001

x \ p	.11	.12	.13	.14	.15	.16	.17	.18	.19	.20
0	.6274	.5997	.5729	.5470	.5220	.4979	.4746	.4521	.4305	.4096
1	.3102	.3271	.3424	.3562	.3685	.3793	.3888	.3970	.4039	.4096
2	.0575	.0669	.0767	.0870	.0975	.1084	.1195	.1307	.1421	.1536
3	.0047	.0061	.0076	.0094	.0115	.0138	.0163	.0191	.0222	.0256
4	.0001	.0002	.0003	.0004	.0005	.0007	.0008	.0010	.0013	.0016

x \ p	.21	.22	.23	.24	.25	.26	.27	.28	.29	.30
0	.3895	.3702	.3515	.3336	.3164	.2999	.2840	.2687	.2541	.2401
1	.4142	.4176	.4200	.4214	.4219	.4214	.4201	.4180	.4152	.4116
2	.1651	.1767	.1882	.1996	.2109	.2221	.2331	.2439	.2544	.2646
3	.0293	.0332	.0375	.0420	.0469	.0520	.0575	.0632	.0693	.0756
4	.0019	.0023	.0028	.0033	.0039	.0046	.0053	.0061	.0071	.0081

x \ p	.31	.32	.33	.34	.35	.36	.37	.38	.39	.40
0	.2267	.2138	.2015	.1897	.1785	.1678	.1575	.1478	.1385	.1296
1	.4074	.4025	.3970	.3910	.3845	.3775	.3701	.3623	.3541	.3456
2	.2745	.2841	.2933	.3021	.3105	.3185	.3260	.3330	.3396	.3456
3	.0822	.0891	.0963	.1038	.1115	.1194	.1276	.1361	.1447	.1536
4	.0092	.0105	.0119	.0134	.0150	.0168	.0187	.0209	.0231	.0256

x \ p	.41	.42	.43	.44	.45	.46	.47	.48	.49	.50
0	.1212	.1132	.1056	.0983	.0915	.0850	.0789	.0731	.0677	.0625
1	.3368	.3278	.3185	.3091	.2995	.2897	.2799	.2700	.2600	.2500
2	.3511	.3560	.3604	.3643	.3675	.3702	.3723	.3738	.3747	.3750
3	.1627	.1719	.1813	.1908	.2005	.2102	.2201	.2300	.2400	.2500
4	.0283	.0311	.0342	.0375	.0410	.0448	.0488	.0531	.0576	.0625

n = 5

x \ p	.01	.02	.03	.04	.05	.06	.07	.08	.09	.10
0	.9510	.9039	.8587	.8154	.7738	.7339	.6957	.6591	.6240	.5905
1	.0480	.0922	.1328	.1699	.2036	.2342	.2618	.2866	.3086	.3280
2	.0010	.0038	.0082	.0142	.0214	.0299	.0394	.0498	.0610	.0729
3	.0000	.0001	.0003	.0006	.0011	.0019	.0030	.0043	.0060	.0081
4	.0000	.0000	.0000	.0000	.0000	.0001	.0001	.0002	.0003	.0004

$n = 5$ (Continued)

p \ x	.11	.12	.13	.14	.15	.16	.17	.18	.19	.20
0	.5584	.5277	.4984	.4704	.4437	.4182	.3939	.3707	.3487	.3277
1	.3451	.3598	.3724	.3829	.3915	.3983	.4034	.4069	.4089	.4096
2	.0853	.0981	.1113	.1247	.1382	.1517	.1652	.1786	.1919	.2048
3	.0105	.0134	.0166	.0203	.0244	.0289	.0338	.0392	.0450	.0512
4	.0007	.0009	.0012	.0017	.0022	.0028	.0035	.0043	.0053	.0064
5	.0000	.0000	.0000	.0001	.0001	.0001	.0001	.0002	.0002	.0003

p \ x	.21	.22	.23	.24	.25	.26	.27	.28	.29	.30
0	.3077	.2887	.2707	.2536	.2373	.2219	.2073	.1935	.1804	.1681
1	.4090	.4072	.4043	.4003	.3955	.3898	.3834	.3762	.3685	.3602
2	.2174	.2297	.2415	.2529	.2637	.2739	.2836	.2926	.3010	.3087
3	.0578	.0648	.0721	.0798	.0879	.0962	.1049	.1138	.1229	.1323
4	.0077	.0091	.0108	.0126	.0146	.0169	.0194	.0221	.0251	.0284
5	.0004	.0005	.0006	.0008	.0010	.0012	.0014	.0017	.0021	.0024

p \ x	.31	.32	.33	.34	.35	.36	.37	.38	.39	.40
0	.1564	.1454	.1350	.1252	.1160	.1074	.0992	.0916	.0845	.0778
1	.3513	.3421	.3325	.3226	.3124	.3020	.2914	.2808	.2700	.2592
2	.3157	.3220	.3275	.3323	.3364	.3397	.3423	.3441	.3452	.3456
3	.1418	.1515	.1613	.1712	.1811	.1911	.2010	.2109	.2207	.2304
4	.0319	.0357	.0397	.0441	.0488	.0537	.0590	.0646	.0706	.0768
5	.0029	.0034	.0039	.0045	.0053	.0060	.0069	.0079	.0090	.0102

p \ x	.41	.42	.43	.44	.45	.46	.47	.48	.49	.50
0	.0715	.0656	.0602	.0551	.0503	.0459	.0418	.0380	.0345	.0312
1	.2484	.2376	.2270	.2164	.2059	.1956	.1854	.1755	.1657	.1562
2	.3452	.3442	.3424	.3400	.3369	.3332	.3289	.3240	.3185	.3125
3	.2399	.2492	.2583	.2671	.2757	.2838	.2916	.2990	.3060	.3125
4	.0834	.0902	.0974	.1049	.1128	.1209	.1293	.1380	.1470	.1562
5	.0116	.0131	.0147	.0165	.0185	.0206	.0229	.0255	.0282	.0312

$n = 6$

p \ x	.01	.02	.03	.04	.05	.06	.07	.08	.09	.10
0	.9415	.8858	.8330	.7828	.7351	.6899	.6470	.6064	.5679	.5314
1	.0571	.1085	.1546	.1957	.2321	.2642	.2922	.3164	.3370	.3543
2	.0014	.0055	.0120	.0204	.0305	.0422	.0550	.0688	.0833	.0984
3	.0000	.0002	.0005	.0011	.0021	.0036	.0055	.0080	.0110	.0146
4	.0000	.0000	.0000	.0000	.0001	.0002	.0003	.0005	.0008	.0012
5	.0000	.0000	.0000	.0000	.0000	.0000	.0000	.0000	.0000	.0001

					$n = 6$ (Continued)					
x \ p	.11	.12	.13	.14	.15	.16	.17	.18	.19	.20
0	.4970	.4644	.4336	.4046	.3771	.3513	.3269	.3040	.2824	.2621
1	.3685	.3800	.3888	.3952	.3993	.4015	.4018	.4004	.3975	.3932
2	.1139	.1295	.1452	.1608	.1762	.1912	.2057	.2197	.2331	.2458
3	.0188	.0236	.0289	.0349	.0415	.0486	.0562	.0643	.0729	.0819
4	.0017	.0024	.0032	.0043	.0055	.0069	.0086	.0106	.0128	.0154
5	.0001	.0001	.0002	.0003	.0004	.0005	.0007	.0009	.0012	.0015
6	.0000	.0000	.0000	.0000	.0000	.0000	.0000	.0000	.0000	.0001
	.21	.22	.23	.24	.25	.26	.27	.28	.29	.30
0	.2431	.2252	.2084	.1927	.1780	.1642	.1513	.1393	.1281	.1176
1	.3877	.3811	.3735	.3651	.3560	.3462	.3358	.3251	.3139	.3025
2	.2577	.2687	.2789	.2882	.2966	.3041	.3105	.3160	.3206	.3241
3	.0913	.1011	.1111	.1214	.1318	.1424	.1531	.1639	.1746	.1852
4	.0182	.0214	.0249	.0287	.0330	.0375	.0425	.0478	.0535	.0595
5	.0019	.0024	.0030	.0036	.0044	.0053	.0063	.0074	.0087	.0102
6	.0001	.0001	.0001	.0002	.0002	.0003	.0004	.0005	.0006	.0007
	.31	.32	.33	.34	.35	.36	.37	.38	.39	.40
0	.1079	.0989	.0905	.0827	.0754	.0687	.0625	.0568	.0515	.0467
1	.2909	.2792	.2673	.2555	.2437	.2319	.2203	.2089	.1976	.1866
2	.3267	.3284	.3292	.3290	.3280	.3261	.3235	.3201	.3159	.3110
3	.1957	.2061	.2162	.2260	.2355	.2446	.2533	.2616	.2693	.2765
4	.0660	.0727	.0799	.0873	.0951	.1032	.1116	.1202	.1291	.1382
5	.0119	.0137	.0157	.0180	.0205	.0232	.0262	.0295	.0330	.0369
6	.0009	.0011	.0013	.0015	.0018	.0022	.0026	.0030	.0035	.0041
	.41	.42	.43	.44	.45	.46	.47	.48	.49	.50
0	.0422	.0381	.0343	.0308	.0277	.0248	.0222	.0198	.0176	.0156
1	.1759	.1654	.1552	.1454	.1359	.1267	.1179	.1095	.1014	.0938
2	.3055	.2994	.2928	.2856	.2780	.2699	.2615	.2527	.2436	.2344
3	.2831	.2891	.2945	.2992	.3032	.3065	.3091	.3110	.3121	.3125
4	.1475	.1570	.1666	.1763	.1861	.1958	.2056	.2153	.2249	.2344
5	.0410	.0455	.0503	.0554	.0609	.0667	.0729	.0795	.0864	.0938
6	.0048	.0055	.0063	.0073	.0083	.0095	.0108	.0122	.0138	.0156
					$n = 7$					
x \ p	.01	.02	.03	.04	.05	.06	.07	.08	.09	.10
0	.9321	.8681	.8080	.7514	.6983	.6485	.6017	.5578	.5168	.4783
1	.0659	.1240	.1749	.2192	.2573	.2897	.3170	.3396	.3578	.3720
2	.0020	.0076	.0162	.0274	.0406	.0555	.0716	.0886	.1061	.1240
3	.0000	.0003	.0008	.0019	.0036	.0059	.0090	.0128	.0175	.0230
4	.0000	.0000	.0000	.0001	.0002	.0004	.0007	.0011	.0017	.0026
5	.0000	.0000	.0000	.0000	.0000	.0000	.0000	.0001	.0001	.0002

n = 7 (Continued)

x \ p	.11	.12	.13	.14	.15	.16	.17	.18	.19	.20
0	.4423	.4087	.3773	.3479	.3206	.2951	.2714	.2493	.2288	.2097
1	.3827	.3901	.3946	.3965	.3960	.3935	.3891	.3830	.3756	.3670
2	.1419	.1596	.1769	.1936	.2097	.2248	.2391	.2523	.2643	.2753
3	.0292	.0363	.0441	.0525	.0617	.0714	.0816	.0923	.1033	.1147
4	.0036	.0049	.0066	.0086	.0109	.0136	.0167	.0203	.0242	.0287
5	.0003	.0004	.0006	.0008	.0012	.0016	.0021	.0027	.0034	.0043
6	.0000	.0000	.0000	.0000	.0001	.0001	.0001	.0002	.0003	.0004

	.21	.22	.23	.24	.25	.26	.27	.28	.29	.30
0	.1920	.1757	.1605	.1465	.1335	.1215	.1105	.1003	.0910	.0824
1	.3573	.3468	.3356	.3237	.3115	.2989	.2860	.2731	.2600	.2471
2	.2850	.2935	.3007	.3067	.3115	.3150	.3174	.3186	.3186	.3177
3	.1263	.1379	.1497	.1614	.1730	.1845	.1956	.2065	.2169	.2269
4	.0336	.0389	.0447	.0510	.0577	.0648	.0724	.0803	.0886	.0972
5	.0054	.0066	.0080	.0097	.0115	.0137	.0161	.0187	.0217	.0250
6	.0005	.0006	.0008	.0010	.0013	.0016	.0020	.0024	.0030	.0036
7	.0000	.0000	.0000	.0000	.0001	.0001	.0001	.0001	.0002	.0002

	.31	.32	.33	.34	.35	.36	.37	.38	.39	.40
0	.0745	.0672	.0606	.0546	.0490	.0440	.0394	.0352	.0314	.0280
1	.2342	.2215	.2090	.1967	.1848	.1732	.1619	.1511	.1407	.1306
2	.3156	.3127	.3088	.3040	.2985	.2922	.2853	.2778	.2698	.2613
3	.2363	.2452	.2535	.2610	.2679	.2740	.2793	.2838	.2875	.2903
4	.1062	.1154	.1248	.1345	.1442	.1541	.1640	.1739	.1838	.1935
5	.0286	.0326	.0369	.0416	.0466	.0520	.0578	.0640	.0705	.0774
6	.0043	.0051	.0061	.0071	.0084	.0098	.0113	.0131	.0150	.0172
7	.0003	.0003	.0004	.0005	.0006	.0008	.0009	.0011	.0014	.0016

	.41	.42	.43	.44	.45	.46	.47	.48	.49	.50
0	.0249	.0221	.0195	.0173	.0152	.0134	.0117	.0103	.0090	.0078
1	.1211	.1119	.1032	.0950	.0872	.0798	.0729	.0664	.0604	.0547
2	.2524	.2431	.2336	.2239	.2140	.2040	.1940	.1840	.1740	.1641
3	.2923	.2934	.2937	.2932	.2918	.2897	.2867	.2830	.2786	.2734
4	.2031	.2125	.2216	.2304	.2388	.2468	.2543	.2612	.2676	.2734
5	.0847	.0923	.1003	.1086	.1172	.1261	.1353	.1447	.1543	.1641
6	.0196	.0223	.0252	.0284	.0320	.0358	.0400	.0445	.0494	.0547
7	.0019	.0023	.0027	.0032	.0037	.0044	.0051	.0059	.0068	.0078

$n = 8$

x \ p	.01	.02	.03	.04	.05	.06	.07	.08	.09	.10
0	.9927	.8508	.7837	.7214	.6634	.6096	.5596	.5132	.4703	.4305
1	.0746	.1389	.1939	.2405	.2793	.3113	.3370	.3570	.3721	.3826
2	.0026	.0099	.0210	.0351	.0515	.0695	.0888	.1087	.1288	.1488
3	.0001	.0004	.0013	.0029	.0054	.0089	.0134	.0189	.0255	.0331
4	.0000	.0000	.0001	.0002	.0004	.0007	.0013	.0021	.0031	.0046
5	.0000	.0000	.0000	.0000	.0000	.0000	.0001	.0001	.0002	.0004

x \ p	.11	.12	.13	.14	.15	.16	.17	.18	.19	.20
0	.3937	.3596	.3282	.2992	.2725	.2479	.2252	.2044	.1853	.1678
1	.3892	.3923	.3923	.3897	.3847	.3777	.3691	.3590	.3477	.3355
2	.1684	.1872	.2052	.2220	.2376	.2518	.2646	.2758	.2855	.2936
3	.0416	.0511	.0613	.0723	.0839	.0959	.1084	.1211	.1339	.1468
4	.0064	.0087	.0115	.0147	.0185	.0228	.0277	.0332	.0393	.0459
5	.0006	.0009	.0014	.0019	.0026	.0035	.0045	.0058	.0074	.0092
6	.0000	.0001	.0001	.0002	.0002	.0003	.0005	.0006	.0009	.0011
7	.0000	.0000	.0000	.0000	.0000	.0000	.0000	.0000	.0001	.0001

x \ p	.21	.22	.23	.24	.25	.26	.27	.28	.29	.30
0	.1517	.1370	.1236	.1113	.1001	.0899	.0806	.0722	.0646	.0576
1	.3226	.3092	.2953	.2812	.2670	.2527	.2386	.2247	.2110	.1977
2	.3002	.3052	.3087	.3108	.3115	.3108	.3089	.3058	.3017	.2965
3	.1596	.1722	.1844	.1963	.2076	.2184	.2285	.2379	.2464	.2541
4	.0530	.0607	.0689	.0775	.0865	.0959	.1056	.1156	.1258	.1361
5	.0113	.0137	.0165	.0196	.0231	.0270	.0313	.0360	.0411	.0467
6	.0015	.0019	.0025	.0031	.0038	.0047	.0058	.0070	.0084	.0100
7	.0001	.0002	.0002	.0003	.0004	.0005	.0006	.0008	.0010	.0012
8	.0000	.0000	.0000	.0000	.0000	.0000	.0000	.0000	.0001	.0001

x \ p	.31	.32	.33	.34	.35	.36	.37	.38	.39	.40
0	.0514	.0457	.0406	.0360	.0319	.0281	.0248	.0218	.0192	.0168
1	.1847	.1721	.1600	.1484	.1373	.1267	.1166	.1071	.0981	.0896
2	.2904	.2835	.2758	.2675	.2587	.2494	.2397	.2297	.2194	.2090
3	.2609	.2668	.2717	.2756	.2786	.2805	.2815	.2815	.2806	.2787
4	.1465	.1569	.1673	.1775	.1875	.1973	.2067	.2157	.2242	.2322
5	.0527	.0591	.0659	.0732	.0808	.0888	.0971	.1058	.1147	.1239
6	.0118	.0139	.0162	.0188	.0217	.0250	.0285	.0324	.0367	.0413
7	.0015	.0019	.0023	.0028	.0033	.0040	.0048	.0057	.0067	.0079
8	.0001	.0001	.0001	.0002	.0002	.0003	.0004	.0004	.0005	.0007

n = 8 (Continued)

x \ p	.41	.42	.43	.44	.45	.46	.47	.48	.49	.50
0	.0147	.0128	.0111	.0097	.0084	.0072	.0062	.0053	.0046	.0039
1	.0816	.0742	.0672	.0608	.0548	.0493	.0442	.0395	.0352	.0312
2	.1985	.1880	.1776	.1672	.1569	.1469	.1371	.1275	.1183	.1094
3	.2759	.2723	.2679	.2627	.2568	.2503	.2431	.2355	.2273	.2188
4	.2397	.2465	.2526	.2580	.2627	.2665	.2695	.2717	.2730	.2734
5	.1332	.1428	.1525	.1622	.1719	.1816	.1912	.2006	.2098	.2188
6	.0463	.0517	.0575	.0637	.0703	.0774	.0848	.0926	.1008	.1094
7	.0092	.0107	.0124	.0143	.0164	.0188	.0215	.0244	.0277	.0312
8	.0008	.0010	.0012	.0014	.0017	.0020	.0024	.0028	.0033	.0039

n = 9

x \ p	.01	.02	.03	.04	.05	.06	.07	.08	.09	.10
0	.9135	.8337	.7602	.6925	.6302	.5730	.5204	.4722	.4279	.3874
1	.0830	.1531	.2116	.2597	.2985	.3292	.3525	.3695	.3809	.3874
2	.0034	.0125	.0262	.0433	.0629	.0840	.1061	.1285	.1507	.1722
3	.0001	.0006	.0019	.0042	.0077	.0125	.0186	.0261	.0348	.0446
4	.0000	.0000	.0001	.0003	.0006	.0012	.0021	.0034	.0052	.0074
5	.0000	.0000	.0000	.0000	.0000	.0001	.0002	.0003	.0005	.0008
6	.0000	.0000	.0000	.0000	.0000	.0000	.0000	.0000	.0000	.0001

x \ p	.11	.12	.13	.14	.15	.16	.17	.18	.19	.20
0	.3504	.3165	.2855	.2573	.2316	.2082	.1869	.1676	.1501	.1342
1	.3897	.3884	.3840	.3770	.3679	.3569	.3446	.3312	.3169	.3020
2	.1927	.2119	.2295	.2455	.2597	.2720	.2823	.2908	.2973	.3020
3	.0556	.0674	.0800	.0933	.1069	.1209	.1349	.1489	.1627	.1762
4	.0103	.0138	.0179	.0228	.0283	.0345	.0415	.0490	.0573	.0661
5	.0013	.0019	.0027	.0037	.0050	.0066	.0085	.0108	.0134	.0165
6	.0001	.0002	.0003	.0004	.0006	.0008	.0012	.0016	.0021	.0028
7	.0000	.0000	.0000	.0000	.0000	.0001	.0001	.0001	.0002	.0003

x \ p	.21	.22	.23	.24	.25	.26	.27	.28	.29	.30
0	.1199	.1069	.0952	.0846	.0751	.0665	.0589	.0520	.0458	.0404
1	.2867	.2713	.2558	.2404	.2253	.2104	.1960	.1820	.1685	.1556
2	.3049	.3061	.3056	.3037	.3003	.2957	.2899	.2831	.2754	.2668
3	.1891	.2014	.2130	.2238	.2336	.2424	.2502	.2569	.2624	.2668
4	.0754	.0852	.0954	.1060	.1168	.1278	.1388	.1499	.1608	.1715
5	.0200	.0240	.0285	.0335	.0389	.0449	.0513	.0583	.0657	.0735
6	.0036	.0045	.0057	.0070	.0087	.0105	.0127	.0151	.0179	.0210
7	.0004	.0005	.0007	.0010	.0012	.0016	.0020	.0025	.0031	.0039
8	.0000	.0000	.0001	.0001	.0001	.0001	.0002	.0002	.0003	.0004

$n = 9$ (Continued)

x \ p	.31	.32	.33	.34	.35	.36	.37	.38	.39	.40
0	.0355	.0311	.0272	.0238	.0207	.0180	.0156	.0135	.0117	.0101
1	.1433	.1317	.1206	.1102	.1004	.0912	.0826	.0747	.0673	.0605
2	.2576	.2478	.2376	.2270	.2162	.2052	.1941	.1831	.1721	.1612
3	.2701	.2721	.2731	.2729	.2716	.2693	.2660	.2618	.2567	.2508
4	.1820	.1921	.2017	.2109	.2194	.2272	.2344	.2407	.2462	.2508
5	.0818	.0904	.0994	.1086	.1181	.1278	.1376	.1475	.1574	.1672
6	.0245	.0284	.0326	.0373	.0424	.0479	.0539	.0603	.0671	.0743
7	.0047	.0057	.0069	.0082	.0098	.0116	.0136	.0158	.0184	.0212
8	.0005	.0007	.0008	.0011	.0013	.0016	.0020	.0024	.0029	.0035
9	.0000	.0000	.0000	.0001	.0001	.0001	.0001	.0002	.0002	.0003

x \ p	.41	.42	.43	.44	.45	.46	.47	.48	.49	.50
0	.0087	.0074	.0064	.0054	.0046	.0039	.0033	.0028	.0023	.0020
1	.0542	.0484	.0431	.0383	.0339	.0299	.0263	.0231	.0202	.0176
2	.1506	.1402	.1301	.1204	.1110	.1020	.0934	.0853	.0776	.0703
3	.2442	.2369	.2291	.2207	.2119	.2027	.1933	.1837	.1739	.1641
4	.2545	.2573	.2592	.2601	.2600	.2590	.2571	.2543	.2506	.2461
5	.1769	.1863	.1955	.2044	.2128	.2207	.2280	.2347	.2408	.2461
6	.0819	.0900	.0983	.1070	.1160	.1253	.1348	.1445	.1542	.1641
7	.0244	.0279	.0318	.0360	.0407	.0458	.0512	.0571	.0635	.0703
8	.0042	.0051	.0060	.0071	.0083	.0097	.0114	.0132	.0153	.0176
9	.0003	.0004	.0005	.0006	.0008	.0009	.0011	.0014	.0016	.0020

$n = 10$

x \ p	.01	.02	.03	.04	.05	.06	.07	.08	.09	.10
0	.9044	.8171	.7374	.6648	.5987	.5386	.4840	.4344	.3894	.3487
1	.0914	.1667	.2281	.2770	.3151	.3438	.3643	.3777	.3851	.3874
2	.0042	.0153	.0317	.0519	.0746	.0988	.1234	.1478	.1714	.1937
3	.0001	.0008	.0026	.0058	.0105	.0168	.0248	.0343	.0452	.0574
4	.0000	.0000	.0001	.0004	.0010	.0019	.0033	.0052	.0078	.0112
5	.0000	.0000	.0000	.0000	.0001	.0001	.0003	.0005	.1009	.0015
6	.0000	.0000	.0000	.0000	.0000	.0000	.0000	.0000	.0001	.0001

x \ p	.11	.12	.13	.14	.15	.16	.17	.18	.19	.20
0	.3118	.2785	.2484	.2213	.1969	.1749	.1552	.1374	.1216	.1074
1	.3854	.3798	.3712	.3603	.3474	.3331	.3178	.3017	.2852	.2684
2	.2143	.2330	.2496	.2639	.2759	.2856	.2929	.2980	.3010	.3020
3	.0706	.0847	.0995	.1146	.1298	.1450	.1600	.1745	.1883	.2013
4	.0153	.0202	.0260	.0326	.0401	.0483	.0573	.0670	.0773	.0881
5	.0023	.0033	.0047	.0064	.0085	.0111	.0141	.0177	.0218	.0264
6	.0002	.0004	.0006	.0009	.0012	.0018	.0024	.0032	.0043	.0055
7	.0000	.0000	.0000	.0001	.0001	.0002	.0003	.0004	.0006	.0008
8	.0000	.0000	.0000	.0000	.0000	.0000	.0000	.0000	.0001	.0001

					$n = 10$ (Continued)					
x \ p	**.21**	**.22**	**.23**	**.24**	**.25**	**.26**	**.27**	**.28**	**.29**	**.30**
0	.0947	.0834	.0733	.0643	.0563	.0492	.0430	.0374	.0326	.0282
1	.2517	.2351	.2188	.2030	.1877	.1730	.1590	.1456	.1330	.1211
2	.3011	.2984	.2942	.2885	.2816	.2735	.2646	.2548	.2444	.2335
3	.2134	.2244	.2343	.2429	.2503	.2563	.2609	.2642	.2662	.2668
4	.0993	.1108	.1225	.1343	.1460	.1576	.1689	.1798	.1903	.2001
5	.0317	.0375	.0439	.0509	.0584	.0664	.0750	.0839	.0933	.1029
6	.0070	.0088	.0109	.0134	.0162	.0195	.0231	.0272	.0317	.0368
7	.0011	.0014	.0019	.0024	.0031	.0039	.0049	.0060	.0074	.0090
8	.0001	.0002	.0002	.0003	.0004	.0005	.0007	.0009	.0011	.0014
9	.0000	.0000	.0000	.0000	.0000	.0000	.0001	.0001	.0001	.0001
	.31	**.32**	**.33**	**.34**	**.35**	**.36**	**.37**	**.38**	**.39**	**.40**
0	.0245	.0211	.0182	.0157	.0135	.0115	.0098	.0084	.0071	.0060
1	.1099	.0995	.0898	.0808	.0725	.0649	.0578	.0514	.0456	.0403
2	.2222	.2107	.1990	.0873	.1757	.1642	.1529	.1419	.1312	.1209
3	.2662	.2644	.2614	.2573	.2522	.2462	.2394	.2319	.2237	.2150
4	.2093	.2177	.2253	.2320	.2377	.2424	.2461	.2487	.2503	.2508
5	.1128	.1229	.1332	.1434	.1536	.1636	.1734	.1829	.1920	.2007
6	.0422	.0482	.0547	.0616	.0689	.0767	.0849	.0934	.1023	.1115
7	.0108	.0130	.0154	.0181	.0212	.0247	.0285	.0327	.0374	.0425
8	.0018	.0023	.0028	.0035	.0043	.0052	.0063	.0075	.0090	.0106
9	.0002	.0002	.0003	.0004	.0005	.0006	.0008	.0010	.0013	.0016
10	.0000	.0000	.0000	.0000	.0000	.0000	.0000	.0001	.0001	.0001
	.41	**.42**	**.43**	**.44**	**.45**	**.46**	**.47**	**.48**	**.49**	**.50**
0	.0051	.0043	.0036	.0030	.0025	.0021	.0017	.0014	.0012	.0010
1	.0355	.0312	.0273	.0238	.0207	.0180	.0155	.0133	.0114	.0098
2	.1111	.1017	.0927	.0843	.0763	.0688	.0619	.0554	.0494	.0439
3	.2058	.1963	.1865	.1765	.1665	.1564	.1464	.1364	.1267	.1172
4	.2503	.2488	.2462	.2427	.2384	.2331	.2271	.2204	.2130	.2051
5	.2087	.2162	.2229	.2289	.2340	.2383	.2417	.2441	.2456	.2461
6	.1209	.1304	.1401	.1499	.1596	.1692	.1786	.1878	.1966	.2051
7	.0480	.0540	.0604	.0673	.0746	.0824	.0905	.0991	.1080	.1172
8	.0125	.0147	.0171	.0198	.0229	.0263	.0301	.0343	.0389	.0439
9	.0019	.0024	.0029	.0035	.0042	.0050	.0059	.0070	.0083	.0098
10	.0001	.0002	.0002	.0003	.0003	.0004	.0005	.0006	.0008	.0010

$n = 15$

x \ p	.01	.02	.03	.04	.05	.06	.07	.08	.09	.10
0	.8601	.7386	.6333	.5421	.4633	.3953	.3367	.2863	.2430	.2059
1	.1303	.2261	.2938	.3388	.3658	.3785	.3801	.3734	.3605	.3432
2	.0092	.0323	.0636	.0988	.1348	.1691	.2003	.2273	.2496	.2669
3	.0004	.0029	.0085	.0178	.0307	.0468	.0653	.0857	.1070	.1285
4	.0000	.0002	.0008	.0022	.0049	.0090	.0148	.0223	.0317	.0428
5	.0000	.0000	.0001	.0002	.0006	.0013	.0024	.0043	.0069	.0105
6	.0000	.0000	.0000	.0000	.0000	.0001	.0003	.0006	.0011	.0019
7	.0000	.0000	.0000	.0000	.0000	.0000	.0000	.0001	.0001	.0003

x \ p	.11	.12	.13	.14	.15	.16	.17	.18	.19	.20
0	.1741	.1470	.1238	.1041	.0874	.0731	.0611	.0510	.0424	.0352
1	.3228	.3006	.2775	.2542	.2312	.2090	.1878	.1678	.1492	.1319
2	.2793	.2870	.2903	.2897	.2856	.2787	.2692	.2578	.2449	.2309
3	.1496	.1696	.1880	.2044	.2184	.2300	.2389	.2452	.2489	.2501
4	.0555	.0694	.0843	.0998	.1156	.1314	.1468	.1615	.1752	.1876
5	.0151	.0208	.0277	.0357	.0449	.0551	.0662	.0780	.0904	.1032
6	.0031	.0047	.0069	.0097	.0132	.0175	.0226	.0285	.0353	.0430
7	.0005	.0008	.0013	.0020	.0030	.0043	.0059	.0081	.0107	.0138
8	.0001	.0001	.0002	.0003	.0005	.0008	.0012	.0018	.0025	.0035
9	.0000	.0000	.0000	.0000	.0001	.0001	.0002	.0003	.0005	.0007
10	.0000	.0000	.0000	.0000	.0000	.0000	.0000	.0000	.0001	.0001

$n = 15$ (Continued)

x \ p	.21	.22	.23	.24	.25	.26	.27	.28	.29	.30
0	.0291	.0241	.0198	.0163	.0134	.0109	.0089	.0072	.0059	.0047
1	.1162	.1018	.0889	.0772	.0668	.0576	.0494	.0423	.0360	.0305
2	.2162	.2010	.1858	.1707	.1559	.1416	.1280	.1150	.1029	.0916
3	.2490	.2457	.2405	.2336	.2252	.2156	.2051	.1939	.1821	.1700
4	.1986	.2079	.2155	.2213	.2252	.2273	.2276	.2262	.2231	.2186
5	.1161	.1290	.1416	.1537	.1651	.1757	.1852	.1935	.2005	.2061
6	.0514	.0606	.0705	.0809	.0917	.1029	.1142	.1254	.1365	.1472
7	.0176	.0220	.0271	.0329	.0393	.0465	.0543	.0627	.0717	.0811
8	.0047	.0062	.0081	.0104	.0131	.0163	.0201	.0244	.0293	.0348
9	.0010	.0014	.0019	.0025	.0034	.0045	.0058	.0074	.0093	.0116
10	.0002	.0002	.0003	.0005	.0007	.0009	.0013	.0017	.0023	.0030
11	.0000	.0000	.0000	.0001	.0001	.0002	.0002	.0003	.0004	.0006
12	.0000	.0000	.0000	.0000	.0000	.0000	.0000	.0000	.0001	.0001

x \ p	.31	.32	.33	.34	.35	.36	.37	.38	.39	.40
0	.0038	.0031	.0025	.0020	.0016	.0012	.0010	.0008	.0006	.0005
1	.0258	.0217	.0182	.0152	.0126	.0104	.0086	.0071	.0058	.0047
2	.0811	.0715	.0627	.0547	.0476	.0411	.0354	.0303	.0259	.0219
3	.1579	.1457	.1338	.1222	.1110	.1002	.0901	.0805	.0716	.0634
4	.2128	.2057	.1977	.1888	.1792	.1692	.1587	.1481	.1374	.1268
5	.2103	.2130	.2142	.2140	.2123	.2093	.2051	.1997	.1933	.1859
6	.1575	.1671	.1759	.1837	.1906	.1963	.2008	.2040	.2059	.2066
7	.0910	.1011	.1114	.1217	.1319	.1419	.1516	.1608	.1693	.1771
8	.0409	.0476	.0549	.0627	.0710	.0798	.0890	.0985	.1082	.1181
9	.0143	.0174	.0210	.0251	.0299	.0349	.0407	.0470	.0538	.0612
10	.0038	.0049	.0062	.0078	.0096	.0118	.0143	.0173	.0206	.0245
11	.0008	.0011	.0014	.0018	.0024	.0030	.0038	.0048	.0060	.0074
12	.0001	.0002	.0002	.0003	.0004	.0006	.0007	.0010	.0013	.0016
13	.0000	.0000	.0000	.0000	.0001	.0001	.0001	.0001	.0002	.0003

$n = 15$ (Continued)

x \ p	.41	.42	.43	.44	.45	.46	.47	.48	.49	.50
0	.0004	.0003	.0002	.0002	.0001	.0001	.0001	.0001	.0000	.0000
1	.0038	.0031	.0025	.0020	.0016	.0012	.0010	.0008	.0006	.0005
2	.0185	.0156	.0130	.0108	.0090	.0074	.0060	.0049	.0040	.0032
3	.0558	.0489	.0426	.0369	.0318	.0272	.0232	.0197	.0166	.0139
4	.1163	.1061	.0963	.0869	.0780	.0696	.0617	.0545	.0478	.0417
5	.1778	.1691	.1598	.1502	.1404	.1304	.1204	.1106	.1010	.0916
6	.2060	.2041	.2010	.1967	.1914	.1851	.1780	.1702	.1617	.1527
7	.1840	.1900	.1949	.1987	.2013	.2028	.2030	.2020	.1997	.1964
8	.1279	.1376	.1470	.1561	.1647	.1727	.1800	.1864	.1919	.1964
9	.0691	.0775	.0863	.0954	.1048	.1144	.1241	.1338	.1434	.1527
10	.0288	.0337	.0390	.0450	.0515	.0585	.0661	.0741	.0827	.0916
11	.0091	.0111	.0134	.0161	.0191	.0226	.0266	.0311	.0361	.0417
12	.0021	.0027	.0034	.0042	.0052	.0064	.0079	.0096	.0116	.0139
13	.0003	.0004	.0006	.0008	.0010	.0013	.0016	.0020	.0026	.0032
14	.0000	.0000	.0001	.0001	.0001	.0002	.0002	.0003	.0004	.0005

$n = 20$

x \ p	.01	.02	.03	.04	.05	.06	.07	.08	.09	.10
0	.8179	.6676	.5438	.4420	.3585	.2901	.2342	.1887	.1516	.1216
1	.1652	.2725	.3364	.3683	.3774	.3703	.3526	.3282	.3000	.2702
2	.0159	.0528	.0988	.1458	.1887	.2246	.2521	.2711	.2818	.2852
3	.0010	.0065	.0183	.0364	.0596	.0860	.1139	.1414	.1672	.1901
4	.0000	.0006	.0024	.0065	.0133	.0233	.0364	.0523	.0703	.0898
5	.0000	.0000	.0002	.0009	.0022	.0048	.0088	.0145	.0222	.0319
6	.0000	.0000	.0000	.0001	.0003	.0008	.0017	.0032	.0055	.0089
7	.0000	.0000	.0000	.0000	.0000	.0001	.0002	.0005	.0011	.0020
8	.0000	.0000	.0000	.0000	.0000	.0000	.0000	.0001	.0002	.0004
9	.0000	.0000	.0000	.0000	.0000	.0000	.0000	.0000	.0000	.0001

					$n = 20$ (Continued)					
x \ p	.11	.12	.13	.14	.15	.16	.17	.18	.19	.20
0	.0972	.0776	.0617	.0490	.0388	.0306	.0241	.0189	.0148	.0115
1	.2403	.2115	.1844	.1595	.1368	.1165	.0986	.0829	.0693	.0576
2	.2822	.2740	.2618	.2466	.2293	.2109	.1919	.1730	.1545	.1369
3	.2093	.2242	.2347	.2409	.2428	.2410	.2358	.2278	.2175	.2054
4	.1099	.1299	.1491	.1666	.1821	.1951	.2053	.2125	.2168	.2182
5	.0435	.0567	.0713	.1868	.1028	.1189	.1345	.1493	.1627	.1746
6	.0134	.0193	.0266	.0353	.0454	.0566	.0689	.0819	.0954	.1091
7	.0033	.0053	.0080	.0115	.0160	.0216	.0282	.0360	.0448	.0545
8	.0007	.0012	.0019	.0030	.0046	.0067	.0094	.0128	.0171	.0222
9	.0001	.0002	.0004	.0007	.0011	.0017	.0026	.0038	.0053	.0074
10	.0000	.0000	.0001	.0001	.0002	.0004	.0006	.0009	.0014	.0020
11	.0000	.0000	.0000	.0000	.0000	.0001	.0001	.0002	.0003	.0005
12	.0000	.0000	.0000	.0000	.0000	.0000	.0000	.0000	.0001	.0001

x	.21	.22	.23	.24	.25	.26	.27	.28	.29	.30
0	.0090	.0069	.0054	.0041	.0032	.0024	.0018	.0014	.0011	.0008
1	.0477	.0392	.0321	.0261	.0211	.0170	.0137	.0109	.0087	.0068
2	.1204	.1050	.0910	.0783	.0669	.0569	.0480	.0403	.0336	.0278
3	.1920	.1777	.1631	.1484	.1339	.1199	.1065	.0940	.0823	.0716
4	.2169	.2131	.2070	.1991	.1897	.1790	.1675	.1553	.1429	.1304
5	.1845	.1923	.1979	.2012	.2023	.2013	.1982	.1933	.1868	.1789
6	.1225	.1356	.1478	.1589	.1686	.1768	.1833	.1879	.1907	.1916
7	.0652	.0765	.0883	.1003	.1124	.1242	.1356	.1462	.1558	.1643
8	.0282	.0351	.0429	.0515	.0609	.0709	.0815	.0924	.1034	.1144
9	.0100	.0132	.0171	.0217	.0271	.0332	.0402	.0479	.0563	.0654
10	.0029	.0041	.0056	.0075	.0099	.0128	.0163	.0205	.0253	.0308
11	.0007	.0010	.0015	.0022	.0030	.0041	.0055	.0072	.0094	.0120
12	.0001	.0002	.0003	.0005	.0008	.0011	.0015	.0021	.0029	.0039
13	.0000	.0000	.0001	.0001	.0002	.0002	.0003	.0005	.0007	.0010
14	.0000	.0000	.0000	.0000	.0000	.0000	.0001	.0001	.0001	.0002

$n = 20$ (Continued)

x	.31	.32	.33	.34	.35	.36	.37	.38	.39	.40
0	.0006	.0004	.0003	.0002	.0002	.0001	.0001	.0001	.0001	.0000
1	.0054	.0042	.0033	.0025	.0020	.0015	.0011	.0009	.0007	.0005
2	.0229	.0188	.0153	.0124	.0100	.0080	.0064	.0050	.0040	.0031
3	.0619	.0531	.0453	.0383	.0323	.0270	.0224	.0185	.0152	.0123
4	.1181	.1062	.0947	.0839	.0738	.0645	.0559	.0482	.0412	.0350
5	.1698	.1599	.1493	.1384	.1272	.1161	.1051	.0945	.0843	.0746
6	.1907	.1881	.1839	.1782	.1712	.1632	.1543	.1447	.1347	.1244
7	.1714	.1770	.1811	.1836	.1844	.1836	.1812	.1774	.1722	.1659
8	.1251	.1354	.1450	.1537	.1614	.1678	.1730	.1767	.1790	.1797
9	.0750	.0849	.0952	.1056	.1158	.1259	.1354	.1444	.1526	.1597
10	.0370	.0440	.0516	.0598	.0686	.0779	.0875	.0974	.1073	.1171
11	.0151	.0188	.0231	.0280	.0336	.0398	.0467	.0542	.0624	.0710
12	.0051	.0066	.0085	.0108	.0136	.0168	.0206	.0249	.0299	.0355
13	.0014	.0019	.0026	.0034	.0045	.0058	.0074	.0094	.0118	.0146
14	.0003	.0005	.0006	.0009	.0012	.0016	.0022	.0029	.0038	.0049
15	.0001	.0001	.0001	.0002	.0003	.0004	.0005	.0007	.0010	.0013
16	.0000	.0000	.0000	.0000	.0000	.0001	.0001	.0001	.0002	.0003

x	.41	.42	.43	.44	.45	.46	.47	.48	.49	.50
0	.0000	.0000	.0000	.0000	.0000	.0000	.0000	.0000	.0000	.0000
1	.0004	.0003	.0002	.0001	.0001	.0001	.0001	.0000	.0000	.0000
2	.0024	.0018	.0014	.0011	.0008	.0006	.0005	.0003	.0002	.0002
3	.0100	.0080	.0064	.0051	.0040	.0031	.0024	.0019	.0014	.0011
4	.0295	.0247	.0206	.0170	.0139	.0113	.0092	.0074	.0059	.0046
5	.0656	.0573	.0496	.0427	.0365	.0309	.0260	.0217	.0180	.0148
6	.1140	.1037	.0936	.0839	.0746	.0658	.0577	.0501	.0432	.0370
7	.1585	.1502	.1413	.1318	.1221	.1122	.1023	.0925	.0830	.0739
8	.1790	.1768	.1732	.1683	.1623	.1553	.1474	.1388	.1296	.1201
9	.1658	.1707	.1742	.1763	.1771	.1763	.1742	.1708	.1661	.1602
10	.1268	.1359	.1446	.1524	.1593	.1652	.1700	.1734	.1755	.1762
11	.0801	.0895	.0991	.1089	.1185	.1280	.1370	.1455	.1533	.1602
12	.0417	.0486	.0561	.0642	.0727	.0818	.0911	.1007	.1105	.1201
13	.0178	.0217	.0260	.0310	.0366	.0429	.0497	.0572	.0653	.0739
14	.0062	.0078	.0098	.0122	.0150	.0183	.0221	.0264	.0314	.0370
15	.0017	.0023	.0030	.0038	.0049	.0062	.0078	.0098	.0121	.0148
16	.0004	.0005	.0007	.0009	.0013	.0017	.0022	.0028	.0036	.0046
17	.0001	.0001	.0001	.0002	.0002	.0003	.0005	.0006	.0008	.0011
18	.0000	.0000	.0000	.0000	.0000	.0000	.0001	.0001	.0001	.0002

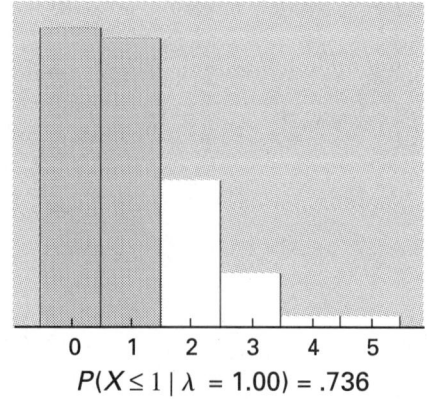

$P(X \le 1 \mid \lambda = 1.00) = .736$

x \ λ	.02	.04	.06	.08	.10	.15	.20	.25
0	.980	.961	.942	.923	.905	.861	.819	.779
1	1.000	.999	.998	.997	.995	.990	.982	.974
2		1.000	1.000	1.000	1.000	.999	.999	.998
3						1.000	1.000	1.000

x \ λ	.30	.35	.40	.45	.50	.55	.60	.65
0	.741	.705	.670	.638	.607	.577	.549	.522
1	.963	.951	.938	.925	.910	.894	.878	.861
2	.996	.994	.992	.989	.986	.982	.977	.972
3	1.000	1.000	.999	.999	.998	.998	.997	.996
4			1.000	1.000	1.000	1.000	1.000	.999
5								1.000

x \ λ	.70	.75	.80	.85	.90	.95	1.0	1.1
0	.497	.472	.449	.427	.407	.387	.368	.333
1	.844	.827	.809	.791	.772	.754	.736	.699
2	.966	.959	.953	.945	.937	.929	.920	.900
3	.994	.993	.991	.989	.987	.984	.981	.974
4	.999	.999	.999	.998	.998	.997	.996	.995
5	1.000	1.000	1.000	1.000	1.000	1.000	.999	.999
6							1.000	1.000

x \ λ	1.2	1.3	1.4	1.5	1.6	1.7	1.8	1.9
0	.301	.273	.247	.223	.202	.183	.165	.150
1	.663	.627	.592	.558	.525	.493	.463	.434
2	.879	.857	.833	.809	.783	.757	.731	.704
3	.966	.957	.946	.934	.921	.907	.891	.875
4	.992	.989	.986	.981	.976	.970	.964	.956
5	.998	.998	.997	.996	.994	.992	.990	.987
6	1.000	1.000	.999	.999	.999	.998	.997	.997
7			1.000	1.000	1.000	1.000	.999	.999
8							1.000	1.000

x \ λ	2.0	2.2	2.4	2.6	2.8	3.0	3.2	3.4
0	.135	.111	.091	.074	.061	.050	.041	.033
1	.406	.355	.308	.267	.231	.199	.171	.147
2	.677	.623	.570	.518	.469	.423	.380	.340
3	.857	.819	.779	.736	.692	.647	.603	.558
4	.947	.928	.904	.877	.848	.815	.781	.744
5	.983	.975	.964	.951	.935	.916	.895	.871
6	.995	.993	.988	.983	.976	.966	.955	.942
7	.999	.998	.997	.995	.992	.988	.983	.977
8	1.000	1.000	.999	.999	.998	.996	.994	.992
9			1.000	1.000	.999	.999	.998	.997
10					1.000	1.000	1.000	.999
11								1.000

x \ λ	3.6	3.8	4.0	4.2	4.4	4.6	4.8	5.0
0	.027	.022	.018	.015	.012	.010	.008	.007
1	.126	.107	.092	.078	.066	.056	.048	.040
2	.303	.269	.238	.210	.185	.163	.143	.125
3	.515	.473	.433	.395	.359	.326	.294	.265
4	.706	.668	.629	.590	.551	.513	.476	.440
5	.844	.816	.785	.753	.720	.686	.651	.616
6	.927	.909	.889	.867	.844	.818	.791	.762
7	.969	.960	.949	.936	.921	.905	.887	.867
8	.988	.984	.979	.972	.964	.955	.944	.932
9	.996	.994	.992	.989	.985	.980	.975	.968
10	.999	.998	.997	.996	.994	.992	.990	.986
11	1.000	.999	.999	.999	.998	.997	.996	.995
12		1.000	1.000	1.000	.999	.999	.999	.998
13					1.000	1.000	1.000	.999
14								1.000

x \ λ	5.2	5.4	5.6	5.8	6.0	6.2	6.4	6.6
0	.006	.005	.004	.003	.002	.002	.002	.001
1	.034	.029	.024	.021	.017	.015	.012	.010
2	.109	.095	.082	.072	.062	.054	.046	.040
3	.238	.213	.191	.170	.151	.134	.119	.105
4	.406	.373	.342	.313	.285	.259	.235	.213
5	.581	.546	.512	.478	.446	.414	.384	.355
6	.732	.702	.670	.638	.606	.574	.542	.511
7	.845	.822	.797	.771	.744	.716	.687	.658
8	.918	.903	.886	.867	.847	.826	.803	.780
9	.960	.951	.941	.929	.916	.902	.886	.869
10	.982	.977	.972	.965	.957	.949	.939	.927
11	.993	.990	.988	.984	.980	.975	.969	.963
12	.997	.996	.995	.993	.991	.989	.986	.982
13	.999	.999	.998	.997	.996	.995	.994	.992
14	1.000	.999	.999	.999	.999	.998	.997	.997
15		1.000	1.000	1.000	.999	.999	.999	.999
16					1.000	1.000	1.000	.999
17								1.000

x \ λ	6.8	7.0	7.2	7.4	7.6	7.8	8.0	8.5
0	.001	.001	.001	.001	.001	.000	.000	.000
1	.009	.007	.006	.005	.004	.004	.003	.002
2	.034	.030	.025	.022	.019	.016	.014	.009
3	.093	.082	.072	.063	.055	.048	.042	.030
4	.192	.173	.156	.140	.125	.112	.100	.074
5	.327	.301	.276	.253	.231	.210	.191	.150
6	.480	.450	.420	.392	.365	.338	.313	.256
7	.628	.599	.569	.539	.510	.481	.453	.386
8	.755	.729	.703	.676	.648	.620	.593	.523
9	.850	.830	.810	.788	.765	.741	.717	.653
10	.915	.901	.887	.871	.854	.835	.816	.763
11	.955	.947	.937	.926	.915	.902	.888	.849
12	.978	.973	.967	.961	.954	.945	.936	.909
13	.990	.987	.984	.980	.976	.971	.966	.949
14	.996	.994	.993	.991	.989	.986	.983	.973
15	.998	.998	.997	.996	.995	.993	.992	.986
16	.999	.999	.999	.998	.998	.997	.996	.993
17	1.000	1.000	.999	.999	.999	.999	.998	.997
18			1.000	1.000	1.000	1.000	.999	.999
19							1.000	.999
20								1.000

x \ λ	9.0	9.5	10.0	10.5	11.0	11.5	12.0	12.5
1	.001	.001	.000	.000	.000	.000	.000	.000
2	.006	.004	.003	.002	.001	.001	.001	.000
3	.021	.015	.010	.007	.005	.003	.002	.002
4	.055	.040	.029	.021	.015	.011	.008	.005
5	.116	.089	.067	.050	.038	.028	.020	.015
6	.207	.165	.130	.102	.079	.060	.046	.035
7	.324	.269	.220	.179	.143	.114	.090	.070
8	.456	.392	.333	.279	.232	.191	.155	.125
9	.587	.522	.458	.397	.341	.289	.242	.201
10	.706	.645	.583	.521	.460	.402	.347	.297
11	.803	.752	.697	.639	.579	.520	.462	.406
12	.876	.836	.792	.742	.689	.633	.576	.519
13	.926	.898	.864	.825	.781	.733	.682	.628
14	.959	.940	.917	.888	.854	.815	.772	.725
15	.978	.967	.951	.932	.907	.878	.844	.806
16	.989	.982	.973	.960	.944	.924	.899	.869
17	.995	.991	.986	.978	.968	.954	.937	.916
18	.998	.996	.993	.988	.982	.974	.963	.948
19	.999	.998	.997	.994	.991	.986	.979	.969
20	1.000	.999	.998	.997	.995	.992	.988	.983
21		1.000	.999	.999	.998	.996	.994	.991
22			1.000	.999	.999	.999	.997	.995
23				1.000	1.000	.999	.999	.998
24						1.000	.999	.999
25							1.000	.999
26								1.000

x \ λ	13.0	13.5	14.0	14.5	15	16	17	18
3	.001	.001	.000	.000	.000	.000	.000	.000
4	.004	.003	.002	.001	.001	.000	.000	.000
5	.011	.008	.006	.004	.003	.001	.001	.000
6	.026	.019	.014	.010	.008	.004	.002	.001
7	.054	.041	.032	.024	.018	.010	.005	.003
8	.100	.079	.062	.048	.037	.022	.013	.007
9	.166	.135	.109	.088	.070	.043	.026	.015
10	.252	.211	.176	.145	.118	.077	.049	.030
11	.353	.304	.260	.220	.155	.127	.085	.055
12	.463	.409	.358	.311	.268	.193	.135	.092
13	.573	.518	.464	.413	.363	.275	.201	.143
14	.675	.623	.570	518	.466	.368	.281	.208
15	.764	.718	.669	.619	.568	.467	.371	.287
16	.835	.798	.756	.711	.664	.566	.468	.375
17	.890	.861	.827	.790	.749	.659	.564	.469

x \ λ	13.0	13.5	14.0	14.5	15	16	17	18
18	.930	.908	.883	.853	.819	.742	.655	.562
19	.957	.942	.923	.901	.875	.812	.736	.651
20	.975	.965	.952	.936	.917	.868	.805	.731
21	.986	.980	.971	.960	.947	.911	.861	.799
22	.992	.989	.983	.976	.967	.942	.905	.855
23	.996	.994	.991	.986	.981	.963	.937	.899
24	.998	.997	.995	.992	.989	.978	.959	.932
25	.999	.998	.997	.996	.994	.987	.975	.955
26	1.000	.999	.999	.998	.997	.993	.985	.972
27		1.000	.999	.999	.998	.996	.991	.983
28			1.000	.999	.999	.998	.995	.990
29				1.000	1.000	.999	.997	.994
30						.999	.999	.997
31						1.000	.999	.998
32							1.000	.999
33								1.000

x \ λ	19	20	21	22	23	24	25
6	.001	.000	.000	.000	.000	.000	.000
7	.002	.001	.000	.000	.000	.000	.000
8	.004	.002	.001	.001	.000	.000	.000
9	.009	.005	.003	.002	.001	.000	.000
10	.018	.011	.006	.004	.002	.001	.001
11	.035	.021	.013	.008	.004	.003	.001
12	.061	.039	.025	.015	.009	.005	.003
13	.098	.066	.043	.028	.017	.011	.006
14	.150	.105	.072	.048	.031	.020	.012
15	.215	.157	.111	.077	.052	.034	.022
16	.292	.221	.163	.117	.082	.056	.038
17	.378	.297	.227	.169	.123	.087	.060
18	.469	.381	.302	.232	.175	.128	.092
19	.561	.470	.384	.306	.238	.180	.134
20	.647	.559	.471	.387	.310	.243	.185
21	.725	.644	.558	.472	.389	.314	.247
22	.793	.721	.640	.556	.472	.392	.318
23	.849	.787	.716	.637	.555	.473	.394
24	.893	.843	.782	.712	.635	.554	.473
25	.927	.888	.838	.777	.708	.632	.553
26	.951	.922	.883	.832	.772	.704	.629
27	.969	.948	.917	.877	.827	.768	.700
28	.980	.966	.944	.913	.873	.823	.763
29	.988	.978	.963	.940	.908	.868	.818

x \ λ	19	20	21	22	23	24	25
30	.993	.987	.976	.959	.936	.904	.863
31	.996	.992	.985	.973	.956	.932	.900
32	.998	.995	.991	.983	.971	.953	.929
33	.999	.997	.994	.989	.981	.969	.950
34	.999	.999	.997	.994	.988	.979	.966
35	1.000	.999	.998	.996	.993	.987	.978
36		1.000	.999	.998	.996	.992	.985
37			.999	.999	.997	.995	.991
38			1.000	.999	.999	.997	.994
39				1.000	.999	.998	.997
40					1.000	.999	.998
41						.999	.999
42						1.000	.999
43							1.000

3 APPENDIX The Normal Table

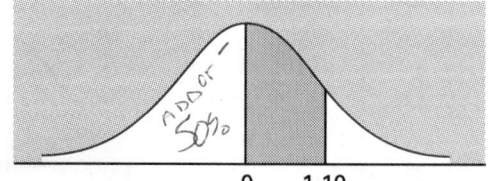

$P(0 < Z < 1.10) = .3643$

z	.00	.01	.02	.03	.04	.05	.06	.07	.08	.09
0.0	.0000	.0040	.0080	.0120	.0160	.0199	.0239	.0279	.0319	.0359
0.1	.0398	.0438	.0478	.0517	.0557	.0596	.0636	.0675	.0714	.0753
0.2	.0793	.0832	.0871	.0910	.0948	.0987	.1026	.1064	.1103	.1141
0.3	.1179	.1217	.1255	.1293	.1331	.1368	.1406	.1443	.1480	.1517
0.4	.1554	.1591	.1628	.1664	.1700	.1736	.1772	.1808	.1844	.1879
0.5	.1915	.1950	.1985	.2019	.2054	.2088	.2123	.2157	.2190	.2224
0.6	.2257	.2291	.2324	.2357	.2389	.2422	.2454	.2486	.2517	.2549
0.7	.2580	.2611	.2642	.2673	.2704	.2734	.2764	.2794	.2823	.2852
0.8	.2881	.2910	.2939	.2967	.2995	.3023	.3051	.3078	.3016	.3133
0.9	.3159	.3186	.3212	.3238	.3264	.3289	.3315	.3340	.3365	.3389
1.0	.3413	.3438	.3461	.3485	.3508	.3531	.3554	.3577	.3599	.3621
1.1	.3643	.3665	.3686	.3708	.3729	.3749	.3770	.3790	.3810	.3830
1.2	.3849	.3869	.3888	.3907	.3925	.3944	.3962	.3980	.3997	.4015
1.3	.4032	.4049	.4066	.4082	.4099	.4115	.4131	.4147	.4162	.4177
1.4	.4192	.4207	.4222	.4236	.4251	.4265	.4279	.4292	.4306	.4319
1.5	.4332	.4345	.4357	.4370	.4382	.4394	.4406	.4418	.4429	.4441
1.6	.4452	.4463	.4474	.4484	.4495	.4505	.4515	.4525	.4535	.4545
1.7	.4554	.4564	.4573	.4582	.4591	.4599	.4608	.4616	.4625	.4633
1.8	.4641	.4649	.4656	.4664	.4671	.4678	.4686	.4693	.4699	.4706
1.9	.4713	.4719	.4726	.4732	.4738	.4744	.4750	.4756	.4761	.4767
2.0	.4772	.4778	.4783	.4788	.4793	.4798	.4803	.4808	.4812	.4817
2.1	.4821	.4826	.4830	.4834	.4838	.4842	.4846	.4850	.4854	.4857
2.2	.4861	.4864	.4868	.4871	.4875	.4878	.4881	.4884	.4887	.4890
2.3	.4893	.4896	.4898	.4901	.4904	.4906	.4909	.4911	.4913	.4916
2.4	.4918	.4920	.4922	.4925	.4927	.4929	.4931	.4932	.4934	.4936
2.5	.4938	.4940	.4941	.4943	.4945	.4946	.4948	.4949	.4951	.4952
2.6	.4953	.4955	.4956	.4957	.4959	.4960	.4961	.4962	.4963	.4964
2.7	.4965	.4966	.4967	.4968	.4969	.4970	.4971	.4972	.4973	.4974
2.8	.4974	.4975	.4976	.4977	.4977	.4978	.4979	.4979	.4980	.4981
2.9	.4981	.4982	.4982	.4982	.4984	.4984	.4985	.4985	.4986	.4986
3.0	.4987	.4987	.4987	.4988	.4988	.4989	.4989	.4989	.4990	.4990

4 APPENDIX Table of Random Numbers

Line	(1)	(2)	(3)	(4)	(5)	(6)	(7)	(8)	(9)	(10)	(11)	(12)	(13)	(14)
1	10480	15011	01536	02011	81647	91646	69179	14194	62590	36207	20969	99570	91291	90700
2	22368	46573	25595	85393	30995	89198	27982	53402	93965	34095	52666	19174	39615	99505
3	24130	48360	22527	97265	76393	64809	15179	24830	49340	32081	30680	19655	63348	58629
4	42167	93093	06243	61680	07856	16376	39440	53537	71341	57004	00849	74917	97758	16379
5	37570	39975	81837	16656	06121	91782	60468	81305	49684	60672	14110	06927	01263	54613
6	77921	06907	11008	42751	27756	53498	18602	70659	90655	15053	21916	81825	44394	42880
7	99562	72905	56420	69994	98872	31016	71194	18738	44013	48840	63213	21069	10634	12952
8	96301	91977	05463	07972	18876	20922	94595	56869	69014	60045	18425	84903	42508	32307
9	89579	14342	63661	10281	17453	18103	57740	84378	25331	12566	58678	44947	05585	56941
10	85475	36857	53342	53988	53060	59533	38867	62300	08158	17983	16439	11458	18593	64952
11	28918	69578	88231	33276	70997	79936	56865	05859	90106	31595	01547	85590	91610	78188
12	63553	40961	48235	03427	49626	69445	18663	72695	52180	20847	12234	90511	33703	90322
13	09429	93969	52636	92737	88974	33488	36320	17617	30015	08272	84115	27156	30613	74952
14	10365	61129	87529	85689	48237	52267	67689	93394	01511	26358	85104	20285	29975	89868
15	07119	97336	71048	08178	77233	13916	47564	81056	97735	85977	29372	74461	28551	90707
16	51085	12765	51821	51259	77452	16308	60756	92144	49442	53900	70960	63990	75601	40719
17	02368	21382	52404	60268	89368	19885	55322	44819	01188	65255	64835	44919	05944	55157
18	01011	54092	33362	94904	31273	04146	18594	29852	71585	85030	51132	01915	92747	64951
19	52162	53916	46369	58586	23216	14513	83149	98736	23495	64350	94738	17752	35156	35749
20	07056	97628	33787	09998	42698	06691	76988	13602	51851	46104	88916	19509	25625	58104
21	48663	91245	85828	14346	09172	30168	90229	04734	59193	22178	30421	61666	99904	32812
22	54164	58492	22421	74103	47070	25306	76468	26384	58151	06646	21524	15227	96909	44592
23	32639	32363	05597	24200	13363	38005	94342	28728	35806	06912	17012	64161	18296	22851
24	29334	27001	87637	87308	58731	00256	45834	15398	46557	41135	10367	07684	36188	18510
25	02488	33062	28834	07351	19731	92420	60952	61280	50001	67658	32586	86679	50720	94953
26	81525	72295	04839	96423	24878	82651	66566	14778	76797	14780	13300	87074	79666	95725
27	29676	20591	68086	26432	46901	20849	89768	81536	86645	12659	92259	57102	80428	25280
28	00742	57392	39064	66432	84673	40027	32832	61362	98947	96067	64760	64584	96096	98253
29	05366	04213	25669	26422	44407	44048	37937	63904	45766	66134	75470	66520	34693	90449
30	91921	26418	64117	94305	26766	25940	39972	22209	71500	64568	91402	42416	07844	69618
31	00582	04711	87917	77341	42206	35126	74087	99547	81817	42607	43808	76655	62028	76630
32	00725	69884	62797	56170	86324	88072	76222	36086	84637	93161	76038	65855	77919	88006
33	69011	65795	95876	55293	18988	27354	26575	08625	40801	59920	29841	80150	12777	48501
34	25976	57948	29888	88604	67917	48708	18912	82271	65424	69774	33611	54262	85963	03547
35	09763	83473	73577	12908	30883	18317	28290	35797	05998	41688	34952	37888	38917	88050
36	91567	42595	27958	30134	04024	86305	29880	99730	55536	84855	29080	09250	79656	73211
37	17955	56349	90999	49127	20044	59931	06115	20542	18059	02008	73708	83517	36103	42791
38	46503	18584	18845	49618	02304	51038	20655	58727	28168	15475	56942	53389	20562	87338
39	92157	89634	94824	78171	84610	82834	09922	25417	44137	48413	25555	21246	35509	20468
40	14577	62765	35605	81263	39667	47358	56873	56307	61607	49518	89656	20103	77490	18062
41	98427	07523	33362	64270	01638	92447	66969	98420	04880	45585	46565	04102	46880	45709
42	34914	63976	88720	82765	34476	17032	87589	40836	32427	70002	70663	88863	77775	69348
43	70060	28277	39475	46473	23219	53416	94970	25832	69975	94884	19661	72828	00102	66794
44	53976	54914	06990	67245	68350	82948	11398	42878	80287	88267	47363	46634	06541	97809
45	76072	29515	40980	07391	58745	25774	22987	80059	39911	96189	41151	14222	60697	59583

Line	(1)	(2)	(3)	(4)	(5)	(6)	(7)	(8)	(9)	(10)	(11)	(12)	(13)	(14)
46	90725	52210	83974	29992	65831	38857	50490	83765	55657	14361	31720	57375	56228	41546
47	64364	67412	33339	31926	14883	24413	59744	92351	97473	89286	35931	04110	23726	51900
48	08962	00358	31662	25388	61642	34072	81249	35648	56891	69352	48373	45578	78547	81788
49	95012	68379	93526	70765	10592	04542	76463	54328	02349	17247	28865	14777	62730	92277
50	15664	10493	20492	38391	91132	21999	59516	81652	27195	48223	46751	22923	32261	85653
51	16408	81899	04153	53381	79401	21438	83035	92350	36693	31238	59649	91754	72772	02338
52	18629	81953	05520	91962	04739	13092	97662	24822	94730	06496	35090	04822	86774	98289
53	73115	35101	47498	87637	99016	71060	88824	71013	18735	20286	23153	72924	35165	43040
54	57491	16703	23167	49323	45021	33132	12544	41035	80780	45393	44812	12515	98931	91202
55	30405	83946	23792	14422	15059	45799	22716	19792	09983	74353	68668	30429	70735	25499
56	16631	35006	85900	98275	32388	52390	16815	69298	82732	38480	73817	32523	41961	44437
57	96773	20206	42559	78985	05300	22164	24369	54224	35083	19687	11052	91491	60383	19746
58	38935	64202	14349	82674	66523	44133	00697	35552	35970	19124	63318	29686	03387	59846
59	31624	76384	17403	53363	44167	64486	64758	75366	76554	31601	12614	33072	60332	92325
60	78919	19474	23632	27889	47914	02584	37680	20801	72152	39339	34806	08930	85001	87820
61	03931	33309	57047	74211	63445	17361	62825	39908	05607	91284	68833	25570	38818	46920
62	74426	33278	43972	10119	89917	15665	52872	73823	73144	88662	88970	74492	51805	99378
63	09066	00903	20795	95452	92648	45454	09552	88815	16553	51125	79375	97596	16296	66092
64	42238	12426	87025	14267	20979	04508	64535	31355	86064	29472	47689	05974	52468	16834
65	16153	08002	26504	41744	81959	65642	74240	56302	00033	67107	77510	70625	28725	34191

5 APPENDIX Student *t*-Table

df	2-sided 20% CI or 1-sided 60% CI	2-sided 40% CI or 1-sided 70% CI	2-sided 60% CI or 1-sided 80% CI	2-sided 80% CI or 1-sided 90% CI	2-sided 90% CI or 1-sided 95% CI	2-sided 95% CI or 1-sided 97.5% CI	2-sided 98% CI or 1-sided 99% CI	2-sided 99% CI or 1-sided 99.5% CI
1	.325	.727	1.376	3.078	6.314	12.706	31.821	63.657
2	.289	.617	1.061	1.886	2.920	4.303	6.965	9.925
3	.277	.584	.978	1.638	2.353	3.182	4.541	5.841
4	.271	.569	.941	1.533	2.132	2.776	3.747	4.604
5	.267	.559	.920	1.476	2.015	2.571	3.365	4.032
6	.265	.553	.906	1.440	1.943	2.447	3.143	3.707
7	.263	.549	.896	1.415	1.895	2.365	2.998	3.499
8	.262	.546	.889	1.397	1.860	2.306	2.896	3.355
9	.261	.543	.883	1.383	1.833	2.262	2.821	3.250
10	.260	.542	.879	1.372	1.812	2.228	2.764	3.169
11	.260	.540	.876	1.363	1.796	2.201	2.718	3.106
12	.259	.539	.873	1.356	1.782	2.179	2.681	3.055
13	.259	.538	.870	1.350	1.771	2.160	2.650	3.012
14	.258	.537	.868	1.345	1.761	2.145	2.624	2.977
15	.258	.536	.866	1.341	1.753	2.131	2.602	2.947
16	.258	.535	.865	1.337	1.746	2.120	2.583	2.921
17	.257	.534	.863	1.333	1.740	2.110	2.567	2.898
18	.257	.534	.862	1.330	1.734	2.101	2.552	2.878
19	.257	.533	.861	1.328	1.729	2.093	2.539	2.861
20	.257	.533	.860	1.325	1.725	2.086	2.528	2.845
21	.257	.532	.859	1.323	1.721	2.080	2.518	2.831
22	.256	.532	.858	1.321	1.717	2.074	2.508	2.819
23	.256	.532	.858	1.319	1.714	2.069	2.500	2.807
24	.256	.531	.857	1.318	1.711	2.064	2.492	2.797
25	.256	.531	.856	1.316	1.708	2.060	2.485	2.787
26	.256	.531	.856	1.315	1.706	2.056	2.479	2.779
27	.256	.531	.855	1.314	1.703	2.052	2.473	2.771
28	.256	.530	.855	1.313	1.701	2.048	2.467	2.763
29	.256	.530	.854	1.311	1.699	2.045	2.462	2.756
30	.256	.530	.854	1.310	1.697	2.042	2.457	2.750
40	.255	.529	.851	1.303	1.684	2.021	2.423	2.704
60	.254	.527	.848	1.296	1.671	2.000	2.390	2.660
120	.254	.526	.845	1.289	1.658	1.980	2.358	2.617
∞	.253	.524	.842	1.282	1.645	1.960	2.326	2.576

← z-table values

6 APPENDIX Percentiles of the χ^2 Distribution

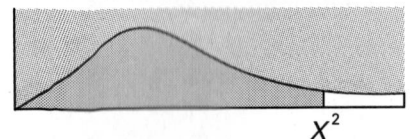

χ^2

df	$\chi^2_{.005}$	$\chi^2_{.01}$	$\chi^2_{.025}$	$\chi^2_{.05}$	$\chi^2_{.10}$	$\chi^2_{.90}$	$\chi^2_{.95}$	$\chi^2_{.975}$	$\chi^2_{.99}$	$\chi^2_{.995}$
1	.000039	.00016	.00098	.0039	.0158	2.71	3.84	5.02	6.63	7.88
2	.0100	.0201	.0506	.1026	.2107	4.61	5.99	7.38	9.21	10.60
3	.0717	.115	.216	.352	.584	6.25	7.81	9.35	11.34	12.84
4	.207	.297	.484	.711	1.064	7.78	9.49	11.14	13.28	14.86
5	.412	.554	.831	1.15	1.61	9.24	11.07	12.83	15.09	16.75
6	.676	.872	1.24	1.64	2.20	10.64	12.59	14.45	16.81	18.55
7	.989	1.24	1.69	2.17	2.83	12.02	14.07	16.01	18.48	20.28
8	1.34	1.65	2.18	2.73	3.49	13.36	15.51	17.53	20.09	21.96
9	1.73	2.09	2.70	3.33	4.17	14.68	16.92	19.02	21.67	23.59
10	2.16	2.56	3.25	3.94	4.87	15.99	18.31	20.48	23.21	25.19
11	2.60	3.05	3.82	4.57	5.58	17.28	19.68	21.92	24.73	26.76
12	3.07	3.57	4.40	5.23	6.30	18.55	21.03	23.34	26.22	28.30
13	3.57	4.11	5.01	5.89	7.04	19.81	22.36	24.74	27.69	29.82
14	4.07	4.66	5.63	6.57	7.79	21.06	23.68	26.12	29.14	31.32
15	4.60	5.23	6.26	7.26	8.55	22.31	25.00	27.49	30.58	32.80
16	5.14	5.81	6.91	7.96	9.31	23.54	26.30	28.85	32.00	34.27
18	6.26	7.01	8.23	9.39	10.86	25.99	28.87	31.53	34.81	37.16
20	7.43	8.26	9.59	10.85	12.44	28.41	31.41	34.17	37.57	40.00
24	9.89	10.86	12.40	13.85	15.66	33.20	36.42	39.36	42.98	45.56
30	13.79	14.95	16.79	18.49	20.60	40.26	43.77	46.98	50.89	53.67
40	20.71	22.16	24.43	26.51	29.05	51.81	55.76	59.34	63.69	66.77
60	35.53	37.48	40.48	43.19	46.46	74.40	79.08	83.30	88.38	91.95
120	83.85	86.92	91.58	95.70	100.62	140.23	146.57	152.21	158.95	163.64

7 APPENDIX   The *F* Distribution

df for denominator	Percentile	\ df for numerator								
		1	2	3	4	5	6	7	8	9
1	.025	0	.03	.06	.08	.10	.11	.12	.13	.14
	.05	0	.05	.10	.13	.15	.17	.17	.18	.19
	.90	39.9	49.5	53.6	55.8	57.2	58.2	58.9	59.4	59.9
	.95	161	200	216	225	230	234	237	239	241
	.975	648	800	864	900	922	937	948	957	963
	.99	4,052	5,000	5,403	5,625	5,764	5,859	5,928	5,981	6,022
	.995	16,211	20,000	21,615	22,500	23,056	23,437	23,715	23,925	24,091
	.999	405,280	500,000	540,500	562,500	576,400	585,940	592,870	598,140	602,280
2	.025	0	.03	.06	.07	.12	.13	.15	.17	.18
	.05	0	.05	.10	.14	.17	.19	.21	.22	.23
	.90	8.53	9.00	9.16	9.24	9.29	9.33	9.35	9.37	9.38
	.95	18.5	19.0	19.2	19.2	19.3	19.3	19.4	19.4	19.4
	.975	38.5	39.0	39.2	39.2	30.3	39.3	39.4	39.4	39.4
	.99	98.5	99.0	99.2	99.2	99.3	99.3	99.4	99.4	99.4
	.995	199	199	199	199	199	199	199	199	199
	.999	998.5	999.0	999.2	999.2	999.3	999.3	999.4	999.4	999.4
3	.025	0	.03	.06	.10	.12	.15	.17	.18	.20
	.05	0	.05	.11	.15	.18	.21	.22	.25	.26
	.90	5.54	5.46	5.39	5.34	5.31	5.28	5.27	5.25	5.24
	.95	10.1	9.55	9.28	9.12	9.01	8.94	8.89	8.85	8.81
	.975	17.4	16.0	15.4	15.1	14.9	14.7	14.6	14.5	14.5
	.99	34.1	30.8	29.5	28.7	28.2	27.9	27.7	27.5	27.3
	.995	55.6	49.8	47.5	46.2	45.4	44.8	44.4	44.1	43.9
	.999	167.0	148.5	141.1	137.1	134.6	132.8	131.6	130.6	129.9
4	.025	0	.03	.07	.10	.14	.16	.18	.20	.21
	.05	0	.05	.11	.16	.19	.22	.24	.26	.28
	.90	4.54	4.32	4.19	4.11	4.05	4.01	3.98	3.95	3.94
	.95	7.71	6.94	6.59	6.39	6.26	6.16	6.09	6.04	6.00
	.975	12.2	10.6	9.98	9.60	9.36	9.20	9.07	8.98	8.90
	.99	21.2	18.0	16.7	16.0	15.5	15.2	15.0	14.8	14.7
	.995	31.3	26.3	24.3	23.2	22.5	22.0	21.6	21.4	21.1
	.999	74.1	61.2	56.2	53.4	51.7	50.5	49.7	49.0	48.5
5	.025	0	.03	.07	.11	.14	.17	.19	.21	.22
	.05	0	.05	.11	.16	.20	.23	.25	.27	.29
	.90	4.06	3.79	3.62	3.52	3.45	3.40	3.37	3.34	3.32
	.95	6.61	5.79	5.41	5.19	5.05	4.95	4.88	4.82	4.77
	.975	10.0	8.43	7.76	7.39	7.15	6.98	6.85	6.76	6.68
	.99	16.3	13.3	12.1	11.4	11.0	10.7	10.5	10.3	10.2
	.995	22.8	19.3	16.5	15.6	14.9	14.5	14.2	14.0	13.8
	.999	47.2	37.1	33.2	31.1	29.8	28.8	28.2	27.6	27.2
6	.025	0	.03	.07	.11	.14	.17	.20	.22	.23
	.05	0	.05	.11	.16	.20	.23	.25	.28	.30
	.90	3.78	3.46	3.26	3.18	3.11	3.05	3.01	2.98	2.96
	.95	5.99	5.14	4.76	4.53	4.39	4.28	4.21	4.15	4.10
	.975	8.81	7.26	6.60	6.23	5.99	5.82	5.70	5.60	5.52
	.99	13.7	10.9	9.78	9.15	8.75	8.47	8.26	8.10	7.98
	.995	18.6	14.5	12.9	12.0	11.5	11.1	10.8	10.6	10.4
	.999	35.5	27.0	23.7	21.9	20.8	20.0	19.5	19.0	18.7

df for denominator	Percentile	df for numerator								
		10	12	15	20	24	30	60	120	∞
1	.025	.14	.15	.16	.17	.17	.18	.19	.19	.20
	.05	.20	.21	.22	.23	.23	.24	.25	.26	.26
	.90	60.2	60.7	61.2	61.7	62.0	62.3	62.8	63.1	63.3
	.95	242	244	245	248	249	250	252	253	254
	.975	969	977	985	993	997	1,001	1,010	1,014	1,018
	.99	6,056	6,106	6,157	6,2.9	6,235	6,261	6,313	6,339	6,366
	.995	24,224	24,426	24,630	24,836	24,940	25,044	25,253	25,359	25,464
	.999	605,620	605,670	615,760	620,910	623,500	626,100	631,340	633,970	636,620
2	.025	.18	.20	.21	.22	.23	.24	.25	.26	.27
	.05	.24	.26	.27	.29	.29	.30	.32	.33	.33
	.90	9.39	9.41	9.42	9.44	9.45	9.46	9.47	9.48	9.49
	.95	19.4	19.4	19.4	19.4	19.5	19.5	19.5	19.5	19.5
	.975	39.4	39.4	39.4	39.4	39.5	39.5	39.5	39.5	39.5
	.99	99.4	99.4	99.4	99.4	99.5	99.5	99.5	99.5	99.5
	.995	199	199	199	199	199	199	199	199	200
	.999	999.4	999.4	999.4	999.4	999.5	999.5	999.5	999.5	999.5
3	.025	.21	.22	.24	.26	.27	.28	.30	.31	.32
	.05	.27	.29	.30	.32	.33	.34	.36	.37	.38
	.90	5.23	5.22	5.20	5.18	5.18	5.17	5.15	5.14	5.13
	.95	8.79	8.74	8.70	8.66	8.64	8.62	8.57	8.55	8.53
	.975	14.4	14.3	14.3	14.2	14.1	14.1	14.0	13.9	13.9
	.99	27.2	27.1	26.9	26.7	26.6	26.4	26.3	26.2	26.1
	.995	43.7	43.4	43.1	42.8	42.6	42.5	42.1	42.0	41.8
	.999	129.2	128.3	127.4	126.4	125.9	125.4	124.5	124.0	123.5
4	.025	.22	.24	.26	.28	.30	.31	.33	.34	.36
	.05	.29	.31	.33	.35	.36	.37	.40	.41	.42
	.90	3.92	3.90	3.87	3.84	3.83	3.82	3.79	3.78	3.76
	.95	5.96	5.91	5.86	5.90	5.77	5.75	5.69	5.66	5.63
	.975	8.84	8.75	8.66	8.56	8.51	8.46	8.36	8.31	8.26
	.99	14.5	14.4	14.2	14.0	13.9	13.8	13.7	13.6	13.5
	.995	21.0	20.7	20.4	20.2	20.0	19.9	19.6	19.5	19.3
	.999	48.1	47.4	46.8	46.1	45.8	45.4	44.7	44.4	44.1
5	.025	.24	.26	.28	.30	.32	.33	.36	.37	.39
	.05	.30	.32	.34	.37	.38	.40	.42	.44	.45
	.90	3.30	3.27	3.24	3.21	3.19	3.17	3.14	3.12	3.11
	.95	4.74	4.68	4.62	4.56	4.53	4.50	4.43	4.40	4.37
	.975	6.62	6.52	6.43	6.33	6.28	6.23	6.12	6.07	6.02
	.99	10.1	9.89	9.72	9.55	9.47	9.38	9.20	9.11	9.02
	.995	13.6	13.4	13.1	12.9	12.8	12.7	12.4	12.3	12.1
	.999	26.9	26.4	25.9	25.4	25.1	24.9	24.3	24.1	23.8
6	.025	.25	.27	.29	.32	.33	.35	.38	.40	.41
	.05	.31	.33	.36	.38	.40	.41	.44	.46	.48
	.90	2.94	2.90	2.87	2.84	2.82	2.80	2.76	2.74	2.72
	.95	4.06	4.00	3.94	3.87	3.84	3.81	3.74	3.70	3.67
	.975	5.46	5.37	5.27	5.17	5.12	5.07	4.96	4.90	4.85
	.99	7.87	7.72	7.56	7.40	7.31	7.23	7.06	6.97	6.88
	.995	10.2	10.0	9.81	9.59	9.47	9.36	9.12	9.00	8.88
	.999	18.4	18.0	17.6	17.1	16.9	16.7	16.2	16.0	15.7

df for denominator	Percentile	\multicolumn{9}{c}{df for numerator}
		1	2	3	4	5	6	7	8	9
7	.025	0	.03	.07	.11	.14	.18	.20	.22	.24
	.05	0	.05	.11	.16	.20	.24	.26	.29	.30
	.90	3.59	3.26	3.07	2.96	2.88	2.83	2.78	2.75	2.72
	.95	5.59	4.74	4.35	4.12	3.97	3.87	3.79	3.73	3.68
	.975	8.07	6.54	5.89	5.52	5.29	5.12	4.99	4.90	4.82
	.99	12.2	9.55	8.45	7.85	7.46	7.19	6.99	6.84	6.72
	.995	16.2	12.4	10.9	10.1	9.52	9.16	8.89	8.69	8.51
	.999	29.2	21.7	18.8	17.2	16.2	15.5	15.0	14.6	14.3
8	.025	0	.03	.07	.11	.15	.18	.20	.23	.24
	.05	0	.05	.11	.17	.21	.24	.27	.29	.31
	.90	3.46	3.11	2.92	2.81	2.73	2.67	2.62	2.59	2.56
	.95	5.32	4.46	4.07	3.84	3.69	3.58	3.50	3.44	3.39
	.975	7.57	6.06	5.42	5.05	4.82	4.65	4.53	4.43	4.36
	.99	11.3	8.65	7.59	7.01	6.63	6.37	6.18	6.03	5.91
	.995	14.7	11.0	9.60	8.81	8.30	7.95	7.69	7.50	7.34
	.999	25.4	18.5	15.8	14.4	13.5	12.9	12.4	12.0	11.8
9	.025	0	.03	.07	.11	.15	.18	.21	.23	.23
	.05	0	.05	.11	.17	.21	.24	.27	.29	.31
	.90	3.36	3.01	2.81	2.69	2.61	2.55	2.51	2.47	2.44
	.95	5.12	4.26	3.86	3.63	3.48	3.37	3.29	3.23	3.18
	.975	7.21	5.71	5.08	4.72	4.48	4.32	4.20	4.10	4.03
	.99	10.6	8.02	6.99	6.42	6.06	5.80	5.61	5.47	5.35
	.995	13.6	10.1	8.72	7.96	7.47	7.13	6.88	6.69	6.54
	.999	22.9	16.4	13.9	12.6	11.7	11.1	10.7	10.4	10.1
10	.025	0	.03	.07	.11	.15	.18	.21	.23	.25
	.05	0	.05	.11	.17	.21	.25	.27	.30	.32
	.90	3.29	2.92	2.73	2.61	2.52	2.46	2.41	2.38	2.35
	.95	4.96	4.10	3.71	3.48	3.33	3.22	3.14	3.07	3.02
	.975	6.94	5.46	4.83	4.47	4.24	4.07	3.95	3.85	3.78
	.99	10.0	7.56	6.55	5.99	5.64	5.39	5.20	5.06	4.94
	.995	12.8	9.43	8.08	7.34	6.87	6.54	6.30	6.12	5.97
	.999	21.0	14.9	12.6	11.3	10.5	9.93	9.52	9.20	8.96
12	.025	0	.03	.07	.11	.15	.19	.21	.23	.26
	.05	0	.05	.11	.17	.21	.25	.28	.30	.33
	.90	3.18	2.81	2.61	2.48	2.39	2.33	2.28	2.24	2.21
	.95	4.75	3.89	3.49	3.26	3.11	3.00	2.91	2.85	2.80
	.975	6.55	5.10	4.47	4.12	3.89	3.73	3.61	3.51	3.44
	.99	9.33	6.93	5.95	5.41	5.06	4.82	4.64	4.50	4.39
	.995	11.8	8.51	7.23	6.52	6.07	5.76	5.52	5.35	5.20
	.999	18.6	13.0	10.8	9.63	8.89	8.38	8.00	7.71	7.48
15	.025	0	.03	.07	.12	.16	.19	.22	.24	.27
	.05	0	.05	.11	.17	.22	.25	.28	.31	.33
	.90	3.07	2.70	2.49	2.36	2.27	2.21	2.16	2.12	2.09
	.95	4.54	3.68	3.29	3.06	2.90	2.79	2.71	2.64	2.59
	.975	6.20	4.77	4.15	3.80	3.58	3.41	3.29	3.20	3.12
	.99	8.68	6.36	5.42	4.89	4.56	4.32	4.14	4.00	3.89
	.995	10.8	7.70	6.48	5.80	5.37	5.07	4.85	4.67	4.54
	.999	16.6	11.3	9.34	8.25	7.57	7.09	6.74	6.47	6.26

df for denominator	Percentile	df for numerator								
		10	12	15	20	24	30	60	120	∞
7	.025	.25	.28	.30	.33	.35	.36	.40	.42	.44
	.05	.32	.34	.37	.40	.41	.43	.46	.48	.50
	.90	2.70	2.67	2.63	2.59	2.58	2.56	2.51	2.49	2.47
	.95	3.64	3.57	3.51	3.44	3.41	3.38	3.30	3.27	3.23
	.975	4.76	4.67	4.57	4.47	4.42	4.36	4.25	4.20	4.14
	.99	6.62	6.47	6.31	6.16	6.07	5.99	5.82	5.74	5.65
	.995	8.38	8.18	7.97	7.75	7.65	7.53	7.31	7.19	7.08
	.999	14.1	13.7	13.3	12.9	12.7	12.5	12.1	11.9	11.7
8	.025	.26	.28	.31	.34	.36	.38	.41	.43	.46
	.05	.33	.35	.38	.41	.42	.44	.48	.50	.52
	.90	2.54	2.50	2.46	2.42	2.40	2.38	2.34	2.32	2.29
	.95	3.35	3.28	3.22	3.15	3.12	3.08	3.01	2.97	2.93
	.975	4.30	4.20	4.10	4.00	3.95	3.89	3.78	3.73	3.67
	.99	5.81	5.67	5.52	5.36	5.28	5.20	5.03	4.95	4.86
	.995	7.21	7.01	6.81	6.61	6.50	6.40	6.18	6.06	5.95
	.999	11.5	11.2	10.8	10.5	10.3	10.1	9.73	9.53	9.33
9	.025	.26	.29	.32	.35	.37	.39	.43	.45	.47
	.05	.33	.36	.39	.41	.43	.45	.49	.51	.53
	.90	2.42	2.38	2.34	2.30	2.28	2.25	2.21	2.18	2.16
	.95	3.14	3.07	3.01	2.94	2.90	2.86	2.79	2.75	2.71
	.975	3.96	3.87	3.77	3.67	3.61	3.56	3.45	3.39	3.33
	.99	5.26	5.11	4.96	4.81	4.73	4.65	4.48	4.40	4.31
	.995	6.42	6.23	6.03	5.83	5.73	5.62	5.41	5.30	5.19
	.999	9.89	9.57	9.24	8.90	8.72	8.55	8.19	8.00	7.81
10	.025	.27	.30	.33	.36	.38	.40	.44	.46	.49
	.05	.34	.36	.39	.43	.44	.46	.50	.52	.55
	.90	2.32	2.28	2.24	2.20	2.18	2.16	2.11	2.08	2.06
	.95	2.98	2.91	2.84	2.77	2.74	2.70	2.62	2.58	2.54
	.975	3.72	3.62	3.52	3.42	3.37	3.31	3.20	3.14	3.08
	.99	4.85	4.71	4.56	4.41	4.33	4.25	4.08	4.00	3.91
	.995	5.85	5.66	5.47	5.27	5.17	5.07	4.86	4.75	4.64
	.999	8.75	8.45	8.13	7.80	7.64	7.47	7.12	6.94	6.76
12	.025	.28	.30	.34	.37	.39	.41	.46	.49	.52
	.05	.34	.37	.40	.44	.46	.48	.52	.55	.57
	.90	2.19	2.15	2.10	2.06	2.04	2.01	1.96	1.93	1.90
	.95	2.75	2.69	2.62	2.54	2.51	2.47	2.38	2.34	2.30
	.975	3.37	3.28	3.18	3.07	3.02	2.96	2.85	2.79	2.72
	.99	4.30	4.16	4.01	3.86	3.78	3.70	3.54	3.45	3.36
	.995	5.09	4.91	4.72	4.53	4.43	4.33	4.12	4.01	3.90
	.999	7.29	7.00	6.71	6.40	6.25	6.09	5.76	5.59	5.42
15	.025	.28	.31	.35	.39	.41	.43	.49	.51	.55
	.05	.35	.38	.42	.45	.47	.50	.54	.57	.59
	.90	2.06	2.02	1.97	1.92	1.90	1.87	1.82	1.79	1.76
	.95	2.54	2.48	2.40	2.33	2.29	2.25	2.16	2.11	2.07
	.975	3.06	2.96	2.86	2.76	2.70	2.64	2.52	2.46	2.40
	.99	3.80	3.67	3.52	3.37	3.29	3.21	3.05	2.96	2.87
	.995	4.42	4.25	4.07	3.88	3.79	3.69	3.48	3.37	3.26
	.999	6.08	5.81	5.54	5.25	5.10	4.95	4.64	4.48	4.31

df for denominator	Percentile	df for numerator								
		1	2	3	4	5	6	7	8	9
20	.025	0	.03	.07	.11	.16	.19	.22	.25	.27
	.05	0	.05	.12	.17	.22	.26	.39	.31	.34
	.90	2.97	2.59	2.38	2.25	2.16	2.09	2.04	2.00	1.96
	.95	4.35	3.49	3.10	2.87	2.71	2.60	2.51	2.45	2.39
	.975	5.87	4.46	3.86	3.51	3.29	3.13	3.01	2.91	2.84
	.99	8.10	5.85	4.94	4.43	4.10	3.87	3.70	3.56	3.46
	.995	9.94	6.99	5.82	5.17	4.76	4.47	4.26	4.09	3.96
	.999	14.8	9.95	8.10	7.10	6.46	6.02	5.69	5.44	5.24
24	.025	0	.03	.07	.12	.16	.20	.23	.25	.28
	.05	0	.05	.12	.17	.22	.26	.29	.32	.34
	.90	2.93	2.54	2.33	2.19	2.10	2.04	1.98	1.94	1.91
	.95	4.26	3.40	3.01	2.78	2.62	2.51	2.42	2.36	2.30
	.975	5.72	4.32	3.72	3.38	3.15	2.99	2.87	2.78	2.70
	.99	7.82	5.61	4.72	4.22	3.90	3.67	3.50	3.36	3.26
	.995	9.55	6.66	5.52	4.89	4.49	4.20	3.99	3.83	3.69
	.999	14.0	9.34	7.55	6.59	5.98	5.55	5.23	4.99	4.80
30	.025	0	.03	.07	.12	.16	.20	.23	.26	.28
	.05	0	.05	.12	.17	.22	.26	.30	.32	.35
	.90	2.88	2.49	2.28	2.14	2.05	1.98	1.93	1.88	1.85
	.95	4.17	3.32	2.92	2.69	2.53	2.42	2.33	2.27	2.21
	.975	5.57	4.18	3.59	3.25	3.03	2.87	2.75	2.65	2.57
	.99	7.56	5.39	4.51	4.02	3.70	3.47	3.30	3.17	3.07
	.995	9.18	6.35	5.24	4.62	4.23	3.95	3.74	3.58	3.45
	.999	13.3	8.77	7.05	6.12	5.53	5.12	4.82	4.58	4.39
60	.025	0	.03	.07	.12	.16	.20	.24	.26	.29
	.05	0	.05	.12	.18	.23	.27	.30	.33	.36
	.90	2.79	2.39	2.18	2.04	1.95	1.87	1.82	1.77	1.74
	.95	4.00	3.15	2.76	2.53	2.37	2.25	2.17	2.10	2.04
	.975	5.29	3.93	3.34	3.01	2.79	2.63	2.51	2.41	2.33
	.99	7.08	4.98	4.13	3.65	3.34	3.12	2.95	2.82	2.72
	.995	8.49	5.80	4.73	4.14	3.76	3.49	3.29	3.13	3.01
	.999	12.0	7.77	6.17	5.31	4.76	4.37	4.09	3.86	3.69
120	.025	0	.03	.07	.12	.16	.20	.24	.27	.29
	.05	0	.05	.12	.18	.23	.27	.31	.34	.36
	.90	2.75	2.35	2.13	1.99	1.90	1.82	1.77	1.72	1.68
	.95	3.92	3.07	2.68	2.45	2.29	2.18	2.09	2.02	1.96
	.975	5.15	3.80	3.23	2.89	2.67	2.52	2.39	2.30	2.22
	.99	6.85	4.79	3.95	3.48	3.17	2.96	2.79	2.66	2.56
	.995	8.18	5.54	4.50	3.92	3.55	3.28	3.09	2.93	2.81
	.999	11.4	7.32	5.78	4.95	4.42	4.04	3.77	3.55	3.38
∞	.025	0	.03	.07	.12	.17	.21	.24	.27	.30
	.05	0	.05	.12	.18	.23	.27	.31	.34	.40
	.90	2.71	2.30	2.08	1.94	1.85	1.77	1.72	1.67	1.63
	.95	3.84	3.00	2.60	2.37	2.21	2.10	2.01	1.94	1.88
	.975	5.02	3.69	3.12	2.79	2.57	2.41	2.29	2.19	2.11
	.99	6.63	4.61	3.78	3.32	3.02	2.80	2.64	2.51	2.41
	.995	7.88	5.30	4.28	3.72	3.35	3.09	2.90	2.74	2.62
	.999	10.8	6.91	5.42	4.62	4.10	3.74	3.47	3.27	3.10

df for denominator	Percentile	df for numerator								
		10	**12**	**15**	**20**	**24**	**30**	**60**	**120**	**∞**
20	.025	.29	.33	.36	.41	.43	.45	.52	.55	.58
	.05	.36	.39	.43	.47	.49	.52	.57	.60	.64
	.90	1.94	1.89	1.84	1.79	1.77	1.74	1.68	1.64	1.61
	.95	2.35	2.28	2.20	2.12	2.08	2.04	1.95	1.90	1.84
	.975	2.77	2.68	2.57	2.46	2.41	2.35	2.22	2.16	2.09
	.99	3.37	3.23	3.09	2.94	2.86	2.78	2.61	2.52	2.42
	.995	3.85	3.68	3.50	3.32	3.22	3.12	2.92	2.81	2.69
	.999	5.08	4.82	4.56	4.29	4.15	4.00	3.70	3.54	3.38
24	.025	.30	.33	.37	.41	.44	.47	.53	.57	.61
	.05	.36	.40	.44	.48	.50	.53	.59	.62	.66
	.90	1.88	1.83	1.78	1.73	1.70	1.67	1.61	1.57	1.53
	.95	2.25	2.18	2.11	2.03	1.98	1.94	1.84	1.79	1.73
	.975	2.64	2.54	2.44	2.33	2.27	2.21	2.08	2.01	1.94
	.99	3.17	3.03	2.89	2.74	2.66	2.58	2.40	2.31	2.21
	.995	3.59	3.42	3.25	3.06	2.97	2.87	2.66	2.55	2.43
	.999	4.64	4.39	4.14	3.87	3.74	3.59	3.29	3.14	2.97
30	.025	.30	.34	.38	.43	.45	.48	.55	.59	.64
	.05	.37	.40	.44	.49	.52	.54	.61	.65	.68
	.90	1.82	1.77	1.72	1.67	1.64	1.61	1.54	1.50	1.46
	.95	2.16	2.09	2.01	1.93	1.89	1.84	1.74	1.68	1.62
	.975	2.51	2.41	2.31	2.20	2.14	2.07	1.94	1.87	1.79
	.99	2.98	2.84	2.70	2.55	2.47	2.39	2.21	2.11	2.01
	.995	3.34	3.18	3.01	2.82	2.73	2.63	2.42	2.30	2.18
	.999	4.24	4.00	3.75	3.49	3.36	3.22	2.92	2.76	2.59
60	.025	.31	.35	.40	.45	.48	.52	.60	.65	.72
	.05	.38	.42	.46	.51	.54	.57	.65	.70	.76
	.90	1.71	1.66	1.60	1.54	1.51	1.48	1.40	1.35	1.29
	.95	1.99	1.92	1.84	1.75	1.70	1.65	1.53	1.47	1.39
	.975	2.27	2.17	2.06	1.94	1.88	1.82	1.67	1.58	1.48
	.99	2.63	2.50	2.35	2.20	2.12	2.03	1.84	1.73	1.60
	.995	2.90	2.74	2.57	2.39	2.29	2.19	1.96	1.83	1.69
	.999	3.54	3.32	3.08	2.83	2.69	2.55	2.25	2.08	1.89
120	.025	.32	.36	.41	.46	.50	.53	.63	.70	.79
	.05	.39	.43	.47	.53	.56	.60	.68	.74	.82
	.90	1.65	1.60	1.55	1.48	1.45	1.41	1.32	1.26	1.19
	.95	1.91	1.83	1.75	1.66	1.61	1.55	1.43	1.35	1.25
	.975	2.16	2.05	1.95	1.82	1.76	1.69	1.53	1.43	1.31
	.99	2.47	2.34	2.19	2.03	1.95	1.86	1.66	1.53	1.38
	.995	2.71	2.54	2.37	2.19	2.09	1.98	1.75	1.61	1.43
	.999	3.24	3.02	2.78	2.53	2.40	2.26	1.95	1.77	1.54
∞	.025	.32	.37	.42	.48	.52	.56	.68	.76	1.00
	.05	.39	.43	.48	.54	.58	.62	.72	.80	1.00
	.90	1.60	1.55	1.49	1.42	1.38	1.34	1.24	1.17	1.00
	.95	1.83	1.75	1.67	1.57	1.52	1.46	1.32	1.22	1.00
	.975	2.05	1.94	1.83	1.71	1.64	1.57	1.39	1.27	1.00
	.99	2.32	2.18	2.04	1.88	1.79	1.70	1.47	1.32	1.00
	.995	2.52	2.36	2.19	2.00	1.90	1.79	1.53	1.36	1.00
	.999	2.96	2.74	2.51	2.27	2.13	1.99	1.66	1.45	1.00

8 APPENDIX Table of Studentized Range Values

Within df	Experiment-wise confidence level	Number of treatment levels													
		2	3	4	5	6	7	8	9	10	11	12	13	14	15
1	.95	18.0	27.0	32.8	37.1	40.4	43.1	45.4	47.4	49.1	50.6	52.0	53.2	54.3	55.4
	.99	90.0	135	164	186	202	216	227	237	246	253	260	266	272	277
2	.95	6.09	8.3	9.8	10.9	11.7	12.4	13.0	13.5	14.0	14.4	14.7	15.1	15.4	15.7
	.99	14.0	19.0	22.3	24.7	26.6	28.2	29.5	30.7	31.7	32.6	33.4	34.1	34.8	35.4
3	.95	4.50	5.91	6.82	7.50	8.04	8.48	8.85	9.18	9.46	9.72	9.95	10.2	10.4	10.5
	.99	8.26	10.6	12.2	13.3	14.2	15.0	15.6	16.2	16.7	17.1	17.5	17.9	18.2	18.5
4	.95	3.93	5.04	5.76	6.29	6.71	7.05	7.35	7.60	7.83	8.03	8.21	8.37	8.52	8.66
	.99	6.51	8.12	9.17	9.96	10.6	11.1	11.5	11.9	12.3	12.6	12.8	13.1	13.3	13.5
5	.95	3.64	4.60	5.22	5.67	6.03	6.33	6.58	6.80	6.99	7.17	7.32	7.47	7.60	7.72
	.99	5.70	6.97	7.80	8.42	8.91	9.32	9.67	9.97	10.2	10.5	10.7	10.9	11.1	11.2
6	.95	3.46	4.34	4.90	5.31	5.63	5.89	6.12	6.32	6.49	6.65	6.79	6.92	7.03	7.14
	.99	5.24	6.33	7.03	7.56	7.97	8.32	8.61	8.87	9.10	9.30	9.49	9.65	9.81	9.95
7	.95	3.34	4.16	4.69	5.06	5.36	5.61	5.82	6.00	6.16	6.30	6.43	6.55	6.66	6.76
	.99	4.95	5.92	6.54	7.01	7.37	7.68	7.94	8.17	8.37	8.55	8.71	8.86	9.00	9.12
8	.95	3.26	4.04	4.53	4.89	5.17	5.40	5.60	5.77	5.92	6.05	6.18	6.29	6.39	6.48
	.99	4.74	5.63	6.20	6.63	6.96	7.24	7.47	7.68	7.87	8.03	8.18	8.31	8.44	8.55
9	.95	3.20	3.95	4.42	4.76	5.02	5.24	5.43	5.60	5.74	5.87	5.98	6.09	6.19	6.28
	.99	4.60	5.43	5.96	6.35	6.66	6.91	7.13	7.32	7.49	7.65	7.78	7.91	8.03	8.13
10	.95	3.15	3.88	4.33	4.65	4.91	5.12	5.30	5.46	5.60	5.72	5.83	5.93	6.03	6.11
	.99	4.48	5.27	5.77	6.14	6.43	6.67	6.87	7.05	7.21	7.36	7.48	7.60	7.71	7.81
11	.95	3.11	3.82	4.26	4.57	4.82	5.03	5.20	5.35	5.49	5.61	5.71	5.81	5.90	5.99
	.99	4.39	5.14	5.62	5.97	6.25	6.48	6.67	6.84	6.99	7.13	7.26	7.36	7.46	7.56
12	.95	3.08	3.77	4.20	4.51	4.75	4.95	5.12	5.27	5.40	5.51	5.62	5.71	5.80	5.88
	.99	4.32	5.04	5.50	5.84	6.10	6.32	6.51	6.67	6.81	6.94	7.06	7.17	7.26	7.36
13	.95	3.06	3.73	4.15	4.45	4.69	4.88	5.05	5.19	5.32	5.43	5.53	5.63	5.71	5.79
	.99	4.26	4.96	5.40	5.73	5.98	6.19	6.37	6.53	6.67	6.79	6.90	7.01	7.10	7.19
14	.95	3.03	3.70	4.11	4.41	4.64	4.83	4.99	5.13	5.25	5.36	5.46	5.55	6.64	5.72
	.99	4.21	4.89	5.32	5.63	5.88	6.08	6.26	6.41	6.54	6.66	6.77	6.87	6.96	7.05
16	.95	3.00	3.65	4.05	4.33	4.56	4.74	4.90	5.03	5.15	5.26	5.35	5.44	5.52	5.59
	.99	4.13	4.78	5.19	5.49	5.72	5.92	6.08	6.22	6.35	6.46	6.56	6.66	6.74	6.82
18	.95	2.97	3.61	4.00	4.28	4.49	4.67	4.82	4.96	5.07	5.17	5.27	5.35	5.43	5.50
	.99	4.07	4.70	5.09	5.38	5.60	5.79	5.94	6.08	6.20	6.31	6.41	6.50	6.58	6.65
20	.95	2.95	3.58	3.96	4.23	4.45	4.62	4.77	4.90	5.01	5.11	5.20	5.28	5.36	5.43
	.99	4.02	4.64	5.02	5.29	5.51	5.69	5.84	5.97	6.09	6.19	6.29	6.37	6.45	6.52
24	.95	2.92	3.53	3.90	4.17	4.37	4.54	4.68	4.81	4.92	5.01	5.10	5.18	5.25	5.32
	.99	3.96	4.54	4.91	5.17	5.37	5.54	5.69	5.81	5.92	6.02	6.11	6.19	6.26	6.33

Within df	Experiment-wise confidence level	Number of treatment levels													
		2	3	4	5	6	7	8	9	10	11	12	13	14	15
30	.95	2.89	3.49	3.84	4.10	4.30	4.46	4.60	4.72	4.83	4.92	5.00	5.08	5.15	5.21
	.99	3.89	4.45	4.80	5.05	5.24	5.40	5.54	5.56	5.76	5.85	5.93	6.01	6.08	6.14
40	.95	2.86	3.44	3.79	4.04	4.23	4.39	4.52	4.63	4.74	4.82	4.91	4.98	5.05	5.11
	.99	3.82	4.37	4.70	4.93	5.11	5.27	5.39	5.50	5.60	5.69	5.77	5.84	5.90	5.96
60	.95	2.83	3.40	3.74	3.98	4.16	4.31	4.44	4.55	4.65	4.73	4.81	4.88	4.94	5.00
	.99	3.76	4.28	4.60	4.82	4.99	5.13	5.25	5.36	5.45	5.53	5.60	5.67	5.73	5.79
120	.95	2.80	3.36	3.69	3.92	4.10	4.24	4.36	4.48	4.56	4.64	4.72	4.78	4.84	4.90
	.99	3.70	4.20	4.50	4.71	4.87	5.01	5.12	5.21	5.30	5.38	5.44	5.51	5.56	5.61

Database I: *Cross-Sectional Demographic and Productivity Data*

Use to answer: (1) Chapter 2, Problem 24; (2) Chapter 3; Problem 24; and Chapter 8, Problem 26

PLANT	GENDER	POSITION	JOBSAT	ATTEND	YRONJOB	TSKSUP	SOCREL	PRDCTY
N	1	1	6.7	93.0	3.0	9.0	6	99.5
N	1	1	7.2	96.5	7.0	9.0	10	98.8
N	1	1	7.9	97.0	10.5	7.0	6	98.7
N	1	1	7.0	96.5	13.0	6.0	5	100.1
N	1	1	5.8	98.1	9.0	7.0	5	98.3
N	2	1	7.3	97.1	11.0	6.0	0	98.5
N	2	1	6.1	98.0	9.0	8.0	5	102.2
N	2	1	7.9	96.0	8.6	7.0	4	99.0
N	2	1	6.8	97.5	10.0	8.0	4	98.6
N	2	1	7.1	95.0	8.0	7.0	5	99.7
N	1	2	5.5	94.0	13.0	6.0	6	95.2
N	1	2	5.4	94.0	5.0	4.0	6	97.3
N	1	2	7.1	90.0	17.0	5.0	6	93.5
N	1	2	5.9	91.0	2.0	4.0	5	95.5
N	1	2	6.0	92.5	15.0	5.0	5	97.0
N	2	2	5.4	93.0	13.0	4.0	5	97.6
N	2	2	5.9	93.0	4.0	4.0	5	95.2
N	2	2	6.2	92.0	5.0	5.0	5	95.9
N	2	2	6.3	90.0	14.0	6.0	4	97.2
N	2	2	5.0	93.5	14.0	5.0	5	97.3
D	1	1	8.5	99.0	0.1	9.0	5.0	105.4
D	1	1	8.4	98.0	4.1	5.0	6.0	105.0
D	1	1	8.5	99.0	7.6	7.0	5.0	106.6
D	1	1	8.6	99.0	8.0	6.0	6.0	104.4
D	1	1	8.4	97.0	9.0	6.0	5.0	105.3
D	2	1	8.2	99.1	8.1	8.0	6.0	108.6
D	2	1	8.0	99.0	6.1	6.0	5.0	106.2
D	2	1	8.1	98.0	5.7	8.0	6.0	106.1
D	2	1	8.0	98.0	7.1	8.0	5.0	104.6
D	2	1	7.6	97.0	8.0	9.0	6.0	106.2
D	1	2	6.5	95.0	10.1	7.0	6.0	105.4
D	1	2	6.5	96.0	2.1	6.0	10.0	105.1
D	1	2	6.5	95.0	14.1	7.0	7.0	102.6
D	1	2	6.5	96.0	2.0	5.0	5.0	102.9
D	1	2	6.7	96.0	12.1	6.0	5.0	105.4
D	2	2	5.7	95.0	10.1	9.0	1.0	100.6
D	2	2	6.0	96.5	3.0	8.0	6.0	103.2
D	2	2	6.1	95.0	1.0	6.0	5.0	105.8
D	2	2	6.2	94.0	11.1	7.0	5.0	104.6
D	2	2	6.5	96.0	11.1	9.0	5.0	102.0

Variable Name	Description of Variable
PLANT	N= Norcross, GA; D=Dallas, TX
GENDER	1= Female; 2 = Male
POSITION	1= Management; 2 = Hourly
JOBSAT	A numerical scale from 0 (highly dissatisfied) to 10 (highly satisfied)
ATTEND	A numerical scale that measures the percentage of time in attendance in plant
YRONJOB	The number of years with COMCEL
TSKSUP	The level of management support in doing a task. Higher scores mean more support.
SOCREL	The level of social relationships within the firm. Higher scores mean more friendly and interactive environments.
PRDCTY	The level of productivity as a percentage of standard. May exceed 100%.

Database II: *Time-Ordered Marketing and Economic Data*

Use to answer: (1) Chapter 2, Problem 25; (2) Chapter 3, Problem 25; (3) Chapter 11, Problem 40; (4) Chapter 13, Problem 15

QTR	TIME	SOM	ADV	RELPR	AVGTRN	ECINDX	NOCOMM
1/87	1	8.0	13.00	1.75	0.5	65	14
2/87	2	14.0	9.10	1.75	1.0	45	15
3/87	3	15.0	11.90	1.74	0.6	60	12
4/87	4	9.1	13.70	1.80	8.0	50	12
1/88	5	11.7	20.80	1.71	8.0	45	17
2/88	6	17.0	13.85	1.65	7.0	40	21
3/88	7	20.8	13.85	1.66	6.0	40	7
4/88	8	6.5	15.90	1.88	1.0	50	14
1/89	9	14.4	24.50	1.60	0.5	55	18
2/89	10	23.0	14.70	1.60	0.5	65	24
3/89	11	24.5	16.20	1.57	6.0	60	15
4/89	12	14.7	29.00	1.58	6.5	65	8
1/90	13	17.6	20.00	1.58	1.5	55	29
2/90	14	29.0	17.50	1.50	1.6	40	18
3/90	15	36.5	18.20	1.50	3.0	40	13
4/90	16	17.5	32.40	1.65	5.0	45	19
1/91	17	19.0	34.00	1.46	5.2	60	18
2/91	18	32.4	20.30	1.60	4.5	60	34
3/91	19	34.0	15.00	1.43	3.6	55	20
4/91	20	20.3	9.00	1.44	2.5	45	4

Variable Name	Description of Variable
SOM	Share of market
ADV	Amount of advertising in tens of thousands of dollars
RELPR	The relative price of COMCEL's phones vs. the mean price of its competitors' phones
AVGTRN	The mean number of training hours per sales employee for the quarter
ECINDX	An index of regional economic activity that ranges from 0 (recession) to 100 (expansion)
NOCOMM	Number of commercials aired per week in the region's highest rated AM station during the quarter

Database III: *Cross-Sectional Economic and Marketing Data*

Use to answer: (1) Chapter 7, Problem 25; (2) Chapter 8, Problem 27; (3) Chapter 11, Problem 39

CITY	SOM	YRSEXP	MEDIA	RELPR	TRAIN	FAX	FAXN	REGION
CHICAGO	12	2	9	2.0	2	35	110	1
CLEVELAND	39	6	13	1.2	9	25	80	1
COLUMBUS	15	2	9	1.8	7	28	78	1
DETROIT	62	6	24	0.9	19	33	93	1
MINNEAPOLIS	56	11	3	1.0	18	30	90	1
ST. LOUIS	23	22	14	1.8	11	25	85	1
ALBANY	11	2	5	2.0	6	45	90	2
BOSTON	16	4	30	2.0	5	55	103	2
HARTFORD	63	17	5	0.6	21	35	67	2
NEW YORK	70	12	7	0.8	24	65	115	2
NEWARK	52	20	27	1.3	16	36	74	2
PORTLAND	31	3	18	1.6	10	42	65	2
ATLANTA	20	3	13	1.5	2	35	100	3
AUSTIN	60	18	16	0.9	18	32	90	3
BALTIMORE	45	6	25	1.5	30	31	93	3
BIRMINGHAM	45	4	28	0.6	5	28	88	3
CHARLOTTE	40	6	17	1.0	12	25	75	3
DALLAS	70	15	32	1.8	20	29	98	3
HOUSTON	55	8	25	1.4	16	31	95	3
JACKSONVILLE	10	1	8	1.7	8	30	92	3
MIAMI	55	13	21	1.1	23	35	100	3
NEW ORLEANS	25	18	16	1.3	10	27	94	3
ORLANDO	25	20	18	0.9	9	38	102	3

CITY	SOM	YRSEXP	MEDIA	RELPR	TRAIN	FAX	FAXN	REGION
WASHINGTON	45	21	6	1.8	10	38	99	3
DENVER	26	4	11	1.7	10	40	100	4
LOS ANGELES	50	18	25	1.6	17	45	100	4
PHOENIX	27	23	19	1.5	11	30	85	4
SAN ANTONIO	72	10	34	0.6	26	25	60	4
SAN FRANCISCO	35	19	20	1.4	11	42	100	4
SEATTLE	10	2	6	1.9	3	39	99	4

CITY	REGION	BUYUSA	CITY	REGION	BUYUSA
CHICAGO	1	75	BIRMINGHAM	3	89
CHICAGO	1	72	BIRMINGHAM	3	86
CHICAGO	1	74	BIRMINGHAM	3	88
CLEVELAND	1	78	CHARLOTTE	3	87
CLEVELAND	1	63	CHARLOTTE	3	80
CLEVELAND	1	75	CHARLOTTE	3	86
COLUMBUS-OHIO	1	70	DALLAS	3	85
COLUMBUS-OHIO	1	64	DALLAS	3	85
COLUMBUS-OHIO	1	68	DALLAS	3	84
DETROIT	1	67	HOUSTON	3	91
DETROIT	1	79	HOUSTON	3	91
DETROIT	1	70	HOUSTON	3	92
MINNEAPOLIS	1	67	JACKSONVILLE	3	84
MINNEAPOLIS	1	74	JACKSONVILLE	3	83
MINNEAPOLIS	1	67	JACKSONVILLE	3	83
STLOUIS	1	74	MIAMI	3	82
STLOUIS	1	73	MIAMI	3	87
STLOUIS	1	73	MIAMI	3	83
ALBANY-NY	2	36	NEW-ORLEANS	3	81
ALBANY-NY	2	41	NEW-ORLEANS	3	90
ALBANY-NY	2	37	NEW-ORLEANS	3	82
BOSTON	2	33	ORLANDO	3	89
BOSTON	2	33	ORLANDO	3	84
BOSTON	2	32	ORLANDO	3	88
HARTFORD	2	34	WASHINGTON	3	86
HARTFORD	2	31	WASHINGTON	3	87
HARTFORD	2	31	WASHINGTON	3	87
NEW-YORK	2	34	DENVER	4	44
NEW-YORK	2	34	DENVER	4	30
NEW-YORK	2	35	DENVER	4	32
NEWARK	2	37	LOS-ANGELES	4	37
NEWARK	2	35	LOS-ANGELES	4	42
NEWARK	2	36	LOS-ANGELES	4	37
PORTLAND-MAINE	2	33	PHOENIX	4	48
PORTLAND-MAINE	2	39	PHOENIX	4	49
PORTLAND-MAINE	2	35	PHOENIX	4	49
ATLANTA	3	86	SAN-ANTONIO	4	43
ATLANTA	3	88	SAN-ANTONIO	4	49
ATLANTA	3	87	SAN-ANTONIO	4	48
AUSTIN	3	88	SAN-FRANCISCO	4	31
AUSTIN	3	82	SAN-FRANCISCO	4	41
AUSTIN	3	85	SAN-FRANCISCO	4	40
BALTIMORE	3	86	SEATTLE	4	42
BALTIMORE	3	85	SEATTLE	4	35
BALTIMORE	3	86	SEATTLE	4	36

CITY	REGION	ACCREC	CITY	REGION	ACCREC
CHICAGO	1	25.7	BIRMINGHAM	3	33.6
CHICAGO	1	24.0	BIRMINGHAM	3	33.8
CLEVELAND	1	29.4	CHARLOTTE	3	33.2
CLEVELAND	1	32.9	CHARLOTTE	3	32.3
COLUMBUS-OHIO	1	33.2	DALLAS	3	36.8
COLUMBUS-OHIO	1	28.0	DALLAS	3	34.3
DETROIT	1	33.4	HOUSTON	3	35.8
DETROIT	1	23.3	HOUSTON	3	34.4
MINNEAPOLIS	1	26.8	JACKSONVILLE	3	36.6
MINNEAPOLIS	1	23.3	JACKSONVILLE	3	35.5
STLOUIS	1	33.6	MIAMI	3	34.9
STLOUIS	1	25.0	MIAMI	3	32.8
ALBANY-NY	2	23.7	NEW-ORLEANS	3	35.9
ALBANY-NY	2	25.6	NEW-ORLEANS	3	35.5
BOSTON	2	26.5	ORLANDO	3	34.6
BOSTON	2	25.5	ORLANDO	3	32.6
HARTFORD	2	27.9	WASHINGTON	3	36.5
HARTFORD	2	24.2	WASHINGTON	3	35.1
NEW-YORK	2	30.5	DENVER	4	28.0
NEW-YORK	2	28.7	DENVER	4	27.6
NEWARK	2	27.8	LOS-ANGELES	4	23.2
NEWARK	2	32.7	LOS-ANGELES	4	24.3
PORTLAND-MAINE	2	28.4	PHOENIX	4	32.7
PORTLAND-MAINE	2	28.9	PHOENIX	4	29.1
ATLANTA	3	35.5	SAN-ANTONIO	4	26.3
ATLANTA	3	34.1	SAN-ANTONIO	4	23.4
AUSTIN	3	35.0	SAN-FRANCISCO	4	27.5
AUSTIN	3	34.6	SAN-FRANCISCO	4	29.1
BALTIMORE	3	36.4	SEATTLE	4	27.2
BALTIMORE	3	34.2	SEATTLE	4	25.6

Variable Name	Description of Variable
SOM	Market share in percentage
YRSEXP	Mean years of experience of sales and service employees
MEDIA	Amount of advertising in tens of thousands of dollars
RELPR	The relative price of COMCEL's phones vs. the mean price of its competitors' phones
TRAIN	Charged expenses for staff training in the previous year in thousands of dollars
FAX	Number of YES responses on the need for FAX capability
FAXN	Sample size for FAX capability survey resulting from a 1-in-k systematic random sample of customers in each city
REGION	COMCEL's sales regions: 1 = Midwest, 2 = Northeast, 3 = South, and 4 = West
BUYUSA	An index of importance on buying American-made products that ranges from 0 (not) to 100 (essential); 3 customer responses: C1, C2, and C3.
ACCREC	Mean age of accounts receivable (in days) of two randomly selected retail outlets: R01 R02

Database IV: *Time-Ordered Productivity and Planned Change Data*
Use to answer: (1) Chapter 10, Problem 25; (2) Chapter 15, Problem 20

DAY	TREATMENT	HRSTOFAIL	s1	s2	s3	s4	s5	SAMPMEAN	SAMPVAR
SEPT7	3	1049	98	97	96	103	104	99.6	13.3
SEPT8	3	1007	98	100	101	96	96	99.2	5.2
SEPT9	3	1057	102	98	104	97	100	100.2	8.2
SEPT10	3	1071	99	95	102	105	98	99.8	14.7
SEPT11	1	908	98	96	95	102	97	97.6	7.3
SEPT14	1	931	96	103	101	97	97	98.8	9.2
SEPT15	1	928	100	98	102	96	100	99.2	5.2
SEPT16	1	907	101	100	95	99	97	98.4	5.8
SEPT17	2	1164	100	97	104	97	102	100.0	9.5
SEPT18	2	1143	111	118	122	95	99	109.0	137.5

DAY	TREATMENT	HRSTOFAIL	S1	S2	S3	S4	S5	SAMPMEAN	SAMPVAR
SEPT21	2	1199	96	103	101	95	102	99.4	13.3
SEPT22	2	1198	102	101	95	96	96	98.0	10.5
SEPT23	1	918	101	100	105	101	105	102.4	5.8
SEPT24	1	924	102	98	104	104	101	101.8	6.2
SEPT25	1	917	105	99	102	96	99	100.2	11.7
SEPT28	1	908	97	96	100	101	101	99.0	5.5
SEPT29	1	914	102	98	96	101	100	99.4	5.8
SEPT30	1	901	99	104	103	99	98	100.6	7.3
OCT1	1	943	86	87	78	86	80	83.4	16.8
OCT2	1	948	89	89	95	93	94	92.0	8.0
OCT5	3	1055	105	97	98	95	101	99.2	15.2
OCT6	3	1017	99	98	99	97	97	98.0	1.0
OCT7	3	1063	96	102	95	100	105	99.6	17.3
OCT8	3	1019	104	98	97	102	102	100.6	8.8
OCT9	2	1173	97	98	105	101	101	100.4	9.8
OCT12	2	1200	105	99	99	103	99	101.0	8.0
OCT13	2	1173	98	96	99	102	103	99.6	8.3
OCT14	2	1142	97	97	102	96	104	99.2	12.7
OCT15	2	1155	105	98	99	105	98	101.0	13.5
OCT16	2	1126	104	96	99	97	101	99.4	10.3
OCT19	2	1129	103	104	97	98	104	101.2	11.7
OCT20	2	1131	100	105	100	99	98	100.4	7.3
OCT21	3	1020	103	101	104	98	103	101.8	5.7
OCT22	3	1041	102	101	95	103	99	100.0	10.0
OCT23	3	1028	101	101	101	98	101	100.4	1.8
OCT26	3	1044	99	100	102	104	98	100.6	5.8

DAY	MACHDOWN	ABSENTHOUR	PERIOD	DAY	MACHDOWN	ABSENTHOUR	PERIOD
SEPT7	12.0	9.0	1	OCT1	27.0	40.0	19
SEPT8	11.8	11.0	2	OCT2	15.0	27.0	20
SEPT9	12.1	9.0	3	OCT5	12.8	15.8	21
SEPT10	12.7	11.5	4	OCT6	10.4	12.0	22
SEPT11	10.5	12.3	5	OCT7	11.8	15.1	23
SEPT14	12.7	14.0	6	OCT8	11.7	16.0	24
SEPT15	12.2	13.5	7	OCT9	11.9	14.3	25
SEPT16	11.9	12.0	8	OCT12	11.1	13.7	26
SEPT17	12.4	14.6	9	OCT13	10.8	15.0	27
SEPT18	11.0	15.0	10	OCT14	11.2	12.5	28
SEPT21	11.6	16.0	11	OCT15	10.2	11.8	29
SEPT22	11.2	15.7	12	OCT16	10.5	13.0	30
SEPT23	12.3	13.0	13	OCT19	10.5	10.2	31
SEPT24	12.7	16.1	14	OCT20	10.9	7.0	32
SEPT25	12.8	16.3	15	OCT21	10.0	8.3	33
SEPT28	11.9	18.0	16	OCT22	10.1	9.0	34
SEPT29	11.1	16.3	17	OCT23	12.3	6.3	35
SEPT30	11.7	44.0	18	OCT26	13.0	5.1	36

Variable Name	Description of Variable
HRSTOFAIL	The number of hours to failure of a phone circuit
TREATMENT	A planned change study: the present circuit and two test circuits under development
	S1–S5: Five samples of productivity during the day; percentage of standard data may exceed 100%
MACHDOWN	Daily total machine downtime in hours
ABSENTHOUR	Daily total number of hours lost due to absenteeism
SAMPMEAN	The daily means of the five samples, S1–S5
SAMPVAR	The daily variances of the five samples, S1–S5

ANSWERS to Selected Odd-Numbered Exercises and Problems

SECTION 1.1

1. a. H
   b. E
   c. O
   d. B
   e. E
   f. O
   g. O and E
   h. O

3. The fourth quarter always has the highest rate of return, averaging about 6.6%. The third quarter always has the smallest return rate, about 2.5%. The returns range from 2.5% to 7%. Average return rate is approximately 4%.

SECTION 2.1

1. a. T
   b. C
   c. C
   d. T

3. For example, a decline in monthly sales for a product (one variable) can suggest a problem; looking at the relationship between the monthly sales and other variables such as own unit price, major competitor's unit price, and monthly number of products returned under warranty can help in diagnosing the causes of the problem.

SECTION 2.2

1.

9	.75	.85					
10	.10	.25	.25	.55	.75	.75	.75
11	.10						
12	.00	.25	.75				
13	.00						

3.

2	3.2	5.1	6.5	8.3						
3	2.5	2.7	3.2	3.5	3.8	4.0	4.5	4.7	6.1	6.6	6.8
4	0.3	1.5	2.6	2.9	5.8					

5. a.

No Test Program

7	06	81						
8	06	12	20	34	89			
9	00	04	06	34	45	67	67	78
10	21							

Test Program

5	50						
6	03	06	57	78	78	78	78
7	04	07	34	60	90		
8	14	90					
9	00						

   b. Yes, distribution has shifted down toward a smaller number of DUIs.

7.

	Freq.	%
	2	6.7
	7	23.3
	7	23.3
	7	23.3
	7	23.3

9. a.

	Cum. Freq.	Cum. %
	0	0
	6	25.0
	16	66.7
	21	87.5
	23	95.8
	24	100.0

   b. Two-thirds of the work groups experienced fewer than 5 accidents.
   c. Deterioration of safety measures

11. b. 10%
    c. No, because the gas prices at 20 stations are not expected to reflect perfectly the gas prices at all the stations

13. d. 10%
    e. No, because the returns for 30 firms are not expected to reflect perfectly the returns for all the firms

SECTION 2.3

1. Was the student absent a lot? Did the student study? Did the student have the prerequisites?

3. Yes; no

5. Skewed toward higher incomes

7. a. Right
   b. One

9. a. Skewed to the right
   b. .7
   c.

Less than 1	48.1
Less than 2	86.7
Less than 3	98.0
Less than 4	99.5
Less than 5	99.8
Less than 6	100.0

   d. 1/2%

SECTION 2.4

1. No upward or downward trend over time

3. Nonstationary

5. Nonstationary; upper trend

7. a. Nonstationary
   b. Slowly increasing, then rapidly increasing, and the 1970s beginning to slow down
   c. Doubles approximately every ten years
   d. Early 1980s; energy harder to find, conservation efforts

9. c. Line graph
  d. It hides the increasing trend toward more satisfied customers.

11. b. No
  c. Increasing trend
  e. No; no

13. b. No
  c. Particularly high readings at hours 4 and 8
  e. No; no

15. a. No
  b. Stationary over first year; decreasing trend over second year; yes

SECTION 2.5

3. a. Mean increases by $.50; standard deviation unchanged
  b. Mean doubles; standard deviation doubles

5. Neither (means equal); bank B

7.

x	f	xf
0	25	0
1	100	100
2	50	100
3	25	75
	200	275

$\bar{x} = \Sigma \dfrac{xf}{n} = \dfrac{275}{200} = 1.375$

9. a. 109, 664.57, 25.78, 72
  b. No

11. With a max. figure of $3000, the mean would have to be $\geq$ $300.

13. .3, .46

15. Not sure; variation about the mean, because most of the salaries could be low with a relatively few very high salaries bringing up the average

SECTION 2.6

1. a. 2.9
  b. 3.21, 1.79
  c. 6
  d. 10

3. If skewed, the balance point is at 100, with more than half of the values on one side of 100 and a tapering off on the other side. From Chebyshev's rule, at least 75% of the data values between 80 and 120. If approximately normal, the balance point is at 100. From the Empirical rule, around 95% of the data values between 80 and 120.

5. a. 16%
  b. 97.5%
  c. 2.5%

7. a. 72.8, 6.00
  b. Around 68%; around 95%; almost all
  c. No, because no values are more than 3 standard deviations from the mean

9. a. 5
  b. $3\frac{1}{3}$
  c. Less than 85 or greater than 125
  d. Less than 99.67 or greater than 110.33

11. a. Around 95%
  b. Almost all

13. 23

SECTION 2.7

1. a. No
  b. The placement of the median value when the values are arranged in order of magnitude
  c. 26

3. a. 37
  b. 12

5. a. 35, 29, 40.5, 11.5
  b. 36.47, 34.91
  c. Smaller than both; very close to median

7.

Freq.	%	Cum. Freq.	Cum. %
2	16.7	2	16.7
5	41.7	7	58.3
3	25.0	10	83.3
2	16.7	12	100.0

  Median = 3

9. a. 109.17
  b. 13
  c. 500
  d. Interquartile range, because it is unaffected by the outlier

11. a. No
  b. You can deduce there must be 11 or 12 observations. The rank of $Q_1 = 3.5 =$(truncated rank of median $+1$)/2 means the truncated rank of the median $= 6$ or 6.5, which implies 11 or 12 observations.

13. a. At most 25%
  b. At most 25%

  Example:
  95 95 100 100 105 105 $\rightarrow \approx$ 0% above 105, 0% below 95
  90 95 100 100 105 110 $\rightarrow \approx$17% above 105, $\approx$ 17% below 95

  c. No; many data sets having different numbers of observations can have the same Q_1, median, and Q_3.

15. a. 50th
  b. 25th
  c. 75th

17.

Less than 1	.481
Less than 2	.867
Less than 3	.980
Less than 4	.995
Less than 5	.998
Less than 6	1.000

Q_1 $= 0$
Median $= 1$
Q_3 $= 1$

SECTION 2.8

1. a. 15
  b. 22.5
  c. 67.5, 127.5

3. a. Skewed
  b. No

5. **a.** Skewed, because the image on the right side of the median is not a mirror image of the image on the left side of the median
    b. No

7. **a.** Help identify outliers
    b. 4, 2.5, 5.5, 3
    c. Yes, 15; look for causes of the high performance as there is a potential opportunity to improve the performance of other salespeople based on what is discovered.

9. Yes; the middle 50% of the values are identical.

11. **b.** Yes, 92.5(Alaska)
    c. Skewed

13. We can't know, but two low scores in a row are more likely to result from an assignable cause, rather than typos or repeat chance events.

SECTION 2.9

1. **b.** Nonstationary; decreasing trend
    c. 44.83, 34.58, 39.71
    d. No
    e. A single mean cannot describe a series where the mean is changing.

3. 5, 6, 7, 8.7, 11.7, 15, 13.7, 13.3, 12.7, 16.7

5. 0, 1, −1, −0.7, .3, 0, 4.3, −5.3, 1.3, −.7; yes (4.3 and −5.3)

7. All data values equal

9. 250, 266.7, 296.7, 323.3, 350, 368.3, 10, −16.7, −6.7, 26.7, −20, 6.7; increasing trend; yes (26.7)

11. 6, −7, −.33, 8.33, −5.67, −1.67, −5, 15, −7.67, 0, −2.33, 4.67, −6.33, 4; yes, period 15, recording 36 complaints.

13. **b.** 30, 61.7, 63.3, 68.3, 41.7, 45, 48.3, 55, 60, 65
    c. 5, −31.7, 56.7, −28.3, 3.3, −5, 1.7, 0, 0, 0
    d. Because it was used in calculating the moving average for those quarters
    e. 30, 35, 40, 45, 40, 45, 50, 55, 60, 65
    f. 5, −5, 80, −5, 5, −5, 0, 0, 0, 0

CHAPTER 2
APPLICATION PROBLEMS

1. **a.** **Machos**   **Status Seekers**

    20 | 000   27 | 500 500
    21 | 000 500   28 | 000 000 000 000 500 500
    22 | 000 000 500 500   29 | 000 000
    23 | 000 500 750

    b. No outliers. Use the mean and standard deviation.
    Machos: Mean = $22,175; SD = $1142.91
    Status Seekers: Mean = $28,200; SD = $ 537.48

    c. The machos have incomes with a lower mean but greater variability than the status seekers.

3. **a.** 2.5%
    b. 2.5%
    c. Staffing levels O.K.; neither percentage above 20%
    d. Less than 10 min.   80
        10 up to 15 min.   10
        15 up to 20 min.   10
        20 up to 25 min.   10
        25 up to 30 min.   10
        30 or more min.   80

5. **a.** Use the median and interquartile range since Houston has an outlier (23%).

	Min.	Q_1	Med.	Q_3	Max.
Atlanta	1.4	2.25	2.9	3.65	11.5
Houston	3.5	5.35	6.2	7.15	23.0

    b. Atlanta: median = 2.9, IQR = 1.4
        Houston: median = 6.2, IQR = 1.8
    c. Yes; Houston gives bigger discounts than Atlanta.
    d. Demand for apartments relative to supply

7. **b.** 9.972, .043, .37, .149
    c. Beyond two standard deviations from the mean (9.88, 10.06); an underfilling problem because such a value is unusually low
    d. Beyond two standard deviations from the mean (.07, .69); an unstable filling process because such a value is unusually high
    e. Look for causes of the suspected problems

9. **a.**

	$\bar{x}$	s
Man./Prof.	.80	.40
Staff	.30	.46
Hourly	.25	.43

    b. Yes; 80% of the managers and professionals want a flexible package, whereas a minority of the other two groups do.
    c. Let individuals choose either a flexible package option or the current benefit package.

11. **b.** 839.6, 799.5, 587
    c. No, because the data are not stationary
    d. 591.7, 497, 414.7, 445, 464.7, 563, 646.7, 920.3, 1059.3, 1185, 1031, 940.7, 945.3, 1003.7, 1187, 1169, 1066, 1185. No; there is an overall increasing trend.

13. **a.** 71.0, 11.0
    c. 45, 99
    d. Look for causes of the extreme numbers of filed grievances at the two plants.

15. **a.** 4.1, 2, 2
    b. Data set is skewed or has outliers.
    c. 7.46, 1

17. **b.** Yes
    c. 62.3, 5.5
    d. Between 51.3 hours and 72.3 hours
    e. Something happened in January or the month before to induce workers to take time off.

19. **b.**

Current Ratio	Cum. %
< 1.00	3.1
1.00 up to 1.50	9.4
1.50 up to 2.00	31.3
2.00 up to 2.50	75.0
3.00 up to 3.5	96.9
3.00 or more	100.0

    d. XYZ's current ratio is in the bottom 3%; should seek reasons why

21. **a.** 7.3, 12.0, 20.0, 32.3, 42.3, 49.3, 50.3, 52.0, 53.7, 57.3, 59.3, 60.0, 58.7, 57.0, 56.0, 55.0
    b. Yes
    c. Improve the current product, get working on a new product.

23. **a.** 34
    c. 35

SECTION 3.1

1. Because diagnosis addresses the question "What affects what."

3. Look for changes in the region or in the company's actions vis-à-vis the region that might account for the decline.

5. Bivariate

7. **a.** Time-ordered
   b. Univariate
   c. Number of salespeople

SECTION 3.2

1. **a.** Quantitative
   b. Quantitative
   c. Categorical
   d. Categorical
   e. Categorical
   f. Quantitative
   g. Categorical
   h. Categorical

3. **a.** Less than 40,000
      40,000 up to 80,000
      80,000 and above
   b. Less than 15,000
      15,000 up to 30,000
      30,000 up to 45,000
      45,000 up to 60,000
      60,000 up to 75,000
      75,000 up to 90,000
      90,000 and above

5. For example: less than 5 years, 5 up to 10 years, 10 or more years

7. No, numbers have no meaning.

9. Low and high
   Low, moderate, and high
   Very low, low, moderate, and high
   Very low, low, moderate, high, and very high

SECTION 3.3

1. **a.**

	Men	Women
n	11	9
$\bar{x}$	3.2	3.7
s	2.6	3.6

   b.

	Men	Women
n	9	11
Median	3	2
IQR	2.5	2

3. **a.**

	Min.	Q_1	Med.	Q_3	Max.
Life	23	31.5	40.5	44	52
Property	29	35	43	51	57

   b. Yes, property group older than life group

5. **a.** Leadership style
   b. Productivity
   c.

	Autocratic	Participative
n	8	8
$\bar{x}$	95.125	103.125
s	1.55	.84
Median	95.0	103.0
IQR	2	1.5

   d.

	Min.	Q_1	Med.	Q_3	Max.
Autocratic	93	94	95	96	98
Participative	102	102.5	103	104	104

   e. Participative leadership leads to greater productivity than autocratic leadership.

7. **a.** Exercise
   b. Drop in cholesterol
   c.

	Exercise	No Exercise
n	8	8
$\bar{x}$	8.05	3.01
s	1.25	.91
Median	8.05	3.35
IQR	2.0	1.2

   d.

	Min.	Q_1	Med.	Q_3	Max.
Exercise	6.3	7.05	8.05	9.05	9.8
No Exercise	1.4	2.35	3.35	3.55	4.2

   e. Exercise leads to a reduction in cholesterol level.

9. Explanatory: previous performance rating (four levels); dependent: salary

11.

	Min.	Q_1	Med.	Q_3	Max.
quality circles firms	10	12	13	14	17
no quality circles firms	5	8	10	12	15

SECTION 3.4

1.

	Yes	No	Total
Managers	15	15	30
Nonmanagers	15	35	50
	30	50	80

3. **a.**

	Auto.	Partic.	Total
Poor Job Climate	150	50	200
Good Job Climate	10	190	200
	160	240	400

   b. (1) 2.5%, (2) 12.5%
   c. 50%
   d. 6.3%
   e. 79.2%
   f. Yes
   g. No; the sample percentage will vary depending on the particular sample of firms selected.

5. **a.**

	Favor	Don't Favor	Total
Democrat	100	400	500
Republican	250	50	300
Independent	250	450	700
	600	900	1500

   b. 40%
   c. 20%
   d. 83.3%
   e. 35.7%
   f. Yes

7. **a.** 30%
   b. 50%
   c. 70%
   d. 48%
   e. Yes

9. **a.**

	Owes Money	Does Not Owe Money
Above Median	6	6
Median and Below	8	4

   b. Yes
   c. We examined a sample of consumers rather than all consumers.

11.

	For	Against	No Opinion	Total
Democrat	12	12	6	30
Republican	12	12	6	30
Independent	16	16	8	40
	40	40	20	100

13.

	For	Against	No Opinion	Total
Democrat	9	15	6	30
Republican	18	6	6	30
Independent	13	19	8	40
	40	40	20	100

60% of Republicans are "For," but only 30% and 32.5% of Democrats and Independents, respectively, are "For."

15. Yes, because 33% of males oppose the death penalty compared to 49% of females.

17.

	Oppose	Favor
Male	700	300
Female	700	300

SECTION 3.5

1. Vertical; horizontal; the dependent variable depends on, or is affected by, the independent variable.

3. **a.** Yes; nonlinear
   b. No
   c. Possible nonlinear relationship in Industry 1; definite nonlinear relationship in Industry 2

5. They are linearly related.

7. **b.** Cities C, F, I, J, M, and P form one cluster; cities A, B, D, E, G, H, K, L, N, and O form another cluster. Look for similarities within and differences between the clusters, and look for changes that may have occurred to determine reasons for clustering.

9. The points would fall on an upward sloping line.

11. Yes; 600

13. **a.** No
   b. Yes; only the incomes of surgeons with Board certification increase with experience.

15. **a.** No
   b. No; hospital type is not related to number of Xrays.

17. **a.** Number of phones
   b. Revenues increase linearly with the number of phones.

SECTION 3.6

1. **a.** Not related in same month
   b. Yes; advertising expenditure leads units sold by 1 month.
   d. Linearly and positively related
   e. An increase (decrease) in advertising expenditures one month is associated with an increase (decrease) in sales the next month.

3. **a.** 120, 150, 100, 170, 200, 140, 210
   b. Yes

5. **a.** Not related in same month
   b. Yes; Y leads C by one month
   d. An increase (decrease) in Y one month is associated with an increase (decrease) in C the next month.

7. Line graphs are designed for time-ordered, not cross-sectioned, data.

9. No; no concurrent or leading relationship is present.

11. **a.** No
   b. Linearly and inversely related
   c. A decrease in the mean hours to failure is associated with an increase in the standard deviation in the hours to failure.

13. **a.** High in quarter 1; low in quarter 2
   c. Somewhat linearly and directly related

SECTION 3.7

1. Variance measures variation in one variable, whereas covariance measures degree to which variation in one variable is associated with variation in another variable; covariance

3. **a.** $\bar{x} = 4$, $s_x = 2.58$, $\bar{y} = 11$, $s_y = 5.16$
   b. 13.33
   c. 1.00
   d. Perfect positive linear relationship between x and y

5. .205, .854, .005

9. **a.** $\bar{x}_{DJ} = 4.36$, $s_{DJ} = 14.27$, $\bar{x}_{IBM} = .73$, $s_{IBM} = 1.83$
   b. A:1, B:2, C:3, D:1; positively
   c. 25.97
   d. .994
   e. No, correlation does not mean causation.

11. **a.** $\text{Mean}_{GPA} = 3.17$; $s_{GPA} = .605$, $\text{mean}_{salary} = 48.571$; $s_{salary} = 3.101$.
   b. A:3, B:2, C:1, D:1; not related
   c. -1.56
   d. $-.16$

13. $r(0) = .9737$; positively linearly related since $r(0)\sqrt{11-0} > 2$

15. **a.** Mean failure time is decreasing, range in failure time is increasing.
   b. Increases
   c. $r(0) = -.9545$; negative, since as the mean decreases, the range increases.
   d. Yes, because $r(0)\sqrt{8-0} > 2$.
   e. Over time, the range is increasing as the mean is decreasing.

CHAPTER 3
APPLICATION PROBLEMS

1. **a.**

	Machos	Status Seekers	Total
Skim Count	30	80	110
Row %	27.3	72.7	100
Col. %	30	80	55
Whole Count	70	20	90
Row %	77.8	22.2	100
Col. %	70	20	45
Total	100	100	200
%	50	50	100

   b. No; 77.8% of the Machos prefer whole milk, whereas only 22.2% of the Status Seekers do.
   c. 200 customers may not be a representative sample.

3. **a.**

	With Inducement	No Inducement
n	6	6
$\bar{x}$	19.0	29.8
s	3.2	3.3

   b. Yes; the accounts with inducements have an average age of 19 days, while the accounts without inducements have an average age of 29.8 days.
   c. Requires two categorical variables (age is quantitative)

5. **a.** Years in residence
  b. Yes; higher years of residence are associated with higher discount.
  c. Requires one categorical and one quantitative variable (both variables are quantitative)

7. **a.**

	Service	Price	
Indeps.	83.3%	16.7%	100%
Chains	20.0%	80.0%	100%
	58.0%	42.0%	100%

  b. Yes; 83.3% of the independents surveyed focus on service, while only 20% of the chains surveyed focus on service.
  c. Requires one categorical and one quantitative variable (the two variables are categorical).

9. **a.**

	Yes	No
n	5	5
$\bar{x}$	59.4	79.4
s	9.3	11.4

  b. Yes; the average number of greviances was around 59 for firms with participative management compared to 79 for firms without it, while the standard deviations are similar.

11. **a.** Row Percentages:

	Low	High	
Programs	40%	60%	100%
No Programs	10%	90%	100%
	25%	75%	100%

  b. Yes; 40% of firms with the programs had row absenteeism, whereas only 10% of firms without the programs had low absenteeism.

13. **a.** Column Percentages:

Underweight Consumers

	Machos	Status Seekers	
Skim	12.5%	17.5%	15.0%
Whole	87.5%	82.5%	85.0%
	100.0%	100.0%	100.0%

Overweight Consumers

	Machos	Status Seekers	
Skim	83.3%	80.0%	81.7%
Whole	16.7%	20.0%	18.3%
	100.0%	100.0%	100.0%

  b. No; most preference is associated with weight, not market segment; for both Machos and Status Seekers, close to 85% of underweight consumers prefer whole milk and close to 82% of overweight consumers prefer skim milk.

15. **b.** $r(0) = -.0242, r(1) = -.1687, r(2) = .4019$
  c. No, $.40\sqrt{12-2} < 2$.

17. **b.** Only in the stereo industry, where ROI is directly linearly related to average product quality

19. **a.** The number of farms is declining while the size of farms is increasing.
  b. Will comprise large agribusiness

21. **b.** Both groups are rising at about the same rate because the scatter diagram roughly falls along a 45 degree line.
  c. Multiple line graphs

23. **a.** No
  b. Profit margins of franchises, amount of financial assistance, etc.

SECTION 4.2

1. a, b, d, e, and h are random experiments because they are actions that, when done repeatedly, yield different outcomes; c, f, and g are not random experiments because they result in a single outcome.

3. **a.** Acceptable, defective
  b. $\dfrac{3}{100} = .03$
  c. $\dfrac{22}{1,000} = .022$
  d. No; the relative frequency based on 1,000 inspections is more likely to be close to the "true" relative frequency than the relative frequency based on 100 inspections.
  e. c

5. **a.** Simple
  b. Compound
  c. Other than 1,500 hours
  d. 2,500 or more hours
  e. None
  f. Common
  g. $\dfrac{40}{400} = .90$
  h. No; the relative frequency based on 100,000 samples is much more likely to be close to the "true" relative frequency than the relative frequency based on 100 samples.
  i. h

7. **a.** Yes, because over repeated selections, the 10 listed outcomes are possible
  b. Yes, because over repeated selections, the number of females can vary from 1 to 3
  c. (1) $\dfrac{3}{10} = .3$ (2) $\dfrac{6}{10} = .6$ (3) $\dfrac{1}{10} = .1$
  d. Because over an infinite number of selections, those outcomes would occur those respective proportions of the time.

9. **a.** $\dfrac{40}{400} = .10$
  b. .12
  c. A random sample is not expected to reflect perfectly the distribution of the number of children in the entire population of U.S. households.

11. Poor because the probabilities should sum to 1

13. **a.** Simple
  b. Finding 0, 2, 3, 4, or 5 defects

15. **a.** Personal
  b. They do not sum to 1.

17. .50, .25, .167, .083

SECTION 4.3

1. 20

3. a, c, e

5. **a.** Because the sum of all probabilities is 1

b. Joint probabilities
c. .472
d. .111

7. a.

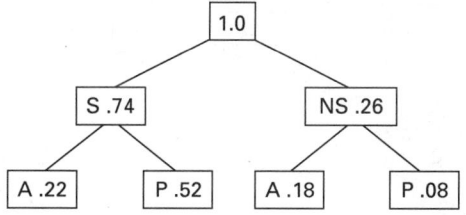

b.

	S	NS	
A	.22	.18	.40
P	.52	.08	.60
	.74	.26	1.00

c. Joint probabilities

d.

	S	NS	
A	1100	900	2000
P	2600	400	3000
	3700	1300	5000

9. a. Row 2 missing probability: .50
Row 3 missing probabilities: .08, .02, .15, .10, .40

b.

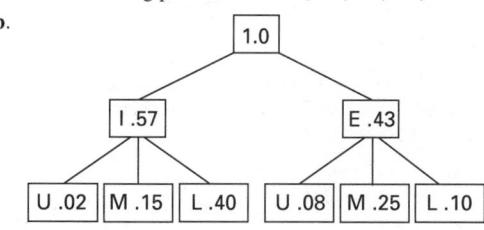

c.

	U	M	L	
E	.08	.25	.10	.43
I	.02	.15	.40	.57
	.10	.40	.50	1.00

d.

	U	M	L	
E	280	875	350	1505
I	70	525	1400	1995
	350	1400	1750	3500

11. a.

	P	NP	
B or Better	.10	.70	.80
C or Worse	.15	.05	.20
	.25	.75	1.00

b. .25

13. a.

	< 2	2–5	over 5	
Yes	.04	.06	.10	.20
No	.20	.40	.20	.80
	.24	.46	.30	1.00

b. .20; .20; .04

c.

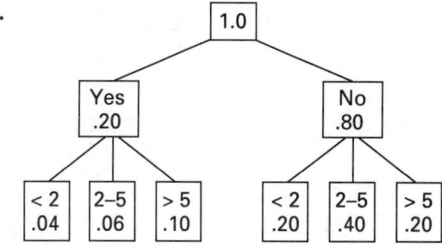

15. A car costing $25,000 is not included (all car costs should be covered).

SECTION 4.4

1. a. Joint
b. Union
c. Neither
d. Union
e. Neither
f. Joint
g. Joint
h. Neither
i. Neither

3. a. Yes
b. No
c. No
d. Yes
e. No
f. Yes

5. a. .065
b. .68
c. Middle Management and Introvert, Lower Management and Introvert

7. a.

	OA	NOA	
P	.24	.16	.40
NP	.38	.22	.60
	.62	.38	1.00

b. .62
c. .76
d. .84
e. 420
f. 310

9. a.

	SQC = No	SQC = Yes	
Below	.35	.15	.50
At/Above	.05	.45	.50
	.40	.60	1.00

b. $P(\text{below}) + P(\text{SQC} = \text{No}) - P(\text{below AND SQC} = \text{No})$
$= .50 + .40 - .35 = .55$
c. $.05 + .45 + .15 = .65$
d. .45
e. 550
f. 650

11. a.

	S	D	
E	.35	.35	.70
I	.15	.15	.30
	.50	.50	1.00

b. $.70 + .50 - .35 = .85$

c. $.15 + .15 + .35 = .65$

13. a.

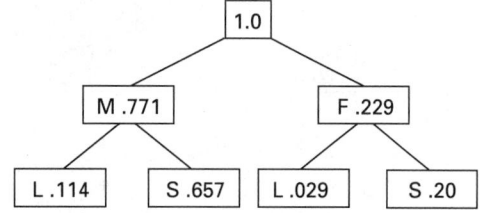

b. .029
c. 3
d. .971
e. $.771 + .857 - .657 = .971$

15. a. .40
b. .60
c. It is the probability of one event OR another event occurring.
d. 0
e. It is the probability of one event AND another event occurring.

SECTION 4.5

1. The occurrence of either one of the events does not affect the probability that the other event will occur.

3. a. Joint, P (highly satisfied AND highly paid)
b. Unconditional, P (highly satisfied)
c. Unconditional, P (highly paid)
d. Union, P (highly satisfied OR highly paid)
e. Conditional, P (highly satisfied | highly paid)
f. Conditional, P (highly satisfied | highly paid)
g. Joint, P (highly satisfied AND highly paid)
h. Conditional, P (highly satisfied | poorly paid)
i. Unconditional, P (poorly paid)
j. Conditional, P (dissatisfied | poorly paid)

5. a. 2
b. 3
c. 3
d. 2
e. 1
f. 3
g. 3

7. a. Conditional
b. Joint
c. Unconditional

9. Equal to, due to independence assumption

SECTION 4.6

1. a. Joint
b. Conditional
c. Conditional
d. Joint

3.

	HP	LP	
High EPS	.40	.20	.60
Low EPS	.10	.30	.40
	.50	.50	1.00

a. $.40/.60 = .667$
b. $.40/.60 = .667$

c. $.30/.50 = .60$
d. $.30/.40 = .75$

5. a.

	NI Up	NI Not Up	
DJI Up	.50	.05	.55
DJI Not Up	.10	.35	.45
	.60	.40	1.00

b. .909
c. .222
d. .60
e. Yes

7. a.

	SQC = No	SQC = Yes	
Below	.35	.15	.50
At/Above	.05	.45	.50
	.40	.60	1.00

b. .25
c. .875
d. .50
e. Yes

9. a. .20
b. .20
c. .20
d. No

11. a. .556
b. .727
c. No

13. a. .15
b. .286
c. No, because knowing the applicant has worked for a company less than 5 years increases the probability the account will be a bad risk

15. a.

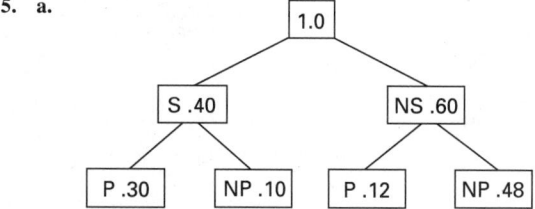

b. .714
c. .828

SECTION 4.7

1. a. .04
b. .855
c.

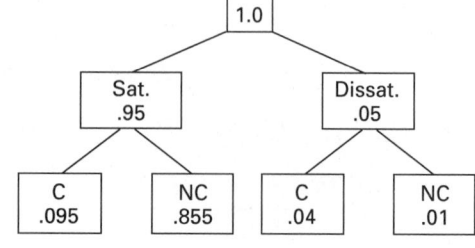

d. .296

3. a.

	B	Not B	
A	.24	.36	.60
Not A	.16	.24	.40
	.14	.60	1.00

	B	Not B	
A	.70	.10	.80
Not A	−.40*	.60	.20
	.30	.70	1.00

*Impossible

	B	Not B	
A	0	.30	.30
Not A	.50	.20	.70
	.50	.50	1.00

b. Yes, manager 2's set
c. Yes; manager 1 does because, for him, $P(A \text{ AND } B) = P(A)P(B)$.

5. a. Yes
   b. .933

	2 New Players hit ≥ 60 HR	2 New Players hit < 60 HR	
Win	63	.02	.65
Don't Win	.07	.28	.35
	.70	.30	1.00

SECTION 4.8

1. Availability error

3. Because they can recall more instances of death due to firearms than death due to falls

CHAPTER 4
APPLICATION PROBLEMS

1. a.

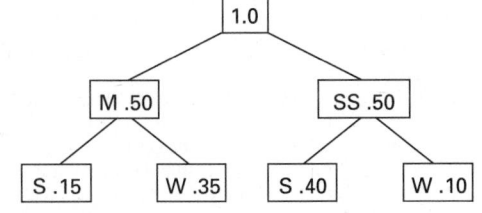

b. .65
c. .50
d. .778
e. Estimated probabilities
f. No; preferring whole milk increases the probability of being a macho
g. Have athletes endorse whole milk

3. a.

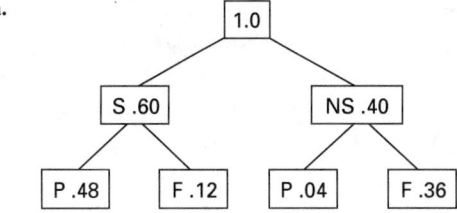

b. .92, .75
c. Good predictor, $P(\text{Success}|\text{Pass})$ is much greater than $P(\text{Success})$

5. a. One
   b. .20, .30, .50 (for example)
   c. .95, .05, .00 (for example)

7. a. Yes

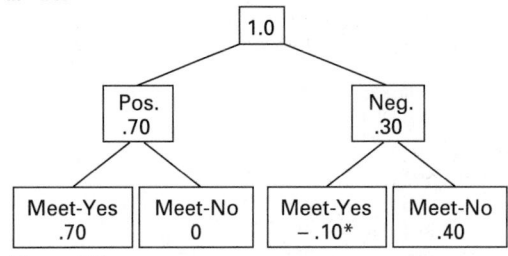

* Impossible

b.

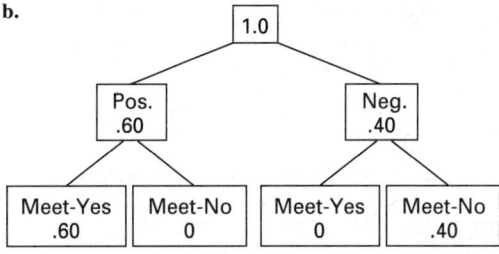

c. The firm will meet its goal if—and only if—the findings are positive.

9. a. Probabilities do not sum to 1.
   b. Multiply each probability by 1.0/.9 to maintain the ordering of the probabilities.

11. a. Yes, since having an SAT score above (below) 1,200 increases (decreases) the probability of having a GPA above 3.5.
   b. Divide number of students with GPAs above 3.5 by 1,500; divide number of students with GPAs above 3.5 and SAT scores above 1,200 by the number of students with SAT scores above 1,200; divide number of students with GPAs above 3.5 and SAT scores below 1,200 by the number of students with SAT scores below 1,200
   c. Relative frequencies, since they are based on many past students

13. a.

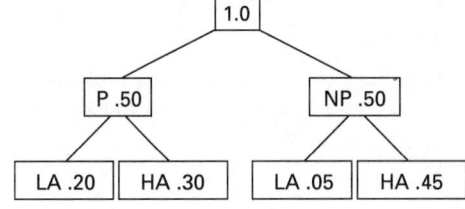

b. .80
c. .25
d. .40
e. No, the probability of having low absenteeism increases if the company runs stress-management programs.

15. c.

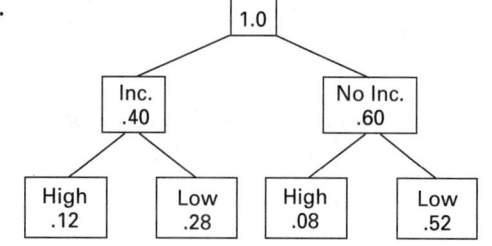

b. .133

17. a. .15
    b. .95
    c. .75
    d. Data show a strong need for capital investment in new computers.

19. a. All probabilities must be equal.
    b. No

21. a. .639
    b. .361
    c. .099
    d. .105
    e. No relationship; the percentages are very close.

23. a. No, P(zero sales of 1,000 units) = .02; rare event, but could happen
    b. Yes, P(zero sales AND zero sales) = (.02)(.02) = .0004

25. a. .875
    b. .75
    c. Yes; P(B or better | group) > P(B or better)

SECTION 5.2

1. a. Yes; discrete; integers from 0 to 100
    b. Yes; discrete; multiples of 6 from 0 to 600

3. a. Not a random variable because every American-made car has one engine
    b. Discrete because there are a countable number of possible percentages
    c. Neither; it is a qualitative random variable.
    d. Continuous because time is continuous
    e. Random and discrete because there are only a finite number of repairs under warranties

5. a. No
    b. No
    c. Yes
    d. No

7. a. $\mu = 1.5$ cars; $\sigma = 1.025$
    b. $\mu = 1.35$ fans; $\sigma = .572$
    c. $\mu = -2.5\%$; $\sigma = 8.292$

9. a. I: $\mu = \$100$; $\sigma = \$2,343.08$
       II: $\mu = \$100$; $\sigma = \$519.62$
    b. II; because its expected outcome is the same, yet it is less risky because of its smaller standard deviation.

11. a. .45, .70, .85, .95, 1.00
    b. .85
    c. .05

13. a. Mean = .87 defects per hour $\sigma = 1.064$ defects per hour
    b. The distribution is skewed (to the right) rather than bell-shaped.

15. b. Midwest National Bank
    c. Mean for Midwest National Bank = 3
       Mean for First South Bank = 2.98
    d. First South Bank, because a higher proportion of the scores are "far away" from the mean
    e. There is more variability in the scores about their average for the First South Bank customers than for the Midwest National Bank customers.
    f. σ for Midwest National Bank = 1.673
       σ for First South Bank = 1.990

SECTION 5.3

1. a. (1) Absent; not absent   (2) 0, 1, 2, 3 . . ., 10
    b. (1) American-made; not American-made
       (2) 0, 1, 2, 3, . . ., 30
    c. (1) In default; not in default   (2) 0, 1, 2, 3, . . ., 10
    d. (1) Defective; not defective   (2) 0, 1, 2, 3 . . ., 10
    e. (1) Order placed; no order placed   (2) 0, 1, 2, 3, 4, 5, 6
    f. (1) High volume; low volume   (2) 0, 1, 2, 3, 4
    g. (1) Audited; not audited   (2) 0, 1, 2, 3, . . ., 10
    h. (1) Incorrect; correct   (2) 0, 1, 2, 3, 40
    i. (1) Late; not late   (2) 0, 1, 2, 3, . . ., 20
    j. (1) Perfect agreement; imperfect agreement
       (2) 0, 1, 2, 3, . . ., 30
    k. (1) Occupied; not occupied   (2) 0, 1, 2, 3, . . ., 20

3. a. .0010
    b. .7290
    c. .2430
    d. The probability of being involved in an auto accident remains the same from year to year, and we are focusing on any single driver.
    e. Historical accident records

5. a. .9039
    b. .0000
    c. .9999
    d. .9039, .0922, .0038, .0001, .0000
    e. ≈ 0
    f. $\mu = .1$ taxpayer audited, $\sigma = .314$ taxpayers audited
    g. $\sigma = 1.118$ taxpayers audited, more variable in the number of taxpayers audited across different groups of 5 taxpayers, which could lead to unequal work loads for IRS employees.

7. a. Neither; R1
    b. Neither; S2
    c. T2; neither
    d. U1; U2

9. a. There is a 34.87% chance that the class mean grade will exceed 70 for all 10 quizzes.
    b. It is virtually impossible that the class mean grade will exceed 70 for only 3 or fewer of the 10 quizzes.
    c. There is a 34.87% chance that the class mean grade will exceed 70 for more than 9 (that is, all 10) quizzes.
    d. There is a .01% (very slim) chance that the class mean grade will exceed 70 for between 2 and 5 (that is, 3 or 4)
    e. There is a 1.6% chance that the class mean grade will exceed 70 for 2,3,4 or 5 of the 10 quizzes.
    h. $\mu = 9$ quizzes, $\sigma = .949$ quizzes
    i. $\sigma = 1.581$ quizzes; outcomes far away from the mean of 5 quizzes with a mean grade exceeding 70 would have a higher probability of occurring, giving rise to more variable results from semester to semester.

11. **a.** .1681
    b. .0284
    c. .3602
    d. $\mu = 3.5$ complete claims, $\sigma = 1.025$ complete claims

13. Xcel's, because the probability of 3 defectives assuming a 30% defective rate is .2668, whereas a probability of 3 defectives assuming a 10% defective rate is considerably smaller (.0574).

SECTION 5.4

1. .0001; it would be highly unusual to sell 0 deluxe phones out of 10 sales of phones, if deluxe phones still account for 60% of sales, so it may be that deluxe phone sales are slipping.

3. 22.62%

5. **a.** .2641; producer risk
   b. .3918; consumer risk
   c. Increase producer risk and decrease consumer risk

7. Yes, because p will vary considerably over subsequent customer selections, and the Bernoulli assumptions would be invalid.

9. **a.** .95
   b. .9499
   c. .9499
   d. No
   e. Yes

11. **a.** .8821
    b. .2228
    c. The producer risk declined a very small amount; consumer risk declined considerably.

13. **a.** .0016
    b. .0039
    c. .0028
    d. They are very rare events.
    e. Look for causes of that pattern.
    f. .125; such a pattern has a 12.5% chance of occurring and so is not unusual, and thus suggests random variation.

SECTION 5.5

1. **a.** Count the number of defects in 1,000 pieces and divide that number by 1,000.
   b. Count the number of misspelled words on 100 pages and divide that number by 100.
   c. For each of 50 lunch hours, count the number of people arriving, and divide the total of these counts by 50.
   d. Count the total number of operations done in the hospital for a single year and record the number of patients who died during the operation. Divide the number of deaths by the number of operations and multiply by 1000.
   e. Count the number of power failures over the past 50 years and divide this count by 50.

3. **a.** .966
   b. .879
   c. .028
   d. .073
   e. .596
   f. .998
   g. .196
   h. .034
   i. .121
   j. .616

5. **a.** $P(X = 3$ given $X = 3)$
   b. $P(X \le 5$ given $\lambda = 3)$
   c. $P(X \ge 3$ given $\lambda = 3)$
   d. $P(1 \le X \le 2$ for $\lambda = .3)$
   e. Count the number of defects in each 100 different 100-yard strips of cable, and divide the total of the counts by 100.

7. **a.** .632
   b. .264
   c. .368
   d. 3
   e. Count the number of errors in each of 50 five-page sections of text, and divide the total of these counts by 50.

9. **a.** $X =$ the number of copiers sold in a 5-day period; possible values; 0, 1, 2, . . .
   Assumptions: The number of copiers sold in one minute is independent of the number of copiers sold in another minute; the probability of any given number of copiers sold is the same for each minute; the probability of a total of 1 copier sold over multiple minutes is approximately proportional to the number of minutes; the probability of 2 or more copiers sold in one minute is close to 0.
   b. A 5-day period
   c. .384
   d. .002
   e. When 9 remain in inventory (will have a 3.2% chance of stockout)

11. **a.** $\mu = 2$ defects, $\sigma = 1.414$ defects
    c. Yes, because such an occurrence would be unusual (.012 probability) if the defect rate is only 2 defects per box.

13. **a.** .050, .149, .224, .224, .168, .101, .050, .022, .008, .003, .001
    c. 3
    d. 3
    e. 1.732
    f. .050; small; it was probably successful.

SECTION 5.6

1. When the continuous variable in question is affected by many independent factors

3. **a.** .6826
   b. .9802
   c. .9902
   d. .9500
   e. .9974
   f. .0013
   g. .9987
   h. .1044
   i. .3239
   j. 0
   k. .9394
   l. .9960
   m. .7983
   n. .0650
   o. .3709
   p. .0013
   q. .0026
   r. .1587
   s. .0228
   t. .5000
   u. 0
   v. .2380
   w. .0228
   x. .4706
   y. .8400
   z. 0

5. **a.** 1,200
   b. 870
   c. 500
   d. 1,000
   e. 400
   f. 1,600
   g. 1,400
   h. 800
   i. 1,329
   j. 608
   k. 1,210
   l. 1,498
   m. 648
   n. 1,010
   o. 958

7. **c.** 2.5, 1.8, 0, 2

9. The second company; the first company

11. 928

13. **a.** 27.99 hours
    b. 32.01 hours
    c. 4.02 hours

15. **a.** 9.5%
    b. ≈ 0%
    c. Low variation makes it easier to meet specifications, assuming that the specs meet consumer wants.
    d. Reduce variation in such aspects of the production process as concentrations of material ingredients, temperature, and amounts filled in the molds, improved supervision, and better machinery.
    e. .56, 1.67

17. **c.** .0013
    d. .1359, .1359

19. It was assumed that the hours to burnout were normally distributed. This could be checked by randomly selecting 100 fuses, testing them for number of hours to burnout, and constructing a relative frequency histogram from the values. The histogram should be bell-shaped with approximately two-thirds, 95%, and all of the values within 1, 2, and 3 standard deviations of the mean, respectively. It was further assumed that the new fuse in question was randomly selected from those produced.

21. **a.** .000147
    b. 9.7502, 9.7498

23. **a.** ≈ 9 weeks
    b. ≈ 12 weeks
    c. 15 weeks
    d. ≈ 18 weeks

25. **a.** 10%
    b. 12.25%
    c. 9%
    d. 17%
    e. 15%
    f. 16.5%

CHAPTER 5
APPLICATION PROBLEMS

1. **a.** .3955
   b. .1562
   c. .3280
   d. Probability of a sale in any neighborhood remains the same on any attempt, implying independence of outcomes.

3. **a.**

X	0	1	2	3	4	5	6	7	8	9	10
P(X)	.050	.149	.224	.224	.168	.101	.050	.022	.008	.003	.001

   b. .034
   c. The number of CD players demanded in one minute is independent of the number of players demanded another minute; the probability of any given number of players demanded in one minute is the same for every minute; the probability of a total of 1 player demanded in several minutes is proportional to the number of minutes; the probability of 2 or more players demanded for one minute is close to 0.

5. **a.** Zenith, because its standard deviation is 1.6% of its mean, while the Apex standard deviation is 6.1% of its mean.
   b. Apex
   c. Zenith
   d. The Zenith distribution is contained within the Apex distribution. High numbers favor Apex, which is more variable. Low numbers favor Zenith, which is tightly clustered around the mean.

7. **a.** The number of product adopters out of 5 awareness-stage-only consumers, with possible values of 0, 1, 2, 3, 4, or 5, and the number of product adopters out of 5 awareness-through-trial-stage consumers with possible values 0, 1, 2, 3, 4, or 5.
   b. .0004, .7373
   c. Get consumers to try the product (e.g., through free trial period or free samples, where appropriate) because around three-fourths of consumers who try it adopt it, whereas only a tiny fraction of consumers merely aware of it adopt it.

9. **a.** .368
   b. .019

11. **a.** Project A: $\mu = \$16.25k$, $\sigma = \$38.304k$
    Project B: $\mu = \$14k$, $\sigma = \$16.248k$
    b. Project A, because its coefficient of variation (standard deviation as a percentage of the mean) is higher

13. **a.** .9772
    b. .50

15. **a.** .6826
    b. .9332
    c. 2%

17. **a.** .007
    b. Something (it could be a purposeful worker slowdown) is reducing the call rate.

19. **a.** .0192
    b. The mean time to replacement decreased, because if it was still 1,900, only around 2% should have failed before 1,600 hours.

21. **a.** .0047
    b. The daily volumes in 1988 are higher than in 1985.

23. **a.** .449, .360, .144, .038, .008, .001
    b. Expected: 45, 36, 14, 4, 0, 0. The manager's belief is supported, $\lambda \approx .8$.
    c. Estimate the number of potatoes in a 100-pound bag and count 10% of them for each bag. Reject a bag if any of the 10% counted are bad, since $P(X > 0|\lambda = .8/10 = .08) = .077$.

25. **a.** Strategy 3
    b. The coefficient of variation is undefined for the first two strategies, and is 115.5% for the third strategy. Strategy 3 is clearly the superior strategy—it has a higher probability of increasing net profit.

SECTION 6.2

1. The percentage of the population that favors brand X would be somewhere between 35% and 45%.

3. The margin of error must increase.

5. a.

Sample	Mean
2,4	3
2,6	4
2,8	5
2,10	6
4,6	5
4,8	6
4,10	7
6,8	7
6,10	8
8,10	9

   b. Since the population mean is 6, the maximum margin of error is 3.

   c.

Sample	Means
2,4,6,8	5
2,4,6,10	5.5
2,4,8,10	6
2,6,8,10	6.5
4,6,8,10	7

   d. The maximum margin of error is 1.
   e. When the sample size increases, the maximum margin of error decreases.

SECTION 6.3

1. The target population is the set of elements of interest. The sampling frame is the physical list of elements or sampling units that will be sampled.

3. Street address

5. More than one frame would be needed. The first frame could be the list of 100 branch offices. Once a sampling unit—a branch office—is selected, then the survey elements, the employees, could be sampled from a second frame of employees from that branch office.

SECTION 6.4

1. See text, pages 302–303.

3. No. Stratified sampling is a survey *design*. Survey *methods* include personal interviews, telephone interviews, and mailed questionnaires.

5. Response error arises because the respondent did not understand the question, did not have the information, or did not answer truthfully. Nonresponse error is introduced into a survey when the element selected from the frame does not respond, either because the element cannot be located or refuses to answer.

7. People who live on the first floor are likely to be older because older people have trouble climbing the stairs. Therefore, the study results could over-represent the characteristics of older people.

9. Selection errors: (1) The target population—all Hispanics—is not represented by the frame. Spanish-speaking people in Miami are mostly Cuban Americans, while those in Western states are mostly Mexican Americans. (2) Some people do not have phones, may have unlisted numbers, or may simply not be listed in the latest version of the telephone directory.
   Must use same diction and voice inflection. Also problem of common understanding of survey wording.
   New immigrants may be suspicious of telephone survey.

SECTION 6.5

1. 480 429 368 475 365
   011 130 119 162 167

3. Ineligible units cause a problem, because the resulting sample will be smaller than desired since ineligibles are discarded.
   Duplicate sampling units cause a problem because the duplicates have a higher chance of selection. This situation could cause the service organization to look worse than if all customers were weighted equally.

SECTION 6.6

1. The variation of the measurement of interest within each stratum is smaller than the variance among the strata; an estimate is needed for each stratum (factory, regional office) as well as an estimate for the whole target population.

3. Proportional allocation considers only the size of each stratum in allocating the total sample. Use when stratum variances similar and sampling cost per stratum similar.

5. Stratified sampling would result in no reduction in the margin of error over simple random sampling unless it is cheaper to survey an item under the stratified plan than the simple random sampling plan.

7. You don't have to know the population size and you don't have to carry around a table of random numbers. "Interview every tenth person walking through the door" is a simple direction for field personnel to follow.

9. Unless the measurement of interest is related to the name of the employee, the population (frame) is random.

11. Small businesses and professional corporations frequently have their home residences listed after the office numbers. This income group would have a greater chance of selection if the next number is selected. The correct procedure is to skip businesses and professional numbers and select the next kth number.

13. a. If the opinions of white- and blue-collar workers are expected to be similar within any factory, but expected to vary by factory, a stratified sampling plan would be considered and each factory would be sampled.

    b. If the opinions are expected to differ by type of worker but not by factory, then one or two factories can be sampled with a large number of workers sampled from each factory.

SECTION 6.7

1. a. Personal interview
   b. Personal interview
   c. Mail questionnaire
   d. Double question!: minimum time—phone; minimum cost—mail

3. Combination of personal interview and telephone

5. The interviewer's facial expressions, etc., affect the answers given. You can determine if your survey has the interviewer bias-problem by reinterviewing the same respondents using different interviewers and comparing the results.

SECTION 6.8

1. **a.** Since respondents have a tendency to compress time (think of the past six weeks as the past month), they may overstate the number of times they visited a shopping mall in the past month.
   b. Personal and potentially embarrassing question
   c. The words "caloric" and "polyunsaturates" may not be familiar to all respondents.
   d. The words "you" and "service" could be ambiguous.
   e. Double question
   f. Ambiguous question. What does "frequent user" mean?
   g. Biased question. People will say they shop at all "upscale" stores, even listing stores that don't exist!

3. For aided-recall form: Pro—Consumer may have considered many other brands but just can't think of the names. Con—Consumer may only have considered the one (s)he bought, but doesn't want to be considered a poor shopper and might say (s)he looked at all brands.

SECTION 6.9

1. Nothing is changed or manipulated, and there is no random assignment of experimental units to treatments in an observational study. Data are simply collected.

3. A properly conducted experiment seeks to show that a factor caused the observed changes in the dependent variable by (1) equalizing experimental units through randomization and (2) controlling for other variables that might affect the dependent variable.

5. Randomization *tends* to equalize groups of experimental units on *all* possible factors.

7. **a.** Despite the random selection, this is not an experiment. The employees were not assigned; they were merely classified.
   b. Other explanations are possible. People who are employed longer usually make more money and have managerial positions. A managerial position may have better working conditions than a nonmanagerial position.

SECTION 6.10

1. A small variation in a factor is likely to produce noticeable effects on the dependent variable. Vary the factor enough so the dependent variable has a chance to reflect the change.

3. Random error is the variation within a treatment caused by all the other variables not considered in the study. Randomization does *not* reduce random error, but tends to equalize it within each treatment.

5. Inconclusive. If accidents go down during selective enforcement, the difference could simply be due to differences in the weather or road construction during the two periods. Consider a control group. Randomly assign high-accident locations to two groups. Put selective enforcement in one and not in the other. Compare the changes before and after for the two groups.

CHAPTER 6
APPLICATION PROBLEMS

1. No. The confidence interval (.48, .54) contains .50.

3. **a.** Population All major airports in the United States
      Sample   Ten randomly selected airports
   b. Population All taxpayers who filed for the year
      Sample   A random sample of taxpayers

   c. Population All hourly, support, and professional workers
      Sample   Randomly selected workers from the groups

5. 24 = MA, Massachusetts
   14 = IN, Indiana
   13 = IL, Illinois
   29 = NH, New Hampshire
   20 = MD, Maryland
   26 = MT, Montana
   46 = VA, Virginia
   12 = ID, Idaho

7. Use stratified sampling with the countries as strata. Use a mailed questionnaire or Fax.

9. **a.** All people who live in New York City who have phones
   b. No. This was a convenience sample. The 100 people were not selected at random from the entire city. Respondents had to be in the shopping mall and select themselves by entering the research booth.
   c. Margin of error has no meaning for a convenience sample. The sample may not be representative of the target population.

11. **a.** Town A already has a fire station; town B does not. Town A has more crime than town B.
    b. Use proportional sampling. Since 70% of the people live in town A, randomly select 700 families from town A for your sample. Randomly select 300 families from town B for your sample.

13. The sample of size 10 contains only 2 men, while the target population contains about 50% men. The makeup of the sample does not mirror the target population. Stratified random sampling should have been used; since women have similar weights and men have similar weights but the average weight of each group is very different.

15. **a.** A large number of the observations could come from his early data entries and overestimate the average over all 5,000 data entries. A large number of the samples could come from his later data entries and underestimate the average over all 5,000 data entries.
    b. The target population is *ordered*. Errors tend to fall systematically as the clerk gains more experience. Use a systematic sampling design.

17. The primary customers of Domino's pizzas are young, single, high school and college students. Amstar's sample excluded these people. The sample was not representative of the target population.

19. **Experimental Factor:**   **Level of feedback**
    Levels: 2 — No feedback, feedback
    Dependent Variable: Level of service measured along a 5-point scale: poor, mediocre, average, good, outstanding
    Experimental Units: Customers who have their cars serviced in our shop

SECTION 7.1

1. A statistic is calculated from a sample. Statistics vary from sample to sample. A population parameter is a constant and is a numerical characteristic of an entire population.

3. **a.** All members of the general public who might use the product
   b. Proportion of the target population who prefer brand A
   c. .40

5. Desired confidence level, variability of the population, sample size, the sample design

7. a. Two target populations — the number of claims processed per day under the old method and under groups of three
b. Long-run mean numbers of claims processed per person under each method
c. The mean numbers of claims produced per day over the sample period under each method

9. a. Parcels delivered
b. Mean delivery time
c. 100 parcels
d. 15.5 hours

11. a. Shift production
b. Shift population mean
c. Five phone sets
d. Shift sample mean
e. Sampling variability

13. a. All scissor buyers
b. Proportion of all scissor buyers who insist on purchasing a Fiskars scissor
c. 500 scissor buyers
d. 30%
e. A sample proportion of scissors preferences will always differ somewhat from the population proportion of scissor preferences.

15. a. Mean number of Hispanics per square mile in San Antonio
b. 2,000 Hispanics per square mile
c. The density of Hispanics in 5 square miles of San Antonio is not expected to reflect perfectly the density of Hispanics in all of San Antonio.

17. a. See text
b. No; the tires are not likely to have the same lifetimes.
c. Improve market share and reduce number of returned tires
d. Would have to wear out all 300,000 tires, leaving none to sell
e. Population mean time to failure and population standard deviation for all 300,000 tires
f. Mean time to failure for the sample, standard deviation for the sample
g. Sampling variability

SECTION 7.2

1. a. 4
b. 1.63
c. Sample means = {2,3,4,3,4,5,4,5,6}; 4
d. 1.155
e. $\mu = \mu_{\bar{x}}$
f. $1.633/\sqrt{2} = 1.155$

3.

Mean	SD
μ	σ
$\mu_{\bar{x}}$	$\sigma_{\bar{x}}$
x	s

5. a. 40
b. 2.921
c. Yes; larger samples reduce standard errors.
d. Yes; the population is normal.

7. No; because managers know what the results would be if they did construct a sampling distribution.

9. 100

11. 49.917 and 50.083 cm; 49.834 and 50.166 cm

13. a. .8413
b. .0668

c. No
d. 52,000 mile
e. 100 miles
f. ≈ 0
g. ≈ 0
h. Yes; the distribution of the sample mean will be normal for samples > 30 according to the central limit theorem.

15. a. .0228
b. .0013
c. .5328
d. .7881
e. .2088
f. 0
g. No; we don't know the distribution of x.
h. Central limit theorem

17. a–d. Answers will vary
e. No, due to averaging small and large incomes in the sample
f. (6) Approximately normal (bell-shaped)

SECTION 7.3

1. You must have a probability (not a convenience) sample; population distribution must be normal or the sample size must be large enough so the sampling distribution is normal; parameter of interest must be fixed. (If the process is a time series, the series must be stationary.)

3. a. Correct
b. Sample standard deviations could either increase or decrease from sample to sample but will be very close to the fixed population standard deviation when $n = 1,000$
c. Reliability coefficient is unaffected
d. Sample means could increase or decrease from sample to sample but will be close to the fixed population mean
e. Margin of error decreases

5. a. .563
b. .486
c. Reduces it
d. 0; If you examine the entire population each time, you get the same mean each time.

7. a. 30.43, 13.61
b. 30.01, 9.49
c. 31.43, 8.12
d. No systematic change in σ; the standard error decreases
e. s estimates σ, which is a constant. As n increases, the standard error decreases

9. a. 44.13, 45.87
b. 43.93, 46.07
c. 43.46, 46.54
Smaller sample sizes increase the standard errors.

11. a. $27,182.50, $4126.81
b. $1305.01
c. ($22,941.22, $31,423.78); we are 99% confident that the mean family income of the blue-collar segment is between $22,941.22 and $31,423.78.
d. Yes, because the lower bound of the CI is above $21,500.
e. Simple random sample from normal population of incomes

13. a. 2,000 hours, 7.5 hours
b. Because 95 out of every 100 CIs will contain the population mean life
c. No, because the upper bound of the CI is lower than 2,000 hours

15. **a.** All cigarettes of brand A
    b. Mean level of nicotine
    c. Levels of nicotine must be approximately normally distributed.
    d. (.494 mg, .506 mg)

17. **a.** 8.25 min, 2.121 min.
    b. .5625
    c. (6.56, 9.94)
    d. Yes, because the upper bound of the confidence interval is less than 11 minutes
    e. Normally distributed

19. 98%

21. 900

23. **b.** Yes
    c. Yes, because there is a stationary mean to be estimated
    d. (29.3, 31.4)

SECTION 7.4

1. **a.** $\bar{x} - t\, s/\sqrt{n}$
   b. $\bar{x} + t\, s/\sqrt{n}$
   c. $\bar{x} \pm t\, s/\sqrt{n}$
   d. $\bar{x} - t\, s/\sqrt{n}$
   e. $\bar{x} + t\, s/\sqrt{n}$
   f. $\bar{x} \pm t\, s/\sqrt{n}$

3. **a.** No. If the population were normal, approximately 95% of the observations would fall within two standard deviations and almost all would fall within three standard deviations. But $650 \pm 2 \times (450)$ is -250 to 1550. Bank loans cannot take on negative values.
   b. With a sample size of $n = 250$, the central limit theorem guarantees that the sampling distribution will be normal.
   c. 13.4% $(1 - .866)$
   d. ($601.67, $698.33)
   e. $609.43 lower bound
   f. $707.36 upper bound

5. $682.30 upper bound

7. No, because the mean could be $12,618 (upper bound), which is greater than $12,500.

9. Yes; .086(upper bound) < .10

11. No; 2.06(lower bound) < 2.20

SECTION 7.5

1. Target population is physically divided into discrete units and an estimate is needed for each unit; variance between strata is greater than variance within strata.

3. $\bar{x}_{ST} = 45.5$, $\text{Var}(\bar{x}_{ST}) = .012$, $45.5 \pm 1.96(.11)$ or (45,27,45.71)

SECTION 7.6

1. No. According to Cochran, if the population proportion is expected to be .05, a sample of size 1,400 is required to ensure the normality of the sampling distribution of proportions.

3. **a.** $.13 \pm 1.645(.0137)$, $(.107, .153)$
   b. Yes. The confidence interval says the percent defective is *at least* 10.7%.

5. **a.** $.287 \pm 1.96\,\sqrt{(.287)(.713)}\,/150$; $(.215, .359)$
   b. No. The estimate applies only to economists listed in the frame.

7. **a.** Yes
   b. .079
   c. (.058, .100)
   d. May be an opportunity to improve the system

9. **a.** Cannot yet tell; $.48 \leq p \leq .56$
   b. Increase the sample size

SECTION 7.7

1. Variance of population, sample design, desired confidence level, required margin of error

3. **a.** 35
   b. 1.014%
   c. 139
   d. To reduce the margin of error by a factor of k, you must increase the sample size by a factor of k^2.
   e. (1.51%, 5.49%)

5. **a.** 65
   b. No, can't estimate a changing mean

7. 1,083

SECTION 7.8

1. Construct a confidence interval for the median when the population is highly skewed and the sample size is less than 30

3. **a.** $(-8.19, 31.52)$
   b. Median
   c. Median because of outlier

5. Yes; use median due to outliers.

7. **a.**

Min.	LF	Q_1	Med	Q_3	UF	Max.
5	40.25	56	60	66.5	2.25	124.00

Outliers: 5, 121, 123, 125

   b. (52, 121); the population median > 50; 52 (lower bound) > 50
   c. Data had 5 outliers

SECTION 7.9

1. **a.** z, t, χ^2
   b. t, χ^2
   c. z, t
   d. χ^2
   e. z, t
   f. z
   g. χ^2

3. 15.66, 33.20
   3.33, 16.92
   6.91, 28.85
   86.92, 158.95
   13.79, 53.67

5. **a.** 3, 2.5
   b. 1.49, 4.51
   c. (1.03, 3.75)

7. population mean

9. **a.** 109.21 ppsi, 140.80 ppsi); we are 95% confident that the standard deviation is between 109.21 ppsi and 140.80 ppsi.
   b. Yes, according to the evidence

11. a. 179.2 min., 9.318 min.
 b. (174.0 min., 184.4 min.); we are 99% confident that the mean delivery time is between 174.0 min. and 184.4 min.
 c. Mean delivery time goal appears to be met, but delivery time variation evidence is inconclusive

CHAPTER 7
APPLICATION PROBLEMS

1. a. $.80 \pm 1.645 \sqrt{((.8)(.2)/800}$; (.779, .821)
 90% confident that unknown population proportion is between .779 and .821
 b. Simple random sample; and sample size large enough so that sampling distribution of sample proportion is normal

3. a. At most $20.5 + (1.282)(7.5/\sqrt{225}) = 21.14$ days
 b. Yes, but the reduction may not be substantial

5. a. At least $1,760 - 1.645; 2,000/\sqrt{400} = 1,595.5$
 b. No

7. a. $.54 \pm 1.96 \sqrt{(.54)(.46)/100}$; (.442, .638)
 Since population proportion could be below or above .50, we *cannot* say that a majority of forecasters believe the deficit will be reduced this year.
 b. Increase the sample size to reduce the margin of error. Ultimately *both* the upper and lower limits will either be above .50 or below .50.

9. a. $\bar{x} = 2.5$ min., $s = .53$ min.
 Est. SE = $.53/\sqrt{10} \cdot \sqrt{(50-10)/(50-1)} = .151$ min.
 $2.5 \pm 1.833 (.151)$; (2.22 min., 2.78 min.)
 90% confident that the average time for all 50 operators to resolve a complaint is between 2.22 min. and 2.78 min.
 b. The workers have improved from 3.2 min. to between 2.22 and 2.78 min. They should be rewarded.

11. 246

13. a. (92%, 104%); 95% confident that the median productivity of all 2,000 work groups is between 92% and 104% of standard
 b. Distribution was not normally distributed.
 c. Yes; one group's productivity (138%) is an outlier.

15. $72.5 \pm 1.645 \sqrt{2.1} = 72.5 \pm 2.38 = (70.12, 74.88)$; 90% confident that the average sales over 2,000 stores will be between 70.12 and 74.88 cartons per week

17. a. Yes
 b. $4,650 \pm 2.262(10.54)$; (4,626 ppsi, 4,674 ppsi); 95% confident that mean impact resistance for the shift is between 4,626 and 4,674 ppsi
 c. $(10 - 1)(1111.11)/19.02 \le \sigma^2 \le (10 - 1)(1111.11)/2.70$
 $22.93 \le \sigma \le 60.86$ ppsi; 95% confident that standard deviation in impact resistance for the shift is between 22.93 and 60.86 ppsi
 d. Shift is meeting average performance standard (4,660 ppsi falls within interval), but is not meeting variability standard (22 ppsi does not fall within the interval on standard deviation).
 e. Diagnose causes for the increased variability.

19. a. At least $54,000 - 2.821(3,162/\sqrt{10}) = 51,179$ miles; 99% confident that new brake pads will last *at least* 51,179 miles.
 b. Limit exceeds 50,000 miles. Switch to new brake pads.
 c. We are not interested in the sample mean only the population mean. Therefore, we must set up a confidence interval.

21. a. At most $.12 + 1.645 \sqrt{(.12)(.88)/2,000} = .132$; At most 13.2%
 b. Blacks were underestimated — potential racial discrimination

23. $.367 \pm 1.96 \sqrt{(.367)(.633)/900}$; (.336, .398)
 Sears can be 95% confident that the proportion of sales made to persons within the city is between 33.6 and 39.8%.

SECTION 8.2

1. Shape: normal, nonnormal, skewed
 Center: mean, median
 Spread: standard deviation, interquartile range

3. a. The log transform cannot be used when any data value is 0. There is no number, x, such that $10x = 0$.
 b. The square root transform cannot be used whenever any data value is negative.

5. a. Sample suggests population is skewed, and $n < 30$.
 b. Log transform is slightly better than square root at eliminating outliers and normalizing the distribution.

7. First distribution unimodal, second bimodal; means similar; variance of the second larger than the first

SECTION 8.3

1. Check for highly asymmetric population

3. a. 2.069 (t)
 b. 2.576 (z)
 c. 1.645 (z)
 d. 1.356 (t)

5. a. 23.043, 1.960
 b. 6146.819, 8.766
 c. 50, 1.961
 d. 94.943, 5.262

7. a. 4.055
 b. 22.580
 c. 3.226
 d. 7.136

9. a. 29.3
 b. 18 df
 c. 2.5
 d. (−1.3, 9.3)
 e. No difference
 f. Normal populations, random sampling, equal variances

11. a. (1.4, 10.6)
 b. Yes, type 2 transistor lasts longer

13. a. (−.9, 1.3)
 b. Yes, no difference in population means

15. a. Yes
 b. $(73.8 - 64.2) \pm 3.355 (4.084) = (-4.1, 23.3)$; At the 99% confidence level, we cannot conclude a difference in the two methods.

SECTION 8.4

1. a. Means, to compare mean tensile strength of the two processes
 b. Proportions, to compare proportions of voters intending to vote for respective candidate
 c. Proportions, to compare proportions of people who must wait more than one minute before and after implementation of QC
 d. Means, to compare mean labor cost per unit before and after training

3. **a.** .055, .107
    b. .022, .057
    c. .006, .009

5. **a.** $.68 - .37 \pm z$(estimated SE)
    b. .030
    c. $.68 - .37 \pm 1.96(.030) = (.251, .369)$
    d. The difference is statistically significant.

7. **a.** (.081, .219)
    b. We are 90% confident that preferred stockholders prefer the proposed change more than common stockholders by between 8.1% and 21.9%.

9. Sample sizes are too small.

11. May not be representative sample

13. Yes, because we are 95% confident that $\hat{p}_{after}$ is between 2.3% and 4.7% lower than $\hat{p}_{before}$.

SECTION 8.5

1. Populations are skewed and sample sizes are small.

3. No, because the interval contains zero

5. **a.** Median 1 = 3.5, Median 2 = 13
    b. Median 2 > Median 1 by between 6 and 32 units

7. **a.** Median C = 73.5   Median N = 68.5
    b. Median N < Median C by between 1 and 10 minutes

9. (−240, 150); CI contains 0; so cannot detect a difference

SECTION 8.6

1. 2.98, .21, 2.74

3. **a.** Yes
    b. Yes

5. $s_1^2 = 1.420$, $s_2^2 = 1.664$; 95% CI for $\sigma_2^2/\sigma_1^2 \approx (.357, 3.906)$
    Note: $F_{12,12}$ used to approximate $F_{13,13}$

7. (.84, 14.81) for 90%; (.65, 20.73) for 95%

9. Some CIs for the difference in population means assume equal population variances.

11. (.55, 6.56); CIs contains 1, so cannot detect a difference

13. **a.** Yes
    b. Before: $\bar{x} = 0$, $s = 2.828$, $s^2 = 8.000$
    After: $\bar{x} = 0$, $s = .816$, $s^2 = .667$
    c. (3.772, 38.690); yes, because we are 90% confident the σ^2_{before} is between 3.772 and 38.690 times as large as the σ^2_{after}.

SECTION 8.7

1. Populations not normally distributed; samples independent; population medians are (nearly) equal

3. Yes, the dispersion of population A > dispersion of population B because the computed M_A > the upper-tabled M-value.

5. **a.** 20.95, 20.70
    b. No, $M = 462.5$
    c. (.59, 10.39); No, CI contains 1.

7. $M_{Yuppies} = \$170.50 <$ lower-tabled M-value of \$198.50; Yuppies have lower income-variability than Dinks

CHAPTER 8
APPLICATION PROBLEMS

1. **a.** Yes, shapes near normal and similar variabilities
    b. (\$5,470, \$6,410); 80% confident that Status Seekers have higher average income level than Machos by \$5,470 to \$6,410

3. **a.** Data skewed; use test for difference between two population medians
    b. (−75, 100); since 0 is in the interval, no difference at the 95% level of confidence

5. Since $M_{FE} = 59.25 < 65.25$, cannot detect difference

7. **a.** (.019, .041); 95% confident that control groups produce between 1.9% and 4.1% more defects than cross-trained groups
    b. Yes, $\hat{p}_{control} - \hat{p}_{cross}$ is positive, and 0 not in CI.

9. (1.64, 16.77); The variance before is between 1.64 and 16.77 times larger than the variance after the campaign. Yes, since 1 is not in the interval.

11. **a.** (.14, .26); Yes; using sports figures generates between 14% and 26% more people who can correctly recall an ad than does the "man-in-the-street" approach.
    b. Cochran's table assures us that the sample size is sufficient.

13. (.59, 3.51); cannot detect a difference between the two population variances since 1 is in interval

15. **a.** (6.21%, 7.79%); 90% confident that workers led by participative leadership have between 6.21% and 7.79% higher productivity than those led by autocratic leadership
    b. Data are not proportions; can take on values greater than 1

17. Using $t(\infty, 80\%) = 1.282$, CI =(188.4, 211.6); 80% confident that vendor A's fixed disk lasts between 188.4 hours and 211.6 hours longer than vendor B's

19. **a.** $\hat{p}_{female} = .78$; $\hat{p}_{male} = .90$
    b. (−.02, .26); cannot detect a difference since 0 is in the interval

21. **a.** $\hat{p}_{black} = .069$; $\hat{p}_{white} = .203$
    b. (.095, .173); Whites are more likely to be assigned nonutility jobs than blacks. The difference in the proportion of whites assigned to nonutility jobs over blacks is between 9.5% and 17.3%.

23. **a.** Lower bound = −9,000; upper bound = 30,000; since CI contains 0, cannot detect a difference.
    b. The difference could be due to factors other than gender — for example, length of service or field of study.

25. M-calculated = 310.5; cannot conclude with 95% confidence that there is a difference in the dispersion of incomes between the two cities.

SECTION 9.2

1. **a.** Hypotheses are made about population parameters, not sample statistics.
    b. The two hypotheses should cover all the possibilities.
    c. Correct
    d. The < should be ≤.
    e. The equal sign should be in the first (null) hypothesis; $\bar{x}$ should be μ.
    f. There should be a constant in place of $\bar{x}$.

3. $H_0: \mu = \$3,500$
    $H_1: \mu \neq \$3,500$

5. a. 1.833
    b. 2.576
    c. 2.326
    d. 2.080

7. a. (1) 10 days
        (2) Correct
    b. (1) Correct
        (2) Upper tailed
    c. (1) 180 feet
        (2) Lower tailed
    d. (1) Correct
        (2) Correct

9. Reject H_0 because $\bar{x} = \$3,250$ is $< \$3,335.50$.

11. a. H_0: $\mu \geq 350$ ppsi
        H_1: $\mu < 350$ ppsi
    b. Type I: Unfairly return a good rope or spend money buying another rope
        Type II: Get injured or die when the rope breaks
    c. .20, because increasing P(Type I) decreases P(Type II).

13. a. $< .025$ if upper-tailed test, $> .975$ if lower-tailed test
    b. $.05 < p < .10$
    c. $.10 < p < .20$ if upper-tailed test, $.80 < p < .90$ if lower-tailed test
    d. $p < .01$

15. a. $\bar{x} = 9.5$, $s = .850$
    b. No, $9.13 < \bar{x} = 9.5 < 10.87$
    c. $.05 < p < .10$

17. a. H_0: $\mu \geq 71$, explore why defect reduction program has not been successful
        H_1: $\mu < 71$, stick with defect reduction program
    b. Type I: Conclude defect reduction program has been successful when it hasn't; cost — waste money on defect reduction program that's not working, fail to explore with ways to reduce defect rate, possibly lose market share if competition improving their defect rate
        Type II: Conclude deficit reduction program has not been successful when it really has; cost — waste money trying to improve an already good program
    c. .01
    d. Yes, $\bar{x} = 61 < 66.07$
    e. $p < .005$

19. a. H_0: $\mu = 32$ oz., make no adjustments to filling machine
        H_1: $\mu \neq 32$ oz., adjust the filling machine
    b. Type I: Conclude the machine is working improperly when it's really fine; cost — unnecessarily incur down-time in production, with the possibility of changing the machine so that it's filling improper amounts.
        Type II: Conclude machine is working fine when its mean fill level is really too high or too low; cost — waste money from using excessive ice cream or lose customers who get too little ice cream
    c. No, $31.32 < \bar{x} = 31.67 < 32.68$
    d. No; hypothesis testing assumes a constant mean.

21. c. $.005 < p < .01$; yes
    d. $.10 < p < .20$; no

23. a. H_0: $\mu \geq 55$; do not implement new procedures
        H_1: $\mu < 55$; implement new procedures

    b. Type I: Conclude new procedures will reduce mean waiting time when they really won't; costs — incur costs switching to the new procedure, ending up with the same, or possibly a longer mean waiting time.
        Type II: Conclude new procedures are no better than the current ones when they really are better; costs — lose an opportunity to reduce mean waiting time, thereby possibly losing customers to competition
    c. 1.826 min.
    d. $\bar{x} < 52.61$ min.
    e. No, $\bar{x} = 54.5 > 52.61$
    f. $.30 < p < .40$

SECTION 9.3

1. a. $\hat{p}$s should be ps
    b. Equal sign should be in null hypothesis
    c. Hypotheses are not mutually exclusive
    d. Should be constants on the right sides of the inequality signs, equal sign should be in null hypothesis
    e. Hypotheses are not mutually exclusive, equal sign should be in null hypothesis

3. a. H_0: $p = .05$
        H_1: $p \neq .05$
    b. H_0: $p \leq .20$
        H_1: $p > .20$
    c. H_0: $p \geq .02$
        H_1: $p < .02$
    d. H_0: $p \geq .10$
        H_1: $p < .10$

5. a. Fail to reject H_0 because $\hat{p} = .46 < .566$; $p > .40$
    b. Fail to reject H_0 because $.208 < \hat{p} = .256 < .272$; $.20 < p < .40$.
    c. Fail to reject H_0 because $\hat{p} = .58 > .542$; $.60 < p < .70$

7. a. H_0: $p \leq .60$; don't build the health club
        H_1: $p > .60$; build the health club
    b. .667; .04
    c. $\hat{p} > .651$
    d. Yes
    e. $.025 < p < .05$; the probability of getting a $\hat{p}$ of .667 or more if the true proportion of employees wanting the health club were .60 or less

9. No, because $\hat{p} = .61$ is not $> .714$

11. Yes, because $\hat{p} = .35 > .329$; $.01 < p < .05$.

SECTION 9.4

1. a. Correct
    b. Null hypothesis is missing an equal sign under $<$
    c. Hypotheses are made about populations, not samples.
    d. Should be a constant on the right side of each expression the hypotheses are neither mutually exclusive nor exhaustive, the equal sign should go in the null hypothesis

3. a. H_0 $\mu_B - \mu_c \leq 0$
        H_1 $\mu_B - \mu_c > 0$
    b. H_0 $\mu_E - \mu_M = 0$
        H_1 $\mu_E - \mu_M \neq 0$
    c. H_0 $\mu_x - \mu_y \geq 0$
        H_1 $\mu_x - \mu_y < 0$
    d. H_0 $\mu_s - \mu_c \leq 0$
        H_1 $\mu_s - \mu_c > 0$

5. **a.** Fail to reject H_0 because $\bar{x}_1 - \bar{x}_2 = 7$ is < 7.288; $.02 < p < .05$
    b. Reject H_0 because $\bar{x}_1, - \bar{x}_2 = -1.7 < -1.041$; $p < .005$
    c. Reject H_0 because $\bar{x}_1, - \bar{x}_2 = \$1.06 > .965$; $.05 < p < .10$

7. Yes, because $\bar{x}_{QS} - \bar{x}_{VI} = -4.6$ min. < -1.76 min.

9. Yes, because $\bar{x}_{PLAN} - \bar{x}_{NOPL} = 1.6\% > 1.24\%$

11. **a.** $1, -1, -2, 3, 0, -2, 3, 0$
     b. $.25, .701$
     c. No, $.25 < 1.33$ (critical value)

13. **a.** $-.03, -.15, -.03, -.36, -.03, 0$
     b. $-.10, .056$
     c. No, $-.10 > -.113$ (critical value)

SECTION 9.5

1. **a.** They are not mutually exclusive.
    b. Hypotheses are made about populations rather than samples, the null hypothesis is missing an equal sign.
    c. They are not exhaustive.

3. **a.** (1) Correct
        (2) Proportions are unitless numbers between 0 and 1, and cannot involve dollars, minutes, miles, ppsi, etc.
    b. (1) Correct
        (2) Correct
    c. (1) Correct
        (2) Correct
    d. (1) Two-tailed rejection region
        (2) Correct

5. No, because $\hat{p}_A - \hat{p}_P = -.002 > -.010$

7. No, because $\hat{p}_{US} - \hat{p}_E = .20 < .238$

CHAPTER 9
APPLICATION PROBLEMS

1. **a.** H_0: $\mu \geq 22$ H_1: $\mu < 22$
    b. Type I: Incorrectly conclude that methods are successful
        Type II: Incorrectly conclude that methods are not successful
    d. Reject H_0, since $\bar{x} = 20.5 < 21.18$ (critical value)
    e. No, only Type I possible
    f. $p < .005$

3. **a.** H_0: $\mu = 5$; H_1: $\mu \neq 5$
    b. Type I: Incorrectly conclude stress level not at optimal level
        Type II: Incorrectly conclude stress level optimal when actually either too high or too low
    c. Reject H_0 since $\bar{x} = 5.35 > 5.219$ (upper critical value)
    d. $p < .01$

5. The claim is supported because $\hat{p}_{NV} - \hat{p}_V = .11 > .097$ (critical value)

7. **a.** H_0: $p \leq .10$; discontinue coupons
        H_1: $p > .10$; continue coupons
    b. Type I: Conclude the coupons led to increased market share when they did not; costs — by continuing with coupons, lose $50 per ticket sold
        Type II: Conclude the coupons were ineffective when they actually led to increased market share; costs — by discontinuing coupons, lose opportunity to increase market share.
    c. Yes, because $\hat{p} = 10.8\%$ is $> 10.5\%$ (critical value)

9. **a.** H_0: $p \geq .15$; start consulting firm
        H_1: $p < .15$; do not start consulting firm
    b. Type I: Conclude percentage has dropped below 15% when it has not; costs — forego venture when it might be successful
        Type II: Conclude percentage is still 15% (or higher) when it has dropped; costs — potentially not enough clients to be successful
    c. Yes, because $\hat{p} = .14$ is not $< .091$ (critical value)
    d. $.30 < p < .40$

11. **a.** H_0: $p \leq .65$; discontinue use of new problem-solving techniques
        H_1: $p > .65$; continue use of new problem-solving techniques
     b. Type I: Conclude new techniques are effective when they actually are not; costs — smaller proportion of ideas implemented than before
        Type II: Conclude new techniques are ineffective when they are effective; costs — forego opportunity to generate good quality improvement ideas
     c. Yes, because $\hat{p} = .733 > .700$ (critical value); reject H_0 and conclude $p > .65$.
     d. $.01 < p < .025$

13. **a.** Yes, since $\hat{p} = .98 > .958$;
     b. $p < .005$

15. Claim is supported since $\hat{p}_{op} - \hat{p}_{res} = .20 > .164$ (critical value)

17. Claim is not supported since p-value is $P(\hat{p} \geq .75) = .5000 > \alpha = .10$

19. **a.** Claim is not supported since $\bar{x} = 74.5 < 74.68$ (critical value)
     b. $.10 < p < .20$

21. **a.** Yes
     b. $\bar{x} = 8.65$, $s = .456$
     c. Yes, since $\bar{x} = 8.65$ minutes < 9.83 minutes (critical value)
     d. $p < .005$

23. **a.** H_0: $\mu_{SG} - \mu_L \leq 0$; do not use small groups
        H_1: $\mu_{SG} - \mu_L > 0$; use small groups
     b. Claim is supported since $\bar{x}_{SG} - \bar{x}_L = 4.8 > 1.93$ (critical value)
     c. $p < .005$

25. **a.** Yes, since $\bar{x}_{LIVE} - \bar{x}_{VIDEO} = 5.8 > 1.41$ (critical value)
     b. Matching was appropriate since high experience/high GPA students given the video training could score higher than low experience/low GPA students given the live lecture training even when the live training method is the superior method because of the greater knowledge or abilities of the high experience/ high GPA students at the outset.
     c. (1) $\bar{x}_{LIVE} = 80.7$, $\bar{x}_{VIDEO} = 74.9$, $\bar{x}_{LIVE} - \bar{x}_{VIDEO} = 5.8$
        (2) $s^2_{LIVE} = 294.46$, $s^2_{VIDEO} = 348.77$
        (3) $s^2_p = 321.61$, $s^2_d = 5.95$, s^2_p is larger
        (4) 8.02
        (5) No, since $\bar{x}_{LIVE} - \bar{x}_{VIDEO} = 5.8 < 13.91$ (critical value)

SECTION 10.1

1. **a.** 1%
    b. Deviation was 4% reject rate on 5-inch drawers and a 6% reject rate on 10-inch drawers
    c. The possible causes include changes in people, technology, organization, or environment.

3. Explanation does not explain cracking on Press 2

5. A problem is always caused by a change.

SECTION 10.2

1. H_0: Mean daily sales is the same for all three strategies (Go with the cheapest strategy).
   H_1: Mean daily sales are not the same for all three strategies (Go with the most effective strategy).

3. H_0: The mean percentage of handsets with scratches is the same for all three temperatures (Go with the cheapest one to maintain).
   H_1: The mean percentage of handsets with scratches is not the same for all three temperatures (Use the temperature with the lowest mean proportion of scratches).

5. No. $IQR_C = 2$, $IQR_{FS} = 1$, $IQR_{PPD} = 1$
   $median_{FS} - median_C = 3$
   $median_{PPD} - median_{FS} = 6$
   $median_{PPD} - median_C = 9$

7. **b.** No. The spread between group means is small, and the spread with each group is large.

9. **a.** $\bar{x}_{500} = 5.7$, $\bar{x}_{550} = .7$ $\bar{x}_{600} = 7.1$
   b. Yes. The spread within each group is small, and at 550° is much smaller than the other means.

SECTION 10.3

1. Variance equals the sum of squares divide by degrees of freedom.

3. **a.** $df_{Total} = 19$, $df_{Within} = 16$, $df_{Between} = 3$
   b. $df_{Total} = 29$, $df_{Within} = 27$, $df_{Between} = 2$
   c. $df_{Total} = 1$, $df_{Within} = 0$, $df_{Between} = 1$
   d. At least two observations per treatment are needed to estimate a variance.

5. **b.** No, the normality assumption does not appear to be met due to skewed distributions, and the equal variance assumptions will not be met due to disparities in the sample variances.

7. **a.** $\bar{x}_A = 2$, $\bar{x}_B = 2$, $\bar{x}_C = 8$, $\bar{\bar{x}} = 4$
   b. SST = 78
   c. SSW = 6, SSB = 72
   d. $df_{Total} = 8$, $df_{Within} = 6$, $df_{Between} = 2$
   e.

Source of Variation	Sum of Squares	df	MS	Variance Ratio
Between	72	2	36.00	36
Within	6	6	1	
Total	78	8		

   f. Yes, since $VR = 36 > F_{.99;\,2,6} = 10.9$

9. H_0: All population mean sales are equal.
   H_1: At least one population mean sales is different from the other two.
   $\bar{x}_1 = 9.00$, $\bar{x}_2 = 12.60$, $\bar{x}_3 = 18.20$, $\bar{\bar{x}} = 13.27$

Source of Variation	Sum of Squares	df	MS	Variance Ratio
Between	214.93	2	107.47	58.62
Within	22.00	12	1.83	
Total	236.93	14		

   Yes, since $VR = 58.62 > F_{.99;\,2,12} = 6.93$

11. H_0: All population mean response rates are equal.
    H_1: At least one population mean response rate is different from the other two.
    $\bar{x}_1 = 16.80$, $\bar{x}_2 = 18.80$, $\bar{x}_3 = 20.40$, $\bar{\bar{x}} = 18.67$

Source of Variation	Sum of Squares	df	MS	Variance Ratio
Between	32.53	2	16.27	1.37
Within	142.80	12	11.90	
Total	175.33	14		

   No, since $VR = 1.37 < F_{.95;\,2,12} = 3.89$

13. **a.** H_0: All population mean labor cost reductions are equal.
    H_1: At least one population mean labor cost reduction is different from the other two.
    $\bar{x}_1 = 0.50$, $\bar{x}_2 = 0.60$, $\bar{x}_3 = 0.70$, $\bar{\bar{x}} = 0.60$
    b. The data of the three treatments show no obvious outliers; no evidence that assumptions are violated
    c.

Source of Variation	Sum of Squares	df	MS	Variance Ratio
Between	.0800	2	.04	200
Within	.0018	9	.0002	
Total	.0818	11		

    Yes, since $VR = 200 > F_{.99;\,2,9} = 8.02$
    d. Use TB and CM or perhaps the CM workshop.

15. **a.** Yes
    b. Yes
    c. Yes
    d. Yes
    e. No, since $8.71 < F_{.999;\,2,12} = 13.0$

17. **a.** H_0: Mean intent to buy is the same for all coffee makers.
    H_1: At least one population mean intent to buy differs from the others.
    b. No, reject H_0 since $VR = 163.00 > F_{.95;\,2,27} = 3.35$

SECTION 10.4

1. The alternative hypothesis is that not all population means are the same. We don't know which population means are different.

3. Increases the CI width, which maintains the probability of a Type I error over all pairwise comparisons.

5. If you did not reject the null hypothesis, you have no evidence that any population means are different.

7. Display1

9. Display is better than free sample, and free sample is better than contest

11. TB and CM is more effective than CM alone, and CM alone is more effective than TB.

SECTION 10.5

1. To compare the locations of three or more distributions, and either the populations are not normally distributed or the variances of the populations are not equal

3. Reject H_0 if $H_{Calc} > 11.34$
   Reject H_0 if $H_{Calc} > 7.78$
   Reject H_0 if $H_{Calc} > 3.84$
   Reject H_0 if $H_{Calc} > 10.60$

5. **a.** All samples have outliers.
   b. H_0: All population medians are equal.
   H_1: Not all population medians are equal.
   $H = 9.18 > \chi^2_{2,.90} = 4.61$. Reject H_0.
   c. Medians for populations 2 and 3 are different; no other differences

7. $H = .04 < \chi^2_{5,.99}, = 5.99$, fail to reject the null hypothesis

9. Reject H_0, since $H = 17.26 > \chi^2_{2,.90} = 4.61$ alone. Diet/ exercise is more effective than exercise alone or diet alone. Cannot conclude any difference between diet alone and exercise alone.

SECTION 10.6

1. 2 independent variables, 2 levels each

3. A main effect for a factor refers to a difference in that factor's level means. Since a 2×2 experiment involves 2 factors, there are potentially 2 main effects.

5. **a.** 4.54; significant main effect for A since VR $= 6.5 > F_{.95;1,15} = 4.54$
b. 5.61; no significant main effect for B since VR $= 1.17 < F_{.99;2,24} = 5.61$
c. 5.645; significant interaction effect since VR $= 7.67 > F_{.975;1,27} = 5.645$ (interpolated)
d. 4.985; no significant interaction effect since VR $= 2.13 < F_{.995;3,45} = 4.985$ (interpolated)

7. **a.** No interaction effect since factor profiles show parallel lines, but there are possible main effects.
b. Possible interaction effect since lines are not parallel; brown/red

9. **a.** The profiles cross; there is a strong interaction.
b. No. Discovery learning is best with students with SATs > 1100; lecture method works better with students scoring < 900.

11. **b.**

Source of Variation	Sum of Squares	df	MS	Variance Ratio
Tag	50	1	50.00	33.33
Train	18	1	18.00	12.00
Interact.	18	1	18.00	12.00
Within	6	4	1.50	
Total	92	7		

c. Reject H_0 of no interaction, since VR $= 12 > F_{.95; 1,4} = 7.71$ Use Computer tag and 40 hours of training.

13. **a.** Possibly, since the profile lines are not parallel. The best dryer brand depends on whether it's gas or electric.
b.

Source of Variation	Sum of Squares	df	MS	Variance Ratio
Type	3.33	1	3.33	0.45
Brand	361.67	2	180.83	24.66
Interact.	11.67	2	5.83	0.80
Within	176.00	24	7.33	
Total	552.67	29		

c. No, since VR $= .80 < F_{.99; 2,24} = 5.61$
d. No, since VR $= .45 < F_{.99; 1,24} = 7.82$
e. Yes, since VR $= 24.66 > F_{.99; 2,24} = 5.61$

15. **b.** Reject the null hypothesis of no interaction. The best combination appears to be 1,250 degrees and 600 ppsi.
d. Reject the null hypothesis of no interaction. The best combination appears to be 1,250 degrees and 600 ppsi.

CHAPTER 10 APPLICATION PROBLEMS

1. **a.** Randomly select, divide into groups, and assign participants
b. Role and case are similar and both better than the lecture

3. **a.** Factorial design
b.

	Lecture	Case
Sensing	85	50
Intuitive	40	85

c. Crossed profiles

5. **a.** 2 factors: need for independence, leadership style
b. Two levels: participative and autocratic
c. 2×2 factorial design to test for interaction
d. For example:

	Low Need	High Need
Partic.	20	100
Auto.	100	30

7. **a.** Displays A and C have outliers on high side. Display B's values show little dispersion and are less than the other two displays.
b. $H = 9.50 > \chi^2_{2,.95} = 5.99$, reject null
c. Displays A and C are better than B; no difference between A and C

9. **a.** Yes
b. No, but need analysis of variance to draw inferences about population means
c. VR $= 18.24 > F_{.95; 2, 12}$, reject null.
d. Plastic and lubricant are better than standard blade; cannot detect other differences.

11. **a.** Crossed profiles
b. VR $= 60 > F_{.95;1, 8}$, reject the null hypothesis of no interaction.
c. Use lecture to teach sensing managers; use case method to teach intuitive managers.

13. **a.** Much spread in means, little spread within groups
b. VR $= 17.33 > F_{.99; 2, 12}$, reject null
c. Brainstorming and Analogy are better than control group; cannot detect other differences

15. **a.** Much spread in means, little spread within groups
b. VR $= 62.67 > F_{.95; 2, 15}$, reject null; letter has highest goodwill.
c. Becomes harassment

17. **a.** 2
b. 200
c. Identify middle- and high-income customers. Randomly select 100 from each target population. Randomly split both groups into 2 subgroups. Assign each subgroup at random to different promotion. Record change in usage before and after the study

19. **a.** Differences between individuals, within sweeteners, etc.
b. Sugar appears to be preferred

21. Spread of rates is small within each country. Spread between countries is large. Conclusion: tentative ranking: France < West Germany < United States

23. **a.** Factorial design
b. For example:

	Low Need	High Need
<20K	$400	$520
30K–50K	$580	$700
>75K	$900	$1,800

Nonparallel profiles

SECTION 11.1

	DV	PV	Tool
1. a.	TV hrs.(quan.)	Age(cat.)	ANOVA
b.	Education(cat.)	Age(cat.)	Chi-sq.
c.	TV hrs.(quan.)	No. in house(quan.)	Regres.
d.	TV hrs.(quan.)	No. in house(quan.) Education(cat.)	Regres.
e.	Network(cat.)	Gender(cat.)	Chi-sq.

3. **a.** 2.85
b. No, 2.85 is the average value for this group.
c. The average GPA increases by .0035 points
e. Has no physical meaning

5. **a.** Categorical: gender (male, female), severity of weather (mild, normal, harsh); Quantitative: age, number of dependent children

   b. Women are more likely to stay home with sick children than men, more severe weather results in more transportation problems and illnesses, older workers are more likely to get sick.

   c. See **b**.

SECTION 11.2

	DV	PV	UA	Obs.	Type
1.	job performance	age, salary years on job	worker	4 pieces of data on each worker	correlational
3.	percent cracked	amount of filler	cabinet	2 pieces of data on each cabinet	experimental
5.	GPA	Math SAT, study hours	Accounting requires basic math skills. The amount of study generally affects performance.		

SECTION 11.3

1. **b.** Yes. As productivity increases, so does salary.
   c. .9424.

3. **b.** No; appears to be an s-shaped curve
   c. .8605. The correlation is high even though the graph and logic suggest a nonlinear relationship.

5. **a.** Does not appear to be a linear relationship between months on job and salary
   b. Does not appear to be a linear relationship between communication level and salary
   c–e. There are two distinct clusters. For males, increasing level of communication related to salary. But not for females. Women may not be treated fairly. .4475, .4471, −.8658. Gender is a stronger predictor than months on the job and level of communication. As gender goes from male = 0 to female = 1, salary goes down.

7. **b.** Yes. Return on stock Y is positively linearly related to movement in NYSE. Stock Y appears to be less volatile than the overall market. When the rate of return for the NYSE increases, so does the rate of return for stock Y, but by a smaller percentage.
   c. .9856; the correlation is very high, suggesting, with the graph, that NYSE is a strong linear predictor of stock Y.

9. **a.**

FINAL	MATHSTAT	GRADECAL
1.000	.9664	.9774
	1.000	.9860
		1.000

Yes; $r_{\text{MATHSAT, GRADECAL}} = .9860$ is near 1.
   b. Yes
   c. Math SAT measures mathematical aptitude and should predict achievement in calculus.

SECTION 11.4

1. SALARY-PRED $= 8.43 + 1.015$PROD
   The intercept of 8.43 is the predicted value of SALARY for a zero PROD, but has no physical meaning. Needed only to make predictions. The slope is 1.015. For a 1 unit increase in PROD, average salary increases by 1.015 or $1,015.

3. For men: SALARY-PRED $= 1974.63 + 45.95$MONTHS
   For women: SALARY-PRED $= 1902.47 + 13.16$MONTHS
   While both sample slopes are positive, the slope for men is much greater than that for women. Men's salaries appear to increase faster than women's.

5. STOCK-PRED $= 1.13 + .56$NYSE
   Stock Y is approximately half as volatile as the market. When NYSE increases by 1%, stock Y increases by .56%.

7. **a.**

	PERF	SKILL	MOTIV
PERF	1.0000	.6381	.7363
SKILL		1.0000	.0000
MOTIV			1.0000

Motivation level is a stronger predictor.
   b. PERF-PRED $= -1.208 + .05417$SKILL $+ .075$MOTIV
   The intercept has no physical meaning; needed only to make predictions
   The slope of .05417 says for a 1 unit increase in SKILL, avg. performance increases by .05417, after controlling for motivation.
   The slope of .075 says for a 1 unit increase in MOTIV, avg. performance increases by .075, after controlling for skill.
   c. PERF $= -1.208 + .05417(80) + .075(80) = 9.126$
   d. The predicted value of 9.126 compares to an actual job performance of 9.0. The two values differ because of the impact of all variables, except skill and motivation, on job performance.

SECTION 11.5

1. **a.** H_0: None of the predictor variables (x_1, x_2, x_3) is statistically related to the dependent variable (y).
      H_1: At least one of the predictor variables (x_1, x_2, x_3) is statistically related to the dependent variable (y).
   b. 3; numerator degrees of freedom is equal to the number of predictor variables — in this case, 3 (x_1, x_2, x_3).
   c. 20; denominator degrees of freedom is $n - k - 1$—in this case, $24 - 3 - 1 = 20$.
   d. 3.10

3. 31.13%; 31.13% of the variation in the dependent variable is accounted for by the predictor variables in the model.

5. H_0: None of the variables are linearly related to credit worthiness.
   H_1: At least one of the variables is linearly related to credit worthiness.

7. **a.** Females:

Source of Variation	SS	df	MS	VR
Regression	144,221.30	1	144,221.30	22.6
Error	44,667.55	7	6,381.08	
Total	188,888.85	8		

Since $F_{.99;1,7} = 12.25, p < .01$.

Males

Source of Variation	SS	df	MS	VR
Regression	1,043,097.2	1	1,043,097.2	46.5
Error	156,902.8	7	22414.7	
Total	1,200,000.0	8		

$p < .01$

   b. $r^2 = .764$ (for females); almost 77% of variation in salaries accounted for by months on job
   $r^2 = .869$ (for males); almost 87% of variation in salaries accounted for by males
   c. 79.88 for females; 149.72 for males

9. a. SALES-PRED $= -2.16 + .28$DISPOSABLE

b.

Source of Variation	SS	df	MS	VR
Regression	80.64	1	80.64	758.71
Error	1.06	10	0.11	
Total	81.70	11		

Since $F_{.90;1,10} = 3.29$. $p < .01$

c. $r^2 = .987$; 98.7% of the total variation in sales can be accounted for by variation in disposable income.

d. .33

e. 39.84

11. b. $(-.405, 1.20)$

c. No, since zero is in the CI

SECTION 11.6

1. No, unless the variables in the equation are correlated with the "true" causal variables

3. Find the residuals and divide each by the square root of MSE. Construct a histogram of the standardized residuals. Approximately 68% should be between -1 and 1. Approximately 95% should be between -2 and $+2$, and almost all should fall between -3 and 3.

5. b. Standardized residuals ($\sqrt{MSE} = .663$)

Class	Tally	Frequency
-3.00 to -2.01	|	1
-2.00 to -1.01	|	1
-1.00 to -0.1	++++ |	6
0 to 0.99	++++ |||	8
1.00 to 1.99		0
2.00 to 2.99		0

Since 14 of 16 residuals are within one standard deviation, the normality assumption may not hold.

c. No. Autocorrelation is usually a problem encountered with time-series data.

7. a. DEFECT-PRED $= .029 - .0007$HOURS

b. No, residuals form curvilinear pattern

SECTION 11.7

1. a. (3.41, 6.39)

b. (4.50, 5.30)

c. PIs set standards for individuals. CIs determine typical satisfaction score for all employees with these characteristics.

3. a. ($2,045.58, $2,443.90)

b. ($2,181.70, $2,307.78)

c. Yes, beyond range of sample

5. a. 14 ($1,988.32, $2,185.22)

b. 26 ($2,181.70, $2,307.78)

c. 40 ($2,315.40, $2,542.68)

d. Narrower in the middle, wider at each end; beyond range of sample

CHAPTER 11 APPLICATION PROBLEMS

1. The unit of association is the worker. The study is cross-sectional and correlational. Nothing is being manipulated or controlled for.

3. $r_{DAYS,AGE} = .0195$ $r^2_{DAYS,AGE} = .0004$
$r_{DAYS,CLOSENESS} = -.8877$ $r^2_{DAYS,CLOSENESS} = .7880$
$r_{DAYS,SALARY} = .1916$ $r^2_{DAYS,SALARY} = .0367$
$r_{DAYS,TRAIN} = -.2036$ $r^2_{DAYS,TRAIN} = .0415$
$r_{DAYS,EQUIP} = -.3951$ $r^2_{DAYS,EQUIP} = .1561$

Only closeness of supervision and equipment age are important predictors by themselves.

5. DAYS $= 11.75 - 1.02$CLOSENESS $+ 0.105$TRAINING $- 0.332$EQUIP
The model will predict the number of days over quota for individual employees, with a margin of error of ± 2 days, approximately 95% of the time.

7. None of the residuals appear to violate the equal variance or independence assumptions. All standardized residuals fell between -1.22 and 2.03, indicating no outliers or violations of the normality assumption.

9. $(-1.25, -.774)$; no, workers should not be closely supervised. For every additional unit of supervision, DAYS that a worker exceeds quota decreases by between .774 and 1.25.

11. GENDER, AGE, SALARY, YEARS, and EDUC appear to be positively and linearly related to job satisfaction. The average job satisfaction score for males appears to be higher than females since the distribution of satisfaction scores is generally higher for males. The same is true for managers in comparison with non-managers. None show a nonlinear relationship.

13. H_0: All population regression coefficients for SALARY, YEARS, AGE, EDUC, EXPER and MANAG are equal to 0.
H_1: At least one of these population regression coefficients is not equal to 0.

SATIS $= 13.018 + .124$SALARY $+ .183$YEARS $- 0.130$AGE $- .464$EDUC $+ 0.154$EXPER $+ 1.467$MANAG

Since VR $= 6.683 > F_{.95;6,43} = 2.336$ reject H_0 and conclude that at least one of the variables is linearly related to job satisfaction

15. 47.95% of the total variation of job satisfaction is accounted for by the six variables in the model.

17. Explanation: The equation tells us that managers are more satisfied than nonmanagers after controlling for the other factors. Satisfaction increases with increases in salary, more years with the firm, and more experience. More education and older workers tend to be less satisfied after controlling for salary years and experience.

Prediction and Control: The equation can be used to predict mean satisfaction scores for a fixed level of the six variables. Prediction limits can also be found. If an employee falls outside the lower prediction limit, the person may have a problem.

19. The unit of association is the group. It is an experimental study because group size is controlled by the experimenter.

21. $r_{PERF,GROUPSIZE} = .608$; $r_{PERF,TRAIN} = .779$; $r_{GROUPSIZE,TRAIN} = .000$
$r^2_{PERF,GROUPSIZE} = .369$; $r^2_{PERF,TRAIN} = .608$; $r^2_{GROUPSIZE,TRAIN} = .000$

By itself, group size accounts for 36.7% of the variation in performance. By itself, training accounts for 60.8% of the variation in performance. Group size and training are uncorrelated because of the balanced design.

23. Both variables are related to the performance measure.
PERF $= 40.92 + 4.81$GROUPSIZE $+ 5.04$TRAIN
Standard error of the estimate $= 2.286$

25. No assumptions are violated.

27. $5.042 \pm 2.262(.330) = (4.296, 5.788)$ Average performance increases by between 4.3 and 5.8 units for each additional hour of training, after controlling for group size.

29. Only SALES appears to be linearly related to HOURS. IN-AUDIT and SALES do not appear to be related to hours.

31. HOURS $= -96.77 + 71.21$SALES $- 0.037$IN-AUDIT $- 90.71$CONTROL

H_0: All population regression coefficients for SALES, IN-AUDIT, and control are equal to 0.

H_1: At least one of these population regression coefficients is not equal to 0.

Since VR $= 128.84 > F_{.95; 3,26} = 2.980$ reject H_0 and conclude that at least one of the variables is linearly related to job satisfaction.

33. Final model uses all these variables. $R^2 = 93.7\%$ indicates that 93.7% of the variation in hours is accounted for by SALES, IN-AUDIT HOURS and CONTROLS.

Variable	t-Value	Two Tail p-Value
SALES	19.14	<.001
IN-AUDIT	-1.26	.2207
CONTROL	-2.43	.0225

35. $-.037 \pm 2.056(.030) = (-.099, .025)$ The number of internal hours appears to have no effect on the number of hours spent by external auditors, after controlling for SALES and CONTROL since 0 is in the interval.

37. a. H_0: All population regression coefficients for DEPOSIT-GROWTH, NET-INTEREST-SPREAD and TAX-STATUS are equal to 0.

H_1: At least one of these population regression coefficients is not equal to 0.

Since VR $= 12.57 > F_{.95; 3,60} = 2.76$ reject H_0 and conclude that at least one of the variables is linearly related to percent premium (or discount)

b. No, since all of the $|t| > 1$.

c. DEPOSIT GROWTH: For every 1% increase in deposit growth, the premium increases by 4.03%

NET INTEREST SPREAD: For every 1% increase in the net interest spread, the premium goes up by 11.2%

TAX STATUS: If the purchase is nontaxable, the premium goes down (discount goes up) by 16.4%

SECTION 12.2

1. Type $= 1$ if is mutual; Type $= 0$ if not mutual or Type $= 1$ if stock; Type $= 0$ if not stock.

3. NUMBER $= 3.77 + .016$SIZE $- 5.122$TYPE $- 0.0003$SIZE $\times$ TYPE; $t = -0.094; p > .30$
The relationship between number of innovations and asset size is the same between mutual and stock companies.

5. APPR $= 1$ if concentration; APPR $= 0$ if multisegment
APPR $= 1$ if multisegment; APPR $= 0$ if concentration

7. E(SALES) $= a + b$FEET $+ c$COMM $+ d$FEET $\times$ COMMd should be positive; for stores where salespeople are on commission, the equation becomes SALES $= (a + c) + (b + d)$FEET. SALES grow faster as FEET increases when salespeople are on commission in comparison to when they are not.

9. a. $50 + .3(80) + 8(0) = 74$
b. $50 + .3(80) + 8(1) = 82$
c. Parallel lines 8 units apart

11. b. AMOUNT-PRED $= 486.263 + 6.363$INCOME, $- 533.757$MARSTAT $- 1.065$ INCOME $\times$ MARSTAT
AMOUNT-PRED$_{married} = 1122.563$ or $\$1,122,563$
AMOUNT-PRED$_{single} = 482.306$ or $\$482,306$
c. Fail to reject; $t = -.83, p > .05$

SECTION 12.3

1. a. Both
b. Linear in parameters only
c. Neither
d. Linear in parameters only

3. Scatter diagrams can be deceiving when squared and interaction terms are appropriate for the model.

5. a. The residuals would show a curved pattern.

SECTION 12.4

1. a. SSR(EDUC) $= 6,863.052$
b. SSR(YEARS) $= 3,232.429$
c. SSR(GENDER) $= 2,001.546$
d. SSR(RACE) $= 1,102.697$
e. SSR(EDUC, GENDER) $= 6,952.499$
f. SSR(YEARS, EDUC, GENDER) $= 8,585.551$
g. SSR(YEARS, EDUC, GENDER, RACE) $= 8,601.526$

3. (1) The effect of RACE on SALARY after controlling for EDUC, YEARS and GENDER
(2) The effect of YEARS on SALARY after controlling for EDUC and GENDER
(3) The effect of GENDER on SALARY after controlling for EDUC
(4) The effect of EDUC on SALARY after controlling for GENDER
(5) The effect of EDUC and GENDER on SALARY after controlling for RACE

5. a. $r_{PRICE, ADS} = .0000$
b. SSR(PRICE,ADS) $= 41.00$
SSR(PRICE) $= 25.00$
SSR(ADS) $= 16.00$
c. SSR(PRICE|ADS) $= 25.00$
d. Same, since PRICE and ADS are uncorrelated.
e. $r_{PRICE, ADS} = .9191$
f. SSR(PRICE,ADS) $= 45.44$
SSR(PRICE) $= 44.10$
SSR(ADS) $= 43.04$
g. SSR(PRICE|ADS) $= 2.4$
h. Different because PRICE and ADS are highly correlated.
i. When variables are highly correlated, the importance of a variable depends on which other variables have already been controlled for.

7. a. 3.68
b. 5.52
c. 3.34

9. a. $t = -.431; p > .30$; fail to reject
b. $(-4.83, 3.00)$; contains zero
c. SSR(F) $= 9,037.989$; df(F)$=43$; MSE(F)$=30.055$
SSR(R) $= 9,032.394$; df(R)$=44$;
$F^* = [(9037.989 - 9032.394)/1]/30.055 = .1862$; fail to reject
d. $t = .4312^2 = .1862$

SECTION 12.5

1. a. All values on upward sloping straight line
b. Scattered about upward sloping straight line
c. Totally scattered
d. Scattered about downward sloping straight line
e. All values on downward sloping straight line

3. c. Y-PRED $= 1.97 + 525x_1 + .792x_2$
Y-PRED $= 4.32 + .769x_1$
Y-PRED $= 3.50 + 929x_2$
d. Stability due to lack of multicollinearity
e. corr$(x_1, x_2) = .2823 <$ corr$(y, x_1) = .6611 <$ corr$(y, x_2) = .8686$

5. No, multicollinearity is present when predictor variables are related.

7. **b.** Set A: $r_{PRICE,ADS} = -.9191$; Set B: $r_{PRICE,ADS} = .0000$

 c. SALES-PRED $= 1,810.0 - 2.1$PRICE
 SALES-PRED $= 553.448 + 1.362$ADS
 SALES-PRED $= 1,272.222 - 1.24$PRICE $+ 0.611$ADS

 d. SALES-PRED $= 1,555.00 - 1.25$PRICE
 SALES-PRED $= 780.00 + 1.000$ADS
 SALES-PRED $= 1,155.00 - 1.25$PRICE $+ 1.000$ADS

 e. Multicollinearity produces unstable sample coefficients.

9. **a.** Since $r_{1.2}^2 = .9986 > R_{y.12}^2 = .9751$; conclude multicollinearity present

 b. y-PRED $= 375.558 + 28.119x_1 - 20.513x_2$

 c. Using x_1 and x_2:
 (236.78, 1,122.75), (140.95, 504.11), (536.02, 895.37)
 versus using x_1 alone: (316.71, 658.61), (153.04, 512.89), (532.76, 891.17)

 d. Yes

CHAPTER 12
APPLICATION PROBLEMS

1. **a.** No. If the combined effect of cigarettes and alcohol is greater than the sum of the individual effects measured separately, an interaction term is needed.

 b. COUNT $= a + b$CIG $+ c$ALCOH $+ d$CIG $\times$ ALCOH (multiplicative) or COUNT $= a + b$CIG $+ c$ALCOH $+ d($CIG $+$ ALCOH) (additive)

3. **a.** Yes. Since the RACE variable was coded 1, the average salary of minorities decreases by the value of the regression coefficient after controlling for the other variables in the model.

 b. An R^2 of between .42 and .52 means that other variables can be found that explain salary in addition to, not instead of, those already in the model. To argue that RACE is not related to salary, the defendants have to find intervening variables (true cause) which, when added to the model and controlled for, reduce the RACE coefficient to close to 0.

5. **a.** No. Even though the t-statistics associated with the TRANS/CLERICAL is less than 1, and the p-value is greater than .05, we cannot make this statement. The regression tells us that this variable is not significant *after controlling for the other variables in the model*. This variable could be related to the error rate if considered by itself. To know if a single independent variable is linearly related to a dependent variable, we would run a simple regression.

 b. $1,000 \times 0.00011 = 0.11\%$. The standard error is 4.237%, which means that the dependent variable was entered as percents not decimals.

 c. Incorrect statement. Even though the parameter estimate for temporaries is much higher than that for the other variable, we cannot compare regression coefficients directly in order to determine their relative importance since ranges of the variables could differ considerably. The variables considered in the equation account for only 35.2% of the variation in error rates. Two-thirds of the variation is due to as yet unknown factors.

7. **a.** Could be nonlinear

 b. PRICE $= 88.176 + 14.159$PRICE $- .797$PRICE^2
 $t = -1.247$; $p = .2399$; The squared term is not significant at the .05 level.

 c. SSR(F) $= 1,285.982$; df(F) $= 12$; MSE(F) $= 26.082$
 SSR(R) $= 1,245.415$; df(R) $= 13$;
 $F^* = [(1285.982 - 1245.415)/1]/26.082 = 1.555 < F_{.95;1,12} = 4.75$

 Fail to reject. Squared term is not significant at the .05 level.

 d. Same conclusion

9. **a.** 2

 b. H_0: The population regression coefficients for the two indicator variables are equal to 0.
 H_1: At least one population regression coefficient is not equal to 0.

 c. VR from the ANOVA table $= 5.003$

 d. TOTAWARD-PRED $= 32,107.74 - 23,871.007$NSS $+ 4,050.227$NSG
 Mean$_{SUR} = 32,107.74$; Mean$_{NSS} = 8,236.74$; Mean$_{NSG} = 36,157.97$

11. $r_{TEST1, SCORE} = .4418$ means $r_{TEST1, SCORE}^2 = .1952$ or 19.52% of the variation in performance score can be explained by TEST1 results alone.

13. **a.** SCORE-PRED $= 57.483 + 18.017$MA $+ 29.317$PHD
 Mean$_{BA} = 57.483$; Mean$_{MA} = 75.5$; Mean$_{PHD} = 86.8$

 b. VR from ANOVA table

 c. H_0: The population regression coefficients for the two indicator variables are equal to 0.
 H_1: At least one population regression coefficient is not equal to 0.

 d. MAS score an average of 18.01 points more than BAS on the performance measure. PHDs perform 29.317 points higher than BAS.

 e. Yes, $t = 3.658$; $p < .001$; MAS perform better than BAS

15. **a.** SSR(F) $= 13,932.538 -$ SSR(R) $= 12,797.457 = 1,135.081$

 b. H_0: $\beta_{MA} = \beta_{PHD} = \beta_{RELATED} = 0$.
 H_1: At least one of these population regression coefficients is not equal to 0.

 c. No, $F^* = (1,135.081/3)/184.185 = 2.054 < F_{.95;3, 52} \approx 2.79$; fail to reject.

17. **b.** SALARY-PRED $= 2,159.350 + 26.626$MONTHS $+ 61.992$COMM $- 227.793$GENDER $- 24.881$MONTHS $\times$ GENDER $- 11.678$COMM $\times$ GENDER

 c. H_0: $\beta_{GENDER} = \beta_{GENDER \times MONTHS} = \beta_{GENDER \times COMM} = 0$.
 H_1: At least one of these population regression coefficients is not equal to 0.

 $F^* = (536.364 - 113.667/3)/1.517 = 92.88 > F_{.95;3, 12} = 3.49$; reject H_0 and conclude the regression equations are different between males and females

 d. H_0: $\beta_{GENDER \times MONTHS} = \beta_{GENDER \times COMM} = 0$.
 H_1: At least one of these population regression coefficients is not equal to 0.

 $F^* = (536.364 - 517.826/2)/1.517 = 6.11 > F_{.95;2, 12} = 3.89$ Reject H_0 and conclude that at least one of the slope coefficients differs between males and females

 e. Yes, the model is significant even though none of the individual variables are significant.

19. H_0: The population regression coefficients for the six predictor variables are equal to 0.
 H_1: At least one population regression coefficient is not equal to 0.

 VR from the ANOVA table $= 23.301 > 2.530$; reject H_0

21.

Dependent	Independent	R^2
JOBSAT	SALARY,YEARS,AGE,EDUC,GENDER,MANAG	85.873%
SALARY	YEARS,AGE,EDUC,GENDER,MANAG	38.311
YEARS	SALARY,AGE,EDUC,GENDER,MANAG	40.911
AGE	SALARY,YEARS,EDUC,GENDER,MANAG	38.671
EDUC	SALARY,YEARS,AGE,GENDER,MANAG	21.811
GENDER	SALARY,YEARS,AGE,EDUC,MANAG	5.253
MANAG	SALARY,YEARS,AGE,EDUC,GENDER	33.538

The rule does not suggest that multicollinearity will be a problem.

23. **a.** Because the deleted variables would not be controlled
   b. Male managers have a higher level of job satisfaction than would be explained by being a manager alone or a male alone; no, only male managers are more satisfied.

SECTION 13.2

1. Assumption of continuity — that recent past is good indication of near future; you can't

3. Quantitative methods: base forecasts on quantitative model (e.g., express sales in one month as a function of advertising level that month, as sales and advertising level the previous month, and use model to forecast next month's sales)
Qualitative methods: base forecasts on intuition, judgment, and accumulated knowledge (e.g., to forecast success of a new product introduction)

5. We are unlikely to have factored in the removal of the Berlin Wall.

7. Judgments are often plagued by inconsistency and error (e.g., overestimating frequencies of wellpublicized events, wishful thinking, selective perception).

9. No historical data for the product

SECTION 13.3

1. **c.** Positive autocorrelation
   d. $\text{SALES}_t\text{-PRED} = 12.069 + .986\text{SALES}_{t-1}$
   e. 3.2%; yes, because forecasting sales to within 3.20% seems adequate
   f. 241.8

3. **c.** Negative autocorrelation
   d. $\text{INVEN}_t\text{-PRED} = 61.49 - .827\text{INVEN}_{t-1}$
   e. 28.9%; no
   f. 16.0

5. **c.** Positive autocorrelation
   d. No
   e. $\text{SALES}_t\text{-PRED} = 10.701 + .904\text{SALES}_{t-1} + .101\text{HS}_{t-2}$
   f. Yes (SALES_{t-1}, $t = 72.90$, $p < .001$; for HS_{t-2}, $t = 5.63$, $p < .001$)
   g. 1.1%
   h. 622.4

7. There is no tendency for the successive changes to be in the same direction (whether positive or negative); no, because knowing the direction of the preceding change does not help you predict the direction of the next change.

9. EPS in one time period is directly related to the EPS one, two, and three time periods earlier.

SECTION 13.4

1. MA4: 8, 11.25, 14.75, 17.75, 21.25, —
Centered moving average: 9.625, 13, 16.25, 19.5, —, —

3. No, because each raw seasonal index is just as likely to be above or below the mean behavior for the year.

5. 90.9, 133.3, 116.7, 187.5

7. 1.2, 1.11, 1.13, 1.02, .98, 92, .97, 1.0, 1.05, 1.07, 1.06, 1.04

9. **a.** Yes
   b. .7856, 1.1680, 1.1108, .9356
   $Y\text{-PRED} = 3.448 + 2.007\text{TIME}$, MAPE = 3.9%
   $Y\text{-PRED} = 7.400e^{.1\text{TIME}}$, MAPE = 14.3%
   $Y\text{-PRED} = 4.284\,\text{TIME}^{.753}$, MAPE = 5.8%
   $Y\text{-PRED} = 2.407 + 2.291\text{TIME} - .014\,\text{TIME}^2$, MAPE = 4.0%
   Choice: linear trend equation
   c. 35.82, 55.60, 55.11, 48.29

SECTION 13.5

1. See text, p.775. The nominal group technique is superior because all ideas are given a chance to be heard. Ideas can be evaluated based on their merit, not on the status of group members.

3. No. Since they are forecasting 15 years into the future, and since many factors influence the demand for insulation, expect that initial estimates would vary considerably. Factors that would affect the demand for R30 insulation include the price of heating oil, the global warming effect produced by the deterioration of the ozone layer, and federal tax policy.

5. Experts of different backgrounds are included in a Delphi study to avoid one-sided views, or what we referred to in Chapter 1 as selective perception.

CHAPTER 13
APPLICATION PROBLEMS

1. **a.** Trend, not seasonal
   b. $\text{EPS}_t\text{-PRED} = 1.441 + .071\text{TIME}$
   c. 3.5%
   d. $2.93, $3.00
   f. $\text{EPS}_t\text{-PRED} = -.019 + 1.05\,\text{EPS}_{t-1}$
   g. 4.0%
   h. No; $3.29
   i. Similarities: both are linear equations for forecasting EPS; their MAPEs are similar in magnitude differences: the equation in **b** is a time series model, equation in **f** is causal; **b** permits forecasts for multiple time periods in the future, **f** permits forecasting only the next time period.

3. **a.** Yes
   b. .8998, .9461, .9551, .9543, .8920, .9346, .9908, 1.0559, 1.1537, 1.0555, 1.1038, 1.0585
   $\text{SALES}_t\text{-PRED} = 1.018e^{.050\,\text{TIME}}$
   c. 1.7%
   d. 18.824 or 18,824; 20.797 or 20,797; 22.062 or 22,062

5. **b.** $\text{NUC}_t = 218.97 + 8.04\text{TIME} - 1.63\text{TIME}^2$
   c. 110, 81, 48, 12, −27, −69, −115, −164, −216
   d. The historical pattern did not extend into the future.

7. The points would be scattered about a positively sloping line because of the significant autoregressive model.

9. **b.** $\text{DISCOUNT}_t\text{-PRED} = .055 + .966\text{DISCOUNT}_{t-1}$; Yes, DISCOUNT_t is significantly related to DISCOUNT_{t-1}
   c. 5.3%
   d. 5.37%

11. b. Individually, NUMBER$_t$ is significantly related to GNP$_t$ ($t = 4.14, p < .01$) and NUMBER$_{t-1}$ ($t = 3.47, p < .05$); due to multicollinearity, neither GNP$_t$ ($t = .90, p > .30$) nor NUMBER$_{t-1}$ ($t = .48, p > .30$) significantly aids in predicting NUMBER$_t$ when used with the other

   c. Final regression model is NUMBER$_t = -5,267.55 + 2.362$GNP$_t$ (GNP$_t$ was used because it is a slightly better predictor of NUMBER$_t$ than NUMBER$_{t-1}$); no, because the residuals appear to randomly fluctuate around 0

13. b. Yes; movie attendence is expected to be higher on weekends than weekdays.

   c. Yes; still a seasonal pattern because the moving average is less than the length of the seasonal pattern

   d. No; because daily variation within a week's span is completely averaged out.

   e. No; because the moving average is a multiple of the seasonal pattern.

SECTION 14.2

1. a. Ratio
   b. Ordinal
   c. Ratio
   d. Interval
   e. Ratio
   f. Nominal
   g. Ordinal

3. a. Nominal
   b. Nonparametric

5. a. Ordinal
   b. Nonparametric

7. a. Ordinal
   b. Nonparametric

7. a. Complaint, nominal
   b. To assess whether their process improvements have had an effect
   c. .70, .22, .05, .02, .01
   d. H_0: The current complaint distribution is the same as that of the past several years.

      H_1: The current complaint distribution is not the same as that of the past several years.
   e. 700, 220, 50, 20, 10
   f. 59.48
   g. Reject H_0; conclude current complaint distribution is not the same as that of the past several years ($\chi^2_{\text{CALC}} = 59.48 > \chi^2_{4, .95} = 9.49$)
   h. Yes; both less than .005

9. b. $\bar{x} \approx 37.88, s \approx 4.692$
   c. H_0: The number of claims processed by the claims processors on a given day are normally distributed.

      H_1: The number of claims processed by the claims processors on a given day are not normally distributed.
   d. $-1.68, -.83, .03, .88, 1.73$
   e. .0465, .1568, .3087, .2986, .1476, .0418
   f. 2.82
   g. Fail to reject H_0; conclude that sampled claims could have been drawn from a normal distribution ($\chi^2_{\text{CALC}} = 2.82 < \chi^2_{3, .99} = 11.34$)
   h. $p > .10$

11. b. $\bar{x} \approx 112.367, s \approx 5.766$
   c. H_0: The number of calories in Howdy Burger burgers is normally distributed.

      H_1: The number of calories in Howdy Burger burgers is not normally distributed.
   d. $-2.14, -1.28, -.41, .46, 1.32, 2.19$
   e. .0162, .0841, .2406, .3363, .2294, .0791, .0143
   f. 19.07
   g. Reject H_0; conclude the number of calories in Howdy Burgers is not normally distributed ($\chi^2_{\text{CALC}} = 19.07 > \chi^2_{4, .95} = 9.49$)

SECTION 14.3

1. a. 9.49
   b. 9.24
   c. 11.34

3. a. No
   b. Yes
   c. No
   d. $< .10, < .05, .10$

5. a. Repayment category, ordinal
   b. To assess whether it has a problem, requiring corrective action
   c. 80%, 14%, 3%, 2%, and 1%
   d. H_0: The repayment category distribution corresponds to the internal standard.

      H_1: The repayment category distribution does not correspond to the internal standard.
   e. 400, 70, 15, 10, 5
   f. 2.03
   g. Fail to reject H_0; cannot conclude the loan repayment process is out of control ($\chi^2_{\text{CALC}} = 2.03 < \chi^2_{4, .95} = 9.49$)
   h. $p > .10$

SECTION 14.4

1. 6.63, 12.59, 18.55

3. Because the larger the chi-square statistic, the more the observed frequencies differ from what the expected frequencies would be if the null hypothesis were true.

5. Reject H_0; conclude number of limited partnerships and annual income are related ($\chi^2_{\text{CALC}} = 27.78 > \chi^2_{1, .99} = 6.63$)

7. a. Fail to reject H_0; cannot conclude that overseas assignment and chances of promotion are related ($\chi^2_{\text{CALC}} = .11 < \chi^2_{1, .95} = 3.84$)
   b. .033

9. a. Reject H_0; conclude type of leadership and worker job satisfaction are related ($\chi^2_{\text{CALC}} = 6.25 > \chi^2_{1, .95} = 3.84$)
   b. .354

11. a. H_0: Level of competition and use of TQM are independent.
      H_1: Level of competition and use of TQM are related.
   b. Fail to reject H_0; cannot conclude level of competition and use of TQM are related ($\chi^2_{\text{CALC}} = 1.33 < \chi^2_{1, .95} = 3.84$)
   c. $p > .10$

CHAPTER 14
APPLICATION PROBLEMS

1. Reject H_0; conclude consumer category and milk preference are related, because $\chi^2_{CALC} = 50.51 > \chi^2_{1,.95} = 3.84$. Status seekers prefer skim milk and Machos prefer whole milk.

3. Reject H_0; conclude type of store and price-or-service orientation are related, because $\chi^2_{CALC} = 19.76 > \chi^2_{1,.95} = 3.84$. Independents emphasize service, and chains emphasize price.

5. Fail to reject H_0; cannot conclude that level of management and personality type are related, because $\chi^2_{CALC} = 1.20 < \chi^2_{2,.95} = 5.99$.

7. a. Reject H_0; conclude that opinion varies by division ($\chi^2_{CALC} = 64.28 > \chi^2_{3,.95} = 7.81$)

   b. That such observed discrepancies would be highly unlikely ($p < .005$) if the 4 divisions really felt the same about flex-time. Divisions 1–3 favor flex-time while Division 4 does not.

9. a. $\chi^2_{CALC} = 13.71$, $p < .005$. Yes, because such observed discrepancies would be highly unlikely if the promotion rates of white males versus women and minorities were the same; $C = .29$

   b. Yes; based on the sample data, we would conclude that for the MBA group, the promotion rates of white males versus women and minorities are the same ($\chi^2_{CALC} = 0$, $p > .995$, $C = 0$) but for the no-MBA group, the promotion rate of white males is higher than that of women and minorities ($\chi^2_{CALC} = 13.91$, $p < .005$, $C = .37$)

11. Reject H_0; conclude the number of customers is not evenly spread over the six working days ($\chi^2_{CALC} = 16.56 > \chi^2_{5,.95} = 11.07$)

13. Yes, because $\chi^2_{CALC} = .55 < \chi^2_{2,.95} = 5.99$, so H_0 cannot be rejected.

15. No, because $\chi^2_{CALC} = 1.58 < \chi^2_{3,.99} = 11.34$, so H_0 cannot be rejected.

SECTION 15.2

1. Improve fitness for use by improving reliability, durability, serviceability and safety

3. Both products conform to engineering and market requirements

5. Inspection can only find defects. It cannot produce better products.

7. Not true. Improving quality must be the goal for all the firm's employees.

SECTION 15.3

1. Under control: there is no systematic pattern
   Not under control: there is a systematic pattern — increasing or decreasing, widening, or a sudden change in level

3. a. Only random variation
   b. Given a USL of 2,100 hours, an overall mean of 2,074.40 hours is far away from the target value.
   c. If the process is not centered

5. a. 616.84 ppsi
   b. 1.29
   c. No

d. LCL = 2,702.50 ppsi, UCL = 2,897.50 ppsi
e. LCL = 28.4 ppsi, UCL = 171.60 ppsi

7. a. 6.51 cm
   b. .77
   c. No
   d. $P(x < 15) + P(x > 20) = .022$

9. a. 1.60 ounces
   b. 1.88
   c. $P(z < -5.64) + P(z > 5.64)$ is essentially 0.
   d. LCL = 20.14 ounces, UCL = 20.86 ounces
   e. LCL = 0 ounce, UCL = 0.52 ounce

11. The mean went out of control in shift 16, but the problem was fixed by the next shift; the standard deviation went out of control in shift 14, but the problem was fixed by the next shift.

13. Customers are unsatisfied with the product even though the C_p is 1.8. The process is not centered and so, many rejects will be produced.

15. From the normal table, the probability is .0026 that this will occur by chance, and thus would signal assignable cause variation.

17. Even if customers are satisfied, firms must strive to improve their product.

19. No, the process exhibits systematic variation.

SECTION 15.4

1. A: Use a mean and standard deviation chart respectively.
   B: Use a p chart.

3. Centerline = .039, LCL = 0, UCL = .097

5. a. 196 per subgroup
   b. 441 per subgroup
   c. 1,764 per subgroup

7. Should equal 0.

9. LCL = 0

SECTION 15.5

1. Final exam: very difficult and at 8:00 A.M.
   Students: not prepared and have an unusually low math ability
   Teacher: poor teacher and is difficult to understand

3. What exactly does "not work properly" mean? When did the problem start? How often does it happen? Where does the CD player not "work properly?"

5. "Why" gets at the problem's causes. It does not help define the problem.

SECTION 15.6

1. a. 80
   b. Accept the lot only if 2 or fewer nonconforming pieces found
   c. Reject the lot

3. Acceptance sampling cannot ensure a steady stream of good raw material.

5. Acceptance sampling stops lots with high percent of defectives from entering the plant; vendor certification increases the chances that vendor ships lots with few or no defectives

CHAPTER 15
APPLICATION PROBLEMS

1. a. There do not appear to be any systematic patterns.
   b. 1.59 seconds; yes
   c. LCL = 100.01 seconds, UCL = 104.55 seconds
   d. LCL = 0 seconds, UCL = 3.32 seconds

3. a. Yes; there do not appear to be any systematic patterns.
   b. Mean: LCL = 94.12, UCL = 105.24
       Standard Deviation: LCL = 0, UCL = 7.73

5. a. LCL = 14.1 search requests, UCL = 21.9 search requests
   b. No

7. a. Yes; on shifts 17–19
   b. No; control not restored until shift 20

9. What: Exactly what is wrong with the opener?
    Where: Exactly where in San Francisco are the complaints? Are there complaints outside of San Francisco?
    When: When did the complaints start? What time of day do the complaints occur? On what days do we receive complaints? When a garage door malfunctions, do all other openers in the wedge malfunction at the same time?
    Extent: Are all three door openers having the problem? What percent of the people in the wedge are complaining? Are other door opener manufacturers having the same problem?

11. What: Exactly what are nicks and burrs?
    Where: Where are the nicks on the panels? All at the same place on each panel? Which stamping lines are experiencing the sudden increase in nicks? Are we getting nicks at the blanking operation?
    When: Exactly what time did the three lines start producing the high percentage of nicks?
    Extent: What are the exact percentages of nicks on the panels from the four lines?

13. a. Sought ways to reduce spelling errors and missing words, which accounted for 85% of the problems; they were successful because now these account for 0% of the problems.
   b. Cannot tell because this information not available from a Pareto chart
   c. They should reduce improper punctuation.

15. Stores in mall: major store became vacant, new mix of stores
    Economy: recession, many local firms closing
    Competition: new mall opened, nearby mall opened a food court
    Weather: many winter storms, several ice storms

17. $P(D = 0 \mid \lambda = 13(.10) = 1.3) = .273$

19. a. There is a cyclical pattern — a sine curve.
   b. No; the director wants a line graph that has an increasing pattern.

INDEX

Acceptance quality level (AQL), 868
Acceptance sampling basics, 867–872
Accurate answers, 314
Additive function, 753
Additive models, 753–756
Administrative issues, 314–315
Alpha level, 543
Alternative generation, 2, 5–10, 13
Alternative hypothesis, 469, 475, 531–532
"Alternative Worldview Method," 316
Amstar Corp. v. Domino's Pizza Inc., 334
Analysis, conjoint, 574
Analysis, exploratory data, 531–538
Analysis of variance (ANOVA)
  experimentation role, 528–531
  exploratory data analysis, 531–535
  hypotheses testing, 543–545
  Kruskal–Wallis nonparametric, 556–561
  one-factor, k-level study, 538–545
  regression model, 620–625
  significant difference testing, 550–554
  two-factor, completely random factorial study, 563–571
ANOVA. *See* Analysis of variance
AQL. *See* Acceptance quality level
Area of opportunity, 261
Assignable cause variation, 5, 12, 844
Asymptotic, 270
Attitude, workers, 7–8, 12, 38–39
Autocorrelation, 641–646, 742
Autoregressive model, 146, 643, 742–745
Autoregressive modeling, 742–744
Availability error, 218
Average, 73–74
"Averaging effect," 350

Balance point histogram, 32
Base rate, error of overlooking, 211
Basic sampling, 300–301
Basic terminology, 322
Bell-shaped histogram, 33–34, 54
Bernoulli process assumption, 244, 256–257
Binomial
  distribution, 244–256
  distribution and problem solving, 253–261
  expression, 246–248
  mean and standard deviation, 249–253
  table, 248
Bivariate data, 100
Box plots, 67–69, 97, 107–110

Brightman, H., 11, 15, 316, 775
Brown, Karen, 6, 15
Budget variance strategy, 3
Bureau of the Census Current Population Reports, 291

Calculating probabilities, 244–246
Categorical cross-sectional data, analyzing, 110–121
Categorical variables, 103, 592, 673–675, 681–684
Centered moving average, 758
Centerline (CL), 843
Central limit theorem, 346–350
Certification, vendor, 867
Chain of Quality, The, 871
Charts, 846–849, 852–861
Chebyshev's rule, 55–56
Chi-square
  calculated, 800–802, 806–807
  distribution, 390–392
  goodness-of-fit test, 798–811
  nonparametric methods, 792–798
  test of independence, 811–818
Circle versus ellipse test, 124
CL. *See* Centerline
Class, 24–26
Classical decomposition method, forecasting, 753–774
Climate study questionnaire, 7–8
Closed-ended questions, 317
Clusters, 127–129, 607
Cluster sampling designs, 309
Cochran, William G., 378
Cochran's rules, 378
Coefficient, correlation, 147
Coefficient, multiple determination, 627
Coefficient, sample regression, 613
Coincident indicators, 149, 744
Column percentage tables, 113
Compensatory rivalry, 328
Complementary event, 177
Compound event, 177
Concreteness error, 218–220
Conditional or column percentage, probabilities, 205–210
Conditional probabilities, 198–199, 202–203
  computing, 202–210
  distinguished from joint, 205
  and row or column percentage tables, 205–206
Confidence intervals
  construction, 385–386, 441–443
  defined, 358
  Dunn, and category probabilities, 802–804

Mann–Whitney nonparametric approach, 432–438
  nonparametric, 384–389
  outliers, 386–388
  population mean and median, 386
  prediction intervals, 649–650
  reducing width, 650–652
  t-based, 358–362, 421–423
  time-ordered data, 363
  Tukey HSD, 551–553
  two-sample t-based, 421–423
  unknown population, 355–368, 376–380, 390–394
Confidence level, 298, 362–363
Conjoint analysis, 574
Consumer Reports, 218–219
Control charts
  for attributes, 852–858
  basic, and problem solving, 843–849
  and quality, 859
  using, 846–849
  for variables, 834–852
Controlled study, 322
Convenience sampling, 305–306
Correlation, 146
Correlational studies, running, 601
Correlation coefficient, 147–148
Counts, 236
Covariance, 148
Cramer, H., 815
Cramer's measure of association, 815–816
Crisis problem. *See* Disturbance problem
Critical values, determining, 475–477
Crosby, P. B., 831
Cross-classify, 816
Cross-sectional data, 20–22, 44–50, 58–64
Cross-tabs tables, 110, 592, 816
Cumulative frequency, 27–29, 59–60
Cumulative percentage, 27–28
Curve fitting, 611–620
Curvilinear regression model, 638
Cyclical pattern, 737, 767–769

Data
  analysis, 13–15, 110, 303, 531–538
  base rate, 211
  bivariate, 100
  collecting for regression study, 600–602
  collection, 4, 7–9, 12–13, 294–335
  cross-sectional, 20–22, 44–50, 58–64, 105–106, 110
  deseasonized, 762
  forecasting, 736–738

Georgia Criminal Justice, 229
interpretation, 4–5, 8–9, 12–13
job attitude, 7–8, 12, 38–39
managerial performance, 296
mean, 45, 53–57
multivariate, 101
nonstationary, 39–44, 71–73
obtaining, 296, 300
organizing and summarizing, 4, 8–9, 12–13, 64
panel, 21
quantitative, 121–122, 134, 834
ranked worker attitude, 249, 387
rescaling, 33–34
statements, 95
time-ordered, 21–22, 38–40, 71, 134–135, 483
transforming, 410–413
univariate, 100
yes/no, 49–50, 852
Data collection
experimental design principles, 321–330
hypothesis testing, 472–473, 496, 500, 506–507
questions, 315–321
random sampling design, 304–306
sampling principles, 296–301
stratified random sampling design, 307–311
surveys, 301–304, 312–315
Dearborn, Dewitt, 5, 15
Decision making, 2, 10–13
normal distribution, 272–278
Decision-making errors, 470–472, 480
Decision rule, 481
Decomposition method, 771
Degrees of freedom (df), 358, 542–543, 569
Delbecq, A., 774
Delphi method, 775–777
Deming, W., 830, 844, 862
Deming chain reaction, 830
Departmental performance, 408
Dependent variables, 106, 322, 592
Descriptive statistics, 18–97
Deseasonalized data, 762
Determination, coefficient of multiple, 627
Deviation, variance, 47–53
Diagnosis, 103
Diagrams
fishbone, 863–865
lagged-variable scatter, 138
probability tree, 186
scatter, 122, 602–611, 688–690, 865
tree, 115–116
Diffusion of treatment, 327–328
Dillman, Don, 312, 320
Discrete probability distribution, 237
Distribution
binomial, 244–261
chi-square, 390–392
discrete probability, 237
normal, 268–284
personal probability, 237

Poisson, 261–268
probability, 612
sample mean, 342–355
sample proportion, 376–377
Disturbance problem, 2, 12
Double moving average, 74
Double-sampling plans, 868
Drucker, Peter, 5, 15
Dunn, Olive, 559
Dunn confidence intervals, 802–804
Dunn's multiple comparisons, 559–561

Element, 300
Empirical rule, 54
Equal variance assumption, 423
Error
availability, 218
avoiding wording, 317–320
concreteness, 218–220
costs, 490, 495–496, 500, 506
decision-making costs, 470–472, 480
judgment, 210–213, 218
margin of, 10, 297–298, 303–304
mean absolute percentage, 747–749
mean and standard distribution, 342–346
noncoherency, 214–217, 214–218
nonresponse, 302
nonstatistical judgment, 218–220
overlooking base rate, 211
prediction, 613
random, 328–329
response, 303
selection, 302
standard of estimate, 625–627
standard of proportion, 356, 377–378
standard of regression coefficient, 628
Type I, 471
Type II, 471
wording, 317–320
Estimated standard error, 356, 419–421, 625–627
Event
complimentary, 177–178
compound, 177
defined, 177
frequency, 178–179
probabilities, 179–180, 199–200
relative frequency, 178
simple, 177
statistically independent, 199–202
Evolutionary operations, 575
Expected frequency, 802
Expected value, 238
Experimental design, 321–322, 326–327, 865–867
Experimental factor, 322
Experimental studies, 600–601
Experimental unit, 322
Experimentation role, 528–531
Experiment, random, 176–177

Experiments vs. nonexperiments, 323–325
Experimentwise error rate, 550
Expert panel, 774–775
Explanatory variables, 106
Exploratory data analysis, 531–535, 565–567
Exponential trend pattern, 764–765
External factors, 316
Extraneous factors, 323
Extra-organizational strategy, 3, 408
Extrapolation, 648
Extra sum of squares principle, 695–705

Factorial study, 563–575
Factor level, 322
Fail to reset region, 474
F-distribution, 439
Finite population correction factor, 363
Fishbone diagrams, 863–865
"Fitness for use," 831
Folsom, Marian B., 11, 15
Forecasting
alternative, 738–741
classical decomposition method, 753–774
classical decomposition model, 753–774
data patterns, 736–738
qualitative, 739–740, 774–777
quantitative, 738–739
regression analysis, 741–753
short-term, 769–770
Frequency counts, 592
Frequency distribution, 24–25
Frequency histograms, 24–25, 59, 862–863
F-tables, 445
Full model, 699

General linear test, 695–705
Graphs, 135, 565
Groocock, J. M., 871
Gryna, F. M., 862

Helmer, O., 775
Histograms
balance point, 32
bell-shaped, 33–34, 55
frequency, 24–25, 59–60, 862–863
mean, 46
probability, 237
relative frequency, 27
rescaling data, 33–34
shape, 31–36
skewed, 34–35, 55–56
symmetric, 32–34
two frequency, 32
Historic strategy, 3
History effect, 327
Homoscedasticity, 636
Honestly significant difference (HSD), 551
HSD. See Honestly significant difference

Hypothesis
  alternative, 469
  defined, 469
  null, 469, 473–479
  problem-solving, 529
  stating, 469, 500
  statistical, 556–557
Hypothesis testing
  analysis of variance, 543–545
  assumptions, 477–479
  introduction, 468
  one population mean, 468–488
  one population proportion, 488–494
  population regression coefficient, 675–678
  two population means, 494–505
  two population proportions, 505–511

Implementation, 2, 11, 13
Indicators, coincident, 149–150, 744
Indicators, leading, 150, 744
Indicator variables, 672–687
Indices, raw seasonal, 758
Indices, typical seasonal, 761
Inductive inference, 114–115
Inferences, beyond parameters, 794–795
Inferences, inductive, 114–115
Information, missing, 6–7
Information needs, diagnosing problem, 315–316
Interaction effect, 566
Interaction variable, 678–681
Internal factors, 316
Interpretation, data, 4–5
Interquartile range, 62–64, 66
Intervening variables, 115–117
Inverse linear relationship, 147

Joint confidence intervals, 631
Joint percentage tables, 112
Joint probability, 185, 205
Juran, J. M., 831, 862

Kepner–Tregoe diagnostic method, 528, 563
Kepner–Tregoe problem analysis, 861–862
Kivenko, Kenneth, 871
Kruskal–Wallis nonparametric analysis of variance, 556–561
Kruskal–Wallis nonparametric test, 539, 558, 793
Kutner, M., 641

Lagged relationships, 136, 146–155
Lagged-variable scatter diagram, 138
Law of large numbers, 179–185
LCL. See Lower control limit
Leading indicators, 150, 744
Least squares method, 613–616
Level of confidence, 298, 362–363
Linear, 603
Linearity, departures, 606
Linear, parameters, 688

Linear regression, simple, 612–613
Linear relationships, 123–124, 147
Linear trend pattern, 764
Linear variables, 688
Line graph, 38–40, 77–78, 136, 140
Logarithmic base 10 transformation, 412
Lower control limit (LCL), 843
Lower limit, 24

Maddala, G. S., 628
Mail questionnaires, 312–314
Main effects, 567
Management Information System (MIS), 296, 300
Managerial actions, 479, 489, 495, 506
Managerial performance, 296
Managerial problem, 2
Mann–Whitney confidence intervals, 435–436
Mann–Whitney nonparametric approach, 432–438
Mann–Whitney test, 793
MAPE. See Mean absolute percentage error
Margin of error, 10, 297, 303–304, 423
Matched-pair design, 499
Mean
  defined, 45, 238
  histogram, 46
  interpreting, 53–57
  median comparison, 60–61, 72–73
  Poisson distribution, 265
  population conditional, 612
  trimmed, 61–62
Mean absolute percentage error (MAPE), 747–749
Mean chart, 846, 849
Mean square (MS), 540
Measure of association, Cramer's, 815–816
Measurement scales, 793–794
Median
  defined, 58–59
  interpreting, 66
  mean comparison, 60–61, 72–73
  moving, 81
  trimmed mean, 58
Mendenhall, William, 302
Mental model, 2, 12, 873
Method, Delphi, 775–777
Method, nominal group, 774
Method of least squares, 613–616
Method, qualitative forecasting, 774–777
Middle data value, 58
MIS. See Management Information System
Missing information, 6–7
Mixed data, 105–110
Mode, 56–57
Models
  additive, 753–756
  full, 699
  mental, 873

multiplicative, 753–756
  restricted, 699
Mood test, 449, 793
Moving average
  double, 74
  outlier impact, 79
  ratio to, 756–761
  single, 73–74
  smoothing, 74–76
Moving median, 81
MS. See Mean square
Multicollinearity, 605, 705–720
Multiple box plots, 107
Multiple comparisons, 550–551
Multiple determination coefficient, 627
Multiple line graphs, 135
Multiple regression, 602, 616–618
Multiple-sampling plans, 868
Multiplicative function, 753
Multiplicative models, 753–756
Multivariate data, 101

National Center for Health Statistics, 230
Neter, J., 641
NGM. See Nominal group method
No-difference null hypotheses, 532
No inspection, 868
Nominal group method (NGM), 774
Noncoherency error, 214–217
Nonconforming, 852
Nonexperiments vs. experiments, 323–325
Nonindependence, 641
Nonlinearity, of regression line, 638–639
Nonlinear models, 691–693
Nonlinear regression, 687–695
Nonlinear relationships, 124–127, 606
Nonnormality, 641
Nonparametric, 384
Nonparametric analysis of variance, Kruskal–Wallis, 556–563
Nonparametric confidence interval, 384–385
Nonparametric methods, 409, 445–451, 792–798
Nonresponse error, 302
Nonsignificant predictor variables, 628–629
Nonstationary time-ordered data, 39–40, 71–73
Nonstatistical judgment errors, 218–220
Nonsymmetric histogram. See Skewed histogram
Normal distribution, 268–284
Null hypothesis
  defined, 469
  exploratory data analysis, 531–532
  testing, and making decision, 473–483, 490, 497, 501, 507–509

Observational study, 323
Obtaining accurate answers, 314

Ogive, 27–29
One- and two-sided intervals, 369
One-factor, k-level study, analysis of
    variance, 538–545
One-factor, two-level completely
    random study, 496
One population
    confidence intervals, 355–373,
        376–380, 390–394
    mean, 468–488
    nonparametric confidence interval,
        384–389
    one-sided confidence intervals,
        368–373
    proportion, 488–494
    sample mean distribution, 342–355
    sample size, 380–384
    statistical inferences, 338–341
    stratified random sampling,
        373–376
One-quarter lagging, 742
One-sided confidence intervals,
    368–373
One-way table, 106
Open-ended classes, 25–26
Open-ended questions, 316
OR, 193. See also Union probability
Ordered target population, 309
Other people's strategy, 3
Ott, Lyman, 302
Outlier
    defined, 35–36
    Empirical rule, 54
    identifying, 66–67
    moving averages, 79
    presence of, 386
    regression model, 641
    super, 97
    trimmed mean, 60–61
Output, statistical software, 96

Paired comparison test, 499
Paired difference test, 499
Panel data, 21
Parameter, 794
Pareto charts, 859–861
Pattern
    cycle, 767–769
    cyclical, 737
    data, 736–738
    detection, 739
    trend, 736, 762–767
Per comparison error rate, 550
Periodic target population, 309
Personal interviews, 312–314
Personal probability, 180–181, 237
Picturing probability, 185–192
"Piggy-backing," 314
Pilot study, 12
Planned change studies, 296, 300,
    321–322
Poisson distribution, 261–268
Population, 10
Population conditional mean, 612
Population mean, 45

Population normality, 423
Population parameter, 338
Population regression coefficient,
    675–678, 698–702
Position bias, 317
Positive linear relationship, 147
Pounds, William, 3, 15, 408
Pounds's strategies, 3
Power trend pattern, 764–765
Prediction, defined, 648
Prediction error, 613
Prediction intervals, 649–652
Predictor variables, 592, 600–601
Probability
    basic concepts, 174–230
    calculating, 244–246
    conditional, 198–199, 202–210
    distributions, 232–292, 235–237
    joint, 185
    joint table, 185–186
    joint and union, 193–198
    personal, 180–181
    picturing, 185–192
    rules, 179–180
    tree diagram, 186–192
    trees, 210–211
    types, 205
    unconditional, 199
    union, 193
    z-scores, 271–272
Probability concepts, 176–185
Probability distribution, 234–235, 612
    binomial distribution, 244–261
    normal distribution, 268–284
    Poisson distribution, 261–268
    problem solving, 234–235
    random variables, 235–244
Probability histogram, 237
Probability tree diagram, 186
Probability trees, 210–218
Problem analysis, Kepner–Tregoe,
    861–862
Problem definition, 528–529
Problem diagnosis, 98–172, 100–101
    in business, 5–10, 13
    defined, 20
    distinguishing from problem
        sensing, 100
    problem-solving model, 2
Problem diagnosis and solving,
    529–531
Problem scanner, 213–214
Problem sensing, 100–101
    and binomial distribution, 255
    in business, 2–5
    distinguishing from problem
        diagnosis, 100
    Poisson distribution, 263
    Pounds's strategies, 3
    statistics role, 3–5, 12–13
Problem solving
    basic control charts, 843–849
    binomials, 253–261
    experimentation role, 528–531
    hypotheses, 529

model, 2–15, 234
    statistical inferences, 338–339
Process capability, 837–843
Process control, 835–837
Product life cycle, 767
Profile graphs, 565
Proportional allocation sampling, 308
Proportion nonconforming chart,
    854–856
Proxy variable, 755
p-value, 476

Quadratic trend pattern, 764, 766
Qualitative forecasting, 739–740,
    774–777
Quality improvement
    acceptance sampling, 867–871
    control charting for variables,
        834–852
    control charts for attributes,
        852–858
    controlling, 858–867
    general principles, 872–873
    manufactured, 831
    strategic importance of, 830
    types of quality, 830–833
    vendor certification, 871–872
Quantitative cross-sectional data,
    121–134
Quantitative data, 834
Quantitative dependent variable,
    593–598
Quantitative forecasting approaches,
    738–739
Quantitative time-ordered data,
    analyzing, 134–146
Quantitative variable, 103, 592
Quartile, 62
Question, closed-ended, 317
Question format, 316–320
Question, open-ended, 316
Questionnaires
    developing, 303
    length, and flexibility, 313
    mail, 312–314
    pretesting, 303
Question writing, 315–321

Ramakrishna, H., 316
Random error, 328–329
Random experiment, 176
Randomization, 325–326
Random numbers table, 305
Random sampling, simple, 375
Random sampling, stratified, 373–376
Random variable, 235–238
    continuous, 236
    discrete, 236
Random variation, 5, 12, 844
Range, defined, 46–47
Range, interquartile, 58, 62–64, 62–67
Ratio to moving average method,
    756–761
Raw seasonal indices, 758
Reducing margin of error, 423

Regression analysis
  analysis of variance, 621–625
  assumptions underlying, 636
  collecting data, 600–601
  curve fitting, 611–618
  curvilinear, 638
  evaluating analysis, 635–648
  evaluating regression model,
    620–635
  extra sum of squares principle,
    695–705
  forecasting, 648–652, 741–753
  indicator variables, 672–687
  limitations, 749–750
  multicollinearity, 705–720
  nonlinear regression, 687–695
  scatter diagrams, 602–608
  variable relationships, 592–598
Regression coefficient errors, 628
Regression line, nonlinearity, 638–639
Regression model. See Regression
  analysis
Regression, multiple, 602, 616–618
Regression, nonlinear, 687–695
Regression, simple linear, 603,
  612–613
Rejection region, 473
Relationship
  detection, 739
  detection tool, 594
  lagged, 136–137
  linear, 124
  nonlinear, 124
  of variables, 592–600
Relative frequency distribution, 26–27
Relative frequency histogram, 27
Reliability coefficient, 358
Representative sample, 312–313
Rescaling data, 33–34
Residual plots, 78–79, 637
Residuals, 78–79, 635, 637, 745–747
Restricted model, 699
Roberts, H., 750
ROI. See Return on investment
RO principle, 325–326
Row or column percentage tables,
  205–206
Row percentage tables, 113
Rules, Empirical and Chebyshev,
  53–55
Rules, planned change studies,
  575–576
Rules of probability, 179–180

s, 356, 358
Sample
  defined, 10, 338
  design, 303
  mean, 45, 53–57, 342–355
  obtaining representative, 312–313
  proportion, 376–377, 488
  range, 46
  regression coefficients, 613
  size, 297–298, 380–384, 472
  standard deviation, 48

statistic, 339
  stratified random, defined, 307
  variance, 47–48
Sampling
  convenience, 305
  designs, 304–306, 309–310
  distribution, 342–346, 418–419,
    439–441
  frame, 301–302
  impact of simple random, 375
  from MIS, 300
  plans, 868
  principles, 296–300
  proportional allocation, 308
  simple random, 304
  stratified random, 373–376
  survey designs, 301
  terminology, 300–301
  units, 301
  without replacement, 297
SAS. See Statistical Analysis System
Scales
  interval, 794
  measurement, 793–794
  nominal, 793
  ordinal or ranking, 793
  ratio, 794
Scatter diagrams, 122, 602–611,
  688–690, 865
Scatter plot, 603
Scheaffer, Richard, 302
Screening procedure, 628
Screening questions, 313
Seasonality, 760
Second-order model, 687
Selection error, 302
Selective perception, 5
Setting confidence level, 362–363, 490
Setting significance level, 472
Shared risk approach, 6
Shewhart, Walter, 843
Short-term forecasting, 769–770
Siegel, Andrew, 412
Significance level, 472, 480
Significance of single predictor
  variable, 630–631
Significant difference testing, 550–554
Simon, Herbert A., 5, 15
Simple correlation matrix, 604–607
Simple event, 177
Simple linear regression, 603,
  612–613
Simple random sampling, 304–306,
  324, 375
Single moving average, 73–74
Single-sampling plans, 868
Skewed histogram, 34–35, 55–56
Skewness, 69
Small expected frequencies, 802, 815
Smoothed line graph, 77–78
Smoothing moving average, 74–76
Software, statistical. See Statistical
  software
Special cause variation, 5
Spread charts, 533–535

Squared deviations, 388
SS. See Sum of squares
SSB. See Sum of squares between
  sample means
SST. See Total sum of squares
SSW. See Sum of squares within
  treatment levels
Standard deviation, 48, 53–57, 239,
  845–846, 849
Standard error of estimate, 625–627
Standard error of mean, 344
Standard error of proportion, 377–378
Standard errors of regression
  coefficients, 628
Stationary time-ordered data, 38–39
Statistical Analysis System (SAS),
  95–97, 170–172, 403–404,
  463–465, 523–524, 587–589,
  664–668, 787–788, 826, 883–884
Statistical dependence, 200
Statistical hypotheses, 556–557
Statistical independence, 200–202
Statistical inferences, 296–300,
  338–341
Statistically related, 620
Statistically significant, 620
Statistical process control, 873
Statistical software. See Statistical
  Analysis System
Statistics
  defined, 2
  descriptive, 18–172
  in decision making, 12
  overview of, 82–94
  software, 95–97
  testing need, 620–621
Statistics and Data Analysis, 412
Stem-and-leaf display, 22–23, 59, 97,
  387
Stevens, S., 793
Stratified random sampling, 307–311,
  373–376
Studies, correlational, 601
Studies, experimental, 600–601
Subpopulation, 616
Summarizing data, 4, 8–9, 12–13, 64
Sum of squares (SS), 540, 568
Sum of squares between sample means
  (SSB), 541
Sum of squares within, 568
Sum of squares within treatment levels
  (SSW), 540
Super outlier, 97
Survey, 20, 296, 300–304, 312–316
Symmetric histogram, 32–34
Symmetry, 69–71
Systematic and cluster designs, 309–310
Systematic sampling designs, 309

Tables
  binomial, 248
  column percentage, 113
  cross-tabs, 110–113, 592, 816
  joint percentage, 112
  joint probability, 185

one-way, 106–107
Poisson, 262
random numbers, 305
row percentage, 113
for studentized range values, 551
Target population
defined, 300, 338
identifying, 302
ordered, 309
periodic, 309
variation, 299
t-based confidence intervals, 358–362
t-based confidence intervals, two-sample, 421–423
Telephone interviews, 312–314
Terminology, basic sampling, 300–301, 322
Tests
chi-square goodness-of-fit, 798–811
chi-square, of independence, 811–818
circle vs. ellipse, 124
Kruskal–Wallis, 793
Mann–Whitney, 793
Mood, 793
paired comparison, 499
paired difference, 499
significant differences between pairs of population means, 550–555
statistical, 620–621
Time-ordered data, 21–22, 38–40, 71, 363
Time-ordered process data, 483
Time series. See Time-ordered data
Total quality management program (TQM), 79
Total sum of squares (SST), 540–542
TQM. See Total quality management program
Transformation, logarithmic base, 10, 412
Transforming data, 410–413
Tree diagram, 115–116
Tregoe method. See Kepner–Tregoe diagnostic method
Trend pattern, 736, 762–767

Trimmed mean, 61–62
Trivial changes, 328
Tukey, John, 551
Tukey HSD confidence intervals, 551–554
Tukey's rule, 539
Two categorical variables, relating, 592–593
Two-factor, completely random factorial study, 563–575
Two frequency histogram, 32
Two populations
comparing, 408–417
Mann–Whitney nonparametric confidence interval, 432–438
mean, 410–411, 417–427, 494–505
nonparametric comparison method, 445–451
normal, 408–409
proportion differences, 505–511
variances, 413–414, 438–445
Two-sided interval, 381–383, 385
Type I error, 471, 521–522, 543
Type II error, 471, 521–522
Typical seasonal indices, 761

UCL. See Upper control limit
Unconditional probability, 199
Unequal variances, 639–640
Union probability, 193
Unit of association, 600–601
Unknown population mean, 355–373
Unknown population median, 384–389
Unknown population proportion, 376–380, 382–383
Unknown population variance, 390–394
Upper control limit (UCL), 843
Upper limit, 24

Validity, 278–284
Van de Ven, A., 774
Variable
categorical, 95, 103, 592, 673–675, 681–684

control charting for, 834–852
defined, 20, 103
dependent, 106, 322, 592
explanatory, 106
indicator, 672–687
interaction, 678
intervening, 114–117
lagged, 138, 146
nonsignificant predictor, 628–629
predictor, 592
proxy, 755
quantitative, 103, 592
random, 235–238
relationships among, 592–600
single predictor, 630–631
types, 103–105
Variance, 47–48
between, 540, 542
Kruskal–Wallis nonparametric analysis of, 556–563
unequal, 639–640
within, 542
Variance ratio, 439–443
Variance within (MSW), 542
Variation, assignable cause, 844
Variation, random, 844
Variation, target population, 299–300
Vendor certification, 871–872

Wall Street Journal, 181
Wasserman, W., 641
WATS line, 314
Weighting constant, 541
Width, and confidence/prediction intervals, 650–652
Within effect, 567
Wording errors, 317–320
Worker attitude survey, 7
Writing questions, 315–321

x-bar, 45

Yes/no data, 49–50, 852

z-scores, and probabilities, 271–272

HINTS FOR WRITING MEMOS FOR END-OF-CHAPTER APPLICATION PROBLEMS

1. Your memo must quickly establish the following:
   - **What** is the problem?
   - **Why** should the reader care?
   - **What** do you want the reader to do?
2. Create informative headings **before** writing your memos. Use "white space" to create a readable and attractive page. For example,

---

Problem

Over the past quarter the reject rate increased from 1% to 4% in the Abilene plant. This increased our rework cost by $70,000. Failure to understand the new quality control procedures caused the jump in the reject rate.

Recommendation

We request $5,250 for Qualtrain Inc. to conduct three one-day workshops for all supervisory and hourly workers.

Supporting Data

On March 12, we interviewed 100 randomly selected workers and supervisors in the Abilene plant and found . . .

---

3. Focus paragraphs clearly—one idea and supporting points. Each paragraph that has more than three sentences should contain a cover sentence that provides an overview. Keep paragraphs to 10 lines or less.
4. Use the active voice. It is more forceful than the passive voice, it reduces the risk of being misunderstood, and it requires fewer words.
5. Use personal pronouns such as **you** and **we**. Personally addressing your audience will produce better responses.
6. Simplify sentences by using lists whenever possible (see hint #1).
7. Avoid long sentences and words, use only one adjective before a noun, and state sentences in positive form. Minimize phrases that begin with **of, with,** or **for.**

From Jerry A. Dibble and Beverly Y. Langford's *Communication Skills and Strategies: Guidelines for Managers at Work,* Atlanta, GA: By the Authors, 1990. Used with permission of the authors.